NATIONAL GEOGRAPHIC

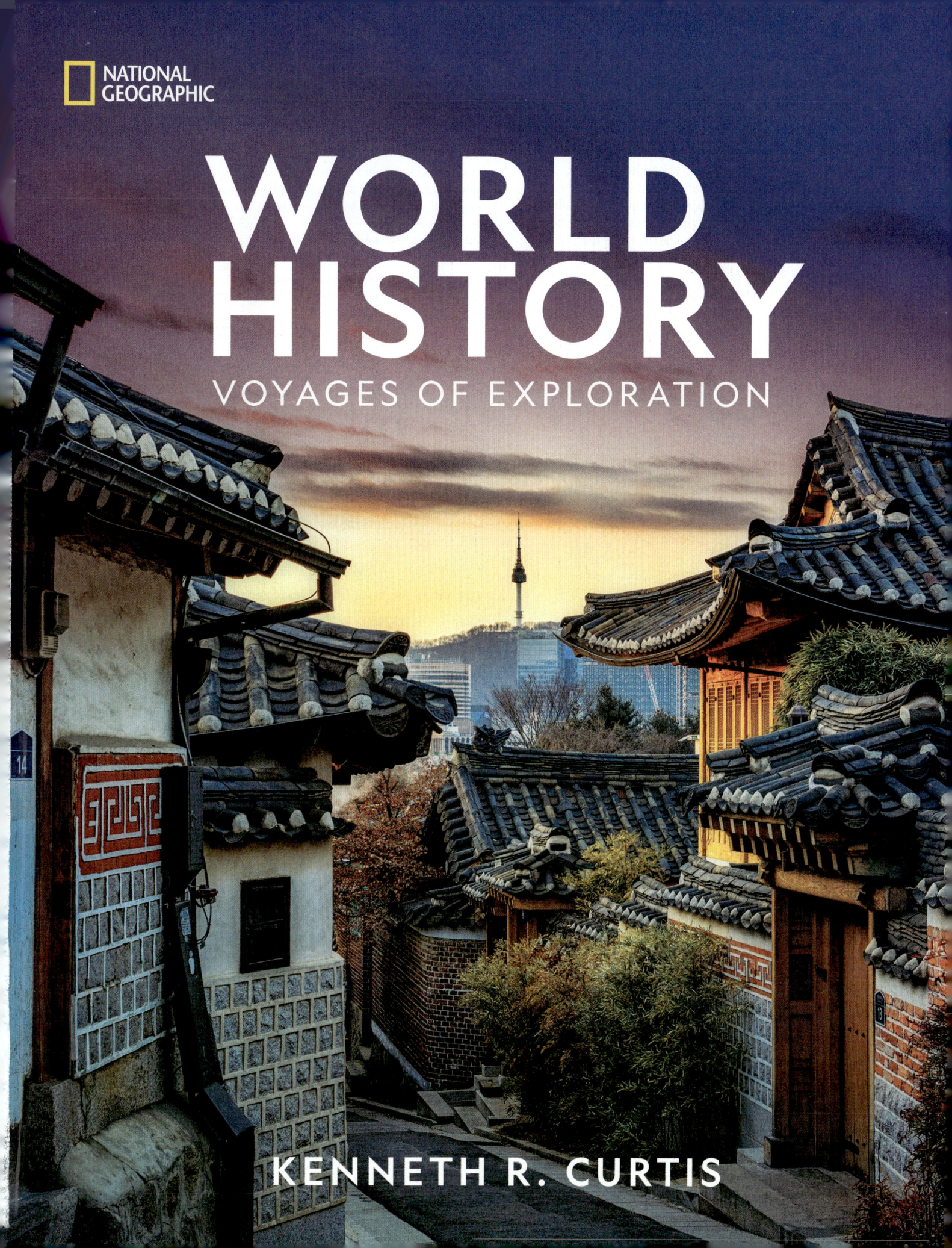

WORLD HISTORY
VOYAGES OF EXPLORATION

KENNETH R. CURTIS

NATIONAL GEOGRAPHIC LEARNING | CENGAGE

Acknowledgments

Grateful acknowledgment is given to the authors, artists, photographers, museums, publishers, and agents for permission to reprint copyrighted material. Every effort has been made to secure the appropriate permission. If any omissions have been made or if corrections are required, please contact the Publisher.

Photographic Credits

Front Cover: Atakorn/iStock/Getty Images

Back Cover: (bkgd) coolbiere photograph/Getty Images, (c) Ossiridian/Getty Images, (c) kathykonkle/DigitalVision Vectors/Getty Images

Acknowledgments and credits continue on page R35.

Copyright © 2021 Cengage Learning, Inc.

ALL RIGHTS RESERVED. No part of this work covered by the copyright herein may be reproduced or distributed in any form or by any means, except as permitted by U.S. copyright law, without the prior written permission of the copyright owner.

"National Geographic", "National Geographic Society" and the Yellow Border Design are registered trademarks of the National Geographic Society ® Marcas Registradas

---

For product information and technology assistance, contact us at Customer & Sales Support, 888-915-3276

For permission to use material from this text or product, submit all requests online at **www.cengage.com/permissions**

Further permissions questions can be emailed to **permissionrequest@cengage.com**

National Geographic Learning | Cengage
200 Pier 4 Blvd., Suite 400
Boston, MA 02210

National Geographic Learning, a Cengage company, is a provider of quality core and supplemental educational materials for the PreK–12, adult education, and ELT markets. Cengage is a leading provider of customized learning solutions with employees residing in nearly 40 different countries and sales in more than 125 countries around the world. Find your local representative at NGL.Cengage.com/RepFinder.

Visit National Geographic Learning online at NGL.Cengage.com

Visit our corporate website at **www.cengage.com**

ISBN: 978-1-337-78682-9

Printed in the United States of America
Print Number: 07   Print Year: 2023

AUTHOR

KENNETH R. CURTIS
Professor of History
California State University Long Beach

Kenneth R. Curtis received his Ph.D. from the University of Wisconsin-Madison in African and Comparative World History. He is Professor of History at California State University Long Beach, where he has taught world history at the introductory level, in special courses designed for future middle and high school teachers, and in graduate seminars. He has worked to advance the teaching of world history at the collegiate and secondary levels in collaboration with the World History Association, the California History/Social Science Project, and the College Board's Advanced Placement World History program. He is coauthor, with Valerie Hansen of Yale University, of *Voyages in World History*, a National Geographic Learning text widely adopted by both college and AP teachers.

SENIOR CONSULTANTS

PEGGY ALTOFF
Past President
National Council for the Social Studies

Peggy Altoff's career includes teaching middle school and high school students, supervising teachers, and serving as adjunct university faculty. Peggy served as a state social studies specialist in Maryland and as a K–12 coordinator in Carrol County, Maryland, and Colorado Springs. She is a past president of the National Council for the Social Studies (NCSS) and served on the task force for the 2012 NCSS National Curriculum Standards.

FREDRIK HIEBERT
Explorer Programs
Archaeologist-in-Residence
National Geographic Society

Fred Hiebert is National Geographic's Archaeologist-in-Residence. He has led archaeological expeditions at ancient Silk Roads sites across Asia. Hiebert was curator of National Geographic's exhibition: *Afghanistan: Hidden Treasures from the National Museum, Kabul*, and its more recent exhibitions, *Tomb of Christ* and *Queens of Egypt*.

NATIONAL GEOGRAPHIC SOCIETY

The National Geographic Society contributed significantly to *World History: Voyages of Exploration*. Our collaboration with each of the following has been a pleasure and a privilege: National Geographic Maps, National Geographic Education and Children's Media, and National Geographic Missions programs. We thank the Society for its guidance and support.

NATIONAL GEOGRAPHIC EXPLORERS AND PHOTOGRAPHERS

National Geographic supports the work of a host of anthropologists, archaeologists, adventurers, biologists, educators, writers, and photographers across the world. The following individuals each contributed substantially to *World History: Voyages of Exploration*.

AZIZ ABU SARAH
Cultural Educator

LYNSEY ADDARIO
Photojournalist

SALAM AL KUNTAR
Archaeologist

ELLA AL-SHAMAHI
Paleoanthropologist and Stand-Up Comic

BUZZ ALDRIN
Astronaut and Author

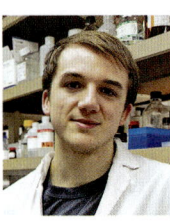

JACK ANDRAKA
Inventor

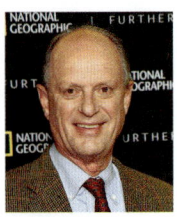

ROBERT BALLARD
Oceanographer

CHRIS BASHINELLI
Cross-Cultural-Explorer

ARI BESER
Filmmaker

JIMMY CHIN
Photographer and Filmmaker

ROBERT CLARK
Photographer

KARA COONEY
Egyptologist and Author

JAGO COOPER
Archaeologist

ADJANY COSTA
Conservationist and Ichthyologist

T.H. CULHANE
Urban Ecologist

GUILLERMO DE ANDA
Underwater Archaeologist

LESLIE DEWAN
Nuclear Engineer

AMELIA EARHART
Aviator

SYLVIA EARLE
Oceanographer

STEVEN ELLIS
Archaeologist

KEOLU FOX
Human Geneticist

KEN GARRETT
Photographer

JERRY GLOVER
Agricultural Ecologist

KAVITA GUPTA
Science Educator

JEFFREY GUSKY
Photographer

DAVID GUTTENFELDER
Photographer

KEVIN HAND
Astrobiologist

PATRICK HUNT
Archaeologist

TERRY HUNT
Archaeologist

JEDIDAH ISLER
Astrophysicist

LYNN JOHNSON
Photographer

YUKINORI KAWAE
Archaeologist

KATHRYN KEANE
Vice President of Public Experiences

PEG KEINER
Educator

AMANDA KOLTZ
Biologist

KATHY KU
Engineer

LOUISE LEAKEY
Paleoanthropologist

MEAVE LEAKEY
Paleoanthropologist

NATALIA LEDFORD
Filmmaker

CHRISTINE LEE
Bioarchaeologist

DANIELLE N. LEE
Biologist

ALBERT LIN
Engineer

CARL LIPO
Archaeologist

GERD LUDWIG
Photographer

JODI MAGNESS
Archaeologist

O. LOUIS MAZZATENTA
Photographer

STEVE MCCURRY
Photographer

KAKENYA NTAIYA
Women's Advocate

SARAH PARCAK
Space Archaeologist

ALAN PARENTE
Creator of Exhibitions and Global Experiences

WILLIAM PARKINSON
Archaeologist

MATTHEW PISCITELLI
Archaeologist

KRISTIN ROMEY
Archaeologist and Writer

JEFFREY ROSE
Paleoarchaeologist

ANDRÉS RUZO
Geothermal Scientist

PARDIS SABETI
Computational Geneticist

ENRIC SALA
Marine Ecologist

PAUL SALOPEK
Writer and Journalist

MAURIZIO SERACINI
Cultural Engineer

NORA SHAWKI
Archaeologist

HAYAT SINDI
Medical Research Scientist

BRIAN SKERRY
Photographer

CHRISTOPHER THORNTON
Archaeologist

NEIL DEGRASSE TYSON
Astrophysicist

MIGUEL VILAR
Molecular Anthropologist

AMI VITALE
Photographer

GENEVIEVE VON PETZINGER
Paleoanthropologist

JON WATERHOUSE
Environmental Steward

TOPHER WHITE
Engineer and Physicist

GRACE YOUNG
Ocean Engineer

v

Wadi Methkandoush archaeological site, Libya

JIMMY CHIN AND THE TYRANNY OF PASSION 1

UNIT 1

Ancient Worlds NEOLITHIC ERA–500 C.E.

UNIT INTRODUCTION 2
UNIT TIME LINE 4
UNIT MAP: EARLY CIVILIZATIONS
c. 3000 B.C.E.–100 C.E. .... ONLINE

THE GLOBAL PERSPECTIVE .... ONLINE
No Walls, No Borders: Nomads

NATIONAL GEOGRAPHIC EXPLORER FEATURE
A National Geographic Nomad

CHAPTER 1
FIRST PEOPLES AND SOCIETIES
NEOLITHIC ERA–5650 B.C.E. 6

SECTION 1 HISTORY IS DISCOVERY
1.1 History Joins Science 8
1.2 NATIONAL GEOGRAPHIC EXPLORER
JEFFREY ROSE Tracing the Paths of Early Humans 12
1.3 The Earliest Migrations 14
1.4 NATIONAL GEOGRAPHIC EXPLORER AND TRAVELER Out of Eden: Paul Salopek Walks Through Time 16
1.5 DOCUMENT-BASED QUESTION
Cave Paintings 20

SECTION 2 THE NEOLITHIC REVOLUTION
2.1 Early Agriculture 22
2.2 MATERIAL CULTURE
The Power of Animals 26
2.3 The First Large Settlements 28

CHAPTER 1 REVIEW 30

CHAPTER 2
EARLY RIVER VALLEY CIVILIZATIONS
3100 B.C.E.–500 C.E. 32

SECTION 1 THE ANCIENT NEAR EAST
1.1 Mesopotamia and City Life 34
1.2 Sumer and the Beginnings of Writing 38
1.3 The Babylonian Empire 40

SECTION 2 KINGDOMS ALONG THE NILE
2.1 African Origins of Egyptian Civilization 42
2.2 The Old and Middle Kingdoms 44
2.3 The New Kingdom and Nubia 48
2.4 PRESERVING CULTURAL HERITAGE
Queens of Egypt 50

Chapter 1, Lesson 1.4

Chapter 2, Lesson 3.1

Chapter 3, Lesson 2.1

SECTION 3 EASTERN MEDITERRANEAN KINGDOMS

3.1 The Hittites and the Assyrians 54
3.2 | **PRESERVING CULTURAL HERITAGE**
     Heritage at Risk 56
3.3 Judaism and the Israelite Kingdoms 58
3.4 | **DOCUMENT-BASED QUESTION**
     Comparing Flood Narratives 62

CHAPTER 2 REVIEW 64

CHAPTER 3

ANCIENT SOUTH ASIA AND CHINA
2600 B.C.E.–207 B.C.E. 66

SECTION 1 FOUNDATIONS OF HINDU SOCIETIES

1.1 Cities Along the Indus 68
1.2 Sanskrit and Epic Texts 70

SECTION 2 THE RISE OF BUDDHISM

2.1 The Buddha's Teachings 72
2.2 | **MATERIAL CULTURE**
     Images of the Buddha 74
2.3 The Maurya Empire 78
2.4 Early Indian Ocean Trade 80

SECTION 3 EARLY DYNASTIES OF CHINA

3.1 China's First Cities 82
3.2 The Zhou Dynasty 84
3.3 Confucianism and Daoism 86

SECTION 4 CHINA'S FIRST EMPIRE

4.1 Qin Rulers Unify China 88
4.2 | **THROUGH THE LENS**
     O. Louis Mazzatenta 90

CHAPTER 3 REVIEW 92

UNIT 1 WRAP-UP 94

vii

UNESCO World Heritage Site, Philippi, Greece

UNIT 2

Far-Reaching Civilizations and Empires 2200 B.C.E.–1279 C.E.

UNIT INTRODUCTION 96	**THE GLOBAL PERSPECTIVE** .... *ONLINE*
UNIT TIME LINE 98	Astronomy: The Search for Meaning and Survival
UNIT MAP: ANCIENT EMPIRES c. 200 C.E. ..... *ONLINE*	**NATIONAL GEOGRAPHIC EXPLORER FEATURE**
	Astronomy with National Geographic

CHAPTER 4
THE PERSIAN EMPIRE
1300 B.C.E.–651 C.E. 100

SECTION 1 ANCIENT IRAN

1.1 **TRAVELER** Herodotus, the World's First Historian 102
1.2 Early Persia 104
1.3 **DOCUMENT-BASED QUESTION** Cyrus the Great and the Jewish Exiles 106
1.4 **NATIONAL GEOGRAPHIC EXPLORER CHRISTOPHER THORNTON** What a Cooking Pot Can Tell Us 108

SECTION 2 THE REIGN OF DARIUS

2.1 Darius and Persia's Golden Age 110
2.2 **MATERIAL CULTURE** Persian Monuments and Scythian Gold 112
2.3 The Greco-Persian Wars 114
2.4 The Legacy of Ancient Iran 116

CHAPTER 4 REVIEW 118

CHAPTER 5
GREEK CIVILIZATION
2200 B.C.E.–200 B.C.E. 120

SECTION 1 EARLY GREECE

1.1 **NATIONAL GEOGRAPHIC EXPLORER WILLIAM PARKINSON** Embracing Our Greek Heritage 122
1.2 Crete and Trading Centers 124
1.3 The Phoenicians and Their Alphabet 126
1.4 The Rise of Greek City-States 128

SECTION 2 THE GOLDEN AGE

2.1 Democracy in Athens 130
2.2 Pericles and Cultural Advances 132
2.3 **A GLOBAL COMMODITY** Gold 134

viii

Chapter 6, Lesson 3.2

Chapter 7, Lesson 2.4

SECTION 3 HELLENISM: A CULTURAL SYNTHESIS

3.1 The Peloponnesian War 138

3.2 Alexander the Great 140

3.3 | **PRESERVING CULTURAL HERITAGE**
Lady Moon at the Crossroads 142

3.4 The Legacy of Ancient Greece 144

CHAPTER 5 REVIEW 148

CHAPTER 6
THE ROMAN EMPIRE AND THE RISE OF CHRISTIANITY 1000 B.C.E.–476 C.E. 150

SECTION 1 THE ROMAN REPUBLIC

1.1 The Emergence of Rome 152

1.2 The Republic Expands 154

1.3 Roman Society 156

SECTION 2 THE ROMAN EMPIRE

2.1 The End of the Republic 158

2.2 Expanding the Empire's Frontiers 160

2.3 Roman Armies and Engineering 162

2.4 Pompeii 164

SECTION 3 THE RISE OF CHRISTIANITY

3.1 | **STATE OF THE WORLD** 1 B.C.E. 166

3.2 | **PRESERVING CULTURAL HERITAGE**
Jerusalem: From History to VR 168

3.3 The Spread of Christianity 174

3.4 | **TRAVELER** Egeria, an Early Christian Pilgrim 176

3.5 | **DOCUMENT-BASED QUESTION**
The Romans and the Christians 178

SECTION 4 WESTERN DECLINE, EASTERN RENEWAL

4.1 Decline of the Roman Empire 180

4.2 Fall of the Western Roman Empire 182

4.3 The Legacy of Ancient Rome 184

CHAPTER 6 REVIEW 188

CHAPTER 7
SOCIETIES IN EAST AND SOUTH ASIA
206 B.C.E.–1279 C.E. 190

SECTION 1 INDIAN CULTURES AND DYNASTIES

1.1 Developments in Hinduism 192

1.2 The Gupta Dynasty 194

1.3 The Chola Kingdom 196

SECTION 2 CHINA'S HAN AND TANG EMPIRES

2.1 | **TRAVELER** Sima Qian, the Grand Historian 198

2.2 Early History of the Silk Roads 200

2.3 Han Expansion and Collapse 202

2.4 The Tang Empire 204

SECTION 3 EAST AND SOUTHEAST ASIAN KINGDOMS

3.1 Kingdoms in Korea and Vietnam 206

3.2 The Emergence of Japan 208

3.3 | **PRESERVING CULTURAL HERITAGE**
Temple Spires Against the Elements 210

CHAPTER 7 REVIEW 214

UNIT 2 WRAP-UP 216

Sheikh Lotfollah Mosque, Isfahan, Iran

UNIT 3

Byzantine and Arab Civilizations

330-1258

UNIT INTRODUCTION 218	**THE GLOBAL PERSPECTIVE** .... ONLINE
UNIT TIME LINE 220	Many Paths to God
UNIT MAP: BYZANTINE AND EARLY MUSLIM EMPIRES 565-750 .... ONLINE	

CHAPTER 8
THE EARLY BYZANTINE EMPIRE 330-1081 222

SECTION 1 CONSTANTINOPLE

1.1 Byzantium's New Rome 224
1.2 Justinian and Theodora 226
1.3 | **PRESERVING CULTURAL HERITAGE**
      "Suspended From Heaven" 228
1.4 | **TRAVELER** Procopius, Plague Witness 232

SECTION 2 CHRISTIANITY IN THE EAST

2.1 The Iconoclasts 234
2.2 Byzantine Growth and Decline 236
2.3 Imprint of an Early Empire 238

CHAPTER 8 REVIEW 240

Unit 3 Time Line

Chapter 8, Lesson 1.2

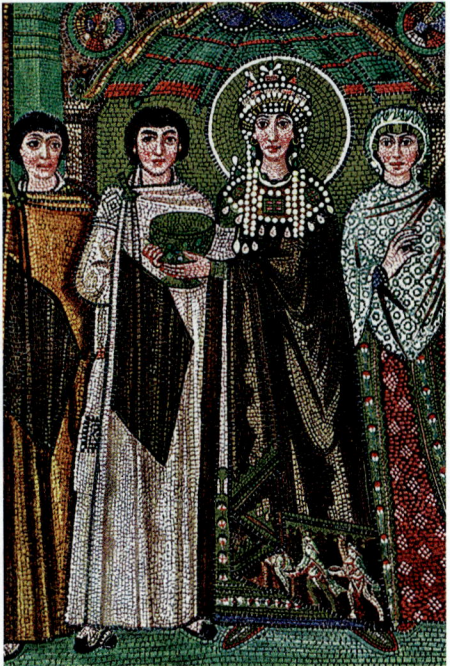

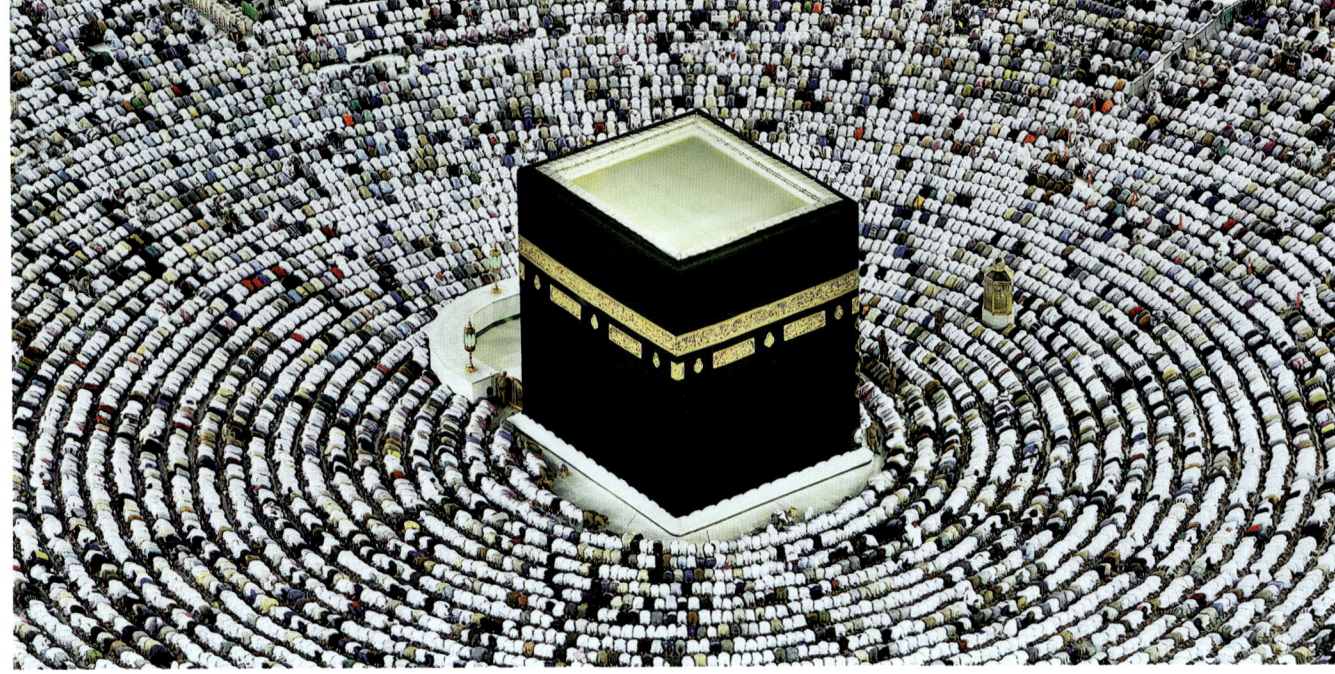

Chapter 9, Lesson 1.1

CHAPTER 9
ARAB EMPIRES AND ISLAMIC EXPANSION 550–1258 242

SECTION 1 ORIGINS OF ISLAM	**2.3	STATE OF THE WORLD** 800 C.E. 254
1.1 The Prophet Muhammad 244	**SECTION 3** THE ABBASID EMPIRE
1.2 The Early Caliphs 246	**3.1** Baghdad, City of Learning 256
**1.3	DOCUMENT-BASED QUESTION** Comparing Calendars 248	**3.2** The Islamic Golden Age 258
	CHAPTER 9 REVIEW 260
SECTION 2 ISLAMIC EXPANSION	
2.1 Conquering the Arabian Peninsula 250	
2.2 The Umayyad Caliphate and North Africa 252	**UNIT 3 WRAP-UP** 262

xi

17th-century Japanese screen depicting Japan's 12th-century Genpei War

UNIT 4

Feudal Europe and Imperial East Asia 481-1500

UNIT INTRODUCTION	264
UNIT TIME LINE	266
UNIT MAP: GROWTH OF THE MONGOL EMPIRE 1206-1294	ONLINE

THE GLOBAL PERSPECTIVE............................ ONLINE
Soldiering: Why We Fight

NATIONAL GEOGRAPHIC EXPLORER FEATURE
Following Soldiers' Traces

CHAPTER 10
EUROPE'S MEDIEVAL ERA 481-1492 268

SECTION 1 WESTERN AND NORTHERN EUROPE
1.1 Christian Rulers in Europe 270
1.2 The Age of Vikings 272
1.3 Conquest and Division 274

SECTION 2 CHANGING LAND, LABOR, AND CULTURE
2.1 Manors, Guilds, and the Growth of Towns 276
2.2 Centers of Learning 278
2.3 Medieval Achievements 280
2.4 | PRESERVING CULTURAL HERITAGE
    Notre-Dame Cathedral 284

SECTION 3 THE CHURCH AND THE CRUSADES
3.1 Changing Roles of the Church 288
3.2 Waves of Crusades 290
3.3 Crusades Within Europe 294

SECTION 4 WANING OF THE EUROPEAN MIDDLE AGES
4.1 Trade, Famine, and Plague 296
4.2 War and Division 298
4.3 | MATERIAL CULTURE Picturing Joan 300

CHAPTER 10 REVIEW 304

CHAPTER 11
EAST ASIA AND CHINESE INFLUENCES 938-1392 306

SECTION 1 THE SONG DYNASTY
1.1 The Rise of Song China 308
1.2 Books, Steel, and Currency 310
1.3 | DOCUMENT-BASED QUESTION
    Knowledge of the World's Islands 312

xii

Chapter 10, Lesson 1.2

Chapter 12, Lesson 2.1

Chapter 11, Lesson 1.1

SECTION 2 KOREA, VIETNAM, AND JAPAN

2.1 Koryo Korea and Vietnam's Ly Dynasty 314
2.2 Shoguns of Japan.................................. 316
2.3 | **MATERIAL CULTURE** Sharing Cultures, Keeping Traditions 318

CHAPTER 11 REVIEW 322

CHAPTER 12
THE MONGOL EMPIRE, MING DYNASTY, AND OTTOMAN RISE
1150–1500 324

SECTION 1 THE MONGOLS

1.1 From Nomads to Conquerors 326
1.2 | **DOCUMENT-BASED QUESTION** Early Accounts of the Mongols 330
1.3 A Fragmenting Empire 332
1.4 | **NATIONAL GEOGRAPHIC EXPLORER AND TRAVELER** Out of Eden: Ten Million Steps ... 334

SECTION 2 CHINA AND SOUTHEAST ASIA

2.1 The Impact of the Mongols 338
2.2 The Ming Dynasty 340

SECTION 3 RISE OF THE OTTOMAN EMPIRE

3.1 The Rise of the Ottomans 344
3.2 | **STATE OF THE WORLD** 1400 c.e. 346
3.3 The Conquest of Constantinople................. 348

CHAPTER 12 REVIEW 350

UNIT 4 WRAP-UP 352

xiii

Maya temple El Castillo, western Belize

UNIT 5

Dynamics in Africa and the Americas 3100 B.C.E.–1532 C.E.

UNIT INTRODUCTION 354	THE GLOBAL PERSPECTIVE .... ONLINE
UNIT TIME LINE 356	Power Objects
UNIT MAP: AFRICAN AND AMERICAN CIVILIZATIONS 1200 B.C.E.–1532 C.E. .... ONLINE	**NATIONAL GEOGRAPHIC EXPLORER FEATURE** Preserving Precious Objects

CHAPTER 13
ACHIEVEMENTS OF AFRICAN SOCIETIES 300–1525 358

SECTION 1 DIVERSE SOCIETIES, POWERFUL KINGDOMS

1.1 Sub-Saharan African Societies 360
1.2 Ghana and Mali 362
1.3 Great Zimbabwe 364
1.4 **TRAVELER** Ibn Battuta, the Longest-Known Journey 366

SECTION 2 TRADE AND CULTURAL INTERACTIONS

2.1 Trans-Saharan Trade 368
2.2 **A GLOBAL COMMODITY** Salt 370
2.3 Africa's Eastern Networks 374
2.4 **PRESERVING CULTURAL HERITAGE** Churches Carved Into Rock 376
2.5 **DOCUMENT-BASED QUESTION** Africa East and West 378

CHAPTER 13 REVIEW 380

Chapter 13, Lesson 2.2

Chapter 14, Lesson 1.4

Chapter 13, Lesson 2.5

CHAPTER 14
CIVILIZATIONS IN THE AMERICAS 3100 B.C.E.–1532 C.E. 382

SECTION 1 FISHING, HUNTING, AND FARMING

1.1 The Settling of the Americas 384
1.2 Early Complex Societies 386
1.3 Classic and Post-Classic Maya Civilization 388
1.4 **NATIONAL GEOGRAPHIC EXPLORER GUILLERMO DE ANDA** Discovering Maya Secrets Underwater 390
1.5 Northern Cultures 392

SECTION 2 MESOAMERICAN AND ANDEAN SOCIETIES

2.1 Toltec and Aztec Civilizations 394
2.2 Andean Cultures and the Inca 396
2.3 Pacific and Caribbean Island Societies 400

CHAPTER 14 REVIEW 404

UNIT 5 WRAP-UP 406

xv

1719 painting by Gaspar van Wittel depicting Naples, Italy

UNIT 6

Global Explorations and Expansions 1296–1850

UNIT INTRODUCTION	408
UNIT TIME LINE	410
UNIT MAP: VOYAGES OF EXPLORATION 1400–1750	ONLINE

THE GLOBAL PERSPECTIVE .... ONLINE
Seafarers: Life on the World's Oceans

NATIONAL GEOGRAPHIC EXPLORER FEATURE
Seafaring with National Geographic

CHAPTER 15
RENAISSANCE AND REFORMATION
1296–1622 412

SECTION 1 THE EUROPEAN RENAISSANCE

1.1 The Rise of Italian City-States 414
1.2 A Cultural Rebirth 416
1.3 Renaissance Arts 418
1.4 **NATIONAL GEOGRAPHIC EXPLORER MAURIZIO SERACINI**
Finding a Lost da Vinci 422

SECTION 2 THE RENAISSANCE IMPACT

2.1 Renaissance Humanism 424
2.2 Raphael's *School of Athens* 426

2.3 **DOCUMENT-BASED QUESTION**
Humanist Writings 428
2.4 **MATERIAL CULTURE**
Renaissances Around the World 430

SECTION 3 THE PROTESTANT REFORMATION

3.1 Martin Luther and the Protestant Reformation 434
3.2 Reforms Across Europe 436

SECTION 4 GLOBAL IMPACT OF RELIGIOUS REFORMS

4.1 Challenges to Habsburg Dominance 438
4.2 The Catholic Reformation 440
4.3 Global Christianities 442

CHAPTER 15 REVIEW 444

xvi

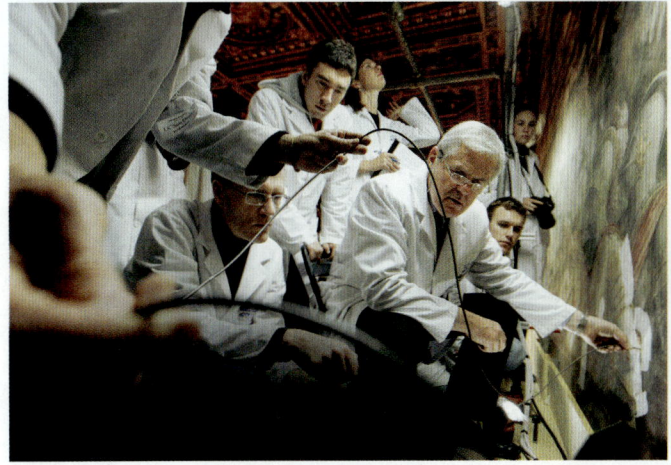

CHAPTER 16
LAND-BASED EMPIRES OF EURASIA
1453–1850 446

SECTION 1 THE OTTOMAN EMPIRE
- **1.1** | **TRAVELER** Evliya Çelebi, Tales from Forty Years of Travel 448
- **1.2** Süleyman and Ottoman Power 450
- **1.3** Safavid Rise and Fall 452
- **1.4** Ottoman Persistence 454

SECTION 2 EMPIRES IN ASIA
- **2.1** Mughal India 456
- **2.2** | **PRESERVING CULTURAL HERITAGE** The Taj Mahal 460
- **2.3** Ming Decline to Qing Power 464
- **2.4** | **DOCUMENT-BASED QUESTION** Voltaire Writes About Qianlong 466
- **2.5** Japan's Tokugawa Shogunate 468

SECTION 3 THE RUSSIAN EMPIRE AND SHIFTING POWERS
- **3.1** Control of the Steppes 470
- **3.2** The Romanov Dynasty 472
- **3.3** Jewish, Tatar, and Armenian Diasporas 476

CHAPTER 16 REVIEW 478

CHAPTER 17
AGE OF MARITIME EXPANSION
1300–1750 480

SECTION 1 EUROPEAN EXPLORATION
- **1.1** Voyages of Discovery 482
- **1.2** Conquests in the Americas 484
- **1.3** | **NATIONAL GEOGRAPHIC EXPLORER PARDIS SABETI** Math Against Malaria 486
- **1.4** The Columbian Exchange 488

SECTION 2 INDIAN OCEAN CONNECTIONS
- **2.1** Portugal's Trade Empire 490
- **2.2** The Dutch East India Company 492
- **2.3** | **DOCUMENT-BASED QUESTION** Trade and Cross-Cultural Encounters 494

SECTION 3 COLONIAL SOCIETIES IN THE AMERICAS
- **3.1** The Spanish Empire in the Americas 496
- **3.2** | **A GLOBAL COMMODITY** Silver 498
- **3.3** The Portuguese and Dutch in the Americas 502
- **3.4** The English Colonies and New France 504

CHAPTER 17 REVIEW 506

CHAPTER 18
AFRICANS IN THE ATLANTIC WORLD
1400–1800 508

SECTION 1 AFRICA, ASIA, AND EUROPE
- **1.1** African History: 1500s to 1700s 510
- **1.2** The Songhai Empire 512
- **1.3** | **PRESERVING CULTURAL HERITAGE** Timbuktu 516

SECTION 2 THE ATLANTIC SLAVE TRADE
- **2.1** | **TRAVELER** Olaudah Equiano, an African Voice 518
- **2.2** The Middle Passage 520
- **2.3** | **A GLOBAL COMMODITY** Sugar 522
- **2.4** Resistance to Slavery 526

CHAPTER 18 REVIEW 530

UNIT 6 WRAP-UP 532

L'Arc de Triomphe, Paris, France

UNIT 7

New Ideas and Revolution 1543-1848

UNIT INTRODUCTION 534
UNIT TIME LINE 536
UNIT MAP: THE AMERICAS c. 1750-1830 ..... ONLINE

THE GLOBAL PERSPECTIVE .... ONLINE
Revolutionary Women

NATIONAL GEOGRAPHIC EXPLORER FEATURE
National Geographic: Women in Science and Exploration

CHAPTER 19
EUROPE IN THE AGE OF SCIENTIFIC REVOLUTION 1543-1848 538

SECTION 1 EUROPE'S STRUGGLE FOR STABILITY
1.1 Power Struggles in France and England 540
1.2 War, Peace, and the Rise of Prussia 542
1.3 The Glorious Revolution 544

SECTION 2 SCIENTIFIC ADVANCES
2.1 Traditions of Inquiry 546
2.2 The Scientific Method 548
2.3 Thinkers and Innovators 550

SECTION 3 PRACTICAL SCIENCE
3.1 Science and Empire 552
3.2 | **TRAVELER** Joseph Banks, Father of Australia 554
3.3 | **MATERIAL CULTURE** Measuring and Mapping 556

CHAPTER 19 REVIEW 560

CHAPTER 20
EUROPEAN ENLIGHTENMENT 1650-1800 562

SECTION 1 REASON AND SOCIETY
1.1 The Age of Reason 564
1.2 | **STATE OF THE WORLD** 1700 c.e. 566
1.3 Civic and Social Reformers 568

SECTION 2 BELIEF IN PROGRESS
2.1 Paris at the Center 572
2.2 | **DOCUMENT-BASED QUESTION** Government and Natural Rights 574
2.3 A New Sense of Confidence 576

CHAPTER 20 REVIEW 578

xviii

Chapter 19, Lesson 1.1

Chapter 20, Lesson 2.2

Chapter 21, Lesson 2.1

CHAPTER 21
POLITICAL REVOLUTION 1750–1830 ... 580

SECTION 1 REVOLUTIONS IN THE WEST
- **1.1** Debate and War in America 582
- **1.2** The French Revolution 584
- **1.3** Haiti's Revolution 588

SECTION 2 NAPOLEON
- **2.1** Napoleon Bonaparte 590
- **2.2** DOCUMENT-BASED QUESTION
  Portraits of Power 594
- **2.3** The Culture of Romanticism 596

SECTION 3 WARS FOR LIBERATION
- **3.1** Simón Bolívar 600
- **3.2** Latin American Wars of Independence 602
- **3.3** The Spread of Revolutionary Ideas 604

CHAPTER 21 REVIEW 606

UNIT 7 WRAP-UP 608

xix

1801 painting by Philip James de Loutherbourg depicting Shropshire, England.

UNIT 8

Industrialization and Imperialism 1615–1928

UNIT INTRODUCTION.. 610
UNIT TIME LINE.. 612
UNIT MAP: COLONIAL POWERS c. 1900 ...... ONLINE

THE GLOBAL PERSPECTIVE........................ ONLINE
A Sense of the World: The Environment in History

CHAPTER 22
INDUSTRIAL REVOLUTION
1615–1928 614

SECTION 1 INDUSTRY AND WORKERS
   1.1 Origins of Industrialization 616
   1.2 Daily Life Transformed 620
   1.3 London's Great Exhibition............................ 622

SECTION 2 GLOBAL CONTEXT AND IMPACT
   2.1 The World Economy Accelerates................. 624
   2.2 Political Ideals 626

SECTION 3 ASIAN TENSIONS IN THE INDUSTRIAL AGE
   3.1 How To Be Modern? 630

   3.2 British India and Indian Revolt..................... 634
   3.3 Rebellions in China 636
   3.4 The Meiji Restoration................................... 638

CHAPTER 22 REVIEW 640

CHAPTER 23
CHANGES IN THE AMERICAS
1803–1924 642

SECTION 1 NORTH AMERICA AFTER INDUSTRIALIZATION
   1.1 Civil War in the United States...................... 644
   1.2 | **A GLOBAL COMMODITY** Cotton............ 646
   1.3 Confederation in Canada 650
   1.4 The Gilded Age 652

xx

Chapter 22, Lesson 3.1

Chapter 23, Lesson 1.1

Chapter 24, Lesson 2.1

SECTION 2 LATIN AMERICA AFTER INDEPENDENCE
2.1 Latin America in the Industrial Age 654
2.2 | **DOCUMENT-BASED QUESTION** Labor and Profit in Latin America 656

SECTION 3 REBELLION AND REFORM
3.1 Indigenous Societies Rebel 658
3.2 Inequality and Reform 662

CHAPTER 23 REVIEW 664

CHAPTER 24
THE NEW IMPERIALISM 1850–1914 666

SECTION 1 DIVIDING AND DOMINATING
1.1 | **TRAVELER** King Khama III, Mission of Diplomacy 668

1.2 A Scramble for Africa 670
1.3 The South African War 674

SECTION 2 TARGETING THE PACIFIC
2.1 Southeast Asia and Austronesia 676
2.2 Imperialist Tactics 678
2.3 | **A GLOBAL COMMODITY** Rubber 680
2.4 Adaptation and Resistance to Empire 684

CHAPTER 24 REVIEW 686

UNIT 8 WRAP-UP 688

xxi

2014 art installation, London, England

UNIT 9

The World Wars 1870–1945

UNIT INTRODUCTION 690	THE GLOBAL PERSPECTIVE .... ONLINE
UNIT TIME LINE 692	Against Inhumanity
UNIT MAP: COUNTRIES INVOLVED IN TWO WORLD WARS 1914–1945 .... ONLINE	**NATIONAL GEOGRAPHIC EXPLORER FEATURE** National Geographic Against Inhumanity

CHAPTER 25
THE FIRST WORLD WAR AND 20TH-CENTURY REVOLUTIONS
1870–1935 694

SECTION 1 TOTAL WAR AND ITS CAUSES
- 1.1 Rivalries, Assassination, Propaganda 696
- 1.2 War on Many Fronts 700
- 1.3 The Course to the End 702
- 1.4 Global Dimensions of Total War 706

SECTION 2 THE GREAT WAR'S CONSEQUENCES
- 2.1 Postwar Treaties and Conflicts 708
- 2.2 **DOCUMENT-BASED QUESTION** The Paris Peace Conference 710
- 2.3 The Armenian Genocide 712
- 2.4 Expanding European Imperialism 714
- 2.5 The "Lost Generation" 716

SECTION 3 REVOLUTIONS IN RUSSIA AND CHINA
- 3.1 Lenin and the Bolshevik Revolution 718
- 3.2 Communist Policy in the New U.S.S.R. 720
- 3.3 China's Republic and Mao's Goals 722

SECTION 4 REVOLUTION IN MEXICO
- 4.1 Instability and Revolt 724
- 4.2 The Campesinos, Zapata, and Villa 726
- 4.3 **DOCUMENT-BASED QUESTION** The Revolution in Murals 728

CHAPTER 25 REVIEW 730

Chapter 25, Lesson 1.3

Chapter 27, Lesson 2.2

CHAPTER 26
ECONOMIC DEPRESSION AND AUTHORITARIAN REGIMES 1908-1939 732

SECTION 1 THE TWENTIES
- 1.1 Over the Air 734
- 1.2 **NATIONAL GEOGRAPHIC EXPLORER AMELIA EARHART** Daring to Fly 738
- 1.3 The Great Depression 740

SECTION 2 DICTATORSHIPS
- 2.1 The Rise of Mussolini 742
- 2.2 Hitler's Scapegoats 744
- 2.3 Stalin's Dictatorship and Purges 746
- 2.4 Totalitarianism in Asia and Latin America 748

SECTION 3 NATIONALISM AND COLONIAL RESISTANCE
- 3.1 Gandhi and India 750
- 3.2 **DOCUMENT-BASED QUESTION** On Progress and Civilization 752
- 3.3 Global Resistance to Colonialism 754

SECTION 4 THE ROAD TO WAR
- 4.1 Japanese Aggression, Italian Invasion 756
- 4.2 Franco and the Spanish Civil War 758
- 4.3 The Hitler-Stalin Pact 760

CHAPTER 26 REVIEW 762

CHAPTER 27
THE SECOND WORLD WAR 1939-1945 ...764

SECTION 1 THE ALLIED AND AXIS POWERS
- 1.1 Germany's Military Might 766
- 1.2 Japan's Rising Sun 768
- 1.3 Allied Momentum 770

SECTION 2 TOTAL WAR
- 2.1 **TRAVELERS** Nancy Wake and Josephine Baker, French Resistance Fighters 774
- 2.2 Wartime Preparations and Policies 776
- 2.3 Civilians, Technology, and the War's Toll 778

SECTION 3 THE HOLOCAUST AND THE LEGACY OF WAR
- 3.1 "The Final Solution" 780
- 3.2 The Holocaust 782
- 3.3 **PRESERVING CULTURAL HERITAGE** Saving the Past 784
- 3.4 Justice and Remembrance 786

CHAPTER 27 REVIEW 788

UNIT 9 WRAP-UP 790

Hong Kong, China

UNIT 10

Global Challenges 1945–PRESENT

UNIT INTRODUCTION 792
UNIT TIME LINE 794
UNIT MAP: FOOD SECURITY AND CLIMATE CHANGE .... ONLINE

THE GLOBAL PERSPECTIVE .... ONLINE
Who We Are: Shared Cultures and Identities

NATIONAL GEOGRAPHIC EXPLORER FEATURE
National Geographic's Global Environmental Citizens

CHAPTER 28
COLD WAR AND GLOBAL UPHEAVALS
1945–1979 796

SECTION 1 SUPERPOWERS IN AN ARMS RACE
1.1 The Yalta Conference and Shifts in Power 798
1.2 American Alliances vs. the Soviet Bloc 800
1.3 The Arms and Space Races 802

SECTION 2 COMMUNISM
2.1 Cuba and Castro 804
2.2 | **PRESERVING CULTURAL HERITAGE**
      Forgotten Art Schools 806
2.3 Mao Zedong and the People's Republic of China 808
2.4 Communes and Chaos 810

SECTION 3 COLONIES SEEK INDEPENDENCE
3.1 Decolonization in Africa 812
3.2 Apartheid in South Africa 814
3.3 The Bandung Generation 816
3.4 The Suez Crisis 818

SECTION 4 WARS IN ASIA AND GLOBAL CRISES
4.1 The Korean War 820
4.2 Two Wars in Vietnam 822
4.3 Strife Around the Globe 824
4.4 | **STATE OF THE WORLD** 1968 C.E. 826

CHAPTER 28 REVIEW 830

Chapter 30, Lesson 3.2

CHAPTER 29
CONFLICTS AND TRANSFORMATIONS
1947–2000 832

SECTION 1 SOVIET COLLAPSE
- **1.1** Glasnost to the Fall of the Berlin Wall............ 834
- **1.2** **THROUGH THE LENS** Gerd Ludwig 838
- **1.3** Post-Soviet Transitions 840
- **1.4** Unrest in Beijing 842

SECTION 2 GLOBAL DEMOCRATIC POSSIBILITIES
- **2.1** Toward Democracy in Latin America 844
- **2.2** **TRAVELER** Nelson Mandela, Anti-Apartheid Activist 846
- **2.3** Nationalist Conflicts 848

SECTION 3 THE MIDDLE EAST
- **3.1** The State of Israel 852
- **3.2** Arab-Israeli Conflicts 854
- **3.3** Revolution and Turmoil 856

SECTION 4 PROMISES AND CHALLENGES OF GLOBALIZATION
- **4.1** Global Human Rights 858
- **4.2** **DOCUMENT-BASED QUESTION** On Nonviolence 860
- **4.3** Economic Challenges 862
- **4.4** **MATERIAL CULTURE** End of a Millennium . 864

CHAPTER 29 REVIEW 868

CHAPTER 30
A GLOBAL 21ST CENTURY
2000–PRESENT 870

SECTION 1 THE POLITICAL PICTURE
- **1.1** September 11 and Aftermath 872
- **1.2** Arab Spring, Syrian Crisis 874
- **1.3** The Future of Southwest Asia 876
- **1.4** Breakdowns and Breakthroughs 882

SECTION 2 THE ECONOMIC PICTURE
- **2.1** Global Financial Crisis 886
- **2.2** The Impact of Globalization 888
- **2.3** **DOCUMENT-BASED QUESTION** Income Inequality 890

SECTION 3 SCIENCE AND TECHNOLOGY
- **3.1** New and Old Energy Sources 892
- **3.2** **NATIONAL GEOGRAPHIC EXPLORERS LESLIE DEWAN AND ANDRÉS RUZO** Reinventing Clean Energy 894
- **3.3** **A GLOBAL COMMODITY** Conflict Minerals 986
- **3.4** The Digital Era in the Balance 898

SECTION 4 VISIONS FOR THE FUTURE
- **4.1** **TRAVELER** Ai Weiwei, A Creative Force in China 900
- **4.2** Women's Leadership and Gender Rights 902
- **4.3** The State of Global Health 908
- **4.4** Food Security 910

CHAPTER 30 REVIEW 916

UNIT 10 WRAP-UP 918

STUDENT REFERENCES R1

NATIONAL GEOGRAPHIC AND SPECIAL FEATURES

MAPS

Additional maps appear online in the Student eEdition.

Early Human Migration: 100,000–14,000 Years Ago	10
Out of Eden Walk, Planned Route	17
Cultural Hearths and the Spread of Agriculture, c. 8000–500 B.C.E.	24
Ancient Mesopotamia, 2500 B.C.E.	34
Ancient Egypt and Nubia, 3000–2000 B.C.E.	42
Jewish Diaspora, c. 586 B.C.E.–500 C.E.	60
Expansion of Ancient Egypt, c. 2575–1070 B.C.E.	65
Indus River Valley Civilization	69
The Maurya Empire	78
Monsoon Winds in the Indian Ocean	80
Ancient China, c. 1300 B.C.E.	83
Shang, Zhou, and Qin Dynasties	93
Herodotus's Journeys, 450–430 B.C.E.	102
The Persian Empire, 500 B.C.E.	110
The Greco-Persian Wars, 490–479 B.C.E.	115
Phoenician and Greek Settlement in the Mediterranean	127
Greek City-States, c. 500 B.C.E.	128
Alexander's Empire, c. 323 B.C.E.	141
The Peloponnesian War, 431–404 B.C.E.	149
Roman Expansion, 264–146 B.C.E.	154
Trade in the Roman Empire, c. 117 C.E.	160
The Spread of Christianity, c. 500 C.E.	174
Egeria's Journeys, 381–384 C.E.	177
Invasions into the Roman Empire, 350–500 C.E.	182
The Gupta Empire and Chola Kingdom	196
Sima Qian's Journeys, 125–120 B.C.E.	199
Silk Roads Main Route, 150 B.C.E.–500 C.E.	201
The Han Dynasty, 206 B.C.E.–220 C.E.	202
Korea and Japan, c. 550 C.E.	209

Title	Page
The Byzantine Empire, 527–565	225
Justinian's Plague, 541–544	233
The Byzantine Empire, c. 1071	236
Growth of the Muslim Empire, 661	250
The Abbasid Empire, c. 850	257
Medieval Europe, c. 500	271
The Schism of 1054	275
The Crusades	292
Trade Routes and Spread of the Plague, 1340s–1350s	297
The Song Dynasty, 960–1279	309
The Geography of Japan	317
The Mongol Empire, 1259	328
The Mongol Empire, 1294	332
Out of Eden Walk: January 2013–October 2017	336
Zheng He's Voyages, 1405–1433	342
The Ottoman Empire, 1481	344
Africa Before 1500	360
Ibn Battuta's Journeys, 1325–1354	367
Trans-Saharan Trade Network	381
Clovis Point Discoveries	385
Early Complex Societies in the Americas	386
North American Civilizations, 1000 B.C.E.–1500 C.E.	392
Toltec and Aztec Civilizations, 900–1500 C.E.	394
Early South American Societies, 600–1532 C.E.	397
Pacific Migration Routes Before 1500	400
Europe, c. 1520	438
Spread of Protestantism, 1600s	442
Evliya Çelebi's Journeys, 1640–1670s	448
Ottoman Expansion, 1451–1683	451
The Safavid Empire, 16th Century	452
Ming and Qing Dynasties, 1405–1783	464
The Mughal Empire, 1526–1707	479
The Voyages of Christopher Columbus, 1492–1504	482
The Columbian Exchange	488
European Presence in the East, 1487–1700	491
Spanish Explorers and Rule, 1513–1598	497
New France and English Colonies in North America, 1754	505
Waldseemüller Map of the "New World," 1513	507
Major African States, c. 1400s–1600s	513
Olaudah Equiano's Journeys, 1755–1789	519
The Triangular Trade, c. 1500–1800	520
Europe, c. 1715	543
Joseph Banks's Journeys, 1768–1771	555

Title	Page
Napoleonic Europe, c. 1810	592
Independence in the Americas, 1804–1839	605
Industrialization in Continental Europe, c. 1850	618
Italian and German Unification, 1858–1871	628
King Khama's Journey, 1895	669
Colonial Presence in Africa, 1897 and 1914	670
Imperialism in Southeast Asia, 1910	676
The Balkans, 1914	697
World War I, August 1914–April 1917	701
Territorial Changes in Europe After World War I	709
Mandates in Africa and Southwest Asia	715
Mandates in the Pacific Islands	715
Where Is Amelia Earhart?	738
Growth of Nazi Germany, 1933–1939	760
German Advances, 1938–1941	766
War in Europe and Africa, 1942–1945	771
War in Asia, 1942–1945	772
Nancy Wake's and Josephine Baker's Journeys, 1942–1945	775
Division of Europe During the Cold War, 1960	801
The People's Republic of China and Taiwan, 1949	809
Achieving Independence in Africa, 1847–1993	812
Division of Korea, 1953	820
Partition of Vietnam, 1954	823
Berlin, 1961	836
Dissolution of the Soviet Union and Aligned Nations	840
Nelson Mandela's Journeys, 1955–1995	847
Arab-Israeli Conflicts, 1947–1967	854
Development of the European Union	862
The British Isles	869
The Middle East	876
Ai Weiwei's Journeys, 1957–2015	901

TIME LINES, CHARTS, MODELS, GRAPHS

Additional visuals appear online in the Student eEdition.

Title	Page
World Events, 200,000 B.C.E.–500 C.E.	4
Dates and Locations of Earliest Cultivation	31
The Eightfold Path	72
The Dynastic Cycle	84
World Events, 2200 B.C.E.–1200 C.E.	98
The City of Athens, c. 400 B.C.E.	131
Gold at a Glance	135
Roman Republic vs. United States	189

xxvii

Roman, Sanskrit, and Western Numerals	195
Factors Contributing to the Collapse of the Han Dynasty	203
Events in Buddhism and Hinduism	215
World Events, 500–1300	220
The Five Pillars of Islam	246
Comparison of the Three Abrahamic Religions	261
World Events, 600–1500	266
European Population, 1000–1450	305
Hierarchical Society in Feudal Japan and Europe	323
World Events, 3100 B.C.E.–1532 C.E.	356
Salt at a Glance	371
World Events, 1300–1650	410
European Literacy Rate, 1475–1750	445
Silver at a Glance	500
The Slave Ship *Brooks*	521
Sugar at a Glance	525
Number of Enslaved People Exported from Africa, 1450–1900	531
World Events, 1543–1859	536
The Scientific Method	549
Time Line of Scientific and Political Events	561
Major Ideas of Enlightenment Thinkers	579
World Events, 1765–1912	612
Economic History of China and Other Major Powers	641
Cotton at a Glance	649
Rubber at a Glance	683
World Events, 1914–1945	692
The Great Powers of World War I	698
Casualties in the Great War	731
Unemployment Rates, 1929–1934	763
World Events, 1945–Present	796
World's Largest Economies, 2018	888
Sampling of Richest and Poorest Countries by Income	890
Greatest and Least Income Inequality Within a Country	891
Countries with Highest and Lowest Happiness Index	891
Selected Breakthroughs in Computer Technology	898
Atmospheric Carbon Dioxide Levels	917

PRIMARY AND SECONDARY SOURCES

Additional primary and sources appear online in the Student eEdition.

"Ethiopia: To Walk the World" by Paul Salopek	17
"Great Rift Valley: Baby Steps" by Paul Salopek	18
"What Explains the Rise of Humans?" by Yuval Noah Harari	31
Epic of Gilgamesh	37
Code of Hammurabi	41
Ten Commandments from the Hebrew Bible	59
Epic of Gilgamesh	63
Book of Genesis from the Hebrew Bible	63
Mahabharata	63
Book of the Dead	65
Ashoka's Fourth Major Rock Edict	79
The Analects of Confucius	86
The Analects of Confucius	93
The Histories of Herodutus	103
Cyrus Cylinder Inscription	107
Book of Ezra from the Hebrew Bible	107
The Histories of Herodutus	117
The Histories of Herodutus	119
The Funeral Oration of Pericles	131
The Republic by Plato	146
Phaedo by Plato	149
Egeria's Travels	176
The Annals by Tacitus	179
Letters of Pliny	179
Edict of Toleration by the Emperor Galerius	179
The Twelve Tables	187
"Sermon on the Mount" from the New Testament	189
Records of the Grand Historian (Shiji) by Sima Qian	198
Lessons for Women by Ban Zhao	215
The Institutes of Justinian	227
The Wars of Justinian by Procopius	233
Epitaph of Basil II	241
The Uthmanis by Al-Jahiz	261
The Canterbury Tales by Geoffrey Chaucer	281
Alexiad by Anna Comnena	292
Account of the Persecution of Jews During the Black Death	305
The Description of Foreign Peoples (Zhu Fan Zhi) by Zhao Rugua	313
Haiku by Ono no Komachi	323
The Complete History by Ibn al-Athir	331
The History of the World Conqueror by Ala-ad-Din Ata-Malik Juvaini	331
Compendium of Chronicles by Rashid al-Din	331
"Uzbekistan: Discovering a Medieval Moon Base in the Heart of Central Asia" by Paul Salopek	335
"What I'm Learning from Walking 21,000 Miles Around the World" by Paul Salopek	337
History of Mehmed the Conqueror by Kritovoulos	349

Entry	Page
The Travels of Marco Polo	351
The Travels of Ibn Battuta	366
Book of Highways and Kingdoms by Abu U-bayd al-Bakri	379
The Book of Duarte Barbosa	379
A Geographical Historie of Africa by Leo Africanus	379
The Travels of Ibn Battuta	381
Popol Vuh	405
"An Oration . . . in Praise of Letters" by Cassandra Fedele	429
The Prince by Niccoló Machiavelli	429
Utopia by Thomas More	429
"Against the Robbing and Murdering Hordes of Peasants" by Martin Luther	435
The Life of Michelangelo by Ascanio Condivi	445
The Book of Travels by Evliya Çelebi	449
Letter to Frederick the Great from Voltaire	467
Letter to the Marquis de Condorcet from Voltaire	467
Letter to King George III from Qianlong	467
Haiku by Matsuo Basho	479
General History of the Things of New Spain by Bernardino de Sahagún	485
Sejarah Melayu (Malay Annals) by Tun Sri Lanang	495
Travels in Persia by Jean Chardin	495
The Ship of Sulaiman by Muhammad Rabi ibn Muhammad Ibrahim	495
A Brief Account of the Destruction of the Indies by Bartolomé de las Casas	507
History and Description of Africa by Leo Africanus	515
The Interesting Narrative of the Life of Olaudah Equiano, or Gustavus Vassa, the African	518
"Go Down Moses"	527
"To the Right Honorable William, Earl of Dartmouth" by Phillis Wheatley	531
Sentence of Charles I, January 27, 1649	542
English Bill of Rights	544
Journal of Joseph Banks	554
Sir Francis Bacon on the Farmers in Ireland	561
Politics by Aristotle	565
The Spirit of the Laws by Charles-Louis Montesquieu	570
A Philosophical Dictionary by Voltaire	570
The Social Contract by Jean-Jacques Rousseau	571
A Vindication of the Rights of Woman by Mary Wollstonecraft	571
Memoirs of Jean François Marmontel	572
The Spirit of the Laws by Charles-Louis Montesquieu	575
A Vindication of the Rights of Woman by Mary Wollstonecraft	575
The Encyclopedia by Denis Diderot	575
Speech to the House of Commons by William Wilberforce	577
An Essay Concerning Human Understanding by John Locke	579
Declaration of Independence	583
Declaration of the Rights of Man and of the Citizen	585
Haitian Constitution, 1801	589
Napoleon's Account of His Coup d'Etat	591
"The Tyger" by William Blake	596
Letter to the Governor of Jamaica from Simón Bolívar	600
Letter to Henry Laurens from Benjamin Franklin	604
Letter to Catherine Macauley from Mercy Otis Warren	607
"London Companion During the Great Exhibition" by R. Beasland	622
The Philosophy of Manufactures by Andrew Ure	641
Exploration of the Valley of the Amazon, 1851–1852, by William Lewis Herndon	657
"A Letter to Striking Workers" by Matías Romero	657
"First Electoral Manifesto of the Argentine Socialist Worker Party"	657
"House Divided" Speech by Abraham Lincoln	665
King Khama III on the Arrival of Europeans in Africa	668
Letter in the New York Herald by Mark Twain	679
"The White Man's Burden" by Rudyard Kipling	679
Letter to the Caliph of Sudan from Menelik II	687
Oral History by British Private Harold Boughton	707
Congress of Damascus Resolution by the General Syrian Congress of Damascus	711
"Eight Points" by Nguyen Ai Quoc	711
"To the World" by the Second Pan-African Congress	711
Ambassador Morgenthau's Story by Henry Morgenthau	713
"Notes on the Next War: A Serious Topical Letter" by Ernest Hemingway	717
"Report on an Investigation of the Peasant Movement in Hunan" by Mao Zedong	723
"Can the Bolsheviks Retain State Power?" by Vladimir Lenin	731
Antonio Gramsci Writing in *Avanti!*, August 1916	743
Hind Swaraj by Mohandas K. Gandhi	753
Jawaharlal Nehru, An Autobiography	753
Speech by Japanese Military Leader Hashimoto Kingoro	763
Speech before the House of Commons by Winston Churchill	767
The Autobiography of the Woman the Gestapo Called the White Mouse by Nancy Wake	774
Night by Elie Wiesel	782

Opening Statement before the International Military Tribunal at Nuremberg 786
"The Four Freedoms" Speech by Franklin D. Roosevelt 789
"Iron Curtain" Speech by Winston Churchill 800
Address by Anthony Eden on the Suez Crisis 819
Speech by Dwight D. Eisenhower on the Suez Crisis 819
Letter to Nikita Khrushchev from John F. Kennedy, 1961 . . . 831
Letter to John F. Kennedy from Nikita Khrushchev, 1961 . . . 831
Nelson Mandela's Address on His Release from Prison 846
Universal Declaration of Human Rights 858
"Guidelines on Christian Conduct During Elections" by Cardinal Jaime Sin 861
Letter from the Gdańsk Prison by Adam Michnik 861
"Purple Reign" by Alison Ozinsky 861
Speech on Globalization by Boutros Boutros-Ghali 869
National Public Radio Interview with Ai Weiwei 901
Declaration from 2017 BRICS Science, Technology & Innovation Meeting 917

DOCUMENT-BASED QUESTIONS

Cave Paintings 20
Comparing Flood Narratives 62
Cyrus the Great and the Jewish Exiles 106
The Romans and the Christians 178
Comparing Calendars 248
Knowledge of the World's Islands 312
Early Accounts of the Mongols 330
Africa East and West 378
Humanist Writings 428
Voltaire Writes About Qianlong 466
Trade and Cross-Cultural Encounters 494
Government and Natural Rights 574
Portraits of Power 594
Labor and Profit in Latin America 656
The Paris Peace Conference 710
The Revolution in Murals 728
On Progress and Civilization 752
On Nonviolence 860
Income Inequality 890

NATIONAL GEOGRAPHIC ADAPTED ARTICLES

"Cities of Silence (Thoughts on the Harappan Culture)" 94
"The Land of the Stars" 216
"The World's Newest Major Religion: No Religion" 262
"Were Viking Warriors Especially Brutal?" 352
"The Real Price of Gold" 406
"The Epic Quest for a Northwest Passage" 532
"Jane Goodall: A Revolutionary Naturalist" 608
"Awash in Plastic" 688
"The Science of Good and Evil" 790
"Navigating the Anthropocene" 918

NATIONAL GEOGRAPHIC EXPLORER/PHOTOGRAPHER FEATURES

Additional Explorer features appear online in the Student eEdition.

Meave and Louise Leakey: Family Traditions 9
Jeffrey Rose: Tracing the Paths of Early Humans 12
Keolu Fox: The Wisdom of Indigenous Peoples 15
Out of Eden: Paul Salopek Walks Through Time 16
Genevieve von Petzinger: Cave Paintings 20
Yukinori Kawae: Strange, Unexplored Places 45
Nora Shawki: Looking for Everyday Life in Ancient Egypt . . . 47
Kara Cooney: When Women Ruled the World 52
Fredrik Hiebert: Heritage at Risk 56
Jodi Magness: Tales Told by Mosaics 61
O. Louis Mazzatenta: Through the Lens 90
Christopher Thornton: What a Cooking Pot Can Tell Us . . . 108
William Parkinson: Embracing Our Greek Heritage 122
Patrick Hunt: Tracing Hannibal's Route 155
Steven Ellis: Excavating the Stories of Ordinary People 165
Christine Lee: Reconstructing Lives 205
Sarah Parcak: Citizen-Science Technology 273
Albert Lin: Searching for Genghis Khan's Tomb 329
Paul Salopek: Out of Eden: Ten Million Steps 334
Matthew Piscitelli: Exploring Peru's Ancient Past 387
Guillermo de Anda: Discovering Maya Secrets Underwater 390
Terry Hunt and Carl Lipo: The "Walking" Statues of Rapa Nui 401
Jago Cooper: Art in the Heart of the Caribbean 403
Maurizio Seracini: Finding a Lost da Vinci 422
Pardis Sabeti: Math Against Malaria 486
Kathy Ku: Just the Beginning 551
Jon Waterhouse and Mary Marshall: Capturing Indigenous Voices 661
Jeff Gusky: The Hidden World of the Great War 705
Amelia Earhart: Daring to Fly 738
Robert Ballard: Discovery on the Sea Floor 769

Ari Beser: The Survivors' Side of the Story 779
Buzz Aldrin: Beyond the Moon 803
David Guttenfelder: Through the Lens 805
Gerd Ludwig: Through the Lens 838
Aziz Abu Sarah: Connecting Cultures 877
Ella Al-Shamahi: Funny Bones 878
Salam Al Kuntar: Protecting Traditions 879
Steve McCurry: Solving a Mystery 880
Leslie Dewan and Andrés Ruzo:
Reinventing Clean Energy 894
Kakenya Ntaiya: Empowering Kenya's Girls 904
Lynsey Addario: A Different Dynamic 906
Hayat Sindi: A Paper Medical Lab 909
Jack Andraka: A Science Fair Discovery 909
T.H. Culhane: Living Off the Grid 912
Jerry Glover: Women and Food Security 914

GLOBAL PERSPECTIVE FEATURES

Global Perspective features appear online in the Student eEdition.

No Walls, No Borders: Nomads .... Unit 1
Astronomy: The Search for Meaning and Survival .... Unit 2
Many Paths to God .... Unit 3
Soldiering: Why We Fight .... Unit 4
Power Objects .... Unit 5
Seafarers: Life on the World's Oceans .... Unit 6
Revolutionary Women .... Unit 7
A Sense of the World: The Environment in History ...... Unit 8
Against Inhumanity .... Unit 9
Who We Are: Shared Cultures and Identities .... Unit 10

PRESERVING CULTURAL HERITAGE FEATURES

Queens of Egypt 50
Heritage at Risk 56
Lady Moon at the Crossroads 142
Jerusalem: From History to VR 168
Temple Spires Against the Elements 210
"Suspended from Heaven" 228
Notre-Dame Cathedral 284
Churches Carved into Rock 376
The Taj Mahal 460
Timbuktu 516
Saving the Past 784
Forgotten Art Schools 806

MATERIAL CULTURE FEATURES

The Power of Animals 26
Images of the Buddha 74
Persian Monuments and Scythian Gold 112
Picturing Joan 300
Sharing Cultures, Keeping Traditions 318
Renaissances Around the World 430
Measuring and Mapping 556
End of a Millennium 864

GLOBAL COMMODITY FEATURES

Additional Global Commodity features appear online in the Student eEdition.

Gold 134
Salt 370
Silver 498
Sugar 522
Cotton 646
Rubber 680
Conflict Minerals 896

STATE OF THE WORLD FEATURES

1 B.C.E.:   Culture and Technology 166
800 C.E.:   Religious Fervor 254
1400 C.E.: Poised for Change 346
1700 C.E.: European Domination 566
1968 C.E.: A Turbulent Year 826

TRAVELER FEATURES

Herodotus: The World's First Historian 102
Egeria: An Early Christian Pilgrim 176
Sima Qian: The Grand Historian 198
Procopius: Plague Witness 232
Ibn Battuta: The Longest-Known Journey 366
Evliya Çelebi: Tales from Forty Years of Travel 448
Olaudah Equiano: An African Voice 518
Joseph Banks: Father of Australia 554
King Khama III: Mission of Diplomacy 668
Nancy Wake and Josephine Baker:
French Resistance Fighters 774
Nelson Mandela: Anti-Apartheid Activist 846
Ai Weiwei: A Creative Force in China 900

Additional features, including videos and image galleries, are available in the Student eEdition.

xxxi

JIMMY CHIN AND THE TYRANNY OF PASSION

It takes a while to make textbooks. If we had been able to go to press as quickly as we would have liked, you'd have been using this book (either in print or ebook form) in February 2019. And if that had happened, you would have seen the person pictured on this page, National Geographic photographer Jimmy Chin, win an Academy Award for Best Documentary Feature.

Jimmy is a man of many talents. He won the Oscar for producing a documentary on Alex Honnold, an American professional rock climber who had completed a "free solo" climb—meaning no ropes, harnesses, or protective equipment—of El Capitan in Yosemite National Park. Jimmy himself is a professional climber, skier, photographer, and now filmmaker.

As writers and editors for a World History textbook for National Geographic, we have access to hundreds of National Geographic Explorers and photographers. All of them are completely brilliant and inspired and doing work that contributes to the common good—either by capturing ideas and images that reveal our world to us in new ways or by using their considerable knowledge and creative skills to innovate new processes and new approaches in their fields.

When several of us were in the audience at a National Geographic Explorers Symposium in 2018, we watched Jimmy Chin talk with another NatGeo photographer about the work that they both do. He used the phrase "the tyranny of passion" and explained that the words aptly describe the way he lives his life.

Jimmy has found in his work something so fundamental to who he is, something he loves so much, that he simply can't *not* do it. His work is so much a part of his thoughts, feelings, and actions that he can't imagine a different life.

The tyranny of passion. Those words have meaning for all of us.

Watch the video of Jimmy that accompanies this textbook. You'll see him talk about how he found what he wants to do with his life. You'll hear him admit that he found a direction that caught him—and his family—by surprise. He's never looked back.

Our message to you, then, is to know that there is something wonderful that you can do with your life, something that draws on your heart and your mind and that you will love to do. You have only to seek it.

Your ideas and your actions are important.

Share them with others.

Be heard.

And along the way, listen to others' voices too.

National Geographic photographer and filmmaker Jimmy Chin hangs from a rope while filming part of his Academy Award–winning documentary, *Free Solo*.

Chin heads up the side of El Capitan in Yosemite National Park. He quietly climbed alongside friend and fellow climber Alex Honnold for four hours to document Honnold's climb up the mountain without ropes.

UNIT 1

CRITICAL VIEWING
These rock engravings of fighting cats at the Wadi Methkandoush archaeological site in Libya are believed to be at least 12,000 years old. Why do you think people created these carvings?

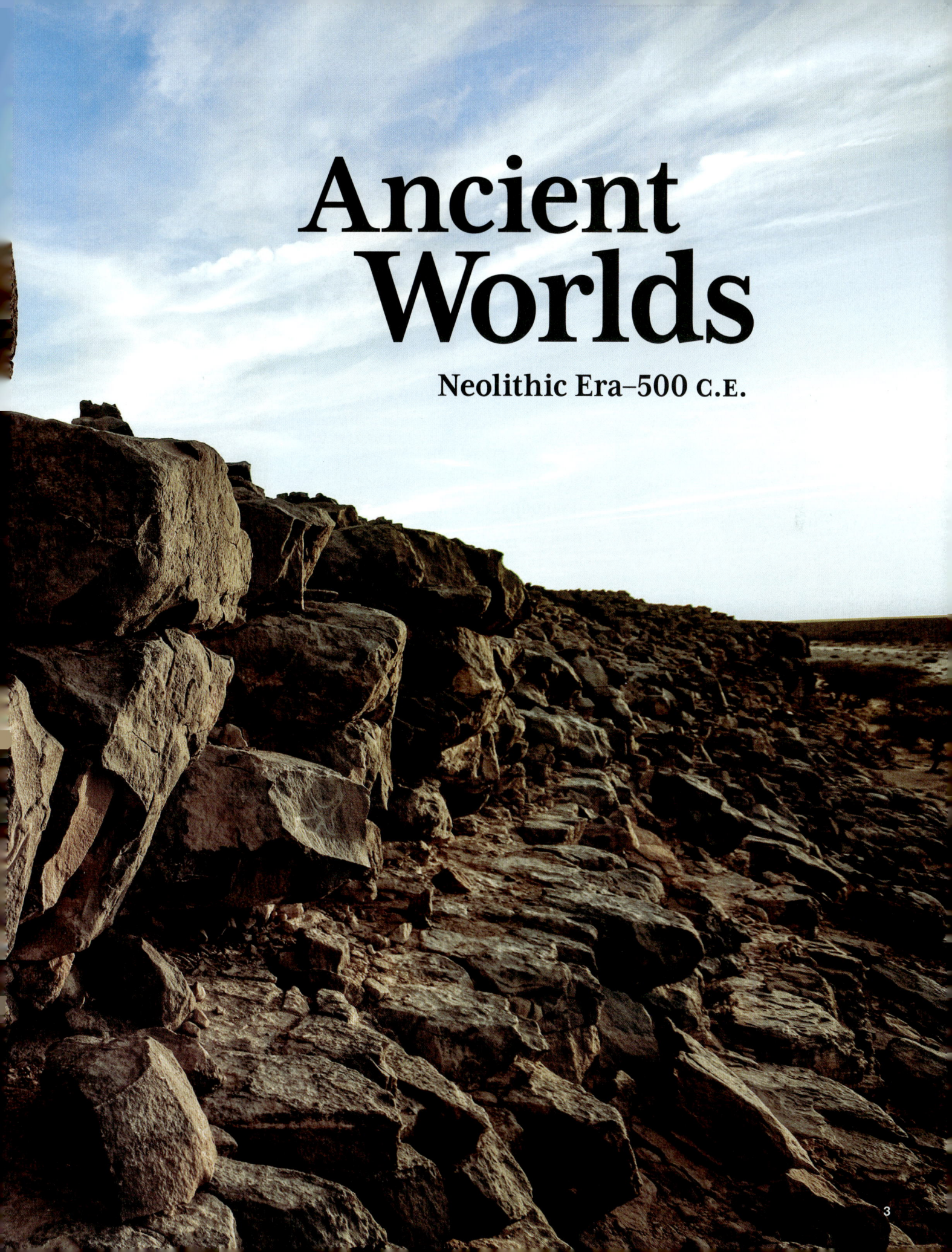

Ancient Worlds

Neolithic Era–500 C.E.

UNIT 1 Ancient Worlds

WORLD EVENTS
200,000 B.C.E.–500 C.E.

8000 B.C.E ASIA People living on the North China Plain begin to cultivate rice, the first domesticated crop in China. *(terraced rice field in southern China)*

200,000 B.C.E AFRICA The first modern humans appear in central and southern Africa. *(Stone Age tool from Morocco)*

60,000 B.C.E EUROPE Modern humans move north and west from the Arabian Peninsula into Europe.

8300 B.C.E ASIA The Natufians establish Jericho, one of the world's oldest known and continuously occupied human settlements.

| 200,000 B.C.E. | 100,000 B.C.E. | 50,000 B.C.E. | 10,000 B.C.E. |

100,000 B.C.E ASIA According to paleoarchaeologist Jeffrey Rose, hunter-gatherers migrate from Africa to the Arabian Peninsula.

12,000 B.C.E ASIA Çatalhöyük is founded in present-day Turkey and grows to house as many as 8,000 people. *(sculpture of embracing couple from Çatalhöyük)*

10,000 B.C.E ASIA The world's first temple—Göbekli Tepe—is built in present-day Turkey. *(stone boar carving from Göbekli Tepe)*

HISTORICAL THINKING

DRAW CONCLUSIONS How do you think the formation of human settlements and the development of agriculture are related?

2334 B.C.E ASIA After conquering the city-states of Sumer, Sargon of Akkad establishes the world's first empire. *(statue of man who could be Sargon the Great)*

3100 B.C.E ASIA Uruk, the first city-state—containing 40,000–50,000 people—thrives in southern Mesopotamia. *(kneeling bull sculpture from Mesopotamia)*

3300 B.C.E ASIA The Sumerians develop the world's first writing system.

2589–2566 B.C.E AFRICA The Egyptian pharaoh Khufu builds the Great Pyramid.

3500 B.C.E ASIA The people of Mesopotamia adopt the use of the wheel.

5,000 B.C.E. — **500 B.C.E.** — **1 C.E.**

7000 B.C.E ASIA Inhabitants of the Indus River Valley develop agriculture, planting wheat, barley, and jujube dates.

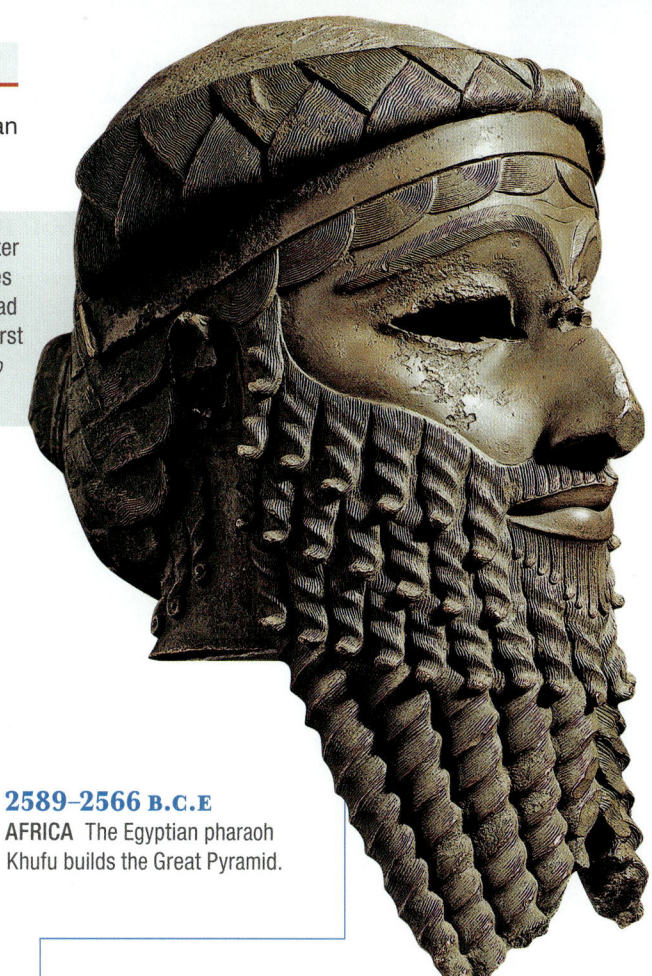

196 B.C.E AFRICA The Rosetta Stone is created.

2100 B.C.E ASIA The *Epic of Gilgamesh*—the world's oldest recorded story—is written. *(engraving of Gilgamesh fighting two snakes)*

100 C.E ASIA Seafaring merchants sail to India from locations around the world, spreading the exchange of goods, Indian culture, and Buddhist thought. *(Buddhist stupa at Sanchi, India)*

CHAPTER 1

First Peoples and Societies

Neolithic Era–5650 B.C.E.

HISTORICAL THINKING How do societies help people survive?

SECTION 1 **History Is Discovery**

SECTION 2 **The Neolithic Revolution**

CRITICAL VIEWING

Abijatta-Shalla National Park in Ethiopia is part of East Africa's Great Rift Valley. What do the physical features shown in the photo tell you about this place?

1.1 MAIN IDEA Historians as well as many types of scientists bring their knowledge and research to understand what happened in the past.

History Joins Science

How do scholars know what happened long ago? Written sources may not exist for some events, and even when written accounts survive, the writer may not have known everything that happened or may have described only part of the story.

TELLING THE STORY OF HUMANKIND

For some world regions, historians work to establish basic facts such as the names of kings or when they reigned. However, most historians today study societies where the basic chronology, or order of events, is already known; in those cases, they bring new questions to the past that reflect the world's changing concerns. As you read, you will learn what historians and scientists think happened in the past and how they came to their conclusions. This text uses B.C.E. and C.E. (*before the Common Era* and *Common Era*) for dates before and after the year 1. Other sources or websites may use the abbreviations B.C. and A.D. for these same time periods.

Ultimately, historians rely on primary sources—documents and **artifacts**, which are objects of historical value made by human beings. Historians read their sources carefully, checking the meaning of different words and grappling with unfamiliar languages from long ago. They also mine these sources for evidence, which they weave into historical arguments. Historians consult fellow historians and other experts, such as linguists, archaeologists, anthropologists, and geographers. However, views of the past are always changing. Sometimes, researchers discover new primary sources and artifacts. Sometimes, historians return to the sources earlier researchers have examined, raise different questions about them, and revise their conclusions. These are all aspects of **historiography**, the art and science of creating a reliable and useful story from bits of information about the past.

"Examining sources" doesn't mean merely going through old documents. Today's high-tech tools can unlock the secrets of the past. For example, archaeologists use LiDAR (light-detection and ranging technology, also known as laser speed guns) to discover the sites of previously unknown ancient cities under thick rain forest vegetation. Scientists may know about other important sites, such as the tomb of an ancient Chinese emperor, but they do not want to disturb the contents. Experts use equipment and methods such as radar, core sampling, and remote sensing to learn more about the tomb without entering it. They do the same to collect data at other fragile sites with little disruption of these sensitive locations. As the ability of scientists to collect and analyze a wider range of information progresses, the understanding of history keeps expanding and increasing.

THE EARLIEST HUMANS

Scientific advances have provided insights into human evolution as well. Scientists believe that the first modern humans appeared in central and southern Africa some 200,000 years ago. *Modern humans* is the term used for early humans who had a physical build, brain size, and appearance similar to that of present-day people. This scientific view is supported by recent research into genetic material, which supplements what historians and other experts can learn from archaeologically excavated remains.

When a woman and a man have a child, most of their DNA, or genetic code, recombines to form a new sequence unique to their baby. (DNA is short for deoxyribonucleic acid.) However, a certain type of DNA, known as mitochondrial DNA, passes directly from the mother to the child. By analyzing mitochondrial DNA, geneticists—scientists who study how the characteristics of living things are controlled by genes—have determined that human beings share a single human female ancestor, known as **mitochondrial Eve**. This woman is believed to have lived in Africa about 200,000 years ago. She was not the first or only modern human female of her time, but she was the first who had daughters who also gave birth to daughters. Every human being alive today has mitochondrial DNA passed down from this individual. We all trace our ancestry to Africa.

8 CHAPTER 1

NATIONAL GEOGRAPHIC EXPLORERS MEAVE AND LOUISE LEAKEY

Family Traditions

National Geographic Explorers Meave Leakey and Louise Leakey (shown digging in Kenya above) are paleoanthropologists, scientists who study fossils of early humans and their ancestors, at the Turkana Basin Institute, a center for human origins research in northern Kenya, near the borders of Ethiopia and South Sudan. Meave, a woman who originally trained to study marine zoology, could not get a job in that field in the 1960s because of her gender. She applied for a position at the Leakey family Primate Research Centre in Kenya, where she discovered her life's work. She also met her future husband, Richard, the son of well-known archaeologists and paleoanthropologists Louis Leakey and Mary Leaky. Working with Richard and their daughter Louise, Meave has made important discoveries about human ancestors dating back millions of years. Louise continues the work of her parents and her grandparents, and her most recent project has been the development of a virtual laboratory. At AfricanFossils.org, users can virtually explore the Lake Turkana site, lab, and fossils as well as download models for 3-D printing.

Human skull and mandible (lower jawbone) found in Morocco

EARLY HUMANS OUTSIDE EAST AFRICA While scientists have long believed that the first modern humans evolved in east Africa's Ethiopia, recent discoveries have challenged that view. Using a technique called thermoluminescence, which measures the release of energy from crystals exposed to extreme heat, scientists estimate that 300,000 years ago, humans made tools found at a site called Jebel Irhoud (JEH-buhl EE-rood), Morocco, in northwestern Africa. Prior African finds had revealed humans dating back nearly 200,000 years. The humans discovered in Morocco shared many characteristics of other modern humans. They had faces much like ours, which might mean they had developed speech; they made tools; and their brains were as large as ours, though a different shape. This discovery led some scientists to suggest that early humans continued to evolve as they spread throughout Africa.

First Peoples and Societies

HUMAN BEHAVIOR AND MIGRATION

Scientists debate when members of our species first acted like modern humans. The ability to plan ahead is an important indicator of human behavior. Additional clues lie in the ability to improve tools, the existence of trade networks, the practice of making art, the ritual of burying the dead, and the ability to speak. Early humans had larynxes, or voice boxes, but they did not begin to speak until sometime between 100,000 and 50,000 B.C.E. Scientists cannot know the exact date because the act of speaking does not produce lasting evidence. Instead, paleontologists have identified certain human activities, such as organizing hunting parties to trap large game, as sufficiently complex to require speech. Speech may have begun because of a genetic mutation, or change in DNA.

Studies of mitochondrial DNA have helped determine when and where modern humans traveled as they spread over the globe. From Africa, modern

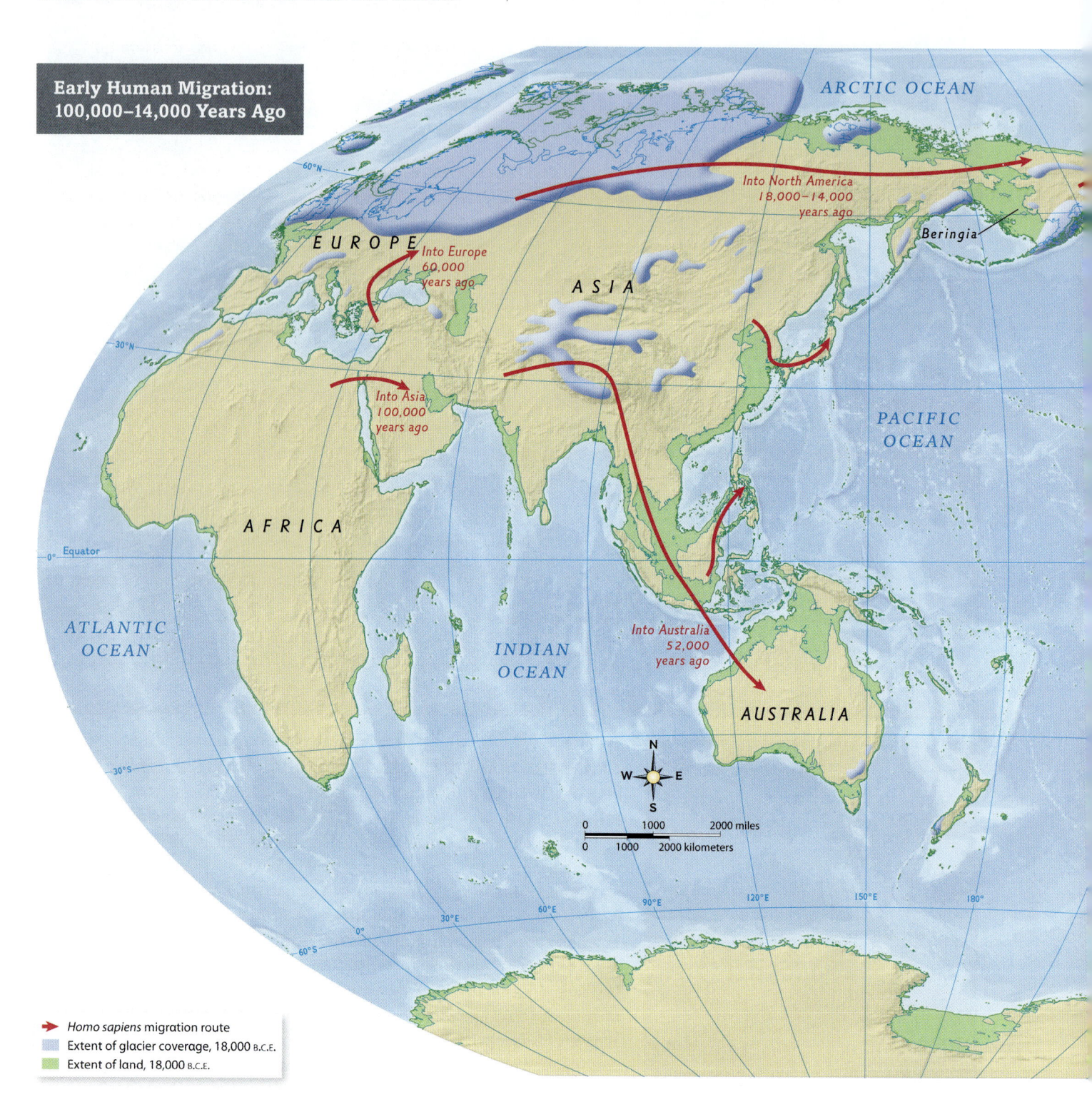

Early Human Migration: 100,000–14,000 Years Ago

- Into North America 18,000–14,000 years ago
- Into Europe 60,000 years ago
- Into Asia 100,000 years ago
- Into Australia 52,000 years ago

Legend:
- *Homo sapiens* migration route
- Extent of glacier coverage, 18,000 B.C.E.
- Extent of land, 18,000 B.C.E.

humans **migrated**, or moved from one region to another, traveling by land and water until they had settled all over Earth. As modern humans left Africa around 100,000 B.C.E. (or perhaps even earlier), they modified tools for new environments. They built boats or rafts to cross bodies of water. Tens of thousands of years ago, water levels were much lower than they are today, so distances between some landmasses were shorter. As you will read later in the chapter, many present-day archaeologists believe that people crossed a land bridge to move from Africa to the Arabian Peninsula.

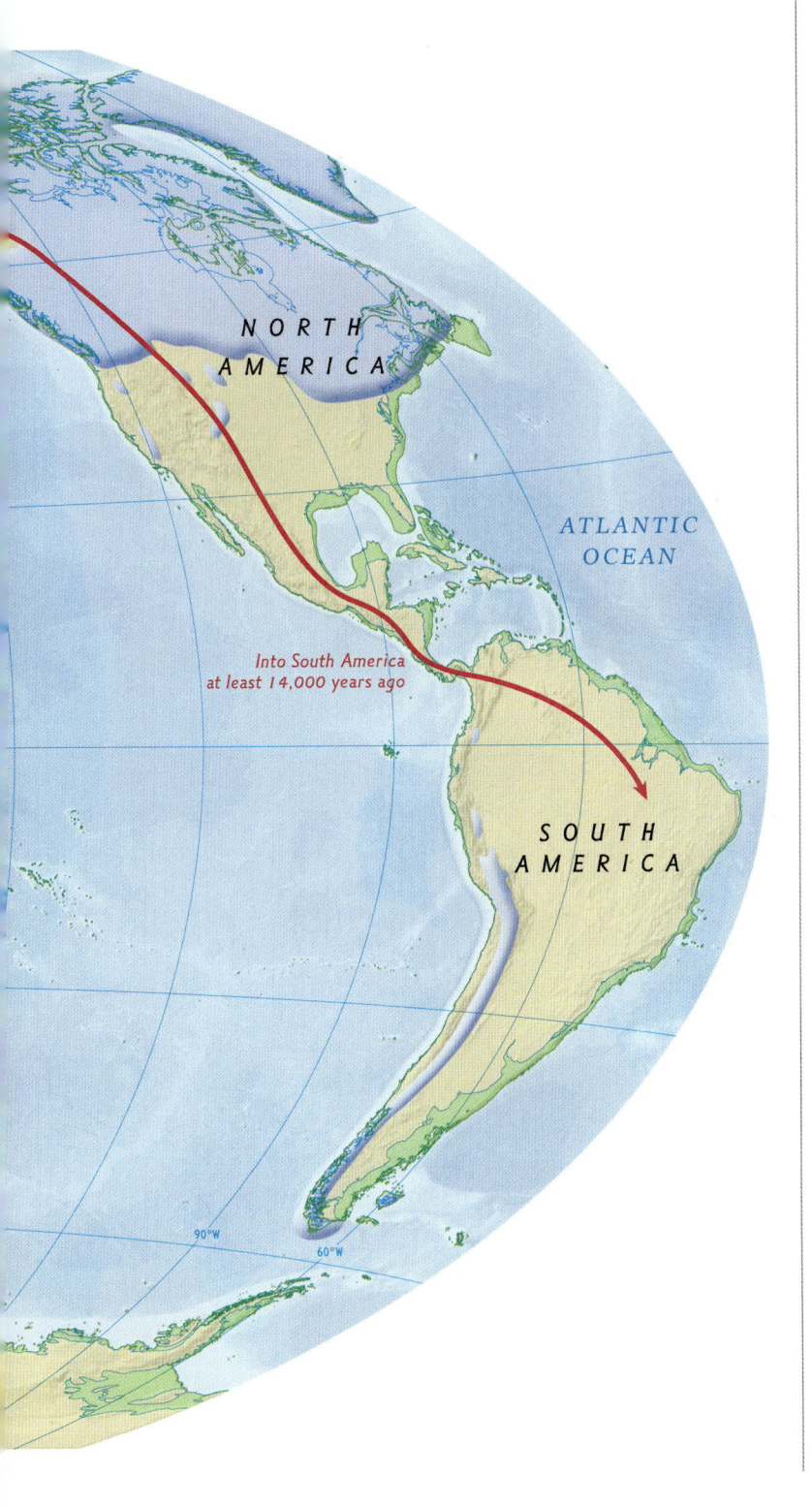

There is evidence that by 74,000 B.C.E. modern humans lived on the Indian subcontinent and by 50,000 B.C.E. had reached Southeast Asia and Australia. The earliest humans to arrive in Australia may have been people fishing from canoes or dugout boats that may have been blown off course by a storm. It's possible that some of the first settlers in South America arrived in a similar manner tens of thousands of years later.

Some early humans went north and west into Europe, starting about 60,000 years ago. Some traveled along the Danube River into eastern Europe; others moved along the coast of the Mediterranean Sea. Archaeological evidence indicates that by 38,000 B.C.E., early humans thought about the future. For example, they made bone needles, which they probably used to make warm clothing for protection in cold European winters. Making clothing out of plant fibers or animal skins is a process that requires many steps and keeps future events or conditions in mind.

The Americas were the last major landmass to be populated by modern humans. The earliest confirmed human occupation dates to about 12,000 B.C.E. One theory is that humans reached the Americas by traveling from Siberia to Alaska over **Beringia**, a land bridge that is now a series of islands in the Bering Sea because today's ocean levels are higher. The first migrations may have occurred in 16,000 B.C.E. or earlier. Part of North America was covered by a sheet of ice more than 1.75 miles thick at that time, but some scientists believe that an ice-free corridor between ice masses allowed movement through present-day Canada. Other scientists suggest that ancient settlers hugged the coast in boats made of animal skins stretched tightly over frames of wooden poles. The ancient site of Monte Verde, Chile, provides clear evidence of human occupation dating from 12,000 B.C.E. You will learn more about this site in a later chapter.

HISTORICAL THINKING

1. **READING CHECK** Why does the understanding of human history keep changing?

2. **IDENTIFY** What factors led to the sequence of migration from Africa to other parts of the world?

3. **DRAW CONCLUSIONS** What can you conclude about the intelligence of early humans based on their long-distance migration?

4. **DESCRIBE** How might early humans have migrated from Beringia through the rest of the Americas?

First Peoples and Societies 11

1.2 NATIONAL GEOGRAPHIC EXPLORER **JEFFREY ROSE**

Tracing the Paths of Early Humans

"If you set out to prove yourself right, you won't learn anything new." —Jeffrey Rose

Jeffrey Rose holds a small stone tool in Zubara, Qatar, one of many areas in Southwest Asia where he conducts his research.

Jeffrey Rose is a paleoanthropologist, a scientist who studies the development of early humans and how this informs us about the meaning of humanity. He spends his days in the southwest Asian country of Oman with his team of experts, sifting through rocks in 100°F heat and learning about the first modern humans who migrated out of Africa. Rose shares, "The evidence from South Arabia has turned the entire story upside down, changing the route, timing, and reason for the expansion out of Africa."

MAIN IDEA National Geographic Explorer Jeffrey Rose's discoveries have changed theories about human migration from Africa.

LOOKING INTO THE PAST

Scientists such as Rose are constantly looking for answers to questions about human migration, including when, where, and why modern humans moved to different areas on Earth. They believe that determining how ancient people adapted to their environments may hold the key to solving some of today's problems, such as adjusting to climate change.

Rose, who became a National Geographic Explorer in 2012, studies the landscape to understand the geography of the world as it was in the past, a way of seeing he says is almost four-dimensional, incorporating the dimension of time into the three dimensions of length, width, and depth. "I'm looking at a sand dune, but it wasn't a sand dune 100,000 years ago," he explains. "It was a lake." Thinking about how the landscape might have looked long ago allowed Rose to make a discovery that has altered what researchers understand about human migration out of Africa.

When Rose began his work, he questioned the theory of many scientists at the time: Humans migrated from Kenya to the southeastern coast of the Arabian Peninsula about 60,000 years ago. The present-day Arabian Peninsula is a desert, and it made sense to think that people who specialized in fishing would have lived along its coast. Rose spent many fruitless months searching the coast for artifacts that would support this theory—and found nothing.

"When you don't find anything," Rose points out, "morale starts to get low, and you feel a tangible sense of despair, which can be really depressing when you're isolated out in the field." Yet not finding anything can also be valuable, as it can indicate that a researcher is looking for the wrong thing or in the wrong place.

Eventually, the missing evidence along the coast led Rose to change course and search inland, where he and his team struck gold (or flint, in this case). They uncovered stone tools made with a special technique developed and widely used by people in the Nile Valley. Never before had tools of this type been found outside of Africa.

A NEW VIEW OF HUMAN MIGRATION

More surprises awaited. To find out how old the artifacts were, Rose used a technique called optically stimulated luminescence (OSL), which measures the last time crystalline materials were exposed to light. The specialized tools he found were more than 100,000 years old—much older than the 60,000 years he expected—and Rose realized he needed to look at the land not as it is today but as it was long ago. Extreme changes in climate explain why Rose found the stone tools inland rather than along the coast. The Arabian Peninsula 100,000 years ago was a fertile grassland and a land of many lakes, an ideal environment for **hunter-gatherers**, people who survive by hunting animals and gathering wild plants.

"I had never thought about modern humans coming from the Nile Valley," Rose says, but in hindsight that seems to be the most obvious scenario. Rose's findings have completely altered claims about modern humans migrating out of Africa. He believes people probably traveled back and forth between Africa and the Arabian Peninsula for tens of thousands of years. As the climate of the peninsula became drier, large animals disappeared, and stone hunting tools became smaller as people were forced to survive on lizards, birds, and rodents. By 70,000 years ago, Rose argues, the climate in the Arabian Peninsula had become so dry that early humans contracted into specific zones called environmental refugia, where they could rely on stable sources of fresh water. Many of these pioneers were forced out of Arabia, kicking off the great human migration beyond the peninsula.

HISTORICAL THINKING

1. **READING CHECK** What did Jeffrey Rose and his team finally find, and why was this discovery important?
2. **IDENTIFY PROBLEMS AND SOLUTIONS** Why is a period of failure sometimes valuable to researchers?

1.3 MAIN IDEA Early modern humans left Africa and settled the rest of Earth over a period of tens of thousands of years.

The Earliest Migrations

For at least 100,000 years, humankind stayed in Africa. Then, sometime around 100,000 years ago, people began to migrate all over the world. By about 14,000 years ago, humans had settled every continent except Antarctica.

THE GREAT HUMAN EXPANSION

People did not start moving from place to place because of crowding. Scientists believe the size of the world's population did not change significantly during this migration. People who stayed in Africa were also on the move—spreading thousands of miles over that continent, the world's second largest after Asia.

This worldwide migration took tens of thousands of years. People moved from areas that were warm to regions that were cold and from grasslands to forests. Their only tools were made of stone, bone, and wood, but they used these tools to obtain food and to survive. There is evidence that humans spent a long time in some areas before moving to another one. For example, modern humans most likely spent about 15,000 years in Beringia as they migrated from Asia to the Americas. Even so, while some people moved, others stayed behind, and eventually humans lived all over the planet.

When this migration began, conditions were ideal. Places that are dry desert today were grasslands with freshwater rivers and lakes and edible plants. The grasslands were home to wild animals, and the open spaces made hunting fairly easy. As modern humans flourished, they **adapted**, or developed characteristics to help them survive in this environment. Long legs were good for walking and running, and an upright posture

CRITICAL VIEWING A zebra herd crosses a savanna in Tanzania. What physical characteristics of this place in Africa would appeal to early humans?

and forward-facing eyes allowed humans to spot and gather plants and hunt game.

People did not plan to settle in distant regions. Those who left Africa and began moving into Asia and Europe had no idea of the size of the landmasses they entered, because the well-watered grasslands stretched as far as they could see. One researcher believes that as people searched for food, they saw inviting new places within a day's journey or so of their settlement. When they returned with their catch, they shared the news about the new territory. Over the course of a generation, or a period of roughly 20 years, people pushed the boundaries of settlement by an average of about 78 miles.

When early humans entered Europe 60,000 years ago, they had to adjust to colder temperatures. Although no clothing has survived from this time, researchers believe these early people made clothing out of animal skins or woven plant material to stay warm. Evidence for this comes from geneticists, who have found the DNA of clothing lice in ancient human remains. Geneticists also tell us that these early human migrants to Europe mingled with the Neanderthals (nee-AHN-duhr-tawls), an extinct species of early humans, who were already living there. People today who have some European ancestry may have inherited Neanderthal DNA as well.

THE STORY OF HUMAN MIGRATION

How do scientists know what these early modern humans were like? This knowledge comes from multiple experts, including archaeologists and paleontologists who analyze tools and fossils. As you read earlier, the location of tools on the Arabian Peninsula was an important discovery. Scientists can also learn a great deal from the shapes of skulls. For example, bones connecting the head to the neck reveal whether a creature walked upright or on all fours. The shape of the face, jaws, and teeth might reveal whether an individual could talk and the kind of foods he or she ate.

Apart from technologies scientists use for determining the ages of bones and artifacts, the field of linguistics, or the scientific study of language, provides valuable information about the spread of people throughout the world. By studying sounds that make up different languages, linguists can trace patterns of migration and settlement.

NATIONAL GEOGRAPHIC EXPLORER
KEOLU FOX

The Wisdom of Indigenous Peoples

National Geographic Explorer Keolu Fox (shown above) is a geneticist who is particularly interested in the ways that indigenous, or native, peoples have adapted to their environments. "There's a treasure trove of information in their DNA that could benefit all of humanity," he says. Fox, who grew up in Hawaii and whose mother is native Hawaiian, believes it is important for scientists to understand the communities that they study. Indigenous people may also offer different points of view that can cast fresh light on scientific inquiry. At the same time, Fox emphasizes that "it's the responsibility of scientific investigators to ensure that 'exploration' of indigenous people's genomes benefits that community as well, financially or otherwise."

The movement of humans from Africa to almost every corner of the globe was a long one. One theme is constant: our ancestors were always on the move. They followed herds, crossed rivers, traveled by boat, and ultimately covered enormous distances at a time when their most powerful weapon was a stone hand ax and the fastest means of moving on land was running. From their beginnings, humans have traveled the world, driven by curiosity and necessity.

HISTORICAL THINKING

1. **READING CHECK** Why did early humans migrate out of Africa?

2. **IDENTIFY MAIN IDEAS AND DETAILS** How can scientists trace early human migration?

3. **DESCRIBE** What evidence shows that early humans made clothing to stay warm after they entered Europe?

1.4 NATIONAL GEOGRAPHIC EXPLORER AND TRAVELER

Out of Eden: Paul Salopek Walks Through Time

"Everybody has a story. They may tell it in a different language, they may whisper it, they may shout it, but they have a story." –Paul Salopek

Embarking on a historic journey, Paul Salopek and guide Ahmed Alema Hessan leave the Ethiopian village of Bouri.

From the earliest moments of human history, our restless ancestors were on the move. National Geographic Fellow and Pulitzer Prize–winning journalist Paul Salopek has become a traveler himself, retracing the paths of human migration over the course of about 10 years. Starting in Africa, in Ethiopia, his 21,000-mile journey takes him through Asia and North America and ends at the tip of South America. Along the way, Salopek is practicing what he calls "slow journalism," relying on personal interaction with people who reveal compelling stories about their lives.

> **PRIMARY SOURCE**
>
> ### JANUARY 2013—ETHIOPIA: TO WALK THE WORLD
>
> I am on a journey. I am in pursuit of an idea, a story, a chimera [something imaginary], perhaps a folly. I am chasing ghosts. Starting in humanity's birthplace in the Great Rift Valley of East Africa, I am retracing, on foot, the pathways of the ancestors who first discovered the Earth at least 60,000 years ago. This remains by far our greatest voyage. Not because it delivered us the planet. No. But because the early *Homo sapiens* who first roamed beyond the mother continent—these pioneer nomads numbered, in total, as few as a couple of hundred people—also bequeathed us the subtlest qualities we now associate with being fully human: complex language, abstract thinking, a compulsion to make art, a genius for technological innovation, and the continuum of today's many races. We know so little about them. They straddled the strait called *Bab el Mandeb*—the "gate of grief" that cleaves Africa from Arabia—and then exploded, in just 2,500 generations, a geological heartbeat, to the remotest habitable fringe of the globe.
>
> Using fossil evidence and the burgeoning science of "genography"—a field that sifts the DNA of living populations for mutations useful in tracking ancient **diasporas** [migrations of people from an ancestral homeland]—I will walk north from Africa into the Middle East. From there my antique route leads eastward across the vast gravel plains of Asia to China, then north again into the mint blue shadows of Siberia. From Russia I will hop a ship to Alaska and inch down the western coast of the New World to wind-smeared Tierra del Fuego, our species' last new continental horizon. I will walk 21,000 miles.
>
> If you ask, I will tell you that I have embarked on this project, which I'm calling the Out of Eden Walk, for many reasons: to relearn the contours of our planet at the human pace of three miles an hour. To slow down. To think. To write. To render current events as a form of pilgrimage. I hope to repair certain important connections burned through by artificial speed, by inattentiveness. I walk, as everyone does, to see what lies ahead. I walk to remember.

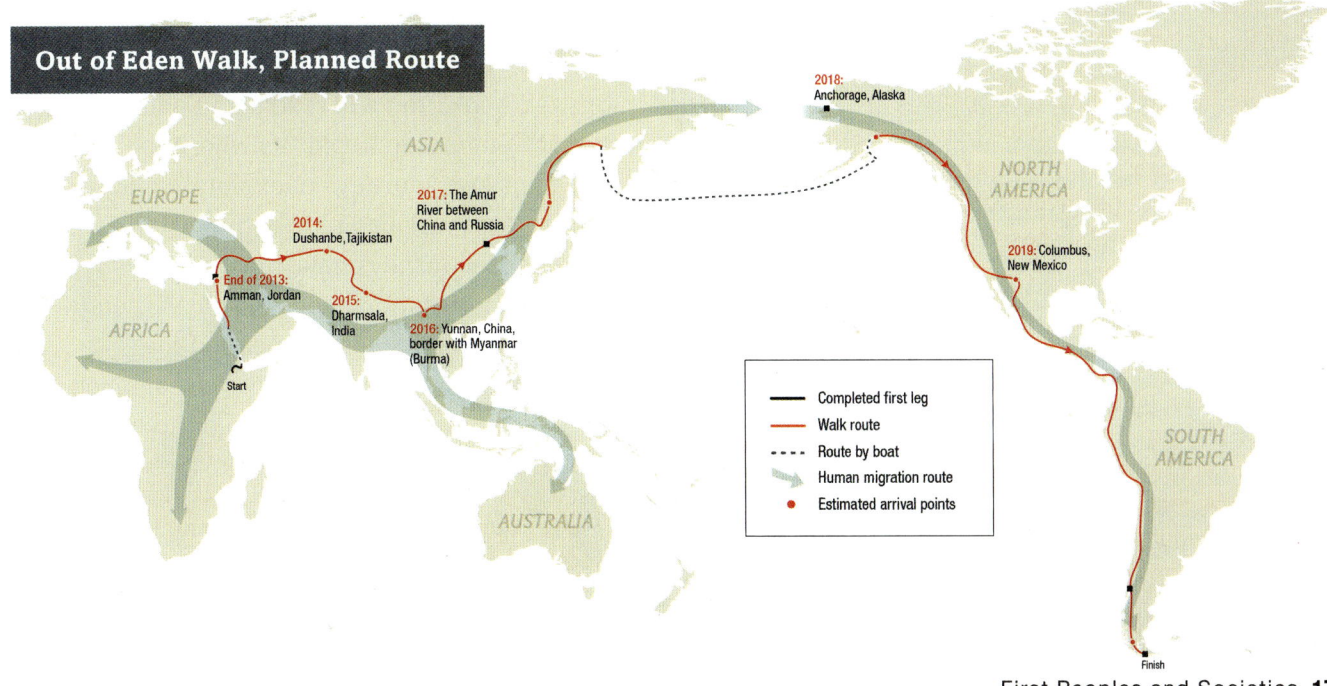

Out of Eden Walk, Planned Route

Salopek's journey begins in Ethiopia at one of the world's oldest human fossil sites, Herto Bouri, and unspools across the scalding Afar Triangle, in the Great Rift Valley. Along this pathway our ancestors headed toward the Gulf of Aden, where they first stepped out of Africa to explore the wider world. As Salopek attests, this ancient pathway remains a conduit of opportunity—and sometimes fatal tragedy—for migrants seeking a better life today.

PRIMARY SOURCE

JANUARY 2013—GREAT RIFT VALLEY: BABY STEPS

"Where are you walking?" the Afar nomads ask.

"North. To Djibouti." (We do not say Tierra del Fuego [in South America]. It is much too far—it is meaningless.)

"Are you crazy? Are you sick?"

In reply, Ahmed Alema Hessan—wiry and energetic, the ultimate go-to man, a charming rogue, my guide and protector through the blistering Afar Triangle—doubles over and laughs. He leads our micro-caravan: two skinny camels. I have listened to his guffaw many times already. This project is, to him, a punch line—a cosmic joke. To walk for seven years! Across three continents! Enduring hardship, loneliness, uncertainty, fear, exhaustion, confusion—all for a rucksack's worth of ideas, palaver, scientific and literary conceits. He enjoys the absurdity of it. This is fitting. Especially given our ridiculous launch.

We broke camp this morning in darkness at Bouri, Alema's smoky home—a village of hackers, of coughers—at the western foot of the Great Rift Valley, in the arid northeast of Ethiopia.

I awoke and saw snow: thick, dense, choking, blinding. Like plankton at the bottom of a sea, swirling white in the beam of my headlamp. It was the dust. Hundreds of village animals churned up a cloud as fine as talc. Goats, sheep, cows, donkeys, and camels—but, sadly, not our camels.

The cargo animals I had requisitioned last October (a key arrangement in a project that has consumed thousands of hours of planning) were nowhere to be found. Their drivers were absent, too. They never showed up. So we sat in the dust, waiting. The sun rose. It began to grow hot. To the east, across the Rift, which is widening by the year by a quarter of an inch, lay our first border: Djibouti.

Are you crazy? Are you sick? Yes? No? Maybe?

The sky above is the color of polished lead.

The Afar Triangle is dreaded as a waterless death march, as a moonscape. Temperatures of 120°F. Saltpans so bright they burn the eyes out. Yet today it rained. And Alema and I have no waterproof tents. We have an Ethiopian flag, which Alema wraps himself in. We lead the two camels ourselves. (Whose are they? I'm not sure. Alema procured them Afar-style, off the cuff.) We inch across an acacia plain darkened to the color of chocolate by the warm raindrops. We tread on a photographic negative. The camels' moccasin-like feet pull up the frail crust of moisture, leaving behind white circles of dry dust.

HISTORICAL THINKING

READING CHECK How does Salopek convey both the very real details of life on foot and his thoughts and feelings about his trek?

What is a Traveler?

In this textbook, you will read about additional National Geographic Explorers who, like Paul, are on their own journeys of exploration and discovery. You will also read about historical figures whose journeys have provided us with much information about the past. Their reactions to the people they met and the places they saw on their journeys reveal much about their home societies as well as about the societies they visited.

Use your History Notebook to comment on what you've read.

Camel-ology

You must allow camels a generous rest at midday. This improves their dispositions. You must avoid walking camels on stones—a camel's foot is not a hard hoof but a smooth pad, soft as a pot holder. (Our older bull, Fares, will take your shoulder between his jaws as you lead him with a rope, and squeeze gently, communicating his distress on sharp rocks.) . . .

While traveling, feed your camels twice a day, morning and night: one lozenge of alfalfa a hand-span thick and one bucket of grain when available. They also will eat orange rinds, banana peels, stale flatbread, plastic bubble wrap encasing laptop computers, the living hair off your scalp, and a thousand different varieties of grasses, thorns, shrubs, and trees. . . .

To pack a cargo camel is to confront a daunting problem of geometry, of architecture: the hump. The placement of the saddle is critical. It cannot be an inch too far forward, or an inch too far back. The camel will complain otherwise. It will roll in the sand. No one hump is like any other hump. Thus, you must achieve loading perfection on just one. . . . It is a pleasing ritual that connects us to these large, fatalistic, self-satisfied animals through our hands.

Paul Salopek and his local guides—along with the camels he would come to know so well—walk through the Afar region of northeastern Ethiopia.

Nearly hidden in the swirling dust, goats make their way back from a day of grazing to their Ethiopian village.

DOCUMENT-BASED QUESTION
1.5 Cave Paintings

Artifacts are important sources of information for scientists who study ancient peoples. What can researchers learn from looking at an object or at paintings that have no words and no date? You've read about technology that helps date artifacts, or tell us how old things are. However, there is more to understanding an artifact than knowing when it was made. Scientists put their skills of observation and deduction to work to understand the messages in artifacts.

"There's something about caves—a shadowy opening in a limestone cliff that draws you in. As you pass through the portal between light and dark, you enter a subterranean world—a place of perpetual gloom, of earthy smells, of hushed silence," says paleoanthropologist and National Geographic Explorer Genevieve von Petzinger (shown above in a cave in western Europe). Von Petzinger has twisted and crawled into dangerous and narrow passageways as much as three-quarters of a mile deep to examine images left behind by ancient peoples. Cave drawings in these hidden chambers reveal that some people had time and energy to create art after meeting their basic needs for survival as early as 63,000 B.C.E.—and perhaps even before.

Von Petzinger studies distinct geometric shapes—dots, lines, rectangles, triangles, ovals, circles—made by early humans. She has found many of the same 32 signs appearing in different caves, sometimes more than a thousand miles apart. The repetition of these symbols over thousands of years, from 10,000 to 40,000 years ago, is a significant forerunner of writing, which first appeared between 4,000 and 5,000 years ago.

ARTIFACT ONE

**Primary Source: Ocher Cave Painting
from Lascaux Caves in Lascaux, France**

Paleolithic painters mixed ocher, a natural clay containing minerals that give it colors ranging from yellow to red, with animal fat and other liquids to make the earliest known paint. Ocher was used to paint these figures on a cave in Lascaux, France, more than 17,000 years ago. Charcoal was also used to create black outlines. Scientists believe that people used the burnt tips of long sticks to draw images on higher levels of the caves.

CONSTRUCTED RESPONSE What steps would the painter of these figures have had to follow to create this art?

ARTIFACT TWO

**Primary Source: Hand Stencils
from Cueva de las Manos in Santa Cruz, Argentina**

Stenciled hands are found in ancient caves in South America, Europe, Africa, Borneo, and Australia. The hands shown here were made between 9,500 and 13,000 years ago. Using data about the relative length of fingers in male and female hands, archaeologist Dean Snow, a National Geographic Explorer, examined eight cave sites in France and Spain over more than a decade. He has determined that about three-quarters of the stenciled hands in those caves belonged to women.

CONSTRUCTED RESPONSE Why are most of the hand stencils found in eight European caves believed to be made by women?

ARTIFACT THREE

**Primary Source: Cave Paintings
from Laas Geel outside of Hargeisa, Somaliland**

Like humanity, art itself started in Africa. Experts found an "art studio" in South Africa that contained tools dating back 100,000 years. Many millennia later in the Horn of Africa peninsula in Laas Geel, artists created these exaggerated paintings of humans and animals. The colorful ocher figures of people, cattle, giraffes, and different types of canines are more than 5,000—and may even be 10,000—years old.

CONSTRUCTED RESPONSE What are the similarities and differences between this cave painting in Africa and the art from France and Argentina?

SYNTHESIZE & WRITE

1. **REVIEW** Review what you have read and observed about modern humans and these cave paintings.

2. **RECALL** On your own paper, list two details you observed looking at each cave painting.

3. **CONSTRUCT** Construct a topic sentence that answers this question: How are the three cave paintings and the materials used to make them similar and different?

4. **WRITE** Using evidence from this chapter and the cave paintings, write an informative paragraph that supports your topic sentence in Step 3.

First Peoples and Societies 21

2.1

MAIN IDEA The transition from hunting and gathering to agriculture was a lengthy process that occurred over thousands of years.

Early Agriculture

You may think that farmers practice a more traditional way of life. Compared with foraging and hunting-gathering traditions, the shift to farming was remarkable. Planting seeds, harvesting crops, and using domesticated animals to help with work meant people lived more closely together in settled communities. This change was so dramatic that it is often called a revolution.

CULTIVATING PLANTS

Archaeologists use the term **Neolithic**, or new stone age, to describe societies that used stone tools and practiced **agriculture**, the cultivation of plant foods and domestication of animals as sources of food and labor. It is not clear why more and more communities chose to adopt agriculture after nearly 200,000 years of hunting and gathering, but climate change or religious beliefs may have been contributing factors. This progression between two different ways of life is sometimes called the **Neolithic Revolution**, and it had a significant impact on the way in which people lived.

The transition took place slowly, and like the process of migration out of Africa, occurred independently in several places. People did not give up hunting and gathering and become farmers in a single generation. Traces of seeds, grasses, and beans have recently been discovered on 23,000-year-old grinding stones in the Huang He region of northern China. Processing foods, or performing a series of actions to change them, was an early precursor to agriculture; people had to use and understand wild plants before they could grow them. Turning foods into flour would have been one of many steps that could lead to the development of agriculture.

Agriculture appeared in northern China about 10,000 years ago, around the same time that agriculture appeared in the area known today as the Middle East. The **Natufians** (nuh-TOO-fee-uhnz)—people who lived in present-day Israel, the Palestinian territories, and southern Syria—were among the earliest people to cultivate, or plant and raise, crops. The first food they

MORTAR
This mortar for grinding materials dates back to 4,000–2,000 B.C.E.

grew was figs; they planted fig trees but did not settle near them. They hunted and gathered as before and visited the fig trees from time to time to collect the fruit. Many other people continued to forage for all their food.

The next crops the Natufians cultivated were grains—wheat and barley. At first, they gathered wild grain. The seeds of wild grain fell easily to the ground because the plants had weak stems, which meant the grain grew back year after year without being planted. Wild grains also had thick husks that protected the seed kernels, but these thick husks made it difficult for humans to remove the seeds. The Natufians chose seeds from plants that were taller and had thinner husks and planted those.

Over time, the wheat and barley the Natufians planted became quite different from the wild plants. The seeds were less likely to fall to the ground, and it was easier for people to remove the kernels. This process of choosing and planting the seeds of grains and other crops to make them more useful continued and

22 CHAPTER 1

CRITICAL VIEWING A shepherd leads sheep between Madaba and Mount Nebo, Jordan. Why do you think the flock is moving through the area instead of stopping?

spread. By 8000 B.C.E., people throughout the eastern Mediterranean, especially those in dryer areas, were growing grain crops. Once they had begun to cultivate crops, the larger size of their villages forced them to continue farming because agriculture could support a larger population than foraging could.

DOMESTICATING ANIMALS

The second element of agriculture was the **domestication**, or taming, of wild animals. Researchers do not know a great deal about how different animals became domesticated, but it seems likely that people began to watch over herds and then feed the animals. The first animals to be domesticated were probably dogs, who are believed to have descended from wolves. In fact, people may have domesticated dogs before they domesticated grains, as there are dog fossils as old as 15,000 years. Current evidence indicates that dogs were domesticated in Asia and Europe at about the same time.

After several thousand years, goats, sheep, and cattle had been domesticated. Archaeologists believe people were riding horses by about 3500 B.C.E. Horse teeth from that era are ground in a way that might indicate

FELINE FRIENDS

While dogs were domesticated with the help of humans, cats may have decided on their own to become our furry companions. One theory is that cats domesticated themselves because their prey—rodents and small animals—lived on the grain stored in farming villages. People long believed that cats were first domesticated in Egypt about 4,000 years ago. However, the discovery of a cat buried with a human dating nearly 10,000 years ago on the Mediterranean island of Cyprus suggests humans and cats may have had close relationships long before that.

Egyptian cat mummy, 672–332 B.C.E.

the use of rope or leather bits in the horses' mouths. Using horses for transportation would have transformed people's lives because a person riding a horse could travel farther and faster than a person on foot could. The ability to move heavier loads over greater distances would have affected the **economy**—or the system for producing and obtaining goods and services—of societies that used horses for transporting people and supplies.

The shift to agriculture nearly always caused a dramatic increase in population size. As villages and families grew larger, people needed to continue farming to feed the larger population. The use of agriculture spread from Africa throughout the world. In addition to wheat and barley, people cultivated other grains such as rice and maize. These changes would have a profound impact on the world as humans progressed from hunting and gathering to a settled agricultural economy. Cultural hearths—or places where new ideas, practices, and technologies began—would soon influence people for generations.

However, this Neolithic transition involved trade-offs. People became smaller and sicker; diets were worse and less varied, and people were more likely to be infected by diseases. There was also much less time for leisure—farming is harder work. Many more people could inhabit a given area, which gave that settled group advantages over other communities. But life for most individuals did not improve as a result of agriculture.

Cultural Hearths and the Spread of Agriculture, c. 8000–500 B.C.E.

HARPOONS
Neolithic communities in Africa used these ivory harpoons to fish more than 6,000 years ago.

HISTORICAL THINKING

1. **READING CHECK** What are the two elements of agriculture?

2. **MAKE INFERENCES** Why might dogs have been the first animals to be domesticated?

3. **DRAW CONCLUSIONS** How did the shift to agriculture affect population size?

4. **INTERPRET MAPS** Along what geographic feature had most agriculture developed by 5000 B.C.E.?

Agriculture established
- by 5000 B.C.E.
- by 3000 B.C.E.
- by 500 B.C.E.
- Cultural hearth, c. 8000–5000 B.C.E.
- Oaxaca

Crops
- Beans
- Corn
- Cotton
- Other grains
- Potato
- Rice
- Sorghum

Animals
- Cattle
- Llama
- Pig
- Sheep

First Peoples and Societies 25

2.2 Material Culture

THE POWER OF ANIMALS

You've learned that early humans domesticated, or tamed, wild animals for practical reasons, including for food, for animal fur or skin, and for the transportation of goods as well as people. And, as you've read, some experts believe that dogs were domesticated before plants were cultivated, which emphasizes their importance as beloved pets. Recall that some cave paintings featured animals as subjects. Humans also saw—and continue to see—animals as spiritual and religious symbols. These complex and varied relationships between people and animals have helped shape the human experience over thousands and thousands of years.

Imaginary Animals Early humans also imagined and depicted animals that did not exist in reality. Representations of the mythical unicorn can be found in art and literature from civilizations as diverse as Mesopotamia, India, China, Greece, and the Islamic world. This detail from a 15th-century tapestry shows the European version of the unicorn: a white horse with a single long horn emerging from its forehead. The image also alludes to the legend that only a maiden can tame this pure creature.

Animals in Religion or Mythology The Toltec civilization, which lasted from about 950 to 1200 C.E. in what is now Mexico, is another society that blended human and animal forms in its spiritual art. This small figure is made of clay that was then covered in mother of pearl. Most experts believe it depicts a warrior wearing a coyote helmet. However, some think it represents a god's face coming out of a feathered snake's mouth.

26 CHAPTER 1

Ancient Egypt Animals figured prominently in ancient Egyptian religious beliefs, with gods and other creatures often portrayed as part animal and part human. For example, a sphinx usually has the body of a lion and the head of a person. However, these sphinxes near the Temple of Amun—who was the king of the gods—near Thebes (now Luxor) each combine a lion's body with a ram's head. Underneath the head and between the paws of each sphinx is a small figure of Ramses II, an important Egyptian pharaoh.

Hanuman Langurs in Jodhpur, India

These animals, also known as gray langurs, are named after the monkey commander in the Hindu epic *Ramayana* who commands an army of monkeys to help save the god Rama's wife. The langurs' black faces, hands, and feet are said to reflect the burns that Hanuman suffered during the rescue. Hanuman langurs are considered sacred to Hindus, so the people of Jodhpur feed the monkeys and allow them to roam freely throughout the city.

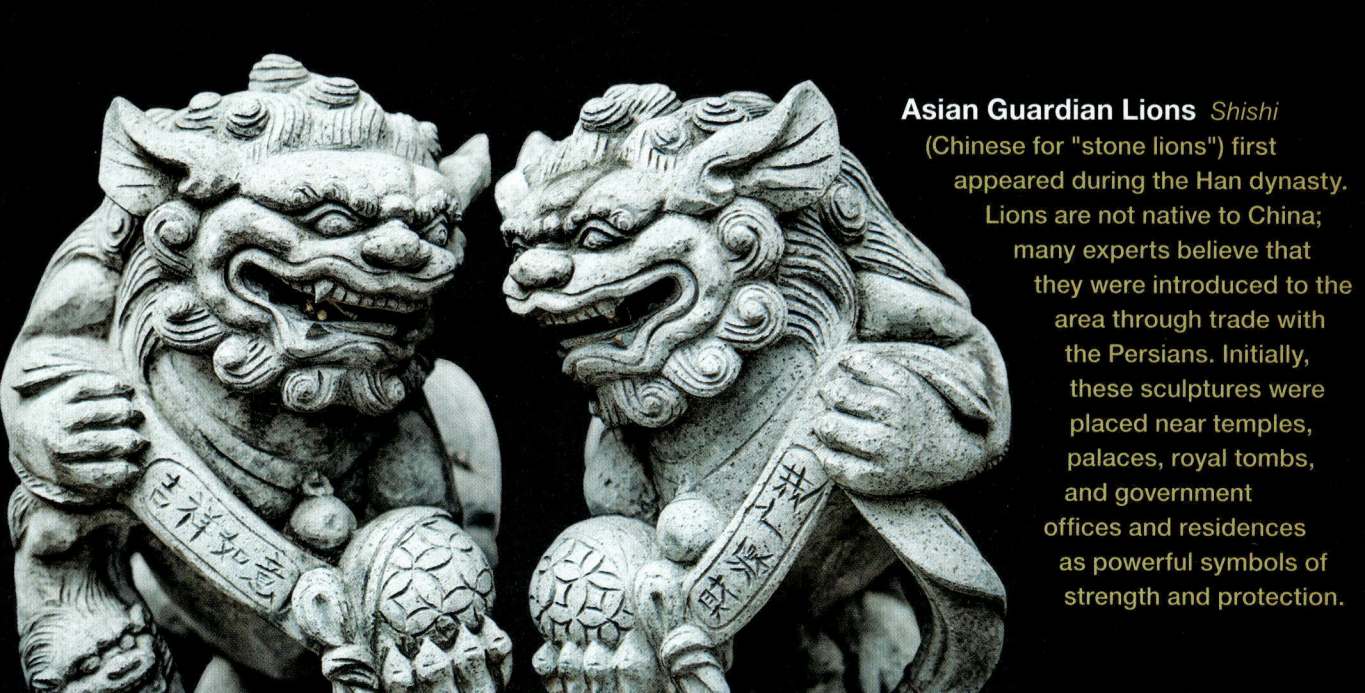

Asian Guardian Lions *Shishi* (Chinese for "stone lions") first appeared during the Han dynasty. Lions are not native to China; many experts believe that they were introduced to the area through trade with the Persians. Initially, these sculptures were placed near temples, palaces, royal tombs, and government offices and residences as powerful symbols of strength and protection.

HISTORICAL THINKING

1. **READING CHECK** What are three relationships that people had and have with animals?

2. **COMPARE AND CONTRAST** How are the animals you read about the same and how do they differ?

3. **MAKE CONNECTIONS** What interaction do you or have you had with animals?

2.3

MAIN IDEA The first large settlements were societies with elements of both hunter-gatherer and agricultural economies.

The First Large Settlements

Determining causes and effects can be difficult when historians are looking at people and events from 10,000 years ago—or more. Archaeological evidence can help. So can investigations of plant life and landforms in the areas being studied. Everyone needs food, fresh water, and safety. Insights into the ways in which people from long ago met those needs can uncover how they lived.

JERICHO AND GÖBEKLI TEPE

Researchers are not sure whether people settled in one place because they had become agricultural or whether they became agricultural because they settled in one place. What is known is that the transition to the Neolithic era brought important changes to human life wherever people adopted agriculture.

One of the world's oldest known continuously occupied human settlements is **Jericho** (JEHR-ih-koh), which began as a Natufian settlement near the Jordan River in the West Bank area of the present-day Palestinian territories. As many as 1,000 people may have lived in Jericho between 8300 and 7500 B.C.E. in mud-brick dwellings with stone foundations. These early people planted wheat and barley and perhaps figs and lentils as well, but they hunted instead of domesticating animals. They also made salt by evaporating water from the Dead Sea. This combination of activities shows the gradual nature of the Neolithic transition.

The residents of Jericho dug a wide ditch and built a wall at least 8 feet high around their settlement for protection from wild animals, human enemies, or possibly both. They also built a 28-foot tower inside the wall that may have served as a lookout post. The ditches, the wall, and the tower all show that one or more leaders coordinated workers and supplies for large-scale construction. These structures indicate a more complex political organization than a band of hunter-gatherers would have had.

The number of people living in Jericho suggests that the rise of agriculture contributed to an increase in population and thus large settlements. However, some scientists argue the opposite. They see the rise of large settlements as causing the shift to agriculture rather than being an effect of it. Evidence from a temple structure at **Göbekli Tepe** in southeastern Turkey could support this view. At least 500 people came together to build an elaborate religious structure on this site some 12,000 years ago. The need to feed this large workforce may have encouraged people in this cultural hearth to cultivate seeds and domesticate animals.

ÇATALHÖYÜK

Settlements of the eastern Mediterranean increased in size gradually. One early example is **Çatalhöyük** (chah-tahl-hoo-YOOK), a settlement in present-day Turkey that was, at its peak, home to as many as 8,000 people. This community developed around 12,000 years ago and lasted more than a thousand years. Houses were so close together that there was no room for streets—or even front doors. People used ladders to enter their homes through the roof and socialized on the flat roofs the way people in today's cities might socialize on sidewalks or in parks.

The people of Çatalhöyük hunted and fished, but most of the food in the settlement came from farming, which created surpluses, or supplies of goods and labor not needed for short-term survival. These surpluses allowed people to focus on other work, such as the creation of new technology and artistic expression. Researchers at the site of Çatalhöyük have discovered pottery, cloth, cups, utensils made of bone, tools, and jewelry. People who made these items could have traded them for other goods.

The dozens of limestone pillars of Göbekli Tepe measure up to 18 feet high and weigh between 7 and 10 tons. These pillars may represent dancing priests, with hands resting above a belt.

Scientists are still exploring Çatalhöyük to understand the people who built it and lived in it. One surprising feature of this community is that the settlement seems to have been located at least six miles from the fields where food crops were grown. Another feature is that the settlement is located right next to the clay soils people used to plaster the walls and floors of their houses as well as to make bowls, bins, and sculptures. Scientists speculate that it was easier for the people who lived at Çatalhöyük to carry lightweight crops over a distance than it was to carry heavy clay.

HISTORICAL THINKING

1. **READING CHECK** How did the first large settlements demonstrate a gradual transition to the Neolithic era?

2. **IDENTIFY MAIN IDEAS AND DETAILS** What are the two different theories on the emergence of large settlements?

3. **ANALYZE CAUSE AND EFFECT** What was one effect of the surpluses at Çatalhöyük?

First Peoples and Societies 29

CHAPTER 1
FIRST PEOPLES AND SOCIETIES
REVIEW

VOCABULARY

Use each of the following vocabulary words in a sentence that shows an understanding of the term's meaning.

1. artifact
2. migrate
3. hunter-gatherer
4. adapt
5. agriculture
6. domestication
7. economy
8. surplus

READING STRATEGY
DETERMINE CHRONOLOGY

Use a sequence chain like the one below to show the order in which humans populated different regions of Earth based on our current understanding. Then answer the question that follows.

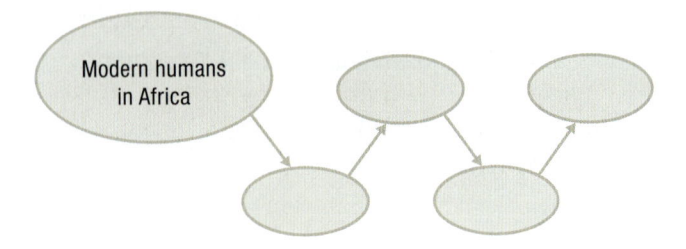

9. Which regions of Earth were last to be populated by human beings, and why?

MAIN IDEAS

Answer the following questions. Support your answers with evidence from the chapter.

10. Name three types of scientists who have contributed to understanding early modern humans and where they lived, and describe the work these scientists do. **LESSON 1.1**

11. What route do some scientists believe early humans used to migrate to the Americas? **LESSON 1.1**

12. What type of environment did early modern humans first inhabit? **LESSON 1.3**

13. What evidence found by geneticists could indicate that early humans in Europe wore clothes? **LESSON 1.3**

14. What were two characteristics of the Neolithic era? **LESSON 2.1**

15. Describe two actions people are believed to have taken to domesticate wheat and barley. **LESSON 2.1**

16. What was an important feature of the Çatalhöyük economy? **LESSON 2.3**

HISTORICAL THINKING

Answer the following questions. Support your answers with evidence from the chapter.

17. **DESCRIBE** What characteristics did early modern humans share with present-day people?

18. **MAKE GENERALIZATIONS** How do we know what early modern humans were like and where and how they lived?

19. **DRAW CONCLUSIONS** What does the domestication of plants and animals suggest about the development of humans?

20. **FORM AND SUPPORT OPINIONS** What do you think were some advantages and disadvantages to a more settled life over the hunter-gatherer one?

21. **SUMMARIZE** Briefly state two different viewpoints of the relationship between agriculture and large settlements.

INTERPRET CHARTS

Look at the chart, which shows the dates and location of the world's earliest cultivation. Then answer the questions that follow.

Date of Earliest Cultivation	Place	Crops and Animals
8400 B.C.E.	West Asia	fig, barley, lentil, wheat, cattle, dog, goat, pig, sheep
8000 B.C.E.	Chang Jiang Basin, China	rice, millet, soybean, pig, dog
8000 B.C.E.	East African Highlands	finger millet, sesame, sorghum, teff grass, cattle
5000 B.C.E.	Southeast Asia	banana, rice, yam, water buffalo, chicken, zebu cattle
5000 B.C.E.	New Guinea	root crops, sugar cane, pig
5000 B.C.E.	Central Mexico	bean, maize, squash, sweet potato, turkey
4000 B.C.E.	Peruvian Andes	bean, peanut, potato, quinoa, guinea pig, llama
3000 B.C.E.	Sub-Saharan Africa	pearl millet, sorghum, rice

22. According to the chart, which crops were found in both Africa and China? What can you infer about the climate of each area?

23. Which animal was domesticated in three different places during a time span of 3,400 years? Why do you think early humans domesticated this animal?

ANALYZE SOURCES

History professor and author Yuval Noah Harari coined the term *Cognitive Revolution* to describe humanity's development of "fictive language"—the ability to speak about fictions—that started around 70,000 B.C.E. Read the excerpt from his June 2015 TED talk and answer the question that follows.

> The real difference between us and other animals is on the collective level. Humans control the world because we are the only animal that can cooperate flexibly in large numbers.... Yet how come humans alone of all the animals are capable of cooperating flexibly in large numbers, be it in order to play, to trade, or to slaughter? The answer is our imagination. We can cooperate with numerous strangers because we can invent fictional stories, spread them around, and convince millions of strangers to believe in them. As long as everybody believes in the same fictions, we all obey the same laws, and can thereby cooperate effectively.

24. According to Harari, what skill separates us from animals, and how do we use this skill?

CONNECT TO YOUR LIFE

25. EXPLANATORY Think about your basic needs and the needs of others in your household or community. Then think about how much time you or others spend working for money you spend on nonessential items, such as video games or designer clothing, and what you or others do with your free time. Compare your thoughts about survival in your world with what you know about survival in the world of ancient hunter-gatherers. Write an essay presenting your thoughts, citing examples from the chapter and your own research. Use the tips below to help you plan, organize, and write your essay.

TIPS

- Define the term *survival* for yourself.
- List what is needed for survival as you have defined it.
- Describe how much time it takes to meet these needs.
- Use two or three vocabulary words from the chapter in your explanation.
- End with a comparison to the challenges faced by early modern humans.

First Peoples and Societies

CHAPTER 2

Early River Valley Civilizations
3100 B.C.E.–500 C.E.

HISTORICAL THINKING How are people today linked to the first civilizations?

SECTION 1 **The Ancient Near East**
SECTION 2 **Kingdoms Along the Nile**
SECTION 2 **Eastern Mediterranean Kingdoms**

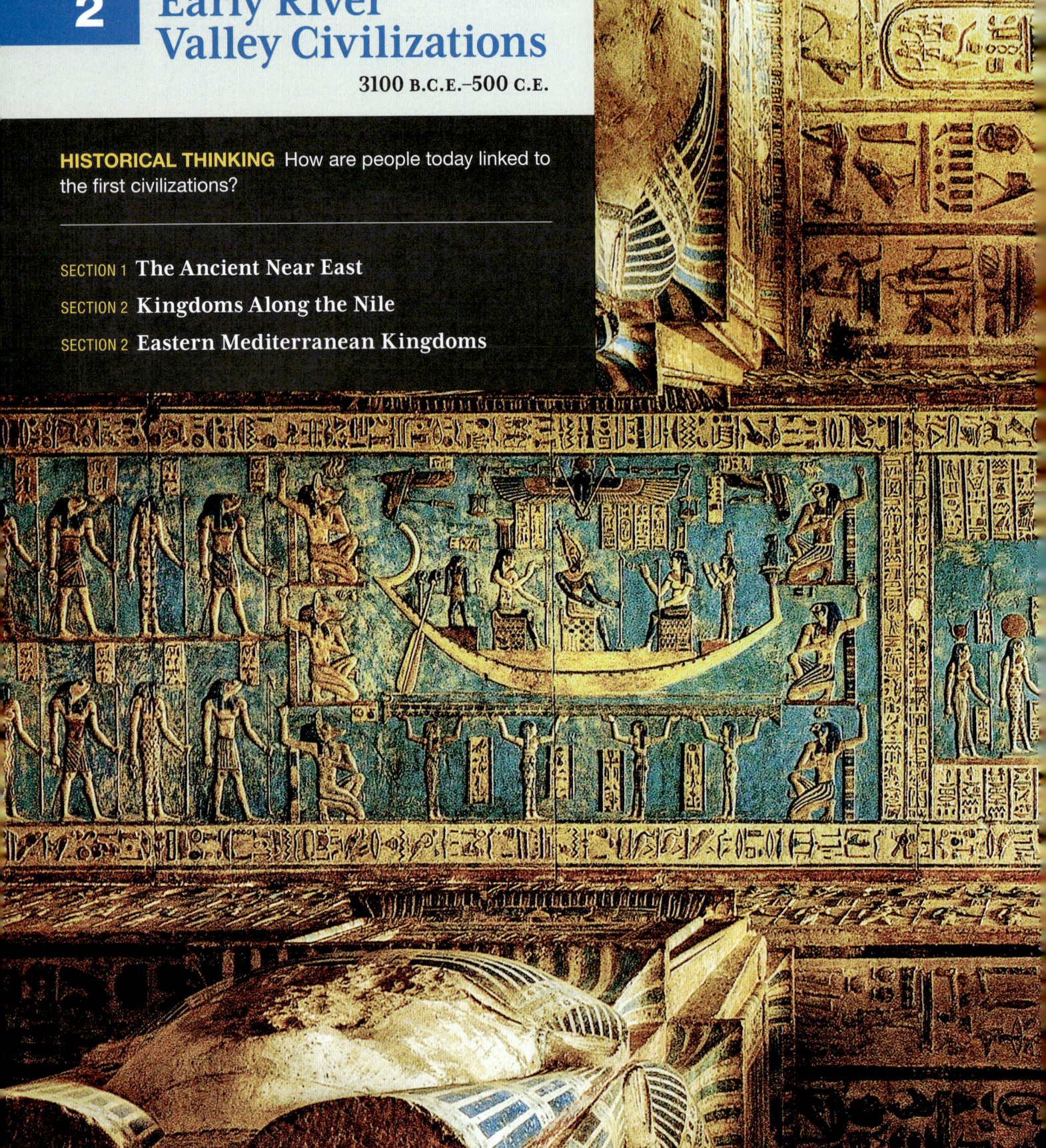

CRITICAL VIEWING

The Temple of Hathor is one of the best-preserved ancient temples in Egypt. Supported by large columns, its ceiling features detailed carvings. What conclusions might you draw about ancient Egyptian civilization based on artistic details in this ceiling?

1.1

MAIN IDEA The development of farming led to the rise of a river valley civilization in Southwest Asia.

Mesopotamia and City Life

You have likely visited large modern cities, or you may live in one. Have you ever wondered when, and why, people first started living in large groups? This development occurred further back in time than you might have imagined, and the success of farming had a lot to do with it.

CITIES ALONG RIVERS

You have read that the development of agriculture caused food surpluses, which led to a population increase in farming settlements such as Çatalhöyük. Eventually, some of these farming settlements grew into large cities. Many of these first cities formed in the southern portion of Southwest Asia—an area that historians have called **Mesopotamia** (meh-suh-puh-TAY-mee-uh). In Greek, the term *mesopotamia* means "between two rivers." It's no wonder then that this name was given to the land between the **Tigris** (TY-gruhs) **River** and the **Euphrates** (yu-FRAY-teez) **River**. Today, the country of Iraq covers much of the river valley region of Mesopotamia.

By 3100 B.C.E., **Uruk**, the first city of about 40,000 or 50,000 people, was thriving in southern Mesopotamia. At Uruk, a complex society took shape as people began to specialize in different occupations. As you will learn in this chapter and the next, complex societies arose along river valleys elsewhere in the world as well, including in Egypt, China, and India. These societies formed in river valleys where the fertile soil and available water caused agriculture to boom, producing food surpluses.

CHARACTERISTICS OF EARLY CIVILIZATIONS

Many historians refer to any advanced and complex society as a **civilization**, though scholars differ somewhat on the defining characteristics. The first civilizations typically developed in cities with populations in the tens of thousands. They arose where there was a food surplus and not everyone had to work to produce food. People started to specialize in various other kinds of work, such as making pottery, building shelters, or keeping records. They created a **division of labor**, or a system in which people perform different jobs to meet the needs of

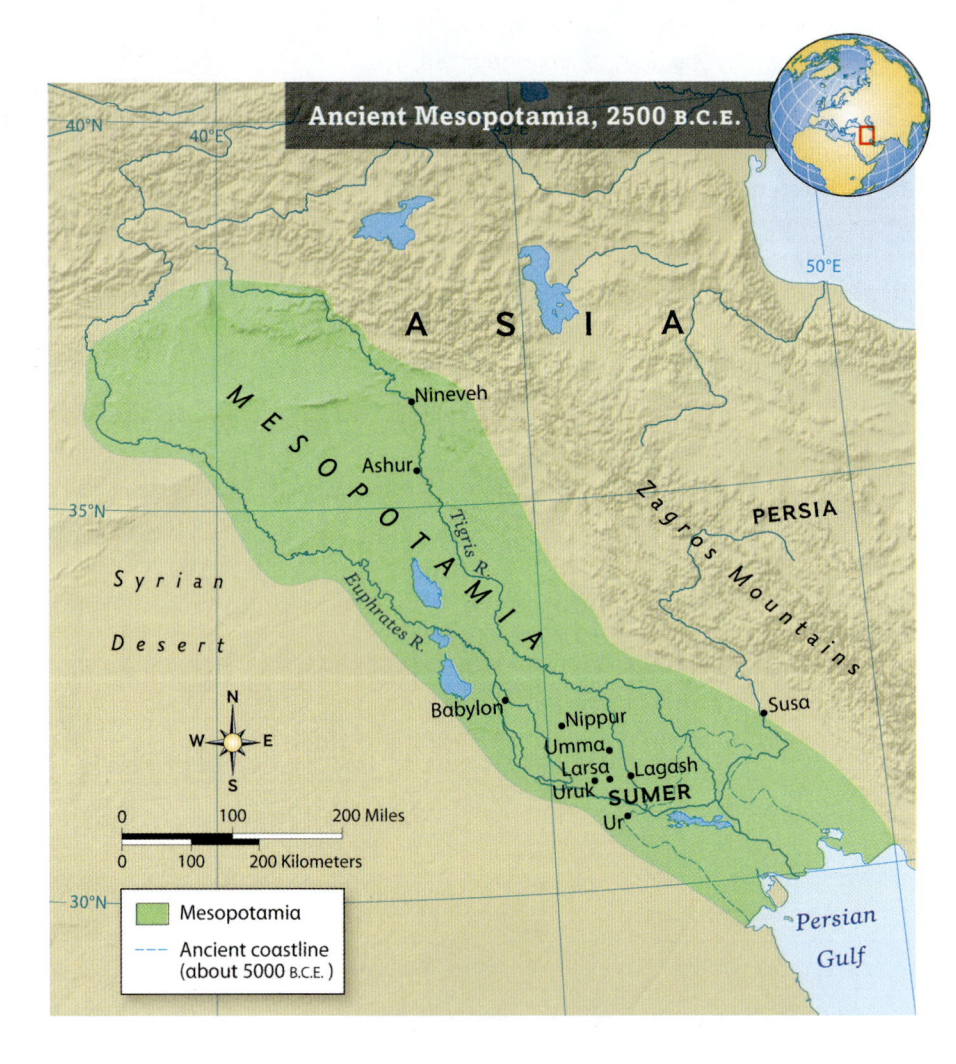

34 CHAPTER 2

a society. This division of labor led to the creation of **social classes**, in which people were grouped by what they did. Some types of work were regarded as more important than others, and the people who did those jobs were in a higher social class, which gave them higher status and more power. Such inequality in civilizations has therefore long meant that the hard work of common people has been exploited to support the power and luxury of privileged ruling classes.

The first civilizations also developed a number of **institutions**, or organizations that are established for a specific purpose and continue over time. Government and religion were the most common types of institutions in early civilizations. Both served to unify communities and provided rules to help people, who were now often strangers to one another in large cities, live together peacefully.

Other features of early civilizations included record-keeping systems for managing information and advances in **technology**, or the practical application of knowledge. The term *technology* refers to any tool or technique that helps people accomplish tasks.

MESOPOTAMIA: A CRADLE OF CIVILIZATION

In some ways, Mesopotamia was an unlikely place to become a birthplace of civilization. The region received little rainfall, which made raising crops difficult. Nor did wild grain grow naturally there.

The swift Tigris River and the slower, meandering Euphrates did bring much-needed water to the region. When the rivers flooded, they deposited **silt**, or especially fine and fertile soil, on the land. The fertile soil was good for growing crops. Yet both rivers were unpredictable, so no one knew just when or where they would overflow their banks. Unexpected floods could destroy wheat, barley, and other crops.

Instead of leaving this harsh environment, the early people of Mesopotamia adapted it to meet their needs. For example, they developed the technological innovation known as **irrigation**, or human-made systems that transport water to where it is needed. They dug canals to bring water from the rivers to their farm fields, and they found ways to store water for future use. To prevent flooding, they built dikes, or walls of dirt, along rivers.

The people of Mesopotamia also came up with the idea of using an ox-drawn plow to help them prepare the soil for planting crops. Neolithic farmers had depended on tools made from bone, wood, or stone. But Mesopotamian farmers began using a new technology—tools made of **bronze**, a mixture of the metals tin and copper—to improve the way they farmed. Bronze plow and axe blades were sharper than stone tools.

Another technological innovation on which the people of Mesopotamia depended was the wheel. Archaeologists do not know exactly when the wheel was invented. They do know that by 3500 B.C.E., many early civilizations had adopted the use of the wheel. By 3000 B.C.E., the people of Mesopotamia were using narrow carts with four wheels to move loads from place to place. By 2500 B.C.E., they were making wheels with spokes. Lighter-weight spoked wheels allowed vehicles to move faster and gave people the ability to transport scarce resources such as timber, stone, and metals over longer distances. The desire for such resources inspired the people of Mesopotamia to become skilled traders.

As the city of Uruk grew larger, it developed into a major economic, cultural, and political center. The bustling city

The development of bronze tools, such as these ax-heads, improved farming methods in ancient Mesopotamia.

Early River Valley Civilizations 35

Characteristics of Early Civilizations

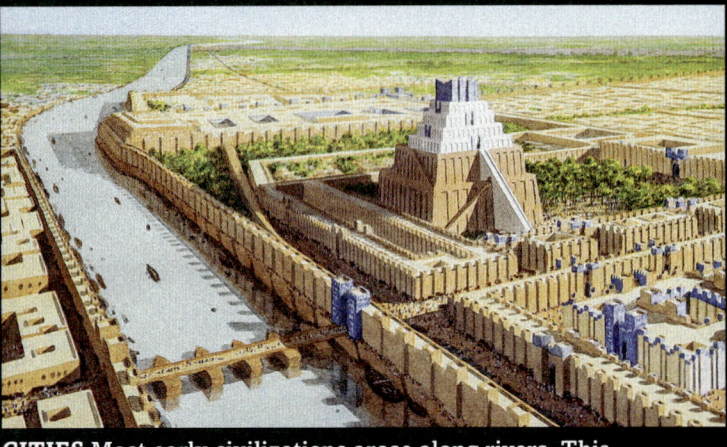

CITIES Most early civilizations arose along rivers. This illustration depicts the city of Babylon in the 500s B.C.E. Babylon became the center of a thriving civilization in Mesopotamia.

RECORD-KEEPING This clay tablet displays an early form of cuneiform, the first writing system. Found in Iraq, the tablet dates from 3000 B.C.E.

INSTITUTIONS These statues from a Sumerian temple show a man and a woman with folded hands. Early civilizations developed institutions such as religion and government to guide the community.

TECHNOLOGY This painting from an ancient tomb in Egypt shows a gardener using a *shaduf*, a device for lifting water. Such innovations in technology were another feature of early civilizations.

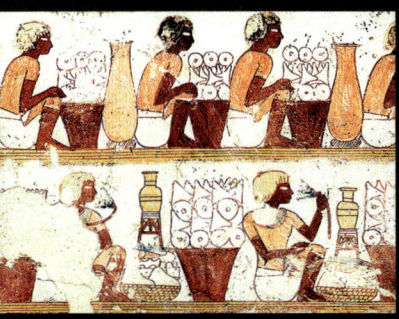

DIVISION OF LABOR Another early civilization developed along the Nile River in Egypt. This Egyptian mural painting from the 1400s B.C.E. comes from the tomb of a royal scribe, a person who learned writing and kept records. People in early civilizations specialized in different jobs, one of which was keeping records.

SOCIAL CLASSES The remains of a doorway at Persepolis in Persia depict a king with two attendants, one holding an umbrella. The division of labor led to the development of social classes, in which some, such as the ruling class, were of higher rank than other classes.

became a **city-state**, in which a ruler governs both the city and the surrounding countryside. In time, other city-states formed in Mesopotamia.

Each Mesopotamian city-state was ruled by a king, who claimed to have a special connection to the gods. This divine leader made most governmental decisions, but he sought the advice of temple priests and wealthy families. A group of administrators enforced laws, ensured that taxes were collected, and kept the city-state running smoothly.

The farms in the surrounding countryside provided each city-state with grain. Uruk had such a large stock of grain that leaders stored it in warehouse-like buildings. With a surplus of grain for food, inhabitants of Uruk were able to specialize in particular jobs. While city residents depended on surplus food grown on surrounding farms, the city provided residents of the farming villages with military protection from raids by neighboring cities.

Like the ancient city of Jericho, the city-state of Uruk had a protective wall, but Uruk's wall was much longer. By about 3000 B.C.E., Uruk's wall stretched about six miles and surrounded about 1,000 acres of land, much of it open farmland. The citizens used an available nearby resource to build the wall. Since the area had few trees or large rocks, they dug up the clay earth around them and crafted sun-dried mud bricks.

How do we know so much about this ancient city? The ruins of temples at the archaeological site where Uruk once prospered provide proof of the importance of religion and the belief in many gods. Large quantities of broken pottery found in one area suggest that potters lived and worked together, as did other craftworkers. The varied sizes of houses unearthed by archaeologists provide evidence of the existence of social classes. Archaeologists also rely on written primary sources to piece together the history of ancient Mesopotamia.

THE *EPIC OF GILGAMESH*

Perhaps the best-known primary source from Mesopotamia is the *Epic of Gilgamesh* (GIHL-guh-mehsh). An **epic** is a long narrative poem that relates the adventures of a legendary or historical hero. Like many ancient literary works, the *Epic of Gilgamesh* was first told orally and then written down in later centuries. Historians consider this epic a valuable resource for understanding ancient Mesopotamia.

Gilgamesh tells the story of the unlikely friendship between two men: Enkidu (EHN-kee-doo), who lives in the wild, and Gilgamesh, an early king of the ancient city of Uruk. While describing Enkidu and Gilgamesh's exploits, the epic reveals details about the benefits of living in a complex society.

Gilgamesh is depicted in the poem as being part god and part man, a common belief about rulers at that time. His travels include visits to the land of the gods and contact with gods and goddesses.

In the next lesson, you will learn more about ancient writing in Mesopotamia. Early writings continue to serve as a key to unraveling the mystery of what life was like long ago.

> Written about 2100 B.C.E., the *Epic of Gilgamesh* is the oldest recorded story in the world. Historians have discovered that a real king named Gilgamesh once ruled Uruk. The epic provides insight into the way that the people of ancient Mesopotamia viewed Gilgamesh.
>
> **PRIMARY SOURCE**
>
> It was he who opened the mountain passes,
>
> who dug wells on the flank of the mountain.
>
> It was he who crossed the ocean, the vast seas, to the rising sun,
>
> who explored the world regions, seeking life. . . .
>
> Who can compare with him in kingliness?
>
> Who can say like Gilgamesh: "I am King!"?
>
> —from the *Epic of Gilgamesh* translated by Maureen Gallery Kovacs

---

HISTORICAL THINKING

1. **READING CHECK** How did the development of farming in Mesopotamia lead to the rise of civilization there?

2. **IDENTIFY MAIN IDEAS AND DETAILS** What are some common characteristics of a civilization?

3. **IDENTIFY PROBLEMS AND SOLUTIONS** What problems did farmers in Mesopotamia face, and how did they solve these problems with technological innovations?

4. **INTERPRET MAPS** Based on the map, what natural resources made Mesopotamia a good site for human settlement?

1.2

MAIN IDEA Ancient Sumer was the site of the world's first empire and the world's first writing system.

Sumer and the Beginnings of Writing

As you have learned, historians use a wide variety of sources, artifacts, and techniques—including methods borrowed from science—to uncover the story of the human past. After written records became available, historians gained a powerful new tool. They now were able to learn about early civilizations directly through the words of the people who lived during the time.

LIFE IN SUMER

In the previous lesson, you learned about the rise of the first city-state, Uruk, in the southern part of Mesopotamia. This region of Mesopotamia is known as **Sumer**. Located along the southern portions of the Tigris and Euphrates rivers, Sumer reached all the way to the Persian Gulf. Around 3000 B.C.E., Sumer featured 12 or more independent city-states, including not only Uruk but also such kingdoms as Lagash, Nippur, Ur, and Larsa.

Like many other people of the time, the Sumerians practiced a religion based on **polytheism**, or the belief in many gods. They believed the various gods controlled different natural forces. For example, the storm-god was thought to control storms and floods.

The fact that every city-state featured a large temple complex is evidence of the strong connection the Sumerians felt to their gods. In the ancient city of Uruk, the temple to Ishtar, the goddess of love and

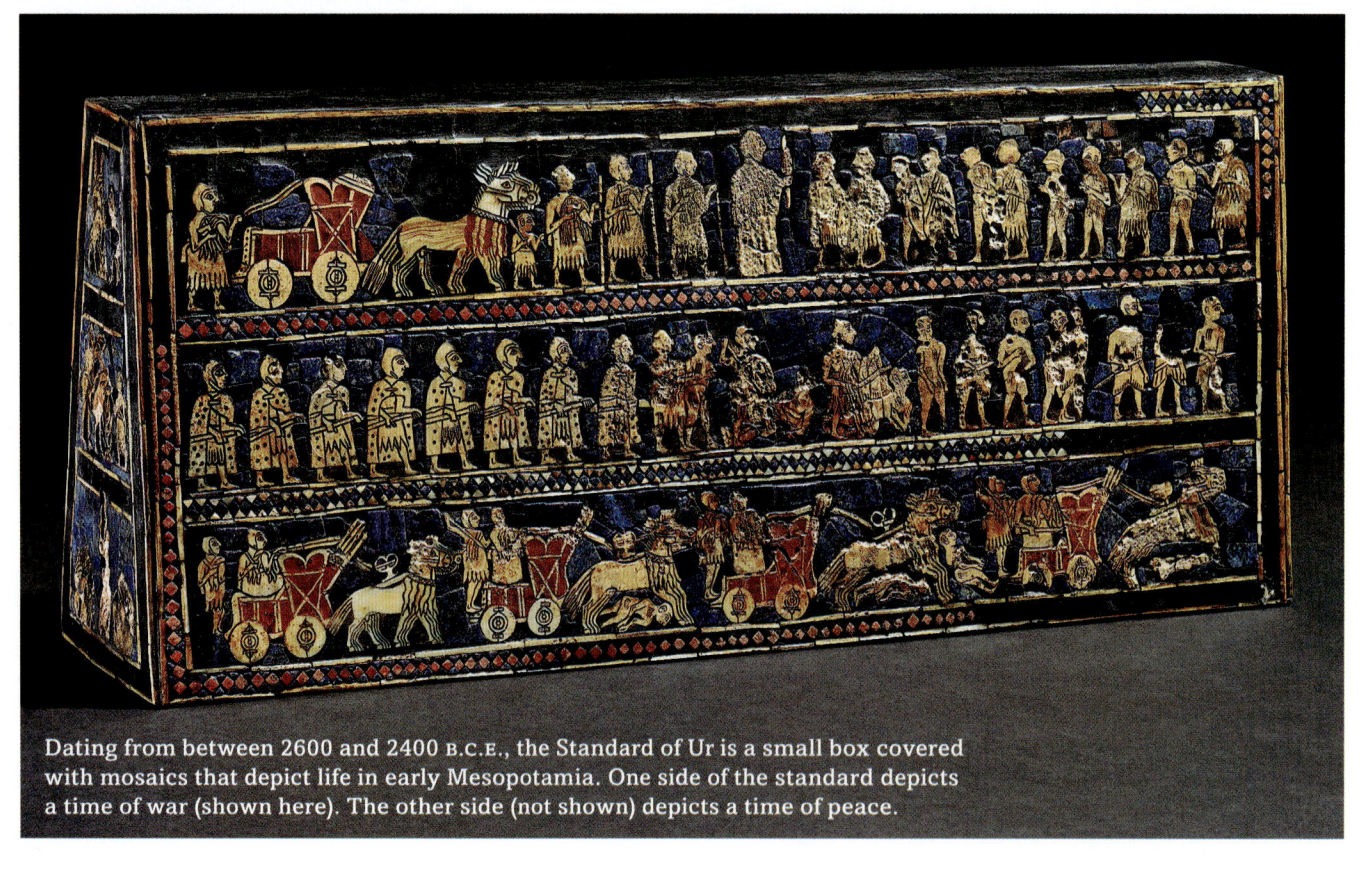

Dating from between 2600 and 2400 B.C.E., the Standard of Ur is a small box covered with mosaics that depict life in early Mesopotamia. One side of the standard depicts a time of war (shown here). The other side (not shown) depicts a time of peace.

38 CHAPTER 2

war, towered over the city. The largest structure in each temple complex was the ziggurat, a mud-brick construction with as many as seven stepped stories, each smaller than the last. The top step contained a temple shrine dedicated to the city-state's most respected god or goddess.

At first, city-states operated independently, with very little close contact. For many years, each had its own ruler. As time passed, trade between city-states increased and so did conflict, including outright warfare. Archaeologists cite the building of higher city walls in the 2000s B.C.E. and a greater number of bronze weapons as evidence of such hostility.

The lack of natural barriers such as mountains made city-states in Sumer prone to attacks from outsiders. The first ruler to conquer all the city-states and unify the region was **Sargon of Akkad**, whose kingdom lay to the north of Sumer. In 2334 B.C.E., after claiming the city-states one by one, Sargon established the world's first empire, or rule by a single power over a diverse group of conquered peoples.

Building on Sumerian achievements, Sargon and his Akkadian descendants ruled over southern Mesopotamia for about 100 years. Trade networks expanded during this time. Based on new discoveries of obsidian, a volcanic black glass, at archaeological sites in the area, researchers believe the Akkadians had trade networks that reached as far as central Turkey.

Eventually, the Akkadians lost control of their sprawling empire, and other rulers conquered the region. But Mesopotamian civilization lasted for about 3,000 years in various forms.

THE EARLIEST WRITING SYSTEM

The people of Sumer developed the world's first writing system, known as Sumerian, sometime around 3300 B.C.E. We still have examples of this early writing system because the symbols were etched into clay, which hardened to provide a permanent record.

Some time after 4000 B.C.E., the Sumerians began using small clay objects of different shapes to keep track of merchandise, such as animals being traded or donated to a temple. Later, they placed these small objects in clay bags and marked the bags to indicate

A cuneiform tablet from about 2300 B.C.E.

their contents. But archaeologists have not been able to decipher the markings.

Sumerians later etched drawings of specific animals into clay. For the first time, a symbol clearly stood for a single object and could not be mistaken for something else. The first written documents depict an item being counted with a tally next to it to show the number of items. Temple accountants used writing to record such transactions as the number and type of animal or the amount of grain donated on successive days. By 3300 B.C.E., a complete writing system of more than 700 signs had emerged.

By 700 B.C.E., the Sumerian symbols had come to stand for sounds rather than objects. Because the Sumerians used a triangle-shaped writing tool to record symbols, this later writing is known as cuneiform (kyoo-NEE-uh-fawrm), meaning "wedge-shaped." From deciphering cuneiform records, historians have learned much about the Sumerian religion and economy.

In addition to a writing system, the Sumerians created a number system to solve economic and architectural problems. Their interests in engineering, astronomy, and calendars led them to develop an exceptionally complex system of mathematics.

HISTORICAL THINKING

1. **READING CHECK** What role did the ziggurat play in Sumerian culture?

2. **MAKE INFERENCES** How did physical features influence empire building in Mesopotamia?

3. **IDENTIFY** How did the Sumerian system of writing develop over time?

Early River Valley Civilizations 39

1.3

MAIN IDEA Hammurabi, ruler of the Babylonian Empire, developed the world's first written code of laws.

The Babylonian Empire

How would you feel if you did not know what laws you had to follow and yet faced punishment for breaking them? For a long time, no clear, written record of laws existed for the people of Mesopotamia. Then one king decided to make a public list of the legal decisions he thought were most important.

CRITICAL VIEWING This segment of a brick wall comes from the Ishtar Gate, one of eight fortified entryways to the ancient city of Babylon. Based on this segment, how does the Ishtar Gate differ from typical gates in modern cities?

HAMMURABI RULES MESOPOTAMIA

After the fall of the Akkadian Empire, Mesopotamia again broke into several different kingdoms. In 1792 B.C.E., **Hammurabi** (ha-muh-RAH-bee) became king of **Babylon**, a city-state along the Euphrates River to the north of Uruk. Under Hammurabi's rule, Babylon grew in power.

Hammurabi focused on improving life for the citizens of the city-state. He initiated a series of **public works**, or construction projects that benefit a community, such as reinforcing city walls and rebuilding old temples and constructing new ones. He also created **alliances**, or partnerships, with other city-states, though turmoil within the region often caused these alliances to fall apart.

Early in his reign, Hammurabi fought to maintain his kingdom's control over the Euphrates River. Later, his focus shifted to threats from neighboring kingdoms, particularly Larsa in the south. Hammurabi strengthened his military, and in time he began a series of conquests. Eventually, he united much of Mesopotamia in the first Babylonian Empire, which would last until 1595 B.C.E. You will learn about the second Babylonian Empire later in this chapter.

CODE OF LAWS

Hammurabi is most remembered for the laws he established. You may have heard the expression "an eye for an eye," which means that if a person harms someone, the punishment will be the same kind of harm. This idea was just one of 282 provisions of Hammurabi's laws, commonly known as **Hammurabi's Code.** These laws encompassed such varied topics as divorce, criminal punishment, commerce, trade, and the treatment of slaves. Hammurabi was not the first ruler to establish a set of laws, but he combined existing laws with new laws of his own to create one organized, written code of laws for all the people of the empire.

Hammurabi's Code was inscribed on an eight-foot stone pillar called a **stela** for everyone to see. However, most Sumerians were not able to read it. The code tells more about the intentions of the rulers than about the actual behavior of the people. Only records of actual court cases can reveal whether people really followed all the laws.

Hammurabi's Code addressed the concept of justice, or fairness under the law. Yet the laws did not treat all people equally. The punishment for many crimes varied depending on the social classes of the people involved. Babylonian society at the time had three main classes. The upper class included the royal family, priests, merchants, and other free men and women who owned land. In the middle were commoners, and at the bottom were slaves. If a man of the upper class put out the eye of his social equal, he himself would be blinded. But if he took out the eye of a commoner, he would only pay a fine. If he put out the eye of a slave, he would compensate the slaveowner, not the slave.

Hammurabi's Code provides historians with insight into life in ancient Mesopotamia, including the roles and status of women. For example, according to the code, a woman was entitled to a share of her parents' property, either as a gift when she married or upon the death of her father. In some cases, women could initiate a divorce, something women in many other ancient societies were not allowed to do. In addition, the code made it clear that people who had been wronged had to work through the legal system. Private retribution, or personal revenge, was not acceptable.

Hammurabi's code also confirms that humankind has been using legal systems to resolve disputes for thousands of years. Although our modern legal system differs in important ways from the one described on Hammurabi's stela, the impact of law in daily life has persisted across time and cultures.

The top of the stela of Hammurabi's code (above) shows Hammurabi receiving a set of laws from the sun god Shamash. Many of the laws describe punishments for criminal offenses. This excerpt from the code concerns the "eye-for-an-eye" punishment, also known as exact retaliation.

PRIMARY SOURCE

196. If a man [of the upper class] put out the eye of another man [of the upper class], his eye shall be put out.
197. If he break another man's bone, his bone shall be broken.
198. If he put out the eye of a freed man [commoner], or break the bone of a freed man, he shall pay one gold mina.
199. If he put out the eye of a man's slave, or break the bone of a man's slave, he shall pay one-half of its [the slave's] value.

—from "The Code of Hammurabi" translated by L. W. King

HISTORICAL THINKING

1. **READING CHECK** How did Hammurabi develop the first Babylonian Empire?
2. **ANALYZE CAUSE AND EFFECT** What were the political and legal impacts of Hammurabi's Code?
3. **COMPARE AND CONTRAST** How is the view of justice in Hammurabi's Code different from that in the laws of the United States today?

2.1

MAIN IDEA People of African origins developed a unique civilization along the Nile River in Egypt.

African Origins of Egyptian Civilization

As in Mesopotamia, civilization in ancient Egypt developed along a river valley where people grew an abundance of crops. But life along the Nile River in Africa differed in key ways from that along the Tigris and Euphrates rivers.

WHO WERE THE EGYPTIANS?

For many years, Westerners who marveled at Egyptian achievements assumed those responsible must have come from outside the continent. Today, historians know that the ancient Egyptians were in fact Africans. Egypt remained an African civilization even as the Nile Valley region became a crossroads of interaction between peoples from Africa, Asia, and Europe. The ancient Egyptians spoke a now lost language that belonged to the Afrasian, or mixed African and Asian, language family. That family includes such modern languages as Amharic (spoken in Ethiopia), Hausa (spoken in Nigeria), and Berber (spoken in Morocco), as well as Hebrew and Arabic.

Between about 6000 and 3500 B.C.E., agriculture had developed in several places in Africa. One such place was the **Sahel**, a semiarid region south of the Sahara. There, the Sudanese people farmed and raised such livestock as goats, cattle, and sheep. At that time, regular rainfall created grasslands that were good for grazing livestock.

Over a long period of time, a decrease in rainfall caused much of the land of the Sahel to become desert. The increase in desert lands led many people to move and settle along the banks of the Nile River in what would become Egypt. They brought their agricultural practices, language, and religion with them. This congregation of a large number of Sudanese farmers along the narrow but lengthy Nile River Valley led to the development of a great civilization in Africa.

LIFE ALONG THE NILE

From its two sources in east-central Africa, the Nile River flows north for more than 4,000 miles. Near its mouth at the Mediterranean Sea, it splits into several branches and forms a triangular-shaped area of low, flat land called a **delta**. Along the course of the river are six steep, unnavigable rapids called **cataracts**.

The low land at the northern end of the Nile became known as Lower Egypt, while the higher land to the south was named Upper Egypt. The smooth flow of the Nile River enabled easy water travel and connected Egyptians living in Lower and Upper Egypt. Beyond Upper Egypt, however, the six cataracts

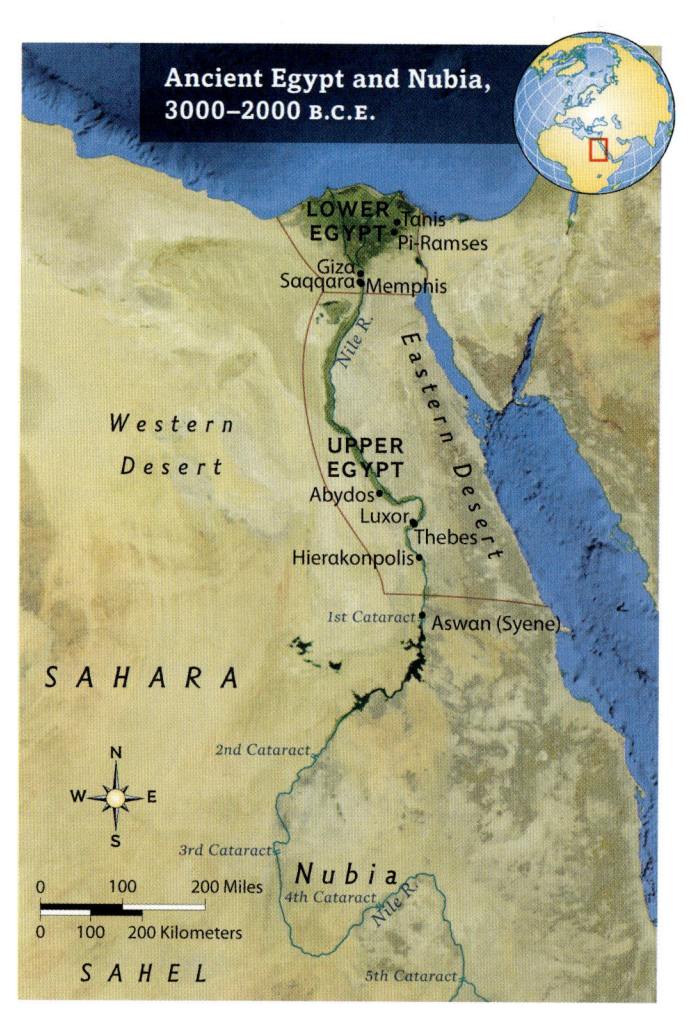

Ancient Egypt and Nubia, 3000–2000 B.C.E.

made travel by boat impossible. This land was known as **Nubia**, which became the home of an ancient kingdom called **Kush**.

Although rivers were the life blood of both Mesopotamia and Egypt, the geography of the two places differed dramatically. The Nile River was much more predictable than the Tigris and Euphrates rivers, so the Egyptians knew when floods would occur. Also unlike Mesopotamia, Egypt had a mild climate and was surrounded by natural barriers—deserts on three sides and the Mediterranean Sea on the fourth. These factors made the Egyptians feel more secure than the people of Mesopotamia. That sense of security even extended to the afterlife. While the less secure Sumerians regarded life after death with horror, Egyptians felt assured in their chances for everlasting life.

Because almost no rain fell anywhere along the Nile, the ancient Egyptians used irrigation to bring water to their farm fields. The area of rich soil along the banks of the Nile became known as *Kemet*, or "the Black Land." Beyond that lay an area of less fertile, red soil called *Deshret*, or "the Red Land." Beyond the red land lay uncultivable desert. Although unsuitable for farming, the desert was a source of both stone and gold.

The Egyptians created a calendar with three seasons based on the predictability of the Nile. During the season of *Inundation*, the Nile flooded. Egyptian farmers, who could not work in the fields, completed construction projects for their leaders. During the season of *Emergence of the Fields from Waters*, farmers irrigated their fields and planted wheat, barley, beans, and peas. During the season of *Drought*, farmers harvested their crops.

Civilization arose in Egypt at about the same time as in Mesopotamia, around 3100 B.C.E. Although Egypt did not have the large cities that were characteristic of Sumer, it was similar in other ways. Egyptian society was also highly stratified, with great differences between the poor and the rich. Large construction projects, like the building of monuments, required the same kind of job specialization. And ancient Egypt shared the belief that the ruler governed with the support of the gods.

Isis (center left), the Egyptian goddess of life, was often associated with the pharaohs of ancient Egypt, who would call upon her to protect them against their enemies.

During certain periods, Upper Egypt and Lower Egypt were united under a single ruler, who as time passed would be revered as the **pharaoh** (FEHR-oh). As a god-king, the pharaoh presided over rituals in honor of the Egyptian gods. Since the pharaoh was often occupied with ritual duties, his chief advisor, called the *vizier*, handled most matters of state.

Historians call the periods during which Egypt was unified under a series of strong rulers *kingdoms*. The times when no one ruler governed the entire land are called *intermediate periods*. In the next lesson, you will learn about the three main kingdoms of Egypt: The Old Kingdom (2686–2181 B.C.E.), the Middle Kingdom (2040–1782 B.C.E.), and the New Kingdom (1570–1069 B.C.E.).

HISTORICAL THINKING

1. **READING CHECK** Why did large numbers of Sudanese farmers move to the Nile River Valley?
2. **COMPARE AND CONTRAST** Identify the similarities and differences in the effects of rivers on the lives of people in ancient Mesopotamia and Egypt.
3. **INTERPRET MAPS** Describe the physical shape of ancient Egypt. What physical features influenced this shape?

Early River Valley Civilizations 43

2.2

MAIN IDEA The Egyptians built massive monuments, developed a writing system, and expanded their territory during the Old and Middle kingdoms.

The Old and Middle Kingdoms

If you were a farmer in ancient Egypt, you would give much of your grain to the pharaoh, who owned the land, and work periodically on one of his building projects. You could not escape these obligations. Your farming community could never survive in the desert, away from the fertile soil along the Nile.

The most famous ancient Egyptian monuments are the three pyramids at Giza (shown here) and the Great Sphinx, a large statue of a lion with a human head.

MONUMENTAL ACHIEVEMENTS

The uniting of Upper and Lower Egypt marked the beginning of the **Old Kingdom**, which lasted from 2686 to 2181 B.C.E., or more than 500 years. During this period, the Egyptians enjoyed prosperity and a stable government. Ancient Egypt had a **monarchy**, or a government ruled by a single person. The Egyptian pharaoh exerted absolute power over all the people.

Rule over Egypt passed from generation to generation of a family. This succession of hereditary rulers, called a **dynasty**, lasted until a family line died out or another family gained power. Through its long history, Egypt had 31 dynasties. Ten different dynasties ruled during the time of the Old Kingdom. The government was based in the capital city of Memphis.

The Old Kingdom is especially remembered for its large, four-sided monuments known as **pyramids**. The pyramids were built as gigantic tombs to hold the bodies of dead pharaohs. The Egyptians believed that each person had a life force, or *ka,* that survived on energy from the body. When a person died, the Egyptians preserved the body with chemicals and

44 CHAPTER 2

NATIONAL GEOGRAPHIC EXPLORER YUKINORI KAWAE

Strange, Unexplored Places

The desire to find answers to difficult questions came early to Yukinori Kawae, shown above at the site of the Great Pyramid. As a junior high school student in Japan, he watched a TV documentary about the Great Pyramid. The documentary posed these questions: Why are the chambers identified by archaeologists located on just one side of the pyramid? Could there be unexplored spaces on the other side? As an adult, Kawae became an archaeologist with a specialization in Egyptology and set out to find answers to such questions.

Using traditional methods at first, Kawae found his task daunting. As he said, "Discussions about pyramid construction can be likened to a crime investigation with scant evidence and insufficient onsite inspection."

Kawae now takes an interdisciplinary approach to archaeology by incorporating computer science, 3-D data surveys, and other technology to find out how the pyramids were built. He and his team of computer scientists and mathematicians rely on data collected by video cameras, scanners, laser beams, and drones at the site of the Great Pyramid. They use the data to make three-dimensional models back at Kawae's lab in Japan. Such models let him "peek" into hidden areas of the pyramid to uncover the mysteries hidden behind the thick stone walls. They may help him answer unresolved questions about the construction methods used to build the pyramids—for instance, how workers managed to raise more than three million stones.

wrapped it to form a mummy. They believed preserving the body this way allowed the life force to continue. They even surrounded the mummified body with food to nourish the person's spirit in the afterlife. From mummifying bodies, the Egyptians developed a detailed knowledge of anatomy and an understanding of the role of the heart in the human body.

A preserved body alone was not enough to ensure a happy afterlife, however. Egyptians believed the dead had to appear before Osiris (oh-SY-ruhs), the god of the underworld. He and other judges would decide whether a dead person deserved entrance to the realm of eternal happiness. According to the Egyptians, the gods weighed each person's heart to determine if the good within the person surpassed the bad.

A pharaoh named Djoser (JOH-sur) ordered the building of the first pyramid in preparation for his afterlife. His vizier, Imhotep, came up with a plan to carry out the pharaoh's vision. This first pyramid looked like a huge, four-sided set of stairs, which is why historians call it a step pyramid. Later, the architectural design would change to create pyramids with smooth sides.

Early River Valley Civilizations

Osiris
God of the underworld

One of the most impressive pyramids, called the Great Pyramid, still stands in Giza (GEE-zuh), near the present-day city of Cairo. The Great Pyramid was built between 2589 and 2566 B.C.E., a period of 23 years, to house the life force of the pharaoh Khufu (KOO-foo).

The building of the Great Pyramid demonstrates both the strong influence of religion and the power of the pharaoh in Egyptian society. About 15,000 to 20,000 laborers, both male and female, worked on the pyramids each year during the flood season. None of these laborers were enslaved. About 5,000 skilled workers and craftspeople worked full-time, while the rest of the laborers rotated in and out.

Using just the limited technology available at the time, the Egyptians created an architectural masterpiece covering an area of 571,211 square feet and standing 480 feet tall. That's twice the area of the U.S. Capitol Building and taller than the Statue of Liberty. The builders used a system of ramps and poles to move an estimated four million stone blocks into position. Some of the blocks weighed as much as nine tons.

Obviously, the Egyptians employed planning, mathematics, and engineering skills to determine how many blocks were required and how to produce the correct slant. The need for exact calculations led the Egyptians to formulate some of the key principles of geometry. In addition, they developed measurement tools, including the cubit, a fixed unit of length of about 18 inches. Careful study of astronomy allowed the Egyptians to create a 365-day calendar of 24-hour days, which they used to keep track of progress on the pyramids.

The pyramid workers lived in special villages, and evidence from an ancient worker village shows that the laborers were well fed and well cared for. The pyramid workers completed other building projects as well, such as the remarkable limestone statue known as the Great Sphinx. This statue depicts a creature with the body of a lion and the head of a human and appears to be guarding three nearby pyramids. Historians now believe that the Sphinx may have been brightly painted at one time.

WRITING SYSTEM

The Egyptians kept written records of such events as the building of the pyramids using picture symbols called **hieroglyphs** (HY-uh-ruh-glihfs). Historians do not know exactly when or how hieroglyphs developed, but the Egyptians credited their god Thoth with their invention. Some of the picture symbols simply represented a single object, such as a house. But other symbols stood for one or more sounds and could be combined to express complex ideas. For this reason, hieroglyphs provided a more comprehensive form of communication than cuneiform.

The Egyptians painted and carved hieroglyphs on tombs, temples, and monuments. For important records and documents, they wrote on a paperlike material called **papyrus** (puh-PY-ruhs), named after the reeds used to make it. Only certain people gained mastery over the more than 800 hieroglyphs in the complex Egyptian writing system. The Egyptian government employed a large number of professional writers, called **scribes**, to keep detailed papyrus records of most transactions, including goods used and traded. The great demand for scribes created a rare chance for social mobility in Egyptian society.

Unlike the clay tablets of the Sumerians, most papyrus scrolls of the Egyptians did not last long. Historians rely mainly on ancient writings in stone for information about Egyptian history and ways of life. An archaeological find called the **Rosetta Stone** unlocked the meaning of Egyptian hieroglyphs. This black granite artifact, which dates to 196 B.C.E., was discovered near Rosetta, Egypt, in 1799 C.E. The stone features an ancient message written not only in Egyptian hieroglyphs but also in Greek and another type of Egyptian writing called *demotic*. Experts were able to use the Greek translation to decipher Egyptian hieroglyphs.

EXPANSION DURING THE MIDDLE KINGDOM

The Old Kingdom eventually broke apart into semi-independent regions ruled by rival dynasties. Egypt then entered the First Intermediate Period, which lasted about 140 years. Then in 2040 B.C.E., a ruler based in the city of Thebes reunited Egypt and began the **Middle Kingdom**, which continued until 1782 B.C.E. During this time, order returned throughout the land, agriculture expanded farther beyond the Nile, building projects resumed, and contacts with other kingdoms and city-states increased.

Like Mesopotamia, Egypt had few natural resources. The pharaohs of the Middle Kingdom increased trade with other regions to obtain scarce natural resources such as wood, gold, silver, and semiprecious stones. Egypt's main trading partners were people living in the lands that are now Syria and Lebanon to the north and in Nubia to the south.

The pharaohs of the Middle Kingdom also ventured out on a path of conquest. They took over land along the eastern Mediterranean Sea and in Nubia. Their control extended south to the area around the Third Cataract, which allowed them to engage in extensive trade with the kingdom of Kush. This connection with Kush enabled the Egyptians to gain valuable trade goods from Ethiopia and other societies to the south. Such items as panther skins, ivory from elephant tusks, and gold were carried through Nubia, overland around the cataracts, and down the Nile to Egypt.

Sometime around the 1700s B.C.E., the Middle Kingdom weakened because of invasions by the Hyksos (HIHK-sohs), a group of people from present-day Turkey. The time that followed has become known as the Second Intermediate Period. Egyptian foot soldiers proved no match against the horse-drawn chariots and the strong bows of the Hyksos. Eventually, the Hyksos claimed complete control of Egypt and ruled over it from 1650 to 1570 B.C.E.

HISTORICAL THINKING

1. **READING CHECK** What were the major achievements of the Old Kingdom and the Middle Kingdom?
2. **MAKE GENERALIZATIONS** What role did religion play in the building of the pyramids?
3. **DRAW CONCLUSIONS** Why do you think Egyptian farmers cooperated in helping construct the pyramids?
4. **MAKE INFERENCES** Why do you think the Egyptians kept so many records on papyrus even though this material was not durable?

NATIONAL GEOGRAPHIC EXPLORER
NORA SHAWKI

Looking for Everyday Life in Ancient Egypt

Since she was a little girl, Egyptian archaeologist Nora Shawki, shown above at a dig site, has been fascinated by the ancient civilization that once flourished in her homeland. After working on numerous excavations unearthing fragments of ancient Egypt, Shawki received a National Geographic Young Explorer Grant in 2015, which has permitted her to plan and direct her own dig at Tell Zuwelen, a settlement near the city of Tanis. Shawki's goal is to learn about the lives of ordinary Egyptians by tracking settlements in the Nile Delta. These settlements have the potential to tell us more about how ordinary people used to live their daily lives. "My research is focused on the ordinary Egyptians rather than the royals," she says. "It's imperative in understanding how the political and economic dynamics worked in ancient Egypt."

Settlement archaeology in the Nile Delta is extremely urgent due to the fact that the delta itself will not be there in the next 40 years due to modern encroachment and looting. Shawki believes she needs to excavate and document as much as possible because once it's gone, it's gone forever. "As an Egyptian, I aim to break boundaries as a female in a male-dominated society and make a change in the way we as the young generation of Egyptians view our own heritage and are able to access it."

2.3 The New Kingdom and Nubia

MAIN IDEA Egypt reached the peak of its power and size during the New Kingdom but was later taken over by Nubia.

The pharaoh Akhenaten (AH-keh-NAH-tehn) and his beautiful queen, Nefertiti (NEHF-ur-tee-tee), were powerful and controversial figures in the New Kingdom. They promoted the worship of Aten, a new form of sun-god, but their religious revolution died with them. When the next pharaoh ascended to the throne, Egyptians resumed worship of the former sun-god, Amun-Ra.

GROWTH DURING THE NEW KINGDOM

After about 80 years of foreign rule, an Egyptian leader named Ahmose (AH-mohz) rebelled, fought the Hyksos, and defeated them. By 1570 B.C.E., Egypt was once again united under the absolute control of a strong monarch. This beginning of the **New Kingdom** ushered in another period of stability along the Nile.

Ahmose and the pharaohs who followed him vowed that, rather than be conquered again, they would be the ones to conquer. Egypt created its first full-time army and marched into Southwest Asia. It took over a swath of territory that included the present-day Palestinian territories, Lebanon, and Syria. It also advanced south into Nubia, gaining access to Nubia's most valuable resource—gold—which the Egyptians associated with immortality and the sun-god Amun-Ra. With the Nubian gold mines under their control, the Egyptians now had unlimited access to the cherished metal.

Determined to keep Nubia under their control, the pharaohs worked to transform Nubia into an Egyptian society. They brought the sons of Nubian chiefs to Egypt. In Egypt, the Nubians studied the Egyptian language and worshipped Egyptian deities. When they returned home, they served Egypt as administrators. Over time, the Nubians adopted Egyptian gods and values while adapting them to their own culture.

Egypt continued to trade with Nubia and other regions during the reign of **Hatshepsut** (haht-SHEHP-soot), the only woman pharaoh of the 18th dynasty. She gained power in 1473 B.C.E. as the guardian for her young stepson but then assumed the duties of pharaoh on her own. Ruling for 15 years, she initiated extensive trade expeditions to gain ebony, ivory, cedar, myrrh trees, and other goods.

During the New Kingdom period, Egypt established a series of alliances with the various powers in the eastern Mediterranean region and occasionally went to war with them. Letters written by the pharaoh Akhenaten, who ruled from 1352 to 1336 B.C.E., show that he communicated with rulers in the eastern Mediterranean lands of Babylonia, Assyria, and Anatolia. Over a period of 500 years, the eastern Mediterranean states engaged in both trade and **diplomacy**, or negotiation between governments.

Akhenaten moved the capital of Egypt to a new site about 200 miles north of Thebes, where he began construction on a city and temples devoted to the worship of Aten. In the past, some scholars concluded that Akhenaten worshipped Aten as the only god. But in fact, he continued to worship other gods as well, though Aten clearly ranked highest.

In the 1330s B.C.E., a nine-year-old boy named **Tutankhamen** (too-tang-KAH-muhn) followed Akhenaten as pharaoh. Tutankhamen ruled for only 10 years and might have been forgotten if not for the discovery of his lavish tomb by British archaeologist Howard Carter in 1922. Unlike most other royal tombs, this one had not been stripped of its treasures by looters. The tomb provided information about the ancient Egyptians' belief in the afterlife.

Tutankhamen's tomb was not a pyramid like the tombs of pharaohs of the Old Kingdom. Like many New Kingdom pharaohs, he was buried in a tomb cut out of rock in an area near Thebes called the Valley of the Kings. The tombs in the valley were built into the landscape to deter robbers. Even so, only Tutankhamen's tomb remained untouched for centuries.

Although New Kingdom pharaohs stopped building pyramids, they continued to construct large temples and other monuments. A long-reigning pharaoh of the 19th dynasty known as **Ramses II**, or Ramses the Great, was the most prolific builder of the New Kingdom. He commissioned hundreds of temples, monuments, and statues. Under Ramses, who ruled from 1279 to 1213 B.C.E., Egypt's power reached its peak.

The many wall paintings that graced Egyptian temples and tombs illustrate the prosperity of the Egyptians and the influence religion had on them. Some paintings show pharaohs interacting with Egyptian gods and goddesses, such as Osiris, Horus, Isis, and Anubis. Others portray leaders performing brave feats in battles or farmers at work in the fields or building pyramids. Such scenes provide historians with insight about the history of the Egyptian people as well as details about their daily lives.

NUBIAN RULE AND DECLINE

The New Kingdom began to weaken after 1200 B.C.E., and Egyptian rulers gradually lost control of Nubia. After 1069 B.C.E., torn by civil war, Egypt was once again split in two. Free of Egyptian rule, the Nubians began to rebuild an independent government based at Napata, a city along the Nile. Then around 747 B.C.E., the Nubians set their sights on the land of Egypt. Believing they were the rightful heirs to the pharaoh's throne, Nubian rulers conquered Egypt.

The high point of Nubian rule occurred under the leadership of King Taharqa (tuh-HAWR-kuh), who reigned from 690 to 644 B.C.E. He revived the practice of building pyramids, which had ended in Egypt about 1,000 years earlier, near the end of the Middle Kingdom. The first Nubian pyramid constructed under King Taharqa stood 160 feet tall and featured a flat, rather than a pointed, top. The Nubians followed other Egyptian traditions, including mummification and the worship of Egyptian gods. Not long after King Taharqa's death, the Nubians lost control of Egypt.

After 332 B.C.E., the Macedonians, who came from the Greek peninsula, gained control of Egypt. The last pharaohs of Egypt were all Macedonians, including the final one, the famous **Cleopatra VII**. Early historians and biographers, who were mostly Roman and male, tended to depict Cleopatra as a woman who relied on her beauty and charm to win special treatment from men. Later historians have suggested that this assessment reflects bias, or prejudice, against women. Some modern historians have pointed out that Cleopatra was an intelligent, accomplished woman who spoke nine languages. They regard her as a shrewd leader whose calculated actions served to secure her power and win the allegiance of the people she ruled. She managed to delay Roman takeover of Egypt until her death in 30 B.C.E. That date marks the end of ancient Egyptian civilization, which lasted about 3,000 years. Egyptian civilization actually rose and fell over a longer period of time than the entire history of the world since then.

Ramses II ruled Egypt from c. 1279–1213 B.C.E.

HISTORICAL THINKING

1. **READING CHECK** How did Egypt increase its power during the New Kingdom period?

2. **DRAW CONCLUSIONS** How did the Egyptians' belief in immortality help shape the relationship between Egypt and Nubia?

3. **ANALYZE PERSPECTIVE** How do the past and present views of Cleopatra VII reflect the changing nature of history over time?

2.4 Preserving Cultural Heritage

Queens of Egypt

You've read about the royal tomb of Tutankhamen and that it and similar burial places for New Kingdom pharaohs are located in the Valley of the Kings. But did you know that there is also a Valley of the Queens? Most women—including royalty—in the ancient world did not hold much power, but Egypt was an exception. Women sometimes ruled with their husbands in political and social realms and sometimes on their own, for example, as the guardian of a younger male heir. And one of them even declared herself king.

In 2019, the National Geographic Society debuted a new exhibition featuring more than 300 artifacts that highlight the women of Egypt with a focus on the New Kingdom through the last queen and pharaoh, Cleopatra VII. We can use these artifacts and other evidence to speculate about what these women were like and how their leadership influenced ancient Egypt.

NEFERTITI

Nefertiti was married to Akhenaten, the 10th pharaoh of the 18th dynasty. Her name translates as "The Beautiful One Has Come" or "A Beautiful Woman Has Come," but she was more than a pretty face. Some historians believe that she co-ruled Egypt with her husband, playing important religious and political roles. Nefertiti also may have assumed some of the pharaoh's duties as he strived to reform his empire under its new religion—the worship of the sun-god Aten. In 1912, workers excavated the now famous painted limestone bust (shown here) near Amarna, Egypt, in the workshop of the court sculptor Thutmose. The personalized features and unique crown helped identify the well-preserved sculpture as Nefertiti.

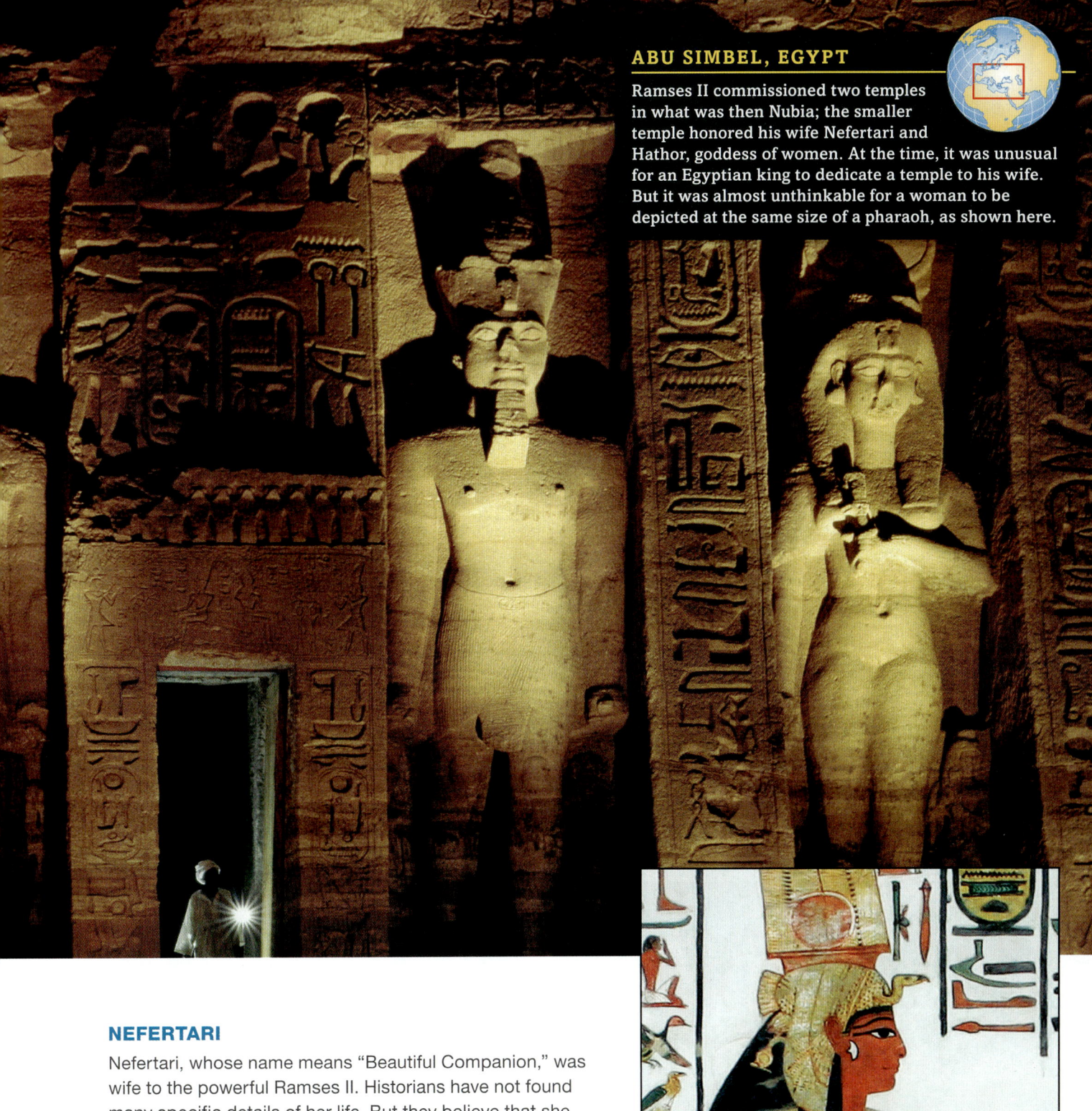

ABU SIMBEL, EGYPT

Ramses II commissioned two temples in what was then Nubia; the smaller temple honored his wife Nefertari and Hathor, goddess of women. At the time, it was unusual for an Egyptian king to dedicate a temple to his wife. But it was almost unthinkable for a woman to be depicted at the same size of a pharaoh, as shown here.

NEFERTARI

Nefertari, whose name means "Beautiful Companion," was wife to the powerful Ramses II. Historians have not found many specific details of her life. But they believe that she was highly educated and participated in both state and religious business. At the main temple at Abu Simbel, one scene shows the royal couple making offerings to the sun gods. In her tomb, wall paintings depict Nefertari both in the company of the gods and as a divine figure, wearing a white gown and a golden headdress. Ramses II was devastated when she died. He said, "Just by passing, she has stolen away my heart." The wall painting shown here, in which Nefertari presents scrolls to the Egyptian god Toth, dates to about 1255 B.C.E.

Early River Valley Civilizations **51**

HATSHEPSUT

You learned that Hatshepsut was the only woman pharaoh of the 18th dynasty. She seized the throne from her stepson Thutmose III by claiming that the god Amun was her father—and Amun wanted Hatshepsut to rule. She insisted, "I acted under his command; it was he who led me." Portraits of Hatshepsut after she declared herself king and consolidated her power feature inscriptions of "His Majesty" as well as the ceremonial garb of the pharaohs, including a royal headdress, kilt, and false beard. After her death, Thutmose III attempted to eradicate all evidence of his stepmother and her reign by destroying her likenesses and monuments and removing her name from the list of kings. Fortunately for us, he was unsuccessful. The limestone statue of the queen shown here dates to about 1479–1458 B.C.E.

TIYE

The daughter of a high-ranking official, Tiye grew up in the royal palace and eventually married Amenhotep III, the ninth pharaoh of the 18th dynasty. Her talent for diplomacy was a definite asset when it came to Egypt's involvement in foreign affairs. In art, Tiye and Amenhotep III are constant companions and partners, with wife and husband depicted at the same height, symbolizing their equality. Letters and inscriptions support this conclusion, as does evidence that Tiye oversaw many important administrative tasks herself. She also advised her son, Amenhotep IV, who later changed his name to Akhenaten. Surviving letters to the pharaoh from foreign rulers encourage Akhenaten to ask his mother for advice. No wonder she gained a reputation as the true power behind the throne! The realistic wood, gold, and silver portrait of Tiye shown here dates to about 1355 B.C.E. It shows the queen in her later years.

NATIONAL GEOGRAPHIC EXPLORER KARA COONEY

When Women Ruled the World

Professor, Egyptologist, and National Geographic Explorer Kara Cooney specializes in craft production, coffin studies, and economies of the ancient world. She has studied nearly 300 coffins in collections all around the world. She was originally drawn to Egyptian art and architecture for the "pretty pictures," but she moved toward the truths of the systems behind the hieroglyphics, sacred texts, and grand monuments.

"I find myself trying to pull the veils away from Egyptian society to see what was really going on," Cooney says. Her 2018 book *When Women Ruled the World* delves into the lives of the six women rulers mentioned in this lesson. "Six powerful queens, five of them becoming pharaohs in their own rights—and yet each and every one of them had to fit the patriarchal systems of power around them, rather than fashioning something new," Cooney points out. "The story of female power in ancient Egypt is a tragedy."

CLEOPATRA VII

Recall that Cleopatra was the last pharaoh to rule Egypt. Her family's claim to the throne dated back to Ptolemy, a Macedonian general who fought for Alexander the Great. (You will read about Alexander and Ptolemy in a later chapter.) Cleopatra ascended the throne at the age of 18 in 51 B.C.E. with her younger brother Ptolemy XIII. The siblings were supposed to rule their empire together, but they soon were at war. Cleopatra allied with Julius Caesar of Rome to regain her royal position. Ptolemy XIII died during the conflict. Although another brother, Ptolemy XIV, was designated as co-ruler, Cleopatra wielded all the power. Her 11-year relationship with the Roman general Mark Antony helped stave off a Roman takeover until her death. The basalt statue of Cleopatra shown here dates from the first century B.C.E.

AHMOSE-NEFERTARI

As the first queen of the New Kingdom from 1539 to 1514 B.C.E., Ahmose-Nefertari worked closely with her husband, Ahmose, to transition from war to peace and reunify Egypt. She held the title of "God's Wife of Amun" or "Wife of the God," in which a woman from the royal family served as a mediator between the god and the king. Ahmose-Nefertari increased the power of this position to gain religious influence as well as political clout and a higher social standing. A God's Wife mirrored the authority of a high priest, and she received payment in the form of property, staff, and many different material goods. Ahmose-Nefertari and her son Amenhotep I were deified after their deaths, and she was worshiped as a goddess of resurrection at the ancient Egyptian village of Deir el-Medina. The wooden statue shown here depicts the queen with braids and in a long linen robe. A vulture pelt and a partial headdress indicate her royal status.

HISTORICAL THINKING

ANALYZE VISUALS Why might the study of artifacts be a better way to learn about the women of ancient Egypt than relying on written documents from that time?

Early River Valley Civilizations 53

3.1

MAIN IDEA Drawing on their military technology and strength, the Hittites and the Assyrians built empires in Southwest Asia.

The Hittites and the Assyrians

Most businesses today are quick to adopt new technology, believing they need any edge they can get to match or beat the competition. The same philosophy held true in ancient times and gave a distinct advantage to two groups—the Hittites and the Assyrians.

THE HITTITE KINGDOM

You have read that the New Kingdom pharaohs communicated and formed alliances with various powers in the eastern Mediterranean region. The **Hittites** (HIH-tyts), who were based in Anatolia, now the country of Turkey, were one of these groups.

Like Egyptian pharaohs, Hittite kings not only led the military and presided over government but also acted as high priests and directed religious practices. The Hittites erected temples to the weather-god Teshub, considered the highest god.

Unlike the Egyptian language, the language of the Hittites belonged to the Indo-European family. Its structure resembled that of Latin, Greek, and Sanskrit, the ancient language of southern Asia. While the Hittite language has not survived, many Indo-European languages are still widely spoken today, including Hindi, Farsi, Greek, Spanish, French, Italian, Irish, German, and English.

The Hittites were the first speakers of an Indo-European language to establish a complex society in western Asia. **Iron**, a heavy metal used to make steel, was the foundation of the Hittite civilization. Iron technology enabled the Hittites to create stronger tools and weapons than the bronze implements used by neighboring peoples. Iron could not be melted and poured into molds like bronze. Instead, skilled

The archaeological site of Hattusha, which was the capital of the Hittite kingdom, preserves the ruins of temples, royal residences, fortifications, gateways, and other types of construction.

metalworkers heated iron and hammered it into the desired shape. The Hittites traded their iron tools and weapons to other peoples, but they kept the process for making them secret.

Advanced iron weapons gave the Hittites an advantage in battle. An iron Hittite sword could crush the skull of an enemy whose head was protected only by a soft bronze helmet. Another new technology, the war chariot, made the Hittites victorious in battle after battle. Two horses pulled a chariot that carried a driver and two warriors into action. During the Battle of Kadesh in 1285 B.C.E., the Hittite ruler commanded 2,500 chariots to defeat the Egyptian army. Later, the two sides signed a peace treaty and promised to aid each other in time of war.

Between 1322 and 1220 B.C.E., the Hittite kingdom reached its largest size, covering all of Anatolia and Syria and the eastern edge of Mesopotamia. But in 1200 B.C.E., the Hittite capital fell to outsiders. Historians are unsure who the invaders were, but ancient Egyptian texts refer to "sea peoples" who attacked parts of the Mediterranean region.

THE ASSYRIAN EMPIRE

The homeland of the **Assyrians** (uh-SIHR-ee-uhnz) was in northern Mesopotamia. Like the Hittites, the Assyrians forged iron weapons that gave them an advantage over their enemies. The Assyrian army also had the first true **cavalry**, or group of soldiers mounted on horseback. Armed with bows and arrows, the Assyrian soldiers rode bareback since saddles and stirrups had not yet been invented.

The Assyrian leaders sought to take over land in order to control trade routes. Unlike previous conquerors in the eastern Mediterranean region, the Assyrians did not immediately take other peoples' territory by force. Because the Assyrian ruler saw himself as the representative of the gods, he believed it was his duty to convince foreign rulers to submit to him voluntarily. Those who surrendered received gentle treatment, but those who resisted were cruelly punished. Soldiers skinned captives alive, gouged out eyes, cut off hands and feet, or impaled victims on stakes. These atrocities served as a warning to those who had not yet been conquered: surrender quickly or else. The Assyrians themselves believed such treatment was justified

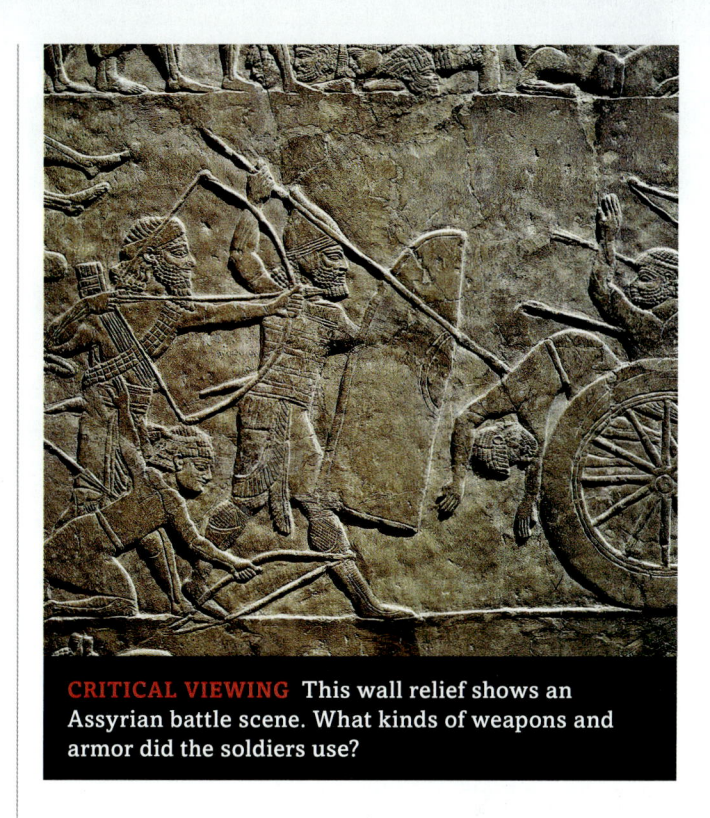

CRITICAL VIEWING This wall relief shows an Assyrian battle scene. What kinds of weapons and armor did the soldiers use?

because the enemy was resisting the gods, not just a human king.

Besides conquering southern Mesopotamia and Egypt, the powerful Assyrian army defeated the kingdom of Israel in 721 B.C.E., which you will learn about in the next lesson. After conquering a region, the Assyrians forced the defeated rulers and skilled craftsmen to relocate to another part of the empire. These forced migrations were originally intended to fill lightly populated parts of the empire. Later, resettlement became a method of demonstrating the ruler's power. Several hundred thousand people were resettled, including many people from Israel who were sent to Assyria.

The Assyrians built a network of roads to connect settlements and established a messenger system to relay messages. They also made the center of government, Nineveh, a showplace, with huge gates, wide streets, canals, an impressive palace, and a library containing more than 20,000 cuneiform tablets. The booming agricultural economy financed such improvements. Yet even the fearsome Assyrians were not indestructible, and their empire fell to a people known as the Chaldeans in 612 B.C.E.

HISTORICAL THINKING

1. **READING CHECK** How did technology help the Hittites and the Assyrians build empires?

2. **FORM AND SUPPORT OPINIONS** Why do you think the Hittites wanted to keep the technology of making iron a secret?

3. **EVALUATE** How would you characterize the Assyrian methods of warfare and rule?

3.2 Preserving Cultural Heritage

HERITAGE AT RISK
By Fred Hiebert

When historians and archaeologists examine past cultures, they turn to monuments from those cultures—the often grand archaeological remains of humanity's built environment—that still exist today. Those aged remnants can reveal a great deal of information about **cultural heritage**, the attributes of a group or society inherited from past generations. Historical monuments and artifacts, or human-made objects, that have been collected contribute to the **human record**, the story of human life on Earth over the centuries.

Dr. Fredrik Hiebert is the archaeologist-in-residence at National Geographic Society. Protecting cultural identity is what his job is all about.

Today, that record is at risk. Historical monuments are vulnerable to external forces such as unchecked human development and harsh climate conditions. In conflict zones, the monuments are sometimes accidental victims of crossfire. And for the same reasons monuments are so beloved by the cultures that produced them, they become a target for those who might attempt to destroy them for political reasons or sell them for profit.

In *World History: Voyages of Exploration*, you will learn about some of the world's most significant monuments, the threats to their survival, and the "culture heroes" who work to preserve them.

HISTORICAL THINKING

ANALYZE VISUALS How do the "before" and "after" photos of Palmyra help explain why that monument might be important to the culture that created it?

ASSYRIAN EMPIRE, c. 645 B.C.E.
Some pieces of cultural identity are preserved in museums. This detail from a gypsum wall panel in King Ashurbanipal's palace in Nineveh (near modern-day Mosul, Iraq) is housed in the British Museum. The sculpture is a **relief**, a technique in which raised figures are just barely more prominent than the background.

PALMYRA

A thriving trade center, Palmyra or "city of palm trees," was an ancient city built between the Mediterranean Sea and the Euphrates River in south-central Syria. The small photo, taken in March 2014, shows the Temple of Bel, the center of religious life in Palmyra. The larger photo shows the temple after it was destroyed by Islamic State militants in September 2015, as a show of force in a war-torn region.

3.3 **MAIN IDEA** The ancient Hebrews developed the concept of belief in one God and established a homeland in Southwest Asia.

Judaism and the Israelite Kingdoms

Stories of men, women, and children forced to flee their homelands frequently appear in the news today. As these people settle in new lands, some will hold on to the traditions of their home countries for at least a generation. One group of people who had to abandon its homeland in ancient times has maintained its core traditions for thousands of years.

Today, many Jews come to pray at the Western Wall, a small remnant of an ancient wall in the Old City of Jerusalem. Some people place slips of paper containing written prayers into cracks in the wall. Jews consider the Western Wall and an elevated plaza in Jerusalem called the Temple Mount especially holy sites.

ORIGINS OF JUDAISM

You have read about rulers or groups who used their military strength to build powerful empires in the Mediterranean region. Conquest is not the only way to unify people and bring change, however. In fact, the introduction of a new religious idea in the region had a powerful impact that is still felt today.

This monumental innovation took place along the eastern shore of the Mediterranean Sea where modern-day Israel, Lebanon, Jordan, and Syria are located. This lightly populated and politically weak region, sometimes called the Levant, was the homeland of the ancient Hebrews. The Hebrews were the first people from the eastern Mediterranean region to practice **monotheism**, or the belief in one God. This belief formed the basis of their religion, **Judaism**, and is explained in their holy book, the Hebrew Bible.

The current text of the Hebrew Bible dates to around 500 B.C.E. Historians regard the text of the Hebrew Bible as a rich source of information about the beliefs of the ancient Hebrews. But the historical accuracy of the stories in the Bible is questionable. By combining analysis of the Bible with archaeological findings, historians can come closer to an accurate understanding of the ancient Hebrew past.

According to the Hebrew Bible, **Abraham**, a Mesopotamian shepherd, was the first person to worship one God. The Bible says that God instructed Abraham to move his family to Canaan, a land in the southern part of the Levant, and offered him a **covenant**, or religious agreement. According to the Bible, if Abraham promised to be faithful to God, then God would grant the land of Canaan to Abraham and his descendants. In other words, Canaan was to be the Promised Land of the Hebrews. The Bible says that Abraham upheld his part of the contract and took his family to Canaan, where they lived as herders and farmers, moving frequently with their flocks.

As the Hebrew population grew, small groups built villages high atop hills. While the Hebrews followed many of the same customs as other peoples in Southwest Asia, their language and religious practices distinguished them from their neighbors.

According to the Hebrew Bible, a drought generations later led to food shortages in Canaan, and so the Hebrews, now known as the Israelites, moved to Egypt. The Bible says that the Egyptian pharaoh enslaved the Israelites and they endured a long period of suffering until God selected a man named **Moses** to lead them out of slavery. Their departure from Egypt and return to Canaan is known as the **Exodus**. According to the Bible, at one point during this 40-year journey, Moses climbed Mount Sinai, where God gave him two stone tablets with a set

The text of the Ten Commandments (shown above in a Hebrew illuminated manuscript) has been translated from its original language into many other languages, including English. Many variations in wording, and even in the way of numbering, exist. The basis of many modern laws, such as the law against stealing, date back to the Ten Commandments, as well as to Hammurabi's Code and other ancient moral and legal codes.

PRIMARY SOURCE

1. I am the Lord Your God, who brought you out of the land of Egypt, out of the house of bondage.
2. You shall have no other gods before Me. You shall not make for yourself any graven image. . . . You shall not bow down to them, nor serve them.
3. You shall not take the name of the Lord Your God in vain; for the Lord will not hold him guiltless that takes His name in vain.
4. Remember the Sabbath, to keep it holy. Six days you shall labor, and do all your work; but the seventh day is a Sabbath unto the Lord Your God. . . .
5. Honor your father and your mother. . . .
6. You shall not murder.
7. You shall not commit adultery.
8. You shall not steal.
9. You shall not bear false witness against your neighbor.
10. You shall not covet your neighbor's house . . . nor anything that is your neighbor's.

—from the *JPS Tanakh*, 1917

Jewish Diaspora, 586 B.C.E.–500 C.E.

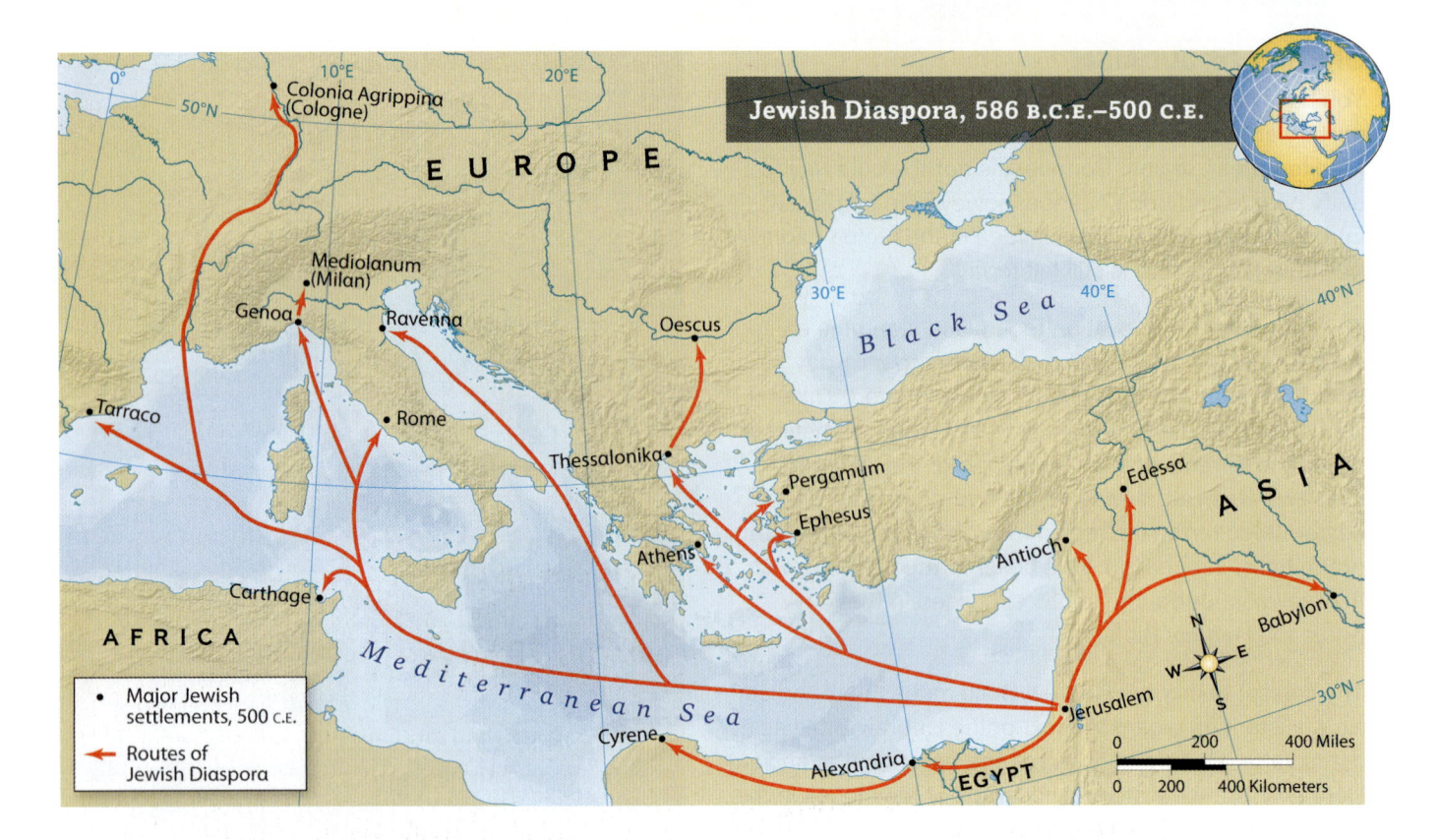

of laws called the Ten Commandments. The Israelites believed that, in this way, God renewed his covenant with them and provided them with guidelines for living a righteous life.

THE ARCHAEOLOGICAL RECORD

No archaeological evidence confirms that a single migration out of Egypt took place. Many scholars think that the story of the Exodus might have grown out of a series of migrations rather than one.

Archaeological excavations have revealed that in 1300 B.C.E., approximately 12,000 to 15,000 people lived in about 300 small villages on previously unoccupied hillsides in the southern Levant. By 1100 B.C.E., the population had grown to 80,000. Most residents had tools made of bronze, flint, and occasionally iron. One piece of evidence suggests that the residents were the Israelites: the lack of pig bones at excavated sites is a sign that the people observed a religious ban on eating pork. This practice is recorded later in the Hebrew Bible.

Archaeologists believe that a complex society first took shape in the region between 1000 and 900 B.C.E. The main evidence, as in Mesopotamia, is the formation of large urban centers with massive walls. At this time, loosely united groups of people became a small kingdom run by non-elected government administrators. The population of the Levant around 1000 B.C.E. has been estimated at 150,000. About 5,000 people lived in the region's largest city, **Jerusalem**, in 700 B.C.E.

Jerusalem was the site of a magnificent temple, which you will learn about later in this lesson.

IMPACT OF THE HEBREW BIBLE

Hebrew monotheism profoundly shaped the teachings of two other major world religions, Christianity and Islam. Today, belief in a single God forms the foundation for all three religions. For the most part, the writings in the Hebrew Bible are the same ones that make up the Old Testament of the Christian Bible. Certain stories from the Hebrew Bible and the Christian Bible also appear in the holy book of Islam, the Quran. These stories include Abraham's covenant with God and Moses' experience on Mount Sinai.

The Torah, which comprises the first five books of the Hebrew Bible, stresses the importance of accepting and honoring God, treating all people with respect and fairness, and caring for the less fortunate. The ethical principles of ancient Judaism had an enormous impact on Christianity, Islam, and later ideas of human rights to which all people are entitled.

THE KINGDOMS OF ISRAEL AND JUDAH

The Israelites who returned to Canaan from Egypt consisted of 12 **tribes**, or extended family units. They had a difficult task in reclaiming Canaan because other people had settled there, including a group called the Philistines. The Israelites soon realized that the 12 tribes would have to band together under a single strong leader to win back the land.

60 CHAPTER 2

According to the Hebrew Bible, **Saul** became the first king of the Israelites in about 1020 B.C.E. and led them in battle against the Philistines. Saul was followed by **David**, who united the 12 tribes, defeated the Philistines, and revitalized the city of Jerusalem. **Solomon**, David's son, oversaw a time of growth and built a magnificent temple in Jerusalem. According to the Bible, the temple housed the Ark of the Covenant, which held the original tablets listing God's commandments. The temple became the central location for all Jews to pray to God.

After Solomon's reign ended, tensions between the northern and southern tribes split the kingdom. The northern region took the name **Israel**, while the southern land became known as **Judah**. Both kingdoms had a form of government called a **theocracy**, in which the legal system is based on religious law.

THE SPREAD OF JUDAISM

You've read that the Assyrian army swept in to conquer Israel in 722 B.C.E. In 586 B.C.E., the Chaldean king Nebuchadnezzar conquered Judah, leaving the Temple in ruins. The people of Judah were forcibly moved to the city of Babylon, an event known as the Babylonian Exile. The word **exile** refers to a forced removal from one's homeland. The Babylonian Exile lasted until 538 B.C.E.

During the years of the Babylonian Exile, the people of Judah recorded the main part of the Hebrew Bible. The name *Jew* literally means a member of the nation of Judah, but it came to refer to all Hebrews.

The Jews became **refugees**, or people forced to leave their homeland because of wars, persecution, or natural disasters. The loss of their homeland led to changes in how the Jewish people practiced their religion. Unable to worship at the Temple, they built the first **synagogues**, or Jewish houses of worship. Jewish religious teachers, called rabbis, led worship services in the synagogues, a practice that continues today.

The Babylonian Exile strengthened the identity of the Jewish people and made it clear that Judaism could survive outside its birthplace. It marked the beginning of the **Diaspora**, the migration of Jews to locations far from their homeland. Over the following centuries, Jewish people would live and practice their religion in places throughout the world.

NATIONAL GEOGRAPHIC EXPLORER
JODI MAGNESS

Tales Told by Mosaics

Determined to find out more about the roots of the Jewish people, archaeologists and other experts turn over every stone, so to speak. Every June, Professor Jodi Magness (left) journeys to an ancient site in Huqoq, Israel, to explore the ruins of a synagogue that dates from the fifth century, when the land was under the rule of the Roman Empire. Within these ancient ruins, Magness and her colleagues have discovered an amazing series of mosaics, artworks created using pieces of stone. Most art in synagogues illustrates biblical stories, but one mosaic discovered by Magness and her team includes pictures of elephants that Magness says represents "the first time a non-biblical story [is] depicted in an ancient synagogue."

Examining the mosaics helps Magness determine when the synagogue itself was constructed. She thinks the mosaic with the elephants might even depict a visit of the conqueror Alexander the Great to Jerusalem.

This mosaic of an elephant comes from an ancient synagogue in Huqoq, Israel.

HISTORICAL THINKING

1. **READING CHECK** Where and how did monotheism develop?

2. **IDENTIFY** What ethical principles are emphasized in the Torah?

3. **IDENTIFY MAIN IDEAS AND DETAILS** How did Judaism influence other major world religions?

4. **MAKE CONNECTIONS** Give two examples of modern laws that are reflected in the Ten Commandments.

Early River Valley Civilizations 61

3.4 DOCUMENT-BASED QUESTION
Comparing Flood Narratives

You may have heard or read the story of Noah and the great flood that appears in Genesis, the first book of the Hebrew Bible. But you may not know that the Hebrew Bible is not the only ancient book that tells a story about a great flood. Like the Hebrew Bible, the *Epic of Gilgamesh* describes a monstrous flood that covers all the land. Striking similarities in the two versions of the flood story suggest that the Hebrew Bible drew on the oral traditions of Mesopotamia.

Other peoples also tell stories of great floods. The early Aztec people, who lived in what is now Mexico, describe a devastating flood that lasted 55 years. There are also stories and legends about a great flood from ancient India, China, and Scandinavia.

The various accounts of floods differ most notably in their depictions of the divine powers that shaped the world. In the *Epic of Gilgamesh*, multiple gods squabble. In the Bible, there is only one God, who sends the flood to punish humanity. In the story from India, the flood is a natural phenomenon and a god saves humanity.

Despite differences among these three accounts, the people who composed them had the same purpose in writing them—to explain how the world came to be as it is and why.

CRITICAL VIEWING

The first scene in this painting depicts Noah supervising the building of the ark. The second portrays God telling Noah to board the ark with his family and animals to be saved. How does the painting convey the importance of saving animals as well as people?

62 CHAPTER 2

DOCUMENT ONE

Primary Source: Epic Poem
from the *Epic of Gilgamesh* translated by Benjamin R. Foster, 2001

The most complete version of the *Epic of Gilgamesh* was written in 700 B.C.E., but it drew on written versions dating back to at least 2100 B.C.E. and even earlier oral traditions. According to the epic, multiple gods squabble and the god Enki warns a man named Utnapishtim that the storm god Enlil is sending the flood to destroy his home city.

CONSTRUCTED RESPONSE What image is created by the use of the words *deluge*, *leveled*, and *tempest*?

> Six days, and seven nights
>
> The wind continued, the deluge and windstorm leveled the land.
>
> When the seventh day arrived,
>
> The windstorm and deluge left off their battle,
>
> Which had struggled . . .
>
> The sea grew calm, the tempest stilled, the deluge ceased.

DOCUMENT TWO

Primary Source: Sacred Text
from the *Jewish Publication Society Hebrew Bible*, 1917

Like the *Epic of Gilgamesh*, the Hebrew Bible had a long history of oral transmission before being recorded in its current version around 500 B.C.E. Some of its earliest content may have circulated orally as early as 1200 B.C.E., when the ancient Hebrews first settled what is now modern Israel. According to the Bible, God decides to punish all of humanity except for a man named Noah and his family.

CONSTRUCTED RESPONSE How is the portrayal of the flood in this excerpt different from the description in the *Epic of Gilgamesh*?

> **17** And the flood was forty days upon the earth; and the waters increased, and bore up the ark [a ship], and it was lifted up above the earth.
>
> **18** And the waters prevailed, and increased greatly upon the earth; and the ark went upon the face of the waters.
>
> **19** And the waters prevailed exceedingly upon the earth; and all the high mountains that were under the whole heaven were covered.
>
> **20** Fifteen cubits upward did the waters prevail; and the mountains were covered.

DOCUMENT THREE

Primary Source: Epic Poem
from *The Mahabharata of Krishna-Dwaipayana Vyasa* translated by Kisari Mohan Ganguli, 1883–1896

The *Mahabharata* is an epic poem of ancient India that provides information on the development of Hinduism and on Hindu moral law. Historians believe that the complete text was written down in 400 B.C.E. but existed in oral form much earlier. According to the flood story in the *Mahabharata*, the god Vishnu, in the form of a fish, warns a man named Manu about an impending flood and tells him how to save himself.

CONSTRUCTED RESPONSE How is this flood narrative similar to the one in the Hebrew Bible?

> And there was water everywhere and the waters covered the heaven and the firmament also. And . . . when the world was thus flooded, none but Manu . . . and the fish could be seen. And . . . the fish diligently dragged the boat through the flood for many a long year and then, . . . it towed the vessel towards the highest peak of the Himavat [Himalaya]. And . . . the fish then told those on the vessel to tie it to the peak of the Himavat.

SYNTHESIZE & WRITE

1. **REVIEW** Review what you have learned about flood narratives of various cultures.

2. **RECALL** On your own paper, make a list of the similarities and differences among the three excerpts you have read.

3. **CONSTRUCT** Construct a topic sentence that answers the following question: Based on the excerpts, what are the similarities and differences among the three flood stories?

4. **WRITE** Using evidence from this chapter and the documents, write an informative paragraph that supports the topic sentence you wrote in Step 3.

CHAPTER 2
EARLY RIVER VALLEY CIVILIZATIONS
REVIEW

VOCABULARY

Match each vocabulary word with its definition.

1. silt
2. technology
3. irrigation
4. ziggurat
5. empire
6. cuneiform
7. pharaoh
8. pyramid
9. monotheism
10. covenant

a. human-made systems of transporting
b. an ancient Egyptian king
c. the belief in one God
d. Mesopotamian writing
e. an Egyptian tomb
f. a religious agreement
g. fertile soil
h. a group of nations or peoples
i. the practical application of knowledge
j. a Sumerian religious structure

READING STRATEGY
DRAW CONCLUSIONS

When you draw conclusions, you make a judgment based on what you have read. Use a chart like this one to draw a conclusion about the importance of rivers to early civilizations. Then answer the question that follows.

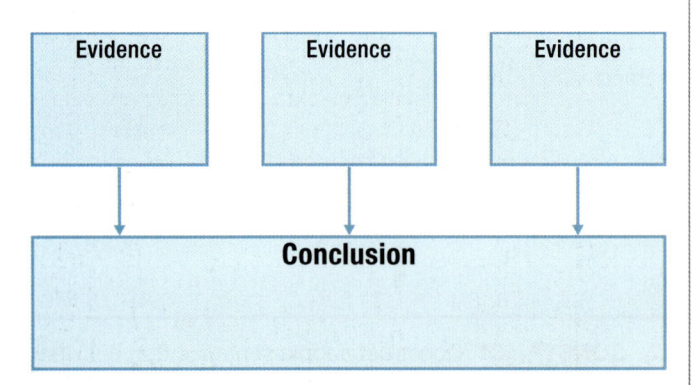

Evidence	Evidence	Evidence

Conclusion

11. Based on your conclusion, explain why the Babylonian and Egyptian empires were so much stronger than the Israelite kingdoms of the eastern Mediterranean.

MAIN IDEAS

Answer the following questions. Support your answers with evidence from the chapter.

12. How are aspects of the culture of ancient Mesopotamia reflected in the *Epic of Gilgamesh*? **LESSON 1.1**

13. How did the ancient Sumerians use cuneiform? **LESSON 1.2**

14. What insight into the roles and status of women can be gained from Hammurabi's Code? **LESSON 1.3**

15. How did the ancient Egyptians excel in mathematics, science, and technology? **LESSON 2.1**

16. Why did ancient Egyptians devote so much time, wealth, and energy to building pyramids? **LESSON 2.2**

17. Why did the pharaohs of the New Kingdom set out to conquer other lands? **LESSON 2.3**

18. Why were the Assyrians particularly brutal in their warfare? **LESSON 3.1**

19. What challenges did the Israelites face as they developed their society? **LESSON 3.3**

HISTORICAL THINKING

Answer the following questions. Support your answers with evidence from the chapter.

20. **MAKE INFERENCES** How did physical features influence the development of civilization in Mesopotamia?

21. **MAKE GENERALIZATIONS** What aspects of ancient Egyptian culture are reflected in its art and architecture?

22. **SYNTHESIZE** What methods have archaeologists used to analyze evidence from early civilizations in Southwest Asia and Egypt?

23. **EVALUATE** Which achievement of ancient peoples do you think had the greatest impact on the world? Explain your answer.

24. **FORM AND SUPPORT OPINIONS** What artistic ideal or visual principle do you think the ancient Egyptian pyramids best demonstrate? Explain your answer.

INTERPRET MAPS

Study the map below, which shows the expansion of Egypt during the New Kingdom. Then answer the questions that follow.

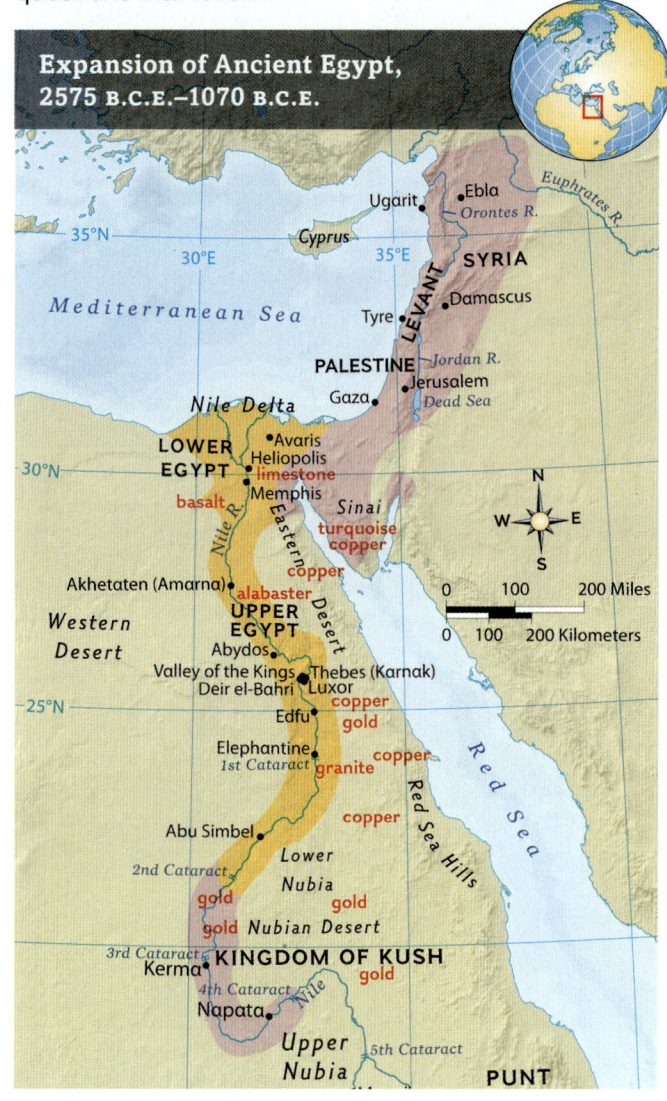

Expansion of Ancient Egypt, 2575 B.C.E.–1070 B.C.E.

25. Based on the map, how did physical features of the region influence the development of Egyptian civilization?

26. Based on the map, what resource was controlled by Kush? How do you think this situation might have affected interactions between Egypt and Kush?

ANALYZE SOURCES

Preparing for the afterlife was so important to the ancient Egyptians that they created a book about it. Compiled in the 1500s B.C.E. but drawing on materials dating back to 2400 B.C.E., the *Book of the Dead* contains detailed instructions for what the deceased should say upon meeting Osiris, the god of the underworld, to gain entry to the afterlife.

> I have not committed evil against men.
>
> I have not mistreated cattle.
>
> I have not committed sin in the place of truth [that is, a temple or burial ground]. . . .
>
> I have not blasphemed a god. . . .
>
> I have not made (anyone) sick.
>
> I have not made (anyone) weep.
>
> I have not killed. . . .
>
> I have not held up water in its season [that is, denied floodwaters to others].
>
> I have not built a dam against running water. . . .

27. What does this passage reveal about the values and morals of the ancient Egyptians?

CONNECT TO YOUR LIFE

28. **INFORMATIVE** Review what you have learned about cuneiform and hieroglyphics. Then think about the kinds of images and symbols you use today to communicate, including the alphabet, emojis, memes, GIFs, and other media. Write an essay describing the similarities and differences among several of these forms of communication.

TIPS

- Review what you have read about cuneiform and hieroglyphics.

- Make a table listing the characteristics of one or two forms of modern communication.

- Draft your essay, describing the forms of communication and identifying their similarities and differences.

- Provide a conclusion that supports the information presented.

Early River Valley Civilizations

CHAPTER 3

Ancient South Asia and China
2600 B.C.E.–207 B.C.E.

HISTORICAL THINKING How did religious and philosophical systems support societies in ancient India and China?

SECTION 1 **Foundations of Hindu Societies**
SECTION 2 **The Rise of Buddhism**
SECTION 3 **Early Dynasties of China**
SECTION 4 **China's First Empire**

CRITICAL VIEWING
Built under the rule of Shi Huangdi, the Great Wall defined his empire. What details in the photo show how the wall would have protected China from invaders?

1.1

MAIN IDEA Agriculture and the domestication of animals along the Indus River led to the development of sophisticated cities and trade among ancient societies.

Cities Along the Indus

Until the early 20th century, we knew little about the ancient cities that developed around the Indus River. That changed when archaeologists went searching for the source of a tiny artifact, a stone seal, and discovered a lost civilization.

CIVILIZATION FORMS AROUND RIVERS

The South Asian landmass is often called the Indian subcontinent and can be divided into three geographic regions. The region to the north is largely uninhabited due to the **Himalaya**, the tallest mountains in the world. In the plains, the **Indus River** flows from the Himalaya to the west, where it empties into the Arabian Sea. The **Ganges** (GAN-geez) **River** flows from the Himalaya to the east and empties into the Bay of Bengal. These river valleys make up the most densely populated region of the subcontinent. The southern peninsula isn't as heavily populated and contains the large Deccan Plateau, a high area with a drier climate.

Like the river valleys of the Tigris and Euphrates rivers in Mesopotamia and the Nile in Egypt, the river valleys of the Indian subcontinent provided water and fertile soil—ideal conditions for agriculture. Sometime around 7000 B.C.E., people of this area began planting wheat, barley, and jujube dates. People domesticated elephants, sheep, and goats and began to build large settlements. By about 2600 B.C.E., cities emerged in the Indus River Valley.

The "Great Bath" at the Indus River Valley city of Mohenjo-Daro shows the Harappan society's sophisticated use of a grid to plan and build a public works structure. Located in present-day Pakistan, these ancient ruins are a UNESCO World Heritage Site.

68 CHAPTER 3

THE RISE AND FALL OF THE HARAPPAN CIVILIZATION

Around the time that Egyptians were building pyramids, the people of the Indus Valley were building their first cities. At its height, the Indus Valley civilization extended over a large area that included parts of present-day Pakistan, India, and Afghanistan. Known today as the **Harappan civilization**, this complex society used a grid for planning large cities and built them with mud bricks of standardized sizes. The cities had open plazas, drainage systems, and avenues several yards wide.

Archaeological excavations of the city of Harappa reveal that it had an area of 380 acres (or 288 football fields) and a population of between 40,000 and 80,000. Archaeologists hoped to find temples or palaces that would help them understand who ruled Harappan society, such as a king or pharaoh. Instead, they found that homes were similar in style. Cities were divided into distinct communities where similar goods have been found. This discovery has led historians to believe that neighborhoods were formed based on people's various occupations.

Unlike other cities of the ancient world, **Mohenjo-Daro** (moh-HEHN-joh DAHR-oh), the second largest Indus Valley settlement, provided drinking water, in-home plumbing, and sewer drains to all its residents, not just a privileged few.

Beginning in 1900 B.C.E., the large urban communities of Harappan society declined. After a long period with little rainfall, Indus River tributaries began to change course or dry up. Many historians believe that change in climate and rainfall were major factors in the decline. They have no written evidence because the Harappan script has not been deciphered. If we ever learn how to read Harappan writing, we will learn much more about this fascinating civilization.

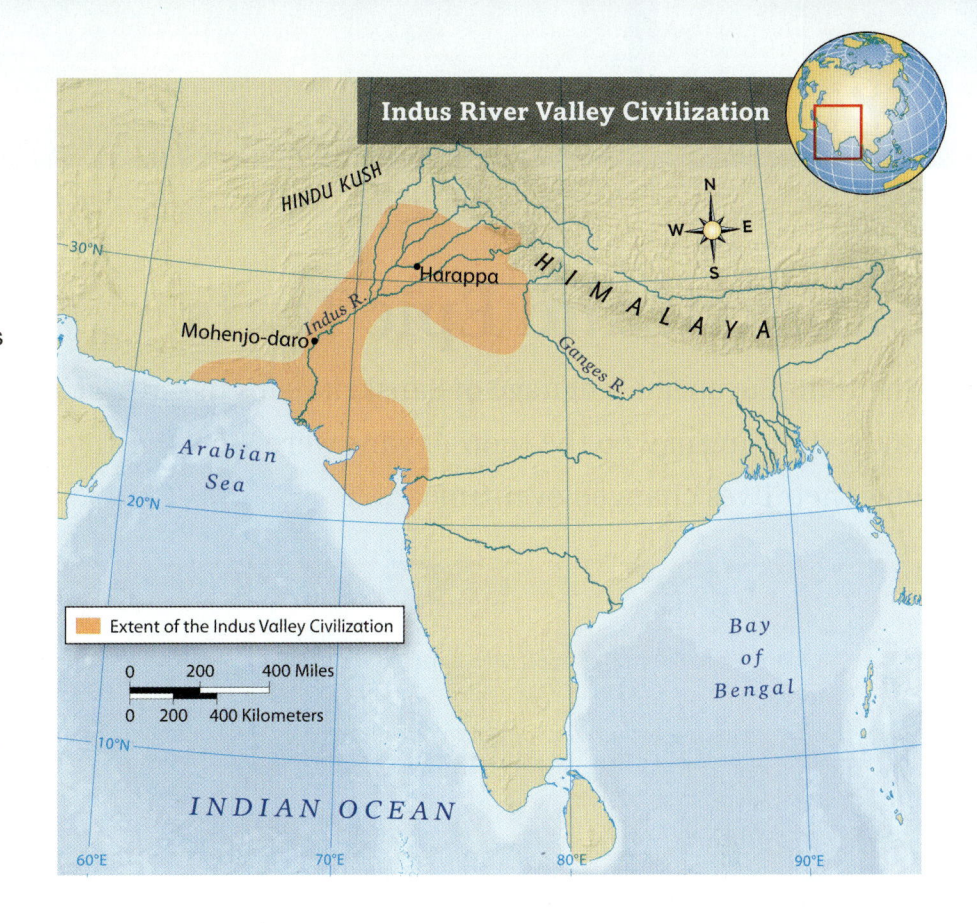

Indus River Valley Civilization

INDO-ARYAN MIGRATIONS

Sometime between 1500 and 1000 B.C.E., several hundred years after the fall of Harappan society, **nomads** arrived in the Indus Valley. The nomads migrated from place to place, using horses and carts to travel across Eurasia. Although they later began to grow crops, early arrivals tended their herds full time.

These migrants called themselves *Aryan*, meaning "noble." Today, historians refer to these people as Indo-Aryans because they spoke **Sanskrit**, an Indo-European language that developed in Central Eurasia. Sanskrit has similar grammatical structures and contains many words related to Latin, Greek, Spanish, French, and English. For example, the word *mother* in English is *mater* in Latin and *matar* in Sanskrit. The Indo-Aryans brought Sanskrit into what is today northern India, but not into southern India or East Asia. The people who live in the region today speak a range of Indo-European languages descended from Sanskrit, including Hindi and Urdu. As you continue reading, you will learn more about Sanskrit's importance in the history and culture of India.

HISTORICAL THINKING

1. **READING CHECK** What important role did rivers play in the development of civilization in the Indus River Valley?

2. **DESCRIBE** What information about the Harappan civilization did archaeologists glean from artifacts and excavations?

3. **EXPLAIN** Why do linguists think Sanskrit is related to Latin and Spanish?

Ancient South Asia and China

1.2

MAIN IDEA Sanskrit hymns and epics reflect the history and culture of ancient India.

Sanskrit and Epic Texts

The Indo-European language of Sanskrit helps us gain a clearer understanding of who the Indo-Aryans were, how they lived, and how their lives changed over time.

CRITICAL VIEWING This finely detailed illustration from an 18th-century edition of the Bhagavad Gita shows Krishna, an avatar of the Hindu deity Vishnu, serving as the chariot driver for Prince Arjuna, as they head into battle. What details in the illustration convey the action that is taking place?

SANSKRIT: THE LANGUAGE OF RELIGION AND SCHOLARSHIP

As you have read, the Indo-Aryans spoke Sanskrit. Although these early migrants had no written language, they passed the language down orally until it was eventually written down around 1000 B.C.E. In time, Sanskrit became India's language of religion and scholarship with texts covering subjects as diverse as poetry, law, and medicine.

Dating back to 1500 B.C.E., Indo-Aryan priests sang hymns that were passed from generation to generation. The collective hymns are called the Rig Veda, which is Sanskrit for "knowledge of the verses." This collection of 1,028 hymns describes numerous gods including Indra, the king of the gods, as well as the god of war, the god of fire, the sun-god, the god of death, and many other minor gods. Elaborate rituals honoring these gods could last several days. The Rig Veda has given historians a glimpse into the **Vedic** (VAY-dihk) religion as well as the everyday life of the Indo-Aryans. (The word *Vedic* can be used to describe both the religion and the society of the Indo-Aryans.)

LITERATURE REFLECTS HISTORY AND CULTURE

The Rig Veda reflects the social roles of men, women, and children in Vedic society. One early hymn shows the variety of occupations in Vedic society, such as carpenters, doctors, and priests. Through other hymns, historians have learned that women in Vedic society shared a similar status with men. Girls could go out unsupervised in public, and, with permission from their parents, were allowed to choose their own husbands. Women could even inherit property, and widows could remarry. Both girls and boys studied the hymns, yet only men were allowed to recite them in public ceremonies.

Later hymns, composed around 1000 B.C.E., reflect changes in Vedic society. By that time, the nomads had settled down and taken up farming. Roles in the society became more fixed, and women's freedoms declined. In addition, people were classified, or organized, into four social groups, called **varna**. Ranked in order of purity, priests, called Brahmins, were at the top. Next came warriors, then farmers and merchants, and finally dependent laborers. Though these categories were flexible in the beginning, much later they developed into a **caste system**, a rigid social hierarchy that dictated the kind of work people could do, who they could marry, and what they could eat.

Another collection of texts, the Upanishads (oo-PAH-nih-shahdz), was composed between 900 and 600 B.C.E. Challenging the old order, these texts introduced new ideas and gods. The Upanishads established the ideas of **reincarnation**, or the rebirth of the soul in different life cycles, and **karma**, the idea that people's actions in this life determine how they will be reborn in the next life. Unlike the gods in the Rig Veda, gods in the Upanishads intervened in human lives and sometimes took human form.

The composition of two great works of epic literature began at approximately the same time. Both were written in Sanskrit. One of these works, the *Mahabharata* (MAH-hah-BAHR-rah-tah), describes a long feud between two clans in more than 100,000 verses. One part of the *Mahabharata*, the Bhagavad Gita (BAH-gah-vuhd GEET-ah), was often read as an independent work. Composed in 200 C.E., it tells the story of a battle between two armies and reflects a conversation between Arjuna, a great warrior, and the god Krishna, who is disguised as a chariot driver. Krishna argues that each person should fulfill his **dharma**, or the way of righteous conduct in life. Krishna urges the warrior to devote himself fully to worshiping him. Krishna's teachings later became fundamental ideas of **Hinduism**. (You will learn more about Hinduism in a later chapter.) The second of these two great epics, the *Ramayana* (rah-MAH-yah-nah), is the tale of the great king Rama who fights to rescue his wife Sita after she is abducted.

In the centuries following their composition, many versions of the *Mahabharata* and the *Ramayana* have appeared throughout South Asia and Southeast Asia. Today these epics have been made into television series popular in those regions.

JAINISM New religious concepts emerged in succeeding centuries. Between the sixth and fourth centuries B.C.E., **Jainism** (JY-nih-zuhm) took shape. Mahavira (shown above), the founder of the Jains, took on a very simple life and traveled by foot for 12 years, debating ideas as he traveled. He was a leading opponent of the caste system that placed Brahmins at the top of the social hierarchy. He died after voluntarily giving up food and water. Jains believe in right faith, right knowledge, and right conduct. They believe that humans must not harm any living beings. For example, to avoid killing insects by mistake, Jains refrain from eating and drinking when it is dark.

HISTORICAL THINKING

1. **READING CHECK** What does the Rig Veda suggest about how women's roles changed over time? What led to the change?

2. **DESCRIBE** What is the principle of karma as introduced in the Upanishads?

3. **MAKE INFERENCES** Why do historians know so much more about the culture of the Indo-Aryans than they do about the culture of the Harappan people?

Ancient South Asia and China 71

2.1

MAIN IDEA The origins of Buddhism lie in the life of Siddhartha Gautama, the Buddha, who sought to find a cure for suffering.

The Buddha's Teachings

Do material possessions, such as the latest smartphone, bring you happiness? Or does your desire to own things only bring you suffering? Would you be willing to give up everything you have to find out? More than 2,500 years ago, a man named Siddhartha Gautama did just that.

THE LIFE OF THE BUDDHA

Born along the southern edge of the Himalaya in today's Nepal, **Siddhartha Gautama** (sih-DAR-tuh GOW-tuh-muh) lived to almost 80 and died around 483 B.C.E. The legend of Siddhartha Gautama's life begins with the story of how his mother dreamed of a white elephant with a lotus flower in its trunk. She consulted oracles, or wise men, who predicted that she would give birth to either a great monarch or a great teacher. Siddhartha's parents raised him inside a walled palace so that he would never see any signs of suffering or illness. He grew up, married, and fathered a child.

One day, while traveling inside the palace park, Siddhartha had four encounters. He came across an elderly man, an extremely ill man, and a dead body being taken away for cremation. Then Siddhartha saw an **ascetic**, or one who chooses a life of poverty, wearing a simple robe and looking happy. These encounters made Siddhartha think about suffering, old age, disease, and death. But seeing the ascetic's happiness gave Siddhartha hope, and he decided to follow the man's example. Siddhartha gave up his wealth and his family to live a life of poverty. After six years of wandering, Siddhartha sat down to meditate under a tree, where he remained for 49 days and attained **enlightenment**, a state of deep understanding and clarity. Through this enlightenment, Siddhartha became the Buddha, "the enlightened or awakened one," and his teachings became the religion of **Buddhism**.

BUDDHIST BELIEFS

The Buddha's first sermon described the path to enlightenment. He told his listeners to avoid extremes of self-denial, such as going without food for long periods of time. He also warned against the complete self-gratification of those who did exactly as they pleased. Instead, he encouraged people to follow the Four Noble Truths: 1) All life is suffering; 2) The cause of suffering is desire; 3) The end of desire means the end of suffering; and 4) Following the Noble Eightfold Path can end suffering.

According to the Buddha, following the Noble Eightfold Path would bring suffering to an end because a person would have attained **nirvana**, a state of blissful escape from suffering. In Buddhism, the term also takes on the meaning of gaining true understanding.

While the Buddha believed in the concept of reincarnation, his teachings marked a major departure from other aspects of the Vedic religion. As you've read, according to the Rig Veda, people could do nothing to change their social class. In contrast, Buddhists suggested that salvation was the result of an individual's actions, not his or her varna. The Buddha encouraged people to leave their families and join him as monks in the Buddhist order. Only those monks who joined the

The Eightfold Path

RIGHT VIEW See and understand things as they really are

RIGHT INTENTION Commit to ethical self-improvement

RIGHT SPEECH Tell the truth and speak gently

RIGHT ACTION Act kindly, honestly, and respectfully

RIGHT LIVELIHOOD Earn a living in a moral, legal, and peaceful way

RIGHT EFFORT Focus your will onto achieving good things

RIGHT MINDFULNESS Value a good mind

RIGHT CONCENTRATION Single-mindedness

CRITICAL VIEWING In this wood carving, the Buddha sits under a bodhi tree, where, according to Buddhist tradition, he meditated for 49 days and gained enlightenment. How would you interpret the expression on the Buddha's face in this carving?

order could attain nirvana. The Buddha's first followers were all men, but Buddhist sources record that the Buddha's aunt asked to join the Buddhist order. The Buddha refused her until his star disciple intervened and persuaded him to change his mind. Later, women did become Buddhist nuns, but they were always subordinate to men. Those outside the order could gain merit by donating food and money. A merchant, a farmer, or even a laborer who made a donation to the order could enhance his or her social standing. Many kings and merchants gave large gifts in the hope of improving their lives, either in this world or in future rebirths.

HISTORICAL THINKING

1. **READING CHECK** Why did Siddhartha Gautama leave his life of luxury?
2. **IDENTIFY MAIN IDEAS AND DETAILS** What are the main ideas presented in the Four Noble Truths and the Noble Eightfold Path?
3. **DRAW CONCLUSIONS** Which aspects of the Buddha's teachings do you think most appealed to people who had previously followed the Vedic religion?

IMAGES OF THE BUDDHA

You've learned that Buddhism originated in India more than 2,500 years ago. Since then, Buddhism has spread all over the world with more than 488 million adherents. As the religion made its way over time into new places, it was reflected in a variety of cultures—each with its own unique style. Depictions of the Buddha, in particular, appeared in different forms and were created with different media as the religion spread from India to East and Southeast Asia and beyond.

The Mogao Caves Dunhuang, China, once a thriving Silk Roads oasis, is home to one of the greatest repositories of Buddhist art in the world. Approximately 492 caves chiseled into the face of a cliff are decorated with murals and adorned with sculptures created over a period of 1,000 years. The variety in the style of the art reflects the different goods that were traded along the Silk Roads and the different cultures that came into contact with each other. Today, the caves are a UNESCO World Heritage Site. This 10-foot-tall statue of a bodhisattva, or future Buddha, was created sometime during the early fifth century C.E. It is believed to be one of the earliest surviving painted sculptures in the Mogao cave complex. The gesture of the statue's left hand symbolizes the granting of wishes or blessings, while the crossed ankles and lions on either side are reminiscent of depictions of royalty. The origin of this artistic style can be traced back to rock caves in present-day Afghanistan, illustrating the cross-cultural nature of the Mogao caves.

Mudras Buddha statues or paintings often depict different hand gestures known as *mudras* (such as the gesture of the bodhisattva on the opposite page). Each mudra has a specific meaning and is used to evoke a particular state of mind. The most common mudra, *dhyana*, signifies meditation. Other mudras include *vyakhyana* or *vitarka* (teaching), *abhaya* (protection), *dharmachakra* (the wheel of dharma), and *varada* (giving or generosity).

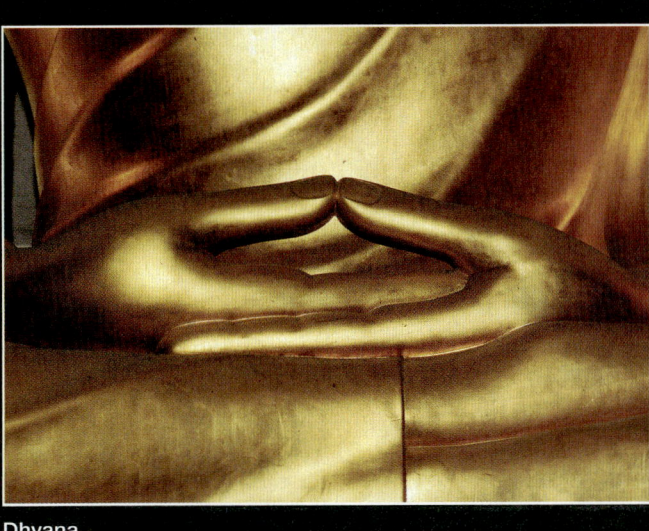

Dhyana

Vyakhyana or Vitarka

Abhaya

Dharmachakra

Varada

The Laughing Buddha

Known as *Budai* in Chinese and *Hotei* in Japanese, the laughing Buddha is often depicted as a chubby, happy monk carrying a large sack. His large belly symbolizes happiness, luck, and generosity. A semihistorical figure, he is believed to have lived in southern China in the 10th century and was eventually recognized as part of the Buddhist pantheon as a future Buddha.

▲ **Boudhanath Stupa** The Boudhanath Stupa in Kathmandu, Nepal, is the center of Tibetan Buddhism in Nepal. (A stupa is a dome-shaped structure built as a Buddhist shrine.) Built in the 14th century, the stupa remains an active sacred site today, as illustrated by the prayer flags streaming from the gold spire. The 13 steps of the spire represent the Buddhist path to enlightenment, while the all-seeing eyes of the Buddha gaze out from each of the four sides at the spire's base. Severely damaged by a massive earthquake that struck Nepal in 2015, the spire was repaired entirely with the help of private donations and local volunteers.

▶ **Chinese Buddha** This bronze sculpture depicts the Buddha seated on a rectangular throne flanked by a pair of small lions. The Buddha's hands form the *dhyana* mudra (the gesture of meditation), and the triangular points emanating from his shoulders represent flames—in this instance a visible manifestation of the body heat associated with meditation. This sculpture is one of the earliest-known iconic images of the Buddha produced in China.

Monumental Buddhist Art Large Buddha statues appear in a variety of cultures touched by Buddhism.

◄ The reclining Buddha shown above is part of the Buddhist temple complex of Mok Khan Lan in Thailand. The reclining Buddha represents the historical Buddha during his last illness as he is about to attain nirvana. To the far left of the reclining Buddha is a statue of the Hindu deity Ganesha, reflecting the overlap of Buddhist and Hindu traditions in Thailand.

◄ This 180-foot-tall Buddha statue was the larger of two monumental statues in the Bamiyan Valley in central Afghanistan. Built along the Silk Roads during the first half of the sixth century C.E., the statues were the largest examples of standing Buddha carvings in the world. Tragically, the statues were declared to be idols by the ruling Taliban and were destroyed in March 2001.

HISTORICAL THINKING

1. **READING CHECK** What are three different ways in which the Buddha has been depicted in art?
2. **ANALYZE VISUALS** How has Buddhist art evolved as it has spread across cultures and the world?
3. **MAKE INFERENCES** How has the Buddhist art you've read about reflected both religious tolerance and intolerance?

2.3

MAIN IDEA Formed by violent conquests, the Maurya Empire later protected and spread its power by projecting an image of respect and peace.

The Maurya Empire

Imagine an experience so dramatic that it completely changes your life. For one king, this dramatic moment happened after a violent conquest. His life changed in a way that would affect his entire empire and how he ruled it.

CHANDRAGUPTA RULES THE MAURYA EMPIRE

In 320 B.C.E., approximately 150 years after the Buddha's death, a general named **Chandragupta Maurya** (chuhn-druh-GUP-tuh MOWR-yuh) defeated another general and gained control of the territory and capital Pataliputra, located along the Ganges. Chandragupta conquered many surrounding kingdoms, establishing an empire that united most of northern India and became the first great Indian empire.

Chandragupta exercised direct control over the area around the Maurya capital and the trade routes linking Pataliputra with outlying trade centers. These trade routes allowed officials to collect taxes from markets in outer regions of the empire. However, unlike the Assyrians and ancient Egyptians, the Mauryans exercised much less direct control over their subjects. Local kings with reduced powers remained in place in many of the regions, and in some areas local assemblies made decisions.

ASHOKA RULES BY EXAMPLE

Chandragupta's grandson, **Ashoka** (uh-SHOH-kuh), began his reign in 268 B.C.E. as a brutal ruler, leading armies on violent campaigns in north and central India. The attack of Kalinga in modern-day Orissa on India's eastern coast was particularly brutal. According to Ashoka's own words, "a hundred and fifty thousand people were deported, a hundred thousand were killed, and many times that number perished." After so much violence, Ashoka felt deep remorse and underwent a dramatic change. He renounced war, converted to Buddhism, and used the fundamental ideas of Buddhism to guide the way he ruled.

Committed to dharma, Ashoka turned to leading by example rather than ruling by force. He strove to demonstrate how a humane leader should rule. By adopting Buddhism as the state religion, Ashoka became a chakravartin (chuhk-ruh-VAHR-TUHN). According to Buddhist beliefs, a chakravartin is an ideal leader who does not leave his family to become a monk but does promote Buddhism. As a chakravartin, Ashoka encouraged cultural unity and strengthened his political power. However, he allowed religious freedom and tolerated other religions. Rather than forcing his subjects to convert to Buddhism, he sponsored religious observances and contributed money for the construction of Buddhist temples, monasteries, and hospitals for both humans and animals. These

78 CHAPTER 3

Ashoka used stone pillars for public announcements. His proclamations were inscribed onto tall columns and erected on roads and in towns across the empire, such as the one shown here in the ancient city of Vaishali in Bihar, India.

services were available to everyone, without regard to religious faith. Ashoka hoped that his subjects would recognize his generosity and willingly acknowledge him as their divine leader. Historians call this type of rule a "ceremonial state."

After Ashoka's death in 232 B.C.E., the Maurya Empire began to break apart. The Mauryans lost control of the last remaining section, the Ganges Valley, around 185 B.C.E. However, Ashoka's legacy continued through the observance and practice of Buddhism. The religion spread throughout the Ganges, northern Indus, and Godavari river valleys. A century later, as kings in Sri Lanka and Afghanistan emulated Ashoka's example, Buddhism extended even farther. Eventually it would become a major world religion with followers in South Asia, Southeast Asia, and East Asia.

Ashoka's inscriptions served several purposes. They showed compassion for Ashoka's subjects and encouraged them to live a life of virtue.

PRIMARY SOURCE

Through his instruction in dharma, abstention from killing and non-injury to living beings, deference to relatives, Brahmins and shramanas [non-Vedic religious followers], obedience to mother and father, and obedience to elders have all increased as never before for many centuries. These and many other forms of the practice of dharma have increased and will increase.

—from the Fourth Major Rock Edict

HISTORICAL THINKING

1. **READING CHECK** How did governing by example help Ashoka build his image and protect his power?

2. **DRAW CONCLUSIONS** What do you think Ashoka hoped to accomplish by carving his beliefs into stone?

3. **EVALUATE** Do you think Ashoka's strategy of spreading Buddhism by example was more or less effective than dictating that all subjects must convert to Buddhism? Why?

2.4 **MAIN IDEA** Commodities and ideas spread across the Indian Ocean by way of an extensive trade network.

Early Indian Ocean Trade

Can you imagine math without decimals? Or food without spices? Early travel and trade in ports throughout the Indian Ocean region gave the world products and ideas that influence our lives to this day.

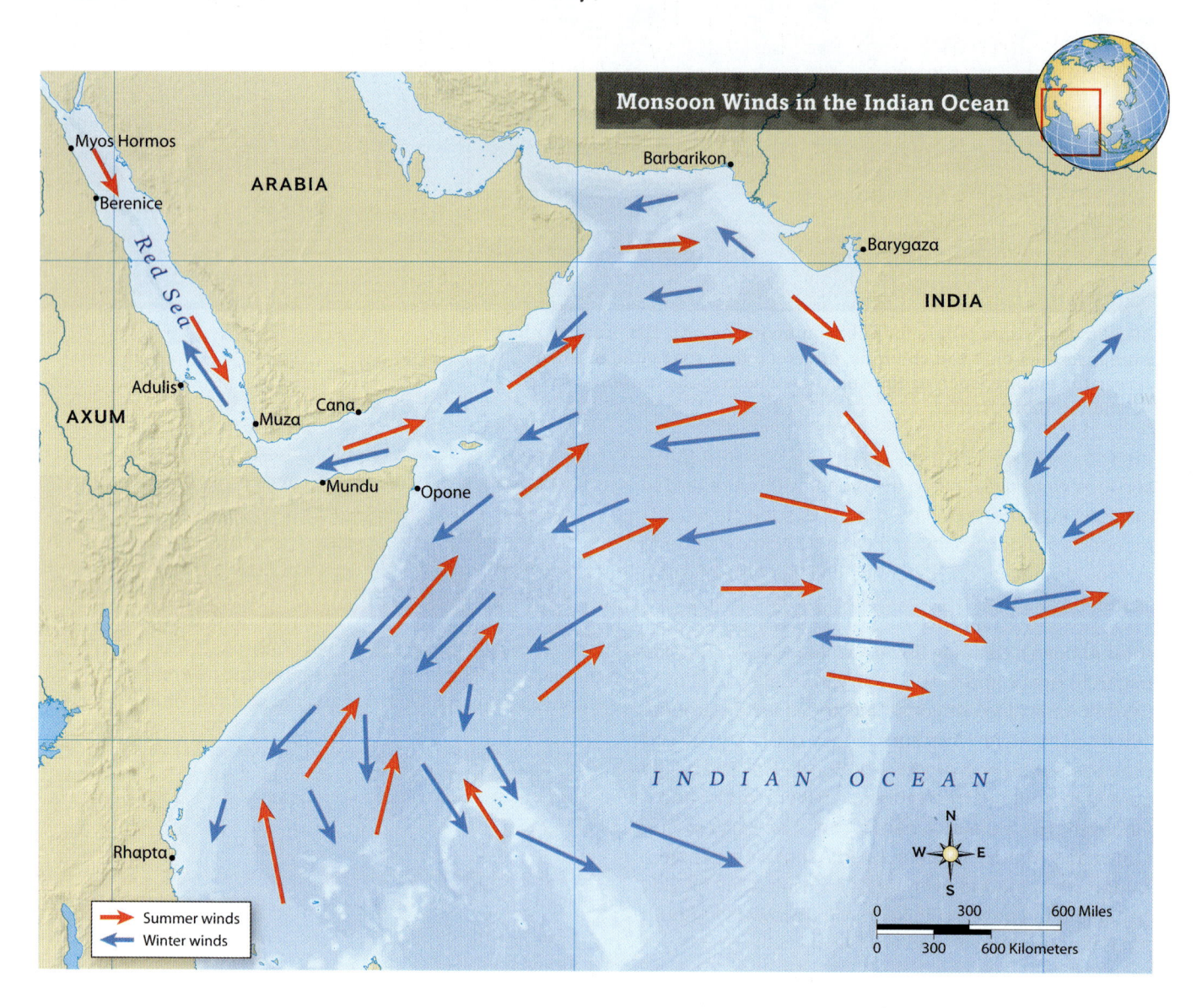

TRAVEL AND TRADE

Because of India's proximity to western Asia, travelers came to India in very early times, bringing new ideas and valuable goods to trade. These same people then carried Indian culture, including Buddhist teachings, out of India along the same paths they had used to bring ideas and products into India.

Land routes through the mountains of the Hindu Kush in the northwest allowed cultural contacts and the movement of valuable goods between South Asia and Central Asia through present-day Afghanistan. The Indo-Aryans probably used these land routes when they entered the Indian subcontinent sometime between 1500 and 1000 B.C.E.

But in ancient times, the most important form of travel between South Asia and the rest of the world was by sea. For instance, people in the Harappan civilization traded with Mesopotamia as early as 2500 B.C.E. DNA evidence indicates that Harappan ships were capable of traveling not just to Mesopotamia but all the way across the Indian Ocean to Australia.

Trade rapidly grew around 100 C.E. when seafaring merchants learned how to use the wind to carry them all the way from the Persian Gulf, southern Arabia, and coastal East Africa to India and back—if they timed it right. From April to October, strong winds called **monsoons** blow northeast toward India. Between November and March, the winds reverse direction and blow southwest, away from India. If merchants caught the winds just right on a summer departure, they could avoid violent storms as they traveled west and return the following winter. By harnessing the strength of these seasonal winds, traders were able to travel more quickly and relatively safely.

THE *PERIPLUS*: AN ANCIENT GUIDEBOOK

Around 50 C.E. a merchant from Egypt wrote a book called the *Periplus*, a Greek word meaning "around the world." Written for merchants, the *Periplus* describes trading ports, distances between ports, and the products traded at each location. The book covers trade throughout the Indian Ocean, but it describes Indian ports as the most important trading destinations.

The author of the *Periplus* instructed his readers to bring money, and lots of it, to India's southwest coast because the markets were chock-full of precious and semiprecious stones, clothing, textiles, coral, pearls, ivory, raw glass, copper, tin, lead, and spices. Initially, most trade was among Indians, Mesopotamians, Persians, and Africans. However, thousands of Roman silver and gold coins have been found on India's south coast. It turns out that one of the most important commodities for Roman traders was peppercorn, which was used to conceal the taste of rancid meat. Roman traders spent so much money on this Indian spice that the Roman emperor eventually banned it as an import.

Glass, such as these jars from ancient Rome, was exported to India from Persia.

DIFFUSION OF MATH, SCIENCE, AND TECHNOLOGY

Early trade in the Indian Ocean involved more than the exchange of valuable goods. People also shared ideas in areas such as mathematics, science, technology, and religion. The spread of ideas from one culture to another is known as **cultural diffusion**. For example, the decimal system, which you'll read more about in a later chapter, was originally used in weights and measures in the Harappan civilization and spread both within India and to other parts of the globe. Traders also shared technological knowledge such as metalworking, shipbuilding, and agricultural techniques.

Medical and veterinary knowledge spread along the same trade routes, too. The holistic medical techniques of Ayurveda and yoga were first practiced in India over 2,000 years ago. Knowledge of veterinary medicine may have been shared among Mesopotamia, ancient Egypt, and India. One ancient Sanskrit text, *Shalihotra Samhita*, describes the veterinary care of horses and elephants.

Perhaps the most widely spread idea from early India, though, was Buddhism, which spread to Southeast Asia and, via land routes, to China and East Asia. In the next lessons, you will learn more about the origins of Chinese civilization.

HISTORICAL THINKING

1. **READING CHECK** What ideas spread from India through early trade in the Indian Ocean?

2. **DRAW CONCLUSIONS** Why is the *Periplus* important to historians who want to learn about trade in the Indian Ocean?

3. **INTERPRET MAPS** What effect did monsoon winds have on trade in the Indian Ocean?

3.1 **MAIN IDEA** China's first cities were built in the Huang He Valley where a complex culture developed.

China's First Cities

Think about the objects you use every day. What do they reveal about you and how you live? Quite a bit, actually. From studying bronze pots, jade weapons, and carved animal bones, archaeologists have learned a lot about China's first cities and the people who lived there.

CRITICAL VIEWING In this majestic aerial photo, the Karst Mountains and Li River surround the city of Guilin in southern China. What do you think it would be like to live here?

EARLY CHINESE CIVILIZATION

As you've read, early civilizations arose around fertile river valleys in Africa and Eurasia. China's civilization was no exception. The ancient people of China built their first cities around the **Huang He** (hwahng huh) and the **Chang Jiang** (chahng jyahng) in an area known as the **North China Plain**. The name *Huang*, which is the Mandarin word for "yellow," refers to the high concentration of fine yellow silt called **loess** that floats on the water and covers the entire Huang He Valley.

Sometime around 8000 B.C.E, people living in the North China Plain began to cultivate rice, the first crop to be domesticated in China. Archaeologists have traced the spread of agriculture north from the Chang Jiang to the Huang He Valley. The earliest known appearance of ancient China's greatest commodity—silk—was around 4500 B.C.E.

THE SHANG DYNASTY

Recent archaeological evidence suggests that China's first dynasty, the Shang, emerged along the banks of the Huang He around 1600 B.C.E. Initially the Shang spread across a series of capitals, but they eventually settled in Anyang. Like the people of ancient Mesopotamia, the Shang built walled cities. They used sun-dried loess as a construction material. They also built canals to control the water flow from the Huang He into the rice, wheat, and millet fields, improving agricultural yields. These construction and farming practices supported a large population of approximately 120,000. Anyang was probably one of the largest cities in the world at its time.

During the Shang dynasty, Chinese artisans mastered the technique of working bronze and created richly decorated pots and ornaments. Many of these bronze objects and vessels were used in ceremonies to honor deceased ancestors. Shang artisans also carved jade, bone, and ivory into intricate figurines, many of which were buried in tombs with the dead.

BONES EXPOSE THE PAST

Archaeologists cannot be certain when people first spoke Chinese, but the first recognizable written Chinese characters appeared on animal bones around 1200 B.C.E. Scholars called the bones **oracle bones** because Shang rulers used them to forecast the future. First, the rulers prayed to their ancestors for advice on the outcomes of future events. Then they heated the bones to the point where they cracked and interpreted the cracks, which they believed revealed the answer. They then recorded on the bone the name of the ancestor, the topic of the question, and the outcome.

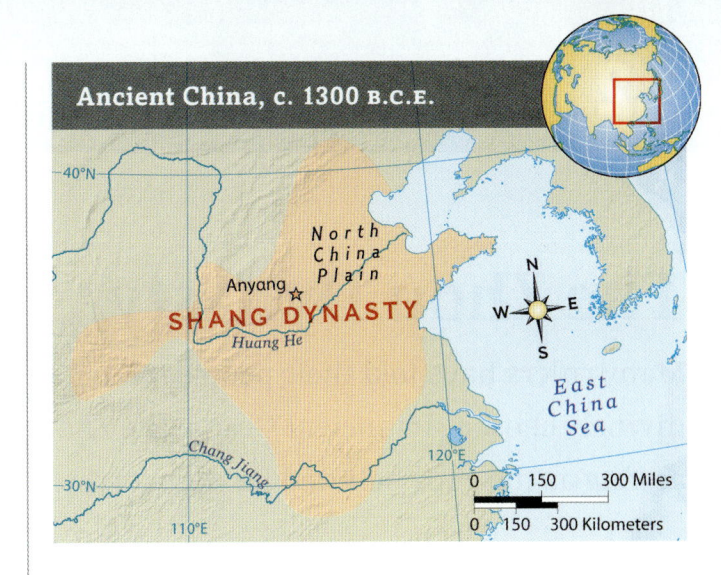

Scholars have deciphered the text on these bones to learn about Shang religion and history. The Shang believed their dead ancestors could intercede in human affairs on their behalf. They also conducted rituals in which they offered food and drink to the ancestors. This type of religion is called **ancestor worship**.

By studying oracle bones and Shang archaeological sites, historians have learned how Shang government and society functioned. For example, Shang rulers exercised direct control over a relatively small area. Their society was hierarchical with a king at the top, warlords next, and farmers at the bottom. Many oracle bones describe battles between the Shang and their enemies. When the Shang defeated an enemy, they took thousands of captives. Some captives became laborers. Others were sacrificed to appease the ancestors.

Over the past century, archaeologists have excavated more than 200,000 oracle bones. The deciphering of these bones marks one of the great breakthroughs in our understanding of ancient Chinese history.

HISTORICAL THINKING

1. **READING CHECK** What role did the Huang He play in the development of the first Chinese cities?

2. **IDENTIFY MAIN IDEAS AND DETAILS** Why was the discovery of oracle bones so important to understanding the Shang dynasty?

3. **DESCRIBE** What were some of the religious practices of the Shang?

3.2

MAIN IDEA The Zhou overthrew the Shang and became the longest lasting dynasty in Chinese history.

The Zhou Dynasty

Many rulers have told their people, and may have believed, that they were divinely chosen. In ancient China, the Zhou believed that a king could rule only as long as the gods believed he was worthy.

THE ZHOU GAIN THE MANDATE OF HEAVEN

After more than 500 years of rule, the Shang dynasty began to weaken, and people from the west overthrew the Shang in 1045 B.C.E. The Zhou (joh) dynasty took over the kingdom and became China's longest ruling dynasty, lasting about 800 years. The Zhou adopted much of the Shang culture, including ancestor worship, writing, and the production of bronze.

However, the Zhou also introduced a new concept that explained how they had been able to conquer the Shang. According to this new concept, known as the **Mandate of Heaven**, a dynasty could rule as long as Heaven believed it was worthy. Worshiped by the Zhou ruling house but not by the previous Shang dynasty, Heaven represented the generalized forces of the cosmos, not a place where people went after death. The Zhou believed that Heaven would send signs—such as terrible storms, famines, unusual astronomical events, or peasant rebellions—before it would withdraw its mandate. After overthrowing a dynasty by force, a new dynasty could justify the actions by claiming to have gained the Mandate of Heaven.

The Mandate of Heaven led to a pattern in the rise and fall of dynasties in China called the **dynastic cycle**. In this cycle a new dynasty arises and people believe it has gained the Mandate of Heaven. Then the dynasty weakens and disasters occur, leading people to believe that the dynasty has lost the Mandate of Heaven. Finally the dynasty is overthrown and a new dynasty emerges. The cycle begins anew with the new dynasty claiming that it has been granted the mandate.

THE WARRING STATES PERIOD

The Zhou people gradually settled more and more territory, expanding their rule to nearly twice the size of the earlier Shang kingdom. The spread of iron tools enabled people to plow the land more deeply and to settle in new areas. Agricultural productivity increased, and the first money circulated around 500 B.C.E.

During the last 500 years of their rule, the Zhou divided their lands among local lords who grew powerful and independent. These local lords fought among themselves and disobeyed Zhou decrees, leading to violence in the final centuries of the dynasty. This time period from 481 to 221 B.C.E. is commonly called the Warring States Period. Armies began to fight battles farther south in different terrain where generals' skills in chariot fighting didn't apply. These generals had to abandon their horse-drawn chariots and lead large armies on foot.

THE DYNASTIC CYCLE

1. The people believe that the gods approve of the new dynasty.
2. The dynasty weakens.
3. Disasters occur.
4. The people believe that the gods no longer approve of the dynasty.
5. The dynasty is overthrown.
6. A new dynasty re-establishes order.

The dynastic cycle developed during the Zhou dynasty.

As local lords continued to gain power through battle, the Zhou king became less of an authority and more of a ceremonial figure. In 221 B.C.E. the last of the Zhou kings was overthrown.

During the violent Warring States Period, people began to think deeply about life and how to develop a more civilized society. Local lords invited philosophers to move to their cities and to discuss ideas freely with other philosophers, ushering in an era of philosophical advancement that became known as "A Hundred Schools of Thought." As you will read, one of these great thinkers, a man named Confucius, would have a profound influence on Chinese philosophy.

CHINA'S BRONZE AGE

The term **Bronze Age** refers to the first use of metal in tools of early societies, such as in Mesopotamia, when farmers began making tools of bronze. China's Bronze Age reached its peak during the Shang dynasty, but the Zhou created new techniques and unique decorative elements as seen in the vessels shown above. They also introduced the practice of writing inscriptions on the bronze, honoring the success of hunters or warriors in battle. Like the Shang, the Zhou used these bronze vessels in weekly ceremonies during which they offered extravagant meals to ancestors.

The process for making bronze vessels required great artistic and technical skills. Zhou artisans used a series of steps to create bronze vessels. First, they made a wax model and carved intricate designs into the wax. Next, they covered the model in clay, leaving small holes. After that, they heated the clay mold so that the wax would melt out through the holes. Once the wax was gone, they poured molten bronze made of copper, tin, and lead into the mold to take the place of the wax. Finally, when the bronze cooled, they broke the clay away from the vessel and used abrasives to sand the bronze and create a shiny surface.

HISTORICAL THINKING

1. **READING CHECK** How did the Zhou use the Mandate of Heaven to justify their rule?

2. **SYNTHESIZE** How did the Zhou build upon the culture and achievements of the Shang?

3. **MAKE INFERENCES** Why do you think people were interested in philosophical questions during the Warring States Period?

3.3 Confucianism and Daoism

MAIN IDEA China's two oldest philosophies originated during a time of instability in Chinese history and helped restore order to society.

What virtues serve as a guide for your own behavior? Kindness? Generosity? Respect for your parents and teachers? In ancient China, the virtues of respect, benevolence, and goodness served as a moral guide for millions of people during an upsetting time.

CONFUCIANISM

Confucius was born in 551 B.C.E. and lived through the Warring States Period of the Zhou dynasty. Confucius made his living by tutoring students, who knew him as Master Kong. He became China's most famous teacher. In reaction to the violence around him, Confucius advocated benevolence, goodness, and virtue, seeking to return to an earlier era, before the Zhou dynasty had fallen into disorder and conflict.

Scholars have not found any texts written by Confucius himself, as bound books did not exist during Confucius' lifetime. However, after Confucius' death, his students collected and recorded the discussions they'd had with him, and these conversations were eventually collected into a book called *The Analects*, which means "discussions and conversations." Students carefully studied *The Analects* because it was thought to be the only text that quoted Confucius directly.

Confucianism is the term used for the philosophy based on the teachings of Confucius. The main tenets, or beliefs, of Confucianism emphasize the role of ritual in bringing out people's inner humanity, or benevolence and goodness. The cornerstone of Confucianism is **filial piety**, or respect for one's parents. According to Confucianism, if children obey their parents and the ruler follows Confucian teachings, then a country in turmoil will right itself because an inspiring example will lead people toward goodness.

DAOISM

Many of Confucius' followers were also familiar with the teachings of **Daoism**, the other major philosophy that arose during the chaotic Warring States Period. The origin of Daoism is uncertain, but legend suggests that it originated with a man named Laozi (low-dzuh), meaning "old master." According to the legend, while traveling to the west on an ox, Laozi was stopped by the guardian of a mountain pass and forced to write down his beliefs. Those writings were said to be the *Dao de Jing*, or *Classic of the Way of Power*.

There are inconsistent accounts of Laozi's actual existence. Historians agree that the *Dao de Jing* is a compilation of teachings by different masters. Daoism emphasizes *Dao*, "the Way," as the path to enlightenment. It urges rulers to allow things to follow their natural course. This concept is often translated as "nonaction," but it is much more. Daoists believe that people should not strive to be in control or to change the world. A person should not boast, argue to prove a point, or try to gain attention. Instead, a person should let go of the stresses of life, live simply, and seek order and balance in his or her life by living in harmony with nature.

Daoists believe that an energy called *qi* is the origin of the cosmos. Qi is made up of yin and yang. Yin represents dark, cold, water, and the earth. Yang represents light, hot, fire, and the heavens. Every human

---

The following excerpt from the first chapter of *The Analects* describes the concept of filial piety.

PRIMARY SOURCE

The Master said: "When the father is alive, watch the son's aspirations. When the father is dead, watch the son's actions. If three years later, the child has not veered from the father's ways, he may be called a dutiful son indeed."

—From *Confucius Analects with Selections from Traditional Commentaries* translated by Edward Slingerland

---

86 CHAPTER 3

A woman prays at Man Mo Temple in Hong Kong. The Daoist temple is open to everyone.

and every object in nature contains both yin and yang. Harmony is achieved through the balance of these complementary forces.

LEGACY OF THE PHILOSOPHIES

Confucianism and Daoism became hallmarks of Chinese traditions and values, influencing everything from government to healthcare to familial roles. The ideals promoted in the philosophies caused leaders to embrace them or reject them wholeheartedly. Starting with the Han dynasty (which you'll learn about in a future chapter), Confucianism served as a unifying force. Confucius' teachings became required reading for all government officials, who had to pass an examination testing their knowledge. In later dynasties, astrologers consulted Daoist sages for advice and for predictions that would legitimize the emperor's decisions.

Daoists believed that meditation, breathing techniques, and special diets could lead to a long life and possibly even immortality. Today Daoists around the world use these practices as well as exercise to achieve emotional harmony and longevity.

Confucianism and Daoism are alive and well in China today, influencing millions of people. Through time, the ideas have often mingled with Buddhism to create a unique and eclectic Chinese philosophy. Thousands of years after their compilations, *The Analects* and the *Dao de Jing* have been translated into many languages and are popular around the world. Chinese medical practices, based on the principles of qi, pharmacology, as well as acupuncture, have also had a global impact.

HISTORICAL THINKING

1. **READING CHECK** How did events in Chinese history influence the development of Confucianism and Daoism?

2. **DESCRIBE** How are Chinese culture and history reflected in *The Analects*?

3. **MAKE CONNECTIONS** Which ideas in Confucianism and Daoism do you think could serve as useful advice for people living today?

Ancient South Asia and China 87

4.1 MAIN IDEA The Qin dynasty unified China and formed an empire.

Qin Rulers Unify China

What does it take to accomplish a lot in a short period of time? Efficiency? Focus? Force? In just 11 years, a cruel but skilled ruler built an empire by creating a system based on merit, forcing his subjects into hard labor, and stifling dissent.

CHINA UNIFIES UNDER AN EMPEROR

China's Warring States Period finally ended in 221 B.C.E when Ying Zheng, the ruler of Qin (chin), defeated the Zhou and other kingdoms. He united the conquered kingdoms, formed an empire, and named himself **Shi Huangdi** (shee hwahng-dee), which means "first emperor."

Chinese historians portray Shi Huangdi as one of the worst tyrants in Chinese history, claiming he murdered his opponents, suppressed all learning, and forced his subjects into hard labor. This view of China's first emperor still prevails today.

Shi Huangdi, the first emperor of China, used cruel methods to bring order to China.

QIN GOVERNMENT AND LAW

Following the practices of his Qin homeland in western China, Shi Huangdi governed according to **Legalism**, a philosophy that emphasized order through strong government and strictly enforced laws. In keeping with Legalism, Qin officials recognized no hereditary titles, not even for members of the ruler's family.

Instead, Qin officials introduced a strict **meritocracy**, a system in which qualified people are chosen and promoted on the basis of their achievement rather than social position. Instead of appointing military and government officials because of their family background, officials sought the most qualified people. The idea of strict meritocracy was unique in the ancient world, and it proved very effective in creating a strong army.

Qin dynasty sources reveal that Shi Huangdi exercised far more control over his subjects than his predecessors. Shi Huangdi initiated several enormous public works projects and enlisted all able-bodied men to build them. Shi Huangdi linked different parts of his empire by building thousands of miles of new roads. He also built canals and irrigation systems. However, the most famous of his public works projects was the Great Wall. He ordered thousands of laborers to link pre-existing dirt walls across the northern border. These stronger walls were meant to protect his empire from the horse-riding nomadic invaders from Central Asia who were to threaten the security of northern China for many centuries. Thus, the wall would be expanded and fortified during the Ming dynasty, which followed the Qin by about 1,500 years.

The Qin dynasty did not last long enough to develop a governmental system for all of China, but it did create a basic **bureaucracy**, or group of administrative government officials. Shi Huangdi appointed a prime

88 CHAPTER 3

The Great Wall as it stands today spans more than 13,000 miles in length. It is one of the largest building projects ever undertaken and was designated as a UNESCO World Heritage Site in 1987.

minister as the top official. Different departments in the capital administered the emperor's staff, the military, and revenue. The Qin divided the empire into districts headed by governors, military commanders, and magistrates.

Evidence from an official's tomb shows that Qin laws were surprisingly detailed, the product of a government concerned with following legal procedures carefully. For example, the Qin established procedures for officials to follow before reaching a judgment and provided clear instructions for investigating cases. Laws also defined fine legal distinctions among different types of crimes. Qin punishments were ruthless, such as the severing of one's foot or nose, but harsh punishments were not unusual in societies elsewhere in the world at the time.

SHORT LIFE, LONG LEGACY

Shi Huangdi lived in a state of fear, believing that his enemies would assassinate him. In preparation for his death, Shi Huangdi forced laborers to create an army of thousands of terra-cotta, or baked clay, warriors to be buried with him and to protect him after his death. You will learn more about the legacy of Shi Huangdi's burial site and the terra cotta warriors in the next lesson.

Shi Huangdi died in 210 B.C.E., just 11 years after he became emperor, and the dynasty fell soon thereafter. However, the Qin name has lived on in the country's name; we call the country "China" because of the Qin.

HISTORICAL THINKING

1. **READING CHECK** How did Shi Huangdi unify his empire?

2. **ANALYZE POINTS OF VIEW** How did Chinese historians portray Shi Huangdi?

3. **IDENTIFY** What are some of the most important accomplishments of the Qin dynasty?

Ancient South Asia and China 89

4.2 Through The Lens

O. LOUIS MAZZATENTA

For over 40 years, National Geographic photographer O. Louis Mazzatenta has traveled extensively and performed many roles at *National Geographic* magazine. Though he retired in 1994, he continues to travel and take photographs. Italy and China are two of his favorite countries to work in because of the abundance of archaeological and historical subjects. "Archaeology is ancient history, but it's made new with the discovery of these things coming out of the earth," explains Mazzatenta.

One of his most thrilling assignments has been capturing the mystery of China's terra-cotta warriors, life-sized clay figures sculpted to stand guard at the tombs of China's first emperor, Shi Huangdi, and Jing Di, the fifth emperor of China's Han dynasty. "As I photographed the soldiers coming out of the ground, they seemed like real people," he says.

What details captured in this photo may have given Mazzatenta that impression?

XI'AN, CHINA

About 7,000 clay soldiers, each with unique expressions and features, have been unearthed from the tomb of Shi Huangdi. Although faded gray now, patches of paint suggest the warriors' clothing was once brightly colored. Archaeologists have also found swords, arrow tips, and other weapons.

Ancient South Asia and China **91**

CHAPTER 3 ANCIENT SOUTH ASIA AND CHINA REVIEW

VOCABULARY

Write one or more sentences that explain the connection between the two concepts.

1. Sanskrit; Vedic
2. reincarnation; karma
3. varna; caste system
4. enlightenment; nirvana
5. oracle bone; ancestor worship
6. Mandate of Heaven; dynastic cycle
7. meritocracy; bureaucracy

READING STRATEGY
DETERMINE CHRONOLOGY

Use a time line like the one below to organize the major events of the 1,500 years of history in this chapter. Place the following events in their correct order along with their dates: birth of Confucius, death of the Buddha, beginning of Maurya Empire, beginning of Shang dynasty, beginning of Zhou dynasty, beginning of Qin dynasty.

8. Of the Chinese dynasties shown on your time line, which two Chinese dynasties began before the Maurya Empire arose in India?

MAIN IDEAS

Answer the following questions. Support your answers with evidence from the chapter.

9. How do the excavations of Harappan cities show that the people of the Indus Valley had developed a sophisticated civilization? **LESSON 1.1**

10. What does the Rig Veda reveal about the lives and beliefs of the Indo-Aryans? **LESSON 1.2**

11. What are some of the actions that Siddhartha Gautama took in his search for an end to suffering? **LESSON 2.1**

12. What effect did the conquest of Kalinga have on Ashoka and his reign? **LESSON 2.3**

13. What are some of the ideas that spread because of early trade across the Indian Ocean? **LESSON 2.4**

14. How did the loess of the Huang He contribute to the development of civilization along the North China Plain? **LESSON 3.1**

15. What difficulties did the Zhou face during the Warring States Period? **LESSON 3.2**

16. What did Confucius teach about the roles of parents and children? **LESSON 3.3**

17. Did the practice of legalism benefit the Qin dynasty? Explain. **LESSON 4.1**

HISTORICAL THINKING

Answer the following questions. Support your answers with evidence from the chapter.

18. **MAKE INFERENCES** What does the *Periplus* reveal about trade in ancient India?

19. **DESCRIBE** How did rulers in India and China seek to justify their methods of governing? Provide one example from each area.

20. **DRAW CONCLUSIONS** How has the discovery of ancient texts aided scholars in understanding early societies in India and China?

21. **COMPARE AND CONTRAST** Compare and contrast the governing strategies employed by Ashoka in India and Shi Huangdi in China.

22. **FORM AND SUPPORT OPINIONS** Would Confucius support Ashoka's practice of governing by example? Explain your reasoning.

INTERPRET MAPS

Study the map of the Shang, Zhou, and Qin dynasties. Then answer the questions below.

23. How did the Qin emperor define his northern border? How did this benefit his empire?

24. What physical features influenced the choice of location for the capitals of these first dynasties?

Shang, Zhou, and Qin Dynasties

ANALYZE SOURCES

One of the main tenets of Confucianism is the practice of filial piety. The following excerpt from *The Analects* describes the importance of this concept. Read the excerpt below and answer the question that follows.

> Master You said: "A man who respects his parents and his elders would hardly be inclined to defy his superiors. A man who is not inclined to defy his superiors will never foment a rebellion. A gentleman works at the root. Once the root is secured, the Way unfolds. To respect parents and elders is the root of humanity."

25. According to the excerpt, how does one's individual roots, or practices from an early age, lead to an orderly and humane society?

CONNECT TO YOUR LIFE

26. **EXPLANATORY** Qin emperor Shi Huangdi undertook a number of large public works projects. Research a large public works project that affects the United States today. Why was this project undertaken? Did it achieve its purpose? Write a paragraph to compare your recent project with a public works project undertaken by Shi Huangdi. Conclude with a statement that evaluates the value of public works projects in your community or state.

TIPS

- Review the discussions of Shi Huangdi's large public works projects in the chapter.
- Conduct research into large public works projects in the United States. Choose one of these projects that interests you.
- Compare one of Shi Huangdi's projects with the U.S. public works project.
- State your main idea about the two projects clearly at the beginning of the paragraph.
- Provide a concluding sentence that evaluates the value of public works projects today.

Ancient South Asia and China 93

Cities of Silence
(Thoughts on the Harappan Culture)

BY PAUL SALOPEK Adapted from "Cities of Silence," Out of Eden Walk dispatch from Kalibangan, Rajasthan, India, August 30, 2018

When it's all said and done, what essence of our days will survive? What shard of human experience endures past the shallows of memory—beyond one generation? Or at most, two? Walking through the world it is impossible not to ask such questions.

The Indus Valley civilization, also called the Harappan culture, was both extraordinarily old and fantastically advanced. The biggest Harappan metropolis ever found is located at Mohenjo-Daro, in Pakistan. In India I visited a smaller and less known site in the desert called Kalibangan. Walking across it today, Kalibangan doesn't look like much. Flat-topped mounds of cobbles and broken bricks rise where the city walls once stood. The sand is littered with millions of 4,000-year-old pottery shards. It is impossible not to step on them. Local shepherds push their cows through the ruin.

National Geographic Explorer Paul Salopek walks across broken 4,000-year-old pottery at the ancient Harappan city of Kalibangan, one of the earliest urban centers in the world.

Kalibangan has architectural features typical of most Harappan cities. A citadel ringed by 20-foot-thick walls protects a complex of fire altars. Most of the population lived, organized in neighborhoods of artisans, on a nearby grid of streets where wooden bumpers once were installed at the corners, presumably to shield buildings from clumsy cart traffic. Kalibangan's most famous relic is an anonymous-looking patch of earth: the oldest plowed field in the world, believed to date back 4,800 years. Even here the technology is elegant: The furrows are cross-plowed at 90-degree angles, presumably allowing intercropping with different seeds, most likely cereals and mustard.

Swaying dizzily under the white desert sun, I dripped sweat from each fingertip and marveled at humankind's capacity for forgetting.

Why is the Indus Valley civilization—by any measure, one of the most accomplished ancient societies in the world—so little known?

Was it because a world-class culture vanished so utterly and mysteriously? By 1800 B.C.E., Harappan cities were being abandoned. Theories explaining their demise range from climate changes that unleashed flooding on the Indus to invasions from Central Asian tribes to an earthquake that may have shifted the course of vital rivers, such as the Saraswati, which exists today only as a ghostly channel of cobblestones in the waterless Thar desert.

Or maybe Harappan culture was simply too peaceful.

The Harappans did not appear to have left us any horror stories, the way violent colonizers like Alexander and the pharaohs did. Instead, the pioneers of urban living bequeathed to us the most efficient brick size, whose dimensional ratio of 1:2:4 is still favored in construction today. Harappa was an antique Switzerland.

"This is not a 'spectacular' civilization," writes Michel Danino in *The Lost River*, a book on the vanished Saraswati River. "[A]s a matter of fact, early archaeologists, especially European ones, complained at times of its 'monotony': no great pyramid, no glorious tomb, no awe-inspiring palace or temple, no breathtaking fresco or monumental sculpture."

I walked on. ∎

UNIT INQUIRY
UNIT 1

Design a Civilization-Building Game

Staging the Question

In this unit, you learned about how and why humans stopped roaming as nomads, settled into the first villages, and formed the earliest civilizations. Each society in the ancient Middle East, the Mediterranean, Africa, and Asia followed its own unique path toward increasingly complex civilizations. At the same time, however, they were all influenced by similar unifying forces, such as religion, and faced similar challenges, such as war. Which factors were the most important to the building—and decline—of the first civilizations?

ASSIGNMENT

List at least five factors that helped early civilizations develop and four challenges the civilizations faced. You might include people, new ideas, and geographic advantages or disadvantages.

Analyze the factors you listed and decide how they contributed to the formation or destruction of a civilization.

Rank the factors in terms of how strongly they influenced the civilizations. You could assign each factor a point value.

Based on your analysis of how early civilizations developed, design a civilization-building game that realistically shows how and why civilizations grow or fail.

Supporting Questions: Begin by developing supporting questions to guide your thinking. For example: How does having a strong ruler affect a developing society? Research the answers in this unit and in other sources, both print and online.

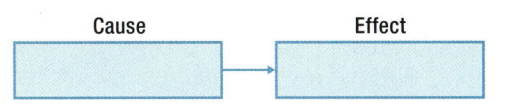

Cause → Effect

Summative Performance Task: Use the answers to your questions to help you determine which positive and negative factors you want to include in your game and how these forces will affect game play. You may format your game in a number of ways, such as a card game, a board game, a role-playing game, or even an online game. Consider researching existing online and board-based civilization-building games for inspiration. You might want to use a graphic organizer like this one to help you plan the steps in your game.

Present: Share your game with the class. You might consider one of these options:

PLAY THE GAME
Gather a group of classmates to play your game. Explain the rules and why certain elements of the game allow players to advance more quickly toward civilization—or set them back further.

PITCH THE GAME
Hold a "pitch session" in which game developers present their games to the class, which acts as the board of directors of a game company. The game developers must explain why their game is realistic and why the company should buy it.

Take Informed Action:

UNDERSTAND Examine current events and identify factors from your game that seem to be at work in societies today.

ASSESS Draw conclusions about why it is important to understand the forces that have contributed to the rise and fall of civilizations.

ACT Make a presentation to share with other classes or in your community about what we gain by studying the forces that shape civilizations.

UNIT 2

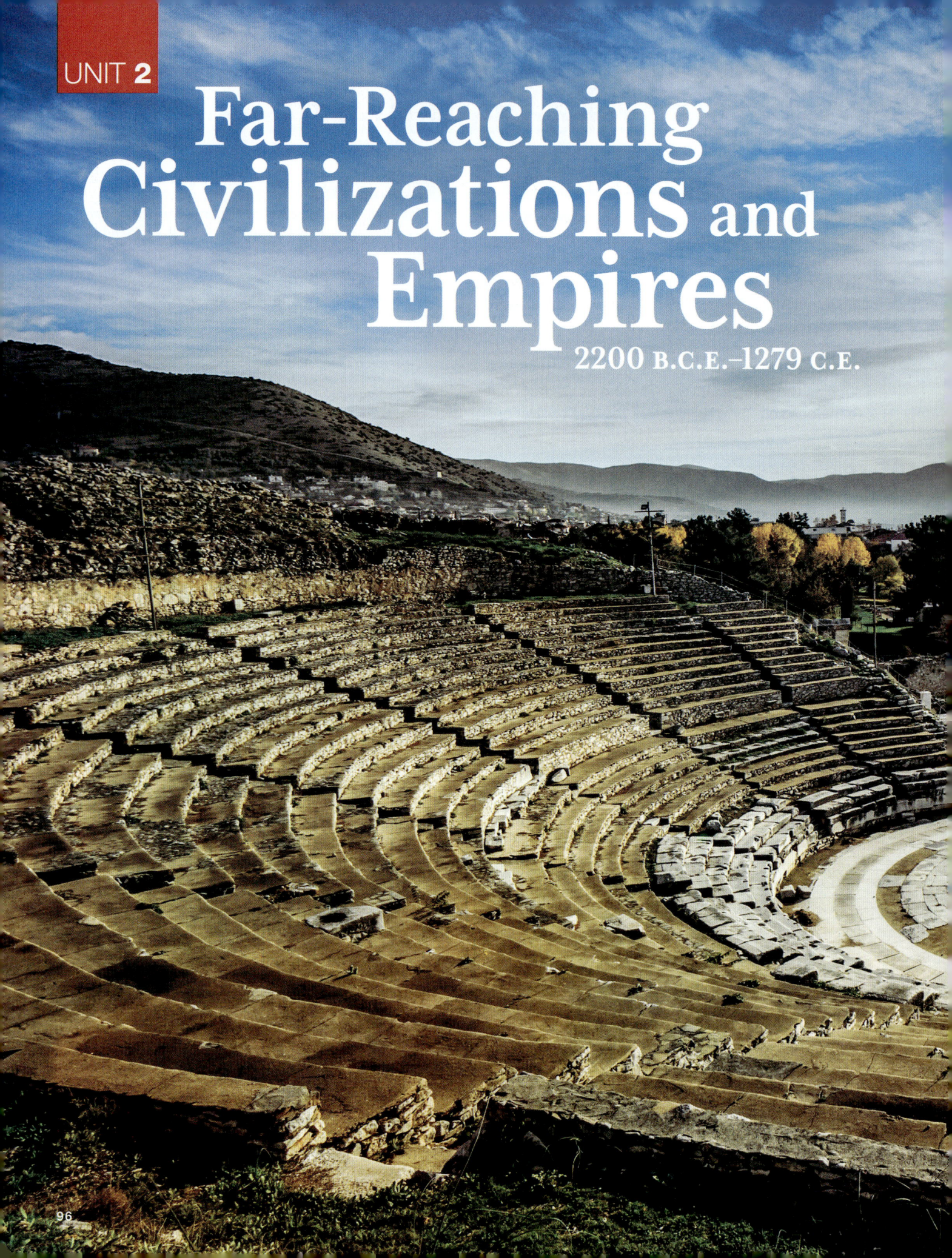

Far-Reaching Civilizations and Empires

2200 B.C.E.–1279 C.E.

CRITICAL VIEWING

The remains of the Hellenistic city of Philippi in northeastern Greece lie along an ancient trade route linking Europe and Asia. Founded in 356 B.C.E. by the Macedonian king Philip II, the city became part of the Roman Empire in 42 B.C.E. Later, the city became a center of Christianity following a visit by the Apostle Paul in 49 C.E. and is now a UNESCO World Heritage Site. What details about this city's history would make it an important site of preservation today?

UNIT 2 Far-Reaching Civilizations and Empires

WORLD EVENTS
2200 B.C.E.–1200 C.E.

c. 760 B.C.E. EUROPE The first important work of Western literature, *The Iliad,* is written. *(Greek amphora depicting the Trojan horse)*

522 B.C.E. ASIA King Darius I ascends the throne of the Persian Empire and ushers in the empire's golden age. *(Persian coin depicting Darius I)*

490 B.C.E. EUROPE Greatly outnumbered Greek forces defeat Persian aggressors in the Battle of Marathon, a major battle of the Greco-Persian Wars.

| 2200 B.C.E. | 1000 B.C.E. | 500 B.C.E. |

2000 B.C.E. EUROPE The first major Phoenician city-states—Tyre and Sidon—arise on the shores of the Mediterranean. *(figurines from the ancient Phoenician city of Byblos)*

509 B.C.E. EUROPE Romans overthrow Etruscan King Tarquin and establish the first republic.

508 B.C.E. EUROPE Cleisthenes establishes the world's first democracy in ancient Greece.

330 B.C.E. ASIA Alexander the Great overthrows the Persian Empire. *(17th-century French painting of Alexander the Great)*

206 B.C.E. ASIA
In China, the peasant leader Liu Bang conquers the Qin to found the Han dynasty. *(Han-era painted warrior with spear)*

HISTORICAL THINKING

ANALYZE CAUSE AND EFFECT How might the failure of the Jewish uprising against the Romans in 70 B.C.E. have contributed to Christianity becoming the official religion of the Roman Empire?

70 C.E. ASIA In Jerusalem, Roman general Titus crushes a Jewish uprising and destroys the city, causing the Jewish people to disperse throughout the empire.

380 C.E. EUROPE Emperor Theodosius declares Christianity the official religion of the Roman Empire. *(mosaic of Jesus Christ)*

649 C.E. ASIA Empress Wu becomes China's first and only female emperor. *(portrait of Empress Wu)*

105 C.E. ASIA The Chinese invent paper.

500 C.E.

1200 C.E.

476 C.E. EUROPE Germanic leader Odoacer leads his army into Rome and conquers the city without a fight, ending the Roman Empire.

320 C.E. ASIA The Gupta dynasty takes control of northern India and ushers in a golden age. *(Gupta-era statue of the Hindu deity Vishnu)*

c. 1000 C.E. ASIA Lady Murasaki Shikibu of Japan writes *The Tale of Genji*, the world's first novel. *(woodcut portrait of Lady Murasaki Shikibu)*

CHAPTER 4

The Persian Empire
1300 B.C.E.–651 C.E.

HISTORICAL THINKING How did the Persians create a well-ordered empire that lasted for 200 years?

SECTION 1 **Ancient Iran**

SECTION 2 **The Reign of Darius**

CRITICAL VIEWING
Columns and sculpted carvings recall the grandeur of the ancient Persian capital of Persepolis, built around 500 B.C.E. What do the ruins of the city suggest about the Persian Empire at that time?

The Persian Empire 101

1.1

MAIN IDEA Herodotus gathered information through his travels and research and produced a work that came to define how history should be written.

Traveler: Herodotus
The World's First Historian

C. 145–87 B.C.E.

A good travel writer uses vivid description and gripping stories to make the history and culture of a place come alive. The historian Herodotus first used these techniques about 2,500 years ago when he wrote about the Persians, Greeks, and other ancient societies.

LIFE AND TRAVELS

Like travelers who write about their experiences today, those of the past introduced their readers to people and places in distant lands. Because the writings of **Herodotus** survived, they have reached across time to enhance our understanding and knowledge of the ancient world. Modern historians still consider Herodotus's book an important source for information about ancient Greece and the Persian Empire. Many scholars have called him the world's first historian.

Little is known about Herodotus's life, including the exact years of his birth and death. Most historians today believe he was born around 484 B.C.E. in Halicarnassus—present-day Bodrum, Turkey—a mostly Greek city within the Persian Empire. At that time, the empire was ruled by a dynasty of kings called the **Achaemenids** (ah-KEE-muh-nihdz). The lands of the Persian Empire, centered in Iran, stretched from Anatolia (the Asian part of modern Turkey) and Egypt across western Asia to northern India and central Asia.

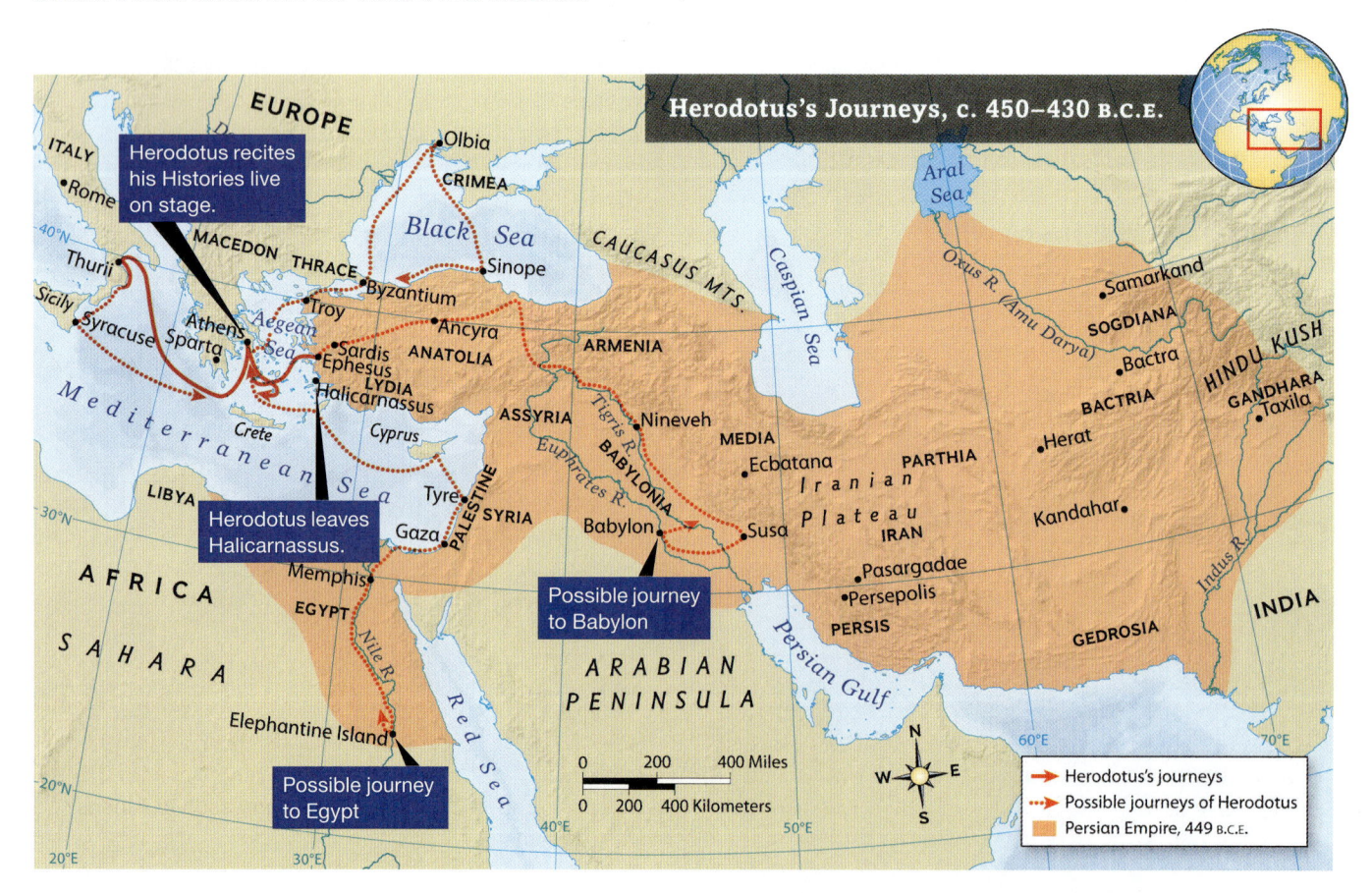

Herodotus's Journeys, C. 450–430 B.C.E.

- Herodotus recites his Histories live on stage.
- Herodotus leaves Halicarnassus.
- Possible journey to Babylon
- Possible journey to Egypt

Legend:
- → Herodotus's journeys
- ⋯ Possible journeys of Herodotus
- ▨ Persian Empire, 449 B.C.E.

102 CHAPTER 4

Herodotus probably lived for a time in Athens, Greece, but he is best known for his extensive travels. Over the course of many years, he journeyed through parts of the Persian Empire, including Anatolia, Lydia, Egypt, Syria, and Babylonia. He also traveled throughout Greece and Italy. His interest in other cultures and keen observational skills made him a savvy traveler. These qualities served him well as a historian.

"GREAT AND MARVELOUS DEEDS"

Herodotus wrote and published his masterpiece, *The Histories*, in Greek around 440 B.C.E. The book is the only one Herodotus produced, and he spent most of his life working on it. From the beginning, *The Histories* was a great success, and Herodotus recited the work before appreciative audiences in Athens. After his death, *The Histories* was divided into nine books. The first five books focus on the rise of the Persian Empire and describe its geography, people, and customs. These books set the stage for Herodotus's history of the **Greco-Persian Wars**, which is the subject of the last four books.

During the wars, the most intense fighting between various Greek city-states and the mighty Persian Empire took place between about 499–479 B.C.E. While Persia was a great empire, the Greeks were largely organized in much smaller city-states, where male citizens actively participated in civic life. Herodotus discusses important battles and provides insight into the leaders of both armies. Although the imperial army of the Achaemenids was far more powerful than those of the much smaller Greek cities, Greek forces were able to repel the imperial invaders twice and, eventually, defeat Persia. In part, Herodotus wrote *The Histories* to understand the Greeks' improbable victory. You will learn more about the Greco-Persian Wars later in this chapter.

Herodotus used methodical research and multiple sources to explain how and why past events occurred. In fact, in ancient Greek, the title of his book means "inquiries" or "research" and is the basis of the English word *history*. Herodotus also distinguished his work by filling his narrative with entertaining stories, dialogue, and speeches by historical figures. He structured the material by weaving themes and morals throughout. For example, to illustrate the moral "pride comes before a fall," Herodotus points out the arrogance and cruelty of the Persian king **Xerxes I** (ZURK-seez) and then describes the king's failure to conquer Greece in 480 B.C.E. Herodotus emphasized the impact of humans on historical events.

On the other hand, he also sometimes stretched the facts to tell a good story. Throughout his book, Herodotus exaggerated the truth, relied on hearsay, invented stories, and made outright mistakes. Many historians who came after Herodotus criticized his work and tried to discredit it. But most scholars today agree that the inaccuracies in *The Histories* do not detract from the book or diminish its significance.

Before Herodotus, travelers wrote disjointed chronicles about people and places that didn't form a unified whole. *The Histories* led to the development of historiography, which as you learned earlier is based on examining sources, selecting details from the sources, and synthesizing those details into a coherent story. As a result of his questions and explorations, Herodotus wrote a narrative that provides a window on the past.

In *The Histories*, Herodotus brought historical events to life. In the first excerpt from his work below, Herodotus calls attention to the fact that his narrative is the result of his inquiry into past events. In the second, he focuses on the Greco-Persian Wars, which he viewed as a conflict between freedom and tyranny. Herodotus illustrates this theme in the excerpt, in which King Xerxes voices his opinion of the freedom enjoyed by the Greeks.

PRIMARY SOURCE

Herodotus of Halicarnassus here displays his inquiry, so that human achievements may not become forgotten in time, and great and marvelous deeds—some displayed by Greeks, some by barbarians [non-Greeks]—may not be without their glory; and especially to show why the two peoples fought with each other. . . .

If, like ours [the Greeks'], their troops were subject to the control of a single man, then possibly for fear of him, in spite of the disparity in numbers, they might show some sort of factitious [false] courage, or let themselves be whipped into battle; but, as every man is free to follow his fancy, it is not conceivable that they should do either.

HISTORICAL THINKING

1. **READING CHECK** What techniques did Herodotus use to hold his readers' attention?

2. **ANALYZE SOURCES** According to Xerxes, what would have happened if the Greek troops had been under the control of one man?

3. **INTERPRET MAPS** How might Herodotus have traveled from Halicarnassus to Athens?

1.2

MAIN IDEA After the Persians overthrew the Medes, the Persian Empire formed under Cyrus the Great, who proved to be a good and tolerant ruler.

Early Persia

The desire to acquire land and exercise power over many people was as great a drive in the ancient world as it has been in modern times. Around the 600s and 500s B.C.E., two groups fought for domination over Iran, an important region in Southwest Asia. History suggests that the best man won.

THE RISE OF THE PERSIANS

Humans had lived on the Iranian Plateau, the region of Southwest Asia that roughly includes the boundaries of present-day Iran, for thousands of years. Some may have been drawn by the abundant pearl oyster beds in the Persian Gulf, the center of pearl trade in the ancient world. Many different cultures arose in the region and developed in relative isolation. Around 1300 B.C.E., however, nomadic groups of Indo-Europeans began migrating there. Two ancient Iranian groups, the Medes (meedz) and the Parsa, grew especially powerful. The Medes settled in an area of northwestern Iran called Media and spoke the Median language. The Parsa—or the Persians, as they came to be known—lived in an area called Persis in southwestern Iran and spoke Persian.

Little is known about Median culture and religion. But historians know that many Persians practiced **Zoroastrianism**, a religion founded by the prophet Zoroaster (also known as Zarathustra) about 3,500 years ago. Zoroastrianism is one of the world's oldest monotheistic religions. Its core teachings are contained in the Avesta, the religion's sacred book. The Avesta describes a supreme god, Ahura Mazda, who created twin spirits of good and evil. The struggle between the two spirits reflects the constant battle humans face in their daily lives.

Both the Medes and the Persians established kingdoms in Iran. In 550 B.C.E., however, the Persian leader **Cyrus II** overthrew the Medes, and the Median Empire came under his control. The Median lands, which included Assyria and its capital of Nineveh, became the first part of the Persian Empire. Cyrus then conquered lands north and west of Persia, including the regions of Lydia, Babylonia, Syria, Palestine, and the Greek city-states on the eastern Aegean Sea. Lydia was an enormously wealthy region. People there had been minting coins from an alloy of gold and silver since around 600 B.C.E.. These Lydian coins were the first metal coins used anywhere in the world.

Remember reading about the Achaemenids? Cyrus was part of that dynasty, which was named for a legendary king. The Persian Empire that Cyrus established is sometimes referred to as the Achaemenid Empire. Cyrus took the title King of Kings, as did all the Achaemenid rulers who came after him. Between 550 and 330 B.C.E., the Achaemenids would rule over about 30 to 35 million people. It was the most diverse empire the world had ever seen. Its subjects came from a mix of cultures, spoke many different languages, and practiced a wide variety of religions. The Persian Empire also contained some of the world's most advanced cities, including Babylon and Susa in southwestern Iran.

THE REIGN OF CYRUS THE GREAT

Cyrus controlled his empire by maintaining a huge army manned not only by Persians but also by peoples of conquered lands, including the Medes. He recruited soldiers from different groups within the empire, so all would share in the wealth that came from further conquests. The new emperor believed doing so would help inspire allegiance, or loyalty, toward his dynasty and his officials. And he was willing to learn from those he conquered. Historians believe Cyrus made a Mede one of his closest advisors.

The Persian leader also adapted cultural traditions from other peoples and borrowed aspects of the governmental systems of other rulers to guide his empire. To administer his lands, Cyrus divided the empire into provinces. Other empires had used this system, but unlike other rulers, Cyrus appointed local people as provincial governors, or **satraps**

104 CHAPTER 4

(SAY-traps). A satrap collected taxes, maintained order within the province, and defended against external threats. The administrative structures Cyrus put into place were so effective that they continued for about two centuries.

While an excellent administrator, Cyrus is most renowned for his tolerance of others' beliefs and practices. He allowed conquered kings to maintain their thrones, and he let his subjects keep their religions, languages, and customs. Cyrus demanded only tribute that defeated people could afford, thus sparing them great hardship. The most famous example of his religious tolerance involved the Jews in Babylonia who, as you have learned, had been held captive there since the conquest of Judah. After Babylonia became part of the Persian Empire, Cyrus freed the Jews. In 539 B.C.E. he allowed them to return to their homeland to rebuild the Jerusalem Temple, which had been destroyed by the Babylonian king Nebuchadnezzar.

Cyrus laid the foundation for Persian civilization. His policy of extending generosity rather than reigning over a repressive regime probably made him a popular leader. In fact, the Persians are said to have called Cyrus their father. As a brave and skilled conqueror and a wise and tolerant ruler, it's no wonder he came to be known as Cyrus the Great.

CRITICAL VIEWING People in this photo are visiting the Tomb of Cyrus, which stands in Pasargadae, the king's ancient capital. The tomb chamber sits atop a massive base. In what way might the design of this tomb, made to contain the remains of a king, be surprising?

HISTORICAL THINKING

1. **READING CHECK** Which two groups founded kingdoms in ancient Iran?

2. **DRAW CONCLUSIONS** How did the policies of Cyrus II help unite and keep peace in his diverse empire?

3. **MAKE INFERENCES** What were the benefits of appointing locals to serve as satraps?

1.3 DOCUMENT-BASED QUESTION
Cyrus the Great and the Jewish Exiles

People often say that history is written by the victors. Cyrus the Great was no exception. He had his bravery and deeds memorialized on a clay cylinder. The Jewish people benefited from Cyrus's victory, but they told the story in their own way.

As you know, Cyrus showed tolerance for the customs and religions of those he conquered. But he wasn't above "blowing his own horn" and taking credit for this policy. He issued the Cyrus Cylinder around 539 B.C.E., after he defeated the Babylonian Empire.

The first part of the cylinder is written in the third person and describes Cyrus's deeds and criticizes the rule of Nabonidus, the Babylonian king. The script claims that the people of Babylon were happy to have Cyrus as their new king. In the second part, Cyrus speaks in the first person and discusses his treatment of the deported people in Babylon.

During Cyrus's rule, royal inscriptions were typically presented in a cylindrical form. And those inscriptions usually praised the bravery and wisdom of the victor and denounced those who were defeated. Many historians believe the portrayal of Nabonidus is exaggerated and unfair. But Cyrus did earn a high reputation for his deeds, and he became a hero to the Jewish people. The Hebrew Bible mentions Cyrus 23 times by name.

CRITICAL VIEWING Dutch artist Jacob van Loo painted *Zerubbabel Showing a Plan of Jerusalem to Cyrus* around 1655. Zerubbabel served as the satrap of the Persian province of Judah under Cyrus and led the first group of Jews from Babylonian captivity to Jerusalem. How would you describe Cyrus's attitude toward Zerubbabel as the satrap points to the plan?

106 CHAPTER 4

DOCUMENT ONE

Primary Source: Artifact
The Cyrus Cylinder, c. 539 B.C.E.

This clay cylinder was created on Cyrus's orders after he conquered Babylon. The Cyrus Cylinder measures about nine by four inches and is covered in Babylonian script. It provides an account of Cyrus's victory, praises Cyrus, and refers to his repatriation of exiled peoples. The cylinder was buried in Babylon's city wall.

CONSTRUCTED RESPONSE
Why do you think Cyrus wanted the cylinder made?

DOCUMENT TWO

Primary Source: Inscription
from the Cyrus Cylinder, c. 539 B.C.E.

The Babylonian rulers sacked temples and forced conquered peoples to resettle in their empire. After his conquest of Babylon, Cyrus allowed these people to return to their homelands. In this excerpt from the Cyrus Cylinder, the script is written as if Cyrus himself were speaking.

CONSTRUCTED RESPONSE How is Cyrus portrayed in this excerpt?

> I am Cyrus, king of the world, great king, mighty king, king of Babylon, king of Sumer and Akkad, king of the four quarters. . . . My vast army marched into Babylon in peace; I did not permit anyone to frighten the people of Sumer and Akkad. . . . As for the citizens of Babylon, . . . I relieved their weariness and freed them. . . . I returned the images of the gods, who had resided there [in Babylon] to their places and I let them dwell in eternal abodes [temples].

DOCUMENT THREE

Primary Source: Sacred Text
from the Book of Ezra

In the Hebrew Bible, the Book of Ezra, chapter 1, verses 1–3, discusses Cyrus and his proclamation regarding the exiled Jews in Babylonia. In this selection from the verses, Cyrus speaks directly to the exiles.

CONSTRUCTED RESPONSE What does Cyrus tell the Jewish exiles to do?

> [T]he Lord stirred up the spirit of Cyrus king of Persia so that he made a proclamation throughout all his kingdom and also put it in writing: "Thus says Cyrus king of Persia: The Lord, the God of heaven, has given me all the kingdoms of the earth, and he has charged me to build him a house in Jerusalem, which is in Judah. Whoever is among you of all his people, may his God be with him, and let him go up to Jerusalem, which is in Judah, and rebuild the house of the Lord, the God of Israel."

SYNTHESIZE & WRITE

1. **REVIEW** Review what you have learned about Cyrus II, his conquest of the Babylonian Empire, and his treatment of the Jewish exiles.

2. **RECALL** On your own paper, write down what the three documents tell you about Cyrus and the Babylonian exiles.

3. **CONSTRUCT** Construct a topic sentence that answers this question: How does the account of Cyrus in the Hebrew Bible compare with the inscriptions on the Cyrus Cylinder?

4. **WRITE** Using evidence from this chapter and the documents, write an informative paragraph that supports your topic sentence in Step 3.

The Persian Empire 107

1.4 NATIONAL GEOGRAPHIC EXPLORER CHRISTOPHER THORNTON

What a Cooking Pot Can Tell Us

"Studying history lets us look back on all that we have accomplished and to consider where we are going now!" —Chris Thornton

Chris Thornton takes a break from working at the archaeological site of Bat in Oman.

Speaking to an audience of fellow archaeologists at Brown University, Chris Thornton posed the question that has motivated generations of researchers: "How do we understand ancient peoples from the materials they left behind?" By examining items such as a humble cooking pot, Thornton seeks to understand what daily life was like in early societies. Although materials such as copper and pottery were essential to everyday life in the past and are frequently found on archaeological digs, they are "frustratingly silent" about the people who used them. Thornton's job is to make these items talk.

MAIN IDEA Working in the field and at National Geographic headquarters, Christopher Thornton helps expand our understanding of the world—both past and present.

IN THE OFFICE AND IN THE FIELD

As the saying goes, Thornton wears many hats. When he's in his office hat, he works in Washington, D.C., as the National Geographic Society's Lead Program Officer for the Committee for Research and Exploration. In this capacity, he manages the process of granting funds to researchers and explorers. "I act as NatGeo's resident 'expert' in six disciplines [anthropology, archaeology, astronomy, geography, geology, and paleontology]," he says, "and serve these six disciplines by helping scholars to get research grants and media attention from NatGeo." On a normal workday, he might be meeting with film producers and explorers in the morning and analyzing the proportion of grants awarded to male and female applicants in the afternoon.

Out in the field, Thornton is the Director of Excavations at the UNESCO World Heritage Site of Bat in the Sultanate of Oman, on the Arabian Peninsula. Bat was a Bronze Age settlement in the region, referred to by ancient Mesopotamian texts as *Magan*. Part of Magan came under Persian control during Cyrus's rule. Archaeologists studied some Magan sites during the 1970s, but very little information was published. When Thornton began working at Bat in 2007, he used up-to-date methodologies, including radiocarbon dating. "Because this region had very limited literacy during the late prehistoric and early historic periods, it needs an archaeologist's eye to investigate and figure out what was going on then," he explains.

RECONSTRUCTING HISTORY

Bat is located at the intersection of several wadis, or dry riverbeds that occasionally fill with water. In the Bronze Age, people settled within wadi systems, which allowed them to survive and farm in the region's dry climate. The same holds true for farmers in present-day Oman.

"One of the key questions I'm trying to answer is how and why people living in arid regions like present-day Oman managed to create relatively large settlements 4,000 years ago," Thornton explains. He believes one clue to the answer lies with copper. He and his team have discovered evidence of copper production and indications of the local use of copper in tools, weapons, and jewelry. According to Thornton, "This suggests that despite the harsh geography of the region, the people of Magan were a very important part of the Bronze Age economic trade networks that led to the rise of cities." In fact, Magan was a major producer of copper for the entire Southwest Asian region for at least 500 years.

Recently, Thornton has been looking to another basic material for clues about life in Bronze Age Bat—pottery. His team has found prehistoric fragments of pottery, or sherds, of cooking pots made in a style that was once thought to exist only in South Asia's Indus Valley. These fragments raise intriguing questions. Are they evidence of a migration of people from the Indus Valley into Magan thousands of years ago? Or do they indicate that the people of Magan admired elements of Indus Valley civilization and imported some of their styles—in the same way that people do today? The pots may also reflect the cultural and technological mixing that took place when Indus Valley people married into Magan families, bringing their cooking techniques with them. At this point, there are many more questions than answers.

Thornton is excited about using contemporary archaeological techniques to study the everyday materials of Bat. By breaking the silence of copper and cooking pots, as well as other items the people of Magan left behind, he hopes to learn how farmers became settlers, and how settlements grew into cities. Ultimately, perhaps, he will help the world understand Magan and the cultural bonds that link it with Oman.

HISTORICAL THINKING

1. **READING CHECK** What does Christopher Thornton do in his two jobs?
2. **ANALYZE CAUSE AND EFFECT** What may have led to the rise of cities in Magan?

2.1

MAIN IDEA Darius I expanded the Persian Empire to its greatest extent and put measures in place to govern and unite its many different peoples.

Darius and Persia's Golden Age

In the ancient world, rulers often used violence to gain power. The Persian Empire was no different—one man used murder, lies, and intrigue to become its leader. In spite of his ruthlessness, however, that leader turned out to be a great one.

SEIZING POWER

After Cyrus's death around 529 B.C.E., his son Cambyses (kam-BY-seez) succeeded him. Cambyses continued his father's conquests and added Egypt and Libya to the Persian Empire. But he only ruled for about seven years. After Cambyses's death in 522 B.C.E., one of his royal bodyguards, a man named **Darius** (duh-RY-uhs), staged a coup, or a sudden overthrow of government. He traveled to Media and, with the help of six Persian noblemen, murdered Bardiya, another son of Cyrus who had assumed the throne several months before. Darius claimed that he had actually killed a priest named Gaumata (GOW-mah-tah), who was impersonating Bardiya.

After the murder, the conspirators discussed what political system they would implement to rule the empire. Some believed the government should be led by a representative form of government or by a group of noblemen. But Darius called for a monarchy, the form of government that had been in place under Cyrus. Although the discussion between Darius and the conspirators took place long before Herodotus was born, the historian presented a lively version in *The Histories* of what they might have said. According to Herodotus, Darius defended his choice by declaring, "One ruler: it is impossible to improve upon that—provided he is the best. His judgment will be in keeping with his character; his control of the people will

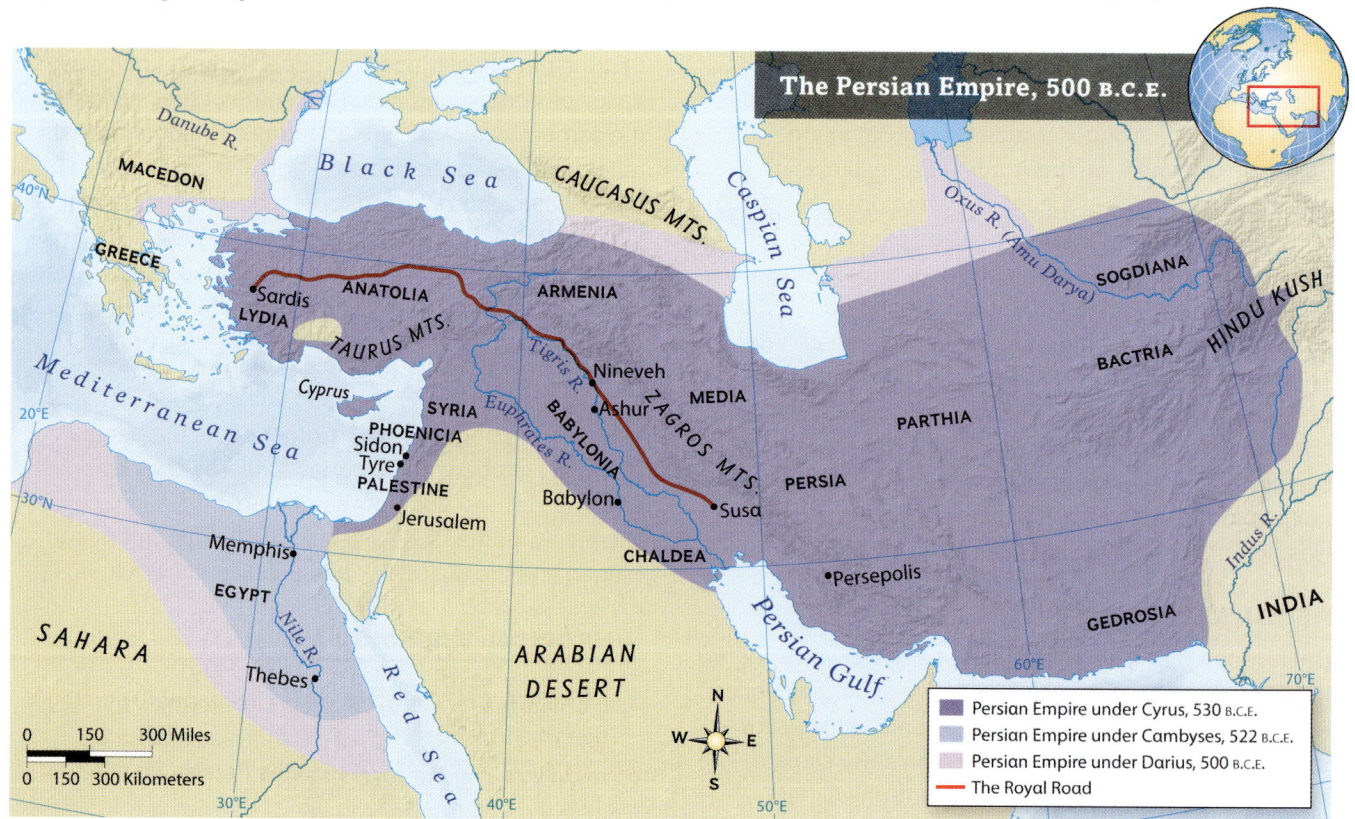

The Persian Empire, 500 B.C.E.

- Persian Empire under Cyrus, 530 B.C.E.
- Persian Empire under Cambyses, 522 B.C.E.
- Persian Empire under Darius, 500 B.C.E.
- The Royal Road

be beyond reproach; his measures against enemies and traitors will be kept secret more easily than under other forms of government."

Darius got his way. Herodotus tells us that the conspirators agreed to select the monarch by seeing whose horse neighed first after the sun came up. Darius won the contest (he cheated) and reigned as King Darius I. And because he was an Achaemenid—Darius was a distant cousin of Cyrus—he continued the Achaemenid Empire.

RULING THE EMPIRE

In spite of the means he used to gain power, Darius was an effective ruler. He expanded the empire until it extended from India in the east to southeastern Europe in the west. The Persian Empire reached its height under Darius and became the largest empire the world had yet seen. Darius followed Cyrus's example by respecting the religious beliefs of others. He also helped carry out Cyrus's decree, which called for the Jews to rebuild the Temple at Jerusalem. And Darius protected his people by introducing a uniform law code for his subjects and appointing judges to administer those laws. Darius also imposed taxes on his subjects, efficiently collecting them through local officials recruited as satraps.

Darius expanded Cyrus's administrative system to maintain control of his huge empire. He divided his lands into 20 satrapies, or provinces, each one run by a centrally appointed satrap. To prevent the satraps from becoming too powerful, Darius appointed inspectors, known as the "eyes and ears of the king," to report problems directly to him.

He also regularized the tax system by requiring each province to pay a fixed amount of revenue based on what its people could afford to pay. Most provinces paid taxes in silver, but Darius allowed some to pay using other commodities. For instance, Egyptians sometimes

This relief of a lion attacking a bull decorates what was the eastern stairway of the Apadana, the largest building at Persepolis.

paid with grain, Indians with gold dust, and Ethiopians with gold, ebony, and elephant tusks. In addition, Darius introduced a single currency and a standardized system of weights and measures.

Understanding that a good government depended on good communication, Darius built the 1,500-mile-long Royal Road, which ran from Susa in Persia to Sardis in Anatolia. Additional roads connected the 20 satrapies. These roads unified the diverse cultures of the empire.

During Darius's reign, the Persian Empire reached its golden age—a period of great cultural achievement. The king carried out ambitious building projects. As a result, Persian architecture flourished. Darius also built a new capital called **Persepolis**. Located in a remote mountainous region in southwestern Iran, Persepolis was mainly used for ceremonial purposes. Darius decorated the capital with palaces and jeweled statues, and Persepolis came to symbolize the magnificence of the Persian Empire. With all his accomplishments, it's no wonder that, like Cyrus, Darius earned the title "the Great."

HISTORICAL THINKING

1. **READING CHECK** How did Darius become king of Persia?

2. **MAKE INFERENCES** How do you think a single form of currency and a standardized system of weights and measures benefited the people of the Persian Empire?

3. **INTERPRET MAPS** What parts of the ancient world did both Cambyses and Darius add to the Persian Empire?

The Persian Empire 111

2.2 Material Culture

PERSIAN MONUMENTS AND SCYTHIAN GOLD

Before the Persians rose to power in Iran, a nomadic people called the Scythians inhabited the region around the ninth century B.C.E. Over the next 200 years or so, however, the nomads migrated to what is now southern Russia and Ukraine, where they founded a powerful empire. The Scythians were great warriors and horsemen. In fact, they were among the first people to harness and ride horses. Unlike the Persians, the Scythians did not leave behind any monuments or written records—they didn't have a writing system. Most of what we know about the Scythians has been gleaned from the artifacts they left behind and from Herodotus. But these items, like the monuments and artifacts of the Persians, have provided great insight into their culture and everyday life.

The Tolstaya Mogila Pectoral

In 1971, a Russian archaeologist excavated a royal Scythian burial mound known as Tolstaya Mogila in present-day southern Ukraine. Dating from the fourth century B.C.E., the mound contained burials of rulers, their families, and their possessions. The greatest find was this beautiful piece of gold jewelry called a pectoral, which would have been worn around the neck. Historians believe Greek artisans made the pectoral for a Scythian ruler.

The pectoral contains three sections that are decorated with a host of animals and scenes from Scythian daily life. This detail from the top section shows two men—possibly chieftains—sewing a sheepskin shirt. A pair of quivers containing the warriors' bows and arrows lies close at hand.

112 CHAPTER 4

Faravahar This winged symbol of Zoroastrianism was carved over a doorway at Persepolis. All parts of the symbol represent different aspects of Zoroastrian philosophy. The circle in the center represents the eternity of the universe and the soul, while the man atop it represents wisdom. The rows of feathers on the wings stand for the three pillars of the faith.

Gold Griffin This Persian gold plaque from the Achaemenid Period features a pair of griffins with a twist: instead of lions' ears, they have those of a bull. Identical feathered wings further balance the design. Rings attached to the back of the plaque suggest that the ornament might have been worn on a belt.

The Oxus Treasure Around 1880, a hoard of Persian artifacts was discovered along the Oxus River in present-day Tajikistan. The Oxus Treasure consists of about 180 pieces of metalwork that have survived from the Achaemenid Empire. The lion heads on the knob of the staff shown here are made from lapis lazuli, a rock prized for its deep blue color.

HISTORICAL THINKING

1. **READING CHECK** What sources have historians used to gather information about the Scythians?

2. **COMPARE AND CONTRAST** How is the artistry of the Persians and the Scythians similar?

3. **DRAW CONCLUSIONS** Based on the artifacts in this lesson, what was important to the Persians and to the Scythians?

The Persian Empire 113

2.4 The Legacy of Ancient Iran

MAIN IDEA Persian rule ended after the Arabs seized control of their lands, but Persia left behind a governmental and cultural legacy.

Nothing lasts forever. The greatest kings die and their monuments crumble to dust. But if those kings and their deeds are great enough, their impact may be felt years—and even centuries—later.

DECLINE OF THE PERSIAN EMPIRE

After his defeat at the hands of the Greeks during the Greco-Persian Wars, Xerxes I withdrew from political life and became an ineffective ruler. In 465 B.C.E., the king and his elder son were assassinated. A series of mostly weak rulers followed, and the Achaemenid Empire began to decline. The next 100 years or so were characterized by rebellions, assassinations, and corruption. It is due to the strong foundation laid by Cyrus, Cambyses, and Darius that the empire endured for so many years. At last, however, a ruler from Macedonia, an ancient kingdom located just to the north of Greece, overthrew the Persian Empire in 331 B.C.E. The young conqueror was called Alexander the Great, and he would adopt many aspects of Persian culture and spread its influences to the west. You will learn much more about Alexander in the next chapter.

Eventually, a group called the Parthians established an empire in Iran and ruled there until 224 C.E., when they were overthrown by the Sasanians. Like the Achaemenids, the Sasanians hailed from Persis. Often called the Second Persian Empire, the Sasanian Empire promoted Iranian art and culture, and Zoroastrianism became the state religion. But unlike the Achaemenids, the Sasanians did not always tolerate those who practiced other religions. Government structures were similar to those of the Achaemenids, however. Provincial officials reported to the Sasanian kings, and the government invested in roads and building projects. The Sasanian Empire ended in 651 after it came under Arab control. Later, many Arabic empires would reflect a strong Persian influence in art, architecture, and poetry.

A LASTING INFLUENCE

In fact, the Persians continued to influence other civilizations for centuries. One of the Persians' greatest legacies was the policy of cultural and religious tolerance that Cyrus II first established in the empire.

CRITICAL VIEWING This gold model chariot is part of the Oxus Treasure. The figures are thought to represent a driver and a satrap as they traveled the Royal Road. What details in this piece convey the skill of the artist?

The policy would serve as a model for other rulers. In addition, because Persian kings respected the many cultures in their empire and allowed them to flourish, the cultures were preserved for the future.

The Persians also brought political order to Southwest Asia. Their well-organized central government was more efficient and humane than any that had been seen before in the region. And the imperial roads helped unite the empire. One of the world's first postal systems even developed on the Royal Road. Similar to the Pony Express, a mail service that arose in the American West in the 1860s, horseback-riding couriers carried letters for the king and other leaders along the road.

As you've learned, many Persians were Zoroastrians. Their devotion to the religion helped keep Zoroaster's teachings alive. And traces of the religion—including the belief in Satan and angels—can be found in later religions, including Christianity and Islam. Zoroastrianism declined in Southwest Asia after the

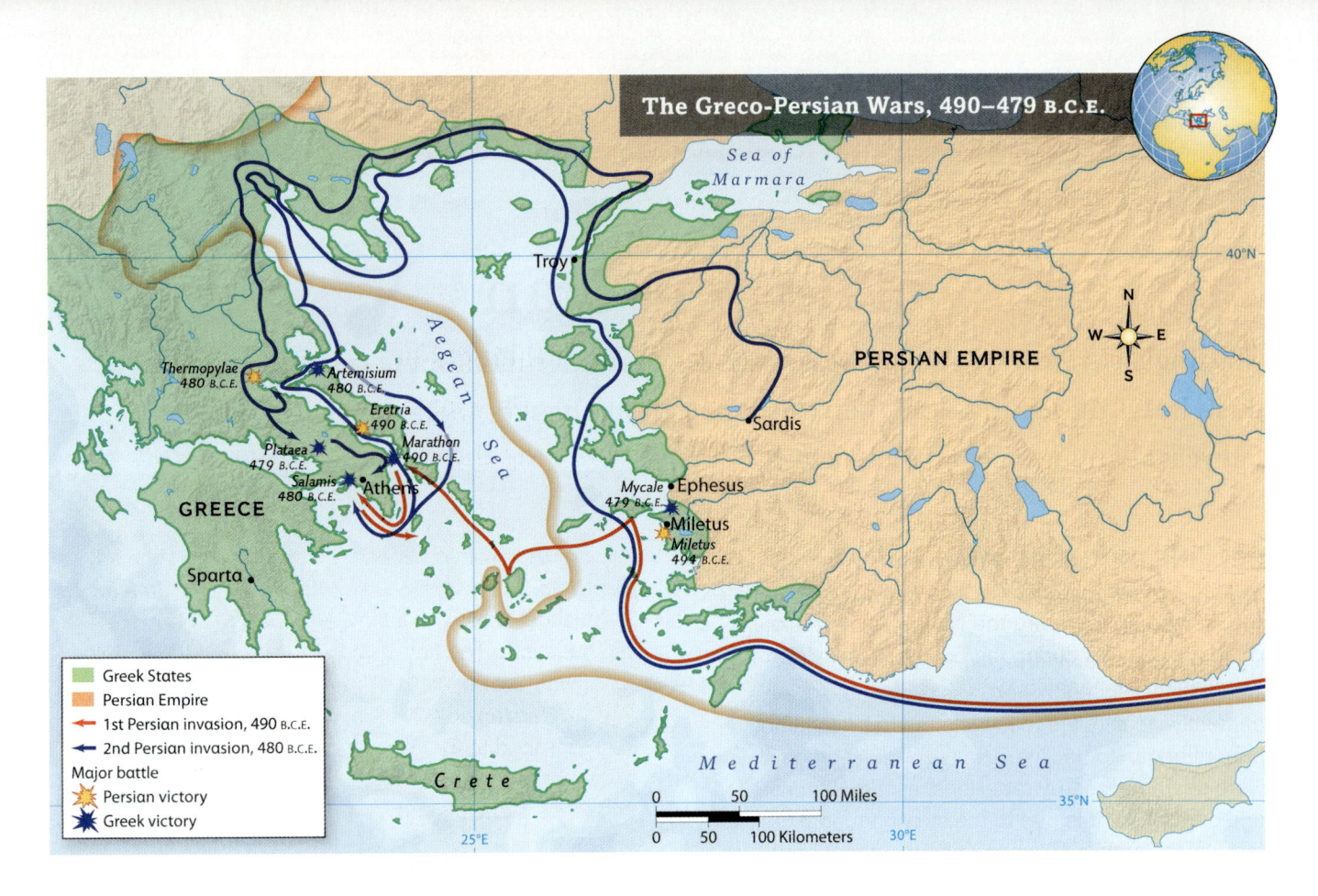

THERMOPYLAE AND SALAMIS

They got their chance 10 years after the Battle of Marathon when Persian armies once again invaded. By that time, Xerxes I, Darius's son and successor, was Persia's king. In 480 B.C.E., Xerxes sent hundreds of ships and more than 150,000 soldiers to Athens. But the size of these forces made progress slow, which gave Athens time to organize alliances with other Greek city-states, including Sparta. Athens took charge of the navy, and Sparta commanded the army.

The first battle was fought at **Thermopylae** (thur-MAHP-uh-lee), an important mountain pass north of Athens. The Spartan king Leonidas led 6,000 Greeks in a fight against more than 100,000 Persian soldiers. The Greeks battled bravely, but Leonidas knew it was hopeless and ordered most of the soldiers to withdraw. However, the king and 300 of his finest Spartan warriors stayed at Thermopylae to protect the retreating army. According to Herodotus, they battled fiercely—using their bare hands when their swords broke. All of them died.

While the Spartans battled at Thermopylae, the Athenians fought in the strait at Salamis. A Greek fleet of about 370 **triremes**, warships with three levels of oars on each side, faced off against about 800 ships of the Persian navy. The Greeks lured the Persians into the narrow strait and sank more than a third of their vessels.

One of the Persian commanders at the Battle of Salamis was Artemisia, queen of Halicarnassus. Although Artemisia was Greek, she was loyal to Xerxes. But during the chaos of battle, she betrayed the Persians after her ship became trapped between the Greek and Persian ships. Thinking quickly, she rammed her ship into a Persian vessel and made her escape. The Greeks believed she was on their side and let her go.

The Persian invaders finally left Greece in 479 B.C.E. after an alliance of Greek armies defeated them at the Battle of Platea. Persia never invaded Greece again, though the war continued off and on for another 30 years. Finally, however, the Greeks and Persians signed the Peace of Callias around 449 B.C.E., bringing the Greco-Persian Wars to an end.

HISTORICAL THINKING

1. **READING CHECK** Why didn't the Battle of Marathon go as the Persians had imagined?

2. **ANALYZE CAUSE AND EFFECT** What led to the Greco-Persian Wars?

3. **INTERPRET MAPS** Near which Greek city-state were most of the major battles fought?

2.4

MAIN IDEA Persian rule ended after the Arabs seized control of their lands, but Persia left behind a governmental and cultural legacy.

The Legacy of Ancient Iran

Nothing lasts forever. The greatest kings die and their monuments crumble to dust. But if those kings and their deeds are great enough, their impact may be felt years—and even centuries—later.

DECLINE OF THE PERSIAN EMPIRE

After his defeat at the hands of the Greeks during the Greco-Persian Wars, Xerxes I withdrew from political life and became an ineffective ruler. In 465 B.C.E., the king and his elder son were assassinated. A series of mostly weak rulers followed, and the Achaemenid Empire began to decline. The next 100 years or so were characterized by rebellions, assassinations, and corruption. It is due to the strong foundation laid by Cyrus, Cambyses, and Darius that the empire endured for so many years. At last, however, a ruler from Macedonia, an ancient kingdom located just to the north of Greece, overthrew the Persian Empire in 331 B.C.E. The young conqueror was called Alexander the Great, and he would adopt many aspects of Persian culture and spread its influences to the west. You will learn much more about Alexander in the next chapter.

Eventually, a group called the Parthians established an empire in Iran and ruled there until 224 C.E., when they were overthrown by the Sasanians. Like the Achaemenids, the Sasanians hailed from Persis. Often called the Second Persian Empire, the Sasanian Empire promoted Iranian art and culture, and Zoroastrianism became the state religion. But unlike the Achaemenids, the Sasanians did not always tolerate those who practiced other religions. Government structures were similar to those of the Achaemenids, however. Provincial officials reported to the Sasanian kings, and the government invested in roads and building projects. The Sasanian Empire ended in 651 after it came under Arab control. Later, many Arabic empires would reflect a strong Persian influence in art, architecture, and poetry.

A LASTING INFLUENCE

In fact, the Persians continued to influence other civilizations for centuries. One of the Persians' greatest legacies was the policy of cultural and religious tolerance that Cyrus II first established in the empire.

CRITICAL VIEWING This gold model chariot is part of the Oxus Treasure. The figures are thought to represent a driver and a satrap as they traveled the Royal Road. What details in this piece convey the skill of the artist?

The policy would serve as a model for other rulers. In addition, because Persian kings respected the many cultures in their empire and allowed them to flourish, the cultures were preserved for the future.

The Persians also brought political order to Southwest Asia. Their well-organized central government was more efficient and humane than any that had been seen before in the region. And the imperial roads helped unite the empire. One of the world's first postal systems even developed on the Royal Road. Similar to the Pony Express, a mail service that arose in the American West in the 1860s, horseback-riding couriers carried letters for the king and other leaders along the road.

As you've learned, many Persians were Zoroastrians. Their devotion to the religion helped keep Zoroaster's teachings alive. And traces of the religion—including the belief in Satan and angels—can be found in later religions, including Christianity and Islam. Zoroastrianism declined in Southwest Asia after the

Arab conquest, but it spread to India and other parts of the world. Today, the followers of Zoroastrianism in India are called *Parsis*, which means "Persians."

The Persians also left behind a legacy in art and architecture. They created beautiful gold and silver coins, jewelry, and decorative objects. Achaemenid artists also excelled at relief sculpture, a work, as you may recall, in which three-dimensional elements project from a flat base. The artists combined Greek and Iranian traditions to carve detailed human and animal figures. Persians also adopted techniques, designs, and materials from across the empire to create a new architectural style. Architects built magnificent cities, temples, palaces, and gardens. The largest building among the royal residences at Persepolis was the Apadana. It was used for receptions and could hold 10,000 people. Much of Persepolis and other ancient Persian cities has been reduced to ruins, but many archaeologists are working today to preserve Iran's cultural heritage. After all—as some historians say—the Persians defined the meaning of empire.

The Persians may have influenced our modern postal service. In the following excerpt from *The Histories*, Herodotus describes the couriers who carried messages on the Royal Road from station to station. The last sentence in the excerpt was adapted by the U.S. Postal Service and became its unofficial motto: "Neither snow nor rain nor heat nor gloom of night stays these couriers from the swift completion of their appointed rounds."

PRIMARY SOURCE

No mortal thing travels faster than these Persian couriers. The whole idea is a Persian invention, and works like this: riders are stationed along the road, equal in number to the number of days the journey takes—a man and a horse for each day. Nothing stops these couriers from covering their allotted stage in the quickest possible time—neither snow, rain, heat, nor darkness.

—from *Herodotus: The Histories* translated by Aubrey de Sélincourt

Fire represents the light and purity of the god worshiped by followers of Zoroastrianism, a religion that developed in ancient Iran. In Zoroastrian temples, like this one in the southwest Asian country of Azerbaijan, the fire is never extinguished.

HISTORICAL THINKING

1. **READING CHECK** Which Persian groups established empires in Iran after the Achaemenids?

2. **EVALUATE** In what ways might the Persians have defined the meaning of empire?

3. **FORM AND SUPPORT OPINIONS** What do you think is Persia's greatest legacy? Explain your answer.

The Persian Empire

CHAPTER 4 THE PERSIAN EMPIRE REVIEW

VOCABULARY

Use each of the following vocabulary words in a sentence that shows an understanding of the term's meaning.

1. satrap
2. coup
3. Zoroastrianism
4. phalanx
5. trireme
6. Greco-Persian Wars

READING STRATEGY
ANALYZE CAUSE AND EFFECT

Use a graphic organizer like the one below to list the causes and effects of the Greco-Persian Wars. Then answer the questions that follow.

Greco-Persian Wars

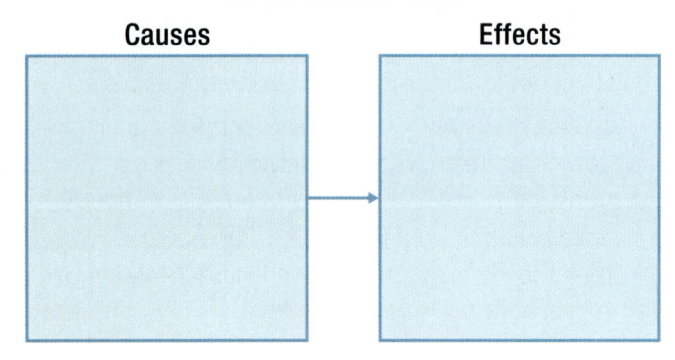

Causes	Effects

7. What happened when Athens sent a few ships to support the rebels in the Ionian Revolt?

8. How did the size of the forces Xerxes sent to Greece impact the Persians' second invasion?

MAIN IDEAS

Answer the following questions. Support your answers with evidence from the chapter.

9. What subjects does Herodotus write about in *The Histories*? **LESSON 1.1**
10. How did Cyrus II administer his lands? **LESSON 1.2**
11. In what way did Cyrus demonstrate his religious tolerance after he conquered Babylonia? **LESSON 1.2**
12. What was the Royal Road? **LESSON 2.1**
13. Why was the phalanx formation an effective strategy in battle? **LESSON 2.3**
14. What happened at the Battle of Thermopylae? **LESSON 2.3**
15. Why is the Sasanian Empire sometimes called the Second Persian Empire? **LESSON 2.4**

HISTORICAL THINKING

Answer the following questions. Support your answers with evidence from the chapter.

16. **MAKE INFERENCES** Why do you think Herodotus's book was an instant success?
17. **EVALUATE** In what way did Cyrus's appointment of a Mede as one of his closest advisors demonstrate great wisdom?
18. **DRAW CONCLUSIONS** How might the inspectors Darius appointed to oversee the satraps have functioned as spies?
19. **SYNTHESIZE** Why were the Greco-Persian Wars significant for both the ancient Greeks and the Persians?
20. **ANALYZE CAUSE AND EFFECT** What happened because weak rulers came to power after Xerxes?
21. **FORM AND SUPPORT OPINIONS** Who do you think was the better leader, Cyrus or Darius? Explain your answer.

INTERPRET VISUALS

After Darius took the throne he had this relief carved into rock on the Zagros Mountains in Behistun, Iran. Darius, the third figure from the left, stands with his foot on Gaumata, who is lying on the ground. Those who opposed Darius's ascension to the throne have been captured and appear before him. Study the relief below. Then answer the questions that follow.

22. How does Darius appear in the sculpture as compared with the rebels standing before him?

23. What message was Darius trying to send to his enemies with this monument?

ANALYZE SOURCES

In *The Histories*, Herodotus presents Artemisia as an advisor and ally of Xerxes during the invasion of Greece. In this excerpt from his work, Herodotus describes Xerxes' reaction after Artemisia sank a Persian ship—the Calyndian—to escape from the Greek triremes at the Battle of Salamis. The "bystander" mistakenly believes Artemisia has sunk a Greek ship. Read the excerpt and then answer the following question.

> For the story goes that Xerxes, who was watching the battle, observed the incident, and that one of the bystanders remarked: "Do you see, my lord, how well Artemisia is fighting? She has sunk an enemy ship." Xerxes asked if they were sure it was really Artemisia, and was told there was no doubt whatever. . . . She was, indeed, lucky in every way—not least in the fact that there were no survivors from the Calyndian ship to accuse her. Xerxes' comment on what was told him is said to have been: "My men have turned into women, my women into men."

24. How did the incident affect Xerxes' opinion of Artemisia?

CONNECT TO YOUR LIFE

25. **EXPLANATORY** Think about the Persian Empire's policy of inclusion and tolerance and how the Persian legacy is relevant to American society. How does the U.S. government reflect inclusion? How does American culture demonstrate tolerance? Do you think our nation could be more inclusive and tolerant? Write an essay explaining how well the Persian example of tolerance is also found in the United States today.

TIPS

- Review what you've learned about tolerance in the Persian Empire and then consider how this policy is also found in the United States. You may wish to jot down your ideas in a graphic organizer.

- State your main ideas clearly and support them with relevant facts, details, and examples.

- Use two or three vocabulary words from the chapter in your essay.

- Provide a concluding statement about the continuation of the Persian legacy.

CHAPTER 5

Greek Civilization
2200 B.C.E.–200 B.C.E.

HISTORICAL THINKING How did the arts, sciences, and government of ancient Greece influence later civilizations?

SECTION 1 **Early Greece**
SECTION 2 **The Golden Age**
SECTION 3 **Hellenism: A Cultural Synthesis**

CRITICAL VIEWING
People bustle through the streets of Plaka, or old town, of Athens, Greece, with the Parthenon and Acropolis overlooking the city. Compare and contrast the buildings. What do they have in common? How are they different?

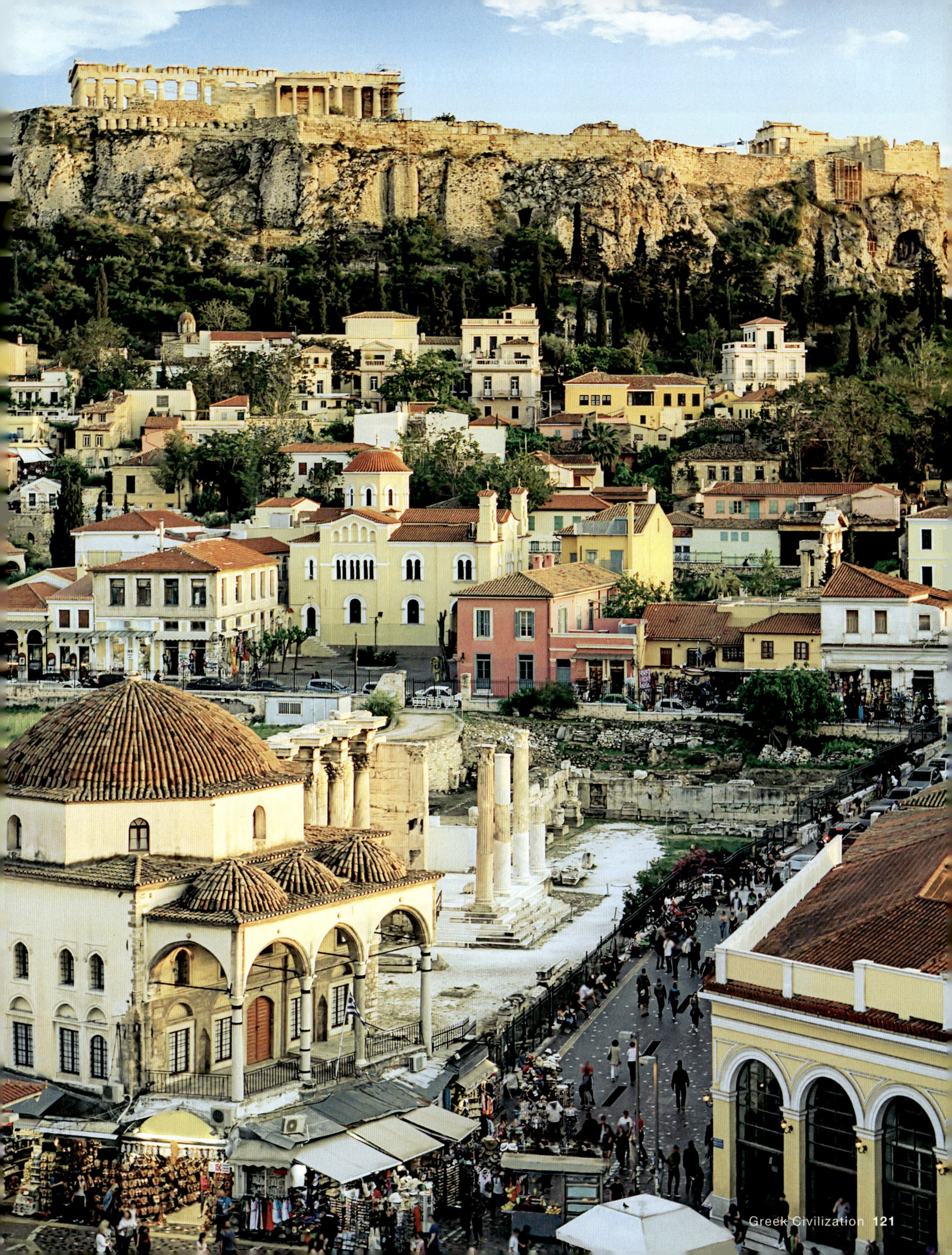

1.1 NATIONAL GEOGRAPHIC EXPLORER **WILLIAM PARKINSON**

Embracing Our Greek Heritage

"To some extent, we're all Greeks." —Bill Parkinson

Parkinson is certain the bodies buried in Alepotrypa Cave were deliberately placed in the position revealed by their skeletons. "Their arms are draped over each other, their legs are intertwined," he says. "It's unmistakable."

Sometimes an archaeological find strikes right at the heart—like the pair of skeletons uncovered near Alepotrypa (ah-leh-POH-trih-pah) Cave in Greece in 2015. Archaeologists were stunned to find the 5,800-year-old bones of a man and woman in their twenties locked in an embrace. The remains raised hard-to-answer questions: Were the couple young lovers? husband and wife? brother and sister? How did they die? "Like most things in Greece, it's complicated," says National Geographic Explorer William Parkinson.

MAIN IDEA
Bill Parkinson studies ancient Greek society, focusing on how early farming villages developed and turned into cities.

SOLVING MYSTERIES

The relationship of the embracing couple—and how they died—may always remain unknown. However, examinations of other skeletons at the cave site suggest the couple lived during a violent time. According to the work of Parkinson's colleague, Dr. Anastasia Papathanasiou, a third of the skeletons show evidence of head trauma, probably caused by rocks or clubs. Archaeologists hope to gain a fuller picture of ancient Greek life from ongoing studies of the site.

Parkinson, a curator at the Field Museum and professor at the University of Illinois at Chicago, is one of those archaeologists. He codirects the Diros Project, a shared Greek and American research venture focused on Alepotrypa Cave, which lies along Diros Bay on the Mani Peninsula in southern mainland Greece. More than 8,000 years ago, Neolithic farmers began using the cave for burials and religious ceremonies. About 6,500 years ago, farmers established a village outside the cave. For unknown reasons, people abandoned the settlement about 5,000 years ago.

Parkinson and his team are working to solve some of the mysteries surrounding this important ancient site. They have gained insight into how early farming villages developed in Greece and are working to piece together how these villages transformed into towns and cities.

Parkinson appreciates Western society's strong connection to the ancient Greeks. "So many aspects of our culture and our civilization derive from what happened over 2,000 years ago in the southeastern corner of Europe," he notes, "from our political systems to many of the sports that still hold the American imagination to much of our language, medicine, philosophy."

NEVER GETTING OLD

Growing up outside Joliet, Illinois, Parkinson liked to search for arrowheads in nearby fields and woods. Originally focused on becoming a journalist when he entered college, he instead became attracted to archaeology for a variety of reasons. For one, much of the work is hands-on. In addition to drawing upon a wide range of skills and knowledge, archaeology is also a "team sport"—one requiring collaboration with many kinds of specialists.

Perhaps the greatest thing about shoveling dirt, Parkinson says, is that it never gets old. He claims, "Nothing can describe how exciting it is to put your trowel in the ground and uncover something nobody has seen for several thousand years." Like the bones of an embracing couple, for example.

What has Parkinson discovered from his fieldwork about the growth of cities from small farming villages? An old theory is that people banded together and formed cities to defend themselves against attackers. According to Parkinson, safety wasn't the only reason. His fieldwork indicates that the early Greeks were drawn to populated places because "there were things going on—in the same way it happens today." And over time, those small beginnings led to the magnificent cities of Greek civilization.

HISTORICAL THINKING

1. **READING CHECK** What attracted William Parkinson to the field of archaeology?

2. **ANALYZE CAUSE AND EFFECT** What has Parkinson's research revealed about the reasons ancient Greek farming villages grew into cities?

1.2

MAIN IDEA Mediterranean cultures that preceded classical Greek civilization prospered from sea trade.

Crete and Trading Centers

You've probably heard people talk about how innovation and productivity are important to a successful economy today. For ancient civilizations, thriving agriculture and trade were the keys to success. One example is a society from about 4,000 years ago on an island in the Mediterranean.

MINOAN SEA TRADE

Geography played an important role in the development of ancient Greek civilization. Greece's mainland consists of a mountainous peninsula extending south into the vast Mediterranean Sea. To its west lies the Ionian Sea and to its east the Aegean Sea. The Aegean, especially, contains many small islands. The much larger island of Crete, the center of the Minoan civilization, sits about 100 miles to the south of the mainland. The **Minoans** are named after King Minos, who according to Greek legend ruled a large empire with many ships. The Minoans did not speak Greek like later peoples who settled in the region did, but the Minoans did engage in long-distance sea trade.

Crete had a limited amount of fertile agricultural land, but it produced enough grain and livestock to feed the population with some left over for trade. The Minoans also crafted textiles, metalwork, pottery, and fine jewelry. By about 2000 B.C.E., they had built large palace complexes with storage areas for farm produce, various raw materials, and craft goods. Their economy was a **redistributive economy**, in which farmers and artisans delivered large amounts of produce and goods to the palace, and palace authorities stored, sorted, and distributed the items to the people as needed.

Many Minoans settled in areas near the palaces, which also served as public meeting places and perhaps religious centers. The palace at **Knossos** became the main center of the Minoan civilization. This structure had indoor plumbing and hundreds of rooms. Colorful **frescoes**, or paintings drawn on wet plaster, covered the walls of the palace and often showed scenes related to seafaring.

CRITICAL VIEWING The Bull-Leaping Fresco, painted about 1550 B.C.E., originally decorated a wall in the palace at Knossos in Crete, Greece. It shows a man flipping over a bull as two women observe. Why do you think the artist chose this subject?

In addition to redistributing food and craft goods, people in the palaces may have also managed the sea trade. Minoan sailors carried foodstuffs, textiles, wood, olive oil, and luxury goods such as jewelry to the Greek mainland, the lands of the eastern Mediterranean, and Egypt. They brought back mainly raw materials: tin and copper for making bronze, as well as gold, silver, gemstones, and ivory.

To keep track of so much activity, early Minoans kept records on clay tablets using script in which pictures represent objects. Later, the Minoans established a writing system in which characters stood for sounds. Today, this script, called Linear A, is still a mystery—nobody has been able to decipher it.

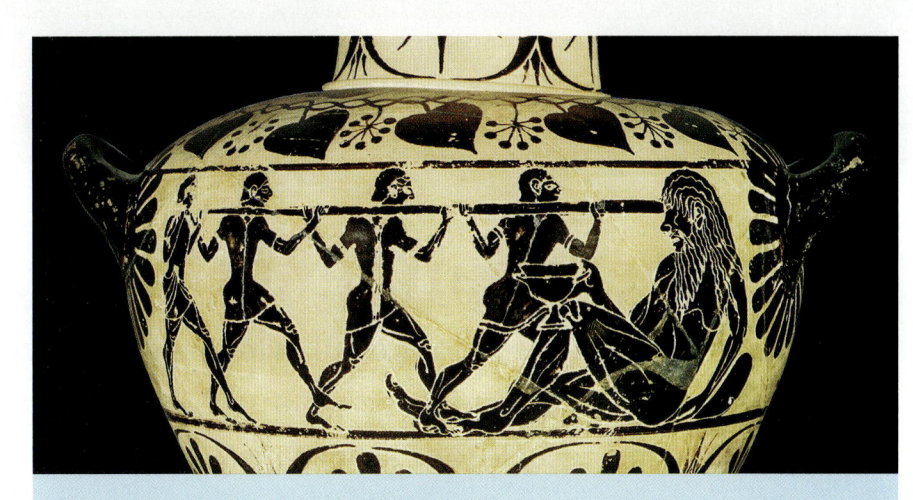

HOMER'S EPICS The characters in Homer's classic epics chase glory on the battlefield and beyond. The *Iliad* tells of events during a period of the Trojan War, including the story line of the great warrior Achilles. The *Odyssey* chronicles the adventures of Odysseus, the king of Ithaca who fought in the war on the side of the Greeks, as he attempts to sail home. Hindered by some gods and aided by others, Odysseus and his crew face obstacles, including dangerous mythical creatures such as the Cyclops shown here.

MYCENAEAN GREECE

Around 1600 B.C.E., Minoan traders sailing to the mainland encountered a Greek-speaking people that we know as the **Mycenaeans**. Their name comes from Mycenae, a city that appears in the epic poem the *Iliad*. Written around 800 B.C.E., the *Iliad* tells how King Agamemnon of Mycenae led a Greek army against Troy, a city located across the Aegean Sea in present-day Turkey. An archaeologist who excavated a palace site in southern Greece in the 1870s thought he had discovered Mycenae. Thereafter, historians referred to the Greek-speaking people who had settled on the mainland as Mycenaeans.

The war described in the *Iliad* was known as the Trojan War, and the story remains a literary classic. However, such a war may or may not have actually taken place. Additionally, although many scholars attribute the *Iliad* and the *Odyssey*, another epic poem, to a writer named **Homer**, some experts believe that *Homer* is merely the name attached to an oral tradition, or a group of stories that are passed down through the generations by people talking with one another.

The *Iliad* did, however, have some basis in fact. Archaeologists have found evidence that the Mycenaeans were, indeed, a warrior people. The graves of wealthy Mycenaean men typically contained bronze weapons and armor. Unlike the palaces of the Minoans, Mycenaean palaces were fortresses surrounded by thick walls. Warriors rode into battle in horse-drawn two-wheeled chariots.

By about 1500 B.C.E., the Minoan civilization was in decline, but historians do not know why. Perhaps the Mycenaeans conquered Crete, or perhaps earthquakes or droughts brought the civilization to an end. Whatever the cause, by 1400 B.C.E. the Mycenaean writing system, known as Linear B, was used for palace records on Crete. This system has been deciphered and has been shown to be an early form of the Greek language.

During the time that the two cultures overlapped, the Minoans exerted a great influence on the Mycenaeans, especially their art. Minoan artifacts and artistic styles appeared throughout the mainland. Like the Minoans, the Mycenaeans had a redistributive economy, and they prospered from a wide-ranging trade network that brought them into contact with other cultures.

Archaeological evidence of the Mycenaeans dates to no later than about 1200 B.C.E. Foreign raiders might have invaded, or infighting among the Mycenaeans might have caused their civilization to collapse.

HISTORICAL THINKING

1. **READING CHECK** How did sea trade affect the Minoan and Mycenaean civilizations?
2. **COMPARE AND CONTRAST** What key characteristics did the Minoan and Mycenaean civilizations share? How did the two cultures differ?
3. **DRAW CONCLUSIONS** How does Homer's *Iliad* reflect the history of ancient Greek civilization?

Greek Civilization 125

1.3 The Phoenicians and Their Alphabet

MAIN IDEA The Phoenicians, a seafaring people from Southwest Asia, employed a new type of writing system, produced a valuable purple dye, and established outposts around the Mediterranean Sea.

Family, friends, and life experiences all help shape your personality and make you who you are. What factors shape a culture? For the ancient Greeks, the list of key influences must include the Phoenicians.

Phoenician script appears on a sarcophagus, or coffin, from the fifth century B.C.E.

PHOENICIAN CITY-STATES

The **Phoenicians** (fih-NEE-shuhnz) occupied a sizable stretch of land along the far-eastern shore of the Mediterranean Sea. This territory included parts of present-day Syria, Lebanon, Israel, and the Palestinian territories. Phoenicia, however, more accurately consisted of a group of independent city-states within that territory. As you have learned, a city-state is a city whose ruler governs both the city and the surrounding countryside. The first major Phoenician city-states—Tyre and Sidon—arose around 2000 B.C.E. Other powerful city-states included Byblos, Aradus, and Berot (modern Beirut). Together, the city-states of Phoenicia dominated the Mediterranean Sea from the ninth to the sixth centuries B.C.E.

The Phoenician city-states prospered mainly from trade. Their trading partners included Egypt, Syria, Mesopotamia, the Greek mainland, and the Aegean islands. People in Phoenicia exported cedarwood, metalwork, fine glass, and cloth colored with a rare reddish-purple dye extracted from snails. They also exported the dye itself, called Tyrian purple after the city-state of Tyre. (The name *Phoenician* comes from the Greek word for the dye.) Phoenician imports included papyrus, silk, spices, horses, precious metals, and gemstones. Although kings ruled most city-states, they often shared political power with merchant families.

The Phoenicians, master seafarers and shipbuilders, sailed west, establishing settlements on the island of Cyprus and the far reaches of the western Mediterranean Sea. By 814 B.C.E., they had built a thriving trading post at **Carthage** (near present-day Tunis) and set up commercial outposts and other small settlements along the North African and Spanish coastlines. Control of these areas gave the Phoenicians access to valuable natural resources, especially precious metals. Some Phoenician sailors voyaged even farther west, passing through the narrow Strait of Gibraltar to reach coastal lands on the Atlantic Ocean.

DIFFUSION OF PHOENICIAN IDEAS

As you have already learned, the exchange of goods has typically also included an exchange of ideas. Participation in a trade network that stretched from the western Mediterranean to Southwest Asia exposed the Phoenicians to a broad range of concepts and viewpoints. The Phoenicians also spread ideas to their trading partners, including the Greeks.

One of those concepts, a new type of writing system developed between 1700 and 1500 B.C.E., was the **alphabet**. In writing based on an alphabet, a single letter represents a single sound. This simplicity helped the writing system spread to other cultures. The alphabet consisted of 22 letters—all of them consonants. Readers supplied vowels on their own. Peoples in various areas of the eastern Mediterranean, including the Phoenicians, likely contributed to the alphabet's development. Early forms of the alphabet found on written records at Byblos have been dated to the 15th century B.C.E.

The exact origins of the alphabet are unknown. It may have evolved from Egyptian hieroglyphics, which included some syllables based on sounds. However, unlike hieroglyphics—a complex system of pictures representing objects, sounds, or ideas that few people other than highly trained scribes could understand—the alphabet was easy to learn and use, which made it accessible to more people. And, unlike cuneiform, it lent itself to writing on papyrus as well as on pottery or stone. In addition, letters could be used in many different combinations to form words, and they could represent nearly any spoken language. The alphabetic system was more flexible than hieroglyphics, cuneiform, or the Mycenaeans' Linear B.

By around 1100 B.C.E., the Phoenician alphabet had settled into a consistent form. The sequence of the 22 letters was set, and lines of alphabetic text were written from right to left. The Mycenaean Linear B writing system seems to have disappeared from Greece around 1200 B.C.E., along with that civilization. The Phoenician system, which arrived in the Aegean lands (Greece) between 950 and 750 B.C.E., took its place.

At first, the Greeks accepted the Phoenician alphabet as it was. They included all its letters, even though some did not represent sounds found in their own language. They also wrote text from right to left. By 700 B.C.E., however, the Greeks had adapted the alphabet to better suit their speech by converting some unused letters into vowels and adding more vowels. In time, they also shifted to a left-to-right form of writing.

The Phoenicians passed along to the Greeks—and others—their knowledge of Mediterranean geography as well. They had an extensive understanding of the Mediterranean Sea and coastal lands. Following the example of the Phoenicians and using what they learned from them, the Greeks established their own colonies in the Mediterranean area during the period 750–550 B.C.E.

Phoenician and Greek Settlement in the Mediterranean

HISTORICAL THINKING

1. **READING CHECK** Why was an alphabetic writing system easier to learn and use than existing writing systems?

2. **INTERPRET MAPS** Which outpost did the Phoenicians likely establish first, Citium or Carthage? Use the map scale to support your answer.

3. **DRAW CONCLUSIONS** Why did some merchant families have considerable power in Phoenician city-states?

Greek Civilization 127

1.4

MAIN IDEA The rise of Greek city-states led to cultural renewal, overseas settlement, and new forms of government.

The Rise of Greek City-States

Life can be difficult. An accident or tragic event can leave a person feeling lost. After the collapse of the Mycenaean civilization, the Greeks seemed lost to history. But they bounced back—and became even stronger.

A PERIOD OF RECOVERY

About 1200 B.C.E., after the Mycenaean civilization fell, the entire population of Greece dropped sharply. Survivors abandoned the palace centers, and agriculture declined. Little evidence exists of social or cultural progress for several centuries. By around 900 B.C.E., however, the population had made a comeback, as had agriculture—assisted by the increasing production of iron tools. Iron had taken the place of bronze as the metal of choice for tools and for weapons.

As you already learned, sometime after the eighth century B.C.E. the Phoenicians introduced the Greeks to their alphabet. This transfer or sharing of information not only gave the Greeks a writing system to replace the one that had largely been lost but also made written language more available to people in general. The oral transmission of poetry and songs had preserved Greek culture through these difficult times, and those forms of expression would soon begin to appear in writing. Recall that the epic works by the poet or group of poets known as Homer were written in the 700s B.C.E.

At about this same time, families began to organize into communities on the Greek mainland and islands. They established borders and exerted control over villages and farms within those borders. They built temples dedicated to a god or goddess within a sanctuary, or sacred area. They set aside land for an **agora**, an open-air marketplace where citizens could gather to discuss politics and other matters of local interest. Later communities often built an outdoor theater and usually surrounded their city center with a wall. These elements came to define the Greek city-state, known to the Greeks as a **polis** (PAW-luhs).

ORGANIZATION AND SPREAD OF CITY-STATES

Recall that mountains cover much of Greece. In ancient times, this terrain made overland travel and communication difficult, so Greeks tended to orient themselves toward the sea. Since mountain ranges divided the landmass, developing city-states were isolated.

Greek City-States, c. 500 B.C.E.

128 CHAPTER 5

Those city-states tended to be located in fertile valleys or on coastal plains, often with no land route directly linking them to other population centers. Unlike the diverse Persian Empire, all Greeks spoke the same language and worshiped the same gods. But isolation limited cooperation among city-states and also made it highly unlikely that a single ruler could control all of them. As a result, there was no unified nation called Greece. Each city-state ruled itself. Most remained small, with perhaps a few thousand people, but each one had its own food sources, court system, and army.

As early as the 800s B.C.E., Greeks began to migrate eastward across the Aegean Sea, settling in coastal Anatolia and nearby islands. There they established trading posts. Over the next 200 years, Greek emigrants formed their own small city-states, not only in the eastern Aegean but along the Black Sea and in what is today southern Italy, Sicily, France, Spain, and northern Africa. These communities remained linked to the metropolis, or "mother city," through trade.

SPARTA AND ATHENS

The evolution of the polis brought with it some novel political ideas. One was citizenship; all residents of a city-state, except foreigners and slaves, were citizens. Another was freedom of speech; citizens could speak freely about political issues. Yet another was the rule of law; citizens were subject to the laws and, whether rich or poor, enjoyed legal equality. (Women, though citizens, lacked certain rights; they could not participate in politics or own property.) Two dominant city-states, **Sparta** and **Athens**, are credited with promoting these and other groundbreaking political concepts.

Until around 600 B.C.E., a group of wealthy landowners or merchants governed most city-states. The warrior society Sparta took a different path. Two military leaders served as its kings but had limited power, and a council of about 30 elders, joined by the two kings, proposed the laws. This "rule by the few" made Sparta an **oligarchy**. An assembly of all free adult men voted on the laws, although they rarely **vetoed**, or voted against, any of them. This assembly marked Sparta as one of the first city-states to grant substantial political rights to its male citizens.

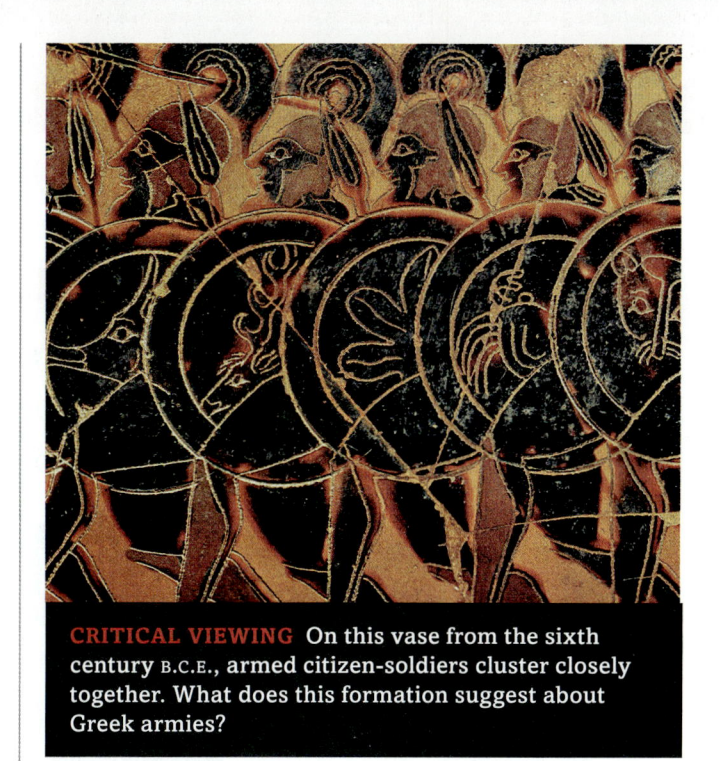

CRITICAL VIEWING On this vase from the sixth century B.C.E., armed citizen-soldiers cluster closely together. What does this formation suggest about Greek armies?

Men who descended from the original Spartans served full-time as citizen-soldiers, or **hoplites**. Spartan hoplites were not permitted to farm or engage in business, but they could vote in the assembly. Male descendants of the first peoples conquered by Sparta could own land and work as artisans and traders. However, unlike citizens, they could not vote in the assembly. Women could not vote either, but they enjoyed more freedoms than women in some other city-states. For example, they ran their husbands' estates when men were away at war. State-owned slaves known as **helots** did the farming and domestic work.

Athens was not a warrior society, but—like Sparta—it could field a powerful army of citizen-soldiers. Recall that when the Persian army invaded in 490 B.C.E., the Athenians beat them back at the Battle of Marathon. Athenians and Spartans later joined forces to repel a second Persian invasion in 480 B.C.E. In the key battle, the Athenian navy destroyed the Persian fleet.

In both Athens and Sparta, citizens had significant rights and freedoms. However, Athenians outdid Spartans by establishing a more open political system: the world's first democracy.

HISTORICAL THINKING

1. **READING CHECK** How did geography impact ancient Greece's attempt to form a united country?

2. **ANALYZE CAUSE AND EFFECT** What factors helped rebuild the ancient Greek civilization?

3. **COMPARE AND CONTRAST** How do the rights of citizens in the Greek polis compare with the rights citizens enjoy today in similar societies?

2.1 MAIN IDEA Athenian political reformers developed a system of government based on democratic ideals.

Democracy in Athens

In a world of pharaohs, kings, and emperors, how did Athens end up ruled by the people? Democracy did not just suddenly appear. It developed slowly, sparked by popular discontent and brought to life by a few reform-minded politicians.

GOVERNMENT REFORMS

By the 600s B.C.E., the sharp rise in agricultural productivity had boosted the population of Athens's peasant farmers. Some free owners of small farms started to demand a greater say in governing the city-state. At this time, every male citizen, whether poor or prosperous, had the right to take part in the assembly, whose main job was to elect the nine **archons**, or chief rulers. However, all candidates for the position of archon were **aristocrats**, people of wealth and high social rank. Athens was not yet a **democracy**, the form of government in which common citizens have a voice in making decisions and choosing leaders.

ELECTED BY LOTTERY Athenians used this machine, known as a *kleroterion*, to elect officials. Each eligible male placed a token with his name on it in one of the slots. A series of balls were then released from a tube to determine whose tokens would be chosen.

Conflict among the archons, along with a declining economy, led to instability in Athens; peasants suffered greatly during this uncertainty and threatened to rebel. In 594 B.C.E., Athenians gave special powers to a single leader named **Solon** (SOH-luhn). To restore peace, he enacted reforms aimed at lessening the financial burden on the poor and increasing political participation. He abolished a tax on crops, canceled debts, and freed peasants and others who had been sold into slavery to pay their debts.

Solon also reformed the political process by establishing four categories of Athenians that had varying levels of political power. Male citizens were assigned to each category based on how much income their land produced. As a result, the wealthiest Athenians in the top two categories filled the most important government roles. Hoplites, including some landowning peasants, gained other positions. As members of a lower class, laborers were not eligible for office, but as citizens, they could vote on substantive issues in the assembly. The matters up for a vote were drafted by a Council of 400, which still consisted mainly of aristocrats. Athens was slowly becoming more democratic.

DEMOCRACY IN ACTION

In 508 B.C.E., additional popular reforms were promoted by an archon named **Cleisthenes** (KLYS-thuh-neez) who established a new form of government. All male citizens over the age of 20—roughly 10 percent of a total population of some 300,000—could join the assembly and had an equal right to speak and to vote on issues of public policy. Democracy was still limited, though, since women and slaves were not allowed to participate.

The City of Athens, c. 400 B.C.E.

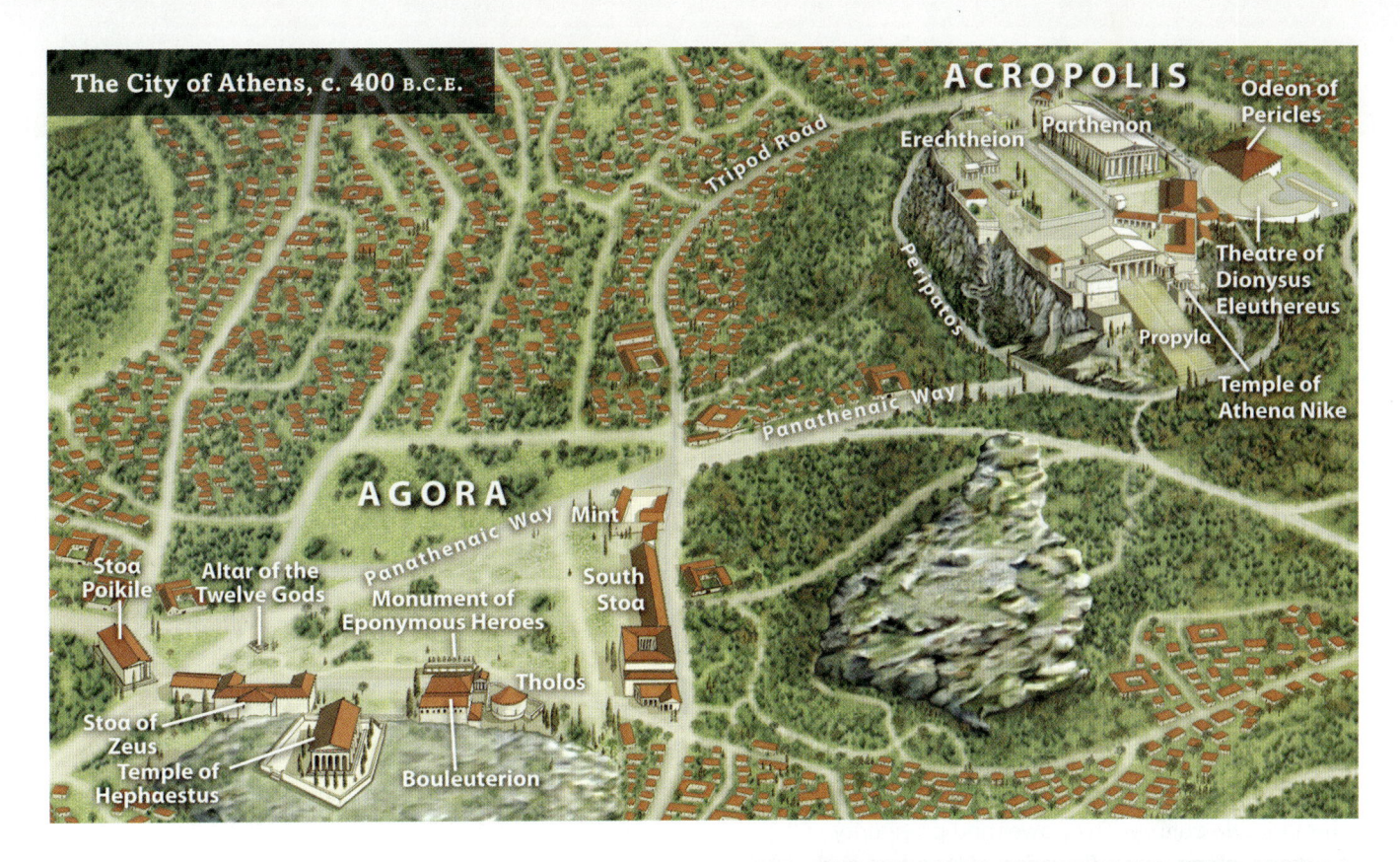

The assembly met outdoors about 40 times a year. At least 6,000 citizens had to attend to ensure a **quorum**, or the minimum number required to conduct the assembly's business. During the assembly, which typically lasted a few hours, citizens voted by a show of hands. A newly formed council prepared the agenda for each assembly. Unlike Solon's council, this Council of 500 represented a cross-section of the Athenian population, not just aristocrats, and its members came from all parts of the city-state. Athens had created the world's first democracy. It is known as a direct democracy because individual citizens participated directly in the making of laws and policies.

In the 450s B.C.E., an Athenian general and politician named **Pericles** (PEHR-uh-kleez) helped expand that democracy. Based on his proposal, members of the council started to receive a small stipend, or living allowance, and so did jurors—the 6,000 citizens over the age of 30 who, in groups of various sizes, had the right to decide legal cases. Pericles believed that individuals had a duty to take part in their political system. Paying citizens for their service made it much more likely that even poor Athenians would be able to participate.

Athenian citizens were proud of their achievements. They had the liberty to participate in decision making, freedom of speech, and political equality. The opportunity existed for every male citizen, whether rich or poor, to offer opinions in the council, speak his mind at the assembly, or judge cases brought before a court.

Around 431 B.C.E., Pericles spoke publicly to honor soldiers who had died in a recent battle. In his speech, Pericles spoke highly of Athenian democracy. The Greek historian **Thucydides** (thoo-SIH-duh-deez) wrote an account of the speech.

PRIMARY SOURCE

In our form of government we are not imitators, but set the pattern for others. We are a democracy. Equality is at the basis of our laws, merit at the basis of our public preferment [advancement, as in rank or office]. The poor and the rich have an equal chance to contribute to the public weal [well-being], as well as to enjoy the honors in the gift of the state. The same spirit pervades throughout the private life of our citizens and we render cheerful obedience both to the written laws of the state and to the unwritten laws of society.

—from *The Funeral Oration of Pericles*

HISTORICAL THINKING

1. **READING CHECK** What significant democratic change did Cleisthenes make to the council?
2. **IDENTIFY** How did Solon try to balance political power between the wealthy and less wealthy?
3. **FORM AND SUPPORT OPINIONS** How do you think people living in Athens felt about the Athenian assembly as established under Cleisthenes? Respond from the perspective of one of the following: an aristocrat, a peasant, a laborer, or a woman.

Greek Civilization

2.2

MAIN IDEA During the time of Pericles, Athenians produced literary works and architecture that reflected their city's impressive artistic innovations.

Pericles and Cultural Advances

From time to time, a society defines what it means to be great. For a period in the fifth century B.C.E., Athens embodied this excellence. This Greek city-state could boast not only a powerful military and a democratic government but also an exceptional culture that left a powerful global legacy.

GOLDEN AGE OF ATHENS

With the Greek victory in the Greco-Persian Wars (490–479 B.C.E.), Athens rose to a position of leadership in an alliance of Greek city-states. Its superiority, however, rested on more than its military and economic strength. In the decades that followed, Athens forged a remarkable culture. The power and prosperity of Athens, along with a flowering of literature and architecture, made this a golden age, a period of great cultural achievement.

In 472 B.C.E., the Athenian playwright **Aeschylus** (EH-skuh-luhs) wrote a play, a tragedy that still survives today. Titled *The Persians,* it explores the story of the Greco-Persian Wars from the point of view of the Persians—and with some sympathy for their fate. Unlike earlier dramas, which had a single character, *The Persians* introduced a second character to the stage. Having two characters onstage allowed the plot to include conflict. Greek dramas also relied on a chorus, a group of players who commented on the action, usually through song.

The Parthenon at the Acropolis, shown here at dawn, is one of the most recognizable buildings in the world.

Hundreds of plays, most of which were tragedies, would appear during this century, including those written by **Sophocles** (SAH-fuh-kleez) and **Euripides** (yoo-RIHP-uh-deez). Sophocles added a third character to his plays and introduced painted scenery. Euripides is known for the strong, heroic women in his dramas. Another literary genre, the Greek comedy, also flourished during this time. Its leading playwright, **Aristophanes** (air-ih-STAH-fuh-neez), poked fun at well-known members of Athenian society through the use of colorful language, nonsense, and satire—humor and sarcasm used to expose or ridicule human foolishness or weakness.

THE PARTHENON AND RELIGION

Sophocles may have modeled one of his characters on Pericles; the two men knew each other and may even have been friends. As you have read, Pericles supported democratic government in the 450s B.C.E. He also promoted the arts, including theater and the fine arts of sculpture and vase painting.

Athena, protector of Athens and goddess of wisdom and war, marches forward on this Hellenistic coin dated to the fourth century B.C.E.

In addition, Pericles used his influence with the assembly to pursue a building campaign in Athens. His goal was to make the city as physically impressive as it was politically powerful. The centerpiece of Athens's reconstruction was the **Parthenon**, built between 447 and 432 B.C.E. This temple honored Athena, goddess of wisdom and war and protector of the city-state, and also served as a memorial to people who had died in the Greco-Persian Wars. A two-room structure surrounded by tall columns, the Parthenon sat atop the Acropolis, a rocky hill jutting up from the center of Athens.

Athena was one of many deities—gods and goddesses—worshiped by Athenians, who also built sanctuaries and other structures to honor Zeus (king of the gods), Hephaestus (god of fire), and Dionysus (god of wine and theater). The Greeks believed their gods and goddesses observed people from high upon Mount Olympus, the tallest mountain in mainland Greece. The ancient Greeks showed their devotion to their deities through animal sacrifices, which took place within a sanctuary.

Women played a central role as priestesses in these rituals. Although women were shut out of the political realm, they could still participate in Greek culture in this meaningful way. The worship of Athena and other powerful goddesses, such as Artemis (goddess of the hunt), Aphrodite (goddess of love), and Demeter (goddess of agriculture), also indicates how much ancient Greek society valued women.

As Greeks, the Athenians and Spartans had much in common culturally and historically. They worshiped most of the same gods and goddesses. They had cooperated to defeat the invading Persians. However, in the late fifth century B.C.E., these two city-states competed to dominate the Greek world. This competition led to conflict.

HISTORICAL THINKING

1. **READING CHECK** How did Pericles influence Athenian culture?

2. **DRAW CONCLUSIONS** What other culture, ancient or otherwise, do you think deserves to be described as "great"? Why?

3. **MAKE GENERALIZATIONS** Why do you think people today still enjoy Greek drama and find beauty in Greek art and architecture?

Greek Civilization 133

2.3 A Global Commodity: Gold

People have probably been obsessed with gold ever since early humans first spied the lustrous metal in streams. Since then, gold has been prized by cultures and civilizations all over the globe. Its malleability made it easy to work with and shape, but gold's beauty, weight, and permanence made it a fitting symbol of rulers and gods. During Greece's golden age, gold became more than a desirable **commodity**, or valuable trade good. Greek traders at this time exchanged their goods for gold but also used coins made of gold and silver as money.

The Greeks founded colonies around the Mediterranean in part to obtain raw materials their homeland couldn't provide, including gold. Laborers toiled deep in the underground gold mines of Thrace, setting fires to break down gold-bearing rocks. The ancient Greek philosopher Aristotle believed that gold formed underground when hardened water was transformed by the sun's rays—a fittingly poetic story for this most precious of metals.

Why did myths and stories arise about gold throughout the ancient world?

WORTH ITS WEIGHT IN GOLD

As good as gold. The streets are paved with gold. These are just a few of the phrases that extol the value of gold. Before it was used as money, gold's fundamental value was accepted by all cultures. In ancient times, when gold's uses were mostly decorative, the Egyptians, Chinese, Indians, and others forced prisoners of war and slaves to mine for the metal. And gold continues to dazzle people today. In this photo, a miner holds aloft a stone extracted from a mine in the Central American country of El Salvador that contains precious gold minerals.

OPEN-CUT GOLD MINE

When gold is close to the surface, miners often use the open-cut, or open-pit, method to extract it. First, the vegetation and soil are cleared away, then the rock layer is blasted, and finally the pit is dug. The walls of the pit are stepped to help prevent rock falls. And engineers build a road along the side of the pit so that trucks can haul the ore and rocks away. The mineral belt in this open-cut mine in Cobar, Australia, is clearly visible.

GOLD AT A GLANCE

USES	Ancient cultures used gold to make jewelry and shrines and images to honor their gods.	For thousands of years, gold in the form of standardized coins was used as money in trade.	Today, gold is used in such fields as medicine, industry, electronics, and dentistry.
VALUE	Gold's rarity and the difficulties involved in finding and extracting it have added to its value and desirability.	The Phoenicians traded to obtain many precious metals but determined that gold was worth four times more than silver.	Gold is measured according to weight and was priced at more than $1,300 per ounce by markets in 2017.
PRODUCTION	Placer mining uses water to separate gold from loose materials such as gravel and sand.	Most gold is mined and extracted from deposits of rocks found deep underground or in open pits.	Copper mines often contain significant amounts of gold in addition to copper.
HISTORY	The first pure gold coins were produced in the 6th century B.C.E. in the ancient kingdom of Lydia under King Croesus, whose wealth was legendary.	Gold discovered in the Sacramento Valley in 1848 sparked a rush of immigrants to the area and spurred statehood for California.	Archaeologists feared that the Bactrian Hoard, a trove of Afghan gold dating from the 1st century C.E., had been stolen, but it was found in 2003.
ECONOMICS	When Mali emperor Mansa Musa traveled to Cairo, Egypt, in the 1300s, he spent so much gold there that its value declined.	Between 1871 and 1914, many nations adopted the gold standard, which linked the value of a country's currency directly to gold.	In 2017, the world's leading producer of gold was China, followed by Australia, Russia, and the United States.

Greek Civilization

What properties of gold do the photos in this lesson demonstrate?

"I HAVE GAZED ON THE FACE OF AGAMEMNON"

Thus wrote Heinrich Schliemann after he uncovered a 3,000-year-old mask in a tomb at the archaeological site of Mycenae. The German archaeologist was sure it was the funerary mask of Agamemnon, the powerful king of Mycenae. Schliemann then found another mask, the one shown here, in the same tomb. However, modern research has dated the masks and determined that they were made about 300 years before the king lived, if he did exist. Both masks were made of a very thin sheet of gold, but the features of the second one were much more defined and portrayed a recognizable face of a man. As a result, this mask is often referred to as the Mask of Agamemnon.

GOLD DIADEM

This woven gold diadem, or crown, was found in the tomb of the Macedonian king Philip II, father of Alexander the Great. It is made of tiny movable parts that would make beautiful sounds when the wind blew through its leaves.

Greek Civilization 137

3.1 | **MAIN IDEA** Continual conflict among the Greek city-states left them vulnerable to an invasion by the Macedonians.

The Peloponnesian War

What seems like a minor dispute can sometimes lead to major trouble. Although Greek city-states repeatedly quarreled with one another, daily life often went on as usual. When the two most powerful city-states went to war, however, the severe consequences rippled throughout the area.

A CLASH OF ALLIANCES

After the Greco-Persian Wars ended, Athens formed the **Delian League** in 478 B.C.E. This alliance included the city-states along the northern and eastern Aegean coast and nearly all of the Aegean islands. The stated purpose of the league was to eliminate the continued Persian threat to the region. By the mid-450s B.C.E., Athens controlled the league. It forced other members to pay tribute in the form of dues to support the Athenian navy.

The other dominant Greek city-state, Sparta, led an alliance known as the **Peloponnesian League**. Sparta had long controlled much of the land on the Peloponnese, a large peninsula at the far south of the Greek mainland. The Spartans believed that they, not the Athenians, should lead the Greeks. The rivalry between Athens and Sparta led to the **Peloponnesian War**, fought from 431 to 404 B.C.E.

The Delian League and the Peloponnesian League squared off in a series of battles. Athens had naval superiority and plenty of money, mainly from tribute, but Sparta could field a stronger army. The two powers invaded each other's territory, clashing both at sea and on land. Key leaders were killed in battle or by disease—in 429 B.C.E., Pericles died as a result of a plague that swept through Athens. In 404 B.C.E., the Spartan-led Peloponnesian League, with the help of Persian armies, finally defeated Athens and the Delian League.

During the conflict, Athens was home to the influential philosopher **Socrates** (SAH-kruh-teez). Socrates was accused of corrupting his students by leading them to question the gods and the authorities. He also became entangled in a political conflict. Just after the war, an oligarchy replaced Athens's democracy. Democratic forces quickly regained control of the government, but some leaders suspected that Socrates had sided with the oligarchy. In 399 B.C.E., after a public trial at which he claimed his innocence, he submitted to execution by drinking a cup of hemlock, a poison.

CRITICAL VIEWING A frieze from the Nereid Monument (390–380 B.C.E.) found near present-day Turkey shows soldiers clashing in combat. What do you notice about the battling warriors?

THE AFTERMATH OF WAR

Nearly all the Greek city-states suffered as a result of the Peloponnesian War. Their armies, including that of Sparta, were severely weakened. The war also drained the Athenian treasury and shattered Athens's navy.

138 CHAPTER 5

Sparta, Athens, and a third city-state, Thebes, had recovered enough by the 370s B.C.E. to continue to attack one another. By the 350s B.C.E., it was clear that none of them had the strength to dominate the Greek world. Exhausted by warfare, the Greeks would find it difficult to respond to an unexpected challenge.

That challenge came from Macedonia, a kingdom in the far-northern mainland with no cities and few farms, mainly populated by Greek-speaking people. Its ruler, **Philip II**, had created a highly skilled army of paid troops. His infantry, or foot soldiers, fought in closely packed units. From the pack they thrust pikes—long poles with sharp spearheads—at the enemy. Philip dreamed of using that army to conquer the Persian Empire, but he first looked southward.

In the 350s and 340s B.C.E., through force of arms as well as bribery, Philip gained the loyalty of much of northern and central Greece. Then, in 338 B.C.E., the Macedonians and their Greek allies defeated a **coalition**, or temporary alliance, of southern Greek city-states. Philip forced people whom he conquered to join his alliance. Greek city-states would keep a measure of political freedom, but never again would they be fully independent actors on the world stage.

The city-states contributed soldiers and other resources to Philip in support of his mission to defeat the Persian Empire. Philip, however, did not live long enough to lead that quest. In 336 B.C.E., a fellow Macedonian assassinated him. It would be up to Philip's son Alexander to carry out his dream.

This 1787 painting by French artist Jacques-Louis David is called *The Death of Socrates*. It shows the philosopher surrounded by his grief-stricken disciples. Socrates continues teaching even as he reaches for the cup of hemlock, a poison that will kill him.

HISTORICAL THINKING

1. **READING CHECK** What were the consequences of the Peloponnesian War and the later conflicts among the Greek city-states?

2. **MAKE INFERENCES** Why do you think the Spartans might have feared the aggressive expansion of Athens's power in the years before the Peloponnesian War?

3. **FORM AND SUPPORT OPINIONS** Do you think the establishment of military alliances may have incited the Peloponnesian War? Why or why not?

Greek Civilization

3.2

MAIN IDEA The conquest of Persia by Alexander the Great led to the mixing and sharing of cultures and ideas across the ancient world, such as the spread of Greek ideas into Asia and Africa.

Alexander the Great

What does it take to persuade thousands of people to leave their homeland and travel to hostile, unknown lands, perhaps never to return? Alexander of Macedonia—later known as Alexander the Great—had both the intelligence and the ambition to seize that chance.

CONQUEST OF PERSIA

Alexander, son of Philip II, set off for Persia in 334 B.C.E. with an army of battle-tested Macedonians and Greeks. They traveled east and then south into Anatolia. The first clash against the Persians at the River Granicus revealed Alexander's leadership style. Wearing armor and a brightly colored cloak, he charged into the fray on horseback at the head of his cavalry. Alexander saw himself as a heroic warrior, and he sought to prove that on the battlefield.

Although Alexander's bravery inspired his troops, his brilliance as a military strategist likely was the key to his success. He led his army through Anatolia and south along the Mediterranean coast to Egypt, where the Egyptians welcomed Alexander after his victory there and treated him as if he were a pharaoh.

Many battles followed as Alexander pursued the Persian king, Darius III. By April of 330 B.C.E., Alexander's army had captured the Persian capitals of Susa and Persepolis. That summer, a Persian official murdered Darius, and Alexander's conquest was complete: the empire was his. Still, Alexander and his soldiers marched on. By the time the military campaign was finished, Alexander had led them on a journey of some 11,000 miles that had taken them as far east as present-day Afghanistan and India. Alexander never returned to Macedonia; in 323 B.C.E., at the age of 32, he developed a fever and died.

GREEK INFLUENCE AND CULTURAL CREATIVITY

The effects of Alexander's conquests lasted far longer than his brief reign. For example, his soldiers had a major impact. Thousands of them stayed in different parts of Southwest and Central Asia, and they often

This Roman marble copy of a Greek bronze original sculpture depicts Alexander as Helios, the god and personification of the sun.

married local women. Over time, these men introduced Greek culture and ideas over a large geographic area, and newly opened trade routes in this region had a similar effect. This process by which Greek culture was diffused throughout the Persian Empire is known as **Hellenization**, which comes from the Greek word for Greece: *Hellas*.

Greek culture, however, did not completely overwhelm Persian culture in the Hellenized areas. Alexander himself had adopted Persian dress and Persian customs. As king of Persia, he modeled his army, administration, and tax system on those of the Persians. He also learned from the experience of earlier Persian kings, including Cyrus the Great. Those kings gained the support of local leaders by preserving their authority and respecting local customs and beliefs.

Alexander's Empire, c. 323 B.C.E.

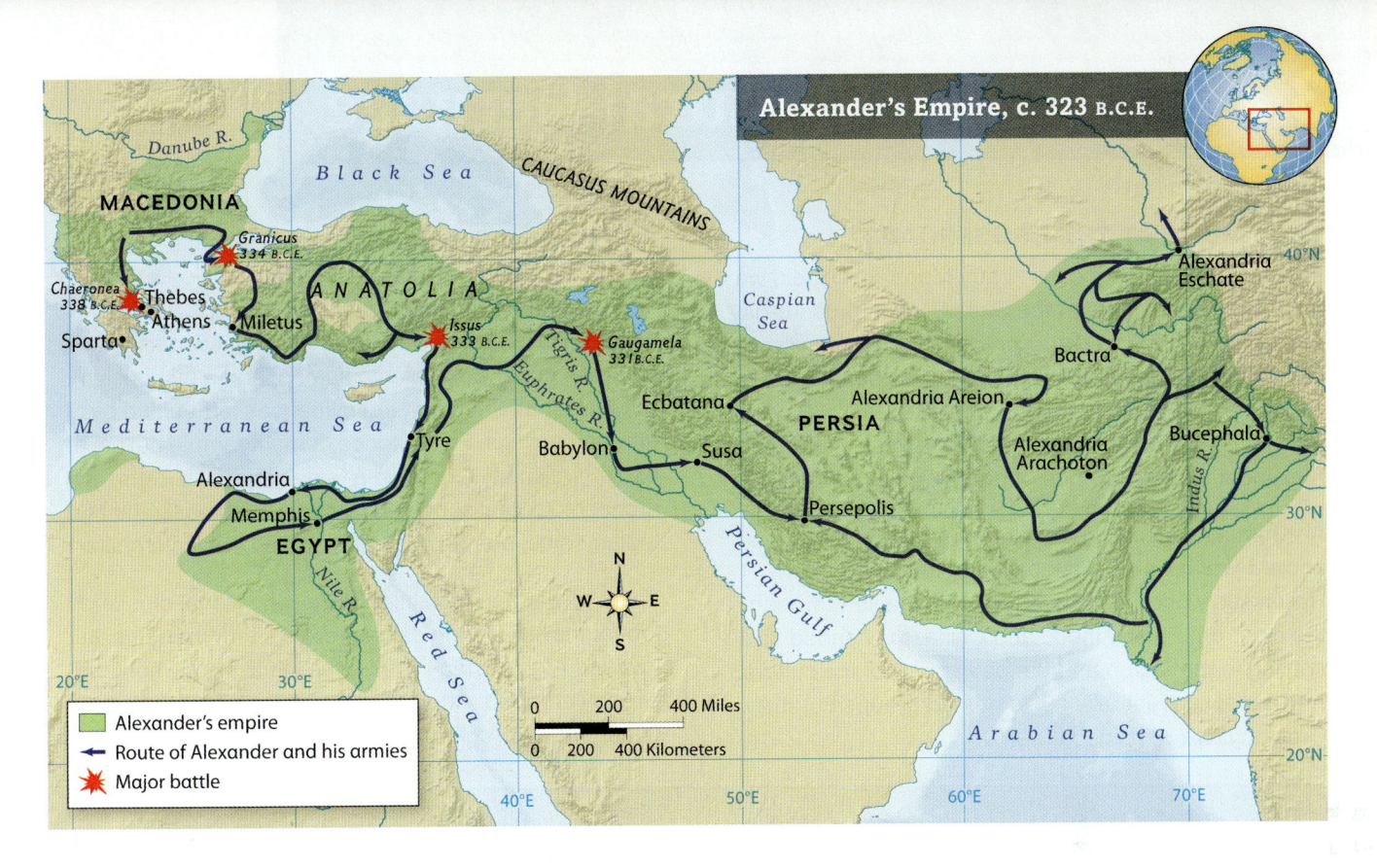

Soldiers who settled in Persia kept many of their Greek ways but not all of them. Archaeologists have unearthed a city in Afghanistan that reflects a creative mix of cultures. Founded in 300 B.C.E., it has all the characteristic buildings of a Greek town. Soil was mounded into an acropolis some 200 feet high, and a semicircular structure served as a theater. The city's palace had rows of Greek columns, but its layout, with huge open spaces, was clearly Persian. Also, temples in the town honored Greek gods as well as those of local civilizations.

Egypt offers an even more striking example, where Greek, Persian, and African cultures intertwined and merged as a result of the Greek conquest. After Alexander died, each of his three generals ruled a main section of the empire. Egypt went to Ptolemy. Like the other generals—and Alexander before them—Ptolemy adopted elements of Persian culture and methods of administration. He established a community of religious worship that merged Greek and Egyptian gods, and he also restored temples that the Persians had destroyed. Ptolemy gave the highest royal posts to Macedonians and Greeks, many of whom had migrated from their homelands. Even though most government tasks, such as collecting taxes, were carried out by local officials, he opened positions in his army to Egyptians.

Ptolemy moved Egypt's capital from Memphis to **Alexandria**. There, he built what became a renowned library. His successors, during what is called Egypt's Ptolemaic period, further developed this city into a major center of learning.

Scholars from many different fields settled in Alexandria. Inspired by one another, they made a number of important scientific breakthroughs. Around 300 B.C.E., a mathematician named **Euclid** (YOO-kluhd) wrote a book titled *The Elements*, which gave the world its first systematic explanation of geometry. Drawing on Euclid's teachings, **Eratosthenes** (air-uh-TAHS-thuh-neez) devised an ingenious experiment to measure the circumference, or distance around, Earth. Applying his knowledge of parallel lines and angles, Eratosthenes came very close to determining the planet's actual circumference. He surprised everyone by showing that Earth is much larger than they had thought.

HISTORICAL THINKING

1. **READING CHECK** What traits helped Alexander lead his army to victory over the Persians?

2. **INTERPRET MAPS** What labels on the map imply that followers of Alexander settled in those places and likely introduced Greek culture?

3. **SYNTHESIZE** Describe the culture that developed in regions of the Persian Empire conquered by Alexander.

Greek Civilization 141

3.3 Preserving Cultural Heritage

LADY MOON AT THE CROSSROADS

Ai-Khanoum, which means "Lady Moon" in Uzbek, was an ancient Greek city on the Oxus River in present-day Afghanistan that was discovered in 1961. Originally part of the Persian Empire, the area was conquered by Alexander the Great in the fourth century B.C.E. However, the city itself wasn't established until 300 B.C.E., after Alexander's death, by one of his generals, Antiochus I.

Ai-Khanoum was an important crossroads of the ancient world—a vital link between India and the Hellenistic world. As different people passed through the city from Persia, India, and China, they ended up settling in the region and becoming part of the culture. Ai-Khanoum eventually fell to nomad groups but the Greek culture remained.

Archaeological findings from this ancient site illustrate a blend of Greek and Asian traditions, key to understanding the Hellenization of the East. The city had the classic features of a Greek city, such as temples to Greek gods, Corinthian columns, and a gymnasium, but it also reflected cultural influences left behind by different groups. For instance, a main temple built in an early Persian style housed a Greek statue of Zeus, and archaeologists discovered artifacts such as Greek and Indian coins, nomadic jewelry, and an Iranian fire altar.

Years of war and instability along with illegal digs and looting have severely damaged the site. When Russia invaded Afghanistan in 1979, the initial excavation had already stopped. After 10 years of war, Soviet troops finally left, but Afghanistan's troubles were far from over.

IVORY STATUETTES, C. FIRST CENTURY C.E.

In the ancient world, ivory was a symbol of luxury. These small sculptures were found in Bagram, a settlement in what is now Afghanistan. Bagram and Ai-Khanoum were both trading outposts on the Silk Roads. The blending of cultural influences in these figures—thought to be furniture ornaments or supports, perhaps for a table—is readily apparent. Each statue features a woman in Hellenistic-style dress standing on the back of a *makara*, a Hindu monster that was half land animal, half sea creature.

Years of instability continued as a civil war progressed, and then in 1996 the Taliban, an extremist Islamic militia, took control. Fighting raged on until 2001.

In 2003, after peace and stability had been re-established, Afghan treasures were revealed, some having been kept safe by the Afghan government who deliberately took them from the National Museum and concealed them. Some of those artifacts came from Ai-Khanoum.

While Ai-Khanoum no longer exists, artifacts remain and efforts are being made to reconstruct the city through computer graphics. In 2005, archaeologists inventoried the Ai-Khanoum collection. It is through these efforts that the cultural legacy of important settlements like Ai-Khanoum can be preserved.

HISTORICAL THINKING

MAKE CONNECTIONS What can preserving an ancient city like Ai-Khanoum tell us about the world?

This first-century-C.E. goblet is a rare example of an almost complete piece of glassware from the era. Discovered in Bagram, it depicts four people surrounded by palm trees, harvesting dates.

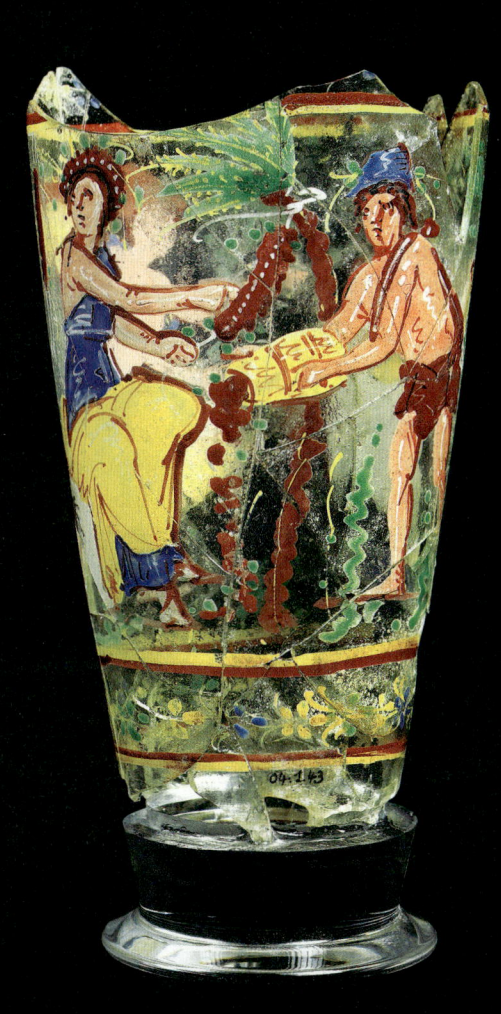

An Afghan worker carefully restores a blue blown-glass vase, also found in Bagram. The carved vessel dates to the first century C.E. and is probably of Greek origin.

On this gilded silver ceremonial plaque from the beginning of the third century B.C.E., Cybèle (the Phrygian goddess of nature) and Nike (the Greek goddess of victory) ride together in a lion-drawn chariot. The disk found in Ai-Khanoum includes symbols from both Anatolia and Greece, showing a synthesis of gods from different regions and religions.

Greek Civilization 143

3.4

MAIN IDEA The ancient Greeks developed a civilization whose impact spread far beyond its borders—and that influence can still be felt today.

The Legacy of Ancient Greece

When people refer to something today as "classical," it suggests that it meets a traditional standard of excellence. Historians also apply the term *classical* to an era in ancient Greece (from 500 to 323 B.C.E.) that set several standards for later civilizations.

GOVERNMENT AND CITIZENSHIP

Democracy, as a system of government, is practiced in many parts of the world today, and any discussion of the sources of modern democracy must refer to ancient Greece. As you have already learned, the Athenians established a direct democracy, a system in which male citizens (a status that excluded foreigners and slaves) had the right to vote in the assembly. Furthermore, according to leaders such as Pericles, these citizens had the responsibility to participate in civic affairs.

Today, democracy still means the participation of common people in government decision-making, just as it did in ancient Athens. Athenians also believed, as every true democracy does today, that all citizens are subject to the rule of law and all enjoy equality before the law. The rights of citizenship, however, have expanded in most present-day democracies to include women, and, since slavery is illegal throughout the world, each individual in a democracy who meets age and residency requirements has rights and a voice.

ART AND ARCHITECTURE

The Parthenon is one of the best examples of classical Greek architecture. This marble temple, perched high atop the Acropolis in Athens, represented the power and wealth of the Greek city-state. Tall columns similar to the Parthenon's can be found in places such as the Supreme Court Building in Washington, D.C., and the British Museum in London. Modern versions of other types of Greek architecture, such as outdoor theaters and sports stadiums, can be found all over the world.

Within the Parthenon stood a magnificent gold and ivory statue of the goddess Athena. A frieze, or horizontal band of sculpted marble showing a festival procession, adorned an inside wall of the temple. Later Greek sculptors preferred to work in bronze. Their sculptures would influence Roman artists, some of whom crafted marble copies of Greek statues.

Greeks of the classical era are also well known for excellence in several styles of painting. Fresco painters applied pigment directly onto walls covered with freshly wet plaster. Paintings on wooden panels included portraits, still lifes, battle scenes, and legendary figures. Another specialized technique in ancient Greece was vase painting. The subject matter of these various painting styles has given historians insight into ancient Greek society.

Alexander the Great was a great supporter of the arts. Through Hellenization, Greek arts spread throughout the lands of the former Persian Empire. At the same time, Greek colonies in southern Italy transferred artistic styles to local cultures—and eventually to Rome and beyond.

LITERATURE AND PHILOSOPHY

As you have already read, historians credit Homer with writing the *Iliad* and the *Odyssey*—two works key to Western civilization and literature—in the 700s B.C.E. Based on observations of other cultures with an oral tradition, scholars believe these epic poems might well be the product of centuries of storytelling, tales passed from generation to generation until they were written down. Whatever their origin, these classical stories still fascinate readers today. Translations in a variety of languages continue to join the hundreds of previous interpretations of these classics.

What would literature be without letters? Although the Greeks did not invent the alphabet, they refined it. Credit for the invention, however, goes to various peoples of the eastern Mediterranean, including the

CRITICAL VIEWING The Hellenistic masterpiece *Winged Victory of Samothrace* dates from the second century B.C.E. The marble statue depicts Nike, the Greek goddess of victory, and was probably built to celebrate a naval triumph. In what ways does the statue celebrate ancient Greek values?

Phoenicians. Over time, the Greeks transmitted their alphabet to other cultures, and it spread throughout much of the world.

The historian Thucydides lived and wrote in the 400s B.C.E. He based much of his *History of the Peloponnesian War* on personal observation—as an Athenian, he served as a general in the war. He also relied on information provided by eyewitnesses. Thucydides therefore set a standard of objective writing for future historians.

Other Athenian writers of this era focused on drama. The playwrights Aeschylus, Sophocles, and Euripides wrote tragedies, such as the *Orestia*, *Antigone*, and *Medea*, that are still performed today—and not just in Greece. The comedies of Aristophanes have also enjoyed revivals through the ages. These dramas are classics, and their universal themes such as pride, personal relationships, and justice remain relevant to modern audiences.

Socrates was not the only famous Athenian philosopher. **Plato** (PLAY-toh) and **Aristotle** (AIR-uh-stah-tuhl) were two thinkers who emphasized the power of human reason to describe the world and to guide proper human behavior. Plato was born around 428 B.C.E. He and his pupil Aristotle addressed a question that still provokes debate today: What is reality? Plato proposed the notion that an ideal reality exists beyond the physical world. Within this invisible world are what he called Forms: perfect versions of universal ideas such as Goodness, Beauty, or Justice. Aristotle disagreed, arguing that the earthly forms were all that existed.

Plato had a vision of the ideal government. It was not a democracy. He favored rule by "guardians," an aristocracy of highly educated people who would promote the common good. He called these people philosophers, a term that means "lovers of wisdom." The ideal rulers would also be politically skilled so that they might better be called philosopher kings or—as Plato added—philosopher queens.

PRIMARY SOURCE

Until philosophers are kings, or the kings and princes of this world have the spirit and power of philosophy, and political greatness and wisdom meet in one, and those commoner natures who pursue either to the exclusion of the other are compelled to stand aside, cities will never have rest from their evils—nor the human race, as I believe—and then only will this our State have a possibility of life and behold the light of day.

—from Book V of *The Republic* by Plato, c. 380 B.C.E.

In his best-known work, *The Republic*, Plato examines the concept of justice as it relates to various systems of government. He explores this and other ideas in dialogues in which his teacher, Socrates, and others engage in back-and-forth discussions of often complex philosophical issues. Plato also tried to identify moral and ethical principles, or general rules of proper conduct or behavior, and sought to define a virtuous way of life.

Aristotle, too, wrote about ethics and virtue, which is moral excellence or "right living." For his book *Politics*, he studied Athens and other Greek city-states as a way of determining what an ideal community of virtuous citizens might look like. Aristotle, who lived from 384 to 322 B.C.E., migrated to Athens from Macedonia and lived long enough to witness the conquest of the southern Greek city-states by Philip II.

Another famous Alexandrian was the Jewish philosopher **Philo Judaeus**, who lived during the later Ptolemaic period, many years after Plato's time. Philo was strongly influenced by Plato, and he kept the earlier philosopher and his teachings in mind as Philo attempted to synthesize Greek philosophy and Jewish scripture. His effort emphasizes the impact of cross-cultural influences during the Hellenistic period.

MATHEMATICS AND SCIENCE

Anyone who has taken a course in geometry knows of the Pythagorean theorem. **Pythagoras** was born around 570 B.C.E. on Samos, an island in the eastern Aegean Sea. As an adult, he settled in a Greek colony in southern Italy, where he studied and taught mathematics. Pythagoras promoted the idea that numbers could explain everything about the world, and modern mathematicians and scientists continue to support and expand upon this idea. Pythagoras is also credited with a breakthrough mathematical analysis of musical harmony. His work in geometry led to advancements in astronomy as well.

As you have already learned, in 300 B.C.E. the Greek mathematician Euclid wrote *The Elements*, which is his treatise that developed geometry in a logical way. Translated from Greek into Arabic and then English, it influenced Muslim and European mathematicians for more than 2,000 years. Among his other accomplishments, Euclid devised a proof of the Pythagorean theorem. Later in the same century, Eratosthenes applied his pioneering work in the field of mathematical geography to measure the circumference of Earth. As you learned earlier, his calculation of Earth's circumference was close to Earth's actual circumference of 24,857 miles. Eratosthenes' work taught the Greeks that the known world occupied only a small section of Earth's northern hemisphere.

Legend has it that in the bath one day, the mathematician **Archimedes** (ahr-kuh-MEE-deez) suddenly shouted "Eureka!" (Greek for "I have found it!") because he had a key insight about the displacement of water as he rose from the tub. Archimedes was born in 287 B.C.E. in the Greek city-state of Syracuse in southern Italy. A genius with numbers, he calculated the approximate value of pi (π)—the ratio of the circumference of a circle to its diameter. Archimedes also excelled as an inventor; one of his inventions, the Archimedes screw, is still in use today. This simple machine, which is used for raising water, consists of a large screw within a pipe. Its users can dip one end of the device into a pond at an angle and then turn the screw to transport the water up the pipe for irrigation or other purposes.

Greek dramas from thousands of years ago remain relevant today. In 2017, a Japanese director presented his version of Sophocles' *Antigone* at an international theater festival in Avignon, France.

HISTORICAL THINKING

1. **READING CHECK** Which two cities in the Greek world, through their political, artistic, literary, or mathematical advances, had the greatest impact on subsequent civilizations?

2. **FORM AND SUPPORT OPINIONS** Of the writers, philosophers, and mathematicians described in this lesson, whose work do you think had the most practical value? Why?

3. **SYNTHESIZE** Much of the art produced by the ancient Greeks—sculptures and panel paintings, for example—has not survived. The same is true of some literature—for example, no original manuscript exists for the *Iliad*. How do we know about these artistic styles? How do we know the story of the *Iliad*?

4. **MAKE INFERENCES** How did the design of the Parthenon reflect Athenian culture?

Greek Civilization 147

CHAPTER 5 GREEK CIVILIZATION REVIEW

VOCABULARY

Match each vocabulary word with its definition.

1. alphabet
2. oligarchy
3. agora
4. polis
5. aristocrat
6. democracy
7. quorum
8. coalition
9. Hellenization

a. a temporary alliance
b. a form of government in which common citizens have a voice in making decisions and choosing leaders
c. a Greek city-state
d. the group of letters that form the individual elements of a writing system
e. a minimum number of people who must be present to conduct a group's business
f. the process by which Greek culture was spread throughout the Persian Empire
g. an open-air marketplace in a Greek city-state
h. a form of government ruled by a few powerful citizens
i. a person of wealth and high social rank

READING STRATEGY
IDENTIFY MAIN IDEAS AND DETAILS

Use a graphic organizer like the one below to identify the supporting details about Greek democracy. Then answer the question that follows.

Greek Democracy
Pay citizens for public service

10. Which members of Greek society were excluded from the democratic political process?

MAIN IDEAS

Answer the following questions. Support your answers with evidence from the chapter.

11. To which regions did Minoan sea traders carry their goods? **LESSON 1.2**
12. What valuable writing system did the Phoenicians introduce to the Greeks? **LESSON 1.3**
13. Why was Sparta considered a warrior society? **LESSON 1.4**
14. How did Athenian citizens participate in their democracy? **LESSON 2.1**
15. Why did Pericles undertake a building campaign in Athens? **LESSON 2.2**
16. How did the Peloponnesian War weaken the Greek city-states? **LESSON 3.1**
17. What effect did Alexander the Great's conquest of the Persian Empire have on Greek culture? **LESSON 3.2**
18. How did Plato's view of reality differ from that of Aristotle? **LESSON 3.4**

HISTORICAL THINKING

Answer the following questions. Support your answers with evidence from the chapter.

19. **MAKE PREDICTIONS** How might history have changed if the Persians had invaded Greece immediately after the Peloponnesian War?
20. **MAKE INFERENCES** Why do you think Pericles is considered one of the greatest Athenians?
21. **MAKE CONNECTIONS** How could artifacts help experts understand how Greek, Persian, and African cultures influence one another?
22. **MAKE GENERALIZATIONS** Discuss how the presence of writers, artists, mathematicians, and scientists can affect a civilization.
23. **FORM AND SUPPORT OPINIONS** Which city-state do you think would have been the more interesting place for a Greek to live, Athens or Alexandria? Explain your answer.

INTERPRET MAPS

Study the map, which shows the Athenian and Spartan alliances during the Peloponnesian War. Then answer the questions that follow.

24. Why do you think Corinth's geographic location made it one of Sparta's most important allies?

25. What information can you gather based on the numbers of Spartan and Athenian victories and their dates? Does this data indicate the winner of the war? Explain.

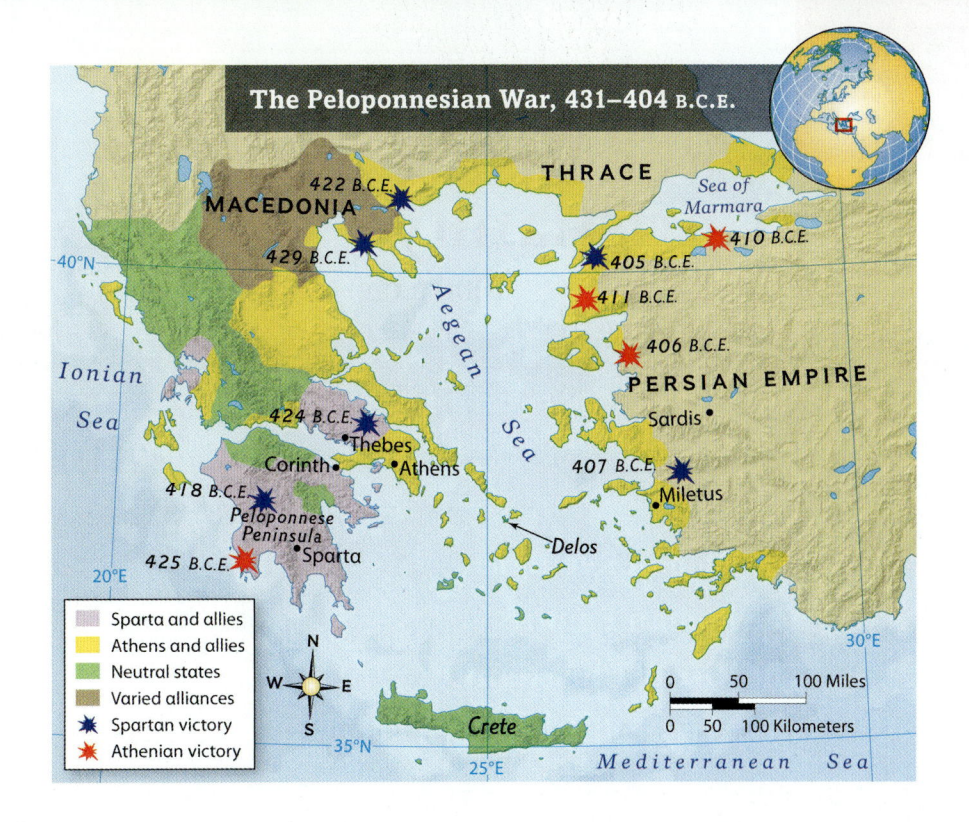

The Peloponnesian War, 431–404 B.C.E.

- Sparta and allies
- Athens and allies
- Neutral states
- Varied alliances
- ✦ Spartan victory
- ✦ Athenian victory

ANALYZE SOURCES

In the *Phaedo*, Plato describes the last hours before the death of Socrates. In this excerpt, Plato describes Socrates' attitude upon seeing his friends. Read the excerpt and answer the question that follows.

> Socrates sat up on his couch and bent his leg and rubbed it with his hand, and while he was rubbing it, he said, "What a strange thing, my friends, that seems to be which men call pleasure! How wonderfully it is related to that which seems to be its opposite, pain, in that they will not both come to a man at the same time, and yet if he pursues the one and captures it, he is generally obliged to take the other also, as if the two were joined together in one head. . . . Just so it seems that in my case, after pain was in my leg on account of the fetter [shackle], pleasure appears to have come following after."

26. What does this incident suggest about Socrates' state of mind before his death? Explain your answer.

CONNECT TO YOUR LIFE

27. **NARRATIVE** Choose one of the figures you read about in this chapter and think of someone alive today who could be regarded as that person's counterpart. Write a few paragraphs to describe the qualities or achievements that earn your respect, and compare and contrast the present-day person with a figure from ancient Greece. Use the tips below to help you plan, organize, and write your essay.

TIPS

- Skim the chapter and choose a figure who intrigues you. Note the characteristics of that person that appeal to you.

- Think of a person in today's world who has some of the same characteristics of the ancient figure you've chosen.

- Describe the two people, noting the qualities or achievements you find worthy of respect.

- Use two or three vocabulary terms from the chapter in your narrative.

- Conclude your narrative with a summary of the ways in which these two individuals are similar and why they are worth our attention.

Greek Civilization 149

CHAPTER 6

The Roman Empire and the Rise of Christianity

1000 B.C.E.–476 C.E.

HISTORICAL THINKING Why did the Roman Empire become one of the most influential in history?

SECTION 1 **The Roman Republic**
SECTION 2 **The Roman Empire**
SECTION 3 **The Rise of Christianity**
SECTION 4 **Western Decline, Eastern Renewal**

CRITICAL VIEWING
The Roman Colosseum opened in 80 C.E., and much of the open-air theater still stands today. Thousands of spectators entered through its arches to watch the brutal games offered as entertainment. In what ways do many modern stadiums resemble the Colosseum?

The Roman Empire and the Rise of Christianity

1.1

MAIN IDEA Rome grew from a small settlement to a powerful republic that conquered the entire Italian Peninsula.

The Emergence of Rome

It has been said that "mighty oaks from little acorns grow." The "little acorn" that was Rome in its early days grew slowly and steadily until it was mighty enough to control all of Italy. And its growth had just begun.

CRITICAL VIEWING The ruins of the Roman Forum, shown here, represent different periods of Rome's history. During the time of the Roman Republic, the Forum became the center of politics. The Roman Senate met in the Forum, but ordinary Romans gathered there, too. How do these ruins convey the Forum's former glory?

THE FOUNDING OF ROME

Rome lies halfway down the west coast of the boot-shaped peninsula of Italy. The tip of the boot looks as if it's about to kick the island of Sicily toward North Africa. To the north, the soaring Alps form a natural barrier. A chain of smaller mountains, the Apennines (A-puh-nynz), runs down the center of the peninsula. The vast Mediterranean Sea, which the Romans would come to call *Mare Nostrum* (MAHR-ay NOHS-truhm), or "our sea," surrounds the peninsula.

By 1000 B.C.E., many small villages had been settled in the seven hills around the **Tiber** (TY-bur) **River**. The villages merged into one large settlement, early Rome, around 750 B.C.E. However, in ancient times, a legend arose about the founding of Rome. According to this story, the twin brothers Romulus and Remus were abandoned on the Tiber. They were rescued by a wolf and raised by a shepherd. The brothers eventually founded a city, and Romulus became its first king in 753 B.C.E. He named the city Rome after himself.

Rome lay at a point where the shallow Tiber could be crossed easily. And the city became a natural stopping point for the trade routes that ran along the river. Rome's fertile soil, mild climate, and access to water allowed agriculture to flourish. Various peoples were attracted to the area, bringing their technologies and cultures with them and helping the city grow in size and power.

By 700 B.C.E., the Greeks had settled in southern Italy and Sicily, and the **Etruscans** controlled a large area just north of Rome. Both groups influenced Rome. The Etruscans were especially skilled in sewage management, engineering, and city planning, and the Romans learned a great deal from them. They also gained an alphabet from the Etruscans and adapted it around 600 B.C.E. to create their first **script**, or form of writing, in their native language—Latin. The words you are reading now use the Latin alphabet.

Around the late 600s, Etruscan kings came to rule Rome. They laid out the city's streets in a grid pattern and built stone houses, temples, and public buildings. The foundations of Rome as one of the great cities of the ancient world had been laid.

THE EARLY REPUBLIC

The Etruscans ruled Rome until 509 B.C.E., when the Romans overthrew King Tarquin, a cruel tyrant who often had his opponents killed. The Romans replaced the monarchy with a new form of government called a **republic**, in which citizens vote for their leaders and the officials that represent them. This differed from the direct democracy established in Athens. Rome was an indirect democracy, which meant the people did not vote directly on laws and policies.

Two executive leaders called consuls ruled the Roman Republic, and they were elected to serve a one-year term. They were primarily tasked with leading Rome's army. The consuls could veto each other's decisions. They also took advice from the **Senate**, which, in the beginning, was composed entirely of wealthy landowners called **patricians**. Roman society at this time was divided into the patricians and the **plebeians**, who included farmers, artisans, and merchants. Most of Rome's citizens were plebeians.

CINCINNATUS During times of crisis, the Romans appointed a **dictator**, who was granted absolute authority. Once the crisis had passed, the dictator was expected to step down. One such dictator was named Cincinnatus. When the Senate called on him to take charge of Rome in 458 B.C.E., he accepted. After Cincinnatus defeated the enemy, he gave up his power. George Washington followed Cincinnatus's example. When Washington was asked to lead the Continental Army during the American Revolution, he, too, accepted the charge. Once the war was won, he resigned his commission.

The Senate formed Rome's legislative branch along with a much less powerful plebeian assembly. Soon after the formation of the republic, plebeians called for a greater voice in the government. In time, they were allowed to elect their own representatives, called **tribunes**. At first, the Senate's opinions on issues carried greater weight than those of the plebeian assembly. In the 400s B.C.E., however, plebeians demanded and gained political and legal equality. The balance of power between the Senate and the plebeian assembly equalized as well.

Plebeians also called for equal treatment under the law. Laws weren't written down, so patricians often interpreted them in ways that would benefit their friends. The plebeians insisted on having the laws carved into bronze tablets and displayed in public for all to see. They got their wish. The laws became known as the **Twelve Tables**, and they protected all Roman citizens.

After 400 B.C.E., the republic continually fought off invaders from the north. In 390 B.C.E., Rome suffered a defeat at the hands of the Gauls, a people from a region of western Europe that included present-day France.

After the city had recovered, the Romans set out to dominate the region. Once an enemy surrendered, Rome's leaders offered citizenship to any man who spoke Latin. Those who did not had to pay taxes and serve as soldiers but could not participate in politics. This policy greatly increased the size and strength of Rome's army, which conquered more territory. By 272 B.C.E., Rome controlled the entire Italian Peninsula.

HISTORICAL THINKING

1. **READING CHECK** What geographic advantages did Rome possess?

2. **DRAW CONCLUSIONS** What does it say about the Romans that the power of their two elected consuls was primarily limited to military affairs?

3. **MAKE INFERENCES** Why did the plebeians want Roman laws to be displayed in public?

1.2

MAIN IDEA Wars between Rome and Carthage launched Rome's conquest of the Mediterranean region.

The Republic Expands

Every road has its bumps. For Rome, the city-state of Carthage was a particularly difficult bump on the road to taking control of the Mediterranean Sea and its surrounding region.

THE PUNIC WARS

You may remember that Carthage began as a trading station for the Phoenicians. By the 400s B.C.E., the North African outpost had developed into an independent city-state. No longer a Phoenician colony, Carthage used its wealth and maritime skills to establish its own empire in the western Mediterranean. By the time the Romans took command of the Italian Peninsula in 272 B.C.E., Carthage controlled much of coastal North Africa and Spain, the islands of Corsica and Sardinia, and the western half of Sicily. The Romans and the Carthaginians fought the first of three **Punic Wars** over this chunk of Sicily. (*Punic* is derived from the Latin word for "Phoenician.")

The First Punic War lasted from 264 to 241 B.C.E. Rome's army consisted mainly of farmers. The Carthaginians hired **mercenaries**, or troops who were paid to fight. However, more clashes took place at sea than on land. Carthage was a major sea power, and so Rome was forced to build its first navy. Roman ships, powered by oarsmen, did well in battle. But stormy seas and inexperienced crews led to shipwrecks costing hundreds of vessels and thousands of sailors' lives.

In spite of these setbacks, the Romans managed to rebuild their navy in time to score a major victory against the Carthaginian fleet off the coast of Sicily. By then, the Carthaginians had had enough. They surrendered

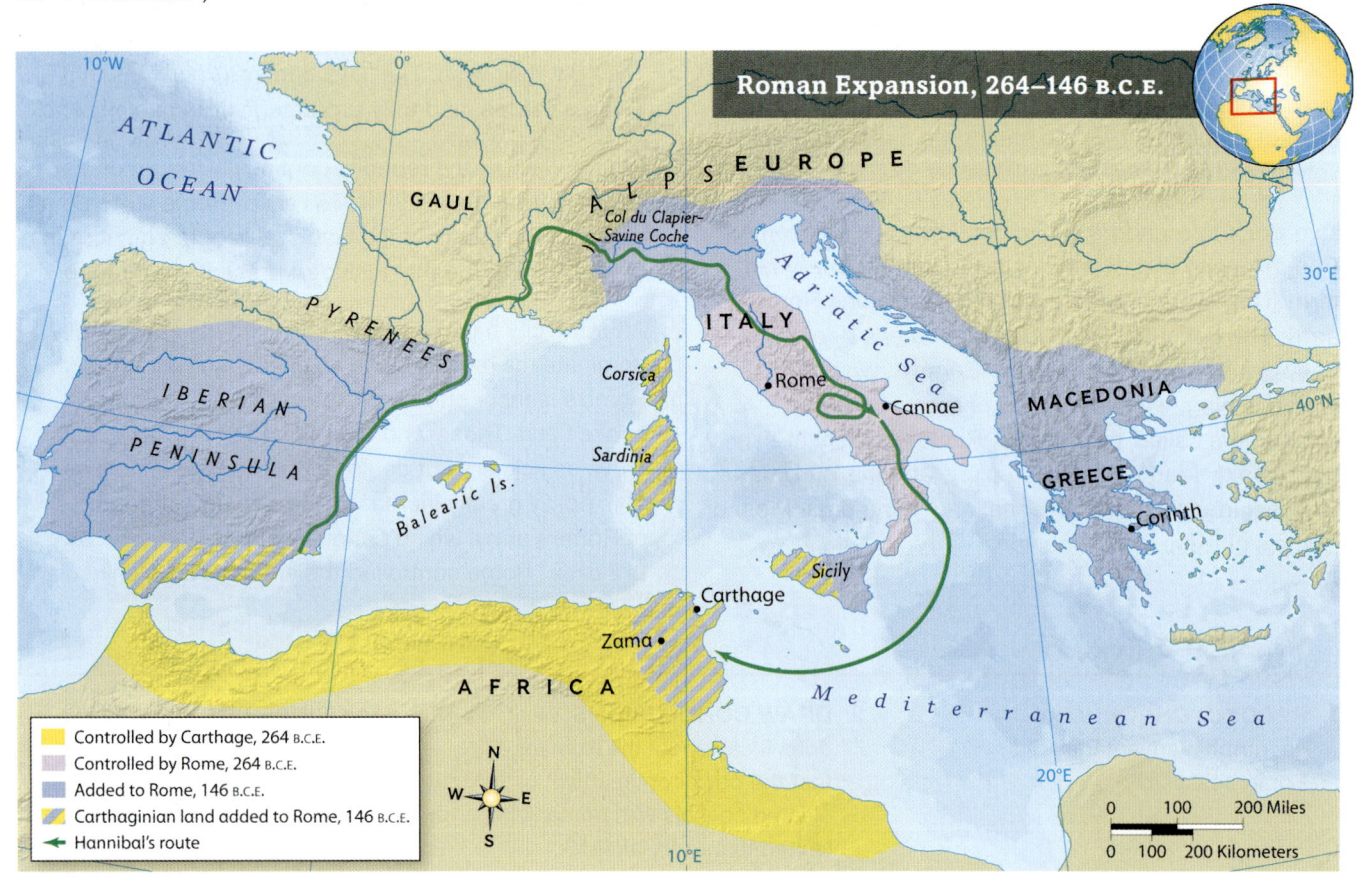

Roman Expansion, 264–146 B.C.E.

- Controlled by Carthage, 264 B.C.E.
- Controlled by Rome, 264 B.C.E.
- Added to Rome, 146 B.C.E.
- Carthaginian land added to Rome, 146 B.C.E.
- Hannibal's route

154 CHAPTER 6

in 241 B.C.E. and gave up Sicily, Corsica, and Sardinia. The peace was short-lived, though. In 218 B.C.E., a Carthaginian general named **Hannibal** sought to avenge Carthage's earlier defeat and attacked a Roman ally in southern Spain. The Second Punic War had begun.

Hannibal's next move was audacious. While the Romans planned a counterattack in Spain, the Carthaginian general decided to invade Italy itself. Starting from his stronghold on the Iberian Peninsula, he headed northeast, leading a force of more than 50,000 soldiers and 37 war elephants on a grueling five-month march. Their route took them through Gaul to the Alps. Crossing the Alps, which are among the world's tallest mountains, was a daring feat—and perhaps foolhardy. Nearly half of Hannibal's men died from starvation or the bitter cold. In spite of these losses, Hannibal's maneuver worked. He took the Romans by surprise and achieved a string of victories as he and his men marched south toward Rome. Hannibal was a brilliant tactician. Even when his outnumbered forces faced the Roman army at Cannae in southeast Italy, Hannibal defeated his foes.

The Romans, however, did not give up. The Roman general Scipio devised a tactic of his own. He invaded North Africa in an attempt to lure Hannibal out of Italy, and it worked. Hannibal returned to defend his homeland. In 202 B.C.E., at the Battle of Zama on the North African coast, Hannibal and Scipio faced off in a brutal fight. Rome defeated Carthage, and the Second Punic War ended in 201 B.C.E. The entire western Mediterranean was now under Roman control.

FURTHER CONQUESTS

Although the Romans had decisively defeated Carthage, they still considered their old enemy a threat. After the Second Punic War was over, Carthage turned its focus to trade and began accumulating great wealth. Some Romans called for the city-state's total destruction. As a result, Rome provoked Carthage into launching the Third Punic War in 149 B.C.E., but it was short-lived. Rome took control of Carthage in 146 B.C.E. The Roman commander sent the survivors to Rome, where they were sold as slaves, and ordered the utter annihilation of Carthage. The city-state ceased to exist. Carthage and its surrounding lands became the Roman province of Africa.

NATIONAL GEOGRAPHIC EXPLORER
PATRICK HUNT

Tracing Hannibal's Route

Hannibal managed to lead his army through the snow-covered Alps. But where did he cross the mountain range? This question has fascinated National Geographic Explorer Patrick Hunt for years. And he might have found the answer. Hunt reconstructed the past by combining an analysis of documents with archaeology. He followed clues provided in the works of the Greek historian Polybius and Roman historian Livy, who wrote accounts of Hannibal's campaign and described the geographic features Hannibal saw and the distances he traveled. Hunt also studied the ways in which the geology of the Alps may have changed in 2,000 years due to erosion and climate change. His research has led him to believe that Hannibal used the Col du Clapier-Savine Coche mountain pass. According to the archaeologist, landmarks on the route and the view from the summit fit perfectly with the descriptions in the ancient texts. Hunt and his team are still looking for physical evidence, including stones that may mark graves. As Hunt says, "An elephant burial would be fantastic!"

Rome was also dealing with another aggressor. During the Second Punic War, Rome was attacked by the army of Macedonia—the homeland of Alexander the Great. Since the Romans had their hands full with Hannibal, they negotiated a peace deal to end the First Macedonian War. After Hannibal's defeat, Rome invaded Macedonia, starting the Second Macedonian War. The Roman army emerged victorious in 197 B.C.E. and later made Macedonia a province. In 146 B.C.E., Rome conquered Greece and made it a colony as well. With its authority extending over much of the Mediterranean, Rome had become a major power in the ancient world.

HISTORICAL THINKING

1. **READING CHECK** What led to the First Punic War?

2. **COMPARE AND CONTRAST** At the beginning of the Punic Wars, how did the Carthaginian and Roman armies differ?

3. **INTERPRET MAPS** How did the Macedonian wars help Rome dominate the Mediterranean?

The Roman Empire and the Rise of Christianity

1.3

MAIN IDEA Roman society was shaped by its patriarchy, classes, religious beliefs, and practical values.

Roman Society

Families around the world have rules. Rules for the children may be intended to keep them safe, teach them how to behave, or clarify what is expected of them. You might find some of the rules governing ancient Roman families a bit harsh.

FAMILY LIFE

Men dominated life in the Roman Republic. Only men could vote, hold public office, join the army, or perform important ceremonies. Rome was a **patriarchy**, or a society in which men have all the power. They were in charge of the family as well. In Roman households, the *paterfamilias* (pah-tur-fuh-MIH-lee-uhs), or male head of the family, made all the decisions. He ruled with complete authority over his wife, children, and extended family members. Laws gave him the power to punish them, sell them into slavery, or even have them killed for serious crimes. Women often did have considerable influence behind the scenes, however, and had the right to divorce and remarry.

CRITICAL VIEWING This fresco from the first century C.E. shows a Roman woman and man holding writing tools and materials. What conclusions can you draw about the couple based on these items?

Roman women were subject to the men in their families—their husbands, fathers, or brothers. Women were considered citizens but had few rights. During the time of the republic, they could not own property or run a business. Most were wives and mothers who performed all of the daily domestic chores. They instructed their daughters in these household skills to prepare the girls for marriage. Most marriages were arranged, and girls could marry as early as 12 years old. The boys in the family often left home at a young age to work or learn a trade.

SOCIAL ORDER

Like the family, Roman society was strictly ordered. Patricians stood at the top of the social ladder. These aristocrats owned most of the land and lived in luxurious country estates, or villas. Unlike the poor, patricians sent their sons to school. Those boys destined for government jobs were later taught by private tutors. Between the ages of 14 and 17, all free boys became citizens.

The plebeians came next in society, and, as you know, made up the majority of Rome's citizens. Some plebeians were well-off and lived comfortably, but many were very poor. Most of the poor plebeians lived and worked on small farms. You've read that Rome's plebeians achieved greater legal and political equality with patricians in the 400s B.C.E. In time, some plebeian families gained significant wealth and political power. But while the social structure of Rome had changed, the gap between rich and poor remained huge.

Slaves were in the lowest class of Roman society. Some prisoners captured in Rome's conquests were enslaved and sent to Rome, but most slaves were bought from foreign traders. Some became household servants. Others toiled in gold and silver mines. But a large proportion of slaves ended up working on farms.

Military campaigns swelled the numbers of slaves in and around Rome. But, as a result of ongoing Roman conquests, foreigners and migrants from the countryside poured into the city as well. Estimates of Rome's population in the second century B.C.E. vary from around 450,000 to as high as 1 million.

Wars and the ever-increasing need for soldiers also had a major effect on Roman agriculture. In the early years of the republic, most Roman soldiers lived and worked on their family farm. They were farmer-soldiers who left their fields when called to defend their city. As the Roman army fought in more distant places, such as Carthage, soldiers had to be away from home for long periods of time. Many of them sold their fields to rich landowners.

These landowners combined their land purchases into large-scale agricultural enterprises where they grew fruits and vegetables, pressed olives into oil, and produced wine. Instead of working the land themselves, they relied on slaves. The rural population shrank, as landless farmers and former farm laborers migrated to the city. There they lived in overcrowded buildings and worked for very low wages—if they were fortunate enough to find employment.

BELIEFS AND VALUES

As Rome expanded, its culture and the Latin language diffused among the peoples it conquered. But the Romans also absorbed the customs and practices of others and adapted them to their own use. Religion is a prime example. Roman gods had a mix of traits drawn mainly from Greek gods. The Roman **pantheon**, or group of many gods and goddesses, included Jupiter, the king of the gods, who was modeled after the Greek god Zeus. Mars, the god of war, had much in common with the Greek god Ares. And Venus, the goddess of love, was as beautiful as the Greek goddess Aphrodite. The pantheon grew as the Romans adopted some of the gods of the people they conquered.

This sculpted head of Mars, the god of war, is from the second century C.E.

Worship of the gods could take place anywhere—even the home. Most Roman houses contained a shrine to a household god, or **lar**. The paterfamilias made daily offerings to the god, who was considered a guardian of the house and family. Priests conducted rituals for more important gods in temples. In addition, Romans celebrated religious festivals throughout the year in hopes that the deities would grant Rome good harvests and success in war. Like the festivals of ancient Greece, those of Rome featured processions, feasts, music, dance, theater, and sports.

But the Romans didn't always share the same values as the Greeks. While the Greeks valued beauty, grace, and elegance, Romans were a more practical people. They preferred such qualities as discipline, strength, and loyalty. These qualities, Romans believed, would help them achieve success. The qualities also reveal an important aspect of the Roman personality known as *gravitas*, or a serious and solemn approach to life. Their values helped the Romans accomplish great things in politics, engineering, and commerce and came to be known as "the Roman Way."

HISTORICAL THINKING

1. **READING CHECK** What powers did the paterfamilias have in Roman families?

2. **COMPARE AND CONTRAST** How did life for rich and poor citizens in Roman society differ?

3. **MAKE INFERENCES** Why do you think discipline, strength, and loyalty were so important to the Romans?

2.1

MAIN IDEA After the Roman Republic became divided by political chaos, the establishment of rule by an emperor ushered in a period of peace and prosperity.

The End of the Republic

Have you ever heard people talk about the "one percent"? They're referring to the very few Americans who own about 40 percent of the country's wealth. The Roman patricians were the one percenters of their day. Their greed helped bring about the end of the republic.

CHAOS IN THE REPUBLIC

You've read that soldiers leaving for far-flung wars sometimes sold their land to the rich. These patricians soon found other ways to acquire land. When the Roman Republic gained territory through military conquests, the government set it aside as public land. However, wealthy landowning families came to control it, using slaves to grow crops for sale.

As more and more small farmers were driven out of business—unable to compete with the large-scale farms—unemployment and poverty became common in the republic. Yet the rich ignored the problems of the poor. Between 133 B.C.E. and 123 B.C.E., two political reformers put forward bills that would take some of the public land from the rich and give it to the poor, but their actions infuriated the Senate. Members of the legislative body had the reformers assassinated.

Julius Caesar's assassination on March 15, 44 B.C.E.—known as the Ides, or middle, of March—captured the imagination of many historians and writers. As a result, that date has come to represent an unlucky or ill-fated day. In the dramatic painting shown here, Caesar reaches out for help just before the senators attack him.

Political turmoil in Rome increased with conflict at home. The army general Marius had been elected consul in 107 B.C.E. He had allowed landless citizens to join the army and paid them for their service. Other generals began instituting the same policy. As a result, soldiers started to switch their loyalty from the state to their generals. Soon, politically ambitious generals marched their armies to do battle against other Roman generals. A series of civil wars broke out as the generals fought for control of Rome. Other crises arose, including a slave rebellion in 73 B.C.E. A slave named **Spartacus** led about 90,000 other slaves against Roman troops in an effort to flee Italy and return to their homelands. Spartacus was killed and his followers defeated.

Finally, a popular general, **Julius Caesar**, won the civil wars in 45 B.C.E., and the Senate agreed to declare him dictator for a six-month period. Many Romans expected Caesar to restore the republic, but instead, he declared himself dictator for life. This act prompted a group of senators to assassinate him in 44 B.C.E.

After 14 more years of civil war, Caesar's great-nephew Octavian became Rome's sole ruler. In 27 B.C.E., Octavian founded a government known as the **principate**, a type of monarchy in which some republican ideals were upheld. Octavian ruled as an emperor and held the position for life. The Senate gave him the name **Augustus**, which means "exalted one."

Augustus brought an end to the republic, weakening the Senate and undermining Roman democracy. But he did bring peace to the empire. His reign began a period of calm and prosperity that lasted for about 200 years. Historians call this period the **Pax Romana**.

PEACE IN THE EMPIRE

Romans were somewhat uneasy about a ruler granted powers for life. It reminded them of the rule of kings. But the people, tired of political chaos, accepted Augustus because he had been legally approved by the Senate, moved slowly and carefully, dressed simply, and lived in a modest palace. The price for Roman citizens was, as you know, a decline in their long tradition of democracy.

During his rule, Augustus initiated many political and social changes. The Senate continued, but the emperor controlled its decisions. Augustus appointed all military leaders and the governors of the important provinces. He also cut the size of the army in half. However, he gave released soldiers grants of land and offered Roman citizenship to many of them. Augustus created a permanent navy and stationed an elite group of soldiers in Rome, called the Praetorian Guard, to provide security in the city. To help ease poverty, Augustus had free handouts of grain distributed to the poor. In addition, he actively encouraged art, literature, and education. And he transformed Rome into an impressive capital by building magnificent monuments. According to his legend, Augustus said, "I found Rome a city of bricks and left it a city of marble."

Roman law changed throughout the principate period. By the mid-100s C.E., the remaining legal distinctions between patricians and plebeians had faded. Nevertheless, Roman courts favored the wealthy and tended to subject the poor to harsher punishments for the same crime. A woman's legal position also changed. Married daughters were entitled to a share of their father's property, which gave them some financial independence. A Roman wife still remained subject to the authority of her husband. However, if her husband died, she was allowed to manage his business.

Experts believe this colossal marble head of Augustus once formed part of a huge statue that included arms, legs, and a torso.

During the time of the republic, as you know, Roman law was set down in the Twelve Tables. In addition, officials developed a set of civil laws for Roman citizens and the law of nations for both foreigners and Romans. Another type of written law consisted of **edicts**. These were the official proclamations of the principles an elected magistrate, or judge, would follow during his tenure. Around 131 C.E., Rome standardized and consolidated the edicts. These proclamations could not be changed by anyone but the emperor. The body of Roman law would later influence the development of law codes in many different parts of the world.

HISTORICAL THINKING

1. **READING CHECK** Why did civil war erupt in the Roman Republic?

2. **MAKE INFERENCES** Why do you think Romans didn't want to return to the rule of kings?

3. **IDENTIFY PROBLEMS AND SOLUTIONS** How did Augustus tackle the problems that had plagued the republic?

2.2

MAIN IDEA Rome extended its imperial frontiers to North Africa in the south and to Britain in the northwest.

Expanding the Empire's Frontiers

When you hear the word *frontier*, you may think of American pioneers in the mid-1800s pushing west in search of gold and a new life. But most pioneers endured only hardship and often faced strong resistance from local peoples. The Romans could probably relate.

NORTH AFRICA

Augustus and many of the rulers who followed him continued to expand the Roman Empire. Rome's army conquered lands and spread the empire's cultural influence farther than ever before. By around 117 C.E., the empire had reached its greatest extent, with territory on three continents—Europe, Asia, and Africa.

As you may remember, Rome established the province of Africa in 146 B.C.E. after defeating Carthage in the Punic Wars. In the century that followed the conquest, large numbers of traders and farmers migrated to the province, and Julius Caesar settled many discharged veterans there. Together, Julius Caesar and Augustus founded 19 Roman colonies in Africa. One of these colonies, the "new" Carthage, grew to become the second largest city in the western part of the empire.

Augustus—then called Octavian—had conquered Egypt in 31 B.C.E. Rome continued to increase its African territory. By the middle of the first century C.E., the empire controlled the entire North African coast. Wealthy Romans recognized the value of the lands there. During and after the reign of Augustus, they established huge and profitable private estates in the provinces. The estates used slave labor to produce wheat, figs, nuts, beans, olives, and wine. Farmers also raised horses, cattle, sheep, and pigs.

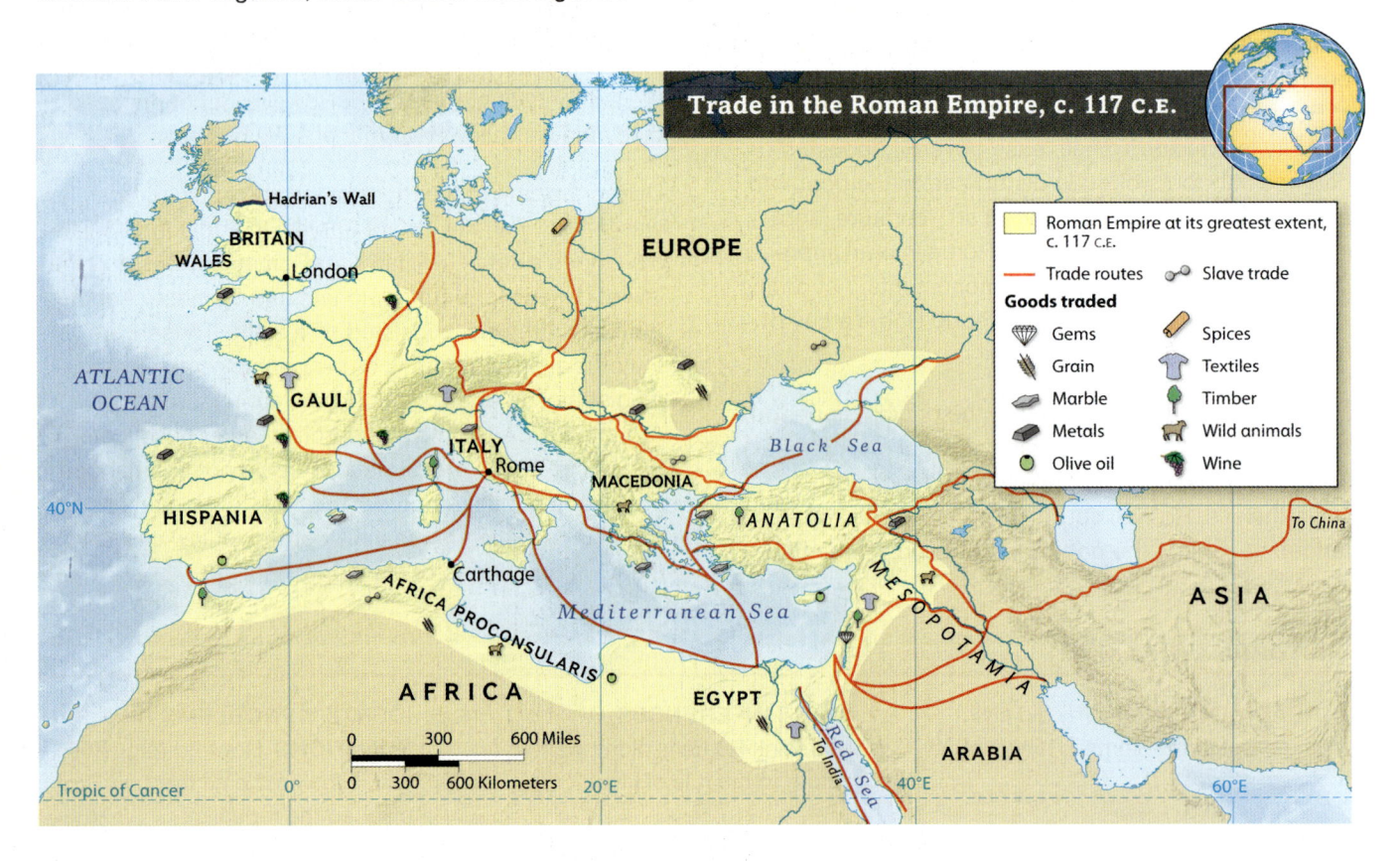

Trade in the Roman Empire, c. 117 C.E.

160 CHAPTER 6

As the empire expanded, roads were built to connect it, and trade flourished. North Africa provided items such as grain and olive oil. European goods included wine and metals. Wild animals came from Africa and Asia. Most of these goods flowed directly into Rome. The city especially needed food to feed its huge population.

A standardized currency in the empire made it easier to conduct trade, and these coins were even accepted outside the empire. Some traders carried currency and goods well beyond Roman borders, sailing to India or traveling the Silk Roads to China. Traders on these journeys often transported their goods in **amphorae**—large two-handled ceramic jars with narrow necks.

BRITAIN

North Africa marked the southernmost edge of the empire, but in time, Rome would set its sights on what would become its northernmost frontier: Britain. In 55 B.C.E., Julius Caesar crossed the English Channel after defeating Gaul and became the first Roman to invade the island. He formed a relationship with several British tribes, but many Romans at that time didn't think the region had any value. Romans also considered the Britons, the indigenous, or native, tribes of Britain, to be barbarians. (Both the ancient Greeks and Romans viewed anyone outside their culture as barbarians.) Augustus maintained the loose alliances established by Caesar, but another emperor had greater ambitions.

In 43 C.E., the emperor Claudius sent four large army units across the channel to conquer Britain. Then around 60 C.E., the Iceni in the southeastern part of Britain revolted against Roman oppression. Queen Boudicca, who ruled the tribe, led the rebellion. Her forces killed about 70,000 Romans and their Briton allies before the Roman army regained control.

Still, some Britons refused to give up. The people of Wales, in the southwest, fought the Romans for decades until they were finally conquered in 78 C.E. The people of the land known today as Scotland, in the north, had greater success. They repeatedly defeated Roman attempts at conquest.

In the 120s C.E., the emperor Hadrian ordered his army to build a wall at Britain's northwestern frontier to keep out invaders. Hadrian's Wall stood about 13 feet high and ran for about 70 miles from coast to coast.

Meanwhile, a measure of peace had been secured in southern Britain. And Roman culture spread through this region as forums, temples, and theaters were built in the towns. The Romans made the wealthier Britons, many of whom received Roman citizenship, responsible for maintaining order in and around the towns. These Britons collected taxes levied by the Romans—largely in the form of grain needed to feed the army.

Roman influence didn't take hold quite as well in Wales and northern Britain. As a result, a strong army presence remained in these regions to maintain Roman authority and squelch uprisings. Of course, the fighting force of the Roman army was enough to deter almost anyone from causing trouble.

CRITICAL VIEWING During the revolt against Britain, Queen Boudicca's troops sacked several cities, including present-day London. In this 18th-century painting, a British artist imagines what Boudicca might have looked like. With what emotions do Boudicca's people seem to regard her?

HISTORICAL THINKING

1. **READING CHECK** What city became the second largest in the western part of the empire?

2. **INTERPRET MAPS** What goods from the Roman Empire were traded in India?

3. **COMPARE AND CONTRAST** How did the conquest of southern Britain compare with that of Wales and the north?

2.3

MAIN IDEA Rome's armies secured an empire, and its engineers built the infrastructure that held it together.

Roman Armies and Engineering

How did the Romans do it? They conquered a vast area, with a diverse and often rebellious population, and managed to defend their empire and build marvelous structures throughout it for centuries. The answer lies with Rome's armies and engineers.

MILITARY MIGHT

Wars in places like Britain were physically demanding, but the Roman army was equal to the challenge. During the republic, the army developed a fighting unit called the legion, which consisted of around 4,200 men. It was the ultimate weapon of ancient warfare.

As you know, the army in the republic was peopled by farmer-soldiers, who fought the republic's battles and then went home. However, soldiers in the Roman Empire were no longer farmers. They were paid professionals known as **legionaries**. At first, many of these soldiers came from Italy, but as the empire grew, army leaders recruited more and more men from the provinces. Legionaries joined young and served for a maximum of 16 years. The soldiers were highly disciplined, and they trained, marched, and fought together. They also took part in intensive fighting drills, which a first century C.E. historian called "battles without bloodshed." All were expected to form a strong sense of duty to their fellow soldiers, to the commanders, and to Rome itself. If a soldier disobeyed an order or retreated during battle, his commander could have him executed for putting his comrades in danger.

The army of the Roman Empire was strictly organized. Legionaries were grouped into 80-man centuries, or units. Six centuries formed a cohort, or division. Ten cohorts, comprising a total of 4,800 soldiers, made up a typical legion. From the time of Augustus through the height of the empire some 200 years later, the Roman army commanded anywhere from 25 to 33 legions. Each soldier was a cog in a vast fighting machine. The Roman battlefield formation resembled the Greek phalanx, with legionaries fighting in tight lines, shields held before them.

A legionary carried a staggering amount of equipment. His helmet, armor, shield, and weapons weighed in at about 50 pounds. And the food, tools, and personal belongings he had to bring as well probably doubled that weight. Many legionaries carried a javelin and wielded a sword and dagger for close fighting. In battle, the Romans sometimes also used a device called a siege engine, a wheeled tower with platforms for weapons and soldiers. Legionaries rolled a tower toward city walls and used its battering rams to knock the fortifications down. Just the sight of a siege engine bearing down on them was sometimes enough to make enemies surrender.

A legion's unique emblem was painted on the front of a legionary's leather-covered wooden shield. The shield's iron boss and rim (in the center) were used as weapons to punch the enemy during battle.

ROADS AND ARCHITECTURE

When the Roman army wasn't fighting, it was often busy building the vast network of roads that connected the empire. The roads not only allowed the army to travel to distant battlefields quickly but also provided messengers, traders, and everyone else in the empire with a faster, safer way to reach their destination.

The first of these extensive roads was the Via Appia, or Appian Way. Built in 312 B.C.E., it ran from Rome to southern Italy. Over time, the army constructed many

CRITICAL VIEWING The towering structure in the center of this photo is an aqueduct, which was built by engineers during the Roman Empire. Aqueducts carried water to citizens throughout the empire, including Spain, where this aqueduct still stands. What does the structure reveal about the skill of Roman engineers?

other major roads that people all over the empire could use to travel to the capital. The web of roadways gave rise to the saying, "All roads lead to Rome." To overcome obstacles along the way, engineers figured out how to build bridges over rivers and tunnels through hills and mountains. At regular intervals, they placed milestones on the roads to mark the distance to major cities. By 300 C.E., about 53,000 miles of roads connected the empire.

Among other materials, engineers used concrete to make bridges and tunnels. An early form of concrete had been in use for centuries. But around the time of Augustus, the Romans developed a more durable type using a secret ingredient—volcanic ash. With this strong new concrete, engineers could build huge, freestanding structures. One of the most famous of these buildings is the Colosseum in Rome. Opened in 80 C.E., the **amphitheater**, or open-air theater with tiers of seats around a central stage, could hold up to 50,000 spectators. The people came to see **gladiators**, usually slaves or criminals, battle wild animals or each other. Other buildings, like the Circus Maximus in Rome, were huge arenas where as many as 250,000 sports fans might gather to watch chariot races. And Rome's Pantheon—the "temple of all the gods"—was completed around 128 C.E. Its unreinforced concrete dome is the largest in the world.

Roman architects drew on Greek architecture for inspiration. But the addition of domes, arches, and vaults—or lengthened arches—resulted in a distinctive Roman style. Arches are featured in the Colosseum and in some of the long stone channels called **aqueducts**. Roman engineers designed aqueducts to carry a steady flow of clean water from hilltops into cities. Most of the water ran through large underground conduits. But Romans also constructed huge arched bridges to carry the water across valleys. It is a testament to the skill of Roman engineers that many of these structures are still standing today.

HISTORICAL THINKING

1. **READING CHECK** Why was the Roman army so successful?

2. **MAKE INFERENCES** Why do you think so many of the structures in Rome were built on such a large scale?

3. **DRAW CONCLUSIONS** What principle did Roman engineers use to deliver water by means of the aqueducts?

The Roman Empire and the Rise of Christianity

2.4

MAIN IDEA A volcanic eruption destroyed Pompeii and left behind a well-preserved site that provides insight into the everyday life of the Roman city.

Pompeii

"Darkness fell, not the dark of a moonless or cloudy night, but as if the lamp had been put out in a dark room." So wrote the Roman historian Pliny the Younger who, on a sunny summer day, watched darkness descend on Pompeii and bury it alive.

CRITICAL VIEWING This plaster cast preserves a Roman citizen who died at Pompeii nearly 2,000 years ago. What does the man's pose suggest about his death?

CATASTROPHE

In the Roman city of **Pompeii**, August 24, 79 C.E., began much like any other day. Men and women headed to work or went to buy a loaf of bread at the local bakery. Mothers walked with their children, and dogs ran through the streets. About 20,000 people lived within the city walls of Pompeii, located by the Bay of Naples in southwest Italy. Like many Roman towns, Pompeii's streets were laid out in an orderly grid pattern, and its citizens enjoyed all the civic comforts the empire provided. Pompeii was an average city resting in the shadow of Mount Vesuvius about a half-mile away. And then something extraordinary—and terrible—happened.

The historian Pliny the Younger was across the Bay of Naples at the home of his uncle when Vesuvius erupted. He looked on in horror as gas mixed with rock and ash shot high into the sky and then rained down on Pompeii. A thick black cloud of smoke and ash blocked out the sun. Terrified citizens ran through the streets.

Fires in the city added to the terror. Lava pouring from the volcano set buildings ablaze. Many Pompeiians were killed by the falling structures and tumbling rocks. Others succumbed to the poisonous gas that filled the air or were suffocated by the smoke and ash. Some people tied pillows on their heads to protect themselves from the rocks or wrapped their tunics over their mouths

164 CHAPTER 6

to keep out the smoke. Recent findings suggest that people also died from the extreme heat created by waves of hot gas and ash.

Lightning, earthquakes, and tidal waves struck Pompeii over the next three days, and many people were buried alive as a blanket of ash nearly 25 feet deep settled over the city. An estimated 2,000 people died, and most of the survivors abandoned the city. Pompeii, with its people and their possessions, remained buried for more than 1,500 years.

FROZEN IN TIME

The city's ruins were first discovered in the late 1500s, but excavation of the site didn't begin until 1748. By the 1800s, archaeologists had discovered that the ash had preserved Pompeii. Household goods, artwork, and jewelry revealed a slice of Roman life. Over the centuries, scientists have uncovered houses containing mosaics and frescoes and graffiti (in Latin!) scrawled on public buildings. They even found an oven with loaves of bread inside. Food scraps retrieved from Pompeii's drainage system indicated that the diet of wealthy Pompeiians included such delicacies as sea urchin and flamingos.

The ash also preserved some of its victims by hardening around the bodies and forming a shell. In time, the bodies decayed and left the shells hollow. A 19th-century archaeologist developed the technique of pouring plaster into these spaces to create exact casts of people and animals captured at their moment of death. The lifelike poses of the victims include a man with his face in his hands, a mother trying to protect a child, and a dog on its back with its paws in the air. Recent researchers have studied the plaster casts using sophisticated CT scanning and made digital 3D reconstructions of the victims' skeletons. The images reveal that the Pompeiians had perfect teeth—probably the result of a healthy diet.

Archaeologists today still investigate the remains of Pompeii. In fact, it is the longest continually excavated site in the world. Nevertheless, about a third of Pompeii still remains buried. But researchers want to take their time uncovering whatever's still hidden under the ash. Their goal is to preserve and conserve the moving artifacts and victims of the city that were frozen in time.

NATIONAL GEOGRAPHIC EXPLORER
STEVEN ELLIS

Excavating the Stories of Ordinary People

In 2005, National Geographic Explorer Steven Ellis became the youngest archaeological director at Pompeii. He wants to use archaeology "to tell the story of ordinary people, the other 98 percent of the population." So Ellis has focused much of his work on a forgotten neighborhood of Pompeii where the working-class people lived. Some of his discoveries, Ellis says, "are changing the way we understand the lives of the sub-elite—for example, the types of food they ate, which were of better quality and variety than is normally supposed." And he's found that, like urban dwellers today, they lived in multicultural neighborhoods, spoke many different languages, and ate at fast-food restaurants. Ellis enjoys digging and discovering artifacts in a part of Pompeii that had been ignored. As he points out, "We're digging in an area where a lot of Pompeiians died during the eruption. They don't have fine art, but they do have bones, seeds, and pieces of pottery that tell us a story."

HISTORICAL THINKING

1. **READING CHECK** What happened to Pompeii on August 24, 79 C.E.?

2. **ANALYZE CAUSE AND EFFECT** What multiple effects occurred as a result of the ash that blanketed Pompeii?

3. **DRAW CONCLUSIONS** Why is it important to uncover the stories of ordinary people who lived long ago?

3.1 State of the World

1 B.C.E.

CULTURE AND TECHNOLOGY

Relative to our fast-paced society, change in the ancient world happened slowly. And historians have limited data from this period to draw on, so dates are not always exact. For these reasons, this first State of the World discussion spans a period of some 200 years: about 100 years before 1 B.C.E. and about 100 years after.

At this point in history, most regions of the world were home to farming societies, nomads, and hunter-gatherers. But major empires flexed their muscles in the Eastern Hemisphere. The two most powerful of these were the Roman and Han empires. As you know, the Roman Empire ruled the Mediterranean. The Han Empire, which arose in 206 B.C.E., became the second great imperial dynasty of China after the Zhou. The Han reached its fullest extent around 1 B.C.E.

Beginning about 25 C.E., the Kushan Empire began to rise in Central Asia and northern India. The Kushans were a group of Iranian nomads whose active trade created a culture that blended Indian, Persian, and Greco-Roman influences. In Southwest Asia, the leaders of the Parthian Empire remained in power but were often forced to fight off aggressors, particularly from Rome.

Important events occurred in the Americas. In North America, farming began around 1 B.C.E. By 100 C.E., the Moche kingdom on the northern Peruvian coast became the first state to develop in South America. On the southern Peruvian coast, the Nasca culture began around 1 C.E. and flourished for about 800 years. Its mysterious geoglyphs—drawings etched into the earth—continue to intrigue researchers.

HISTORICAL THINKING

INTERPRET MAPS What conclusion can you draw about the five largest cities in the world around 1 B.C.E.?

Nasca Lines The Nasca, whose culture flourished from around 200 B.C.E. to 600 C.E., etched drawings in the ground that were often so large, they could only be seen from the air. Some historians believe the lines marked the course of underground water sources.

FIVE LARGEST CITIES

Rank	City	Population (thousands)
1	Rome	800
2	Chang'an	420
3	Alexandria	400
4	Seleucia	400
5	Antioch	270

*Population in thousands (approximately)

WORLD POPULATION

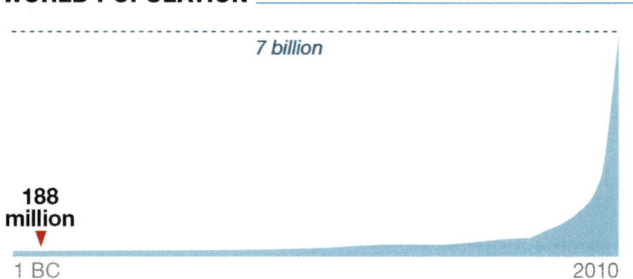

1 BC: 188 million
2010: 7 billion

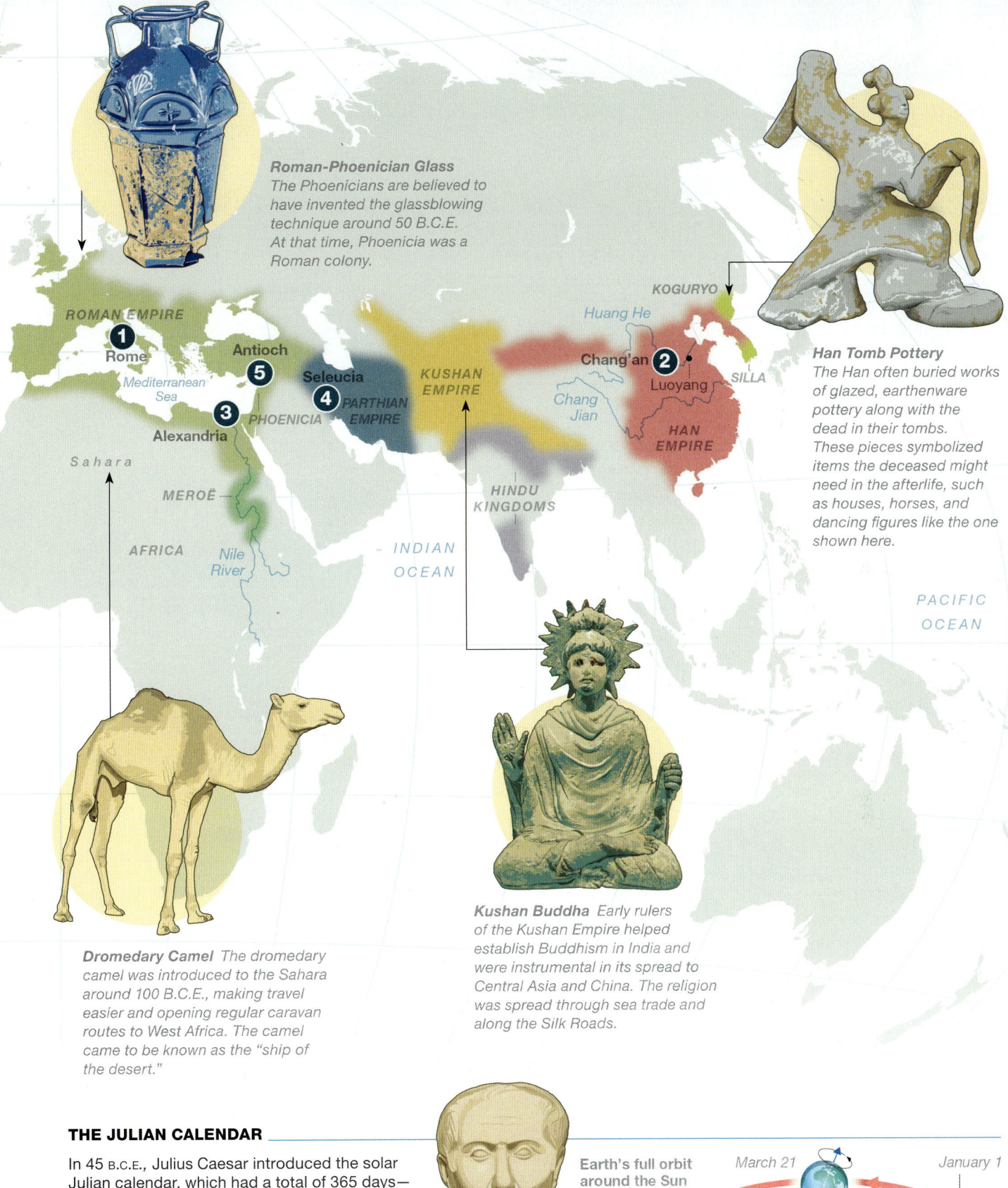

Roman-Phoenician Glass
The Phoenicians are believed to have invented the glassblowing technique around 50 B.C.E. At that time, Phoenicia was a Roman colony.

Han Tomb Pottery
The Han often buried works of glazed, earthenware pottery along with the dead in their tombs. These pieces symbolized items the deceased might need in the afterlife, such as houses, horses, and dancing figures like the one shown here.

Dromedary Camel The dromedary camel was introduced to the Sahara around 100 B.C.E., making travel easier and opening regular caravan routes to West Africa. The camel came to be known as the "ship of the desert."

Kushan Buddha Early rulers of the Kushan Empire helped establish Buddhism in India and were instrumental in its spread to Central Asia and China. The religion was spread through sea trade and along the Silk Roads.

THE JULIAN CALENDAR

In 45 B.C.E., Julius Caesar introduced the solar Julian calendar, which had a total of 365 days—366 days in a leap year—divided into 12 months. It became fully operational in 8 B.C.E. That same year, the Senate proposed changing the month of Quintilis to July, in honor of Julius Caesar, and the month of Sextilis to Augustus (August), in honor of Rome's current emperor. March was the first month of the year. The Gregorian calendar in use today is based on the Julian calendar.

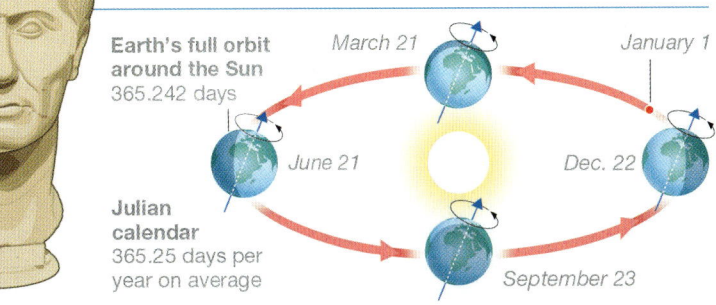

Earth's full orbit around the Sun
365.242 days

Julian calendar
365.25 days per year on average

The Roman Empire and the Rise of Christianity 167

3.2 Preserving Cultural Heritage

RESTORING THE EDICULE

This view of the Holy Edicule captures light from the candles of the hundreds of pilgrims who visit the Church of the Holy Sepulchre every day. The 2016 conservation project has ensured that this testament to time will endure for many thousands of pilgrims still to make the journey.

Jerusalem: From History to VR

Dr. Fredrik Hiebert is the in-house archaeologist for the National Geographic Society. He's visited many monuments to human achievement, but none has had a greater impact on him than the Church of the Holy Sepulchre in the Old City of Jerusalem, the epicenter of many world religions and events. Below, Dr. Hiebert shares his unique experience in the church.

THE CHURCH OF THE HOLY SEPULCHRE

The church originally dates to 325 c.e., established by the first Christian emperor of Rome, Constantine. Today it is located in the old Christian quarter, where visitors and pilgrims walk through a mazelike covered bazaar that gives way to the brilliant sunlight of the courtyard in front of the church.

At the core of the church is a large shrine, the Edicule or "little house." Over the centuries, the church and the shrine have been subject to damage from earthquakes and invasions and are under threat of fire from pilgrims' candles. In October 2016, National Geographic was invited to document the restoration of the Holy Edicule, where, according to Christian tradition, Jesus' body was laid following his crucifixion.

THE CONSERVATION PROJECT

To restore the Edicule, the church turned to a conservator from the National Technical University of Athens, Professor Antonia Moropoulou, famous for conserving the Hagia Sophia in Istanbul, Turkey. The conservation team used high-tech, noninvasive techniques to peer inside the walls of the Edicule and injected its walls with liquid mortar to reinforce the structure. The upper floors of the church were transformed into a masonry lab where stone slabs were cleaned and repaired—sometimes to reveal painted frescoes under layers of black candle soot. An iron support structure built in 1947 to support the walls of the Edicule was also removed, setting the monument free for the first time in 70 years.

Throughout the night of October 26, 2016, a team of conservators worked to slide off the white slab of marble that covered the top of the inner shrine of the Edicule—something that had not happened for centuries. Peering down into that unseen chamber was a remarkable experience, a chance to look through history. Aside from the dust that had accumulated over the centuries, under the top slab was another partially preserved marble slab engraved with a simple cross. Beneath that was hewn limestone, likely the original bedrock, venerated for generations as the Holy Rock that all of Jerusalem was built on.

The conservation of this shrine is a reminder of the fragile nature of our treasured monuments. Sites that have withstood earthquakes, war, and fire need the stewardship of the world to survive for future generations. National Geographic is one of many organizations committed to preserving the stories and places that are essential parts of understanding our shared past.

Telling the Story

by Kristin Romey

Kristin Romey is an editor and writer covering archaeology and culture for National Geographic. She documented the historic restoration of the Edicule for the magazine. Here, she describes the experience.

Getting assigned the Church of the Holy Sepulchre story for National Geographic was a pretty good stroke of luck, but being able to share it with our readers took a lot of hard work. In 2016, Dr. Fredrik Hiebert heard about an upcoming project to restore the Edicule at the Church of the Holy Sepulchre in Jerusalem. We decided it would make a great story for National Geographic and ended up spending almost a year traveling back and forth between Washington, D.C., and Jerusalem to report on the conservation work. The project resulted in four National Geographic digital exclusives, a television segment, and the cover story for our December 2017 magazine issue.

For me, the work of reporting begins long before I talk to the people involved in a story. With this assignment, I started by reading up on the history of the Church of the Holy Sepulchre and the tomb that's purported to be the final resting place of Jesus. I learned that the church was built around the tomb in the fourth century and that the

A picture taken on November 4, 2016, shows the Edicule being strengthened as part of the conservation work done by Moropoulou and her team.

church had been destroyed and rebuilt several times throughout the centuries. This made me wonder: Is the tomb, which is a site of worship for millions of people today, the same one that was first identified in the 330s?

Then I had to delve into the complicated history of the six Christian denominations that claim ownership of a part of the Church of the Holy Sepulchre: the Greek Orthodox Church of Jerusalem, the Roman Catholic Church, the Armenian Orthodox Church, the Syriac Orthodox Church, the Ethiopian Orthodox Church, and the Coptic Christians. There's a ladder on an outside ledge of the church that allegedly hasn't been moved since the 18th century, just because two of the Christian denominations can't agree on whom the ladder belongs to. The family that holds the only key to the church doors is Muslim because the Christian denominations don't trust one another to be the keyholder. So I knew I had to be ready to deal with some unusual situations when I first traveled to Jerusalem.

Like any reporting assignment, this one had its high and low points. The best parts were when I was interviewing the various stakeholders in the church and learning about the different Christian traditions. The Armenians claim theirs is the oldest official Christian country, for instance, while the Franciscan Catholics pride themselves on being the archaeologists of the Holy Land. Many Palestinian Christians worship in the Greek Orthodox Church, which has had a presence in the region as a patriarchate since the fifth century.

Since the Church of the Holy Sepulchre is open every day of the week, the conservators had to do most of their work on the Edicule after the church was closed to visitors for the night, often working until the church reopened at 5 a.m. the next morning. We had this enormous, ancient church complex—absolutely bustling during the daytime—all to ourselves at night, save for a few dozen monks who actually lived inside the church. At first it was magical to explore the nooks and crannies, inspect other 2,000-year-old tombs tucked into side chapels, and marvel at Crusader-era graffiti carved into the walls. After the eighth or ninth night, however, things could get a bit repetitive (there was only so much sandblasting I could watch the conservators do). The church could get quite cold, and we were stuck in there until the Muslim family came with the key in the morning and opened the door to let us out. So it wasn't always a glamorous assignment.

The biggest highlight was the night they opened the tomb. We were given exclusive media access to the opening, but the church authorities wouldn't tell us exactly when it would occur. They just said to be in Jerusalem during a specific week in October 2016 and be prepared to get to the church at a moment's notice. Only the conservation team, me, our National Geographic film team and photographer, and a small group of high-ranking church representatives were to be present. No news about the tomb was to be made public until it was opened, examined, and resealed, a project that could take up to 60 hours.

I remember I was eating dinner when I got a call to hurry, that it was happening, and that the church doors would remain unlocked for only five minutes. I raced through the streets of Jerusalem's Old City, excitedly thinking about my exclusive story, and got inside the Church of the Holy Sepulchre just in the nick of time. The first thing I saw inside the church were several dozen priests of different denominations, all with their cell phones raised toward the tomb. I quickly realized that while many were taking photos, others were live-streaming the tomb-opening on social media! I knew I had to work fast to make sure that National Geographic could keep its exclusive and be the first media outlet to cover the story.

Fortunately, I had already written most of the background information on the history of the church and the tomb, so I pulled up the text on my cell phone and quickly fleshed out the story of the tomb-opening and the atmosphere inside the church as it happened. Then I went to the top authorities inside the church to plead my case and ask to be allowed to publish the story as soon as possible—and not have to wait until the tomb was resealed. "It's already all over Facebook!" I exclaimed, waving at the crowd of priests holding up their cell phone cameras at the tomb. Finally, the authorities relented, I emailed the text to my editor back in Washington D.C., and within a day the headlines had gone around the world.

Being a journalist comes with a lot of responsibility: It's your job to get your facts right and tell your story in a way that's not only entertaining and interesting but also completely accurate. And if you do good journalism, the karma comes back to you. Not only did millions of people learn about the legacy of the Church of the Holy Sepulchre and the importance of the Edicule, but also the conservation team was pleased with how National Geographic explained their complicated scientific studies to the public. As a result, they gave us the final exclusive discovery from their work: the latest dating results on mortar that bound the earliest parts of the Edicule. It turns out that the building constructed in the fourth century is the same Edicule that pilgrims and tourists flock to today. That's a pretty much unbroken 1,700-year-old history for one of Christianity's most important monuments, and that's pretty cool.

Visitors take part in National Geographic's immersive exhibition *Tomb of Christ: The Church of the Holy Sepulchre Experience*, which virtually transports visitors to the Church of the Holy Sepulchre.

This fly-in view of the Edicule shows what visitors see as part of the VR experience.

Building a Virtual World

When the National Geographic museum team prepares a new exhibition, Creative Director Alan Parente is usually on the front lines. Parente has headed up the design work for some of the museum's most popular shows, including *Peruvian Gold* (2015) and *The Greeks: Agamemnon to Alexander* (2016). But the *Tomb of Christ* exhibition in 2017 offered new opportunities—and new challenges. Parente shared his experience with National Geographic Learning.

NGL: What was the team's primary goal in developing the *Tomb of Christ* exhibition?

ALAN: This exhibition raised exciting new questions about museum exhibitions in general. With so much change in design technology, as a team we stepped back to ask, "How do we best study a place?" And we knew we wanted to make as much information as possible accessible to as many people as possible—to let people study a place, to really experience it, without having to travel there. So the chance to let visitors experience the Church of the Holy Sepulchre through VR and 3-D technology was a great opportunity for us. We wanted both to teach and to thrill.

NGL: How did you go about creating this virtual experience?

ALAN: It can be a complex process, but ultimately it is only as good as the data and imagery you have available to create it—the difference between something that looks real or animated. Our team used advanced tools like LiDAR to gather extensive data and high-resolution cameras to film the location. LiDAR is remote sensing technology that can be used to create 3-D models and maps that are accurate to the millimeter. In theory, we could 3-D print these places at full size if we wanted to. These tools not only provide incredibly accurate data, they guarantee a beautiful user experience—as close to real as you can get without being there.

NGL: What special challenges did the Church of the Holy Sepulchre offer?

ALAN: We had to consider the historical and religious significance of the church. This is a cultural site that draws hundreds of thousands of pilgrims and tourists each year, and we were mandated to conduct our work without interrupting visitors' experiences. This meant deploying a very small team working simultaneously in relatively short periods of time—even in the middle of the night. And the structure of the Edicule itself was a challenge.

NGL: In what way?

ALAN: The Edicule was somewhat fragile after centuries of pilgrims' attention. There's an expression that we can "love a place to death." These historical monuments aren't built to withstand that much traffic. And that's what's so great about the possibilities of VR—we can make the site accessible to so many more people without risking more damage to the site itself. And it allows us to tell stories in brand new ways, like changing lighting, getting camera angles and close-ups that would be impossible for a real-life visitor, even taking you back and forth in time.

NGL: How has the *Tomb of Christ* exhibition been received by the public?

ALAN: It was our second-most popular show! But best, I think it surprised our visitors. People came in expecting one type of exhibition—maybe one with artifacts, for example—and instead found something very different. Many people came in specifically because it was the Church of the Holy Sepulchre, but these new technologies and methods of storytelling are usable for all kinds of locations. Our explorers are out there capturing data all over the globe that will let us take visitors along with them. The bottom line is VR is an exciting new way to help visitors explore aspects of human history in a new way. ∎

HISTORICAL THINKING

FORM AND SUPPORT OPINIONS Do you think it is a good idea to use VR to help people explore historic sites? What are some of the benefits? What are some of the drawbacks?

3.3

MAIN IDEA Christianity was based on the teachings of Jesus and spread by his followers.

The Spread of Christianity

A great teacher can change lives. Jesus had this power. His message of love and everlasting life brought hope and joy to his followers and laid the foundation of a religion that continues to influence the world today.

The Spread of Christianity, c. 500 C.E.

- Boundary of Roman Empire, c. 395 C.E.
- Christian areas, c. 325 C.E.
- Christian expansion, c. 500 C.E.

TEACHINGS OF JESUS

The Romans captured Jerusalem in 63 B.C.E. and brought the Jewish people under their control. For many years, Roman emperors allowed the Jews to worship their God, just as they tolerated the practices of many other religions in the empire. But when the Roman rulers began to enforce emperor worship, the Jews resisted and rose up against Rome. The Jews were defeated in 70 C.E., and the future emperor Titus destroyed Jerusalem and the temple. Many of the Jewish people left the city and scattered throughout the empire. Their dispersion helped spread a new religion that was gaining ground in the Jewish community. The religion was **Christianity**, and it was based on the teachings of a Jew from Nazareth named **Jesus**.

Most of what we know about Jesus and his teachings comes from the four Gospels, which were written after his death by four of his disciples, or followers: Matthew, Mark, Luke, and John. The books are part of the Christian Bible's New Testament. Through these sources, we know that Jesus worked as a carpenter and began to speak openly about his new ideas when he was about 30 years old, around 28 C.E. The Gospels also claim that Jesus could perform such miracles as healing the sick and bringing the dead back to life.

Jesus taught that obedience to God's laws was more important than following the laws of men. This Judeo-Christian view of law differed from the Greco-Roman view, which insisted that laws were made by citizens.

174 CHAPTER 6

Both cultures asserted that everyone should follow laws, but the Judeo-Christian tradition influenced democratic law with its principles of equality and ethical behavior. In Greco-Roman culture, philosophers upheld the power of reason and logic, while Judeo-Christian adherents put their faith in God. And while the Judeo-Christian tradition taught that it is the duty of every individual to live a moral life and practice charity and love toward all, the Greco-Roman world emphasized the civic duty of the individual citizen to vote and contribute to public life.

Jesus' teachings appealed to ordinary people. He declared that God loved everyone equally—not just the wealthy and powerful. Jesus also promised that those who loved God and sought his forgiveness for their sins would go to heaven after death. To his disciples, Jesus was Christ, "the anointed one." That is, they believed Jesus was the Messiah, the one who would free them.

SPREADING THE MESSAGE

As Jesus traveled through the Roman province of Judea preaching his message, he chose his closest disciples, known as the **Twelve Apostles**, to help him spread it. Like Jesus, the apostles stressed the importance of living a simple life and helping the less fortunate. After Jesus was denounced, or condemned, by some conservative Jewish authorities for his new ideas, he was arrested by the Romans as a dangerous popular leader. Jesus was executed by crucifixion.

After Jesus' death, his apostles and other followers continued to spread his teachings. Traveling on the Roman road network, they carried Christianity to Jewish communities throughout the empire. They also began encouraging Gentiles, or non-Jews, to worship with them. Soon, Christianity split from Judaism, developed its own identity, and grew rapidly. But Roman authorities still didn't realize that Christianity was separate from Judaism, which allowed Christians to operate without attracting much attention from the Romans.

Nevertheless, the Romans sometimes persecuted, or punished, Christians for their beliefs. One of the fiercest of these persecutors was **Paul**, a Greek-speaking Jew from Anatolia born around the same time as Jesus. But Paul became Christianity's greatest champion. According to the New Testament, Jesus appeared as the Son of God to Paul in a vision. Soon after, Paul converted to Christianity and began spreading Jesus'

CRITICAL VIEWING *The Last Supper,* painted by Italian artist Leonardo da Vinci in 1498, depicts the moment when Jesus announces to his 12 closest followers that one of them will betray him. Jesus is seated in the middle of the table. Judas, his betrayer, is the second man to Jesus' right. What emotions are vividly expressed by the followers in this moment?

teachings himself. In fact, he became a **missionary**, a person who travels to another country to do religious work.

Paul traveled throughout the eastern Mediterranean, Greece, and Italy and established several churches in these regions. He also reached out to Christian communities through his **epistles**, or letters, in which he answered questions, resolved issues, and generally kept up the spirits of persecuted Christians. Paul was often arrested for his activities, but he always escaped to preach again.

In 64 C.E., the Roman emperor Nero blamed Christians for a devastating fire that swept through Rome. By then, the Romans had realized that Christianity was a separate religion and that it was becoming increasingly popular. Fearing that it might destabilize the empire, Nero made the practice of Christianity illegal. He had thousands of Christians massacred, including Paul, according to traditional belief. Because anyone could be put to death for simply being a Christian, worshipers met in secret and buried their dead in underground chambers called **catacombs**. The suffering of Christians would continue for more than 250 years, but their courage and determination ensured Christianity's survival and later growth as the world's largest religion.

HISTORICAL THINKING

1. **READING CHECK** Who was Jesus?

2. **INTERPRET MAPS** Where did Christianity spread outside of the Roman Empire?

3. **DESCRIBE** What are key beliefs of the Judeo-Christian culture?

3.4

MAIN IDEA A traveler historians call Egeria made a pilgrimage to the eastern Mediterranean and wrote a descriptive account of her travels to various biblical sites.

Traveler: Egeria
An Early Christian Pilgrim

C. LATER 4TH CENTURY–EARLY 5TH CENTURY C.E.

Egeria is a woman of mystery. We don't know when she was born or when she died. We're not even entirely sure that Egeria was her name. What we do know is that around 379 C.E. she set off for Jerusalem for the trip of a lifetime.

PILGRIMAGE

Most historians believe Egeria was born in the second half of the fourth century to a well-to-do family in the Galicia region of Roman Spain. Although she bore a pagan name—Egeria is the name of a water spirit in the polytheistic religion of ancient Rome—she had a strong Christian faith. As a young woman, Egeria decided to leave home and take a **pilgrimage**, a journey to a holy place.

Like Paul a few hundred years before, Egeria took to the Roman roads on a religious journey. Unlike Paul, she didn't set out to spread Jesus' teachings, and she didn't have to worry about being arrested. In 312, Rome put an end to the persecution of Christians. And in 380, Christianity became the official religion of the Roman Empire. (You'll learn more about this surprising turn of events later in the chapter.) Traveling mostly by foot, Egeria went to visit sites in the Holy Land and beyond. Egeria had studied the Bible thoroughly. She wanted to visit biblical sites and talk about biblical events with the local Christians she would meet along the way.

Egeria's primary destination was Jerusalem, at the time a center of Christian thought and a holy city for both Christians and Jews. She remained there for three years, likely from 381 to 384. During her stay in Jerusalem, she took trips to other biblical sites in the region, including a lengthy expedition south to Mount Sinai on Egypt's Sinai Peninsula. In Egypt, Egeria also visited Alexandria and sailed south on the Nile River as far as Thebes. Her homeward trip took her north along the coast of Syria to present-day Turkey and the city of Constantinople, now Istanbul.

A LETTER HOME

Near the end of her pilgrimage, Egeria wrote a long letter to a circle of women in her hometown, based on notes she had kept during her travels. She addressed the letter to her *sorores*, Latin for "sisters." This term could mean that she herself was a sister, or nun, in a religious society. But it might just have been the way she addressed her female Christian friends. Egeria wrote expressively, mainly in Latin but with occasional Greek phrases. She offered detailed descriptions of what she saw, perhaps to help her friends imagine what she was experiencing.

The fragment of Egeria's letter that has survived begins with her trip to Mount Sinai. In the following excerpt from her letter, Egeria describes the view from Sinai's summit. Note that she refers to the eastern Mediterranean as the Parthenian Sea and uses the term *Saracens* to indicate the Arabs of the Sinai Peninsula.

PRIMARY SOURCE

I want you to be quite clear about these mountains, reverend ladies my sisters, which surrounded us as we stood beside the church looking down from the summit of the mountain in the middle. They had been almost too much for us to climb, and I really do not think I have ever seen any that were higher (apart from the central one which is higher still) even though they only looked like little hillocks to us as we stood on the central mountain. From there we were able to see Egypt and Palestine, the Red Sea and the Parthenian Sea (the part that takes you to Alexandria), as well as the vast lands of the Saracens—all unbelievably far below us.

—from *Egeria's Travels* by John Wilkinson, 1999

Egeria also discussed her encounters with monks and clergy. She visited several of the Christian churches in Jerusalem. Egeria described the daily services in one by writing that all the doors of the church "are opened before cockcrow [very early morning] each day." And after the monks and men and women "who are willing to wake at such an hour" arrive, "they start the morning hymns and the bishop with his clergy comes and joins them."

Only the middle part of her letter, which includes descriptions of her trips to Palestine and Egypt, survived. In the 11th century, this fragment of the letter was copied in a manuscript and preserved in an Italian monastery. The manuscript lay forgotten in the monastery for about 700 years until it was rediscovered in the late 1800s.

Egeria's account of her travels is among the earliest written by a Christian on a pilgrimage to the Holy Land. Her letter has been a treasure trove for scholars, who have studied it to learn about the evolution of the Latin language in the later period of the ancient world. Religious scholars have also gleaned information about the development of Christian church services in the fourth century. But most of all, Egeria's observations during her travels and her religious passion strike a common chord with the many pilgrims who have since followed in her footsteps.

HISTORICAL THINKING

1. **READING CHECK** Why did Egeria undertake her pilgrimage?

2. **COMPARE AND CONTRAST** How do Egeria's travels in the Roman Empire compare with those of Paul?

3. **INTERPRET MAPS** According to the maps, what possible route did Egeria take to Jerusalem?

3.5 DOCUMENT-BASED QUESTION
The Romans and the Christians

You probably take freedom of religion for granted. It's a basic right in the United States. The Roman Empire didn't go quite that far. It did tolerate many gods, including those worshiped by conquered peoples. But in time, the Romans came to require that people worship the emperor. Both Jews and Christians believed in one single almighty God, and many were willing to die rather than worship another.

The Temple of Saturn, shown here, has stood in the Roman Forum since around 497 B.C.E. It was dedicated to the Roman god of agriculture. The temple was restored in 42 B.C.E. and then again before 380 C.E. The second restoration was designed to demonstrate Rome's continuing resistance to Christianity.

Emperor worship began with the death of Julius Caesar, when he was officially recognized as a god. Once Augustus became emperor, he allowed people in some parts of the empire to build temples to him. However, in Rome and throughout Italy, an emperor was traditionally only worshiped—often with sacrificial offerings—after his death. Members of an emperor's family were also worshiped.

Roman rulers believed emperor worship helped unify the empire and center the people's loyalty on the ruler. When Christianity became too big to ignore, the Christian refusal to honor the emperor with sacrifices at public festivals was seen as endangering the empire. As you know, Nero blamed the Christians after fire destroyed much of Rome in 64 C.E. Nero may have made them his scapegoat because he was responsible for the fire.

Following Nero's persecution of the Christians, the emperor Trajan, who ruled from 98 to 117, determined that a person could be punished if proven guilty of being Christian. Many Romans also objected to Christianity's ceremonies. The Roman historian Tacitus suggested that Christians were "hated because of their outrageous practices." One such practice, Holy Communion—the consumption of bread and wine believed by Christians to be the body and blood of Jesus—led to charges of cannibalism.

DOCUMENT ONE

Primary Source: Book
from *The Annals* by Tacitus, 109 C.E.

The Annals is a history of the Roman Empire from the reign of Tiberius to that of Nero. In this work, Tacitus refers to Jesus and Christians only once—and by so doing, provides convincing evidence for most scholars that Jesus really did exist. In the following excerpt, Tacitus first discusses the execution of Jesus ("Christus") and then refers to the fire in Rome for which Christians were held responsible.

CONSTRUCTED RESPONSE How does Tacitus characterize Christianity?

> Christus, from whom the name [Christian] had its origin, suffered the extreme penalty during the reign of Tiberius at the hands of one of our procurators, Pontius Pilate, and a most mischievous superstition, thus checked for the moment, again broke out not only in Judea, the first source of the evil, but even in Rome. . . . Accordingly, an arrest was first made of all who pleaded guilty; then, upon their information, an immense multitude was convicted, not so much of the crime of firing the city, as of hatred against mankind.

DOCUMENT TWO

Primary Source: Letter
from *Letters of Pliny* by Gaius Plinius Caecilius Secundus, C.E. 112

From 111 to 113, Pliny the Younger, then a respected Roman politician, served as the governor of a province in Anatolia. A number of Christians had appeared in his court, and Pliny wrote to Emperor Trajan to explain his method for punishing them.

CONSTRUCTED RESPONSE What method did Pliny use to determine whether Christians should be punished?

> [T]he method I have observed towards those who have been brought before me as Christians is this: I asked them whether they were Christians; if they admitted it, I repeated the question twice, and threatened them with punishment; if they persisted, I ordered them to be at once punished: for I was persuaded, whatever the nature of their opinions might be, a contumacious [rebellious] and inflexible obstinacy [stubbornness] certainly deserved correction.

DOCUMENT THREE

Primary Source: Official Proclamation
from the Edict of Toleration issued by Emperor Galerius, C.E. 311

Gaius Galerius Valerius Maximianus was a Roman emperor from 305 to 311. Galerius persecuted Christians mercilessly—until 311 when he came down with a painful disease. Some historians speculate that Galerius issued his Edict of Toleration because he feared the Christian God was punishing him for his persecutions.

CONSTRUCTED RESPONSE How does Galerius characterize Christians and himself?

> After the publication, on our part, of an order commanding Christians to return to the observance of the ancient [Roman] customs, many of them, it is true, submitted in view of the danger, while many others suffered death. Nevertheless, since many of them have continued to persist in their opinions and we see that in the present situation they neither duly [properly] adore and venerate [honor] the gods nor yet worship the god of the Christians, we, with our wonted clemency [customary mercy], have judged it is wise to extend a pardon even to these men and permit them once more to become Christians and re-establish their places of meetings.

SYNTHESIZE & WRITE

1. **REVIEW** Review what you have learned about the Roman Empire, Roman religion, and Christianity.

2. **RECALL** On your own paper, write down the main idea expressed in each document.

3. **CONSTRUCT** Construct a topic sentence that answers this question: How did Roman authorities and writers view Christianity?

4. **WRITE** Using evidence from this chapter and the documents, write an informative paragraph that supports your topic sentence in Step 3.

The Roman Empire and the Rise of Christianity

4.1

MAIN IDEA As the Roman Empire declined in the third and fourth centuries, far-reaching political and religious changes took place.

Decline of the Roman Empire

When you hear today that a company is too big to fail, that means it's too important to the economy to be allowed to fail. That concept didn't exist in ancient Rome. The empire was becoming too big to manage from Rome, and things began to fall apart.

ROMAN WORLD IN CRISIS

For about 200 years, the Roman Empire ran relatively smoothly, largely under the rule of the so-called "Five Good Emperors." The five were Nerva, Trajan, Hadrian, Antoninus Pius, and Marcus Aurelius, whose reigns spanned the years from 96 to 180 C.E. They were strong rulers who had managed to maintain order in the empire. But with its diverse geography and cultures, the vast empire was becoming increasingly difficult for an emperor to govern.

Defending it was challenging, too. During the last years of Marcus Aurelius's rule, wars broke out on Rome's northern and eastern borders. In the north, Germanic tribes launched raids along the Danube River. In the east, Rome fought the powerful Parthian Empire from Persia. Conflicts on these two fronts strained the empire's money and resources.

After the death of Marcus Aurelius, the empire descended into civil war, as warring groups fought over who would be emperor. While Roman soldiers battled both at home and abroad, invaders plundered riches from unguarded Roman provinces. As the empire became increasingly unsafe, people blamed their leaders. Between 235 and 285, more than 25 different emperors ruled, many of whom were either replaced or murdered. In the Iberian Peninsula, France, and Britain, the people broke from Rome to form a separate Gallic Empire. They preferred the rule of local leaders.

A DIVIDED EMPIRE

At last, in 284, the throne was seized by **Diocletian** (dy-uh-KLEE-shun), who came up with a plan for keeping the empire alive. The new emperor put an end to the principate and, in 285, divided the empire in two: the Western Roman Empire and the Eastern Roman Empire. Diocletian set up a rule by four emperors called a **tetrarchy**. Diocletian ruled the Eastern Roman Empire, and his trusted friend Maximian ruled the Western Roman Empire. Diocletian named the two junior emperors.

Diocletian and Maximian began to institute reforms. They strengthened the army by increasing the number of soldiers to 400,000 men and creating new forces that could be sent to put down trouble wherever it broke out. They also divided the provinces into smaller, more manageable units. In an effort to promote unity, Diocletian and Maximian enforced emperor worship and the use of the Latin language, although Greek was commonly used in the eastern empire. To increase revenue, the emperors regulated the tax system and stabilized the currency. After 20 years, and with the empires recovering, Diocletian and Maximian stepped down and let the junior emperors take over.

The tetrarchy did not last long after that, however. **Constantine**, the son of a former senior emperor of the Western Roman Empire, began a quest for power and sparked a civil war. Constantine became the emperor of the Western Roman Empire in 312 and emperor of both empires in 324. However, he was more interested in the Eastern Roman Empire.

By that time, Rome and the west had weakened considerably. The east had a larger population and produced more food, taxes, and soldiers than the west. So Constantine decided to move the imperial capital from Rome to the ancient Greek city of Byzantium in the Eastern Roman Empire. He renamed the city Constantinople, which means "city of Constantine." The capital was located on the strategically important Bosporus, a narrow stretch of water between Europe and Asia. Constantine rebuilt the city on a monumental scale similar to that of Rome, and so it was sometimes known as "New Rome." He also continued the reforms begun by Diocletian and Maximian, thereby earning the title "Constantine the Great."

CHRISTIANITY RISES

As you know, after Christianity continued to grow in the Roman Empire, emperors began to perceive the religion as a threat. Christians suffered persecution for hundreds of years. In 303, Diocletian's junior emperor, Galerius, launched a particularly violent persecution of Christians. He imprisoned church leaders, destroyed churches, and executed those who would not sacrifice to Roman gods. You may remember that Galerius ended Christian persecution with the Edict of Toleration in 311.

In 312, on the eve of a battle for control of the empire, the fate of Christianity changed even more dramatically. According to legend, Constantine had a vision of the Christian cross in the sky before battle. As a result, he had the cross painted on his soldiers' shields, and they marched into battle as "Christian soldiers." Constantine won the battle, became emperor, and converted to Christianity. In 313, he issued the Edict of Milan, legalizing Christianity.

In 325, Constantine summoned a group of Christian leaders to meet in the city of Nicaea (nye-SEE-uh), in Anatolia, not far from the new capital. The leaders drew up a basic statement of faith, known as the Nicene Creed. The creed defined God as a Holy Trinity: the union of Father, Son (Jesus), and Holy Spirit. It also established common Christian sacraments, or religious ceremonies, including Baptism.

This meeting began the practice of gathering Christian leaders together to discuss beliefs and practices, which were then communicated to churches throughout the empire and beyond. Each church was led by a priest, and groups of churches were overseen by a bishop. According to biblical tradition, the first bishop was the apostle Peter, who was killed during the persecutions in 64 C.E. Another bishop named Augustine, who served in the port city of Hippo in northern Africa from 396 to his death in 430, continues to influence Christian thought today. In time, the bishop of Rome became the most important bishop, or pope, and led the unified Roman Catholic Church.

In 380, the emperor Theodosius declared Christianity the official religion of the Roman Empire. Christianity eventually replaced the polytheistic Roman traditions and became a powerful, organized religion.

The *Colossus of Constantine*, carved around 315, was originally placed near the Roman Forum and showed the emperor seated on a throne. The statue was about 40 feet high. Today, only these marble fragments remain, including Constantine's huge head and hand, and are exhibited in the courtyard of a museum in Rome.

HISTORICAL THINKING

1. **READING CHECK** Why was the Roman Empire in crisis?

2. **COMPARE AND CONTRAST** In what ways were the Western and Eastern Roman empires similar and different?

3. **MAKE INFERENCES** Why do you think Constantinople was a strategic location for Roman trade?

The Roman Empire and the Rise of Christianity 181

4.2

MAIN IDEA Both external and internal factors brought the Western Roman Empire to an end.

Fall of the Western Roman Empire

In spite of the problems that plagued the Western Roman Empire, most people probably couldn't imagine the world without it. But danger stood just outside the empire's frontiers. It was the beginning of the end.

INVADING TRIBES

After Constantine's death in 337, his sons came to power, but they soon plunged the empire into another civil war. Theodosius, who, as you know, made Christianity the official religion of Rome, reunited the empire. But after his death in 395, the division of the eastern and western empires became permanent.

Meanwhile, Germanic tribes from northern Europe—the Goths (comprising two branches, the Ostrogoths and the Visigoths) and the Vandals—continued to try to cross into the western empire along the Danube-Rhine border. They came in search of better farmland and so migrated south toward the Roman frontier. However, the Romans considered the tribes barbarians and resisted their request to settle on Roman soil.

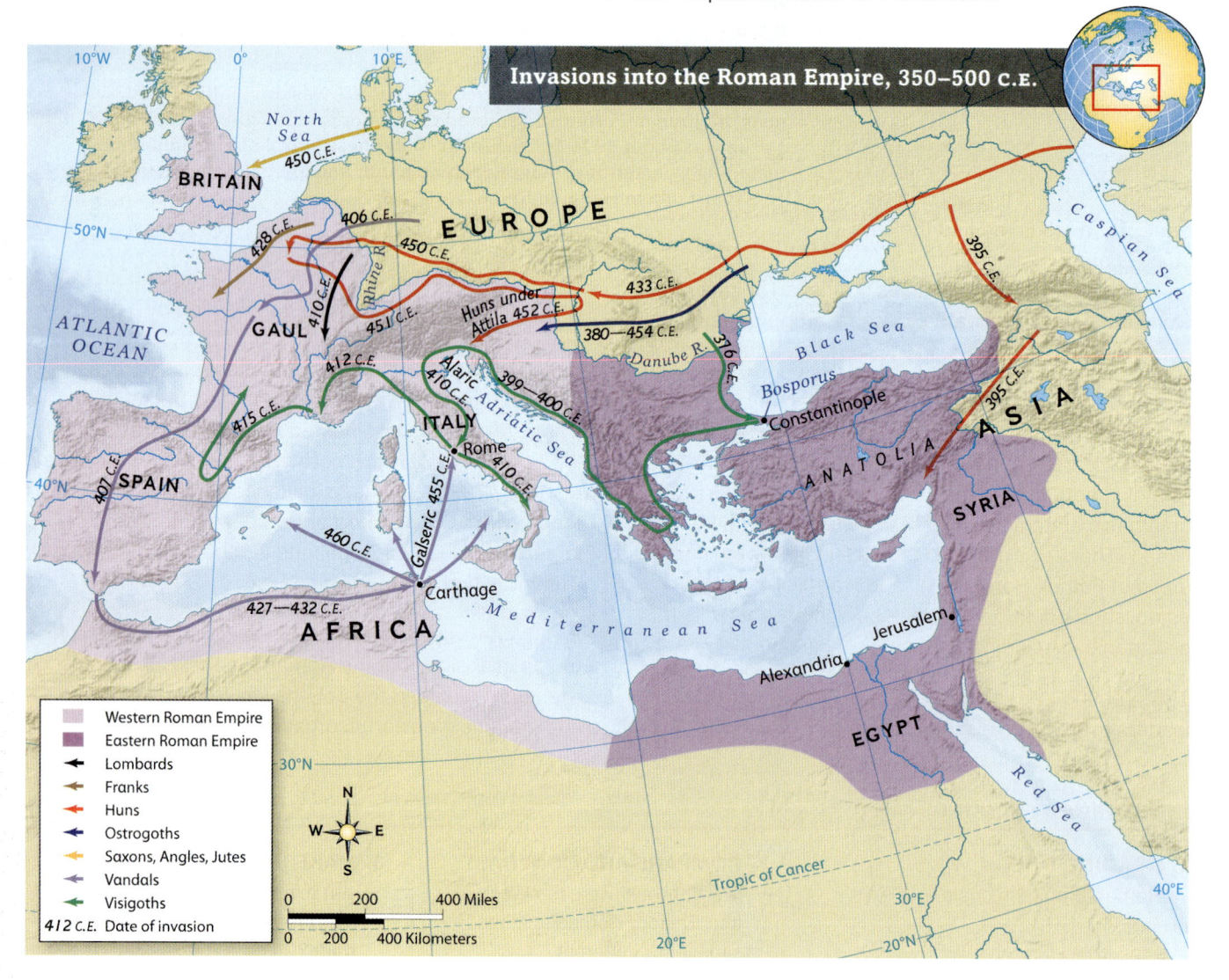

Invasions into the Roman Empire, 350–500 C.E.

Legend:
- Western Roman Empire
- Eastern Roman Empire
- Lombards
- Franks
- Huns
- Ostrogoths
- Saxons, Angles, Jutes
- Vandals
- Visigoths
- 412 C.E. Date of invasion

182 CHAPTER 6

The Goths' request became more urgent in the 370s when the Huns, a nomadic group from Central Asia, threatened the tribe's homeland. The Huns' skill with horses and bows made them a ferocious fighting force. After the Goths were forced to cross the Danube into the Western Roman Empire, a Roman commander attacked them, inciting war. In the early 400s, the Vandals, with as many as 80,000 soldiers, invaded Gaul and then Spain. With few Roman soldiers at their command, the Roman emperors had to enlist "barbarian" fighters to defend the empire.

And then the unthinkable happened. On August 24, 410, Alaric, the chief of the Visigoths, led his army into Rome. Alaric had been trained in the Roman army. Over three days, he and his soldiers completely sacked Rome. About 6,000 Roman soldiers came to defend the city, but they were quickly defeated. This was the first time since the fourth century B.C.E. that a foreign army had entered the city. It would not be the last time.

New invaders appeared again and again, as other Germanic tribes, including the Lombards, Franks, Angles, Saxons, and Jutes, went on the attack against the western empire. Roman armies fought back but to no avail. Province after province fell to the invaders. The Vandals crossed the Mediterranean to North Africa, where they captured Carthage in 439. Angles, Saxons, and Jutes crossed the sea into Britain. Ostrogoths and Lombards streamed into northern Italy and Gaul, where they settled. Led by their ruler, **Attila**, the Huns attacked Gaul in 451 but were defeated by the Romans and the Visigoths. A year later, Attila invaded Italy and sacked several cities. In 455, Vandal forces sailed to Italy. They occupied Rome for two weeks.

END OF THE WESTERN EMPIRE

For the next 20 years or so, different Germanic groups gained control of Rome. Finally, in 476, the Germanic leader Odoacer entered the city with his army. Unopposed, he removed the final Roman ruler of the western empire, a 16-year-old named Romulus, and became the first king of Italy. The Roman Empire was over. The Western Roman Empire was broken up into many Germanic kingdoms. The Eastern Roman Empire, with its capital at Constantinople, remained powerful and united. Later known as the Byzantine Empire, it would continue imperial traditions for nearly 1,000 years.

So what led to the fall of the Western Roman Empire? Historians have been debating the question for centuries. Most agree that the internal problems that weakened Rome had existed for many years and rendered the empire vulnerable to the invaders.

Perhaps the main reason for Rome's fall was its financial woes. Constant warfare ruined Rome's economy and disrupted its trade. The Vandals struck a major blow when they claimed North Africa and seized control of the Mediterranean. Because of the empire's inadequate agricultural production, people suffered food shortages. They also faced higher taxes. The empire expected its citizens to pay for all the expensive wars being fought. Both the rich and the poor suffered as a result of the failing economy, but the poor suffered more. Unrest arose as the gap between the two classes widened.

Rome's declining economy also undermined defense. In the early 400s, the Roman army consisted of an estimated 350,000 troops stationed at frontier outposts and 150,000 mobile troops. To maintain the army's strength, soldiers had to be paid. But decreasing revenues sometimes meant no recompense for soldiers. When they weren't paid, they didn't fight.

The army suffered from a lack of manpower for another reason. After expansion ended in the second century, the influx of conquered people and slaves to the empire began to come to a halt. The economy, in part, depended on slave labor, and the army relied on those taken in war to fill its ranks. In time, the army had to hire Germanic peoples to fight Rome's battles. And these soldiers felt little, if any, loyalty toward the empire.

After the division of the empire, the west began to suffer politically as well. Ineffective and corrupt leaders created instability in the western empire. No longer able to trust the leadership of their government, ordinary citizens began to look out for themselves rather than the empire. The Roman virtue of civic responsibility no longer seemed very important.

The Roman Empire lasted about 500 years and, for much of that time, dominated the Mediterranean. Rome fell, but it left a legacy in such areas as law and government, culture and language, and architecture and engineering. This legacy continues to influence much of the world today.

HISTORICAL THINKING

1. **READING CHECK** What happened on August 24, 410?

2. **INTERPRET MAPS** Which groups invaded the Eastern Roman Empire?

3. **DRAW CONCLUSIONS** How did bringing Germanic peoples into the Roman army sometimes backfire on Rome?

4.3

MAIN IDEA Ancient Rome left a lasting legacy in the arts, sciences, religion, and government.

The Legacy of Ancient Rome

How, you may wonder, can an ancient civilization influence our lives today? Let us count the ways. From the words we speak to the laws that govern us, Rome's legacy is everywhere.

LANGUAGE AND LITERATURE

You may remember that the early Romans adapted the Etruscan alphabet to develop a Latin one. As the Roman Empire grew, Latin writing spread to northern Europe. Over time, five Romance languages—French, Spanish, Italian, Portuguese, and Romanian—developed from Latin. The English language uses the Latin alphabet, and many English words have Latin roots, including *subway* (*sub-* is a Latin prefix meaning "under") and *statement* (the suffix *-ment* is used to form a noun from a verb). Furthermore, the English language adopted Latin words such as *campus*, *census*, and *stadium*. Legal documents are rich with Latin text, including common expressions such as *ex post facto*, *per se*, and *quid pro quo*, and the language also makes appearances in science papers and memorial inscriptions.

The Romans also left a legacy in poetry. For the Romans, the ultimate poem was the epic. This long poetic form, based on Greek traditions, recounts a hero's adventures. The most celebrated Roman epic is the *Aeneid* by the poet **Virgil**. Written between 30 and 19 B.C.E.—during the early years of the Roman Empire—the work tells the story of Aeneas, a mythical Roman hero said to have fled to Italy from his Trojan homeland to become the legendary father of the Romans.

Public speaking, or **oratory**, was highly prized in ancient Rome as well. A young male patrician's education typically included training in the art of argument and persuasion. The Roman statesman **Cicero**, who served as a consul in 63 B.C.E., was one of Rome's greatest orators. Serious students of debate and public speaking still study his speeches today.

CRITICAL VIEWING When he served as a consul of the Roman Republic in 63 B.C.E., Cicero stood before the Senate and denounced Catiline, a senator who had plotted to overthrow the republic. The event is depicted in this 19th-century painting by Italian artist Cesare Maccari and shows Catiline sitting alone while Cicero attacks him. What details in the painting convey Cicero's skill as a public speaker?

184 CHAPTER 6

CRITICAL VIEWING The exterior of the Pantheon is relatively plain, but the interior, shown here, is lined with colored marble and is dominated by its great concrete dome. No one knows what method Roman engineers used to support the Pantheon's dome. The oculus, or "eye"—the opening you see here in the center of the dome—provides the structure's sole source of light. How would you describe the dome?

MATHEMATICS AND PHILOSOPHY

Math may not come to mind when you think about ancient Rome, but the Roman numeral system was superior to any other that had been known in Europe up to that time. Roman numerals used the symbols I (1), V (5), X (10), L (50), C (100), and D (500). The symbol M, for 1,000, emerged after the fall of Rome. These numerals made simple math problems easier to solve. The Romans probably adopted the numerical system from the Etruscans. But while the Etruscans read their numbers from right to left, the Romans read theirs from left to right. Roman numerals are no longer used in mathematics—they were replaced by Arabic numerals around the 10th century—but are sometimes seen on public buildings, among many other uses.

Greek ideas inspired much of Roman philosophy. As you know, the Romans were practical people, so ethical and scientific arguments interested them more than theory and speculation. They were especially influenced by the Greek Stoic philosophy, which stressed civic duty and an acceptance of one's circumstances. Both ancient Greek and Roman philosophy taught moral and ethical principles—in particular, living a good and virtuous life. Similar values formed the basis of Judaism and Christianity and were central to the development of Western political thought. Their example had a deep influence on Thomas Jefferson, George Washington, and other founders of the United States.

ART, SCIENCE, AND TECHNOLOGY

The Romans took a realistic approach to art as well. Their statues and paintings portrayed subjects realistically. Like people today, many Romans decorated their homes with these works of art—although we usually display photos and paintings rather than heavy statues. In wealthier homes, mosaics and frescoes might have ornamented the floors and walls. Frescoes can be compared to modern murals and even some street art.

The Roman Empire and the Rise of Christianity

Erected in Rome in 315 C.E., the Arch of Constantine celebrates the emperor's victory in 312 when he fought for control of the empire. At about 70 feet high, the monument is Rome's largest surviving triumphal arch.

Roman artists frequently carved a relief, a sculpture with figures raised against a flat background, on monuments, tombs, and important public buildings. The sculptures often featured soldiers in battle, heroes and heroic deeds, and symbols of patriotism—universal themes that modern reliefs convey, including those at the National World War II Memorial in Washington, D.C.

With their improved form of concrete, Romans constructed all-weather roads, bridges, and buildings that can still be seen today. European roads still follow Roman routes and sometimes cross original Roman bridges. When building streets for a new town, Roman city planners took its geography and climate into account. They usually designed cities in a grid pattern, creating a network of intersecting horizontal and vertical lines. Many modern towns and cities use this pattern.

Roman architects used their durable concrete to create monuments and aqueducts throughout the empire. The columns, arches, and domes they included in these structures are also seen in the U.S. Capitol and other buildings. And many of today's stadiums are modeled on the design for Rome's Colosseum. Even some of the sports played in today's arenas resemble Roman gladiator games, in which opponents were pitted against each other. Of course, while modern athletes sometimes get hurt during a game, they no longer fight to the death.

RELIGION AND GOVERNMENT

One of Rome's most enduring legacies is its impact on religion. You probably remember that Constantine the Great had legitimized Christianity in 313, and Theodosius made it the official religion of the Roman Empire in 380. With the legalization of their religion, Christians quickly organized and spread their faith throughout the empire. The city of Rome soon became the home of the Roman Catholic Church. The church would go on to exert an enormous influence on European and global history. Today Christianity is the largest religion in the world.

In the Judeo-Christian legal tradition, all people are equal before God and before the law. And both the Hebrew Bible and the New Testament state that, when someone is accused of a crime, several witnesses must be brought forward to testify. A single witness is not enough to convict the person charged. The Romans had similar ideas, and these political concepts still influence the justice systems of many countries today, including that of the United States. The U.S. Constitution enforces equality before the law and declares that a person accused of a crime is innocent until proven guilty and has a right to a trial by a jury of peers, or fellow citizens.

The structure of the U.S. government also reflects elements of the Roman Republic's government, including representative assemblies and the system of checks and balances. And the Roman ideal of civic duty is encouraged in the United States and elsewhere. By the way, *civic* comes from the Latin word *civis*, meaning "relating to a citizen." It turns out that the Romans and their Latin language still influence the way we live today.

The Twelve Tables stated the rights and duties of citizens of the Roman Republic. These excerpts from the first and ninth tables detail some of the laws concerning trial proceedings and public law. Which of these laws are reflected in U.S. law today?

PRIMARY SOURCE

Table I. Proceedings Preliminary to Trial

1. If the plaintiff summons the defendant to court, the defendant shall go. If the defendant does not go, the plaintiff shall call a witness thereto. Only then the plaintiff shall seize the defendant.

7. If they agree not on terms, the parties shall state their case before the assembly in the meeting place or before the magistrate in the marketplace before noon. Both parties being present shall plead the case throughout together.

Table IX. Public Law

1–2. Laws of personal exception shall not be proposed. Laws concerning capital punishment of a citizen shall not be passed . . . except by the Greatest Assembly . . .

6. For anyone whomsoever to be put to death without a trial and unconvicted . . . is forbidden.

HISTORICAL THINKING

1. **READING CHECK** How has Latin influenced the English language?

2. **DRAW CONCLUSIONS** How might a philosophy that includes the idea of accepting one's circumstances help maintain the social order?

3. **MAKE INFERENCES** Why do you think many modern stadiums have been modeled on the Colosseum?

4. **EVALUATE** Why is it important to have several witnesses testify when someone is charged with a crime rather than rely on the testimony of a single witness?

The Roman Empire and the Rise of Christianity

CHAPTER 6 THE ROMAN EMPIRE AND THE RISE OF CHRISTIANITY
REVIEW

VOCABULARY

Write a sentence to explain the connection between each of the following pairs of vocabulary words.

1. republic; dictator
2. patrician; plebeian
3. legionary; mercenary
4. gladiator; amphitheater
5. missionary; pilgrimage

READING STRATEGY
COMPARE AND CONTRAST

Use a comparison chart like the one below to compare and contrast the role and rights of men and women in Roman society. Then answer the questions.

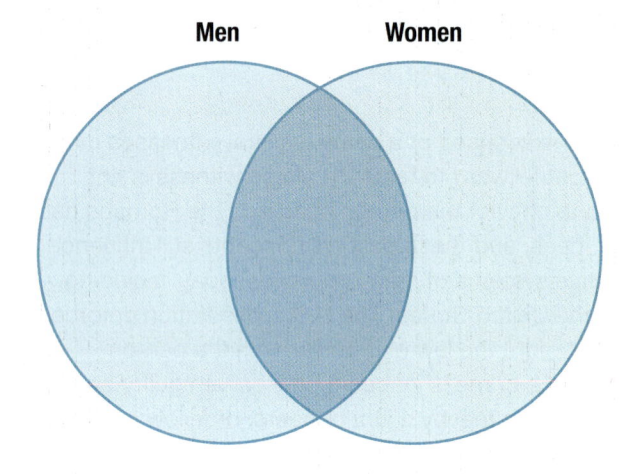

Men | Women

6. How did the roles of men and women differ?
7. What rights did men and women share?

MAIN IDEAS

Answer the following questions. Support your answers with evidence from the chapter.

8. How did the government of the Roman Republic differ from that of ancient Greece? **LESSON 1.1**
9. What surprise tactic did Hannibal use against the Romans during the Second Punic War? **LESSON 1.2**
10. What three classes made up the social order in the Roman Republic? **LESSON 1.3**
11. What did Julius Caesar do soon after he gained control of Rome? **LESSON 2.1**
12. Why did the emperor Hadrian build a wall in Britain? **LESSON 2.2**
13. How did the Roman Empire connect its far-flung lands? **LESSON 2.3**
14. How did the apostle Paul spread the story and teachings of Jesus? **LESSON 3.3**
15. What new type of government did Diocletian put in place? **LESSON 4.1**
16. How did the declining economy undermine the defense of the Western Roman Empire in the 300s and 400s? **LESSON 4.2**

HISTORICAL THINKING

Answer the following questions. Support your answers with evidence from the chapter.

17. **EVALUATE** How did Cincinnatus demonstrate the Roman virtue of civic duty?
18. **MAKE PREDICTIONS** What do you think might have happened if Julius Caesar had restored the republic?
19. **SYNTHESIZE** Why was concrete a critical material in the Roman Empire?
20. **COMPARE AND CONTRAST** How did the lives of slaves differ from those of patricians and plebeians in Roman society?
21. **DRAW CONCLUSIONS** What did Jesus' teachings have in common with democratic values?
22. **ANALYZE CAUSE AND EFFECT** What happened as a result of the division of the empire and the political and cultural shift toward the east?
23. **MAKE INFERENCES** Why do you think the Romans embraced the Greek epic poem?
24. **FORM AND SUPPORT OPINIONS** Do you think the Roman people were better off during the time of the republic or the empire, or were their lives similar during both periods? Explain your answer.

188 CHAPTER 6

INTERPRET CHARTS

Study the chart below, which compares the government of the Roman Republic with that of the United States. Then answer the questions that follow.

Roman Republic vs. United States

Government	Roman Republic	United States
EXECUTIVE BRANCH	Led by two consuls elected for a one-year term; led government and army; could veto each other's decisions; took advice from the Senate	Led by a president elected for a four-year term; heads government and military; has veto power over legislation; takes advice from Cabinet members
LEGISLATIVE BRANCH	• Senate of 300 members • Senate advised consuls and set policies • Plebeian assembly made laws and elected representatives	• Congress made up of Senate and House of Representatives • Senate of 100 members • House of Representatives of 435 members • Laws approved by both groups • Congress with power to override a presidential veto
JUDICIAL BRANCH	• Eight judges oversaw courts and governed provinces	• Supreme Court of nine justices • Supreme Court interprets the Constitution and federal law
LEGAL CODE	Twelve Tables basis of Roman law • Twelve Tables established laws protecting citizens' rights • Edicts made by magistrates	U.S. Constitution basis of U.S. law • Constitution established individual rights of citizens and powers of government • Congress has the power to propose and pass amendments to the Constitution

25. What legislative check on the executive branch is part of the U.S. government but was not part of the Roman Republic's government?

26. How is the Constitution similar to the Twelve Tables?

ANALYZE SOURCES

According to the Gospel of Matthew, Jesus gathered his disciples on a mountain, where he "opened his mouth and taught them." In this excerpt from the Sermon on the Mount, as the teachings came to be known, Jesus addresses persecuted Christians. Read the excerpt and answer the question that follows.

> Blessed are those who are persecuted for righteousness' sake, for theirs is the kingdom of heaven. Blessed are you when men revile [insult] you and persecute you and utter all kinds of evil against you falsely on my account. Rejoice and be glad, for your reward is great in heaven, for so men persecuted the prophets who were before you.
>
> —Matthew 5:10–11

27. What impact do you think these teachings had on those who suffered persecution?

CONNECT TO YOUR LIFE

28. EXPLANATORY Just as many diverse people searching for security and opportunity in ancient times became Roman citizens, many people today want to leave their homeland for a chance at a better life in other countries. Do you think today's immigrants to the United States should be allowed to settle here? Or should they be kept from entering the country? Write a brief essay explaining your views on immigration today.

TIPS

- Review how foreigners were regarded by Romans at various times during the republic and the empire. What did the Romans gain and suffer in their dealings with foreigners?

- Conduct research on our country's policy toward immigration today, and consider the advantages and disadvantages of admitting immigrants.

- Use two or three vocabulary terms from the chapter in your explanation.

- Provide a concluding statement that summarizes your views on immigration.

The Roman Empire and the Rise of Christianity

CHAPTER 7

Societies in East and South Asia
206 B.C.E.–1279 C.E.

HISTORICAL THINKING How did societies in East and South Asia influence one another's cultures over time?

SECTION 1 **Indian Cultures and Dynasties**
SECTION 2 **China's Han and Tang Empires**
SECTION 3 **East and Southeast Asian Kingdoms**

CRITICAL VIEWING
Mount Fuji, the highest mountain in Japan, is located on the island of Honshu. Based on details in the photo, why do you think many Japanese people consider Mount Fuji to be sacred?

Societies in East and South Asia 191

1.1

MAIN IDEA As texts, beliefs, and practices evolved, Hinduism spread in India and throughout the world.

Developments in Hinduism

Have your beliefs changed as you've grown older? What influenced those changes? The religious beliefs brought by the Indo-Aryans changed over time and these changes evolved into the religion we know as Hinduism.

Hindus make pilgrimages to Varanasi, an ancient city on the Ganges River, where they bathe in the river's water, which is believed to have purifying powers.

DEVELOPMENTS AND CENTRAL IDEAS

As you've read previously, the Rig Veda told stories of Indo-Aryan gods and goddesses. Hinduism grew out of these Indo-Aryan beliefs and developed slowly over many centuries. However, the term *Hinduism* wasn't used until the 19th century when the British of colonial India coined the term to refer to traditions and practices not associated with Islam, Jainism, or Christianity. Unlike Buddhism, Hinduism has no single founder, and it doesn't have an agreed upon set of beliefs. Because Hindus worship different Hindu deities, many people didn't consider themselves to be members of a single religious community until the 1800s.

The Upanishads, which you read about in an earlier chapter, introduced the concept of **Brahman** as a universal spirit. Hindus believe Brahman created the universe and exists in everything—a belief that became central to Hinduism. As new scriptures such as the Sanskrit epics the *Mahabharata* and the *Ramayana* appeared, Hindus began to see all Hindu deities as expressions of Brahman. Vishnu and Shiva became two of the most venerated, or revered, deities. These deities take many avatars, or forms with various names. In some cases, artists depict them as having four or more arms. This depiction represents **omnipotence**, or unlimited power, and the ability to overcome evil by performing multiple feats at once.

192 CHAPTER 7

CRITICAL VIEWING Most Hindu temples in India are dedicated to one deity. In southern India, the towers of a temple have a pyramid shape and are decorated with sculptures of mythological figures. The Meenakshi Temple (far left) in the city of Madurai is one of the oldest Hindu temples in India. Temples in the United States are often dedicated to multiple deities. They serve as both places of worship and community centers. Today, there are more than 450 Hindu temples in the United States. The BAPS Shri Swaminarayan Mandir (left), located in Atlanta, Georgia, is the largest Hindu temple in the United States. How are the two temples alike? How are they different?

Hindus believe the human soul is eternal and that after death people undergo reincarnation, in which their souls are reborn in different bodies over different life cycles. The things people do during their lifetimes affect their karma (the sum of their good and bad actions) and determine the kind of life into which each person will be reborn. The ultimate goal of a Hindu is to end this cycle of birth and rebirth by living selflessly and overcoming material desires.

RELIGIOUS PRACTICES

Hindu worship has both public and private aspects. Temples are the center of public worship. Hindus carry out private worship in their homes, where they express devotion to a personal deity.

Hindu rites are further classified into daily worship in the home, worship during religious holidays, and pilgrimages. Each year many Hindus travel to the Ganges River to bathe in its holy waters. They believe the river has purifying powers that will wash away sins. They also scatter the cremated remains of their loved ones there, believing the waters will elevate the loved ones' karma and assist the dead in reincarnation.

Pilgrims from around the world visit temples, shrines, and palaces in Varanasi, one of the oldest cities in the world. Located on the banks of the Ganges, it is revered as the home of Shiva. Varanasi is also an important city for India's Muslims and has ancient Buddhist ruins as well. The city is also a center of learning for those who study ancient Sanskrit texts.

THE SPREAD OF HINDUISM

The beliefs and rituals that would later be called Hinduism were primarily practiced in India. By 1 C.E., merchants and missionaries had carried the religion into present-day Nepal, Bhutan, and Sri Lanka. From there, they continued to spread Hinduism east throughout Southeast Asia.

Today Hinduism is growing in Britain, the United States, and Canada as immigrants from India move to these areas. There are approximately one million Hindus living in Britain and two million living in the United States. As the third largest religion in the world, after Christianity and Islam, Hinduism has nearly one billion practitioners worldwide.

HISTORICAL THINKING

1. **READING CHECK** What new religious concept about Brahman changed Hindus' beliefs about Hindu deities?

2. **DESCRIBE** Describe private and public worship in the Hindu religion and explain the role of pilgrimages.

3. **COMPARE AND CONTRAST** What are some of the similarities and differences between Hindu temples in India and the United States? Why are they different?

Societies in East and South Asia

1.2

MAIN IDEA Literature, art, mathematics, and science flourished during India's Gupta dynasty.

The Gupta Dynasty

Who first discovered that the planet Earth is round and orbits around the sun? Where did the numbers you use in math come from? You might be surprised to learn that these ideas first came from India during the Gupta dynasty.

RISE OF THE GUPTAS

After the fall of the Maurya Empire, India experienced a period of upheaval that lasted for approximately 500 years. During this time, various dynasties arose in different regions of South Asia. One of the most powerful was the Gupta dynasty, which controlled much of northern India between 320 and 600 C.E.

An admirer of the earlier Maurya Empire, the founder of the Gupta dynasty, **Chandragupta I**, took the name Chandragupta from the Maurya founder and governed from the former capital at Pataliputra. Unlike the Maurya rulers, Gupta rulers followed Hindu practices and sponsored the building of temples at which Brahmin priests led public worship. However, they tolerated other religions and included Buddhists among their court advisors.

Chandragupta I ruled the Gupta dynasty from 320 to 330. Both he and his son Samudragupta conquered neighboring kingdoms to expand the northern territory. However, they allowed the defeated kings to continue ruling their kingdoms as long as they provided military assistance or paid **tribute**, a tax required of conquered people.

This large-scale sculpture in the Udayagiri Caves dates to the early fifth century. It depicts the myth of Vishnu in the form of an avatar, rescuing goddess Earth from the cosmic ocean.

Gupta rulers divided the land into provinces governed by high imperial officers. This decentralized power gave more autonomy to the provinces, but they eventually began to seek independence. These internal struggles were compounded by foreign invasions. By approximately 600, invasions and independence movements had so weakened the dynasty that the Gupta were unable to retain control, and the dynasty fell apart after 300 years of rule.

RELIGION REFLECTED IN ART, LITERATURE, AND ARCHITECTURE

The classical Gupta dynasty is widely considered to have been the golden age in India when architecture and art flourished. Before the Gupta, temples were built of wood or brick, but Gupta dynasty builders constructed freestanding temples out of stone. Cave temples embellished with Hindu paintings and sculptures were also carved into sandstone hills at Udayagiri.

The Gupta rulers supported writers as well. The work of poet and playwright **Kalidasa**, considered the greatest of India's Sanskrit authors, reflects the sophisticated values of the Gupta dynasty and makes use of the literary possibilities of the Sanskrit language. In one of his poems, he wrote: "Yesterday is but a dream, Tomorrow is only a vision. But today well lived makes every yesterday a dream of happiness, and every tomorrow a vision of hope." Little is known about Kalidasa's life, and yet he had a significant impact on the work of writers who followed him.

ADVANCES IN MATHEMATICS, ASTRONOMY, AND METALLURGY

The oldest representation of the zero as a symbol was found on an ancient manuscript from the Gupta period, and a Gupta-era mathematician developed rules in rhymed verse for multiplying and dividing by zero. Independently, on the other side of the globe, the Maya of present-day southern Mexico and Central America started using the zero at roughly the same time.

The great mathematician and astronomer Aryabhata wrote books in which he furthered development of the decimal system, calculated pi to 3.1416, and calculated area and volume. One of his books explained that Earth is round and rotates around the sun. **Hindu-Arabic numerals** (1, 2, 3, . . . etc.) also came from Sanskrit of this period. These numerals are often called *Arabic* because Arab traders brought them to the west where they eventually replaced Roman numerals.

Gupta **metallurgy**, metal technology, also improved during this period. The Gupta imported gold to create beautifully crafted coins and used iron to construct tall pillars, such as the Iron Pillar of Delhi. This 23-foot tall pillar, erected around 400 C.E., is made of iron so pure that it has never rusted. It would be more than 1,000 years before metalworkers in other parts of the world would have the skill to create such a large object out of iron.

Roman, Sanskrit, and Western Numerals

Roman first used c. 900-800 B.C.E.	Sanskrit first used c. 450 B.C.E.	Western Arabic today
	•	0
I	⌒	1
II	२	2
III	३	3
IV	४	4
V	५	5
VI	६	6
VII	७	7
VIII	८	8
IX	९	9

HISTORICAL THINKING

1. **READING CHECK** Describe two advancements in literature and two advancements in mathematics during the Gupta dynasty.

2. **ANALYZE CAUSE AND EFFECT** What factors caused the decline and fall of the Gupta dynasty?

3. **INTERPRET CHARTS** How do the numerals in Sanskrit compare to our numerals today? Why did the Hindu-Arabic numerals replace the Roman numerals in the west?

1.3 **MAIN IDEA** Religion and politics merged and produced a better quality of life in the nearly forgotten Chola kingdom.

The Chola Kingdom

If you could build a structure that both honors your heroes and represents you, what would it look like? The rulers of the Chola kingdom are remembered for huge temples that not only convey a deep devotion to their gods, but also promote their own power.

LIFE UNDER THE CHOLA KINGDOM

While historians remember the Gupta period as the golden age in India, they hardly remember the Chola kingdom at all. Yet, the Chola kingdom of southern India, established in 907, rivals the Gupta Empire in its contributions to architecture, education, religion, and governance. The kingdom promoted dance and music at services in the temples. The Chola spoke Tamil, a Dravidian language that is unrelated to Sanskrit and other Indo-Aryan languages, and children learned to read and write Tamil. The Chola built colleges, and students were well educated in mathematics, astronomy, and literacy, as well as religion. In fact, the literacy rate was 20 percent, the highest in the world at the time.

Large irrigation projects also improved the Chola economy. The Chola built a 1,079-foot-long dam to divert water to six canals to irrigate thousands of acres. This dam, known as the Kallanai dam, is one of the oldest irrigation systems in the world that is still in use.

Despite the achievements of the Chola, not everyone was satisfied. By this time, the caste system had become much more rigid. The poor and the outcast had no chance of escape. One Hindu sect called the Lingayats questioned the ideas of reincarnation, rejected the caste system, cautioned against child marriage, and encouraged widows to remarry, a practice that was not allowed in the Chola world. People who expressed these ideas were forced to flee the kingdom. The Lingayats' ideas predated the social reform movements of the 19th century, and centuries later, their movement for greater social equality has lived on. These reformers continue to challenge ancient beliefs and practices in southern India today.

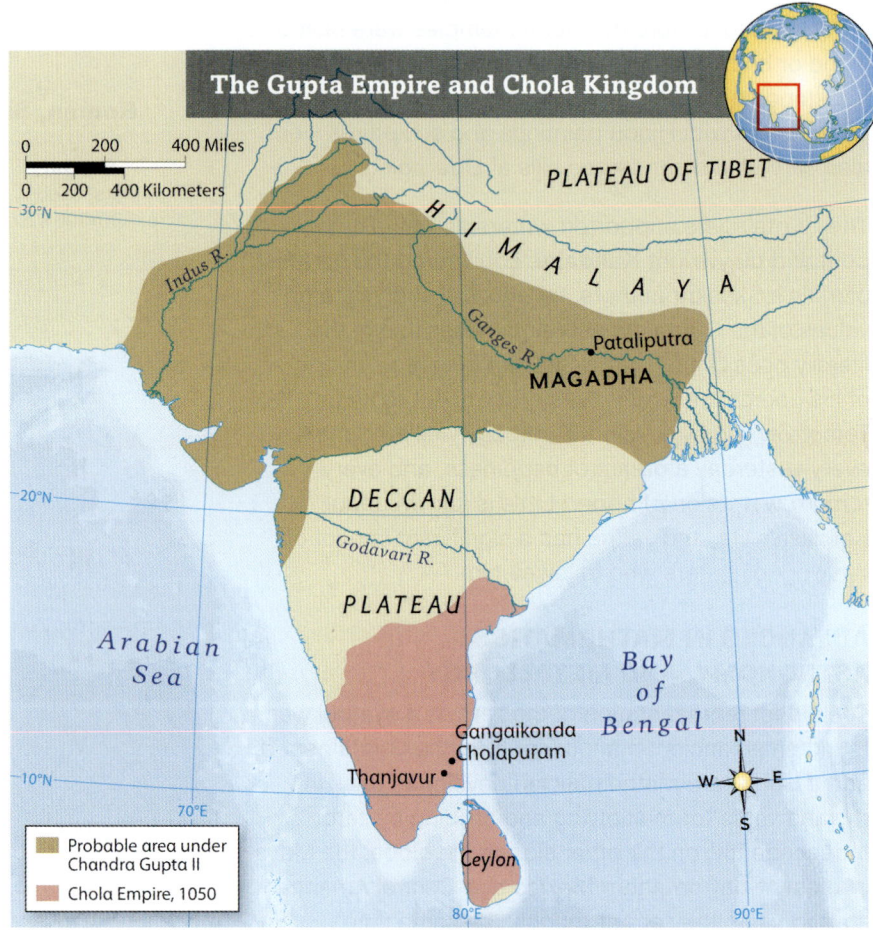

TEMPLES MIX RELIGION AND POLITICS

The Chola kingdom is renowned for its many elaborate temples, which displayed the kings' devotion to Hindu rituals. These architectural masterpieces lined the rivers

The Chola temples in Tamil Nadu, including the Brihadisvara Temple at Thanjavur shown here, are UNESCO World Heritage Sites. The Brihadisvara Temple is decorated with sculptures depicting Hindu deities.

and filled Chola cities. Today, a visitor to Tamil Nadu will find nearly a hundred temples in the Chola capital of Thanjavur alone.

The most famous of these Chola temples still stands over 200 feet tall, the tallest building of its time. The Chola king Rajaraja commissioned the temple and dedicated it to the deity Shiva in 1010. Frescoes depicting the king and the deity line the interior walls of the temple, and inscriptions provide details about Rajaraja's victories and accomplishments. The temple reveals the king's dedication to Shiva, as well as his belief that, as king, he was Shiva's representative on Earth.

After Rajaraja died, his son Rajendra moved the capital east and built his own temple. While Rajendra's structure is smaller than his father's, its graceful, curved tower and exceptional cast bronze and stone sculptures show a very high level of craftsmanship.

SUCCESS IN GOVERNMENT

The Chola ruled from 907 to 1279, longer than any other Indian kingdom. Chola leaders controlled the immediate vicinity of the capital and possibly the other large cities in the district. Elected district councils governed villages surrounding the cities and those in more distant areas. Every household was given one vote in elections, and subcommittees oversaw local matters. The Chola expanded south onto the island of Sri Lanka and out into the Indian Ocean. There they allowed local leaders to continue to rule, but they encouraged local rulers to build Hindu temples and to adopt Chola principles of government. The kingdom's stability may be attributed to this practice of self-government.

In 1257, the Chola were defeated by their neighbors, the Pandyas, in the southwest, and the kingdom finally fell in 1279.

HISTORICAL THINKING

1. **READING CHECK** What do the Chola temples reveal about their kings?

2. **ANALYZE CAUSE AND EFFECT** How did Chola government principles impact the success of the kingdom?

3. **EVALUATE** Why might historians question the inscriptions on temple walls describing Rajaraja's victories and accomplishments?

Societies in East and South Asia

2.1

MAIN IDEA A Chinese historian who wrote about the rise and fall of ancient Chinese societies influenced writers and historians who followed him.

Traveler: Sima Qian
The Grand Historian c. 145–87 B.C.E.

If there had been a Lifetime Achievement Award in ancient China, Grand Historian Sima Qian would have been the ideal nominee. He took on a lifelong mission: writing the whole of Chinese history.

FINDING PATTERNS

Around 90 B.C.E., Sima Qian (SUH-mah CHEE-en) completed a history of China called *Records of the Grand Historian,* or *Shiji*. He described thousands of years of Chinese history in an account of more than 500,000 words, the equivalent of 50 thick books in English. Later historians valued his records and point of view. He presented events through the eyes of the people who lived through them and produced a gripping story that is still popular in China.

Sima Qian searched for patterns in the ways in which important rulers and generals of past political eras made decisions. Which decisions led to success and prosperity? Which led to defeat and decay? He included lively descriptions of assassins, merchants, court actors, and bandits. His history brought all these people to life through his empathy, or ability to understand the feelings and actions of others.

PRIMARY SOURCE

I have traveled to the northern border and returned by the Direct Road. As I went along I saw the towers of the Great Wall, which Meng Tian had constructed for the Qin. He cut through the mountains and filled up the valleys . . . Truly he made free with the strength of the common people! Qin had only recently destroyed the feudal states; the hearts of the people of the world were not yet at rest and the wounded were not yet healed. Tian was a renowned general, yet he did not take this opportunity to urge that the ills of the common people be attended to.

—from *Ssu-ma Ch'ien, Grand Historian of China* by Burton Watson, 1958

TRAVELS AND WRITINGS

As a young man, Sima Qian traveled throughout China. He saw the Great Wall, and he ends his biography of the general Meng Tian, who oversaw the building of the Great Wall, by noting that the general "made free with," or exploited, "the strength of the common people" and did not worry about their "ills," or problems. In other words, they were not treated well.

The Great Wall Sima Qian saw was not the massive structure of today. It was made of pounded dirt that stretched for miles and was dotted with watchtowers. Centuries later, workers built a wall of brick and stone over the dirt foundations.

Sima Qian lived during the reign of Emperor Wu of the Han dynasty. The emperor sent **delegations**, groups to represent him, to gather information on people and territories outside his empire. One delegation traveled for years into unknown lands, even through the Taklamakan Desert, whose name means "those who enter do not return." These explorations found the early routes of the Silk Roads that allowed trade between China and Central Asia.

Emperor Wu heard tales of horses with celestial, or heavenly, powers and thought such beasts would be useful for his military goals. They might also reveal secrets of immortality, or living forever. He sent soldiers on long-distance treks to find and capture these horses.

Sima Qian did not write about Emperor Wu. That would have been dangerous. *Shiji* was a personal project that covered China's history only to the Qin period, the first Chinese dynasty. In judging the strengths and weaknesses of its rulers, Sima Qian wrote: "Evil destroys the doer, but good endures, through the sons of the father, the subjects of the ruler, the disciple of the teacher. It is the function of the historian to prolong the memory of goodness by preserving its record for all ages to see."

Sima Qian was Grand Historian for 20 years. In his court post, he kept a **chronicle**, or factual daily record, of events and ceremonies. He fell from royal favor when he spoke in defense of a general who had angered the emperor. This was **treason**, the crime of betraying the government. Sima Qian had to leave the court, but he continued writing *Shiji*. The story goes that after he died, his daughter hid his writing to protect it. When *Shiji* was brought into the open years later, it changed the way Chinese writers recorded their history and brought belated fame and honor to Sima Qian.

Sima Qian, like Herodotus and other travelers who came before him and those who have continued to journey, extended human understanding across regions with limited contact with each other. Their questions and explorations help us develop a fuller picture of the past as well as the present state of humanity.

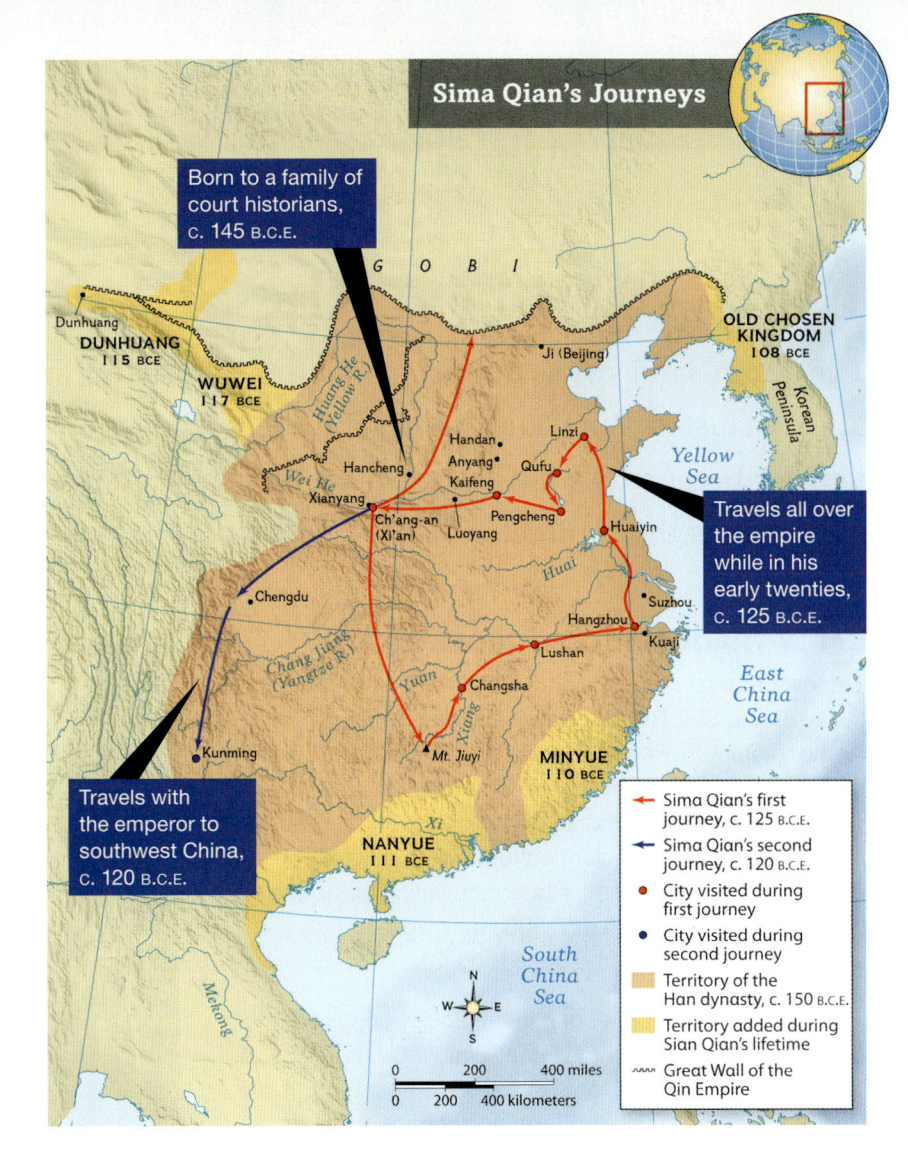

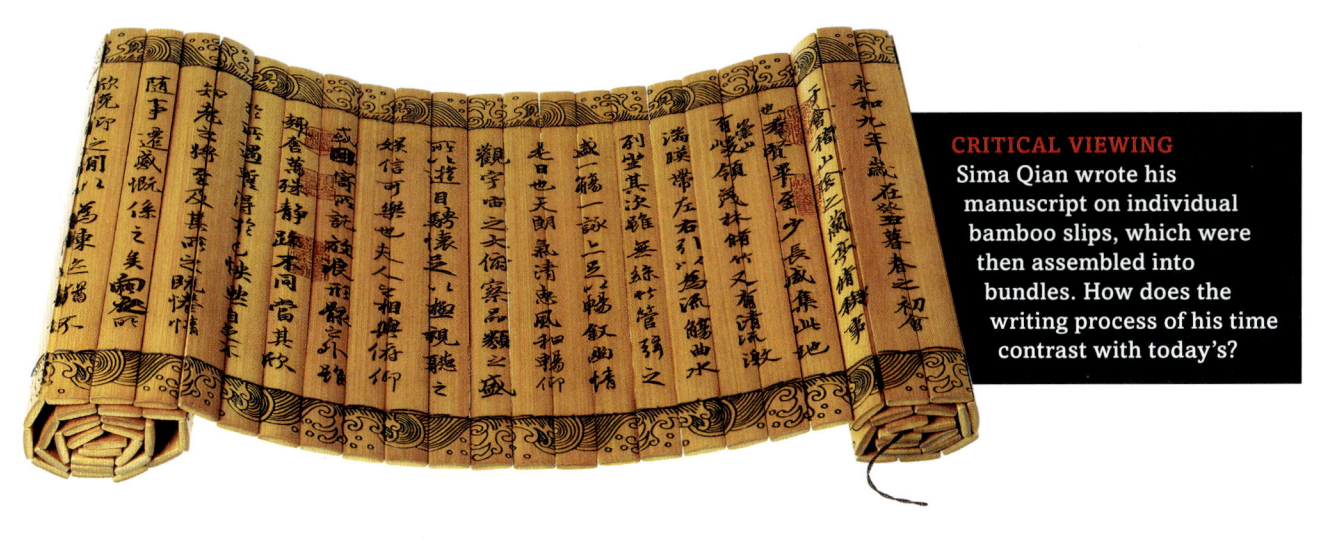

Sima Qian's Journeys

- Born to a family of court historians, c. 145 B.C.E.
- Travels all over the empire while in his early twenties, c. 125 B.C.E.
- Travels with the emperor to southwest China, c. 120 B.C.E.

Legend:
- Sima Qian's first journey, c. 125 B.C.E.
- Sima Qian's second journey, c. 120 B.C.E.
- City visited during first journey
- City visited during second journey
- Territory of the Han dynasty, c. 150 B.C.E.
- Territory added during Sian Qian's lifetime
- Great Wall of the Qin Empire

CRITICAL VIEWING
Sima Qian wrote his manuscript on individual bamboo slips, which were then assembled into bundles. How does the writing process of his time contrast with today's?

HISTORICAL THINKING

1. **READING CHECK** How was Sima Qian's *Shiji* different from the writing he did as Grand Historian?

2. **IDENTIFY MAIN IDEAS AND DETAILS** What words in the primary source excerpt support the idea that Sima Qian showed empathy?

3. **ANALYZE** What was one result of sending delegations outside the empire's boundaries?

4. **FORM AND SUPPORT OPINIONS** What impact might Sima Qian's travels have had on his approach to writing history?

Societies in East and South Asia 199

2.2

MAIN IDEA The Silk Roads, a series of ancient trade routes, facilitated the spread of goods and ideas throughout the Asian continent and beyond.

Early History of the Silk Roads

The desert sand swirls in your face and the scorching sun leaves you parched and exhausted. But your caravan of traders trudges onward despite the difficult journey because of what awaits you at the market—silk, spices, gold, and jewels, glittering in the sunlight.

EARLY TRADE ROUTES ACROSS ASIA

The overland routes through Central Asia are known today as the **Silk Roads**. National Geographic Archaeologist-in-Residence, Fredrik Hiebert, describes the Silk Roads as "a metaphor for ancient trade that went east and west." Based on his discoveries, Hiebert has concluded that ancient cultures were always connected and that traders began traveling along the Silk Roads about 4,000 or 5,000 years ago—much earlier than historians had once thought.

The 4,000-mile routes began in the ancient city of Chang'an and followed the Great Wall of China. Originally a network of local overland routes, the Silk Roads eventually joined to form a vast network that connected China with the rest of Asia, Europe, and Africa. The Silk Roads also included maritime, or sea, routes that allowed traders to sail to the Mediterranean Sea and Europe. Other maritime routes led across the Indian Ocean to Arabia and East Africa and across the Pacific Ocean to Korea, Japan, and Southeast Asia.

Chinese goods may have traveled thousands of miles along the Silk Roads, but few traders made the entire journey from one end of the route to the other. The trip over the rugged terrain would have taken at least six months. Chinese traders, traveling in caravans of camels, traded their goods somewhere around Kashgar, near the Han Empire's western border, passing their goods along to Central Asian nomads. The nomads, in turn, may have gone on to trade the goods with other merchants from Asia, Africa, and Europe.

The Silk Roads depended on strong governments to protect travelers and allow trade to flourish. Beyond China, empires in Persia and Rome protected the routes. When the Han dynasty declined after 204, trade fell off until the time of the Tang dynasty in the 600s.

CRITICAL VIEWING The Mogao Caves are located near an ancient Silk Roads oasis town in China. Hundreds of Buddhist paintings such as this one adorn the walls of the caves. How might these paintings have influenced traders and travelers and helped spread Buddhism?

THE SPREAD OF GOODS

In addition to silk, Chinese merchants also traded paper, decorative lacquerware, and objects made of iron or bronze. In exchange for these goods, Chinese merchants often sought gold, silver, olive oil, and especially Central Asian horses.

All along the Silk Roads in China, market towns sprang up. Some of these Central Asian markets, in turn, grew into great cities. In these market towns, a dazzling variety of goods filled the stalls: Central Asian rugs and blankets; Indian spices, such as cinnamon and pepper; Korean celadon; and European wool and honey.

Traders from these and many other places used different currencies, and many had no money at all. As a result, the traders often bartered for other goods. In fact, at the high point of the Silk Roads trade, Chinese armies stationed in Central Asia bought goods from the local people using their pay, which they often received in bolts of silk because of coin shortages.

THE SPREAD OF IDEAS AND INVENTIONS

The Silk Roads were conduits not just for traders, but also for religious pilgrims, soldiers, and refugees fleeing dangerous areas. These travelers exchanged ideas, technologies, languages, and religions, and ideas spread from one culture to another, a process called cultural diffusion. In this way, for example, Chinese ideas about papermaking, metalwork, and farming techniques began to spread beyond China's borders, even reaching, in time, as far as western Europe.

Chief among the new ideas brought to and absorbed by China was Buddhism. Indian merchants introduced Buddhist ideas to Chinese traders and even established Buddhist shrines along the Silk Roads. Sea trade routes also helped spread religious ideas. The routes connected Southeast Asia with both India and China, facilitating travel by missionaries and followers. The regions closest to China, particularly Vietnam, became predominantly Buddhist, like China. Rulers of other regions, including Cambodia, patronized both Buddhism and Hinduism, as did most rulers in India.

By the year 600, Buddhism was firmly implanted in the Chinese countryside. Eventually, it became an important part of Chinese life with many Chinese blending Buddhist practices with Confucian beliefs. Thanks to the Silk Roads and maritime trade, other ideas also reached China, including Greek and Indian styles in sculpture, painting, and temple building—all of which enriched Chinese culture and civilization.

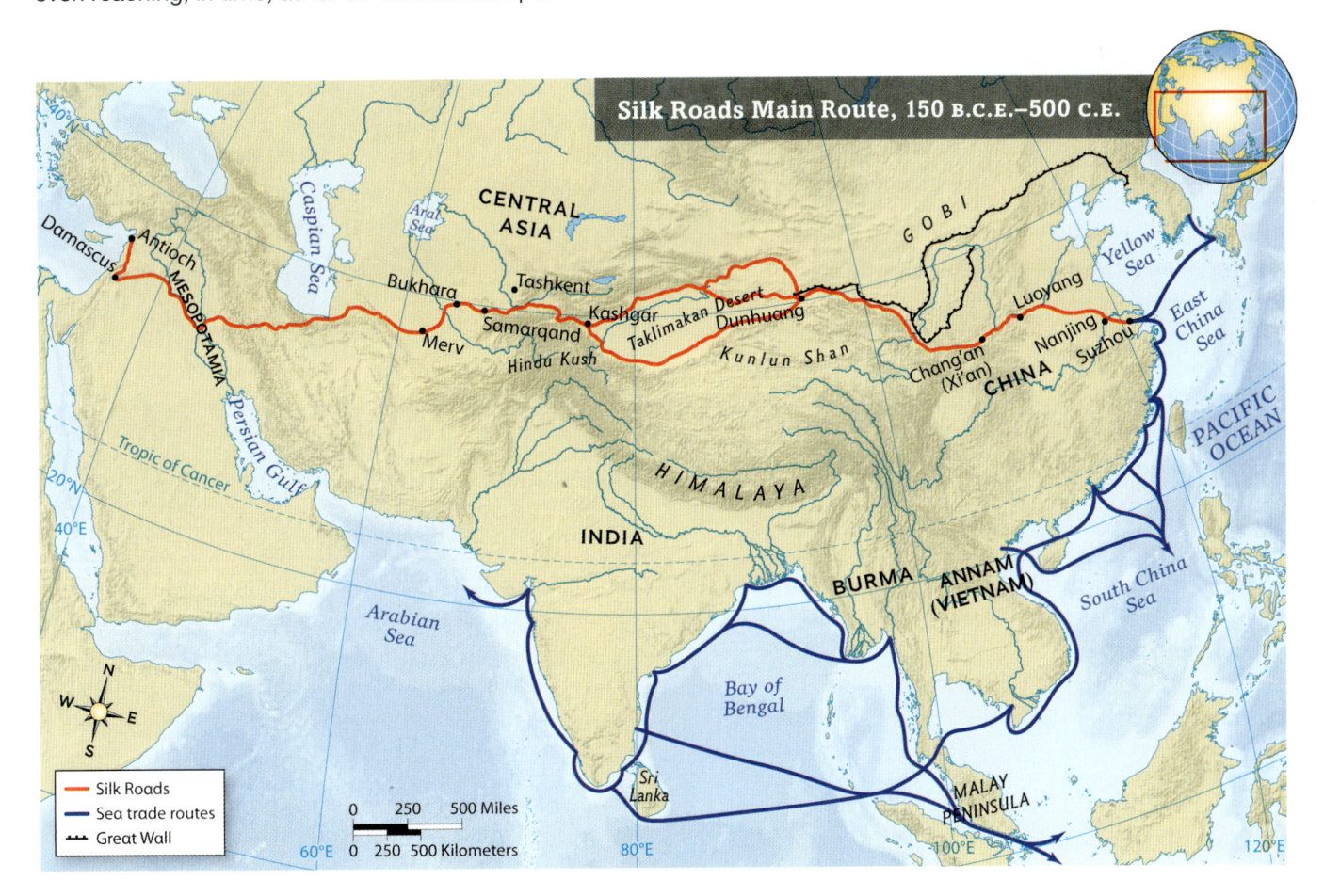

HISTORICAL THINKING

1. **READING CHECK** What were some of the goods and ideas exchanged on the Silk Roads?

2. **INTERPRET MAPS** What geographic features made traveling along the Silk Roads difficult and even dangerous?

3. **MAKE INFERENCES** What role do you think the early Silk Roads played in China's prosperity?

Societies in East and South Asia 201

2.3 MAIN IDEA The Han dynasty expanded Chinese territory, the economy, and education, but rebellions and invasions led to its decline.

Han Expansion and Collapse

Imagine if your teachers told you to memorize everything they said and then recite it back to them. That was what education was like before the Han Chinese invented paper.

QIN FALL AND HAN RISE

After the death of Qin emperor Shi Huangdi in 210 B.C.E., some regions rebelled against the weak, unpopular second Qin emperor. An ambitious peasant by the name of Liu Bang (lee-oo bahng), who had served as a low-ranking official under the Qin, sided with the rebels. Liu Bang was charismatic, and the peasants elevated him to leader of one of the competing rebel groups. After defeating a rival rebel leader, Liu Bang successfully overcame the Qin to found the Han dynasty in 206 B.C.E. Liu Bang, one of only two emperors born as a peasant, ruled until 195 B.C.E.

When Han forces took power, they faced the immediate problem of staffing a government large enough to govern the empire. They continued the Qin Legalist structure of a central government with the emperor at the head and a prime minister as the top official. Underneath the prime minister were three main divisions: tax collection, military supervision, and personnel recruitment. As the Chinese empire expanded to include diverse peoples, the Han Chinese majority was named after this early dynasty.

In 140 B.C.E., Emperor **Wudi** came to the throne. He became one of the most powerful Han emperors. In 124 B.C.E., he established the Imperial Academy to encourage the study of Confucian texts. Like others before him, Emperor Wudi believed that knowledge of Confucian ritual, history, poetry, and the *Analects* would produce more virtuous, and thus better, officials. Before promoting officers, the central government tested the officers' knowledge of the Confucian classics.

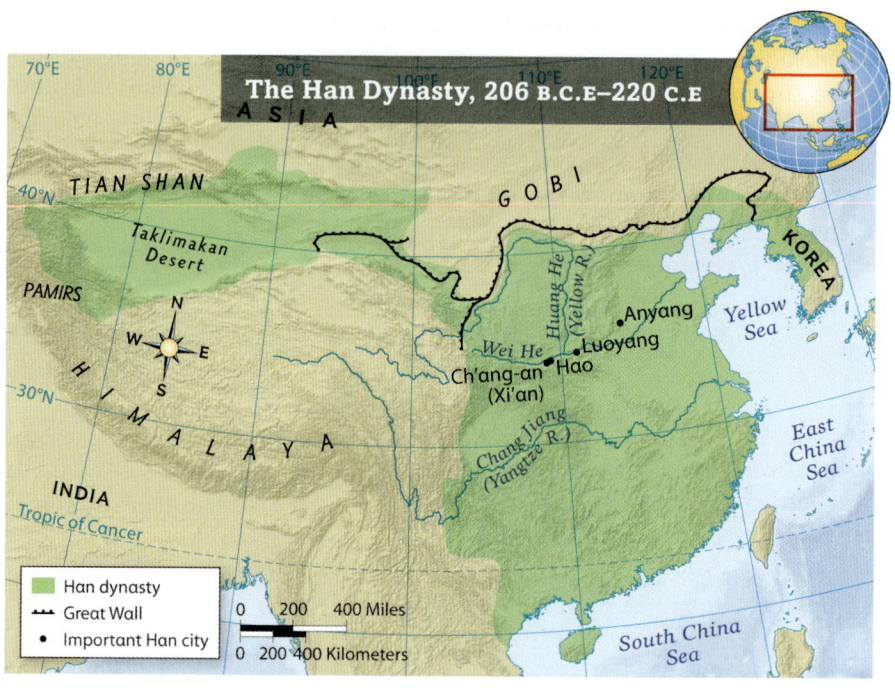

PAPER AND MATHEMATICS

Paper was first discovered by simple ragpickers who washed and recycled old fabric, left fibers on a screen, and accidentally discovered how to make paper. Initially, the Chinese used paper to wrap fragile items, but they quickly saw that paper was a good surface for writing that was cheap to make. By 200 C.E., it was commonly used for books and letters instead of the silk or bamboo slips used earlier.

With the adoption of paper as the primary writing material, the culture of learning in China shifted from an oral one to a written one. Before the invention of paper, students and poets memorized texts and recited them orally, but by the end of the Han dynasty students read books and poets composed poems on paper. Buddhist monks also benefited from the new invention. They wrote prayers on slips of paper and distributed them to large numbers of devoted followers.

Paper became one of China's most important inventions because it was cheap to produce, durable, and lightweight. Around the world, societies that had previously written on other materials shifted to paper almost as soon as they encountered it.

China's mathematics were also influential. One work called *Jiuzhang Suanshu (Nine Chapters on the Mathematical Art)* was written during the Han dynasty. The text provided arithmetic, algebraic, and geometric algorithms for everyday problems such as land surveying, tax collection, civil engineering, and wage distribution. Historians disagree on the origin of the text, but many believe it was written around 200 B.C.E. Used as a textbook in China and neighboring countries for 2,000 years, it is often compared with *The Elements*, which was written by the Greek mathematician Euclid.

EXPANSION OF THE HAN DYNASTY

During the long reign of Emperor Wudi, the Han dynasty expanded its empire west into the Taklimakan Desert, east into present-day Korea, and south into present-day Vietnam. However, officials living in the **garrison towns**, where soldiers of the empire were based, had little control over the people native to the region.

The Han dynasty gained much of its northwestern territory between 201 and 60 B.C.E. in wars against the Xiongnu, a nomadic people who moved across present-day Mongolia in search of grass to feed their sheep and horses. The Xiongnu had a strong army with brilliant horsemanship. In battle after battle, the Xiongnu used their military strength to threaten and weaken the Han.

In 139 B.C.E., Emperor Wu dispatched the envoy Zhang Qian to Central Asia to create an alliance against the Xiongnu. Although Zhang Qian failed in his mission, he visited local markets and learned about trade with outside societies. The information he brought back to Emperor Wudi opened the Silk Roads as trade routes through which China could trade silk for animal hides and semiprecious gems, such as lapis lazuli and jade.

FACTORS LEADING TO COLLAPSE

The Han dynasty ruled for 400 years, with only one interruption when a usurper founded his own short-lived dynasty. Natural disasters such as earthquakes, floods, and locust plagues were worrisome, but corruption and internal conflicts strained the dynasty even further. Confucian officials and military leaders vied for power. Exhausted by taxes, reduced plots of land to farm, and new policies of strict control, peasants rebelled. In 184 C.E., a large group of peasants attempted to overtake the capital.

External forces also threatened the Han. Continued invasions from the Xiongnu and other neighbors weakened the dynasty and drained military funds. Strained relations with neighbors also disrupted trade along the Silk Roads, causing further economic shortfalls. Continuous internal and external conflicts further weakened the dynasty until the last emperor **abdicated**, or gave up, his throne in 220 C.E.

Factors Contributing to the Collapse of the Han Dynasty and the Roman Empire

	Han Dynasty	Roman Empire
INTERNAL FACTORS	• Corruption • Economic decline • Peasant rebellions • Power plays as officials and military leaders vied for power	• Corruption • Economic decline • Religious divisions and intolerance • Power plays as military leaders vied for power • Civil war and division • Iron contamination of water pipes
EXTERNAL FACTORS	• Locust plagues • Earthquakes and floods • Trade disruption along the Silk Roads • Invasions from Xiongnu and other neighbors	• Mosquito infestations and malaria • Trade disruption due to war • Invasions from Huns, Vandals, and Goths

HISTORICAL THINKING

1. **READING CHECK** How did the Han expand Chinese territories? How much influence did they have on those new lands?

2. **INTERPRET MAPS** How does the size of the Han dynasty compare to that of the former Qin dynasty?

3. **COMPARE AND CONTRAST** How was the decline and collapse of the Han dynasty similar to and different from that of the Roman Empire?

2.4

MAIN IDEA Expansion and trade led to prosperity and advancement under the Tang dynasty.

The Tang Empire

Today in our global economy, millions of products are imported and exported through a complex system of trade with other countries. Centuries ago, the people of Tang China benefited from trade along the Silk Roads and the Grand Canal.

A Tang artisan portrayed a whimsical camel and its sleepy driver in this porcelain sculpture created c. 7th–9th century C.E.

CHINA REUNITES

The Han dynasty ended in 220, and China experienced more than 300 years of disunity before the founder of the Sui (sway) dynasty reunified China in 589. The Sui dynasty lasted only until 618, barely 30 years. But a Sui general, Li Yuan, wrested power from rivals to found the Tang dynasty, which lasted nearly 300 years. **Taizong** (ty-johng), who was the second Tang emperor, is probably the dynasty's most famous. He ruled from 626 to 649 and extended the borders of the Tang empire far into Central Asia and south into Vietnam, an expansion that protected China's trade along the Silk Roads. It also protected the dynasty from invasions by nomadic Turkish-speaking people.

One of Taizong's greatest accomplishments was a comprehensive law code, the Tang code, that was designed to help local magistrates govern and solve disputes. The Tang code also described the equal-field system, which was the basis of the Tang dynasty tax system. Based on a census, or an official count of the population, the equal-field system divided land according to rank and determined how much each individual would pay in taxes. This system gave Tang officials an unprecedented degree of control over their 50 million subjects. The first half of the Tang dynasty was one of the most prosperous and peaceful eras in Chinese history.

After Taizong's death, a woman who called herself **Emperor Wu** held power for a short time. She was the only woman to rule China as emperor in her own right. Emperor Wu promoted *The Great Cloud Sutra*, a Buddhist text that prophesied a kingdom ruled by a woman would be transformed into a Buddhist paradise.

Although few women were literate at the time, a small number of women were educated in the palace school, and Emperor Wu hired them as scribes. After serving five years as a Tang emperor, Emperor Wu proclaimed a new dynasty named the Zhou (jow). However, in 705, she was overthrown in a palace coup and the Tang dynasty was restored.

After a period of relative stability, a general led the army in a mutiny against the Tang emperor in 755. The Tang suppressed the rebellion, but they never regained full control of the provinces. Court officials began to take control, and regional leaders gained power. After a long period of decline, the Tang dynasty fell in 907. It would not be long, however, before the new Song dynasty re-established imperial control in 960.

THE SPREAD OF BUDDHISM

Beginning in the Han dynasty, Buddhism began to spread to China via the Silk Roads. Initially Buddhism was slow to take hold because it encouraged followers to leave their families and remain celibate, or unmarried. This was in conflict with Confucian respect for parents and family. However, in 310 a local ruler converted to Buddhism and granted Buddhists land to build monasteries. By the year 600, Buddhism had become established in China.

Buddhist art and architecture flourished as Tang leaders embraced Buddhism and donated money and land to Buddhist monasteries. Emperor Taizong combined Buddhist ideals with Confucian policies to create a new model of governance. The Tang support of Buddhism continued until late in the dynasty when weakened leaders began to criticize Buddhism and other "foreign" religions. During the reign of Emperor Wuzong from 841 to 846, imperial hostilities toward Buddhism led to the destruction of some 5,000 monasteries. But this was only a temporary setback. Buddhism was now so strong in China that it survived far into the future.

TANG INFLUENCES

International trade boomed in Tang China, and the capital of Chang'an became a **cosmopolitan** city, a diverse place with people, goods, and ideas from around the world. Traders brought music and dance from the west. Equestrian sports, or those performed on horseback, came from the north.

During the Tang dynasty, the wood buildings characteristic of Chinese architecture became more elaborate. Tang builders added curved tile roofs, towers, raised walkways, and bright tiles on floors. Gardens featured ponds and bridges. Many Buddhist temples and monasteries were also built during this time, and many survived the anti-Buddhist backlash.

The Tang were known for their visual arts, which were imported and copied by Korean and Japanese Buddhists and artisans. Tang poetry was also highly valued in Korea and Japan, where it was studied by men of the higher classes.

Perhaps the Tang advancement with the widest influence was woodblock printing. Artisans carved Chinese characters into woodblocks, which were then coated with ink and pressed onto sheets of paper. Woodblock printing led to a communications revolution. People turned to books to learn about everything from cooking to mathematics, agriculture, warfare, and medicine. Buddhists promoted the art of printing, and Buddhist texts spread the religion. Woodblock printing spread the Chinese writing system to Korea, Vietnam, and Japan, and Chinese writing carried the influence of Tang ideas and arts throughout these societies.

NATIONAL GEOGRAPHIC EXPLORER
CHRISTINE LEE

Reconstructing Lives

What can a scientist learn from a 5,000-year-old skeleton? Christine Lee, a **bioarchaeologist**, or a scientist who studies human remains from archaeological sites, has learned a lot—what people ate, what diseases they had, and what types of injuries they suffered. She explains that the way bodies are buried reveals whether a society was peaceful or chaotic and leads to an understanding of their belief systems.

While studying the skeletons of women, Lee was able to determine when the practice of foot binding increased in China. During the Song dynasty, elite men saw small feet as a sign of wealth and glamour. Only very wealthy women had bound feet during the Song dynasty. As you will learn, the practice increased dramatically during the Ming and Qing dynasties.

This pit of human skulls was found during the excavation of Zhengzhou, a city from the Shang dynasty about 3,750 years ago.

HISTORICAL THINKING

1. **READING CHECK** What are some of the ideas that the Tang imported and exported through trade with neighboring countries?

2. **DESCRIBE** What does the bioarchaeological study of human skeletons reveal about life in China's past?

3. **DETERMINE CHRONOLOGY** Create a flowchart showing how Buddhism spread to China, how it grew in China, and how it expanded outside of China.

Societies in East and South Asia 205

3.1

MAIN IDEA Heavily influenced by the Chinese, the people of Korea and Vietnam fought to maintain their own identity.

Kingdoms in Korea and Vietnam

How long would you tolerate someone telling you what to do? The Koreans and Vietnamese struggled against Chinese political control for hundreds of years. While they borrowed freely from China, they still hung on to aspects of their culture that made them unique.

THE THREE KINGDOMS

From approximately 57 B.C.E. through 668 C.E., the Korean Peninsula was divided into small chiefdoms. The greatest of these chiefdoms were the Koguryo (koh-gur-YOO) in the north, the Paekche (pahk-chay) in the southwest, and the Silla (SIHL-uh) in the southeast. These three kingdoms vied for territory and influence from 313 to 668 C.E., an era known as the Three Kingdoms period.

The Han of China conquered the Koguryo in northern Korea and sent officials and merchants to live in four commanderies, or military cities. The largest of these, Lelang, was near present-day Pyongyang. The Koguryo regained control of the four cities one by one, expelling the last Chinese from Lelang in 313.

As the Sui and Tang dynasties took power in China, the Korean rulers sent officials to China to learn about

Sunrise breaks over the mountains in Bukhansan National Park, Seoul, South Korea.

206 CHAPTER 7

Chinese culture and governance. The kings of Koguryo and Paekche adopted Buddhism in the 370s and 380s, believing that combining Confucian education with Buddhism would strengthen their kingdoms. However, Buddhism was a contentious issue among the Silla. Many in the Silla kingdom opposed the religion, but King Pophung was determined to build a shrine to the Buddha. In 527, according to legend, a miracle silenced the opposition, when a Buddhist official survived execution, bleeding milk rather than blood.

The Sui and Tang dynasties attempted to take over Korea but failed in several attacks on the peninsula. Then in 660, the Silla joined forces with the Tang to defeat the Paekche and Koguryo. They succeeded and unified Korea in 668. However, the Tang saw the unification as an opportunity to **depose**, or remove from power, the Silla and take control of the entire peninsula. The Silla held out against the Chinese army and navy and defeated Chinese forces to unify Korea again in 676.

For the most part, the Silla followed Tang government principles. However, they rejected the equal-field system, which distributed lands to every household. Instead, the Silla granted entire villages to aristocratic families who appointed officials and paid their salaries. Like the Tang, the Silla used civil service exams, but only members of the highest-ranking families were allowed to take them. The Silla entered a period of decline after 780, when different branches of the royal family fought for control of the throne, and no one ruled for long.

THE PEOPLE OF VIETNAM

While Korea marked the northern extent of Chinese influence, Vietnam marked the southern. Under different dynasties, the Chinese ruled Vietnam from 111 B.C.E. to 938 C.E. During this time, the Vietnamese embraced Buddhism, Confucianism, and Daoism, calling this combination of beliefs the Three Teachings. But they never gave up their traditional practice of ancestor reverence and spirit worship. Throughout their history, they repeatedly rebelled against Chinese control and refused to identify as Chinese. In fact, they built temples in honor of heroes who fought the Chinese, such as **Trung Trac** and **Trung Nhi**, two sisters who organized an army that pushed the Han back and formed an independent state near the Red River in northern Vietnam in 40 C.E. Three years later, the Chinese regained control, but today these sisters are two of Vietnam's greatest heroes.

Statues of the heroic Trung sisters hold a place of honor in the Hai Ba Trung Temple in Hanoi.

A DIFFERENT CULTURE IN THE SOUTH

In the southern part of Vietnam, people lived quite differently from their neighbors in the north. The Champa kingdom formed in 192 C.E. Its people, known as the Cham, practiced Hinduism and adopted cultural traditions from India.

Skilled sailors, the Cham traded widely, and goods from their kingdom have been found in Taiwan, the Philippines, and Malaysia. Within southern Vietnam, excavations have uncovered rare gold, agate, and glass beads from India, Iran, and the Mediterranean.

Like their neighbors in the north, the Cham continuously fought off invasions from the Chinese as well as attacks from other countries in Southeast Asia.

HISTORICAL THINKING

1. **READING CHECK** Which aspects of Chinese culture and governance did the Koreans adopt? Which did they reject? Why?

2. **SEQUENCE EVENTS** Create a timeline of events in Korea from 313 to 676 C.E.

3. **DRAW CONCLUSIONS** What do the temples dedicated to heroes reveal about Vietnamese culture and beliefs?

3.2

MAIN IDEA Korea and China strongly influenced the culture and government of Japan.

The Emergence of Japan

You may learn a lot from textbooks, but what can you learn from a novel? Quite a bit. The world's first novel was written by a Japanese woman around 1000, and it reveals much about Japanese culture at that time.

CRITICAL VIEWING An 1853 woodblock print triptych, a three-paneled artwork, by Japanese artists Utagawa Toyokuni and Utagawa Hiroshige illustrates a snowy winter scene from *The Tale of Genji*. Prince Genji, depicted on the right, is the central character in the novel. How do the artists use images of nature to express Genji's feelings and the action taking place?

EARLY JAPAN

Japan is an island chain, or **archipelago**, made up of four large islands and many smaller ones. Its closest neighbor, South Korea, is only 120 miles away, and that proximity explains the mainland's influences on Japan. For example, Japan adopted Korea's practices in growing rice. As an archipelago, however, Japan long escaped invasions and migrations, forming a unique culture that developed largely from one ethnic group.

Japan has no indigenous writing system, so archaeologists have pieced together its early history from archaeological materials and later sources. One of those sources explains that the Yamato clan was directly descended from the sun-goddess Amaterasu.

A **clan** is a group of people with a common ancestor. The earliest known religion of Japan, **Shinto**, included the worship of the spirits of trees, streams, and mountains, as well as of deceased rulers.

During the 300s and 400s, the Yamato was one of many clans that ruled different regions of Japan. However, by the sixth century, these clans had united under the leadership of a Yamato emperor. According to legend, the Yamato line has run unbroken from 660 B.C.E. until today, the oldest line of monarchs in the world.

As the Koguryo, Paekche, and Silla kingdoms fought for dominance on the Korean peninsula, many Koreans fled instability by migrating to Japan. These refugees

208 CHAPTER 7

introduced Korean military practices, methods of government, and a writing system that used Chinese characters. The Yamato modeled their government on the Korean form and adopted Chinese characters and Korean military practices. They also allied with the Paekche kingdom against the Silla.

For nearly 50 years, Paekche rulers pressured the Yamato to adopt Buddhism, but the Japanese hesitated to adopt the new religion. One clan related to the Yamato, the Soga, supported Buddhism, though. In 587, an armed conflict broke out between the Soga and clans opposed to Buddhism. After the victory of the Soga, the Japanese court converted to Buddhism. The Soga appointed **Prince Shotoku** as **regent**, which meant that Prince Shotoku would rule in the place of the Soga family.

Along with Buddhism, Prince Shotoku studied the teachings of Confucius and, beginning in 600, sent several delegations to China to learn from the newly formed Sui dynasty. The delegations, which included officials, Buddhist monks, students, and translators, brought back political, artistic, economic, and religious ideas that would influence Japan for centuries.

Prince Shotoku died in 622, but Chinese influence continued. Successive Japanese rulers sought to implement the Tang blueprint for rule, including a written law code. In doing so, they sought to strengthen their country and enhance their own rule, because a Chinese-style emperor had much more power than a Japanese chieftain.

In 710, the Japanese moved their capital to Nara, their first Chinese-style city with gridded streets, walls, and gates. After 710, the Japanese adopted Chinese building practices, using tiled roofs and stone bases for timber columns so that they did not rot.

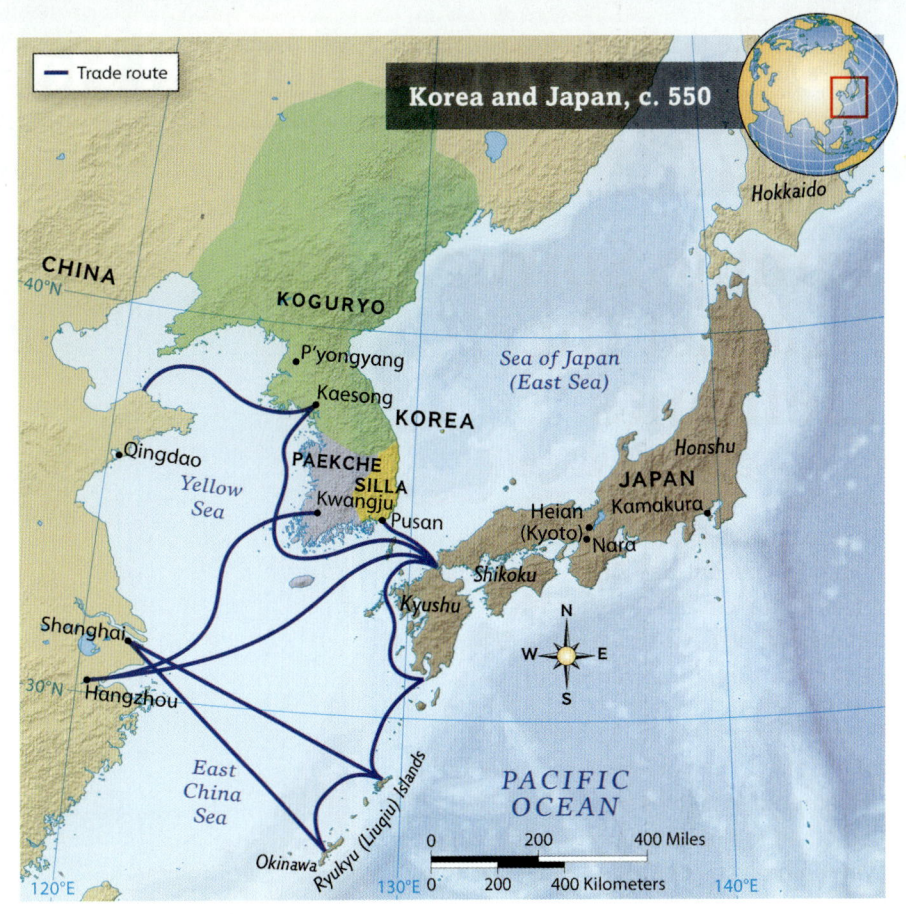

THE WORLD'S FIRST NOVEL

During the fifth century, Japan adopted the Chinese writing system. However, Japanese was from a different language family than Chinese. Chinese characters, called *kanji*, did not capture the full meaning of the Japanese language. In the ninth century, the Japanese developed a syllabic alphabet, called *kana*. Each kana character represented a syllable, so Japanese words could be written as they were pronounced.

Aristocratic men continued to use kanji, but aristocratic women were forbidden from using these characters, so they used kana instead. One woman named **Murasaki Shikibu** used kana to write *The Tale of Genji*, the world's first novel. The book describes the life of Prince Genji and his descendants. Shikibu's book describes fashion, entertainment, and romance in a world that valued skill in poetry, music, and calligraphy. The novel provides a wealth of insight into daily lives, such as the courtship of young men and women of the aristocracy and life at the emperor's court around 1000.

HISTORICAL THINKING

1. **READING CHECK** How did China and Korea influence the culture and politics of Japan?

2. **MAKE INFERENCES** What do Japanese kana and *The Tale of Genji* reveal about the lives of Japanese people around 1000?

3. **INTERPRET MAPS** Which Japanese island provided a convenient port of entry from the Korean peninsula to the Japanese archipelago?

Societies in East and South Asia 209

3.3 Preserving Cultural Heritage

Temple Spires Against the Elements

The Khmer Empire, one of the most successful and sophisticated kingdoms in Southeast Asia's history, made the city of Angkor in present-day Cambodia its capital. It was in that city that Angkor Wat, a massive temple complex, was built in the 12th century by King Suryavarman II.

One of the greatest works of Khmer architecture, Angkor Wat is an important part of Cambodian culture and history. Originally dedicated to the Hindu god Vishnu, Angkor Wat features sculptural reliefs with Hindu motifs and ancient Khmer scenes along the temple walls. Later, during the reign of King Jayavarman VII (1181–1220), a new capital was built, Angkor Thom, dedicated to Buddhism. Angkor Wat then also became a Buddhist temple and much of the Hindu art was replaced with Buddhist art. Today, both styles can be seen throughout the temple.

ANGKOR WAT

Built to honor the Hindu god Vishnu, the central temple at Angkor Wat is a five-towered pyramid. Each tower is shaped like a lotus bud, which in Hinduism represents beauty and purity. Today, the temple complex is threatened by sinking ground due to increased tourism and depleted water levels.

Strangler fig trees and creeping lichens devour ruins at Ta Prohm—another temple located northeast of Angkor Wat.

By the early 15th century, the once grand Angkor kingdom fell. Researchers found that Angkor's demise wasn't due to enemy invaders but to the changing climate. Long droughts followed by heavy monsoon rains destroyed the city's infrastructure and the empire collapsed.

Once the Khmer Empire fell, Angkor was abandoned and eventually covered up by the jungle—not to be discovered again until the mid-19th century. Restoration efforts began in the early 20th century but were halted in the 1970s and 1980s because of political instability and wars in Cambodia.

After withstanding the tests of time and war, the Angkor complex—and Angkor Wat—was designated a UNESCO World Heritage Site in 1992. Yet once again, environmental issues plague the Angkor region and endanger the stability and structure of Angkor Wat.

Once Cambodia became safe to visit, tourists flocked to Siem Reap, the resort city near the Angkor region. The increasing number of people has taxed the city's systems and resources—especially water. As water levels have dropped, archaeologists have noticed some sinking and movement in some of the structures in Angkor.

These environmental issues combined with previously poor preservation efforts are threatening the future of Angkor Wat. While the structure is somewhat stable now, archaeologists, architects, restoration specialists, museum curators, and conservationists are working to prevent even greater damage from occurring. Preserving Angkor Wat's cultural heritage is truly a global effort. The World Monuments Fund, a U.S. conservation group, is working with Cambodian professionals and other conservation groups from around the world to protect the historic site from the elements.

HISTORICAL THINKING

ANALYZE CAUSE AND EFFECT In what ways can the environment affect cultural heritage?

A Buddhist monk stands outside the temple at Angkor Wat. Over hundreds of years, the Cambodian jungle has reclaimed the area, and tree roots cover many of the stone structures.

Societies in East and South Asia 213

CHAPTER 7 REVIEW
SOCIETIES IN EAST AND SOUTH ASIA

VOCABULARY

Complete each of the following sentences using one of the vocabulary words from the chapter.

1. Believers of Christianity, Islam, and Hinduism often believe in their God's _____, or unlimited power.

2. The fact that the Iron Pillar of Delhi has never rusted is evidence of Gupta expertise in _____.

3. Conquered people often have to pay _____ to their conquerors.

4. The Tang dynasty tax system was based on a _____, or an official count of the population.

5. Filled with people from around the world, the Chinese capital of Chang'an was very _____.

6. A _____ is more interested in human skeletons and teeth than in pieces of pottery or bronze.

7. The ruling Soga family appointed a _____ to run the government in their place.

8. Four large islands and many small islands make up Japan's _____.

READING STRATEGY
DRAW CONCLUSIONS

When you draw conclusions, you make a judgment based on what you have read. Use a chart like this one to draw a conclusion about the influence of Han and Tang China on Korea, Vietnam, and Japan. Then answer the question.

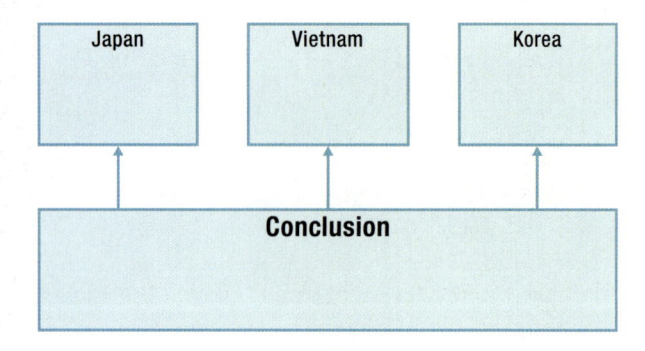

Japan	Vietnam	Korea

Conclusion

9. Why do you think Korea, Vietnam, and Japan resisted China's control while embracing some elements of its influence?

MAIN IDEAS

Answer the following questions. Support your answers with evidence from the chapter.

10. What are two dimensions of Hindu religious practice? **LESSON 1.1**

11. Why is the Gupta dynasty considered to be India's golden age? **LESSON 1.2**

12. In what ways did the Chola kings merge religious devotion and political advancement? **LESSON 1.3**

13. Why was Zhang Qian's travel through Central Asia important to China's economy? **LESSON 2.3**

14. What events contributed to the prosperity of the Tang dynasty? **LESSON 2.4**

15. Which traditions did the Koreans and Vietnamese keep even after adopting many Chinese ways? **LESSON 3.1**

16. What geographic factor influenced Japan's acceptance of Korean and Chinese cultural and political ideas? **LESSON 3.2**

HISTORICAL THINKING

Answer the following questions. Support your answers with evidence from the chapter.

17. **EXPLAIN** Why did the Hindus depict deities as having more than two arms? How did this depiction help followers understand the deities?

18. **COMPARE AND CONTRAST** How were the Gupta dynasty and the Chola kingdom similar? How were they different?

19. **IDENTIFY PROBLEMS AND SOLUTIONS** What problems did the Tang emperors face? How did they solve them? Which were they unable to solve?

20. **ANALYZE CAUSE AND EFFECT** How did alliances with the Tang influence the outcome of the Three Kingdoms period in Korea?

21. **FORM AND SUPPORT OPINIONS** Do you think *The Tale of Genji* is a reliable resource for researching Japanese history? Why or why not?

INTERPRET TIME LINES

Study the time line of events in Buddhism and Hinduism. Then answer the questions that follow.

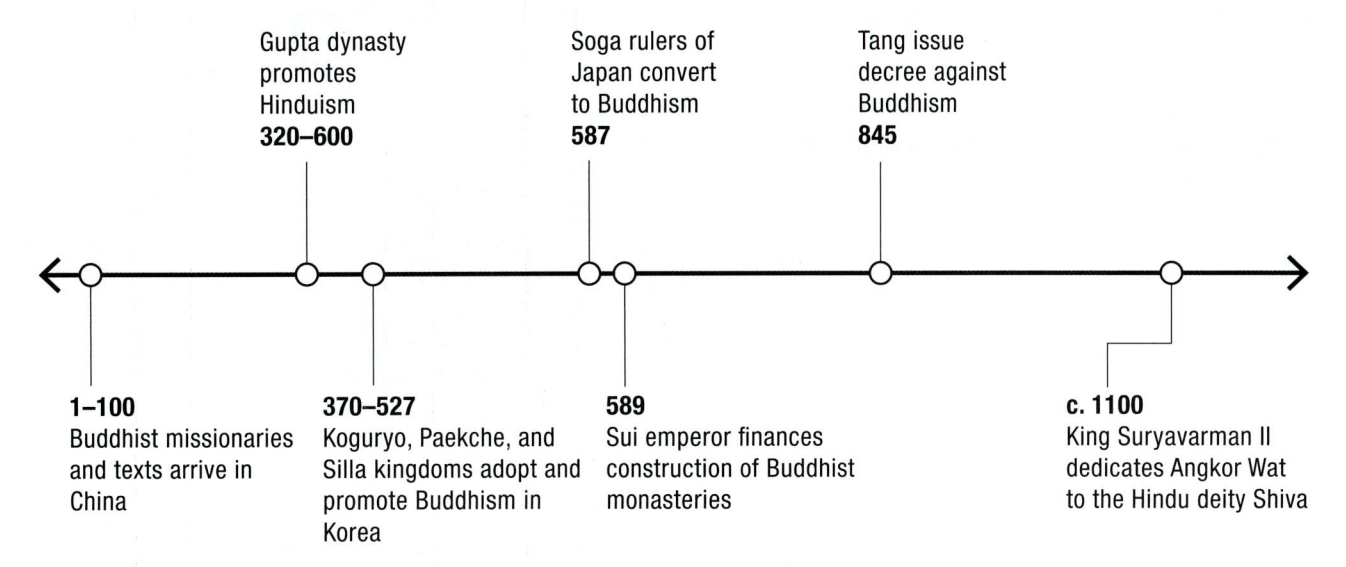

Above the line:
- **320–600** Gupta dynasty promotes Hinduism
- **587** Soga rulers of Japan convert to Buddhism
- **845** Tang issue decree against Buddhism

Below the line:
- **1–100** Buddhist missionaries and texts arrive in China
- **370–527** Koguryo, Paekche, and Silla kingdoms adopt and promote Buddhism in Korea
- **589** Sui emperor finances construction of Buddhist monasteries
- **c. 1100** King Suryavarman II dedicates Angkor Wat to the Hindu deity Shiva

22. How long did Buddhism prosper in China before the Tang backlash?

23. Which event shown on the time line do you think most contributed to the spread of Buddhism and Hinduism?

ANALYZE SOURCES

The daughter of a Han poet and historian, Ban Zhao wrote a book that taught young Chinese women how to be worthy wives. She also delivered strong messages to men. Read the two excerpts below and answer the question that follows.

> If a husband does not control his wife, then the rules of conduct manifesting his authority are abandoned and broken. If a wife does not serve her husband, then the proper relationship between men and women and the natural order of things are neglected and destroyed. . . .
>
> Yet only to teach men and not to teach women—is that not ignoring the essential relation between them? . . . It is the rule to begin to teach children to read at the age of eight. . . . Only why should it not be that girls' education as well as boys' be according to this principle?
>
> —from *Lessons for Women* by Ban Zhao

24. How did the teachings of Ban Zhao both limit women and promote their advancement?

CONNECT TO YOUR LIFE

25. **INFORMATIVE** Chinese influence did not end with East Asia. Research China's influence on your life, either through ancient inventions used around the world today, current systems of trade and economy, or cultural influences in food and medicine. Then write a short essay describing this influence.

TIPS

- Review Chinese advances in government, technology, and other fields described in this chapter or earlier lessons.
- Investigate the present-day influence of China on global trade and the economy.
- Decide whether you want to write about past or present influences and do further research based on your decision.
- Use two or three vocabulary terms from this chapter in your essay.
- Conclude your essay with a statement that summarizes the influence of China on your life today.

NATIONAL GEOGRAPHIC | CONNECTION

The Land of the Stars

BY NADIA DRAKE Adapted from "How 'The Land of the Stars' Shaped Astronomy (and Me)" by Nadia Drake, news.nationalgeographic.com, August 2, 2016

My father may have dedicated a lifetime to studying the heavens, but my mother comes from the land of the stars. In the Middle East, the night sky's stories have been known for millennia, told by those who named its lights, aligned their tombs and temples with its shifting shapes, and divined the movements of the worlds wandering our solar system.

I came to the Middle East for the first time not knowing what to expect yet anticipating the awakening of a sleepy part of myself. I'd grown up hearing Arabic and knowing the recipe for proper tabbouleh, but Lebanon was a place I'd only seen in my dreams.

As the mountains and buildings of Beirut emerged from the haze, I felt like I was coming home. I was that youth whose universe was right there among the salt and the cedars and the centuries of richness and strife, staring wide-eyed at a realm where the first twinklings of the stars were recorded.

I've always felt like a bit of an impostor Arab. My blondish hair and bluish eyes don't fit the stereotypical image of my darker-eyed kin—but walking the streets of Beirut meant seeing that so many Lebanese women look just like me. It was an observation that offered solace, and I felt like I belonged—a nearly impossible privilege in a part of the world where wars are fought to make "belonging" even a smidge more possible. But there I was.

One evening, we camped in the Wadi Rum desert near Jordan's southern border. Also known as the Valley of the Moon, the Wadi Rum is moody and otherworldly in a harsh and commanding way. There, lumpy sandstone walls erupt from scorched, reddish sands crisscrossed by herds of camels and Bedouin shepherding tourists around in rickety Jeeps.

Too hot to sleep, I wandered outside and found myself completely distracted by one of the most dazzling skies I'd ever seen. A half moon bright enough to cast shadows obliterated the stars until it sank behind a ridge—and then, in the Valley of the Moon, those stars started screaming for attention.

Stars sprinkle the night sky over the Wadi Rum desert in Jordan.

I settled into the sand and lay there silently for hours, transfixed by the lights tracing paths across the sky. Antares, the red supergiant beating at the heart of Scorpius, soon emerged, and then the entire scorpion's tail curled across the sky and dipped into the stream of stars that is the Milky Way. Cygnus glittered overhead, next to the starfield where NASA's Kepler telescope has made such monumental planet discoveries. In the north, Cassiopeia clung to her throne, while in the south, the Sagittarius teapot pointed to the spot where a supermassive black hole churns away in the core of our galaxy.

I can only imagine how captivating this evening light show must have been during the ages when Earth's skies were uncontaminated by artificial lights. It's no wonder cultures all over the planet have their own version of its stories, their own solutions to its mysteries. What did the ancient Arabs think these shapes in the sky represented?

The Middle East is far from perfect, as is every place on Earth. Conflict disfigures the region in profoundly troubling ways. Yet if you ever doubt that we are all connected, just look up: Twinkling overhead are the same exact stars humans all over the world have gazed at forever, beckoning to us and inviting us to solve their riddles. ■

UNIT 2 Curate a Museum Exhibit

Staging the Question

In this unit, you examined three civilizations that had a tremendous influence on later cultures. One theme that unites the Persians, Greeks, Romans, and Han dynasty is the drive to further human knowledge in numerous realms. All four cultures made remarkable advances in astronomy and other sciences, writing, visual and performing arts, economics, engineering, and various other fields. By scrutinizing Persian, Greek, Roman, and Chinese artifacts and writings, researchers have learned a great deal about each civilization's attainments in learning. What can we learn about a culture from studying its advancements?

ASSIGNMENT

Select five artifacts or images from either the Persian, Greek, Roman, or Han empire. You may choose images from this unit or from your own research.

Identify the fields of knowledge—such as science, art, economics, or engineering—that each object or image represents.

Explain how each object or image illustrates the civilization's understanding of the fields it represents.

Use the objects and the information you learned about them to create a museum exhibit about the Persians, Greeks, Romans, or Han dynasty.

Supporting Questions: Begin by developing supporting questions to guide your research. For example: How does this object help me understand the importance of writing to the Persian empire? Research the answers in this unit and in other sources, both print and online. You might want to use a web like this one to record the answers to your questions about each artifact.

Summative Performance Task: Write an explanatory label for each object or image you chose. Your labels will tell museum visitors how each item represents the civilization's advancements in at least one field of learning. Write two or three paragraphs for the exhibit introduction explaining why you chose these particular artifacts and sharing your ideas about how the civilization was changed by its advancements in knowledge.

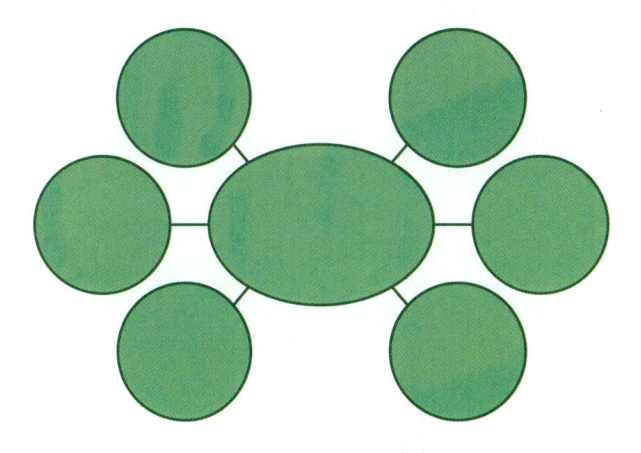

Present: Share your exhibit with the class. You might consider one of these options:

MAKE A GALLERY
Combine your exhibit with those of other students who focused on the same civilization. Curate your gallery by choosing artifacts that fit together logically to illustrate the civilization's advancements in at least three fields. Display your exhibit in the classroom or create an online gallery.

GIVE AN EXPLORER LECTURE
Watch lectures by National Geographic Explorers online, then follow their model to write your own Explorer lecture. Create an online slideshow of the artifacts you selected and give your lecture to the class. Use gestures and expressions to convey an Explorer's enthusiasm for the topic.

Take Informed Action:

UNDERSTAND Conduct research online or on social media to learn about artifacts from ancient civilizations that are in danger of destruction.

ASSESS Choose an artifact and think about how it illustrates the culture's understanding of certain fields of knowledge.

ACT Comment on the posts or articles you found about the artifact, sharing your arguments about why it should be preserved.

Far-Reaching Civilizations and Empires 217

UNIT 3

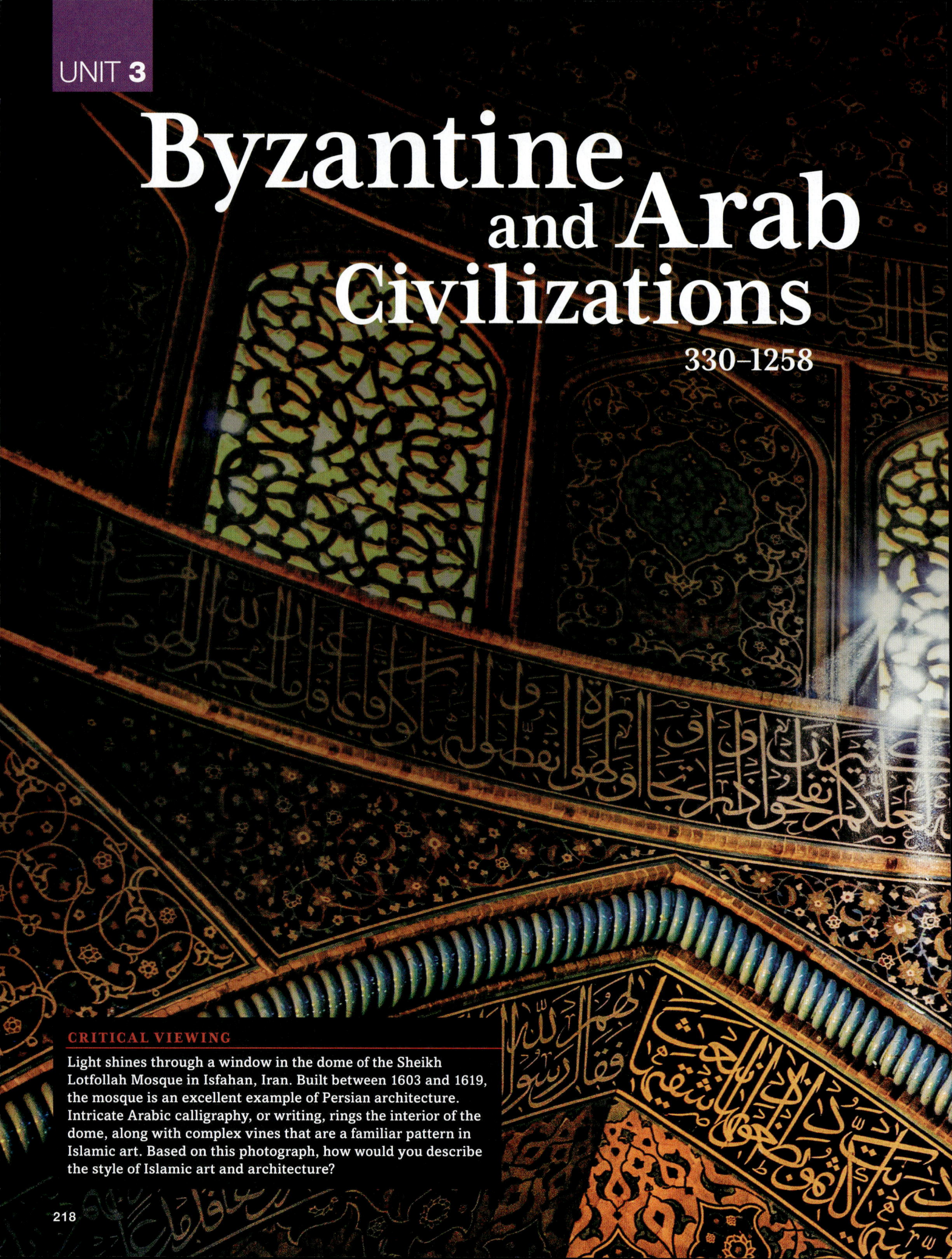

Byzantine and Arab Civilizations

330–1258

CRITICAL VIEWING

Light shines through a window in the dome of the Sheikh Lotfollah Mosque in Isfahan, Iran. Built between 1603 and 1619, the mosque is an excellent example of Persian architecture. Intricate Arabic calligraphy, or writing, rings the interior of the dome, along with complex vines that are a familiar pattern in Islamic art. Based on this photograph, how would you describe the style of Islamic art and architecture?

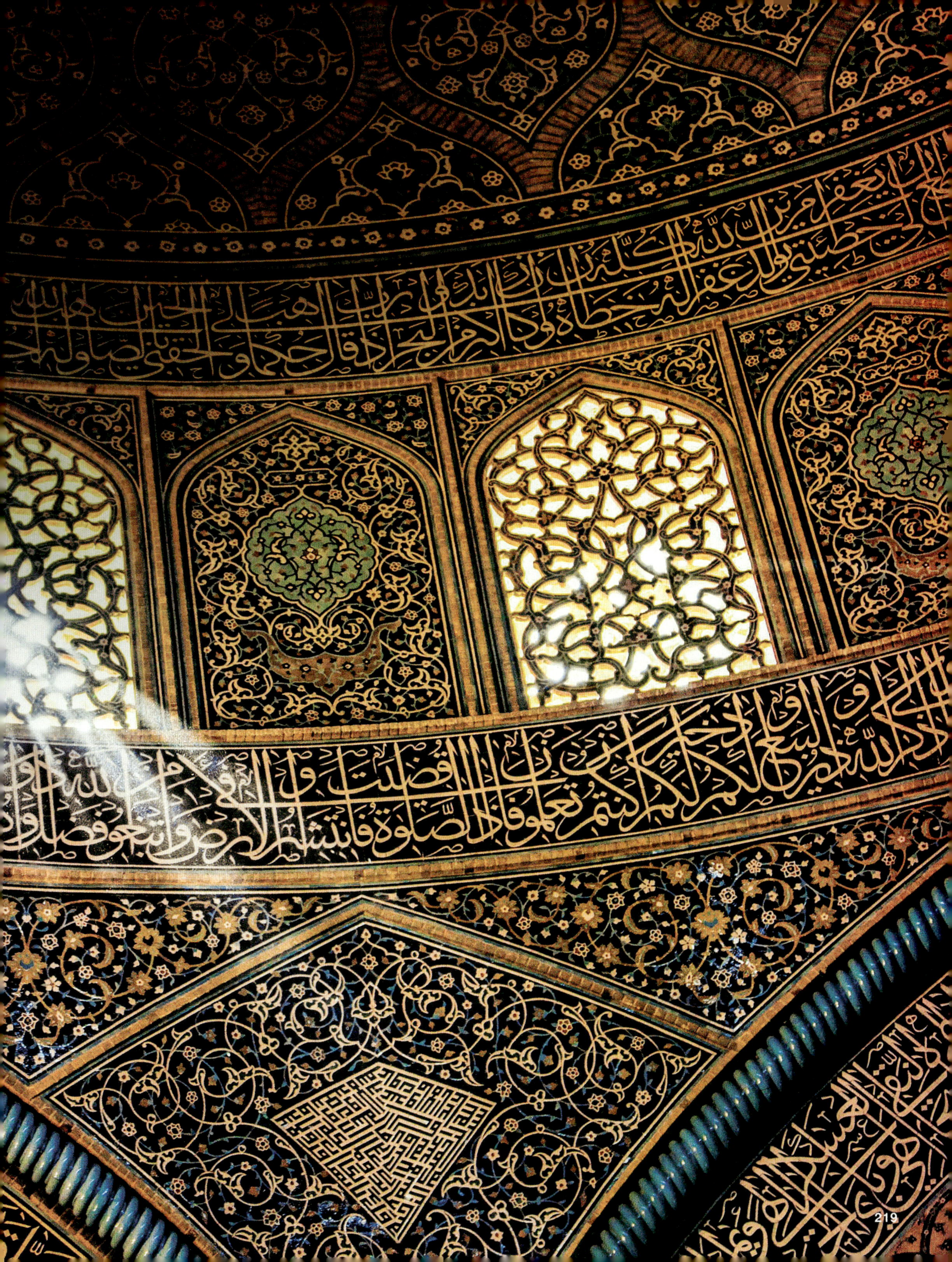

UNIT 3 Byzantine and Arab Civilizations

WORLD EVENTS 500–1300

532 EUROPE The Hagia Sophia, Constantinople's most significant church, is destroyed in a riot and is rebuilt by Justinian. *(Hagia Sophia, present-day Istanbul, Turkey)*

527 EUROPE The emperor Justinian I begins his 38-year rule of the Byzantine Empire. *(Byzantine pectoral with coins and medallion, c. 539)*

632 ASIA After the death of Muhammad, rivals for the succession lead to the split of Islam into two denominations—Sunni and Shiite.

500 | 600 | 700

530 EUROPE The general Belisarius is victorious over the Persian Sasanians, expanding the eastern boundaries of the Byzantine Empire. *(Persian short sword and scabbard, c. 6th–7th century)*

670 AFRICA Muslim troops begin their conquest of North Africa, capturing valuable lands and expanding the reach of the Muslim empire.

622 ASIA Muhammad and his followers migrate from Mecca to Medina, another city on the Arabian Peninsula, to establish an Islamic community. *(ceramic plaque representing the mosque of Medina, c. 17th century)*

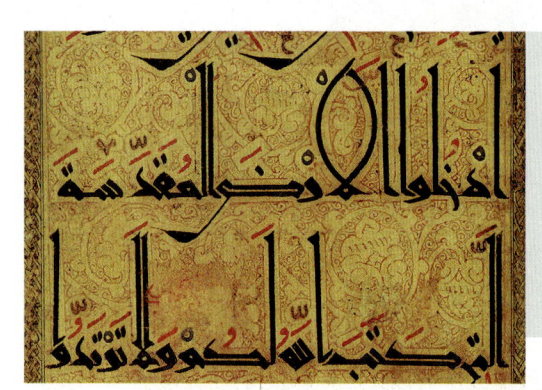

c. 613 ASIA Muhammad, a merchant in the city of Mecca on the Arabian Peninsula, experiences revelations from God that inspire him to spread the teachings of Islam. *(folio from a Quran manuscript, c. 1180)*

HISTORICAL THINKING

COMPARE AND CONTRAST How do the religions of Christianity and Islam compare in terms of growth during this period?

744 ASIA The Abbasids, a family claiming to be direct descendants of Muhammad's uncle Abbas, gain control of the Muslim empire after the assassination of the caliph. *(piece of column from a building in the former Abbasid capital of Raqqa, Syria, c. mid-700s)*

c. early 800s ASIA The caliph Al-Mamun rules the Muslim empire and champions scientific advances, inviting scientists to study in Baghdad at a center known as the House of Wisdom. *(Indian miniature of Caliph Al-Mamun, c. 1593)*

762 ASIA The Abbasid caliph Mansur establishes a new capital at Baghdad, which becomes an important center for learning and trade.

867 EUROPE The Macedonian dynasty ushers in the golden age of the Byzantine Empire, during which the arts and literature flourish and knowledge of mathematics expands.

1258 ASIA Muslim leaders no longer control the territories that were once united under the Abbasid empire.

800 // **1000** // **1300**

1071 EUROPE The decline of the Byzantine Empire is hastened after Byzantines are first driven out of southern Italy and later defeated at a battle in present-day Turkey.

1054 EUROPE The Christian Church formally splits into the Orthodox Church in the east and the Roman Catholic Church in the west, an event known as the East-West Schism. *(Byzantine icon of the Virgin Mary, c. 1100)*

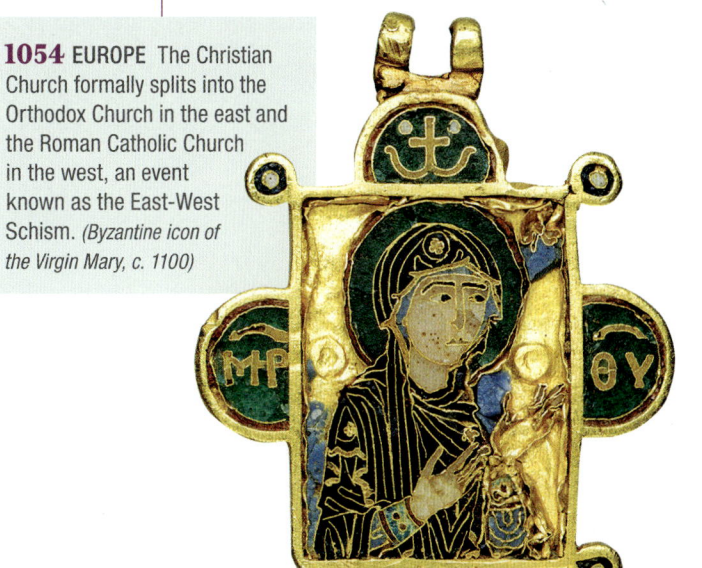

c. 860 EUROPE Construction of the Alhambra, a building that is considered a remarkable architectural achievement in Islamic Spain, begins in the city of Granada. *(view of the Alhambra, Granada, Spain)*

CHAPTER 8

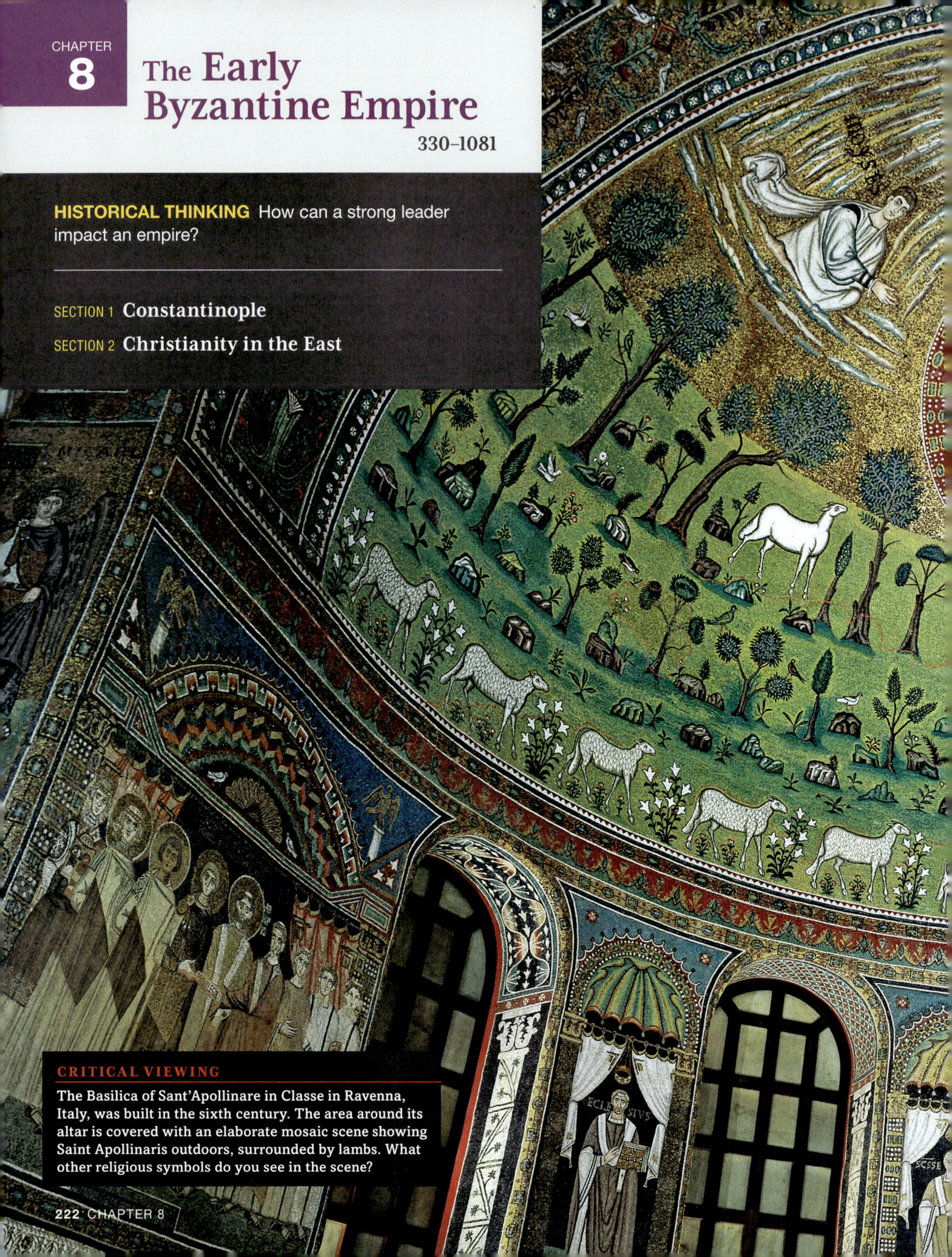

The Early Byzantine Empire
330–1081

HISTORICAL THINKING How can a strong leader impact an empire?

SECTION 1 **Constantinople**

SECTION 2 **Christianity in the East**

CRITICAL VIEWING
The Basilica of Sant'Apollinare in Classe in Ravenna, Italy, was built in the sixth century. The area around its altar is covered with an elaborate mosaic scene showing Saint Apollinaris outdoors, surrounded by lambs. What other religious symbols do you see in the scene?

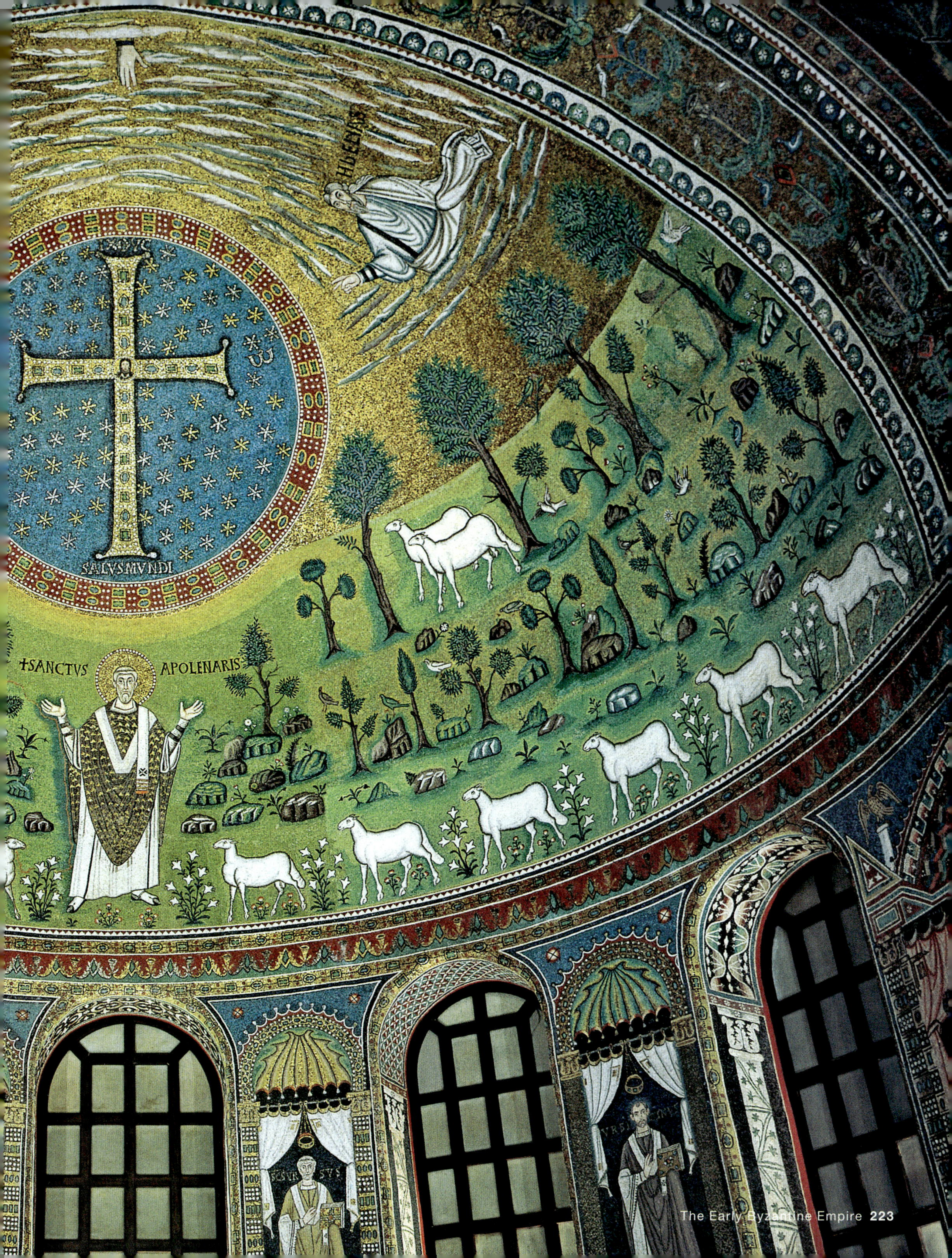
SALVSMVNDI
+SANCTVS
APOLENARIS

1.1 MAIN IDEA The Byzantine Empire was well located for trade but also vulnerable to attack.

Byzantium's New Rome

Empires don't last forever. But some reorganize and reinvent themselves, becoming something new. This is what happened with the Roman Empire. After the fall of Rome and the western empire, the eastern empire continued on for another thousand years as the Byzantine Empire.

CONSTANTINOPLE CONNECTS EAST AND WEST

As you have read, the emperor Diocletian divided the Roman Empire in 285 and appointed separate rulers to the eastern and western halves. The Eastern Roman Empire became known as the Byzantine Empire because its capital was built on the old Greek town of Byzantium. By 330, the emperor Constantine had transformed Byzantium into a grand "New Rome." He named the city Constantinople, which means "city of Constantine" in Greek. Today it is called Istanbul.

While the Western Roman Empire was torn apart by invading Germanic tribes, the Byzantine Empire managed to survive similar attacks. A series of strong emperors fought off enemies and strengthened the empire, which allowed it to continue the traditions of Roman civilization for another thousand years after the collapse of the Western Roman Empire. The people that historians call Byzantines, most of whom spoke Greek, proudly called themselves Romans.

Constantinople occupied one of the ancient world's most important geographic locations. At the heart of the empire was the small but important land link between Asia and Europe that permitted trade between east and west. The empire itself reached into both continents, with its center in present-day Greece and Turkey.

The Bosporus, a strait that runs through Istanbul, Turkey, still serves as a link between Europe and Asia—much as it did during the Byzantine Empire, when the city was known as Constantinople.

The Byzantine Empire, 527–565

Constantinople was also located on the Bosporus, a strait that links the Black and Mediterranean seas. The city served as a major trade center for goods traveling by land and sea from Europe, Asia, and Africa. It also attracted people from Europe, Asia, and Africa, who came to trade goods from their homelands and ended up living in the thriving city. These immigrants gave Constantinople the cultural diversity for which it was famous.

THE EMPIRE EXPANDS

The Byzantine Empire's location brought problems as well as advantages. Although Constantinople was well protected, the rest of the empire was surrounded by enemies. To the north and west were Germanic kingdoms forcefully pressing on the empire's borders. To the east was an age-old enemy, the powerful and hostile Persian Empire.

The rich resources and great wealth of the Byzantine Empire made it a tempting target for raids and invasions. With no strong geographic barriers to prevent invasion by enemies, the empire was dangerously exposed, and its borders were constantly under attack by invading neighbors.

The Byzantine Empire needed strong leadership to hold it together in the face of so many threats. Over a thousand years, its borders grew and shrank depending on the ability of its rulers and the eagerness of its enemies to wage war. At its greatest extent, the empire completely encircled the Mediterranean Sea.

The greatest Byzantine ruler was one of its earliest—**Justinian**, who reigned from 527 until his death in 565. He not only recaptured lost Byzantine lands but also reconquered large areas of the old Western Roman Empire. His armies defeated the Persians and reconquered North Africa, the Italian Peninsula, and parts of present-day Spain. For a brief time, Justinian reunited the Eastern and Western Roman empires. He built up the strength of the Byzantine Empire, even while Rome was being overrun by invaders. Justinian's legacy of leadership remained influential throughout the time of the Byzantine Empire and beyond.

HISTORICAL THINKING

1. **READING CHECK** Why was Constantinople's geographic location an advantage for trade?

2. **DRAW CONCLUSIONS** Why was the Byzantine Empire a prime target for invasions?

3. **INTERPRET MAPS** How did the Byzantine Empire expand during Justinian's lifetime?

1.2

MAIN IDEA The Byzantine Empire reached new heights under the rule of Justinian and Theodora, who left a legacy of law and government despite the devastation of the plague.

Justinian and Theodora

Antony and Cleopatra, Henry VIII and Anne Boleyn, John and Jackie Kennedy—power couples don't always have it easy, but they always have influence. Justinian and Theodora were one of the world's first power couples.

RISE OF JUSTINIAN AND THEODORA

The emperor Justinian I rose to power in 527 and ruled for 38 years. A native of Thrace, a region north of Greece, Justinian was the child of peasants and grew up speaking the local language and Latin. He was adopted by his predecessor, his uncle Justin I, and raised in Byzantium, where he studied law, theology, and Roman history. Even before he was named emperor, he served by his uncle's side as virtual co-emperor.

In 520, Justinian met his future wife, **Theodora**. Not much is known about her early life except that she was an actress and her father was a bear keeper at the Hippodrome, or circus. A Roman law from Constantine's time almost stood in the way of their marriage because of the difference in their social ranks. There are benefits to supreme power, though. Justinian simply had the law changed and married the woman he loved. When Justinian gained the throne, Theodora was proclaimed empress. They ruled together for more than 20 years.

Theodora was Justinian's most trusted and influential advisor. She was intelligent and politically skilled and used her considerable influence to recognize the rights of women, a controversial idea in male-dominated Byzantine society. She was responsible for passing strict laws that protected women and gave them more benefits when seeking a divorce. When Justinian became severely ill during the plague, a deadly epidemic disease, and was unable to govern, Theodora served as the sole ruler of the empire. Historians have also noted that Justinian passed only a few important laws after Theodora's death, indicating that she may have been the major strategist of the pair.

BYZANTIUM UNDER JUSTINIAN

Justinian believed it was his duty to restore the Roman Empire to its historical boundaries. He achieved his goal with the help of a brilliant general named **Belisarius**. After expanding the eastern boundaries of the empire with a victory over the Persian Sasanians in 530, Belisarius reconquered the Vandal kingdom in North Africa and parts of Spain and retook most of Italy from the Goths, reaching Rome in 540. Justinian and Belisarius were successful in large part because, like the Persians and Western Romans before them, they recruited soldiers from diverse groups, including Goths, Armenians, Arabs, and Persians.

In this mosaic, the empress Theodora is surrounded by her attendants. Theodora is depicted wearing jewels, a crown, and a royal purple robe.

This sixth-century mosaic shows Justinian in the center with religious leaders on the right and government officials on the left.

Even as he expanded his empire, Justinian faced internal threats. In January 532, residents of Constantinople rioted against his policies. The riot lasted a week and burned or destroyed half the city, including the Hagia Sophia, the city's most important church. The military killed as many as 30,000 people in its efforts to put down the uprising. Justinian rebuilt the Hagia Sophia, which is regarded today as the most important structure of the Byzantine Empire.

Justinian was a devout Christian who provided funding for many churches and monasteries. He also developed the empire's infrastructure with new bridges and forts. Justinian's building projects were so numerous that his biographer wrote an entire volume just on that subject.

THE CODE OF JUSTINIAN

Justinian's *Corpus of Civil Law*, familiarly known as the **Code of Justinian**, eclipsed all his other achievements. When Justinian became emperor, he undertook an ambitious project to create a unified set of clear and consistent laws across the empire. Like Hammurabi long before him, Justinian created a legal system to bring peace and stability to his domain.

He appointed a commission of legal experts to review all known laws. From 529 to 534, this commission gathered all the laws of the Roman Empire, which numbered around three million. They edited, adapted, and revised those laws to create a manageable law code. Obsolete or confusing laws were eliminated and new laws concerning slavery and women's rights were added. (The code is 1,500 pages long in its modern edition.)

Justinian ended up with four books of law: one of laws borrowed from the older Roman Empire, one a collection of opinions by legal experts, one textbook for law students, and finally a collection of new laws devised by Justinian himself. The Code of Justinian includes laws on subjects ranging from religion, trade, and property to marriage and adoption. One of the most important principles of Justinian's code is one still used in our courts today—"No one suffers penalty for merely thinking." Justinian's *Corpus* preserved the core of Roman law not simply for sixth-century judges and lawyers, but for all time.

PLAGUE AND THE END OF AN ERA

In spite of Justinian's many achievements, the heights of his reign were followed by years of **stagnation**, or lack of growth and development, due in part to the ravages of the plague. The first recorded outbreak of what came to be known as Justinian's plague occurred in 541 in the Egyptian port of Pelusium at the mouth of the Nile. Rats in shipments of grain sent as tribute to Constantinople carried the disease across the Mediterranean the next year. The death toll from the plague may have been as high as one-quarter of the empire's population during Justinian's reign. Over the next 200 years, at least 15 outbreaks devastated the empire and millions died throughout the region.

The final outbreak of plague hit Constantinople in 747 and ended in 767. In the following years, a slow revival began. However, society had changed. Before the plague, the Byzantine Empire had been an urban society in which people met at the marketplace to discuss their affairs or enjoy theater and circus performances. By 600, urban life had faded. In Constantinople alone, 230,000 out of 375,000 people had died. On a positive note, the empire's scholars never stopped preserving Greek learning, systematizing Roman law, and writing new Christian texts.

Theodora died in 548, and historians mark the last period of Justinian's rule from 550 onward as the point where the Eastern Roman Empire gave way to the **medieval** Byzantine Empire, which lasted from about 500 to 1500. This new phase was marked by struggle and loss of territory.

> One of Justinian's goals in creating his code of laws was to reorganize and standardize confusing Roman laws. The following excerpt, from the *Institutes*, defines the concept of civil law for new law students.
>
> **PRIMARY SOURCE**
>
> Civil law is thus distinguished from the law of nations. Every community governed by laws and customs uses partly its own law, partly laws common to all mankind. The law which a people makes for its own government belongs exclusively to that state and is called the civil law, as being the law of the particular state. But the law which natural reason appoints for all mankind obtains equally among all nations, because all nations make use of it. The people of Rome, then, are governed partly by their own laws, and partly by the laws which are common to all mankind.

HISTORICAL THINKING

1. **READING CHECK** What was Justinian's main military goal?

2. **IDENTIFY PROBLEMS AND SOLUTIONS** How did Justinian address the problem of a disorganized and oversized legal code?

3. **EVALUATE** Why is Theodora considered a major figure of the Byzantine Empire?

1.3 Preserving Cultural Heritage

"Suspended From Heaven"

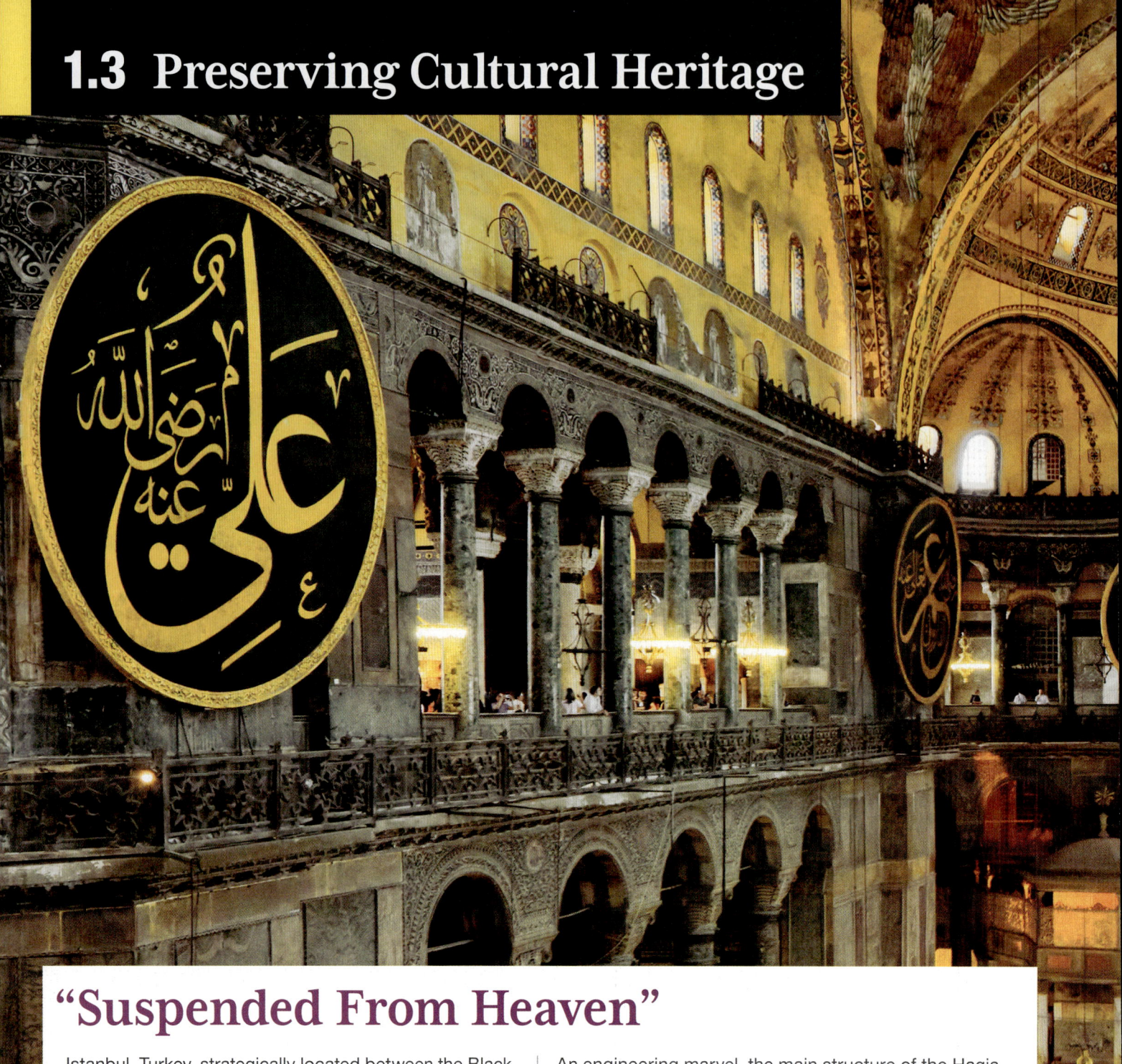

Istanbul, Turkey, strategically located between the Black Sea and the Sea of Marmara and straddling Europe and Asia, has been home to significant political, religious, and artistic history. A bridge between the East and the West, it's no wonder that the Byzantines chose what was then called Constantinople as the capital of their empire.

It was in Constantinople in 532 that the Byzantine emperor Justinian I commissioned the Hagia Sophia, a Christian church and one of the finest examples of Byzantine architecture. *Hagia Sophia*, which means "Divine, or Holy, Wisdom" in Greek, was built in a short time—about 6 years—and completed in 537.

An engineering marvel, the main structure of the Hagia Sophia consists of a central dome that rests on top of four huge arches supported by four giant columns and two semi-domes. Forty arched windows encircle the center dome, which gives it the appearance of floating over the church as if it is, in the words of the writer Procopius, "suspended from heaven."

The complicated construction of the main structure made it prone to problems. In 558, an earthquake destroyed the first dome, which was then rebuilt in 562. The surviving main structure is the original that was first constructed between 532 and 537.

ISTANBUL, TURKEY

This view of the interior of the Hagia Sophia from the upper level shows the altar (back center) and the sultan's loge (back left), where the Ottoman sultan would go to pray.

The Early Byzantine Empire 229

The Hagia Sophia's central dome is 182 feet from ground level and 102 feet in diameter.

The original interior of the Hagia Sophia was minimally decorated, but as new Byzantine rulers came into power, they filled the walls with mosaics and frescoes depicting art and religious life in the Eastern Roman Empire. For almost a thousand years, the church served as the center of Eastern Christianity.

Then in 1453, the Ottomans conquered Constantinople and converted the Hagia Sophia into a mosque. Minarets were added around the perimeter of the building and the mosaics and frescoes were plastered over. It remained a mosque until the fall of the Ottoman Empire. In 1934, the Turkish government secularized the building, made it into a museum, and began to restore the original mosaics. However, in 2020 a Turkish court revoked the building's status as a museum, and the government issued a decree allowing the Hagia Sophia to be used as a mosque once again.

The Hagia Sophia represents the interconnected histories of Rome, Byzantium, and the Ottomans, with both Christian and Islamic art decorating the walls. However, the integrity of the building is threatened by successive earthquakes.

While Istanbul's strategic location made it an ideal place for an empire's capital, it also makes it vulnerable to earthquakes. Istanbul lies on the North Anatolian Fault, a crack in Earth's crust that spreads in a line from east to west across the northern part of Turkey. Typically when an earthquake occurs along this fault line, the stress migrates west. Based on this pattern, scientists have determined that Istanbul, home to the Hagia Sophia, is also at risk. Unfortunately, they can't predict when the next earthquake may hit or how large it may be.

After one of the largest earthquakes struck the town of Izmit in 1999, the Turkish government made earthquake safety a priority on their agenda. Today, scientists monitor the structural integrity of the Hagia Sophia and test potential earthquake damage to assess the risks.

HISTORICAL THINKING

FORM AND SUPPORT OPINIONS Do you believe ancient buildings like the Hagia Sophia are important to preserve? Why or why not?

The interior of the Hagia Sophia, which has served as a church, a mosque, and a museum, contains both Byzantine mosaics and Arabic calligraphy, illustrating a blend of two different cultures.

The Early Byzantine Empire 231

1.4

MAIN IDEA Procopius chronicled the history of Justinian's reign over the Byzantine Empire.

Traveler: Procopius Plague Witness c. 500–554

Today every major political leader is followed by photographers, video crews, and reporters who record their every move. But what about the leaders of the distant past? How do we know about their lives?

EMBEDDED WITH THE BYZANTINE ARMY

Just as Herodotus created a record of the Greco-Persian Wars, the traveler and writer Procopius (pruh-KOH-pee-uhs) recorded Justinian's expansion of the Byzantine Empire. Not much is known about the early life of Procopius except that he was born in Palestine in about 500 and that he learned Greek and studied law. As a young man, he traveled to Constantinople and went to work as a legal advisor and secretary to General Belisarius. During his 13 years with Belisarius and the Byzantine army, Procopius traveled throughout the empire, witnessed its expansion, and learned about its inhabitants. He was with the general during campaigns against the Sasanians in Persia, the Vandals in North Africa, and the Goths in Italy.

Over the course of his life, Procopius wrote three books. *The Wars of Justinian* is about the wars to defend and expand the empire. *Buildings* is about Justinian's public works and was probably commissioned by the emperor. Procopius's final book was called *The Secret History* and was in fact kept a secret and published only after his death. Here, Procopius describes Justinian, Theodora, and Belisarius as corrupt and untrustworthy people with low morals. Today, many historians do not take it very seriously as a historical source. Some speculate that it was a way for the author to "let off some steam" and no one knows for certain why Procopius wrote the book.

In all his work, Procopius wrote for his contemporaries, not for historians of the future. Some of what he recorded came from his own observations. Other information came from the people he met. He followed the style of other classical historians such as Herodotus and Thucydides. Like Herodotus, Procopius must be read critically, but he is the source of the most extensive information about Justinian's world. Like Thucydides, Procopius is most accurate when he is relaying his personal observations, rather than in his historical writing.

CRITICAL VIEWING This Iranian miniature shows Sasanian soldiers laying siege to a Byzantine fortress during the second war between the two empires. Based on this image, what weapons did the Sasanian army use?

232 CHAPTER 8

Justinian's Plague, 541–544

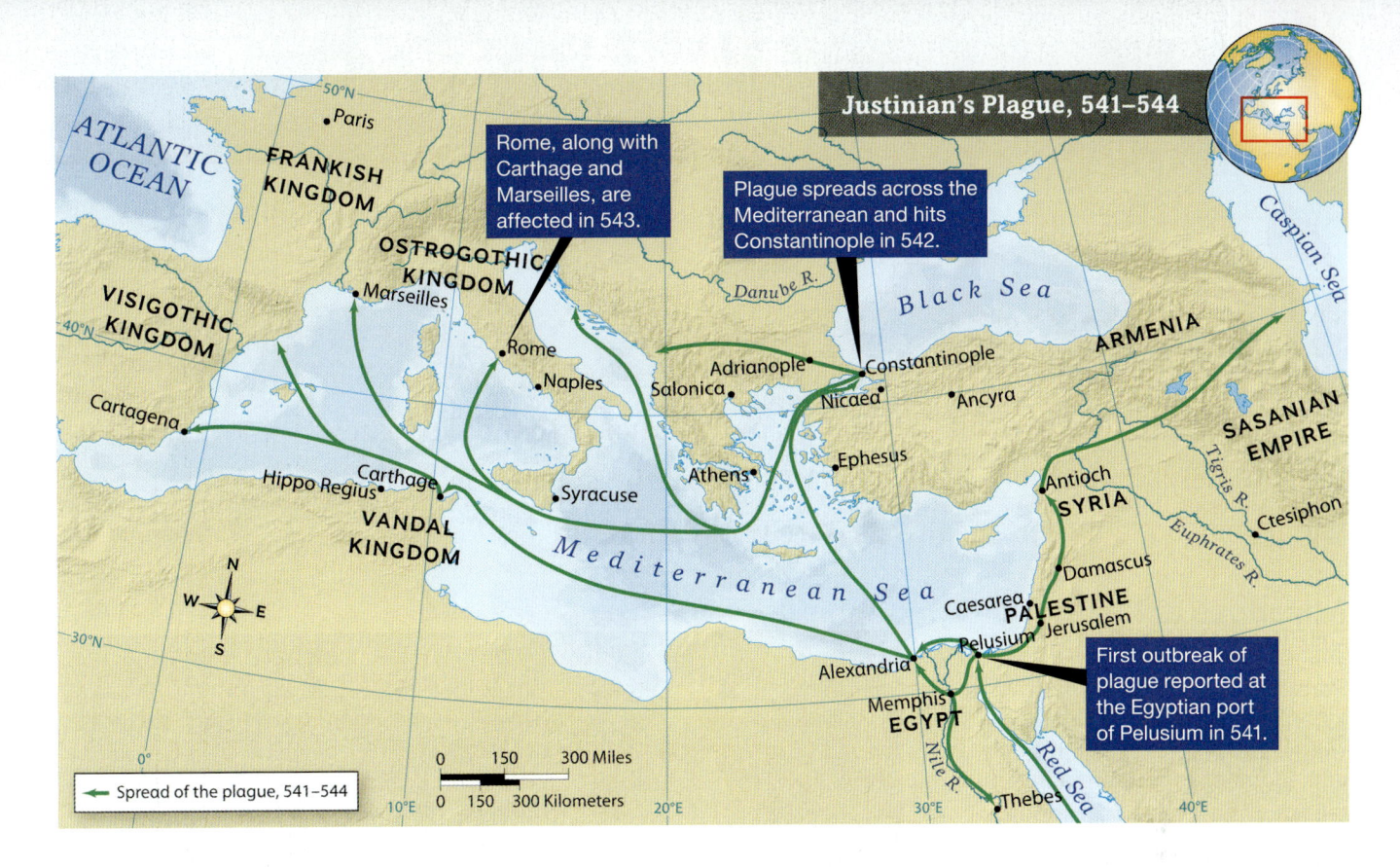

- Rome, along with Carthage and Marseilles, are affected in 543.
- Plague spreads across the Mediterranean and hits Constantinople in 542.
- First outbreak of plague reported at the Egyptian port of Pelusium in 541.

→ Spread of the plague, 541–544

WITNESS TO JUSTINIAN'S PLAGUE

Much of what historians know about the plague during Justinian's reign comes from Procopius. Procopius returned to Constantinople around 541, just before the plague's outbreak. He observed that the disease first appeared in towns along the coast and then moved inland, but he did not know why. Only in the late 19th century did scientists realize that black rats living on ships were the main agents responsible for spreading the disease.

In *The Wars of Justinian*, Procopius describes scenes where there are so many bodies needing to be buried that all rites and rituals are ignored. Rival clans and factions put aside their differences to carry each other's dead. Justinian's government paid men to remove bodies. First, the people placed the bodies in tombs. Then all the tombs filled up. Trenches were dug for the bodies, and soon there was no more space for trenches. Finally, bodies were taken to the towers of a citadel in the outskirts of Constantinople and placed there. According to Procopius, more than half the city died of plague.

In the absence of accurate population statistics, historians have to estimate the deaths resulting from the plague. As you have read, the deaths in the empire's large cities were massive. High estimates put the death toll from the plague at one-fourth of the empire's population—of 26 million subjects, only 19 million survived.

PRIMARY SOURCE

During these times there was a pestilence [epidemic], by which the whole human race came near to being annihilated [utterly destroyed]. Now in the case of all other scourges [afflictions] sent from heaven some explanation of a cause might be given by daring men. . . . But for this calamity it is quite impossible either to express in words or to conceive in thought any explanation, except indeed to refer it to God. For it did not come in a part of the world nor upon certain men, nor did it confine itself to any season of the year, so that from such circumstances it might be possible to find subtle explanations of a cause, but it embraced the entire world, and blighted [destroyed] the lives of all men . . . respecting neither sex nor age.

—*The Wars of Justinian* by Procopius

HISTORICAL THINKING

1. **READING CHECK** How do we know so much about the Byzantine Empire during Justinian's reign?
2. **DRAW CONCLUSIONS** Why did Procopius believe the reason for the plague must be "referred to God"?
3. **IDENTIFY DETAILS** How did Procopius convey the number of people who died during the plague?

The Early Byzantine Empire

2.1

MAIN IDEA The Byzantine Empire and Christian Church faced more than a century of discord over the use of icons.

The Iconoclasts

A typical smartphone or tablet screen has many colored squares with graphic symbols and letters. We call them icons, and chances are that you know immediately what a lot of them mean. People of the ancient Byzantine Empire had icons, too, but their meanings were very different.

CHRISTIAN ICONS

As Christianity grew and spread in the sixth and seventh centuries, a Christian culture grew with it. Art, in the form of **icons**, or sacred or religious images, was an important part of that culture. The word *icon* comes from the Greek word *eikōn*, which means "image, figure, or likeness." An icon is historically an image of Christ, the saints, the Virgin Mary, or an angel—all important people to Christians.

Icons were not produced as art, but rather as sacred objects; the artists were generally unknown, the works unsigned. Many icons were thought to have appeared miraculously, not created by an artist. These icons in particular were believed to have special powers, such as answering prayers, healing the sick, and offering protection. Icons were **venerated**, or honored and adored, in homes and churches and carried through the streets in religious processions.

Icons were important in the Christian Church during a time of instability and economic and societal change for the empire. Starting in 541 as a result of the plague, the population declined, cities shrank, the economy contracted, and tax revenues plummeted.

In the early seventh century, the structure of the empire began to change. Because the government could no longer afford to pay soldiers, local militias consisted of part-time soldiers who farmed the land during peacetime. Conquered people were moved into less populated rural areas. The tradition of separate civil and military powers that had existed since Constantine's time was replaced by a combined military and civil power structure. The empire was divided into military districts, each headed by a governor who heard legal disputes, collected taxes, and commanded the militia.

In the middle of the seventh century, Arabs conquered lands that had previously been held by the Byzantine Empire, including Syria, Palestine, Egypt, and much of North Africa. Most of Italy was lost, while the Balkans north of Greece fell to the Avars and the Slavs, who lived north of Constantinople.

A woman lights candles in front of a religious icon at a Greek Orthodox church in Istanbul, Turkey. At one time, these icons were banned in the eastern branch of the Christian Church.

During this period, the upper and lower classes began to lead almost identical lives. Fewer people knew Latin, so the most common language, Greek, was more widely used. Some people owned more land than others, but they now worked the land alongside their poorer dependents. Slavery declined as well because no one could afford to feed slaves. Most farmers were peasants who worked the land themselves with two oxen and a plow and grew only enough food for their own families.

Icons served as a powerful source of solace to the Byzantine people during this time of change. Some scholars believe icons held the Byzantine identity and empire together. In 626, an icon of the Virgin Mary was credited with saving Constantinople from a Persian attack. But attitudes began to change and by the beginning of the eighth century, the veneration of icons had become controversial.

THE ICONOCLASTIC CONTROVERSY

The Second Commandment of the Hebrew Bible forbids the creation of graven, or engraved, images. In Judaism and Islam, this commandment is interpreted to forbid portrayals of religious figures. Christians have had a variety of interpretations. In the eighth century, some Eastern Christians began to believe that icons violated the Second Commandment. They may have been influenced by neighboring Muslims, or they may have been reacting to the growing power and wealth of the Christian Church. The people opposed to these images were known as **iconoclasts**, or "image breakers." They supported iconoclasm, which is the rejection or destruction of religious images. The people who venerated icons were known as iconophiles.

The split sharply divided the empire for over a century and caused rifts within the Christian Church. The first period of iconoclasm was from 726 to 787. It was started by the emperor Leo III, who banned the worship of icons. In 730, he ordered the destruction of all icons, including the largest icon in Constantinople, the golden Christ, which hung above his own palace gates. This action angered people so much that—according to one version of events—a mob of women killed the man who removed it. One of the most vocal religious leaders who defended icons against Leo's attacks was John of Damascus, a scholar and monk. He argued that there was a difference between veneration and worship.

This Byzantine icon shows the Virgin Mary holding the Christ-child. Mary's hand directs the viewer to the child, who holds out his hand in a blessing.

After the emperor Leo III, the Byzantine rulers went back and forth. Constantine V, Leo's successor and son, was also an iconoclast. He went even further, burning down a monastery on Mount Olympus and actively persecuting iconophiles. After Constantine, the iconophiles experienced a brief period of relief under the reign of Empress Irene in the late 700s. Emperor Leo V reinstated iconoclasm in 815. Similar to prior iconoclastic emperors, Leo V attacked the monks who produced icons. Many icon painters had their foreheads branded as a warning to others. The prohibition against the veneration of icons remained in place until 843, when the mother of Michael III, an iconophile serving as regent for her son, ended the controversy. Icons became an integral part of Byzantine Christianity.

The years when icons were banned in the Byzantine Empire increased an existing rift between the Christian Church in the east and west, which was never healed. At the same time, the controversy helped define Byzantine identity and the eastern branch of the Christian Church. The church came out of the controversy newly unified, and the patriarch, or bishop of Constantinople, became even more independent of papal authority in Rome.

HISTORICAL THINKING

1. **READING CHECK** How did attitudes toward icons start to change in the eighth century?

2. **MAKE INFERENCES** Why do you think icons became important to the Byzantine people during a time of economic and societal change?

3. **ANALYZE POINTS OF VIEW** Why does John of Damascus make a distinction between *worship* and *venerate*?

2.2 MAIN IDEA
In the tenth century, the Byzantine Empire reached its golden age and spread Christianity into eastern Europe and Russia before beginning to decline.

Byzantine Growth and Decline

What makes an empire great? Is it the breadth of its territory? The power of its rulers? Or the beauty and innovation of its arts and sciences? As you have read, the Byzantine Empire experienced great heights, but another glorious period was still to come. Yet the empire eventually weakened and faced a long, slow decline.

REVITALIZING THE EMPIRE

After the Iconoclastic Controversy ended in 867, a new dynasty arose that changed the fortunes of the empire and led it into a golden age. The Macedonian dynasty was founded by Basil I who, like Justinian, came from humble peasant beginnings. His successors began reconquering territory that had once made up the extended Byzantine Empire.

More than 100 years after Basil I gained the throne, a descendant, **Basil II**, conquered the Bulgarian Empire and added parts of Syria, Mesopotamia, and Armenia, among others, to his territory. The Byzantine Empire was again a major power in the region. On the home front, Basil II worked to control the growing power of the regional governors and their families who had become a landed aristocracy. He required that land taken from peasants be returned, and he changed the system of taxation so the responsibility for paying more in taxes fell to the large landowners.

The Macedonian dynasty in general and Basil II's rule in particular are considered the golden age of the Byzantine Empire. Some scholars even call it the Byzantine or Macedonian Renaissance. Arts of all kinds were funded and promoted, literature flourished, and scholars, such as Leo the Mathematician, expanded on Greco-Roman knowledge.

The Byzantine Empire, c. 1071

EXTENDING THE FAITH

The period following the Iconoclastic Controversy was an important period for the eastern branch of the Christian Church as it expanded into new regions. This extension of the faith was to have revolutionary consequences that still shape our world today.

In 863, at the request of the ruler of Moravia (present-day Czech Republic), two Byzantine Greek brothers, Cyril and Methodius, became missionaries to the Slavic people of eastern Europe. Chosen because they spoke a Slavic dialect, Cyril and Methodius

236 CHAPTER 8

proved to be enormously successful. The brothers and their missionary successors ultimately reached out and converted the Bulgarians, Serbs, and Rus peoples (Russians).

But Cyril and Methodius's importance reaches far beyond the spread of religion. To reach the people he wanted to convert, Cyril translated the Bible into local languages, inventing an alphabet made up of a combination of Greek and local letters. This became the precursor of the modern Cyrillic alphabet. Today, over 50 languages, including Russian, use an alphabet derived from the Cyrillic. Byzantine trade and culture traveled the same paths as the missionaries, adding to the wealth of the Byzantine Empire and influencing Russian and eastern European art and architecture.

Cyril and Methodius's work of translating the Bible further increased tensions between the western and eastern branches of the Christian Church, as many leaders in the western branch believed the Bible should only be written in Latin. This and other tensions would eventually lead to a formal division of the church into the Orthodox Church in the east and the Roman Catholic Church in the west. You will learn more about this split in a later chapter.

THE DECLINE

After the rule of Basil II ended, the Byzantine Empire went into steep decline. Large landowners took back control and regained power. More than ten emperors ruled in the 56 years between 1025 and 1081. Then, shortly after the split of the Christian Church, the Byzantine Empire faced a new enemy, the Latin Christians of western Europe.

In 1071, the Byzantines experienced what is known as the "Double Disasters." First, the Normans, Viking descendants who had settled in northern France, drove the Byzantines out of southern Italy. Then, in August, the Seljuk Turks, skilled horsemen from Central Asia, captured the emperor in a massive defeat for the Byzantines at the battle of Manzikert. After 1071, Byzantine emperors ruled a much smaller empire with a much-weakened army.

This fresco of Saint Basil performing a religious ceremony is located in the Church of St. Sophia in Macedonia. Initially part of the First Bulgarian Empire, the church was built after the region's official conversion to Christianity.

HISTORICAL THINKING

1. **READING CHECK** Why was the period of the Macedonian dynasty called the Byzantine Empire's golden age?

2. **IDENTIFY PROBLEMS AND SOLUTIONS** How did Cyril address the problem of converting the Slavs?

3. **INTERPRET MAPS** What area was still part of the Byzantine Empire after 1071?

2.3

MAIN IDEA The Byzantine Empire had an impact on the development of western European, Islamic, and Slavic civilizations.

Imprint of an Early Empire

For many years, a famous historian named Edward Gibbon was the leading authority on the ancient Roman world. He wrote that the Byzantine Empire was corrupt, decadent, immoral, and overly bureaucratic. Essentially, he portrayed it as being the opposite of the enlightened and efficient western Europe. He was wrong.

INFLUENCING EAST AND WEST

Historians now realize the important role played by the Byzantine Empire in preserving the traditions of the classical age. The empire was an essential link that passed Greco-Roman knowledge and culture to the medieval west and also to the Islamic east, for example to Arabia and Persia. The people of the Byzantine Empire protected Greco-Roman knowledge and culture for future generations, developed artistic and architectural styles that influenced artists and builders of the Muslim Golden Age and the European Renaissance (about which you'll learn more later), and gave birth to a branch of Christianity that developed into the Russian, Serbian, and Greek Orthodox Churches.

The empire began as a literal "New Rome," an extension of the Roman Empire, under Constantine, but as the centuries passed the main language shifted from Latin to Greek and a unique tradition and culture developed.

LASTING LEGACIES

Although at times the Byzantine Empire ruled over most of the Mediterranean world, one of its most lasting legacies is not armed conquest but diplomacy. Many Byzantine leaders were adept treaty makers and developed a tradition of negotiating and making deals with their neighbors, often playing one against another.

One reason the empire maintained its power during periods of both decline and ascent was that its economic and financial system remained strong throughout. Some historians believe that the reliability of its gold currency was possible because it was introduced at the same time that trade increased with West Africa, which made gold more available. The empire also traded with China and developed one of the only silk industries outside China after smuggling out some silkworms around 560.

Most famously, the Byzantine Empire preserved and improved upon the legal codes of the Romans. The Code of Justinian formed the foundation for much of European law and still influences international law today. The emperor Leo III created a new law code in 726, the *Ecloga*. The *Ecloga* revised Roman law to incorporate Christian principles and it was written in Greek, so it

CRITICAL VIEWING This mosaic adorns a huge arch in the Basilica of San Vitale in Ravenna, Italy. The arch shows Jesus and the apostles. Why do you think Jesus is shown at the top of the arch with a different orientation than the images of the apostles?

could be read by more people. The *Ecloga* became part of the legal institutions of the Slavic world, for example in Russia.

The Byzantine Empire developed an influential artistic culture. Its distinctive style is well represented by the remarkable mosaics—groups of tiny colored stone cubes set in mortar to create a picture or design—found in churches such as the Hagia Sophia. Byzantine mosaics were known for their exceptional quality and craftsmanship. Large expanses of gold-backed glass created a rich glow, and natural stone cubes helped create vibrant, detailed scenes. Byzantine artists used techniques from Greece and Rome in painting and mosaic and mixed them with Christian themes, developments that would capture the attention of Renaissance painters a few centuries later. Furthermore, Byzantine art and culture traveled with missionaries and traders to the Slavic world where it had an enormous influence.

WOMEN IN BYZANTIUM

As you have seen, powerful women like Theodora had a strong impact on Byzantine history even if they were still legally inferior to men. In fact, women in the empire had more rights than in many other societies both before and after the Byzantine era.

Under Byzantine law, a woman could be the guardian of an emperor who was still a child and serve as a de facto ruler or regent. Because of this law, Theodora possessed a leadership role in the running of Justinian's empire, and the empress Irene restored the use of icons and plotted against her own son to hold onto her position as emperor.

Throughout the empire, a woman could become the legal head of her household and gain control of her family's resources when her husband died. All Byzantine women, even married women, could sign contracts and make their own wills. The United States did not grant women these kinds of property rights until the 19th century.

HISTORICAL THINKING

1. **READING CHECK** Why is the Byzantine Empire considered important to the later development of western Europe?
2. **COMPARE AND CONTRAST** What are the similarities and differences between the Code of Justinian and the *Ecloga*?
3. **DRAW CONCLUSIONS** How do you think the rights granted to women in the Byzantine Empire affected women's quality of life? Explain your reasoning.

Byzantine Mosaics

REALISTIC ANIMALS Mosaics often contained realistic animals, such as the sheep shown here.

DAZZLING GOLD Many mosaics contained shiny pieces of gold leaf to create a sparkling effect.

INTRICATE PATTERNS The mosaic floor of the Basilica San Vitale contains intricate patterns.

CHAPTER 8
THE EARLY BYZANTINE EMPIRE
REVIEW

VOCABULARY

Choose the vocabulary word that best completes each of the following sentences.

1. An outbreak of a deadly _____ resulted in loss of life and a struggling economy.

2. The Byzantine economy experienced _____ after the reign of Justinian.

3. The _____ period in European history lasted from about 500 to 1500.

4. The _____ of the Virgin Mary glowed beautifully in the candlelight.

5. People would adore and _____ pictures of religious figures.

6. An _____ believed that images of religious figures went against the Second Commandment.

7. Byzantine _____ were part of the empire's artistic legacy.

READING STRATEGY
MAKE INFERENCES

Complete a graphic organizer like the one below to make an inference about the Byzantine Empire and its success. Tell what you know about the subject in the "I Know" section. Write your inference in the "And So" section. Then answer the question that follows.

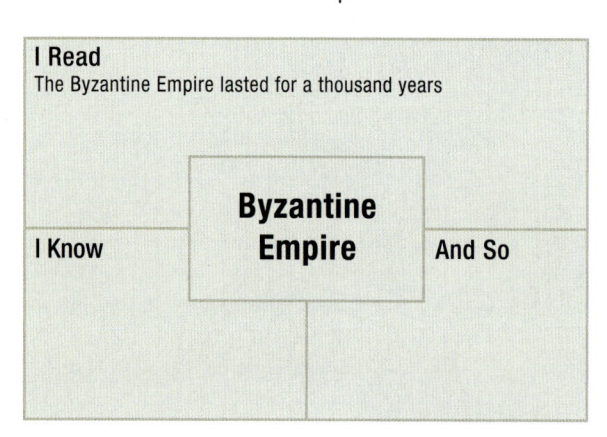

I Read		
The Byzantine Empire lasted for a thousand years		
I Know	**Byzantine Empire**	And So

8. What caused the downfall of the Western Roman Empire, and what can you infer about the Eastern Roman Empire in contrast?

MAIN IDEAS

Answer the following questions. Support your answers with evidence from the chapter.

9. What was important about Constantinople's location? **LESSON 1.1**

10. Why was the Justinian Code an important legacy of Justinian's reign? **LESSON 1.2**

11. What did iconophiles want? **LESSON 2.1**

12. What qualities marked the golden age of the Macedonian dynasty? **LESSON 2.2**

13. How did the Byzantine Empire impact the Slavic world? **LESSON 2.3**

HISTORICAL THINKING

Answer the following questions. Support your answers with evidence from the chapter.

14. **EXPLAIN** How did trade with West Africa influence the Byzantine economy?

15. **DRAW CONCLUSIONS** Why are Procopius's writings important to modern historians?

16. **MAKE GENERALIZATIONS** How did Byzantine laws of inheritance influence women's lives? Did that make any significant difference to the historic course of the empire? Provide support from the text in your answer.

17. **EVALUATE** Write a few sentences arguing for or against use of the term *golden age* to describe the Macedonian dynasty.

18. **ANALYZE CAUSE AND EFFECT** What is the connection between Egyptian grain and the spread of the plague?

19. **FORM OR SUPPORT OPINIONS** Was the translation of the Bible into the Slavic languages truly important in the conversion of the Slavs to Christianity? Why or why not?

20. **DRAW CONCLUSIONS** How did Christianity both unify the Byzantine Empire and help form the Byzantine identity?

INTERPRET VISUALS

Study the icon. Then answer the questions that follow.

21. How does the use of gold leaf affect the painting?

22. Why might gold leaf have been such an essential part of the style of icons?

Saint Michael, c. 14th century

ANALYZE SOURCES

Basil II ruled Byzantium during its golden age, and unlike most emperors, he was buried outside the city of Constantinople at the Hebdomon Palace complex. The epitaph below was found in later manuscripts, not on or near his tomb. Read it and answer the questions that follow.

> Other past emperors
> previously designated for themselves other
> burial places
> But I Basil, born in the purple chamber,
> place my tomb on the site of the Hebdomon [Palace]
> and take sabbath's rest from the endless toils
> which I satisfied in wars and which I endured.
> For nobody saw my spear at rest,
> from when the Emperor of Heaven called me
> to the rulership of this great empire on earth,
> but I kept vigilant through the whole span of my life
> guarding the children of New Rome
> marching bravely to the West,
> and as far as the very frontiers of the East.
> The Persians and Scythians bear witness to this
> and along with them Abasgos, Ismael, Araps, Iber.
> And now, good man, looking upon this tomb
> reward it with prayers in return for my campaigns.
>
> —Epitaph of Basil II

23. According to the epitaph, what did Basil think was the most important achievement of his reign?

24. What does the use of the term "New Rome" tell us about Byzantine identity in the 11th century?

CONNECT TO YOUR LIFE

25. **NARRATIVE** The plague in Constantinople lasted 20 years and changed the city in profound ways. Write a story in which you are a traveler who has left the city before the outbreak of the plague and then returned after it is over, 20 years later.

TIPS

- Review the lesson that describes the plague and then imagine yourself being one of the people who witnessed this event.

- Use sensory details to describe the city before and after the plague: think of sounds, smells, tastes, and feelings as well as what you would see.

- Use vivid language to help readers visualize the scene.

- Include two or three vocabulary terms from the chapter in your narrative.

- Conclude your narrative by expressing an emotional response to the changes.

The Early Byzantine Empire 241

CHAPTER 9

Arab Empires and Islamic Expansion
550–1258

HISTORICAL THINKING How does religion affect world civilizations?

SECTION 1 **Origins of Islam**
SECTION 2 **Islamic Expansion**
SECTION 3 **The Abbasid Empire**

CRITICAL VIEWING

The Great Mosque of Córdoba in what is now Spain is one of the best-known examples of Muslim architecture. What generalizations can you make about the art and architecture of Islam based on this photo of a prayer hall?

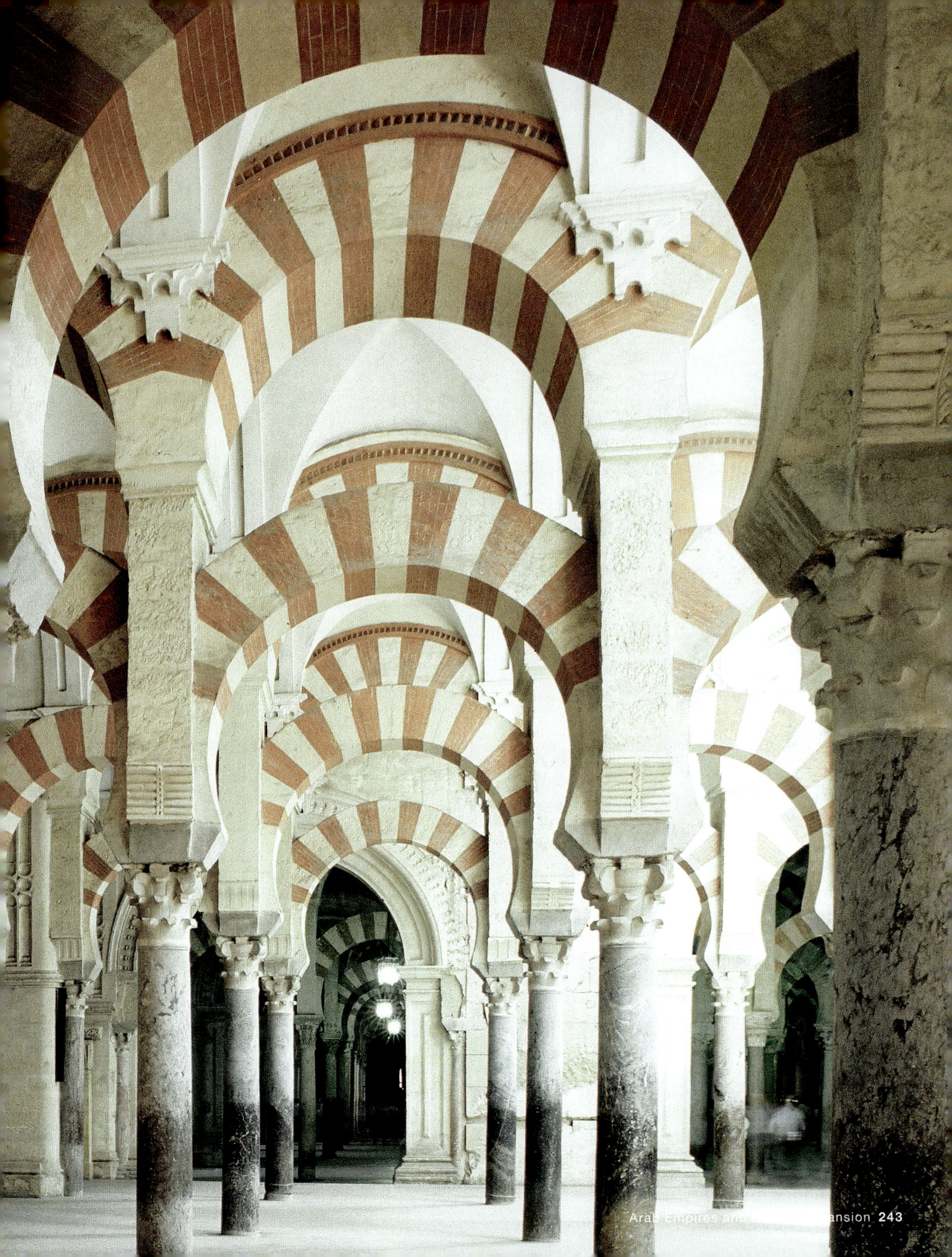

1.1

MAIN IDEA Muhammad introduced Islam to the people of the Arabian Peninsula and united them as one.

The Prophet Muhammad

Think about leaders who have affected your life or the lives of others. Leaders can cause political change, social change, or spiritual change. Long ago, the actions of Muhammad led to all of these changes at the same time.

ORIGINS OF ISLAM

Imagine living in the dry, scorching desert of the Arabian Peninsula. The land was so parched that it was difficult to farm there. Instead, many people who lived in the region herded animals such as sheep, cattle, camels, and goats. These people were known as the **Bedouin** (BEH-duh-wuhn), an Arabic word meaning "desert dweller." Living a nomadic life, they moved with their herds to find locations where water and grazing land were available at different times of the year. Luckily, **oases**, isolated places with water where plants can grow, dotted the land, and the Bedouin could find not only water but also areas of grasses for their animals.

The Bedouin traveled together in clans, or groups of people with a common ancestor. Each clan elected its own **sheikh** (SHAYK) to lead them as they conducted their day-to-day affairs. Like most of the people on the peninsula, the clan members communicated with one another in Arabic.

By the time of the Roman Empire, cities such as **Mecca** rose up around the oases and became trade centers where people from Persia, Egypt, the Byzantine Empire, and elsewhere exchanged goods. Arabs, Jews, and Christians lived together and interacted with and influenced one another. The Arab people, who practiced polytheism, believed that their deities lived in objects found in nature, such as trees or rocks. One of the most revered objects was a large black rock in a cube-shaped shrine called the Kaaba (KAH-buh), which was—and still is—located in Mecca.

Many Arabs traveled to Mecca to pray to one of the gods represented in the Kaaba. This steady stream of visitors brought wealth to the merchants and leaders of this prosperous city, which provided the setting for the introduction of the religion of **Islam**. The word *Islam* translates from Arabic to English as "submission to the will of God." In fact, the central idea of Islam is that entry to heaven and an afterlife is attainable only through full surrender to God. Today, Islam is one of the world's major religions, with more than 1.5 billion followers called **Muslims**.

Like Jews and Christians, Muslims are monotheistic. You learned that monotheism is the belief in one God, and the concept of God's forgiveness of sin. Because all three religions honor Abraham as the first religious prophet, they are known as Abrahamic religions. All three religions accept Moses as a prophet as well, but they disagree about other prophets. Only Muslims accept Muhammad as a prophet, and Muslims see Jesus as a prophet rather than as the Son of God as Christians do. Also, while Judaism, Christianity, and Islam all include rituals as part of worshiping God, the rituals vary from religion to religion. For example, both Muslims and Jews follow a set of dietary restrictions. Although these rules differ between each religion, Islam and Judaism share at least one common ban in their diets: followers are forbidden from eating pork.

LIFE AND LEADERSHIP OF MUHAMMAD

Considered a prophet by Muslims, **Muhammad** is credited with introducing Islam to the Arab people. Muslims do not call Muhammad the founder of Islam because they believe God's teachings are timeless, and therefore Islam has no definite origin. Instead, Muslims believe that Muhammad, who was born around 570, was the last messenger of Allah, the Arabic word for God. Historians have learned most of what they know about Muhammad from the writings of others in the centuries following his death. The religious texts of Islam provide few details about his life.

Muhammad was a successful merchant in Mecca and about 40 years old when he began visiting a secluded cave to pray. He was concerned that people focused too much on wealth rather than on the welfare of others.

Muslims from all over the world journey to pray at the Kaaba in Mecca, Saudi Arabia. (The word *Kaaba* means "cube" in Arabic.) The shrine contains a holy rock called the Black Stone.

Around 613, he had a series of visions that included a figure. Muslims believe that Allah spoke to Muhammad through the angel Gabriel, who called on Muhammad to spread the message of submission to God. Followers see Muhammad's teachings as the direct result of his hearing the word of God.

After his religious revelations, Muhammad began spreading the word of Islam, and his wife Khadijah (ka-DEE-juh) and cousin Ali were among his early followers. Khadijah met and hired Muhammad to work as an agent for her successful trading business and soon asked him to marry her. She had a reputation for being generous, sharing her wealth, and caring for the poor. Khadijah believed in Muhammad's revelations immediately and supported him as he preached his ideas.

Muhammad's message was not well-received in much of Mecca at first; leaders feared the growing belief in Islam might have a negative effect on religious pilgrimages to their city and cause losses of income. At the same time, some people in **Medina** (muh-DEE-nuh)—another oasis city that was 210 miles away—grew enthusiastic about Islam and hoped its message might bring an end to feuding among various Arab clans. Feeling unsafe in Mecca, Muhammad and his supporters moved to Medina in 622. This migration of Muhammad and his followers from Mecca to Medina, called the **Hijrah** (HIHJ-ruh), marked a turning point in Islam. All dates in the Islamic calendar are calculated from the year of the Hijrah.

In Medina, Muhammed and other Muslims established an Islamic community called the umma (OO-muh).

Muhammad encouraged Arabs to submit to God, accept Muhammad as God's messenger, pledge loyalty to the umma, and give up their old clan rivalries. In these ways, Islam unified the people of Medina and later the entire Arabian Peninsula. The community was open to everyone who chose to believe. Women gained more status under Islam, with the right to own and inherit property. Strict rules regulated the treatment of slaves.

Meccan leaders worried about the growing strength of Islam. They prepared to attack Medina, but they did not realize that Muhammad had his own military force. He believed that Allah had given him instructions to fight if necessary to expand Islam. Muslim troops swept into Mecca, conquering the city and dedicating the Kaaba to the worship of Allah alone. This conquest's long-term effects included the rapid spread of Islam from Mecca and Medina through the rest of Arabia. By the time of Muhammad's death in 632, most Arabs had converted to Islam. Today, all Muslims are expected to make the **hajj**, or pilgrimage to the holy city of Mecca, if possible.

HISTORICAL THINKING

1. **READING CHECK** How did Muhammad unite the Arab people?
2. **ANALYZE CAUSE AND EFFECT** What were the effects of geography on the settlement and interaction of people who lived on the Arabian Peninsula during Muhammad's time?
3. **DRAW CONCLUSIONS** Why do you think Muhammad opened the doors of his umma to everyone?

Arab Empires and Islamic Expansion

1.2

MAIN IDEA The period following the death of Muhammad brought both growth and division to the Muslim people.

The Early Caliphs

Sometimes when people lose a leader, they fear that their lives will change. Although Muhammad's death brought uncertainty about the future of Islam, strong leaders followed in Muhammad's footsteps and spread his ideas.

BASIC BELIEFS OF ISLAM

During Muhammad's lifetime, a group of followers committed his teachings to memory. Soon after his death, they compiled his ideas and principles to form the Quran (kuh-RAN), the holy book of Islam. Muslims believe the Quran is the direct word of God as revealed to Muhammad.

Other written texts important to Muslims are hadith (huh-DEETH), accounts of Muhammad's words and actions from those who knew him. A collection of customs called the Sunna (SOO-nuh) describes Islamic practices in detail. These three sacred sources—the Quran, hadith, and the Sunna—form the basis of Islamic law, or **sharia** (shuh-REE-uh). Sharia focuses on a wide variety of topics ranging from family life to prayer to business. It controls not only the religious parts of life but political and social aspects as well. For example, sharia expressly prohibits consuming alcohol and gambling.

The Five Pillars of Islam

Faith To believe "There is no God but God, and Muhammad is his messenger."

Prayer To pray five times a day in the direction of Mecca

Alms To pay a fixed share of one's income to support the poor

Fasting To refrain from eating and drinking during the daytime hours of the month of Ramadan

Pilgrimage To make the hajj to Mecca at least once in your lifetime, if possible

The Prophet's Mosque in Medina in present-day Saudi Arabia contains the tomb of Muhammad and is a holy site for Muslims.

CRITICAL VIEWING A group of people in Kolkata, India, pray on a city roof and in the streets. According to the Five Pillars of Islam, in what direction should these Muslims face during prayer?

In addition, the Quran and hadith outline the basic requirements of Islamic faith, which have become known as the Five Pillars of Islam. Following the Five Pillars of Islam shows that a Muslim is willing to make Islam an integral part of his or her life.

Early Muslims felt a connection to Jews and Christians, who also practiced monotheism and had holy texts that contained similar teachings to those found in the Quran. These "people of the book" who lived in Muslim regions sometimes benefited from special privileges, such as lower taxes. Those who believed in multiple gods did not receive these advantages.

In the early days of Islam on the Arabian Peninsula, Muslim traditions began to take shape. Like Muslims today, early believers prayed in a **mosque**, or Muslim place of worship, under the direction of a religious teacher known as an imam (ih-MAHM). Muslims are expected to face Mecca, kneel, and pray five times a day.

Muhammad's death caused the young Muslim community to think carefully about how Islam would continue—and who would lead it. The umma decided that the prophet's father-in-law Abu Bakr (uh-boo BA-kuhr) would serve as the first **caliph** (KAY-luhf), or successor to Muhammad. Under Abu Bakr's leadership, Muslim troops conquered all the Arabian Peninsula and moved into Egypt, Iraq, and Syria.

Abu Bakr was followed as caliph by another "companion of the Prophet" who had known Muhammad. Later, the transition from one caliph to the next was not always smooth, but the decision to install a caliph as the successor of Muhammad had the effect of ensuring the growth and longevity of Islam.

SUNNI AND SHIITE SPLIT

Disagreements about leadership of the umma emerged soon after Muhammad's death. Both the third caliph, Uthman, and the fourth caliph, Ali, were assassinated. Ali and his wife Fatima were both related to Muhammad and considered by many—but not all—to be the rightful heirs to the Muslim empire. Following Ali's death, a family known as the **Umayyads** (oo-MY-uhdz) seized power, and it began a dynasty in which a member of the family would always be caliph. Some Muslims strongly opposed these actions, and conflicting opinions led to a rift in Islam.

One group, called the **Shiite** (SHEE-yt), believed that all caliphs must be direct descendants of Muhammad through Ali, and still grieved the death of Ali's son Hussein at the Battle of Karbala in 680. In contrast, the majority of Muslims, called the **Sunni** (SOO-nee), thought that any devout Muslim could rise to become caliph. Because of this belief, the Sunni supported the Umayyads and acknowledged Umayyad caliphs as legitimate rulers. These two branches of Islam—Sunni and Shiite—still exist to this day.

HISTORICAL THINKING

1. **READING CHECK** How did the rule of the first caliphs bring about both growth and division?
2. **FORM AND SUPPORT OPINIONS** Which of the Five Pillars of Islam is the hardest to comply with, and why?
3. **IDENTIFY MAIN IDEAS AND DETAILS** Why did Jews and Christians living under the rule of the Muslim empire sometimes receive special benefits?

Arab Empires and Islamic Expansion

1.3 DOCUMENT-BASED QUESTION
Comparing Calendars

How do you know whether you are busy or free next Wednesday? You may have written a note in a paper calendar or planner. Or you might check a calendar app online or on your phone. People have been consulting calendars for more than 4,000 years. The earliest calendars helped farmers know when to plant and harvest crops.

The Egyptians were among the earliest people to develop a calendar, which they used to keep track of their three seasons. Consulting their calendar let them know when the Nile River would flood and when they could plant and harvest wheat. People today owe a debt to the ancient Egyptians for developing an early solar calendar, which was based on where the sun appeared in the sky at different times.

As the Egyptian civilization declined, the Romans also developed a calendar based on the way the sun seemed to move. Remember that at the time, people believed that the sun revolved around Earth. This calendar, known as the Julian calendar, would be the basis of the Gregorian calendar that is commonly used today. This calendar is remarkable because it addresses not only the relationship between Earth and the moon but also between Earth and the sun.

Another example of a civilization that made many advances in astronomy is the Maya civilization, which flourished in what is now Mexico at about the same time as the Muslim empire. Careful observations of the sun's place in the sky allowed Maya astronomers to create an extremely accurate 365-day calendar. They kept track of the seasons with this calendar, but they used a 260-day calendar for religious purposes. You will learn more about the Maya in a later chapter.

In contrast, the earliest calendars of Southwest Asia used the phases of the moon to create a lunar calendar. (The word *lunar* comes from the Latin word for *moon*.) The Sumerians, the Hebrews, and astronomers in the Muslim empire all devised lunar calendars. Present-day Jewish and Muslim calendars are still based on the movement of the moon, which is why Jewish and Islamic holidays occur on different days from year to year.

In this image from a 16th-century Ottoman manuscript, an astronomer uses a compass and an armillary sphere to study the movements of the sun. An armillary sphere is an astronomical device used to show the position of the stars and planets.

ARTIFACT ONE

Primary Source: Islamic Calendar Detail
from a calendar almanac, signed and dated by Katib Muhammad Ma'ruf Na'ili, 1224 A.H./1810 C.E.

In the Islamic calendar, like this one from Turkey, each of the 12 lunar months includes 29.5 days, which totals 354 days. Astronomers today use a solar year of 365.25 days. Because the Islamic calendar does not account for the extra days, each day falls at a slightly different time each year. For example, the first day of Ramadan, the holy month of fasting, falls 10 or 11 days earlier than it did the previous year.

CONSTRUCTED RESPONSE Why do you think this Islamic calendar appears to be so complex?

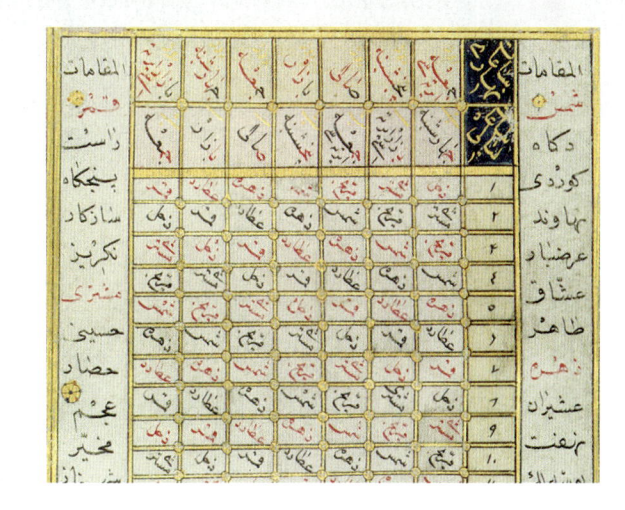

ARTIFACT TWO

Primary Source: Gregorian Calendar Detail
from the Prague Orloj (Prague astronomical clock), 15th century

Many nations around the world use the Gregorian calendar, in which one revolution of Earth around the sun marks a year (365 days) and one revolution of the moon around Earth is a month (29.5 days). This calendar dial from the astronomical clock in Prague displays the 12 months with zodiac signs and symbols in its inner circle. The rotating outer circle includes every day of the year, with the current day appearing at the top.

CONSTRUCTED RESPONSE How does this calendar differ from most calendars used in the United States today?

ARTIFACT THREE

Primary Source: Chinese Calendar Detail
from Song dynasty calendar, 960–1279

The Chinese calendar was based on cycles of 12 for months and also for years. Each period was associated with a different animal: rat, ox, tiger, rabbit, dragon, snake, horse, sheep, monkey, rooster, dog, and pig. In this calendar, the 12 cycles can be seen around the yin and yang symbol. Today, the Chinese still use their traditional calendar for religious festivals but generally use the Gregorian calendar on a day-to-day basis.

CONSTRUCTED RESPONSE What does the shape of the calendar reveal about how the ancient Chinese perceived the passage of time?

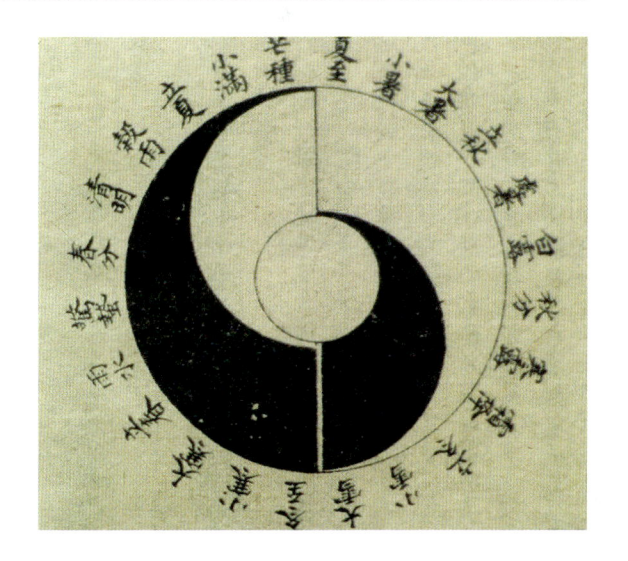

SYNTHESIZE & WRITE

1. **REVIEW** Review what you have read and observed about the calendars of various cultures.

2. **RECALL** On your own paper, list two details you learned by reading about one of the calendars described and two details you observed by looking at that calendar.

3. **CONSTRUCT** Construct a topic sentence that answers this question: How are the three calendars similar to and different from one another?

4. **WRITE** Using evidence from this chapter and the documents, write an informative paragraph that supports your topic sentence in Step 3.

Arab Empires and Islamic Expansion

2.1

MAIN IDEA The caliphs who followed Muhammad as leaders of Islam formed a powerful empire that stretched across the Arabian Peninsula—and beyond.

Conquering the Arabian Peninsula

Conquered people do not simply fade away. They must find ways to adapt to life under their new leaders. Groups who fell under the control of the Muslims felt not only political impacts but social and economic effects as well.

EARLY CONQUESTS

Earlier, you learned that Abu Bakr and the caliphs who immediately followed him formed a powerful army that set out to conquer non-Muslim lands. The main goals of the invasions were to expand the umma, spread the message of Islam, increase Islamic influence in regional affairs, and gain wealth. The Muslims were helped in their efforts by the fact that other ruling powers in the area had weakened and had little will to resist. In some cases, the people were eager to escape their current oppressors and imagined a better life under Muslim rule.

The Muslim army was divided into units of 100 and subunits of 10. The Muslims developed a successful strategy for defeating their enemies. First, their infantry, or foot soldiers, advanced with bows and arrows and crossbows. Next, their cavalry galloped in on horseback to overpower their opponents. The troops were led into battle by the caliph, who headed the army.

Overpowering city after city, the Muslims soon ruled the entire Arabian Peninsula. The army then headed south and gained control of Egypt by 642. By 650, the Muslims controlled an even larger swath of territory from Libya to Central Asia. Soon, they were ruling over more non-Arab people than Arabs. Everywhere they claimed land, they erected mosques for the worship of God.

Writings left behind by defeated peoples tell tales of great destruction at the hands of Arab armies. However, archaeologists have yet to uncover proof of this supposed devastation, so some experts believe that the Muslim invaders attempted to preserve as much of the conquered cultures as they could so that their own empire would flourish.

UNITING DIVERSE PEOPLES

Early Arab leaders knew conquest alone would not create a stable empire. Whenever they seized a new region, they immediately began the sometimes lengthy process of making the vanquished people feel included in the new regime. Occasionally, this process of pacifying the people took several generations.

The Arabs levied, or charged and collected, the same tax rates on conquering and conquered people alike. The only catch was that the conquered people had to convert to Islam to receive this tax break. Once they became Muslims, they received similar

Growth of the Muslim Empire, 661

- Lands under Muslim control at the time of Muhammad's death, 632
- Lands conquered by Muslims under first four caliphs, 632–661

250 CHAPTER 9

In this 11th-century illustration, Arab foot soldiers—wearing blue head coverings and carrying round shields—attack a Byzantine general and his deserting troops.

rights to those born into the religion. After all, Islam stressed the equality of all believers before God. All Muslims, whether converts or born to Muslim parents, paid two types of taxes. A tax on land required that Muslims pay the government one-tenth of their yearly harvest. As specified in the Five Pillars of Islam, Muslims paid alms through a *zakat* (zuh-KAHT) tax to help the needy or serve God. Non-Muslims paid a fixed *jizya* (JIHZ-yuh) tax, which was higher than taxes paid by Muslims.

The empire's armies divided conquered people into three groups. As you have read, those who converted became Muslims. Those who continued to practice Judaism or Christianity were granted the status of "protected subjects." The Arabic word for a protected person is *dhimmi* (DIH-mee); through **dhimmitude**, protected status was awarded to certain non-Muslims. Later, Zoroastrians also received *dhimmi* status, joining Jews and Christians. Polytheists formed the lowest group and received less protection than the other two groups. The granting of *dhimmi* status to certain non-Muslims is a special characteristic of Islam.

Almost all religions distinguish between believers and those outside their religions. However, very few award privileges to some nonbelievers but not to others.

Conquered people under Muslim rule had more freedoms than most defeated people of the time. Jews and Christians were allowed to continue practicing their religion even though they sometimes suffered for their beliefs. In fact, the Muslims who controlled the conquered regions did not press them to convert. Later, however, Jews and Christians faced many restrictions, such as not being able to ride on horseback or build new houses of worship.

For many vanquished people, conversion to Islam seemed the best choice. Becoming a Muslim would definitely impact one's political, social, and economic future in positive ways. Some converted to avoid paying the *jizya* tax, and others converted to Islam because they came to believe in the main principles of the religion. Other incentives to conversion to Islam included stronger trade connections and access to literacy and education in Arabic.

HISTORICAL THINKING

1. **READING CHECK** Why did the Muslim caliphs set out to conquer the Arabian Peninsula?

2. **INTERPRET MAPS** How might the conquest of Egypt have benefited the Muslim caliphs?

3. **DRAW CONCLUSIONS** What might have happened if strong caliphs had not begun a path of conquest?

Arab Empires and Islamic Expansion

2.2

MAIN IDEA The Umayyads initiated a time of change and expansion for the Muslim empire.

The Umayyad Caliphate and North Africa

Religion can bring people together—but it can also divide them. In the case of the early Muslims, a division led to changes within the empire. However, strong leadership allowed the empire to strengthen and expand rather than wither away, and Islam became part of daily life in many areas of Asia, Africa, and Europe.

BUILDING, EXPANSION, AND SOUND GOVERNMENT

Muhammad had left no directive about who should succeed him as the leader of the Islamic community. A civil war, now known as the first *fitnah*, broke out between the Shiite and Sunni factions in 656. The *fitnah* ended in 661 with a victory for the Umayyads, who ruled until 750. Muawiya (moo-AH-wee-ya), the fifth caliph, was the first leader of the Umayyad dynasty.

The Umayyads moved their capital from Medina to **Damascus**, Syria. Although this action outraged many Muslims, the Umayyad leaders believed they could rule their growing empire more capably from this location. They also made Arabic the official language even though they were no longer headquartered on the Arabian Peninsula. As people who spoke languages like Persian and Greek converted to Islam, these new Muslims needed to learn the Arabic language. In Islam, daily prayers must be said in Arabic, and the Quran can only properly be read in that language.

The Umayyads fashioned the Great Mosque of Damascus from a former Christian church. Architects created a large space where Muslim worshipers could pray toward Mecca. The Great Mosque contained a number of firsts for an Islamic building—a place to wash one's hands and feet, a large courtyard, and a tall, slender tower called a **minaret** from which specially trained Muslims issued the call to prayer. No artwork showing human figures or living animals appeared in the building, reflecting Islamic beliefs. The Muslims honored and followed the Ten Commandments, including the Second Commandment: "You shall not make for yourself a graven image."

While some Muslims believed Muawiya was more interested in wealth than in advancing Islam, he did succeed in reuniting Muslims and expanding the empire. He and his successors influenced Asia, Africa, and Europe politically, economically, and socially through their conquests. They pushed into North Africa in the years between 670 and 711 and captured the land called Maghreb, meaning *west* in Arabic, the location of the present-day countries Morocco, Algeria, and Tunisia. Farms in the Maghreb provided the entire Mediterranean region with grain, olive oil, and fruit. The area was also a center for the transport of gold and other trade goods from sub-Saharan Africa across the Mediterranean Sea.

The Muslim conquest of North Africa changed the ways of life and beliefs of the people who lived there. Formerly under the control of the Romans, North Africa had become primarily Christian. Over time, Arabic culture, the Arabic language, and the religion of Islam took root and dominated the region.

From Africa, Umayyad forces crossed the Strait of Gibraltar to take control of parts of the Iberian Peninsula. Additional regions of Southwest and Central Asia fell to the invaders as well. Muslim troops also headed southeast into the Indian subcontinent. Local armies prevented the Umayyads from advancing farther, but the Muslim empire had grown to cover more than four million square miles.

Muawiya and later caliphs realized they needed a strong government to maintain their large domain. They ruled with a firm hand and organized a bureaucracy, which you learned is a group of administrative government officials. The appointed officials ran different bureaus, or

The Dome of the Rock on the Temple Mount in Jerusalem was completed in 691. This gold-domed Islamic mosque, one of the earliest surviving Islamic monuments, stands where Judaism's First Temple was destroyed in 587 B.C.E. Important Christian sites are also nearby.

departments. The caliphs also selected loyal governors to oversee distant provinces. The Umayyads made it clear they intended to leave a lasting mark. They issued their own coined money and built the monumental Dome of the Rock in Jerusalem, alongside Jewish and Christian buildings.

ESCAPE TO THE IBERIAN PENINSULA

After losing control of the empire to rival Muslims in 750, some Umayyads fled to the Iberian Peninsula. There, an Umayyad prince named Abd al-Rahman set up the independent Islamic state of al-Andalus (al-an-duh-LUS). The new Umayyad capital of **Córdoba** had gardens, fountains, paved streets, and running water. Gold and other raw materials flowed into the city, where they were transformed into finished products.

By the year 1000, Córdoba had become a leading center of Islamic learning where many people, including Jews and Christians, could interact in relative harmony. Although the Muslim government practiced **religious tolerance**, or the acceptance of the beliefs and practices of others, non-Muslims faced a number of restrictions. They were required to wear a badge and were prohibited from owning weapons. But scientists, doctors, mathematicians, architects, writers, and artists of various religions came to Córdoba to study and work. The prominent Jewish philosopher and physician Maimonides—who was born in Córdoba—was widely respected by Muslim and Christian scholars as well as by Jews living throughout the Mediterranean.

HISTORICAL THINKING

1. **READING CHECK** What lands did the Umayyads add to the Muslim empire?

2. **IDENTIFY MAIN IDEAS AND DETAILS** How did the Muslim conquest of North Africa affect Jews, Christians, and others in the region who did not practice Islam?

3. **CATEGORIZE** How did Muslim expansion affect North Africa politically, socially, and economically?

2.3 State of the World

800 C.E.

RELIGIOUS FERVOR

Around 800, several great empires and states were thriving. By that time, the Muslim power that had defeated the Umayyads—the Abbasid dynasty—had become the wealthiest state in the world. Charlemagne, the king of the Franks, had united much of western Europe under his rule, and the region enjoyed more peace and prosperity than it had since the fall of the Western Roman Empire. On Central America's Yucatán Peninsula, Chichén Itzá was a vibrant urban center of the Maya civilization. The kingdom of Ghana in West Africa, with its lucrative gold trade, had also become rich and powerful by 800.

Religion played a key role in the rise and fall of at least two of these states. You've read that the Umayyad caliphate fell, in part, because many Muslims disapproved of the secular, or nonreligious, nature of the state. A mystical Islamic practice called **Sufism**, a mystical tradition with the goal of bringing the believer as close as possible to God, arose in reaction to the Umayyads' secularism. Charlemagne's campaigns to expand his empire was largely driven by his desire to spread his Christian faith. In 800, the pope crowned Charlemagne the first emperor of the Holy Roman Empire, a complex of lands in western and central Europe.

Throughout Asia, Buddhism continued to spread. During Japan's Heian period, which began in 794, Buddhism grew in popularity and combined elements of the country's traditional Shinto religion. In 791, Buddhism became the state religion in Tibet. China's Tang dynasty was heavily influenced by Buddhism. However, the dynasty fell into decline around 800. When its rule ended in 907, Chinese emperors began to favor Daoism and Confucianism over Buddhism.

HISTORICAL THINKING

INTERPRET MAPS What reactions might the religious structures shown on the map have stirred among people who lived around 800?

Temple of Kukulkan Built between 800 and 900 by the Maya, the Temple of Kukulkan demonstrates the civilization's architectural abilities and knowledge of astronomy. The pyramid contains 365 steps, one for each day of the year in the Maya calendar. And, as the sun sets at the spring and autumnal equinoxes, a shadow in the shape of a snake descends one of the staircases.

FIVE LARGEST CITIES

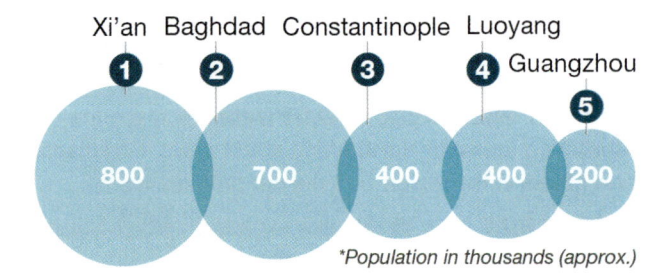

1. Xi'an — 800
2. Baghdad — 700
3. Constantinople — 400
4. Luoyang — 400
5. Guangzhou — 200

*Population in thousands (approx.)

WORLD POPULATION

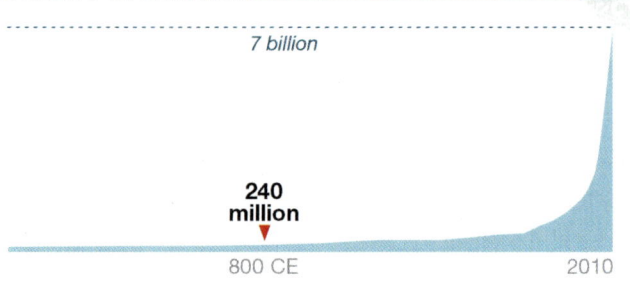

800 CE: 240 million
2010: 7 billion

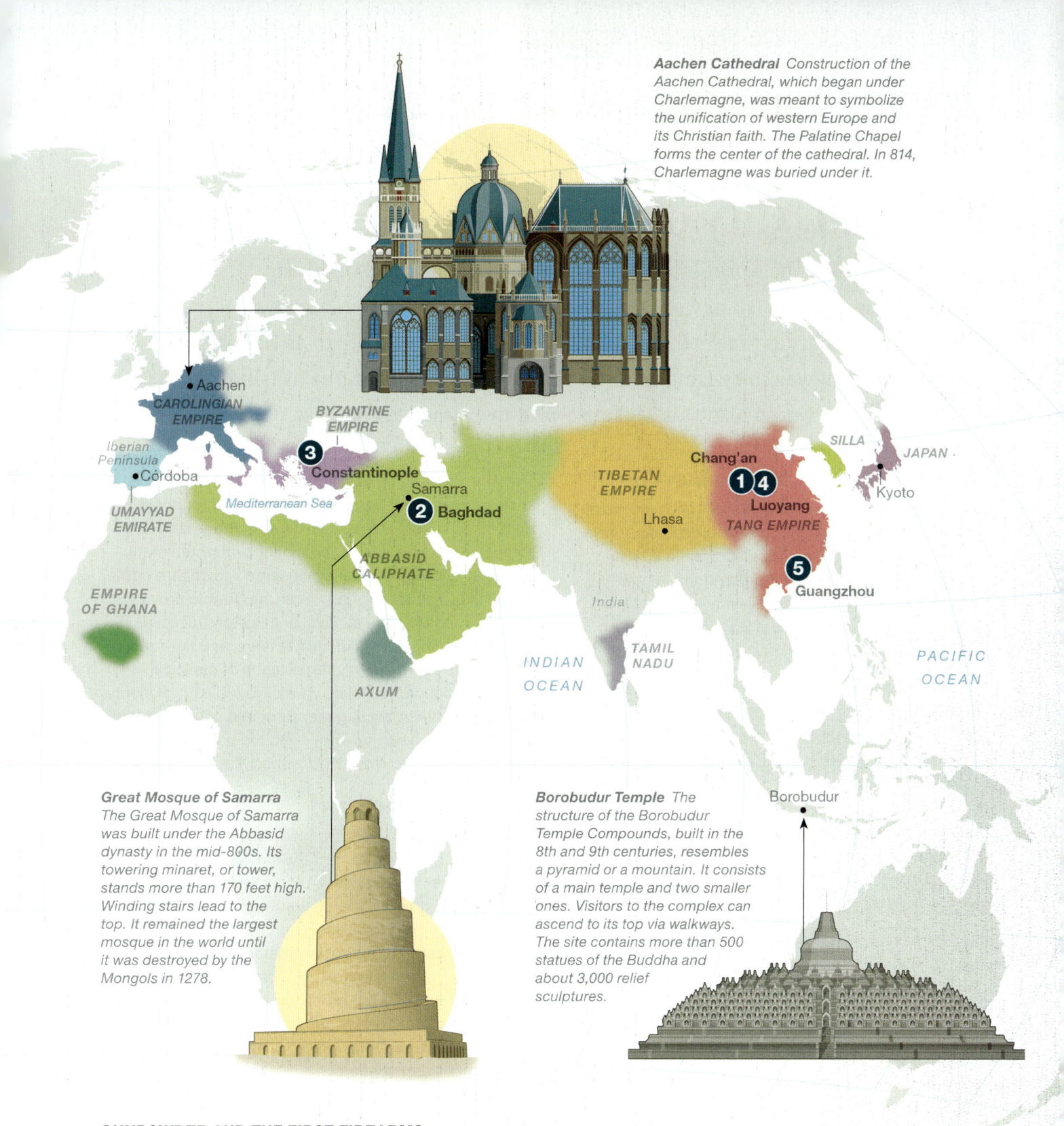

Aachen Cathedral Construction of the Aachen Cathedral, which began under Charlemagne, was meant to symbolize the unification of western Europe and its Christian faith. The Palatine Chapel forms the center of the cathedral. In 814, Charlemagne was buried under it.

Great Mosque of Samarra The Great Mosque of Samarra was built under the Abbasid dynasty in the mid-800s. Its towering minaret, or tower, stands more than 170 feet high. Winding stairs lead to the top. It remained the largest mosque in the world until it was destroyed by the Mongols in 1278.

Borobudur Temple The structure of the Borobudur Temple Compounds, built in the 8th and 9th centuries, resembles a pyramid or a mountain. It consists of a main temple and two smaller ones. Visitors to the complex can ascend to its top via walkways. The site contains more than 500 statues of the Buddha and about 3,000 relief sculptures.

GUNPOWDER AND THE FIRST FIREARMS

Historians believe the earliest use of gunpowder occurred around 850 in China, during the Tang dynasty. The Chinese are thought to have been the first to develop black powder, a chemical mixture that explodes when ignited. At the time, Chinese scientists were actually seeking a potion that would grant people immortality. When they discovered black powder's explosive qualities, the Chinese used it primarily in fireworks. In time, of course, they recognized gunpowder's potential in warfare.

The fire-lance, first used in the 10th century, was an early gunpowder weapon. In the beginning, the Chinese used the weapon to surprise an enemy with its explosive discharge.

Chinese fire-lance
- Bamboo shaft
- Slow-burning cord
- Two-foot tube attached with cord and filled with gunpowder

Arab Empires and Islamic Expansion   255

3.1

MAIN IDEA The Abbasid dynasty, which ruled the Muslim empire from the city of Baghdad, increased trade, strengthened government, and united diverse peoples.

Baghdad, City of Learning

Islamic law divided the world into two distinct parts. The areas that had accepted the religion of Islam were known as Dar-al-Islam, or the "abode of Islam." Bordering areas that had not accepted Islam were referred to as Dar-al-Harb, or "abode of war." The Umayyads had increased the size of Dar-al-Islam, but a new dynasty would lead this Muslim world to a time of greatness.

A NEW CAPITAL FOR A NEW DYNASTY

When Syrian soldiers assassinated the Umayyad caliph in 744, the **Abbasids**, a family claiming descent from Muhammad's uncle Abbas, seized power. In 762, an Abbasid caliph named Mansur ordered that a new capital be built along the Tigris River in Mesopotamia. Mansur specified that the city of **Baghdad** be built in the shape of a circle.

The city's location at the crossroads of Africa, Europe, and Asia dramatically increased trade. Ships sailed to India and China loaded with Arabian horses and locally produced goods such as cloth and carpets. The ships also carried foreign goods, including African ivory and Southeast Asian pearls, and returned with spices, medicines, silk, and other fine cloth. The trade conducted by the Baghdad merchants impacted all three continents by introducing an array of new products to those regions.

Under the Abbasids, non-Arab Muslims, such as Persians, rose in status and gained the same rights as Arab Muslims. Muslims, Christians, Jews, and Zoroastrians lived side by side and interacted with one another daily. The Abbasids lifted some of the restrictions on non-Muslims and created a more equal society. Some people in the new capital became used to the finer things in life, such as large houses, perfectly tailored clothing, and other luxuries. Other peoples from the far reaches of the empire—Africans, Turks, and Persians—also moved to Baghdad, and a variety of languages, including Arabic, Persian, Greek, and Hebrew, could be heard throughout the city. However, there was not full equality for everyone. Baghdad was also a center for the slave trade and had a slave market where captured people were bought and sold.

The Abbasid caliphs developed a strong interest in past knowledge and encouraged the translation of books from other cultures, especially Greek, into Arabic. The libraries that stored these translations attracted many scholars, and Baghdad soon became known as a center of learning. Translating early texts into Arabic proved to be instrumental to the survival of this early information. Often, the original texts did not survive, and the Arabic translations provided an interpretation of the initial material. Baghdad scholars carefully studied astronomy, medicine, mathematics, geography, and other subjects described in the books. They used the past knowledge they researched to make discoveries of their own.

ABBASID GOVERNMENT

The Abbasid caliph portrayed himself as hand-selected by God. He oversaw the military, the bureaucracy, and the courts. An executive officer known as a vizier managed the government so that the caliph could concentrate on the royal court and its ceremonies. Regional governors supervised distant lands, and mercenaries and enslaved Turks formed the army. The Abbasids continued the bureaucracy of the Umayyads but also introduced ideas about governing from other areas, particularly Persia. Many Persians were appointed as administrators within the bureaucracy, and as a result a number of Persian ideas and customs became a part of general Muslim culture.

The Abbasids created a judicial system based on Islamic law. The caliph appointed a **qadi** (KAH-dee), or judge, for Baghdad and each of the empire's provinces. The judges were selected from a group of well-educated men who knew Islamic law and who usually had the final say in legal matters. The judges' enforcement of sharia shows the continuing close connection between religion and government.

The Abbasid Empire, c. 850

Map legend:
- Extent of Abbasid Empire, 786–809
- Other Muslim dynasties
- Islamic expansion, 750–850
- Byzantine Empire

ABBASID SOCIETY

Most people in the Abbasid empire could change their status. For example, non-Muslims could convert to Islam, and slaves could gain freedom. Islam guaranteed specific rights to women, such as the right to divorce. However, these rights were inferior to those of men. Under sharia, women inherited property from their fathers but only one-fourth of their brother's share. In general, the higher the status of their husbands, the more women were restricted.

Anyone related to Muhammad, including the Abbasids, had the most prestige. The highest-status person was the caliph. Visitors had to kiss the ground in front of his throne, and an executioner stayed close, ready to kill anyone who displeased the Muslim leader.

The bulk of Muslim society consisted of workers in the city and farmers in the countryside. Young boys studied at a mosque, while many girls learned at home. Boys of promise trained to become members of a well-educated elite or merchants. Merchants were highly respected in Baghdad because trade was so important to the city's economic success. Also, merchants often donated money for the upkeep of mosques and to assist the needy.

Some slaves in the Abbasid empire came from eastern Africa and central Asia, but the largest number came from the Slavic areas of central and eastern Europe. In fact, the English word *slave* comes from the Latin word for *slav* because so many enslaved people were Slavic.

Building on the Indian Ocean trading networks you read about, Muslim merchants traveled to coastal East Africa and Southeast Asia. Trade exchanges, rather than conquest, introduced people of these regions to Islam and had an enormous impact for centuries to come.

In time, Abbasid caliphs found it increasingly difficult to control their sprawling empire. Regional governors often kept the taxes they collected for themselves. As a result, the central government did not have enough money to maintain itself. A group from Persia known as the Buyids took over the government in 945. They allowed the caliph to remain as a **figurehead**, or leader in name only. The once-strong Abbasid empire broke apart into different regions, but the Islamic culture and religion remained. Though no longer part of a single empire, the territory would remain under Muslim control until 1258.

HISTORICAL THINKING

1. **READING CHECK** What major impacts did the Abbasid caliphs have on the people who lived in their empire?

2. **INTERPRET MAPS** What were the geographic advantages and disadvantages of Damascus and Baghdad as centers of trade?

3. **EVALUATE** Why did the Abbasid caliphs hold the point of view that merchants were an important part of Muslim society?

3.2 **MAIN IDEA** The Islamic Golden Age was a time of significant achievements for the Muslim people.

The Islamic Golden Age

Some civilizations—including the Muslim empire—are known for their impressive achievements in learning and innovation, which ushered in an era of celebrated accomplishments. This period of great advancement in the arts and sciences during Abbasid rule has been dubbed the Islamic Golden Age.

ARCHITECTURE AND ART

One achievement of the Muslim empire was the construction of elaborate mosques and their minarets and gigantic domes. The mosques provided central places for Muslims to pray, but they were also beautiful and perfectly embodied the artistic ideals of Muslim artists and worshipers. In addition, their imposing size showcased the empire's tremendous power.

These early Muslim mosques were richly decorated but void of the human figures prohibited by Islam. Instead, the walls and archways contained abstract designs in repeating patterns, including geometric shapes and floral images, in the art style called **arabesque**. Muslim artists purposefully duplicated designs to show the universal theme of the infinity of God's creation. In addition to geometry, mathematical patterns such as symmetry and algorithms influenced the style. **Calligraphy**, or a form of elegant handwriting, transformed quotations from the Quran into elaborate art.

The mosaics on the exterior of the Umayyad Mosque in Damascus, Syria, include trees growing naturally from the columns. This composition portrays part of the paradise that Muhammad promised his followers would enter after their deaths.

LITERATURE

Early Muslim people immensely enjoyed poetry, admiring it more than other forms of literature. Many poets wrote about love. The Persian mathematician and poet **Omar Khayyam** is credited with popularizing quatrains, or four-line rhyming poems. His works centered on love and other topics, including the meaning of life and the relationship between Allah and humans. *The Rubaiyat of Omar Khayyam* has been translated into every major language.

Rumi was another influential poet from the Muslim world. He was Persian, practiced Sufism, and was famous for his "spiritual couplets." Rumi largely wrote in the Iranian language of Farsi, but he sometimes wrote in Arabic and Turkish as well.

Khayyam also composed an important book about mathematics. Other Muslims wrote about mathematics,

258 CHAPTER 9

geography, history, medicine, and astronomy as well as fiction. A series of popular stories was compiled under the title *The Thousand and One Nights*. This well-known collection centers around a princess, Scheherazade, who must entertain a ruthless king with a different fascinating story each night to keep herself alive.

Although early Muslims loved the adventures of *The Thousand and One Nights*, the most important Islamic book remained the Quran. Muslims began to study the Quran at an early age, learning Arabic to do so if that was not their native language. All Muslims marveled at the beauty of what they considered the word of God.

SCIENCE AND MATHEMATICS

Islamic scholars used sophisticated devices to determine the direction of Mecca for prayer. Muslims improved a Greek instrument known as the **astrolabe** that allowed users to calculate their location on Earth using the date, time of day, and angle of the sun. Later, sailors from many different cultures would use the Muslim astrolabe to find their way around the world.

Early Muslim astronomers used observatories to study the position of the stars at different times. The information they gathered helped set the dates for religious ceremonies. This knowledge also allowed the development of an accurate world map and gave geographers the information they needed to calculate the circumference of Earth.

Al-Mamun, a caliph who ruled during the early 800s, strongly encouraged innovation in astronomy and other fields of science. He invited scientists to Baghdad, where they studied in a large library. In the House of Wisdom, as the building in which they worked was known, scribes also translated books into Arabic. Under Abbasid rule, different schools, or groups of scholars, discussed and debated proper application of sharia.

Islam's emphasis on caring for those less fortunate, including the sick, led to many advances in medicine. Muslim, Christian, and Jewish doctors developed new medical procedures and wrote books that served as guides for other physicians in newly built hospitals across the empire.

In the 1000s, al-Zahrawi of al-Andalus wrote a medical encyclopedia that was the leading medical textbook in Europe for nearly 500 years. Physician and philosopher **al-Razi** is considered the greatest physician of this era. In *The Comprehensive Book on Medicine*, he carefully describes a variety of diseases and their treatments.

A renowned thinker as well as physician, Ibn Sina used Greek, Persian, and Indian texts to write an encyclopedia in the early 1000s that included many medical facts. He also explained how and why God created an imperfect world and how science and religion support each other. Another philosopher, **Ibn Rushd**, studied Greek philosophy. Writing in Córdoba in the 1100s, he attempted to show how the logic of the Greek philosophers Plato and Aristotle could relate to religious teachings. Ibn Rushd's ideas later influenced Christian and Jewish philosophers.

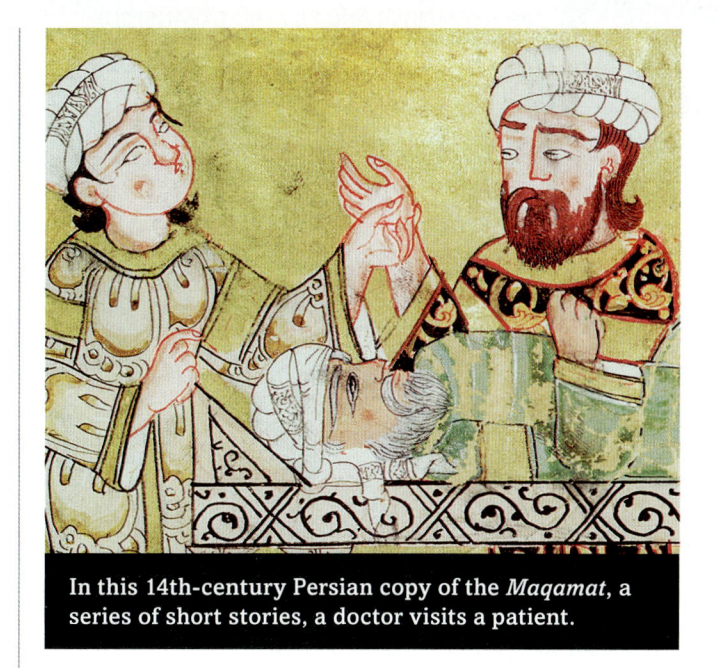

You have read that Muslim scholars carefully examined ancient Greek mathematics texts and also made new scientific advances. These scholars looked at the innovations of other cultures as well. From the people of India, they borrowed the numbering system in use throughout much of the world today, now known as the Hindu-Arabic number system. Adopting the use of the numerals 1, 2, 3, 4, 5, 6, 7, 8, 9, and 0 allowed Muslim mathematicians to make amazing strides in their field. The mathematician al-Khwarizmi not only popularized the decimal system among Muslims but also built on Greek ideas to create *al-jabr*, or algebra. His mathematical texts made their way to Europe, allowing Europeans to learn about the number system developed in India.

In this 14th-century Persian copy of the *Maqamat*, a series of short stories, a doctor visits a patient.

HISTORICAL THINKING

1. **READING CHECK** In which fields of study did the Muslims excel during the Islamic Golden Age?
2. **ANALYZE CAUSE AND EFFECT** What were the effects of religion on Muslim achievement during the Islamic Golden Age?
3. **FORM AND SUPPORT OPINIONS** Which Muslim accomplishment do you think had the greatest effect on the larger world? Explain.

CHAPTER 9
ARAB EMPIRES AND ISLAMIC EXPANSION
REVIEW

VOCABULARY

Complete each of the following sentences using one of the vocabulary words from the chapter.

1. Muslims are required to make a _____ to Mecca.
2. Following Muhammad's death, Abu Bakr became the first _____ to lead the Muslim people.
3. Both the Quran and hadith serve as the basis for Islamic law, or _____.
4. The traditional act of awarding protected status to some non-Muslims is known as _____.
5. During the Abbasid dynasty, each province had a _____ who enforced Islamic law.
6. After the Abbasids lost control of their empire, the caliph became a mere _____ with no power.
7. Geometric shapes and floral images are examples of the Muslim art style called _____.
8. Quotations in elaborate handwriting known as _____ often decorate mosque walls.
9. Sailors from around the world used the Muslim _____ to calculate their location on Earth.

READING STRATEGY
DETERMINE CHRONOLOGY

Use a time line like the one below to organize major events in the origins and spread of Islam. Then answer the question below.

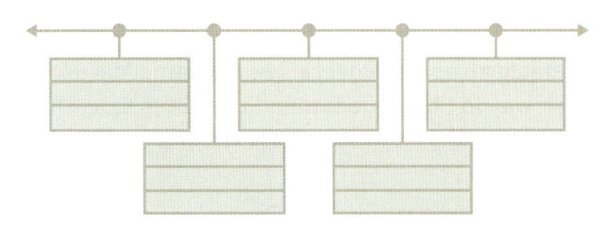

10. In what year did the Hijrah occur?

MAIN IDEAS

Answer the following questions. Support your answers with evidence from the chapter.

11. How did the religion of Islam gain its first followers in the Arabian Peninsula? **LESSON 1.1**
12. What caused Muslims to split into two groups, Shiites and Sunnis? **LESSON 1.2**
13. What impact did the expanding Muslim empire have on Asia, Africa, and Europe? **LESSON 2.1**
14. How did the Umayyad conquest of North Africa change the Muslim empire? **LESSON 2.2**
15. How did Islam influence law and government in the Abbasid empire? **LESSON 3.1**
16. How did each of these people contribute to the Islamic Golden Age: Ibn Sina, Ibn Rushd, al-Razi? **LESSON 3.2**

HISTORICAL THINKING

Answer the following questions. Support your answers with evidence from the chapter.

17. **COMPARE AND CONTRAST** Why do you think some Arab people readily accepted Islam and others were resistant to it?
18. **IDENTIFY MAIN IDEAS AND DETAILS** How do Muslims, Christians, and Jews differ in their beliefs about prophets?
19. **ANALYZE CAUSE AND EFFECT** What effects did the introduction of the position of caliph have on the Muslim people?
20. **DISTINGUISH FACT AND OPINION** What is one fact and one opinion about the life of Christians and Jews under Muslim rule?
21. **MAKE INFERENCES** Why and how did Muslim architects change the design of the church they converted into the Great Mosque of Damascus?
22. **IDENTIFY PROBLEMS AND SOLUTIONS** What problems do you think the Abbasid caliphs' way of governing may have caused, and how do you think this affected their empire?
23. **DRAW CONCLUSIONS** How did lifting restrictions on Christians and Jews likely affect the Abbasid empire?
24. **EVALUATE** How important was the Islamic Golden Age to the world? Explain.

INTERPRET CHARTS

Study the chart below, which compares the three Abrahamic religions. Then answer the questions that follow.

Comparison of the Three Abrahamic Religions

CATEGORY	JUDAISM	CHRISTIANITY	ISLAM
Name of God	Hebrew: Yahweh	Various languages: God, Gott, Dieu, Dios, Deus, Mungu, Alaha	Arabic: Allah
Founder	Abraham	Jesus	No founder, but spread by Muhammad
Sacred Texts	Hebrew Bible (including the Torah), Talmud	Christian Bible (Old Testament—similar to Hebrew Bible—and New Testament)	Quran, Hadith, Sunna
Origination	Southern Levant (Israel, Palestinian territories, Jordan)	Southern Levant	Arabian Peninsula
Great Prophets	Noah, Abraham, Moses, Joshua	Noah, Abraham, Moses, Joshua	Noah, Abraham, Moses, Joshua, Jesus
Major Branches	Orthodox, Conservative, Reform	Catholic, Orthodox, Protestant	Shia, Sunni

25. In addition to Abraham, what other important figures do all three religions have in common?

26. Which religions share a sacred text?

ANALYZE SOURCES

Al-Jahiz (776–868) was a scholar during the Muslim empire. This excerpt from *The Uthmanis* describes his thoughts about Muslim succession following the death of Muhammad. Read the excerpt and answer the question that follows.

> Which is better for the community, to choose its own leader or guide, or for the Prophet to have chosen him for us? Had the Prophet chosen him, that would of course have been preferable to the community's own choice, but since he did not, it is well for it that he left the choice in its own hands. . . . Had God laid down the procedure for the nomination of the Imam [Caliph] in a detailed formula with his own precise directions and clear signs, that would indeed have been a blessing. But since He did not make specific provision [for the office of Caliph], it is preferable for us to have been left in our present situation. How can anyone oblige or constrain God to establish an Imam according to a formula simply because in your view such a solution would be more advantageous and less troublesome, and better calculated to avoid error and problems.

27. Does al-Jahiz's argument support the Sunni or Shiite view of how a caliph should be chosen?

CONNECT TO YOUR LIFE

28. ARGUMENT Often, people complain about government bureaucracy. However, you have read how the Umayyad dynasty used a bureaucracy to successfully govern its large empire. Many other governments, ancient and modern, have employed bureaucracies. Write an essay in which you make an argument for or against government bureaucracy, citing examples from the chapter and your own research. Use the tips below to help you plan, organize, and write your essay.

TIPS

- List pros and cons of a bureaucracy.
- State your position for or against government bureaucracy.
- Use information from the chapter as well as examples of bureaucracy to support your ideas.
- Address counterarguments.
- Use two or three vocabulary terms from the chapter in your essay.
- Conclude your argument with a sentence summarizing your position.

NATIONAL GEOGRAPHIC CONNECTION

The World's Newest Major Religion:
No Religion

BY GABE BULLARD Adapted from "The World's Newest Major Religion: No Religion," by Gabe Bullard, news.nationalgeographic.com, April 22, 2016

Around the world, when asked about their feelings on religion, more and more people are responding with a *meh*. The religiously unaffiliated, called "nones," are growing significantly. They're the second largest religious group in North America and most of Europe. In the United States, nones make up almost a quarter of the population. In the past decade, U.S. nones have overtaken Catholics, mainline Protestants, and all followers of non-Christian faiths.

There have long been predictions that religion would fade from relevancy as the world modernizes, but all the recent surveys are finding that it's happening startlingly fast. France will have a majority secular—or nonreligious—population soon. So will the Netherlands and New Zealand. The United Kingdom and Australia will soon lose Christian majorities. Religion is rapidly becoming less important than it's ever been, even to people who live in countries where faith has affected everything from rulers to borders to architecture.

But nones aren't inheriting the Earth just yet. In many parts of the world—sub-Saharan Africa in particular—religion is growing so fast that nones' share of the global population will actually shrink in 25 years as the world turns into what one researcher has described as "the secularizing West and the rapidly growing rest." (The other highly secular part of the world is China, where the Cultural Revolution tamped down religion for decades, while in some former Communist countries, religion is on the increase.)

Within the ranks of the unaffiliated, divisions run deep. Some are avowed atheists. Others are agnostic, which means they do not claim to have faith or disbelief in God. And many more simply don't care to state a preference. Organized around skepticism toward organizations and united by a common belief that they do not believe, nones as a group are just as internally complex as many religions. And as with religions, these internal contradictions could keep new followers away.

A billboard created by a coalition of atheist and agnostic groups appears in Sacramento, California, in 2010.

If the world is at a religious precipice, then we've been moving slowly toward it for decades. Fifty years ago, *Time* asked in a famous headline, "Is God Dead?" The magazine wondered whether religion was relevant to modern life in the post-atomic age when communism was spreading and science was explaining more about our natural world than ever before.

We're still asking the same question. But the response isn't limited to yes or no. A chunk of the population born after the article was printed may respond to the provocative question with, "God who?" In Europe and North America, the unaffiliated tend to be several years younger than the population average. And 11 percent of Americans born after 1970 were raised in secular homes.

Scientific advancement isn't just making people question God, it's also connecting those who question. It's easy to find atheist and agnostic discussion groups online, even if you come from a religious family or community. And anyone who wants the companionship that might otherwise come from church can attend a secular Sunday Assembly or one of a plethora of Meetups for humanists, atheists, agnostics, or skeptics.

The groups behind the web forums and meetings do more than give skeptics witty rejoinders for religious relatives who pressure them to go to church—they let budding agnostics know they aren't alone. ∎

UNIT INQUIRY
UNIT 3 — Argue Before the Emperor

Staging the Question

In this unit, you learned that religion permeated most aspects of both public and private life in the Byzantine and Muslim empires. Government and laws were dictated by religious beliefs, and people could be penalized for not professing Christianity or Islam. You have also read that the Byzantine and Muslim emperors practiced different levels of religious tolerance—willingness to allow people under their rule to follow different religions. Perhaps the emperors made these choices for reasons of faith, or perhaps they had practical purposes. How can religious tolerance help or hinder a ruler trying to effectively govern an empire?

ASSIGNMENT

Research the policies on religious tolerance in the Byzantine and Muslim empires.

Analyze how these policies affected people and institutions within the empires.

Draw conclusions about how religious tolerance helped rulers expand their empires and govern effectively—or how it held them back from those goals.

Develop a claim about the value of religious tolerance to an empire, and construct an argument supporting your claim.

Supporting Questions: Begin by developing supporting questions to guide your research. For example: What was the level of religious tolerance under Emperor Justinian? Who was helped or harmed by Justinian's policy? Research the answers in this unit and in other sources, both print and online.

Summative Performance Task: In this unit, you learned that both the Byzantines and the Muslims valued oration and debate. Make a case for or against religious tolerance to present before a Byzantine or Muslim emperor. Write your claim, and then list your reasons and the supporting examples you found in your research. You might want to use an organizer like this one to help you organize your argument.

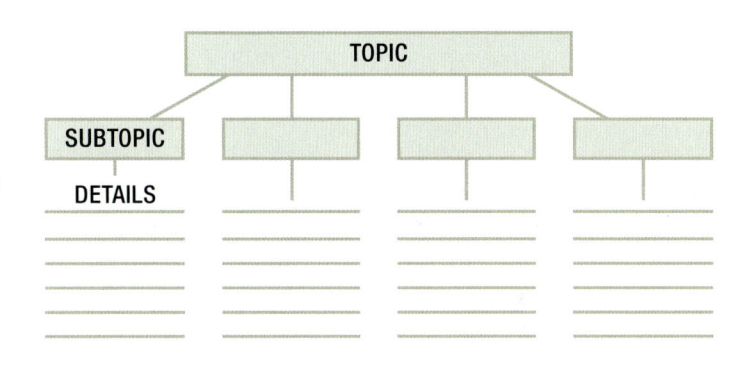

Present: Share your argument with the class. You might consider one of these options:

HOLD A DEBATE
Form a team with other students whose claims are similar to yours. Debate your ideas against a team that has an opposing view. Have the teacher or another student act as the emperor who listens and judges the debate.

HOLD AN ORATORS' FORUM
Take turns with your classmates giving an oration, or persuasive speech, as if you are speaking in an open forum before the emperor. Use your organizer to give your speech; do not write it out word for word. Practice beforehand so that you can speak expressively and with confidence.

Take Informed Action:

UNDERSTAND Identify and describe an example of religious intolerance by a government in current or recent news.

ASSESS Determine whether this behavior is doing harm to individuals or to the country in general.

ACT Draft a letter to your government representatives encouraging them to speak out against the instance of religious intolerance that you identified.

UNIT 4

CRITICAL VIEWING

This detail from a 17th-century Japanese screen depicts a clash between samurai from Japan's Taira and Minamoto clans during the 12th-century Genpei War in which the Minamoto eventually defeated the Taira for control of Japan. The struggle between the two clans was recorded in an epic called *The Tale of the Heike* sometime before 1330. This work is often likened to a Japanese *Iliad*. What does the existence of both the screen and the epic suggest about the role of the Genpei War in feudal Japan?

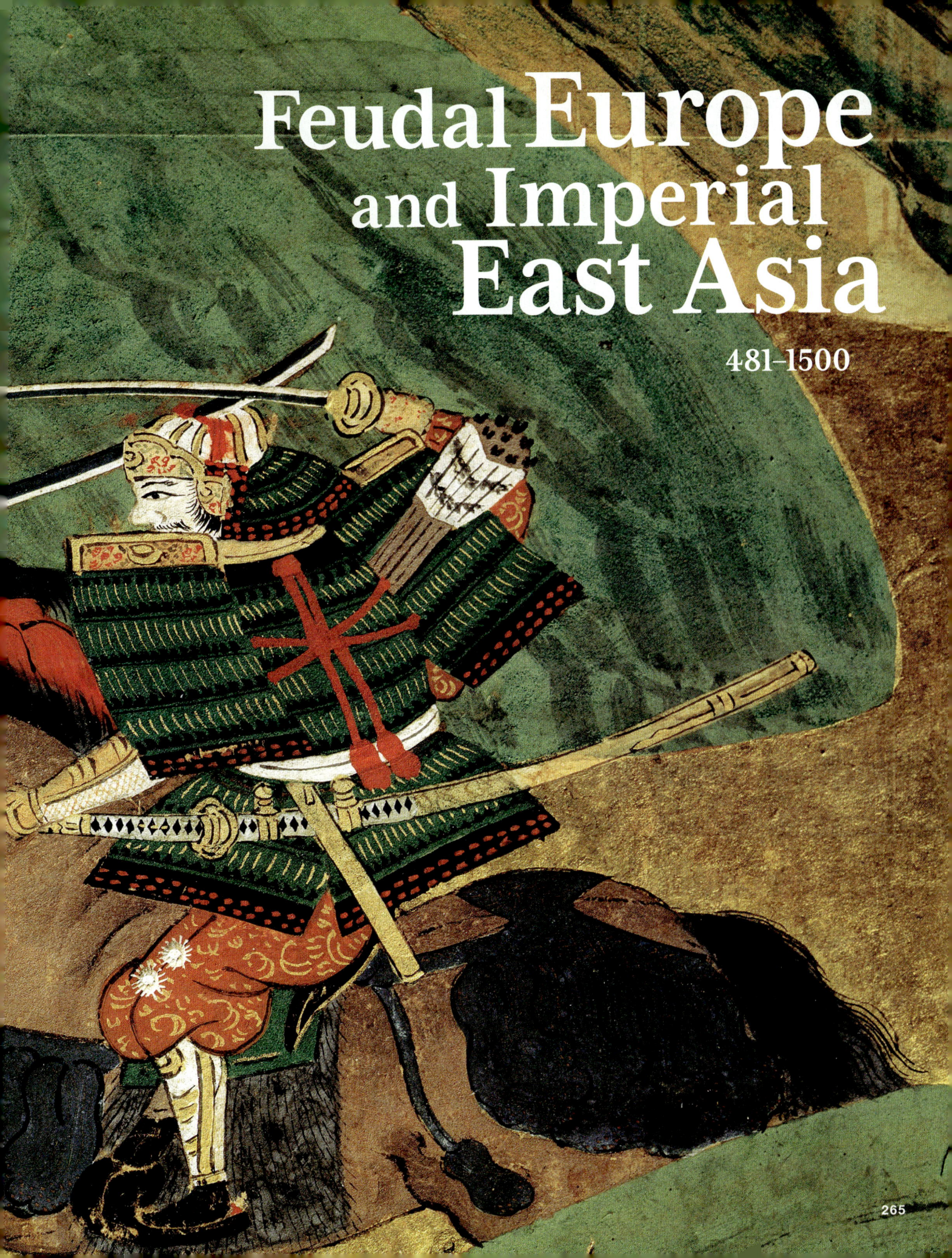

Feudal Europe and Imperial East Asia

481–1500

UNIT 4: Feudal Europe and Imperial East Asia

WORLD EVENTS 600–1500

1054 EUROPE
The western and eastern branches of the Christian Church split into two separate churches, known respectively as the Roman Catholic Church and the Eastern Orthodox Church. *(Eastern Orthodox icon of Saint Christopher)*

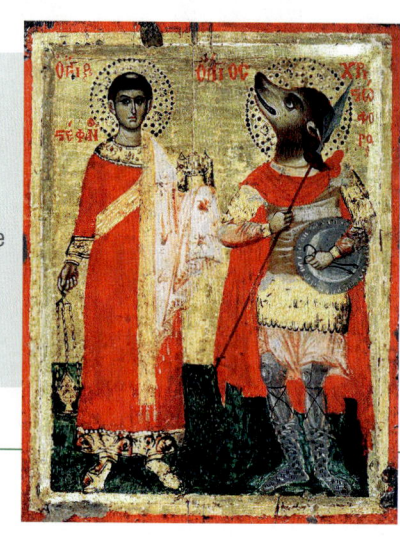

1095 EUROPE
The first of a series of religious wars, called the Crusades, begins between Christians and Muslims over the control of sacred sites in the Holy Land. *(wax seal with Crusader, c. 14th century)*

800 EUROPE
Pope Leo III crowns Charlemagne emperor of the Romans.

976 ASIA The Song dynasty reunites northern and southern China.

c. 1040 ASIA Chinese bookmaker Bi Sheng invents the movable type process of printing books.

845 EUROPE
Vikings sail up the Seine River to raid Paris. *(Viking helmet pendant, c. 10th century)*

936 ASIA
The Koryo dynasty defeats the Silla kingdom and rules the Korean Peninsula. *(Korean celadon stoneware, c. 13th century)*

HISTORICAL THINKING

DRAW CONCLUSIONS What preceding event in Europe might have amplified the death toll caused by the plague?

c. 1315 EUROPE Crop failures throughout northern Europe lead to food shortages, resulting in the Great Famine of 1315–1322. *(The Triumph of Death by unknown artist, c. 1446)*

c. 1100 ASIA The Song dynasty produces the world's first paper money.

1142 ASIA After years of fighting, the Southern Song and the Jurchen sign a peace treaty.

1215 EUROPE King John of England signs the Magna Carta, a written set of laws that guarantees the rights of the English barons.

1337 EUROPE England and France engage in battles over control of France, marking the beginning of the Hundred Years' War. *(Joan of Arc by Dante Gabriel Rossetti, 1882)*

1212 ASIA Genghis Khan and his army invade northern China. *(statue of Genghis Khan at Mongolian parliament building)*

1348 EUROPE Originating in Asia, the plague reaches London and kills millions across Europe. *(illustration of rat leaving a ship)*

1453 ASIA Under Mehmed II, the Ottomans conquer Constantinople, bringing an end to the Byzantine Empire.

CHAPTER 10

Europe's Medieval Era
481–1492

HISTORICAL THINKING What should be the relationship between church and state?

SECTION 1 **Western and Northern Europe**
SECTION 2 **Changing Land, Labor, and Culture**
SECTION 3 **The Church and the Crusades**
SECTION 4 **Waning of the European Middle Ages**

CRITICAL VIEWING

The island of Mont-Saint-Michel, which lies off the coast of Normandy, France, served as the site of a medieval monastery and town. Based on the structure of the town, what might you conclude were important concerns in medieval society?

Europe's Medieval Era 269

1.1

MAIN IDEA The European rulers Charlemagne and Otto the Great formed powerful empires and promoted Christianity in Europe.

Christian Rulers in Europe

Americans have always maintained, in the words of Thomas Jefferson, "a wall of separation between Church & State." No such wall existed in Europe during the period following the fall of Rome. In fact, European kings formed close alliances with popes and became leaders in the Christian Church as well.

EMERGENCE OF CHARLEMAGNE

Europe's medieval period, also known as the **Middle Ages**, lasted from about 500 to 1500. The Latin roots of the word *medieval* literally mean "middle age." During this time, Europe underwent many political and cultural changes and emerged as a distinct cultural region.

You may recall that after the fall of the Western Roman Empire in 476, various Germanic tribes spread into the former Roman lands of Europe. For the most part, these settlers kept their own traditions, though they eventually adopted the Roman religion, Christianity.

One of these Germanic tribes was the Franks, who occupied what is today northern France, Belgium, and western Germany. Early in the medieval era, the Franks and other tribes engaged in almost continual warfare. As they had against the Romans, Germanic warriors banded together behind a leader to conduct raids into enemy territory. Ambitious leaders gained the loyalty of many warriors. One Frankish leader, Clovis, established a kingdom in northeastern Gaul, which is now France, in 481. A few years before his death, Clovis became the first Frankish leader to convert to Christianity, after which many of his people converted, too.

Descendants of Clovis ruled the Frankish kingdom until the mid-700s. But by 725, Charles Martel, a palace official from another powerful family, had gathered an army and gained control of the kingdom, though he never called himself king. The Carolingian dynasty, named after Martel, overthrew the former dynasty in 751. The Carolingian dynasty's territory would expand greatly under Martel's grandson, who became known as **Charlemagne**, or "Charles the Great."

Charlemagne emerged as king of the Franks in 768 and soon launched a series of military campaigns against neighboring Germanic tribes, including the

This painting shows Charlemagne being crowned king of the Lombards by the pope in 774.

Lombards and the Saxons. The pope in Rome, Pope Leo III, supported Charlemagne's aggression against the Lombards, who occupied northern and central Italy and posed a threat to papal lands around Rome. Charlemagne eventually conquered not only the Lombard kingdom in Italy but also parts of Spain and much of Germany. Under Charlemagne, the Franks came to dominate much of Europe. In 800, the pope crowned Charlemagne emperor of the Romans, a title that would later be known as Holy Roman Emperor.

The alliance between Pope Leo III and the Carolingians benefited both sides. In Charlemagne, the pope gained a protector and a strong promoter of Christianity. From the pope, Charlemagne gained religious authority that solidified his role as king. As a religious leader, Charlemagne sponsored a series of councils aimed at improving and unifying the Roman Catholic Church.

270 CHAPTER 10

Medieval Europe, c. 500

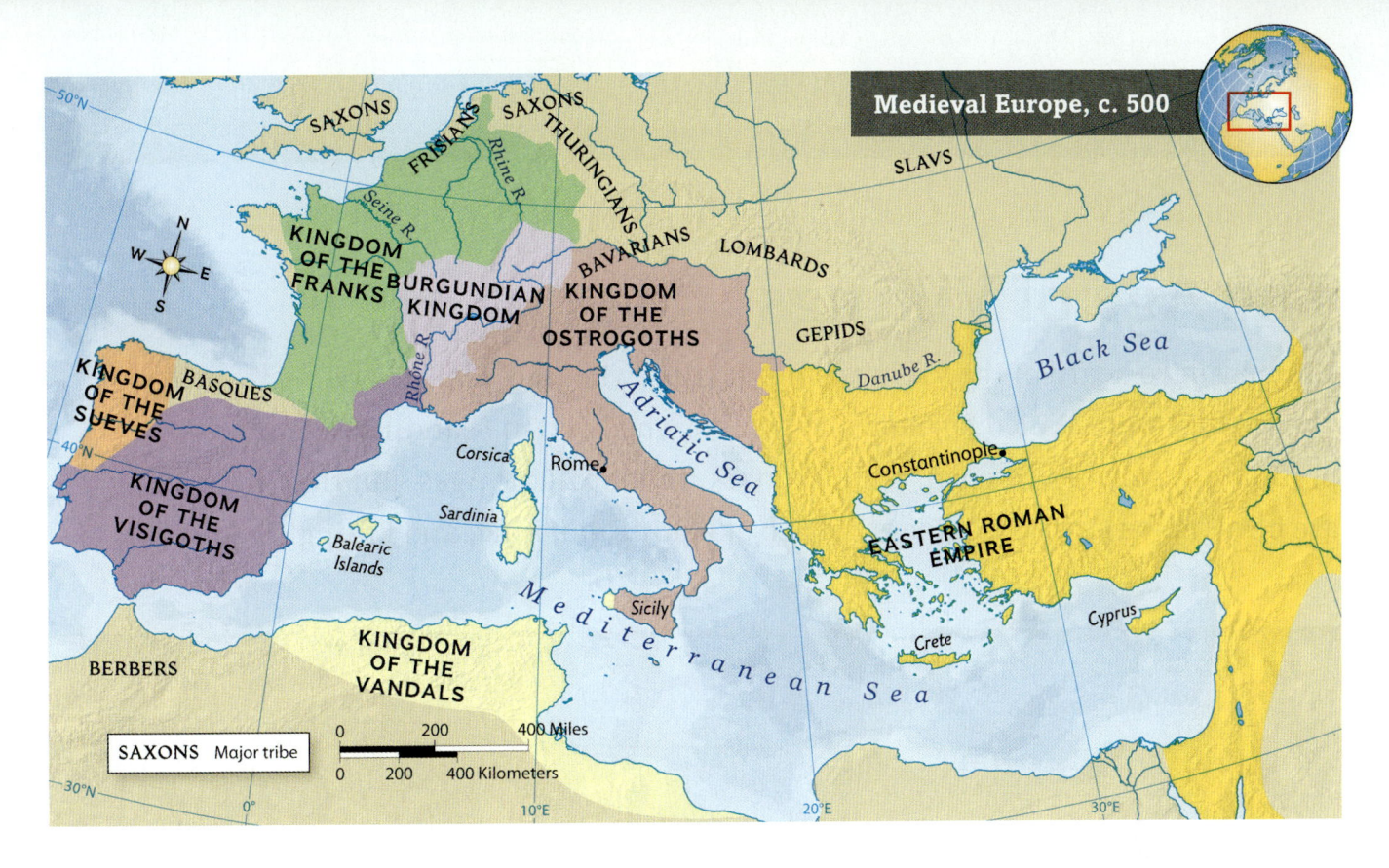

Reforms enacted in these councils had the force of law throughout the lands Charlemagne controlled. He also encouraged learning by establishing schools in his royal court and in **monasteries**, which were Christian communities of men living under religious vows.

Charlemagne's conquests and the pope's support marked the kingdom of the Franks as a true European empire—a potential heir to the fallen Roman Empire. After Charlemagne died in 814, however, the empire he had formed soon fell apart.

OTTO THE GREAT

In 843, Charlemagne's empire was split into three kingdoms—West Francia, Middle Francia, and East Francia. The kingdom of East Francia, which included much of modern-day Germany, consisted of several **duchies**. A duchy is a territory ruled by a duke or duchess. In 936, the various dukes elected the duke of Saxony as king of the Germans. Named Otto I, he would earn the title **Otto the Great**.

In the first years of his rule, Otto attempted to exert strict control over the other German dukes, which provoked rebellions. But he was able to quash the rebellions and restore order in the kingdom. In addition to overcoming internal threats to his power, Otto also had to deal with enemy invasions. The biggest external threat came from the Magyars, a people from the Hungarian plains. Since the early 900s, the Magyars had made several incursions into German lands. In 955, during one of their raids, Otto won a decisive victory that ended the Magyars' attacks.

Like Charlemagne, Otto extended the frontiers of his kingdom. In 951, he marched south into Italy and claimed the title of king of the Lombards. A decade later, in 962, Otto marched into Italy again, this time to help the pope fend off an attacker. Shortly after Otto reached Rome, the pope crowned him Holy Roman Emperor.

Through a treaty, Otto gained the power to ratify papal elections. In 963, he took that power a step further. Feeling betrayed when the pope made a treaty with one of his enemies, Otto replaced the pope with a candidate he chose himself. Similar power struggles between popes and emperors would be a regular feature of European politics for centuries to come.

HISTORICAL THINKING

1. **READING CHECK** When did Charlemagne rise to power, and what were his major achievements?

2. **COMPARE AND CONTRAST** How was the reign of Otto the Great similar to that of Charlemagne?

3. **INTERPRET MAPS** How did the kingdom of the Franks compare in size with other European kingdoms around 500?

Europe's Medieval Era

1.2

MAIN IDEA During the Middle Ages, Viking raiders plundered communities along the coasts and rivers of Europe and ventured to North America.

The Age of Vikings

You may have heard of the Vikings but not know who they really were. The Vikings were skilled farmers and traders who lived in Scandinavia, or present-day Norway, Sweden, and Denmark, in the Middle Ages. But the Vikings are best known as brutal raiders, skilled at looting, burning, and killing.

CRITICAL VIEWING The annual Viking festival in Wolin, Poland, is one of the largest events in which Europeans dress as Viking and Slav warriors to reenact medieval battles between the two groups. Based on this reenactment, how would you describe medieval battle conditions?

VIKING RAIDS

While the German king Otto I was fighting off an invading Magyar force in the mid-900s, a group of invaders from the north, the Vikings, plagued much of the rest of Europe. These fearsome warriors sailed their longboats out of Scandinavia in search of valuable goods they could steal. For more than two centuries, starting in the late 700s, they terrorized the European continent.

Small Viking fleets sailed west across the North Sea to present-day Scotland, Ireland, and England. There they targeted monasteries because these communities often contained large amounts of silver and other treasures.

Larger bands of Vikings also plundered and burned towns along the coasts of Germany, France, Spain, and islands in the western Mediterranean Sea. They often made quick strikes, staying just long enough to steal much of a town's wealth—and killing anyone who tried to stop them.

The Vikings were not restricted to coastal routes. Their longboats were constructed not only to withstand sea travel but also to navigate shallow rivers. As a result, the Vikings could raid wealthy inland towns. In 845, they used their longboats to sail up the Seine River to Paris. The citizens of Paris avoided being plundered only by paying off the Vikings with 7,000 pounds of silver.

Across the Baltic Sea from Scandinavia lay a region inhabited mainly by Slavs—present-day Russia. In the early 800s, Vikings from Sweden crossed the sea and followed rivers into this region. These Vikings engaged in trading as well as raiding. Later, some Vikings followed rivers south all the way to the Black Sea and Constantinople, where they traded furs and slaves for spices and silks from as far east as China.

A traditional Russian chronicle says that in the late 800s a Viking founded Kievan Rus (KEE-ehf-uhn ROOS), a state centered on the trading town of Kiev in present-day Ukraine. Historians still debate whether the Vikings had any role in this event. They also disagree about whether the people known as the Rus were Slavs or Vikings or a mix of peoples. But whoever they were, the Rus gave Russia its name.

VIKING SETTLEMENTS

Some Vikings chose to settle down and farm the lands they had previously raided. Danish Vikings settled in northern and eastern England in the late 800s, while Norwegian Vikings settled in Scotland and Ireland. In the tenth century, another Viking group from Denmark settled in Normandy, in present-day France.

Over time, British and French kings built fortresses and enlarged their armies to resist Viking incursions. In other places, Viking settlers **assimilated**, or integrated, into local populations. The Slavic lands of Russia fairly quickly absorbed the Vikings from Sweden. Viking settlers in Normandy eventually merged into the culture of Western Francia, the westernmost Frankish kingdom.

At a time when most sailors stayed within sight of a coastline, the seafaring Vikings set out across the open Atlantic Ocean. By the 870s, Scandinavians had settled in Iceland, a large island more than 800 miles west of Norway. In the late 900s, a Viking leader named Erik the Red led approximately 400 to 500 followers an additional 200 miles west to Greenland in search of fertile land.

Tales of the adventures of Erik the Red appear in *The Vinland Sagas*, orally transmitted stories written down sometime after 1200. The Scandinavians called the land of North America *Vinland*, which means "land of wild grapes." Erik the Red's son, **Leif Eriksson**, headed toward Vinland around 1000. He and 40 companions sailed from Greenland to Newfoundland, becoming the first Europeans to visit what is today Canada.

The remains of a Viking settlement have been unearthed at L'Anse aux Meadows in southern Newfoundland. Some archaeologists believe that more Viking settlements will be uncovered in the years to come, some perhaps as far south as New England.

NATIONAL GEOGRAPHIC EXPLORER
SARAH PARCAK

Sarah Parcak searches for Viking artifacts at Point Rosee in Newfoundland.

Citizen-Science Technology

The search for Viking settlements in North America has benefited from the expertise of Sarah Parcak, a National Geographic Explorer. Known as a space archaeologist, Parcak examines high-resolution satellite images for possible historic sites hidden just below Earth's surface. "We're using satellites to help map and model cultural features that could never be seen on the ground because they're obscured by modernization, forest, or soil," Parcak explains.

This technology led her to a spot in Newfoundland known as Point Rosee. An archaeological dig at the spot has turned up Viking-style turf walls and signs of ironworking.

Parcak also uses satellite technology to protect ancient sites, and she wants to create a global network of citizen-scientists to help her. Using an online satellite imagery program, volunteers can help stop looters from stealing valuable artifacts. They can also join the hunt for as-yet-undiscovered sites.

HISTORICAL THINKING

1. **READING CHECK** Why did early Viking raiders target monasteries?
2. **IDENTIFY MAIN IDEAS AND DETAILS** What methods have archaeologists used to learn about the Vikings?
3. **ASK AND ANSWER QUESTIONS** What questions do you have about the Vikings, and where might you find answers to your questions?

Europe's Medieval Era

1.3

MAIN IDEA In the mid-1000s, a Norman ruler conquered England and a division occurred in the Christian Church.

Conquest and Division

Ruling a large group of people with differing interests is never an easy task. But a strong leader managed to do just that in medieval England. The Christian Church, however, moved in the opposite direction—and became divided.

WILLIAM THE CONQUEROR

The Danish Vikings who invaded England in 866 and settled in the north and east did not dominate England. They continually vied with the Anglo-Saxons, a mix of Germanic peoples from present-day Denmark and northern Germany, for control of the island. The Anglo-Saxons had invaded England in the 400s and pushed out the Romans. More than four centuries later, in the 900s, the tables had turned. The Anglo-Saxons were the ones battling "barbarian" invaders.

Meanwhile, the Viking settlers across the English Channel thrived. A steady stream of Scandinavians migrated to the Viking colony in Normandy. In the 900s, after people from Normandy, called Normans, conducted a series of destructive raids inland, the French king accepted the colony as a legal—and largely independent—duchy. The Normans, in turn, adopted the French language and the Christian religion. Normandy had stabilized, but England was still in a state of upheaval.

By 954, an Anglo-Saxon king had conquered the Danes and established his rule over all of England. But in the early 1000s, a new group of Viking invaders overpowered the Anglo-Saxons. Several Scandinavians ruled as kings of England until 1042, when an Anglo-Saxon noble with family ties to Normandy gained the throne. This king promised that, upon his death, the English throne would go to William, Duke of Normandy. But the English nobility chose instead to elect an Anglo-Saxon, Harold, as king.

This decision did not please William, who believed he was the rightful heir to the throne. In September 1066, he sailed for England with an army to claim the crown. Harold, the new king of England, already had his hands full with yet another Viking invasion. On September 25, Harold met and defeated a large force of Viking warriors

CRITICAL VIEWING The Bayeux Tapestry, a work of embroidery produced around 1092, depicts more than 70 scenes leading up to the Norman conquest of England. In this scene, the Norman cavalry rides toward the site of the Battle of Hastings. How are these Norman soldiers equipped?

in northern England. Just three days later, William and his Norman army landed on the southeast coast of England.

Harold rushed his forces southward to meet this new threat. The two armies clashed near the town of Hastings. In the Battle of Hastings, the Normans defeated the Anglo-Saxons, and Harold died on the battlefield. Thus, William gained the English throne and the title **William the Conqueror**.

William the Conqueror now reigned over all of England as well as Normandy. In his first few years in power, he put down several rebellions, often brutally. He brought in loyal friends to serve as his closest officials and redistributed Anglo-Saxon lands to Normans. French became the official language of the court.

A Christian, William strongly supported the church and the pope. He insisted, however, on filling high church positions in England with Normans. Later Norman kings, who ruled for another 70 years, also demanded a role in church matters.

THE SCHISM OF 1054

As you have learned, relations between the western, or Roman, church and the eastern, or Byzantine, church began to deteriorate in the fifth century. The churches used different languages in their services—Latin in the Roman church and Greek in the Byzantine. With the rise of the Carolingian dynasty in the mid-700s, the pope in Rome allied politically with the Frankish rulers, not the Byzantine emperors.

By 1000, the Roman and Byzantine churches had begun to diverge further. Members of the Roman church recognized the pope in Rome as their leader, while members of the Byzantine church recognized the patriarch of Constantinople. Doctrines and practices varied as well. For example, Byzantine priests were required to have beards, but Roman priests were not.

In 1054, a bishop in a Byzantine province wrote to an Italian bishop criticizing certain practices of the western church. These practices included using unleavened bread, or bread without yeast, during a service called communion and failing to fast on Saturdays. In two lengthy letters to the patriarch in Constantinople, the pope in Rome defended these practices. But the pope made the inflammatory assertion that he had the right to rule over all bishops, even those of the eastern church.

The pope and the patriarch argued until they finally expelled each other from membership in the Christian Church, a punishment called **excommunication**. As a result, the western and eastern churches split into two separate religions, which are now called Roman Catholicism and Eastern Orthodoxy. Historians refer to this event as the **Schism of 1054**.

HISTORICAL THINKING

1. **READING CHECK** How did William the Conqueror rise to the throne of England?

2. **COMPARE AND CONTRAST** How did the western Christian Church differ from the eastern Christian Church?

3. **INTERPRET MAPS** What lands were under the authority of the Eastern Orthodox Church after the Schism of 1054?

Europe's Medieval Era 275

2.1

MAIN IDEA Increased agricultural production in medieval Europe led to population growth, which supported the expansion of towns and commerce.

Manors, Guilds, and the Growth of Towns

Not all revolutions involve armies. Some result from many ordinary people changing the way they do things, often as a result of new technology. That's how one revolution got its start in the medieval era.

LAND AND LABOR

In early medieval times, European economies relied on agriculture, and so fertile land had great value. Large landowners, who were typically nobles or church leaders, established a system called **manorialism** to organize their land and the peasants who worked it.

Manorialism was an economic, social, and political system. The landowner's estate, or manor, produced grains, meats, and crafted goods that supported the peasants, the landowner, and others. Occupants of the manor lived together in a community, where they interacted socially. The landowner, or lord, had legal authority over the manor, essentially serving as its ruler.

Among its cultivated fields, orchards, and pastures, the typical European manor included a variety of buildings. The lord and his family lived in the manor house, usually a fortified stone structure, or castle. Peasants lived in one-room huts. Most manors also had barns, a church, a mill for grinding grain, and a workshop. Thus, the manor was a nearly self-sufficient farming village.

Some peasants farmed small tracts of land of their own. But by the year 1000, most peasants were **serfs**, agricultural workers who were bound to the land of their lord. Serfs were not free to leave the lord's land without his permission. If lords sold their land, they did not take their serfs with them. The serfs stayed with the land.

Each year, the serfs had to turn over a large share of the crops they raised to their lord. They were also required to work the lord's personal fields and do other tasks. In return for their service, the lord promised to protect them against raiders, robbers, and other dangers.

To protect their manors, powerful landowning nobles often commanded the service of horse-riding warriors called **knights**, who were skilled in the use of swords, crossbows, and other weapons. A knight became a lord's **vassal**. A vassal gave military service and pledged loyalty to a lord in exchange for land to live on. This system of defense emerged after the Frankish and other European kingdoms broke down, leaving it up to powerful local lords to provide people with protection and security.

Traditionally, this legal system has been described as **feudalism**. Yet historians today often avoid the term because no one alive between 1000 and 1350 used the word. The term came into use only after 1600.

Around 1200, manorialism began to fade away. Landowning nobles in western Europe came to rely on free, rent-paying peasants to work their lands. By then, agricultural innovations were increasing productivity. In eastern Europe, however, serfdom continued. Russian peasants remained serfs for centuries to come.

Farmers before 1000 had learned that leaving a third or more of their fields unplanted each year increased soil fertility, as did manure from cattle. Greater fertility meant larger harvests. Farmers later found that rotating crops from year to year—planting different crops that absorbed different nutrients from the soil—allowed them to keep their fields under continuous cultivation.

New technology also expanded yields. A heavier plow, with wheels, allowed peasants to till even the tough clay soils of northern Europe. Attaching iron to a wooden plow blade improved soil cultivation. A newly designed collar helped horses pull the plows more efficiently, while iron horseshoes protected the animals' hooves.

The application of these new methods and technologies resulted in a substantial increase in grain production. This expansion of the food supply led to a population boom in Europe. Between 1000 and 1340, Europe's population nearly doubled, to around 75 million.

Rothenburg ob der Tauber, which lies along the Tauber River, is one of the best-preserved medieval towns in Germany.

THE COMMERCIAL REVOLUTION

As populations grew, so did towns. European towns rose up around local markets that displayed such goods as butter and cheese, textiles, and soap produced by individual households. At first, shoppers traded for the goods they needed. After 1000, with the renewed minting of coins, they began making purchases with money.

As the availability of money increased, so did **commerce**, or the buying and selling of goods on a large scale. Farmers could now sell their food surpluses for money in the growing towns and cities. Artisans and merchants, too, earned money for the goods they sold.

New institutions arose to accommodate these changes. One was the **guild**, an association of artisans or merchants formed to set quality standards, establish prices for goods, and help businesses flourish. Guilds often amassed enough wealth and power to take control of a town's government.

Another new institution was banking. Banks began appearing in northern Italy around 1200, after African discoveries increased the gold supply in the Mediterranean. Business people needed a safe place to keep the money they accumulated and used to run their businesses. Besides protecting deposited money, banks made loans and invested in business ventures. Banking spread from Italy across the Mediterranean and into northern Europe. By 1300, banking networks served international traders, encouraging further commercial expansion.

In search of larger infusions of **capital**, or money for use in starting a business, merchants began to form partnerships with investors. A merchant would open and manage a business, and the investor would supply the capital and share in the profits. Larger associations of merchants attracted multiple investors. As international trade expanded, a wealthy merchant class arose.

This shift from an economy based on self-sufficient agriculture to one based on international trade is referred to as the **Commercial Revolution**. This revolution advanced the right of individuals to own and manage private property, encouraged competition, and supported the quest for profit.

The Commercial Revolution was just getting started in the late Middle Ages. Its impact would be felt well into the 18th century.

HISTORICAL THINKING

1. **READING CHECK** What factors contributed to the growth of the Commercial Revolution?
2. **DESCRIBE** What were the main characteristics of the economic system of manorialism?
3. **DRAW CONCLUSIONS** How did individuals benefit from the Commercial Revolution?

2.2

MAIN IDEA During the Middle Ages, the Roman Catholic Church sponsored schools for European youth, universities evolved, and religious scholars developed a philosophy that combined faith and logic.

Centers of Learning

Have you read any good books lately—written in Latin? Teenagers who attended school in the Middle Ages were expected to read and write Latin. The language of the Romans remained a key element in a classical education for a long time—until the late 1800s in the United States.

EDUCATION AND THE CHURCH

Large medieval manors generated wealth and provided stability and security for their residents. A traditional practice, aimed at preventing these large estates from being split up, allowed that only the eldest son could inherit a father's property. The other sons in the family often left the manor to get an education and pursue careers. Daughters either married and moved to their husband's property or continued to live with their family.

Three social classes existed in medieval Europe. Known as the three orders of society, they were the nobles, the peasants, and the **clergy**, or religious leaders appointed by the church to perform ceremonies and explain church teachings. Led by the pope, the clergy included priests, who headed individual churches, and bishops, who oversaw groups of churches.

In the Middle Ages, the church took the main responsibility for educating European youth. Some students attended schools located within monasteries, where monks served as teachers. A monk was a member of a religious order who lived and worked in a monastery, typically following a simple life devoted mainly to prayer and spiritual contemplation. Women who joined similar religious orders were called nuns.

The University of Oxford in England, one of the world's great universities, was established in the 1100s. Many European universities were founded during the Middle Ages, including the University of Bologna in Italy and the University of Paris in France.

They lived and were educated in convents. Like monks, nuns spent much of their time praying and reading, writing, and illustrating religious books. In monastery and convent schools, called monastic schools, the teaching focused on the Christian Bible and its moral lessons.

In addition to being centers of education, Christian monasteries and convents had social, economic, and political importance. They provided charitable support for the poor, sick, and aged. Many monasteries owned large tracts of land, often donated by wealthy landowners. Monasteries contributed to the economy by marketing their surplus agricultural and craft goods. They ruled themselves, and their political independence and power was sometimes threatening to kings.

In addition to monasteries and convents, other centers of learning emerged in towns and cities. Run by priests, these schools were located in a **cathedral**, the principal church of a district administered by a bishop. Cathedral schools originally prepared students to become priests and church administrators, but they later taught those who wanted other careers as well. The schools accepted only males, mostly the sons of nobles.

The curriculum of the cathedral schools was much broader than that of the monastic schools. Cathedral schools focused on classical learning, which was based on the Greek and Roman educational system. All students studied three subjects: grammar, rhetoric, and logic. Cathedral schools also offered courses in arithmetic, geometry, astronomy, and music.

Some cathedral schools expanded and became universities. In the early 1100s, the university at Bologna in Italy became a center for the study of law. Founded around 1200, the University of Paris in France drew students eager to study a variety of disciplines, including religion. As commerce expanded, European towns and cities needed lawyers, accountants, and others with business skills, while the church needed religious scholars. Universities filled both sets of needs.

SCHOLASTICISM

European universities maintained a strong focus on Christianity, with its fixed beliefs and reliance on faith. But they also fostered interest in the natural sciences, which called for the application of logic and reasoning. The two areas of study often presented conflicting ideas.

Some Roman Catholic scholars began looking for a way to unify the study of religion and the study of worldly subjects. They found a way in a philosophy that came to be known as **Scholasticism**. Proponents of Scholasticism sought knowledge, whether religious or otherwise, by applying human reason and logic.

The Italian scholar **Anselm of Canterbury**, considered the founder of Scholasticism, attended a monastic school in Normandy in the 1050s and later became a monk. In the late 1070s, Anselm wrote two lengthy works that presented his ideas about faith and reason. He concluded that the existence of God can be determined through reason alone. In 1093, the Norman king of England appointed Anselm to the top religious post in England—archbishop of Canterbury.

Bernard of Clairvaux, an influential French monk, opposed the application of logic to religious matters. Bernard was a **mystic**, a person who seeks knowledge of God through devotion or meditation. He criticized Scholastics like Anselm for their reliance on logic.

A German nun named **Hildegard of Bingen** was also a mystic. However, she applied reason and logic to the study of the natural sciences, focusing on identifying plants that had medicinal powers. A multitalented woman, she composed poetry and music and wrote persuasively about the equality of men and women. She founded a convent and traveled throughout Germany, preaching to large groups.

One of the greatest Scholastics, the Italian priest **Thomas Aquinas** taught at the University of Paris. He based his philosophy partly on the works of the Greek philosopher Aristotle. Aquinas tried to bridge the gap between faith and reason in *Summa Theologica*, in which he explains the reasoning for all the church's main teachings. One of the key arguments addresses the question, "Is there a God?" Aquinas states that somebody had to be the first to set events in motion, "and this is what everyone takes to be a God."

In *Summa Theologica*, Aquinas also presents his philosophy of natural law, a set of moral principles derived from nature. Human beings, he argues, are creatures guided by reason, and so laws or rules of morality should reflect their rational nature. Natural law comes into play, he states, whenever a person uses reason to do what is good and avoid what is evil.

HISTORICAL THINKING

1. **READING CHECK** What social, economic, and political roles did Christian monasteries and convents have in the medieval era?
2. **COMPARE AND CONTRAST** What were the main differences between monastic schools and cathedral schools?
3. **MAKE INFERENCES** How does Thomas Aquinas use reason to explain the existence of God?

2.3

MAIN IDEA The medieval era in Europe featured great achievements in the arts, advances in technology and science, and the development of democratic ideas in government.

Medieval Achievements

For many years, historians used the term *Dark Ages* to describe the period immediately after the fall of the Roman Empire. Citing the frequent warfare and disappearance of urban life, they viewed it as a bleak period, a time of ignorance and barbarity. Today, historians rarely use the term and instead tout the achievements that occurred as the Middle Ages progressed.

WRITING

In medieval Europe, Christianity served to unify people socially and politically, with the clergy, the nobles, and the peasants all following the same religion. Not surprisingly, most writers of the time focused on Christian topics and themes, producing works that ranged from scholarly essays to romantic poetry. Until fairly late in the Middle Ages, they wrote in Latin, the language of the Roman Catholic Church.

Before the mid-1100s, few people outside the church could read or write Latin. Monks and nuns learned Latin in the monastic schools and were expected to study the Bible and other religious writings. Because they were literate, many of them played a key role in the spread of literature by serving as scribes. Working alone or together in a scriptorium, a room in a monastery set aside for writing and copying manuscripts, scribes copied biblical and other texts onto sheets of parchment. They often included beautiful illuminations, or decorations produced with brightly colored inks, and bound the manuscripts into books. An illuminated manuscript often contained large, ornamental capital letters as well as detailed illustrations and designs.

This detail from the *Peterborough Psalter* shows David, a king of the Israelites in the Bible, playing the harp. The psalter, or book of psalms, was made in England in the early 1300s.

Nearly all monasteries and convents had a library for storing manuscripts, as did universities. Some manuscripts were available for lending to scholars, and a few libraries even arranged for interlibrary loans. Religious and scholarly works filled a large portion of a library's shelves. These works included histories and biographies, collections of letters and sermons, and books of philosophy and science.

280 CHAPTER 10

A shift away from Latin toward the vernacular, or the language spoken by ordinary people, led to an increase in fictional works in the form of heroic and romantic poetry. The first epic in English, *Beowulf*, appeared as a manuscript around 985. The story had been part of the Germanic oral tradition for about two centuries. Set in Denmark, *Beowulf* tells the tale of a heroic prince who slays an evil monster.

Two medieval writers of vernacular poetry were **Dante Alighieri** and **Geoffrey Chaucer**. Dante, an Italian who was inspired by his love for a woman, completed *The Divine Comedy* around 1321. Written in Italian, the long narrative poem tells of the author's travels through hell, purgatory, and heaven. Chaucer, an English writer, finished *The Canterbury Tales* around 1400. This poetic work offers amusing and colorful descriptions of a group of pilgrims, including a monk, a merchant, and a knight, who journey to a shrine in Canterbury, England, and tell tales along the way.

Geoffrey Chaucer wrote *The Canterbury Tales* in Middle English, which is the form of English spoken between about 1100 and 1400. In this excerpt, the author describes a nun who tries to impress others with her courtly manners.

PRIMARY SOURCE

Original	Translation
At mete wel y-taught was she with-alle;	At meals she was well taught indeed;
She leet no morsel from hir lippes falle,	She let no morsel fall from her lips,
Ne wette hir fingres in hir sauce depe;	Nor wet her fingers deep in her sauce;
Wel coude she carie a morsel, wel kepe,	She well knew how to carry a morsel and take good care
That no drope ne fille up-on hir brest.	That no drop fell upon her breast.

—from the Prologue to *The Canterbury Tales* by Geoffrey Chaucer, c. 1400, translated by Larry D. Benson

ART AND ARCHITECTURE

The medieval period saw a return to Roman-influenced styles of art and architecture in Europe. By around 950, the turmoil caused by the barbarian invasions had subsided, and the Roman Catholic Church had regained its influence. About 1000, the Romanesque style in art and architecture emerged, fusing Roman, Byzantine, and Germanic traditions. New cathedrals—featuring massive stone walls, rounded arches, and small windows and decorated with religious sculptures and paintings—arose in France, Germany, Italy, England, and Spain.

By the mid-1100s, the architectural style of cathedrals began to shift from Romanesque to Gothic. The Gothic cathedrals featured pointed arches, tall and thin walls, and large windows that let in great amounts of light. This style emerged in the monastery church at Saint-Denis in France, which was rebuilt starting in 1140. Throughout Europe, the construction of Gothic cathedrals was financed not only by the church but also by guilds flush with profits from the Commercial Revolution.

Art historians often point to the Cathedral of Notre Dame at Chartres, near Paris, as one of the best examples of a Gothic cathedral. Reconstructed after a fire in 1194, its structural changes included the use of flying buttresses, which are exterior, arched supports for walls. This innovation permitted artisans to construct the high, arched ceilings found in Gothic cathedrals. It also allowed walls to be thinner and much taller—so tall that a viewer at street level would see a structure soaring as if to the heavens. The cathedral's many stained-glass windows filtered all the light that entered, creating a warm glow inside.

ADVANCES IN TECHNOLOGY AND SCIENCE

The construction of soaring cathedrals in the medieval era called for advanced engineering skills. Europeans applied new skills and technologies not only in architecture but also in agriculture and industry.

To produce more food, Europeans opened new land to cultivation and farmed land more intensely than they had before. Earlier in this chapter, you read about some of the agricultural innovations that increased productivity, such as the use of manure as a soil fertilizer and the practice of crop rotation. One popular rotation of turnips, clover, and grain took advantage of different nutrients in the soil each year.

Once grain was harvested, it had to be ground into meal or flour. As early as 500, but particularly after 1000, farmers began to harness the power of water in flowing

CRITICAL VIEWING Begun in 1063, the Cathedral of Santa Maria Assunta in Pisa, Italy (top), is a prime example of Romanesque architecture. Westminster Abbey, one of the most important Gothic buildings in England, was begun in 1245. How does Westminster Abbey differ in style from the Cathedral of Santa Maria Assunta?

rivers to operate mills. Water mills were first used to grind grain and then were adapted to other uses, such as sawing wood and sharpening or polishing iron. By 1100, at least 5,000 water mills existed throughout England, or one mill for every 35 families. Europeans also developed their own version of a Persian invention, the windmill, for use in places that lacked flowing water.

Science also advanced during the Middle Ages. The English philosopher Roger Bacon was an early proponent of experimental science. In the mid-1200s, Bacon undertook experimental research in areas ranging from astronomy to optics, the science of light. From his studies of light and the eye, Bacon predicted the invention of glasses and developed a pinhole camera for observing an eclipse of the sun. He was far ahead of his time in proposing motorized ships and carriages and flying machines.

MAGNA CARTA AND PARLIAMENT

Political changes also occurred during the Middle Ages. Although William the Conqueror established a strong monarchy in England after his invasion in 1066, the dominance of English kings did not mean all was quiet throughout the land. Disputes frequently occurred between the king and the church, lords and their vassals, and merchants and their customers.

During the 1100s, not just in England but throughout Europe, people increasingly used the law to resolve disputes. The University of Bologna, in Italy, offered courses in law, based in part on Byzantine and Roman legal texts. Working in monasteries, guilds, and universities, Europeans began to write down previously unwritten laws.

In 1215, a dispute arose between England's King John and his barons, or landholding nobles. The rebellious barons complained of high taxes and claimed that the king, as their lord, had failed to preserve their rights and privileges as vassals in England's feudal system. The dispute ended only after the barons forced the king to put his seal on a written set of laws.

The main purpose of this set of laws, called the **Magna Carta**, or "Great Charter," was to define the obligations

This stained glass window in the Mansion House, the official residence of the mayor of London, depicts King John signing the Magna Carta in 1215.

of the king to his barons. But the document's 63 clauses also established fundamental principles that would become the basis for English constitutional law. Those principles, later incorporated into the legal systems of other countries, supported the rise of modern constitutional government.

The Magna Carta limited the king's authority and established that the law applied to everyone, including the king. It guaranteed a free man's right to a trial by his peers—and within a reasonable amount of time. The legal procedure that prevents the government from holding a person indefinitely, without appearing before a judge, is known today as **habeas corpus**.

Another clause established that the king could not impose new taxes without getting the approval of the barons and high church officials. Thus, the Magna Carta signaled the beginning of a transfer of power from the king to a lawmaking body, called **Parliament** in England. Later events during the Middle Ages advanced the development of Parliament and solidified the role of aristocratic landowners in governing England.

HISTORICAL THINKING

1. **READING CHECK** What technological advances in agriculture occurred during the Middle Ages in Europe?
2. **MAKE INFERENCES** How do the works of Dante Alighieri and Geoffrey Chaucer reflect the importance of religion in medieval society?
3. **IDENTIFY MAIN IDEAS AND DETAILS** How did the Magna Carta contribute to the rise of modern democratic institutions and procedures?
4. **DRAW CONCLUSIONS** An important principle of the American legal system is that "justice delayed is justice denied." How is this idea reflected in the Magna Carta?

2.4 Preserving Cultural Heritage

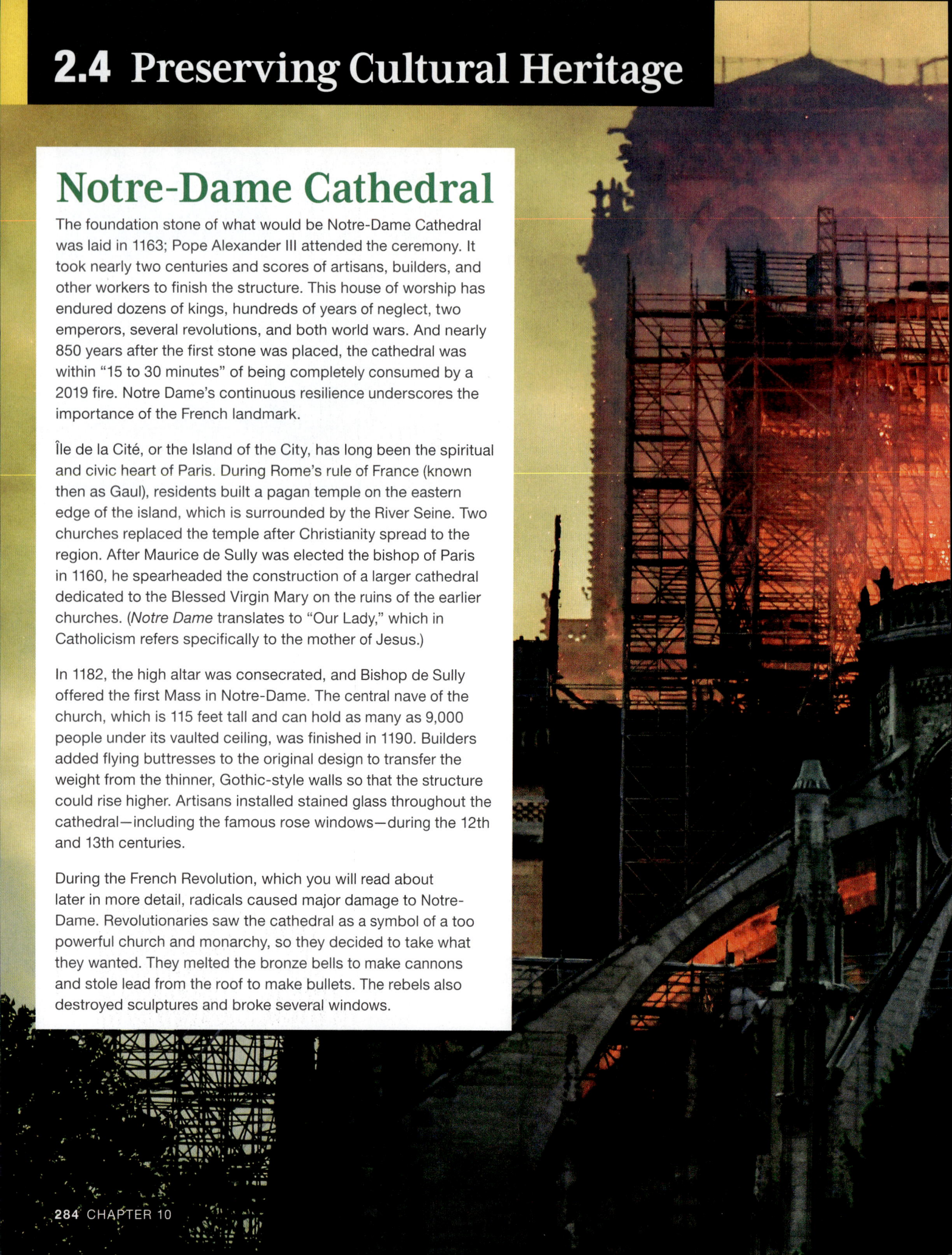

Notre-Dame Cathedral

The foundation stone of what would be Notre-Dame Cathedral was laid in 1163; Pope Alexander III attended the ceremony. It took nearly two centuries and scores of artisans, builders, and other workers to finish the structure. This house of worship has endured dozens of kings, hundreds of years of neglect, two emperors, several revolutions, and both world wars. And nearly 850 years after the first stone was placed, the cathedral was within "15 to 30 minutes" of being completely consumed by a 2019 fire. Notre Dame's continuous resilience underscores the importance of the French landmark.

Île de la Cité, or the Island of the City, has long been the spiritual and civic heart of Paris. During Rome's rule of France (known then as Gaul), residents built a pagan temple on the eastern edge of the island, which is surrounded by the River Seine. Two churches replaced the temple after Christianity spread to the region. After Maurice de Sully was elected the bishop of Paris in 1160, he spearheaded the construction of a larger cathedral dedicated to the Blessed Virgin Mary on the ruins of the earlier churches. (*Notre Dame* translates to "Our Lady," which in Catholicism refers specifically to the mother of Jesus.)

In 1182, the high altar was consecrated, and Bishop de Sully offered the first Mass in Notre-Dame. The central nave of the church, which is 115 feet tall and can hold as many as 9,000 people under its vaulted ceiling, was finished in 1190. Builders added flying buttresses to the original design to transfer the weight from the thinner, Gothic-style walls so that the structure could rise higher. Artisans installed stained glass throughout the cathedral—including the famous rose windows—during the 12th and 13th centuries.

During the French Revolution, which you will read about later in more detail, radicals caused major damage to Notre-Dame. Revolutionaries saw the cathedral as a symbol of a too powerful church and monarchy, so they decided to take what they wanted. They melted the bronze bells to make cannons and stole lead from the roof to make bullets. The rebels also destroyed sculptures and broke several windows.

PARIS, FRANCE

In the early evening of April 15, 2019, a fire broke out in Paris's Notre-Dame Cathedral. Hundreds of firefighters battled for more than 12 hours in an attempt to save the iconic building, as well as the treasures inside, and to keep the blaze from spreading throughout the city. When the flames were finally extinguished, nearly all of the roof was destroyed. Gone, too, was the spire that had been over 300 feet tall.

An open square created in the 19th century allows observers to see the cathedral's entire grand facade, including the two towers that stand 226 feet tall and include Gothic stone carvings of biblical figures.

The Catholic Church regained control of the cathedral after the revolution, and French author Victor Hugo's 1831 novel *The Hunchback of Notre-Dame* renewed the public's interest in the building. In 1844, French Gothic architect Eugène-Emmanuel Viollet-le-Duc was chosen to lead the effort to restore the structure to its former glory; it took him nearly 25 years to complete the project. Viollet-le-Duc also added several new elements—the soaring spire, statues of the Twelve Apostles, and Notre-Dame's famous and fearsome stone gargoyles.

In 1914, Notre-Dame was slightly damaged when 50 bombs were dropped on Paris during World War I. And when Charles de Gaulle made his way to the French capital in 1944 to liberate France from Germany in World War II, several bullets struck the cathedral. But the blaze of April 2019 outpaced any other previous threats to the Gothic structure. At the time, Notre-Dame was undergoing a $6.8 million renovation to repair cracks in the stone, and workers had removed copper statues of evangelists and apostles from the roof a week before the tragedy. Other items that remained when the smoke cleared were all three rose windows, the Grand Organ, St. Louis's tunic, and the Holy Crown of Thorns, believed to be worn by Jesus at his crucifixion.

Unfortunately, other treasures and relics were forever lost to the flames. But the people of France—and the world—will not be defeated by this setback. Soon after the blaze, architects and other designers offered sketches of possible options to replace the cathedral's roof and other missing parts. And French president Emmanuel Macron said, "The fire at Notre-Dame reminds us that our history never stops and we will always have challenges to overcome." He also vowed, "We will rebuild it together. It will undoubtedly be part of French destiny and our project for the years to come."

HISTORICAL THINKING

INTEGRATE VISUALS How do the photos and history of Notre-Dame Cathedral reflect France's history?

Flames from the fire did not reach Notre-Dame's famous 18th-century Great Organ. However, each of the 8,000 pipes—a few of which date back to the 13th century—and the instrument's wind chest and electrical system needed to be cleaned of dust. The western rose window also survived. The first and smallest of the cathedral's three rose windows was completed about 1225 and restored between 1844 and 1867.

3.1

MAIN IDEA Beginning in the 1000s, reformers attempted to establish more uniform beliefs and practices within the Roman Catholic Church.

Changing Roles of the Church

There's an old saying that money opens doors. In medieval Europe, money could buy a person a position in the church, like that of a bishop or even pope.

STRUCTURE OF THE CHURCH

By 1000, the European countryside was blanketed with churches, each one the center of a parish in which the clergy lived alongside the **laity**, or members of the church who are not clergy. Many churches, especially the cathedrals, owned valuable lands that brought them wealth, but others had little land of their own. The laity were expected to pay a **tithe**, or 10 percent of their income, to their local parish priest. He, in turn, performed the sacraments, or holy rituals, for them, including baptism and marriage. The priest also celebrated Mass, in which he administered the sacrament of the Eucharist, or Holy Communion. In this sacrament, Roman Catholics eat bread and drink wine that they believe become the body and blood of Jesus.

The clergy fell into two categories: the secular clergy and the regular clergy. The **secular** clergy did not belong to a monastic order or live in a monastery. They lived out in the community and worked with the laity as local priests or as teachers in cathedral schools. Regular clergy lived in monasteries and followed the rules of their monastic order, most of which were modeled on the Benedictine Rule, a guide for monastic life written by an Italian monk named Benedict around 530 C.E. The Benedictine Rule called for strict obedience to the abbot, or head of the monastery, and required that monks remain unmarried, have few possessions, wear simple clothing, and follow a daily schedule of prayer and work.

Sacra di San Michele, an abbey built between 983 and 987, sits on top of Mount Pirchiriano in Italy. Like other churches devoted to St. Michael, including Mont-Saint-Michel in France (shown at the beginning of this chapter), Sacra di San Michele was constructed on a hard-to-reach site.

MONASTIC REFORMS

The Roman Catholic Church had started out as many individual churches that developed their own **doctrines**, or official beliefs, and practices. As time passed, official church councils sought to standardize doctrines and practices. Although the pope in Rome was the supreme authority in church matters, the monastery system allowed a variety of practices to flourish.

One monastery at Cluny, in eastern France, was the largest in Europe, with holdings in land and money greater than those of the church in Rome. Cluny's abbot was more powerful than anyone in the church except the pope. By the late 1000s, some 300 monks lived at Cluny. In addition, about 1,000 monasteries, home to 20,000 monks, were associated with Cluny. But Cluny's growth meant the abbot was too busy to visit most of these monasteries, and monastic discipline suffered.

In 1098, several monks broke away from Cluny and began a new order, the Cistercians, and called for a return to enforcement of the Benedictine Rule. Unlike the Cluny monasteries, each Cistercian monastery had its own abbot. All abbots met at regular intervals to ensure that everyone followed the same regulations. Cistercian monks lived more simply than those at Cluny. They wore clothes of undyed wool, ate only vegetarian foods, and built undecorated churches.

Some reformers urged monks to live exactly as Jesus and his followers had, not in monasteries with their own incomes but on the streets as beggars dependent on ordinary people for contributions. Between 1100 and 1200, these reformers established at least nine begging orders. Their members were known as friars. The new begging orders explicitly rejected what they saw as lavish spending by the church.

An Italian Catholic named **Francis of Assisi** founded the most important begging order, the Franciscans, which had some 28,000 members by 1326. Franciscans were not allowed to live in a permanent dwelling or to keep any money, books, or extra clothes. Another begging order, the Dominicans, arose in Spain in the early 1200s. Its founder stressed education and sent some of his followers to attend universities.

St. Francis of Assisi, shown on the right, is the patron saint of animals and ecology. He felt a connection and brotherhood with all living creatures.

PAPAL AND SECULAR STRUGGLES

By the early 1000s, the practice of buying and selling church offices had become widespread in Europe. In 1046, three men competed to become pope. One of them had bought the position from an earlier pope. The ruler of Germany, Henry III, intervened in the dispute and paved the way for a German bishop to assume the papacy. The new pope, Clement II, then crowned Henry as the new Holy Roman Emperor. Henry had effectively taken control of the papacy, which allowed him to arrange for the appointment of three later popes.

In 1075, however, Pope Gregory VII renewed that struggle. He declared that only popes could invest bishops, or formally install them in office, and the penalty for breaking this rule would be excommunication. The pope and the next Holy Roman Emperor, Henry IV, soon clashed when they put forward rival candidates for bishop of Milan, Italy.

Pope Gregory excommunicated Henry, who later sought and received the pope's forgiveness. In 1075, the pope drafted 27 declarations asserting the independence of the church from secular rulers. Pope Gregory had regained control of his office.

HISTORICAL THINKING

1. **READING CHECK** What reforms in monastic life did the Cistercians make?

2. **DRAW CONCLUSIONS** Why was the buying and selling of church offices a serious problem?

3. **MAKE PREDICTIONS** Do you think the "victory" of Pope Gregory VII ended the struggle for power between popes and kings? Why or why not?

Europe's Medieval Era

3.2

MAIN IDEA Starting in 1096, Christians launched a series of military expeditions against non-Christians with the aim of conquering Palestine.

Waves of Crusades

You've probably heard the saying "The ends justify the means." Christians of the Middle Ages relied on similar reasoning when they launched violent attacks against non-Christians in the name of Jesus, the "Prince of Peace."

BYZANTINE EMPIRE UNDER ATTACK

In 1095, **Pope Urban II** addressed a large meeting of church leaders, telling them that the Byzantine emperor had requested help against the Seljuk Turks, a nomadic tribe from Central Asia. At the time, the Byzantine Empire was shrinking, much of its territory having been captured by Arab Muslims. The Seljuks had begun to carve out a Seljuk empire in central Anatolia that would extend south into Syria and Palestine. They also initiated a quest to topple Constantinople, the heavily fortified Byzantine capital. Meanwhile, the Normans of France had attacked the Byzantine Empire and aimed to conquer Constantinople, too.

The Byzantine Empire, in spite of its wealth and well-trained military, seemed unable to adequately defend itself. Part of the problem was a lack of consistent and competent leadership. Over a span of 50 years before 1081, the empire had gone through 13 rulers, many of them inept. The year 1081, however, brought the Byzantine leader **Alexius Comnenus** to the throne.

Alexius stopped the advance of the Normans in western Greece in 1085. He also achieved a **truce**, or a temporary halt of warfare, with the Seljuks and other Muslim Turks on the empire's eastern border. But the Seljuks remained within striking distance of Constantinople—and they had control of Palestine, called the Holy Land by Christians. The Holy Land included the city of Jerusalem and the area around it, where Jesus had preached and died. Christians, Jews, and Muslims all believed the land rightfully belonged to them.

FIRST CRUSADE: A CALL AND A RESPONSE

The Holy Land, and especially Jerusalem, had long attracted Christian pilgrims who wanted to visit the sites where Jesus had lived and died and was buried. Muslims, too, considered several sites in Jerusalem sacred, including the Dome of the Rock, from which the prophet Muhammad reportedly ascended into heaven. After taking control of the region, the Seljuk Turks blocked Christian pilgrimage routes to the Holy Land.

Pope Urban II was concerned about the threat Muslims posed to the Holy Land and to the Byzantine Empire. He had heard stories of pilgrims being harassed and holy places being damaged or destroyed. In his speech to the meeting of church leaders, he called for what historians refer to as the First **Crusade**, a Christian military expedition to invade and conquer Palestine. He asked Europe's nobles, the warrior class, to march against the Muslim "infidels," or unfaithful ones. The word *Crusader* referred to anyone belonging to a large, volunteer force fighting against Muslims. The Crusaders wore a cross on their clothing.

Pope Urban II had determined that warfare designed to defend Christians and sacred Christian sites served a holy purpose. Such a **holy war**, he believed, was morally justified. In his speech, the pope declared that all Crusaders who died en route to the Holy Land could be certain that God would forgive their sins. The Crusaders, he said, were pilgrims, and God forgave all pilgrims' sins.

Some 50,000 combatants responded to the pope's plea. Out of these, several armies of volunteer fighters were organized. The first force set out in August 1096 under the leadership of **Godfrey of Bouillon**, a German duke. A Norman leader known as Bohemond led another group. Both armies marched overland to Constantinople. The Byzantines had not forgotten the earlier Norman attacks on their empire. **Anna Comnena**, the emperor's daughter, later wrote a history of the period, in which she praised the Norman leaders for their courage in battle but criticized them as cunning, or devious, schemers. Emperor Alexius, fearing trouble from the Normans, hurried the Crusaders away from his capital and on their way to Jerusalem.

CRITICAL VIEWING In this detail from an illuminated manuscript, Christian soldiers amass for the siege of Antioch in 1098 during the First Crusade. How would you characterize these volunteer troops?

Europe's Medieval Era 291

The Crusades, 1096–1270

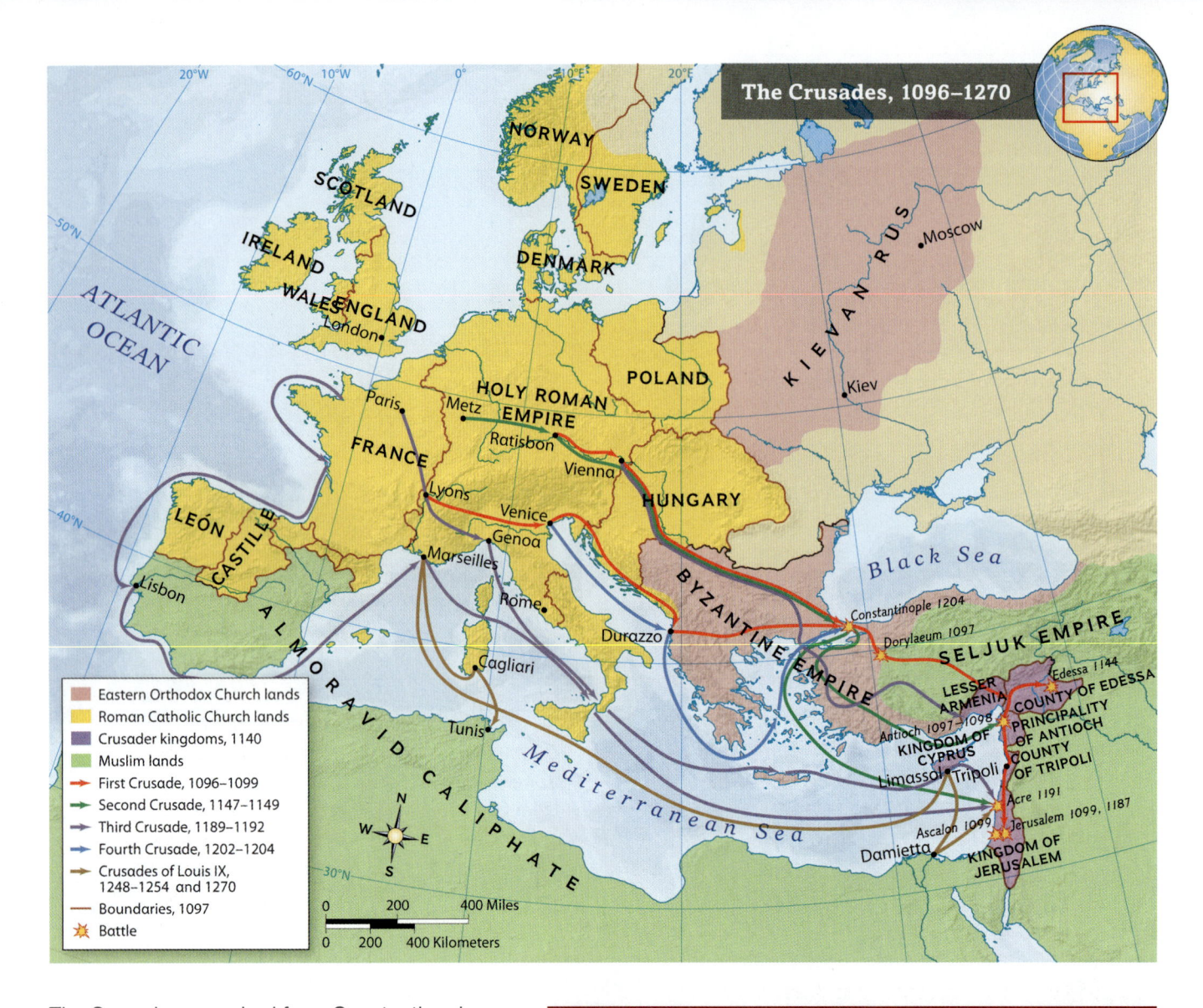

The Crusaders marched from Constantinople southwest across Anatolia toward the historically Christian center of Antioch in Syria. They conquered Antioch in 1098 after an eight-month siege. The following year, they accomplished their main goal by capturing Jerusalem, and Godfrey of Bouillon became the ruler of Palestine. After this victory, the Crusaders massacred thousands of the city's Jewish and Arab residents. Although the Crusaders succeeded in conquering Jerusalem, they would hold it for only 88 years.

DEFEAT AND MORE CRUSADES

By 1140, the Crusaders had set up four small states in the Holy Land: the Kingdom of Jerusalem, the County of Tripoli, the Principality of Antioch, and the County of Edessa. Together, these states became known as the Latin East, because the Crusaders spoke Latin. Of all the Crusader states, Edessa, bordering Seljuk lands,

---

In *Alexiad*, her work about her father's reign as Byzantine emperor, Anna Comnena described the Norman leader Bohemond and his father, Robert Guiscard. She characterized these two Norman nobles as equally tough, warlike, and despicable.

PRIMARY SOURCE

Now, Bohemond took after his father in all things, in audacity, bodily strength, bravery, and untamable temper; for he was of exactly the same stamp as his father, and a living model of the latter's character. Immediately on arrival, he fell like a thunderbolt, with threats and irresistible dash upon Canina, Hiericho, and Valona [three Byzantine sites], and seized them, and as he fought his way on, he would ever devastate and set fire to the surrounding districts. He was, in very truth, like the pungent smoke which precedes a fire, and a prelude of attack before the actual attack. These two, father and son, might rightly be termed "the caterpillar and the locust"; for whatever escaped Robert, that his son Bohemond took to him and devoured.

—from *Alexiad* by Anna Comnena, c. 1148, translated by Elizabeth A. Dawes

was the most vulnerable to Muslim attack. In 1144, the Seljuk Turks conquered Edessa.

The loss of Edessa alarmed Christians and moved a new pope to call for a Second Crusade. Bernard of Clairvaux, a monk you read about earlier, depicted the Crusade as a road to salvation in his preaching, which stimulated widespread support. His eloquent sermons prompted the kings of both France and Germany to lead large armies to Edessa in 1147.

The Second Crusade failed completely. After discovering that the Turks had killed the Christian inhabitants of Edessa, the Crusaders gave up on trying to recapture the state. They decided instead to lay siege to Damascus, a fortified Muslim city in Syria. They retreated after four days, however, when it became clear they could not conquer the city. The failure of the Second Crusade dismayed Christians and greatly encouraged Muslims.

The Muslim ruler **Saladin**, founder of a new dynasty in Egypt, joined with the Seljuks to dislodge the Crusaders. In 1187, Saladin's army retook Jerusalem. The Crusaders in Jerusalem who weren't killed were held for ransom or sold into slavery. Saladin's troops restored the mosques as houses of worship and removed the crosses from all Christian churches, though Muslims later allowed Christian pilgrims to visit the city.

Subsequent major Crusades failed to recapture Jerusalem. In the Third Crusade launched in 1189, England's King **Richard the Lionheart** sailed to the Holy Land with his army, landing at Acre, just north of Jerusalem. Richard exemplified the Code of Chivalry, a code of honorable conduct that called for knights to be skilled at combat, brave, fair, and courteous. Richard demonstrated this code in the courtesy he showed his Muslim opponent Saladin, and it may have been mutual respect that allowed these powerful men to negotiate a peace treaty in 1192. Acre fell to the Crusaders, as did several other seaports to the north and the island of Cyprus. The Third Crusade was generally a success, though Jerusalem remained in Muslim hands.

Europeans decided to make a further attempt to retake Jerusalem and launched the Fourth Crusade in 1202. However, the Crusade leaders agreed to first take part in a plot to unseat the Byzantine emperor in Constantinople, for which they would be paid by a Byzantine prince who sought the throne. Although they were successful, the expected payment for their deed did not materialize, and so the Crusaders sacked the magnificent city in 1204, killing all who opposed them. They took everything that could be taken, including not only valuable works of religious art, rare books, and precious manuscripts, but even doors and tiles from roofs. Many of the stolen objects were destroyed or lost, though some can still be found in cities in Italy, France, and Germany. As a result of the Fourth Crusade, Constantinople and its population declined dramatically.

Saladin developed a reputation among Muslims as a firm but generous ruler. He demonstrated his great military leadership in the struggle against the Christian Crusaders.

During this period, many minor Crusades also took place, but most of them were short-lived and never reached the Holy Land. In 1248 and again in 1270, Louis IX of France led two Crusades. The first, aimed at conquering Muslim Egypt, ran afoul of Baybars, a Turkish slave who was then commander of Egypt's army and later ruler of Egypt and Syria. The conflict ended in many Crusader deaths and the capture and ransom of Louis. The next Crusade ended in North Africa, where Louis and many of his troops died of disease.

HISTORICAL THINKING

1. **READING CHECK** What factors led Pope Urban II to call for the First Crusade?
2. **EVALUATE** Did the Crusades align with the teachings of Jesus? Explain your answer.
3. **DRAW CONCLUSIONS** How did the plight of the Byzantine Empire change from the First through the Fourth Crusade?
4. **INTERPRET MAPS** On which Crusade did the armies travel entirely by land?

3.3

MAIN IDEA During the Middle Ages, the Catholic Church launched attacks against Jews and Muslims in Europe as well as its own members who held unacceptable views.

Crusades Within Europe

History is full of examples of groups whose members believed they were superior to others and committed brutal acts against those outside their group. The Crusaders were one example. You won't have to look hard to find many others.

ATTACKS ON NON-CHRISTIANS

The main goal of the major Crusades was to free Palestine from the Muslims, who had "invaded the land of the Christians," according to Pope Urban II. The restoration of Muslim power in Palestine and the threat of Turkish armies to the Byzantine Empire led the pope to feel justified in waging a holy war. However, that war led to attacks on people who had nothing to do with Palestine or the Byzantine Empire.

Many European Christians believed that Christianity was superior to other religions and, in fact, was the one true religion. Infused with the spirit of holy war, they sometimes attacked perceived enemies of Christianity in Europe. At times they acted on their own, and at other times in direct response to a pope's command.

Anti-Semitism, hostility toward and discrimination against Jews, was widespread in Europe during the Middle Ages. Many European Christians looked down on Jews, who were banned from certain occupations, denied citizenship, and prevented from marrying Christians. Jews often resided in **ghettos**, separate areas of cities in which they were required to live. Christians resented Jews who made their living as moneylenders, even though Jews were pushed into moneylending because they were restricted from working in many other occupations.

Before 1096, however, European Christians had largely tolerated Jews and respected their right to practice their own religion. That year, as preparations began for the First Crusade, a French preacher named Peter the Hermit started gathering an army of eager Christian soldiers. Consisting mainly of peasants and urban poor led by knights, this army, called the People's Crusade, set off for the Holy Land. While marching through the Rhine River region of Germany, the Crusaders attacked a number of towns with large Jewish communities. They carried out **pogroms**, or organized massacres, in which they slaughtered several thousand Jews—men, women, and children. They threatened to kill others unless they converted to Christianity. Later Crusader armies carried out similar pogroms as they traveled through Europe.

In 1212, Pope Innocent III approved a Crusade against non-Christians in Spain. Historians refer to this Crusade and other military campaigns against the Muslims of Spain and Portugal as the **Reconquista** (ray-kohn-KEE-stah), a Spanish word meaning "reconquest." In 711, Arabs had invaded Spain from North Africa and established Muslim states there. Before 1200, Christian rulers had recovered isolated cities in the region, such as Toledo in Spain and Lisbon in Portugal. A decisive Crusader victory in 1212 began a string of conquests until only a single state, Granada, remained under Muslim control by 1249. Two centuries later, the Christian monarchs **Isabella and Ferdinand** of Spain completed the Reconquista. In 1492, after a 10-year, state-sponsored Crusade, they conquered Granada.

In the same year, the Spanish monarchs completed what they called the "purification" of Spain. They gave Jews the option of converting to Christianity. Jews who refused to convert were expelled. Likewise, numerous Muslims living in Spain were exiled, and many moved to North Africa. The anti-Semitism of the Spanish leaders was not unique in Europe. The English and French monarchies, for example, had earlier given in to religious prejudice and banished their Jewish populations.

PURIFYING THE CHURCH

During the time of the Crusades, various popes launched campaigns against enemies *within* the church as well as those outside. These campaigns aimed to rid the church of **heretics**, or church members who hold religious views contrary to official doctrine.

One way that popes chose to eliminate heretics was through an **Inquisition**, a judicial procedure that evolved into a special court for hearing charges against accused heretics. Unlike other church courts, which operated according to established legal norms, an Inquisition used anonymous informants, forced interrogations, and torture to identify heretics. Offenders who refused to renounce their beliefs could be sentenced to life imprisonment or death. The church established a series of Inquisitions beginning in 1231.

Both a Crusade and an Inquisition were used to extinguish the heretical Christian sect known as the Cathars, which arose in southern France in the 11th century. The Cathars considered the spiritual world good and the material world evil. They accused the Roman Catholic Church of becoming too materialistic and losing sight of its spiritual mission. The Cathars also questioned some of the sacraments and viewed Jesus as an angel and not as the Son of God, which the church taught. The Cathars flourished over the next century, attracting followers in France, Germany, and Italy and gaining the support of many nobles and clergy. One French subgroup of Cathars, the Albigensians, grew especially influential. They criticized the church as corrupt, arguing that its priests shirked their religious duties to pursue wealth and political power.

In 1209, Pope Innocent III called for a Crusade against the Cathars, and nobles from northern France undertook what became known as the Albigensian Crusade. Over the next 20 years, the Crusaders slaughtered large numbers of Cathars, including bishops and other clergy. In 1231, Pope Gregory IX directed an Inquisition against the Cathars. Many of those who would not renounce their beliefs were imprisoned, tortured, or burned to death. The church succeeded in putting an end to Catharism by the late 1300s.

LEGACY OF THE CRUSADES

The quest to conquer Palestine, the original goal of the Crusades, ended in failure in 1291, when Muslim forces captured the last of the coastal towns in the region held by Crusaders. Palestine, including Jerusalem, remained firmly in the hands of those the church considered infidels. Moreover, the Crusaders had further weakened the Byzantine Empire and made it more vulnerable to aggressors.

CRITICAL VIEWING Ferdinand and Isabella of Spain completed the Reconquista by retaking Granada, the last territory held by Muslims in Spain. What details stand out in this wedding portrait of the Catholic monarchs?

The Fourth Crusade's assault on Constantinople, in which the Crusaders treated Eastern Orthodox Christians as if they were Muslim enemies, created a genuine and lasting schism between Roman Catholics and Eastern Orthodox adherents. Byzantines regained control of Constantinople in 1261, but it was no longer the beautiful and prosperous capital of a powerful Eastern empire.

The Crusades also solidified the hostility between Christians and Muslims. The brutally violent behavior of Roman Christians toward Muslims and Orthodox Christians would not quickly be forgotten, and neither would their behavior toward Jews.

The Crusades did give Europeans a closer connection with the eastern Mediterranean region. Some Crusaders found much to admire and copy in the Islamic world. Even the Europeans who stayed home were affected by imports from Muslim regions, such as eyeglasses, new medical ideas, and a more flexible number system. Other imports that originated in China, such as paper, also came to Europe via the Islamic world. The increased trade with the eastern Mediterranean region contributed to the growth of the merchant class in Europe.

HISTORICAL THINKING

1. **READING CHECK** What were the main effects of the Crusades?
2. **COMPARE AND CONTRAST** How were the Crusades and the Inquisitions similar? How were they different?
3. **SEQUENCE EVENTS** List the main events of the Reconquista in chronological order.

4.1

MAIN IDEA In the 1300s, a prospering Europe was devastated by a food shortage and a deadly disease.

Trade, Famine, and Plague

In the 1300s, Europeans did not know the cause of a deadly disease that was wiping out almost the entire population of some towns. Many people thought it was God's punishment for their sins. Doctors blamed it on bad air. The real cause wouldn't be discovered for hundreds of years.

THE SPICE TRADE

By 1300, Europe was prosperous and peaceful. Nearly all the Crusaders had come home from the Holy Land, bringing back new information about the world beyond Europe. They also brought back a taste for spices.

Merchants from Italian city-states sailed to such ports as Acre in Palestine, Alexandria in Egypt, and Constantinople. There they loaded their ships with silks, gems, and other goods. But spices dominated their cargoes. Europeans were consuming more and more of such spices as pepper, cinnamon, and nutmeg. They used the spices to enhance the flavor of foods and to treat illnesses. The growth in trade would have an unexpected downside, however, as Christian and Muslim societies became exposed to a deadly disease.

THE GREAT FAMINE

Until the early 1300s, Europeans generally had sufficient food to eat. Improved agricultural techniques had steadily increased crop yields enough to feed the ever-growing population. Local shortages sometimes occurred, but they did not last long. But then disaster struck. Crop failures throughout northern Europe led to food shortages, resulting in the **Great Famine of 1315–1322**. A famine is an extreme shortage of food in a country or large geographic region.

In the period leading up to the famine, a small shift in climate brought cooler temperatures and more rain to Europe, especially in the north. In 1315 and 1316, spring rains kept peasants from plowing all of their fields. Much of the seed they planted rotted in the ground, and further heavy rains ruined the crops that did sprout.

A poor harvest two years in a row forced peasants to take drastic measures. They killed and ate their draft animals—the horses and oxen they used to pull their plows—and gobbled the seed they had saved for planting in the spring. Still, many of them starved, and even nobles and clergy began dying from lack of food.

The weather improved in 1317, but the lack of seed grain and draft animals, along with the physical weakness of the malnourished peasants, meant that food stocks could not be restored quickly. Many people continued to die of starvation, and thousands of peasants fled their fields to beg in the cities. This and other changes accelerated the decline of the manorial system.

The Great Famine lasted seven years, during which more than 10 percent of the population of northern Europe died. The supply of food did not return to normal until around 1325.

CRITICAL VIEWING In this 16th-century painting *The Triumph of Death*, Flemish painter Pieter Bruegel portrays death as an army of skeletons. What aspects of life in the Middle Ages does this painting bring to mind?

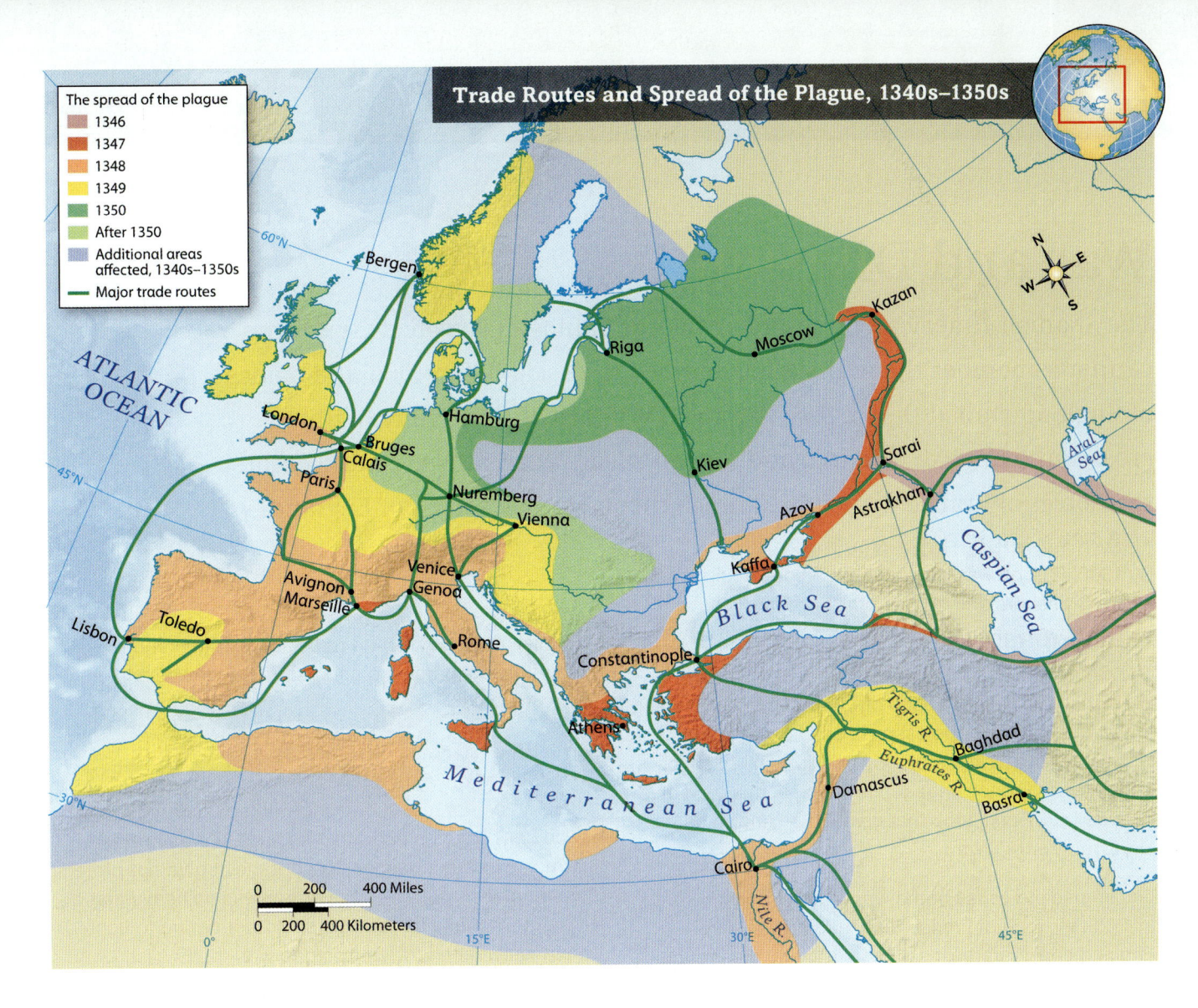

Trade Routes and Spread of the Plague, 1340s–1350s

The spread of the plague:
- 1346
- 1347
- 1348
- 1349
- 1350
- After 1350
- Additional areas affected, 1340s–1350s
- Major trade routes

THE BLACK DEATH

The Great Famine was followed by an even worse disaster. In 1347, a merchant ship sailed out of a Black Sea port carrying rats infected with plague, a highly contagious disease that had spread along the trade routes crossing central Asia. The ship transported its deadly cargo back to several Mediterranean ports, from which the disease spread inland to Arabia, North Africa, and Western Europe over the next four years.

The plague was carried not only by rats but also by the fleas that bit them. It came in two main forms, bubonic and pneumonic. A person bitten by an infected flea contracted the bubonic form, marked by egg-sized, painful boils that turned black. Droplets from that person's cough or sneeze could infect people who inhaled them. Those people got the pneumonic form.

The plague was called the **Black Death**, after the black boils. But it was mainly the pneumonic form that spread death throughout Europe from 1347 to 1351, reducing the population from around 75 million to 55 million.

Some scholars link the high death rate from the plague with the Great Famine, arguing that European peasants had not fully recovered physically from the famine when the plague hit. Thus, they were less able to combat the disease. A related theory holds that peasants had been weakened by their diet on the manor—mainly grains and such legumes as beans and peas. Large swaths of woodland, once habitat for game animals, had been turned into farmland. The loss of hunting land meant peasants no longer consumed enough protein from meat to keep them healthy.

HISTORICAL THINKING

1. **READING CHECK** What caused a large drop in the population of Europe in the first half of the 1300s?

2. **ANALYZE CAUSE AND EFFECT** What were the causes and effects of the Great Famine of 1315–1322?

3. **INTERPRET MAPS** What does the map in this lesson indicate about the relationship between trade routes and the spread of the plague across Western Europe?

Europe's Medieval Era

4.2

MAIN IDEA War between France and England and a schism in the Roman Catholic Church added to the turmoil in Europe during the 1300s and 1400s.

War and Division

The Spanish-American philosopher George Santayana wrote, "Those who cannot remember the past are condemned to repeat it." In 1066, the nobles of England denied the English throne to William of Normandy. William crossed the English Channel and started a war. Nearly three centuries later, the nobles of France denied the French throne to Edward III of England. How do you think he reacted?

THE HUNDRED YEARS' WAR

The Great Famine and the plague created turmoil throughout Europe for much of the 14th century. Adding to the widespread hopelessness and fear, the continent was also plunged into a bloody conflict. The rulers of England and France engaged in a long series of battles between 1337 and 1453 that came to be known as the **Hundred Years' War**.

The immediate cause of the war was a political dispute. In 1328, the king of France died, and Edward III of England considered himself next in line to the French throne. But the nobles of France selected his cousin as king instead. In 1337, reasserting his claim, Edward sent an army across the English Channel to France, sparking a war that would continue for more than a century.

The roots of the war went far beyond a straightforward dispute over who should rule France, however. England and France had long been bitter rivals. By the 1330s, the two countries were engaged in many complicated territorial disputes. English kings had large landholdings in France but had trouble controlling them. French kings sought to extend their rule over all of France, but they faced challenges from French princes. France backed Scotland in its quest to gain independence from England. England aligned itself with Flanders, a province of France whose prosperous commercial centers sought the status of independent city-states.

France, with a population of some 15 million, was far richer than England, which had only around 4 million people. France's larger population and wealth allowed it to field bigger armies and hire foreign soldiers. The war took place entirely on French soil. Between battles, English troops launched raids across the French countryside, capturing and plundering towns and burning crops.

The Hundred Years' War marked a shift in the technology of warfare. The era of heavily armored knights on horseback fighting with spears and swords was coming to an end. Knights had donned heavier armor to protect themselves, but they could not protect their horses. Moreover, the armor was so heavy that a knight who fell off his horse could not get up to fight an assailant on foot. Early in the war, the English won significant victories because they used a new type of longbow, 6 feet tall, that shot metal-tipped arrows farther and more accurately than the crossbows then in use.

By the final years of the war, both sides had turned to gunpowder, a Chinese invention that had spread to Europe in the 1200s. In the 1400s, it powered primitive cannons that shot stones, bolts, or lead bullets. Although difficult to aim accurately, these new weapons could destroy the walls surrounding a castle or town under siege and make it possible to overtake the site. The French army used gunpowder weapons in conjunction with crossbows to finally defeat the English in 1453. They expelled English forces from all of France except the northern port of Calais, located just across the English Channel.

The Hundred Years' War significantly changed the political structure of France and England. At the beginning of the war, the two kingdoms consisted of patchworks of territory ruled by a king who shared power with his nobles. By the end of the war, the two countries had become centralized monarchies governed by kings with considerably more power.

While the English and French kings **consolidated**, or unified and strengthened, their power, they also consulted with advisory groups in their countries, particularly on the subject of taxes. As you have read, this advisory group was called Parliament in England and included nobles, clergy, and later other subjects of the king. The French equivalent was called the Estates-General. The newly centralized monarchies in France and England proved effective at governing, and the existence of representative assemblies helped kings gain the allegiance of their subjects. Those ruled by these monarchies began to feel a sense of national identity.

THE GREAT SCHISM OF 1378

As the Hundred Years' War wore on, a crisis of authority erupted in the Roman Catholic Church. In 1378, a political rivalry resulted in the election of more than one pope, causing a split within the church.

CRITICAL VIEWING The Battle of Poitiers, which took place in France in 1356, was an early victory for the English in the Hundred Years' War. In this painting of the battle, John II of France surrenders to Edward, Prince of Wales, who was called the Black Prince. What symbol, long associated with the French crown, appears on the cloak of the French king?

The rivalry occurred between French and Italian leaders in the church. The French bishop who became Pope Clement V in 1305 decided not to reside in Rome, a city beset by political turmoil. In 1309, at the urging of the French king, he moved the papacy to Avignon, a city within a region of southern France controlled by the papacy. The Avignon papacy continued, through six additional French popes, until 1377. During this time, the papacy functioned fairly normally. The popes promoted missionary work and sought an end to the Hundred Years' War. But many Catholics believed the French kings controlled the Avignon popes and that greed had corrupted the papacy.

In 1377, a newly elected French pope returned the papacy to Rome, but he died the next year. Pressured by the people of Rome, the College of Cardinals—the senior clergy who elect the pope—chose an Italian as his replacement. But some of the French cardinals, opposed to the new pope, elected their own pope. This French "antipope" took up residence in Avignon. This period of two popes in the Roman Catholic Church became known as the **Great Schism of 1378**.

In the years that followed, popes and antipopes declared each other—and all opposing cardinals, bishops, and priests—to be heretics. The Great Schism not only divided the church leadership in two, it also split the population and countries of Europe nearly evenly as well.

In 1409, realizing that the schism was a disaster for the church, the opposing groups of cardinals met to find a solution. But they only made matters worse by electing yet another pope. Finally, in 1417, at the Council of Constance, all the cardinals agreed on a way to solve the problem they had created. They pushed aside all three popes and elected a new one, an Italian acceptable to all, who would reside in Rome.

HISTORICAL THINKING

1. **READING CHECK** What event started the Hundred Years' War?

2. **ANALYZE CAUSE AND EFFECT** What were some political effects of the Hundred Years' War?

3. **SEQUENCE EVENTS** How did the Great Schism of 1378 start, and how did it end?

4.3 Material Culture

PICTURING JOAN

Far into the Hundred Years' War, a teenage peasant named Joan of Arc claimed to hear divine voices calling upon her to save France from being taken over by the English. She marshalled French troops to an important victory against the English at the city of Orléans in 1429 and boosted the morale of the French. Captured a year later, she was imprisoned by the English, tried for heresy, and then burned alive in 1431. While **Joan of Arc**—or Jeanne d'Arc in French—was a real person, the portrayals of her life approach mythic proportions. No portrait of Joan of Arc from her lifetime has survived. But her image has been represented in myriad ways over the centuries to serve a variety of political, religious, and commercial purposes.

Jeanne D'Arc During Her Lifetime This sketch is the only existing image of Joan of Arc made during her lifetime. A clerk drew it in the margins of the Paris Parliament's register after receiving news of the French victory at Orléans. The clerk depicted Joan with flowing hair and dressed in a long skirt. In fact, Joan wore men's clothing and cut her hair short for battle.

The Struggle Over Gender This miniature from the 15th century depicting Joan in a soldier's armor contrasts with images of her in women's clothing with long, flowing hair. Artists had to decide: should Joan be portrayed as a woman or as a warrior? In the 1400s, it was considered not only shocking but also heresy for a woman to wear men's clothing.

Political Symbol French political parties on both the right and the left have used Joan of Arc as a symbol to espouse their views.

This 19th-century statue of Joan of Arc by the French sculptor Prosper d'Épinay stands in the Notre-Dame de Reims Cathedral in France. After the French victory at Orléans in 1429, Joan attended the coronation of Charles VII in the Reims Cathedral. The sculpture depicts Joan wearing a smock covered with fleurs-de-lis, an emblem of the French monarchy, over her armor. A replica of her banner appears behind her.

This 1926 statue of Joan stands in Rouen, France, where Joan was burned at the stake. The statue was created by the French sculptor Maxime Réal del Sarte, who was active in Action Française, a right-wing nationalist organization that promoted the restoration of the monarchy and Roman Catholicism as the state religion in France in the early 1900s. The organization used Joan as its symbol.

Europe's Medieval Era 301

The Martyr After imprisoning Joan in Rouen, France, the English found her guilty of heresy and ordered her burned at the stake.

This 1824 oil painting by the French painter Hippolyte-Paul Delaroche depicts Joan being interrogated in prison by Cardinal Henry Beaufort, an English statesman and Bishop of Winchester. The painting emphasizes Joan's holiness, showing her with folded hands, her face lit up, and her eyes looking upward. The charges against Joan included breaking divine law by dressing as a man and carrying weapons.

In this 1843 oil painting, the German artist Hermann Anton Stilke portrays Joan on a pyre at Rouen, with a cross strapped to her waist and her eyes looking to the heavens. The pope annulled Joan's conviction in the 1450s. Viewed by many as a Christian martyr, she was officially declared a saint in 1920.

The Maid Joan of Arc preferred to be called "the maid," and she was often referred to as "The Maid of Orléans." Many painters have portrayed her as a simple country girl, who, being inspired by God, was able to persuade the future king of France to allow her to lead an army. This 1879 oil painting by the French painter Jules Bastien-Lepage depicts Joan in her family's garden with Saints Michael, Margaret, and Catherine appearing and encouraging her to fight against the English.

Joan on Film This poster for the 1948 American movie *Joan of Arc* shows the Swedish actress Ingrid Bergman in the role of Joan. Bergman appears in characteristic Joan of Arc attire—dressed in armor and holding a sword. The film portrays Joan as a strong, spiritual woman guided by her faith. Bergman was in her thirties when she played the teenage hero.

Hero of Two World Wars Government posters used Joan of Arc as a patriotic symbol. This World War I poster encourages American women to aid their country by buying stamps. The poster shows Joan in armor but with makeup and a modern hairstyle to appear more feminine.

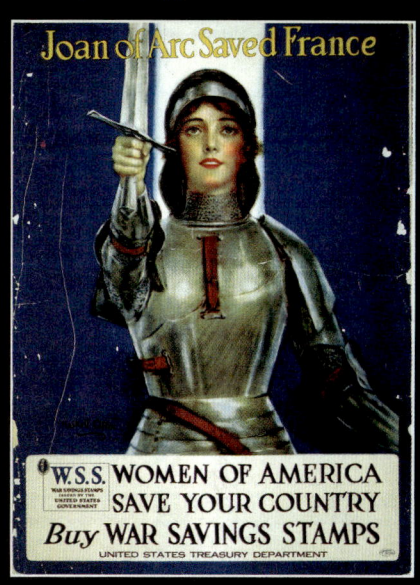

Feminist Icon This 1912 poster uses Joan's image to promote *The Suffragette*, a newspaper of the Women's Social and Political Union (WSPU). The WSPU was a militant political organization that campaigned for women's suffrage in the United Kingdom.

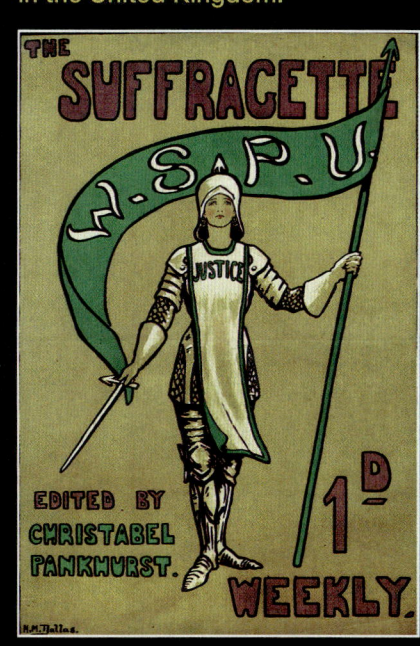

HISTORICAL THINKING

1. **READING CHECK** How did Joan of Arc become a national hero and symbol of France?

2. **COMPARE AND CONTRAST** Choose two visual depictions of Joan of Arc from this lesson and tell how they are alike and how they differ.

3. **MAKE INFERENCES** Why might the English have felt particularly threatened by Joan of Arc?

Europe's Medieval Era 303

CHAPTER 10 EUROPE'S MEDIEVAL ERA
REVIEW

VOCABULARY

Use each of the following vocabulary words in a sentence that shows an understanding of the term's meaning.

1. serf
2. vassal
3. commerce
4. capital
5. clergy
6. vernacular
7. holy war
8. pogrom

READING STRATEGY
IDENTIFY PROBLEMS AND SOLUTIONS

Identifying problems faced by people of the past and noting their solutions can help you understand the way history unfolded. Complete the Problem-and-Solution Chart to analyze the way European peasants solved the problem of producing more food on agricultural land during the Middle Ages.

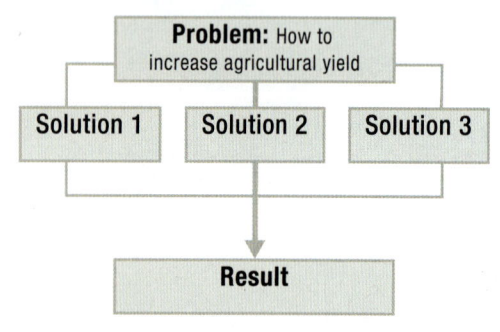

Problem: How to increase agricultural yield

- Solution 1
- Solution 2
- Solution 3

Result

9. How did solutions to the problem of increasing agricultural yield impact Europe's population in the years between 1000 and 1340?

MAIN IDEAS

Answer the following questions. Support your answers with evidence from the chapter.

10. How did Christianity spread through Europe? **LESSON 1.1**

11. How did William of Normandy gain the title "Conqueror"? **LESSON 1.3**

12. What economic changes did the Commercial Revolution bring to Europe? **LESSON 2.1**

13. Why were Scholastics considered unifiers? **LESSON 2.2**

14. How did reformers try to change the Roman Catholic Church in the 1000s? **LESSON 3.1**

15. What was the main goal of the First Crusade? **LESSON 3.2**

16. How did the Great Famine of 1315–1322 accelerate the decline of the manorial system? **LESSON 4.1**

17. How was the government of England similar to that of France after the Hundred Years' War? **LESSON 4.2**

HISTORICAL THINKING

Answer the following questions. Support your answers with evidence from the chapter.

18. **MAKE INFERENCES** Why was Hildegard of Bingen an unusual woman for her time?

19. **ANALYZE CAUSE AND EFFECT** What were the results of increased participation in government by the nobles of England during the medieval era?

20. **MAKE GENERALIZATIONS** How did monasteries and convents contribute to European culture and society during the Middle Ages?

21. **DRAW CONCLUSIONS** How did the Roman Catholic Church both unify and divide people during the Middle Ages?

22. **SEQUENCE EVENTS** Write the following events in chronological order, from earliest to latest: the First Crusade; the writing of the Magna Carta; Charlemagne's alliance with the pope; the end of the Hundred Years' War; the Great Famine.

23. **FORM AND SUPPORT OPINIONS** What do you consider the best and worst aspects of the life of a serf during the Middle Ages?

INTERPRET VISUALS

Study the graph of Europe's population between 1000 and 1450. Then answer the questions that follow.

24. Describe the population trends that occurred in Europe between 1000 and 1450.

25. What events contributed to the population decline that occurred in Europe after 1340?

European Population, 1000–1450

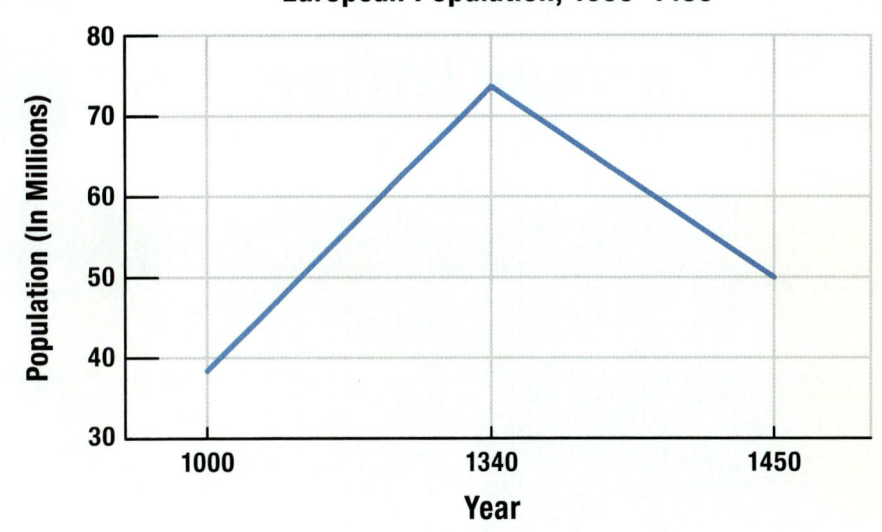

Source: Josiah C. Russell, "Population in Europe" in Carlo M. Cipolla, ed., The Fontana Economic History of Europe, Vol. I: The Middle Ages (Glasgow: Collins/Fontana, 1972) 25–71

ANALYZE SOURCES

During the time of the Black Death, many Europeans blamed Jews for causing the plague. In 1349, a German member of the clergy wrote an account of pogroms against Jews throughout Germany. This excerpt from his account focuses on one German town. Read the excerpt and answer the questions that follow.

> The persecution of the Jews began in November 1348, and the first outbreak in Germany was at Sölden, where all the Jews were burnt on the strength of a rumor that they had poisoned wells and rivers, as was afterwards confirmed by their own confessions and also by the confessions of Christians whom they had corrupted and who had been induced by the Jews to carry out the deed. And some of the Jews who were newly baptized said the same. Some of these remained in the faith but some others relapsed, and when these were placed upon the wheel [a type of torture] they confessed that they themselves sprinkled poison or poisoned rivers.
>
> —from "The Persecution of the Jews," in *The Black Death*, translated and edited by Rosemary Horrox, 1994

26. According to this excerpt, what did the people of Sölden believe was causing people to die from the plague, or the Black Death?

27. On what evidence was the guilt of the Jews based? How do you think this evidence was obtained?

CONNECT TO YOUR LIFE

28. **INFORMATIVE** This chapter describes the gradual transfer of law-making power from the king to a representative body in England between the 1200s and the 1400s. Review this information and identify two principles established during the period that are reflected in current laws in the United States. Write a short essay explaining how these principles continue to protect the rights of people today.

TIPS

- Reread the section on the Magna Carta and Parliament and note the changes to English law that occurred between 1215 and 1430.

- Select two changes or principles that you consider important and locate a section of your state constitution or the U.S. Constitution that expresses the same idea or furthers the idea.

- Write a topic sentence describing the connection between English law of hundreds of years ago and certain legal protections you enjoy today.

- Using evidence from the text or your research, support your topic sentence with relevant facts or examples.

Europe's Medieval Era 305

CHAPTER 11

East Asia and Chinese Influences
938–1392

HISTORICAL THINKING How does one culture adopt influences from other cultures and adapt them to its own?

SECTION 1 **The Song Dynasty**
SECTION 2 **Korea, Vietnam, and Japan**

CRITICAL VIEWING

The Matsumoto Castle in Nagano is the oldest existing castle in Japan. Built in the late 1500s of wood and stone and set against the Japanese Alps, the feudal castle is noted for its many unique architectural elements, including a pavilion for viewing the moon. What are some other distinctive features of the castle?

1.1 **MAIN IDEA** China entered a time of significant prosperity and growth during the Song dynasty.

The Rise of Song China

People often say that adversity makes a person stronger. For the Song, the humiliation of admitting weaknesses and paying tribute to their conquerors eventually led to a time of great prosperity and commercial success.

THE SONG DYNASTY RISES

As you've read, after the Tang dynasty came to an end, China fell into chaos until 960, when the Song dynasty was founded and restored order. By 976, the Song had united both north and south China and established its capital at Kaifeng in the Huang He Valley.

The Song founder kept in place the Tang political structure, with the emperor at the top of a central bureaucracy that oversaw local government. However, the Song believed that generals had exercised too much power in the Tang dynasty. So the Song initiated a period of greater civilian rule with power residing in the hands of bureaucrats rather than with generals.

The Song dynasty faced a problem common to earlier dynasties: keeping peace with the nomads to the north, in this case the Kitan. To counter this threat, the Song formed an alliance with the Jurchen who had formed the Jin dynasty. With their help, the Song defeated the

CRITICAL VIEWING This photo shows a busy street in modern-day Kaifeng, the former capital of the Northern Song. What would it be like to live in a city among centuries-old buildings? How might such an environment, made up of the past and present, influence your daily life?

Kitan in 1125. However, the Jurchen immediately turned and attacked the Song. They built siege towers that rose over the walls of Kaifeng, the Song capital. Then the Jurchen used the Chinese invention of gunpowder to fight the Chinese. They also employed a more technologically complex use of gunpowder. Rather than tying gunpowder to arrows to shoot at the enemy as the Chinese had, the Jurchen shot bombs made of bamboo shells containing gunpowder and porcelain shards. Unable to devise an effective defense, the residents of Kaifeng surrendered in January 1127.

THE SONG DYNASTY IS FORCED SOUTH

Taking control of northern China, the Jurchen modeled their government after the Song and ruled 40 million Chinese. Refusing to live under the Jurchen, 500,000 Song Chinese fled south in one of the largest migrations in human history. The Jurchen captured the former Song emperor, but one of the emperor's sons joined the migration south, became the new emperor, and formed a new capital at Hangzhou. Historians now refer to the period when the Song capital was in Kaifeng as the Northern Song and the period when the Song capital was in Hangzhou as the Southern Song.

At first, life in the south was extremely difficult for those who fled as well as for those who were already there. The north and south were distinct cultural regions with many differences. Northerners were accustomed to eating noodles and bread, whereas rice was the main staple in the south. Also, the northern and southern **dialects**, or regional variations in language, were different, so northerners and southerners couldn't understand each other. The huge influx of new residents into southern cities changed the **demographics**, or the characteristics of the population. Hangzhou had been a small, regional city, but within a few years its one million residents had built it into a worthy successor of the former capital at Kaifeng. By the end of the 12th century, Hangzhou had become the largest city in the world.

For the next 14 years, the Southern Song fought to regain control of the north and to keep the Jurchen from invading the south. Finally, in 1142 the Southern Song and the Jurchen signed a peace treaty. But the terms of the treaty were humiliating to the Song. They were forced to pay a tribute of 250,000 ounces of silver and 250,000 bolts of silk each year to the Jurchen. They also became the first Chinese dynasty to formally accept another dynasty as a "superior state."

The payments, however, stimulated trade and economic growth in the Song dynasty because the Jurchen used the tribute money to buy large quantities of Chinese goods. The Southern Song rebuilt their economy and became one of the richest societies in the world. China's farmers realized that they could grow more food in southern China than they had in the north, so they began to grow cash crops to sell at markets. Peasants turned into part-time or full-time artisans and sold pottery, baskets, and textiles. Commercial growth through markets, as well as advances in technology, book publishing, currency, and education, all led to an improved quality of life for many Chinese.

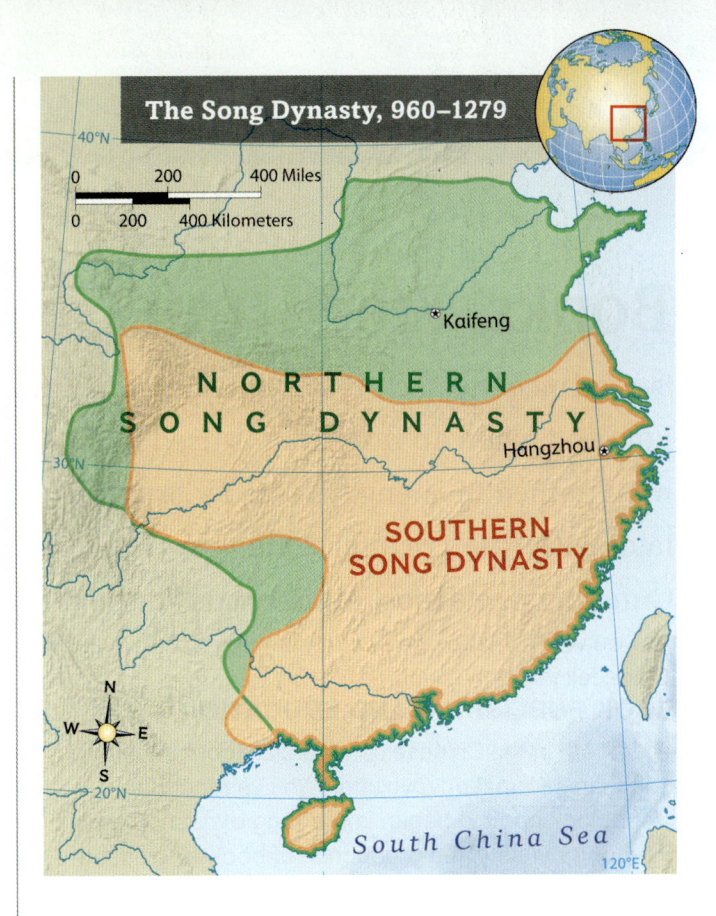

Life was better, and so was travel. Improvements in mapmaking, boat building, and navigational instruments allowed Song ships to sail on deepwater routes to Vietnam and Cambodia for the first time. Through increased trade, the Song learned much more about the peoples and products of the outside world. China's economic transformation affected the whole region, and Song coins circulated widely throughout Korea, Japan, and Vietnam.

HISTORICAL THINKING

1. **READING CHECK** In what ways did China prosper under the Song dynasty?

2. **IDENTIFY PROBLEMS AND SOLUTIONS** What problems did war with the Jurchen pose to the Song? What solutions did the Song develop as a result?

3. **MAKE CONNECTIONS** How do the challenges that the Southern Song faced with large migrations compare with immigration issues the world faces today?

1.2

MAIN IDEA Rapid growth in commerce led to great achievements in publishing, agriculture, education, and metalworking in Song China.

Books, Steel, and Currency

Sometimes the person who invents something doesn't get the credit for it because how and when an invention is used makes a big difference. In 1040, a Chinese man named Bi Sheng invented a process for printing books. More than 400 years later, a German printer, Johannes Gutenberg, invented a similar process. Today, Gutenberg gets most of the credit for developing the printing press.

BOOK PUBLISHING AND EDUCATION

The boom in the Chinese commercial economy brought about an information revolution. You've read that woodblock printing began in the Tang dynasty. During the Song dynasty, the production of books increased dramatically. Shortly after 1040, the Chinese bookmaker Bi Sheng invented a printing process that involved arranging **movable type**—individual clay characters—into a frame to form a page. This process was tedious since the Chinese language has thousands of different characters, but for large print runs of more than 100,000 copies, the innovation of movable type made sense.

The low cost of books and economic growth produced a boom in education. Parents who could afford it hired tutors for their sons in hopes that their sons would pass civil service exams and get prestigious government jobs. Although women were not allowed to take civil service exams, many women did learn to read and write, and women took pride in educating their children and managing household finances.

During the Song dynasty, civil service examinations were held every three years. To assure that no preference was given to known students, the candidates' names were removed from the exams and the answers were recopied so that a candidate's handwriting could not be recognized. Those students with the highest scores would move on to the next level of exams. The best students advanced as far as the palace examinations, which the emperor gave orally.

At the time of the Song dynasty's founding, civil service exams had already been in use for more than a thousand years. But it was only in the Southern Song era that the literacy rate increased such that 1 in 250 people took the exams, and government appointments became almost fully merit-based, or awarded by test scores. As a result, the Song era saw a major shift from government by aristocracy to government by merit-based bureaucracy.

COMMERCIAL REVOLUTION

In northern China, farmers grew wheat and millet, but rice was the most plentiful crop in the south where there was much more rain. Farmers planted rice seeds in small gardens, and then they transported the rice plants to the fields. The farmers used pumps and water wheels to regulate the flow of water into rice fields. Once the plants took root, farmers flooded the fields with water until the crop ripened. In the late 10th century, southern farmers imported a strain of rice from Vietnam that had a shorter growing season and produced two crops a year. With this type of rice, farmers doubled their yields, which helped feed the rapidly growing population.

During the Song dynasty, there was an increase in all goods, not just rice. Iron production surged as well, and metalworkers made both wrought iron, softer iron formed into shapes with tools, and cast iron, which was melted and poured into molds. Cast iron was so hard it could not be worked with a hammer. Song-era blacksmiths also learned to produce steel, one of the strongest metals known, by heating sheets of iron together in a superhot furnace.

Demand for iron goods increased so much that individual workshops could not meet it. Metalworkers worked full time in factory-like spaces where they cast iron armor, weapons, tools, and fittings such as nails and locks that were used for buildings and bridges.

These large-scale foundries housed hundreds of workers who produced identical items in large quantities

In this painting from the Song dynasty, students take the civil service examination at the imperial palace in Kaifeng.

and at low prices. By 1078, China was producing 125,000 tons of iron, or 3.1 pounds per person. It wasn't until 1700, just before the Industrial Revolution, that Europe matched this level of production.

Farmers and foundries sold their goods at markets, and people needed a way to pay for their purchases. In response, Song authorities increased the money supply. During the previous Tang dynasty, **currency**, money in circulation, consisted of round bronze coins with square holes. Carrying strings of heavy bronze coins became cumbersome for merchants and buyers alike, especially for large transactions. Sometime around 1000, the Song government introduced the world's first paper money. Over time, the use of bank seals and increasingly complex designs helped discourage counterfeiting. Paper money allowed people to buy and sell in larger quantities, further contributing to economic growth.

During the Northern Song dynasty, Kaifeng was one of the three largest cities in the world, and Kaifeng's residents lived at a density of 32,000 people per square mile. Along with its many markets, Kaifeng had 72 major restaurants, each standing three floors high and licensed by the government. Just as in ancient Rome, residents of Kaifeng and other Song cities could enjoy public restaurants and stopping for meals, noodles, or snacks at small stands and major restaurants.

RELIGIOUS LIFE

Prosperity also allowed the Chinese to give money to many different religious institutions. Many educated Chinese were drawn to the teachings of **Neo-Confucianism**. Traditional Confucianism had focused on society, ritual, and morality. But Neo-Confucians sought self-development through the study of four Confucian classics known as *The Four Books*. Followers learned to examine everything in the world around them to discover an underlying pattern and understand the all-inclusive life force called *qi*. The ultimate goal of Neo-Confucian education was to attain sagehood, which was a state of ultimate wisdom. By the 17th century, Neo-Confucianism had gained a wide following in Japan, Korea, and Vietnam as well as in China.

HISTORICAL THINKING

1. **READING CHECK** How did the expansion of markets lead to advances in education, agriculture, and the production of iron and steel?

2. **SYNTHESIZE** Why was it necessary to double crop yields in southern China after 1126? How did the Chinese accomplish this?

3. **ANALYZE CAUSE AND EFFECT** What events in the Tang dynasty led to the use of paper currency during the Song dynasty?

East Asia and Chinese Influences 311

1.3 Knowledge of the World's Islands

DOCUMENT-BASED QUESTION

How much can you really learn about the world from reading books and talking with others? Is it necessary to travel to other countries to learn about them? Without ever setting foot on another country's soil, Song official Zhao Rugua (JOW ROO-gwah) wrote a two-volume book all about the lands and cultures of the world.

Zhao Rugua was the director of overseas trade in China's largest international trade port, Quanzhou (chwahn-joh). In this position, he met many foreign and domestic traders and talked to them about the places they visited, the people they met, and the goods they traded. Zhao never traveled outside of China, but he learned from others and from written records, including Muslim geographers' accounts that he probably heard about from Muslim travelers.

Around 1225, Zhao combined the information he obtained into a two-volume book he titled *The Description of Foreign Peoples*. The first volume tells about the location of each country, its people, and its products. The second volume is a catalogue of products from each country.

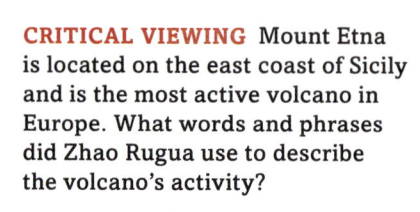

CRITICAL VIEWING Mount Etna is located on the east coast of Sicily and is the most active volcano in Europe. What words and phrases did Zhao Rugua use to describe the volcano's activity?

312 CHAPTER 11

DOCUMENT ONE

Primary Source: Book
from *Zhu Fan Zhi* by Zhao Rugua, c. 1225

In this excerpt, Zhao describes his impressions of the African islands of Pemba and Madagascar.

CONSTRUCTED RESPONSE

Which parts of this description seem credible? Which do not? Why?

This country is in the sea to the southwest. It is adjacent to a large island. There are usually on the great island great peng birds that are so large that they cover the sun when they fly by and the sun's shadow shifts so much that it gives a different reading on the sundial. If the great peng bird finds a wild camel, it swallows it. If one should happen to find a peng feather, after cutting off the hollow quill, you can use it to make a water pail.

The products of the country are big elephants' tusks and rhinoceros horns.

. . . Enticed by offers of food, [the people of this country] are caught and then carried off to be sold as slaves in the Arab countries where they command a high price. They work as gatekeepers. People say that they do not miss their families.

DOCUMENT TWO

In this excerpt, Zhao describes the kingdom of northern Taiwan.

CONSTRUCTED RESPONSE

Taiwan is a mere 150 miles from Quanzhou, yet Zhao's description was actually recycled from earlier documentation written in the 600s. What information in the excerpt explains why the Chinese had little contact with Taiwan?

The country of northern Taiwan is some five or six days' sail east of Quanzhou. . . . The king's residence is called Poluotan Cave; around it [are] three separate wooden palisades surrounded by running water and protected by thorn hedges, and the palace roof has many carvings of birds and animals. . . .

Their soldiers are armed with weapons of every kind, such as knives, pikes, bows and arrows, and swords; they use drums, and make armor from bear and leopard skins. . . .

They have no unusual goods; the locals tend to be robbers, which is why traders do not go there. Still, the locals . . . collect yellow wax, locally mined gold, buffalo tails and jerked leopard meat and take it to the Philippines to sell it.

DOCUMENT THREE

In this excerpt, Zhao describes the island of Sicily off the coast of the Italian Peninsula. The mountain he refers to is Mount Etna, which still erupts today.

CONSTRUCTED RESPONSE

What information has Zhao included about Madagascar and Taiwan but omitted from his information about Sicily?

The country of Sicily is near the border with Rome. It is a sea island one thousand li [roughly 0.33 miles] in breadth. The clothing, customs, and language of the people are the same as those of Rome. This country has a mountain with a very deep cavern in it that emits fire the four seasons of the year. When seen from afar it looks like smoke in the morning and fire in the evening; when seen up close it is a wildly roaring fire. . . .

Once every five years fire and stones break out and flow down to the seacoast and then flow back again. The trees in the woods through which this stream of fire flows are not burned, but the stones it meets in its course turn to ashes.

SYNTHESIZE & WRITE

1. **REVIEW** Review what you have learned about Chinese trade with the "outside world" during the Song dynasty.

2. **RECALL** On your own paper, list details about each country's land, people, and products.

3. **CONSTRUCT** Construct a topic sentence that answers this question: Was Zhao Rugua's book a valuable resource for Chinese merchants who were traveling abroad during the late Song dynasty?

4. **WRITE** Using evidence from this chapter, information about the author, and the excerpts, write an argumentative paragraph that supports your topic sentence in Step 3.

2.1

MAIN IDEA Korea and Vietnam continued to adopt and adapt Chinese ways while prospering as somewhat independent countries.

Koryo Korea and Vietnam's Ly Dynasty

Have you ever admired someone you also disliked? Korea and Vietnam both admired China and adapted many Chinese ideas and practices to meet their own needs. But they also maintained a strong aversion to Chinese control.

KOREA UNDER THE KORYO DYNASTY

Although the Chinese considered Korea to be part of China, the Koreans did not. After the defeat and withdrawal of the Chinese in 676, the Korean Silla kingdom ruled. But in 936, the Koryo kingdom defeated the Silla and founded the dynasty from which Korea takes its name. Starting with King Taejo, whose title means "Great Founder," the Koryo dynasty modeled the structure of its central government on China's Tang dynasty and divided the region into administrative districts as China had. It also followed Chinese practice in sponsoring Buddhism while adopting Confucianism. Taejo applied a traditional Korean emphasis on nature by assessing the life forces of trees and streams in selecting sites for his cities and palaces.

The Koryo king also used a Chinese-style exam to recruit officials by merit and to reduce the influence of powerful families who formed a hereditary local aristocracy. This policy succeeded for over 200 years, but in 1170, aristocratic families and their military supporters overthrew the Chinese-style administration and implemented their own. As a result, Koryo kings continued to rule as figureheads, but Koryo's professional bureaucracy came almost entirely from its hereditary nobility.

Trade continued between Korea and China even during politically unstable times. Korea exported precious metals and edible goods in exchange for Chinese silks, books, and ceramics. Koryo potters also imported advanced Chinese techniques, but they introduced an important innovation to Chinese celadon wares. Improving on the porcelain-making process used in China, Korean potters built high-firing kilns, ovens for pottery, to make their pale green, inlaid celadon pots. Many people considered Korean celadon to be the finest porcelain in the world.

Similarly, woodblock printing reached new levels of sophistication in the hands of Korean printers. Between 1237 and 1248, Korean monks carved Buddhist teachings onto approximately 80,000 woodblocks known collectively as the Tripitaka Koreana. Koreans also adopted the technology of printing with movable type. However, rather than carving characters into separate clay blocks, the Koreans improved the process and used metal type. The world's earliest book printed with movable metal type was made in Korea in 1377.

Some religious texts had been brought back from China by Korean monks. For example, a monk named Uichon went to China to study in 1085, and he later donated some of his 5,000 books to the Tripitaka Koreana. Uichon was hoping to find a way to bridge two schools of Buddhist thought, one which believed that the study of texts was most important, the other placing emphasis on meditation.

In 1402, shortly after the end of the Koryo dynasty, royal astronomers, or scientists who study stars and planets, designed Korea's earliest surviving map of East Asia. The map shows China as the largest country in the world. But it distorts the size of Korea, making it look much larger than its actual size. This may have been the first time a map showed north at the top, a common practice today. Yet this map, like all maps that try to translate the shape of Earth to a flat piece of paper, reflects the culture of those who made it.

THE LY DYNASTY RISES IN VIETNAM

As the Tang dynasty weakened in China, resistance to Chinese control grew in Vietnam. Vietnamese general Ngo Quyen (noh kwehn) revolted in 939, defeating the Chinese by planting iron-tipped stakes in a riverbed to sink China's warships. He claimed independence for Vietnam and named himself king. China acknowledged

A monk holds one of the 80,000 woodblocks from the Tripitaka Koreana collection, which is kept at the Haiensa Temple in present-day South Korea. These are a replication of the original blocks, commissioned in 1237. The originals were destroyed by the Mongols in 1232.

the independence of the new **Dai Viet** state in exchange for tribute payments. This began 1,000 years of independence for Vietnam.

Ngo's rule lasted for 30 years, and the rulers who followed him built up the military to defend Vietnam against China's Song dynasty. To assure that the Chinese would not attempt a takeover, the Vietnamese sent a delegation to China. However, the Song rulers refused to recognize Vietnam's independence until 1009 when the Ly (lee) dynasty came to power.

Even as an independent state, the Ly dynasty acknowledged the superiority of the Chinese emperor, and periodically sent delegations to present the emperor with gifts. The Chinese emperor bestowed gifts on the emissaries in return. Trade between the Chinese and Vietnamese continued as it had for the previous 1,000 years. The Vietnamese exported medicines and resources such as timber and elephant tusks, which the Chinese used to carve ornaments and jewelry.

Chinese-educated scholars of the Ly dynasty argued that the Vietnamese king ruled Vietnam because he, like the Chinese emperor, held the Mandate of Heaven. Vietnamese kings credited local spirits with protecting the royal house, but at the same time, they reinforced Buddhism as the state religion.

The Ly dynasty's rulers moved the Vietnamese capital to what is now Hanoi, established a strong central government based on Chinese law and Confucian values, and recruited a professional army.

Dedicated to the study of Confucian texts, the Ly dynasty king founded a temple of literature in 1070, and by 1076, the government had set up an imperial academy. Following a centralized curriculum, students studied for civil service exams similar to those used in China.

Along with establishing the government, army, and education, the Ly dynasty worked on its **infrastructure**, or transportation networks. Ly dynasty builders built a successful road system and a system of canals that improved year-round rice farming. The Ly dynasty remained in power until 1225.

HISTORICAL THINKING

1. **READING CHECK** How did the Koreans improve upon some of the technology they adopted from China?
2. **ANALYZE CAUSE AND EFFECT** What events in China may have caused Ngo Quyen to seek independence for Vietnam?
3. **IDENTIFY** What are some of the major accomplishments of the Ly dynasty?

East Asia and Chinese Influences 315

2.2 | **MAIN IDEA** During Japan's feudal period, power shifted from the hands of the emperor to those of landowners and warriors.

Shoguns of Japan

Just how loyal should you be to your teacher, your parents, or a boss? In feudal Japan, a warrior would give his life for his lord. This dedication to the lord was even stronger than the warrior's loyalty to a family member or the emperor himself.

JAPAN'S GEOGRAPHY

The physical geography, or **physiography**, of Japan affected many aspects of life in this nation and still does today. As you may recall, Japan is an archipelago made up of four large islands and many smaller ones. The islands are actually the peaks of mostly submerged mountains. Japan's mountains are part of a vast network of volcanoes and intense earthquakes that line both sides of the Pacific in what is known as the **Ring of Fire**. Thick forests comprise another large portion of the Japanese islands' geography. Japan's terrain of rugged mountains and dense forests may have inspired Japan's ancient religion, **Shinto**, which means "way of the gods." Followers of Shinto believe that spiritual powers called *kami* reside in anything in nature that inspires a sense of religious wonder. Followers of Shinto regard mountains as especially important, particularly Mount Fuji, near Tokyo, which has long been considered sacred.

CRITICAL VIEWING The mountainous Shakotan Peninsula on the west coast of Hokkaido, Japan, projects into the Sea of Japan. From details in this aerial photo, what impact do you think Japan's physical geography has on where and how people live?

The Geography of Japan

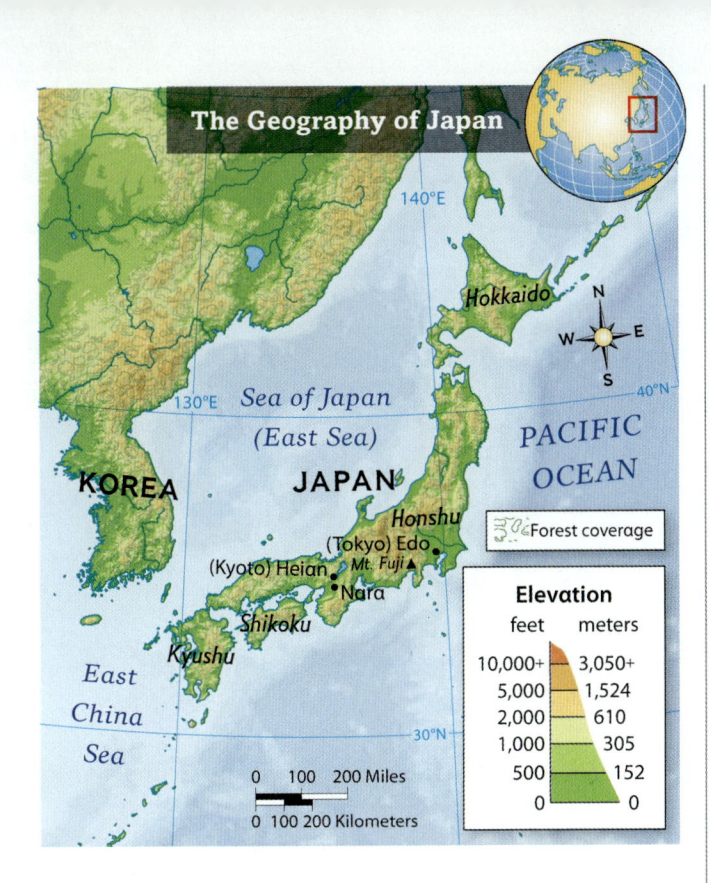

Japan's landscapes are breathtaking, but the space available for agriculture and construction is very limited. Only about 12 percent of Japan's total land is available for farming, and Japan's population is crowded onto a few coastal plains. However, Japan's temperate climate is ideal for growing rice, a major staple of the Japanese diet. Fish and other seafood are also central to Japanese cuisine since most people live near the ocean.

During the 9th and 10th centuries, Japan continued to trade with China and Korea. Japan's main export was lumber from its vast forests. Because Japan did not mint its own coins at the time, Chinese Song dynasty coins became the unofficial currency.

FEUDALISM IN JAPAN

Partially due to the scarcity of land, the **daimyo** (DY-mee-oh), or wealthy landowners, gained power and built up strong alliances to protect their property. As their power increased, the central government and the emperor's power faded. Around the time that the Song dynasty came to rule in China, Japanese warrior clans under daimyo were gaining power. They forced the Japanese emperor to retire to the capital, which had moved from Nara to Kyoto in 794. He remained in Kyoto as a figurehead, and his responsibilities were limited to religious and ritual functions.

Each daimyo retained an army of warriors called samurai. In Japan at this time, real power lay with the daimyo in the countryside, loyally served by their samurai. Meanwhile, the emperor was only a shadowy figure, while the **shogun**, or general, had little real authority. The situation was similar to the feudalism of medieval Europe, where knights were bound as vassals to their lords, who dominated rural society. Powerful daimyo commanded the allegiance of lesser lords, armies, and peasants, creating rival clans that battled for control of Japan.

The Minamoto clan ruled during what is known as the Kamakura period (1185–1333), named for its capital of Kamakura, a city just outside present-day Tokyo. Political power rested in the hands of the Minamoto leader, Yoritomo. He became shogun, who claimed to govern on behalf of the emperor while struggling to command the daimyo. The shogun discontinued the use of Chinese-style civil service examinations, opting instead to appoint members of powerful clans to office. Still, scholars continued to study both Buddhist and Confucian texts, many of which were imported from China.

In 1333, the Ashikaga clan toppled the Minamoto and moved the capital back to Kyoto. However, political power was decentralized and the Ashikaga shoguns had little control over the daimyo who ruled their own rural domains. Since each daimyo had a separate army of samurai, incessant warfare spread chaos throughout the islands. The introduction of gunpowder weapons in this period, as in Europe and western Asia, was making warfare even more deadly. Still, the Ashikaga remained in power for more than 200 years until 1573.

The samurai warriors followed a strict code of behavior called *bushido* (BUSH-ih-doh), or "way of the warrior." Like the knight's code of chivalry in Europe, bushido promoted loyalty, bravery, and honor. Most samurai practiced a form of Buddhism known as **Zen Buddhism** because of its emphasis on self-discipline, inward contemplation, and fearlessness. The Shinto value of devotion to family and ruler and the Confucian emphasis on service to state and country also influenced the code.

HISTORICAL THINKING

1. **READING CHECK** What were the official roles of the shogun and the emperor? What were their roles in reality?

2. **ANALYZE CAUSE AND EFFECT** How did Japanese physiography influence the country's religion, economy, and rise of the daimyo?

3. **COMPARE AND CONTRAST** In what ways were Japanese samurai similar to European knights? In what ways were they different?

2.3 Material Culture

SHARING CULTURES, KEEPING TRADITIONS
You've learned about Chinese influences in East Asia during the 10th–14th centuries. As Chinese influence grew in East Asia, the people of Japan, Korea, and Vietnam adopted and adapted many aspects of Chinese culture, including new ideas and technology. However, as they adapted Chinese ideas to suit their own needs and cultures, they often made significant improvements that led to new discoveries and traditions.

Japanese Gardens In the ancient Shinto tradition of worshiping kami and seeking harmony with nature, the earliest Japanese gardens were considered sacred places. The Japanese developed many varieties of gardens, but they can be categorized into two distinct types: strolling gardens and viewing gardens. Strolling gardens feature carefully designed landscapes along a walking path. The garden shown here is a moss garden, one of the many viewing gardens at Kennin-ji, a Zen Buddhist temple built in Kyoto in 1202. Zen Buddhism greatly influenced Japanese garden traditions. The main purpose of Zen viewing gardens is to create a calm state of mind for meditation. Zen Buddhism inspired Japanese gardeners to create landscapes that represent the world in miniature, using simple elements, such as stone and gravel, to stand for something larger. In a dry landscape garden, for instance, gravel raked in various ways might represent the ocean and larger stones might symbolize hills and mountains, while arrangements of smaller stones might portray a waterfall or a stream.

Japanese Writing System In this 1897 Japanese woodblock print by Toyohara Chikanobu, a young woman practices *kanji*, the Japanese word for Chinese characters. As you'll recall from an earlier chapter, the Japanese adopted the Chinese writing system in the fifth century. Four centuries later, they developed a syllabic alphabet called *kana* that better captured the full meaning and inflection of the Japanese language.

Japanese Tea Ceremony The photograph above shows a *chawan* of matcha tea. A chawan—a bowl used for preparing and drinking tea—is one of the traditional utensils used in the Japanese tea ceremony, as is the *chasen*, or bamboo tea whisk, shown beside the chawan. Introduced by a Japanese Zen Buddhist priest, the tea ceremony is a ritual rooted in the principles of Zen Buddhism, focusing attention on the beauty of simple, everyday activity. It wasn't until the 17th century that tea from China and Japan arrived in Europe, eventually becoming a traditional beverage in Britain and Russia, too.

Korean Celadon Pottery Korea imported a porcelain-making process first developed during the Song dynasty in China. Sometime after 1150, Korean potters improved the Chinese process by using iron pigments and high-firing kilns to create the unique and coveted pale blue-green color of celadon. Popular items of Koryo celadon pottery included vases, bowls, and jugs, as well as ceramic pillows with cut-out designs, such as the one shown here.

East Asia and Chinese Influences

Confucianism in Vietnam Built in 1070 during the Ly dynasty, the Temple of Literature, shown here, is located in Hanoi, Vietnam. Dedicated to the Chinese philosopher Confucius, the temple features statues and altars dedicated to Confucius and his disciples. In 1076, the Imperial Academy—Vietnam's first university—was established inside the temple. Students studied Chinese literature, history, and philosophy. The government also held civil service examinations here, and the emperor himself asked the questions. The temple is an example of how Ly dynasty rulers and their Chinese-educated scholars adopted and promoted Confucian values and principles in education, government, and society.

Japanese Buddhism This four-panel Japanese folding screen (c. 1700) by Ogata Korin depicts Raijin, the thunder god (above), and his brother Fujin, the wind god (right). Often portrayed together, Raijin and Fujin are Shinto gods, or kami. In Japan's Shinto religion, the brothers are viewed as protectors of Japan. As Buddhism spread from China to Japan, Shinto kami came to be seen as protectors of Buddhism, too. In time, certain Buddhist and Shinto rituals integrated, and Shinto gods were incorporated into Japanese Buddhist traditions.

European Chinoiserie The term *chinoiserie* (SHEEN-wahz-ree) refers to a style in European arts and crafts that became popular in the 17th and 18th centuries. *Chinoiserie* is borrowed from the French word *chinois*, meaning "Chinese." Reflecting an increased interest in China and East Asia, European craftsmen created works that were fanciful interpretations of Chinese styles and motifs rather than authentic adaptations of Chinese art.

▲ In keeping with the chinoiserie decorative style, Chinese landscape scenes adorn the walls of the Troja Palace in Prague, the capital of the Czech Republic.

◄ This secretary, or writing desk, is an excellent example of French chinoiserie with its pagoda-shaped top, front panels in imitation lacquer, and charming tea-drinking scenes.

HISTORICAL THINKING

1. **READING CHECK** What is one example of a culture adapting and improving upon an idea or technology from China?

2. **COMPARE AND CONTRAST** In what way is the chinoiserie style different from other adaptations of Chinese culture?

3. **MAKE CONNECTIONS** Which example of cultural adaptation included in this lesson do you find most interesting? Why?

East Asia and Chinese Influences 321

CHAPTER 11 REVIEW
EAST ASIA AND CHINESE INFLUENCES

VOCABULARY

Match each vocabulary word with its definition.

1. dialect
2. demographics
3. movable type
4. currency
5. infrastructure
6. physiography
7. daimyo
8. shogun

a. the general and military ruler of Japan
b. individual tablets arranged in a frame for printing
c. money in circulation
d. the characteristics of a particular population
e. a wealthy landowner
f. networks for transportation
g. a regional variation in language
h. the physical geography of a place

READING STRATEGY
COMPARE AND CONTRAST

Comparing and contrasting characteristics of different societies can help you better understand the similarities and differences between them. In a Venn diagram like the one below, list ways in which the effect of Chinese culture on Korea and Japan were similar and different. Then answer the question below.

Effect of Chinese Culture on Korea | Similarities | Effect of Chinese Culture on Japan

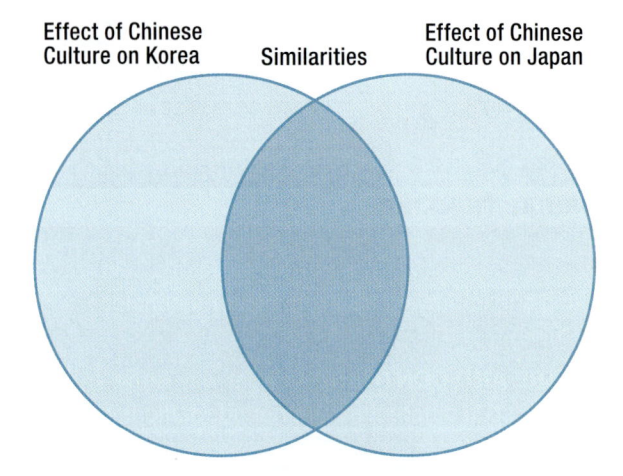

9. Compare and contrast the effect of Chinese culture on Korea and Japan. How was the effect similar? How was it different?

MAIN IDEAS

Answer the following questions. Support your answers with evidence from the chapter.

10. How did tribute payments to the Jurchen eventually help the Southern Song prosper? **LESSON 1.1**

11. How did farming practices change over the course of the Song dynasty? **LESSON 1.2**

12. What effect did woodblock printing have on education in Song China? **LESSON 1.2**

13. What changes did women and children, particularly young boys, experience during the Song dynasty? **LESSON 1.2**

14. How was China able to produce extremely large quantities of iron? **LESSON 1.2**

15. How do Korea's accomplishments during the Koryo dynasty reflect Chinese influence? **LESSON 2.1**

16. How did Vietnam avoid a Chinese takeover during the Ly dynasty? **LESSON 2.1**

17. What was the role of the samurai in feudal Japan? **LESSON 2.2**

HISTORICAL THINKING

Answer the following questions. Support your answers with evidence from the chapter.

18. **SYNTHESIZE** How did Song inventions help Zhao Rugua write books that facilitated trade between China and other countries?

19. **FORM AND SUPPORT OPINIONS** What qualities and advances were women admired for in the Song dynasty? Does this show that women were held in high esteem or that they were subservient? Support your opinion.

20. **DRAW CONCLUSIONS** Why did common people give more money to religious institutions during the Song dynasty?

21. **COMPARE AND CONTRAST** How was life for the Koryo king in 1170 similar to the life of emperors in feudal Japan?

22. **SEQUENCE EVENTS** Create a flow chart to show how power shifted from the Japanese emperor to the shogun.

INTERPRET CHARTS

The following chart shows the structure of society in feudal Japan and feudal Europe. Study the chart and then answer the questions that follow.

Hierarchical Society in Feudal Japan

Emperor	Figurehead with a religious role
Shogun	General with absolute power
Daimyo	Landowners
Samurai	Noble warriors (vassals)
Peasants, artisans, and merchants	Lowest class

Hierarchical Society in Feudal Europe

The Pope	Religious ruler
King	Ruler of a regional country
Nobility	Landowners
Knights	Noble warriors (vassals)
Peasants and Serfs	Lowest class

23. How were the roles of the Japanese emperor and the Pope similar? How were they different?

24. Who held more power, a shogun or a king?

ANALYZE SOURCES

Ono no Komachi is known as one of Japan's greatest poets. Read the poem below and answer the questions that follow.

> Watching the wan moonlight
>
> illuminate tree limbs,
>
> my heart also brims,
>
> overflowing with autumn.
>
> —Ono no Komachi (c. 833–857)

25. What emotions does this poem convey?

26. How does this poem reflect Shinto ideas as well as universal themes?

CONNECT TO YOUR LIFE

27. **EXPLANATORY** Two of the great innovations of the Song dynasty were the book and paper currency. Write a short paragraph describing how your life and society at large would be different if these innovations had not been introduced.

TIPS

- List ways paper currency and books affect your life today. Review the lesson on Song contributions to better understand how they changed life for people of the time.

- Draft a main idea statement that expresses your view of the importance of these innovations.

- Use evidence from the text and your own experience to support your main idea.

- Use two or three vocabulary terms in your paragraph.

East Asia and Chinese Influences 323

CHAPTER 12

The Mongol Empire, Ming Dynasty, and Ottoman Rise
1150–1500

HISTORICAL THINKING How did nomads from Central Asia build great empires?

SECTION 1 **The Mongols**
SECTION 2 **China and the Ming Dynasty**
SECTION 3 **Rise of the Ottoman Empire**

CRITICAL VIEWING

The Hall of Supreme Harmony dominates Beijing's Forbidden City, a huge complex of buildings that once served as the center of Chinese imperial power and government. What details in the photo help indicate the size of the hall?

1.1 MAIN IDEA Led by Genghis Khan, the Mongols conquered much of Asia and eastern Europe and ruled the largest land empire in history.

From Nomads to Conquerors

You've read about the Persian Empire and the Roman Empire, but there was another one that topped them both in size and might: the Mongol Empire. The Mongols swept across Asia in one of history's most impressive conquests.

NOMADIC LIFE

Before the 13th century, the Mongols were a loose collection of independent nomadic tribes from the **steppes**—or vast, grassy plains—beyond the Great Wall, northwest of China. These grasslands were perfect for raising sheep, goats, yaks, and horses. The Mongols' lives were centered on these herds and the products they obtained from them. They made their clothes out of sheep, goat, and yak wool. They ate the animals' meat and made cheese from their milk. The nomads traded these animal products for grain, wood, silk and cotton textiles, and metal products such as knives, daggers, and spears. Mongol tribes traveled with their herds, roaming the steppes and living in portable felt tents called **gers**.

Horses were essential to the Mongols' culture and identity. Children quickly became skilled riders who could shoot a bow and arrow while riding on horseback. Mongol horses were small and stocky and had incredible

Many Mongolians in rural areas still live in gers, and urban dwellers also head to the countryside to spend time in the felt tents. Gers, like the ones shown here on the Mongolian steppes, are often set up in valleys for protection from the wind.

stamina. They could run for six miles without stopping and pull carts loaded with goods. Most important, the fast, agile horses were the Mongols' best weapon in warfare.

Traditionally, the men looked after the horses, built the gers and carts, and led their herds to new grazing areas. Mongol women had more freedom than women in most sedentary societies. For example, they ran the households when the men were away. Women also set up and took down the gers, milked the animals, and prepared the food. Mongol women often sat beside their husbands during meetings, participating in decision-making. As a result, women had the power to influence decisions at all levels of society.

Mongols belonged to clans, groups of people recognizing a common ancestor. Men served as both herders and soldiers. Different clans were united by chiefs and often fought in battles against rival clans. They also conducted raids to steal cattle or capture prisoners. Although differences in wealth existed among the families, there was no strict social order. And they were treated fairly by their chief, who periodically collected taxes by claiming one of every hundred animals in a herd.

CRITICAL VIEWING Standing more than 130 feet high, this stainless-steel statue of Genghis Khan is the tallest equestrian statue in the world. Visitors can walk through the horse's neck and chest and stand on the animal's head. How does the statue convey Genghis Khan's power?

GENGHIS KHAN

A man named Temujin (TEE-moo-juhn) would become a political leader in the early 1200s. He was born around 1162 as the son of a chieftain of a small Mongol tribe. When Temujin was nine, his father was poisoned by someone from another nomadic group. Temujin sought to claim his position as the new leader, but his people refused to acknowledge him. He and his mother and siblings were ostracized, or banished, from the tribe and survived for a time by eating fish and wild plants rather than the traditional nomad diet of meat and milk.

When he grew older, Temujin began forming alliances with other clans and building an army. Temujin trained his soldiers and used strict discipline to create a powerful military machine. As he gathered more followers, he weakened their loyalty to a particular clan by dividing the soldiers into units composed of men from various clans. Temujin wanted his soldiers to be loyal only to him.

By 1206, Temujin had defeated his rivals and united the nomadic tribes under his leadership. That same year, the Mongol chieftains gave him the title **Genghis Khan** (JEHNG-gihs KAHN), which means "universal ruler." The title conferred upon him divine status. And that may have been what compelled Genghis Khan to set out to conquer the world. He and the Mongols believed it was his destiny.

Actually, we don't really know very much about Genghis Khan and his motives. The main source for information on the ruler is a book called *The Secret History of the Mongols*, an oral history dating from around 1228 and written down about 100 years later. Historians have theorized about Genghis Khan's life and why he set off on his conquests. Some scholars believe that, with a growing population, the Mongols needed more food and grazing land. Others claim that trade disputes with China meant that the Mongols had to expand to obtain the goods they couldn't produce.

Whatever the reason, Genghis Khan and his army invaded northern China in 1212. Their approach must have been a terrifying sight. As drums sounded the charge, thousands of soldiers galloped toward the enemy. The Mongols designed improved stirrups of leather and metal that allowed them to control their

The Mongol Empire, Ming Dynasty, and Ottoman Rise 327

The Mongol Empire, 1259

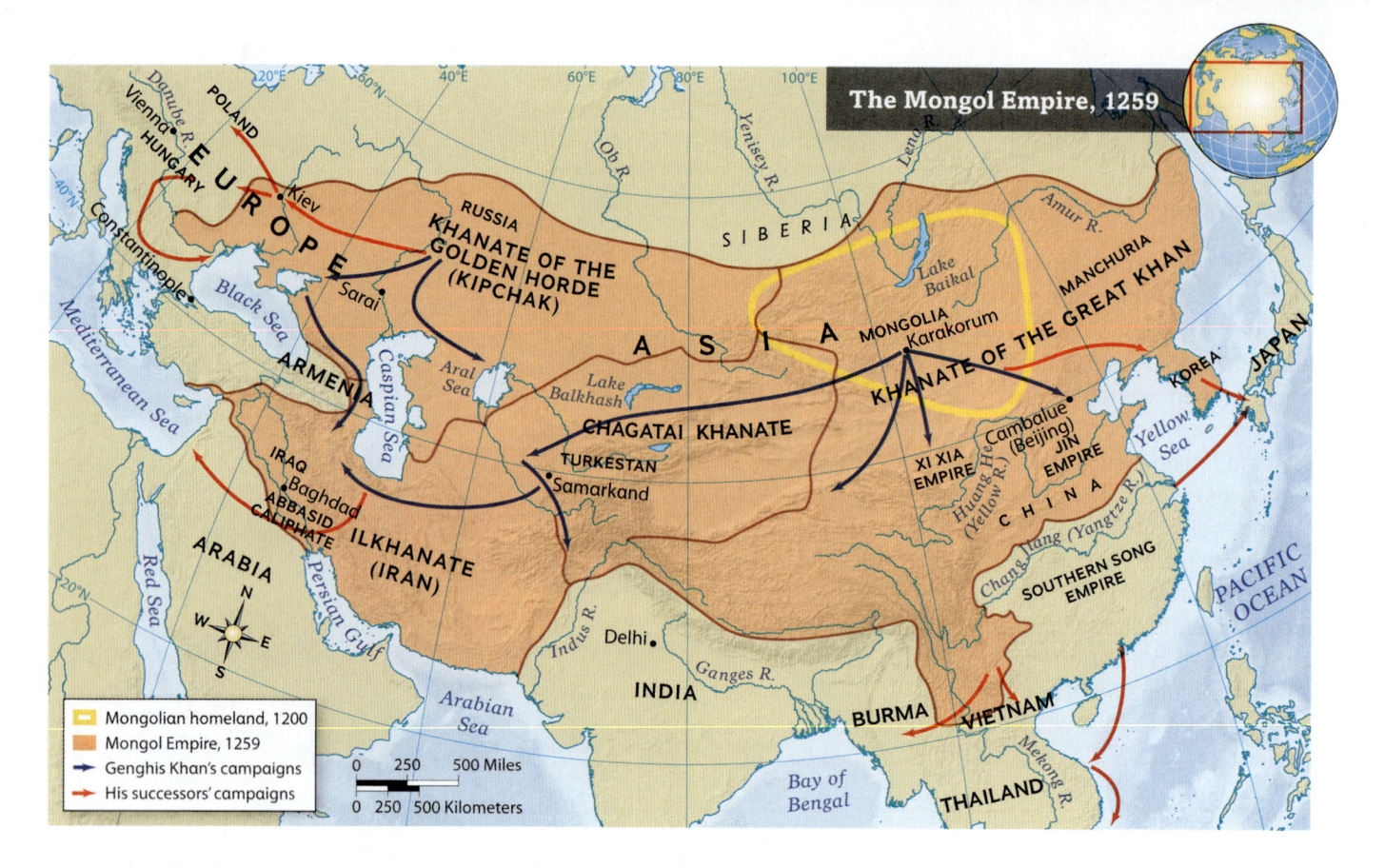

Map legend:
- Mongolian homeland, 1200
- Mongol Empire, 1259
- Genghis Khan's campaigns
- His successors' campaigns

horses with their legs, leaving their arms free to fire wave after wave of arrows at their foes. Genghis Khan also devised brilliant tactics to outwit the opposition. One of his favorites was to pretend to withdraw his troops. When the opposing army pursued them, other Mongol units would suddenly appear and overwhelm the army. And, of course, the Mongols depended on their horses. A Mongol soldier traveled with three or four horses so that each animal could get a break from carrying the rider—and the warrior could keep moving.

The Jin dynasty in China had fortified the Great Wall against Mongol attack, but it made no difference. After taking the Jin capital in 1215, Genghis Khan turned west. In 1218, he began his conquest of Central Asia and seized lands as far west as the Caspian Sea. Meanwhile, he sent other warriors into southern Russia where they defeated the Kipchaks, a group of nomadic people. Soon after, Genghis Khan returned to invade northwestern China. While on campaign there, Genghis Khan died in 1227. The exact cause of his death is a mystery.

THE GREAT KHAN

Before his death, Genghis Khan divided his empire into four **khanates**, or areas ruled by khans—one for each of his sons. But he intended the empire to remain a single entity with a single leader. In 1229, Genghis Khan's third son, **Ogodei** (AH-gah-day), took the title Great Khan and became the ruler of the Mongol Empire.

Ogodei, along with his brothers, had joined his father in battle and commanded troops during the invasions across Central Asia.

Following in his father's footsteps, Ogodei began to expand the empire. He launched a series of simultaneous campaigns in Asia and Europe. In 1234, the Mongol armies consolidated Genghis Khan's victories in China and overthrew the Jin dynasty. That same year, the Mongols occupied the northern part of Korea. Ogodei also sent soldiers to Iran, Iraq, and Russia where they sacked Kiev, the Russian capital, in 1240. Then in 1241, they marched through Hungary, defeated mounted European knights in battle in Poland, and crossed the Danube River heading for the city of Vienna. It seemed that western Europe would fall to the Mongols as well, but suddenly the Mongol armies retreated. The Europeans did not know why, but it was because of the death of Ogodei. Mongol custom dictated that they return to Karakorum, their capital, to choose a new leader. They never returned.

After the overthrow of the Jin dynasty, Ogodei decided to spare the people and lands of the northern Chinese region from destruction. As a result, Ogodei preserved Chinese culture in north China and benefited from the technologies that had developed there. The Mongols also learned new governmental techniques from the Chinese. In fact, they often profited from the knowledge and skills of those they defeated by bringing

Albert Lin teamed up with other National Geographic Explorers as part of his Valley of the Khans Project. Here, he lays out a grid at an archaeological site in the forests of Mongolia.

NATIONAL GEOGRAPHIC EXPLORER   ALBERT LIN

Searching For Genghis Khan's Tomb

Genghis Khan wanted his burial site to remain a secret, and he got his wish. That didn't stop National Geographic Explorer Albert Lin from trying to find it, though. He began his search for Genghis's tomb in 2009. But since, as Lin says, "Mongolian custom warns that disturbing Genghis Khan's burial site will unleash a curse that could end the world," he figured out how to look for the tomb without using a shovel. Instead, Lin used noninvasive computer-based technologies, such as satellite imagery, ground-penetrating radar, and remote sensors. He also tried crowdsourcing, inviting volunteers to examine satellite images online and tag anything that warranted further investigation. Lin didn't find Genghis Khan's tomb, but the explorer remains undaunted and continues to apply similar approaches in his other undertakings. As he says, "The most exciting thing about science is the unknown—anything is possible."

astronomers, engineers, metallurgists, artisans, and merchants to Karakorum. In addition, the Mongols left many local governments intact and allowed conquered peoples to practice their own religions and customs. Some of the people who demonstrated great loyalty to the empire were even permitted to join the Mongol armies.

Under Ogodei's rule, the Mongol Empire expanded to its greatest extent. After his death, however, the rulers of the khanates struggled for power, and the empire began to fall apart.

HISTORICAL THINKING

1. **READING CHECK** Who were the Mongols?
2. **INTERPRET MAPS** Why do you think the Mongols made Karakorum the capital of their empire?
3. **MAKE PREDICTIONS** What might have happened if Ogodei hadn't died during the Mongol army's invasion of Europe?
4. **DRAW CONCLUSIONS** Why was it wise to allow conquered peoples to keep their local government and practice their religions?

1.2 DOCUMENT-BASED QUESTION
Early Accounts of the Mongols

Barbarians. Plunderers. Ferocious Mongol hordes. These are just some of the terms used to describe the invading Mongol armies. But most of these descriptions were penned by early Arab, Persian, and central Asian historians. Recent scholars have challenged this view. While it's certainly true that the Mongols were often brutal during their conquests—by some accounts, the Mongols killed more than 40 million people—studies now suggest that this violence may have been exaggerated. Perhaps there's another side to their story.

It seems there was some method to the Mongols' madness. When they galloped onto the battlefield, they were ready for action. If the opposing army and local people put up a fight, the Mongols were merciless. They slaughtered everyone in their path and leveled the town. However, if the Mongols were offered no resistance, the people were allowed to live.

Genghis Khan may have encouraged foreigners to fear him. He called himself "the punishment of God" and was said to be pleased when others perceived him as such. Sometimes, when he and his army appeared, the frightened townspeople surrendered immediately. The terror his words and presence inspired saved their lives. The Mongols were a pragmatic, or practical, people. If they laid waste to a town, they'd have to rebuild it. And the destruction would interrupt commerce and trade, which the Mongols valued and depended on.

The Mongols were pragmatic about governing as well. Genghis Khan tried to unite the people in his empire both politically and culturally. He established a set of laws that he enforced equally for all his subjects. And as you've read, the Mongols believed in religious freedom. They usually spared the lives of the religious leaders in the lands they invaded. Artisans often enjoyed favored status as well. Genghis also advocated literacy. The leader had the first Mongol writing system created and had it taught to his people.

In this 14th-century Persian miniature depicting the Battle of Ain Jalut, the Mongols—in black caps—battle the Egyptian army in Palestine. The Mongols lost the 1260 battle, which put an end to their effort to conquer Southwest Asia.

DOCUMENT ONE

Primary Source: Book
from *The Complete History* by Ibn al-Athir, c. 1231

The Arab historian Ibn al-Athir spent much of his life in Mosul, a city in present-day Iraq. His chief work, *The Complete History*, is a history of the world. One of the sections in the work deals with the Mongols. In this excerpt from the book, the historian describes what he calls "the announcement of the death-blow of Islam and the Muslims" delivered by the Mongol army.

CONSTRUCTED RESPONSE What words does Ibn al-Athir use to convey the brutality of the Mongols?

> For some years I continued averse [unwilling] from mentioning this event, deeming it so horrible that I shrank from recording it. . . . [T]his thing involves the description of the greatest catastrophe and the most dire calamity . . . which befell all men generally and the Muslims in particular. . . . For truly those whom they [the Mongols] massacred in a single city exceeded all the children of Israel. Nay, it is unlikely that all mankind will see the like of this calamity, until the world comes to an end and perishes. . . . These Mongols spared none, slaying women and men and children. . . . The hurt was universal; and which passed over the land like clouds driven by the wind.

DOCUMENT TWO

Primary Source: Book
from *The History of the World Conqueror* by Ala-ad-Din Ata-Malik Juvaini, 1256

Persian historian and official Ala-ad-Din Ata-Malik Juvaini served at the Mongol court in Persia. His book, *The History of the World Conqueror*, is considered one of the most complete histories of Genghis Khan and his successors. In the following, Juvaini discusses the empire-wide postal system established by Genghis. Note that a yam is a relay station that appeared every 20 or 30 miles along the system's route where a rider could eat, sleep, or get a fresh horse.

CONSTRUCTED RESPONSE What conclusions can you draw about the Mongol postal system?

> When the extent of their [Mongol] territories became broad and vast, . . . it became essential to ascertain [determine] the activities of their enemies, and it was also necessary to transport goods from the West to the East. . . . Therefore throughout the length and breadth of the land they established yams and made arrangements for the upkeep and expenses of each yam. . . .
> [M]essengers need make no long detour in order to obtain fresh mounts while at the same time the peasantry and the army are not placed in constant inconvenience. . . . Every year the yams are inspected, and whatever is missing or lost has to be replaced by the peasantry.

DOCUMENT THREE

Primary Source: Book
from *Compendium of Chronicles* by Rashid al-Din, c. 1314

Rashid al-Din was a doctor, historian, and chief minister for the Mongol ruler of Iran. His *Compendium of Chronicles* includes the history of the Mongol Empire. In the excerpt below, Rashid al-Din provides his observations of Ogodei, the Great Khan, while the author was a government official.

CONSTRUCTED RESPONSE How does the historian portray Ogodei?

> During the seven years [1235–1241] Ogodei enjoyed life and amused himself. He moved from summer camp to winter camp and vice versa, serene and happy. . . . At every opportunity, he allowed his sublime [inspiring] thoughts to overflow lavishly into the most just and charitable of good deeds, into the eradication [elimination] of injustice and enmity [hatred], into the development of cities and districts, as well as into the construction of various buildings. He never neglected any measure designed to strengthen the framework of peace, and to lay the foundation of prosperity.

SYNTHESIZE & WRITE

1. **REVIEW** Review what you have learned about the Mongols and their conquests.

2. **RECALL** On your own paper, write down the main idea expressed in each document.

3. **CONSTRUCT** Construct a topic sentence that answers this question: How did early historians represent the Mongols?

4. **WRITE** Using evidence from this chapter and the documents, write an informative paragraph that supports your topic sentence in Step 3.

1.3 **MAIN IDEA** After the Mongol Empire split into four khanates, Kublai Khan, the ruler of the Khanate of the Great Khan, brought all of China under his control.

A Fragmenting Empire

Family feuds rarely end well. When Genghis Khan's descendants squabbled over who would be sole ruler of the Mongol Empire, it broke into four dominions. The ruler of one of them would be the greatest khan since Genghis.

The Mongol Empire, 1294

DIVISION OF THE EMPIRE

As you've read, a struggle for power erupted after Ogodei's death in 1241. At last, 10 years later, Mongke, one of Genghis Khan's grandsons, asserted himself as Great Khan. Mongke continued to expand the empire. His armies marched through Southwest Asia where they conquered Iran, Iraq, and Syria. In 1258, the Mongols killed the last Abbasid caliph in Baghdad, bringing an end to the Abbasid Empire. Mongol soldiers also headed east and advanced against China. In 1257, Mongke himself took charge of the army in China. Two years later, however, he died.

Mongke had been a relatively kind and popular ruler. He brought economic stability to the empire and instituted measures that protected ordinary civilians. He was also the last of the Great Khans to hold the enormous empire together. Mongke's brothers fought for control, and **Kublai Khan** (KOO-bluh KAHN) emerged the victor. In 1260, he declared himself the Great Khan. By that time, the Mongol Empire had fractured into four khanates: the Golden Horde, or Kipchak Khanate; the Chagatai Khanate; the Ilkhanate; and the Khanate of the Great Khan.

The Golden Horde stretched from Hungary to the steppes of Siberia and included the Russian principalities of Kiev and Moscow. Chagatai Khan, a son of Genghis Khan, ruled the central Asian khanate that bore his name and was succeeded by his grandson.

332 CHAPTER 12

The Ilkhanate, centered in Iran and including the former Abbasid capital of Baghdad, was less successful. Its economy was impoverished by the high taxes imposed by its Mongol rulers.

KUBLAI KHAN

Kublai Khan seized control of the Khanate of the Great Khan, which included Mongolia, Korea, Tibet, and northern China. But he was determined to add to his empire by conquering all of southern China. Remember reading about China's Song dynasty? The leaders of the dynasty fought off Kublai's forces during much of the 1270s but finally surrendered in 1279. As a result, Kublai Khan became ruler of all China, the first to unite the lands in more than 300 years. He was also the first foreigner to rule the entire country. As China's new emperor, Kublai moved his capital to the site of modern Beijing and founded a new dynasty called Yuan (YOO-AHN). He would try to further extend his empire to Japan and, later, into Southeast Asia, but these attempts failed.

Under the Yuan dynasty, the Chinese government continued much as before, with a strong central state built around a bureaucracy. But each Chinese official had to report to a Mongol or other Central Asian superior. Because the number of Chinese in the empire far exceeded the number of Mongols, Kublai feared putting too much power in their hands. For the most part, the Mongols lived apart from the Chinese.

Many Chinese hated Mongol rule and resented being subjects of a "barbarian" king from Central Asia. Kublai forced Chinese peasant farmers to work on his extravagant building projects, particularly in his capital. Beijing became a wealthy city filled with magnificent palaces and gardens—all for the enjoyment of rich foreigners. And many of the farmers were forced off their land when they couldn't pay their taxes. Aware of Chinese unrest and fearful of rebellion, the Yuan dynasty enforced laws that restricted the activities of the local people.

This painting from a French illustrated manuscript from around 1400 shows the departure of Marco Polo and his father and uncle from Venice in 1271. In the painting, Polo, dressed in a light pink robe and portrayed as an older man, speaks to a group of dignitaries before he boards the boat that will take him to the court of Kublai Khan.

Still, Kublai Khan was an effective leader. He extended the Grand Canal initially built during the Qin dynasty to Beijing and built roads along its banks. Grains and other goods moved from the south of China to the north on these land and water routes. Above all, Kublai encouraged foreign trade. Caravan routes across Central Asia—including the Silk Roads—were largely safe, thanks to the **Pax Mongolica**, or Mongol peace. This period of peace, which continued from the mid-1200s to the mid-1300s, was due to the law and order imposed by the Mongols across Eurasia.

Kublai also invited foreign merchants to visit China. The most famous of these was the Venetian trader **Marco Polo**, who traveled as a teenager with his father and uncle along the Silk Roads and arrived at Kublai Khan's court around 1275. Polo came to be employed by Kublai Khan and was sent on government missions throughout China and beyond. After serving the emperor for nearly 20 years, Polo returned home greatly impressed with Kublai Khan's wealth and power.

HISTORICAL THINKING

1. **READING CHECK** What happened after Mongke's death?

2. **ANALYZE CAUSE AND EFFECT** Why did the Chinese feel like second-class citizens under Kublai Khan's rule?

3. **INTERPRET MAPS** Why was it important to the Mongols to make sure the routes of the Silk Roads were safe?

1.4 NATIONAL GEOGRAPHIC EXPLORER AND TRAVELER

Out of Eden:
Ten Million Steps

"We walk on. At dawn we inch steadily toward our own blue shadows that stretch, bending, far behind us: shades that slip backwards over the desert horizon. We will meet them one day." –Paul Salopek

The stone ruins of the Beleuli caravanserai Salopek mentions in his journal stand on an Uzbek steppe that was once the scene of a busy marketplace.

In Chapter 1, you read about Paul Salopek's long walk to retrace the path of human migration from Ethiopia to the southernmost tip of South America. He began his trek in January 2013. Three and a half years later, Salopek had traveled 3,600 of the planned 21,000 miles. He found himself on the Ustyurt Plateau of Uzbekistan, following the path of the Silk Roads, the historic trade routes between East Asia and the Mediterranean. There, in land once conquered by Genghis Khan, Salopek visited the ruins of one of many ancient travelers' inns that dotted the landscape and noted the irony of the fact that the ruthless Mongols had built such peaceful, practical rest stops.

PRIMARY SOURCE

JULY 2016—UZBEKISTAN: DISCOVERING A MEDIEVAL MOON BASE IN THE HEART OF CENTRAL ASIA

We are moving slowly through the world.

The sun melts a hole in the sky: white-hot as the focused beam of a magnifying glass. The steppe is sweltering. Cloudless. Windless. We create our own paltry wind by walking.

There are three of us. Aziz Khalmuradov, my Uzbek guide, limps behind on blister-broke feet. The donkey wrangler, Jailkhan Bekniyazov, is dizzy with some mysterious ailment—sunstroke, or perhaps extreme homesickness. We slog eastward 15 or 20 miles a day across the burning steppe. . . . The planet creaks underfoot, carrying us forever toward sunrise. Toward Khiva—the old mud-walled khanate. Toward the unimaginable cold of Siberia. Toward Beleuli.

Beleuli: a stone ruin. A Silk Road caravanserai [inn for travelers] lost on the grasslands of Karakalpakstan. Built in late 13th century. A pioneering artifact of globalization. A work of art. A cautionary tale.

"The construction was clever," Shamil Amirov, an archaeologist with the Karakalpak branch of the Academy of Sciences of Uzbekistan, tells me. "Beleuli was extremely remote. So they built it for self-sufficiency."

The outpost's defensive walls were turreted to protect treasure-laden caravans against local nomad attacks. To catch the stray breezes, passing merchants occupied second-floor apartments above a grand central square. (The ground-level rooms served as stables for camels, horses, donkeys—the cargo animals.) There were market stalls, craftsmen's workshops, baths, soldiers' barracks. Shipments of gold, spices, silks, medicines, carpets, porcelain, and other luxury goods packed the warehouses. At the center of Beleuli's courtyard: a public drinking reservoir the size of a hotel swimming pool.

Beleuli was a medieval moon base.

Wheat was sown nearby on the banks of seasonal ponds. These crops supplied the caravanserai's bakery and fed its cattle herd. Most impressive of all, a system of stone-domed cisterns, called sardobas, stored scarce rainwater. This water was collected—via a complex network of underground brick gutters—from erratic steppe thunderstorms. While Beleuli's traders sipped clean water from faucets, London's 40,000 unwashed citizens waded through ankle-deep slops.

Who conceived Beleuli?

The answer is improbable: the Mongols. Warrior-nomads. The supposed destroyers of civilizations, the horsemen of apocalypse, the urbanite's nightmare, the human locusts.

Having destroyed the powerful Central Asian trading empire of Khorezm in 1221, Genghis Khan's hordes began to impose their own taxes on the commerce bumping through the region by camelback from India, China, and Europe. Pillage and mass slaughter were dandy. But business was business. To promote this lucrative traffic, the Mongol overlords ordered a string of travelers' inns, spaced a day's camel ride apart, to be built across the Ustyurt Plateau, an immense wilderness of salt flats and prickly grasses that isolated the rich Central Asian cities of the Oxus River from the mercantile hub of the Caspian Sea. (Today the Ustyurt Plateau, straddling Uzbekistan and Kazakhstan, is more desolate than ever.) In effect, the Mongols bankrolled a primordial interstate highway system, complete with fortified truck stops.

HISTORICAL THINKING

READING CHECK Why does Salopek express surprise that the caravanserai was conceived and built by the Mongols?

Crossroads Revival

More a network than a single path, the Silk Roads emerged over centuries of interaction and trade. Routes shifted as empires rose and fell; traffic declined after the rise of maritime trade. Regional powers now want to revive these historic commercial lifelines to better connect Asia with Europe and beyond.

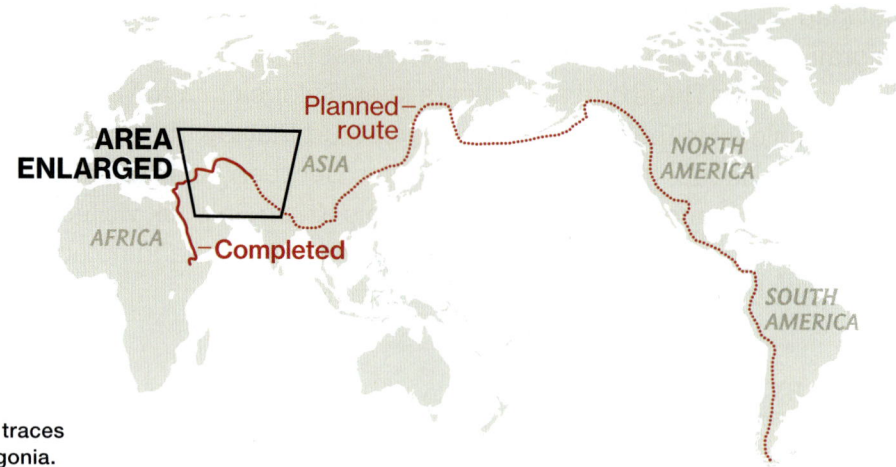

Paul Salopek's 21,000-mile journey on foot traces human migrations from East Africa to Patagonia.

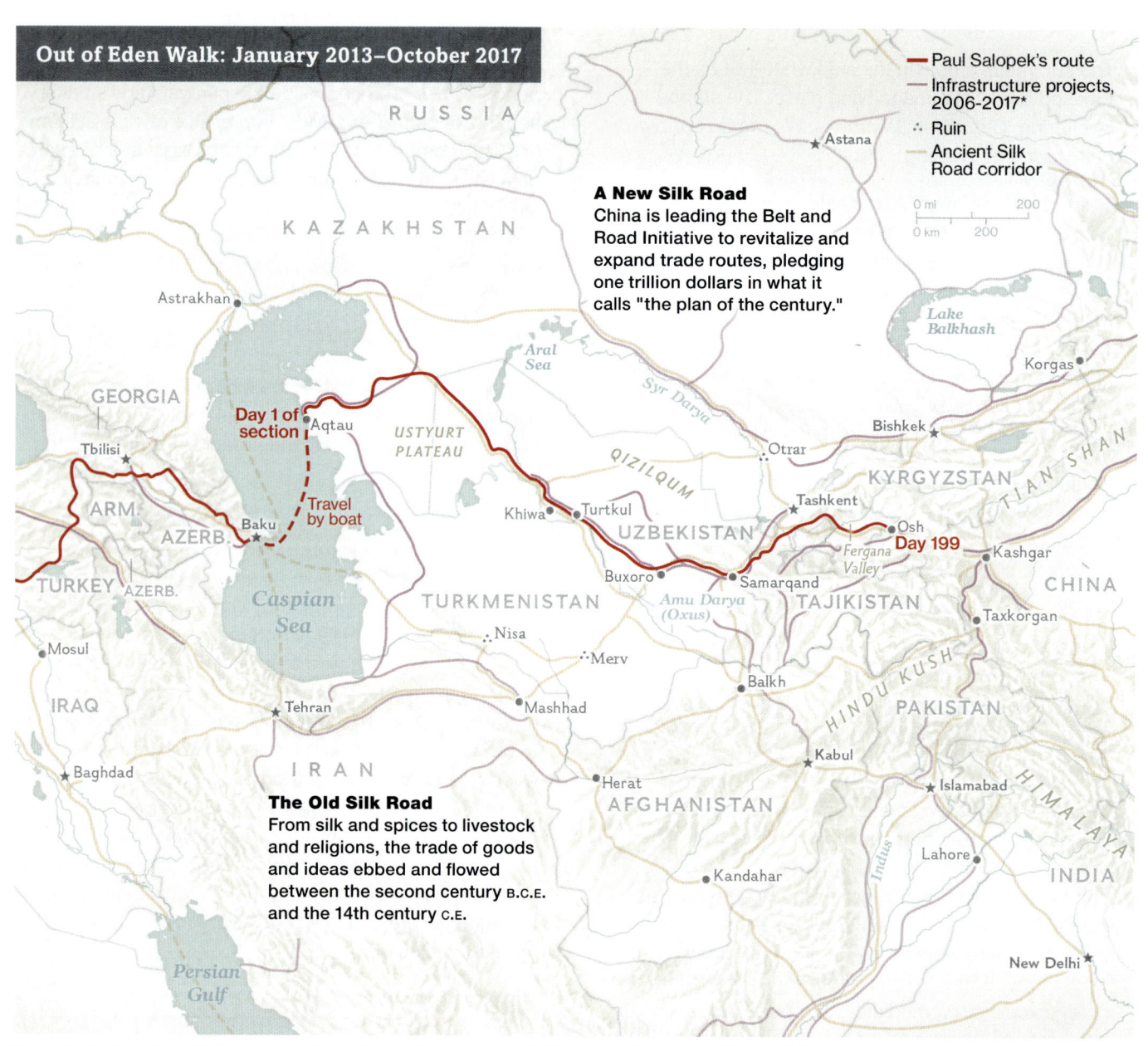

Out of Eden Walk: January 2013–October 2017

A New Silk Road
China is leading the Belt and Road Initiative to revitalize and expand trade routes, pledging one trillion dollars in what it calls "the plan of the century."

The Old Silk Road
From silk and spices to livestock and religions, the trade of goods and ideas ebbed and flowed between the second century B.C.E. and the 14th century C.E.

*Includes belt and road initiative as well as other projects. Lauren C. Tierney and Ryan T. Williams, NGM Staff.
SOURCES: Patrick Wellever, Reconnecting Asia Project, Center for Strategic and International Studies

Salopek's original plan was to complete his 21,000-mile journey in seven years. But three years into the odyssey, it was clear that he would need more time. The weather, the terrain, and the politics of a given region had slowed his pace. Salopek revised his plans, expecting the entire journey to take about a decade. But the delays did not dampen Salopek's spirits. In fact, for this slow journalism project, the deliberate pace is the point.

> **PRIMARY SOURCE**
>
> ### APRIL 2016—WHAT I'M LEARNING FROM WALKING 21,000 MILES AROUND THE WORLD
>
> Naturally, since setting out from the Horn of Africa in 2013, walking has made my legs and heart stronger. But more important, it's limbered up my mind. Spanning nations, continents, and time zones on foot—day after day, month after month—has altered the way I experience life on the planet.
>
> I've learned quickly, for instance, that the poorest parts of the globe are the most congenial to foot travel. In Ethiopia, where few people own cars, everybody walks. Even the smallest child could guide me through complex landscapes still netted by human trails. In more affluent and motorized countries, by contrast, people lose connection not only with their environment but with the shape of the world itself. Cars annihilate time and distance. Locked inside bubbles of metal and glass, confined to narrow strips of asphalt, we become drugged with speed. . . . On foot in car-crazy Saudi Arabia, I discovered the pointlessness of asking directions. . . .
>
> Walking across the Earth, I have relearned the old ceremony of departures and arrivals. (Making and striking campsites, packing and unpacking rucksacks, an antique and comforting ritual.) I have absorbed landscapes through my taste buds, by gleaning farmers' harvests. And I have reconnected with fellow human beings in ways I could never conceive as a reporter crisscrossing maps by jet and car. Out walking, I constantly meet people. I cannot ignore them or drive by them. I greet them. I chat with strangers five, ten, twenty times a day. I am engaged in a meandering, three-mile-an-hour conversation that spans two hemispheres. In this way walking builds a home everywhere.
>
> ### HISTORICAL THINKING
>
> **READING CHECK** According to Salopek, how has walking enhanced his experience as he travels across the world?

One step at a time, Paul Salopek is exploring lands that early humans, Silk Road traders, and Central Asian armies once traveled. In this 2016 photo, Salopek walks along the Caspian Sea in Kazakhstan with his traveling companion—a cargo pony named Alex Moen.

2.1 | **MAIN IDEA** The Mongol Empire fell and left a lasting impact on Asia and Europe.

The Impact of the Mongols

All things—both good and bad—must come to an end. This old adage certainly seems to apply to great empires. The Mongol Empire was ending, but its impact would resound throughout much of the world.

END OF THE EMPIRE

Kublai Khan's treatment of the Chinese led to hostility among the people. Some formed secret societies and plotted rebellion. But Kublai was a strong leader who knew how to control his kingdom. After his death in 1294, however, the Yuan dynasty gradually declined. Seven emperors ruled China over the next 40 years, but none of them possessed Kublai's leadership skills.

During the 1360s, rebellions broke out in China, and Zhu Yuanzhang (JOO YOO-AHN-JAHNG), the son of a peasant, became the rebels' leader. In 1368, they drove the Mongols out of China, bringing the Yuan dynasty to an end. Zhu declared a new dynasty, the Ming, or "brilliant," dynasty, and chose for himself the title **Hongwu** (HUNG-WOO), which roughly translates as "vastly martial." You'll learn more about the Ming dynasty in the next lesson.

By the time the Yuan dynasty collapsed, most of the other khanates had disintegrated as well. In the 1330s, the government of the Ilkhanate fell apart. The Chagatai khans ruled Central Asia until the 1370s when the Turkish conqueror Timur—also known as **Timur** the Lame—proclaimed himself ruler of the western part of the khanate. After his conquest, khans with no real power occupied the throne. The khans who ruled the Golden Horde in Russia stayed in power the longest. They ruled Russia for 250 years. Russian leader **Ivan III** finally led Russia to independence from Mongol rule in 1480. The great Mongol Empire had come to a close.

CRITICAL VIEWING Markets still thrive in some of the cities and towns along the Silk Roads. The women in this photo are selling food at a market in Samarkand, Uzbekistan. What other traditions are evident in the photo?

MONGOLIAN INFLUENCE

The Mongol Empire was gone but not forgotten. Its influence was felt long after the Mongols retreated to the steppes of Central Asia. Perhaps the Mongols' greatest legacy was linking Europe and Asia through trade. Merchants from Europe, China, Southwest Asia, and India traveled the Silk Roads and traded ideas as well as goods. Although many Mongols practiced shamanism, a worship of nature spirits, they were open to the religious beliefs of others. Different religions gained followers along the routes. Islam became the dominant religion of people along the Silk Roads and was adopted by Mongols in several of the khanates. Unfortunately, disease was sometimes carried along the trade routes. Some scholars believe the terrible plague that devastated western Asia, North Africa, and Europe in the 1300s may have arrived in lands along the Mediterranean Sea, in part, via the Silk Roads.

Contacts between Europe and Asia also spread new ideas in science. Paper production and gunpowder, both Chinese innovations, reached Europe during this period. The Chinese adopted Islamic medical advances in treating wounds, while Indian scientists learned to question the idea of a geocentric, or Earth-centered, universe from Muslim astronomers.

Cross-cultural exchanges took place in the arts. Muslim artists were influenced by artistic techniques from China and India. Human figures, featured in both countries' artistic works but traditionally forbidden in Islamic art, began to appear in Muslim creations, particularly Persian miniatures. In addition, influenced by Indian narrative art, murals in mosques sometimes depicted stories from sacred Islamic texts. In Europe, artists began using the Chinese dragon in their works. The Mongols themselves had a great impact on the arts. Chinese painting, ceramics, and literature flourished under the rule of Kublai Khan. And Ogodei brought artists and architects to build and decorate his capital at Karakorum. Russian architecture was influenced by Central Asian styles, though after the rule of the Golden Horde, Russian leaders remained suspicious of the nomadic societies to their south and east.

The network of roads built by the Mongols across Eurasia also brought the East and West into contact. Craftsmen, scientists, engineers, and merchants from Europe could travel as far as China for the first time.

This blue-glazed Persian jar was probably bartered on the Silk Roads around 1280.

And the postal system established by Genghis Khan functioned as the central nervous system of the huge empire. The Mongols used the postal relay stations to provide visiting **envoys**, or diplomatic representatives, with guides, guards, food, and shelter.

During Mongol rule, European merchants carried Asian goods to their home markets where demand for these items, especially silk, quickly rose. But traveling over land to obtain the products took a lot of time. Eventually, Europeans would begin to search for a sea route to China. This search, in part, led to the European Age of Exploration in the 1400s, which you will read about later. In their quest for the sea route, Europeans were aided by the descriptions of places and distances in Marco Polo's book. Some of the information was used to create maps of the East. And the Italian explorer Christopher Columbus is said to have taken Polo's writings with him when he set off on the voyages that led him to the Americas.

HISTORICAL THINKING

1. **READING CHECK** How did the Yuan dynasty fall?

2. **ANALYZE CAUSE AND EFFECT** How do you think Islam spread along the Silk Roads?

3. **SYNTHESIZE** In what way are the Mongols, Marco Polo, and later European exploration connected?

2.2

MAIN IDEA The Ming dynasty restored Chinese rule and initiated a period of political and cultural power and influence.

The Ming Dynasty

Sometimes, unlikely leaders emerge during times of crisis. Hongwu—a peasant and, for a time, a monk—had led China's rebellion and seized power. Now he was determined to restore Chinese traditions and Chinese government.

RETURN TO CHINESE RULE

Hongwu set out to restore China to greatness, but he proved to be a **despotic**, or tyrannical, ruler. After Hongwu's prime minister plotted to overthrow him, the emperor had the minister executed and abolished the office. Hongwu engaged a number of "grand secretaries" to handle routine administrative matters, but the emperor exercised direct control over his empire.

Because Hongwu had been born a poor peasant himself, he protected the interests of farmers. He rebuilt China's agricultural system and supported the growth of manufacturing. He also cut government spending and punished corruption within his administration. Although Hongwu distrusted scholars, he based his rule on the principles of the Tang and Song dynasties and restored Confucian values. He believed that an efficient government depended on a bureaucracy filled with

Powerful dragons were frequently depicted on works of art made during the reign of the Ming emperor Yongle. This box, made to hold a Buddhist scripture, was created for use at court.

Confucian scholars. The emperor established schools across China to train students to take the civil service examination and prepare for government service. But to prevent the scholar-officials from gaining too much power, Hongwu enforced strict rules and severely punished them for the slightest infraction.

Hongwu expanded his empire to include part of Manchuria, located in present-day northeastern China. He also demanded tribute from states whose foreign affairs he controlled, including Korea. The emperor sent his ambassadors to the city of Samarkand in Central Asia to demand tribute, but they were imprisoned by Timur who, as you may recall, ruled the western part of the Chagatai Khanate at that time. Timur was actually planning to invade China itself, but the great conqueror died in 1405, and the mission was canceled.

After Hongwu's own death in 1398, his son Zhu Di (JOO DEE) became the next ruler of Ming China. Zhu Di came to power in 1403 and took the name **Yongle** (YUNG LOH), meaning "perpetual happiness." Like his father, Yongle was a suspicious, ruthless, and tyrannical ruler. He established a sort of secret service agency to search out and report to him any treasonous activity in the empire. And although Yongle had little interest in high culture, the emperor sponsored the publication of a huge body of Chinese literature that filled more than 11,000 volumes called *The Great Canon of the Yongle Era*.

THE FORBIDDEN CITY

Soon after Yongle became emperor, he authorized the transfer of the imperial capital from Nanjing to Beijing. As the capital during the Yuan dynasty, Beijing was associated with "barbarian" rulers, but it placed Yongle near his supporters. The location also allowed him to keep an eye on the northern defenses. And Beijing was well protected: it was surrounded by 14 miles of 40-foot walls.

In the heart of the new capital, Yongle commissioned the construction of the Imperial Palace, a huge complex of buildings that would be the center of imperial power and government for the next 500 years. The Imperial Palace was also known as the **Forbidden City** because few people were allowed to enter it and then only with the emperor's permission.

An estimated one million workers labored for almost 15 years to complete the complex, which contained hundreds of buildings. Some of the buildings were residences for the imperial family and their more than 100,000 servants. For defense purposes, the Imperial Palace was surrounded by a wall more than 30 feet high and a moat about 170 feet wide.

The rectangular, symmetrical, and compass-aligned design of the Forbidden City was said to be in perfect harmony with the world. Even the colors used in the complex had symbolic meanings. For example, yellow, which the Chinese believed represented the earth, the producer of all life, was used in the glaze for roof tiles. And red, a color the Chinese associated with power, happiness, wealth, and honor, appears throughout the complex. Dragons were a symbol of the emperor's **omnipotence**, or unlimited power. Artists carved a coiled dragon in the ceiling of the Hall of Supreme Harmony, the Forbidden City's tallest building. The building also housed the emperor's golden Dragon Throne.

While the Imperial Palace was being built, Yongle oversaw another construction project. You probably remember that Kublai Khan had extended the Grand Canal. To make the transport of grain to Beijing even more efficient, Yongle extended the Grand Canal even farther and deepened and widened it. In the process, his engineers built a dam to divert water from a river to the Grand Canal and dug reservoirs to control water levels.

THE VOYAGES OF ZHENG HE

Like Hongwu, Yongle sent ambassadors to receive tribute from leaders in Southeast Asia and Central Asia and, for a time, Japan. However, Yongle also wanted to expand his empire. In 1406, his forces occupied the southeast Asian state of Dai Viet, which you read about earlier. The following year, Yongle claimed Dai Viet as a province. Resistance to the Chinese soon erupted and continued for years. The Ming dynasty finally left Dai Viet in 1428 and abandoned its direct rule there.

As you have read, the Indian Ocean had long been a zone of interaction, with people and commodities moving between Africa, Arabia, Iran, India, and Southeast Asia. Now the Yongle emperor decided to follow those routes on a grand tribute-seeking mission. For about 300 years, China's navy had been expanding, and the Ming dynasty had overseen technological advances in shipbuilding. The accuracy of Chinese navigation was also the best in the world. Yongle wanted to display his naval power, so in 1405, he ordered the first in a series of seven voyages to Asia and Africa. He selected a young Chinese Muslim called **Zheng He** (JUNG HUH) to command the expeditions.

China had developed an extensive sea trade to obtain spices and other items, but the expeditions were about more than exploration and trade. Zheng He's main mission was to glorify Yongle by asserting Chinese control over trade routes and weaker countries. On

Zheng He's Voyages, 1405–1433

This map shows the main and subsidiary, or secondary, routes of Zheng He's seven expeditions. Note that the map labels include place names from the 1400s as well as present-day names.

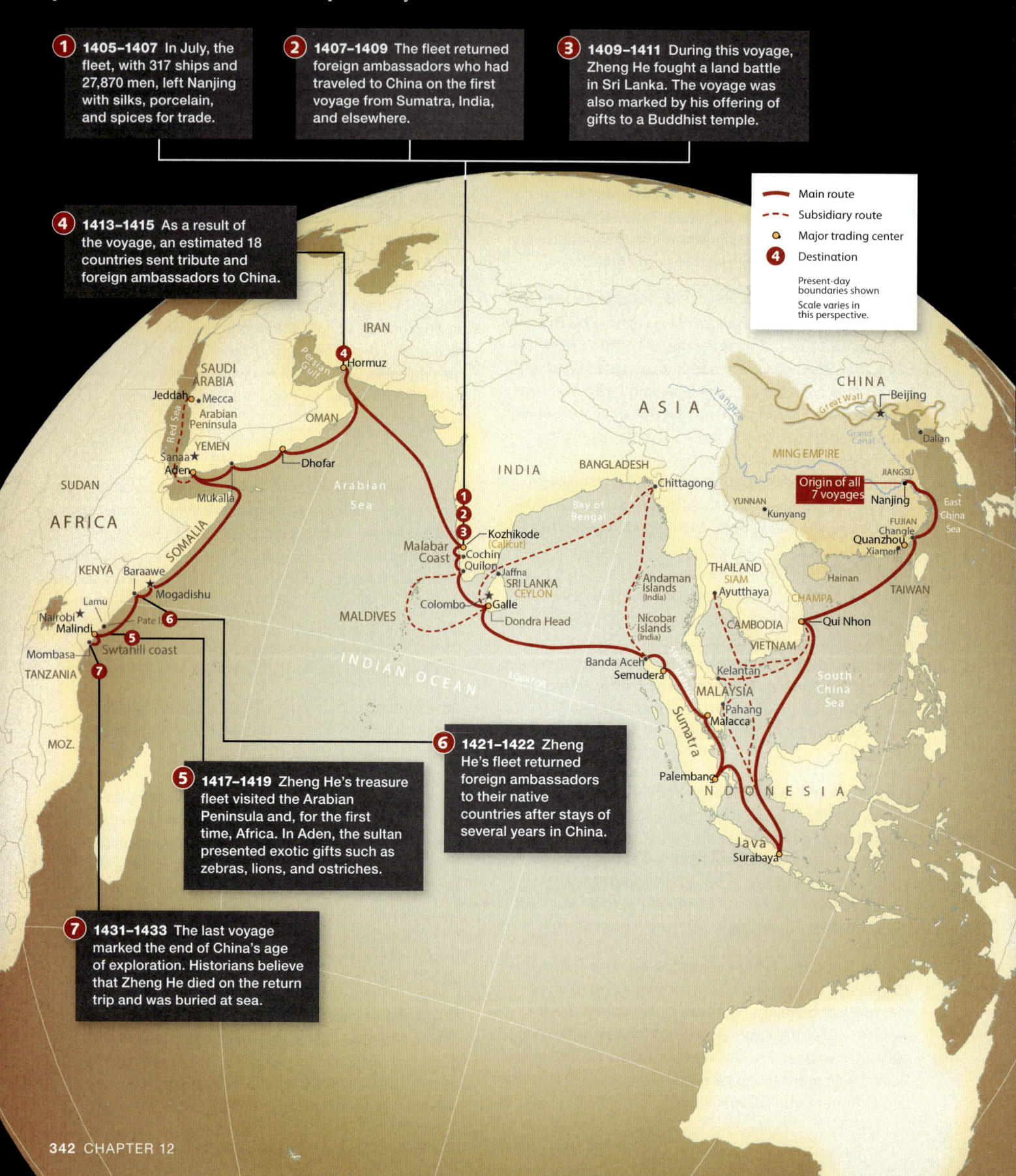

1 **1405–1407** In July, the fleet, with 317 ships and 27,870 men, left Nanjing with silks, porcelain, and spices for trade.

2 **1407–1409** The fleet returned foreign ambassadors who had traveled to China on the first voyage from Sumatra, India, and elsewhere.

3 **1409–1411** During this voyage, Zheng He fought a land battle in Sri Lanka. The voyage was also marked by his offering of gifts to a Buddhist temple.

4 **1413–1415** As a result of the voyage, an estimated 18 countries sent tribute and foreign ambassadors to China.

5 **1417–1419** Zheng He's treasure fleet visited the Arabian Peninsula and, for the first time, Africa. In Aden, the sultan presented exotic gifts such as zebras, lions, and ostriches.

6 **1421–1422** Zheng He's fleet returned foreign ambassadors to their native countries after stays of several years in China.

7 **1431–1433** The last voyage marked the end of China's age of exploration. Historians believe that Zheng He died on the return trip and was buried at sea.

Legend:
- Main route
- Subsidiary route
- Major trading center
- **4** Destination

Present-day boundaries shown. Scale varies in this perspective.

342 CHAPTER 12

his first expedition, Zheng He led a fleet of more than 60 ships manned by more than 27,000 sailors. His expeditions included treasure ships to carry tribute and trade items back to China. At more than 400 feet long and 160 feet wide, the treasure ships were far bigger than any other ships at that time.

For three decades, Zheng He sailed some 40,000 miles around Southeast Asia, India, Southwest Asia, and East Africa. He returned with tribute that included such exotic items as gold, gems, rare spices, giraffes, and zebras. Although the expeditions mainly served to fuel Yongle's vanity, they also helped expand China's connections to other Asian and African societies. On his seventh and final journey, Zheng He left the main fleet for a personal journey. Following the example of his grandfather and his father, he went to Arabia to visit the holy sites of Mecca and Medina. As a Muslim, it was his duty to perform the hajj pilgrimage.

A CONSERVATIVE TURN

Zheng He died during his seventh voyage in 1433. Two years later, a new emperor, Zhengtong (JUNG-TUNG), took power and stopped all future voyages. Zhengtong claimed the expeditions were too expensive. He also believed that the Chinese were the most civilized people on Earth and had nothing to learn from foreigners. After Yongle, conservative Ming emperors tried to restore what they saw as the glories of the imperial Chinese tradition in governance and the arts. As part of that conservative turn, they gave up on the sea voyages, returning to the long imperial tradition of focusing on defense of the interior border with Central Asia.

To prevent another invasion of nomadic horsemen, Ming rulers strengthened the Great Wall. They extended the stone wall to a length of about 5,500 miles and built 25,000 watchtowers along it. Most of the Great Wall that stands today was constructed during the Ming dynasty.

Many Ming artists also took a conservative approach by focusing on the revival of traditional artistic styles. Many Chinese artists carved small decorative items out of wood and jade and produced beautiful porcelain vases. Ming dynasty artists particularly excelled in painting and pottery. The paintings reflected the artists' personal styles, and ceramics combined new developments with old traditions. One new technique involved the use of a blue overglaze, which was applied on top of an already glazed piece and is sometimes called "blue and white." This style was imitated in Vietnam, Japan, and, around the 17th century, in Europe, where all fine porcelain became known as "china."

Yongle had strengthened and stabilized China's economy when he rose to power, and it continued to be robust for many years. Even in the late 1500s, the magnificence, wealth, and power of the Ming impressed foreign visitors. But by 1600, the old cycle of imperial decline had begun. The court became corrupt, pirates raided the coasts, bandits came down from the mountains, and people lived in greater poverty and insecurity. It seemed the Ming dynasty was losing the Mandate of Heaven.

A EUROPEAN IN MING CHINA The Italian missionary Matteo Ricci arrived in China in 1582, having sailed around Africa and stopping for several years in India. His goal was to convert the Chinese to Christianity, and he hoped to do it from the top down by convincing elite scholar-officials that his faith was compatible with Confucianism. Ricci learned Chinese and wrote a book showing how one could convert to Roman Catholicism and remain a good Confucian. He was an accomplished mathematician and cartographer, but what Ming officials most appreciated was Ricci's ability to memorize a long list of information and then flawlessly repeat it—even backwards! That was a very useful talent in a society where officials had to pass difficult examinations to move up the ranks. For his part, Ricci noted with approval that, in Ming China, the highest status went to men of learning (like himself) rather than, as in Europe, to military leaders: "[T]he entire kingdom is administered by ... Philosophers. The responsibility for orderly management of the entire realm is wholly and completely committed to their charge and care...." In the end, Matteo Ricci made only a few converts before he died in China in 1610.

HISTORICAL THINKING

1. **READING CHECK** How did Hongwu establish an efficient government?

2. **MAKE INFERENCES** Why do you think Yongle built the Imperial Palace?

3. **INTERPRET MAPS** What conclusion can you draw from the fact that the final destination of Zheng He's first three expeditions was India?

4. **MAKE PREDICTIONS** What might have happened if China had not ended its maritime expeditions?

3.1

MAIN IDEA The Ottoman Turks were Central Asian nomads who gave rise to a dynasty and, later, a mighty empire.

The Rise of the Ottomans

When you hear about nomads from Central Asia seeking to forge an empire, you probably think of the Mongols. But in the 14th century, the nomads were Turks, and they were on a religious mission.

TURKISH ORIGINS

In the 10th century, Turkish peoples from central Eurasia began migrating to Southwest Asia. Many of these nomadic groups had converted to Islam. One of the Islamic groups, the Seljuks, grew in number and power and captured Baghdad from the Persians in 1055. The Seljuks expanded across much of Southwest Asia and, in 1071, marched on the Byzantine Empire. By the early 12th century, the Seljuks occupied most of Anatolia.

By the late 1100s, however, the Seljuk empire had weakened. When the Mongols stormed across Asia in the early 1200s, the invading armies reached Anatolia and defeated the Seljuks. A small Seljuk kingdom continued as a Mongol province for a time, but the dynasty finally died out in 1293. Around that time, as you may remember, the Mongol Empire was also beginning to decline, and small Muslim-ruled states emerged in northwestern Anatolia.

A large number of Turks inhabited Anatolia. Many of these Anatolian Turks saw themselves as **ghazis** (GAH-zees), or warriors for Islam. The ghazis were led by a commander, or emir, and were bound by a strict Islamic code of conduct. Between 1300 and 1326, a powerful ghazi named Osman developed the small Turkish state that his father had founded along the frontier of the Byzantine Empire. **Osman** became the leader of the Ottoman Turks. *Ottoman* comes from the Arabic form of his name—Uthman—and would be the name of his dynasty and the empire that would eventually arise.

The Ottoman Empire, 1481

- Ottoman Turks, 1300
- Acquisitions, 1300–1359
- Acquisitions, 1359–1451
- Acquisitions, 1451–1481

344 CHAPTER 12

CRITICAL VIEWING After his defeat at the Battle of Ankara, Sultan Bayezid is taken prisoner and brought before Timur in this 16th-century miniature painting from India. What details in the painting convey Bayezid's defeat and Timur's triumph?

OTTOMAN EXPANSION

The Ottomans set out to conquer poorly defended areas along the Byzantine frontier. Osman united nomadic tribes and city-dwelling Muslims who wanted to expand the amount of territory under Islamic rule. After the death of Osman in 1326, his son, Orhan, began hiring Christian mercenaries to join the fight and lessen Ottoman dependence on the nomads. Orhan captured important towns in northwestern Anatolia and declared himself **sultan**, meaning "strength" or "one with power."

Throughout the 1300s, the Ottomans took over territories in western Anatolia and southeastern Europe. In 1361, the Ottomans captured Adrianople (ah-dree-uh-NOH-puhl), the second most important city in the Byzantine Empire after Constantinople, and made it their capital. They also defeated other Turkish states and gained eastern Anatolia. As the Ottomans established their new empire, their wise treatment of those they conquered helped gain peoples' trust. The Ottomans appointed local officials to govern the territories and improved the lives of the peasants. Most Muslims were required to fight in Ottoman armies, but non-Muslims were not. In exchange for this exemption, however, they had to pay a tax.

You have read about Timur, who had earlier taken over the Chagatai khanate from the Mongols. Now he turned west and, in 1402, briefly halted further Ottoman expansion. The Ottomans were preparing to invade Constantinople when they learned that Timur was advancing on Anatolia. The two armies clashed at the Battle of Ankara in central Anatolia, and the Ottomans were soundly defeated. Timur captured Sultan Bayezid (BAY-uh-zihd), who commanded the Ottoman army. According to legend, Timur kept Bayezid in a golden cage until the sultan's death in 1403. Timur's empire ended after his death in 1405, while the Ottomans continued to expand.

And so, what was the secret to the Ottomans' success? For the most part, the answer is gunpowder, which, as you may recall, was invented by the Chinese. The technology had been passed along to Europe and the Islamic world through trade on the Silk Roads. Instead of sending in the cavalry, with soldiers on horseback shooting bows and arrows as the Mongols had, the Ottomans employed infantry soldiers carrying muskets. Under a powerful sultan, the Ottomans would also use gunpowder to fire cannons that could blast down city walls to achieve one of their greatest victories.

HISTORICAL THINKING

1. **READING CHECK** Who was Osman?
2. **COMPARE AND CONTRAST** How did the motivation behind Mongol and Ottoman expansion differ?
3. **INTERPRET MAPS** Which city was situated in the center of the Ottoman Empire by 1481?

3.2 State of the World

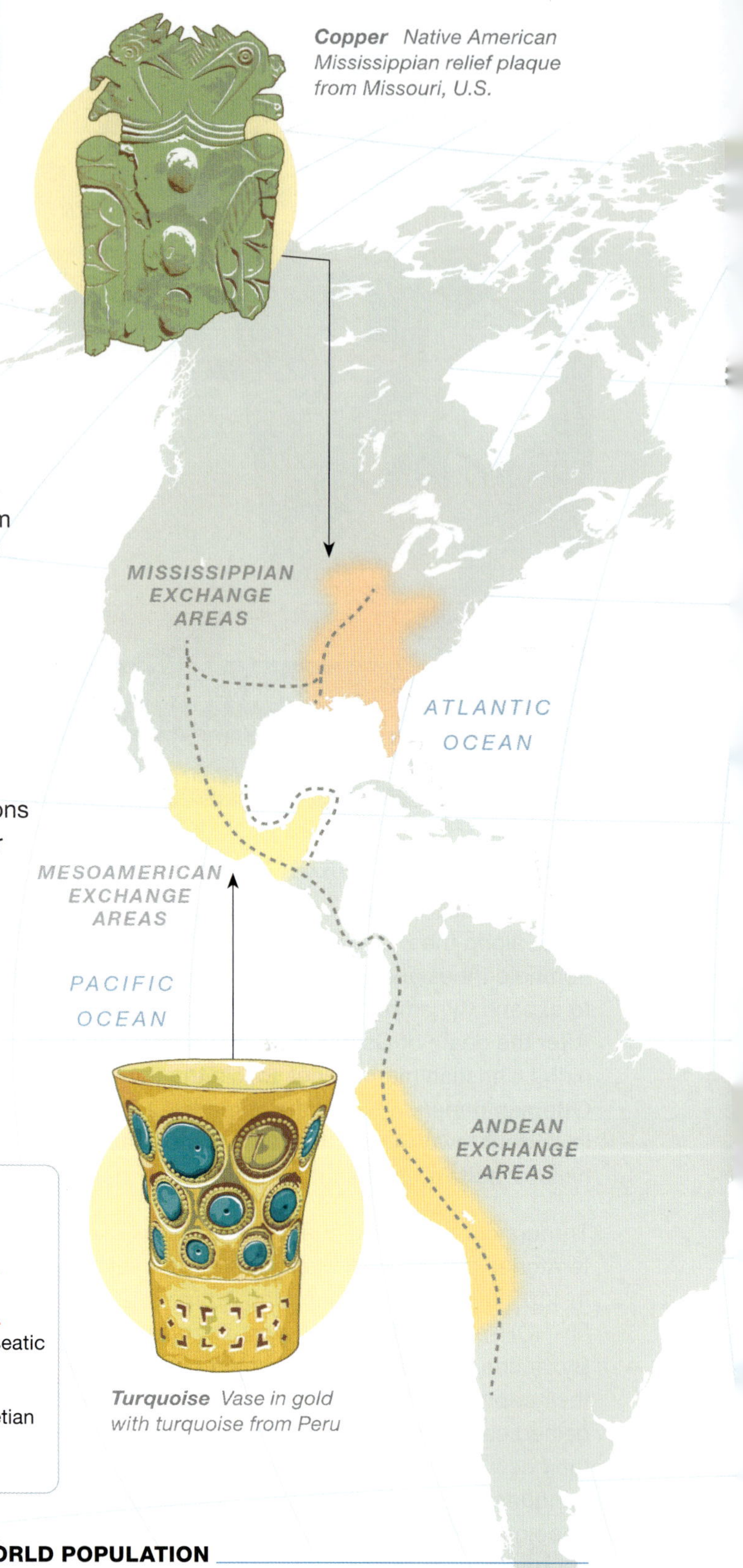

Copper Native American Mississippian relief plaque from Missouri, U.S.

1400 C.E.

POISED FOR CHANGE

By 1400, change was in the air. Revolutionary ideas about the importance of the individual took hold in Italy and began to sweep through western Europe. The movement would bring about far-reaching changes in art, religion, and government that continue to reverberate today. In other parts of the world, great civilizations arose. The kingdom of Kongo emerged in west central Africa and, in time, ruled over more than half a million people. In central Mexico, the Aztec created a state that would later expand into an empire and become the region's dominant power.

Meanwhile, some countries began to explore the world beyond their borders. After China threw off Mongol rule, the Ming dynasty commissioned Zheng He to undertake a series of voyages throughout Asia and East Africa. But after the expeditions concluded, China turned its focus inward. Portugal, on the other hand, looked outward. Its kings sent explorers to the West African coast to find a sea route that would allow them to tap into the spice trade with Southeast Asia. Eventually, they established trading posts along Africa's coastline that dealt in both goods and slaves—a development that would transform Europe, Africa, and the Americas.

Before Portugal expanded its influence, Europe, Asia, and Africa were connected by a network of trade routes that converged on Southwest Asia. The trade strengthened the political power and cultural influence of the Muslim world in 1400—for a while.

Trade routes
The Silk Road
Chinese
Arab
Indian Ocean Trade
Hanseatic
Genoese and Venetian
Others

Turquoise Vase in gold with turquoise from Peru

MISSISSIPPIAN EXCHANGE AREAS
MESOAMERICAN EXCHANGE AREAS
ANDEAN EXCHANGE AREAS
ATLANTIC OCEAN
PACIFIC OCEAN

HISTORICAL THINKING

INTERPRET MAPS Which goods shown on the map were traded in Muslim-dominated areas?

FIVE LARGEST CITIES

Nanjing	Vijayanagara	Cairo	Paris	Hangzhou
1	2	3	4	5
480	400	300	275	235

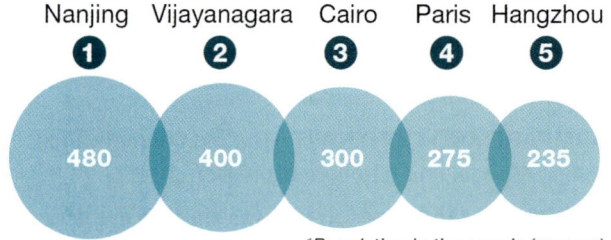

*Population in thousands (approx.)

WORLD POPULATION

1% of the world's population lived in the largest cities (from 80,000 people to nearly 500,000). Most were in Asia.

54.3% of the world's population in 2016 lived in cities.

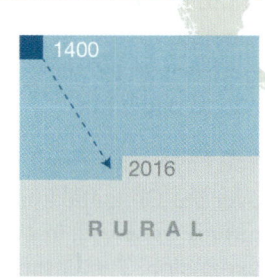

1400 → 2016
RURAL

346 CHAPTER 12

Fur Europe

Silk China

THE SILK ROADS
The Mongols revitalized the ancient Silk Roads and made the routes more secure. As a result, great expeditions, including Marco Polo's, could traverse areas that had once been plagued by tribal wars and bandits.

EUROPEAN TRADE AREA

Moscow
London
Kiev
④ Paris
Genoa Venice
Constantinople
Merv
Samarkand
Dunhuang
Beijing
Nanjing ① ⑤
Xi'an
Nagasaki
Hangzhou
Tangier Algiers
Mediterranean Sea
Baghdad
③ Cairo
Delhi
Calcutta
CHINESE TRADE AREA
MUSLIM-DOMINATED TRADE AREA
Muscat
Surat
INDIAN TRADE AREA
PACIFIC OCEAN
Timbuktu
Aden
Calicut
② Vijayanagara
Angkor
SWAHILI CITY STATES
Mombasa
Malacca
Spice Islands
INDIAN OCEAN
Kilwa
GREAT ZIMBABWE

Gold

INDIAN OCEAN TRADE
Spices from Indonesia's Spice Islands were the most valuable commodity traded on these maritime routes, which came under Arab control in the Middle Ages.

Ivory Box made of ivory and bitumen, from Egypt

WORLD POPULATION

390 million

By 1400, the world's population was lower than it had been 100 years earlier due to the bubonic plague, often called the Black Death. About **55% of the dead had lived in Asia** and only **0.5% in North America**.

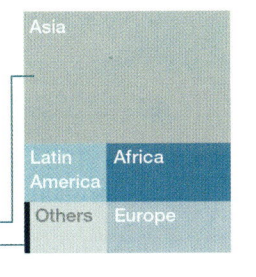

Asia
Latin America
Africa
Others
Europe

THE BLACK DEATH

at least 75 million

The Black Death was a devastating pandemic that killed millions across large portions of the world in a very short time. Originated by fleas and lice, it spread along the trade routes.

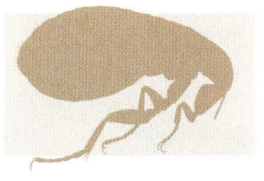

The Mongol Empire, Ming Dynasty, and Ottoman Rise

3.3 **MAIN IDEA** The Ottoman conquest of Constantinople marked the end of the Byzantine Empire and the start of a major Islamic empire.

The Conquest of Constantinople

By the mid-15th century, Constantinople had been reduced to a shadow of its former glory. And it was surrounded by Ottoman territory. The Ottomans wanted to take advantage of its isolation and vulnerability.

CRITICAL VIEWING The Ottomans battle the Byzantines at Constantinople in this painting called *First Turkish Attack on Constantinople in 1453* by Italian artist Palma il Giovane. How would you describe the battle as depicted in this painting?

348 CHAPTER 12

MEHMED THE CONQUEROR

By 1450, all that remained of the Byzantine Empire was the city of Constantinople, but its fortified walls presented a seemingly impregnable, or indestructible, barrier. Still, it was a tantalizing target. The city's population had fallen from about a million people in ancient times to only around 50,000 in the 1400s. And through Constantinople, the Byzantines controlled the Bosporus and the trade and traffic on the waterway. In religious terms, the city was still the center of the Orthodox Christian faith.

The Ottomans had tried to seize Constantinople in 1422, but their bid was unsuccessful. Then in 1451, a young sultan rose to power who was determined to accomplish the feat. His name was **Mehmed II**, and he came to be known as Mehmed the Conqueror. "Give me Constantinople," he declared early in his reign.

Mehmed carefully prepared his attack. He constructed a castle on the Bosporus and placed armed guards inside it ready to shoot at ships attempting to bring provisions to Constantinople. He also had a powerful cannon built that could bring down the city's walls. The cannon was 26 feet long and could shoot 1,200-pound boulders.

In 1453, at the age of 21, Mehmed launched his assault. The Ottomans began by firing their cannons at Constantinople's walls. At the same time, their fleet attempted to enter the city's harbor. But the Byzantines had blocked access to the Golden Horn, the inlet to the Bosporus, with a chain. Mehmed devised a plan to circumvent the problem. At night, he had his army pull 70 ships out of the Bosporus, haul them over a hill on greased logs, and then refloat them in the waters of the Golden Horn.

While Mehmed commanded a force of as many as 100,000 soldiers and a large fleet of ships, the opposition army numbered only about 8,000. Nevertheless, the Byzantines held off the Ottomans for over seven weeks. At last, however, the Turks broke through the city's walls. Many civilians as well as soldiers died on both sides during street-to-street fighting. Constantinople had not seen such bloodshed since the horrible violence of the Fourth Crusade in 1402. But Mehmed was now in control. After permitting several days of looting, he ordered his soldiers to allow the remaining inhabitants to return to their homes in peace. The Byzantine Empire had finally come to an end.

REBUILDING ISTANBUL

After Constantinople fell, Mehmed rode on a white horse to the Hagia Sophia, the city's cathedral, to deliver prayers of thanks for his victory. He soon converted the church to a mosque, underscoring the Muslim takeover of the city. Mehmed also set about rebuilding Constantinople, which he renamed Istanbul and made the new Ottoman capital. He constructed a great mosque and eight colleges around it. For nearly 100 years, the schools were renowned for their excellence in teaching the sciences. Borrowing from and building on the long tradition of Arab scholarship, learning in mathematics and astronomy reached an even higher level during the Ottoman Empire under Mehmed.

The great conqueror opened Istanbul to everyone: Muslims, Jews, Christians, Turks, and non-Turks. An envoy from Venice arrived in the city within months of the conquest to renew trade with the new ruler. A well-read man himself, Mehmed drew Italian and Greek scholars to his court and collected works in Greek and Latin for his palace library. He also hired Italian architects to help rebuild Istanbul.

The Ottoman conquest of Constantinople—the last remnant of the Eastern Roman Empire—shifted the military balance in western Eurasia away from Christian rulers and toward Muslim rulers. But Mehmed saw himself as the successor of the Roman emperors as well as a champion of Islam. His victory helped pave the way to the growth of one of the greatest empires in history.

The Greek historian Kritovoulos served as an official under Mehmed and wrote a history of the conquest of Constantinople. Although the historian wasn't present at the siege, he describes here how Mehmed may have felt upon seeing the sacked city.

PRIMARY SOURCE

When he saw what a large number had been killed, and the ruin of the buildings, and the wholesale [total] ruin and destruction of the City, he was filled with compassion and repented not a little at the destruction and plundering. Tears fell from his eyes as he groaned deeply and passionately: "What a city we have given over to plunder and destruction."

—from *History of Mehmed the Conqueror* by Kritovoulos

HISTORICAL THINKING

1. **READING CHECK** How did Mehmed prepare for his attack on Constantinople?

2. **ANALYZE CAUSE AND EFFECT** What happened as a result of Mehmed's victory?

3. **ANALYZE SOURCES** How does Kritovoulos's description of Mehmed contrast with what you've read about the conqueror's actions in Constantinople?

CHAPTER 12 REVIEW
THE MONGOL EMPIRE, MING DYNASTY, AND OTTOMAN RISE

VOCABULARY

Match each vocabulary word below with its definition.

1. steppe
2. ger
3. khanate
4. envoy
5. omnipotence
6. despotic
7. ghazi
8. sultan

a. a Muslim ruler
b. an area of the Mongol Empire
c. a vast, grassy plain
d. a warrior for Islam
e. a diplomatic representative
f. unlimited power
g. nomadic tent
h. tyrannical

READING STRATEGY
ANALYZE CAUSE AND EFFECT

Use a cause-and-effect chart like the one below to describe the impact of the Mongol invasions. Then answer the questions.

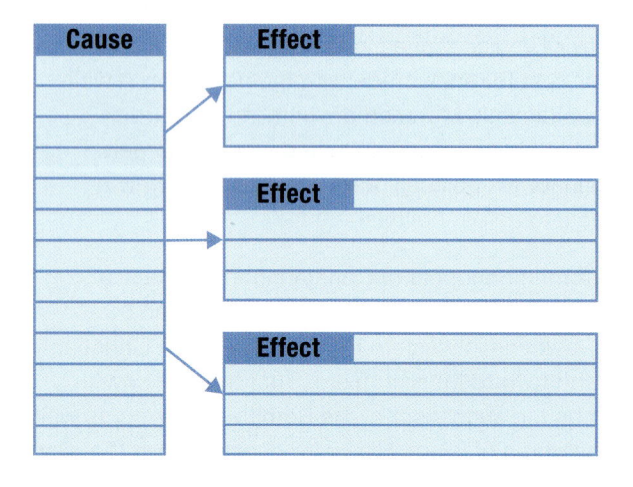

Cause	Effect
	Effect
	Effect

9. What happened in 1241 as a result of Ogodei's death?

10. How did Ogodei's decision to spare the people and lands of northern China from destruction affect the region culturally?

MAIN IDEAS

Answer the following questions. Support your answers with evidence from the chapter.

11. Who was Genghis Khan? **LESSON 1.1**

12. How did Kublai Khan treat the Chinese after he founded the Yuan dynasty? **LESSON 1.3**

13. How did the Mongol Empire link Europe and Asia through trade? **LESSON 2.1**

14. Why did later Ming emperors put an end to the voyages of exploration? **LESSON 2.2**

15. What defeat briefly interrupted Ottoman expansion? **LESSON 3.1**

16. What surprise tactic did Mehmed II use to enter Constantinople's harbor? **LESSON 3.3**

HISTORICAL THINKING

Answer the following questions. Support your answers with evidence from the chapter.

17. **MAKE INFERENCES** Why do you think Genghis Khan wanted his burial site to remain a secret?

18. **ANALYZE CAUSE AND EFFECT** What impact did the Mongol invasion of Southwest Asia have on the Abbasid Empire?

19. **DRAW CONCLUSIONS** Why was Kublai Khan's decision to move his capital to Beijing significant?

20. **FORM AND SUPPORT OPINIONS** What do you think is the Mongol Empire's greatest legacy? Explain your answer.

21. **EVALUATE** How did Zheng He's expeditions help expand China's dominance over maritime global trade in Asia?

22. **SYNTHESIZE** How did China indirectly help the Ottoman Turks establish an empire?

23. **MAKE CONNECTIONS** Why did Mehmed II want to be seen as the heir to the Roman emperors?

INTERPRET VISUALS

This full-size replica of one of Zheng He's treasure ships stands in Nanjing, China. The people in the foreground of the photo help convey the ship's immensity. Study the photo. Then answer the questions that follow.

24. How did local people probably react when they saw Zheng He's treasure ships pulling into their port?

25. What does the size of the treasure ship suggest about what Ming emperor Yongle expected from the expeditions?

ANALYZE SOURCES

Marco Polo's stories about his travels and adventures were gathered into a book around 1300, and it was an instant success. In this excerpt from the book, Polo describes the trade that flowed through Beijing during the Yuan dynasty. Read the excerpt and then answer the following question.

> You may take it for a fact that more precious and costly wares are imported into Khan-balik [Beijing] than into any other city in the world. Let me give you particulars. All the treasures that come from India—precious stones, pearls, and other rarities—are brought here. So too are the choicest and costliest products of Cathay [China] itself. . . . This is on account of the Great Khan [Kublai] himself, who lives here, and of the lords and ladies and the enormous multitude of hotel-keepers and other residents and of visitors who attend the courts held here by the Khan.

26. What impression of Beijing and Kublai Khan does Polo convey?

CONNECT TO YOUR LIFE

27. **EXPLANATORY** Mehmed II rebuilt Constantinople to make it an important center of art, education, and business. Review the measures he took to accomplish this, and then think about a city or region today that has suffered from war or a natural disaster. What did people do to rebuild that area? What do you think they might have learned from Mehmed's actions in Constantinople? Write a short essay explaining what local people and the government have done to rebuild a ravaged area and what actions or policies of Mehmed they might have adopted.

TIPS

- Review Mehmed's actions and policies when he rebuilt Constantinople.
- Do research to learn what was done recently to rebuild an area that was damaged or destroyed by war or a natural disaster.
- Consider which of Mehmed's actions and policies might have helped in the modern-day rebuilding.
- Use two or three vocabulary terms from the chapter in your essay.
- Provide a concluding statement that summarizes your ideas on how adopting Mehmed's actions and policies might have helped.

The Mongol Empire, Ming Dynasty, and Ottoman Rise

NATIONAL GEOGRAPHIC CONNECTION

Were Viking Warriors Especially Brutal?

BY CHRISTOPHER SHEA Adapted from "Did the Vikings Get a Bum Rap?" by Christopher Shea, news.nationalgeographic.com, September 28, 2014

You've read about the motivations and characteristics of soldiers throughout history. Many accounts of warriors in medieval times focus on their brutality. The Vikings of Scandinavia have especially been portrayed as monstrous warriors who launched raids throughout Europe, supposedly decimating towns and needlessly slaughtering priests.

But according to Anders Winroth, a Yale history professor and author of the book *The Age of the Vikings*, the Vikings were no more bloodthirsty than other warriors of the period. They suffered from bad public relations, however, partly because they attacked a society more literate than their own. Therefore, most accounts of them come from their victims. Moreover, because the Vikings were pagan, Christian writers cast them as a devilish outside force.

This illustration shows the stereotype of Viking marauders wreaking mayhem, even on clergy. The scene depicts the monastery at Clonmacnoise, Ireland.

To be sure, scholars have for decades been stressing aspects of Viking life beyond the warlike. They point to the craftsmanship of the Norse (a term that refers more generally to Scandinavians) and the ingenuity of their ships. They also highlight their trade with the Arab world, their settlements in Greenland and Newfoundland, and the fact that the majority of them stayed behind during raids. But Winroth wants to put the final nail in the coffin on the notion that the Vikings were the "Nazis of the North," as British journalist Patrick Cockburn has argued.

It used to be routine for scholars to claim that the Vikings killed some of their victims by means of the so-called blood eagle. The form of an eagle reportedly was carved onto a victim's back, the rib cage severed, and the lungs pulled out the back. But Winroth holds strongly to the view that this story comes from a misreading of Norse verse. Norse poetry is full of birds, including eagles, that feast on the bodies of one's enemies. Authors of Scandinavian sagas, writing centuries after the Viking raids, turned an eagle cutting into a man's back into an eagle being carved on the back.

Winroth also wants us to rethink the berserkers, the supposedly near-psychopathic warriors in the front line of Viking attacks. The berserkers were said to be immune to pain. More colorful accounts add that they chewed on their shields and ate burning coals. Winroth argues that references to berserkers first appear in the poetry of 13th- and 14th-century Iceland. In the poetry, the berserkers are plainly described as people who lived "once upon a time."

Winroth proposes that "the Vikings were sort of free-market entrepreneurs." Rather than being primed for battle by an irrational love of mayhem, the Vikings went raiding mainly for pragmatic reasons. They sought to build personal fortunes and enhance the power of their chieftains. As evidence, Winroth enumerates cases in which Viking leaders negotiated for payment, or tried to, rather than immediately attack.

Winroth believes the Vikings need to be seen in context. For a historian, he says, putting people in the context of their times humanizes them. And that's good, even when we're talking about people best known as warriors who plundered villages and slaughtered monks. ∎

UNIT INQUIRY
UNIT 4 Broker a Peace Treaty

Staging the Question

In this unit, you followed the rise of several combative dynasties. The kings and nations you have read about went to war for varying reasons. According to one chronicler, Genghis Khan fought for the sheer joy of it, saying, "Man's greatest good fortune is to chase and defeat his enemy, seize his total possessions, leave his married women weeping and wailing." Like Charlemagne, Osman, and others, however, Genghis Khan was an astute ruler as well as a warlord and most likely had more complex motivations. But was war the only choice? By examining the causes of war, how can cultures in conflict make peace?

ASSIGNMENT

Identify the root causes for the wars and conquests described in this unit. Choose one of the conflicts to explore in greater depth.

Research the causes of the war, as well as the resources each side in the war controlled.

Synthesize ideas for how the warring nations could exchange resources or find other ways to make peace.

Develop a peace plan for two warring empires or nations from this unit, laying out terms that would allow each side to gain what it had sought through conflict.

Supporting Questions: Begin by developing supporting questions to guide your research. For example: What did the Song have that the Jurchen needed? Were there other reasons for the Song and Jurchen to fight? Research the answers in this unit and in other sources, both print and online. You might want to use a graphic organizer like this one to record your answers.

Summative Performance Task: Develop a peace plan that you will present to both powers in the war. Include specific details about the conditions each side will have to accept and explain the advantages each side will gain by agreeing to them. Use what you know about the causes of the war to help you create peace terms that will appeal to the combatants.

Present: Share your plan with the class. You might consider one of these options:

MAKE A PRESENTATION
Create a slideshow or video to present before an international body such as the United Nations, laying out the peace terms and their advantages. Include graphics, photos, or other visuals to support your points.

BROKER A TREATY
Meet with classmates who are acting as representatives for the warring powers. Explain the points of your plan, and negotiate the final terms of the peace.

Take Informed Action:

UNDERSTAND Understanding the causes of a disagreement can lead to a peaceful solution, even when there is no war involved. Identify a disagreement in your school or community.

ASSESS Determine the causes of the disagreement and think of solutions that address these causes.

ACT Create a "peace plan" to solve the disagreement and present it to the two sides. You may meet with representatives of both sides, write a letter, or communicate your plan in some other way.

Feudal Europe and Imperial East Asia 353

UNIT 5

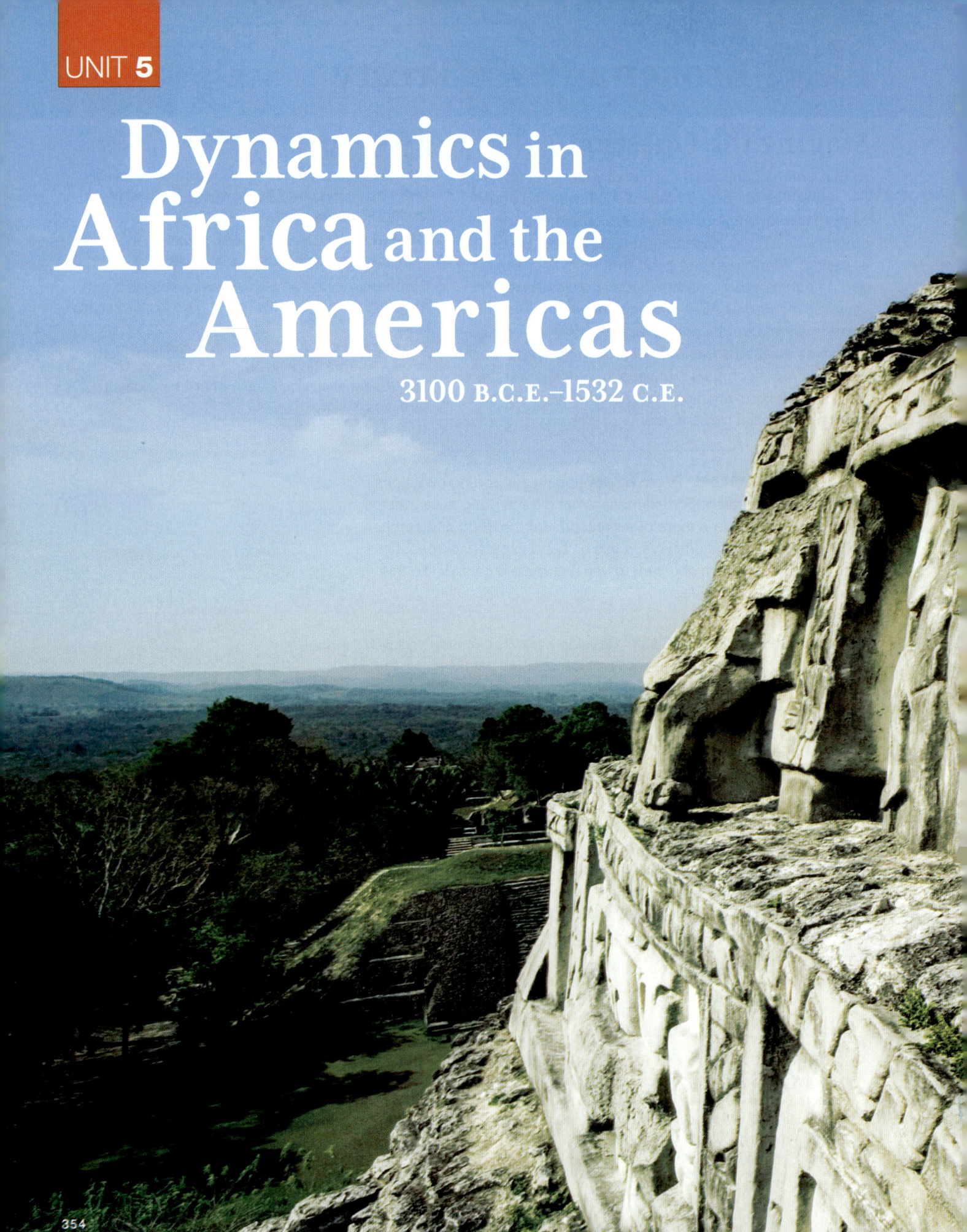

Dynamics in Africa and the Americas

3100 B.C.E.–1532 C.E.

CRITICAL VIEWING
In western Belize, stone carvings adorn the Maya temple El Castillo ("The Castle") at the Xunantunich archaeological site. This structure at Xunantunich, which is ancient Mayan for "stone woman," stretches to 130 feet above the main plaza. Based on the details in this photograph, what can you infer about the Maya people and their religion?

UNIT 5 Dynamics in Africa and the Americas

WORLD EVENTS 1500 B.C.E.–1600 C.E.

c. 1000 C.E. AMERICAS The Mississippian culture builds the prehistoric city of Cahokia in present-day Illinois. *(flint clay artifact called the Rattler Frog Pipe, c. 1000–1250)*

c. 1200 B.C.E. AMERICAS The Olmec develop their civilization in Mesoamerica. *(Olmec colossal stone head, c. 1200 B.C.E.)*

c. 500 C.E. AFRICA Ghana becomes the first great trading state in West Africa.

1500 B.C.E. // 1200 B.C.E. // 1 C.E.   200 C.E.   400 C.E.   600 C.E.

400s C.E. AFRICA Bantu speakers from West Africa migrate to sub-Saharan Africa.

700 C.E. AMERICAS The Anasazi expand their territory and begin to live in small villages in what is now the southwestern United States. *(ancestral Pueblo earthenware jar, c. 1300)*

250 C.E. AMERICAS The Maya Classic Period begins. *(earthenware head of Oaxaca, Maya corn god, c. 500)*

HISTORICAL THINKING

DRAW CONCLUSIONS Which event is most likely connected to the death of Inca emperor Huayna Capac?

1250 C.E. AFRICA The Mamluk gain control of Egypt and establish the Mamluk Empire, reinstituting Muslim rule. *(brass Mamluk candlestick, c. mid-14th century)*

1230 C.E. AFRICA Sundiata establishes and rules the Empire of Mali in West Africa.

c. 800 C.E. AFRICA The Indian Ocean trade network begins with small trading settlements on the African and Asian coasts.

1450 C.E. AMERICAS The Inca build Machu Picchu in the Andes.

1492 C.E. AMERICAS Christopher Columbus makes the first of several voyages to the Americas. *(painting of a man said to be Christopher Columbus, 1519)*

1527 C.E. AMERICAS The Inca emperor Huayna Capac dies from smallpox or the measles, a disease introduced to the Americas by Europeans.

1300s C.E. AFRICA The Shona establish the capital city of Great Zimbabwe in southern Africa. *(carved soapstone Zimbabwe bird)*

1352 C.E. AFRICA Ibn Battuta travels to Mali and recounts information about the trans-Saharan trade network.

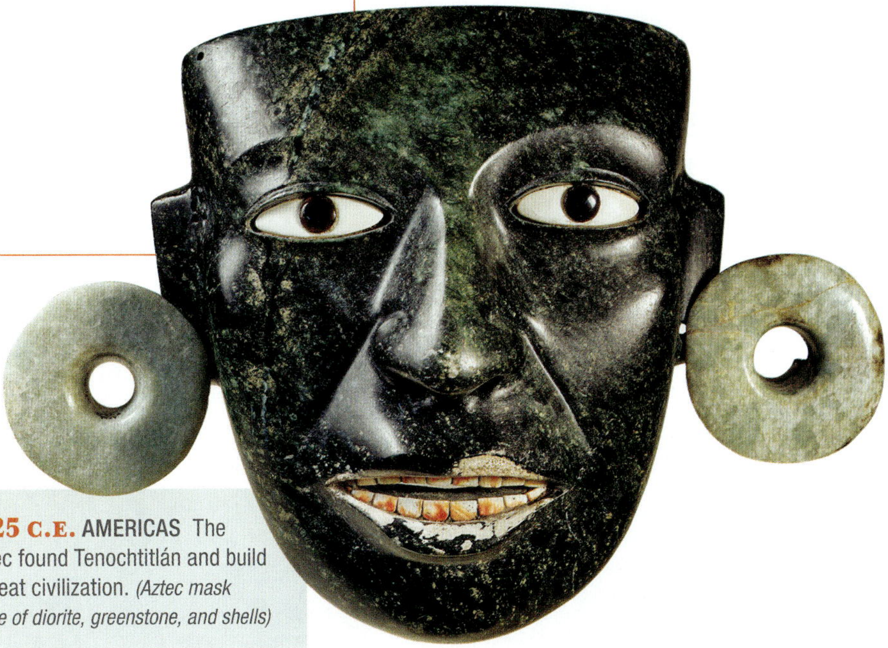

1325 C.E. AMERICAS The Aztec found Tenochtitlán and build a great civilization. *(Aztec mask made of diorite, greenstone, and shells)*

CHAPTER 13

Achievements of African Societies
300–1525

HISTORICAL THINKING How did African societies influence other cultures?

SECTION 1 **Diverse Societies, Powerful Kingdoms**

SECTION 2 **Trade and Cultural Interactions**

CRITICAL VIEWING
The Great Mosque of Djenné is an important religious site in Mali. What materials were used to construct the mosque?

1.1

MAIN IDEA Speakers of the Bantu language family migrated throughout sub-Saharan Africa, bringing with them a knowledge of farming and ironworking.

Sub-Saharan African Societies

When you think of Africa, do you think of the Sahara? This vast desert divides the enormous continent into two parts: North and East Africa and sub-Saharan Africa. More than 2,000 years ago, a group of people in western Africa started migrating throughout sub-Saharan Africa, spreading their language and culture.

SUB-SAHARAN AFRICA AND BANTU MIGRATIONS

Africa is a large continent with an area greater than that of the United States, Europe, and China combined. It is also a land of varying climate zones. The northern coast of Africa borders the Mediterranean Sea and is separated from southern regions by the mighty Sahara. Immediately to the south of the Sahara is a semidesert region called the **Sahel**. South of the Sahel is the **savanna**, an area of fertile grasslands, followed by rain forest, more savanna, and the Kalahari Desert near the southern tip of Africa.

You have already learned about Africa's earliest civilizations in Egypt and Nubia, and you have heard about African participation in Indian Ocean trade. You have also read about the spread of Islam in North Africa. In fact, much of what we know about early North and East Africa comes from accounts by Arab travelers.

Historians know less about early sub-Saharan Africa since few Arab travelers entered the region before the year 1000. Instead, they must look at evidence from archaeological excavations, oral traditions, and the distribution of languages. Africans today speak nearly 2,000 languages, or about one-third of all the world's languages. They fall into a few main language categories. Speakers of Arabic in North Africa and of Amharic in East Africa, for example, speak languages that are part of the wider Afrasian family. Many West Africans speak languages of the Niger-Congo family. The **Bantu** languages are part of that family, and Bantu speakers would have a huge impact on sub-Saharan Africa.

Bantu means "people" and is a general name for many different peoples of Africa who speak more than 500 different languages yet share a common ancestry. By studying the different Bantu languages, linguists, people who study human speech, know that the Bantu originated in western Africa around present-day Nigeria and Cameroon. Research suggests that speakers of Bantu languages began moving east and south from their original homes as early as 1000 B.C.E. Over generations, these Bantu societies developed differences

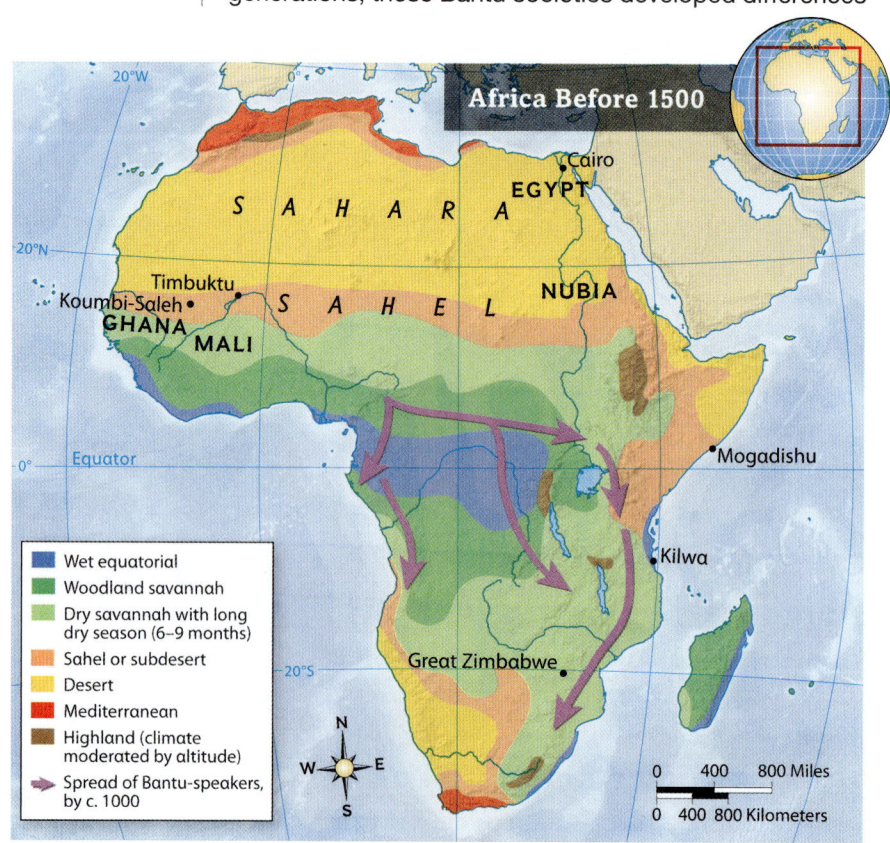

Africa Before 1500

Legend:
- Wet equatorial
- Woodland savannah
- Dry savannah with long dry season (6–9 months)
- Sahel or subdesert
- Desert
- Mediterranean
- Highland (climate moderated by altitude)
- Spread of Bantu-speakers, by c. 1000

360 CHAPTER 13

in their speech, culture, and mode of living. For example, those groups who moved south into the rain forest focused on crops that were successful in a warm and humid atmosphere. Those who moved east encountered cattle-herding peoples in the Nile River Valley from whom they borrowed a focus on cattle-herding. In western and southern Africa, farming and cattle-herding went together.

Bantu societies were skilled in agriculture and ironworking and brought these technologies with them as they migrated. As you have learned, farming supports much denser populations than hunting and gathering. That is why the Bantu moving both south into the rain forest and east across savanna lands either absorbed the ancient hunting and gathering societies they found in those places or forced such foragers to move to more remote areas. By the 400s, Bantu societies had come to southern Africa, a frontier of settlement almost 4,000 miles in distance.

CRITICAL VIEWING The Sahel has a dry season (left) and a wet season (right). How is the land different during the two seasons?

EARLY AFRICAN WAYS OF LIFE

All African societies, including those of Bantu speakers, used oral traditions to remember the past as a guide to the present. In some West African societies, there was even a special class of oral historians known as **griots** who passed historical knowledge from father to son across the centuries. When historians began studying the stories of the griots in the 20th century, they found that they could learn a great deal about the African past that had previously not been known.

The core of African life lay in the village. Usually, residents of a village belonged to a **lineage**, descendants from a common ancestor. The residents' lineage defined their rights and responsibilities. It was the elders of the lineage who made the most important decisions. Over time, groups of lineages might come together to form clans, larger networks that might include thousands of people. Similarly, related clans might sometimes band together and accept a chief or king as their common leader. However powerful African kings might become, for many people the most important thing was still their lineage and clan.

Like most farming societies, African villages were patriarchal. Men had more power and authority than women. Men usually did jobs that were considered more prestigious, such as hunting, working with metals, going on military conquests, looking after cattle, and trading. Women more often did the tough day-to-day work of farming, gathering wild fruits and vegetables, carrying water, gathering wood, and preparing meals. But it was also true that in many village societies, older women, as elders, had a voice in decision-making. Women often had their own councils where they made decisions to protect women's interests. In some African kingdoms, there was even an official role for the Queen Mother, a person nearly equal in power to the king.

A man with many children and great wealth was a "great man." Great men often became leaders of clans or groups of clans that formed chiefdoms or kingdoms. Further conquest might expand the kingdom even further. In the next lesson, you will learn about two powerful kingdoms that grew out of this practice—Ghana and Mali.

HISTORICAL THINKING

1. **READING CHECK** How did farming techniques and ironworking skills spread throughout sub-Saharan Africa?

2. **INTERPRET MAPS** Look at the map in this lesson. In what ways did the sub-Saharan lands on which Bantu-speaking peoples settled vary?

3. **MAKE INFERENCES** Why did men take on the more prestigious tasks in sub-Saharan African society?

Achievements of African Societies 361

1.2

MAIN IDEA Trade allowed the kingdom of Ghana and the Mali Empire to thrive in West Africa.

Ghana and Mali

Location! Location! Location! is often said to be the key to economic success. The early history of West Africa supports the idea that people can profit from their location. West African kingdoms and empires flourished based on their ideal trade positions.

THE RISE OF THE KINGDOM OF GHANA

Around 300, a people called the Soninke (sah-NEENG-kay) lived in small agricultural villages in West Africa. Their location was ideal for economic growth. To the north lay mines filled with salt, important for flavoring food and maintaining health. Directly south were mines filled with gold. Both gold and salt proved to be valuable commodities and brought wealth to the Soninke.

Over time, Soninke clans joined together under a strong leader to form the kingdom of Ghana. By the 500s, the kingdom's location on the Niger River allowed its people to become **intermediaries**, or go-betweens, in the salt–gold trade. The king of Ghana established a taxation system for collecting fees for all goods going in and out of the lands he ruled. He carefully monitored the amount of gold that flowed through his lands. All gold nuggets were possessions of the king, and only gold dust could be traded. In this way, Ghana gained a **monopoly**, or sole control, over gold and its trade and became a wealthy empire by 800.

In the mid-1000s, the Muslim historian al-Bakri reported that the capital of Ghana, Koumbi-Saleh (KUHM-bee SAHL-uh), was actually two towns in one. One part was Islamic, filled with mosques as well as Muslim traders and scholars. The other part was where the king, nobles, and the common people practiced a polytheistic religion, involving a belief in many gods. The common people made their living mainly through farming, fishing, herding, and craftmaking. Though often rich, traders in Ghana received little respect because they did not produce a product.

In the 11th century, the Almoravid dynasty in the north was on the rise. From their base in Morocco, the Almoravids competed with Ghana for control of valuable resources like salt. The kings of Ghana resisted Almoravid attacks, but by 1075 they lost control of Koumbi-Saleh and the kingdom went into sharp decline.

SUNDIATA AND THE MALI EMPIRE

The people under the control of Ghana had begun to rebel as the kingdom weakened. Among them were the Malinke (meh-LING-kay), whose rulers would later establish an even more powerful kingdom. It was the griots, custodians of Malinke oral traditions, who kept alive the story of **Sundiata** (sun-JAHT-ah), a sickly prince who gained the strength to lead his people to victory.

The story begins with Sundiata's mother, Sogolon. Sogolon had married the Malinke king, but she delivered a disabled son who could not even raise himself from the ground. She and Sundiata suffered humiliating insults and were finally driven away. Then one day, according to the griots, a blacksmith with magical powers gave young Sundiata an iron rod that he used to raise himself and stand. Sundiata returned and took his father's kingdom, Sogolon was showered with wealth, and the Mali Empire rose to power.

Starting from these beginnings in about the 1230s, the Mali Empire grew until it stretched from West Africa's Atlantic coast to the rich lands of the upper Niger River, where the city of **Timbuktu** became a center of trade and learning. After Sundiata, a ruler, or **mansa**, converted to Islam, and the later emperors of Mali oversaw the religious, political, and economic aspects of the large empire. While the mansas practiced Islam, they did not force their subjects to convert to Islam and many subjects retained their traditional religion. To keep political order, the mansas hired well-educated Muslims as administrators. Local rulers who sent tribute were allowed to retain much of their authority. Yet the

362 CHAPTER 13

The village of Goumina sits on an island in the middle of the Niger River in Mali. Like their ancestors, people here still rely on the river to flood every summer to irrigate their rice crop and to supply them with transportation to trading centers along the river.

mansa's standing army made sure no one overstepped the central government's power.

Both the farming of crops such as millet, rice, and sorghum and the herding of sheep, goats, and camels were important economic activities in Mali. However, trade brought riches to the mansas and allowed them to maintain the government. All trade items that passed through the empire were heavily taxed, including the goods that crossed the Sahara, as you will learn later in this chapter.

HISTORICAL THINKING

1. **READING CHECK** What led the people of Ghana and Mali to gain profits through trade?

2. **COMPARE AND CONTRAST** How were the empires of Ghana and Mali similar and different?

3. **DRAW CONCLUSIONS** Why did Muslim mansas allow the people of Mali to keep their traditional religions rather than force the people to convert to Islam?

Achievements of African Societies

1.3 **MAIN IDEA** The wealthy trading empire known as Great Zimbabwe demonstrated its strength and power through the construction of impressive stone structures.

Great Zimbabwe

Consider how various peoples of the past have demonstrated their authority and strength. Some formed fierce armies, while others built ornate palaces. Some spread news of great feats through messages on stelae. The early rulers of southeastern Africa announced the power of their kingdoms through massive stone structures.

These ruins are the remains of the Great Enclosure from the ancient capital city of Great Zimbabwe.

GREAT STONE HOUSES

As you have already read, groups of Bantu speakers migrated throughout sub-Saharan Africa. One group settled as far south as the high plateau beyond the Zambezi River. There, the **Shona** people established the state that reached its greatest extent in the early 1300s. Its center was the imposing capital city known as Great Zimbabwe. That spot was likely chosen as the location of the capital because of its mild climate and fertile soil as well as its strategic position. **Great Zimbabwe** was situated along a much-traveled trade route that carried gold and other items. Taxes collected on goods that passed through Great Zimbabwe brought enormous wealth to its leaders.

Like many other Bantu settlers in sub-Saharan Africa, the Shona lived as cattle herders and farmers. They made efficient use of iron tools in their day-to-day life. Before 1000, most people lived in small villages of houses made from wood beams. Then some villagers became rich enough to build their own stone structures. By the 13th and 14th centuries, the population of the region had reached 10,000. The villages built some 300 stone enclosures, or areas surrounded by walls, across the plateau. The word for these enclosures in the Shona language is *Zimbabwe*, or "place of stone houses." This word is the source of the name of the present-day nation of Zimbabwe where the structures are located. The largest of these enclosures, Great Zimbabwe, prospered for about 250 years.

After 1450, the inhabitants of Great Zimbabwe deserted their walled complex. Perhaps they had depleted natural resources by cutting down forests for fuel to make iron. Perhaps their population grew too large for the area. The shifting of trade routes also contributed to the demise of Great Zimbabwe.

STUDYING THE RUINS

The ruins of Great Zimbabwe cover almost 1,800 acres near the present-day city of Masvingo. One point of interest at the site is the Great Enclosure, a large circular wall that is 15 feet thick and more than 30 feet in height. It is the largest single stone structure in sub-Saharan Africa built before 1500. One estimate holds that it might have taken 400 workers four years to complete the project. In any case, the remains of the wall show the skill of those who built it. It is made of evenly cut granite blocks placed so closely together that mortar was not necessary. The Great Enclosure was reserved for the ruler and other elites, keeping them separate from the common people.

Since the people of Great Zimbabwe did not keep written records, oral traditions and archaeological finds provide the only sources of information about their way of life. Of special interest to scholars is the discovery of a hoard, or a hidden supply of stored items, unearthed at one of the smaller enclosures. The hoard included Chinese ceramics, beads from India, and colorful Persian plates. Other artifacts at the site indicate that skilled Shona craftworkers created fine gold jewelry. All these findings provide evidence of participation in trade networks. In fact, East African traders were exporting the gold of Great Zimbabwe to Indian Ocean markets and bringing valuable goods back in return. Archaeologists have found fine porcelain from Ming China at the site of Great Zimbabwe, reminding us of the voyages of Zheng He.

Africans are proud of the architectural achievement of Great Zimbabwe, so much so that when they gained their independence and had a chance to pick a new name, the people of this region chose *Zimbabwe*.

SHONA SCULPTURE

The only surviving sculptures from Great Zimbabwe are stylized birds carved out of soapstone. The birds resemble fish eagles, a common species in the region. Today the people of Zimbabwe are entranced by the birds made long ago, and an image of a bird even appears on Zimbabwe's national flag.

HISTORICAL THINKING

1. **READING CHECK** For what reason are the people of Great Zimbabwe most remembered today?

2. **MAKE INFERENCES** Why did the Great Enclosure require so many workers and take four years to complete?

3. **ASK AND ANSWER QUESTIONS** What are three questions about Great Zimbabwe that you might like to research?

Achievements of African Societies

1.4

MAIN IDEA Ibn Battuta traveled extensively throughout the Muslim world, learning fascinating details of the people and places he encountered.

Traveler: Ibn Battuta
The Longest-Known Journey 1304–1368

No two places are alike, even if they share many characteristics and are united under a single ruler. Sometimes, it is only possible to discern the differences and similarities through first-hand observation. World travelers do just that. They make extended trips to discover what makes each place on Earth unique and what ties various places together.

WHERE HE WENT

Ibn Battuta (IB-uhn bah-TOO-tuh) is remembered today for his invaluable descriptions of the Muslim world. As a 20-year-old legal scholar, the young Muslim had no idea that he would become a world traveler. At first, he embarked from his home in Tangier, Morocco, to make the hajj pilgrimage to Mecca, fulfilling one of the five pillars of Islam. It was only after this pilgrimage that he decided to continue traveling with no fixed destination and no set time of return. He spent the next 29 years following the trade routes that knit the Islamic world together. After his journey, Ibn Battuta dictated his adventures to another writer to create a book called *The Travels*.

In all, Ibn Battuta traveled about 75,000 miles throughout the *dar-al Islam*, Arabic for "abode of Islam." His journey led him to Egypt, Muslim-ruled areas of Spain, Arabia, Persia, and south into India. He traveled along China's Pacific coast with Muslim sea merchants, and he toured the northern and eastern coasts of Africa. He explored deep into West Africa. He traveled on foot, rode camels and donkeys, and sailed by boat.

To finance his journey, Ibn Battuta relied on donations from other Muslims. The Five Pillars encouraged donations not only to the poor but also to travelers. Ibn Battuta's dependence on Muslim support kept him from venturing beyond the realm of Islam. For example, he never visited the majestic Great Zimbabwe, which you read about in the last lesson. But he did visit the African Muslim cities on the Indian Ocean coast. You will read more about them later.

> In this excerpt from *The Travels*, Ibn Battuta describes his first stop in Mali at Taghaza, an important center of the salt trade.
>
> **PRIMARY SOURCE**
>
> After 25 days we arrived at Taghaza. This is a village with nothing good about it. One of its marvels is that its houses and mosque are of rock salt and its roofs of camel skins. It has no trees, but is nothing but sand with a salt mine. They dig in the earth for the salt, which is found in great slabs lying one upon the other as though they have been shaped and placed underground. A camel carries two slabs of it. Nobody lives there except the slaves . . . who dig for the salt. They live on the dates imported to them, . . . on camel-meat, and on anili [a type of grain]. . . .

WHAT HE SAW

During his long journey, Ibn Battuta frequently accompanied Muslim merchants on established land and sea routes. His reports include descriptions of trade items, trade processes, and the people he met along the way. It appears that he mainly encountered rulers, high-ranking judges, and religious leaders. His account includes many details about political events, ways of governing, and social interactions with male Muslims. Little is mentioned of local economies or the ways of life of women and non-Muslims.

Ibn Battuta was the first traveler to record an eyewitness description of sub-Saharan Africa. Some of the details you read earlier about the Mali Empire are known only because of Ibn Battuta's eyewitness

366 CHAPTER 13

Ibn Battuta's Journeys, 1325–1354

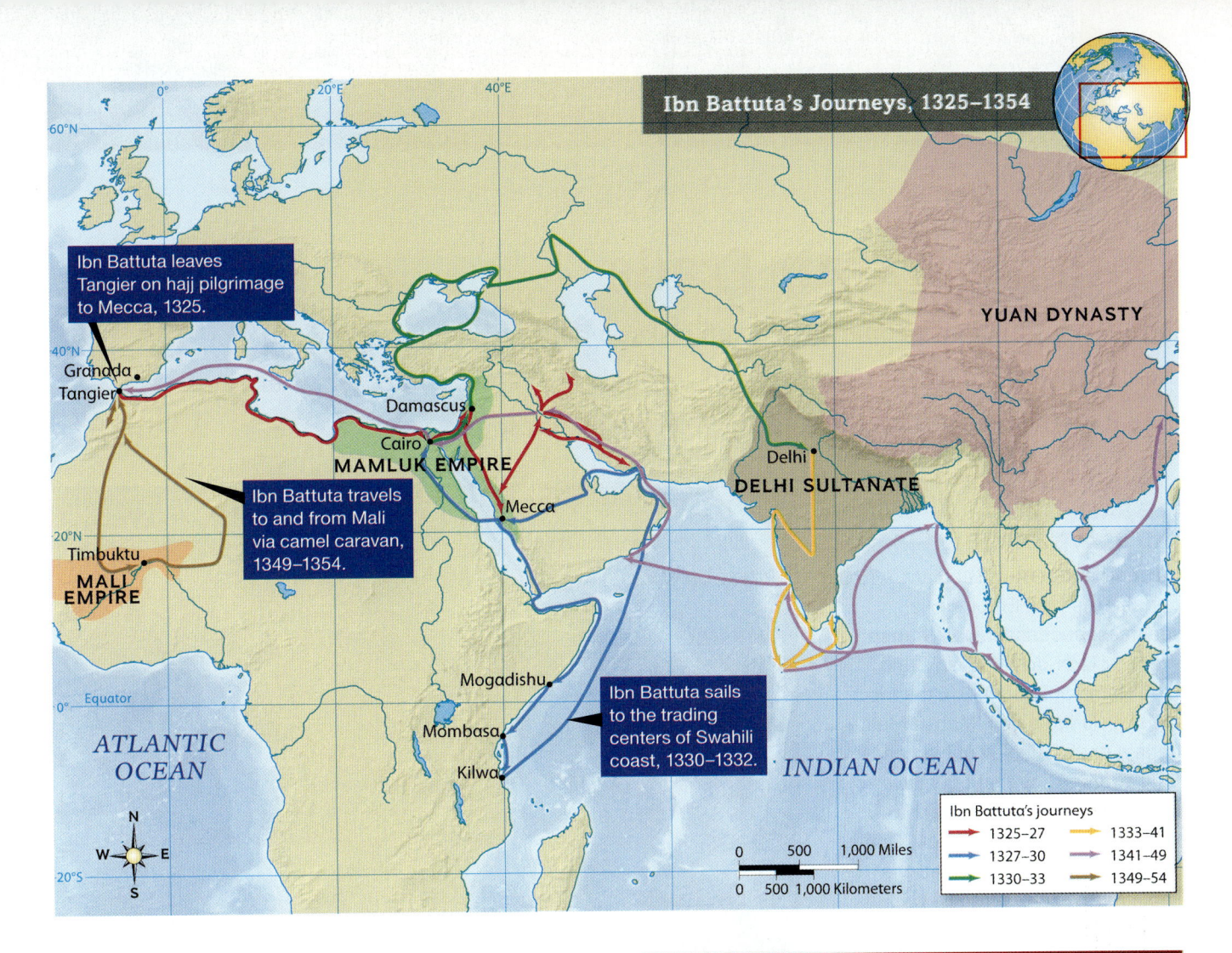

account. For example, Ibn Battuta describes a grueling 25-day trip to get to Mali with a **caravan**, or group of people who travel together. He also describes the city of Timbuktu.

A devout Muslim, Ibn Battuta was shocked at the way in which the people of Mali practiced Islam. For example, he disapproved of the fact that women were not secluded. Yet he was pleased that many people worshiped at mosques and memorized the Quran. He did approve when he saw that children who failed at their Quranic lessons were sternly punished.

You read in a previous chapter that the people of Arabia were the first people to practice Islam. Ibn Battuta believed this region was a model for how Islam should be practiced.

Many legs of Ibn Battuta's journey would not have been possible 300 years earlier. By 1450, however, West and East Africa were important stops along trade routes within the broader Islamic world. You will learn more about these early trade routes as you read the next lesson.

Ibn Battuta's account of a 1348 visit to Damascus, Syria, portrays the suffering caused by the Black Death, or plague. As you know, the plague caused many deaths in Europe as well.

PRIMARY SOURCE

The entire population of the city joined in the exodus, male and female, small and large; the Jews went out with their book of the Law and the Christians with their Gospel, their women and children with them; . . . in tears and humble supplications, imploring the favor of God through His Books and his Prophets.

HISTORICAL THINKING

1. **READING CHECK** Why has Ibn Battuta gained a place in history?
2. **INTERPRET MAPS** Did Ibn Battuta visit West Africa before or after he visited China?
3. **MAKE GENERALIZATIONS** In what ways are the reports of Ibn Battuta biased?
4. **EVALUATE** How trustworthy do you think *The Travels* is as a historical source?

Achievements of African Societies 367

2.1

MAIN IDEA The robust trade in salt, gold, and slaves over Saharan trade routes brought wealth to West and North Africa.

Trans-Saharan Trade

Throughout history, people have taken risks in hopes of receiving rewards for their efforts. Traders in Africa trekked through the harsh Sahara for weeks at a time to gain wealth from the trade of West African resources.

THE SALT, GOLD, AND SLAVE TRADE

You read about how Sundiata founded the Mali Empire. His wealthiest successor was **Mansa Musa** (MAHN-sa MOO-sa), who ruled from 1307 to 1332. On a trip to Cairo during a hajj, Mansa Musa made a grand display of his riches. Early sources say that 500 slaves marched in front of him, each carrying a gold walking stick. One hundred camels transported the leader's travel money—700 pounds of gold—which he spent freely. In Cairo, legend says, he spent so much that he flooded the market with gold and seriously reduced the value of the Egyptian currency.

Mansa Musa had gained his wealth through taxes on trade that passed through the empire along the **trans-Saharan trade network**, a set of well-established trade routes across the Sahara. Crossing the Sahara to reach Mali required weeks of travel over scorching sand. Travelers from the north risked this trip because of the salt and gold they could acquire in Mali. Some towns in Mali seemed to overflow with salt, which was highly valued in places where it was scarce. In other locations, gold was a prized commodity. Mining gold was profitable but dangerous as mines often collapsed. However, farmers were willing to do it to add to their income.

In addition to exchanging salt and gold, the people of Mali also participated in the slave trade. An estimated 5,500 slaves crossed the desert yearly. The slave traders of Mali did not enslave people from their own country. Instead, they captured people in the forest belt to the south and sold them across the desert to Arab traders.

Other people of West Africa envied Mali's wealth. Armored soldiers on horseback captured major cities, including Timbuktu. By 1450, the neighboring Songhai (SAHNG-gy) people, who had also gained riches through trade, had conquered Mali and claimed rulership over many West African societies. You will learn more about the Songhai people in a later chapter.

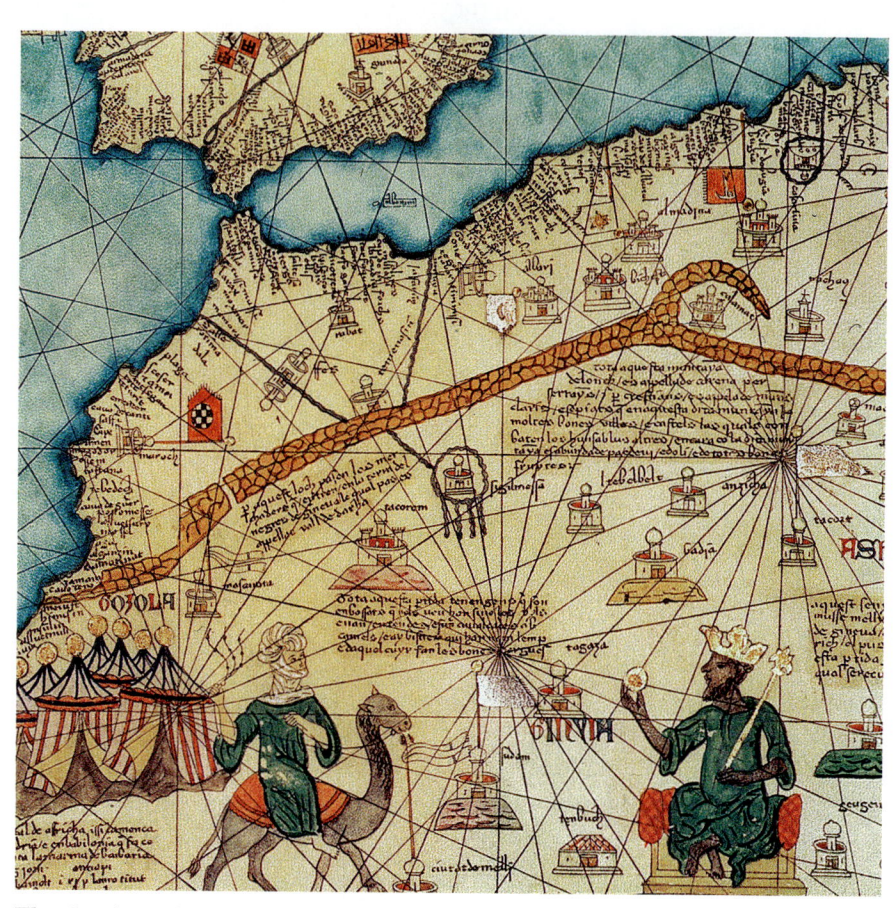

The *Catalan Atlas* shows trade routes of various places in Africa. Mansa Musa (right) is shown as a prominent figure on the atlas.

MAMLUK TRADE NETWORKS

You learned about the ruler Saladin who had founded a new dynasty in Egypt in the 12th century and retook Jerusalem from the Crusaders. His dynasty was replaced by the Mamluks (MAM-looks). They started as enslaved Turkish soldiers. Once the Mamluks converted to Islam, they were granted freedom, and some gained high positions in the military and in government. In 1250, they gained control of Egypt and established their own dynasty. Soon after, the Mamluk Empire extended to include Syria. The Mamluks would retain control of these lands until 1517.

As converts to the faith, the Mamluks took the defense of Islam very seriously, reviving the faith after the Mongol sack of Baghdad in 1258. The new government of the Mamluks was based in Cairo and led by a sultan. Many Muslims, especially Muslim scholars, poured into the city. With its many colleges, called *madrasas*, Cairo replaced Baghdad as the cultural center for Islam. It grew to become one of the largest cities of the day with a population of more than 400,000 people. It was this impressive city that was visited by both Mansa Musa and Ibn Battuta.

During this time, North Africa continued to be the end African destination for salt, gold, and slaves from West Africa. From there, other traders transported the trade items and enslaved people to markets in Europe and Asia across the Mediterranean. Traders also transported goods to locations on the Indian Ocean by way of the Red Sea. In return, products such as Chinese silk and spices from India reached North Africa.

Eventually, such problems as drought, government corruption, and the bubonic plague caused severe economic distress. To keep his government going, the Mamluk sultan increased taxes on trade. Traders looked elsewhere for the items they desired. By the early 1500s, the Mamluks had lost control of their lands.

HISTORICAL THINKING

1. **READING CHECK** Why was salt important to the people of Mali?
2. **IDENTIFY** Which historical figure is most often used as an example of Mali's wealth? Why?
3. **MAKE INFERENCES** What might have led the people of Mali to take part in the African slave trade?

Mamluk Artifacts

This glass lamp was once used in a madrasa, or school, in Cairo in the 14th century during the time of the Mamluk Empire.

This steel armor was worn by horses to protect their heads.

This globe was used to burn incense. The smoke would escape through the tiny holes.

2.2 A Global Commodity: Salt

For centuries, salt was a scarce and precious commodity. Traded across continents, it established the wealth of empires for much of human history. You've already read that in the 12th century, merchants traveled to Timbuktu on the trans-Saharan caravan route to trade a measure of gold for an equal weight of salt. (Imagine such an exchange today!) Mighty African empires even went to war to control sources of salt.

Although salt is no longer scarce, in present-day Africa, traditional camel caravans still make the 500-mile trek between Timbuktu and the continent's salt mines to move this simple but vital substance. Today, there are an estimated 14,000 uses for salt, the most important of which is keeping us alive. No wonder it's a treasured commodity—and one that has profoundly shaped and influenced history.

What factors might influence the changing value of a commodity like salt throughout history?

BACK TO THE SALT MINES

A salt miner in Uganda displays a handful of salt harvested from Lake Katwe. Work in salt mines can be dangerous and physically demanding, as evidenced by the film of salt covering this worker's skin. The modern expression "back to the salt mines," a reference to reluctantly returning to one's job after time away, acknowledges the unpleasantness of salt mining and possibly the fact that some countries forced prisoners to toil in salt mines as a punishment.

SALT AT A GLANCE

LIFE	• Life-sustaining salt consists of two important elements: sodium and chloride.	• Sodium aids communication between cells and allows muscle and nerve function.	• Chloride regulates blood pressure and acidity and is used to make stomach acid.
VALUE	• Salt exists only in small amounts on Earth's surface, but is no longer scarce because it is inexpensive and easy to produce.	• Salt is used to preserve food and in medication, although too much salt can be unhealthy. It's also a key ingredient in PVC plastic.	• Production of salt has increased to meet worldwide demands. China and the United States produce the most salt.
PRODUCTION	• Salt can be mined from underground deposits left behind by ancient seas and harvested from the ocean through evaporation.	• Solution mining injects water into salt deposits, removes the solution, and evaporates the water to yield salt.	• Solar recovery methods use energy from the sun to produce salt. The sun and wind provide energy to evaporate water from salt.
HISTORY	• The camel was introduced to Saharan trade around 200 C.E., marking the start of the salt trade.	• Ancient Rome's Via Salaria, or "salt road," was one of the oldest salt trade routes.	• Wagons of "white gold" made the 62-mile journey along the Old Salt Road across Europe during the Middle Ages.
ECONOMICS	• The salt trade built the wealth of countries and empires and financed the construction of the Great Wall of China.	• Salt was used to pay Roman soldiers and traded for slaves in ancient Greece—a lazy slave was "not worth his salt."	• Today, China leads the world in salt production, and international trade of this commodity is minimal due to global availability.

Achievements of African Societies

This aerial photograph shows vast salt flats in the African country of Senegal. Pools of mineral-colored salt water rest in holes dug by salt collectors, awaiting the miracle of evaporation. Algae can also give salty water its unique color.

The workers in this photograph appear dwarfed by the task in front of them. Consider the challenges they face while toiling in an environment such as this on a daily basis, including the African heat and the demanding physical tasks involved in processing salt. Salt harvesters do their best to protect their skin from the scorching sunlight and the harsh effects of salt as they prepare this commodity for transport to markets far and wide.

What do the photos in this Global Commodity lesson reveal about the process for harvesting salt and the impact of the salt industry on human lives?

Achievements of African Societies 373

2.3

MAIN IDEA Muslim kingdoms and city-states in Africa primarily dominated Indian Ocean trade in the 1200s through the 1500s.

Africa's Eastern Networks

While African resources flowed through North Africa to Europe across the Mediterranean, another trade network bustled to the east. This set of trade routes spanned the Indian Ocean and was driven primarily by Muslim traders and sultans.

The fort at Kilwa, shown here, was built by the Portuguese after they arrived in East Africa in 1498 and took control of the region's trade.

INDIAN OCEAN TRADE

Varied lands and people surrounded the Indian Ocean long ago. The East African coast, the southern edge of the Arabian Peninsula, the Persian Gulf, and the west coast of India had various languages, cultures, and political units. Yet all the city-states and larger political units surrounding the large body of water joined together as part of the Indian Ocean trade network. Just as rulers of North and West Africa taxed overland trade, so too did the sultans of these coastal regions tax Indian Ocean sea trade. Sultanates, the territories governed by the sultans, could be as small as a single city-state or a large kingdom. For example, small Muslim sultanates dotted East Africa's coast while an enormous Muslim kingdom prospered in northern India.

The people of these three regions traveled the Indian Ocean on ships called **dhows** (dows), boats with triangular sails that were common in the Arab world. These early vessels carried goods between ports, much like camels of the desert. Dhows had no deck, so passengers sat and slept next to the ships' cargo. Indian ocean winds powered the boats as they beat against their large sails. Little human labor was required on these voyages, so traders and their families staffed their own boats. As people of three regions traveled to other lands, they often intermarried, bringing about a mixing of cultures.

One such culture was that of the **Swahili** (swah-HEE-lee) people. The ancestors of the Swahili were Bantu-speaking migrants who settled on the coast. As they interacted with traders from other lands, they borrowed words from Arabic, Farsi, and the Indian language Gujarati. The Swahili converted to Islam and began to focus more on trade than farming.

One of their important trading cities was **Kilwa**, located on a small island off the coast of present-day Tanzania. Among Kilwa's main exports were gold from interior regions like Great Zimbabwe, elephant tusks, and slaves. Many goods from Africa's interior traveled to ocean ports, then to Kilwa, and on to their final destination. Kilwa was just one of about 40 East African trading settlements where African resources were traded for goods such as spices, beads, silk and cotton cloth, and porcelain from other locations. Those who participated in trade were highly regarded in society.

This Ethiopian miniature illustrates the legendary meeting of King Solomon and the Queen of Sheba.

THE KINGDOM OF ETHIOPIA

Another East African society with wider connections was the kingdom of Ethiopia. In this mountainous region, the rulers had long been Christians. Though later encircled by Muslim-dominated societies, they held fast to their ancient Coptic form of the Christian faith, which was connected to the Eastern Orthodox Church. Ethiopian priests, monks, and nuns still use their own sacred script, called Ge'ez (gee-EHZ), for religious purposes. When Christian pilgrims arrived in Jerusalem during the Middle Ages, they found Ethiopian visitors there as well.

One of the most famous churches in all of Africa is St. George's Church at Lalibela, built by an Ethiopian king in the 1200s. Instead of building the church upward, the king had his architects design the Lalibela church to be dug out of the living rock, below ground. You will learn more about this church and others like it in the next lesson.

The Christian kings of Ethiopia even traced their ancestry back to the Hebrew Bible. The Queen of Sheba, they claimed, was Ethiopian, and when she returned home after visiting Jerusalem, she delivered a child, the son of King Solomon, and called him **Menelik** (MEH-nuh-lihk). Menelik was the legendary founder of a line of emperors who ruled Ethiopia until the 1970s.

HISTORICAL THINKING

1. **READING CHECK** How did trade affect the people living in areas that bordered the Indian Ocean?

2. **DRAW CONCLUSIONS** Why were East Africans who participated in trade highly regarded in society?

3. **MAKE INFERENCES** Why was it important for the kings of Ethiopia to trace their lineage to the Hebrew Bible?

2.4 Preserving Cultural Heritage

CHURCHES CARVED INTO ROCK

Lalibela, a town north of Addis Ababa in Ethiopia, is home to 11 monolithic churches, each formed from a single large block of stone. These Christian churches are a vital part of Ethiopian history and culture, yet they are under threat. Without immediate attention, the churches—and their history—may deteriorate.

The town, which was named for King Lalibela, became the center of Ethiopian Christianity during the 12th century. After the capture of Jerusalem by Muslim forces in 1187, King Lalibela commissioned the churches and declared the town to be a new Jerusalem.

The churches were carved from volcanic rock below Earth's surface. Trenches were carved in a rectangle isolating a single stone block. The block was then carved inside and out, creating the churches from the top down rather than from the ground up. The roofs of each of the churches are level with the ground. Long underground tunnels provide passageways from one church to another.

These churches are still in use today, and the town is visited every year by hundreds of thousands of religious pilgrims. Preservation efforts for the site started as early as the 1960s, with the World Monuments Fund (WMF) working with conservators to document information, stabilize construction, and raise international attention for the protection of the site. In 1978, UNESCO designated the churches as a World Heritage Site.

As transportation conditions to Ethiopia improved, the number of visitors to Lalibela increased. This growth in tourism along with water filtration problems has caused damage and structural problems.

In 2007, temporary shelters were built over four churches to address water problems caused by rain. However, it was later discovered that the shelters caused additional damage to the churches. In 2018, a group was commissioned to study the current state of conservation and make recommendations for further actions to ensure that the Lalibela churches—and Ethiopia's cultural heritage—are preserved now and for the future.

HISTORICAL THINKING

DRAW CONCLUSIONS How do human interaction and the environment affect cultural sites like the churches of Lalibela?

A priest stands at the entrance to the Church of Gabriel-Raphael. The entrance to this church is up at the top of the structure instead of down at the bottom.

LALIBELA, ETHIOPIA

The Church of Saint George is one of 11 rock-hewn monolithic—or carved from a single stone—churches in this Ethiopian town. The church is formed in the shape of a cross and extends 40 feet down below the surface.

DOCUMENT-BASED QUESTION
2.5 Africa East and West

A variety of factors affected life in West Africa and along the Swahili Coast between 1000 and 1500, including climate, available resources, basic beliefs, and cultural diffusion. The term *Swahili Coast* refers to the East African lands along the Indian Ocean where people developed the Swahili language and built Muslim trading cities.

Political, social, and religious aspects of life in various parts of Africa influenced building styles in particular. Places where Islam was well established, such as North Africa, the cities of the Sahel, and the Swahili Coast, became home to many mosques, some of which were large and impressive. African rulers also became used to sturdy and elaborate palaces. In addition, the multiroom houses of traders and other wealthy individuals provided visual confirmation of their high status in society. Stone proved to be the ideal resource for such imposing structures, though Swahili structures were also built of coral cut from Indian Ocean reefs.

Less-wealthy people made do with whichever resources were available in their area. Traditional building materials such as mud, wattle, grasses, tree branches, and even salt formed many one-room homes in much of West and East Africa. Wattle is formed by interweaving poles, branches, and reeds. Originally, many people in sub-Saharan Africa resided in circular homes with dome-shaped roofs. Later, Africans began building rectangular homes with flat roofs, an idea they borrowed from Arab visitors.

Wood was abundant in some parts of Africa and therefore was the main resource for doors used not only in African homes but also sold as export items. Swahili craftsmen were experts at carving intricate designs for these doors. The most ornate doors featured ebony wood with inlays of ivory. East African merchants also found a good market for the mangroves they harvested from coastal wetlands. These were in high demand in Arabia, where there is very little local wood for use in construction.

CRITICAL VIEWING The Sankore (sayn-KOHR) Mosque still stands in Timbuktu. It has features you will find in mosques anywhere. But the architects of Mali also brought their own culture and building knowledge to the task, for example including beams within its thick mud walls. These beams can be seen protruding through the walls of the mosque. What do you think the inside of the mosque looks like based on its appearance from the outside?

DOCUMENT ONE

Primary Source: Book
from *Book of Highways and of Kingdoms*
by Abu U'bayd al-Bakri, 1068

Al-Bakri provided early descriptions of Ghana in his *Book of Highways and of Kingdoms*. He did not actually travel to West Africa, so his account is based on observations of others. Geographers and historians today rely on the descriptions of al-Bakri to gain much of their knowledge of Ghana long ago.

CONSTRUCTED RESPONSE What can you infer about the king's attitude toward Muslim merchants based on the architecture of the town?

> The city of Ghana consists of two towns situated on a plain. One of these towns, which is inhabited by Muslims, is large and possesses 12 mosques, in one of which they assemble for the Friday prayer. . . . In the environs are wells with sweet water, from which they drink and with which they grow vegetables. The king's town is six miles distant from this one and bears the name of Al-Ghaba. Between these two towns there are continuous habitations. The houses of the inhabitants are of stone and acacia wood. The king has a palace and a number of domed dwellings all surrounded with an enclosure like a city wall. In the king's town, and not far from his court of justice, is a mosque where the Muslims who arrive at his court pray.

DOCUMENT TWO

Primary Source: Book
from *The Book of Duarte Barbosa* by Duarte Barbosa, 1518

Searching for new sea-trade routes to southern India, the Portuguese came into contact with booming East African trading cities such as Kilwa. They were shocked to find such well-developed communities. Duarte Barbosa, a Portuguese government official, traveled throughout the Indian Ocean region to see for himself the richness of that trade.

CONSTRUCTED RESPONSE Why is Duarte Barbosa so impressed with Kilwa?

> Going along the coast from the town of Mozambique, there is an island which is called Kilwa, in which is a Muslim town with many fair houses of stone and mortar, with many windows after our fashion, very well arranged in streets, with many flat roofs. The doors are of wood, well carved with excellent joinery. Around it are streams and orchards and fruit-gardens with many channels of sweet water. It has a Muslim king over it. From this place they trade with Sofala, whence they bring back gold. Before the King our Lord sent out his expedition to discover India, the Muslims of Sofala, Cuama, Angoya and Mozambique were all subject to the King of Kilwa.

DOCUMENT THREE

Primary Source: Book
from *A Geographical Historie of Africa* by Leo Africanus, 1526

Leo Africanus grew up in Muslim-ruled Grenada in Spain and went with his father on a diplomatic mission to the Songhai Empire. Determined to learn more about the world, he traveled throughout North Africa and into West Africa. In his book, he describes in detail the trading city of Timbuktu, which, at the time of his writings, featured majestic mosques and was a center of learning where books were highly valued.

CONSTRUCTED RESPONSE Why do you think the houses of Timbuktu were made of clay-covered wattles with thatched roofs rather than stone?

> The houses of Timbuktu are huts made of clay-covered wattles with thatched roofs. In the center of the city is a temple built of stone and mortar, and in addition there is a large palace where the king lives. The shops of the artisans, the merchants and especially weavers of cotton cloth are very numerous. Fabrics are also imported from Europe to Timbuktu, borne by Berber merchants.
>
> The women of the city maintain the custom of veiling their faces, except for the slaves who sell all the foodstuffs. The inhabitants are very rich, especially the strangers who have settled in the country.

SYNTHESIZE & WRITE

1. **REVIEW** Review what you have read and observed about the construction of houses in early East Africa and West Africa.

2. **RECALL** On your own paper, list key details about the architecture at each of the three locations described.

3. **CONSTRUCT** Construct a topic sentence that answers this question: How are the three types of houses described in the primary sources similar to and different from one another?

4. **WRITE** Using evidence from this chapter and the documents, write an informative paragraph that supports your topic sentence in Step 3.

Achievements of African Societies 379

CHAPTER 13 REVIEW
ACHIEVEMENTS OF AFRICAN SOCIETIES

VOCABULARY

Use each of the following vocabulary words in a sentence that shows an understanding of the term's meaning.

1. griot
2. lineage
3. intermediary
4. monopoly
5. mansa
6. caravan
7. trans-Saharan trade network
8. dhow

READING STRATEGY
IDENTIFY MAIN IDEAS AND DETAILS

Use a graphic organizer like the one below to list a main idea and details about each of the following: Mansa Musa, Ibn Battuta, and Sundiata. Then answer the question that follows.

Main Ideas	Details

9. Use the details you listed to describe how one of the people mentioned above contributed to the growth of a kingdom or an empire of sub-Saharan Africa.

MAIN IDEAS

Answer the following questions. Support your answers with evidence from the chapter.

10. In what different ways were African societies governed? **LESSON 1.1**
11. How did Ghana and Mali profit from trade? **LESSON 1.2**
12. What have archaeological finds revealed about Great Zimbabwe? **LESSON 1.3**
13. How did Ibn Battuta's Islamic faith affect his travel? **LESSON 2.1**
14. What was the purpose of the trans-Saharan trade network? **LESSON 2.2**
15. Why was the Indian Ocean trade network significant in history? **LESSON 2.4**

HISTORICAL THINKING

Answer the following questions. Support your answers with evidence from the chapter.

16. **EXPLAIN** How did the different climates of sub-Saharan Africa affect the economy of the region?
17. **MAKE INFERENCES** Why might historians want to verify the information found in the stories of griots through architectural findings?
18. **ANALYZE CAUSE AND EFFECT** What was the effect of the Bantu migrations on hunter-gatherer societies in southern and eastern Africa?
19. **CATEGORIZE** How did both internal and external factors lead to the break-up of the Ghana empire?
20. **FORM AND SUPPORT OPINIONS** Did Sundiata or Mansa Musa have a greater effect on Mali? Explain your answer.
21. **EVALUATE** How closely can a modern-day traveler follow in Ibn Battuta's footsteps? Explain.
22. **DRAW CONCLUSIONS** Why did the Mamluks convert to Islam and support its expansion?
23. **MAKE INFERENCES** Why did Ethiopian kings connect their dynasty to the Hebrew Bible?

INTERPRET VISUALS

Study the map at right, which shows the trans-Saharan trade network. Then answer the questions below.

24. Was the Sahara a barrier to trade in North and West Africa? Why or why not?

25. Based on the map, which resource appears to be available in the largest amount?

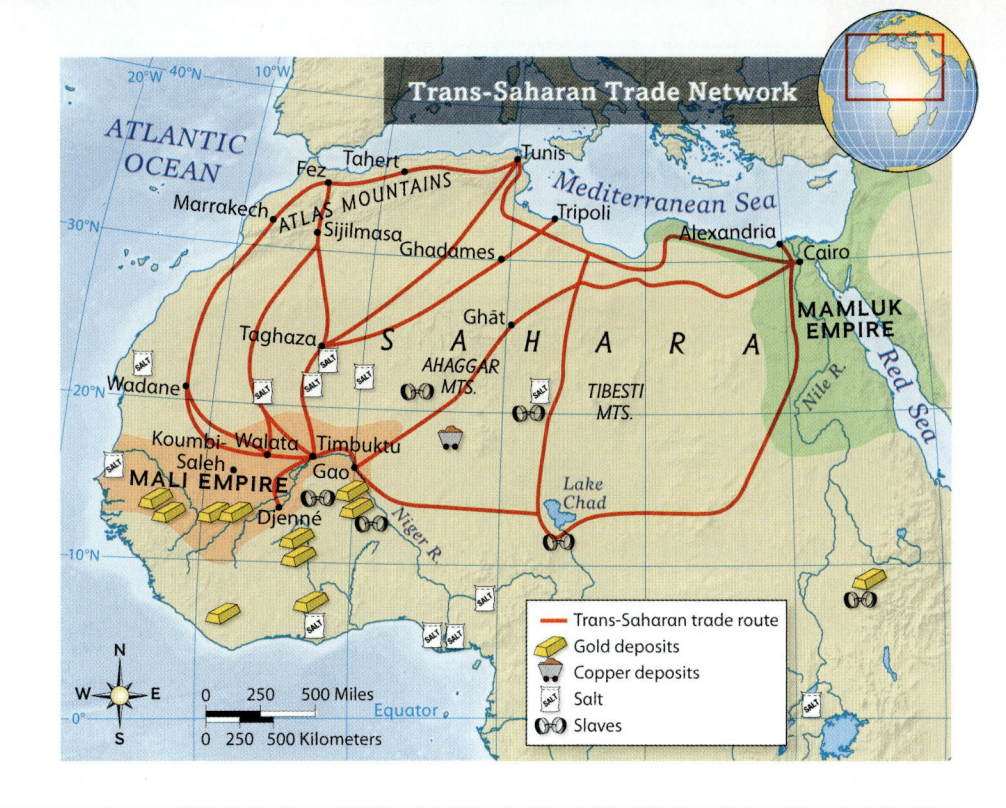

Trans-Saharan Trade Network

Legend:
- Trans-Saharan trade route
- Gold deposits
- Copper deposits
- Salt
- Slaves

ANALYZE SOURCES

In this excerpt, Ibn Battuta describes a visit to the royal court of Mali, where he observes griots orally relaying history to the king. He uses the word *sultan* for the Mali king since earlier rulers of the empire had converted to Islam. Read the excerpt and then answer the questions that follow.

> Each of them is inside a costume made of feathers resembling the green woodpecker on which is a wooden head with a red beak. . . . They stand before the Sultan in this laughable get-up and recite their poems. . . . They say to the Sultan: "This platform, formerly such and such a king sat on it and performed noble actions, and so and so did such and such; do you do noble acts which will be recounted after you?"
>
> —from *The Travels of Ibn Battuta*, 1350–1351

26. What attitude does Ibn Battuta hold toward the griots?

27. Why might he have formed this attitude?

CONNECT TO YOUR LIFE

28. **ARGUMENT** In 2012, Islamist rebels, who believe that the government should impose a strict form of religious law, pushed back the army of the government of Mali and temporarily took over the city of Timbuktu. To impose their extreme version of the faith, they attacked holy sites they saw as lacking in purity. Research to find out more about these rebels and then think about the following: Can you think of other times when wars have been fought to force people to believe and behave in a certain way? Is it ever justified for religious leaders to use violence to impose their own version of religion on other people? Write a short argument stating your position, using present-day or past examples.

TIPS

- List possible examples and choose one or two to use in making your argument.
- Summarize your viewpoint clearly before you present your points in more depth.
- Include reasons and specific details to support your position.
- Counter the strengths of an opposing viewpoint with your own position.

Achievements of African Societies 381

CHAPTER 14

Civilizations in the Americas
3100 B.C.E.–1532 C.E.

HISTORICAL THINKING How did early American societies emerge and interact before European contact?

SECTION 1 **Fishing, Hunting, and Farming**
SECTION 2 **Mesoamerican and Andean Societies**

CRITICAL VIEWING

This view from the Pyramid of the Moon in Teotihuacán in modern Mexico shows tourists descending steps to the Avenue of the Dead. The Pyramid of the Sun looms in the background. What generalization can you make about the people who lived here more than 2,000 years ago?

1.1

MAIN IDEA Descendants of the early humans who crossed the Beringia land bridge fanned out across the Americas from north to south, adapting to diverse environments.

The Settling of the Americas

Imagine finding lands and waters untouched by human beings. How would you and the people with you survive in these new places? The first people to set foot in North and South America, the last continents to be settled by humankind, accepted that challenge and developed a myriad of distinct cultures.

HOW THE FIRST AMERICANS LIVED

As you have read, the story of how and when humans came to the Americas is ever evolving. New discoveries constantly challenge what experts think they know. The best evidence for the first wave of migration comes from far down the west coast of the Americas at a settlement called **Monte Verde**, in what is now Chile. The Rocky Mountains and the Andes Mountains form a bony spine running along the western edge of the Americas. This barrier kept the first settlers in the coastal zones west of the mountain chain. Early humans probably traveled down the west coast of North and South America in small boats. These vessels were likely not that different from those used by early humans to sail to Australia.

Although no human remains have been found at Monte Verde so far, experts have discovered the 14,000-year-old footprints of a child. The site is under a layer of peat, which preserved organic materials such as wood, skin, and plants that almost never survive. This unusual preservation means that scholars know exactly which tools the first Americans used. When hunting, Monte Verde's residents used stone flakes on wooden sticks, spear points, and bolos—long strings with stones tied at both ends. The main weapon used to kill large game was the *atlatl*. The atlatl was a powerful two-part spear-thrower that people used over thousands of years.

The people who lived in Monte Verde hunted mastodon, a relative of the modern elephant that became extinct about 9000 B.C.E. They also foraged along the coast for shellfish, which could be eaten raw, and many other types of food. In the initial stages of migration, the settlers found a coastal environment much more hospitable than an inland one. Hunting parties could leave for long periods, knowing that people left behind had ample food supplies.

By 11,000 B.C.E., small bands of people had settled all of the Americas. For weapons, they used atlatls as well as wooden sticks with sharp slivers of rock, called microblades, attached to the shafts. Studies of different sites have determined that while the people in these regions shared many common traits, different technological traditions also existed in different North American regions. Each group left behind distinct artifacts, usually a spear point of a certain type.

Like the residents of Monte Verde, these later peoples combined hunting with the gathering of wild fruits and seeds. They lived in an area stretching from present-day Oregon to Texas, with heavy concentration in the Great Plains. They hunted a wide variety of game using atlatls tipped with stone spear points called **Clovis points**. Archaeologists call these characteristic artifacts Clovis points because the first such spear points were found in Clovis, New Mexico.

DIVERSE ENVIRONMENTAL ADAPTATIONS

The migrations to the Americas ended when the world's climate warmed quickly at the end of the last Ice Age. After 8300 B.C.E., the sea level rose. By 7000 B.C.E., most of Beringia was underwater once again. After 7000 B.C.E., the ancestors of modern American Indians dispersed over North and South America and began settling in diverse environments. Hunting, farming, gathering, and fishing were the principle activities that sustained these communities.

Hunting was common across the Americas. In fact, in some environments, it was the primary source of food. In the polar north, the ancestors of people like the Inuit developed great skills in hunting sea mammals such as whales and walruses. American Indians in the Clovis tradition hunted huge megafauna like wooly mammoths

Clovis Point Discoveries

Legend:
- Coastline at 75m below current sea level
- Glacial ice 12,000 years before present
- Glacial ice 13,000 years before present

CLOVIS POINT DISTRIBUTION
- 1–4
- 5–12
- 13–24
- 25–54
- 88–142

No sites reported finding 55–87 Clovis points.

Makers of Clovis spear points chose glassy rocks of striking colors to craft finely worked stone points.

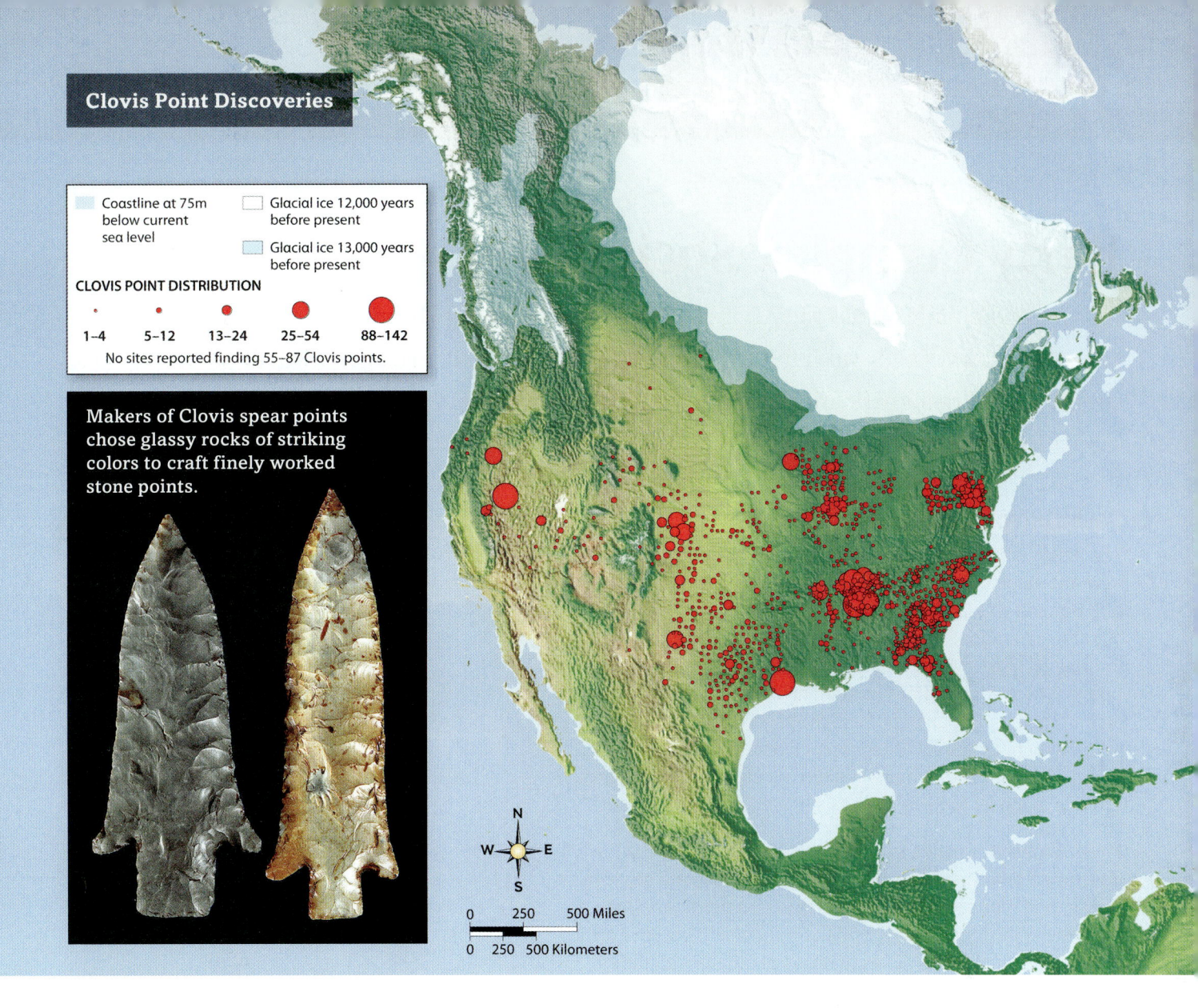

across the Great Plains. They were so successful that scientists believe that prehistoric people hunted these giant creatures into extinction, a reminder that humans not only adapt to environments but change them as well.

In other areas, farming became a common way of life after several separate Neolithic revolutions. As you will learn, farming sustained large populations and powerful empires in Mesoamerica—the region that stretches from today's Mexico into Central America—and in the Andes of South America. Woodland communities along the eastern seaboard also included skilled farmers and hunters. In the Mississippi River Valley and the Great Lakes region of North America, indigenous communities combined farming, hunting, fishing, and the gathering of foods such as honey, wild rice, and berries.

In some environments, aquatic resources were key to sustaining the population. Fishing and the gathering of seafood played a central role in the livelihoods of people in places such as the Amazon River basin, the swamps and bayous of what are now the states of Louisiana and Florida, and along the Pacific coast.

While adapting to varying environments, First Nations communities (as they are called in Canada) also developed hundreds of distinctive cultures, languages, and modes of living. Long separated from the peoples of the Eastern Hemisphere, the earliest Americans undertook their historical journeys in a unique geographic laboratory.

HISTORICAL THINKING

1. **READING CHECK** How and when did the first humans settle in the Americas?
2. **MAKE INFERENCES** What makes Monte Verde an important archaeological site?
3. **COMPARE AND CONTRAST** What were the similarities and differences between the ways in which the first Americans adapted to their various environments?

Civilizations in the Americas

1.2

MAIN IDEA The first humans who lived in the Americas developed agriculture and complex societies similar to others around the world.

Early Complex Societies

Indigenous peoples from the Arctic to Patagonia successfully adapted to varied surroundings and habitats. It was only in places where agricultural surpluses led to significant population density, however, that we find the transition to complex societies.

FOUNDATIONS OF COMPLEX SOCIETIES

The history of farming in the Americas began independently from the Neolithic revolution in Eurasia, and it is nearly as old. Squash was first domesticated in the Americas about 10,000 years ago. Soon, the people of Mesoamerica began to grow **maize**—which is similar to corn—squash, and beans. These foods offer excellent nutritional benefits when eaten together. Because of this advanced nutrition, by 2500 B.C.E., the population of Mesoamerica had increased by about 25 times. Mesoamericans did not start to domesticate animals, such as turkeys, until much later, around 800 B.C.E.

In the Andes Mountains in South America, agriculture developed differently. While Andean people also ate squash, beans, and maize, the main diet staple was potatoes. Over time, they developed many types of potatoes to improve their diets. Also, by planting different crops at different altitudes, Andean farmers increased their food security: if one crop failed, others might still grow well.

Around 4000 B.C.E., the Andeans domesticated the llama, the alpaca, and the capybara, a mammal that resembles a modern guinea pig but weighs 145 pounds or more in adulthood. Llamas and alpacas were used for their wool and as pack animals. Capybaras were raised for their meat. Unlike people in other parts of the world, early Americans never used the wheel or the plow to help them farm.

The earliest complex societies in the Americas developed in present-day Peru in the Andean region of South America, which extends from the Amazon rain forest in the east to the Pacific coast in the west. The earliest large urban community, Caral, arose in about 3100 B.C.E., around the same time cities first appeared in Mesopotamia. Caral's social classes were revealed in its architecture. Wealthy people lived in large dwellings on top of pyramids, artisans resided in smaller houses at the base of pyramids, and unskilled laborers had much simpler homes at the edge of the city. About 20 smaller towns have been found near Caral.

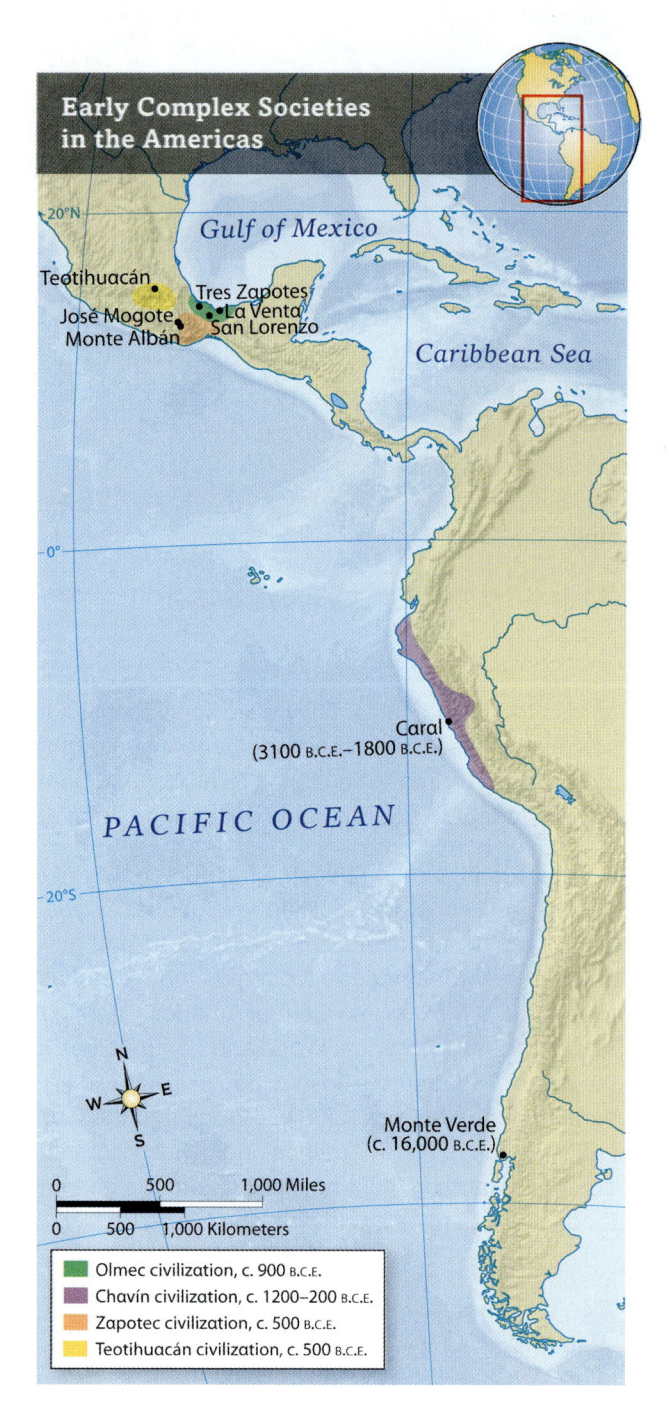

Early Complex Societies in the Americas

- Olmec civilization, c. 900 B.C.E.
- Chavín civilization, c. 1200–200 B.C.E.
- Zapotec civilization, c. 500 B.C.E.
- Teotihuacán civilization, c. 500 B.C.E.

Teotihuacán, José Mogote, Monte Albán, Tres Zapotes, La Venta, San Lorenzo

Caral (3100 B.C.E.–1800 B.C.E.)

Monte Verde (c. 16,000 B.C.E.)

Several hundred years after the decline of Caral in 1800 B.C.E., the Chavín civilization developed. The Chavín people built cities with large temples and stone sculptures and developed a religion that would influence later Andean civilizations. The most famous Chavín site is Chavín de Huantar, which had a population of 2,000–3,000 people and stretched out over 100 acres. No one is certain why the Chavín civilization declined, but earthquakes or drought may have played a part.

LEGACIES OF THE OLMEC, ZAPOTEC, AND TEOTIHUACÁN

The Olmec civilization developed in Mesoamerica at about the same time as the Chavín. The Olmec are considered the first advanced technological culture in the Americas. Their civilization consisted of at least five cities in the coastal region of what are now the Mexican states of Veracruz and Tabasco. Scholars are still learning about the Olmec, but they consider the Olmec the **mother culture** of the Mesoamerican societies that followed.

Scholars do know that the Olmec had social classes, a basic writing system, and an organized religion. The Olmec traded extensively and as far south as present-day Nicaragua. They drank chocolate, built pyramids, played ball games, and created incredible works of art, including small sculptures and colossal stone heads.

Several cultures that traded with the Olmec developed their own complex civilizations, including the Zapotec. The Zapotec lived in the southern highlands in the Oaxaca Valley and built the cities of San José Mogote and Monte Albán. Like other Mesoamerican civilizations, Zapotec cities had plazas, pyramids, palaces, and an astronomical observatory. Like other mountain peoples, the Zapotec built **terraces**, or stepped platforms, in the hills to create more room for their crops.

Another important Mesoamerican culture was centered in the city of **Teotihuacán**, which lasted from 200 B.C.E. to 650 C.E., and is the earliest known civilization in the Valley of Mexico. This area would later become home to the Toltec and Aztec cultures, both of which were heavily influenced by Teotihuacán. The largest city in the Americas before 1500, Teotihuacán covered 8 square miles and had a population of 200,000. Most people lived in one-story apartment compounds that were divided among several families. The outsides of the compounds had no windows and were painted white, while the interiors were covered with colorful frescoes. The city had a plumbing system that drained wastewater into underground channels that drained into canals.

Sometime around 600 C.E., major buildings in Teotihuacán were set on fire and artworks destroyed. The damage may have been the work of invaders, as it seems the city had no military fortifications. Many scholars, however, believe that the violence shows a revolt by the poor against the wealthy elite. In any case, Teotihuacán's population began to decline. By 750, the city was abandoned.

NATIONAL GEOGRAPHIC EXPLORER MATTHEW PISCITELLI

Exploring Peru's Ancient Past

About 5,000 years ago, the first complex societies in the Americas developed in a region along the north central coast of modern-day Peru called Norte Chico, or "Little North." In four river valleys in the region, people established permanent farming villages and built monumental structures for conducting religious ceremonies. Archaeologist and National Geographic Explorer Matthew Piscitelli works to investigate and preserve what remains of these settlements. In his research, he incorporates scientific tools such as drones and radar to map sites and identify buried structures.

Archaeologists have discovered about 30 large settlements with stepped platform mounds and sunken circular plazas in Norte Chico. According to Piscitelli, these large-scale structures served as religious centers that attracted visitors from outlying areas. He regards the Norte Chico settlements as a mother culture that greatly influenced cultures that followed. The Norte Chico culture set the stage for later Andean cultures, including the mighty Inca Empire.

HISTORICAL THINKING

1. **READING CHECK** What major crops did the earliest societies in the Americas develop, and why were they so important to the development of complex civilizations?
2. **INTERPRET MAPS** Why do you think ancient American civilizations developed along coastal areas?
3. **DRAW CONCLUSIONS** Why would the existence of large buildings or extensive irrigation projects be a sign of a complex society?

1.3

MAIN IDEA The Maya, a complex urban society that existed in Mesoamerica from 1500 B.C.E. to 1500 C.E., was a sophisticated civilization that in its Classic and Post-Classic periods rivaled that of Greece and China.

Classic and Post-Classic Maya Civilization

In 2018, scientists scanned a section of the Guatemalan lowlands and digitally removed the forest cover. They discovered something that amazed the world: huge numbers of previously unknown buildings, raised roads, quarries, irrigation systems, and terraced fields. All these features were created by the Maya, an ancient American culture that flourished for thousands of years.

ECONOMY AND POLITICS

For many years, experts understood that the Maya developed an advanced civilization that, starting in 1500 B.C.E., thrived for more than three millennia on the Yucatán Peninsula between the Gulf of Mexico and the Caribbean Sea. The Maya built a series of independent city-states, developed an accurate calendar, and were constantly at war with one another—or so archaeologists thought. The structures revealed by the land scans in 2018 showed that Maya city-states did not only interact through war. In fact, scientists now believe that Maya society was more interconnected and densely populated than anyone had realized.

The understanding of Maya society is still defined by its cities and architecture, however. Some Maya cities from the Classic Period (250–900 C.E.) include Copán, Tikal, Chichén Itzá (chee-CHEHN eet-SAH), and Palenque (pah-LEHNG-kay). Each city had a large central plaza that was used both as a market and for religious ceremonies, a palace, government buildings, temples, pyramids, and at least one ball court. The Maya ball game dated back to the Olmec and was a central part of Maya life. The ball game was not only an entertainment; it also had significant religious meaning.

To feed people in these cities, the Maya conquered the landscape, learning to control water to their advantage; they built canals, reservoirs, and dykes—or dams—even in swampy areas that modern scientists thought were uninhabitable. Their raised roadways were passable even during floods. Like the Zapotec, they terraced fields. And like earlier Mesoamerican peoples, the Maya practiced **slash-and-burn agriculture**, a method of clearing fields for planting in which people cut down trees, burned them, and used the ash as fertilizer.

This colorful fresco in a Maya temple in Bonampak, Mexico, shows a procession of musicians. The temples that contain these murals were suddenly abandoned around 800, a time when work on many other monuments stopped abruptly, marking the end of the Classic Period.

Maya city-states were ruled by kings who believed that they were descended from the gods. However, these rulers were not always completely independent of one another. In some cases, a ruler could be a vassal to a more powerful king. And queens were religiously important and could hold power in their own right. Recent analysis reveals a tradition of warrior queens, shown on carvings as armed for battle. On one, a queen known as Ix Naah Ek' wears the helmet of the Maya god of war. On other carvings, women are depicted standing on the heads of conquered enemies.

Pacal the Great was one of the most impressive Maya kings. He ruled the city of Palenque in present-day southeastern Mexico, near the Guatemalan border. Before Pacal ascended the throne at age 12, Lady Sak K'uk, his mother, served as regent. Pacal ruled his city for almost 70 years and took Palenque from a small, relatively unimportant place to one of the greatest cities in Mesoamerican history. Today, only a small part of the city has been studied.

Maya society was strictly divided into classes. The nobility included priests, warriors, and scribes. Below the nobility came merchants, artisans, and architects. Next were the farmers, who made up the majority of the population. The lowest class was made up of enslaved people. They were usually acquired through war, did much of the agricultural work, and sometimes served as sacrifices to the gods.

PEOPLE, CULTURE, AND TECHNOLOGY

Maya civilization seems to have been defined by warfare. Leaders of individual city-states battled one another to extend their territory, power, and influence. The Maya also needed captives to use in the frequent blood sacrifices demanded by their religion. Sometimes the people of a city, especially the king and queen, provided the blood themselves, but most often the blood was provided by sacrificing warriors who had been captured in battle.

The Maya were skilled artists who created beautiful works of pottery, sculpture, weaving, and painting. They worked with gold and copper but no other metals. They were the only ancient American civilization to develop a complex system of writing, which they used on stelae, in tomb art, and in folded books made of tree-bark paper called **codices**. (The singular term is *codex*.) Their writing also recorded their sophisticated mathematical and scientific calculations.

> **THE POPOL VUH** Much of the Maya belief system is recorded in the oral epic *Popul Vuh* (POHP-uhl voo), or "The Council Book," which is the most complete surviving pre-Columbian text in the Americas and tells the story of the origins of the gods, humanity, and the Maya people. It was written down after the Spanish conquest, using Roman script but the Mayan language. Recently, archaeologists discovered sections of the story inscribed on stelae, proving that at least parts of the epic were written down before the Spanish arrived.

At the time, the Maya numerical system was more advanced than any in the world. The Maya understood the concept of zero and were able to calculate sums into the hundreds of millions. Astronomers built observatories and used their mathematical skills to track the movements of the sun, moon, and stars. They observed the stars and planets so closely that they could predict eclipses. The Maya also created a complex ritual calendar as well as a 365-day solar calendar that is nearly as accurate as the one used today.

The Maya were great writers. Though many of their works included mathematical and scientific calculations, the Maya also wrote about their gods and their history. They left inscriptions on temples, in pyramids, on pottery, and in codices. It took hundreds of years of study for experts to discover how to read the Mayan script, which is made up of about 800 glyphs.

After about 800 C.E., the Maya entered an era of decline, which could have been the result of their unending wars. Another cause may have been environmental. The tropical environment around the main cities is highly sensitive and can easily be overfarmed. Competition for scarce land and food may have fed into the vicious cycle of warfare. A long drought between 800 and 1050 may have played a role as well. The urban-temple complex revived between 910 and 1500 but never achieved its former glory. Today, about 10 million Mayan speakers live in Guatemala, Honduras, Belize, El Salvador, Mexico, and the United States.

HISTORICAL THINKING

1. **READING CHECK** Why are the Maya considered one of the world's great civilizations?

2. **EVALUATE** How did the carvings of queens reveal their role in Maya society?

3. **ANALYZE CAUSE AND EFFECT** How might overfarming have contributed to the decline of the Maya civilization?

1.4 NATIONAL GEOGRAPHIC EXPLORER GUILLERMO DE ANDA

Discovering Maya Secrets
Underwater

"The sacred geography of the Maya is important because it's exactly why we are doing our work." –Guillermo de Anda

Archaeologist Guillermo de Anda descends into the Holtún cenote in Chichén Itzá, Mexico.

Guillermo de Anda is not a typical archaeologist. He doesn't excavate remains covered by dirt at a dry and dusty site. Instead, he puts on a wetsuit and rappels several stories into caves full of water. De Anda then straps on his underwater gear, organizes any necessary scientific equipment, and swims back to the time of the Maya. It's dangerous and precise work. "We have a saying that it's easier to train someone to be an archaeologist than to be a cave diver," he says.

MAIN IDEA National Geographic Explorer Guillermo de Anda's explorations of underwater caves in Mexico have revealed new information about the Maya and their way of life.

PRAYING FOR RAIN

Scientists such as de Anda use the latest technology to investigate new environments and provide new information about the first peoples of the Americas. One such environment is the **cenote**, a large natural pool or open cave. The Maya believed caves served as portals between the world of the living and the underworld. There, they practiced sacred ceremonies, including human sacrifices and communication with the dead.

De Anda specializes in mapping and exploring cenotes and underwater caves to research the Maya. In 2010, he explored the Holtún cenote. This cenote is located 1.6 miles northwest of El Castillo, the large Maya pyramid at Chichén Itzá. He found carefully arranged human skeletons and items such as pottery, fragments of carved figures, a flint knife, and the remains of birds, dogs, and stingrays. Some experts believe that the Maya sacrifices and gifts were an appeal to the rain god Chaak to provide needed rainfall for their crops.

According to the *Popul Vuh*, the Maya cosmos had four sides and four corners. El Castillo stands in the middle of four cenotes: Holtún, Xtoloc, Kanjuyum, and the Sacred Cenote. In February 2018, de Anda and his team began an attempt to reach a hidden, blocked cenote under the pyramid itself. He believes a successful excavation could lead to evidence of a "fifth direction" or other clues to Maya beliefs and rituals.

PLUNGING INTO THE PAST

Accessing and studying cenotes requires a lot of experience and a lot of preparation in challenging conditions. "You also have to stay a long time under the water," de Anda explains. "Sometimes we will spend six or seven hours in the water. That's the most demanding part because you still have to go back, you're tired, cold, hungry."

In addition to their scuba gear, underwater archaeologists also have to contend with bulky technology that helps them gather information. One such tool is ground-penetrating radar, or GPR. GPR can be used to find and map hidden tunnels or caves, including cenotes. Thermal imaging and LiDAR can detect some of the estimated 3,000 cenotes in southern Mexico that are concealed by dense forests. Researchers also mount sonar equipment on kayaks and use laser-scanning and photogrammetry to generate 3-D versions of the caves.

In January 2018, de Anda and a team of archaeologists discovered a passage that links the flooded cavern systems of Sac Actun and Dos Ojos. This flooded freshwater cave in the Yucatán Peninsula is now the world's largest and measures 215 miles long. It contains important evidence of the Maya as well as the very first Americans.

In March 2019, de Anda and other specialists announced the discovery of a cave system under Chichén Itzá that contains well-preserved ritual items dating back more than a thousand years. To reach the cave known to locals as Balamkú, or Jaguar God, de Anda had to crawl on his stomach for hours through incredibly narrow tunnels. "When I get to the first offering," he notes, "I realized I was in a very very very sacred place." He adds, "You almost feel the presence of the Maya who deposited these things in there." Continuing studies may provide additional clues to the rise and fall of this mighty civilization. "Balamkú will help rewrite the story of Chichen Itzá," de Anda claims.

HISTORICAL THINKING

1. **READING CHECK** Why are the discoveries of Guillermo de Anda and his team important?

2. **ANALYZE CAUSE AND EFFECT** What is the effect of technology on the work of de Anda and other archaeologists?

1.5 MAIN IDEA Early modern humans who migrated and settled in present-day Canada and the United States also developed complex societies.

Northern Cultures

What was North America like when Europeans arrived? For generations, students were taught it was an empty, wild land sparsely populated with small bands of Native Americans hunting and fighting one another. The truth is quite different—and far more interesting.

EARLY NORTH AMERICANS

Millions of Native American people lived across vast territories in what are now the United States and Canada. They were organized into hundreds of different societies.

Many early North American archaeological sites are located along the rivers of the midwestern United States. The Adena culture, the oldest known complex society, built large **earthworks**, or constructions of soil and rocks, along the Ohio River Valley in Ohio and Illinois between 500 B.C.E. and 100 C.E. No evidence demonstrates that the Adena raised crops, but they did trade with other groups and engaged in mound-building.

The Hopewell people, who established themselves between 200 B.C.E. and 500 C.E., were both farmers and mound-builders. They grew crops and built large earthworks in the valleys of the Ohio, Illinois, and Mississippi rivers. The Hopewell had a larger trade network than the Adena, and archaeologists believe that the Hopewell mounds were also well-known religious sites that attracted Native American pilgrims.

Between 800 and 1450, the Mississippian culture developed one of the first urban societies in North America. This society was centered around the Mississippi River Valley, but it reached as far east as present-day Georgia and as far south as New Orleans. The Mississippian people built large urban centers and were the first known group in the Americas to use bows and arrows.

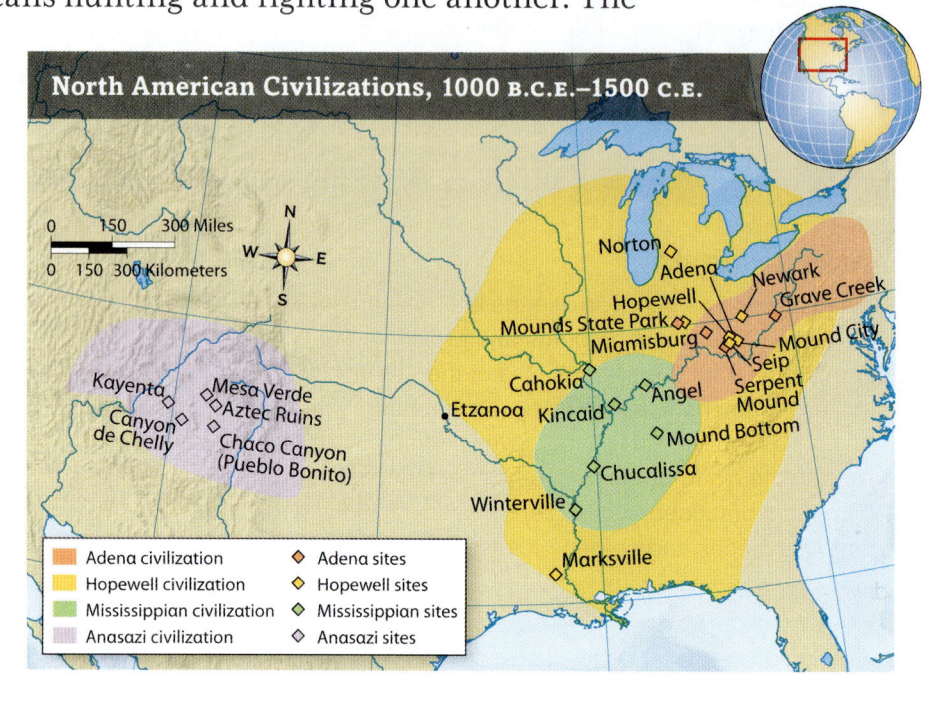

More than 100 different Mississippian sites have been discovered. These towns and cities followed a plan similar to that used by the Maya, with temples and mounds around a central plaza. Recent investigations have focused on evidence of cultural and archaeological influences flowing from the Yucatán Peninsula to places such as **Cahokia**, the largest of the Mississippian cities.

Located in present-day Illinois, experts claim that Cahokia sprang up between 1000 and 1100, its population swelling from about 7,000 to 15,000. The Cahokians built houses, an expansive plaza as large as 45 football fields, and more than 100 mounds. The largest mound—Mound 38—stands nearly 100 feet high and has a base larger than that of the Great Pyramid of Giza in Egypt.

Recent studies have shown that Cahokia was a place of pilgrimage and an astronomical site. It may have been used for complex calculations, showing that the people of Cahokia—perhaps learning from the Maya—may have had the advanced knowledge to predict eclipses.

392 CHAPTER 14

Archaeologists recently found evidence of another ancient city in the Midwest. Etzanoa is located between the Arkansas and Walnut rivers near Wichita, Kansas. It is thought to have flourished between 1450 and 1700 and been home to at least 20,000 people. Ancestors of the Wichita people, the people of Etzanoa were farmers and buffalo hunters from today's Oklahoma and Texas who traded meat and hides to the Pueblo people in return for cotton, obsidian, and turquoise.

THE ANASAZI

The Pueblo peoples—Hopi, Zuni, Acoma, and Laguna—located in what is now the southwestern United States have a long and intriguing history. Their predecessors were the ancestral Pueblo, or Anasazi, who flourished between 100 and 1600. One of the most famous civilizations in North America, the Anasazi originated in present-day Colorado, Arizona, Utah, and New Mexico. At their height, they may have lived in thousands of different communities connected by a 400-mile network of roads and spread over almost 30,000 square miles.

Anasazi villages and towns show signs of contact with the Mesoamerican cultures, particularly in the design of their ball courts. The Anasazi used irrigation to farm, and their craftspeople made distinctive pottery, cotton and feather clothing, and turquoise jewelry. Early Anasazi lived in caves or pit houses carved out of the ground. Starting in about 700, they expanded their territory and began to live in small villages. Their buildings were made with bricks and mortar and had log roofs. Some of these buildings had as many as 100 connected rooms.

The Chaco culture thrived between 850 and 1250 during a particularly mysterious period of Anasazi history centered around Chaco Canyon, New Mexico. The Chacoans were skilled astronomers and used advanced water control and collection techniques. They erected huge stone buildings called "great houses." The great houses were often oriented to the sun and moon and were within direct view of one another, which enabled quick communication over long distances. It is possible that these great houses were not villages but political, religious, or trading centers that were populated only at particular times or for specific events. No one is certain.

After 1150, the Anasazi abandoned the towns and great houses and started to live in large communities built into the sides of cliffs. The most famous Anasazi cliff city is **Mesa Verde**, in Colorado. After only about 50 years, the Anasazi began to vacate their cliff homes. No one is sure why the Anasazi moved to the cliffs or why they left them. One recent theory is that the Anasazi were driven out by internal strife. Whatever the reason, the Anasazi deserted their cliff dwellings and moved to other parts of the Southwest, including the White Mountains of Arizona and the Rio Grande Valley

CRITICAL VIEWING The ancient Pueblo built individual dwellings connected to one another, as shown here in Mesa Verde. Based on details from the photograph, why do you think the people chose to build Mesa Verde where they did?

HISTORICAL THINKING

1. **READING CHECK** In what types of environments did the oldest complex societies develop in North America?
2. **COMPARE AND CONTRAST** How were many North American civilizations similar to and different from Mesoamerican cultures?
3. **INTERPRET MAPS** Where were most of the mound builders' sites located, and why?

2.1

MAIN IDEA In the 10th and 12th centuries, two new cultures—first the Toltec and then the Aztec—arose and created complex social structures in what is now the Valley of Mexico.

Toltec and Aztec Civilizations

Kingdoms come and go, but beliefs and traditions continue. The feathered serpent god traveled through the centuries taking bits of knowledge and culture with him. Born among the Olmec, he visited San José Mogote and Teotihuacán before he settled among the Toltec and then the Aztec, where he was called Quetzalcoatl (kweht-suhl-kuh-WAH-tuhl).

CHARACTERISTICS OF THE TOLTEC

A new Mesoamerican society, the Toltec, began to rise about the 10th century C.E. The Toltec conquered the city of Teotihuacán around 900, which began a period of wealth and local influence that lasted until about 1100. Some archaeologists believe the Toltec were descendants of the Teotihuacán people, and others think they migrated to central Mexico from the north.

The Toltec were excellent potters, metalworkers, and warriors. Once they were established in the area, they built a capital called Tollan. Ultimately, the city covered around five square miles and was home to 30,000–40,000 people. The remains of the city reveal at least two large pyramids, a palace, and a ball court. Dwellings were organized into groups of homes around a central courtyard surrounded by a wall. Each courtyard contained an altar in the center.

No one is certain why the Toltec civilization weakened and ended around 1100. Reasons for the decline may have been environmental or political. The city of Tollan was certainly lost through violent overthrow; it was burned, buried, and later looted by the next dominant group in the Valley of Mexico, the Aztec. These people adopted much of Toltec culture and technology, and even though they migrated from the north, they claimed to be the Toltec's descendants.

THE AZTEC EMPIRE

Around 1325, a people known as the Mexica traveled to the Valley of Mexico from what is now western Mexico. When they arrived, they found some 50 established city-states. Because the area was already occupied, the Mexica were forced to settle in the surrounding swampland and on an island in the middle of Lake Texcoco. They called their city **Tenochtitlán**.

After they had been in the region for about 100 years, the Mexica formed an alliance with the Texcoco and Tlacopan city-states. This Triple Alliance became what historians call the Aztec. Under the rule of **Moctezuma**, the Mexica became the dominant group in the Triple Alliance, and Tenochtitlán became the center of the Aztec Empire.

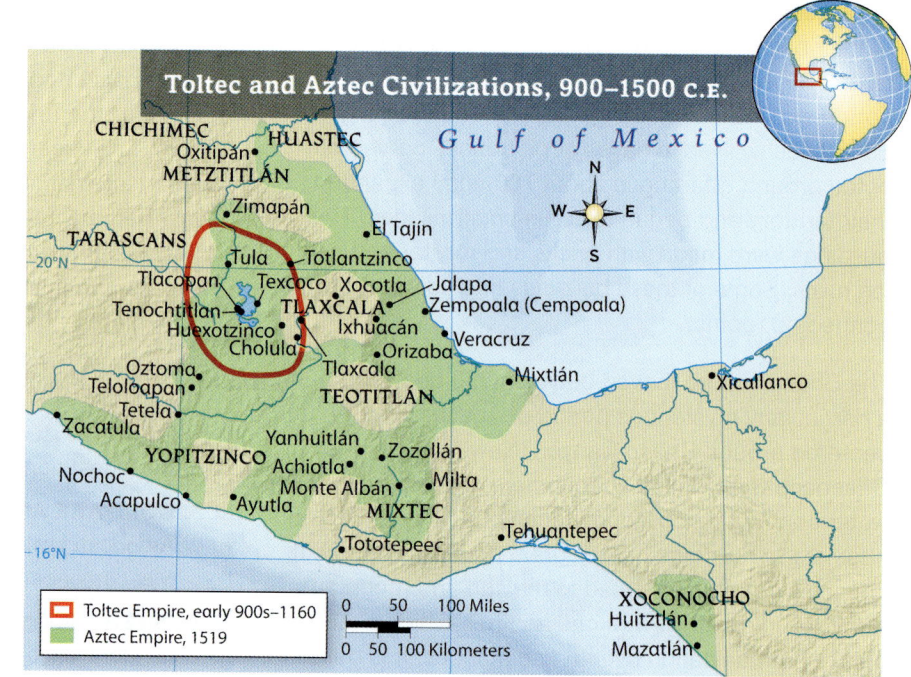

Toltec and Aztec Civilizations, 900–1500 C.E.

- Toltec Empire, early 900s–1160
- Aztec Empire, 1519

At its height, Tenochtitlán contained 60,000 homes, covered an area of five square miles, and had a population of around 200,000 people. Residents traveled large canals by canoe, and **chinampas**—artificial islands created to raise crops—supplied ample food. Reservoirs held fresh water, and flower gardens were everywhere. The central marketplace offered cooked and uncooked food, enslaved people, and luxury goods made from gold, silver, and feathers.

By 1500, the Aztec had conquered 450 city-states and ruled over a population of between 6 and 11 million. They maintained their military by drafting all adult men from among their own as well as conquered people. Once the Aztec defeated a people, they demanded tribute and chose sacrificial victims from the conquered. Not surprisingly, the Aztec faced frequent rebellions.

Like many other societies in the Americas, the Aztec engaged in human sacrifice, but they have become known for killing unusually high numbers of people at one time. The term for human blood in the Aztec language was "precious water," and the Aztec believed that their gods needed that precious water to keep the soil fertile, the harvest plentiful, and the seasons regular.

Aztec society was strictly organized. The Aztec leader was considered a god. Next in the hierarchy were local rulers, then nobles and priests, and finally commoners, serfs, and slaves. The position of emperor was not strictly hereditary, though it often stayed within the same family. A group of nobles, priests, and successful warriors chose each new leader and could depose him if they did not approve of his rule. While there was some flexibility, everyday life was generally extremely structured and rule-oriented. Crafts were specialized, and sons were trained in the professions of their fathers.

Although the Aztec were fierce warriors, they were skilled farmers, successful traders, expert architects, and accomplished artists as well. Aztec priests were also the scientists and in many cases the scribes of the society. Both boys and girls went to school, and some scholars believe that the Aztec were the first society with **compulsory education**, or education required by law, for all boys under the age of 16.

CRITICAL VIEWING Quetzalcoatl (at right in the main panel) devours a person in this image from the Codex Borgia, which scholars think the Aztec wrote before the arrival of European explorers. Which details in the illustration help you identify Quetzalcoatl?

Gender relations in Aztec society were complex. On a public level, this was a decidedly male-dominated culture with war, politics, and blood rituals as the special domain of men. But modern scholars acknowledge the parallel institutions in which women had significant power as doctors, priestesses, teachers, merchants, and skilled artisans. In Tenochtitlán, it seems that a shared system of childcare freed mothers to take on specialized roles.

The Aztec Empire had many characteristics found in other empires both nearby and on the other side of the world. Like the Maya, the Aztec had complex ritual and solar calendars, worshiped a feathered serpent god, built large stone monuments, and played a ritual ball game. Like many societies in Africa and Eurasia, ordinary Aztec people were required to pay tribute to their leaders by contributing a share of their crops, performing labor, or providing other goods. The Aztec also shared similarities with another American empire that ruled farther south at the same time: the Inca.

HISTORICAL THINKING

1. **READING CHECK** What influence did the Toltec have on the Aztec?
2. **MAKE CONNECTIONS** How did the Aztec manipulate their environment to help increase their power?
3. **DRAW CONCLUSIONS** Why did the Aztec face many rebellions from the people they conquered?

2.2

MAIN IDEA The Andean region in South America was home to a variety of fascinating, elaborate civilizations as well as one of the largest empires in the world: the Inca.

Andean Cultures and the Inca

For a long time, historians and other scholars claimed that a writing system was essential to a complex culture. Yet one great empire—the Inca—managed a population of millions over far-reaching, difficult terrain without having a conventional written script.

EARLY SOUTH AMERICAN SOCIETIES

In what is now northern Bolivia, archaeology shows an ancient tradition of intensive agriculture supporting the earthworks, canals, raised fields, and causeways that indicate the beginnings of complex societies. The Andean region contains extreme climates—including oxygen-poor high altitudes, steamy jungles, and dry coastal deserts—and many different societies developed in the vicinity.

The Paracas and the Topará peoples created **geoglyphs**. Geoglyphs are large geometric designs and shapes drawn on the ground, created by scraping away dark surface dirt and rocks to reveal lighter-colored soil. The geoglyphs made by the Paracas and the Topará date from 500 B.C.E. to 200 C.E. From 200 to 700 C.E., the Nasca people produced their own glyphs now known as the Nasca Lines. These designs were made in a variety of shapes including spirals, fanciful animals, and humanlike figures. Some archaeologists believe people walked the patterns in spiritual rituals.

Other early Andean societies include the Moche (MOH-chay), who flourished between 100 and 700 C.E. They were best known for the sophisticated pottery and metalworking they left behind. The militaristic Wari may have invaded and brought down—or helped bring down—both the Moche and the Nasca, while the neighboring Tiwanaku (tee-WAH-nuh-koo) culture built their city-state on reclaimed marshland, like the Aztec's Tenochtitlán. The Chimú (chee-MOO) people stabilized their empire by allowing people they defeated to retain some control over local governments. They also made a very early form of the telephone.

These early cultures all developed road systems and established trading networks, some more extensive than others. They built irrigation and canal systems and raised or terraced their fields. These civilizations survived for hundreds of years because they transformed their environment by controlling or collecting water and increasing agricultural productivity.

This feline ceramic bottle from the Wari people dates from the 900s to the 1100s.

All of these societies also had skilled artisans. Expert weavers made exquisite textiles, architects built impressive cities, sculptors carved stone statues, and craftspeople made jewelry from jade and decorations from gold and silver. Sometime around 700 to 800, the peoples of the Andes Mountains combined tin and copper to make bronze and also added copper and silver to gold to make an alloy that was easier to work with than pure gold. They used different quantities of metals to make different colors. Unlike the peoples of Eurasia, the Andeans never used these metals for weapons or tools.

Around 1400, a new culture arose in the Andes. From its capital city high in the mountains, this society created an empire that would eclipse all others.

THE INCA EMPIRE

The Inca civilization, which lasted from 1400 to 1532, started in the same region as the Wari and Tiwanaku, whom the Inca greatly admired. The Inca capital, **Cusco** (KOO-skoh), was located in the Andes at 11,300 feet. With an estimated peak population of up to 150,000, the city had vast plazas, parklands, shrines, fountains, and canals. Later, as the empire expanded, a second capital was established at **Quito** (KEE-toh).

396 CHAPTER 14

Archaeologists believe the Inca moved to Cusco around 1400. The first great ruler was **Pachacuti** (pah-chah-KOO-tee), who seized the throne from his brother in a coup in 1438 and began to expand the Inca domain at an amazing speed. In only 100 years, Pachacuti and his successors conquered large chunks of present-day Peru, Ecuador, Bolivia, Argentina, and Chile to rule over a population of about 10–12 million.

Compared with other world empires, the Inca were remarkably centralized and authoritarian. Rather than accept tribute but otherwise leave conquered peoples with their own languages and customs, the Inca overpowered them. They held the gods of conquered people hostage by taking images of those deities to Cusco. They built their own temples on sites sacred to the people they defeated. They resettled thousands, forcing people to move to regions far from their original homes. And they encouraged submission by treating those who surrendered more gently than those who resisted.

The Inca integrated people they conquered into their empire. Vanquished people were forced to perform labor and serve in the military. In fact, most of the soldiers in the Inca army were defeated people. The Inca kept local leaders in power but required them to give up their lands and swear loyalty to the emperor. They also allowed these leaders to serve in the central government—though only at lower levels—as long as the leaders learned Quechua (KEH-chuh-wuh), the Inca language.

The Inca did not have an orderly system of succession, and this flaw weakened their empire. Each time an Inca ruler died, all the male relatives who hoped to succeed him launched an all-out war until a single man won.

CHARACTERISTICS OF INCA RELIGION, CULTURE, AND SOCIETY

The Inca believed in many gods, with the most powerful being Inti, the sun god. The Inca were certain that they were chosen people who derived from Inti and that the emperor was a direct descendant of Inti. Below the gods were ancestor spirits and *wak'a*, spirits who inhabited places such as streams, caves, rocks, and hills. The Inca also believed that their nobles lived after death. Rulers and close family members were mummified. These mummies were removed from their tombs during important ceremonies, given food and drink, and consulted about important issues.

Like the Maya and the Aztec, the Inca developed a complex, organized ritual calendar. The Inca also practiced human sacrifice like other Andean and Mesoamerican societies did. Scholars believe Inca sacrifices were not as frequent as those in Mesoamerican societies and usually occurred in times of hardship, such as droughts or floods, or during unusual astronomical events, such as eclipses. Occasionally, events demanded a larger number of sacrifices, such as when a ruler died. One source gives the largest number of Inca people killed at a single time as 4,000.

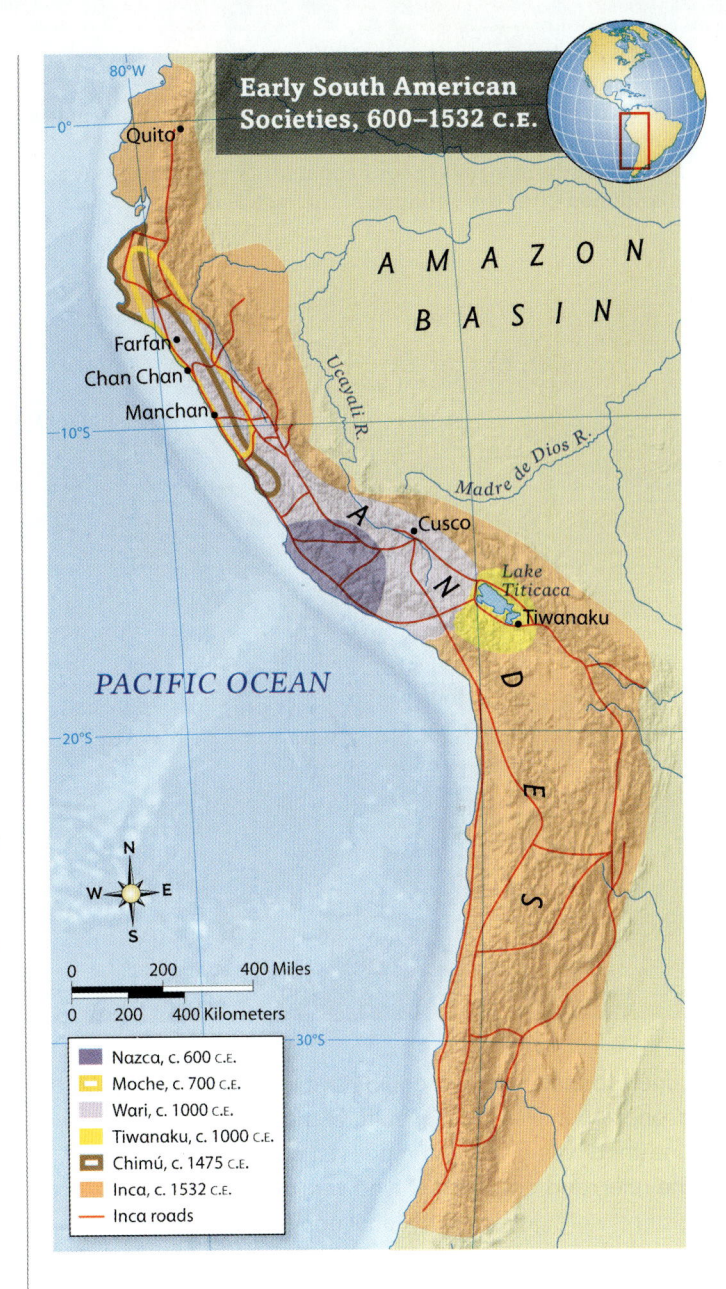

Inca society was strictly organized. The aristocracy was divided into three tiers: the close relatives of the emperor and previous rulers, more distant relatives, and leaders of conquered peoples. During his reign, the emperor lived as a god among his subjects. Even so, he had to maintain support from the nobles, who could overthrow him at any time.

The ordinary people of the Andes lived in family groups. Each group farmed land in several connected ecological

Early South American Societies, 600–1532 C.E.

Legend:
- Nazca, c. 600 C.E.
- Moche, c. 700 C.E.
- Wari, c. 1000 C.E.
- Tiwanaku, c. 1000 C.E.
- Chimú, c. 1475 C.E.
- Inca, c. 1532 C.E.
- Inca roads

Civilizations in the Americas

Machu Picchu, which stands 8,000 feet above sea level, embodies the Inca talent for engineering. The site's even stone houses on multiple levels are connected by man-made waterways and more than 100 stairways. Built around 1450 as a summer palace for Pachacuti, Machu Picchu was abandoned after the collapse of the Inca Empire.

zones so that everyone could have food even if the crops in one zone failed. All agricultural produce was divided—one-third was given to the priests, one-third went to the ruler, and one-third stayed with the farmer. Family groups were governed by local nobles, including women.

Like the Aztec, the Inca had parallel spheres for men and women. For example, men controlled the cult of the sun god, associated with war, while women led the lunar cult, responsible for fertility. "Chosen women" were sent from the provinces to special schools in Cusco where they learned leadership skills in the women's sphere, as well as legends of the Inca gods.

INCA ACHIEVEMENTS

Like other Andean societies, the Inca adapted to prosper in extreme landscapes. They terraced the land for agriculture, transported water over long distances, built underground water systems, and adorned their cities with impressive fountains. The Inca Empire stretched across multiple environments, from the Pacific Ocean, through a coastal plain fertile for agriculture, to the steepest mountains, and to the tropical rain forest on the other side. Trade across such diverse terrains with different crops and natural resources made the Inca rich.

The Inca are particularly famous for their incredible architecture. Like the master stonemasons of Great Zimbabwe in Africa, Inca builders created huge structures with blocks of stone fitted together so well that mortar, a mixture used to keep larger materials together, was not necessary. One of the most famous examples of Inca architecture is the mountain-top city of **Machu Picchu** (mah-choo PEE-choo).

Another major legacy of the Inca Empire was its impressive road system. While some roads in the region were built as early as 1000 B.C.E., it was the Inca who linked existing roads with new roads to create one huge highway network. While other empires—the Persians, the Romans, and the Chinese—had impressive engineering systems, none but the Inca had the skill to build at such high altitudes. With no wheel, the Inca constructed roads across deserts, deep chasms, and mountains taller than 16,000 feet.

Most of the traffic on these roads was by foot, with llamas carrying small loads. These routes included rest stations and a messenger system. Inca messengers most likely switched off often to travel so quickly. These roads allowed not only the rapid deployment of the Inca army but also allowed efficient delivery of messages between the capital and provinces, reinforcing the centralization of Inca power in spite of enormous spaces and difficult terrain.

The Inca mathematical system was quite advanced and almost identical to the one used today. The Inca developed an agricultural calendar and calculated the correct days to plant and harvest, as well as when to celebrate important festival days. They also produced beautiful textiles, pottery, and metal sculpture. They were influenced by the Chimú as well as other Andean cultures, but their work was more technically advanced than the art of previous societies.

Much about the Inca remains a mystery because they did not have a writing system. However, they did develop the **quipu** (KEY-poo), a series of knotted strings that the Inca used to keep records, including business accounts, population censuses, and calendars. Interestingly, recent theories claim that some quipu also include historical and religious stories and songs.

Despite its accomplishments, the Inca Empire was not as strong or stable as it appeared. Conquered people resented their heavy labor obligations, but if they failed to cooperate, the Inca sent loyal subjects as colonists to take their land. If they still rose up, Inca officials would move troublemakers to distant regions. Succession disputes also destabilized the empire. It is possible that the Inca might have withstood or even overcome these failings, but by 1500, they faced a new and unexpected enemy: diseases brought by Europeans to the Americas.

HISTORICAL THINKING

1. **READING CHECK** Why is the Inca Empire considered a major world empire?

2. **INTERPRET MAPS** What physical features limited the expansion of early South American civilizations?

3. **IDENTIFY** How did earlier Andean civilizations influence the Inca?

4. **ANALYZE CAUSE AND EFFECT** What effect did the road system have on the Inca Empire?

2.3

MAIN IDEA Peoples of the Pacific and the Atlantic traveled great distances, bringing complex societies to ocean islands.

Pacific and Caribbean Island Societies

Imagine being at sea in a simple canoe with everything you need to survive onboard. You are surrounded by the sea. There is no land in sight—and you have no idea when you might see any. This is what great Polynesian explorers and settlers experienced.

POLYNESIAN SOCIETIES

Sometime before 300 C.E., the first settlers reached present-day Hawaii, traveling the great distance from the Marquesas Islands without a clear idea of what might lay ahead. By this time, Polynesian sailors had developed a strong form of double canoe, two wooden frames lashed together with rope. These sail-driven vessels could carry tons of cargo and travel over a hundred miles a day. The Polynesians carried with them not just food and water but breadfruit and taro seedlings for planting and the pigs they relied on for meat. With deep knowledge of the ocean environment, Tahitian navigators headed into the unknown, eventually establishing communities on the Hawaiian Islands.

Sometime after 400, the first settlers reached Rapa Nui (RAH-puh NOO-ee), also known as Easter Island. Their final migration, in 1350, was to New Zealand, where they became the Maori (MAW-ree). Experts believe the Polynesians also reached the coast of South America

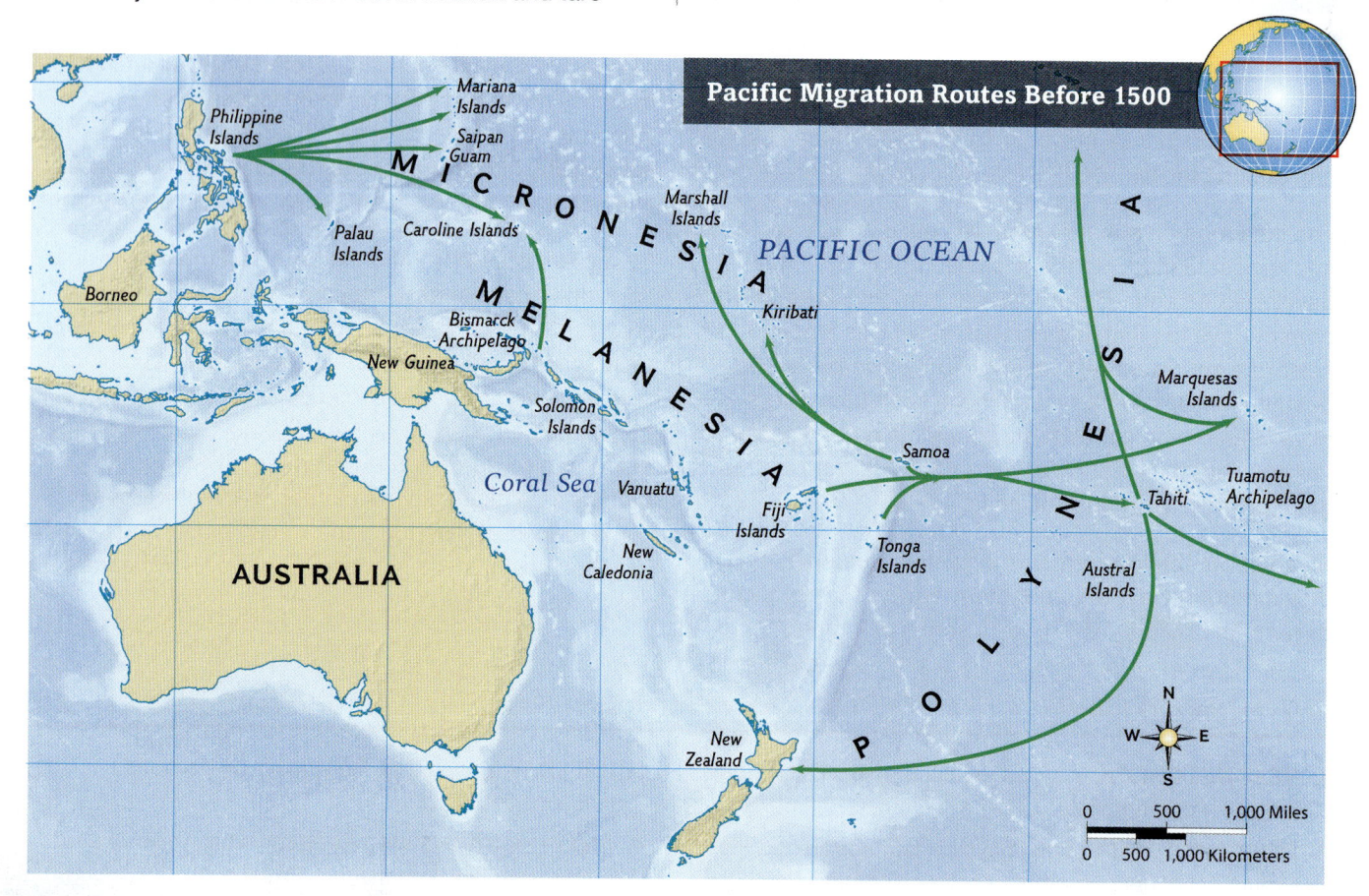

Pacific Migration Routes Before 1500

400 CHAPTER 14

In 2011, a team of 18 people in Hawaii put Hunt and Lipo's walking technique to the test and moved a 10-foot, 5-ton moai replica 100 yards in only 40 minutes.

NATIONAL GEOGRAPHIC EXPLORERS TERRY HUNT AND CARL LIPO

The "Walking" Statues of Rapa Nui

Rapa Nui's mysterious moai have captured people's imaginations for centuries. "This whole business of giant statues really cries out for an explanation: what on Earth is going on here?" asks National Geographic Explorer Terry Hunt. How did the inhabitants of Rapa Nui transport more than 500 of these multi-ton religious figures across the small island's rough terrain?

Early theories included dragging the statues with ropes on tree trunks or using an inverted wooden V to move the moai. But ancient stories said the statues walked. So later approaches involved placing the statues upright and moving them with a twisting motion or on a ledge over wooden rollers. Hunt and fellow National Geographic Explorer Carl Lipo offer a new approach. "Ultimately, the evidence of how the statues were moved can be found on the statues themselves," Lipo explains. "They were engineered to move. The details of the statues were telling us about transport." Hunt and Lipo said three small groups could have walked a moai: two on the sides to rock the statue forward and one, from behind, to stabilize it.

In 2011, 18 people in Hawaii put this technique to the test and moved a ten-foot, five-ton moai replica 100 yards in only 40 minutes. Walking is currently the best explanation of how ancient Rapa Nui people transported the statues and is consistent with Rapa Nui oral traditions.

Terry Hunt

Carl Lipo

Civilizations in the Americas 401

These giant stone figures on Rapa Nui, or Easter Island, portray ancestral leaders. When alive, a ruler would commission a statue of himself that remained horizontal. After leaders died, the statues were placed in an upright position.

at some point because sweet potatoes, a South American plant, have been found on Polynesian islands as well. And chickens, which were domesticated by the Polynesians, were also in South America before the Spanish arrived.

That Rapa Nui was settled at all is as amazing as it is unlikely; it is truly a speck in a wide sea. It lies 1,300 miles southeast of its nearest neighbor, Pitcairn Island, and is only 14 miles across at its widest point. It was probably settled by a small party of Polynesians blown extremely far off their original course. Rapa Nui is well known around the world because of its ancient moai (MOW-eye) statues that resemble humans with large heads.

The Polynesians were master shipbuilders, navigators, sailors, and fishermen. They had no navigational instruments, so they relied on their expert knowledge of astronomy. They used observation not only of the stars but also of clouds, waves, and bird flight patterns to navigate across vast distances in all types of weather. The Polynesians established trading networks but also warred with one another, depending on island proximity.

Polynesian communities ranged from a few houses around a lagoon to large protected villages on the larger islands. The more people lived in one area, the stronger the chiefs became, and the more elaborate their religious rituals. Polynesian law was based on what the Hawaiians called *kapu*. Kapu was a long list of taboos that regulated each person's behavior. If a person of low rank ate food prepared for a chief, for example, or if a woman entered a warrior's canoe, he or she could face severe punishment.

Considering the extensive distances between some of the islands, the culture of Polynesia is exceptionally unified. Polynesians separated by thousands of miles share many of the same words. Tools and artistic styles are also remarkably similar across the many islands.

CARIBBEAN ISLAND SOCIETIES

Like the Polynesians, the people of the Caribbean islands in the western Atlantic had to migrate by sea to find new homes. However, they did not have to travel nearly as far. Central and South America are separated from their closest island neighbors by only 200–500 miles, compared with the thousands of miles that separate the islands of Polynesia.

Today, the Caribbean islands are usually divided into three groups: the Greater Antilles (including Cuba, Hispaniola, Jamaica, and Puerto Rico), the Lesser Antilles (including Grenada in the south to the Virgin Islands in the north); and the Bahamian Archipelago. There were three main waves of migration to the Caribbean islands. The first wave came from Central America to Cuba and Hispaniola in about 5000 B.C.E. The people who settled there used stone tools, hunted, and foraged. In about 1000 B.C.E., a different group came from South America. They settled these same islands and later expanded into the Bahamian Archipelago. These people were farmers and fishers, and they also made pottery. Many historians believe these are the ancestors of the Taíno people first encountered by Christopher Columbus. Finally, from about 250 B.C.E. to 1450 C.E., groups began to migrate to the Lesser Antilles from the Orinoco river delta in present-day Venezuela.

Ultimately, the peoples of the Caribbean became two closely related groups who both spoke a language called Arawak (A-ruh-wahk). The Island Caribs lived in the Lesser Antilles, while the Taíno lived in the Greater Antilles and the Bahamas. Like the Polynesians, Caribbean peoples were expert navigators and seafarers. They, too, fought with one another but also developed complex trade networks. They had expert astronomical knowledge, built thatched buildings, grew crops, and developed skills such as weaving and making pottery and baskets.

While they shared many characteristics, civilizations in the Caribbean islands were culturally diverse. In general, Island Caribs lived in smaller, less permanent villages, had more communal societies, and were influenced culturally by South American peoples. The Greater Antilles islands, on the other hand, were more densely populated. The Taíno had bigger, more permanent towns and more hierarchical societies, and their villages were led by chiefs. There is evidence they traded with and were influenced culturally by Mesoamerican societies.

HISTORICAL THINKING

1. **READING CHECK** What skill made both Polynesian and Caribbean migrations possible?
2. **INTERPRET MAPS** Which Pacific island served as a base for possible migrations to present-day North America, South America, and New Zealand?
3. **SYNTHESIZE** How do the locations of the Caribbean island groups relate to which mainland cultures influenced them?

NATIONAL GEOGRAPHIC EXPLORER
JAGO COOPER

Art in the Heart of the Caribbean

On the tiny island of Mona, 41 miles west of Puerto Rico, anthropologist and National Geographic Explorer Jago Cooper researches cave art created by indigenous peoples as early as the 12th century. The images are painted or carved (like the one shown above). They include people, animals, and patterns that twist across the rock surfaces. Cooper, the British Museum's curator of the Americas, says, "These finger-fluted designs reflect the spiritual beliefs of the indigenous people."

He explains, "For the millions of indigenous peoples living in the Caribbean before European arrival, caves represented portals into a spiritual realm, and therefore these new discoveries of the artists at work within them captures the essence of their belief systems and the building blocks of their cultural identity."

Mona is one of the most cavernous areas in the world. Cooper points out that the Caribbean people "deliberately explored caves that were difficult to access." As of 2016, Cooper and his team found extensive evidence of pre-Columbian iconography on the walls and ceilings in more than 25 caves on the island. Cooper is also investigating similar art in Cuba and the Dominican Republic.

CHAPTER 14
CIVILIZATIONS OF THE AMERICAS
REVIEW

VOCABULARY

Use each of the following vocabulary words in a sentence that shows an understanding of the term's meaning.

1. terrace
2. slash-and-burn agriculture
3. geoglyph
4. cenote
5. earthworks
6. codex
7. chinampa
8. maize

READING STRATEGY
MAKE INFERENCES

Complete a graphic organizer like the one shown to make an inference about why it is important to scholars to decipher Inca quipu. Summarize what you've read in the "I Read" section. Tell what you know in the "I Know" section. Then write your inference in the "And So" section.

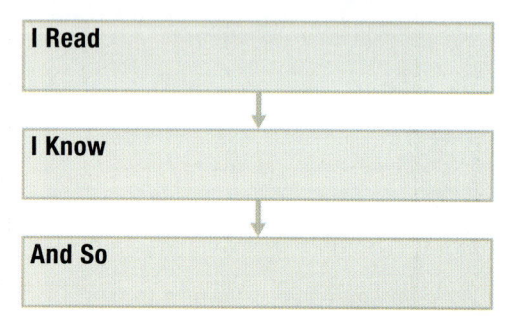

I Read

I Know

And So

9. Why is it so difficult for researchers to decode Inca quipu?

MAIN IDEAS

Answer the following questions. Support your answers with evidence from the chapter.

10. What did the Caral, Chavín, Olmec, Zapotec, and Teotihuacán have in common? **LESSON 1.1**

11. How did the Maya use advanced mathematics? **LESSON 1.2**

12. What links the Anasazi culture to Mesoamerica? **LESSON 1.5**

13. Why are the Aztec considered a complex civilization? **LESSON 2.1**

14. How did early Andean civilizations express themselves through art? **LESSON 2.2**

15. What are the three main groups of the Caribbean islands? **LESSON 2.3**

HISTORICAL THINKING

Answer the following questions. Support your answers with evidence from the chapter.

16. **IDENTIFY** How did the closing of the Beringia land bridge affect the civilizations of the Americas?

17. **MAKE PREDICTIONS** How do you think the practice of human sacrifice will influence how Europeans interpret American civilizations?

18. **IDENTIFY PROBLEMS AND SOLUTIONS** In what ways did American civilizations modify their environments, and how do those modifications help people understand those civilizations?

19. **SYNTHESIZE** How did different physical environments affect the lack of knowledge about ancient American civilizations when compared with Eurasian civilizations from the same era?

20. **MAKE CONNECTIONS** What were the legacies of the Olmec, Zapotec, and Teotihuacán societies? Support your answer with specific examples.

21. **FORM AND SUPPORT OPINIONS** In your opinion, which civilization—Maya, Aztec, or Inca—was greater than the others, and why?

22. **COMPARE AND CONTRAST** What are three similarities between American and Eurasian civilizations?

23. **DRAW CONCLUSIONS** What were two main reasons that civilizations in the Americas declined? Use examples from the chapter.

INTERPRET VISUALS

Study the images of a Maya pyramid (top) and an ancient Egyptian pyramid (bottom). Then answer the questions that follow.

24. How are the pyramids similar, and how are they different?

25. What difficulties did people face when building these pyramids?

ANALYZE SOURCES

In this excerpt from the *Popol Vuh*, the hero twins—who often represent pairs such as life and death, sky and earth, day and night, or sun and moon—do some work for their grandmother. Read the excerpt and answer the question that follows.

> Then they [Hunahpu and Xbalanque] began to work, in order to be well thought of by their grandmother and their mother. The first thing they made was the cornfield. "We are going to plant the cornfield, grandmother and mother," they said. "Do not grieve; here we are, your grandchildren, we who shall take the place of our brothers," said Hunahpu and Xbalanque.
>
> At once they took their axes, their picks, and their wooden hoes and went, each carrying his blowgun on his shoulder. As they left the house they asked their grandmother to bring them their midday meal.

26. What conclusions can you draw about corn and how it was farmed in ancient Maya society?

CONNECT TO YOUR LIFE

27. **NARRATIVE** You have read that the Inca were weakened by unknown European diseases. Put yourself in the place of someone from the empire, such as a member of the royal family, a conquered subject who has taken part in a rebellion, a priest, or a local leader. Write a story in which you are a main character and explore what you may have thought or done when an unknown illness affected your community. Use the tips below to help you plan, organize, and write your story.

TIPS

- Choose your role carefully, considering the different interests of various people at that time.
- Identify your character's thoughts and feelings about the illness and what may happen next.
- Use vivid language to describe the location, events, and the other characters in the story.
- Include realistic dialogue in your narrative.
- Use two or three vocabulary terms from the chapter.
- End the narrative with a prediction of future events on the part of your character.

NATIONAL GEOGRAPHIC CONNECTION

The Real Price of Gold

BY BROOK LARMER Adapted from "The Real Price of Gold" by Brook Larmer, *National Geographic*, January 2009

No single element has excited and tormented the human imagination more than the shimmering metal known by the chemical symbol Au. For thousands of years, the desire to possess gold has driven people to extremes, fueling wars and conquests, girding empires and currencies, leveling mountains and forests. Gold is not vital to human existence; it has, in fact, relatively few practical uses. Yet its chief virtues—its unusual density and malleability along with its imperishable shine—have made it one of the world's most coveted commodities. It has long been a symbol of beauty, wealth, and immortality. Nearly every society through the ages has invested gold with an almost mythological power.

At this improvised mine in Ghana, a 13-year-old boy sluices for gold.

For all of its allure, gold's human and environmental toll has never been so steep. Part of the challenge, as well as the fascination, is that there is so little of it. In all of history, only 16,000 tons of gold have been mined, barely enough to fill two Olympic-size swimming pools. More than half of that has been extracted in the past 60 years. Now the world's richest deposits are fast being depleted, and new discoveries are rare. Most of the gold left to mine exists as traces buried in remote and fragile corners of the globe. It's an invitation to destruction. But there is no shortage of miners, big and small, who are willing to accept.

At one end of the spectrum are the armies of poor migrant workers converging on small-scale mines. According to the United Nations Industrial Development Organization (UNIDO), there are between 10 million and 15 million so-called artisanal miners around the world, from Mongolia to Brazil. Employing crude methods that have hardly changed in centuries, they produce about 25 percent of the world's gold and support a total of 100 million people. It's a vital activity for these people—and deadly too.

In the Democratic Republic of the Congo in the past decade, local armed groups fighting for control of gold mines and trading routes have routinely terrorized and tortured miners. They have used profits from gold to buy weapons and fund their activities. In the Indonesian province of East Kalimantan, the military, along with security forces of an Anglo-Australian gold company, forcibly evicted small-scale miners and burned their villages to make way for a large-scale mine. Thousands of protestors against expansion of a mine in Cajamarca, Peru, faced tear gas and police violence.

The deadly effects of mercury are equally hazardous to small-scale miners. Most of them use mercury to separate gold from rock, spreading poison in both gas and liquid forms. UNIDO estimates that one-third of all mercury released by humans into the environment comes from artisanal gold mining.

At the other end of the spectrum are vast, open-pit mines run by the world's largest mining companies. Using armadas of supersize machines, these big-footprint mines produce three-quarters of the world's gold. They can also bring jobs, technologies, and development to forgotten frontiers. Gold mining, however, generates more waste per ounce than any other metal, and the mines' mind-bending disparities of scale show why. The mining gashes in the earth are so massive they can be seen from space. But the particles being mined are so microscopic that, in many cases, more than 200 could fit on the head of a pin. At a mining operation in eastern Indonesia, extracting a single ounce of gold—the amount in a typical wedding ring—requires the removal of more than 250 tons of rock and ore.

And so the real cost of gold keeps rising. ∎

UNIT INQUIRY — UNIT 5
Make a Documentary About Power Objects

Staging the Question

In this unit, you learned about some objects and commodities—such as masks, gold, and enigmatic stone carvings—that possessed power or significance in Africa and the Americas. The Global Perspective further explored the nature of power objects and why they matter so deeply to the people who create them. As you have discovered, these items can explain much about an early society, including what qualities it valued, what the people's religion taught them about the world, and what they viewed as wealth. What do our own society's power objects say about us?

ASSIGNMENT

Research the power objects treasured by at least three of the civilizations discussed in this unit.

Identify at least three items that you believe are power objects of your own culture.

Compare these modern-day power objects with those of the earlier civilizations. Consider what each society's power objects say about its culture's priorities and beliefs.

Make a documentary film about some modern-day power objects and their significance. Use the insights you gained from analyzing historical artifacts.

Supporting Questions: Begin by developing supporting questions to guide your research. For example: Does this object exemplify religious or secular beliefs? Research the answers in this unit and in other sources, both print and online. You might want to use a matrix like this one to record your answers.

	Object 1	Object 2	Object 3
Religious Meaning			
Monetary Value			
Other Significance			

Summative Performance Task: Make a documentary about the modern-day power objects you chose. In the script, explain what the objects say about the culture they embody, and discuss their similarities with historical power objects. You may include video clips or images of the present-day and historical objects, interviews with people discussing present-day objects, and any other footage that supports your ideas.

Present: Share your documentary with the class. You might consider one of these options:

POST IT ONLINE
Post the documentary on a class website and invite your classmates and friends to view it. Invite viewers to share their feedback and questions with you. Respond to the feedback and questions you receive.

VIEW IT IN CLASS
Work with your teacher to schedule a class viewing of the documentary. After the viewing, ask classmates for their reactions and lead a class discussion about modern-day power objects.

Take Informed Action:

UNDERSTAND Think about the value of understanding your own culture's power objects. Identify the ideas you learned from the present-day power objects that you believe are important to share.

ASSESS Choose the power object that most clearly stands for your culture. Think about the best place to share information about the object.

ACT Create an informational poster about the power object to display in your school, the public library, or another place in your community. You may also look for opportunities to screen your documentary.

UNIT 6

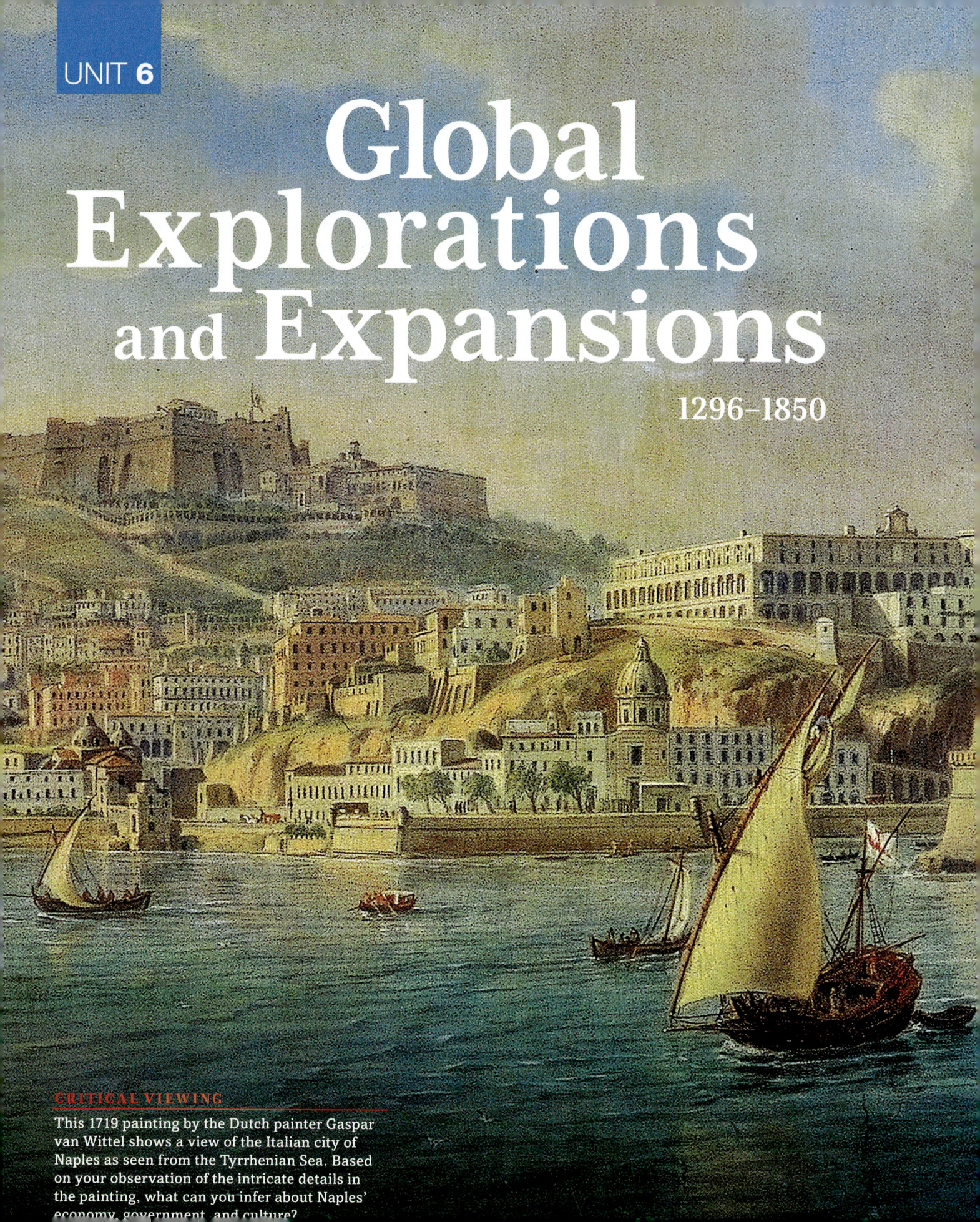

Global Explorations and Expansions

1296–1850

CRITICAL VIEWING
This 1719 painting by the Dutch painter Gaspar van Wittel shows a view of the Italian city of Naples as seen from the Tyrrhenian Sea. Based on your observation of the intricate details in the painting, what can you infer about Naples' economy, government, and culture?

409

UNIT 6 Global Explorations and Expansions

WORLD EVENTS 1300–1650

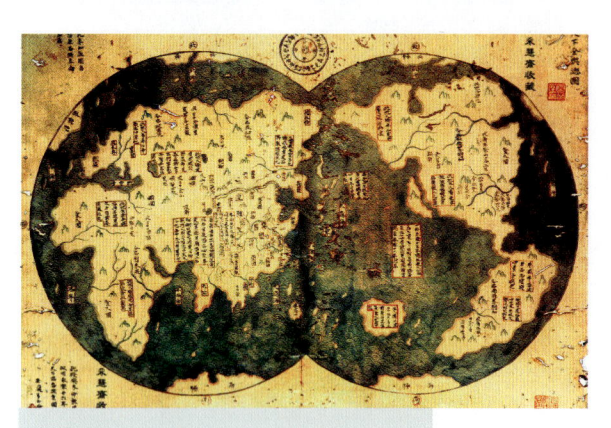

c. 1464 AFRICA The Songhai Empire begins in West Africa under ruler Sunni Ali. *(tomb of Sunni Ali in Timbuktu, Mali)*

1405 ASIA Chinese explorer Zheng He makes the first of seven voyages to India, Arabia, and Africa. *(copy of a map of the world drawn by Zheng He in 1421)*

1455 EUROPE The printing press developed by Johannes Gutenberg is used to print a Bible.

1501 ASIA The Safavid Empire rises in present-day Iran under Shah Ismail I.

1517 EUROPE Martin Luther nails his 95 theses to a church door in Wittenberg, Germany, triggering the Reformation.

c. 1300 EUROPE The Renaissance begins in the city-state of Florence in Italy. *(marble bust by Italian artist Donatello, c. 1415)*

1532 AMERICAS Spanish soldiers led by Francisco Pizarro conquer the Inca Empire. *(gold Inca llama, c. 1400–1532)*

HISTORICAL THINKING

DETERMINE CHRONOLOGY What earlier event might have helped make the founding of Jamestown possible?

1492 AMERICAS Christopher Columbus embarks on the first of his four voyages to the Americas. *(compass possibly used by Columbus)*

1545 EUROPE During the Catholic Reformation, church leaders gather for the Council of Trent.

1556 ASIA Mughal leader Akbar the Great expands his empire in Muslim India. *(Mughal coin, c. 1556)*

1607 AMERICAS Jamestown, located in the colony of Virginia, becomes the first permanent English settlement in North America. *(silver ear-picker found at Jamestown)*

1603 ASIA Ieyasu Tokugawa unifies Japan under a shogunate.

1613 EUROPE The Romanov dynasty begins in Russia and rules until 1917.

1644 ASIA The Manchus found the Qing dynasty, the last of China's imperial dynasties. *(Qing dynasty rockwork lion sculpture)*

c. 1650 AFRICA More than 40 trading posts in West Africa provide slaves for the Atlantic slave trade. *(relief from slave prison at trading post in Ghana)*

CHAPTER 15

Renaissance and Reformation
1296–1622

HISTORICAL THINKING Can tradition coexist with transformation?

SECTION 1 **The European Renaissance**
SECTION 2 **The Renaissance Impact**
SECTION 3 **The Protestant Reformation**
SECTION 4 **Global Impact of Religious Reforms**

CRITICAL VIEWING
This fresco of the Virgin Mary surrounded by saints adorns the ceiling of a chapel in the Church of the Gesù in Rome. Completed in 1564, the church is the primary church of the Jesuits, a religious order that emerged during the Catholic Reformation. What are characteristics of the artistic style of the painting?

Renaissance and Reformation 413

1.1

MAIN IDEA Through banking, trade, and fighting, Italy's city-states grew in size, power, and wealth, with Florence taking the lead by the end of the 1400s.

The Rise of Italian City-States

Imagine a time when political power seemed up for grabs. In the 1300s, Italy was divided into smaller kingdoms, city-states, and papal territories. Regions battled for land and resources or to control trade. Wealthy families battled for control as well.

EXPANDING CITY-STATES

Though growing in wealth, Italy in the 1300s could be violent and unstable. Farmland for growing olives, grapes, or wheat surrounded walled towns and cities. Some cities had to raise armies to defend themselves against attack from other cities. They fought to take over successful industries or a region's natural resources. Over time, stronger cities controlled larger areas.

In times of turmoil and in times of peace, Italian merchants carried on their centuries-old trade with northern Europe, northern Africa, and societies across Asia. As city-states grew wealthier into the 1400s, traders imported luxury goods for the rich. Carpets, gems, tulips, horses, and expensive dyes for brilliant colors in fabrics and paint came from bazaars, or large outdoor markets, in Muslim cities along the Mediterranean.

Controlling trade connections was essential to Italy's city-state economies. The city-states of Venice, Milan, Rome, and Florence were among the most powerful. Venice, a major port city, built a coastal trading empire that included many islands and trading stations along the Mediterranean as well as a colony in Constantinople. Milan, ruled by aggressive dukes, allied itself with France to take over northern and central Italy. Popes had been forced out of Rome by those who wanted a government that was independent of the church. The effort failed. When popes returned to govern, they used new ideas in mathematics and learning, along with growing wealth in trade, to rebuild the city.

Florence prospered through banking and wool and silk manufacturing. A republic, Florence was governed by members of guilds, organizations of people in the same field of work. The guilds for lawyers, bankers, or silk weavers had more power than guilds for stone masons, blacksmiths, or saddle makers. Workshops and offices hired apprentices, who were workers training to learn a craft or discipline. Those who achieved mastery could join a guild and open their own workshops. Without a king, duke, or ruling dynasty, Florence relied on the active participation of its citizens to achieve stability.

FLORENCE'S DOME

City leaders of Florence turned to art and architecture to display the city's growing success. The city's centerpiece, its cathedral, had been under construction since 1296. Work slowed when plague spread in the mid-1300s, devastating Italy, western Asia, and North Africa. The disease reduced Florence's population from 120,000 to 50,000. But by 1418, all but the cathedral's dome had been completed. The dome would have to be huge—138 feet across at its base, which was more than 170 feet off the ground. How could workers haul up materials to begin construction? What would keep the dome from collapsing? The master builders of Florence had no solutions, so city leaders announced a public competition. Competitors had to build a model and describe how the dome could be accomplished.

Filippo Brunelleschi (broo-nuhl-LEHS-kee) had apprenticed as a goldsmith but pursued architecture instead. He studied mathematics and lived in Rome briefly to examine classical Roman buildings and ruins. For the dome competition, he described his ideas for a crane and a giant hoist, or lift, for safely moving workers and materials. These inventions and his model, with its Roman influences, were brilliant. He was given the job. Even before the dome was completed in 1436, Brunelleschi became the most sought-after architect in Florence.

Structures symbolizing a city's identity were meant to be seen from miles around. They were a source of pride for the people in the street and farmers in the valleys. Florence's cathedral is called *il Duomo* in Italian.

(*Duomo* is Italian for "cathedral.") The cathedral had been planned to show off one of Europe's most powerful cities. Now with its magnificent dome, Florence could claim an architectural wonder.

THE MEDICI FAMILY

Florence's greatest family, the Medici (MEHD-ih-chee), controlled Europe's wool manufacturing and banking. Bankers who spoke multiple languages, knew the values of coins in different societies, and could negotiate and calculate exchange rates were essential to growth in trade. The Medici established banks in Venice, Rome, London, and other cities.

The economy of Florence weakened after the plague, and guilds became less powerful. In 1434, Cosimo de Medici took over the government. He was a **patron** of artists, which meant he gave artists financial support. He promoted the Medici reputation with art, building projects, and pageantry, or grand public displays. Cosimo admired Plato and learning from ancient Greece. He founded a public library in Florence, the first in western Europe since ancient times.

By the time control of Florence passed to Cosimo's grandson, **Lorenzo de Medici**, the former republic was, in effect, ruled by a Medici prince. Lorenzo became known as "the Magnificent" for his learning and his support of scholars and artists, but some citizens of Florence were upset that the Medici had undermined their republic by establishing a ruling dynasty. By the end of the 1500s, the absolute rule of the Medici would bring an end to the cultural and political conditions that once made Florence a center of artistic achievement.

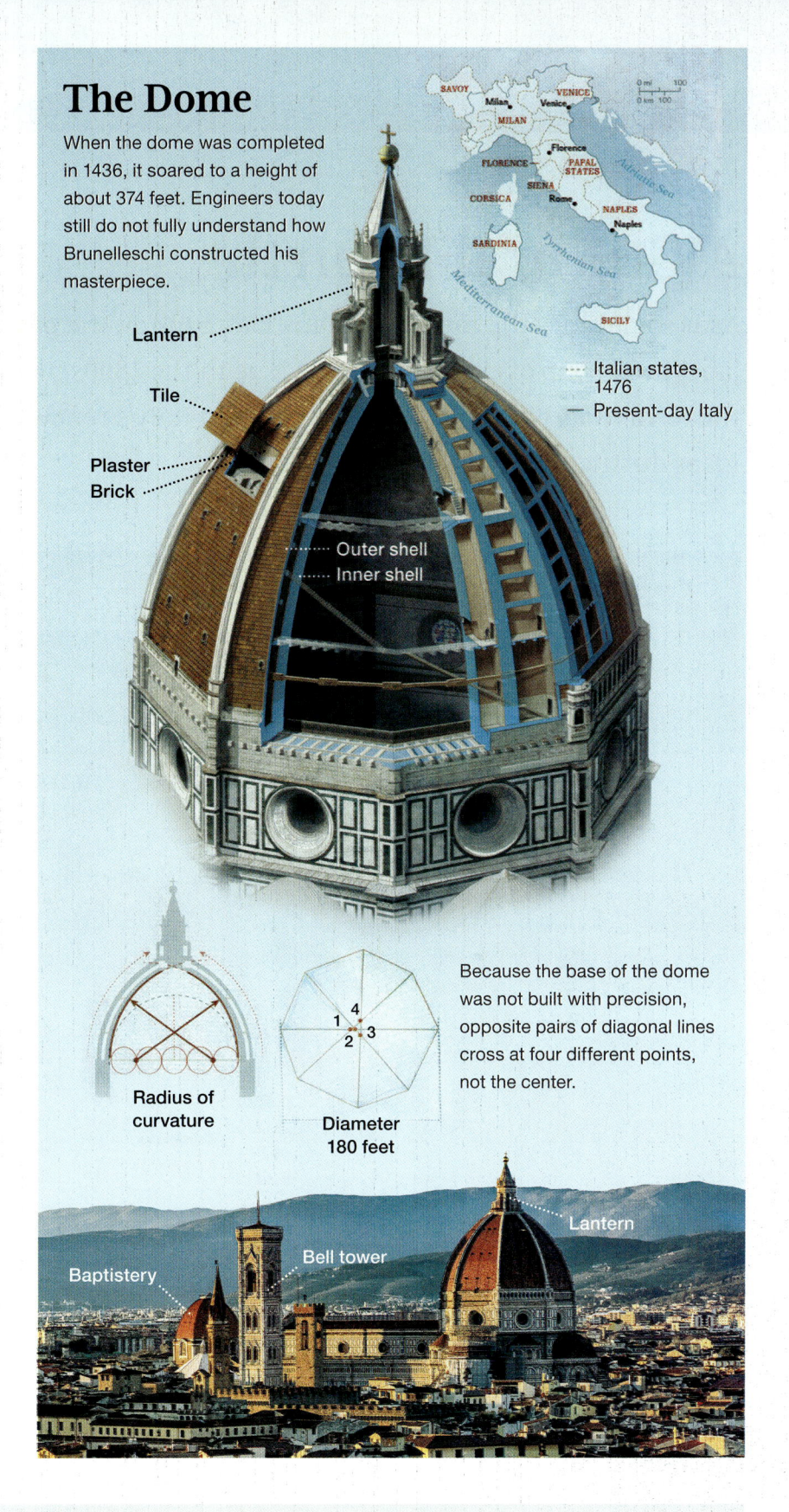

The Dome

When the dome was completed in 1436, it soared to a height of about 374 feet. Engineers today still do not fully understand how Brunelleschi constructed his masterpiece.

Lantern
Tile
Plaster
Brick
Outer shell
Inner shell

Italian states, 1476
Present-day Italy

Radius of curvature

Diameter 180 feet

Because the base of the dome was not built with precision, opposite pairs of diagonal lines cross at four different points, not the center.

Baptistery
Bell tower
Lantern

HISTORICAL THINKING

1. **READING CHECK** How did Florence stand out from the other major city-states?

2. **IDENTIFY PROBLEMS AND SOLUTIONS** How was engineering important to the solution of the dome's design?

3. **DRAW CONCLUSIONS** Why do you think banking was essential to trade at this time?

1.2

MAIN IDEA Ideas and goods from North African and Asian societies, along with a revolution in mass printing, led to a series of cultural changes in Europe.

A Cultural Rebirth

As is sometimes the case, historians look back on the past and give a name or label to a group of events. This was true in the 1800s, when historians applied the term *renaissance*, meaning "rebirth," to Italy's renewed interest in ancient ideas during the 14th and 15th centuries.

Many of the Renaissance artist Giotto's paintings portray the life of St. Francis, an Italian monk known for his care of the poor and animals. In this fresco, St. Francis (with a halo at right), addresses the throned sultan Al-Kamil, ruler of Egypt, Palestine, and Syria.

TRADE AND CULTURE

The European Renaissance, which lasted from the 1300s into the 1600s, had international roots. As you have already read, scholars in cities such as Córdoba, Baghdad, and Timbuktu had been translating classical Greek writings for hundreds of years. While Arab and Jewish scholars studied these texts to make advances in science and mathematics, European Christian scholars focused on religion.

Through trade with Asian and African societies, Italians became aware of these translated works. They learned, too, about texts that described Chinese inventions and Muslim medicine and astronomy. Italian scholars traveled to Christian monasteries and to libraries in Muslim cities in search of classical writings, even if only in fragments. Works by the philosophers Aristotle and Plato, the mathematicians Euclid and Ptolemy, and the great Roman orator Cicero generated excitement and

416 CHAPTER 15

were in demand. Italians founded academies, or Greek-style schools, and read classical writings that explored how to be ethical in society and what was harmonious or ideal in art and architecture.

Asian goods were also valued. Intricately painted ceramics and silks woven with gold threads came into Venice from Mongol and Ottoman trading sources. Wealthy Italians also prized thick, hand-knotted carpets in geometric designs. Some commissioned painters to include luxury goods in their portraits. A **commission** was a request for a specific art or design project, usually from a rich patron. A painting showing an expensive carpet, whether spread on a table or hung from a window during a festival, signaled the patron's high status or prestige.

Trading cities were sources of fascination. However, most Italian painters never saw Ottoman cities and their busy bazaars. Painters may have based their images of these places on stories from travelers, traders, and soldiers. One artist who drew on such stories was **Giotto**, who lived in the 1300s.

Giotto was one of the earliest and most influential of the Italian Renaissance painters. Although his work had Byzantine influences, Giotto portrayed people with expressive faces and natural postures in realistic backgrounds and settings. Painters who followed him admired him for "painting from life." This opened the way for the three-dimensional characteristics of Renaissance painting.

THE PRINTED WORD

As you have already learned, China and Korea had used woodblock printing and movable type since the 11th century. Printers coated the blocks with ink and pressed them into paper. In the 1200s, Spanish Muslims were the first Europeans to follow the ancient Chinese technique for making paper. They shredded and soaked cloth rags, pressed the fibers into single sheets, and then let them dry. Scribes wrote on this paper, and bookbinders sewed pages together to form books.

This labor-intensive method of bookmaking changed in the mid-1400s. A German printer, **Johannes Gutenberg**, made metal castings of individual letters of the German alphabet. This metal type could be rearranged, inked, pressed, and reused. The metal letters could print multiple copies without breaking or wearing out. Gutenberg's method was soon used to print thousands of books far more cheaply and quickly than copying books by hand.

The printing press came to Italy in 1465. By 1500, Italy had 73 workshops for printing and selling books, and throughout Europe several million books had been produced. Many were printed in the vernacular European languages—such as German, Italian, Spanish, French, and English—rather than in Latin. Before that, most writings had been documents of the church, written in Latin. As people read or heard works read in their native language, they began to think of themselves as German, French, Italian, or Spanish.

Printing presses provided greater access to printed materials. As a result, more people learned to read, even in rural areas, and they shared books, and the stories and information within them, at social gatherings. The technological advance of the printing press allowed ancient and global ideas and creative expression to reach new readers. The revolution in print materials transformed learning and communication in Europe.

GUTENBERG'S BIBLE The first book Gutenberg printed on his new press was a Latin Bible. The Gutenberg Bible, as it came to be called, contained 1,286 pages with about 42 lines on each page. It was remarkable for its neat, even letters and hand-painted illustrations of nature. Gutenberg printed 180 copies of his Bible, of which about 50 survive today.

HISTORICAL THINKING

1. **READING CHECK** Why did many painters include carpets in their pictures?

2. **DRAW CONCLUSIONS** How might Giotto's painted figures have affected viewers who had only seen religious stories in earlier art?

3. **ANALYZE CAUSE AND EFFECT** What was one effect of the use of vernacular languages in printed books on those who read them?

1.3

MAIN IDEA Italian and northern European artists learned about one another's work and tried out their innovative methods and materials.

Renaissance Arts

Imagine a world in which no one has heard of superstar artists and musicians. But that's how it was in Europe until the 15th century, when some Renaissance artists became the superstars of their day.

"TRUTH TO NATURE"

During the Renaissance, rediscovered classical writings in math, science, and philosophy fueled a new direction in the arts, called a "truth to nature," or **naturalism**. Renaissance artists strove for accuracy in their depictions of people or of the natural world.

Leonardo da Vinci is famous for being an artist, a scientist, an inventor, and a keen observer of the natural world. Maybe you have heard or read about a "renaissance man" or "renaissance woman." Those terms refer to someone who has many talents, and they come from Leonardo's time. To develop oneself as fully as possible was a Renaissance goal.

In 1465, when he was about 15, Leonardo traveled to Florence to train to be a painter. Throughout his life, until his death in 1519, he traveled to escape political upheavals or to compete for commissions. The Duke of Milan, whose court rivaled the splendors of the Medici court in Florence, hired him as a military engineer. Leonardo also lived in Rome and in France. In 1517, the royal court in France gave him the title "First Painter, Engineer, and Architect of the King."

In Florence, artists were trained to draw as the first stage of making a painting. But Leonardo's drawings accomplished far more. He drew plant life, the flight of birds, and images of **anatomy**, or the interior and exterior structures of living things. His drawings showed how water moves and how machines work. He sketched his ideas for a parachute, an adding machine, a giant crossbow, flying machines, and elaborate theatrical displays. His many inventions, whether for entertainment or military use, were not all built but were remarkably far ahead of their time.

In his paintings, Leonardo based his choices of color on his observations, such as the effects of light in the atmosphere. Nearer objects were their true color, he wrote, but distant objects were bluer, as if in a mist or haze. His ideas influenced painters throughout Italy. Leonardo's *Last Supper* and the portrait *Mona Lisa* are today two of the most famous images of European art.

ART THAT INSPIRES AWE

About 25 years younger than Leonardo, **Michelangelo Buonarroti** also studied in Florence. He was educated at the Medici Palace and became a painter, sculptor, architect, and poet. At 23, he completed his first sculpted masterpiece in marble, the *Pietá*, or "Pity," in which Mary mourns the death of her son Jesus. Six years later, Michelangelo finished his 13-foot sculpture, *David*, the larger-than-life statue of the young man who killed a giant, according to the biblical account. This second marble masterpiece was a commission from the supporters of a renewed republic that had temporarily expelled the Medici family. *David* became a symbol of victory over tyranny. Both sculptures made Michelangelo famous. Proud and competitive, he was said to care more for his work as an artist than for money or celebrity.

In 1508, he accepted a commission to paint, in fresco, the ceiling of the Sistine Chapel in Rome. *Pittura a fresco* is an Italian term meaning "painting freshly." In fresco painting, artists ground minerals into powders to create pigments of different colors. They mixed the pigments with water and then brushed the mixture onto a damp, newly plastered surface. When dry, the color was chemically bound to the surface.

Michelangelo spent about four years working on the ceiling. Much of that time he spent lying on his back on a scaffold. He painted Old Testament figures in active poses. Among them are prophets, whom he painted holding books or reading. Michelangelo's human forms

LYBIAN SIBYL (detail of Sistine Chapel Ceiling)
This sibyl, or female prophet, faces the church altar. The twist of her body and the placement of her foot make her appear as though she is about to stand, the kind of realistic "action" in paint Michelangelo was known for. The sketch is known as a study. Completed in red chalk, it demonstrates the artist's approach as he worked out the figure's pose.

were unmatched by any other artist in their intensity and power. One dramatic section is as widely recognized as Leonardo's great *Mona Lisa*. Titled *Creation of Adam*, a figure who represents God reaches out toward Adam to convey the spark of life.

NORTHERN PAINTERS

Italian artists influenced artists in the Netherlands, Germany, and other northern European regions. These artists did not abandon their tradition of precision, attention to detail, and mastery of landscapes. Their work, in turn, influenced Italians.

Jan van Eyck (yahn vahn IKE) of the Netherlands was an early northern Renaissance artist. He perfected the technique of mixing pigments with oil. Thin layers or glazes of oil paint caught the light, giving colors a jewel-like quality not possible in fresco painting. Lorenzo de Medici collected van Eyck's paintings. Leonardo, along with many other Italian artists, adopted and experimented with oil the painting technique.

In the 1300s and 1400s, artists sometimes included themselves in a group of figures in a painting, but van Eyck may have been the first to simply paint himself. *Portrait of a Man* shows him in a red chaperon, or head covering. His gaze, the roughness of his skin, and the glint in his eyes look real. Van Eyck was proud of his work. He wrote on the frame of the portrait, "As I can . . . Jan van Eyck made me on 21 October 1433."

Albrecht Dürer (AHL-brekht DYOO-ruh) of Nuremberg, Germany, was the first northern artist to apply the innovations of Italian artists to his own work. Born in 1471, his life overlapped that of many of Italy's famous artists. At 23, he traveled to Venice, painted watercolors of the great works he saw, and later returned to Italy to stay longer and learn more. In his writings, he said, "art was extinct until it came to light again [in Italy]."

Dürer was an accomplished maker of woodblock prints and engravings and is credited with elevating these techniques to a fine art. He noticed that many artists in Italy were literate and well read and had a higher social position than artists in Germany did. He wanted to bring the desire for scientific knowledge to Germany and raise artistic standards. He succeeded for himself and influenced many others.

SPANISH RENAISSANCE

El Greco ("the Greek") was born in Crete in 1541. As a young man, he moved to Venice to study art. Later, he chose to paint in nearby Toledo, an ancient city with a history of Roman occupation and rule by Arabic-speaking Christians and Muslims.

Self-Portrait Holding a Medallion, c. 1556

PAINTED FROM A MIRROR Michelangelo's monumental works brought him great fame. Another northern Italian artist, Sofonisba Anguissola (ah-gwih-SOH-lah), has been called Europe's first famous woman artist. Because women weren't allowed to study anatomy at this time, female artists tended to paint portraits. Anguissola gained renown for her self-portraits.

Anguissola's father sent her drawings to Michelangelo and her paintings to potential patrons. Her exceptional skill attracted the attention of King Philip II of Spain, and in 1559 at age 27, she moved to the Spanish court in Madrid. For ten years, she painted royal portraits. Such portraits asserted the importance, even majesty, of a ruler. Rulers chose virtuosos, or those of exceptional skill, who could duplicate in paint the look of velvet, brocade, silk, lace, or gems to emphasize their wealth. Anguissola continued painting self-portraits into old age.

The self-portrait shown here is a miniature, an artwork designed to be worn or carried.

CRITICAL VIEWING Van Eyck's *Madonna of Chancellor Rolin* (above left, 1435) introduces the illusion of space by including a background scene, while El Greco's *View of Toledo* (above right, c. 1599–1600) introduces emotion through the somber clouds in the sky. What are some differences between the two painting styles?

Toledo's population was a mix of Jewish and Catholic Spaniards, and the town was full of scholars and poets. El Greco received commissions to paint for churches and monasteries. He had brought the Renaissance to Spain, but his style rejected naturalism. For example, he did not use realistic colors, nor did he apply the ancient Greek and Roman ideals for human proportions. Instead, he elongated, or distorted, his figures, giving them a restless and emotional quality that many critics praise.

OTTOMAN CONNECTIONS

Just as trade connected Italy to the Ottomans, so did the arts. In the late 1400s, the Venetian artist Gentile Bellini went to the Ottoman court. Sultan Mehmed II wanted an artist to use Italian techniques to paint and cast bronze medals of his image so it could be seen throughout Europe.

Then in the early 1500s, the sultan invited Leonardo to submit drawings for a bridge to cross the Golden Horne, part of the Bosporus that runs through present-day Istanbul. Another drawing was submitted by the military engineer Mimar Sinan, who was to become the greatest architect in Ottoman history. Living at the same time as Michelangelo, Sinan created mosques whose domes seem to float in the air while flooding interior spaces with light. We see the flow of ideas across cultures when Michelangelo used the Byzantine architecture of Istanbul as inspiration for the dome of Saint Peter's Basilica in Rome and when Sinan was then influenced by Michelangelo in his design of the magnificent Süleymaniye Mosque.

HISTORICAL THINKING

1. **READING CHECK** How did observations of the natural world bring change to the arts of Italy?

2. **MAKE INFERENCES** Why do you think artists like Leonardo and Michelangelo had to be competitive?

3. **DESCRIBE** What elements of van Eyck's paintings astonished viewers?

4. **IDENTIFY MAIN IDEAS AND DETAILS** What evidence indicates that artists in Renaissance Italy and the Ottoman Empire influenced one another?

1.4 NATIONAL GEOGRAPHIC EXPLORER **MAURIZIO SERACINI**

Finding a Lost da Vinci

"You simply have to go beyond what your eyesight can do." —Maurizio Seracini

CRITICAL VIEWING A team of researchers, led by Maurizio Seracini, pass an endoscope through a hole in a Giorgio Vasari mural to see if a lost Leonardo da Vinci masterpiece is behind it. Based on details in this photograph, how would you describe the techniques being used to solve this art mystery?

At the Palazzo Vecchio in Florence in 1504, the two greatest artists of the Italian Renaissance faced off—but this was not a duel. It was a battle with pencils and brushes. Leonardo da Vinci, an artist in his early 50s known through all of Europe, had been commissioned to paint a mural on a wall in the enormous Hall of 500 in the Palazzo. The young artist Michelangelo had been commissioned to paint another mural on the same wall. The two men couldn't stand each other. This was a competition to show the world who was the better artist.

MAIN IDEA National Geographic Explorer Maurizio Seracini uses high-tech methods to analyze art masterpieces.

FINDING THE LOST DA VINCI

Michelangelo drew a detailed, full-size version of his planned scene. But before he started to paint, the pope summoned him to Rome to work on another project. Leonardo's painting, called *The Battle of Anghiari*, was completed, but the paint didn't dry properly and some of it began to drip down the wall. Even so, the painting was much admired, but some 50 years after Leonardo completed his work, artist Giorgio Vasari was hired to paint over it. The artwork was lost forever. Or was it?

Fast-forward hundreds of years. National Geographic Explorer Maurizio Seracini grew up in Florence, then moved to California to attend college, where he received a degree in bioengineering. In the 1970s, Seracini, at the request of his former professor and famed Leonardo historian Carlo Pedretti, applied his understanding of technology to solve the mystery of the lost da Vinci masterpiece. While studying Vasari's mural, Seracini spotted a nearly invisible Italian motto in the upper corner. It read "*cerca trova*," which translates to "seek and you shall find." Seracini began to suspect that Leonardo's painting was behind Vasari's. Unfortunately, the technology of the 1970s wasn't sophisticated enough to tell.

THE ART DETECTIVES

In 2000, Seracini used 3-D modeling and thermography to reconstruct the Hall of 500 at the time of Leonardo, which allowed him to pinpoint the spot that would have been painted by the artist back in 1504. This spot coincided exactly with the "cerca trova" clue. A radar scan also indicated that there was a small air gap behind this section of the wall. Had Vasari built a wall over Leonardo's masterpiece to protect it before he painted his own mural? The answer seemed impossible to determine without causing harm to Vasari's work.

Turning again to technology, Seracini, with the help of a group of physicists, developed two noninvasive devices that would be able to detect the presence of chemicals in the paint traditionally used by Leonardo. However, getting permission from the city of Florence to use this technology proved difficult because the devices emitted a small amount of radiation. Instead, in 2011 the city decided to send in a team of art restoration experts to drill small holes into parts of the mural that were already damaged. The government then asked Seracini to use an endoscopic camera, a tiny device on a flexible tube, to explore the space behind the wall. Seracini and his team found places behind the mural that looked as if they had been stroked with a brush. The team also retrieved fragments of pigment similar to those used by Leonardo in other paintings. However, Seracini's exploratory work on the mural was stopped in 2012, when local authorities refused to allow the drilling of any new holes.

Today, Seracini lives in Florence and focuses on his company, Editech, which he founded in 1977. It was the first company in Europe to apply engineering sciences to the study of cultural heritage and the authentication of works of art. In addition to the Leonardo mural, he has studied more than 4,000 works of art, including *The Adoration of the Magi*—another Leonardo masterpiece. He determined that the work was completed by another artist who painted over Leonardo's original sketch, changing the layout considerably.

Over the years, Seracini has collaborated with several major museums to solve art mysteries. In many ways, his work could be said to have been inspired by that nearly invisible clue he saw in a corner of Vasari's mural: *cerca trova*—seek and you shall find.

HISTORICAL THINKING

1. **READING CHECK** What evidence did Seracini find that made him think there might be another painting behind the Vasari mural in the Hall of 500?

2. **ANALYZE CAUSE AND EFFECT** What effect does the need to preserve artwork have on the need to study it? Explain how both relate to Seracini's work.

2.1

MAIN IDEA The ideals of Renaissance humanism as expressed by Petrarch and Erasmus influenced education, art, and writing for centuries to come.

Renaissance Humanism

What qualities do we admire in people today? Many admire those who work to help others, serve in the military, or protect local communities. During the 14th and 15th centuries, the movement known as humanism explored the question of what makes a good person.

PETRARCH AND EARLY HUMANISM

Around 1350, a group of Italian scholars pioneered a new intellectual movement called **humanism**. Humanists studied texts of Greek and Roman thinkers, and these works inspired them to value active participation in public life. They moved the focus away from a life of contemplation and prayer to one that promoted human relationships within society. They admired political and military action as well as devotion to God and the church. Humanists also valued eloquent language and its ability to both persuade and delight.

One of the earliest humanist writers was the Italian historian, poet, and philosopher **Petrarch** (PEH-trahrck), who lived from 1304 to 1374. He came from a well-educated family who introduced him to the classical Latin writers Cicero and Virgil when he was young. Orphaned as a young man, Petrarch at first spent his family's money on clothes, shoes, and hairstyles, but once he ran out of money, he began to think seriously about a profession.

Petrarch wanted work that would allow him to think deeply, and eventually he became a priest. However, his life changed when he saw a woman in church. He called her Laura. No one knows whether that was really her name, whether Petrarch ever spoke to her, or even if she really existed! Nonetheless, Petrarch wrote a series of love poems to Laura in the sonnet form in Italian. A sonnet is a 14-line poem that follows a particular rhyme scheme, or pattern. It was unusual for a serious writer in Italy to write in Italian rather than Latin in the 1300s, and Petrarch had many readers. Sonnets became one of the most popular forms of poetry in Europe.

Apart from his love poems, what drove Petrarch was his effort to answer his questions about how to live a good life. The church at this time was full of conflict and

In 1341, Petrarch was crowned with a wreath of laurels, echoing a traditional Roman ceremony. Today, poets are sometimes recognized for their work with the title *poet laureate*.

corruption, so he did not feel he could rely on church leaders for guidance. Instead, he turned to the Latin writers he had admired as a boy, especially Cicero. He traveled throughout Europe, searching the libraries of old monasteries for forgotten Latin manuscripts. Inspired by these sources, Petrarch wrote letters and imaginary dialogues, or conversations, between himself and Cicero. Like his love poems, these were read throughout Europe. Petrarch's humanist writings inspired the formation of universities in England, Scotland, Ireland, Italy, Germany, and Scandinavia.

ERASMUS AND THE CHURCH

Desiderius Erasmus was born in 1469 in Rotterdam, Holland—nearly 100 years after Petrarch's death. Like Petrarch, Erasmus admired Greek and Latin philosophers, and he wrote one of the first books printed on Europe's printing presses—the Greek New Testament with his Latin translation next to the Greek text. At this time, most educated Europeans could read Latin, so the Latin translation allowed more people to read the New Testament themselves for the first time. Erasmus traveled even more widely than Petrarch, attending university in Paris and then going to England where he became a tutor in the royal court. This position took him to Rome, where he saw what he considered the excessive grandeur of Pope Julius II. He began to write **satire**, humorously critical observations, about Rome and the church. His satirical book *The Praise of Folly*, printed in 1511, was the best-selling book in Europe for several years. Even the pope laughed at the way Erasmus poked fun at human weakness and institutions while ultimately affirming Christian ideals.

Erasmus argued for the importance of education and believed that it should not be controlled by the church. His elegant writing style and ability to see many sides of an issue influenced writers such as the English writer William Shakespeare and the French essayist Michel de Montaigne. Writing some 75 years after Erasmus, Montaigne is credited with having invented the personal essay, a form he used to explore his personal character in order to better understand the human condition.

Portrait of a Young Woman as a Sybil, c. 1620

HUMANISM AND WOMEN Humanist writers looked to classic Latin and Greek authors for inspiration. As you've read, sculptors, architects, and painters turned to the statues and buildings of ancient Greece and Rome for inspiration. Born in 1593, the painter Artemisia Gentileschi was trained by her father. She was the first woman to become an official member of the artistic academy of Florence and received commissions from the Medici family and Charles I of England.

Gentileschi's painting expresses many humanist ideas. For example, her figures seem to express human emotions and appear in realistic settings. Gentileschi worked to overcome the limitations society placed on women in her time, not only in her professional activities but also in her choice of subjects. Of her 60 surviving paintings, 40 portray women.

HISTORICAL THINKING

1. **READING CHECK** What was Petrarch looking for as he visited libraries in different parts of Europe?

2. **IDENTIFY** What poetic form did Petrarch use for his love poems to Laura?

3. **DRAW CONCLUSIONS** Why do you think Erasmus was so popular, even though he criticized many institutions of his time?

Renaissance and Reformation 425

2.2

MAIN IDEA Italian Renaissance artists captured the era's interest in Greek antiquity while adopting a technique called linear perspective—an innovation in Western art.

Raphael's *School of Athens*

Outdoor schools? Not a bad idea in Greece's mild climate. The famous academies of ancient Greece were not buildings but open-air gatherings. But in this painting from 1511, Plato, Aristotle, and other notable philosophers interact in an imaginary scene set in Rome.

HUMANIST LEARNING

In the early 1500s, Italy's cultural center shifted south from Florence and Venice to Rome. The church used its great wealth to become an important patron of the arts. Pope Julius II, who had hired Michelangelo to paint the Sistine Chapel, brought another Florentine artist to Rome, the young and accomplished **Raphael**. The pope commissioned Raphael to paint large frescoes in his papal offices and rooms. The most famous of these works is the *School of Athens* painted in Julius's library. In the painting, philosophers ponder, write, debate, and teach in the pursuit of truth. But instead of an outdoor olive grove, the gathering is set in St. Peter's Basilica. Julius wanted to show the importance of ancient wisdom to Christian beliefs. In his view, a learned individual—one who studied the classics, including poetry and mathematics—could better understand religious ideas.

Raphael's composition leads viewers' eyes to Plato and Aristotle at its center. Plato points up. To him, truth was found in ideals that existed beyond the senses. Aristotle gestures toward the earth; he finds truth in observing the world. Raphael provided no key to the identity of all the ancient figures, nor to their faces, some of which resembled artists he knew. He also included himself in the painting—on the far right. By the time of his death at age 37 in 1520, he was famous for his art and oversaw a large number of apprentices in his workshop.

PERSPECTIVE

School of Athens is painted on a flat wall about 25 feet wide, yet it gives the illusion of depth. Painters made figures, objects, and architectural features appear closer or farther away using mathematical calculations. The architect Brunelleschi, whom you read about earlier in this chapter, had developed the technique a hundred years earlier. Called **linear perspective**, it allowed artists to determine the placement and size of figures on a flat plane, making them appear as if positioned in three dimensions. Today, architects and animators use computer software to create and alter perspective in 3-D.

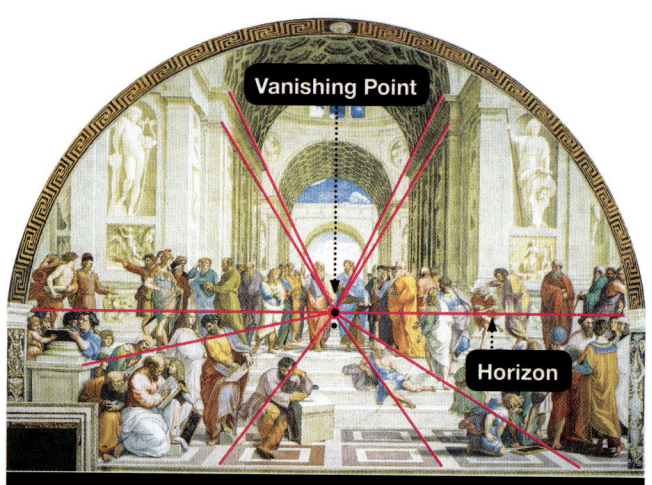

To create linear perspective, all parallel lines in a painting converge in a single vanishing point on the horizon, creating the illusion of depth.

HISTORICAL THINKING

1. **READING CHECK** Why did Pope Julius II commission the *School of Athens*?

2. **INTERPRET VISUALS** According to Raphael's painting, in what ways did classical thinkers share knowledge?

3. **SYNTHESIZE** How does the architectural structure in the painting show linear perspective?

CRITICAL VIEWING Raphael was only 27 when he completed this fresco, which celebrates the classical period. How does *School of Athens* express the ideals of humanism and Renaissance art?

PYTHAGORAS
This Greek mathematician sits before a slate showing ratios for musical tones. He believed numbers held the key to all aspects of the universe.

IBN RUSHD
Also known as Averroes, this Arab philosopher lived in Spain during the 12th century and sparked interest in Aristotle prior to the Renaissance.

EUCLID
Euclid wrote *Optics and Elements*, books on geometry and mathematics, around 300 B.C.E. He holds a compass over a slate with a geometric drawing on it.

SOCRATES
Socrates talks with figures representing people from different cultures, emphasizing the universal appeal of his philosophy.

ZOROASTER
The ancient Iranian astronomer and philosopher Zoroaster, often viewed as the founder of monotheism, holds a sphere showing the fixed stars.

PTOLEMY
Ptolemy, a Greco-Roman mathematician and astronomer, holds the sphere of Earth. The figure facing the viewer on his right is the painter Raphael.

Renaissance and Reformation 427

DOCUMENT-BASED QUESTION
2.3 Humanist Writings

It's one thing to worry about what people will think of you if you say what's on your mind. It's another thing to fear for your life. Renaissance humanist writers had to be careful not to offend the powerful. They created works that are praised for their elegance and depth and are still read today.

Humanists believed the works of ancient Greece and Rome offered important moral values and fresh perspectives. They may have been right because the ideas of humanism had a broad influence, starting in Italy in the 14th century and affecting all of Europe by the 16th century.

The goals of a humanist education were to teach people to contribute to the common good by taking part in public life. Humanists valued practical careers over contemplation. Eloquence, or the ability to speak and write well, was also important and led to the creation of the field of studies known today as the humanities.

Humanists did not reject religion but rather sought to combine classical and Christian ideas. Northern European humanists, in particular, saw humanist learning as a way to bring about reform within the church.

CRITICAL VIEWING Paintings of the Virgin Mary in classic art usually show her holding the baby Jesus. This 1505 painting by the Italian artist Vittore Carpaccio shows Mary sitting in a garden reading a book. She is dressed in the clothing of a 16th-century Italian noblewoman. How does Carpaccio's painting reflect humanist views of education?

DOCUMENT ONE

Primary Source: Speech
from "An Oration . . . in Praise of Letters" by Cassandra Fedele, c. 1487–1521

Born in 1465 in Venice, Italy, Cassandra Fedele was a prodigy, a young person of unusual talent, who appeared before groups of learned men to display her knowledge while still a teenager. As a woman, she had to find ways to express her extensive learning without threatening powerful men who felt they knew how women should behave.

CONSTRUCTED RESPONSE Based on the excerpt, what qualities would Fedele value in a prince?

> The study of literature refines men's minds, forms and makes bright the power of reason, and washes away all stains from the mind, or at any rate, greatly cleanses it. It perfects its gifts and adds much beauty and elegance to the physical and material advantages that one has received by nature. States, however, and their princes who foster and cultivate these studies become much more humane, more gracious, and more noble. For this reason, these studies have won for themselves the sweet appellation, "humanities."

DOCUMENT TWO

Primary Source: Book
from *The Prince*, by Niccolò Machiavelli, completed 1513, published posthumously (after his death) 1532

Machiavelli was a supporter of the republic in Florence and was tortured and expelled from the city when the Medici family retook control. He then tried to regain his place by writing *The Prince*, advising the Medici on how best to rule the city. The book was controversial because it described the reality of politics in harsh terms. Thus, today the term *Machiavellian* means "scheming and unscrupulous."

CONSTRUCTED RESPONSE According to this excerpt, why is it safer for a ruler to be feared than loved?

> Upon this a question arises: whether it be better to be loved than feared or feared than loved? It . . . is much safer to be feared than loved. . . . Because [men] are ungrateful, fickle, false, cowardly, covetous, and as long as you succeed they are yours entirely; they will offer you their blood, property, life, and children, as is said above, when the need is far distant; but when it approaches they turn against you. And that prince who, relying entirely on their promises, has neglected other precautions, is ruined; because . . . men have less scruple in offending one who is beloved than one who is feared.

DOCUMENT THREE

Primary Source: Book
from *Utopia* by Thomas More, 1516

Thomas More, born in London in 1478, was an advisor to Henry VIII of England and a friend of Erasmus. But being a humanist did not always mean acting humanely. Henry VIII ordered many executions, and Thomas More had people burned at the stake. In *Utopia*, his most famous book, More describes an imaginary island.

CONSTRUCTED RESPONSE In this excerpt, how does the imaginary Utopia reflect humanist ideals?

> It is ordinary to have public lectures every morning before daybreak, at which none are obliged to appear but those who are marked out for literature; yet a great many, both men and women, of all ranks, go to hear lectures of one sort or other, according to their inclinations: but if others that are not made for contemplation choose rather to employ themselves at that time in their trades, as many of them do, they are not hindered, but are rather commended, as men that take care to serve their country. After supper they spend an hour in some diversion, . . . where they entertain each other either with music or discourse.

SYNTHESIZE & WRITE

1. **REVIEW** Review what you have learned about the values of humanism.
2. **RECALL** On your own paper, list two details about each of the writers mentioned above and two details about each of the excerpts.
3. **CONSTRUCT** Construct a topic sentence that answers this question: Does education in the humanities make people more ethical? Why or why not?
4. **WRITE** Using evidence from this chapter and the documents, write an informative paragraph that supports your topic sentence in Step 3.

2.4 Material Culture

RENAISSANCES AROUND THE WORLD

You've learned about the European Renaissance, in which a rebirth of interest in classical writings sparked innovations in art, literature, and other fields. But that's not the only renaissance in history. Revivals of past traditions have occurred across time in societies all over the world. Sometimes the work of a previous era inspires just one person or a few people, whose creative work then ignites a general resurgence of interest in a past tradition. A revival may spread from one creative field to another—from musicians to writers to artists—with creative expression exploding in all directions.

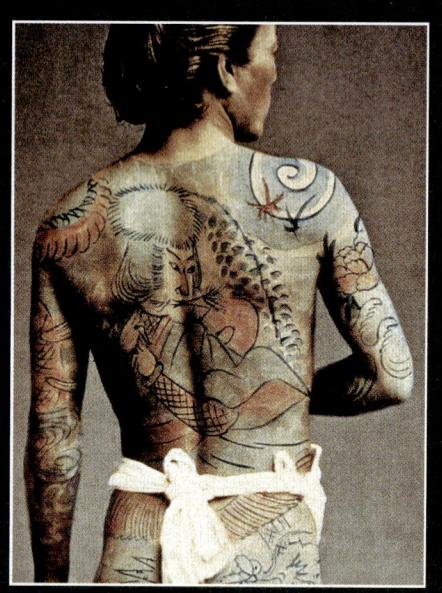

Tattoo Art A global resurgence of tattoo art has occurred in such places as North and South America, Europe, the Pacific Islands, and Japan since the 1990s. Today, tattoos are popular body decorations and even the subject of museum exhibitions. The roots of tattooing extend across the globe and back to prehistoric times. The image on the right shows 1,600-year-old tattoos on the arm of a female mummy found in Peru.

This photo shows traditional, elaborate full-body Japanese tattoo art, or *irezumi*, from about 1880. Tattooing experienced a rebirth in Japan during the Edo period (1603–1868).

In the photo above, Filipino artist Apo Whang-Od, known worldwide as a master of traditional tattoo art, practices the 1,000-year-old art of *batok*, in which a sharp thorn fastened to a stick is dipped in black ink and tapped into the skin with a bamboo mallet. This form of tattoo art is currently experiencing a revival in popularity in the Philippines, as well as among island cultures in Samoa, Hawaii, and New Zealand.

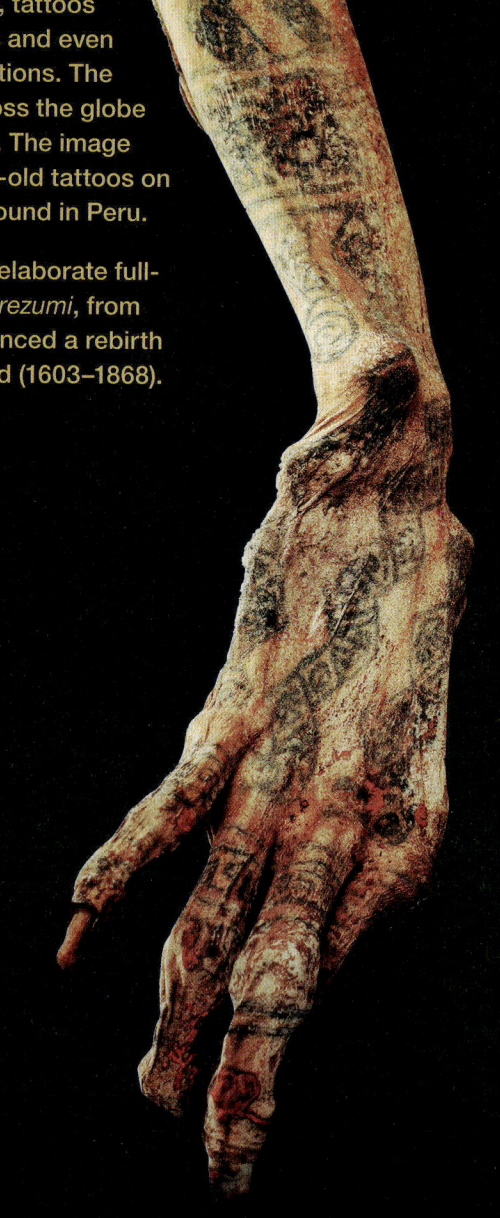

430 CHAPTER 15

▼ **Acoma Pueblo Pottery** The revival of Acoma Pueblo pottery in New Mexico in the late 1900s resulted largely from the work of one potter, Lucy Lewis. Lacking formal art training, Lewis took her inspiration from ancient pots and pottery shards found in her community, the Acoma Pueblo. Known for her black-on-white designs, Lewis specialized in small pots like those shown here.

▼ **Japanese Folk Crafts Movement** The Japanese folk crafts movement of the late 1920s was the brainchild of Japanese philosopher Soetsu Yanagi, who was inspired by Korean pottery. He promoted appreciation of Japan's folk art, which he called *mingei*, or "art of the people." Examples of mingei include the 19th-century iron kettle shown here.

◀ **China's Golden Age** China's "Renaissance," or golden age in literature, art, and technology began during the Tang dynasty (618–907 C.E.) as Tang rulers sought to bring back the glory of the Han dynasty (206 B.C.E.–220 C.E.). This glazed horse sculpture demonstrates the artistry and skill of craftspeople in the Tang period. War horses were the pride of the Tang and represented the dynasty's military expansion and artistic achievement.

▼ **Hawaiian Cultural Renaissance** A Hawaiian cultural renaissance in the late 1960s and the 1970s featured renewed interest in traditional Hawaiian music and dance as well as language and voyaging. Traditional Hawaiian musical instruments that might be used during the performance of the hula, a dance, include this sharkskin drum and two kinds of ukuleles.

The Harlem Renaissance The Harlem Renaissance was an explosion of African-American artistic expression in the 1920s and 1930s that began in New York City's Harlem neighborhood and spread across the country. Musicians, writers, and artists drew upon earlier African-American traditions and their African heritage to produce distinctive works of music, literature, and art.

For example, musician Louis Armstrong (right) used his trumpet to transform jazz into fine art. Artist Aaron Douglas incorporated traditional African imagery into his modern artwork (below, left). And writer Zora Neale Hurston blended black folklore and dialect in her novel *Their Eyes Were Watching God* (below, right).

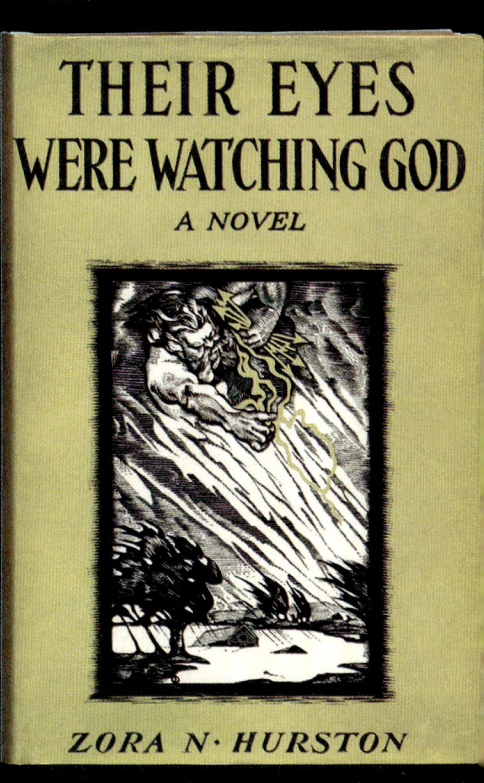

HISTORICAL THINKING

1. **READING CHECK** What is a renaissance?

2. **COMPARE AND CONTRAST** How do the renaissances you've read about differ and how are they alike?

3. **MAKE CONNECTIONS** What experience do you have with a contemporary renaissance?

3.1

MAIN IDEA Angered by the way the Roman Catholic Church was raising money, Martin Luther published 95 theses that led to a series of changes known as the Protestant Reformation.

Martin Luther and the Protestant Reformation

An impressive building may inspire awe and appreciation in those who see it. Yet others may object to the cost of such a structure. That's how one German monk felt when he visited Rome and saw St. Peter's Basilica under construction.

LUTHER'S 95 THESES

In 1450, the pope ordered that work begin on St. Peter's Basilica in Rome. Drawing on the artistic and architectural advances of the Renaissance, St. Peter's would be a fitting symbol for the Catholic Church. At the time, the church was richer and more powerful than any king or emperor in Europe. The magnificent structure would take 200 years to complete, but in 1517, well before it was completed, the German monk **Martin Luther** would do something that would dramatically alter the religious, political, and social landscape of Europe.

Luther was angry about the way money was being raised to build the great basilica. Catholics were encouraged to buy **indulgences**, or special pardons, from the archbishop to save their own souls as well as those of deceased loved ones. Luther's studies of the Bible led him to believe that faith in God was the only way to save souls. He wrote a list of 95 theses, or ideas, criticizing the sale of indulgences and other church practices. In thesis 86, for example, he said, "Why does not the pope, whose wealth is today greater than the riches of the richest, build just his one church of St. Peter with his own money, rather than with the money of poor believers?"

According to legend, Luther nailed his list to the door of Wittenberg's largest church. Then he did something even more courageous: he had copies printed in German and Latin. He mailed a copy to the archbishop, who passed it along to the pope. Church officials dismissed the ideas of the man they thought of as just another small-town monk. But thanks to the printing press, Luther's ideas gained widespread attention, and he became a best-selling author.

This 1529 double portrait by artist Lucas Cranach the Elder commemorates the marriage of Martin Luther to Katharina von Bora.

In addition to criticizing indulgences, Luther believed priests should be allowed to marry and have families. In 1525, he married a former nun, Katharina von Bora, whom he praised for her business sense and managerial abilities. Many historians believe Katharina's abilities helped make Luther successful.

EARLIER INFLUENCES

Luther's ideas led to the changes known today as the Reformation, a political and religious challenge of papal authority. His ideas did not come out of nowhere. Scholars had questioned the power and practices of the church for more than 100 years before Luther printed his 95 theses.

One early critic was the theologian **John Wycliffe**. Wycliffe lived and wrote in Oxford, England, in the late 14th century. As Luther would more than 100 years later, Wycliffe came to believe that the Bible, not the pope, was the source of God's word. He arranged for the Latin Bible to be translated into English so more people could read it. Like Luther, Wycliffe believed priests should be able to marry and that the church should give up its power and wealth.

Soon after Wycliffe published his arguments, his ideas attracted the attention of **Jan Hus**, a priest and philosopher from Prague, in the kingdom of Bohemia (present-day Czech Republic). Hus was impressed by Wycliffe's views toward the reform of Catholic clergy. At that time, the church and its high-ranking officials owned property in Bohemia. Yet many priests were poor, and peasants were forced to pay taxes to the church. Eventually declared a heretic, Hus was burned at the stake in 1415.

Like Hus and Wycliffe, the humanist Desiderius Erasmus, whom you learned about earlier, was critical of the wealth of the Catholic Church. He also disapproved of princes who fought wars over minor insults and priests who supported those wars to advance their own careers. Erasmus agreed with many of Luther's criticisms, but he didn't like Luther's combative tone. As a humanist, Erasmus valued tolerance for diverse opinions, and he did not think it right to punish people for their beliefs.

AN OUTLAW AND A HERO

After his publication of the 95 theses, Luther continued to write extensively. Wittenberg became the publishing center of Germany, with one-third of the books published there written by Luther and another one-fifth by his followers.

> In spite of his radical ideas about religion, Martin Luther believed it was a Christian's duty to obey legitimate authority. When the German peasants rebelled in 1524, Luther was appalled by their behavior. He responded by writing a pamphlet to distance himself (and his reform movement) from the peasants' cause and align himself with the nobility.
>
> **PRIMARY SOURCE**
>
> Since the peasants, then, have brought both God and man down upon them . . . since they submit to no court and wait for no verdict, but only rage on, I must instruct the worldly governors how they are to act in the matter with a clear conscience.
>
> First, I will not oppose a ruler who . . . will smite and punish these peasants without offering to submit the case to judgement. For he is within his rights, since the peasants are not contending any longer for the Gospel, but have become faithless, perjured, disobedient, rebellious murderers, robbers and blasphemers. . . .
>
> —from "Against the Robbing and Murdering Hordes of Peasants," by Martin Luther, 1525

Luther wrote about every aspect of life. He wrote pamphlets offering spiritual inspiration and analysis of the Bible, but he also urged German nobles to take over the lands held by the Catholic Church. In 1520, Luther was given a chance to recant, or take back, his criticisms of the church. Luther refused. He was declared an outlaw, but he also became a hero to many German nobles, shopkeepers, artisans, and students.

German peasants, in particular, were inspired by Luther to question many aspects of their lives. They had been forced to pay high taxes to landowners. They questioned whether babies should be baptized since they were too young to understand the meaning of the ritual. They questioned private property. They wanted to choose their own priests and wanted the right to overthrow princes. In 1524, the peasants rebelled. At first, Luther acknowledged that some demands were valid, but as the uprising spread and mob violence grew, he urged princes to strike down those he described as "murderers and robbers." Armies attacked, and as many as 100,000 died in the uprising known as the Peasants' War. Luther had chosen to support the princes over the common people.

HISTORICAL THINKING

1. **READING CHECK** What new technology helped spread Martin Luther's ideas throughout Europe?

2. **ANALYZE CAUSE AND EFFECT** Why did Wycliffe support the translation of the Bible into English?

3. **MAKE INFERENCES** What are some possible reasons why Martin Luther chose to side with the nobility against the peasants in the 1525 revolt?

Renaissance and Reformation

3.2

MAIN IDEA The Protestant Reformation brought radical changes to Europe as more people left the Roman Catholic Church and formed new religions.

Reforms Across Europe

Reforms can make things better, but not every change is an improvement. Some religious reformers took extreme positions that led to intolerance or violence.

THE REFORMATION SPREADS

Not all the Europeans who left Catholicism became "Lutherans." Other reformers developed a variety of alternative church structures, rituals, and beliefs. Over time, followers of Luther and these other reformers became known as **Protestants** for their protests against the Roman Catholic Church.

Even before Luther published his 95 theses, another reformer, **Ulrich Zwingli**, was preaching directly from the Bible and questioning the teaching and practices of the Catholic Church. Like the Byzantine iconoclasts you read about earlier, Zwingli believed statues and other religious art were idols, or false gods, and should be destroyed.

By 1519, Zwingli had become the priest of the largest church in Zurich, Switzerland, where he preached powerful sermons. By 1524, he had convinced the city council to allow the destruction of all religious art in Zurich's churches. Teams of artisans destroyed religious objects and painted church interiors white to symbolize purity. Zwingli and his followers wanted to create communities that did not allow people to sin. The Swiss reformers created their own institutions—courts, schools, and charities—to carry out their vision of Christian society.

While Luther changed the religious environment of Germany and Zwingli changed Switzerland, **John Calvin** would have the greatest impact on Europe's religious world. Admired as a man of determination and insight, Calvin was also criticized for his coldness and his austere depiction of God. His doctrine that an elect group of believers chosen by God were the only true Christians would lead to the creation of Puritanism in England and would shape the culture of the English colonies in North America.

After fleeing persecution in France in 1536, Calvin set out to create a Protestant Rome in Geneva, Switzerland. His church had far more power over people's lives than Zwingli's church. Everyone in Geneva was required to attend religious services. People who arrived late or fell asleep could be punished and even imprisoned.

Calvin and his pastors tried to guide followers toward the "correct" form of Christianity. Church officials regulated clothing and hairstyles, and parents could not give their children names associated with Catholic saints. Innkeepers were expected to report on visitors who played dice or cards, sang indecent songs, stayed up late, or committed blasphemy by speaking disrespectfully about sacred things. Extreme penalties were imposed for offenders.

Geneva became an international city as Protestants who were persecuted in other areas of Europe sought refuge there. They brought wealth and industries which, along with Calvin's planning, transformed Geneva into a modern city with hospitals and educational institutions. Today, many international organizations are headquartered there.

Other reformers took the ideas of Luther, Zwingli, and Calvin and adapted them further. One group, the Anabaptists, rejected the Catholic and Protestant view that churches should answer to state or civil authorities. They also believed that people should be rebaptized as adults, when they could exercise their own free will. A man called John of Leyden carried the Anabaptist perspective to an extreme. He turned Münster, Germany, into an armed encampment of baptized believers in an episode that ended in his execution and continued persecution of moderate Anabaptists.

ENGLAND BREAKS WITH ROME

While theologians and philosophers triggered reformations in Germany and Switzerland, in England the king broke with the Roman Catholic Church for political reasons. **Henry VIII** was a devout Catholic who opposed the changes Luther promoted. But in 1527, Henry asked the pope to annul, or rule invalid, his marriage of 25 years. He and Queen Catherine of

The difference between Catholic and Protestant beliefs and rituals is clearly demonstrated by church architecture. Note the sharp contrast between the Spanish colonial church of Santa Maria Tonantzintla (left) in Mexico and that of the Old Whaling Church in Massachusetts (below). The Spanish church reflects the Catholic preference for ornate interiors associated with elaborate rituals, while the colonial English church reflects the simplicity of Calvinism.

Aragon, the daughter of Spain's Ferdinand and Isabella, had produced only one surviving child, a daughter. The Roman Catholic Church did not allow divorce, and Henry felt he needed a son to inherit the throne.

The pope did not want to offend Catherine's powerful nephew, the Holy Roman Emperor Charles V, and refused to annul Henry's marriage. Henry declared himself head of the new Church of England so he could put Catherine aside and marry Anne Boleyn, one of Catherine's ladies-in-waiting. This new church kept nearly all the practices and rituals of the Catholic Church but rejected the pope's authority. The Church of England created the Book of Common Prayer, which established a **liturgy**, or form of worship, that has influenced Protestant churches throughout the English-speaking world. Over time, Henry made further changes, such as abolishing monasteries and seizing their land and property. In England, the Reformation led to an increase in the power of the monarchy.

HISTORICAL THINKING

1. **READING CHECK** How did Zwingli feel about Luther's efforts to reform the Catholic Church? Explain.

2. **MAKE INFERENCES** Why did the people of Zurich destroy religious art in their churches?

3. **ANALYZE CAUSE AND EFFECT** What caused Henry VIII to break with the Roman Catholic Church and form the Church of England?

Renaissance and Reformation 437

4.1

MAIN IDEA Efforts to maintain Roman Catholic control of Europe led to military as well as religious challenges.

Challenges to Habsburg Dominance

Sometimes the winner of a game, an election, or a power struggle seems obvious. But history is full of unexpected outcomes. New factors and unanticipated circumstances can turn everything upside down.

THE HABSBURGS

Originally from central Europe, the Habsburg dynasty extended its rule through a series of strategic marriages between 1452 and 1515. As a result, the Habsburgs held more thrones than any other family in Europe in the 1500s, but religious strife and competition among emperors, kings, and princes challenged the dominance of the Habsburgs.

By 1516, when 16-year-old **Charles I** took the throne, the Habsburgs ruled the Netherlands, southern Italy, and Spain. Very soon, control of the silver and gold of the Spanish Empire would make the Habsburgs one of the wealthiest dynasties in the world.

With extensive territory in Europe and the wealth of the Americas at their disposal, it seemed that the Habsburgs might be able to create a Catholic empire and achieve political unity in western Europe. In 1520, the pope crowned Charles as Holy Roman Emperor after he was elected to that position by the archbishops and princes who ruled the German-speaking lands. As Holy Roman Emperor, he was now Charles V and the principal defender of the Catholic faith. But Charles faced challenges to the considerable power of the Habsburgs. France, which was creating a strong centralized government that gave the king sweeping powers, was making efforts to conquer parts of Italy and was a powerful rival in the west.

The Protestant Reformation also created problems. The wave of challenges to the Catholic Church that swept through German-speaking Europe led to decades of inconclusive warfare among princes loyal to the pope and those who called themselves Lutherans. Religious division became a fixture of western Europe.

In 1555, Charles finally gave up his attempt to impose Catholicism through military means and agreed to a peace, recognizing the principle that princes could impose either Catholicism or Lutheranism within their own territories. Exhausted, Charles abdicated, or gave up, his throne, retired to a monastery, and split his inheritance between his brother Ferdinand, who took control of the Habsburgs' central European territories, and his son Philip, who became king of Spain. The Habsburgs had failed to hold Europe together.

438 CHAPTER 15

RELIGIOUS AND POLITICAL CONFLICTS

Charles's son **Philip II** ruled over a magnificent court at Madrid in Spain, the Spanish empire in the Americas, and the new southeast Asian colony of the Philippines. However, even with the vast riches of New Spain, wars severely strained the treasury, and increased taxes led to unrest. Philip's determined efforts to impose Catholicism led to religious conflicts. For example, in 1568, the *moriscos*, Arabic-speaking residents of Spain who had been forced, like the Spanish Jews, to convert to Catholicism in 1492, rebelled when the church imposed stricter rules. It took two years for Philip's forces to crush the uprising; Philip then ordered all the moriscos who had survived to leave Spain.

Religious differences also drove Philip's war on the Calvinists in his Dutch provinces. He tried to seize their property, but they armed themselves and rebelled against him.

Protestant England was another constant source of concern for Philip. Under the rule of Queen Elizabeth I, England harassed the Spanish at every turn. England provided aid to Calvinist rebels in Spain's Dutch provinces, and English pirates raided Spanish treasure ships in the Caribbean. In 1588, Philip sent a great naval armada to invade England. Poor weather, along with clever English strategy, led to the defeat of the Spanish Armada. The English took their victory as a sign that God was indeed on their side.

Religious differences affected one of Spain's chief rivals, France. French Protestants, largely Calvinists known as Huguenots (HYOO-guh-nahtz), were a small but prosperous minority. Catholic persecution of Huguenots reached its extreme in 1572, with the Saint Bartholomew's Day massacre. Huguenot leaders were assassinated, and tens of thousands of Protestants were killed. More than 25 years later, in 1598, the Edict of Nantes gave French Protestants in certain cities limited rights.

Challenges remained, however. The expanding Ottoman Empire threatened the Habsburgs in central Europe and on the Adriatic coast of Italy. Meanwhile, religious tensions increased, not just between the rulers of Spain and England. Competition between Catholic and Lutheran rulers in German-speaking lands, as well as struggles for power by Europe's major powers, brought about the catastrophic Thirty Years War.

From 1618 to 1648, Catholic and Protestant armies rampaged across central Europe. In some areas, as much as 30 percent of the population was killed as a result of famine and disease, a loss almost as great as that of the Black Death 300 years earlier. Religious intolerance, combined with greed and lust for power, had turned central Europe into a blood bath.

The humanists' emphasis on peaceful contemplation and toleration for diverse views had been largely forgotten. But by 1648, leaders realized that no military solution was possible and agreed to a peace that recognized that the religious divisions of Europe would be permanent.

Philip II (left) of Spain married Mary I of England (right) in 1554. Until her death in 1558, the two kingdoms maintained friendly relations and Catholicism was restored as England's official religion. However, when Mary's sister and heir, Elizabeth I, took the throne, the country returned to Protestantism.

HISTORICAL THINKING

1. **READING CHECK** What was the primary goal of the Habsburg dynasty when Charles I took the throne in 1516?

2. **IDENTIFY MAIN IDEAS AND DETAILS** What three challenges did Charles I face in his efforts to bring about political and religious unity?

3. **IDENTIFY PROBLEMS AND SOLUTIONS** Why did Philip II try to invade England in 1588?

4.2

MAIN IDEA The Catholic Church recognized problems within the church as well as the threat of the Protestant Reformation and undertook its own reforms.

The Catholic Reformation

Do the ends justify the means? In the 16th and 17th centuries both Protestants and Catholics used cruel methods to convince people of what they each thought was the religion that would save their souls.

THE COUNCIL OF TRENT

Some had pushed for reforms and changes within the Roman Catholic Church before 1517, but once Luther published his 95 theses, the growth of Protestantism became a threat the church could not ignore. This movement to reform and strengthen the Roman Catholic Church from within became known as the Catholic Reformation or the Counter-Reformation. In 1545, the pope called for a meeting in the city of Trent in northern Italy to begin the formal process of reforming the church from within. A group of bishops met 25 times over a period of 18 years in what became known as the **Council of Trent**. These meetings laid out the rituals and structures of the modern Roman Catholic Church. They also clearly defined the differences between Catholics and Protestants.

The Roman Catholic Church published a list, or index, of forbidden books. This list included works by humanist writers such as Erasmus and Machiavelli, as well as translations of the Bible into languages other than Latin. The church also used the Inquisition to enforce conformity. As you may recall, the Inquisition was a group of institutions that investigated people to make sure they were following the teachings of the Catholic Church. The most famous was the Spanish Inquisition, originally created to persecute Jews and Muslims.

After the Protestant Reformation, the Spanish Inquisition was also used to track down Protestants in Spain. After the Council of Trent, it hunted down corrupt priests. The Inquisition was not any crueler than some Protestant-controlled regimes that punished those who did not conform to the religious views of those in power. Europe in the 16th and 17th centuries had little room for freedom of speech, and those who believed they were rooting out people who threatened the religious order, whether Catholic or Protestant, were often cruel.

Through the Council of Trent, the Catholic Church tried to create a truly universal church that would address the spiritual needs of all people, no matter what their language or where they lived. The church conducted all worship in Latin and reduced the number of church holidays and ceremonies. It standardized the rituals

A prisoner is tortured by the Spanish Inquisition while monks await his confession, c. 1500. Individuals were often punished and even killed by the Inquisition for exercising free thought and speech.

440 CHAPTER 15

used for worship and prayer. The church worked to increase activities that provided charity and expand opportunities for **piety**, or devotion to the church. It also established new rules to reduce corruption among clergy and the monastic orders.

CATHOLIC REFORMERS

Ignatius of Loyola set aside his life as a Spanish noble to live as a beggar. He developed the idea that through simple meditation and prayer, people might come closer to God, and through his book *Spiritual Exercises*, he began to gain disciples, or followers. Convinced of the need for a solid education in order to carry out God's will, he became a university student. Ignatius's perspective was not always welcomed by the Catholic Church; he faced imprisonment and trials, but by 1540, the pope approved of the formation of a new order, or religious community, to be known as the Society of Jesus. Members of the order were called Jesuits.

Gian Lorenzo Bernini sculpted *The Ecstasy of Saint Teresa* in marble and bronze in the mid-1600s. It depicts Teresa of Ávila overwhelmed by a religious vision.

Jesuit schools became one of the most effective defenses against the Protestant Reformation. Many parts of Europe, including Poland and parts of Germany, returned to Catholicism because of Jesuit schools. Jesuits also emphasized caring for the poor and the sick. They wrote and published widely, providing European readers with reasonable arguments for their religious views. The Jesuits became one of the most active missionary arms of the Catholic Church, spreading the faith to the Americas, Africa, and Asia, and across Europe.

Teresa of Ávila was a Spanish nun and mystic, or person who seeks a direct connection to God. At the age of 13, Teresa was placed in a convent. Although it was founded as an order that emphasized prayer and withdrawal from the world, it had become a retreat that allowed wealthy young women to live in comfort. Teresa began to have religious visions, gave up her worldly goods, and started a new order with women who had been moved by her teaching. Her order required a vow of poverty and gave all the nuns equal status regardless of their prior rank. It also required withdrawal from the world and obedience. Parents of daughters who joined Teresa's convent were suspicious. They feared they would lose contact with their daughters or that their family fortunes would be given away. Teresa and her followers faced persecution, yet her following grew until the church finally recognized her order. Teresa of Ávila and Ignatius of Loyola were **canonized**, or recognized as saints by the Catholic Church, on the same day in 1622.

HISTORICAL THINKING

1. **READING CHECK** Who called the series of meetings known as the Council of Trent, and what was the outcome of those meetings?

2. **DRAW CONCLUSIONS** How did the use of Latin reflect the structure of the Roman Catholic Church?

3. **COMPARE AND CONTRAST** Compare and contrast the efforts of the Inquisition and the Jesuits to strengthen the Catholic Church.

4.3

MAIN IDEA The Protestant Reformation and the Catholic Counter-Reformation had global effects on religion, politics, and settlement.

Global Christianities

Conflicts over religion occurred at the same time Europeans were expanding trade networks and land claims to areas beyond Europe. This expansion offered new opportunities to spread religious ideas.

DIVERSE CHRISTIAN PRACTICES

Since ancient times, Christian communities have developed diverse rituals and interpretations of the Bible. The Armenian Church and Coptic Christianity in Ethiopia, for example, both have unique sacred languages and rituals inherited from long ago.

The diversity of Christian practices led to conflict in the 11th century when, as you have learned, the Roman Catholic and Eastern Orthodox branches of Christianity finalized a split that had been brewing for centuries by excommunicating one another. Roman Catholics recognized the authority of the pope in Rome and used Latin as the official church language. Orthodox communities, many with Greek as their church language, recognized the patriarch of Constantinople as leader. The Orthodox Church became very influential in Russia, where it deeply affected social and political life. It was not until 1965 that the Roman Catholic and Orthodox churches recognized one another as valid by lifting their mutual excommunications.

Such splits are part of the evolution of most major religions. Divisions among Buddhists followed the death of the Buddha around 483 B.C.E. In the 600s, following the death of Muhammad, Islam split into Sunni and Shiite groups over disputes about leadership. As in Europe, where political competition was fueled by religious disagreement, differences between Sunnis and Shiites deepened and led to political and military competition in the Islamic world.

Similarly, the deep and bitter divisions that led to religious warfare in Europe at the time of the Protestant and Catholic reformations would also have wider consequences, as missionaries spread their interpretations of the faith using new maritime connections to Africa, Asia, and the Americas.

REFORMATIONS AROUND THE GLOBE

Although the Protestant Reformation started in western Europe, its effects were felt far beyond that region. Some Protestant groups fled the continent to avoid persecution, such as Calvinists fleeing from France and England. Some of these Puritans became known as Pilgrims. The Pilgrims were English **dissidents**, or people who were at odds with the official religion. They left Holland, where they had been living to avoid persecution and sailed to Plymouth, Massachusetts, on the *Mayflower*. Soon after, a much larger group of English settlers arrived to form the Massachusetts Bay Colony farther up the coast. Inspired by Calvin and his followers, who had tried to make Geneva into a city that reflected their beliefs, these Puritans planned to create a haven for what they considered to be a "purified" form of Christianity.

The Catholic Counter-Reformation had an even larger global impact in the 16th century. Roman Catholic

Spread of Protestantism, 1600s

- Anglican
- Calvinist
- Lutheran

442 CHAPTER 15

CRITICAL VIEWING As Catholic missionaries traveled throughout the world as a result of the Counter-Reformation, they established churches in the Americas, Africa, and Asia, such as this 18th-century Roman Catholic Church in southern China. How would you compare the style of this church to other churches you've seen pictured in this chapter?

missionaries from Spain and Portugal carried their religion into the Americas. In 1524, the first Franciscan friars arrived in Mexico. The Franciscans became the most important missionary order among the Aztec. They searched for parallels between native beliefs and Christian teachings; at the same time, they suppressed practices such as human sacrifice.

Before long, Aztec converts to Catholicism began making the new religion their own. For example, in 1531 a peasant named Juan Diego reported that he had seen a vision of the Virgin Mary, who had appeared to him on the very site of an earlier shrine to the Aztec goddess of fertility. The Catholic Church recognized his vision as authentic, and the cult of the Virgin of Guadalupe was born. Her dark-skinned image became central to the Mexican practice of Catholicism. Historians use the term **religious syncretism** to describe this merging of indigenous religious rituals and ideas with conversion to a new faith. Another example of religious syncretism is when African converts to Christianity brought their traditions into the new faith, for example, by keeping their old gods but now calling them "saints."

It is true that indigenous peoples sometimes suffered from missionary efforts, as when Jesuits converted people in Brazil to Catholicism and resettled them in villages where they might be killed by disease or sold into slavery. In South Africa and North America, Calvinist settlers deprived indigenous peoples of land and resources. Still, a final outcome of the global expansion of Christianity in the 17th century was a rich and diverse set of faith traditions across the world.

HISTORICAL THINKING

1. **READING CHECK** What were the possible financial benefits to rulers who became Protestants?

2. **INTERPRET MAPS** How did the spread of the Lutheran and Calvinist branches of Protestantism differ from that of the Anglican branch?

3. **ANALYZE CAUSE AND EFFECT** What were the effects of the Reformation and the Counter-Reformation on settlement in the Americas?

Renaissance and Reformation 443

CHAPTER 15 RENAISSANCE AND REFORMATION REVIEW

VOCABULARY

Use each of the following vocabulary words in a sentence that shows an understanding of the term's meaning.

1. patron
2. humanism
3. linear perspective
4. indulgence
5. Protestant
6. liturgy
7. piety
8. dissident

READING STRATEGY
COMPARE AND CONTRAST

Use a Venn diagram like the one below to compare and contrast the Protestant Reformation and the Catholic Reformation. Then answer the questions that follow.

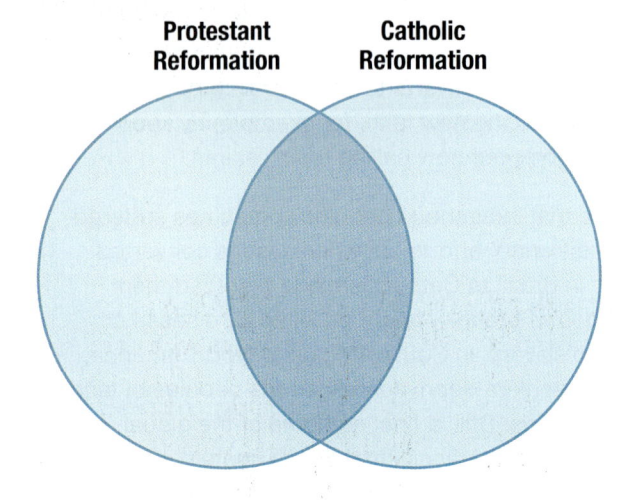

Protestant Reformation | Catholic Reformation

9. Which Reformation movement (Protestant or Catholic) benefited most from the development of the printing press and increased literacy?

10. Which Reformation movement (Protestant or Catholic) employed schools most effectively to further its goals?

MAIN IDEAS

Answer the following questions. Support your answers with evidence from the chapter.

11. What did Italy's city-states hope to gain in their battles with each other in the 1300s? **LESSON 1.1**

12. Why did Renaissance artists sometimes include carpets in their commissioned paintings? **LESSON 1.2**

13. What were some ways that Leonardo da Vinci used science and mathematics in his art? **LESSON 1.3**

14. What sources did Petrarch turn to for moral guidance in the 1300s? **LESSON 2.1**

15. What technique did artists use to make objects look closer or farther away in their paintings? **LESSON 2.2**

16. Why did Niccolò Machiavelli write *The Prince*? **LESSON 2.3**

17. Why did Zwingli and his followers destroy statues and religious art in Zurich's churches? **LESSON 3.2**

18. How did Jesuit schools impact the Protestant Reformation? **LESSON 4.2**

HISTORICAL THINKING

Answer the following questions. Support your answers with evidence from the chapter.

19. **ANALYZE CAUSE AND EFFECT** How did widespread use of the vernacular in printed books affect Europeans?

20. **MAKE GENERALIZATIONS** Discuss the ways that three different humanist writers expressed the ideals of humanism in their work.

21. **DRAW CONCLUSIONS** Why was Martin Luther so successful in spreading his ideas?

22. **COMPARE AND CONTRAST** Discuss the similarities and differences between the goals and methods of the Protestant Reformation and the Catholic Reformation. In your opinion, was one of these efforts more successful? Why or why not?

23. **ANALYZE CAUSE AND EFFECT** How were Protestants and Catholics impacted by advances in maritime technology?

INTERPRET VISUALS

Study the graph below, which shows the estimated rates of literacy in Europe between 1475 and 1750. Then answer the questions that follow.

European Literacy Rates, 1475–1750

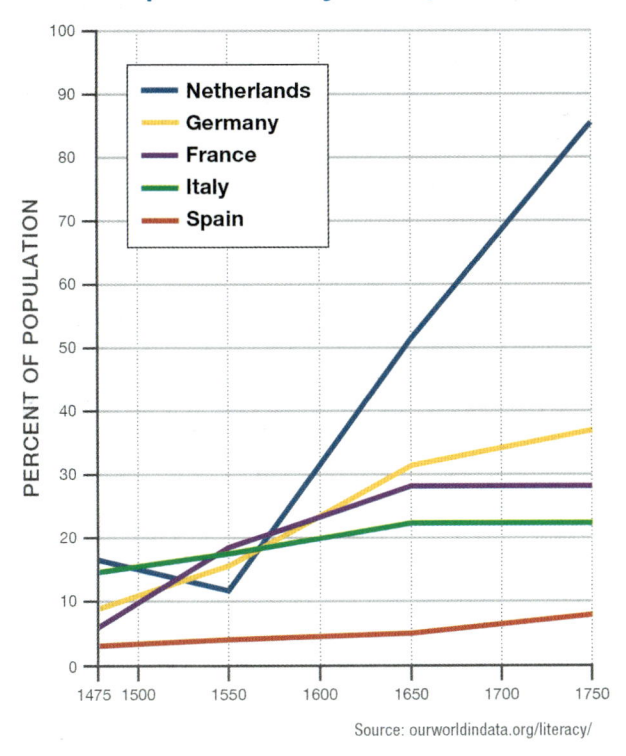

- Netherlands
- Germany
- France
- Italy
- Spain

Source: ourworldindata.org/literacy/

24. Which two nations had the highest rates of literacy in 1475? Which two had the highest in 1750?

25. How would you describe the change in rates of literacy in Germany between 1550 and 1650? In the Netherlands in this same period?

ANALYZE SOURCES

One of Michelangelo's students, Ascanio Condivi, wrote a biography of his teacher that was published in 1553. In this excerpt, Condivi describes the physical strain of painting the Sistine Chapel ceiling and its effect on Michelangelo. Read the excerpt and answer the question that follows.

> After he had accomplished this work, because he had spent such a long time painting with his eyes looking up at the vault, Michelangelo then could not see much when he looked down; so that, if he had to read a letter or other detailed things, he had to hold them with his arms up over his head. . . . From this we may conceive how great were the attention and diligence with which he did his work.

26. According to his biographer, how did the work of painting the ceiling of the Sistine Chapel affect Michelangelo's vision?

CONNECT TO YOUR LIFE

27. **ARGUMENT** In a statement that many view as the guiding principal of humanism, the writer Petrarch said, "It is better to will the good than to know the truth." Do you think this statement served as a guide for political and religious leaders of the Renaissance and Reformation? Is it a statement that could be used as a guide for moral and ethical living today? Write an essay presenting your answers to both questions, citing examples from the chapter and your own research.

TIPS

- Review the discussions of the Renaissance, humanism, and the Reformations in the chapter.
- Choose two or three figures from the chapter who you think might exemplify or contradict Petrarch's statement. Conduct additional research into these figures if necessary.
- Use two or three vocabulary words from the chapter in your argument.
- Think about your own life and the behavior of leaders you admire today. Does this statement serve as a guide in our present-day world? Why or why not?

CHAPTER 16
Land-Based Empires of Eurasia
1453–1850

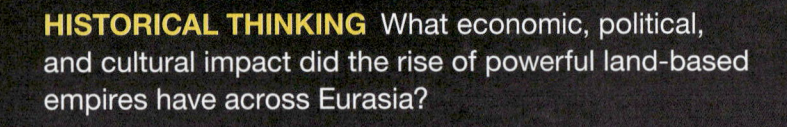

HISTORICAL THINKING What economic, political, and cultural impact did the rise of powerful land-based empires have across Eurasia?

SECTION 1 **The Ottoman Empire**
SECTION 2 **Empires in Asia**
SECTION 3 **The Russian Empire and Shifting Powers**

CRITICAL VIEWING

Mughal emperor Shah Jahan built the Taj Mahal in India in the mid-1600s as a tomb and monument for his wife. The Taj Mahal is considered the finest example of Mughal architecture and one of the most beautiful buildings ever created. What feelings does the building's exterior evoke?

Land-Based Empires of Eurasia

1.1

MAIN IDEA Evliya Çelebi, an adventurous Ottoman voyager, traveled throughout the Ottoman Empire and beyond during the 17th century.

Traveler: Evliya Çelebi
Tales from Forty Years of Travel 1611–1682

If you could travel anywhere, would you explore your own country, trek to allied lands, or venture into hostile territory? The most famous Ottoman traveler spent most of his time touring the Ottoman Empire, but he also set forth into enemy lands in Iran and Europe.

Evliya Çelebi's Journeys

- Takes part in Battle of St. Gotthard, 1664
- Shipwrecked en route to Trebizond, early 1640s
- Travels to Iran, 1655–1656
- Performs hajj pilgrimage to holy sites of Islam, 1671–1672

The Travels of Evliya Çelebi
- Journeys, 1640–1670s
- Possible journey, 1663
- The hajj, 1671–1672
- City visited by Çelebi
- Other city
- Boundaries, ca. 1680

448 CHAPTER 16

BEGINNING A LIFE OF TRAVEL

At the age of 20, Evliya Çelebi (ehv-lee-yuh chuh-LEH-bee) dreamt of a visit from the Prophet Muhammad. Normally, if a person saw the Prophet Muhammad in a dream, he or she would ask for a blessing. Instead, Çelebi asked for the chance to travel. In the dream, the prophet responded, "Thou shalt travel through the whole world and be a marvel among men. Of the countries through which you will pass, of their castles, strongholds, wonderful antiquities, . . . the extent of their provinces and length of the days there, draw up a description which will be a monument worthy of thee."

Çelebi was the son of the chief goldsmith of the powerful sultan of the Ottoman Empire. He had impressed the sultan with his artful recitation of the Quran. Even though Çelebi lived a privileged life in Constantinople, he was passionately curious about the world outside of his home. "I longed," he wrote, "to set out for the Holy Land toward Baghdad and Mecca and Medina and Cairo and Damascus." Çelebi visited those places and many more, which was a great feat in the 17th century. He traveled in luxury, accompanied on each trip by an entourage of men and slaves, cases of fine clothing, libraries of books, and numerous mules and camels. Today Çelebi is recognized as the greatest of all the Ottoman travelers. In 2014, Turkey's Ministry of Culture and Tourism sponsored the country's first 3-D animated movie, *Evliya Çelebi: The Fountain of Youth*. But long before the film was made, the Turkish phrase for a person who feels a constant urge to travel was *Evliya Çelebi gibi*, or "He is like Evliya Çelebi."

RECORDING HIS ADVENTURES

As Çelebi traveled, he recorded his adventures in his *Book of Travels*. After his trips, he returned with both true and fictionalized tales to entertain the sultan and the court.

Early in his travels, Çelebi survived a shipwreck while crossing the Black Sea during a storm. He and his companions retreated to a lifeboat and survived by using their turbans as paddles. However, after this event, Çelebi refused to travel by open sea.

Evliya Çelebi also traveled beyond the Ottoman Empire to Europe and Iran. In Europe he participated in wars between Ottoman forces and the Holy Roman Empire. While in Iran, he described the tense relationships between the Safavid dynasty and the Ottoman rulers.

Çelebi first began to record his adventures after touring his own city of Constantinople. There he watched a parade celebrating an anticipated victory against the Safavid dynasty of Iran.

PRIMARY SOURCE

This procession of the imperial camp begins its march at dawn and continues the whole day until sunset and amounts to the number of 200,000 men all passing like a thundering sea, . . . Nowhere else has such a procession been seen or will be seen. Such is the crown and population of that great capital Constantinople, which may God guard from all celestial and earthly mischief, and let her be inhabited until the end of the world.

—from *The Book of Travels* by Evliya Çelebi

When Çelebi was 60 years old, he made a pilgrimage to the holy cities of Mecca, Medina, and Jerusalem. He described his experience and the proper Muslim ritual for entering Medina.

PRIMARY SOURCE

After one hour of traveling we arrived at the top of a hill. When one reaches this point and turns south one sees the orchards and gardens of Medina and the dome of the Mosque of the Prophet reaching to the sky. From the gleam of the gilded pinnacle on the dome, the plain of Medina becomes light upon light and one's eyes are dazzled. Here the sincere lover gets off his horse or camel or mule and says the following prayer: Peace and blessing be upon you, O Messenger of God; peace and blessing be upon you, O Beloved of God; peace and blessing be upon you, O lord of the first ones and the last ones; and peace be upon the apostles of God. . . . If the pilgrim feels strong enough, he proceeds from here as far as Medina by foot, a five-hour downhill stroll. If he is handicapped or old, he remounts his horse or camel or mule or donkey and continues the journey, repeating again and again the noble blessings on the Prophet.

—from *The Book of Travels* by Evliya Çelebi

HISTORICAL THINKING

1. **READING CHECK** According to Çelebi's own writing, what three cities were his top priority travel destinations? Did he ever visit these places?
2. **ANALYZE POINT OF VIEW** What does Çelebi's description of the royal procession in Constantinople tell readers about his opinion of his own city?
3. **DESCRIBE** What ritual do pilgrims observe as they enter Medina?
4. **ASK AND ANSWER QUESTIONS** Historians claim that Çelebi fabricated many of the details of his travels. What questions might they have asked to lead them to that belief?

1.2 MAIN IDEA The Ottoman Empire spread far and wide under Süleyman's leadership.

Süleyman and Ottoman Power

Which would you rather have: political and military power, wealth for a luxurious life, or a virtuous life of religious devotion? The powerful Ottoman sultan Süleyman I managed to have it all: a huge military, too much money to count, and a deep devotion to his religion.

OTTOMAN EXPANSION AND MILITARY POWER

Having used gunpowder weapons such as cannons to seize control of Constantinople in 1453, the Ottomans grew in military strength. Over the next 100 years, the Ottoman armies pushed further into Europe and North Africa as well as Arab and Persian lands.

The heart of the Ottomans' power was cavalry warfare, attacks carried out by fighters on horseback. After the conquest of Constantinople, which gave the Ottomans access to both the Black Sea and the Mediterranean, they constructed a navy as well. The Ottomans' greatest force, however, was their elite enslaved soldiers from conquered Christian lands. These soldiers, called **janissaries**, trained year-round and became highly skilled at using gunpowder weapons. While a sultan may not have been able to trust his own brothers or sons because they may well have been vying for his power, the janissaries were completely loyal. They were constantly aware that they had no family to protect them, and if they disobeyed, they would be killed. By the 16th century, the janissaries not only served in the military, they also played a central role in the administration. Even the sultan's chief minister was a slave.

On the Persian frontier, the Ottomans faced pushback from the rising Safavid dynasty. In fact, well before Evliya Çelebi's birth, the Turkish Ottomans and the Iranian Safavids were already struggling for the geographic heart of the Islamic world. Adding to their military competition were religious differences. The Ottomans, who controlled the holy sites of pilgrimage in Arabia, were members of the dominant Sunni branch of Islam. The Safavids, on the other hand, had come to embrace the Shiite tradition.

Süleyman I was the 10th sultan of the Ottoman Empire.

SÜLEYMAN, THE MAGNIFICENT

The Ottomans' master strategist was the sultan **Süleyman I**, who came to power in 1520. As a strong military leader, Süleyman greatly expanded the empire.

Süleyman's court reflected the ethnic diversity of his empire. Turkish was the language of the government and the military, Arabic was the language of religion and philosophy, and Persian was the language of poetry and the arts. Süleyman and the members of his court led luxurious lives. Visitors from around the world brought so many gifts that at some point they just piled up with no one looking at them. Süleyman seldom wore an item of clothing twice, and observers wrote that four servants

Ottoman Expansion, 1451–1683

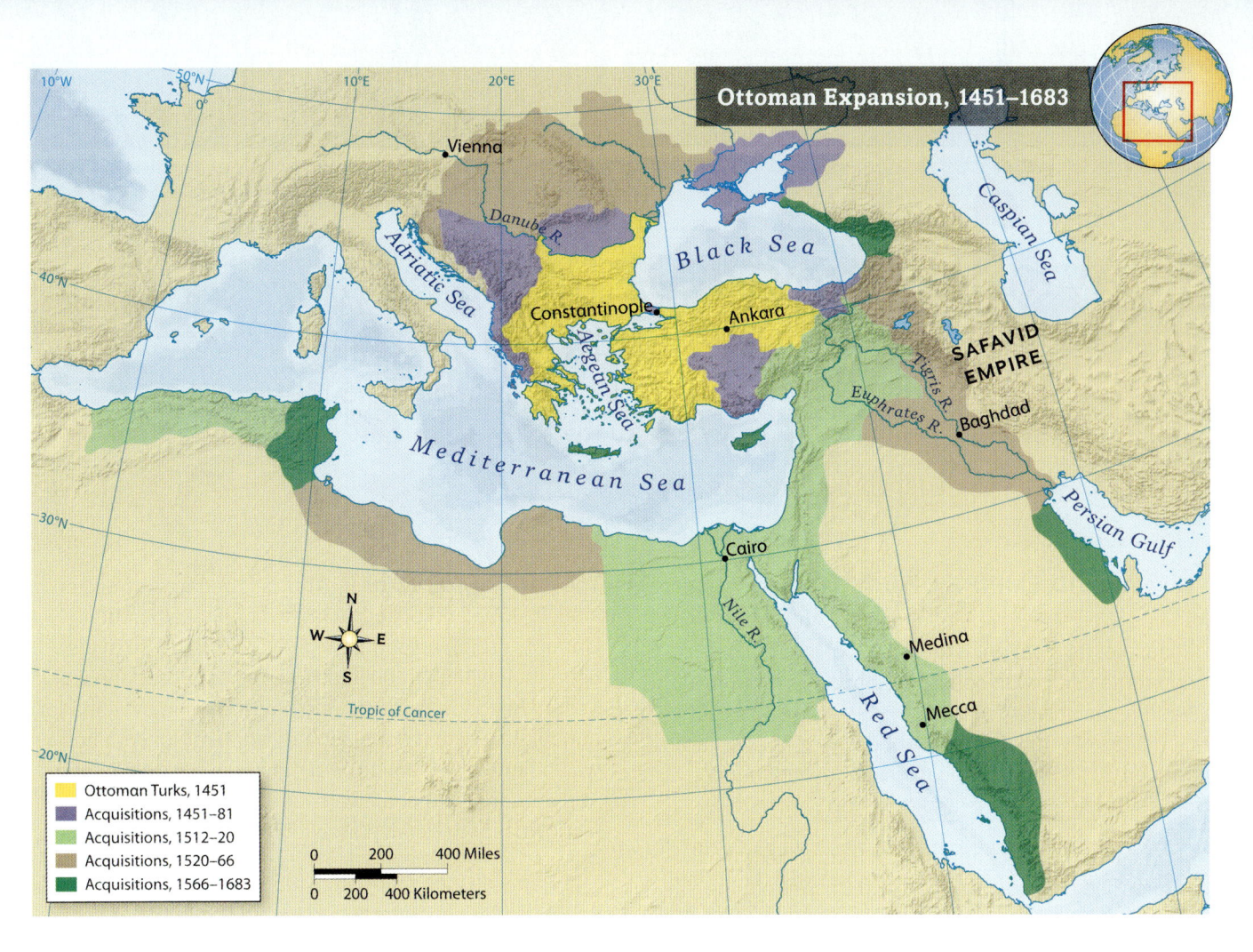

Legend:
- Ottoman Turks, 1451
- Acquisitions, 1451–81
- Acquisitions, 1512–20
- Acquisitions, 1520–66
- Acquisitions, 1566–1683

accompanied the sultan at all times in case he desired a drink of water, needed a jacket, or became tired. The sultan also employed his own personal coffeemaker. This lavish lifestyle led the Europeans to call him "Süleyman the Magnificent." However, within the empire he was known as "Süleyman the Lawgiver" because his laws covered such details as the types of clothing that people of different social positions should wear. These laws helped keep stability in the empire and were later used in other parts of the world to form constitutions.

Süleyman was a devoted Muslim who centralized religious authority and sponsored the building of religious schools and mosques. You have read about the sublime works of Sinan, the sultan's favorite architect. Nevertheless, he did not impose religious laws on minority cultural and religious traditions. Instead, he provided legal protections for minorities by allowing them to practice their own religions, govern their own affairs, and maintain their own courts. The only requirement was that they remained loyal and paid their taxes promptly.

Under Süleyman, the Ottomans aggressively expanded into Europe, northern Africa, and western Asia. They dominated Islam's holy pilgrimage sites in Jerusalem, Mecca, and Medina, and they regained control of Baghdad from the Safavids. The Ottoman navy defeated Christian fleets in the Red Sea, the Persian Gulf, and the Indian Ocean. As you have already read, the Ottomans marched into the German-speaking lands of central Europe, but Austria's Habsburg dynasty pushed Süleyman's forces back when they attempted to lay siege to Vienna in 1529. After Süleyman's death in 1566, a united European fleet defeated the Ottomans in 1571. Still, the Ottomans refused to give up on Europe. Nearly a century later, they again threatened to take Vienna. By that time, the Ottomans held firm control of much of southeastern Europe and were a major player in the European balance of power.

HISTORICAL THINKING

1. **READING CHECK** How did the Ottomans gain power to spread throughout eastern Europe, northern Africa, and Arab lands?

2. **IDENTIFY SUPPORTING DETAILS** What details in the text explain why the Europeans gave Süleyman the title "the Magnificent"? What details explain why the Ottomans called him "Süleyman the Lawgiver"?

3. **INTERPRET MAPS** Along what bodies of water did the Ottoman Empire extend?

Land-Based Empires of Eurasia

1.3

MAIN IDEA The Safavid Empire controlled Iran as a prosperous Shiite state that opposed the Ottomans.

Safavid Rise and Fall

"The enemy of my enemy is my friend" is a saying that has been around for a very long time. But the saying is as true today as it was in the 16th century, when the Safavids of Iran befriended the European Habsburgs to fight together against the Ottomans.

THE SAFAVID EMPIRE OF IRAN

Iran has a long history of influence in Southwest Asia. Because of its location at the center of international trade routes, Iran was constantly under threat from invaders, including Alexander the Great in 330 B.C.E. Much later, other invaders swept down from Azerbaijan, conquered the Persian-speaking lands, and founded the Safavid Empire, which lasted from 1501 until 1722.

The Safavids were members of an Islamic sect that captured the cities of Baghdad and Basra from the Ottomans. As you've read, they adopted Shiite beliefs and imposed them on conquered subjects, including Sunni Muslims and followers of Persia's ancient Zoroastrian faith. The Ottomans retook Baghdad, but the Shiites, who had long been a suppressed minority group, now controlled a large Islamic state.

The greatest Safavid ruler, **Abbas I**, became shah, or king, in 1597 and built the Safavid capital at Isfahan. Under his rule, the economy thrived and the Safavids used their wealth to build palaces, mosques, schools, hospitals, roads, bridges, and new irrigation systems for agriculture. With a population of a half million, Isfahan was a huge city teeming with mosques and public baths. The gardens of Isfahan were legendary, and the city was a showcase for Persian architecture and engineering.

The Safavids also made Iran into a cultural center. Shiite scholars were encouraged to immigrate to the area, and Persian verse influenced poets as far away as East Africa and India. Craftsmen, artists, and traders moved to Iran and sold their work in vast markets. Persians traded silks, carpets, and ceramics by sea, and Europeans eagerly imported these products.

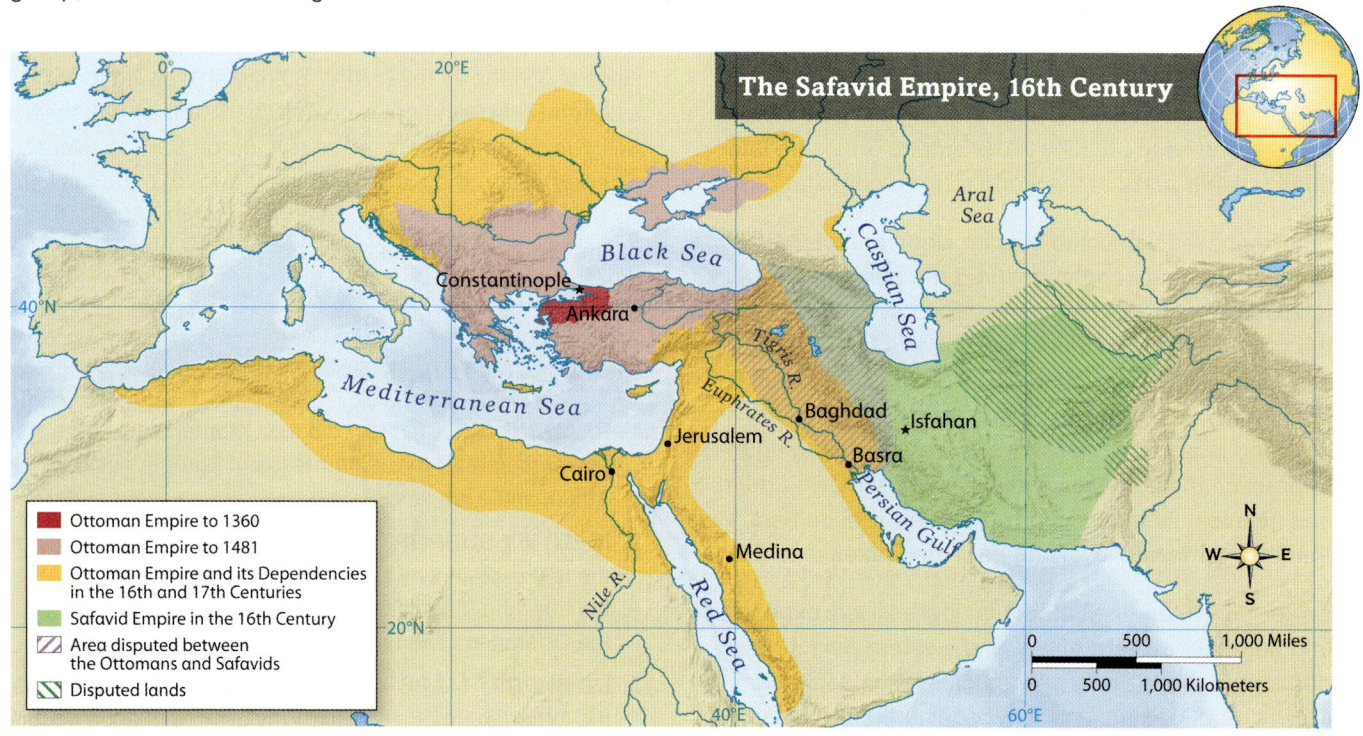

The Safavid Empire, 16th Century

Legend:
- Ottoman Empire to 1360
- Ottoman Empire to 1481
- Ottoman Empire and its Dependencies in the 16th and 17th Centuries
- Safavid Empire in the 16th Century
- Area disputed between the Ottomans and Safavids
- Disputed lands

452 CHAPTER 16

The Safavids built the Shah Mosque in Isfahan, Iran, during the reign of Abbas I. A masterpiece of Persian architecture, engineering, and craftsmanship, the mosque features a magnificent dome decorated with colorful mosaic tiles and calligraphy.

The Safavid Empire was a theocracy in which the ruler was also a religious leader. Under the shah, officials were appointed based on skill rather than heredity, but most were from the nobility. The social structure was organized like a pyramid with the shah and the royal class at the top, followed by the nobility and the clergy, and then rich merchants and urban artists. Commoners were the lowest group. During Abbas's rule, women were treated with respect. A tradition began where the unmarried aunts and daughters of the Shah were admired as patrons of the arts and of religious pilgrims.

The Safavids were constantly at battle with the Ottomans over the lands around Mesopotamia. So although they were antagonistic toward anything Christian or European, the Safavids formed an alliance with the European Habsburgs. Through this alliance, Abbas acquired guns, cannons, and training that his professional soldiers used against the Ottomans.

DECLINE IN LEADERSHIP

Shah Abbas neglected to groom a worthy successor, and after his death in 1629, the quality of leadership declined. The next shah, Süleyman I, was an ineffective ruler who was much more concerned with entertainment and a decadent lifestyle than governance. Corruption spread throughout his court, angering the Shiite clerics who had previously supported the Safavid Empire.

The last Safavid shah attempted to reverse the trend and regain support of the clergy. Like the Puritans in Europe, he imposed harsh conditions on public morality, banning music, coffee, and public entertainment, and he restricted women to their homes. However, people rejected these harsh restrictions, and support for the empire declined even further. The Safavid Empire fell easily to Afghan invaders who descended on Isfahan in 1722, leaving the city in ruins.

HISTORICAL THINKING

1. **READING CHECK** How did the similarities and differences between the Safavids and Ottomans lead to their constant struggle for power?

2. **INTERPRET MAPS** What lands were in dispute between the Safavids and the Ottomans?

3. **ANALYZE CAUSE AND EFFECT** How did the lives of women change after Shah Abbas died? Why did this change occur?

1.4 **MAIN IDEA** In the 17th century, signs of economic decline began to appear in the Ottoman Empire, but it remained a powerful political and cultural force.

Ottoman Persistence

How much effort do you put into having artistic handwriting or choosing an attractive style of type? During the Ottoman Empire, calligraphy, among other art forms, was highly valued—even as the empire began to show signs of weakness.

While the Safavids were defeated in 1722, the Ottomans persisted as a significant power into the mid-18th century. Their empire continued to include much of southeastern Europe with the same political order.

As a sign of their enduring strength, the Ottomans continued to attack Vienna. More than 100 years after Süleyman's first attack in 1529, Ottoman forces made another attempt in 1638. It wasn't until 1739, though, that the Ottomans finally defeated the Habsburgs, who were forced to cede territory to Constantinople. By that time, however, Ottoman power had waned. Rather than expanding the empire, Ottoman military leaders focused their energies on defending the empire's borders against emerging powers, especially Russia.

Ottoman political strength continued following Süleyman's death. Unlike Safavid Iran, where the quality of the shah's leadership was such a determining factor, Ottoman administrative reforms had created stronger and more reliable institutions for both civilian and military affairs. A clear example occurred in 1648 when both court officials and ordinary citizens of Constantinople grew dissatisfied with a sultan who ignored matters of state, or his official duties, while spending lavishly on a decadent lifestyle. He was assassinated. However, unlike Safavid Iran, where weak leadership led to dynastic decline, Ottoman institutions were strong enough to allow a smooth transition to more effective leadership.

This fresco in Florence, Italy, depicts Süleyman's attack on Vienna in 1529.

THE ARTS AND THE ECONOMY

The Ottomans had a long tradition of creating exquisite works of art. During the 16th century, Süleyman hired as many as 120 artists, including painters, textile artists, and architects. Perhaps the most admired artists, however, were the calligraphers, or handwriting artists. Calligraphers trained for many years to create Arabic scripts that symbolized the harmony of God's creation. Quotations from the Quran formed the bulk of the calligraphic text, but artists also used other religious texts, poems, short expressions of wisdom, and words of praise for the Ottoman rulers. Their graceful scripts **embellished**, or decorated, book pages as well as tiles, ceramics, and the walls of buildings.

Painters worked alongside calligraphers in creating illustrated books such as the Quran. Calligraphers used gold or colorful inks as they wrote the text, leaving space for illustrations. You may recall that many Muslims believe the representation of human figures or animals to be forbidden, so artists painted complex floral and geometric patterns known as arabesques to embellish religious texts.

Calligraphers and painters also decorated silk and other textiles. Before the mid-16th century, the Ottomans had imported raw silk from Iran. However, as relations between the two empires deteriorated, the Ottomans were forced to create their own silk. The city of Bursa in present-day Turkey became the silk capital where weavers produced a large variety of silks and velvets. Artists employed by Süleyman I wove gold and silver threads into fabrics worn by the sultan and others of the imperial palace. They created large floral designs that could be seen from afar for use in royal processions.

In the 17th century, the Ottoman economy began to weaken. Ottoman agricultural and commercial production was still substantial, but economic expansion no longer kept up with population growth. Also, the flow of silver into Europe from the Americas caused **inflation**, or increased prices, in the Ottoman economy and a weakened balance of trade. It now became difficult to fund further investment in the arts.

These economic difficulties compelled the court to reduce the number of royal artists and royal commissions. Royal workshops continued to produce

This red satin prayer rug, embroidered with gold and silver thread, dates from the 19th-century Ottoman Empire.

calligraphy and books, and the royal architects continued to build mosques. However, textile art was pushed out of the royal palace. Private workshops continued the art, producing the quality of silk fabrics that had been reserved for the royal court. These textiles became available in markets where they were purchased by upper-class Ottomans and European merchants. The textiles were highly valued in Europe where royalty and priests used the fine fabrics for both state and religious ceremonies.

Despite such challenges, however, the Ottomans persisted as a large and stable state, central to the balance of power in western Asia, central Europe, and North Africa.

HISTORICAL THINKING

1. **READING CHECK** Describe signs of weakness in the Ottoman military and economy in the 17th century.

2. **MAKE GENERALIZATIONS** Why did calligraphy and illustrated books remain a priority in Ottoman art?

3. **MAKE INFERENCES** Why were Ottoman textiles popular in Europe?

2.1 MAIN IDEA Through the practice of tolerance, the Mughal dynasty was able to maintain a stable government in India.

Mughal India

A strong army can conquer a nation, but what does it take to keep people of very different beliefs from revolting? A great Mughal emperor found a solution when he implemented a policy of religious tolerance.

THE DELHI SULTANATE

Islam arrived on the Indian subcontinent via trade with the city-states of East Africa and through invasions by Turks from Central Asia. By the early 1200s, most of northern India was under Muslim rule in the Delhi sultanate, named for its capital city of **Delhi**. The sultanate lasted for three centuries and is credited with preventing the Mongols from invading South Asia.

Five different dynasties ruled the Delhi sultanate between 1210 and 1524. Government officials in Delhi believed the most qualified person in the sultanate, even if not a royal relative, could become sultan. This system of succession led to a free-for-all fight for control whenever a sultan died. One victorious sultan, Muhammad bin Tughluq (TOO-gluhk), conquered most of India. Only parts of southern India remained free of his control. The new sultan staffed his administration solely with foreigners, who he believed would remain loyal if other Muslims tried to overthrow him.

RISE OF THE MUGHAL DYNASTY

Muslim rule in India reached its peak with the Mughal dynasty, which was founded in 1526 by the Turkic prince Babur, who conquered lands in Afghanistan and India, ending the Delhi sultanate. The dynasty reached its height under the emperor **Akbar I**, whose armies controlled most of the Indian subcontinent. Akbar became one of the most powerful men in the world, ruling 100 million subjects from Delhi.

The Mughal state was well positioned to take advantage of expanding trade along the Indian Ocean. The Mughals exported dyed cotton textiles, sugar, pepper, diamonds, and other luxury goods. Imperial mints, factories with government authorization to produce currency, created hundreds of millions of gold, silver, and copper coins.

Akbar invested in roads to help traders move goods to market. The Mughals also granted tax-exempt status to new settlements to encourage people to move into previously underutilized lands. These settlements transformed the eastern half of Bengal (present-day Bangladesh) from tropical forestland into a densely populated rice-producing region.

Agriculture was the ultimate basis of Mughal wealth and power. Taxes on agricultural lands provided 90 percent of the income that paid for

One of Delhi's most recognizable landmarks, Qutb Minar is a high tower with inscriptions from the Quran written on its red and tan sandstone facade. Begun before the founding of the Delhi sultanate, the tower was completed during the reign of the first sultan. As was common practice, the builders used pieces of destroyed Hindu and Jain temples to build both the tower and the nearby mosque.

Mughal art was dominated by miniatures—tiny, detailed illustrations that appeared in books or as individual works. This miniature of a horse is from the 17th century.

Mughal armies. The Mughals sent tax clerks out to the provinces to survey the lands and divert revenue, or income for the government, to Delhi. The Mughals also continued the practice of allocating 10 percent of tax income to local rulers who had been in place before the Mughal conquest. By recognizing local rulers, the Mughals were able to incorporate existing Indian authorities into their government while maintaining control from the top.

RELIGIOUS TOLERANCE

As Muslims, the Mughals faced a difficult challenge in ruling over the Hindu majority of India. They had conquered by force, but maintaining control of a people with such different beliefs was a more difficult challenge.

Akbar's solution was to develop a policy of tolerance and inclusion. He canceled the special tax that Islamic law allows Muslim rulers to collect from nonbelievers. He also granted Hindu communities the right to follow their own social and legal customs. Hindu princes and rural aristocrats were incorporated into the Mughal administrative system. The Hindus were accustomed to a social system in which people paid little attention to matters outside their group. So Akbar presented the ruling Muslims as simply another caste with their own rituals and beliefs. In this way, the Mughals achieved a stable social order.

Akbar's successor Jahangir and his remarkable wife, **Nur Jahan**, continued Akbar's policy of religious tolerance. Jahangir was a weak ruler, so his wife took charge and kept Mughal power intact. Since women were secluded in separate quarters, Nur Jahan could not appear at court in person. Instead she issued government decrees through trusted family members. Taking a special interest in women's affairs, she donated land and dowries, or property that girls could use to start their married lives, to orphans. She was from an Iranian family, and she patronized Persian-influenced art and architecture, building many of the most beautiful mosques and gardens in north India.

Nur Jahan was also interested in commerce. She owned a fleet of ships that took religious pilgrims and trade goods to Mecca. Her policies facilitated both domestic and foreign trade even more than Akbar's had. During her time, India had a strong influence on the wider world. Indian merchants, sailors, bankers, and shipbuilders played important roles in Indian Ocean markets. The ports of Mughal India teemed with visitors from Europe, Africa, Arabia, and Southeast Asia.

Jahangir recognized and was grateful for his wife's crucial contributions. While Mughal coins were normally stamped with the name of the emperor, Jahangir had coins minted in Nur Jahan's name.

Jahangir's successor and son Shah Jahan held his wife, Mumtaz Mahal, in great regard as well. Following her death, he had an extensive **mausoleum**, or tomb, built in her honor. The mausoleum, the Taj Mahal, often called a work of "poetry in stone," became one of the most admired and magnificent buildings in the world.

MUGHAL DECLINE

Mughal India was at its height when Aurangzeb (ow-rang-ZEHB) became emperor in 1649. He called himself *Alamgir*—"world seizer"—to express his goal of extending Mughal power even further. Indeed, when he died many years later in 1707, the empire was at its greatest extent.

The problem was that in order to sustain his rule, Aurangzeb was forced to spend almost all his time away from the capital of Delhi on military campaigns. Regional rulers across India were testing the emperor's authority, for example, by withholding tax revenue and using it to engage in Indian Ocean trade and to purchase gunpowder weapons.

Aurangzeb managed to hold them in check but at a huge cost. His devotion to Islam and his imposition of the special tax on nonbelievers increased tensions with Hindus and other religious minorities. And the costs of his wars emptied the Mughal treasury. After his death, invasions from Iran and Afghanistan weakened Mughal power. As you will see, it was the British who would later benefit from Mughal decline.

In this 16th-century painting from the Mughal dynasty, Akbar I converses with people of different religious beliefs, including Muslim scholars and Jesuits, missionaries from a Catholic religious order.

HISTORICAL THINKING

1. **READING CHECK** How did Akbar's policy of religious tolerance help the Mughals maintain control of India?

2. **ANALYZE CAUSE AND EFFECT** What was the result of the Mughal policy of granting tax-exempt status to new settlements?

3. **DESCRIBE** How did Nur Jahan's foreign and domestic trade policies support the diffusion of cultures?

4. **MAKE INFERENCES** How did the large size of the Mughal Empire eventually contribute to its decline?

Land-Based Empires of Eurasia

2.2 Preserving Cultural Heritage

The Taj Mahal

The Taj Mahal in northern India is considered the greatest work of Mughal architecture, blending Indian, Persian, and Islamic styles. It is also considered one of the most beautiful buildings in the world—one that over three million people come to visit each year.

An enormous mausoleum complex, the Taj Mahal was built in Agra, India, along the banks of the Yamuna River, commissioned in 1632 by Mughal emperor Shah Jahan after the death of his beloved wife Mumtaz Mahal.

In 1631, Mumtaz Mahal died in childbirth. According to legend, Shah Jahan and his wife had been inseparable since their marriage in 1612. Grief-stricken, Shah Jahan ordered the building of the most beautiful tomb in the world as an enduring monument to the love of his wife.

Construction began in 1632 and over 20,000 workers from India, Persia, the Ottoman Empire, and Europe worked to build the magnificent complex. The five main structures of the complex consist of the main gateway, the garden, a mosque, a *jawab*, or guesthouse mirroring the mosque, and the mausoleum.

AGRA, INDIA

Goat shepherds walk with their flocks on the other side of the Yamuna River, across from the Taj Mahal. The heavily polluted river has become a breeding ground for mosquito-like bugs, whose excrement is leaving green stains on the mausoleum's marble.

CHAPTER 16

The Taj Mahal rises up behind workers from the Archaeological Survey of India, the organization charged with cleaning the mausoleum's facade. India's Supreme Court has called preservation of the structure a "hopeless cause" due to government failures to cut down on pollution.

It took two decades to complete the work. The white-marble mausoleum was completed around 1638 while the remaining buildings and decoration work continued. Shah Jahan intended to build a second mausoleum across the river where his remains would be buried, but before that could be done he was overthrown by one of his sons. He was then imprisoned in the Agra Fort, which had a view of the Taj Mahal.

Notable for its white marble facade, the Taj Mahal's interior is decorated with semiprecious stones and carvings of verses from the Quran. After Mughal rule ended, the iconic white marble mausoleum suffered from neglect and deterioration. Major restoration was carried out in the early 20th century in an effort to preserve India's cultural heritage, and the Taj Mahal was designated a UNESCO World Heritage Site in 1983.

As both industrial development and tourism increased in India, air pollution from neighboring factories and vehicle emissions from increasing traffic threatened the facade of the marble building. Actions have been taken to combat the growing air pollution as well as the vast amounts of visitors. In 1996, the Supreme Court of India ordered environmental protections for the Taj Mahal. As a result, some factories were closed while others installed pollution-control equipment. A buffer zone around the complex and a ban of nearby vehicular traffic has also helped decrease pollution.

Today, the Archaeological Survey of India continues to manage the site and works with the World Monuments Fund to restore and preserve the Taj Mahal, maintaining it as the most magnificent example of Mughal architecture.

HISTORICAL THINKING

EVALUATE Industrialization plays a key role in growing economies in less-developed countries, but it also has consequences for the environment. Should industrial development be strictly regulated to protect cultural sites like the Taj Mahal? Why or why not?

Land-Based Empires of Eurasia

2.3 MAIN IDEA By exploiting Ming weaknesses, the Manchurians took over China, pushed back northern adversaries, and established one of the most prosperous empires in the world.

Ming Decline to Qing Power

If you were rich and famous, would you need to try to please others? One Chinese emperor didn't think so. He ruled over a huge and extremely powerful country. He felt no need to pay attention to smaller countries on the other side of the world.

MING FALL AND QING RISE

By the beginning of the 17th century, Ming China, which you read about in an earlier chapter, was starting to show signs of weakness. The Chinese economy relied on silver from Spanish America, but as supplies of silver fell, inflation, or increased prices, triggered a decline in purchasing power. In other words, people were able to buy less with the same amount of money.

This economic crisis occurred at the same time as a government crisis. The aging emperor had lost interest in governing, and without his oversight, corruption increased. While officials vied for power, the country's affairs went unattended. Irrigation works were left unfinished and roads became unsafe as bandits robbed merchants. Peasants began to revolt. These weaknesses made China vulnerable to invasion, and in 1644 armies from neighboring Manchuria overran Beijing, deposed the Ming dynasty, and established the Qing (chihng) dynasty.

The Qing were Manchu (mahn-CHOO), or from Manchuria, and had a different language and identity than the majority Han Chinese. They never fully assimilated into Chinese culture, but they continued many of the policies and philosophies of previous dynasties with the hope that the Chinese people would endorse their rule. They maintained Confucianism as the official ideology and retained the Chinese system of ministries and the examination system.

When the emperor **Kangxi** (KAHNG-shee) ascended the throne in 1661, Ming resistance continued in the south. However, Kangxi, who had been educated by Christian Jesuit tutors, brought knowledge of cannons and the mathematics to use them to successfully

Ming and Qing Dynasties, 1405–1783

Qing Empire
- Qing homeland
- Dominant by 1644
- Dominant by 1659
- Acquired From Russia, 1689
- Dominant by 1783
- Principal tributary states
- Ming Empire
- Great Wall

464 CHAPTER 16

suppress the rebels and to annex the island of Taiwan. He oversaw tremendous economic expansion. Farmers improved agricultural productivity by planting crops such as peanuts, potatoes, and maize from the Americas, and the Chinese population boomed—a sign of prosperity. Over six decades, Kangxi established the Qing as masters of one of the greatest empires the world had known.

QING TRADE AND FOREIGN RELATIONS

The emperor **Qianlong** (CHEE-ahn-lawng) ruled during the empire's greatest prosperity and territorial expansion. China exported luxury goods such as silk and porcelain, and, in return, vast quantities of silver poured into Qing China. Farmers added new crops, and artists and small-scale **entrepreneurs**, people who organize and operate businesses, expanded the glassmaking and coal-mining industries. Cotton textile production also emerged as a major commercial industry at this time, helping 18th-century China retain its position as the largest industrial economy in the world.

Pearls, silk, and silver and gold thread adorn the pheasant featured in this example of embroidery, or decorative needlework, from the 18th-century Qing dynasty.

Territorial expansion was one of the greatest Qing achievements. Through both diplomacy and force, the Qing dynasty added 600,000 square miles to its empire. However, the Qing were not interested in asserting cultural superiority over the societies they acquired, and Korea and Vietnam remained self-governing through rituals such as annual tribute missions to Beijing in recognition of the Qing as their overlords.

The Russians, who you will read more about later in this chapter, were also expanding territory during this time, and the Qing worried that the Russians might threaten China. After some skirmishes, the Russians and the Chinese agreed to a treaty. The Qing recognized Russian claims west of Mongolia, and the Russians disbanded settlements to the east.

Unlike the Russians who came over land, other Europeans came by sea. The Qing restricted European trade to a single port in south China. They also allowed Europeans to trade only with state-approved firms, which gave the Qing exclusive control over the market. They easily fixed prices and amassed huge profits.

The Chinese trade structure frustrated the British, who were the greatest maritime commercial power of the time. With the goal of opening access to the vast Chinese market, King George III sent a mission to China to negotiate formal diplomatic relations in 1792. However, when British representatives refused to recognize Emperor Qianlong as superior to King George, negotiations broke down. The Qing controlled the largest and wealthiest empire in the world. And as Qianlong noted in his response to the British: "We have never valued ingenious articles, nor do we have the slightest need of your country's manufactures." The Qing had no need to look beyond their own imperial borders for resources.

HISTORICAL THINKING

1. **READING CHECK** What were some of the greatest Qing accomplishments?

2. **INTERPRET MAPS** By how much did the Qing Empire expand from the size of the previous Ming dynasty?

3. **MAKE INFERENCES** How did Qing trade practices with Europeans turn the balance of trade in China's favor?

Land-Based Empires of Eurasia 465

2.4 DOCUMENT-BASED QUESTION
Voltaire Writes About Qianlong

Today's technology can help us connect with people in faraway lands pretty quickly. But how much can you really know about someone you have never met? In the 18th century, news of Qianlong's rule of China traveled far, and France's most famous philosopher became a fan of China's emperor.

Well before Qianlong became emperor, his grandfather and father had groomed him for the role. He had a fine education in which he gained skills in writing, art, philosophy, and government. He published more than 44,000 poems and sponsored the compilation of China's greatest works of philosophy. While he held the throne, the arts and humanities flourished in China.

Qianlong's successful rule made an impression on Europe's greatest thinkers. Voltaire was a contemporary of Qianlong and the most outspoken philosopher of his time in France. He used satire, wit, and reason to criticize European corruption and injustice. Although he was in regular contact with the greatest intellectuals of Europe, Voltaire held a man he had never met in the highest regard. In his eyes, Qianlong was a great philosopher king who ruled over a model state. In 1764, Voltaire wrote, "One need not be obsessed with the merits of the Chinese to recognize that their empire is the best that the world has ever seen."

Emperor Qianlong ruled China from 1736 to 1796.

DOCUMENT ONE

Primary Source: Letter
from a letter by Voltaire to Frederick the Great, King of Prussia, 1772

In 1770, Qianlong's 3,000-word poem "Ode to Mukden" was translated into French. As one of the greatest essayists and poets of Europe, Voltaire read and admired the translated poem. The king of Prussia, on the other hand, was not known to be much of a poet. However, when Voltaire wrote this letter, he was seeking financial support from King Frederick the Great.

CONSTRUCTED RESPONSE Why does Voltaire compare Frederick the Great's writing to Qianlong's? Do you think Voltaire really believes that King Frederick's writing is better than Qianlong's? Explain your answer.

> I do not know if the emperor of China has some of his discourses recited in his Academy, but I defy him to write better prose, and, with regard to his verses, I am acquainted with a king of the North [Frederick] who can write better ones without too much trouble. . . . Know that the king's poem on the Confederates is infinitely superior to the poem of Moukden [Mukden].

DOCUMENT TWO

Primary Source: Letter
from a letter by Voltaire to the Marquis de Condorcet, 1770

Voltaire was a strong advocate of religious tolerance. He criticized Christians for not being accepting of other faiths. In China, Christian missionaries were sometimes forbidden from preaching and converting Chinese people. However, Qianlong had several Jesuit missionaries as his personal friends. In this letter, Voltaire quotes a dialogue between Qianlong and the Chinese minister of state to argue a point.

CONSTRUCTED RESPONSE How does this anecdote support Qianlong's beliefs about religious tolerance?

> [When] a Minister of State accus[ed] a mandarin [Chinese official] of being a Christian, the Emperor Kien-long [Qianlong] asked:
> "Does his province complain of him?"
> "No."
> "Does he render justice impartially?"
> "Yes."
> "Has he failed in his duty towards the state?"
> "No."
> "Is he a good father to his family?"
> "Yes."
> "Why then dismiss him for a mere nothing?"

DOCUMENT THREE

Primary Source: Letter
from a letter by Qianlong to King George III of Britain, 1793

Chinese products were in high demand in Europe. However, Europeans found it difficult to convince Qing officials to open up their markets. In an attempt to persuade China to open up to freer trade, King George sent an ambassador to China. This excerpt is from Qianlong's response.

CONSTRUCTED RESPONSE In what way does Qianlong's response to King George further opinions similar to those of Voltaire?

> . . . [O]ur Celestial Empire possesses all things in prolific abundance and lacks no product within its own borders. There was therefore no need to import the manufactures of outside barbarians [societies outside China] in exchange for our own produce. But as the tea, silk, and porcelain which the Celestial Empire produces are absolute necessities to European nations and to yourselves, we have permitted, as a signal mark of favor, that foreign *hongs* [merchant firms] should be established at Canton, so that your wants might be supplied and your country thus participate in our beneficence [generosity].

SYNTHESIZE & WRITE

1. **REVIEW** Review what you have learned about Voltaire and Qianlong.
2. **RECALL** On your own paper, list details about Qianlong from what Voltaire has written and from Qianlong's own words.
3. **CONSTRUCT** Construct a topic sentence that answers the following question: Was Voltaire's belief that Qianlong was a benevolent and wise leader accurate?
4. **WRITE** Using evidence from this chapter and the documents, write an informative paragraph that supports your topic sentence in Step 3.

2.5

MAIN IDEA Japan's Tokugawa shoguns brought peace and stability, but their tight grip on society slowed prosperity and isolated Japan from much of the world.

Japan's Tokugawa Shogunate

When things feel chaotic, do you ever feel the need to pull back and take control? This is what the Tokugawa shoguns tried to do when they felt Japanese society was changing too fast.

STABILITY AND PROSPERITY

The 16th century was a time of violence and insecurity in Japan, and as the nation entered the 17th century, the Japanese emperor remained secluded in Kyoto. The Tokugawa (toh-koo-gah-wah) shoguns who ruled from the political capital at Edo, today's Tokyo, had the real political power. These shoguns took control and formed a shogunate—a government ruled by shogun generals—that brought peace and stability to the Japanese islands. Still, the provincial lords, the daimyo, retained substantial authority within their own domains.

Under the Tokugawa, the economy flourished as farmers and fishermen improved their processes and increased their yields. The shoguns and daimyo developed an efficient tax system based on precise appraisals of the land and population. Some of this new tax revenue went toward the improvement of roads and irrigation works, further stimulating economic growth.

Internal trade expanded as Japanese cities and commercial centers grew and peasants geared their production toward urban markets. By 1720, Edo had grown from a small village to a city of more than a million people.

This peacetime economy altered roles for samurai warriors and for women. While samurai remained loyal to their daimyo lords, some positioned themselves as intellectual and cultural leaders. They established schools, wrote Confucian treatises, and patronized the arts. Women's roles began to change, too. Elite women contributed to Japanese literature, including experimenting with a form of poetry called *haiku*. Women from merchant and artisan families claimed some mobility and economic opportunities. Some participated as performers or audience members in theater and dance. Samurai and women enjoyed the new form of drama called *kabuki*.

These artistic trends and societal changes worried the Tokugawa leaders because they wanted to maintain a more traditional society. They demanded that people return to traditional ways of living and ordered them to dress in clothing and live in houses appropriate to their social status.

CHALLENGES, REFORM, AND DECLINE

By the 18th century, the Tokugawa shoguns faced numerous challenges. The population had grown to more than 30 million. While population growth had been a sign of prosperity early in the shogunate, it became a problem in a country with limited farmland. Urban centers grew and encroached on farmland, and constant construction in urban areas depleted Japan's timber resources. Wood became more expensive, and heavy logging led to soil erosion.

The Tokugawa shogun **Yoshimune** (YOH-shih-muhn) supported the use of fertilizer to refresh exhausted soil, but the problem of limited land for agriculture and timber only escalated. The economy took a downturn, and hundreds of thousands perished in a terrible famine in the 1780s.

To curb unnecessary ==consumption==, or spending, Yoshimune issued edicts emphasizing frugality. But his edicts did not change people's behavior. He sponsored reforms to curb corruption, reduce imports, and support fishing, and he increased government control over commerce. But these policies undermined new business development, and Japanese business gradually became more regulated and less inventive.

These troubles resulted in a rural uprising. It was becoming clear that the Tokugawa shoguns' policies were inadequate to solve Japan's problems.

JAPAN REJECTS THE EUROPEAN WORLD

The shoguns' conservative policies were most evident in foreign affairs. In the 17th century, Tokugawa leaders outlawed Christianity because the shoguns were alarmed by the early success of Christian missionaries. A series of seclusion edicts strictly limited contact with Europeans. The Tokugawa allowed only one Dutch trading expedition per year. During that expedition, no Bibles or other Christian texts were allowed to enter the country.

The seclusion edicts only applied to Europeans. Trade with Chinese and Korean merchants grew, and overall, Japanese foreign trade increased. Through the Dutch trade expedition, some scientific and philosophical books from Europe reached Japan, and European knowledge became known as "Dutch learning." But for the most part, Japanese thinkers relied on China to learn of advances in science and philosophy.

Some Tokugawa thinkers even downplayed Chinese influence. They rejected Buddhism and Confucianism and elevated Shinto since that was Japan's indigenous religion. The practice of **nativism**, favoring Japanese tradition and ideas rather than those of outsiders, spread. Unlike China, Russia, and Britain, Japan opted out of empire building.

In the early 1790s, Americans and Russians arrived in Japan, hoping to re-establish trade relations. The Japanese responded by attacking their vessels, forcing them to flee. Their commitment to seclusion would later be challenged with an ultimatum from these foreign powers: open your doors to foreign trade, or we will use advanced weapons to destroy them.

This woodblock print by the Japanese artist Utagawa Hiroshige is from his series *One Hundred Famous Views of Edo*. First published in 1856–1859, the series made Hiroshige one of the most popular *ukiyo-e* artists of all time. *Ukiyo-e*, which is Japanese for "pictures of the floating world," was an art style that flourished during the Tokugawa period.

HISTORICAL THINKING

1. **READING CHECK** Why did the Tokugawa shoguns decide to seclude Japan from Europeans?
2. **IDENTIFY PROBLEMS AND SOLUTIONS** Why did population growth become a problem in the 18th century, and how did the Tokugawa government seek to solve the problem?
3. **ANALYZE CAUSE AND EFFECT** What was one effect of the Tokugawa government's attempts to increase control over commerce?

3.1

MAIN IDEA A strong, centralized Russia formed from a diverse populace of people living along the Eurasian steppes.

Control of the Steppes

Have you ever heard the saying "Absolute power corrupts absolutely"? In the case of one Russian monarch, power led not only to corruption but also to a reign of absolute terror.

LIFE ON THE STEPPES

The Eurasian steppes extend approximately 5,000 miles across Europe and Asia from Hungary to Manchuria. The steppe region consists largely of grasslands; few trees grow there, and the soil isn't well suited for farming. These are the lands of nomadic herders like the Mongols, whose great empire you learned about earlier.

Most people lived north of the steppes in the forests, where they raised herds and grew crops on small family farms. Treeless arctic plains called **tundra** and land called **taiga** that was covered with scattered stands of evergreen shrubs lay beyond the forests. People in this region survived by fishing and hunting reindeer, bear, and walrus.

Some of the people living in the region called themselves the Rus, the root of the word *Russia*, which became another name for the area. This multiethnic group spoke many different languages. But starting in around 500, the Slavs, who occupied much of the territory along the southwestern coast of the Black Sea, moved north and east, carrying their language with them. The Slav language is related to Russian, Ukrainian, Polish, and Czech.

Children race horses across the steppes during the summer Naadam Festival, an annual celebration of nomadic culture in Mongolia.

470 CHAPTER 16

TAKING CONTROL OF THE STEPPES

West of the Slav region were the Magyars, Christian converts known to their neighbors as Hungarians. Two Turkish-speaking communities were also in the area—the Khazars, who lived near **Kiev** and who had converted to Judaism, and the Bulgars, converts to Islam.

Before 930, the Rus paid tribute to rulers like the Khazars and the Bulgars. However, the Rus evolved into early states called principalities. As trade grew, so did the populations of the Rus principalities, with Kiev becoming the largest. After signing a trade treaty with the Byzantine Empire, the Kievan Rus began to eliminate their political rivals, including the Khazars and the Bulgars.

Unlike the other groups, the Rus had not chosen a religion. However, since the middle of the ninth century, Byzantine missionaries had been active among the Rus. Earlier you read about the Byzantine missionary Cyril and how he created the Cyrillic alphabet using a combination of Greek and local languages to provide a written language for the Slavs. The Christian scriptures were then translated using this alphabet, called Old Church Slavonic.

Prince Vladimir of Kiev, who emerged as the leader of the Kievan Rus, converted to Christianity in 987 after he married the sister of a Byzantine emperor. He then ordered all the inhabitants of Kiev to come to the riverbank where he surprised them by performing a mass baptism. Thus, Christianity became the religion of the Rus.

Conquest by the Mongols in the 1230s left the city of Kiev devastated. The principality of Muscovy (Moscow) eventually emerged as Kiev's successor, and Ivan III defeated other Russian families to become the undisputed leader of the region.

By the time **Ivan IV** came to power in 1533, what became known as Russian Orthodox Christianity had taken deep root in Russia. Ivan IV took the title **tsar**, a version of the Latin term *Caesar*, because he considered Russia a continuation of the old Roman Empire. Claiming that God had granted him the divine right to rule, he centralized power and extended Russia's frontiers. He also maintained a large buffer around Russia to protect it from invasion. Ivan's accomplishments came with a price, though. He was known as "Ivan the Terrible" because of his cruelty. For example, when he heard that members of the nobility in the town of Novgorod were plotting against him, he had the entire town destroyed, executing thousands of the town's innocent inhabitants. He also formed an elite force to torture and kill anyone who disobeyed him. In a fit of rage, he even murdered his own son, heir to the throne.

CRITICAL VIEWING This 1897 oil painting by Victor Mikhailovich Vasnetsov portrays Ivan IV. What can you infer about the tsar from details in the painting?

HISTORICAL THINKING

1. **READING CHECK** Describe the religious diversity in the steppes before the 10th century.

2. **DESCRIBE** How did the Slav language come to dominate the vast region of the steppes?

3. **IDENTIFY SUPPORTING DETAILS** Describe some of the events that gave Ivan IV the title "Ivan the Terrible."

3.2

MAIN IDEA The Romanov dynasty in Russia sought to become more European while maintaining its oppressive treatment of the serfs.

The Romanov Dynasty

How difficult is it to live up to your values? Most of us have good intentions, but when it comes down to practice, we often fall short. This is what happened to the Russian empress Catherine the Great. She hoped to grant the Russian people more freedoms, but she found that the cost was too high.

RISE OF THE ROMANOVS

It was Russia's fear of disorder and instability that allowed Ivan IV to rule without limitation. But Ivan's death ushered in a "time of troubles" because, as you've read, he killed his own son and failed to leave a clear successor. After 30 years of instability, Russian nobles offered royal power to a noble named Mikhail Romanov. With his ascent in 1613, the Romanov dynasty began, and it endured for a long time. Like the Ottoman Empire and the Qing dynasty, Romanov rule in Russia lasted into the 20th century.

The Romanovs continued Russia's imperial expansion. Animal furs had become fashionable, and profit lured Russian traders to the east, where they traveled across the Ural Mountains into frigid Siberia in search of animal pelts. Although Russians were trading furs on a substantial scale, agricultural surpluses were the main source of revenue for the tsars and the nobility. Peasants worked the fields to provide this revenue stream. While most European countries had given up serfdom, serfs continued to live in oppressive conditions in Russia. Russian peasants were tightly bound to their villages, and the aristocracy increasingly saw these serfs as property to be bought and sold.

Tsar **Peter the Great** visited western Europe as a young monarch in 1697, and he returned to Russia with the realization that it had fallen behind. He was determined to bring Russia up to par with its European counterparts. To bring about rapid transformation, Tsar Peter accumulated greater power for himself by bringing the nobles more tightly under his control. He forced his royal court to dress in the latest European fashions, and he ordered Russian aristocrats to shave off their long beards so they would look more European. Any Russian man who wanted to keep his beard would have to pay a "beard tax" and carry a receipt that read: "the beard is a superfluous [unnecessary] burden." Tsar Peter's beard policy showed who was in charge and made it clear that change in Russia would flow in one direction: from the top down.

To further Russia's transformation, Peter also brought in the latest military technology from Europe. In a spectacle of military power, he created a regular standing army, larger than any in Europe, as well as a powerful navy fleet. He also sponsored a new educational system to train more efficient civilian and military bureaucrats. Still, the situation of the serfs did not improve. Their heavy taxes paid for the Russian military, and their sons fought in Peter's armies. At the serfs' expense, Peter extended Russian frontiers in wars against Sweden and Poland and laid the groundwork for later conquests of Muslim steppe societies. For all the elegance of Peter's new capital, his insistence on expansion and absolute power left Russia's policies little changed from those of Ivan the Terrible.

EUROPEAN AND ASIAN INFLUENCES

With great expense Peter built the new capital city of St. Petersburg on the Baltic Sea to serve as Russia's "window on the West." He used European architectural styles in St. Petersburg, emulating the elegant baroque buildings of Rome and Vienna. Peter's palace in St. Petersburg was originally planned as the main residence of the Romanov family, but later Romanovs moved the capital back to Moscow. They returned to the "Winter Palace" for winter retreats in the milder climate of St. Petersburg.

A little over a hundred years earlier, in the 1550s, Ivan the Terrible built St. Basil's Cathedral in Moscow to commemorate his conquest of Kazan, a city ruled by Muslims. Some scholars theorize that St. Basil's "onion dome" architecture was inspired by Kazan's central mosque, which was destroyed by Ivan's armies. However,

472 CHAPTER 16

The Cathedral of Vasily the Blessed, known as St. Basil's Cathedral, is located in Red Square in Moscow. Completed in 1560, the cathedral was ordered by Ivan IV to be built in 1552. In 1860, during restoration, the cathedral was painted with the bright, striking patterns of color for which it is known. Today, the cathedral is a museum and a UNESCO World Heritage Site.

CRITICAL VIEWING The Winter Palace in St. Petersburg, Russia, once the official residence of the Romanov family, is now part of a complex of buildings that house the Hermitage Museum. How does the architectural style of the palace compare to that of St. Basil's?

dome roofs were characteristic of Byzantine architecture as well, and St. Basil's Cathedral was built with red brick, probably inspired by Italian Renaissance architecture. Russian culture thus absorbed diverse influences, both from Europe to the west and Asia to the east.

REFORM AND REPRESSION UNDER CATHERINE THE GREAT

Catherine the Great was a German princess who married into the Romanov family. Her husband, Peter the Great's grandson, was overthrown in 1762, within a year of taking the throne. However, within hours of the coup, Catherine had herself declared empress. In a short time, she accumulated enough personal power to become one of the dominant figures of 18th-century Eurasian politics.

Catherine continued Russian expansion, adding approximately 200,000 square miles to the country. As Catherine consolidated control over vast new territories, she developed policies that benefited Russia while seeming to be tolerant of the cultures of conquered regions. Rather than encouraging Siberians to convert to the Russian Orthodox Church, she prevented the church from converting them. This policy benefited her regime because converts to Orthodoxy had tax protections, so too many converts meant diminished tax revenues. In Crimea, Catherine protected the rights of Muslims. She understood that the best way to maintain stability was to work with local Muslim leaders.

From the beginning of her rule, Catherine sought to reform Russia. She had studied the ideas of European philosophers, such as Voltaire, and hoped to reorganize the government using liberal ideas. She labored over issues such as the legal code, town planning, and agriculture. She also pushed for the education of both boys and girls, and she supported science and the arts. Although ending serfdom had been part of her plan for reform, Catherine needed the loyalty and service of the landowning nobles to carry out her reforms. In the end, she increased the nobility's power over the serfs, and even expanded serfdom into areas where peasants had previously been free.

Catherine shared Peter the Great's intention to make Russia a European state, and she adopted laws and attitudes that reflected that position. European demand for Russian grain increased, providing a profitable market for Russian landowners. To produce more grain, the Russian nobility made increasingly harsh demands on the serfs. These aristocrats, who lived in elegant townhouses and country estates, saw European luxuries as essential to their lifestyles, and they treated the serfs like slaves.

As the serfs' situation deteriorated, unrest led to rebellion. By the 1770s, rebels who promised an end to serfdom, taxation, and **conscription**—forced enrollment in the military—had gained a following. They looted estates and murdered nobles, but as they neared Moscow, their leader was captured and the rebellion was defeated. After she had crushed the rebels, Catherine tightened her grip on the populace, suppressing those who sought better treatment for the serfs, even though she had originally professed those same ideas.

This bronze statue of Peter the Great stands in Senate Square in St. Petersburg, surrounded by the buildings of the civil and religious governing bodies of pre-revolutionary Russia.

HISTORICAL THINKING

1. **READING CHECK** What did the Romanov tsars Peter the Great and Catherine the Great do to make Russia more European?

2. **ANALYZE LANGUAGE USE** What does the phrase "window on the West" mean with regard to the construction of St. Petersburg?

3. **COMPARE AND CONTRAST** How did Catherine the Great's policies toward newly conquered peoples contrast with her policies toward the serfs?

4. **MAKE PREDICTIONS** What problems do you think the situation with the serfs will create for Russia's future?

3.3

MAIN IDEA The Jewish, Tatar, and Armenian people spread throughout Eurasia where they faced prejudice and abuse and where they were, at times, welcomed.

Jewish, Tatar, and Armenian Diasporas

What would it take to convince you to move to a place with a completely different language and culture? Members of the Jewish, Armenian, and Tatar communities left their homes for a variety of reasons, often not by their own choice.

MEMBERS OF THE JEWISH COMMUNITY PETITION THE TSARINA

One of Catherine the Great's innovations was to invite **petitions**, or formal written requests, from her subjects. People who felt local and provincial officials were misusing their power believed the tsarina would surely correct the injustices if only she knew about them. Catherine encouraged this attitude and invited her subjects (serfs were not included) to submit petitions. One of these was submitted by a group of Jewish leaders in Belarus. You may recall that the Babylonian Exile, which lasted from 586 to 538 B.C.E., marked the beginning of the Jewish Diaspora, in which the Jewish people migrated to different locations around the world. The Jews in Belarus were known as *Ashkenazim* (ahsh-kuh-NAH-zuhm). They spoke Yiddish, a German-derived language mixed with Hebrew and, in the east, with words from Slavic languages. Members of the Ashkenazim were broadly scattered. Many lived in peasant villages within the Russian Empire, while those living farther west were more likely to live in cities and engage in commerce. Many Ashkenazim lived apart from other religious groups, partly by their own preference and partly because of exclusion by Christians. They followed their own traditions and married within their own group. The European Jews remained culturally distinctive in their music, cuisine, folktales, and Yiddish language.

They both contributed to and borrowed from the majority communities. However, the Ashkenazim were vulnerable and insecure. In their petition to Catherine the Great, the Ashkenazim explained that after they joined the Russian Empire, they had been allowed to continue to invest in and run certain wholesale and retail businesses. However, a decree by the governor-general of Belarus forbade them from continuing these businesses. The petition explained that many Jews were left completely impoverished.

So many petitions flowed into St. Petersburg that it is unlikely that Catherine had time to read them, and the difficulties the Ashkenazim experienced were not resolved. Loss of business was just one result of the deep prejudices Jews faced. All across Europe, Jewish communities faced terrifying intimidation and abuse. They often suffered theft of property and sometimes even violent attacks from their Christian neighbors. You previously learned how Jews were attacked during the Crusades and how the Jews of Spain were expelled by Christian rulers in 1492.

THE TATARS

The nobility of a group of Muslim, Turkish-speaking people called the Tatars also petitioned Catherine the Great. In the 16th century, the Tatar home, the Kazan region, had been conquered by Ivan the Terrible. Ivan had slaughtered much of the Muslim population and forced many survivors to convert to Orthodox Christianity.

Catherine allowed the Tatars to build new mosques, and she accepted petitions from Tatar nobles. The petition of 1767 described insults Tatars had suffered based on their faith and rank, and they also requested that their region remain Muslim. Catherine initially allowed the Tatars some freedoms and control of their lands, but this didn't continue and Tatar peasants were forced into serfdom.

THE ARMENIAN DIASPORA

The Armenians, who originated in western Asia, are followers of an ancient Orthodox Christian faith. Like the Jews, their diaspora covered a wide area of Eurasia that included Russian and Ottoman lands. Many Armenians

476 CHAPTER 16

This portrait of Catherine the Great, was painted by Fedor Stepanovich Rokotov, c. 1770.

also lived in India and Iran. They had distinct Armenian neighborhoods in Constantinople, Jerusalem, Agra, Isfahan, and other cities.

Push and pull factors influenced Armenians to immigrate to places outside their homeland. **Pull factors** entice people to immigrate to new lands. In the late 1500s, the emperor Akbar I invited Armenian merchants to live in Mughal India. He understood that Armenians were skilled at handicrafts and commerce, so he created incentives to attract Armenians to India. He exempted them from paying taxes on the products they imported or exported. He also allowed them to move around India and conduct businesses in areas where other foreigners were not allowed.

Perhaps the biggest **push factor** that caused people to leave Armenia was its location. The Armenian homeland was bordered by the feuding Ottoman and Safavid empires. Partly to secure his border with the Ottomans, the Safavid shah Abbas I forced as many as 150,000 Armenians to move to a separate quarter of Isfahan. By moving Armenian merchants into Isfahan, Shah Abbas was able to advance Iran's silk trade. Although Armenians were forced to live away from their homeland, they were allowed to build churches and look after their own community affairs.

During the Romanov dynasty, many Armenians moved from Isfahan to Russia to take advantage of Russia's growing economy. Armenians were at the center of a commercial network stretching across the Indian Ocean. They had business interests all the way from the Mediterranean to the South China Sea.

HISTORICAL THINKING

1. **READING CHECK** Describe some of the abuses faced by the Jewish, Tatar, and Armenian people.

2. **COMPARE AND CONTRAST** How did the European Jews, Tatars, and Armenians differ from their neighbors?

3. **IDENTIFY** What are some of the push and pull factors that influenced Armenian migration?

Land-Based Empires of Eurasia 477

CHAPTER 16 LAND-BASED EMPIRES OF EURASIA REVIEW

VOCABULARY

Match each of the following vocabulary words with its definition.

1. janissary
2. shah
3. mausoleum
4. entrepreneur
5. tundra
6. taiga
7. tsar
8. petition
9. push factor
10. pull factor

a. a king in Iran
b. a highly trained soldier and slave in the Ottoman army
c. an incentive that attracts people to a new country
d. land covered with evergreen trees in the far north
e. a formal written request
f. a condition that causes people to leave their country
g. a person who organizes and operates a business
h. a large tomb
i. treeless arctic plains
j. the ruler of imperial Russia

READING STRATEGY
DRAW CONCLUSIONS

When you draw conclusions, you make a judgment based on what you have read. Use a chart like this one to draw a conclusion about the qualities of effective leaders of land-based empires in Eurasia in the 17th and 18th centuries.

Leader	Details
Conclusion	

11. Which of these leaders strengthened their empires through tolerance of religious and cultural groups other than their own?

MAIN IDEAS

Answer the following questions. Support your answers with evidence from the chapter.

12. How did Çelebi fulfill the wishes of the Prophet Muhammad from his dream? **LESSON 1.1**

13. How did Süleyman I treat communities of different religions once they became part of the Ottoman Empire? **LESSON 1.2**

14. In what ways was the Safavid society prosperous? **LESSON 1.3**

15. In what ways did the Ottoman Empire persist into the 17th and 18th centuries? **LESSON 1.4**

16. How were the Mughals different from most of their subjects in India? **LESSON 2.1**

17. How did the Qing prevent the Russians from expanding into China? **LESSON 2.3**

18. What was French philosopher Voltaire's opinion of Qianlong? Why did he hold this opinion? **LESSON 2.4**

19. How did the lives of women and samurai change during the Tokugawa shogunate? How did the Tokugawa respond to these changes? **LESSON 2.5**

20. How did Ivan IV centralize control of Russia? **LESSON 3.1**

21. Describe the condition of the serfs under Peter the Great and Catherine the Great. **LESSON 3.2**

HISTORICAL THINKING

Answer the following questions. Support your answers with evidence from the chapter.

22. **COMPARE AND CONTRAST** How did the Ottomans and the Safavids differ? How were they similar?

23. **ANALYZE CAUSE AND EFFECT** What pull factor did Akbar I use in India to entice immigrants to move into underdeveloped lands?

24. **SYNTHESIZE** What common difficulties did the Mughals in India and the Qing in China have in ruling their countries? How effective were they in dealing with these difficulties?

25. **DESCRIBE** In the Ottoman Empire, Christian children were enslaved to become janissaries. In Russia, the serfs were treated as slaves. Describe how the slaves were treated under each society.

INTERPRET VISUALS

Study the map of the Mughal Empire. Then answer the questions below.

26. What river formed a natural barrier to the north at the extent of the Mughal Empire in 1530?

27. What major bodies of water had the Mughal Empire expanded to by 1605?

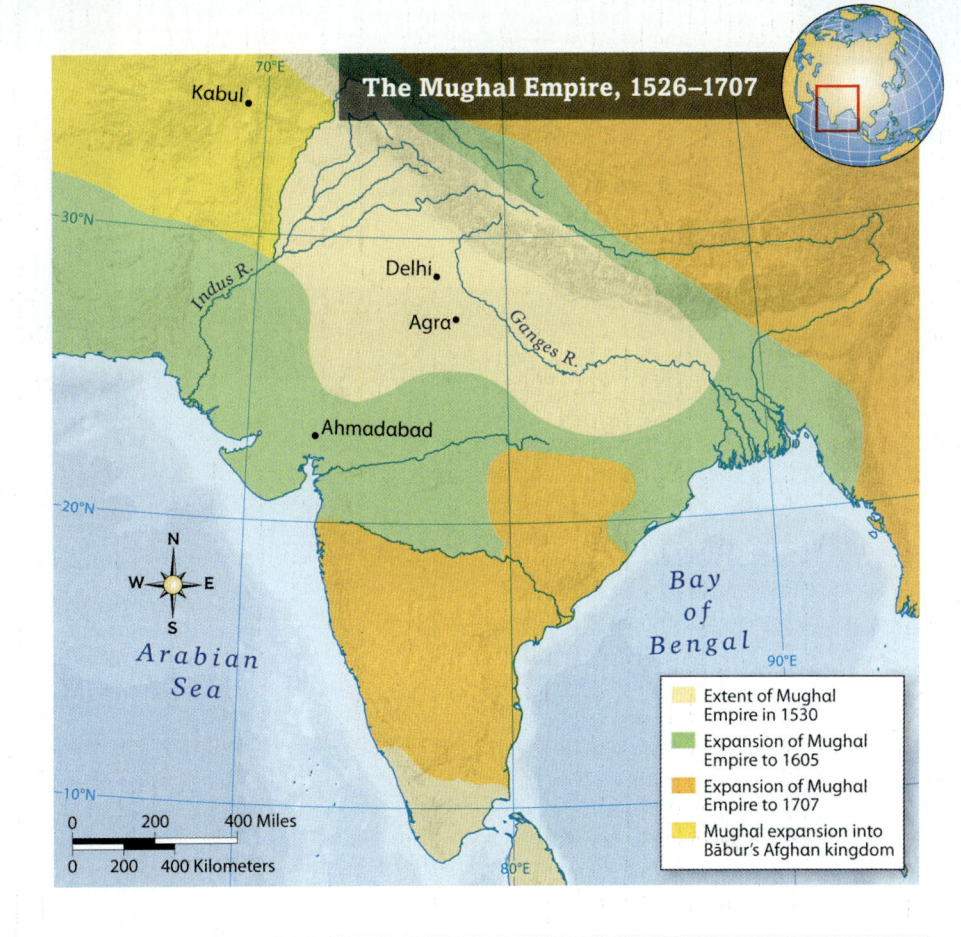

ANALYZE SOURCES

Matsuo Basho (1644–1694) was probably the most famous of all haiku poets. In this form of poetry, each haiku has 17 syllables in three unrhymed lines of 5, 7, and 5 syllables. In this poem, Basho describes common images from life in 17th-century Japan. Read the poem and answer the question that follows.

> An ancient pond,
>
> the frog leaps:
>
> the silver plop and gurgle of water.
>
> —Matsuo Basho, translated by Michael R. Burch

28. What universal, timeless theme is expressed in this haiku?

CONNECT TO YOUR LIFE

29. **INFORMATIVE** You've read about the ways that Ottoman, Safavid, Mughal, and Russian monarchs expressed their power and values through architecture. Research an impressive new building that has been completed in the last 10 years in the United States. Find out who paid for the building and how the building is meant to be used. What values and traditions does the style of the building express? Prepare an informative presentation with text and photos.

TIPS

- Reread the sections on architecture from this chapter.

- Research recent buildings in the United States. Choose a building you can visit, if possible, or choose one you find especially interesting.

- Identify the people or organizations that paid for the building. Find out about the architect and why he or she was chosen to design this building.

- Think about the goals for the building, both practical and symbolic. Do you think the building fulfills those goals? Why or why not?

- Conclude your presentation with a statement that sums up the values and traditions represented by this building.

Land-Based Empires of Eurasia 479

CHAPTER 17

Age of Maritime Expansion
1300–1750

HISTORICAL THINKING How did European exploration transform the world socially, politically, and economically?

SECTION 1 **European Exploration**
SECTION 2 **Indian Ocean Connections**
SECTION 3 **Colonial Societies in the Americas**

CRITICAL VIEWING
The ships shown here were built to replicate those that sailed during Europe's Age of Exploration beginning in the late 15th century. What qualities might the explorers who sailed on ships like these have possessed?

Age of Maritime Expansion 481

1.1 MAIN IDEA European navigators set off on voyages of exploration to discover a sea route to Asia.

Voyages of Discovery

"Here are dragons." "Land unknown." These warnings sometimes labeled unexplored parts of the world on early European maps and globes. A voyage to these places could be filled with danger. But by the mid-1400s, some navigators were ready to take their chances.

GOLD, GOD, AND GLORY

Around 1450, western Europe was ready to expand. The Renaissance had inspired curiosity about the world, and merchants were eager to find new trading opportunities and markets. But, as you know, the Ottoman Empire controlled the trade routes to Asia where many of the luxury items Europeans desired, including silk and spices, came from. To secure a share of this profitable trade, Europe's leaders and merchants sponsored numerous sailing expeditions to search for an alternative sea route to Asia.

Remember Zheng He, the Chinese admiral who led maritime expeditions to ports in Asia and Africa during the Ming dynasty? His fleets of treasure ships traveled along well-known trade routes across the Indian Ocean. However, between about 1450 and 1750, a period sometimes called the Age of Exploration, European navigators explored largely uncharted waters in the Atlantic. Their explorations were motivated by factors that historians often refer to as "gold, God, and glory." "Gold" represents the profits merchants hoped to gain through the trade of spices, slaves, and precious metals. "God" indicates the European desire to spread Christianity and seize Muslim lands. "Glory" denotes the drive to create an empire and gain political power.

Portugal took the lead in European exploration. In 1419, **Prince Henry the Navigator**, the son of Portugal's king, established a navigation school on the Atlantic coast in Sagres, Portugal. There, sailors learned to navigate a course by the stars and by using technological tools such as the magnetic compass and the astrolabe and quadrant, devices for measuring latitude that had been borrowed from Arab prototypes. They also learned shipbuilding and, in particular, how to build a **caravel**. The caravel was a light ship with triangular sails and was also borrowed from Arab mariners. Caravels were quick, easy to maneuver, and could sail into the wind, which earlier European ships could not do.

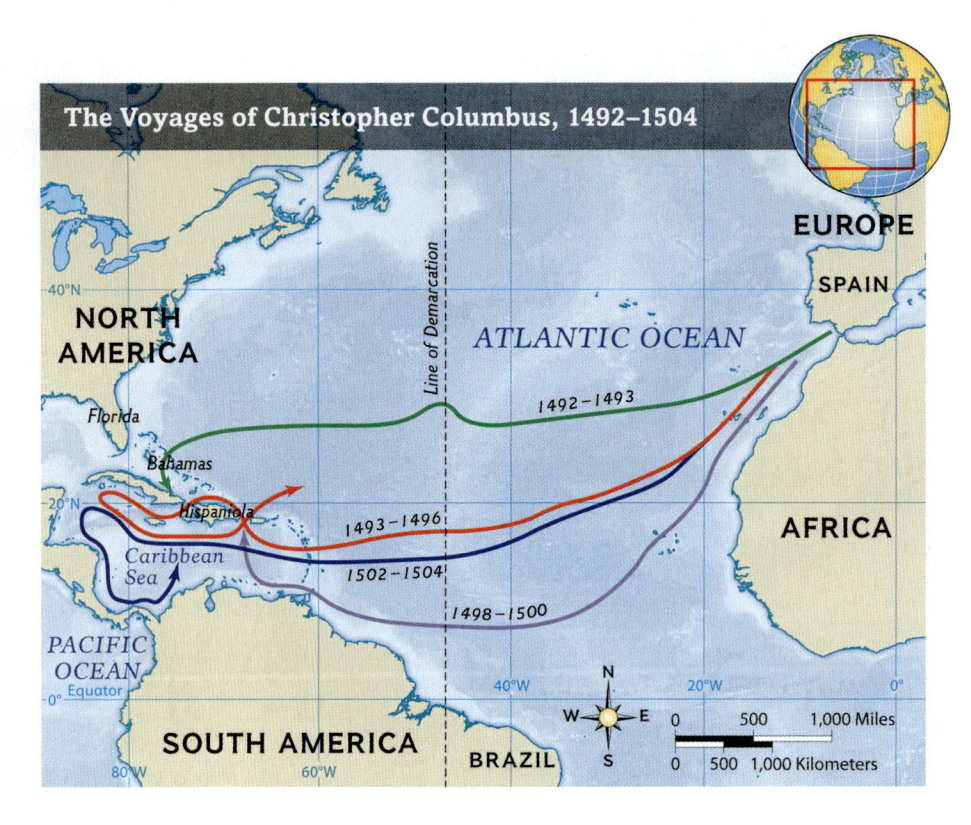

CHRISTOPHER COLUMBUS

Italian navigator **Christopher Columbus** used caravels during his historic voyage to the Americas. He thought he could find a faster sea route to Asia by sailing west across the Atlantic Ocean. So, in the 1480s, Columbus

OCTOBER 12, 1492

When land was sighted on October 12, Columbus must have been relieved. The voyage had taken longer than expected, and his crew was threatening mutiny. Convinced he had reached Asia, Columbus called the local Carib and Taino people he encountered there "Indians." But Columbus had greatly underestimated Earth's circumference and, as a result, the distance from Europe to Asia. So he unexpectedly found an area unknown to Europeans: the Americas.

CRITICAL VIEWING American artist John Vanderlyn's 1846 painting, *Landing of Columbus*, depicts a romanticized view of the explorer upon his arrival in the West Indies. Members of Columbus's crew express varying emotions and reactions, while local inhabitants watch them warily from behind a tree. How do the figures in the painting convey the motivating factors of gold, God, and glory?

petitioned both the Spanish and the Portuguese monarchs to fund his voyage, but they rejected his proposal. Finally, in 1492, King Ferdinand and Queen Isabella of Spain agreed. You may remember that these monarchs expelled thousands of Jews and Muslims from Spain and Portugal that same year. Spain also conquered the kingdom of Granada in 1492, which helped Ferdinand and Isabella finance Columbus's expeditions.

Columbus departed Spain on August 3, 1492, with three ships, the *Niña*, the *Pinta*, and the *Santa Maria*. In October, he and his fleet arrived in the Bahamas, off the coast of Florida. From there, Columbus sailed to the islands of the Caribbean—believing the entire time he was exploring islands south of China—and claimed them for Spain. Meanwhile, Ferdinand and Isabella petitioned the pope to allow them to colonize the lands Columbus seized for Spain. Spain's economy was based on **mercantilism**, a system in which government protects and regulates trade to create wealth at the expense of rival powers. Under this system, the Spanish would maintain the sole right to trade with their colonies.

But Portugal competed with Spain over who would control the lands. In 1494, the two countries agreed to the **Treaty of Tordesillas** (tawr-day-SEE-yahs), which established a boundary, called the **Line of Demarcation**, that passed vertically through the Atlantic Ocean and Brazil. Portugal gained possession of the easterly lands, including Brazil, while Spain would receive any newly encountered lands to the west.

Columbus made three more voyages to the Caribbean islands. Although he didn't find a route to Asia or the riches he dreamed of, he did open up a "new world" to European exploration and colonization. Spain would be the first to capitalize on the opportunities it provided.

HISTORICAL THINKING

1. **READING CHECK** What did sailors learn in Prince Henry's school in Portugal?

2. **ANALYZE CAUSE AND EFFECT** What led Europeans to explore the Atlantic between 1450 and 1750?

3. **INTERPRET MAPS** Why do you think Columbus assumed he had sailed to Asia?

1.2 **MAIN IDEA** In the 1500s, Spain invaded the Americas and conquered the Aztec and Inca empires.

Conquests in the Americas

An uneven fight isn't necessarily determined by numbers. Relatively small Spanish forces—but armed with the latest military technology (and, unknowingly, deadly diseases)—were able to bring the two most powerful empires in the Americas to their knees.

CORTÉS AND THE AZTEC

As Europeans continued their exploration of the Western Hemisphere, they realized that Columbus had not reached Asia but rather lands they would call *America*. After the Treaty of Tordesillas divided these lands, Spanish navigators were quick to explore their new territory. In 1513, **Vasco Núñez Balboa** crossed through Panama with his crew, and they became the first Europeans to see the Pacific Ocean. Balboa claimed everything he saw for Spain. About six years later, **Ferdinand Magellan** led an expedition that would be the first to circumnavigate, or travel all around, the world.

By 1543, Spain had conquered lands that extended south to Chile, north to Florida, and west to California. The Spanish soldiers and adventurers who led the conquest of the Americas came to be called conquistadors (kahn-KEE-stuh-dawrz). One of the most successful of the conquistadors was **Hernán Cortés**, who launched an invasion of Mexico in 1519 with about 500 men.

After landing on the coast of Mexico, Cortés learned of the gold-rich Aztec Empire and marched inland to conquer it. On the way to the Aztec capital of

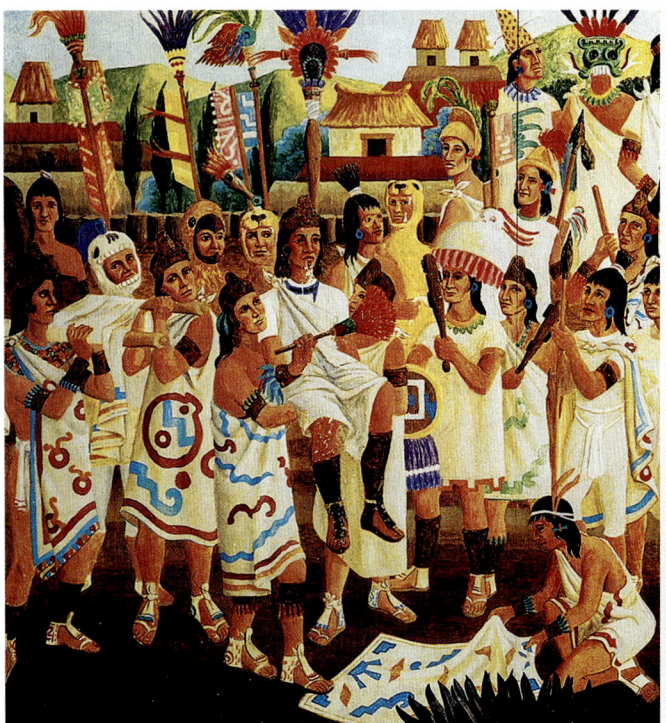

CRITICAL VIEWING This mural (painted at a later date) depicts the 1519 meeting of Spanish leader Hernán Cortés and Aztec ruler Moctezuma in Tenochtitlán. Cortés, riding a white horse, appears on the right, while Moctezuma, on the left, is carried by his servants. How does the portrayal of the Spanish soldiers compare with that of the Aztec?

484 CHAPTER 17

> In 1547, Spanish historian Bernardino de Sahagún interviewed people who had witnessed the invasion of Mexico by Cortés and his army. In the following excerpt from one of those interviews, an eyewitness describes Moctezuma's amazement and terror when he saw the conquistadors' weapons.
>
> **PRIMARY SOURCE**
>
> It especially made him faint when he heard how the guns went off at the Spaniards' command, sounding like thunder. . . . And when it went off, something like a ball came out from inside, and fire went showering and spitting out. . . . And if they shot at a hill, it seemed to crumble and come apart. . . . Their war gear was all iron. They clothed their bodies in iron, they put iron on their heads, their swords were iron. . . . And their deer [horses] that carried them were as tall as the roof.
>
> —from *General History of the Things of New Spain*, by Bernardino de Sahagún, 1569

Tenochtitlán, he recruited allies from some local societies who were unhappy with Aztec rule, as well as the Aztec practice of human sacrifice. A key role in the campaign was played by a young Nahua-speaking woman known as La Malinche, who learned Spanish after joining Cortés's troops and served as his translator.

The Aztec ruler Moctezuma received the Spanish courteously while Aztec officials debated what to do. They were intimidated by the Spanish who, though few in number, were armed with steel weapons, cannons, and horses—all unknown to the Aztec. Also, the bearded and light-skinned Cortés seemed to resemble their feather-serpent god Quetzalcoatl, who, according to legend, had left long ago but promised to return. Cortés used Moctezuma's hesitation against him. He seized the king and forced the Aztec to fight.

Cortés demanded and received gold and other treasure but could not hold onto Tenochtitlán. After a series of bloody battles, Cortés finally laid siege to the magnificent capital city in 1521. The Aztec fought fiercely, but they were weakened by smallpox, a deadly disease brought to the Americas by the Spanish. In the end, Cortés and his army destroyed Tenochtitlán. Spain would eventually build Mexico City on its ruins.

PIZARRO AND THE INCA

Smallpox also played a role in the Spanish conquest of the Inca. In the 1520s, the conquistador **Francisco Pizarro** set off for South America and the gold and silver of the Inca Empire. Like Cortés, Pizarro and his army of about 200 men had the advantage of superior weapons and horses. And the Inca had been weakened by a deadly smallpox epidemic before Pizarro arrived. In addition, a bitter civil war had divided the ruling dynasty. In 1532, the newly appointed Inca emperor, **Atahualpa** (ah-tuh-WAHL-puh), invited Pizarro and his soldiers to a meeting in the northern part of present-day Peru.

Atahualpa, accompanied by about 5,000 of his warriors, received the Spaniards peacefully. He and Pizarro exchanged gifts, and the Inca ruler probably felt safe. But then Pizarro's men opened fire on the mostly unarmed Inca and took Atahualpa prisoner. The Inca ruler offered his captors one room filled with gold and two filled with silver in exchange for his release. Pizarro took the treasure and then executed Atahualpa. The highly centralized Inca Empire began to disintegrate.

The Inca in other parts of the empire continued to resist the Spanish until 1572, when the last Inca ruler was executed. Through military conquest, Spain built one of the richest and most powerful empires in the world in the 1500s.

This silver figurine probably represents a llama, which provided the Inca with food, wool, and transportation. Historians believe figurines like this one were used in sacred rituals and may have been buried along with sacrifices.

HISTORICAL THINKING

1. **READING CHECK** Who were the conquistadors?

2. **COMPARE AND CONTRAST** How was Cortés's conquest of the Aztec similar to Pizarro's conquest of the Inca?

3. **ANALYZE SOURCES** What weapons and equipment does the eyewitness describe in the excerpt?

Age of Maritime Expansion 485

1.3 NATIONAL GEOGRAPHIC EXPLORER PARDIS SABETI

Math Against Malaria

"Science is infectious." —Pardis Sabeti

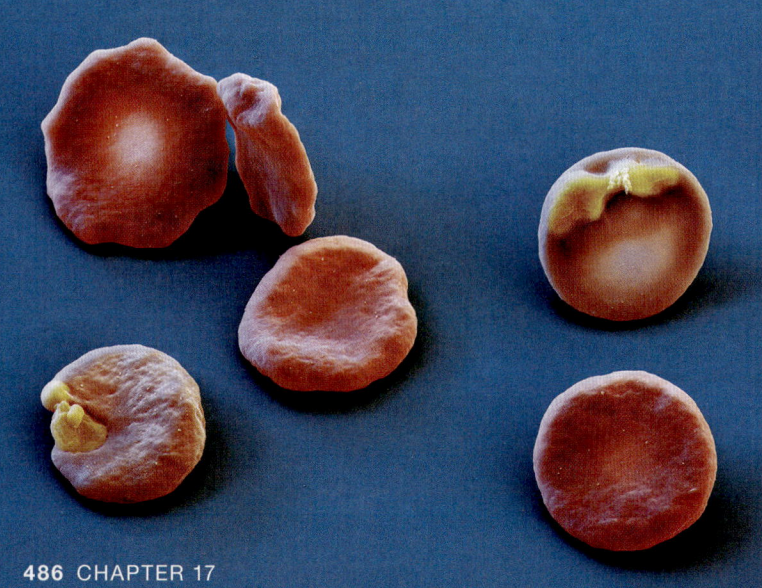

Pardis Sabeti (above) is a musician, teacher, volleyball player, and research scientist who specializes in the study of infectious diseases. She divides much of her time between working at Harvard University and collecting virus samples in West Africa. Shown here in the genome center at the Broad Institute of MIT and Harvard, Sabeti collaborates with colleagues all over the world to prevent major outbreaks of deadly diseases.

Four of these red blood cells (left) are healthy, but the other two, tinged with yellow, have been infected with malaria. The infection began when a malaria-carrying mosquito bit its victim and the malaria parasite entered the bloodstream. Sabeti believes the microbes that cause malaria and other infectious diseases are continually evolving in a struggle to survive human defenses.

It wasn't that long ago that the concept of an epidemic killing a million people seemed like ancient history. However, the 2019 coronavirus outbreak changed everything. Just the mention of a novel, or new, virus can send shivers down the spines of health officials throughout the world. But the difference between today and the past is that modern science can limit and sometimes even prevent the spread of diseases. National Geographic Explorer Pardis Sabeti uses mathematics in her battle against diseases, including malaria.

> **MAIN IDEA** Scientist Pardis Sabeti uses her math skills to understand epidemics.

UNDERSTANDING DISEASE

As you have read, the conquistadors' cannons helped them destroy the powerful Aztec and Inca empires. But the conquistadors had a secret weapon, unknown even to them: smallpox. The ability of European invaders to conquer the Americas had as much to do with deadly diseases as it did with superior weapons. That's because many Europeans had developed an immunity, or a natural resistance, to diseases like smallpox. The indigenous peoples, however, had no such immunity. Smallpox swept through entire regions, decimating a large percentage of the population.

Malaria also played a role in the settlement of the Americas. Brought with the slave trade from Africa, it proved deadly to indigenous peoples and Europeans in the Caribbean. But many Africans had been exposed to the disease in childhood and developed some immunity. As a result, even today, the population of the Caribbean is largely of African descent.

One key to preventing an epidemic is knowing what causes the disease. By 1900, for example, scientists knew that malaria was caused by mosquito bites. Another key is taking steps to eliminate the cause—in the case of malaria, by eliminating standing water where mosquitoes can breed. A third key is vaccination. Today, vaccines provide immunity to a host of diseases such as smallpox and polio. No vaccine, however, has yet proven effective against malaria, which kills more than one million people every year.

Enter Pardis Sabeti. When Sabeti was two years old, she and her family fled from Iran just before the country's 1979 revolution and settled in Florida. While at school, Sabeti fell in love with math. In medical school, she also developed a love of research and data analysis. She would combine these interests to fight malaria and other infectious diseases.

ANALYZING DATA

Sabeti is one of a new breed of scientist, called a computational geneticist, who uses computers to analyze the genetic data of people and diseases. When Sabeti was in graduate school, she developed a groundbreaking algorithm, or a procedure for solving a problem or analyzing data using a computer. She uses her algorithm to analyze a specific gene, the part of a cell that controls growth, appearance, and traits. The information helps her discover how infectious diseases change over time and spread. Sabeti's algorithms can also reveal how people adapt to or resist a disease through changes in their biology. This knowledge can aid scientists in developing strategies for dealing with disease.

While analyzing data gleaned from people who had been exposed to malaria, Sabeti made an important discovery. She explains, "I realized I'd found a trait that had to be the result of natural selection—a trait that likely helped the population I was looking at cope with malaria better than others. It was an amazing feeling because at that moment I knew something about how people evolved that nobody else knew."

Sabeti has done fieldwork in Sierra Leone and other African countries affected by malaria, Lassa fever, and the Ebola virus. Much of the time, however, she can be found in her research lab. There, Sabeti and her colleagues put their math skills to work analyzing data. Their goal is to find better treatments for diseases such as malaria—and eventually, perhaps, a cure.

HISTORICAL THINKING

1. **READING CHECK** Why were the native populations of the Americas vulnerable to diseases like smallpox?

2. **MAKE INFERENCES** Why was Sabeti excited to discover a trait that helped some people cope with and resist malaria?

3. **DRAW CONCLUSIONS** How does fieldwork help Sabeti further understand the infectious diseases she analyzes?

1.4 The Columbian Exchange

MAIN IDEA After Columbus arrived in the Americas, a global exchange of plants, animals, people, and diseases crossed the Atlantic Ocean.

Do you like apples, citrus fruit, or grapes? These foods came to our shores through a worldwide movement of goods across the Atlantic that began more than 500 years ago. You might think about that the next time you bite into an apple.

A GLOBAL FOOD EXCHANGE

Columbus's first voyage in 1492 brought the so-called "Old World," the Eastern Hemisphere of Europe, Asia, and Africa, into contact with the "New World," the Western Hemisphere of the Americas. (Of course, the land was only new to the Europeans; diverse indigenous societies had been settled across those lands for thousands of years.) The encounter coincided with improved methods of sea travel and the European desire to explore, settle, and exchange with new lands. The creation of regular interchange between the Eastern and Western hemispheres, and the integration of previously isolated peoples into global networks, is known as the **Columbian Exchange**, named after Columbus. The exchange resulted in a transfer of foods, crops, animals, technology, and medicines between the two hemispheres.

The Europeans who traveled to the Americas intentionally brought food and crops well known to them, such as wheat, barley, grapes, and apples, and livestock including cattle, pigs, chickens, sheep, and horses. All of these plants and animals flourished in the Americas. Wheat became one of the most important crops in North America. And horses brought by the Spanish changed the lives of Native Americans by making buffalo hunting much easier and safer.

Europeans also brought crops from Africa and Asia to the Americas. Sugarcane thrived in the Caribbean islands and Brazil. Later in this book, you will learn more about the enslaved people brought from Africa who did the harsh work in the cane fields to create huge profits for European plantation owners. By the end of the 1600s, rice had become a staple crop in the Carolinas. Enslaved Africans would also be forced to work the rice fields.

Foods from the Americas traveled to Europe, Africa, and Asia as well. Ships returned to Europe with beans, corn (also called maize), peppers, tomatoes, potatoes, turkeys, and much more. Many of these foods became

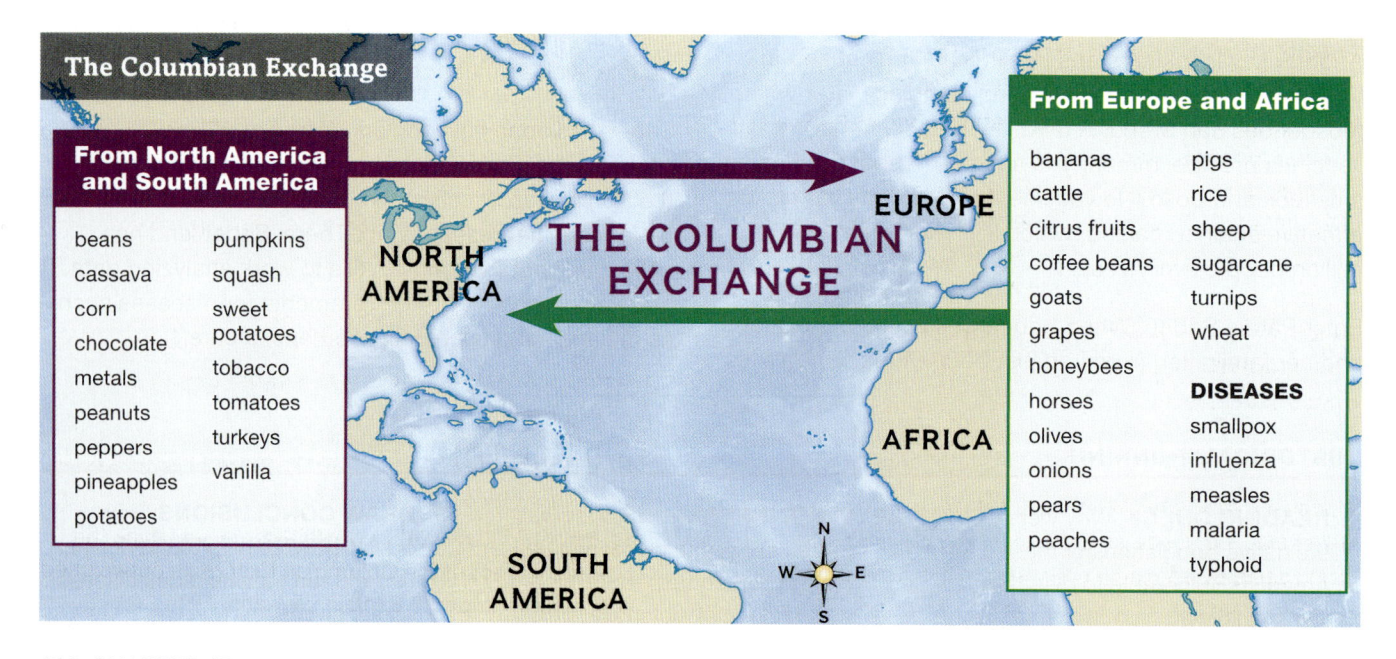

The Columbian Exchange

From North America and South America

beans	pumpkins
cassava	squash
corn	sweet potatoes
chocolate	tobacco
metals	tomatoes
peanuts	turkeys
peppers	vanilla
pineapples	
potatoes	

From Europe and Africa

bananas	pigs
cattle	rice
citrus fruits	sheep
coffee beans	sugarcane
goats	turnips
grapes	wheat
honeybees	
horses	**DISEASES**
olives	smallpox
onions	influenza
pears	measles
peaches	malaria
	typhoid

CRITICAL VIEWING The Monument to the Discoveries in Lisbon, Portugal, celebrates the country's leading role in European exploration. Prince Henry the Navigator stands at the top of the monument followed by Portuguese explorers, mapmakers, and artists. How does the monument's design convey the impression that the statue is on the point of setting out to sea?

staples of European diets. West Africans came to rely on American food crops, such as corn, peanuts, squash, and sweet potatoes. And Asian farmers cultivated corn, tomatoes, peppers, peanuts, and sweet potatoes.

Two of the crops from the Americas—corn and potatoes—played an especially important role in Europe, Asia, and Africa. Both produced higher yields than wheat and grew in fields that were hard to cultivate. By the 1700s, corn and potatoes had reached as far as India and China, and populations in both places increased significantly. Today about 30 percent of the foods eaten worldwide originated in the Americas. This early food trade led to our global cuisine. Who could imagine Italian food without tomato sauce, New Zealand without lamb, or Thai food without chili peppers? Kitchens around the world reflect the Columbian Exchange.

NEGATIVE IMPACTS OF THE EXCHANGE

Not everything that traveled in the exchange was beneficial, however. In addition to goods, Europeans introduced deadly new diseases to the Americas for which the Native Americans had no immunity. You have read that the conquistadors spread smallpox when they arrived. Colonizers also brought other diseases, including typhoid, measles, and influenza. As a result, the indigenous population of Central America fell from about 25 million to 2.5 million between 1519 and 1565. And historians estimate that, within about 150 years of Columbus's voyages, epidemics of infectious diseases had killed up to 90 percent of the native population, a pattern that would later be repeated in Australia and Polynesia. With these deaths, the world also lost valuable indigenous knowledge in areas such as agriculture and medicine. For good and bad, the Columbian Exchange transformed the world.

HISTORICAL THINKING

1. **READING CHECK** What led to the Columbian Exchange?
2. **DRAW CONCLUSIONS** In what way did the Columbian Exchange encourage slavery?
3. **FORM AND SUPPORT OPINIONS** Do you think the positive impact of the Columbian Exchange outweighed the negative impact? Explain your answer.

Age of Maritime Expansion

2.1

MAIN IDEA Portugal built a powerful trading empire in the Indian Ocean.

Portugal's Trade Empire

Europeans knew that whoever found a direct sea route to Asia would become fabulously wealthy. The competition was intense, but Portugal would win out and become "Lord of the Seas"—for a time, anyway.

FINDING A ROUTE TO INDIA

The Portuguese had a special incentive to explore the Atlantic Ocean since geography separated them from Mediterranean trade. Remember reading about Prince Henry and his navigation school? Henry also began funding caravel expeditions to explore Africa's western coast. By 1460, Portuguese explorers were trading with Africans from new coastal trading posts, sending spices, gold, and slaves to European markets.

Then, in 1487, Portuguese explorer **Bartholomeu Dias** sailed around the Cape of Good Hope on the Atlantic coast of present-day South Africa. By doing so, he proved that a sea route around Africa to India was possible. About 10 years later, another Portuguese navigator, **Vasco da Gama**, began exploring the east African coast and crossed the Indian Ocean to India, where he marveled at the merchant ships filled with spices, silks, and precious gems. Da Gama returned to Portugal with Asian spices and knowledge of sea routes and Indian Ocean ports.

Portuguese mariners had a more accurate sense of geography than Columbus, and their success in connecting Europe directly with Asia had a very different outcome. Columbus's connection across the Atlantic was brand new, and the Spanish quickly overwhelmed indigenous societies in the Americas. In the Indian

CRITICAL VIEWING The Cape of Good Hope was once believed to be the southernmost tip of Africa. It marked the spot at which Dias began sailing east rather than south and would have given him hope that he was on course for India. Based on the photo, what challenges did Dias face as he sailed around the cape?

490 CHAPTER 17

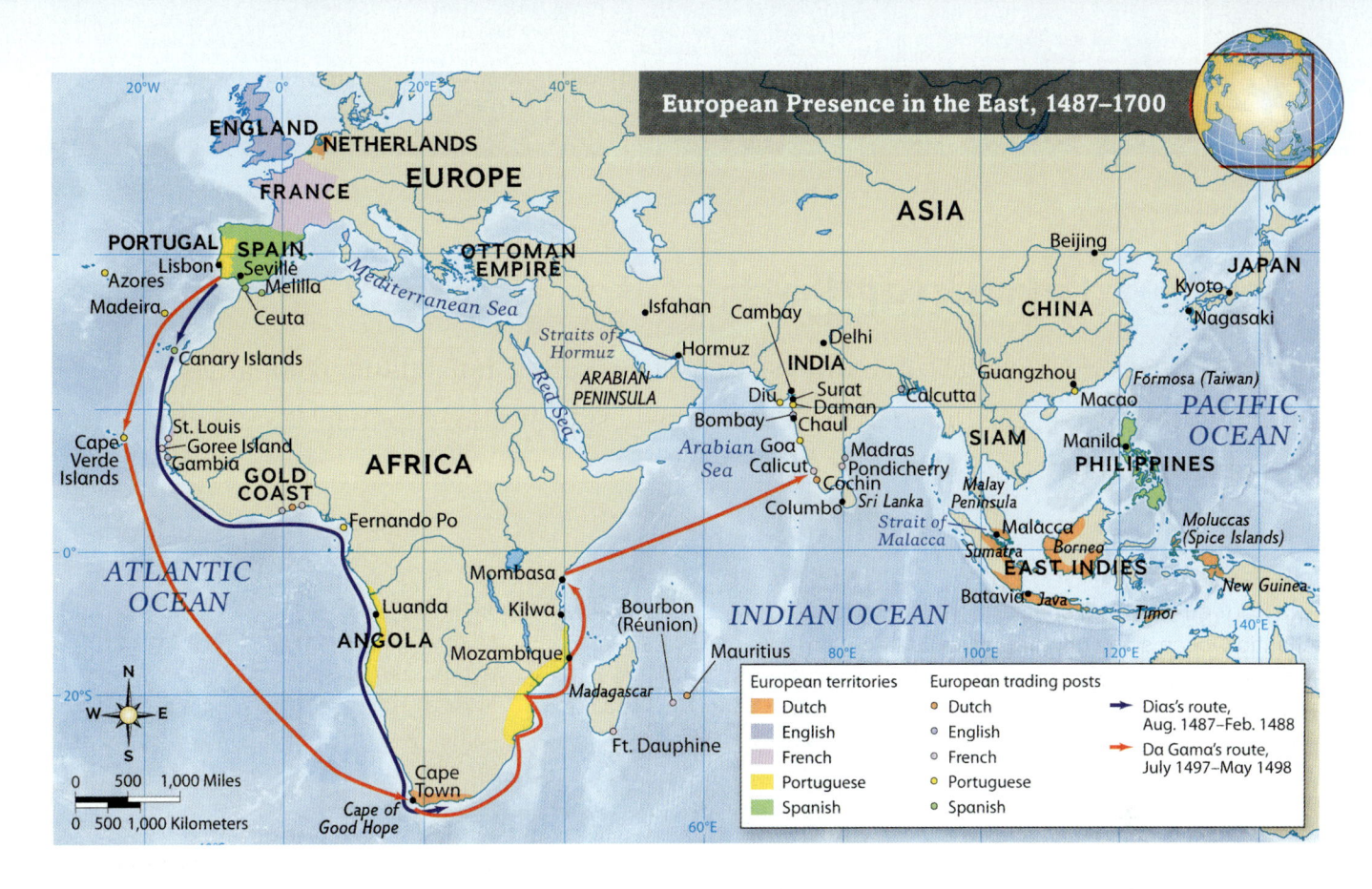

Ocean, however, the Europeans were entering an established trade network surrounded by powerful land-based empires like the Mughal Empire of India.

The problem for the Portuguese was that they did not have anything of value to offer Asian markets. Their only advantage over Asian competition was their powerful cannons. That is how they defeated a fleet of Muslim ships off the coast of India in 1509 and took control of important trade routes.

BUILDING A TRADE EMPIRE

After the battle, the Portuguese extended their power. In 1510, they captured Goa on India's west coast and made it their chief port. From Goa, they took over important "choke points" of trade, places that Asian and African merchants had to pass through to conduct their business. In 1511, the Portuguese attacked and captured Malacca on the west coast of the Malay Peninsula. The city gave Portugal control of the Strait of Malacca and the Moluccas, islands so rich in spices they were called the Spice Islands.

In 1514, Portugal gained control of the Strait of Hormuz, which provided the only sea passage from the Persian Gulf to the Indian Ocean. Seizing the waterway meant Portugal could charge Muslim traders a fee for passage through the straits between Iran and India. In Africa, the Portuguese diverted the gold trade to their own ships, using their cannons to destroy the old city of Kilwa, and joined forces with Ethiopian Christians to secure trade around the Red Sea. In East Asia, the Portuguese established a strongly fortified trading post on Macao on the eastern coast of China in the 1550s. By the 1570s, they had reached all the way to Japan.

Portuguese merchants profited handsomely from the trade. They purchased luxury items in Asia for about one-fifth the cost the Muslim traders had charged. As a result, prices for these items on the European markets were lower, and more people could afford them. Portugal would remain unrivaled until other, equally aggressive European powers would muscle their way into the Indian Ocean trade.

HISTORICAL THINKING

1. **READING CHECK** Why did Portugal want to find a direct sea route to India?

2. **INTERPRET MAPS** By 1700, which European power had taken control of the East Indies from the Portuguese?

3. **ANALYZE CAUSE AND EFFECT** How did Portuguese merchants and European buyers benefit as a result of Portugal's domination of Indian Ocean trade?

2.2

MAIN IDEA The Dutch East India Company gained control of the spice trade in the East Indies.

The Dutch East India Company

In the business world, large companies sometimes "swallow up" smaller companies. In the Indian Ocean, the Dutch made it their business to swallow up their Portuguese competitors.

THE RISE OF THE DUTCH

Portugal tried to keep its sea route to Asia a secret, but it soon attracted the attention of other European countries. Navigators from other countries began to sail to Asia in the early 1600s, and the Netherlands and England became the key challengers to Portugal's pioneering role in developing European trade in the Indian Ocean.

In the mid-1500s, the Netherlands was a collection of provinces governed by the Catholic rulers of Habsburg Spain. In 1568, the provinces began waging a war of independence against the Spanish. Seven of the northern provinces won their independence in 1609 and formed the Dutch Republic. However, fighting continued for many years until Spain finally recognized full Dutch independence in 1648.

Dutch merchants in the 17th century were among the most successful traders in the world. The shipowner and his family in the painting shown here are dressed in the typical Dutch style of the time and are posed before the trading vessels that provided them with great wealth.

The Dutch based their economy on the fishing and shipbuilding industries and soon became a major sea power. Around 1650, they commanded a fleet of about 16,000 ships, the largest in the world. In the 1590s, the first Dutch traders arrived in the Indian Ocean and explored the Spice Islands. They returned to the Netherlands loaded with pepper, cloves, cinnamon, nutmeg, and other spices and made huge profits when they sold the goods.

Soon the Dutch and other Europeans began making the long sea voyage to India. Both England and the Netherlands formed an East India Company to regulate their trade in the region. Established in 1602, the **Dutch East India Company** was richer and more powerful than England's company. It became Europe's largest commercial enterprise of the 17th century. A charter granted by the government gave the Dutch East India Company exclusive control over Dutch trade with Asia. The company also had the right to build forts, form armies, establish colonies, and make treaties.

The Dutch East India Company operated as a **joint-stock company**, which means that it sold shares of stocks to investors who became partners in the venture. In this new form of business enterprise, investors shared losses as well as profits. Innovations in banking and insurance also gave the Dutch a more stable infrastructure for investment. These institutions would later be valuable in the development of **capitalism**, in which businesses are privately owned and exist to make profits. But the Dutch East India Company was not based on free-market principles. Like other European powers, the Dutch practiced mercantilism and stressed government control over trade monopolies.

Today, the Netherlands is the world's largest producer of tulips with over 70 percent of the market. One of the best places to see Dutch tulips is the Keukenhof, the largest flower park in the world. More than seven million flower bulbs are planted here each year.

DUTCH ENTERPRISE

Over time, the Dutch East India Company eroded Portugal's position in the Indian Ocean by taking over strategic points of trade. In 1619, the company established its headquarters at Batavia (present-day Jakarta) on the island of Java in the East Indies. From there, the Dutch conquered several nearby islands. Dutch warships regularly squared off against Portuguese vessels and won most of the battles. Then in 1641, the Netherlands seized Malacca and the Spice Islands from Portugal. By 1700, the Dutch controlled the spice trade and the Indian Ocean trade routes.

The Dutch ruled some of these areas in Asia directly, such as the Banda Islands where they grew valuable nutmeg. Often the Dutch saw more opportunity in inserting themselves as middlemen into existing markets. For example, India was the world's biggest producer of cotton textiles. Using their faster ships with large cargo capacity, the Dutch profited by transporting such goods around the Indian Ocean as well as by selling the cloth in Europe.

They had also established a colony at Cape Town on the southwestern coast of Africa. This outpost provided fresh water and other services to Dutch ships that rounded the Cape of Good Hope. In time, the colony became part of the slave trade. The Dutch East India Company used slave labor on its settlements, and many of the enslaved people came from South Asia.

In the early 1600s, the Dutch East India Company got involved in the search for the **Northwest Passage**, a sea route from the Atlantic Ocean to the Pacific by way of a series of arctic northern Canadian islands. Such a route would have significantly shortened the voyage between Europe and Asia. In 1609, while under contract with the company, English explorer **Henry Hudson** searched for the passage but failed to find it. He did, however, sail up what is now the Hudson River to present-day Albany, New York. Along the way, he traded for furs with Native Americans. This trade was so lucrative that the Dutch established a post in the area.

With all the goods flowing into and out of the Netherlands—tulips were a hot commodity—Amsterdam, its capital, became a leading center of commerce. Meanwhile, however, other European countries continued to battle for a foothold in the Indian Ocean trade.

HISTORICAL THINKING

1. **READING CHECK** Why were the Dutch in a good position to compete with the Portuguese in the Indian Ocean?
2. **COMPARE AND CONTRAST** In what way was the Dutch East India Company similar to an independent country?
3. **ANALYZE CAUSE AND EFFECT** What was one effect of the Dutch East India Company's search for the Northwest Passage?

Age of Maritime Expansion 493

DOCUMENT-BASED QUESTION

2.3 Trade and Cross-Cultural Encounters

When someone discovers the next great thing, everyone wants to get in on the action. You've learned that the Portuguese and the Dutch established lucrative trade-based empires in the Indian Ocean. Eventually, other European maritime powers followed with their own merchant fleets. As Europeans traveled the Indian Ocean, some of them wrote down their views of the people they encountered. The Muslims and Asians did, too. Impressions on all sides weren't always flattering.

The Dutch established a few substantial settlements along the Indian Ocean, including those on the island of Java in today's Indonesia. For the most part, though, Europeans in the Indian Ocean limited their enterprises to "factories," as they called their trade settlements along the coast. But when they traveled inland to regions such as the Ottoman and Mughal empires or Safavid Iran, they discovered that they had to play by the rules of local leaders.

As Europeans competed for trade and wealth with local competitors in these inland regions, they left records of their cultural encounters. Likewise, Asians recorded accounts of European behavior. These reports frequently revealed the prejudices on both sides. Many Asians referred to Europeans as "Franks" and accused them of being greedy and violent. Europeans tended to view Muslims and other Asians as lazy and deceitful. Their views enforced negative stereotypes that would persist for many years.

Spices displayed in sacks are still sold in traditional open-air markets in India, just as they were when Europeans worked the Indian Ocean trade. Spices shown in this photo include cloves, cardamom, nutmeg, and turmeric.

494 CHAPTER 17

DOCUMENT ONE

Primary Source: Book
from the *Sejarah Melayu (Malay Annals)* by Tun Sri Lanang, 1612

Tun Sri Lanang was the Chief Minister of the Kingdom of Johor (in present-day Malaysia), which was founded by refugees from Malacca after the Portuguese conquest of 1511. About 100 years later, the sultan commissioned Tun Sri Lanang to rewrite and compile the *Malay Annals*, a history of their leaders before the conquest. In this excerpt from the work, Tun Sri Lanang describes the Portuguese attack on Malacca in 1511, led by Portugal's Viceroy, Alfonso d'Albuquerque.

CONSTRUCTED RESPONSE How does Tun Sri Lanang characterize the Portuguese attack on Malacca?

> And the Franks [Portuguese soldiers] engaged the men of Malacca in battle, and they fired their cannon from their ships so that the cannon balls came like rain. . . . The Franks then fiercely engaged the men of Malacca in battle and so vehement [violent] was their onslaught [attack] that the Malacca line was broken, leaving the king on his elephant isolated. And the king fought with the Franks pike to pike, and he was wounded in the palm of the hand. . . . And Malacca fell. The Franks advanced on the King's hall and the men of Malacca fled.

DOCUMENT TWO

Primary Source: Memoir
from *Travels in Persia, 1673–1677* by Jean Chardin, 1686

French jeweler Jean Chardin traveled twice to the Safavid Empire in Iran, where he learned the Persian language and formed strong opinions about the people. While in the capital of Isfahan, Chardin negotiated a deal to create jewelry for the shah. After Chardin returned from his second visit, he detailed his observations of Safavid Iran in *Travels to Persia, 1673–1677*. In this excerpt from the memoir, Chardin relates his impressions of the Persian people.

CONSTRUCTED RESPONSE According to Chardin, what do the Persians expect to receive in exchange for a favor?

> As civil as that nation is, they never act out of generosity. . . . And they cannot conceive that there should be such a country where people will do their duty from a motive of virtue only, without any other recompense [reward]. It is quite the contrary with them; they are paid for everything, and beforehand too. One can ask nothing of them, but with a present in one's hand. . . . The poorest and most miserable people never appear before a great man, or one from whom they would ask some favor, but at the same time they offer a present, which is never refused, even by the greatest lords of the kingdom.

DOCUMENT THREE

Primary Source: Memoir
from *The Ship of Sulaiman* by Muhammad Rabi ibn Muhammad Ibrahim, translated by John O'Kane, 1972

In 1686, Muhammad Rabi was the leader of a diplomatic mission to Siam, known today as Thailand. Muhammad Rabi wrote an account of the mission, focusing on the Iranians who resided in Siam at that time and their role in its trade and political affairs. He also discussed the European traders who had joined the Malay, Chinese, and Iranian merchant communities in Siam. In the following excerpt from his book, Muhammad Rabi describes an influential Frenchman at the Siamese court.

CONSTRUCTED RESPONSE How does Muhammad Rabi portray the Frenchman?

> [T]he king was not able to find an Iranian to act as prime minister [and] the only candidate who remained was that Frank [the Frenchman] who had originally worked as a sailor. . . . The Frank minister has succeeded in penetrating into the king's affections to such an extent . . . that there is never a moment in public or in private when he is not at the king's side. To the world at large this Christian minister displays a record of service, integrity, thrift and sincerity. . . . However, it is a fact every year he sends huge sums of money from the king's treasury abroad to the Frank kingdoms, supposedly for business purposes. Up until now there have been absolutely no visible returns from that money.

SYNTHESIZE & WRITE

1. **REVIEW** Review what you have learned about the Indian Ocean trade.
2. **RECALL** On your own paper, write down the main idea expressed in each document.
3. **CONSTRUCT** Construct a topic sentence that answers this question: Why do you think Europeans, Asians, and Muslims formed negative impressions of each other during their cross-cultural interactions?
4. **WRITE** Using evidence from this chapter and the documents, write an informative paragraph that supports your topic sentence in Step 3.

3.1

MAIN IDEA Spain pushed deeper into North America and colonized new lands where a hierarchical class system developed.

The Spanish Empire in the Americas

Spanish explorers faced a perilous journey when they sailed for the Americas. But, if successful, they knew Spain would be rewarded with great riches. The same cannot be said for the indigenous peoples they conquered.

NORTHERN EXPANSION

While Cortés and Pizarro were conquering Mexico and Peru, other Spanish conquistadors defeated the Maya in Yucatán and Guatemala. But the Spanish didn't limit their American explorations to Mesoamerica and South America. Soon they began moving north into the present-day United States. In 1513, **Juan Ponce de Léon** (PAWN-say DAY lay-OHN) was the first European to set foot in Florida, and he claimed it for Spain. Over the next 30 years or so, more Spanish explorers pushed deeper into North America in search of new territories and treasures.

One of the largest of these expeditions was led by **Francisco Vásquez de Coronado** from 1540 to 1542. Coronado and his men explored what is now California and parts of the Southwest. They hoped to find the legendary Seven Cities of Cibola (SEE-boh-lah), a kingdom said to be rich in silver and gold. But they found only Native Americans who resisted Spanish rule.

As a result, the Spanish monarchy had Catholic priests explore and colonize some of the new lands. Priests had accompanied explorers during American

CRITICAL VIEWING In *Defeat of the Spanish Armada*, a painting by 18th-century English artist Charles Robinson, the British navy fires on the Spanish fleet. The British victory in 1588 dealt a severe blow to the Spanish Armada and to Spain. How does the artist portray the Spanish sailors of the armada?

colonization from the beginning. While the explorers traveled in search of wealth, the priests sought to convert the indigenous peoples to Christianity. To that end, the clergymen established missions, or religious settlements, where they preached Christianity and provided food and shelter. By 1629, more than 25 missions dotted what is now New Mexico.

Some priests brutally punished the Native Americans who would not adopt Christianity. **Bartolomé de Las Casas**, a Spanish priest himself, spoke out against these abuses but to little effect. Some Native Americans converted but didn't entirely abandon their traditions. Instead, they combined their own practices with Christian teachings. As you have learned, this blending of different belief systems is called religious syncretism.

By the mid-1500s, Spain had established an American empire. The king of Spain was the ultimate authority. A group of advisors, called the Council of the Indies, regulated trade, appointed officials, and made laws. The king also divided his territory in the Americas into two **viceroyalties**, or colonies: New Spain, which included portions of Central and North America; and Peru, which covered portions of South America. A **viceroy**, a colonial leader appointed by the king, ruled each viceroyalty. The viceroys governed from their capitals—Mexico City in New Spain and Lima in Peru.

SOCIAL ORDER

A strict hierarchy developed in Spanish colonial society. At the top were Spanish-born settlers called *peninsulares*. They were closely followed by the *criollos* (cree-OH-yohs), Spaniards who were born in the Americas. These two groups were small but held the most power. Next came **mestizos**, people of mixed Spanish and Native American ancestry. Indigenous peoples and enslaved Africans were at the bottom. They made up the largest group but had the least power.

The Spanish government gave the wealthiest colonists large tracts of farmland called **haciendas**. On Caribbean islands, most haciendas were sugarcane plantations. A hacienda included a grant, or **encomienda**, that allowed owners to force Native Americans to labor for them. Under this system, Native Americans farmed, ranched, and mined for the Spanish throughout the Americas. In return for their labor, native peoples received protection from their enemies rather than payment. But Spanish landlords often abused the indigenous people, forcing them to work under harsh conditions, especially in the mines, where many died. In response to criticism of the treatment of Native Americans, the Spanish government put an end to the encomienda system in 1542. But abuse of indigenous workers on farms and in mines continued.

Spanish Explorers and Rule, 1513–1598

- Juan Ponce de León, 1513
- Álvar Núñez Cabeza da Vaca, 1528
- Hernando de Soto, 1539–43
- Francisco Vásquez de Coronado, 1540–42
- Juan Rodríguez Cabrillo, 1542
- Juan de Oñate, 1598

As the Spanish colonies in the Americas developed and thrived, the population of some of its cities steadily increased. Mexico City and Lima grew especially large, and so did some mining towns in South America. By 1580, the population of Potosí, the capital of Bolivia, topped 150,000, making it the largest city in the Americas. Mexico also produced one of the outstanding writers of the Spanish colonial period, a nun and self-taught poet and playwright named Sor Juana Inés de la Cruz. She had served the viceroy's wife and learned Latin. Further studies were not allowed for women, so she joined a convent in Mexico City in the late 1600s, where she was free to write poetry and study philosophy for the rest of her life. Her poems are still popular today.

Spain dominated colonization in the Americas until 1588, when the English defeated the Spanish Armada, a fleet of warships sent by Spain to attack England. After the defeat, other European powers gained momentum and started to take advantage of Spain's vulnerability and establish their own colonies in the Americas.

HISTORICAL THINKING

1. **READING CHECK** How did the king of Spain control his colonial empire in the Americas?

2. **ANALYZE CAUSE AND EFFECT** What happened after Spanish explorers failed to find riches in what is now the southwestern United States?

3. **INTERPRET MAPS** Why might the distance between the two viceroyalties have caused problems for Spain?

3.2 A Global Commodity: Silver

People in the ancient world discovered silver around 4000 B.C.E.—long after gold and copper—and valued its beauty and ability to reflect light. Silver is the lightest of the precious metals and soft. It can be stretched thinner than a strand of hair. It can also be polished to a brilliant shine that only contact with sulfur can dim. The Inca called silver "tears of the moon" for the metal's milky luster. Silver is rare, and very little of the metal had been mined before 1492. That's the year Spain began its conquest of the Americas and plunder of their resources, including silver.

In the mid-1550s, huge deposits of silver in mines in present-day Mexico, Bolivia, and Peru allowed Spain to begin a lucrative trade with China that lasted 250 years. Once a year, a ship known as the Manila galleon made the long voyage back and forth between Acapulco, Mexico, and Manila, in the Spanish colony of the Philippines, to exchange silver for Chinese goods such as silk and porcelain. During this period, the three mines produced 85 percent of the world's silver.

How do you think silver both connected and divided the world during the age of maritime expansion?

A SILVER LINING

Silver often plays second fiddle to gold, but it contains special properties that set it apart from other precious metals. Silver is the best conductor of heat and electricity, and it reflects light better than any other element. As a result, it is used to make mirrors, telescopes, and microscopes. Of course, silver is also beautiful. Silversmiths, like the one at work in Cambodia in this photograph, fashion decorative objects and jewelry from the metal—just as they did in ancient times.

Age of Maritime Expansion

How do the items shown here reflect silver's versatility?

SPANISH COLONIAL COINS

Spain began minting silver coins in 1537, following its conquest of the Americas. The Spanish coins shown here, called reales, were issued in 1723 and are stamped with King Philip V's name. Holes were punched in coins used as currency in Spain's colonies. Spanish reales were used in English colonies as well. Half of the coins in circulation in colonial America were probably reales. In fact, Spanish money would be used as legal tender in the United States until 1857.

SILVER AT A GLANCE

USES	• Like gold, silver was used in the ancient world to make jewelry, artwork, and objects for religious rituals.	• Silver became the most used material for coinage in history because it was perfect for smaller denominations.	• Silver is an essential element in modern technology, medicine, and health-care products.
VALUE	• In ancient Egypt, silver was sometimes valued over gold since sources of silver in the region were more rare.	• Silver became so tied to currency that, in some countries, the word for *silver* and *money* is the same.	• The price of silver rose to an average of about $35 an ounce in 2011 but fell to about $19 in 2016.
PRODUCTION	• Silver is rarely found in a pure state and usually combines with ores such as lead and copper.	• Silver-bearing deposits of ores are mined and then smelted or ground to separate the silver.	• In the 1500s, miners in South and Central America crushed and mixed silver-bearing ore by having mules tread over it.
HISTORY	• The Greek silver-lead mine of Laurium, near Athens, was the best-known mine of the ancient world and was worked by slaves from 500 B.C.E. to 100 C.E.	• Silver goods retained their luster longer until the Industrial Revolution of the 18th and 19th centuries, when more sulfur was released into the atmosphere.	• By 1892, $397 million worth of silver had been mined from Nevada's Comstock Lode, which is the equivalent of more than $9 billion today.
ECONOMICS	• In the 16th century, the flow of silver in Spain resulted in inflation in that country and in much of Europe, with sharp increases in the price of food.	• In 1792, the United States based its currency on the value of silver, and silver coins were not removed from circulation until 1967.	• In 2017, the world's four leading producers of silver were Mexico, Peru, China, and Russia.

SILVER CAULDRON

This silver cauldron, or large pot, was found in 1891 in a bog in the Danish town of Gundestrup. Made around the first century B.C.E., the silver vessel is decorated with people, animals, and unknown gods. Experts believe an ancient people known as the Thracians, who lived in the area of present-day Bulgaria and Romania, made the cauldron. But they have no idea how it got to Denmark.

INCA SILVER

Like the Peruvian societies that came before them, the Inca were known for their beautiful metalwork. Unfortunately, the Spanish melted down almost every artifact of silver or gold. Pieces that survive include this large silver beaker featuring a human face wearing a headdress (far right). Beakers like this one were often used as drinking vessels during Inca rituals.

Standing at just slightly more than four inches tall, this silver female figurine (right) shows a woman with arms and hands held close to the chest. The figure is adorned with inlaid stones.

3.3

MAIN IDEA Portugal and the Netherlands established profitable colonies in Brazil, the Caribbean, and the mainland of North America.

The Portuguese and Dutch in the Americas

Spain was the first to stake a claim on land in the Americas—but it wouldn't be the lone colonizer for long. In the scramble for land in the Americas, Portugal and the Netherlands didn't want to be left out.

THE PORTUGUESE IN BRAZIL

Remember reading about the Treaty of Tordesillas at the beginning of this chapter? According to the terms of the treaty, Portugal received Brazil, one of the areas that remained outside of Spanish control. But the Portuguese didn't explore Brazil until they stumbled across it when they sailed too far west on a trip to India. In 1500, the Portuguese navigator **Pedro Álvares Cabral** landed in Brazil long enough to claim it for Portugal.

At first, the Portuguese had limited interest in Brazil. The only resource the region seemed to provide was brazilwood, a tree that produced a red dye. The tree gave Brazil its name. But after the French began trading with Brazil's native people, Portugal decided to assert its authority over the area and established its first Brazilian colony in 1532. The Portuguese king divided the colony into administrative districts and appointed a governor to rule over each one.

Colonists began arriving and so did priests, who converted many of the indigenous people to Christianity. The Portuguese priests in Brazil tried to protect local people from cruel treatment at the hands of colonial settlers but had little success. The Portuguese government encouraged colonists in Brazil to set up plantations for growing sugarcane. Sugar, as you know, was a luxury in Europe, so Portugal would make great profits by its sale. However, growing and processing sugarcane was labor-intensive and dangerous. So the plantation owners used slave labor to do the work.

In the beginning, the owners enslaved native Brazilians to grow their sugarcane. Some of the indigenous people fled into the heavily forested interior of Brazil, but the Portuguese recaptured many of them. Eventually, the Portuguese imported African slaves to work on the sugarcane plantations. Portugal had already been using enslaved Africans on its sugar plantations in West Africa and now brought that practice to Brazil. By 1600, about 15,000 enslaved Africans labored on Brazil's sugar plantations. Resistance was widespread among the African slaves. Some even managed to escape to Brazil's interior and form independent farming communities. Most weren't so lucky. Over time, Portugal would import a total of nearly four million slaves. You will learn more about the slave trade later in this book.

Meanwhile, Portuguese colonists pushed further into Brazil. In 1695, gold was discovered in southeastern Brazil, triggering a gold rush. With enslaved Africans providing the labor, Brazilian mines produced enormous amounts of gold. By 1760, gold rivaled sugar as Portugal's main export. And the search for more gold led to the discovery of diamonds. Brazil became Portugal's most important overseas colony.

THE DUTCH IN NORTH AMERICA

As you know, the Dutch were conducting a booming trade in the Indian Ocean and Europe by the early 1600s. They wanted to get in on the equally lucrative opportunities available in the Americas. To that end, the Netherlands formed the Dutch West India Company in 1621. You've read about the Dutch East India Company, which regulated trade in the Indian Ocean. Its counterpart was granted a monopoly on trade with the Americas, the Caribbean islands, and Africa.

The Dutch West India Company was also determined to wage war on the economies of Spain and Portugal. In 1628, Piet Heyn, the company's director and an admiral, captured a Spanish treasure fleet filled with gold and silver from the Americas. He received a hero's welcome when he returned home. The company used some of the treasure to challenge Portugal's hold on Brazil. In 1630, the Dutch seized an area in northeastern Brazil

CRITICAL VIEWING The upper levels of Elmina Castle, located in present-day Ghana, provided luxurious accommodations for European traders and ship captains. Below, however, filthy cells in the dungeons housed enslaved people before they were shipped across the Atlantic. Why do you think cannons were mounted and pointed toward the sea?

and took over its sugar plantations there. The Dutch company also sponsored a fleet of ships that captured Elmina Castle, a Portuguese fort on the coast of West Africa, and used it to transport slaves to Brazil and the Caribbean. Elmina became a key outpost for the growing slave trade. The Dutch colony in Brazil flourished for nearly 25 years until the Portuguese won it back in 1654.

Meanwhile, the Dutch West India Company established several colonies in the Caribbean, including a group of five islands called the Netherlands Antilles. The islands were captured from Spain in 1634. Like other European colonizers, the Dutch built sugar plantations on these Caribbean islands and forced enslaved Africans to supply the labor.

You've learned that when the Dutch East India Company sent Henry Hudson to find the Northwest Passage, he only got as far as present-day New York state. The fur trade that Hudson had begun in the region gradually expanded, and the Dutch West India Company was authorized to set up a colony there. As a result, in 1624, the company established New Netherland off the tip of what the Native American inhabitants called Manna-hata Island (today's Manhattan) and built **New Amsterdam** (today's New York City) as its capital. Dutch presence on the mainland of North America didn't last long, however. In 1664, the English seized New Netherland without a struggle. By that time, the English and French had come to dominate colonial America.

HISTORICAL THINKING

1. **READING CHECK** What made Brazil Portugal's most important colony?

2. **MAKE INFERENCES** Why did the Dutch West India Company want to undermine the Spanish and Portuguese economies?

3. **ANALYZE CAUSE AND EFFECT** What happened as a result of Henry Hudson's attempt to find the Northwest Passage?

Age of Maritime Expansion

3.4

MAIN IDEA England and France established colonies in North America that developed differing economies and relationships with the indigenous peoples.

The English Colonies and New France

The English government established colonies in North America in hopes of finding gold, silver, and a viable sea route to Asia. None of those things turned up, but many of those who settled in the colonies found freedom, work, and a new home.

ENGLISH COLONIES

Due to wars and internal problems during the late 1400s and much of the 1500s, England couldn't compete with other European countries in overseas exploration and colony-building. By the end of the 16th century, however, England had expanding agricultural and mining industries, land shortages, and an increasingly mobile population. These factors set the stage for England to challenge its European rivals.

CRITICAL VIEWING This aerial photo of Jamestown shows the original fort and settlement site. Archaeologists reconstructed the fort and erected fences to mark the dimensions of the original buildings. The colonists built the fort on an island to defend Jamestown against the Spanish. Why might the colonists have feared an attack by Spain?

504 CHAPTER 17

In 1607, a group of English colonists landed at Chesapeake Bay on the mid-Atlantic coast of North America. There they founded **Jamestown**, England's first permanent settlement in the Americas. They named the surrounding land Virginia, and tobacco became the colony's chief crop. To grow their tobacco, planters began to use indentured servants, people who pledged to work for four to seven years in exchange for ocean passage and living costs. Slavery was also introduced to Jamestown. The first slaves, African captives taken from a Portuguese ship by English raiders, arrived in 1619.

Other colonies were soon founded along the Atlantic coast. Slavery would expand throughout the Southern Colonies. As cash crops such as tobacco, cotton, indigo, and rice flourished, a plantation system and distinct social classes arose.

Slavery was not widely practiced in the New England Colonies, which began with the arrival of the Pilgrims and the Puritans, who were seeking religious freedom. More settlers soon arrived for economic reasons. As fishing, whaling, and shipbuilding industries developed, New England became the center of colonial trade.

The Middle Colonies were known for their tolerance. This policy was primarily a legacy of Dutch settlers who had welcomed Jews and Protestants and people from Sweden, Finland, and Norway. The population of these colonies grew as a result of a thriving agricultural industry. And cities, including Philadelphia and New York, became economic and cultural centers.

NEW FRANCE

One year after English colonists arrived in Jamestown, French explorer **Samuel de Champlain** sailed up the St. Lawrence River and founded **Quebec** in present-day Canada. Quebec would be the base of France's colonial empire in North America, known as New France. The colonists began a valuable trade in furs with First Nations communities such as the Algonquin. While the English colonists sought to expand their share of territory and push Native Americans off the land, the French established good relationships with their Algonquin trading partners and even forged alliances with them. French fur traders often traveled into the interior and married local women. Their children often spoke both French and indigenous languages.

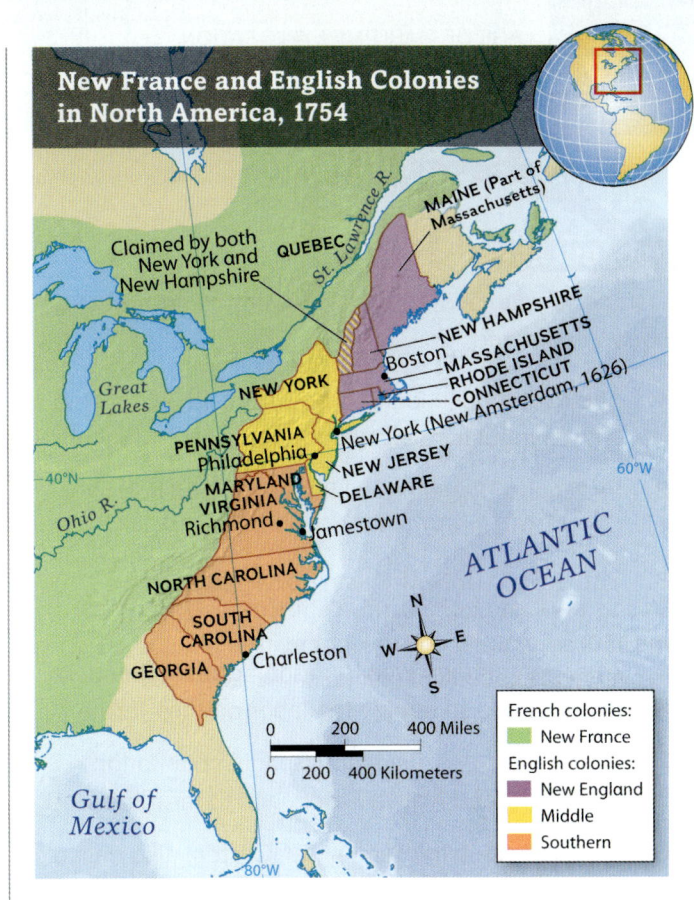

Other French explorers pushed deeper into the North American continent. In 1673, Jacques Marquette and Louis Joliet paddled through the Great Lakes and upper Mississippi River. Their account of the extraordinary natural resources they saw there led the French to create a 4,000-mile-long network of trading posts along the bodies of water. Explorer Sieur de La Salle traveled the Illinois and Mississippi rivers and claimed all the land along the rivers for French king Louis XIV in 1682. By the early 1700s, New France covered much of what is today the midwestern United States and eastern Canada.

Despite the size of its territory, however, the population of New France remained sparse. The English wanted to extend their settlements to the west and had their eyes on the lands of New France. In 1754, the **French and Indian War** broke out between France and its Native American allies on one side and England and the American colonists on the other. England would win the war, and New France would lose most of its colonies. But the outcome for the American colonists would not be what they had expected.

HISTORICAL THINKING

1. **READING CHECK** Why were indentured servants and enslaved people brought to Jamestown?

2. **INTERPRET MAPS** How would you describe the location of the English colonies in relation to New France?

3. **ANALYZE CAUSE AND EFFECT** What led to the French and Indian War?

CHAPTER 17 AGE OF MARITIME EXPLORATION REVIEW

VOCABULARY

Complete each sentence below with the correct vocabulary word.

1. The Portuguese learned how to build a light ship with triangular sails called a _____.

2. Ferdinand Magellan led the first expedition to _____ the world.

3. The _____ of New Spain governed from his capital in Mexico City.

4. After Jamestown was founded, tobacco planters used _____ to supply the labor on their farms.

5. Under the _____ system, Spanish plantation owners forced Native Americans to farm the land.

6. The Spanish explorer Hernán Cortés, also called a _____, conquered the Aztec.

7. Wealthy Spaniards owned large agricultural estates known as _____.

READING STRATEGY
ANALYZE CAUSE AND EFFECT

Use a cause-and-effect chain to identify the multiple causes and effects of the Indian Ocean trade empire established by Portugal. Then answer the questions.

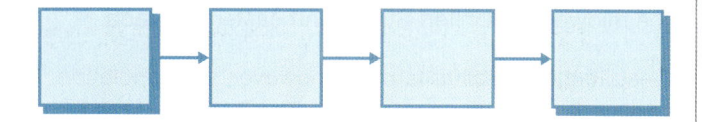

8. How did the legacy of Prince Henry impact the establishment of Portuguese trade in the Indian Ocean?

9. What happened as a result of Portugal's seizure of the Straits of Hormuz?

MAIN IDEAS

Answer the following questions. Support your answers with evidence from the chapter.

10. What did Christopher Columbus hope to achieve on his voyages? **LESSON 1.1**

11. Who brought about the end of the Aztec and Inca empires? **LESSON 1.2**

12. What were some of the positive and negative impacts of the Columbian Exchange? **LESSON 1.4**

13. Why was the 1498 voyage of Vasco da Gama important to Portugal? **LESSON 2.1**

14. What was the purpose of the Dutch East India Company? **LESSON 2.2**

15. Which groups made up the social order in Spanish colonial society? **LESSON 3.1**

16. Why did the Portuguese have limited interest in Brazil when they first colonized it? **LESSON 3.3**

17. How did raising tobacco help Jamestown succeed? **LESSON 3.4**

HISTORICAL THINKING

Answer the following questions. Support your answers with evidence from the chapter.

18. **ANALYZE CAUSE AND EFFECT** What happened as a result of Columbus's voyages?

19. **FORM AND SUPPORT OPINIONS** Do you think the Spanish would have been able to conquer the Aztec and Inca if the native peoples had not been infected with disease? Why or why not?

20. **DRAW CONCLUSIONS** Aside from the desire for wealth and power, what else probably encouraged the Portuguese to take away much of the Indian Ocean trade from the Muslims?

21. **MAKE INFERENCES** Why do you think some of the Native Americans in New Spain combined their spiritual traditions with Christian teachings?

22. **SYNTHESIZE** In addition to taking over profitable Spanish colonies in the Americas, what might have motivated Dutch attacks on Spain?

23. **COMPARE AND CONTRAST** How did the Dutch attitude toward settlers in North America compare with their attitude toward those they colonized elsewhere?

INTERPRET MAPS

German cartographer Martin Waldseemüller drew this map of the New World in 1513. The map shows Florida in the top left corner with the Caribbean islands of Cuba (Isabella) and Haiti and the Dominican Republic (Spagnolla) beneath it. Spain and Africa appear on the right, and the area labeled with the Latin words *terra incognita*, meaning "unknown lands," represents Brazil. Study the map, and then answer the questions below.

24. How does Waldseemüller depict the physical relationship between North America and South America?

25. What does the map suggest about European knowledge of the Western Hemisphere in 1513?

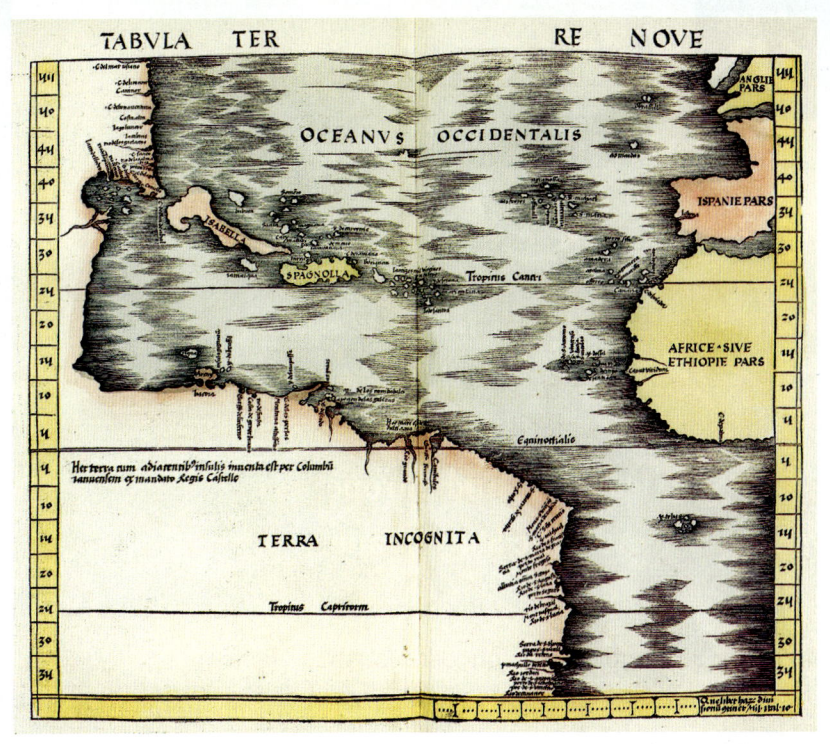

Waldseemüller Map of the "New World," 1513

ANALYZE SOURCES

The Spanish missionary Bartolomé de Las Casas witnessed the harsh treatment of indigenous people at the hands of Spanish settlers. In 1542, he wrote *A Brief Account of the Destruction of the Indies*, detailing what he had seen. In this excerpt, Las Casas summarizes the Spaniards' brutality toward indigenous people on the Caribbean island of Hispaniola.

> The Spaniards first assaulted the innocent Sheep . . . like most cruel Tygers, Wolves and Lions hunger-starv'd, studying nothing, for the space of Forty Years, after their first landing, but the Massacre of these Wretches, whom they have so inhumanely and barbarously butcher'd and harass'd with several kinds of Torments, never before known, or heard . . . . [O]f Three Millions of Persons, which lived in Hispaniola itself, there is at present but the inconsiderable remnant of scarce Three Hundred.

26. How does Las Casas characterize the Spanish settlers and the indigenous people in Hispaniola?

CONNECT TO YOUR LIFE

27. **EXPLANATORY** Between 1450 and 1750, Europeans explored lands unknown to them. The expeditions were dangerous and filled with challenges and hardships. What would you like to explore: outer space, the oceans, Antarctica? Think of where you'd like to go, and then plan your expedition. Consider how you'd get there, what challenges you might face, and what you would want to find or accomplish on your expedition. Write a brief essay explaining where you'd go, how you'd get there, and what the purpose of your expedition would be.

TIPS

- Review what you've read about the experiences of the Spanish, Portuguese, Dutch, French, and English explorers.

- If necessary, do research to learn about the place you've chosen to explore.

- Decide what the goal of your expedition would be. Do you want to study conditions on another planet, discover new life forms, find evidence of climate change? Reflect on the ways in which your goal compares with those of the explorers in this chapter.

- Use two or three vocabulary terms from the chapter in your essay.

- Provide a concluding statement summarizing your trip and comparing your expedition to those conducted by early European explorers.

CHAPTER 18

Africans in the Atlantic World
1400–1800

HISTORICAL THINKING How have elements of African cultures spread around the world?

SECTION 1 **Africa, Asia, and Europe**
SECTION 2 **The Atlantic Slave Trade**

CRITICAL VIEWING
This young girl in Mali is wearing a traditional Songhai headdress. The Songhai built a large empire in West Africa in the 1400s and 1500s. What does this headdress suggest about cultural links to the past in present-day Mali?

Africans in the Atlantic World 509

1.1

MAIN IDEA Between the 1500s and 1700s, Africa continued to develop as a politically and culturally diverse continent with expanding international trade networks.

African History: 1500s to 1700s

Since ancient times, Africans had formed trade connections with other peoples across the Mediterranean, the Red Sea, and the Indian Ocean. Through the centuries, these trade networks kept expanding, spreading both goods and ideas across the continent and to other parts of the world.

CRITICAL VIEWING People buy and sell goods at a street market in Ibadan, Nigeria. What can you infer about the city's economy based on evidence in the photo?

A DIVERSE CONTINENT

By the 1500s, Africa's geographic diversity—its deserts, grasslands, and rain forests—had been matched by its variety of political systems for a very long time. Some Africans formed small bands of hunter-gatherers, while others lived in kingdoms led by powerful monarchs. In many agricultural communities, ruling dynasties developed along with a complex hierarchy.

In almost all African societies, clan elders played a key role in negotiating consensus, or general agreement, on community decisions. African villages ruled by a distant chief or king retained their own ways of keeping peace and administering justice.

Over time, interaction among various African peoples brought about cultural and economic changes. For example, in the Great Lakes region of east-central

510 CHAPTER 18

Africa, Bantu-speaking people migrating from the west brought knowledge of grain agriculture and gained access to cattle in exchange. In the societies that resulted from this migration, farming provided most of the food, while cattle were viewed as signs of wealth and social status. Supported by agricultural surpluses and dominated by clans wealthy in cattle, a number of powerful kingdoms, such as Rwanda and Buganda, emerged in the 1600s.

In the Great Lakes region and other parts of Africa, high population density was connected to more centralized politics. That was not true in the Igbo (ee-BWOH)-speaking region of West Africa, however. In this rich agricultural area, with its vibrant markets and trade, powerful kings never emerged. Instead, the people preferred a system in which men and women gained titles and authority based on their achievements rather than on their social rank at birth.

The growth of external markets and the spread of Islam persisted in Africa through the 1500s. Though the Muslim-ruled empire of Mali collapsed in about 1450, trade persisted. West African goods such as gold and leather were transported across the Sahara in return for commodities from the Mediterranean region. From West African cities on the **Niger River**, goods then flowed on this "water highway" into Africa's rain forests. The continual stream of both goods and ideas, as well as religious pilgrims and teachers, reinforced the spread of Islam across much of West Africa.

African trade across the Indian Ocean continued even after the Portuguese disrupted coastal trade with their assault on the East African port of Kilwa in the early 1500s. Muslim Swahili merchants still carried on a lively trade with peoples in India and around the Persian Gulf. In fact, African merchants traded brightly patterned Indian cotton textiles deep into the interior of the continent in the 16th century.

Beginning in 1696, Arab sultans of Oman began to exert control over East African ports. Swahili princes and aristocrats generally accepted the authority of the Arab sultans while continuing to regulate the day-to-day affairs of their own city-states. Traditional Swahili arts and crafts, such as poetry and jewelry, continued to thrive, blending Islamic and African themes.

CHRISTIANITY IN AFRICA

Christianity had been part of North African life since ancient times. As you learned, the Ethiopian Coptic Church, connected to the Eastern Orthodox Church, was already more than 1,000 years old when the Portuguese arrived along Africa's eastern coast in 1498. The many monasteries that had been built in the region were evidence of the strong presence of Christianity.

By this time, Islam was spreading throughout the region. As a result, the Ethiopian and Portuguese Christians formed a military alliance against the expanding Muslim kingdom. The alliance was not a great success. The Portuguese leader was killed in a battle with Muslim forces. In addition, because the Ethiopians had their own Christian beliefs and rituals, they refused to accept the Catholic interpretations of European priests.

A new frontier of Christianity in Africa opened in the Kongo kingdom of Central Africa. King Nzinga, the ruler of the kingdom, converted to Roman Catholicism after the arrival of the Portuguese. Nzinga exchanged ambassadors with the pope and sent his son to school in Lisbon. His alliance with the European Christians became strained, however, when Portuguese slave trading disrupted Kongo society. Nzinga complained to the king of Portugal, but the slave trade continued.

In the mid-1600s, the Kongo kingdom collapsed. A Christian reformer named **Kimpa Vita** quickly stepped in to provide direction to the Kongo people. She declared that she had been visited by Saint Anthony and had spoken with God, who said that the people must unite under a new king. Kimpa Vita taught that Jesus and his apostles were Africans who had lived and died in Kongo, and she mixed Christian beliefs with African religious traditions. Her teachings were popular with many Africans, but Portuguese missionaries regarded her as a heretic. She was captured by rivals, tried for witchcraft, and burned at the stake.

European settlers introduced yet another form of Christianity to the continent. In the 1600s, Dutch Calvinists and French Huguenots brought Protestant Christianity to southern Africa. However, another two centuries passed before significant numbers of southern Africans converted to Christianity.

HISTORICAL THINKING

1. **READING CHECK** How did Muslim traders affect the cultures of North, East, and West Africa?

2. **IDENTIFY MAIN IDEAS** What was one common feature of the political systems in almost all African societies?

3. **COMPARE AND CONTRAST** What were the differences and similarities in Christian beliefs introduced in eastern, central, and southern Africa?

1.2

MAIN IDEA In the 1500s, leaders of the Songhai Empire gained control of interregional and trans-Saharan trade and established an effective system of government in West Africa.

The Songhai Empire

What happens when a large, successful company goes out of business? Usually, another company eagerly steps in to fill the void. That's just what happened when the prosperous West African empire of Mali disintegrated. Another group quickly claimed control of regional trade.

EMERGENCE OF SONGHAI

You've read that first Ghana and then Mali grew powerful because of an active trans-Saharan trade network. In the mid-1400s, the once-mighty Mali Empire declined because of weak rulers and struggles over **succession**, or the process by which a new leader is chosen to follow an outgoing leader. Groups of people began breaking away, and the Mali Empire lost control of several major cities, including Timbuktu, in 1433. Then in the 1460s, soldiers on horseback with iron breastplates beneath their battle tunics attacked Mali from the north and south. They were the elite forces of a group of West African people called the Songhai (SAHNG-gy).

The Songhai ruled from their capital city of Gao, southeast of Timbuktu along the Niger River. The Songhai leader **Sunni Ali**, in power from 1464 to 1492, built a powerful cavalry that quickly won the reputation of being undefeatable as it set out to conquer surrounding lands. On water, his war canoes controlled

CRITICAL VIEWING In Gao, Mali, Muslims take part in evening prayer near the tomb of Askia Muhammad the Great, an emperor who championed Islam in the Songhai Empire. What is unusual about the tomb's appearance?

512 CHAPTER 18

Major African States, c. 1400s–1600s

the Niger River. The professional army's many victories allowed Sunni Ali to build the Songhai Empire. In spite of these achievements, Muslim historians portray Sunni Ali as a harsh and unjust ruler because he mistreated the Muslim scholars of Timbuktu during his conquest.

The same was not true of **Askia Muhammad the Great**, who claimed control of Songhai in 1493 after Sunni Ali's death and is remembered as a great supporter of Islam. *Askia* became the name of the Muslim dynasty that Muhammad established and the title of its rulers. Muhammad followed the example of Mansa Musa by showing off his wealth as he made a pilgrimage to Mecca.

Although Muhammad championed Islam and mandated that the empire's laws be based on Islamic law, the faith spread slowly within the Songhai Empire. Most West Africans lived in small agricultural villages and continued to worship African gods and follow traditional rituals. Eventually, some aspects of Islam blended with traditional West African beliefs, but few villagers became Muslim. Even in cities such as Timbuktu, where many Africans were Muslim, religious syncretism took place. Muslim visitors from other lands often thought Africans did not adhere closely enough to Islamic principles. They particularly criticized the relaxed attitude of Africans toward the veiling of women.

Africans in the Atlantic World 513

A scholar reads Islamic manuscripts from the 13th century at the Ahmed Baba Institute of Higher Learning and Islamic Research in Timbuktu. About 4,000 ancient manuscripts were burned by radical Islamist militants in Timbuktu before the militants were driven out by French forces in 2013.

TRADE AND GOVERNMENT

Trade both north and south expanded even farther under the Songhai Empire. For example, kola nuts from the forest regions in the south were exchanged for valuable salt from mines in the Sahara region. In turn, gold was traded north for such commodities as ceramics, glass, and Islamic texts.

The Songhai also traded people. At first, the Songhai relied on captured slaves to serve as loyal soldiers and as skilled craftworkers. The supply of enslaved people then increased as Songhai armies conquered new territory, and a larger number of slaves were sold in North African markets.

Within the Songhai Empire, people used cowrie shells as a currency for local trade. Cowrie are a type of snail, and their beautiful shells were highly valued in Africa during the 1400s and 1500s. The Songhai people used fixed amounts of cowrie shells to pay for cloth, food, and other goods.

To strengthen his empire's control of trade, Muhammad shrewdly planned his battles and conquests. He pushed back against the Tuareg people who lived in the desert north of Timbuktu to prevent them from claiming Sahelian trade routes. He conquered Taghaza in northern Africa to gain access to its salt mines and expanded his empire into the Sahara as far as he could. He also defeated the Mossi people of what is now Burkina Faso and the people of present-day Niger and incorporated them into his empire. In addition, he forged new trade connections with the Hausa people who lived to the east of Songhai lands.

Gaining wealth through trade was just one way Muhammad ensured the success of the Songhai Empire. To make sure his government could effectively oversee his growing empire, he established a bureaucracy. Each department within the bureaucracy had a different responsibility, such as handling finances, administering justice, waging war, and regulating agriculture.

Muhammad also controlled his sprawling empire by dividing it into provinces. Generally, each province followed the borders of a particular conquered land. Muhammad installed relatives or close followers as governors of the provinces. These loyalists obeyed his every command. Taxes paid by the conquered territories added to the empire's wealth.

SUPPORT FOR LEARNING

Muhammad and other Songhai rulers used some of the empire's wealth to support Islamic arts and sciences. The Sankore Mosque in Timbuktu, with its impressive library, became a center of intellectual debate, drawing scholars from far and wide. Sankore University was established around the mosque and became a leading center of learning. Timbuktu also became famous for its book market, where Arab and African Muslim scholars could find finely bound editions of books they sought. The opportunity to both trade and gain knowledge drew many Muslims to Timbuktu.

Today, the site of the Sankore Mosque is protected as a UNESCO World Heritage Site. In 2013, however, Islamists, who believe in a strict legal interpretation of Islam, destroyed some of Timbuktu's precious manuscripts. They wanted to wipe out all records that demonstrated the blending of African and Islamic cultures. Fortunately, a number of similar manuscripts had already been moved to another location for safekeeping.

END OF AN EMPIRE

The wealth of Songhai's gold and salt mines inspired the envy of the ruler of Morocco in northern Africa. In 1591, he dispatched his army, equipped with firearms from Europe, to conquer Songhai. With the advantage of superior weapons and aided by internal disputes within Songhai, the Moroccans won an easy victory. The invaders forced Timbuktu scholars to flee the city. Later, the Songhai Empire broke up into smaller kingdoms, chiefdoms, and sultanates.

Never again would a large-scale African state rise to such dominance in the Sahel. Saharan people other than the Moroccans would ultimately gain control of trans-Saharan trade, however.

Even before the demise, or downfall, of Songhai, Europeans were building small settlements along the West African coast. European merchants were looking for ways to control not only the gold trade but also the booming slave trade. The Atlantic Ocean would emerge as an important connection to Europe and the Americas, bringing drastic changes for Africans.

Writing under the name Leo Africanus, a young diplomat who visited Songhai during Askia Muhammad's reign published a description of the empire at its peak. In this excerpt from his writing, he describes the city of Timbuktu. The name Barbarie refers to Berber lands in northern Africa.

PRIMARY SOURCE

Here are many shops of craftsmen and merchants, especially those who weave linen and cotton cloth. To this place Barbarie merchants bring cloth from Europe. All the women of this region except maidservants go with their faces covered and sell all necessary kinds of foods. . . .

The rich king of Timbuktu has many articles of gold, and he keeps a magnificent and well-furnished court. When he travels anywhere he rides upon a camel which is led by some of his noblemen. . . .

Here there are many doctors, judges, priests, and other learned men, that are well maintained at the king's cost. Various manuscripts and written books are brought here out of Barbarie and sold for more money than any other merchandise. . . .

The inhabitants are people of a gentle and cheerful disposition and spend a great part of the night in singing and dancing through all the streets of the city. They keep great store of men and women slaves.

—from *History and Description of Africa* by Leo Africanus, translated by J. Pory and edited by R. Brown, 1896

HISTORICAL THINKING

1. **READING CHECK** What were some major achievements of Askia Muhammad the Great?
2. **EXPLAIN** How did Islam spread in West Africa?
3. **INTERPRET MAPS** What trend do you notice about the locations of the various African civilizations?
4. **ANALYZE CAUSE AND EFFECT** What factors contributed to the fall of the Songhai Empire?

1.3 Preserving Cultural Heritage

TIMBUKTU

Once a prosperous center for trade and learning, Timbuktu is a historically significant city in the West African country of Mali. Its location where the Sahara and the Niger River meet made it an important city along the trans-Saharan trade routes.

In 2012, Tuareg rebels backed by Islamic militants took control of the northern part of Mali. The militants soon replaced the Tuareg and imposed strict sharia, or Islamic, law. They ordered that many of Timbuktu's monuments, tombs, and artifacts be destroyed.

French troops backed by the United States and the European Union drove out the Islamist forces from Timbuktu in 2013. As the rebels fled, they set fire to several buildings, including libraries that housed thousands of ancient texts, with the oldest manuscript dating to around 1204.

Work to repair the resulting damage began immediately. Not all the historic manuscripts were destroyed. A librarian and several others had packed and hidden away many of the manuscripts for safekeeping. To preserve its cultural heritage, Mali's sites were included on the 2014 World Monuments Watch. The French and Malian governments, along with UNESCO, created a plan for the restoration of the sites destroyed by the conflict.

In 2016, The Hague's International Criminal Court (ICC) brought a Malian rebel leader to trial for his alleged crimes. This trial marked the first prosecution of cultural heritage destruction as a war crime. He was found guilty and ordered to pay for the damage.

HISTORICAL THINKING

DESCRIBE What is the historical significance of Timbuktu and what would be lost if the city was not preserved?

A museum guard displays a burnt ancient manuscript in its box at the Ahmed Baba Institute.

TIMBUKTU, MALI

A door and some rubble are all that remain of a mausoleum destroyed by Islamist fighters in a cemetery in Timbuktu, Mali, in 2013. These same fighters set fire to dozens of ancient manuscripts at the Ahmed Baba Institute, the city's biggest and most important library.

2.1

MAIN IDEA An enslaved African sailor wrote an influential firsthand account of the horrors of slavery, which he witnessed during his sea travels.

Traveler: Olaudah Equiano
An African Voice c. 1745–1797

In the Atlantic slave trade, millions of Africans were forced to sail across the Atlantic to be sold into slavery. Many were destined for the sugar plantations of the West Indies. Much of what we know about their horrific journeys and difficult lives comes from the writings of an enslaved sailor working on a merchant ship that crossed the Atlantic.

EARLY LIFE AND TRAVELS

In 1789, British antislavery activists were eagerly discussing a new book by a former African slave named **Olaudah Equiano** (oh-LOW-duh ehk-wee-AHN-oh). In his **slave narrative** called *The Interesting Narrative of the Life of Olaudah Equiano, or Gustavus Vassa, the African*, Equiano vividly described the ordeal of slavery from a first-person point of view.

Equiano was born around 1745, when the Atlantic slave trade was at its height. Hundreds of thousands of captive Africans crossed the Atlantic on sailing ships every year. According to his narrative, Equiano was 11 years old when he was captured and forced onto a slave ship headed to the West Indies. In his narrative, he describes the horrors of the infamous **Middle Passage**, the journey by slave ships across the Atlantic from West Africa to the Americas.

Equiano continues his narrative by describing his sale to a British naval officer. Rather than working on a Caribbean sugar plantation like many African captives, Equiano spent much of his early life aboard ships. Later, he was sold to a Philadelphia merchant who conducted business in the West Indies. Aboard ship, Equiano learned reading, writing, and mathematics. He tended to his enslaver's business, which sometimes included trading in slaves. Life as a sailor allowed him more independence than most slaves had, yet he longed for true freedom.

Eventually, Equiano won his freedom through a combination of good fortune and business sense. His final owner was a member of the Society of Friends, or Quakers. The Quakers had strong doubts about whether Christians should own other people. The slaveholder agreed to Equiano's **manumission**, or release from slavery, if Equiano could pay his own purchase price. He allowed Equiano to conduct his own trades in his spare time to earn money.

In this excerpt from his autobiography, Olaudah Equiano describes his impressions as he was first brought onto a slave ship.

PRIMARY SOURCE

The first object which saluted my eyes when I arrived on the coast was the sea, and a slave ship . . . These filled me with astonishment, which was soon converted into terror . . . [T]hey made ready with many fearful noises, and we were all put under deck . . . now that the whole ship's cargo were confined together, [the stench of the hold] became absolutely pestilential [deadly]. The closeness of the place, and the heat of the climate, added to the number in the ship, which was so crowded that each had scarcely room to turn himself, almost suffocated us. . . This wretched situation was again aggravated by the galling of the chains, . . . and the filth of the [latrines], into which the children often fell, and were almost suffocated. The shrieks of the women, and groans of the dying, rendered the whole a scene of horror almost inconceivable.

—from *The Interesting Narrative of the Life of Olaudah Equiano, or Gustavus Vassa, the African*, 1789

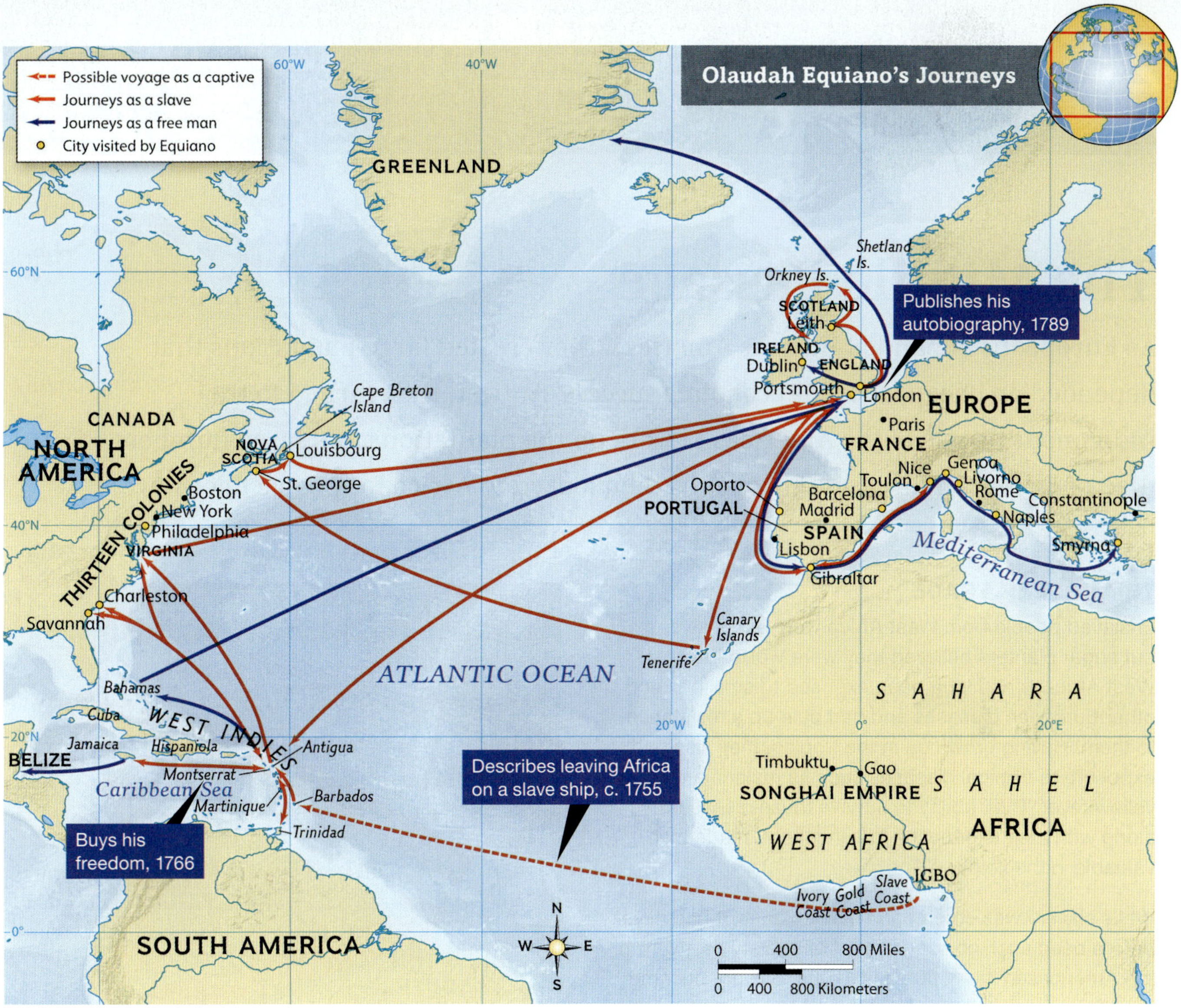
Olaudah Equiano's Journeys
Possible voyage as a captive
Journeys as a slave
Journeys as a free man
City visited by Equiano
GREENLAND
CANADA
NORTH AMERICA
THIRTEEN COLONIES
NOVA SCOTIA
Cape Breton Island
Louisbourg
St. George
Boston
New York
Philadelphia
VIRGINIA
Charleston
Savannah
Bahamas
Cuba
Jamaica
Hispaniola
WEST INDIES
Antigua
Montserrat
Martinique
Barbados
Trinidad
BELIZE
Caribbean Sea
Buys his freedom, 1766
SOUTH AMERICA
ATLANTIC OCEAN
Describes leaving Africa on a slave ship, c. 1755
Shetland Is.
Orkney Is.
SCOTLAND
Leith
IRELAND
Dublin
ENGLAND
Portsmouth
London
Publishes his autobiography, 1789
EUROPE
Paris
FRANCE
Nice
Toulon
Genoa
Livorno
Rome
Naples
Constantinople
Smyrna
Oporto
PORTUGAL
Barcelona
Madrid
SPAIN
Lisbon
Gibraltar
Mediterranean Sea
Canary Islands
Tenerife
SAHARA
SAHEL
Timbuktu
Gao
SONGHAI EMPIRE
WEST AFRICA
AFRICA
Ivory Coast
Gold Coast
Slave Coast
IGBO
60°W
40°W
20°W
0°
20°E
60°N
40°N
20°N
0°
N
S
E
W
0 400 800 Miles
0 400 800 Kilometers

After paying the man who had enslaved him and gaining his freedom, Equiano moved to London, where he lived as a free man and often set off on new sea adventures. In his later years, he wrote about his experiences and lectured to audiences about the evils of slavery. As an antislavery activist, he hoped his actions would help turn the tide of public opinion against slavery.

IMPORTANCE OF HIS WRITINGS

Historians have confirmed the accuracy of Equiano's account of his adult activities. However, some scholars question the accuracy of his retelling of his earliest life. Some evidence, though inconclusive, suggests that Equiano was actually born in the Americas and may have used other slaves' stories to create his description of Africa and the voyage across the Atlantic. This possibility serves as an important reminder to be cautious when using memoirs to learn about history.

Still, Equiano's *Interesting Narrative* is important to the study of history because it provides a firsthand account of life under slavery in the 1700s. As one of the first slave narratives, the book aided the cause of **abolition**, the movement to end slavery, as did Equiano's speaking tours. Equiano's earnings from the book made him the wealthiest black man in England at the time.

HISTORICAL THINKING

1. **READING CHECK** What is the significance of *The Interesting Narrative of the Life of Olaudah Equiano, or Gustavus Vassa, the African*?
2. **INTERPRET MAPS** Use the map to describe Equiano's journeys as a slave.
3. **COMPARE AND CONTRAST** How was Equiano's experience different from that of most enslaved Africans in the 1700s?

2.2

MAIN IDEA The trip over the Middle Passage, in which slaves were transported from West Africa to the Americas, was the largest forced migration in human history and one of the most brutal.

The Middle Passage

As Europeans expanded into the Americas, they created large plantations that depended on cheap labor for economic success. At first, they turned to the indigenous people of the Americas to work on the plantations, but large numbers died of European diseases. Europeans then looked to Africa for people to enslave.

TRIANGULAR TRADE

Enslaved people from West Africa were expensive, but sugar planters believed they were worth the cost. West Africans had long been exposed to smallpox and other European diseases and had built up a resistance to them. Having grown up in the tropics, they also had exposure to tropical diseases such as malaria and yellow fever. Their ability to survive these diseases, along with their experience in agriculture, made them valuable in the fields.

While slavery was common in many places, it had never before been such an integral part of society as it was in the Americas in the 1600s and 1700s. Slavery became central to every aspect of social and economic life in the Americas. In West Africa, many groups had traditionally enslaved their captured enemies, but now they gained wealth by selling slaves to Europeans. Unlike earlier enslaved people, who were often incorporated into their captor's society through marriage, these Africans were stripped of all rights and had little hope of escaping bondage.

The Atlantic slave trade was part of a network often called the **triangular trade**, which connected Europe, Africa, and the Americas from the 1500s through the 1800s. The network is named for the shape the trade route formed. On the first leg of the route, European ships loaded with manufactured goods such as guns and cloth sailed into West African ports. After exchanging these goods for enslaved Africans, European traders then set off on the second leg of the journey, the Middle Passage. This part of the route took enslaved West Africans to the Americas, where they were traded for products such as sugar, tobacco, rum, and timber. On the third leg of the trade network, ships loaded with these products returned to Europe, where the products were sold or exchanged for cloth or guns, and the cycle began again.

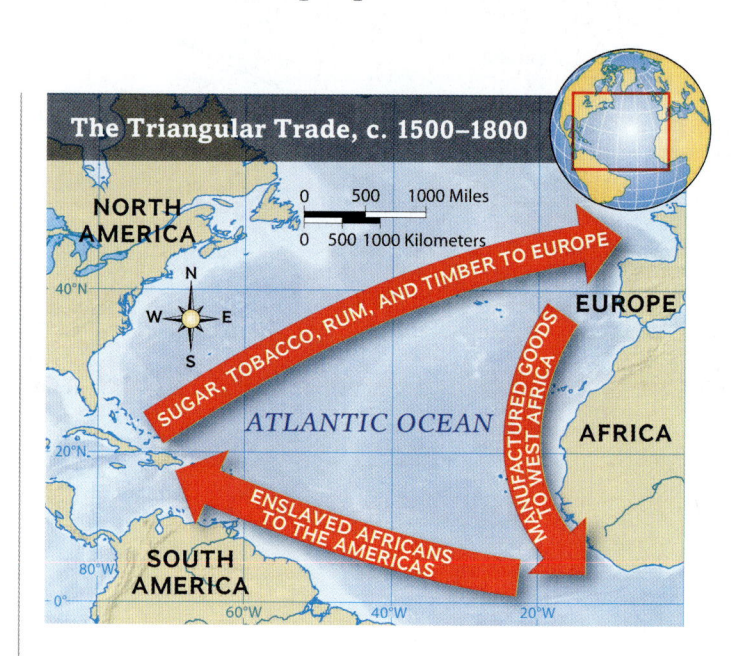

The Europeans who controlled the triangular trade made huge profits. Indian Ocean trade was also connected to this Atlantic trade network because Europeans often included such commodities as Asian textiles as trade items. The largest profits in this slave-based system of sugar production and trade went to Europeans who owned the ships and plantations. But African merchants and kings also profited and increased their local power.

HORRORS ABOARD SLAVE SHIPS

The most horrific part of the triangular trade was the Middle Passage, in which humans were transported as if they were inanimate trade items. European slave traders often rationalized, or attempted to justify, their inhumane treatment of Africans by claiming that, as Christians, they were rescuing Africans from "paganism." As more Africans converted to Christianity, those profiting from

PLAN OF LOWER DECK WITH THE STOWAGE OF 292 SLAVES
130 OF THESE BEING STOWED UNDER THE SHELVES AS SHEWN IN FIGURE B & FIGURE 5.

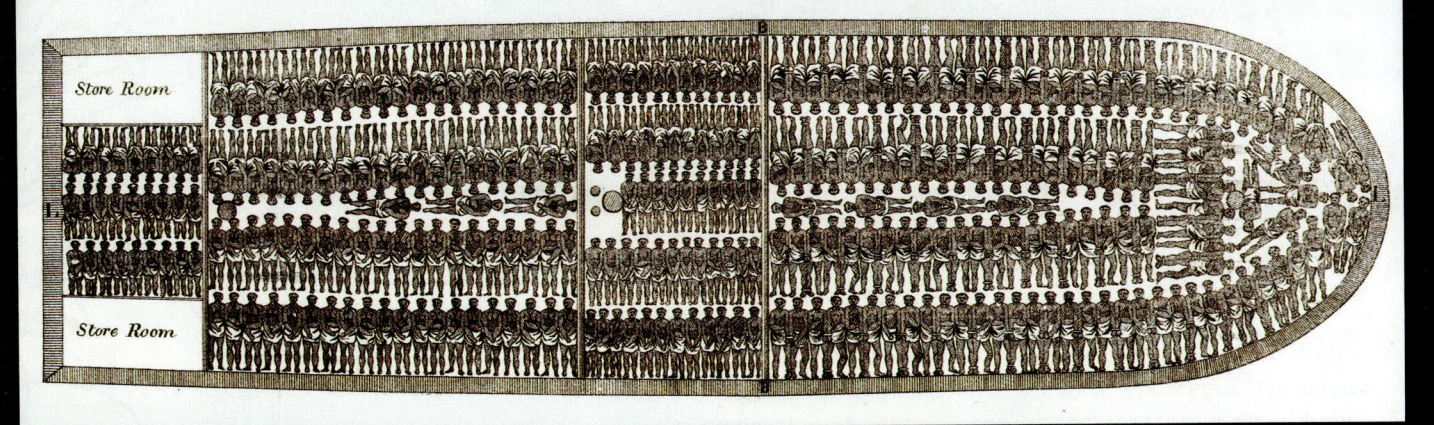

The Slave Ship *Brooks*

Abolitionists used these diagrams of the British slave ship *Brooks* in their campaign against slavery. The diagram above illustrates how captive Africans were tightly packed into the cargo hold while the cross-section at right shows how little headroom captives had, just 2 feet, 7 inches or less. The diagram at the far right provides a closer view of captives crammed into the ship.

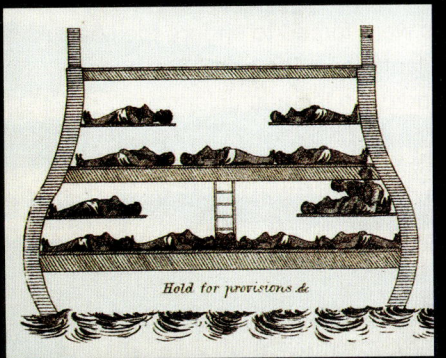

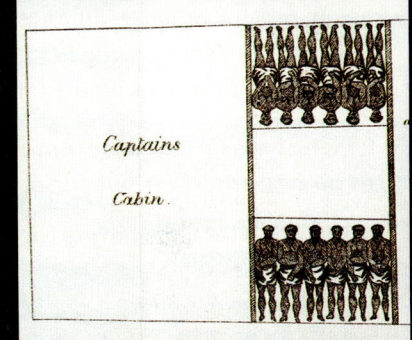

---

slavery turned to **racism**, the belief that the color of a person's skin makes them superior or inferior, to justify their motives.

Enslaved Africans experienced brutal conditions aboard a ship during the Middle Passage. Below the ship's deck, African men lay shackled in a hunched position, so close together they could hardly move. Women and children were allowed more movement because captors believed they were less likely to rise up in rebellion. Small groups of slaves were regularly taken above deck and forced to move their arms and legs wildly to prevent loss of muscle.

On a typical ship, about 400 to 600 slaves were squeezed into the slave quarters, which grew unbearably hot and filled with noxious air. Any slave who showed the slightest hint of rebelling was beaten severely. Many enslaved Africans died of diseases such as dysentery, scurvy, and smallpox. A typical trip took from about 3 to 12 weeks, and as many as 20 percent of the captives did not survive. Slave traders simply regarded such loss as part of the cost of running a business.

In all, more than 12 million Africans endured the long and harrowing voyage across the Atlantic. An unknown number died while held in captivity at the European slave forts or on the journey from their homes to the coast. The slaves transported over the Middle Passage had little idea of what to expect when they reached their destination. Most would face harsh conditions as enslaved workers on plantations.

Great Britain, France, Holland, and other European nations gained great wealth through the triangular trade, but by the late 1700s, many people began to speak up against the evils of African enslavement. Some were motivated by their belief in the value of all human life, others by Christian religious conviction. Many Christians could not reconcile slavery with their belief that all people should be treated with love and charity. Eventually, Parliament would ban British participation in the slave trade, as you will read about later.

HISTORICAL THINKING

1. **READING CHECK** What was the Middle Passage?
2. **MAKE INFERENCES** Why did slave traders pack so many enslaved Africans on the ships that traveled to the Americas?
3. **INTERPRET MAPS** How did the triangular trade reflect the structure of the colonial economy?

2.3 A Global Commodity: Sugar

For many people, their first taste of sugar marks the beginning of a lifelong love affair with it. Early in the ancient world, sugarcane only grew in New Guinea, an island in the South Pacific Ocean, but it eventually spread to India and Southwest Asia. After the Arabs turned sugar production and processing into an industry during the Middle Ages, demand for sugar increased. The problem was, the supply of sugarcane was limited because it grew best in a hot, tropical climate.

In part, European explorers sailed to the Americas in search of places to cultivate sugarcane. They discovered that Brazil and the Caribbean islands were perfect for that purpose. But the work involved in growing, harvesting, and processing the cane was brutal. As a result, millions of enslaved Africans were forced to endure the Middle Passage and labor on sugarcane plantations. By the 1700s, sugar—the oil of its day—was a hot commodity on the triangular trade.

In what ways can a commodity such as sugar impact the lives of people all over the world?

A SPOONFUL OF SUGAR

The man shown here is ready to harvest sugarcane on a plantation in present-day Brazil. It's no easy task to farm sugarcane by hand—the tall stalks often grow more than 10 feet high, and farmers can't relax after the stalks are gathered. Sugarcane has to be processed within hours after it's cut. Otherwise, bacteria in the soil can feed on the stalk's sucrose, or natural sugar, and cause significant production loss. Harvesting and processing sugarcane can go on for months. All to satisfy the world's sweet tooth.

Africans in the Atlantic World 523

A SWEET SNACK

Some people cut off the tough outer layer and chew on fresh sugarcane stalks like those pictured here. When you chew on a stalk, you can savor the sweet juice, but you have to spit out the stringy fibers. Chewing on sugarcane is probably healthier than eating refined sugar. And many people consume far too much of the processed product. The U.S. government suggests an average intake of about 13 teaspoons of sugar per day, while most Americans consume about 25.

HEALTH	• Fruit sugar, which is stored as fat, allowed our earliest ancestors to survive harsh winters and food shortages.	• By 500 C.E., sugar was used in India as a medicine to treat headaches and other ailments.	• Today, doctors believe that excessive sugar consumption can lead to obesity, high blood pressure, and Type 2 diabetes.
PRODUCTION	• Powerful presses crush sugarcane stalks to extract the sugar from them.	• Sugar beets are sliced and then immersed in hot water to extract the sugar.	• As the juices extracted from sugarcane and sugar beets cool, pure sugar crystals form.
VALUE	• During the Middle Ages, sugar was as expensive as nutmeg, saffron, and other luxury spices.	• By 1750, the price of sugar fell, making it affordable for the middle classes and, in time, the poor.	• In the modern world, sugar is inexpensive and found in many foods but has no nutritional value.
HISTORY	• When the Persians invaded India in the 6th century B.C.E. and discovered sugarcane, they called it "the reed which gives honey without bees."	• In the 700s C.E., Arab armies conquered Persia and spread what they learned about sugar production to other lands.	• Europeans got their first taste of sugar during the Crusades, which began in the 11th century, when soldiers brought home food from Muslim regions.
ECONOMICS	• In the 1400s, when only the very wealthy could afford sugar, the Spanish queen Isabella I gave her daughters a box of sugar as a special gift.	• During the triangular trade, the sale of sugar made up one-third of Europe's economy, and British colonists called it "white gold."	• With the development of sugar beet farming in the 19th century, sugar became widely affordable, and its consumption skyrocketed.

What do the photos in this lesson reveal about the process of refining sugar and the impact of the sugar industry on human lives?

MODERN SUGARCANE PROCESSING

Instead of a windmill, workers today use a machine like this one in India to press and extract sugarcane juice. Though not a fruit or vegetable juice, the liquid from raw sugarcane is consumed by many people, especially in areas where the plant is grown. Unlike processed sugarcane products, this liquid is said to have health benefits, such as boosting the immune system and fighting infection.

2.4

MAIN IDEA During the years of the Atlantic slave trade, enslaved Africans relied on a variety of strategies and resources to resist, cope with, and escape from slavery in the Americas.

Resistance to Slavery

It's almost impossible to imagine what it would be like to be captured suddenly and then face a lifetime of slavery. Undoubtedly, a person would have to draw upon every possible resource to carry on. Among the resources Africans called upon were music, religion, and their sense of community.

SLAVE LABOR ON PLANTATIONS

As you have learned, from the 1500s to the late 1700s, Europeans developed a large-scale form of agriculture in the Americas: the plantation system. Africans became unwilling participants in an enterprise that depended on slave labor to produce agricultural products.

Over time, many successful sugar planters in the Caribbean became absentee owners who used their profits to build impressive country houses, including some of the finest estates in France and Britain. The work of overseeing slave labor usually went to lower-status European immigrants, who were often harsh supervisors. The life of a slave on a sugar plantation was grueling. Enslaved Africans performed all the backbreaking work of planting, weeding, harvesting, and processing sugarcane. They were treated more like machines than human beings, and many were literally worked to death. Sunday was their only day of rest.

Later, other types of plantations, such as tobacco plantations in Virginia and rice and indigo plantations in the Carolinas, would grow prosperous through the labor of enslaved Africans. As you will learn, a big change came in the late 1700s with the beginning of the Industrial Revolution. British factories needed more and more raw cotton to make clothing and other products, and by the early 1800s, Native Americans were being driven off the land to make way for cotton plantations, which relied on slave labor.

This illustration from 1667 depicts the manufacturing of sugar by enslaved Africans on a Caribbean plantation.

WAYS OF RESISTING BONDAGE

Everywhere in the Americas, enslaved Africans looked for ways to resist their captivity and escape bondage. Slaveholders and overseers were always on the lookout for any resistance—and they reacted to it brutally. In his autobiography, Olaudah Equiano tells of a slave trader who cut off the leg of a slave for running away.

Usually, enslaved Africans found more subtle ways to express their defiance. Although these smaller acts did not lead to freedom, they helped enslaved men and women cope with their situation. Slaves sang songs and told stories based on African cultural traditions. Often, the songs and stories ridiculed plantation owners, using coded language the slaveholders could not understand. Slaveholders knew that Africans frequently used drums to communicate, so they banned the musical instruments from their quarters. Despite this, enslaved people were still able to relay messages through rhythm. Slaves also purposely slowed down their work, broke farm tools, and feigned illness as ways to impede, or hinder, the plantation owners' financial success. However, such resistance often resulted in a beating.

Religion also served as a survival aid. Praying alone or with others helped restore dignity and provide hope for a better life. In areas with large African populations, enslaved people merged their existing beliefs with Christianity. For example, in Brazil and Cuba, Yoruba gods called *orishas* were transformed into Catholic saints. In British North America, enslaved people focused on aspects of Christianity most closely connected to their plight. They sang hymns of liberation and were inspired by biblical stories, such as that of Moses leading the enslaved Israelites to freedom.

ESCAPING TO FREEDOM

Enslaved people who managed to escape to freedom needed help to survive and to avoid recapture. Options for escaped slaves included joining pirate groups in the Caribbean, settling among Native American populations, or forming their own **autonomous**, or self-governing, communities.

As early as the 16th century, escaped slaves banded together to form their own communities. Called **maroon communities**, these self-governing groups of escaped slaves were common in the Caribbean and in coastal areas of Central and South America. The word *maroon* comes from a Spanish word meaning "wild or untamed," but it came to be used as a name for an escaped slave.

The largest and most powerful maroon community was Palmares in Brazil. Founded in the early 17th century, it had tens of thousands of residents who

Harriet Tubman was a former slave who helped hundreds of enslaved Africans in North America escape to freedom in the 1800s. She often used coded songs to communicate with freedom seekers. On one trip, she used the following song to announce her return to a group she had left in hiding and to tell them it was safe to approach her.

PRIMARY SOURCE

Oh go down, Moses,
Way down into Egypt's land,
Tell old Pharaoh,
Let my people go.

Oh Pharaoh said he would go cross,
Let my people go,
And don't get lost in the wilderness,
Let my people go.

You may hinder me here, but you can't up there,
Let my people go,
He sits in the Heaven and answers prayer,
Let my people go!

—from *Harriet: The Moses of Her People* by Sarah H. Bradford, 1886

Maroon communities still exist in the Caribbean and in parts of South and North America. At the annual Accompong Maroon Festival in Jamaica (shown above) community members commemorate the signing of a peace treaty between the maroons and the British in 1739, which recognized the maroons' freedom.

defended themselves against the Portuguese until the Portuguese defeated them in 1694. Significant maroon communities also developed in Venezuela, Guyana, and Florida. In some places, escaped slaves assimilated into indigenous communities. In Florida, for example, Africans who escaped from slavery in the Carolinas and Georgia formed an alliance with the Creek, a Native American tribe. Escaped Africans who lived among Native Americans in Florida and intermarried with them came to be known as Black Seminoles.

SLAVERY'S IMPACT ON AFRICA

As early as the 16th century, the Atlantic slave trade had brought conflict to some West African societies, such as the Kongo kingdom. Over the next two centuries, the demand for African slaves dramatically increased as the Caribbean sugar industry grew. Few West African communities escaped slavery's effects on their social, economic, and military institutions.

The Asante kingdom was one society whose leaders took part in the Atlantic slave trade. Asante was a growing power in the rain forest region of 18th-century West Africa. Asante rulers captured many prisoners as they expanded their kingdom through warfare. Before the rise of the Atlantic slave trade, some war captives would have been sent home through prisoner exchanges or redeemed for ransom. Others would have been kept as household servants and farmworkers. With the rise of the Atlantic slave trade, however, the Asante exchanged captured slaves for valuable imported goods, such as rum, cloth, and guns.

The kings of Dahomey, another West African kingdom, were more aggressive in using the slave trade to advance state interests. They traded enslaved people for guns to build a military advantage over their neighbors. Other rulers then found that they needed to conduct a similar trade for their own self-defense. They felt forced to sell Africans from neighboring societies in order to protect their own people.

This vicious cycle was reinforced by differing European and African gender preferences. Europeans preferred to buy young males, who fetched high prices because they could do hard physical labor. In contrast, West Africans preferred female slaves, who were valued as agricultural and domestic workers. In addition, female slaves could give birth to children and add to the population and labor force of a village or clan. Leaders of societies like the Asante and Dahomey could doubly benefit from the slave trade by exchanging imprisoned men for imported goods while keeping captive women for their own social and economic benefit.

Thelma Maiben-Owens, a present-day resident of Africatown, takes photos of her ancestors' graves at the Old Plateau Cemetery in Mobile, Alabama.

THE *CLOTILDA*

Even though the United States banned the import of enslaved Africans in 1808, plantation owners continued to make illegal slave runs to provide labor for the booming cotton industry. In 1860, an Alabama plantation owner named Timothy Meaher chartered a schooner called the *Clotilda* and enlisted its captain, William Foster, to sail to the kingdom of Dahomey, where Foster bought approximately 110 Africans. The *Clotilda* and its human cargo sailed back to Alabama, entering Mobile Bay under the cover of night. Once the slaves were unloaded, the *Clotilda* was taken up the Mobile River, burned, and sunk.

After being freed by Union soldiers in 1865, the *Clotilda*'s survivors used money they had earned to buy land just north of the city of Mobile. They created a settlement called Africatown, where they formed a society based on that of their homeland. Many of the survivors' descendants still live there today and grew up hearing stories of the ship that brought their ancestors to Alabama.

In May 2019, the Alabama Historical Commission announced that a shipwreck discovered in a remote area of the Mobile River was almost certainly the *Clotilda*. The discovery was funded by the National Geographic Society—with Dr. Fredrik Hiebert, archaeologist-in-residence, as part of the survey team—and confirmed by archaeological analysis of the sunken vessel against existing records and registration documents.

In the spring of 2020, the U.S. government allocated money to conserve the site of the *Clotilda*. It remains to be determined whether the ship will be raised and restored or left at the bottom of the river as a national slave ship memorial, but its discovery has brought validation and renewal to the residents of Africatown.

The Atlantic slave trade transformed West African society, uprooting men, women, and children from their homes. The fabric of family life in Africa began to unravel as more and more people were taken away. Life became difficult and insecure as African villagers began to fear capture. The loss of population through the export of slaves harmed economic growth. Productivity suffered as Africa lost many of its young, most able workers. The amount of money gained by the sale of an enslaved person was far less than that individual may have contributed to Africa's economy over a lifetime of work. In general, the destabilization of Africa's society and economy set the stage for the entry of outside countries into the affairs of the continent.

HISTORICAL THINKING

1. **READING CHECK** In what ways did enslaved Africans resist their captivity?
2. **DRAW CONCLUSIONS** How did Asante and Dahomey doubly benefit from the Atlantic slave trade?
3. **COMPARE AND CONTRAST** How did slavery differ for male and female captives?
4. **ANALYZE CAUSE AND EFFECT** How were the economy and social structure of West African societies impacted by the Atlantic slave trade?

CHAPTER 18 AFRICANS IN THE ATLANTIC WORLD REVIEW

VOCABULARY

Match each vocabulary term with its correct definition.

1. slave narrative
2. Middle Passage
3. succession
4. maroon community
5. autonomous
6. manumission
7. triangular trade
8. abolition
9. racism

a. a trade network connecting Europe, Africa, and the Americas between the 1500s and the 1800s
b. self-governing
c. the release from slavery
d. the movement to end slavery
e. the process by which a new leader is chosen to follow an outgoing leader
f. a written account of the life of a former slave
g. the belief that a particular race of people is superior to other races
h. a self-governing group of escaped slaves
i. the journey by slave ships across the Atlantic Ocean from West Africa to the Americas

READING STRATEGY
IDENTIFY MAIN IDEAS AND DETAILS

Use a graphic organizer like the one below to identify details that support the main idea about the Atlantic slave trade. Then answer the question that follows.

Main Idea
The Atlantic slave trade had a devastating impact on family and community life in West Africa.

- Detail
- Detail
- Detail

10. How did the Atlantic slave trade affect family and community life in West Africa?

MAIN IDEAS

Answer the following questions. Support your answers with evidence from the chapter.

11. How did Christianity spread to Central and South Africa? **LESSON 1.1**
12. Why were Sunni Ali and Askia Muhammad important in West Africa's history? **LESSON 1.2**
13. According to the slave narrative written by Olaudah Equiano, what were conditions like on the Middle Passage? **LESSON 2.1**
14. How did European expansion into the Americas affect Africa? **LESSON 2.2**
15. Why did escaped slaves band together in maroon communities? **LESSON 2.4**

HISTORICAL THINKING

Answer the following questions. Support your answers with evidence from the chapter.

16. **COMPARE AND CONTRAST** How did Africans and Europeans differ in their response to Kimpa Vita's ideas?
17. **MAKE INFERENCES** Why do you think cowrie shells were used as currency in West Africa?
18. **SYNTHESIZE** What political, social, and economic impacts did Islam have on Africa?
19. **ANALYZE CAUSE AND EFFECT** How did Askia Muhammad build a successful empire?
20. **DRAW CONCLUSIONS** Why did many slaveholders react brutally to slave resistance?
21. **DESCRIBE** How did the treatment of enslaved people in West Africa change over time?
22. **MAKE GENERALIZATIONS** How did the practice of slavery conflict with religious and political principles in the United States?
23. **FORM AND SUPPORT OPINIONS** Do you think Olaudah Equiano's narrative is a reliable source for learning about slavery in the Americas? Support your answer with evidence.

INTERPRET VISUALS

Study the table at right and answer the questions below.

24. During what period of time were the largest number of slaves exported from Africa? Why?

25. Slavery was abolished in the United States in 1865. How does the table reflect that fact?

The Atlantic Slave Trade: Number of Enslaved People Exported from Africa, 1450–1990

Period	Number of Slaves	Percent of Total
1450–1500	81,000	0.6%
1501–1600	338,000	2.6%
1601–1700	1,876,000	14.6%
1701–1800	6,495,000	50.7%
1801–1900	4,027,000	31.4%
Total	12,817,000	100.0%

ANALYZE SOURCES

Phillis Wheatley (1753–1784) was the first African-American poet to have her work published. Born in West Africa, Wheatley was enslaved as a young girl and sold to a family of Boston Quakers who provided her with a good education. One of the enduring themes of her poetry was freedom for all. In this excerpt from her 1773 poem "To the Right Honorable William, Earl of Dartmouth" Wheatley interrupts her argument for American independence to explain her own desire for freedom. Read the excerpt and answer the questions that follow.

> Should you, my lord, while you peruse my song,
> Wonder from whence my love of Freedom sprung,
> Whence flow these wishes for the common good,
> By feeling hearts alone best understood,
> I, young in life, by seeming cruel fate
> Was snatch'd from Afric's fancy'd happy seat:
> What pangs excruciating must molest [disturb],
> What sorrows labor in my parent's breast?
> Steel'd was that soul and by no misery move'd
> That from a father seiz'd his babe belov'd:
> Such, such my case. And can I then but pray
> Others may never feel tyrannic sway?

26. Who is Wheatley referring to as "Steel'd was that soul and by no misery move'd"?

27. According to the poem, why does Wheatley feel uniquely qualified to argue for independence?

CONNECT TO YOUR LIFE

28. **ARGUMENT** Current genetic research indicates that the concept of race has no biological basis. It is merely a human construction. Do you think that knowledge of this research will put an end to racism? Write an essay stating your opinion and explaining the reasons for it.

TIPS

- Conduct responsible online research to review what genetic researchers say about the concept of race.

- Form and clearly state your opinion on the effects of this research on the existence of racism in today's society.

- Provide reasons from your research and your own experience to support your opinion.

- Write a conclusion that summarizes your argument.

NATIONAL GEOGRAPHIC | CONNECTION

The Epic Quest for a Northwest Passage

BY GREG MILLER Adapted from "These Maps Show the Epic Quest for a Northwest Passage" by Greg Miller, news.nationalgeographic.com, October 20, 2016

You've read about how the spirit of seafaring propelled European and African empires as they expanded. Had the Northwest Passage existed during this time of growth, it would have been a real game-changer.

It had to be there: an ocean at the top of the world. The ancient Greeks drew it on their maps, and for centuries, the rest of Europe did too. Since the 1500s, countless men have died trying to find a maritime shortcut across the Arctic that would open up new trade routes to Asia. Now, thanks to a warming planet, the long-sought Northwest Passage actually exists, at least for part of the year.

This 1872 map erroneously shows the Gulf Stream and other warm currents feeding an open sea around the North Pole.

The idea of a northern ocean passage dates back at least to the second century C.E. Ptolemy and other ancient Greek geographers believed Earth had four habitable zones balanced by two uninhabitable frigid zones—often thought to be water—at the top and bottom of the globe. But it wasn't until the early 16th century, after the voyages of Columbus, that the idea of a Northwest Passage really took hold among Europeans. Columbus, after all, had sailed west looking for a sea route to the East. Instead, he found a continent blocking the way. The Northwest Passage would be a way around this continent.

Maps from this period are filled with the wild imaginings of mapmakers, from nonexistent bays and islands to sea monsters. Early explorers also occasionally adjusted the facts. The Englishman Martin Frobisher made three voyages in search of the Northwest Passage in the late 1500s. He didn't find it. But he pretended to have discovered more straits than he did.

Perhaps the most famous attempt to find the Northwest Passage was the expedition led by Sir John Franklin in 1845. A British Navy officer, Franklin had led two previous expeditions to the Arctic. But this time the expedition didn't return on schedule, and Franklin's wife, Lady Jane, began pressing the British government to send a search party, which they did in 1848. Newspaper reports on the hunt for the missing expedition gripped the British public, but all searchers found were graves of men who had died early on and a few scattered notes and relics. The two boats in the expedition had become trapped in ice, and all 129 men, including Franklin, had perished. Over 160 years later, the wreckage of the two boats, the H.M.S. *Erebus* and *Terror*, was finally located.

Unbeknownst to Franklin and other explorers, their expeditions coincided with what scientists call the Little Ice Age, a period of several centuries of unusual cold in the Arctic. As temperatures began to climb toward the end of the 19th century, the long sought Northwest Passage finally opened up.

The Norwegian explorer Roald Amundsen completed the first journey entirely by boat through the Northwest Passage in 1906. It took three years and two winters on the ice. More recently, it's been getting easier. As polar ice has melted, the route has become more accessible. In 2016, a cruise ship carrying 1,700 people became the first passenger liner to complete the passage. The melting of Arctic sea ice has raised the possibility of new trade routes and energy production, as well as the potential for territorial conflicts and environmental damage to a relatively untouched part of Earth.

For better or worse, a new chapter in the storied history of the Arctic is just beginning. ∎

UNIT INQUIRY — UNIT 6: Design a Conqueror's Toolbox

Staging the Question

In this unit, you learned how and why nations sought to expand their territories and influence through trade, conquest, and the exploration of land and sea. In Africa, Asia, and Russia, land-based empires pushed their borders outward in aggressive quests to control and incorporate new lands. Meanwhile, European powers vied for supremacy over the seas in a bid to dominate trade and establish colonies in Asia and the Americas. Advances in seafaring technology tempted rulers toward plans for expansion into distant realms. How did the most successful empires use the tools at their disposal to explore new territories and expand their existing territories?

ASSIGNMENT

Choose three nations in this unit that successfully expanded their territory and influence on land and sea.

Evaluate the methods used by the nations' rulers to promote exploration and expansion.

Think about how each nation used the resources at its disposal.

Based on your analysis of the most effective strategies for expansion, create a conqueror's toolbox of items and ideas that would allow a nation to most efficiently become an empire.

Supporting Questions: Begin by developing supporting questions to guide your research. For example: What new technology can you use to support exploration and expansion of your empire? Research the answers in this unit and in other sources, both print and online. You might want to use a graphic organizer like this one to record your questions and answers.

Summative Performance Task: Use the answers to your questions to help you determine which items you will include in your conqueror's toolbox. You can include tangible items such as maps or navigation tools. To create tools for implementing ideas and strategies, write instruction sheets or manuals with text and illustrations.

Present: Share your toolbox with the class. You might consider one of these options:

CREATE A VIRTUAL TOOLBOX
Find images of the tangible items you want to put in the toolbox and assemble them on a web page. Write a caption for each item, explaining why it is an essential tool for expanding an empire. Write at least two instruction sheets for expansion strategies and link them to your web page.

HOLD AN ACADEMIC POSTER SESSION
Create a poster featuring images of the tools with captions, and print copies of your instruction sheets. Display your poster and instruction sheets alongside those of your classmates and take time to review and comment on each other's toolboxes.

Take Informed Action:

UNDERSTAND Identify and describe a country in the news today that is using tools or strategies such as the ones you described to dominate or conquer other countries.

ASSESS Examine the consequences of this country's actions and its effects on the territories it is trying to dominate.

ACT Share your concerns by researching organizations that oppose such expansions and finding out what types of support they need. Then find a way to offer your support.

Global Explorations and Expansions 533

UNIT 7

CRITICAL VIEWING

The French flag—also known as the Tricolor—unfurls under the Arc de Triomphe in the middle of Paris. France adopted the blue, white, and red design after the French Revolution in 1789 and again after the revolution of 1830. Emperor Napoleon commissioned the arch in 1806 to celebrate a military victory. Based on this information, what can you infer about the importance of these two symbols to the nation of France?

New Ideas and Revolution
1543–1848

UNIT 7 New Ideas and Revolution

WORLD EVENTS
1543–1859

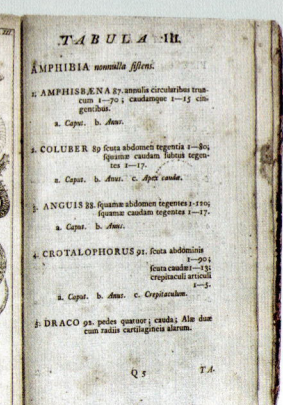

1735 EUROPE Carl Linnaeus publishes *Systema Naturae* in which he describes a system for classifying plants and animals. *(pages from an edition of Systema Naturae)*

1643 EUROPE Louis XIV begins his reign as king of France and rules as an absolute monarch. *(symbol of Louis XIV, the Sun King, on the gate of the courtyard at Versailles)*

c. 1750 EUROPE The Industrial Revolution begins. *(an early loom)*

1543 EUROPE Nicolaus Copernicus publishes his theory that the sun is the center of the universe.

1632 EUROPE Italian astronomer Galileo Galilei publishes *Dialogue Concerning the Two Chief World Systems*, arguing against the prevailing church view that Earth is the center of the universe and supporting Copernicus's sun-centered model.

1690 EUROPE Englishman John Locke publishes *Two Treatises of Government*, declaring that humans are born free and equal.

1650 AFRICA More than 40 trading posts in West Africa provide slaves for the Atlantic slave trade. *(Elmina Castle, a historic slave fortress, in Ghana)*

HISTORICAL THINKING

MAKE INFERENCES How might Locke's declaration that humans are born free and equal have influenced later events?

1776 AMERICAS The American colonies declare their independence from British rule. *(mural of the adoption of the Declaration of Independence at the National Archives)*

1859 EUROPE English naturalist Charles Darwin publishes *On the Origin of Species*, which explains his theory of evolution. *(portrait of Darwin in 1877)*

1799 EUROPE Napoleon Bonaparte seizes control of the French government. *(bicorn hat that once belonged to Napoleon)*

1821 AMERICAS Venezuela, with the help of Simón Bolívar, and Mexico gain independence from Spain.

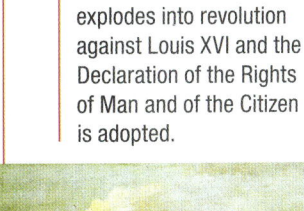

1800 — **1900**

1789 EUROPE France explodes into revolution against Louis XVI and the Declaration of the Rights of Man and of the Citizen is adopted.

1848 EUROPE Nationalism stirs unrest and revolution across Europe.

1857 ASIA Indian soldiers revolt against British rule in India.

1768 EUROPE Botanist Joseph Banks and Captain James Cook of Great Britain begin a three-year journey around the globe, collecting plant and animal specimens and carrying out astronomical observations. *(painting of the H.M.S. Endeavour, Captain Cook's ship)*

1804 AMERICAS Haiti wins independence from France. *(Haitian flag with the city of Port-au-Prince in the background)*

537

CHAPTER 19

Europe in the Age of Scientific Revolution
1543–1848

HISTORICAL THINKING How can scientific advances challenge previously accepted ideas and lead to new knowledge?

SECTION 1 **Europe's Struggle for Stability**

SECTION 2 **Scientific Advances**

SECTION 3 **Practical Science**

538 CHAPTER 19

CRITICAL VIEWING
The luminous Milky Way, thousands of light years from Earth, stretches across the night sky. Powerful telescopes, such as this large radio telescope system in Chile, help astronomers observe and discover more about the stars and planets. What details in the photograph convey the scale of the universe?

Europe in the Age of Scientific Revolution 539

1.1

MAIN IDEA Religious and political differences caused discord both within and between France and England.

Power Struggles in France and England

If you had the power to tell people how to live and what to believe, would you do it? Louis XIV of France did just that. He amassed tremendous power, insisted on Catholicism as France's religion, and had his subjects fund his building projects and wars.

FRENCH AND ENGLISH DISCORD

The English and French monarchies had been great rivals since the Middle Ages. Though, as ambitious monarchs in both countries claimed ever greater power, their plans were complicated by religious differences within their own realms as well as conflicts with nobility who resented losing some of their own authority. In the end, both countries found paths to political stability but followed very different models of government. In France, **absolute monarchy** gave the king unquestioned and limitless power. In England, the powers of a monarch were limited by a **constitutional monarchy** that balanced power between a monarch and Parliament.

The discord between France and England was so much a part of the 16th century that English poet and playwright William Shakespeare wrote the conflict into many of his plays. In *Henry VI*, Shakespeare writes, "'Tis better using France than trusting France," and one of the characters describes the French king as "weak of courage and in judgment."

Shakespeare's plays marked the pinnacle of the English Renaissance in theater. His works depict the intrigues of kings and nobles as well as the lives of common people. English audiences, including Queen Elizabeth and her successor King James, were captivated by Shakespeare's work. Across the English Channel, however, the French were not so pleased. Reading the plays 100 years after Shakespeare's death, the French philosopher Voltaire expressed his opinion: Shakespeare's works were "contrary to good taste" and Shakespeare was "a savage."

The Armada Portrait of Elizabeth I commemorates the great sea battle of 1588, when the English fleet defeated the Spanish Armada, which had been sent to invade England and overthrow the queen. In the painting, two windows behind Queen Elizabeth depict the outcome of the battle. In the left window, a message of Elizabeth's victory appears. In the right window, the Spanish Armada is shown sinking as the English fleet returns to shore.

540 CHAPTER 19

QUEEN ELIZABETH

Under the major influence of **Elizabeth I**, English society entered the 17th century in relative peace and with increasing national confidence. Elizabeth supported the Church of England established by her father, Henry VIII. As you have read, Henry VIII formed the church after the pope refused to annul his marriage to his first wife. He formed the Church of England to defy the pope's authority, but he retained many Catholic rites and traditions, including powerful bishops.

When Henry's oldest daughter, Mary, took the throne before Elizabeth in 1553, she tried to return England to a Catholic state and brutally persecuted Protestants. Elizabeth brought back Protestant rule, but she was more interested in stability than in religious dogma. She worked closely with Parliament and brought peace through compromise with Catholics.

Elizabeth never married and had no children, so a relative, James Stuart, took the throne as **James I** upon her death in 1603. Unlike Elizabeth, James clashed with Parliament. He believed he had a God-given right to rule as an absolute monarch, and he was unwilling to share power with Parliament. Shortly after James became king, a group of church leaders met to request a new translation of the Bible, as existing versions had many errors. James assembled a group of about 50 translators and scholars, and in 1611 the King James Bible was the result. Even so, English Protestants, especially the English Calvinists, who were Protestant reformers known as Puritans, grew discontented with the opulent Stuart court and the luxurious lives of English bishops.

CATHOLICISM AND ABSOLUTE MONARCHY

Unlike the English, the French were predominantly Catholic. As you read earlier, however, following the murder of tens of thousands of French Protestant Huguenots in the St. Bartholomew's Day massacre of 1572, the 1598 Edict of Nantes allowed Protestants to worship in specified cities.

But **Louis XIV**, who ascended the throne as a five-year-old child in 1643, would become a monarch of legendary power over the following 72 years. He emphasized the Catholic nature of his kingdom as well as his divine right to rule without limits. His motto was "One King, One Law, One Faith." As a child ruler, Louis even relied on a cardinal, a high official in the Catholic Church, to guide his kingdom. Having established the Catholic Church as the "one faith," he revoked the Edict of Nantes, triggering the exodus, or flight, of about 200,000 French Protestants to areas of Calvinist control such as Switzerland, the Netherlands, and Cape Town in South Africa.

Elsewhere in Europe, Protestants objected to Louis's treatment of the Huguenots. But Louis was the envy of all who aspired to absolute power. His huge Palace of Versailles displayed his power and wealth, and he entertained with extravagant banquets and first-rate theater and music.

Jean-Baptiste Colbert Presenting Members of the Royal Academy of Science to Louis XIV was painted c. 1667 and hangs in Versailles. What details in the painting convey Louis XIV's power as an absolute monarch?

HISTORICAL THINKING

1. **READING CHECK** In what ways were England and France different in terms of religion and government?

2. **ANALYZE POINTS OF VIEW** How did Shakespeare's plays reflect discord between France and England? In what ways did they show bias?

3. **EVALUATE** Which form of government do you think was most effective in leading the country to a prosperous future, Queen Elizabeth's or King Louis XIV's? Why?

1.2

MAIN IDEA As civil war plagued England, the Thirty Years' War raged through northern Europe, leading to Prussia's rise as the strongest German state.

War, Peace, and the Rise of Prussia

Things are seldom as simple as they seem. In the case of the Thirty Years' War, the Catholics were fighting the Protestants. Then France, a staunchly Catholic state, joined the war on the side of the Protestants.

A TIME OF WARS

You remember that James I of England had clashed with Parliament. His son, Charles I, followed a similar path. He pursued war against Spain and supported Protestant rebels in France. However, Parliament blocked his ability to finance his wars and presented a petition against him. In retaliation, Charles disbanded Parliament for 11 years. When Parliament reconvened in 1640, it sought to limit the king's power. Tensions exploded, and Charles arrested several leaders of Parliament on charges of treason, or the crime of betraying one's country. The people of London reacted with violence, and the king fled, triggering the English Civil War.

Oliver Cromwell, a Puritan and member of Parliament, organized opposition to the king's forces. He and the Puritans fought to rid the Church of England of Catholic influences, destroying statues and stained glass windows much as the followers of Ulrich Zwingli had done in Switzerland more than a century earlier. After seven years of fighting, Charles I was captured and beheaded in 1649.

While war raged in England, religious hostilities spread across other countries in Europe. In Spain, Philip II aggressively imposed Catholic **orthodoxy**, established beliefs and practices, on his subjects. He killed or expelled Spain's *moriscos*, people whose families had converted from Islam to Catholicism during the 1492 expulsion of Jews and Muslims. As you have learned, he also waged war against the Dutch provinces, though by 1609 they had gained their independence.

In 1618, the Holy Roman Emperor, Ferdinand II, revoked a policy of tolerance toward Protestants, inciting the catastrophic **Thirty Years' War**. As you have learned, this was the final and most violent of Europe's religious wars. The Holy Roman Empire was supported by Catholic Habsburg rulers in Spain and Austria against the Protestant forces of Denmark and Sweden. France did not fit this pattern because although the kingdom was Catholic, it was competing with the Habsburgs for power and therefore sided with the Protestant coalition. Armies rampaged through German towns and countryside. Around eight million people perished. Rural communities suffered the most with losses of up to 30 percent of their population.

By 1644, all sides were exhausted and sent representatives to Westphalia in northern Germany to discuss peace. It took them four years to reach an agreement, but in 1648 the Peace of Westphalia finally brought some stability to Western Europe. The treaty redrew political and religious maps of Europe, splitting the area into separate states that, whether Catholic or Protestant, recognized one another's **sovereignty**, or right to control their own affairs. One important feature of the Peace of Westphalia was that ambassadors sent to represent one kingdom at the court of another could not be arrested or disturbed, meaning that diplomacy could continue even during times of conflict. After 1648, the era of Habsburg dominance and religious warfare had come to an end.

THE RISE OF PRUSSIA

Following the defeat of the Habsburgs in the Thirty Years' War, five kingdoms emerged to dominate the balance of power in Europe: England, France, Prussia,

---

After finding Charles I guilty of treason during the English Civil War, Parliament sentenced him with the following words.

PRIMARY SOURCE

For all . . . treasons and crimes this court does adjudge that he, . . . Charles Stuart, as a tyrant, traitor, murderer, and public enemy to the people of this nation, shall be put to death by the severing of his head from his body.

—from the sentence of Charles I, January 27, 1649

Russia, and Austria. Spain was no longer one of Europe's great powers.

The Protestant-dominated German-speaking lands were divided into numerous territories after the war, with Prussia emerging as the strongest German state. Frederick William I made his kingdom a pioneer in military technology and organization. He used the latest cannons and muskets and developed a professional army of well-trained troops. Precision marching and constant drilling were the hallmarks of the Prussian military. The landowning rural aristocracy cooperated in taxing the peasants, which gave Frederick William and his successors the resources to expand the military and make Prussia, with its capital at Berlin, a powerful force.

The competition between France and England would go global, with competing colonial and trade interests in North America, the West Indies, and South Asia. France's Louis XV built on his father's accomplishments and invested in both a large army and a naval force strong enough to challenge the English. However, maintaining such military forces decade after decade came at a great expense. For their part, the English used their island location to advantage with a clear focus on their navy and merchant shipping.

Austria, which had held a leading role among German states, was threatened by Prussia's rise. It sought to bolster its position through an alliance with France, while the Prussians allied themselves with Britain. By the mid-18th century, this tangle of alliances would turn local squabbles into international conflicts.

Meanwhile, as you have learned, Russia emerged as a great military power under the Romanov rulers Peter the Great and Catherine the Great. Although partly an Asian empire, Russia's huge military would make it an important player in the European balance of power as well.

HISTORICAL THINKING

1. **READING CHECK** In what ways were both England's Civil War and the Thirty Years' War about religion? In what ways were they about politics?

2. **INTERPRET MAPS** After the Thirty Years' War, which powers became dominant in Europe in 1715? Why?

3. **IDENTIFY** What types of technology did the Prussian king use to boost the state's power?

Europe in the Age of Scientific Revolution 543

1.3

MAIN IDEA In an era of upheaval, the English Parliament ousted the king and limited the monarchy's power even as a change in climate brought famine, disease, and social unrest to other parts of Europe and beyond.

The Glorious Revolution

Imagine if the U.S. Congress asked Canada to help overthrow the U.S. president because they didn't like the president's religion. That's pretty much what happened in England in 1688. Parliament asked the Dutch to help them overthrow the king.

RELIGIOUS CONFLICT AND REVOLUTION

Like Prussia and France, England was a powerful force in the late 1600s. After Charles I's execution, Oliver Cromwell took power and instituted a series of radical reforms. He abolished the monarchy and the Church of England and organized a republic in which citizens were allowed to vote for representatives. But he also instituted highly unpopular reforms. For example, Puritans thought plays were sinful, so Cromwell closed all the theaters. Many Londoners resented the reforms.

After Cromwell died in 1658, Parliament invited Charles's son, Charles Stuart, home from exile to re-establish the monarchy, a time period known as the Restoration. A patron of the arts, Charles II ended the unpopular restrictions on theaters. He also founded the Royal Observatory and supported the Royal Society to promote scientific research. But the Stuarts were seen as too tolerant of Catholics—some of them even were Catholic. Terrified the Stuarts would make England a Catholic state, Parliament enlisted the support of the Dutch in what is called the Glorious Revolution of 1688. Dutch forces supported Parliament in overthrowing the last Stuart king. Protestant princess Mary and her Dutch husband William were installed as the new monarchs. The ascension of **William III and Mary II** to the English throne made permanent the Protestant character of the English monarchy and the Church of England.

William and Mary were required to approve the **English Bill of Rights**, which guaranteed a number of important freedoms, such as freedom of speech in Parliament and the right to a trial by jury. Restrictions on individual liberties remained for working people, the middle class, Catholics, and women, but the document set an important precedent for England and the world, and by the 18th century, the balance of power between king and Parliament provided a stable foundation for England.

The English Bill of Rights and its predecessor, the Magna Carta, had tremendous influence on the founders of the United States. Americans looked to the British documents as they drafted the Declaration of Independence and their own Bill of Rights. The following are some of the rights guaranteed in the English Bill of Rights, written in 1689. Do they sound familiar?

PRIMARY SOURCE

- It is the right of the subjects to petition the king, . . . prosecutions for such petitioning are illegal;
- The raising and keeping of a standing army . . . in time of peace, unless it be with consent of Parliament, is against the law;
- The subjects which are Protestant may have arms for their defense . . . as allowed by law;
- The election of members of Parliament ought to be free;
- The freedom of speech . . . in Parliament ought not to be . . . questioned . . . ;
- Excessive bail ought not to be required, nor excessive fines imposed, nor cruel and unusual punishments inflicted;
- Jurors ought to be duly impanelled [appropriately chosen]. . . .
- All . . . fines . . . before conviction are illegal and void;
- For redress of all grievances, and for the amending, strengthening, and preserving of laws, Parliaments ought to be held frequently. . . .

THE LITTLE ICE AGE

In an age of upheaval, the English Parliament took charge to limit the monarchy's power. In England during its Civil War and in many other societies in the mid-1600s, changes in climate had brought famine, disease, and social unrest.

The Houses of Parliament and Big Ben, the clock tower at the northern end, lie along the Thames River in London, England.

According to climate historian Geoffrey Parker, "An intense episode of global cooling coincided with an unparalleled spate of revolutions and state breakdowns around the world." While Europeans saw religion as the source of these clashes, Parker and other climate historians looking at the miserable harvests of the 1640s point to a more basic cause of conflict: hunger.

By the late 16th century, the climate of the northern hemisphere had become progressively colder and unpredictable. Cooler and erratic temperatures caused poor harvests and rising prices in grain. The cost of wheat doubled in some places from the beginning to the middle of the 17th century.

Glaciers in Japan and in the Alps engulfed farms and villages and closed a gold mine in Austria. Cod off the Scottish coast moved south to warmer waters. Drier conditions in North American prairies made farming difficult, and some Native Americans shifted from farming to hunting.

Many people died from malnutrition, famine, and disease. Others rebelled. Poor harvests meant diminished tax revenues in England, France, China, and the Ottoman Empire. The turmoil weakened leaders and contributed to decades of war and violence.

Then, late in the 1600s, warmer temperatures and better harvests returned. Perhaps it is not a coincidence that the end of the Little Ice Age saw the return of stability to places like England, with the success of its Glorious Revolution, and China, with the rise of the powerful Qing dynasty.

HISTORICAL THINKING

1. **READING CHECK** Why did Parliament oust the Stuart king?

2. **MAKE CONNECTIONS** Which of the rights from the English Bill of Rights are included in the U.S. Bill of Rights?

3. **ANALYZE CAUSE AND EFFECT** According to climate historians, what effect might climate have had on global turmoil in the 17th century?

Europe in the Age of Scientific Revolution

2.1

MAIN IDEA A long history of scientific inquiry predated the Scientific Revolution but not without interruptions.

Traditions of Inquiry

Generally, scientists build upon the work of others, challenging it, expanding on it, and documenting new findings. But the scientists aren't the only ones challenging scientific research. New ideas have often been resisted. And sometimes they are outright forbidden.

BEFORE THE SCIENTIFIC REVOLUTION

In the 17th century, people didn't have the scientific knowledge and historical data available to help them analyze climate change like that experienced during the Little Ice Age. For most Europeans at the time, the Christian faith, whether Catholic or Protestant, still held most of the answers to basic questions about relationships between God, humanity, and the natural world.

However, scientific pursuits are as old as the human desire to understand the world. The ancient Greek scholar Aristotle studied the heavens in the fourth century B.C.E. and concluded that Earth was the center of a universe of revolving spheres. People accepted this **geocentric theory** for hundreds of years. Many early scientists used mathematics as a basis for scientific inquiry. As you have learned, Eratosthenes used rays of sunlight and geometry to calculate the circumference of Earth as 24,427 miles. His calculations were off by less than two percent. The actual circumference is 24,857 miles.

After the collapse of the Western Roman Empire in 476, the Greek tradition of classical learning was lost in Europe, and Europeans contributed little to scientific inquiry. Greek science was still studied in the Byzantine Empire, however, and science thrived in Muslim-ruled cities like Baghdad, Cairo, and Córdoba. Here, Muslim and Jewish scholars built on Greek writings. Between the 600s and 1100s, Muslim scholars studied scientific theories from Greece and other regions of the world. They advanced mathematical understanding by adopting the decimal system, the number zero, and Hindu-Arabic numerals, as you've already read. The knowledge they gained from the study of stars led to advances in navigation and the development of more accurate calendars.

Translations of Greek texts, along with the advanced knowledge of Byzantine, Jewish, and Muslim scholars spread to Europe around 1200. Inspired in part by the work of the Muslim scientists, the Franciscan monk Roger Bacon began to study **optics**, light and vision, and astronomy during the Middle Ages. He believed that the study of science and the natural world would help people understand God. He argued for a change to the Christian calendar so that it would more accurately reflect time for religious holidays. However, the Franciscan order considered his studies to be contrary to religious tradition. Rather than encourage his research, the Roman Catholic Church imprisoned Bacon. The calendar didn't change for another 300 years.

Thomas Aquinas was more successful in adapting Greek learning to medieval Christianity. As you have learned, Aquinas combined Aristotle's writings with those of early church writers to create a philosophical foundation for the Catholic faith. For example, Aquinas determined that since both Aristotle and the early Christians agreed that Earth was the center of the solar system, the geocentric view was supported by both reason and faith.

COPERNICUS AND GALILEO

As European Christians questioned their faith during the Reformation and Renaissance, they also challenged Aquinas's understanding of the physical world. Both mathematics and observation of the natural world struck at the heart of that intellectual system, challenging the church's assumptions about the natural world.

In the 16th century, most people believed Aristotle's teachings that the sun and other planets revolved around Earth. However, in 1543, a Polish astronomer and mathematician, **Nicolaus Copernicus**, proposed the revolutionary idea that the sun was actually the center of the solar system. According to his **heliocentric theory**, Earth and other planets revolved around the sun. This theory used mathematics to propose heliocentrism as a simpler explanation for planetary movement, but it introduced a huge problem. To believe this theory, people would have to admit that Aristotle and the Catholic Church had been wrong. Knowing that his work would be controversial, Copernicus delayed publication of his book and dedicated it to the pope. He died soon after it was published.

Despite the controversy, the Italian mathematician **Galileo Galilei** took Copernicus's heliocentric theory very seriously. He invented a telescope and pointed it at the heavens, where he discovered spots on the sun, craters on the moon, and other indications that the heavens were not perfect and unchanging as the church had claimed. He contradicted Aristotle and Aquinas by observing that a body in motion would stay in motion unless acted upon by an external force. This insight would later prove essential to new understandings of planetary motion. Most importantly, Galileo confirmed Copernicus's theory that the sun was the center of the solar system. Church authorities argued that the heliocentric theory contradicted the teachings of the Bible regarding God's creation. They arrested and tried Galileo as a heretic and forced him to renounce his support for the heliocentric theory.

Galileo was placed under house arrest and forbidden from publishing scientific research, but the Scientific Revolution that he and Copernicus helped launch could not be so easily suppressed. By the 18th century, the use of scientific observation and the application of mathematics were becoming increasingly common, especially among the elite of northern Europe. Aided by royal and aristocratic patronage, they began to pursue the "new science."

A visual representation of the Greek geocentric theory appears above (top) in a 13th-century French miniature. Below it is a visual representation of Copernicus's heliocentric theory, which shows the sun at the center of the universe.

HISTORICAL THINKING

1. **READING CHECK** What were some early scientific and mathematical discoveries in ancient Greece?

2. **DESCRIBE** What was the heliocentric theory? Why was it revolutionary?

3. **MAKE CONNECTIONS** Why were Greek and Muslim advances in mathematics essential to the development of the "new science"?

Europe in the Age of Scientific Revolution **547**

2.2

MAIN IDEA Sir Francis Bacon and René Descartes proposed new approaches to scientific research.

The Scientific Method

When you think of a scientist, you probably think of someone who conducts experiments. But observations and experiments are relatively new to science. In the 16th and 17th centuries, the pursuit of truth through experimentation was revolutionary.

In this 19th-century painting, the English physician and scientist William Gilbert shows Queen Elizabeth I and her court his experiment on electricity. The first to use the term *electricity*, Dr. Gilbert established the magnetic nature of Earth.

THE "MODERNS"

In the 17th century, an intellectual debate divided western European thinkers into two camps: the "ancients" and the "moderns." The ancients based their beliefs about medicine, mathematics, and astronomy on the ideas of classical authors such as Aristotle.

The moderns rejected the idea that classical authors and Christian theology were infallible. They argued that human reason provided the key to knowledge. The moderns believed that God created humans with reason so humans could observe and accurately describe God's creation.

Sir Francis Bacon was one of the moderns who applied reason and advanced an **inductive approach** to science. Inductive reasoning involves working from carefully controlled observations of natural phenomena toward larger truths. Bacon urged scientists to gather data by following specific steps. This new approach to science would become the **scientific method**, a logical procedure for developing and testing ideas.

The French scientist **René Descartes** applied reason using a **deductive approach**. This method involved moving from general principles to specific truths. Descartes argued that philosophy had to be firmly grounded in reason, and he emphasized systematic doubt as a key to knowledge. His famous saying, "I think, therefore I am," expressed his belief that his ability to reason was proof of his existence. Descartes also argued that he had to doubt the existence of God before he could prove that God did, in fact, exist.

SCIENTIFIC RATIONALISM

The ideas promoted by Bacon and Descartes became known as **scientific rationalism**. In this school of thought, observation, experimentation, and mathematical reasoning replaced ancient wisdom and church teachings as the source of scientific truth. Scientific rationalism provided a procedure for establishing proof for scientific theories, and it laid a foundation for formulating theories on which other scientists could build.

Building upon previous research had become easier by the 17th century. After the mid-1400s, when the printing press came into wide use, books were more easily available. In fact, many people believe the 1543 publication of Copernicus's book *On the Revolution of the Heavenly Spheres* sparked the Scientific Revolution.

Along with books, universities and scientific societies played an important role in spreading ideas such as scientific rationalism. Perhaps the most important scientific society was the Royal Society of England. Many of England's greatest scientists were members.

As ideas spread, scientific rationalism extended beyond science. Bacon was a politician, so he applied the principles to government, arguing that the direction of government should be based on actual experience. As you will learn, the thinkers of the European Enlightenment were optimistic that reason would provide the key to improving human society as well.

THE SCIENTIFIC METHOD The ideas of Bacon and Descartes eventually led to a new approach to scientific inquiry. "All our knowledge begins with the senses, proceeds then to the understanding, and ends with reason. There is nothing higher than reason," wrote the German philosopher Immanuel Kant. The scientific method is a logical approach to forming a **hypothesis**, an unproven theory, which might answer a question and can be tested. Generally, the steps are as follows:

Step 1: Observe and Question A scientist makes an observation, gathers information, and forms a question about a subject.

Step 2: Hypothesize The scientist proposes a hypothesis.

Step 3: Experiment The scientist designs and conducts an experiment to test the hypothesis.

Step 4: Analyze Data The scientist records and carefully examines the data from the experiment.

Step 5: Evaluate and Share Results The scientist judges whether the data do or do not support the hypothesis and publishes the results of the experiment.

HISTORICAL THINKING

1. **READING CHECK** What new ideas did Sir Francis Bacon and René Descartes propose?

2. **IDENTIFY SUPPORTING DETAILS** How did scientists share knowledge during the Scientific Revolution?

3. **ANALYZE CAUSE AND EFFECT** What was the effect of the Scientific Revolution on broader areas of society?

2.3

MAIN IDEA As the church and society became more accepting of science, mathematicians, scientists, and philosophers from many parts of Europe contributed to the advances of the Scientific Revolution.

Thinkers and Innovators

After seeing what happened to Galileo, would you be willing to stand up for science? Many people did. In fact, in 18th-century Europe studying science was all the rage. Women scientists pushed against gender norms as well as religious pressures.

THINKERS AND INNOVATORS AT WORK

During the Renaissance, the Flemish physician **Andreas Vesalius** dissected human corpses to create careful descriptions of human anatomy. Before Vesalius, people turned to the Greek physician Galen for information. Galen, who lived at the time of the Roman Empire, had dissected many birds and other animals, but dissecting a human body was forbidden by Roman law. Therefore, Galen's theories about the human body were based largely on speculation. Although many Christians objected to the dissection of dead bodies, Vesalius's books revolutionized biology and medicine.

Using a Copernican framework of the sun at the center of the solar system, **Johannes Kepler** analyzed the orbit of the planet Mars. Kepler's calculations showed that the planets move in elliptical rather than circular paths. This contrasted with Aristotle's and Christian teachings that all celestial motion was circular. Therefore, Kepler reinforced Galileo's challenge to Christian teachings. However, Kepler presented his findings as God's harmonious plan for the universe.

When French mathematician **Blaise Pascal** was a teenager, he started work on a device that would help his father calculate taxes. The Pascaline, or Arithmetic Machine, uses wheels and dials to add and subtract. Some people consider it the first digital calculator. Later, Pascal conducted experiments on atmospheric pressure and pressure applied to liquids. The Pascal principle explains that pressure applied to a confined liquid will transmit throughout the liquid, regardless of where the pressure is applied.

The Irish chemist **Robert Boyle** also studied air pressure. In 1662, he and English scientist Robert Hooke discovered that the volume of a gas decreases with increased pressure and that the inverse is also true. This finding is known as "Boyle's law."

Englishman **Isaac Newton** was one of the most important scientists of the Scientific Revolution. He followed Descartes's and Bacon's lead in using reasoning and experimentation. He used beams of light and prisms to observe how light splits into a spectrum of colors, proving that the colors were a property of light. He also used his studies of light to invent a new telescope that uses mirrors to reflect light and create a sharper image.

Newton is best known for his studies of gravity. He used deductive reasoning to propose a universal law of attraction between objects based on their mass and distance. He then used inductive reasoning in the experiments he conducted to support his theory. With this theory and his three laws of motion, Newton created a complete mechanical explanation of motion in the universe. He explained that gravity keeps planets in place as they orbit the sun. His work is the foundation of modern physics and led to scientific advances ranging from steam engines to space rockets.

By the time of Newton's death in 1727, the earlier tensions between science and Christian faith had lessened. An English poet even celebrated Newton with the lines: "Nature and Nature's laws lay hid in night / God said, 'Let Newton Be!' and all was light."

WOMEN IN SCIENCE AND MATHEMATICS

Even before **Laura Bassi** completed her doctorate, the Bologna Academy of Sciences admitted her as an honorary member for her work in physics. After she attained her degree in 1732, the University of Bologna in Italy offered her a position. She would be the first woman professor of physics, and she later became chair of experimental physics.

Fascinated by the work of Isaac Newton, Bassi based many of her lectures on Newtonian physics. She is one of the scientists credited with introducing

Newton's ideas to Italy. She is also recognized for her research on electricity and its uses in medicine.

A contemporary of Bassi, another woman of Bologna, **Maria Gaetana Agnesi** was also a child prodigy. As a teenager, she participated in philosophical discussions with well-known intellectuals. However, she is best recognized for her work in mathematics. Agnesi's algebra book, *Analytical Institutions*, was translated into many languages, and it included relatively new subjects, such as integral and differential calculus. The French Academy of Sciences wrote that it was "the most complete and best made treatise." Even the pope recognized the value of her work and appointed Agnesi professor of mathematics at the University of Bologna. However, she turned down the position, choosing instead to dedicate her life to charity.

The German astronomer **Caroline Lucretia Herschel** started scanning the heavens after she and her brother William, an astronomer, moved to England. Together, they identified 2,500 new star clusters and nebulae, clouds of gas and dust in outer space. Herschel also made many discoveries on her own, the most famous of which were eight comets she discovered between 1786 and 1797. Because of her contributions to astronomy, Herschel received the Gold Medal of the Royal Astronomical Society and became an honorary member of the Royal Society. Many of the comets she discovered are named after her.

NATIONAL GEOGRAPHIC EXPLORER KATHY KU

Just the Beginning

In 2010, American college student Kathy Ku arrived in the East African nation of Uganda to teach. She became aware that both she and her host family frequently got sick because they were drinking dirty water.

One way to treat the contaminated water was to set it out in clear plastic bottles in the sun, but Ku found this method literally distasteful. "I took a swig of the water and essentially spit it back out because it tasted like burnt plastic, and it was really warm as well. It's a very effective way of treating your water, but I thought there had to be a better solution that people would actually like to use."

The problem of making unclean water drinkable lodged itself in Ku's mind and would not go away, even after she returned to college. At age 19, Ku designed a ceramic water filter. To develop her idea more fully, Ku took a year off during her junior year. Her goal was not just to bring water filters to Uganda but to have them constructed there using locally sourced clay and sawdust.

Ku's vision became a reality in 2014, the year her first water-filter factory began operating. The factory has since moved into a bigger and better space near Kampala, Uganda's capital and largest city. The new facility has the capacity to produce 10,000 water filters a month. "We have provided 100,000 people with access to clean drinking water," says Ku. "But there's still much more to do!" For more on Kathy Ku and her work, check out National Geographic's website.

HISTORICAL THINKING

1. **READING CHECK** Many scientists were devout Christians. How did they reconcile their religious and scientific ideals?

2. **FORM AND SUPPORT OPINIONS** Was the work of Bassi, Agnesi, and Herschel more important to the advancement of science or the advancement of women? Why?

3. **EVALUATE** Which of these thinkers and innovators do you think contributed most to the field of science? Why?

3.1

MAIN IDEA Advances in plant science led to an agricultural revolution that benefited wealthy farmers but led to inequality in Britain and in its colonies around the world.

Science and Empire

Progress is good, right? Maybe not always. As British scientists applied scientific advances to agriculture, some people were winners, but many others struggled to survive.

BOTANICAL SCIENCE AND "IMPROVEMENT"

People have always studied ways to use plants for medicine as well as for food. With the rise of modern **botany**, the science of plants and plant life, scientists began to systematically collect and categorize **flora**, or plants, from around the world.

One of these scientists was **Carl Linnaeus**. In 1735, he published *Systema Naturae* in which he describes a system for organizing species into hierarchical categories. The Linnaean system classifies plants by the hierarchy of species, genus, family, order, class, phylum, and kingdom. Linnaeus also developed a two-name system of Latin names for organisms. The first name indicates the genus and the second the species.

With the support of Britain's George III, farmers derived practical economic lessons from Linnaeus's botanical work. In agriculture, this improvement meant using scientific methods to increase the productivity of existing farmland and to cultivate unused land.

By the 18th century, agricultural improvement brought about an agricultural revolution. Wealthy farmers in Great Britain invested in windmills to pump water from marshes, and they also began to rotate crops and crossbreed farm animals. Through these practices, more land was available for planting, and food production became more efficient. The resulting increase in food supply would be necessary as people began to move to cities during the Industrial Revolution.

EMPIRE AND POVERTY

This agricultural revolution brought efficiencies in production, but it led to greater inequality. Previously, English farm families had all shared common access to pastures and woodlands. But new laws, known as enclosure laws, allowed the wealthy to acquire common lands as private property. The rationale was that these landowners would farm the land more efficiently.

CRITICAL VIEWING This hand-colored engraving of a sunflower by botanical illustrator John Miller appeared in a 1777 English translation of a botanical treatise by Carl Linnaeus. Why do you think the artist paid such close attention to detail?

However, these laws meant that rural families lost access to the commons, as common lands were known, that they had once used for grazing cattle or sheep or for hunting. When they could no longer sustain themselves, many farming families went to work for the rich, while others drifted to cities or took jobs mining coal.

Therefore, what was known as improvement for some led to poverty for others. The price of bread increased and laws barred the poor from hunting wild game. As affordable food sources were taken away, rural people lost their **food security**, or their assurance that they would be able to obtain the food needed for

Originally established in 1759, Kew Gardens in London, England, housed more than 3,400 plant species by 1769. Sir Joseph Banks, whom you will learn about in the next lesson, managed the gardens from 1772 to 1819 and brought back plant specimens from all over the world.

good health. People resisted both in the cities and countryside, but laws were on the side of the upper class. The people in Parliament and the courts were from the landowning and wealthy classes. The interests of the poor were not represented.

Outside Great Britain, botany played a pivotal role in globalizing the practical application of science. British scientists brought new plant specimens from around the world to be examined, catalogued, and cultivated.

Throughout the expanding empire, British governors and commercial enterprises established botanical gardens as part of the effort to achieve improvement on a global scale. For example, when the Royal Navy needed timber for ships, British botanists identified South Asian mahogany as ideal for its height and durability. Breadfruit from Polynesia became an inexpensive yet nutritious food for slaves in the West Indies.

The British Empire used science to justify its dominance as well as to expand it. When confronted with the wealth produced by European science and technology, people in other parts of the world questioned the value of their own traditions and beliefs. In some places, such as Africa, conquest was so rapid that people had no time to make choices or to adjust. The prevailing belief among Europeans was that there was no need to take indigenous interests into account. Instead, they believed that the process of improvement gave them rights over land anywhere in the world. "Economic botany" one scientist wrote, referring to the idea that plants could be used to increase wealth, "would help to banish famine in India and win the love of the Asiatics for their British conquerors." Instead, Britain's empire was based on racial inequality, and Indians would suffer many famines under British rule.

HISTORICAL THINKING

1. **READING CHECK** What were some examples of agricultural advancements in the 18th century?

2. **IDENTIFY SUPPORTING DETAILS** How did Carl Linnaeus contribute to the science of botany?

3. **FORM AND SUPPORT OPINIONS** Who benefited and who suffered as agricultural improvement was implemented? Why?

3.2

MAIN IDEA The observations of Joseph Banks and James Cook taught Europeans about the rest of the world, but they also contributed to European empire building.

Traveler: Joseph Banks
Father of Australia 1743–1820

If you had the chance to sail around the world, what would you bring home as a souvenir? The botanist Joseph Banks wasn't your everyday tourist. He brought back thousands of plant species and drawings of plants and animals.

JOSEPH BANKS AND JAMES COOK

From 1768 to 1771, botanist Joseph Banks sailed the Pacific Ocean aboard the *Endeavour* in search of flora and **fauna**, or animals. He brought back drawings and specimens of 1,400 plants and 1,000 animals previously unknown in Europe. He dried the plants between pages of books and systematically classified and catalogued his findings. His work greatly expanded European knowledge of the natural world.

Although botany was central to Banks's mission on the *Endeavour*, he was also very interested in the people he encountered. He kept careful notes of his interactions with native peoples of Tierra del Fuego (the southern tip of South America), the Polynesians of the Pacific, and the **Aborigines**, the original inhabitants of Australia.

When Banks learned that Tahitians understood the speech of the Maori of New Zealand, he realized that there was a family connection between the two peoples. Through these encounters, Banks became a pioneer of **ethnography**, the study of the linguistic and cultural relationships between peoples.

While Banks studied plants and animals and learned about the people he encountered on his travels, the *Endeavour*'s captain, James Cook, carried out important astronomical observations that helped solve the problem of identifying a ship's **longitude**, or east-west position.

Cook also used his mathematical and navigational skills to chart the oceans. He was assisted in this endeavor by a Tahitian high priest named Tupaia, who also helped Banks understand Polynesian language and culture. As you have learned, Polynesian sailors were masters at using wind, currents, and stars to find their way.

Tupaia came from a family of navigators and was able to supplement Cook's instruments and charts with a local understanding of winds and currents. By charting the Pacific Ocean, Cook facilitated future European voyages to such places as Hawaii, New Zealand, and Australia.

SCIENCE AT THE SERVICE OF EMPIRE

The *Endeavour* returned to England in 1771 after a three-year journey. The surviving crewmen were among the few at that time who had sailed around the world, and Captain Cook became an instant celebrity.

While Cook would make two more journeys, Banks never again traveled outside Europe. However, he came home dreaming of "future dominions," and he became

---

The Polynesian people fascinated Banks and his shipmates. In this excerpt from his journal, Banks describes a ritual they witnessed and participated in just after they stepped ashore on the island of Tahiti.

PRIMARY SOURCE

Though at first they hardly dared approach us, after a little time they became very familiar. The first who approached us came crawling almost on his hands and knees and gave us a green bough [branch]. . . . This we received and immediately each of us gathered a green bough and carried it in our hands. They marched with us about half a mile and then made a general stop and, scraping the ground clean . . . every one of them threw his bough down upon the bare place and made signs that we should do the same. . . . Each of us dropped a bough upon those that the Indians had laid down, we all followed their example and thus peace was concluded.

—from Joseph Banks's journal

554 CHAPTER 19

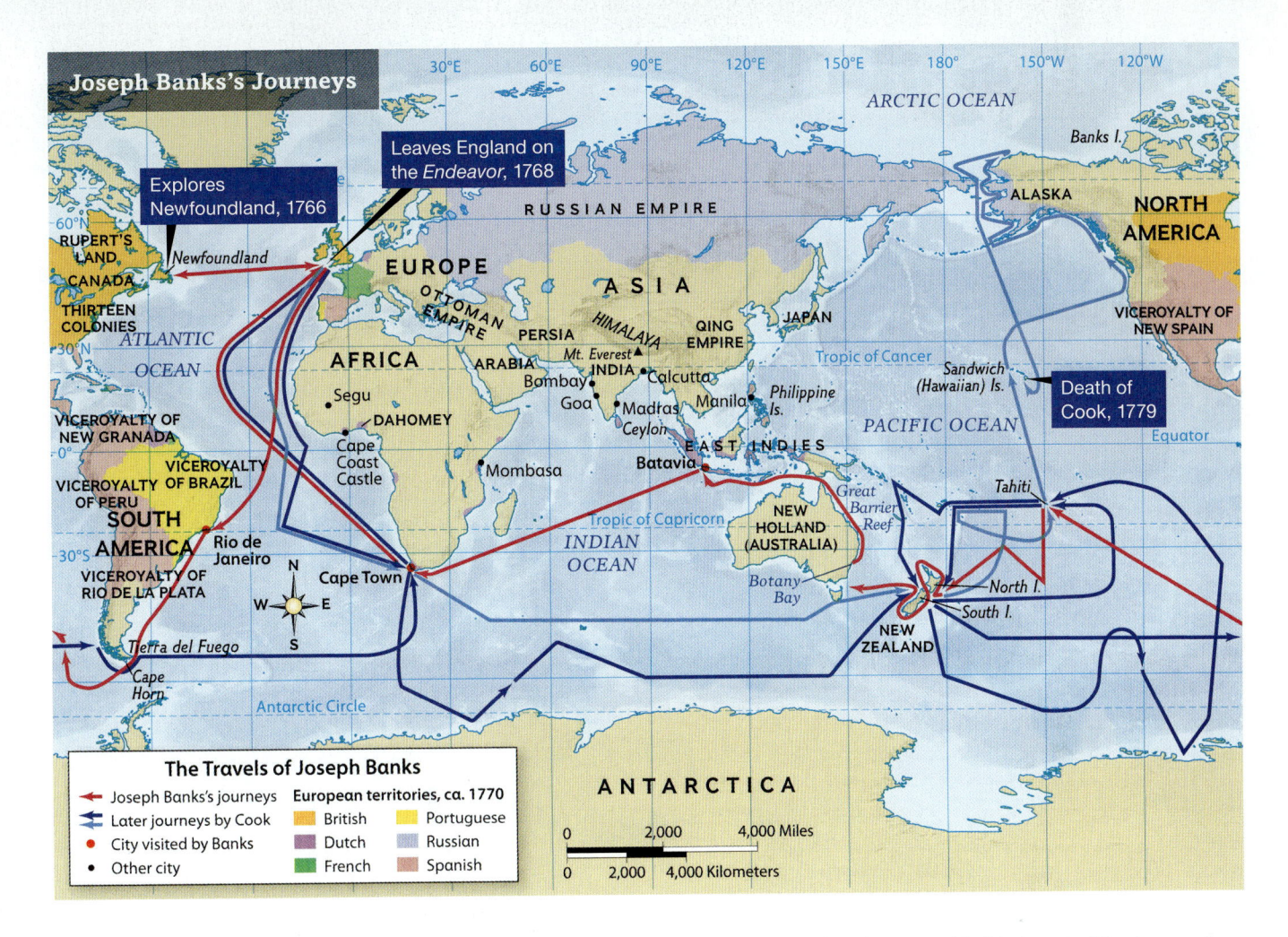

an influential advocate of British settlement in Australia. In fact, he is sometimes called "the Father of Australia" for the role he played in the foundation of the colony of New South Wales.

You read about the long competition between France and Britain. Louis XIV had founded the French Academy of Sciences, and later kings also supported scientists to advance their military and empire. But the most prestigious scientific establishment of the day was Britain's Royal Society. Joseph Banks served as president of the Royal Society from 1778 to 1820. He focused on economic botany, which linked science to technological and economic development.

Through his role at the Royal Society, Banks promoted the introduction of Merino sheep to New South Wales, where Botany Bay is named in his honor. Wool exports from these sheep strengthened the colony's economy, and the British founded new colonies across Australia. Banks believed these developments exemplified the successful outcome of applied practical science.

Unfortunately, British settlement had a devastating impact on the Aborigines. Before European contact, Aborigines lived in small bands, using their deep understanding of local environments for hunting and gathering. Many were pushed off their traditional lands as the British fenced off vast landholdings for sheep. In the 19th century, more than half of the Aboriginal population died from diseases introduced by European settlers.

HISTORICAL THINKING

1. **READING CHECK** What goals did Banks and Cook have for their voyage in the Pacific?

2. **ANALYZE POINTS OF VIEW** Some Australians call Joseph Banks "the father of Australia." Why? What opinion do you think Aborigines might have of Banks? Why?

3. **DESCRIBE** How did the work of Banks and Cook in the Pacific further the progress of science?

4. **FORM AND SUPPORT OPINIONS** Do you think Banks's work in the Pacific was more beneficial or more devastating in the long run? Support your opinion with evidence from the text.

Europe in the Age of Scientific Revolution 555

3.3 Material Culture

MEASURING AND MAPPING

In the late 18th and early 19th centuries, increased sophistication in the measurement of time and the mapping of space firmly linked science and empire. Europeans' acquisition of more detailed information on world geography was an essential step toward worldwide control. However, cartography, or the art and science of making maps, was established long before European dominance. From ancient Babylon to the medieval Muslim empire, mapmakers depicted places both near and far. At first, they did not have proper tools or measuring devices to properly chart locations. They often worked with earlier maps, which were not always correct. Many maps of previous eras were thematic, more focused on the artwork or illustrations instead of accuracy. Still, as centuries passed, several individuals and societies improved instruments and calculations to develop precise and detailed representations of our world.

Oldest Map of the World This clay tablet—one of the oldest surviving world maps—dates to approximately the sixth century B.C.E. and measures only 3.2 by 4.8 inches. The world is shown as a circle enclosed by a saltwater ring (translated as "Bitter River"), with several triangles beyond that border. The map also includes cuneiform, which you learned is the earliest known form of writing. Babylon is shown within the circle as a rectangle to the right of a line representing the Euphrates, even though the river flowed through the city. This portable artifact is less of an accurate depiction of the geography of the area and more of a symbolic portrayal of how Babylonians centered themselves in the world.

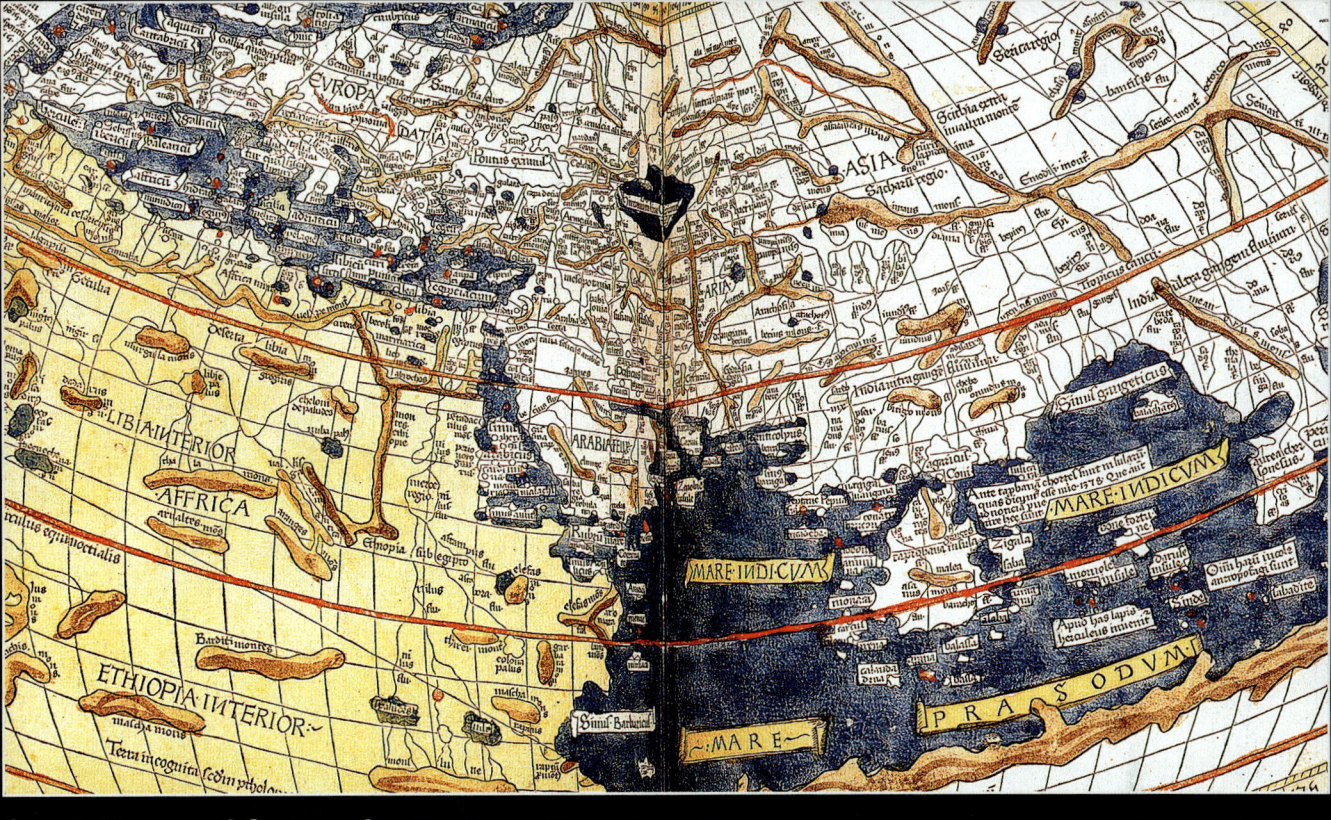

Greek Maps and Geography The Greco-Roman astronomer and mathematician Ptolemy was one of the first to work on a more realistic portrayal of the world. He applied geometry and other math to calculate more than 8,000 locations in Europe, Africa, and Asia. His methods were reintroduced to the Western world in the 13th century. Byzantine scholars translated and applied his techniques to produce maps (such as the one shown above). Experts now know that Ptolemy's calculations were incorrect. However, Ptolemy's influence on cartography cannot be underestimated.

Astrolabe The astrolabe—a sophisticated instrument that allowed users to calculate their location on Earth—was first developed by the Greeks. In the Middle Ages, these devices reached the Islamic world. There, scholars improved astrolabes so that Muslims could determine the location of Mecca. By measuring the date, time of day, and angle of the sun, Muslims could determine their position and pray in the correct direction. The astrolabe also functioned as a slide rule, one of the world's first handheld mathematical calculators. Sailors from many different cultures used the upgraded Muslim mariner's astrolabe to find their way around the world.

Europe in the Age of Scientific Revolution 557

Kangnido Originally produced in 1402, the map known as Kangnido is the earliest known Asian map and oldest surviving Korean map. This 1470 reproduction includes fairly realistic portrayals of the Korean Peninsula and the islands of Japan. Less accurate is the large mass of land in the map's center, which represents China and the Indian subcontinent. Europe, Africa, and the Arabian Peninsula are even more ill-defined, crammed into the left side of the map. No originals of the Kangnido survive.

Tabula Rogeriana Although the Tabula Rogeriana was commissioned by and named after a royal Christian patron, it was produced by Muslim mapmaker Al-Idrisi in 1154. Al-Idrisi was a scientist and scholar who joined the court of King Roger II of Sicily sometime after 1138. Al-Idrisi had traveled extensively through Central Asia, Africa, and Europe. He later blended traditions from Christianity, Islam, Judaism, and Greece to develop the most accurate map of its time. The Tabula Rogerina contains two maps: a small one that has curved parallels and a larger one (pictured here) comprised of 70 separate regional sections, with Sicily dead center. Unlike modern maps, south—not north—is at the top.

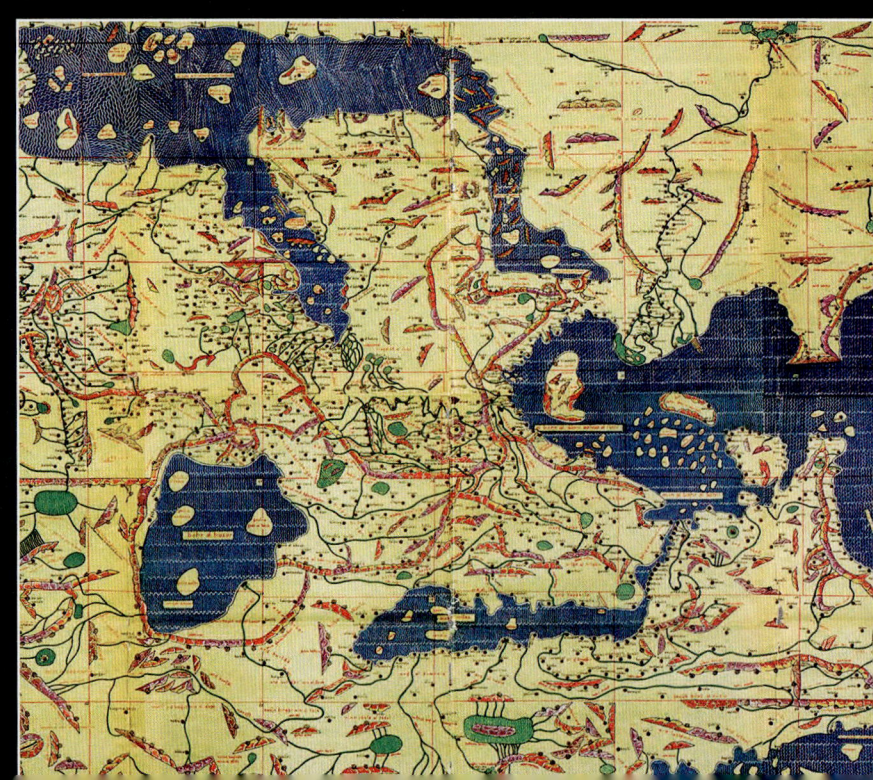

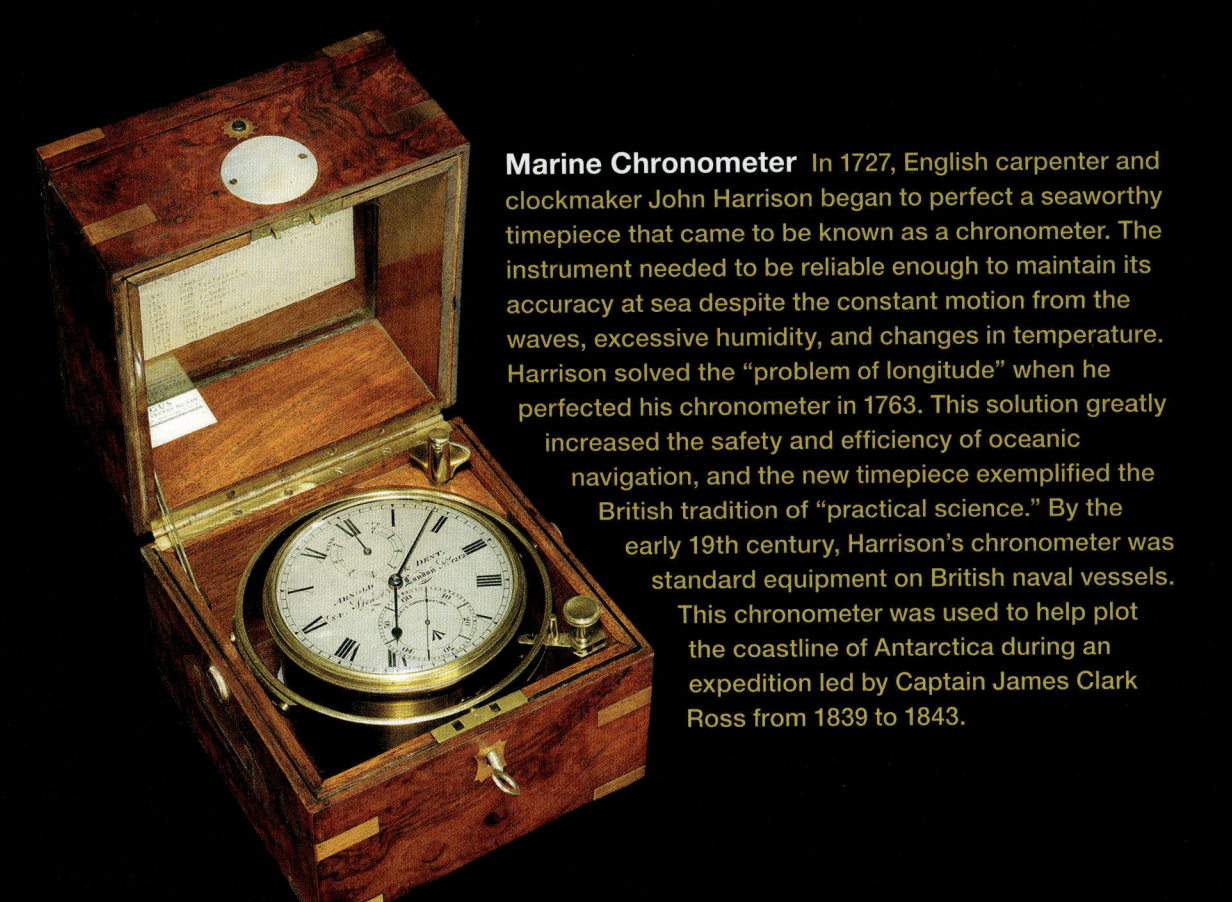

Marine Chronometer In 1727, English carpenter and clockmaker John Harrison began to perfect a seaworthy timepiece that came to be known as a chronometer. The instrument needed to be reliable enough to maintain its accuracy at sea despite the constant motion from the waves, excessive humidity, and changes in temperature. Harrison solved the "problem of longitude" when he perfected his chronometer in 1763. This solution greatly increased the safety and efficiency of oceanic navigation, and the new timepiece exemplified the British tradition of "practical science." By the early 19th century, Harrison's chronometer was standard equipment on British naval vessels. This chronometer was used to help plot the coastline of Antarctica during an expedition led by Captain James Clark Ross from 1839 to 1843.

GIS/Digital Maps Geographic information systems, or GIS, are computer systems designed to collect, store, check, manage, analyze, and display geographical data, usually in a digital format. These digital maps can serve a general purpose, or they can depict themes based on a specific location or spatial relationship. GIS can compare and contrast many types of information to discover how locations or themes relate to one another. For example, a digital map could combine data about places that produce pollution and areas that are sensitive to pollution. This map could help experts determine which regions are most at risk. A GIS software program called IDRISI, named after the Muslim scholar, was developed at a Massachusetts university in the 1980s. This system is now known as TerrSet.

DATA SOURCE
Street data
Buildings data
Traffic data
Integrated data

DATA LAYERS

HISTORICAL THINKING

1. **READING CHECK** How did maps and measuring instruments change over time?

2. **COMPARE AND CONTRAST** How are the maps and measurement tools you've read about different, and how are they similar?

3. **MAKE CONNECTIONS** What experience do you have with modern maps?

Europe in the Age of Scientific Revolution

CHAPTER 19 REVIEW
EUROPE IN THE AGE OF SCIENTIFIC REVOLUTION

VOCABULARY

Write one or more sentences that explains the connection between the two concepts.

1. absolute monarchy; constitutional monarchy
2. geocentric theory; heliocentric theory
3. ethnography; Aborigine
4. flora; fauna
5. scientific method; hypothesis
6. inductive approach; deductive approach
7. botany; food security

READING STRATEGY
IDENTIFY PROBLEMS AND SOLUTIONS

Identifying problems faced by individuals and nations and tracking their solutions can help you understand the way history unfolds. Complete the Problem-and-Solution Chart to analyze several problems faced during this period of European history. For example, how did England achieve religious and political stability? How did German-speaking nations resolve religious conflicts? How did British scientists solve the longitude problem? You may also choose another problem from the chapter. Then answer the question.

Problem:
Event 1:
Event 2:
Event 3:
Solution:

8. What possible problem was created by the stated solution?

MAIN IDEAS

Answer the following questions. Support your answers with evidence from the chapter.

9. What was the main source of instability in England during the 16th and 17th centuries? **LESSON 1.1**

10. Which countries gained power during the Thirty Years' War? Which countries lost power? **LESSON 1.2**

11. What were William and Mary required to accept when they became king and queen of England? **LESSON 1.3**

12. Why was Galileo Galilei imprisoned? **LESSON 2.1**

13. How did Sir Francis Bacon's approach to scientific inquiry differ from René Descartes's approach? **LESSON 2.2**

14. How were Vesalius, Kepler, Newton, and Bassi influenced by scientists who came before them? **LESSON 2.3**

15. How did the Scientific Revolution lead to expansion of the British Empire? **LESSON 3.1**

16. How did Joseph Banks and James Cook contribute to science through their voyage on the *Endeavour*? **LESSON 3.2**

HISTORICAL THINKING

Answer the following questions. Support your answers with evidence from the chapter.

17. **IDENTIFY** In what ways did monarchs and the church support the Scientific Revolution?

18. **FORM AND SUPPORT OPINIONS** If scientists of the 16th and 17th centuries knew more about climate change, do you think they could have prevented some of the turmoil in the world during the time of the Little Ice Age? Why or why not?

19. **ANALYZE CAUSE AND EFFECT** Describe how ideas from the Renaissance and Reformation led to the Scientific Revolution.

20. **EXPLAIN** How did scientific theories and methods of the Scientific Revolution challenge earlier beliefs and church orthodoxy?

21. **IDENTIFY PROBLEMS AND SOLUTIONS** What types of problems did the study of science create in the British Empire? How effective were the British solutions?

INTERPRET VISUALS

Study the time line of scientific and political events. Then answer the questions that follow.

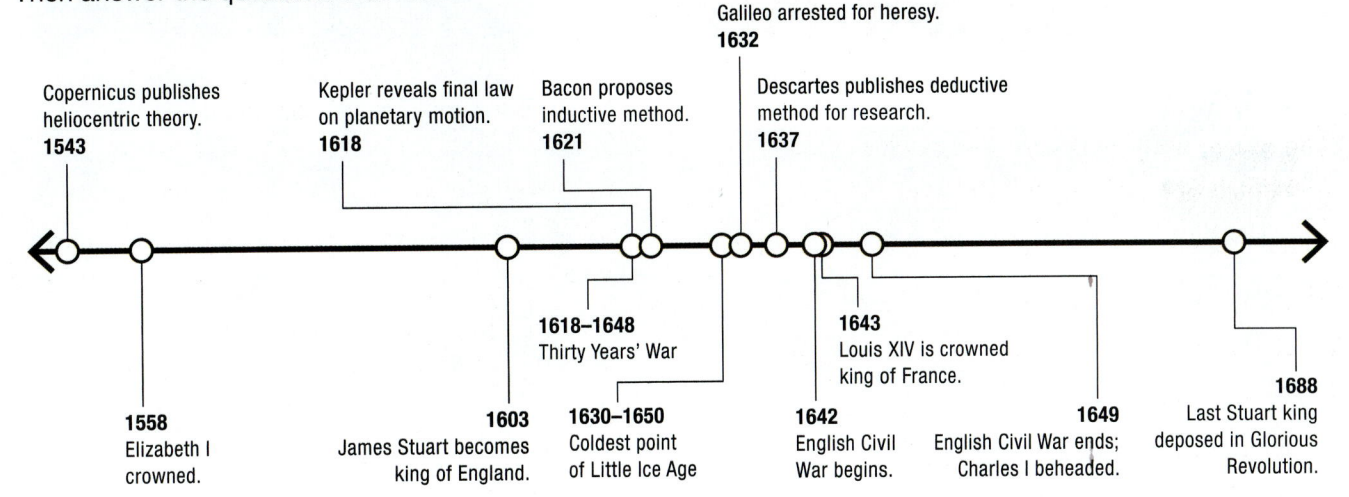

- Copernicus publishes heliocentric theory. **1543**
- Kepler reveals final law on planetary motion. **1618**
- Bacon proposes inductive method. **1621**
- Galileo arrested for heresy. **1632**
- Descartes publishes deductive method for research. **1637**
- **1558** Elizabeth I crowned.
- **1603** James Stuart becomes king of England.
- **1618–1648** Thirty Years' War
- **1630–1650** Coldest point of Little Ice Age
- **1642** English Civil War begins.
- **1643** Louis XIV is crowned king of France.
- **1649** English Civil War ends; Charles I beheaded.
- **1688** Last Stuart king deposed in Glorious Revolution.

22. What was the difference in the political climate between England and France in the early 1640s?

23. What kind of weather was Europe experiencing around the time Galileo was arrested? What was happening in Germany during this same period?

ANALYZE SOURCES

English scientists believed nothing should stand in the way of scientific progress. Read the following quotation from Sir Francis Bacon about farmers in Ireland and answer the questions that follow.

> We shall reclaim them [the lands] from their [the farmers'] barbarous manners . . . populate, plant and make civil all the provinces of that kingdom.
>
> —Sir Francis Bacon

24. What practice is Sir Francis Bacon referring to in this quote? What is he suggesting should be done in the Irish provinces?

25. What attitude does this statement convey about the rural farmers of Ireland?

CONNECT TO YOUR LIFE

26. INFORMATIVE This chapter describes the effect a changing climate had on people living in Europe during the Little Ice Age. Use reliable Internet and print sources to learn about current scientific research into one aspect of climate change. Write a short essay to inform others of the measures being advocated to prevent further climate disruption.

TIPS

- Revisit the information on the Little Ice Age in this chapter. Summarize the information and use it to open your essay.

- Take notes on one aspect of present-day climate change. Consult at least three reliable sources linked to major university, museum, or research institutions.

- Be sure to attribute any quotations or ideas to the appropriate people or institutions.

- Conclude with a paragraph that sums up the current thinking on climate change and what steps should be undertaken to lessen its impact.

CHAPTER 20

European Enlightenment
1650–1800

HISTORICAL THINKING How were enlightened ideas a break from the past?

SECTION 1 **Reason and Society**
SECTION 2 **Belief in Progress**

CRITICAL VIEWING

The General Staff Building in St. Petersburg, Russia, was built in the early 19th century and served as the headquarters of the Russian armed forces and several ministries. A triumphal arch connects two wings of the building and is topped by a sculpture symbolizing victory. The building is an example of neoclassical architecture, a style that arose during the Enlightenment and was influenced by that movement's admiration of classical Greece and Rome. What architectural elements of the building reflect classical influence?

1.1 **MAIN IDEA** The philosophical movement known as the Enlightenment began when thinkers began to re-evaluate old ideas about society.

The Age of Reason

Ideas can be dangerous, especially when they question long-held beliefs and the authority of leaders. But in the 17th century, some European philosophers contested established thought and used what they called the "light" of human reason to bring about change.

ROOTS OF THE ENLIGHTENMENT

As you know, the Scientific Revolution ushered in a new way of viewing the natural world. Scientists, including Galileo, Francis Bacon, and Isaac Newton, used not only observation and experimentation but also logic and reason to try to answer their questions about the universe. The Scientific Revolution helped inspire European thinkers in the mid-1600s to challenge traditional ideas about religion, government, and society. They believed people should use reason—the power of the human mind to think and understand in a logical way—to help them understand the physical world and their place in it.

CRITICAL VIEWING Louis XIV of France built his palace at Versailles to demonstrate his power as an absolute monarch. The palace's Hall of Mirrors, shown here, celebrates the king's reign and the economic prosperity of the French upper classes. How does the style of the room contrast with Enlightenment ideals?

These thinkers sparked an intellectual movement called the Enlightenment, also known as the Age of Reason. Rather than simply accept what religious and political figures had to say, Enlightenment philosophers encouraged others to use reason and experience to gain knowledge and shatter the "darkness" of ignorance. Their revolutionary political ideas challenged and often opposed traditional and entrenched institutions, beliefs, and social orders.

The Enlightenment had its deepest roots in the classical world of ancient Greece and Rome. Remember reading about the ancient Greek philosophers Plato and his student Aristotle? Their philosophical ideas differed in many respects, but they generally agreed on the evils of **tyranny**, a state of government in which rulers have unlimited power and use it unfairly. Plato called tyranny the "worst disorder of a state." He asserted that tyrants and their states lacked reason and order. The best government, Plato believed, was one led by an aristocracy of philosophers who would promote the common good. Aristotle contended that tyranny could corrupt monarchy. He wrote that powerful monarchs often acted only in their own selfish interest, not for the common good.

During the Renaissance, classical ideas and culture were revived, and these would later influence Enlightenment thinkers. The Protestant Reformation, the result of questioning the authority and practices of the Catholic Church, also had a significant impact on the movement.

THE SOCIAL CONTRACT

Two English philosophers of the 1600s, **Thomas Hobbes** and **John Locke**, helped lay the foundation of enlightened thought with the notion of a **social contract**. This was an agreement between rulers and the ruled to cooperate for mutual social benefits in pursuit of an ordered society, with clearly defined rights and responsibilities for each. But the two men came to very different conclusions about government and human nature.

Hobbes witnessed the terrible violence of the English Civil War and the Thirty Years' War and, as a result, took a dim view of people. In his 1651 work, *Leviathan*, he described humans as naturally selfish and wicked. Free to do what they liked, he wrote, people's lives would be "solitary, poor, nasty, brutish, and short." Hobbes maintained that, for the sake of peace, individuals must hand over their rights to a strong ruler.

Locke took a more optimistic view of humankind. He claimed that people had the ability to reason and learn for themselves, and they could use their acquired knowledge to benefit society. In his 1689 book, *Two Treatises of Government*, Locke proposed his own social contract. A key component of the contract was the idea that all people are born free and equal with **natural rights**, such as life, liberty, and property. It was the duty of government to protect these rights, Locke declared. But if it failed to do so, the people had the right to overthrow the ruler and establish a new government. In fact, Locke had been involved in England's Glorious Revolution, and his ideas influenced the English Bill of Rights.

The concept of natural rights was not new, but in the late 1600s, only certain privileged classes enjoyed these inherent rights. Locke's call for natural rights was, in part, a rejection of the unlimited authority of the absolute monarchs who ruled in Europe during the 1600s and 1700s. The European king who best characterized absolute rule was Louis XIV of France, whom you've read about. He enforced his will and subdued any challenges to his authority. Still, absolute monarchs were not just found in Europe. Most states and empires in the world at that time were ruled by one leader, variously called a king, tsar, sultan, emperor, shah, or prince.

Locke's ideas greatly influenced other philosophers—especially in France. And, as you'll learn later, his ideas would have a lasting impact on political thought.

In *Politics*, a work of political philosophy, Aristotle set out to investigate the factors that comprise a good government and those that combine to form a bad one. The following excerpt from the work discusses some of these factors.

PRIMARY SOURCE

It is evident, then, that all those governments which have a common good in view are rightly established and strictly just, but those who have in view only the good of the rulers are all founded on wrong principles, and are widely different from what a government ought to be, for they are tyranny over slaves, whereas a city is a community of freemen.

—from *Politics* by Aristotle, 350 B.C.E.

HISTORICAL THINKING

1. **READING CHECK** What inspired the Enlightenment?
2. **COMPARE AND CONTRAST** How did the views of Hobbes and Locke differ with regard to rulers and the ruled?
3. **ANALYZE SOURCES** According to Aristotle, what do the ruler and the ruled become when a government focuses only on the good of the ruler?

European Enlightenment

1.2 State of the World

1700 C.E.

EUROPEAN DOMINATION

The modern era, which began with humanism and the European Renaissance, matured during the Enlightenment in the 1700s. Around that time, the world also witnessed the increasing expansionist power of western European nations. Mighty empires still held sway in the east. China's Qing Empire, for example, reached its peak around the middle of the 18th century. But the great gunpowder empires—Safavid Persia, the Ottoman Empire, and Mughal India—had either ended or fallen into decline by then.

European ascendancy was greatly aided by the Industrial Revolution, a period beginning around 1750 when businesses started to produce goods in factories. The Industrial Revolution created a shift in how Europe's trade was conducted. Instead of buying colonial goods, industrialized nations looked for markets to sell their machine-made items. And in their drive to acquire new colonies, they no longer sought precious metals and spices. Now European nations wanted raw materials for their factories.

Like the gunpowder empires, countries such as Spain, France, and Great Britain (which formed in 1707 with the union of England and Scotland) used their superior weapons to impose their will on the people they colonized. They then restructured the colony's economy and government to serve the needs of industrialization. Their technical expertise and power led the Europeans to regard those they colonized as inferior. The pattern of racism that developed would have an enduring impact on the colonies.

HISTORICAL THINKING

INTERPRET MAPS How did European domination of the global trade network probably affect non-European empires?

Sugar cane Caribbean

FIVE LARGEST CITIES

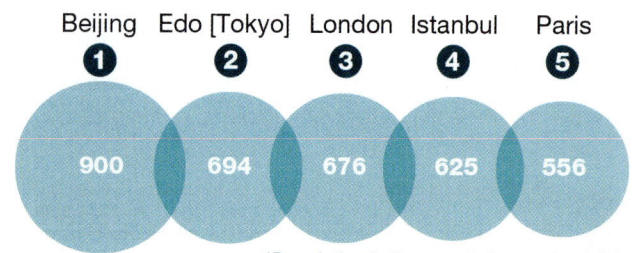

Beijing	Edo [Tokyo]	London	Istanbul	Paris
❶	❷	❸	❹	❺
900	694	676	625	556

*Population in thousands (approximately)

WORLD POPULATION

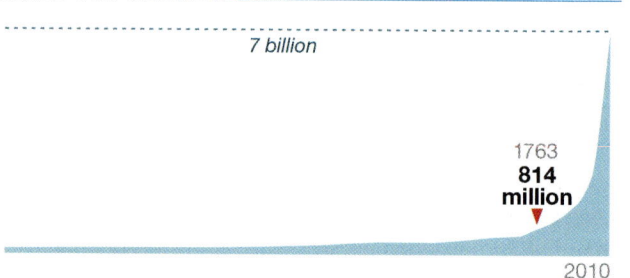

7 billion

1763
814 million

2010

566 CHAPTER 20

Silver Spain

Spices East Indies

Slave shackles Africa

Cotton India

Salt Africa

Economic areas
- European
- Islamic
- Russian
- Chinese
- Indian

Trade routes
- British slave trade triangle
- Other British
- Spanish
- Portuguese
- Dutch
- Other

NEWCOMEN STEAM ENGINE

In 1712, British inventor Thomas Newcomen devised a steam engine to drain water from deep mines. The engine used atmospheric pressure to perform the work and replaced the costly teams of horses previously employed to power a pump. Newcomen's invention was inefficient, but it was safe and reliable. Scottish inventor James Watt would improve on Newcomen's ideas and create what would be called the first modern steam engine—an invention that would power the Industrial Revolution.

1. The boiler, closed by a valve, generates steam continuously. The piston is kept up at the top of the cylinder because of the weight of the mine pump rod.
2. The valve opens and steam fills the cylinder.
3. The valve closes trapping steam inside the cylinder.
4. A pipe sprays cool water inside the cylinder, so the steam condenses rapidly, leaving very little pressure inside.
5. The atmosphere's pressure pushes the piston down, lifting the pump rod at the other end of the beam.

European Enlightenment 567

1.3

MAIN IDEA Enlightenment philosophers challenged powerful institutions and called for reform.

Civic and Social Reformers

What problems do you think need to be fixed in American society, and how would you address them? Europe's enlightened thinkers believed they could apply reason to solve problems in government, religion, education, and economics.

Enlightened thought wasn't only spread through publications. By the late 1600s, coffeehouses had become popular places to exchange Enlightenment ideas, especially in London. For a penny, a man—and coffeehouses only admitted men—could sit by the fire, drink a cup of coffee, and join the conversation. As a result, the coffeehouses of the 17th and 18th centuries came to be known as "penny universities."

THE PHILOSOPHES

The Enlightenment reached its height in France in the mid-1700s with a group of social critics known as **philosophes** (fee-luh-ZAWFS), the French word for philosophers. A philosophe named **Charles-Louis de Secondat, Baron de Montesquieu** (mahn-tuh-SKYOO) wrote about political liberty. Like Locke, Montesquieu agreed that liberty was a natural right. During his travels in England, he had observed the English form of government and been impressed with what he called its separation of powers. As a result, Montesquieu advocated for the separation of government into three branches—executive, legislative, and judicial—in his 1748 book, *The Spirit of the Laws*. Doing so, he said,

568 CHAPTER 20

would prevent any individual or group from seizing control of all the power.

One of the most popular and influential of the philosophes was a writer who went by the pen name **Voltaire**. He used satire to poke fun at religious leaders, the wealthy, and government. His witty attacks on aristocrats at the French court sometimes landed him in trouble. Voltaire was jailed twice and exiled to England for several years. Nevertheless, he continued to fight for social reforms, including religious tolerance and freedom of speech.

Jean-Jacques Rousseau (roo-SOH) is another great philosophe whose views, though, were often at odds with many other Enlightenment thinkers. While most of the movement's philosophers believed in the power of reason and science to improve the world, Rousseau claimed that civilization had corrupted people's natural goodness and destroyed their liberty. He wrote, "Man is born free, and everywhere he is in chains." Like Hobbes and Locke, Rousseau proposed a social contract. Unlike these earlier thinkers, however, Rousseau's contract was an agreement among individuals to create their own government. In his 1762 work, *The Social Contract*, he called for a direct democracy in which people would give up some of their freedom for the common good. Under Rousseau's social contract, all people would be equal, and there would be no kings or titled nobility.

WOMEN OF THE ENLIGHTENMENT

Even though Rousseau maintained that everyone should be equal, he drew the line at granting this right to women. He supported reforming childhood education, but he believed girls should mainly be instructed in how to be good wives and mothers. For all their progressive ideas, most of the philosophes, in fact, relegated women to their traditional societal roles.

Some women in the 1600s pushed back against this characterization of them. English philosopher, writer, and scientist **Margaret Cavendish** criticized the restrictions on women's freedom and said they resulted from nothing more than the "conceit men have of themselves." Although she had no formal schooling herself, Cavendish was a prolific, or highly productive, writer. In several of her works, she encouraged the equality and education of women. Cavendish wrote scientific treatises as well, a rare accomplishment for a woman at that time.

Another Englishwoman, **Mary Astell**, also addressed the lack of educational opportunities for women in *A Serious Proposal to the Ladies*, published in 1694. In other writings, Astell challenged the reasoning of some male Enlightenment thinkers. For example, questioning Locke's rejection of absolute rule, she wrote, "If absolute sovereignty [rule] be not necessary in a state, how comes it to be so in a family?" And to Rousseau's assertion that "man is born free," she countered, "If all men are born free, how is it that all women are born slaves?"

The most famous and outspoken female social critic of the 1700s was the English writer **Mary Wollstonecraft**. In her 1792 work, *A Vindication of the Rights of Woman*, she argued that because women have the ability to reason, they deserve the rights that men enjoy, including education. She wrote, "How many women waste life away . . . who might have practiced as physicians, regulated a farm, managed a shop, and stood erect, supported by their own industry?" Wollstonecraft also encouraged women to enter such male-dominated domains as medicine and politics.

ECONOMIC LIBERTY

Enlightenment thinkers even influenced economics. As you know, many European countries in the 1600s and 1700s based their economy on mercantilism, a system in which the government closely controlled commerce. A Scottish economist named **Adam Smith** promoted the idea of free markets in his 1776 book *The Wealth of Nations*. He believed businesses and industries should regulate their activities without government interference. This economic policy is called ==laissez-faire== (LEH-say-FEHR), which is French for "let do" but, in this context, is often translated as "leave us alone."

Laissez-faire capitalism, which you learned is a system in which businesses are privately owned and exist to make profits, would create a free-market economy in which the people selling and buying products would determine what goods were needed and what price should be paid for them. Smith reasoned that this economic liberty would ensure economic progress and produce more wealth for all.

In his book, Smith supported his ideas with what he called the three natural laws of economics. The first was the law of self-interest. Smith declared that people worked for their own good: to earn money and acquire the things they needed. Competition, the second law, guaranteed that companies would try to make better products that would appeal to buyers. And these products would be regulated by the third law—the law of supply and demand. In a free-market economy, according to this law, a greater supply of goods would lower the demand for them and lower their price. Conversely, low supply and high demand would cause prices to rise.

Enlightenment Thinkers

CHARLES-LOUIS MONTESQUIEU
Montesquieu first became famous for *Persian Letters,* a work in which he satirized Parisian society, mocked the rule—just ended—of Louis XIV, and criticized Catholicism. However, Montesquieu is best remembered for *The Spirit of the Laws,* considered one of the great works in the history of political theory. The masterpiece, consisting of 31 books, surprised most people at that time, who considered Montesquieu to be brilliant but rather superficial.

In this excerpt from *The Spirit of the Laws,* Montesquieu explains how a lack of separation of powers—specifically with regard to the judiciary power—enfringes on a person's liberty.

PRIMARY SOURCE

[T]here is no liberty, if the judiciary power be not separated from the legislative and executive. Were it joined with the legislative, the life and liberty of the subject would be exposed to arbitrary control; for the judge would be then the legislator. Were it joined to the executive power, the judge might behave with violence and oppression. There would be an end of everything, were the same man or the same body . . . to exercise those three powers, that of enacting laws, that of executing the public resolutions, and of trying the causes of individuals.

VOLTAIRE
Voltaire, portrayed here as a young man, was a prolific writer who produced poetry, prose, plays, satires, and thousands of letters. In his best-known work, *Candide,* Voltaire pokes fun at religion, government, and philosophers. However, some historians believe Voltaire's greatest contribution was introducing the ideas of Isaac Newton to France and much of Europe. The philosophe popularized the story that Newton formulated the laws of gravity when the scientist saw an apple fall from a tree.

Voltaire's *A Philosophical Dictionary* contains a series of articles, some of which are critical of religion and other institutions. In this excerpt from the dictionary, Voltaire takes aim at those theologians, or religious scholars, who tried to restrict freedom of expression.

PRIMARY SOURCE

In general, we have as natural a right to make use of our pens as our language, at our peril, risk, and fortune. I know many books which fatigue, but I know of none which have done real evil. Theologians, or pretended politicians, cry: "Religion is destroyed, the government is lost, if you print certain truths or certain paradoxes [contradictory statements]. Never attempt to think, till you have demanded permission from a monk or an officer. It is against good order for a man to think for himself."

Smith believed the interplay among self-interest, competition, and supply and demand would result in what he called the "invisible hand" of the market to control and regulate itself. *The Wealth of Nations* is considered by many experts to be the most influential book on market economics ever written, and Adam Smith is often called the "father of modern economics."

SPREAD OF ENLIGHTENMENT IDEAS

As you know, some of the philosophes were punished for their views. In France, it was illegal to criticize the government or the Catholic Church. But that didn't stop enlightened thinkers from publishing their beliefs. As a result, their ideas spread throughout Europe and beyond in books, magazines, newspapers, pamphlets—and letters. Voltaire wrote thousands of them, and these were often shared with an ever-expanding audience.

No publication helped spread Enlightenment ideas as much as the set of books that comprised the *Encyclopedia,* largely created by French philosophe **Denis Diderot** (DEE-duh-roh). Diderot and other Enlightenment philosophers and scholars contributed

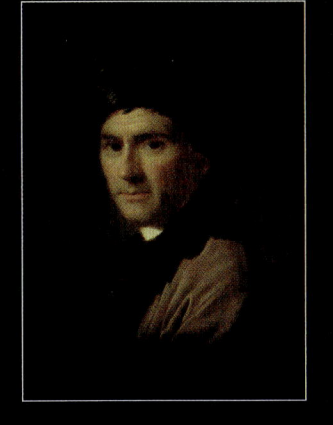

JEAN-JACQUES ROUSSEAU
While Rousseau believed people were naturally good, he didn't believe they were naturally intelligent. As a result, Rousseau suggested that people entrust a great lawgiver to develop their constitution and set of laws. To convince people to accept the laws, Rousseau said the lawgiver could claim he'd been guided by divine inspiration. Rousseau's reforms revolutionized music as well as society. He promoted freedom of expression in music and inspired such musicians as Austrian composer Wolfgang Amadeus Mozart.

A key idea of Rousseau's *Social Contract* is the concept of the "general will," which looks to the welfare of the whole and not the individual. Rousseau argues that, under the social contract, a person gains freedom by submitting to the general will.

PRIMARY SOURCE

Whatever benefits he had in the state of nature but lost in the civil state, a man gains more than enough new ones to make up for them. His capabilities are put to good use and developed; his ideas are enriched, his sentiments made more noble, and his soul elevated to the extent that—if the abuses in this new condition did not often degrade him to a condition lower than the one he left behind—he would have to keep blessing this happy moment which snatched him away from his previous state and which made an intelligent being and a man out of a stupid and very limited animal. . . .

MARY WOLLSTONECRAFT
Wollstonecraft called not only for equal educational opportunities for women but also for their social equality. She tried to live according to her beliefs. In a male-dominated world, Wollstonecraft worked as an editor, reviewer, and writer. Wollstonecraft died shortly after giving birth to a child she named Mary. Her daughter would become Mary Shelley, after marrying English poet Percy Shelley, and wrote the novel *Frankenstein*.

Wollstonecraft believed Enlightenment ideas must also apply to women. In this excerpt from *A Vindication of the Rights of Woman*, she attacks Jean-Jacques Rousseau for his views on women's education—namely that women should be taught to make themselves agreeable to men.

PRIMARY SOURCE

Rousseau declares that a woman should never, for a moment, feel herself independent, that she should be governed by fear to exercise her *natural* cunning, and made a coquettish slave in order to render her a more alluring object of desire, a *sweeter* companion to man. . . . He [Rousseau] carries the arguments, which he pretends to draw from the indications of nature, still further, and insinuates that truth and fortitude, the corner stones of all human virtue, should be cultivated with certain restrictions, because, with respect to the female character, obedience is the grand lesson which ought to be impressed with unrelenting vigor. What nonsense!

articles on topics including natural law, the history of philosophy, and social theory. The first volume of the *Encyclopedia* was published in 1751. Although the French government banned the work, Diderot continued with his project until the final volume was produced in 1772. Translations of the *Encyclopedia* into English, German, Spanish, and Italian spread Enlightenment ideas across Europe and around the world.

Women weren't invited to write for the *Encyclopedia*. But, as you'll see, some women in Paris found their own way to spread Enlightenment ideas in their homes.

HISTORICAL THINKING

1. **READING CHECK** What government reform did Montesquieu propose?
2. **COMPARE AND CONTRAST** How did Rousseau's social contract differ from John Locke's?
3. **MAKE INFERENCES** Why do you think Mary Astell used the words of male Enlightenment philosophers to make her points?
4. **DRAW CONCLUSIONS** How did Adam Smith's ideas on economics reflect enlightened thought?

2.1 MAIN IDEA In the 18th century, Paris became the intellectual center of the Enlightenment.

Paris at the Center

Today, many people debate their ideas on social media. Enlightened thinkers probably would have enjoyed trading views online, too. But instead, they networked in person. And Paris was the best place to do it.

THE CITY OF LIGHT

In the 1700s, philosophers, artists, and scientists from all over Europe and the Americas flocked to Paris to study and discuss ideas. Because the brightest minds of the Enlightenment gathered there (and also because it was one of the first European cities to adopt street lighting), Paris earned the nickname *La Ville-Lumière*, or "The City of Light."

You've read that Enlightenment ideas were disseminated through print media, such as letters, newspapers, pamphlets, and the *Encyclopedia*. But the Enlightenment also spread by word of mouth. Ideas were intensely discussed in the drawing rooms of wealthy Parisian women who organized regular social gatherings called **salons**. There, guests debated the latest Enlightenment contributions to philosophy, science, art, and literature. The women who hosted the salons chose the topics for discussion and controlled the flow of conversation. As you know, women at this time received little formal education, so the salons served as a socially accepted substitute for learning.

One of the best-known salon hosts was Marie Thérèse Geoffrin (joh-FREHN). Her salons had theme nights. Art was the theme on Mondays. Wednesdays were reserved for literature. But Geoffrin was a strict host. She never allowed any discussion of politics or religion at her salons. A generous patron of enlightened thinkers, Geoffrin also helped finance Diderot's vast project. Another popular host, Sophie de Grouchy (grew-SHEE), promoted equal rights for women at her gatherings. And she collaborated with her husband, Nicolas de Condorcet, on his works supporting educational reform and the abolition of slavery. Condorcet supported women's rights and racial equality, arguing that prejudices against women and Africans came from ignorance and would be ended by reason.

Guests at the Parisian salons ranged from nobles and bishops to painters and politicians. Well-known philosophes, including Voltaire, Montesquieu, and Diderot, were frequent visitors. American statesman **Benjamin Franklin** also regularly attended salons when he served as America's first ambassador to France. He once came to the salon of Marie Paulze-Lavoisier (luh-vwah-see-AYE) who was an artist known for her finely detailed scientific illustrations.

FREEDOM OF THOUGHT AND SPEECH

Salons did not welcome people of the working-class majority, but high-ranking members of the **bourgeoisie** (burzh-wah-ZEE), or middle class, were often invited to attend. However, they were expected to observe upper-class rules on proper behavior. The gatherings helped break down social and intellectual barriers but only if middle-class guests remembered to flatter their hosts and address aristocrats deferentially.

The French writer Jean François Marmontel contributed articles to the *Encyclopedia* and penned several books, including one containing his memoirs. In this excerpt from that work, Marmontel describes how salon host Julie de Lespinasse brought her guests together and encouraged conversation.

PRIMARY SOURCE

[The] circle was formed of men who were not at all acquainted with each other. She had taken them here and there in society, but so well matched that when they were there they found themselves in most perfect harmony. . . . Nowhere was conversation more lively, more brilliant, nor better regulated than at her house.

—from *Memoirs of Jean François Marmontel* by Jean François Marmontel, 1827

Lights illuminate the Pont Neuf, the oldest standing bridge in Paris. To ensure the safety of Paris at night, Louis XIV had candle-lit lanterns hung in the streets, primarily during the winter. The city first installed gas streetlights in the 1820s.

Salon hosts and guests may have made an exception for Voltaire, who was born into the middle class. His wit, intelligence, and dazzling conversation made him a favorite. But his views, particularly on religion, sometimes scandalized his audience. For instance, Voltaire championed **deism**, a religious philosophy that supports the idea of "natural religion." Deists believe that people are either born with a certain amount of religious knowledge or can acquire it using reason. They believe God created the universe but, after doing so, had no further involvement in it, allowing the world to run according to natural laws. Deism spread through Europe and across the Atlantic, where the philosophy would influence the founders of the United States.

As a deist, Voltaire believed organized religion hindered free and rational inquiry, and many philosophes rejected the core beliefs of Christianity. Nevertheless, most of them tolerated the right of others to express their religious views and ideas. Voltaire defended a Protestant family—in Catholic France—against persecution and religious intolerance in his 1763 essay, "A Treatise on Tolerance." In the essay, he wrote, "Think for yourself and let others enjoy the privilege to do so, too." The following more famous quotation has been attributed to Voltaire, but it was actually written by a 20th-century biographer of the philosophe: "I disapprove of what you say, but I will defend to the death your right to say it." Nevertheless, it sums up Voltaire's attitude—and that of many other Enlightenment thinkers—toward free speech.

HISTORICAL THINKING

1. **READING CHECK** What occurred at Parisian salons?

2. **EVALUATE** How did salons empower the women who hosted them?

3. **MAKE CONNECTIONS** How did the beliefs of deists support Enlightenment thought?

European Enlightenment 573

2.2 DOCUMENT-BASED QUESTION
Government and Natural Rights

What is the primary role of government? To keep its people safe? Provide economic regulation? Maintain services and infrastructure? The Enlightenment gave rise to the ideas that people should be the basis of government and that they create government to protect natural rights. As a result, many enlightened thinkers became civic reformers. A few even rejected the idea of monarchy and aristocracy altogether and called for popular rule through a republican form of government.

As you've read, Enlightenment philosophers claimed that natural rights, including life, liberty, and property, were inherent in human beings. Civic reformers argued that these rights should be protected by rulers through the social contract. In return, individuals would agree to cede, when necessary, some of their freedom.

These ideas arose, in part, in resistance to absolutism, the rule of absolute monarchs in Europe. Concern about the dangers of their tyranny led Charles-Louis Montesquieu to argue for a separation of powers and embrace representative governments of limited power as the ideal form of government. In his works, Denis Diderot opposed the political establishment by promoting religious tolerance and freedom of thought. Mary Wollstonecraft called for a radical reform of the national education system for the benefit of women and all society.

While Voltaire championed liberty, he didn't think democracy was the ideal form of government. He believed people were basically selfish and incapable of self-control and needed the guidance of a wise monarch. And actually, in time, a few absolute monarchs began to govern more wisely. Influenced by the Enlightenment and its philosophers, some kings and queens took a new path and became more tolerant rulers.

Voltaire is buried in the Pantheon of Paris, where many great French citizens have been laid to rest. His tomb is shown here. Voltaire's coffin is inscribed with the following: "Poet, philosopher, historian, he made the human mind to soar and prepared us to be free."

DOCUMENT ONE

Primary Source: Book
from *The Spirit of the Laws* by Charles-Louis Montesquieu, 1748

Montesquieu begins *The Spirit of the Laws* with an explanation of the laws that govern the physical world and animals. He then goes on to discuss the laws that govern humans when they live together in society. In this excerpt from his work, Montesquieu describes the laws and government best suited for societies.

CONSTRUCTED RESPONSE According to Montesquieu, what is the best form of government?

> Better is it to say, that the government most conformable [similar] to nature is that which best agrees with the humor and disposition [state of mind and character] of the people in whose favor it is established. The strength of individuals cannot be united without a conjunction [joining] of all their wills. . . . Law in general is human reason, inasmuch as it governs all the inhabitants of the earth. . . . They [the laws of each nation] should be adapted in such a manner to the people for whom they are framed.

DOCUMENT TWO

Primary Source: Book
from *A Vindication of the Rights of Woman* by Mary Wollstonecraft, 1792

Mary Wollstonecraft believed women should receive the same educational opportunities as men and have the same civil and political rights as well. In *A Vindication of the Rights of Woman*, she argues that, as a result of men's subjugation, women do not live in a "natural state." Here, Wollstonecraft explains what might happen if women had equal rights.

CONSTRUCTED RESPONSE In Wollstonecraft's view, how would women benefit from achieving the same rights as men?

> Asserting the rights which women in common with men ought to contend [strive] for, I have not attempted to extenuate [excuse] their [women's] faults; but to prove them to be the natural consequence of their education and station in society. If so, it is reasonable to suppose that they will change their character, and correct their vices and follies, when they are allowed to be free in a physical, moral, and civil sense. Let woman share the rights, and she will emulate [imitate] the virtues of man; for she must grow more perfect when emancipated [freed].

DOCUMENT THREE

Primary Source: Book
from *Denis Diderot: The Encyclopedia Selections* translated by Stephen Gendzier, 1967

Unlike encyclopedias today, Denis Diderot's volumes were meant not only to provide information but also to guide opinion. In fact, Diderot claimed that the aim of the work was "to change the way people think." The following excerpt from the *Encyclopedia* is drawn from the entry on government.

CONSTRUCTED RESPONSE According to the writer, what is the greatest good of the people?

> [T]he good of the people must be the great purpose of the government. The governors are appointed to fulfill it; and the civil constitution that invests them with this power is bound therein by the laws of nature and by the law of reason. . . . The greatest good of the people is its liberty. Liberty is to the body of the state what health is to each individual. . . . A patriotic governor will therefore see that the right to defend and to maintain liberty is the most sacred of his duties.

SYNTHESIZE & WRITE

1. **REVIEW** Review what you have learned about the Enlightenment and the views of enlightened thinkers on government and natural rights.

2. **RECALL** On your own paper, write down the main idea expressed in each document.

3. **CONSTRUCT** Construct a topic sentence that answers this question: How did Enlightenment philosophers apply their ideas about natural rights to government?

4. **WRITE** Using evidence from this chapter and the documents, write an informative paragraph that supports your topic sentence in Step 3.

2.3

MAIN IDEA The Enlightenment influenced some European monarchs and had a lasting impact on government, religion, and the social order.

A New Sense of Confidence

Imagine you were an absolute ruler with plenty of power and wealth to spare. Would you want to give any of it up? Well, that's just what some European monarchs chose to do during the Enlightenment.

Frederick the Great was a generous patron of the arts and an accomplished musician. In this 1852 painting, *Flute Concert with Frederick the Great in Sans Souci*, he performs an evening concert at his palace. Austrian composer Wolfgang Amadeus Mozart wrote three pieces for the Prussian king.

ENLIGHTENED DESPOTS

Do you remember reading about the power of the Catholic Church during the Middle Ages? Its authority surpassed that of kings and queens. But with the decline of medieval order, monarchs began to assume more power. By 1600, as you know, some ruled as absolute monarchs, with unlimited authority and almost no legal limits. They claimed to rule by divine right, mandated, they believed, by the will of God.

At the same time, though, a growing middle class was pressing for more of a voice in government—especially in England. In 1689, the English Bill of Rights guaranteed basic rights to English subjects, and Parliament limited the king's power. (Still, many centuries would pass before most people were allowed to vote.) And, as you've read, the English philosophers John Locke and Thomas Hobbes began writing about the rights and responsibilities of rulers and the ruled, paving the way for enlightened thought.

William Wilberforce, a member of the British House of Commons, worked to put an end to the slave trade. After introducing many resolutions and bills to Parliament, he finally succeeded in his struggle in 1807. In this excerpt from a speech he made to Parliament in 1789, Wilberforce explains why the British slave trade should be abolished.

PRIMARY SOURCE

As soon as ever I had arrived thus far in my investigation of the Slave Trade, I confess to you, Sir, so enormous, so dreadful, so irremediable [irreversible] did its wickedness appear, that my own mind was completely made up for the abolition. A Trade founded in iniquity [evil], and carried on as this was, must be abolished, let the Policy be what it might, let the consequences be what they would, I from this time determined that I would never rest till I had effected its abolition.

—from William Wilberforce's speech in the House of Commons, May 12, 1789

When the Enlightenment spread in the 1700s, some monarchs embraced the new ideas and made reforms in their countries. Because they never surrendered their complete authority, they became known as **enlightened despots**, absolute rulers who applied certain Enlightenment ideas. You've already read about the reign and reforms of one of these enlightened rulers: Catherine the Great of Russia. A favorite of the philosophes, Catherine exchanged letters with Voltaire and read many of the Enlightenment thinkers' latest works. However, as you know, she failed to follow through on many of her reforms, and the Enlightenment ultimately had little impact on Russia.

Frederick the Great, who ruled Prussia from 1740 to 1786, was another enlightened despot. While Louis XIV of France had declared, "I am the state," Frederick said, "I am the first servant of the state." The Prussian king introduced religious tolerance, reduced censorship of the press, and reformed the country's legal system. However, although Frederick believed serfdom was wrong, he did not take steps to abolish it because he needed the support of wealthy landowners.

Like Frederick, **Joseph II** of Austria promoted religious freedom, freedom of the press, and legal reforms during his reign from 1780 to 1790. Many of these reforms had begun under Joseph's mother, Maria Theresa. But while practical reasons guided Maria Theresa, Joseph was driven by Enlightenment ideals. Joseph also freed the serfs under his rule and had landowners pay peasants for their labor. These changes made Joseph unpopular with the aristocracy, and most of his reforms were dismantled after his death.

IMPACT OF THE ENLIGHTENMENT

The impact of the Enlightenment wasn't limited to monarchs and their reforms. New ideas also influenced ordinary people. The ideas of equality, representation, and rights inspired people because they emerged in a world dominated by hierarchy, inequality, and lack of representation and rights. The argument for a more democratic form of government, with people taking an active role in it, promoted the rise of individualism. And the claim that people should question their own religious beliefs led to a more secular outlook. Encouraged to depend less on the authority of the church and their rulers, people began to think for themselves and use reason to judge right from wrong.

Many Enlightenment thinkers also railed against injustice. While Montesquieu approved of slavery, Voltaire, Rousseau, Wollstonecraft, and others urged an end to the institution and the Atlantic slave trade. Rousseau wrote, "The words *slave* and *right* contradict each other, and are mutually exclusive." Wollstonecraft called the slave trade "an atrocious insult to humanity." As you've learned, France and Britain controlled much of the slave trade in the 18th century. Enlightened thinkers' opposition to slavery may have encouraged politicians and lawmakers to demand its abolition.

Philosophers of the Enlightenment advocated reform, but they lived in a world of ideas. They weren't active revolutionaries. Yet their assertion that a government should be overthrown if it failed to protect an individual's rights resonated with many people. In the 18th and 19th centuries, this notion would inspire democratic revolutions in the American colonies, France, and other parts of the world. Although the Enlightenment would not lead to a perfect world, it would give many western Europeans confidence that their lives would improve and the belief that reason could bring progress.

HISTORICAL THINKING

1. **READING CHECK** Why did some European monarchs in the 18th century come to be known as enlightened despots?

2. **MAKE INFERENCES** Why do you think many Enlightenment thinkers believed the slave trade should be abolished?

3. **SUMMARIZE** How did the Enlightenment and the social contract affect ordinary people?

CHAPTER 20 EUROPEAN ENLIGHTENMENT REVIEW

VOCABULARY

Match each vocabulary word below with its definition.

1. bourgeoisie
2. tyranny
3. philosophe
4. enlightened despot
5. natural rights
6. salon
7. laissez-faire
8. social contract

a. an absolute ruler who made reforms
b. an agreement between rulers and the ruled
c. a state of government in which rulers use unlimited power unfairly
d. an economic system opposed to government regulation of business
e. the middle class
f. a gathering at which guests discussed Enlightenment ideas
g. life, liberty, and property
h. a thinker during the Enlightenment

READING STRATEGY
MAKE INFERENCES

Use a cluster diagram like the one below to make inferences about the Enlightenment. Then answer the questions.

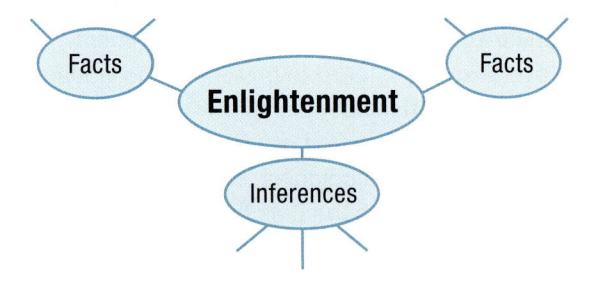

[Cluster diagram: Enlightenment in center, connected to Facts, Facts, and Inferences]

9. Why do you think the French government banned Denis Diderot's *Encyclopedia*?

10. Why did the reforms introduced by Austrian ruler Joseph II make him unpopular with the aristocracy?

MAIN IDEAS

Answer the following questions. Support your answers with evidence from the chapter.

11. According to the philosophes, who were the recipients of natural rights? **LESSON 1.1**

12. What did Mary Wollstonecraft and other female Enlightenment thinkers advocate for women? **LESSON 1.3**

13. According to Adam Smith, how would competition help control the market? **LESSON 1.3**

14. How did salons help spread Enlightenment ideas? **LESSON 2.1**

15. Who were some of the enlightened despots? **LESSON 2.3**

16. Why did the Enlightenment result in a more secular outlook among some people? **LESSON 2.3**

HISTORICAL THINKING

Answer the following questions. Support your answers with evidence from the chapter.

17. **FORM AND SUPPORT OPINIONS** How do you think Louis XIV of France reacted to the Enlightenment? Explain.

18. **COMPARE AND CONTRAST** How did Rousseau's view of civilization differ from that of other enlightened thinkers?

19. **MAKE INFERENCES** Why did civic reformers argue for representative governments?

20. **EVALUATE** Why did deism appeal to some of the enlightened thinkers?

21. **ANALYZE CAUSE AND EFFECT** How did salons impact the Enlightenment?

22. **DRAW CONCLUSIONS** How did the Enlightenment encourage people to believe that reason could improve their lives and bring progress?

23. **FORM AND SUPPORT OPINIONS** What is the most important legacy of the Enlightenment?

INTERPRET CHARTS

Study the chart at right, which summarizes the major ideas of Enlightenment thinkers. Then answer the questions below.

24. What form of government encompasses all of these ideas?

25. In your opinion, which is the most important Enlightenment idea? Explain your answer.

Major Ideas of Enlightenment Thinkers

Enlightenment Thinker	Idea
John Locke	Government established to protect people's natural rights: life, liberty, and property
Charles-Louis Montesquieu	Government separated into three branches: executive, legislative, judicial
Voltaire	Enforce policy of religious tolerance and freedom of expression
Jean-Jacques Rousseau	People create own government and give up some of their freedom for the common good
Mary Wollstonecraft	Grant equality and education for women

ANALYZE SOURCES

In *An Essay Concerning Human Understanding*, published in 1690, John Locke states that people acquire knowledge through their perceptions and experiences and then use reason to form ideas. In this excerpt from the introduction to the work, Locke discusses the unwillingness of people to embrace new ideas. Read the excerpt and then answer the question that follows.

> Truth scarce ever yet carried it by vote [never was accepted by the majority of people] anywhere at its first appearance: new opinions are always suspected, and usually opposed, without any other reason but because they are not already common. But truth, like gold, is not the less so for being newly brought out of the mine. It is trial and examination must give it price, and not any antique fashion; and though it be not yet current by the public stamp, yet it may, for all that, be as old as nature, and is certainly not the less genuine.

26. Why do you think Locke compared truth to gold?

CONNECT TO YOUR LIFE

27. **EXPLANATORY** You have read about the lasting impact of Enlightenment ideas. Ideas about religious tolerance, representative government, and freedom of expression would result in spreading democracy around the world. Think about how these and other enlightened ideas affect your own life. Then write a short essay explaining the impact of Enlightenment ideas on your life today.

TIPS

- Review the Enlightenment thinkers and ideas discussed in this chapter.
- Choose two or three enlightened ideas that have had the greatest impact on your own life.
- Use at least two or three vocabulary words from the chapter in your essay.
- Conclude your essay by summarizing the impact of Enlightenment ideas on Americans today.

CHAPTER 21

Political Revolution
1750–1830

HISTORICAL THINKING What factors can lead to revolution?

SECTION 1 **Revolutions in the West**

SECTION 2 **Napoleon**

SECTION 3 **Wars for Liberation**

CRITICAL VIEWING

Near the Patowmack Canal in Virginia, National Geographic photographer Ken Garrett captures an evening reenactment of an American Revolution skirmish. What conclusions can you draw about warfare during the 18th and 19th centuries based on details in this photograph?

Political Revolution 581

1.1 MAIN IDEA Enlightenment ideas inspired American colonists to declare independence and establish their own republic.

Debate and War in America

The principles of the Enlightenment spread to different parts of the world, including the Americas. Enlightenment concepts such as John Locke's call for protection of the basic rights of "life, liberty, and property" fueled the American colonists' desire for independence from Britain.

THE AMERICAN WAR FOR INDEPENDENCE

For many years, the British ruled their colonies in North America relatively peacefully. At the end of the French and Indian War, however, the colonists' joy over the British victory soured when Britain issued the Proclamation of 1763, limiting colonial westward expansion. The British wanted to avoid further conflict with French settlers and Native Americans.

Uneasiness grew as the British imposed additional taxes on the colonists to cover the costs of the war. Colonists bitterly resented these taxes because they had no representatives in Parliament who could vote in favor of or against them. Many people began to call themselves "Americans." They adopted the slogan "No taxation without representation!" and formed **militias**, or volunteer armies.

Fighting broke out in April 1775 when British soldiers marched on Concord, Massachusetts, to destroy militia supplies. Several weeks later, members of the Continental Congress met to determine future actions, one of which was to appoint **George Washington** commander of the Continental Army. On July 4, 1776, Congress approved the **Declaration of Independence** written by **Thomas Jefferson**.

The declaration built on John Locke's Enlightenment idea of a social contract. Locke believed that subjects could overthrow leaders who did not honor their side of the contract. Using Locke's logic, Jefferson argued that an American rebellion was justified. Jefferson

CRITICAL VIEWING *Washington Crossing the Delaware*, painted by Emanuel Leutze in 1851, honors the moment the American general George Washington and his troops sailed across the Delaware River on the night of December 25–26, 1776, to surprise German forces on the other side. Based on this image, how do you think the artist viewed Washington and the Continental Army?

included Locke's idea of **popular sovereignty**—the belief that government authority arises from the people themselves—as well. And Jefferson also incorporated ideas from the English Bill of Rights, which outlined the basic rights of British citizens.

Revolutionary leaders also drew upon the political philosophy of **William Blackstone**, a British attorney whose lectures on British **common law**, or laws determined by earlier court decisions, were published as *Commentaries on the Laws of England*. They cited this work as a basis for the argument that Americans were not merely subjects of the king but also British citizens with fundamental rights, and that taxation without consent was unfair.

Rebellious colonists became determined to create a republic with a government in which they had a voice. Their fight for independence during the American Revolution was long and difficult. The makeshift Continental Army was pitted against the well-equipped and well-trained British "redcoat" soldiers. A key turning point was the American victory at the Battle of Saratoga, after which France threw its support behind the colonists. In 1781, the Americans finally defeated the British army at the decisive Battle of Yorktown.

CONSEQUENCES OF THE REVOLUTION

The first attempt to form a confederation of the former colonies was unsuccessful. National leaders such as **James Madison** argued that the individual states would have to give up more of their power to a central government. In 1787, delegates met at the Constitutional Convention in Philadelphia, where they wrote the Constitution of the United States of America. Their goal was to create an American republic in which the people vote for their leaders. The delegates planned a government based on **constitutionalism**, an approach to government that strictly defines and limits its powers.

Madison and other founders incorporated ideas of the Enlightenment into the U.S. Constitution. Inspired by Montesquieu's belief in the separation of powers, they created three branches of government: executive, legislative, and judicial. Each branch could check and balance the powers of the other branches.

Compromise was the hallmark of the Constitution. For example, delegates from large and small states agreed on a two-house legislature called Congress. The House of Representatives would have representatives based on a state's population, and the Senate would have an equal number of senators for each state. The delegates also agreed to balance the powers of individual states with **federal** powers, or the shared authority of the states united in a single nation. Their resulting Constitution remains the supreme law of the United States and has lasted more than 230 years.

The issue of slavery required negotiation as well. Leaders from southern states argued that enslaved people should count in a state's population when calculating the number of representatives and electoral college votes. Northern delegates disagreed; they thought slaves should not be counted because they could not vote. The sides reached a compromise: when creating congressional districts, five enslaved African Americans would count as three free persons. Slavery remained legal, with 40 percent of southerners and many people in the North held in bondage.

Congress amended the Constitution in 1791 by adding a **Bill of Rights** that guaranteed civil liberties, such as freedom of religion, freedom of the press, and freedom of assembly. However, most states restricted the vote to white men who owned property. As in Europe, the Enlightenment idea that "all men are created equal" was not applied to everyone. Women, Native Americans, and most free black people were denied many basic rights.

Historians debate whether the American Revolution was a true "revolution" because a rearrangement of social and economic power did not take place. For the French Revolution that followed, there is no such debate.

The Declaration of Independence details the colonists' grievances and makes a stirring announcement of universal values.

PRIMARY SOURCE

We hold these truths to be self-evident, that all men are created equal, that they are endowed by their Creator with certain inalienable Rights, that among these are Life, Liberty and the pursuit of Happiness.—That to secure these rights, Governments are instituted among Men, deriving their just powers from the consent of the governed.

HISTORICAL THINKING

1. **READING CHECK** How did the nation's founders incorporate Enlightenment ideas as they established the United States?

2. **IDENTIFY MAIN IDEAS AND DETAILS** Why did the American colonists protest taxes that were imposed to cover the costs of the French and Indian War?

3. **MAKE CONNECTIONS** Did the phrase "all men are created equal" apply to the United States after its revolution? Explain.

1.2 MAIN IDEA After years of oppression, French commoners worked together to seize power from the upper classes.

The French Revolution

Change can happen slowly—or it can explode suddenly and dramatically. Drastic developments quickly swept through France as its common people rebelled against the ruling classes during the French Revolution. This turning point would impact governments and societies throughout Europe and change the course of history.

RULE UNDER LOUIS XVI

Combined social and economic issues led French citizens to topple the monarchy during the French Revolution of 1789. Three distinct social classes, or **estates**, existed in France at the time. The First Estate consisted of the Catholic clergy, the Second Estate included the nobility, and the Third Estate contained everyone else.

The Third Estate included the bourgeoisie, which you learned is the middle class. The bourgeoisie in France was made up of highly educated and often property-owning professionals, such as doctors, lawyers, and merchants. However, the majority of the Third Estate were peasants who lived in rural farming villages.

The Third Estate had far fewer rights than the other classes did. The Catholic Church owned much of the property in France, so the church and its clergy enjoyed many special advantages. The nobles of the Second Estate benefited from privileges as well. Both the First Estate and the Second Estate were exempt from direct taxation, while the Third Estate was burdened with heavy taxes.

Just as the American colonists admired the Glorious Revolution and its English Bill of Rights, so did the overburdened French middle class. Members of the French bourgeoisie also felt **disenfranchised**, or without rights or the ability to influence their government. They wanted their government to reflect the ideas of Montesquieu, Rousseau, and other Enlightenment thinkers by recognizing the French bourgeoisie's rights.

In the early 18th century, a period of prosperity had boosted birth rates and made France the most populous

CRITICAL VIEWING In this political cartoon from the 18th century, the First and Second Estates—personified by a clergyman and an aristocratic military officer, respectively—crush a man representing the Third Estate under a large stone that represents taxation. What conclusion can you draw about the three estates from this image?

584 CHAPTER 21

country in Europe. But fighting and losing the French and Indian War had been expensive, and in the 1780s, bad harvests and higher taxes caused suffering for this vast population. Many people fled their farms for Paris and other cities, where they faced overcrowding and unemployment. Like the American colonists, they believed they were being mistreated by their king.

The absolute monarch **Louis XVI** ruled over his 24 million French subjects from his spectacular palace at Versailles, 12 miles outside Paris. Though wealthy and powerful, he was a poor decision maker, and he often relied on his wife and queen, **Marie Antoinette**, for advice. Many people believed that the queen was under the influence of her relatives in Austria, and she was known for her extravagant tastes. Much of the nobility and the Third Estate distrusted her. Some spread a rumor that when she was told the people of France had no bread, Marie Antoinette cruelly replied, "Let them eat cake!"

OVERTHROWING THE MONARCHY

Like Britain before the American Revolution, France had accumulated a lot of war debt. Funding the French and Indian War and supporting the American rebels had emptied the French treasury, and the common people were crushed by taxes.

In 1789, Louis and his ministers reluctantly convened an Estates-General to address their economic woes. Each of the three orders of French society sent representatives to the rarely held assembly. Third Estate delegates hoped to create a representative legislative body. However, each estate had only one vote on each issue; the First and Second Estates sided together, so none of the Third Estate's proposals were accepted. Furious, the Third Estate delegates formed their own National Assembly and pledged to hold meetings until a constitutional monarchy was formed. Recall that a constitutional monarchy is a government in which the monarch shares power with a parliament. Rather than give in to this demand, Louis XVI ordered 18,000 troops to defend his palace at Versailles. The French Revolution had begun.

The common people of Paris soon joined the fight for rights. Working-class men called *sans-culottes*—because they wore trousers instead of the lavish clothes of the rich—stormed the Bastille. The Bastille was a building in Paris that served as both a jail and armory, or place where government weapons are stored. Thomas Jefferson, then the U.S. minister to France, was in Paris at the time. He most likely noticed that commoners took a greater role in the French Revolution than the common people in America had during the American Revolution. In the former British colonies, the privileged and well educated led the rebellion. Jefferson described the storming of the Bastille in a letter: "They took all the arms, discharged the prisoners & such of the garrison as were not killed in the first moment of fury, carried the Governor & Lieutenant governor to the Grave (the place of public execution) cut off their heads, & sent them through the city in triumph to the Palais royal."

Louis XVI quickly recognized the National Assembly. It immediately declared equality before the law, eliminated special rights for nobles, and dismissed all feudal obligations. The assembly's **Declaration of the Rights of Man and of the Citizen** stated that "men are born and remain free and equal in rights" and "the natural and inalienable rights of man" are "liberty, property, security, and resistance to oppression." Government positions were open to all, and taxes were assigned more equally. Freedom of thought and religion were granted, and mandatory payments to the Catholic Church ended.

The National Assembly vowed to work with Louis XVI to establish a new constitutional monarchy. However, some 20,000 Parisians—mostly women—who distrusted the king and were also angry about the high price of bread advanced toward Versailles. This "March of the Women" forced the king and his family to relocate to Paris, where revolutionaries could better watch them. Farmers throughout France stormed noble estates, causing many aristocrats to flee the country.

Following the example of the Constitutional Convention in the United States, the National Assembly formed a Legislative Assembly to draft a new set of basic laws, which Louis XVI promptly rejected. He was captured and held prisoner in his Parisian palace. Although other European rulers attempted to come to Louis's aid and overthrow the revolution, French citizens thwarted an Austrian attack. The French monarchy was doomed.

The Declaration of the Rights of Man and of the Citizen includes many statements of liberty.

PRIMARY SOURCE

Law is the expression of the general will. Every citizen has a right to participate personally, or through his representative, in its foundation. It must be the same for all, whether it protects or punishes. All citizens, being equal in the eyes of the law. . . .

French artist Jean-Pierre Houël's *Storming of the Bastille* captures the scene after commoners attacked the Paris prison on July 14, 1789.

REVOLUTIONARY DESPOTISM

The National Assembly dissolved itself in 1791 in favor of a National Convention. This new legislative body began writing a republican constitution and ordered the execution of Louis XVI and Marie Antoinette in January 1793. The French Constitution of 1793 granted all male citizens full voting rights, even non–property-owners. In this way, it was more radical than the U.S. Constitution.

Most French revolutionaries, similar to American rebels, only recognized the rights of free men, not of women or enslaved people. However, in her *Declaration of the Rights of Women*, author Olympe de Gouges argued, "The exercise of the natural rights of women has only been limited by the perpetual tyranny that man opposes to them; these limits should be reformed by the laws of nature and reason." Some revolutionaries decreed that enslaved people should be freed, raising hopes for freedom and equality among those held in bondage in the French Caribbean.

The **Jacobins**, a radical faction, took control of the government, ushering in a time of extreme violence. Their leader was former lawyer **Maximilien Robespierre**, who won followers because of his support of liberty and equal rights and his determination to defend France from outside attack.

Robespierre wanted to transform society into a "Republic of Virtue" in which corruption and inequality would be eliminated—through intense fear, if necessary. When the Jacobins confiscated land, however, many of the bourgeoisie resisted. And when Jacobins attacked the power and property of the Catholic Church, many conservative peasants in rural France opposed them.

Fearful of losing control, Robespierre sacrificed liberty in favor of **despotism**, the oppressive rule by a leader with absolute power. His Committee of Public Safety began a Reign of Terror in which more than 17,000 people were executed. More than 300,000 citizens were arrested. Some were imprisoned without trial and tortured.

The symbol of the French Revolution became the **guillotine** (gee-yuh-TEEN), a machine with a sharp blade designed to behead people. Joseph Guillotin, a doctor, devised the guillotine as a rational Enlightenment device that would make public executions less violent. Ironically, his invention was identified with the cruelty and despotism of revolutionary terror.

By July 1794, the tables had turned. Robespierre and many other Jacobins lost their own heads to the sharp blade of the guillotine. One journalist wrote, "the revolution was devouring its own children." The National Assembly reasserted its power and created a new constitution with a limited electorate and a separation of powers. Although France appeared to be on its way to a stable representative government, the nation would face years of upheaval.

The American Revolution and the French Revolution differed in several ways. Americans fought to break away from a governing country, while the French wanted internal change. Many historians believe the Americans had a clearer goal—the colonists wanted to establish a new nation. The French, instead, wanted to create a society of perfect equality. However, both revolutions inspired other people, including French colonists in what would become Haiti, to fight for liberty and independence.

The blade on this 18th century guillotine reads *Armées de la République*, which translates to "Armies of the Republic."

HISTORICAL THINKING

1. **READING CHECK** How did the Third Estate differ from the First and Second Estates before the French Revolution?

2. **ANALYZE CAUSE AND EFFECT** What were three main causes of the French Revolution?

3. **IDENTIFY MAIN IDEAS AND DETAILS** What political reforms did the National Assembly establish in France?

4. **SEQUENCE EVENTS** In what order did the following actions take place: the meeting of the National Convention, the establishment of the National Assembly, and the adoption of a constitution?

Political Revolution 587

1.3

MAIN IDEA Enslaved people in the French colony of Saint-Domingue rebelled against their bondage and won freedom as the new independent nation of Haiti.

Haiti's Revolution

For people trapped in slavery, a better life seemed impossible. However, on a French island in the Caribbean, enslaved people took action to make their dreams of liberty come true.

UPRISING IN SAINT-DOMINGUE

The colony of Saint-Domingue, which occupied the western half of the island of Hispaniola in the Caribbean Sea, was France's richest overseas possession, or territory controlled by outsiders. Tending to vast sugarcane fields, half a million enslaved Africans toiled on the colony's plantations under harsh conditions.

News of the 1789 French uprising sparked hints of revolution in Saint-Domingue. The first to call for more rights were the *gens de couleur*, free men and women of mixed race. These literate artisans and farmers were slaveholders and had some wealth. Gens de couleur sought the same rights as the white plantation owners, and by 1791 civil war broke out between the two groups.

When he was growing up, African-American artist Jacob Lawrence did not see any black heroes in textbooks. So he decided to paint some. As a young man, Lawrence created a series of 41 panels about the Haitian Revolution, which included the famous rebel general Toussaint L'Ouverture. Decades later, in the 1990s, Lawrence revisited these images. *L'Ouverture (The Opener)* epitomizes Lawrence's distinctive style.

Neither faction wanted to end slavery, but their conflict led to a large slave uprising led by a man who was called Boukman because he could read. He was a priest in the *voudon* religion, which combined West African and Roman Catholic rituals and beliefs, and he was able to summon thousands of slaves to revolt in the summer of 1791. Like the French peasants who burned the manors of aristocratic landholders, Boukman's slave army attacked the planters' estates. The **insurgents**, or rebel fighters, marched on the city of Le Cap and slaughtered many white planters and gens de couleur until planter forces captured and executed Boukman.

TOUSSAINT L'OUVERTURE AND INDEPENDENCE

In 1792, the French government sent an army to restore order, but a new Saint-Domingue commander emerged. Because he was enslaved, we know little about his family or childhood, but we do know that he received a French education during his time in a slaveholder's house. The name this man is remembered by, **Toussaint L'Ouverture** (TOO-san LOO-vuhr-tyur), refers to the "opening" he made in the enemy lines. His military, political, intellectual, and diplomatic strengths would help free the colony from the French.

Toussaint knew how to organize slaves and simultaneously form alliances with whites, gens de couleur, and foreign forces. By 1801, his army controlled most of the island. He supported a new constitution that granted rights to all and named Toussaint governor-general for life.

By this time, France's government had shifted from a republic to a dictatorship. A French military unit was dispatched to crush Toussaint's army. Toussaint fought off the threat for several months and then agreed to meet with French officers to make a peace treaty. The officers betrayed him and sent him to prison in France, where he died after harsh treatment.

After Toussaint's death, the French lost the war—and disease played an important role. People born in Saint-Domingue had built up resistance to malaria and yellow fever, tropical diseases spread by mosquitoes. Soldiers fresh from France, however, were vulnerable to these illnesses. Toussaint had been aware of this, so he often forced the French to camp in swampy ground, where many soldiers became sick and died. To avoid additional casualties, the French removed their forces from the island. Saint-Domingue became the independent nation of Haiti in 1804.

Slaveholders in the United States were terrified of the Haitian example of the enslaved rising up to overthrow the people who had forced them into bondage. So the United States placed a trade embargo on the new country. And even though Haiti officially established itself as a black-ruled republic in 1820, the United States did not recognize Haitian independence for years to come. Britain and France also refused to accept Haiti as a free nation.

Although the rebels who spearheaded the Haitian Revolution found inspiration in the American and the French revolutions, the Haitian Revolution differed from the other two. The Haitian Revolution expressly addressed the unfairness of the colonial social hierarchy based on race. And only the Haitians immediately abolished slavery, granting liberty and basic human rights to people of all races. After their victory in 1783, Americans did not grant rights to people of African heritage, Native Americans, or women. Likewise, the French did not offer suffrage to women. However, all three revolutions resulted in a written constitution and the establishment of a republic—though France's republic would not last long.

The following excerpts are from the 1801 Haitian constitution endorsed by Toussaint L'Ouverture.

PRIMARY SOURCE

Art. 3—There can be no slaves on this territory; servitude has been forever abolished. All men are born, live, and die there free and French.

Art. 4—All men can work at all forms of employment, whatever their color.

Art. 5—No other distinctions exist than those of virtues and talents, nor any other superiority than that granted by the law in the exercise of a public charge. The law is the same for all, whether it punishes or protects.

HISTORICAL THINKING

1. **READING CHECK** Why is Toussaint L'Ouverture considered a hero to the people of Haiti?

2. **DRAW CONCLUSIONS** Why do you think the United States failed to recognize Haiti's independence?

3. **COMPARE AND CONTRAST** Which revolution—American, French, or Haitian—had the greatest impact on its society? Explain your response.

Political Revolution 589

2.1

MAIN IDEA Napoleon Bonaparte restored stability to post–revolutionary France, initiated reforms, and attempted to conquer Europe before his eventual and total defeat.

Napoleon Bonaparte

Certain individuals make extremely powerful impacts—some positive, some negative—on the world. For better or worse, the French leader Napoleon Bonaparte affected Europe so strongly that the era of his rise, rule, and collapse is sometimes called the "Age of Napoleon."

CRITICAL VIEWING *The Coronation of Napoleon* by French artist Jacques-Louis David shows the newly crowned emperor placing a crown on the head of his wife, Josephine, in front of a large crowd. The 1807 canvas is more than 20 feet high and 32 feet wide. What does the portrayal of the ceremony and the size of the painting tell you about how Napoleon viewed himself?

THE RISE OF A NEW LEADER

The French Revolution quickly moved through three distinct stages. As you learned, the focus at first centered around establishing a constitutional or limited monarchy. Once that proved impossible, revolutionary leaders sought to fundamentally transform French society and turned to democratic despotism under the Jacobins. Finally, amid the turmoil, an emerging military genius would create a French empire.

Despite efforts by the National Convention, France remained sharply divided from 1795 to 1799. The new republic's executive branch, the Directory, faced conspiracies by both Jacobins and monarchists. Meanwhile, French armies collected victories under the young general **Napoleon Bonaparte**, whose troops captured northern Italy from the Austrians in 1796. Then, in 1799, two members of the Directory plotted with Napoleon to launch a successful coup, or sudden overthrow, of the French government.

Like George Washington, Napoleon looked to ancient Rome for inspiration. However, while Washington admired the Roman Republic, Napoleon followed Rome's imperial example and transformed France's republic into his empire. Most French people were proud of Napoleon's military successes and eager to emerge from the turmoil of the revolution, so they continually voted to approve Napoleon's growing power. In addition, Napoleon encouraged his political opposition to join his administration. He also restored papal authority to gain the support of Catholics, especially in the countryside. As a result, he faced little opposition when he crowned himself Emperor Napoleon I in 1804.

Napoleon appeared to be the enlightened despot Enlightenment philosophes had hoped for. (Recall that an enlightened despot was an absolute ruler who applied certain Enlightenment ideas.) To many French citizens, Napoleon embodied the **ideology**, or basic beliefs, of the French Revolution. His domestic policies brought order to France and seemed to have the interest of its people at heart. Napoleon started the Bank of France to stabilize the economy and enforced the more rational use of the metric system of weights and measures to improve trade.

Most importantly, the new emperor created the **Napoleonic Code**, a clear and organized system of laws that recognized the legal equality of all French citizens. Napoleon made sure that these laws addressed Enlightenment ideals such as personal liberty, freedom of religion for Protestants and Jews, and the rule of law. Still, the growth of executive power under Napoleon lessened the separation of powers emphasized earlier by Montesquieu. And the Napoleonic Code reduced rights for women and reestablished slavery in French colonies.

Napoleon proved to be a master of **propaganda**, information used by a government to make people think or act in a particular way. He commissioned artwork to show himself as an infallible leader in the spirit of the Roman Empire and issued collectible medals touting his fame. He also ordered that newspapers must publish articles slanted in his favor. All such propaganda efforts were aimed at gaining the approval of the public.

FRENCH NATIONALISM

Determined to expand his empire, Napoleon led military campaigns throughout Europe. Many historians point out that these campaigns provided the French people with a national identity. A sense of **nationalism**—or belief that individuals are bound together by ties of language, culture, history, and often religion—developed in France. Previously, French nobles had refused to believe that they had any affiliation to the lower ranks of society. French peasants and commoners felt a connection to their local community but not the French state in Paris. As soldiers fighting for France, common people began to see themselves as citizens of a nation rather than merely subjects of a king. Napoleon made the most of France's growing nationalism and promised French citizens glory, if not representative government.

Bringing together the people of France enabled Napoleon to create a political structure known as a **nation-state**. A nation-state is a state mostly made up of people of one nationality, sharing common traits

---

> In his own account of the 1799 coup, Napoleon glosses over his role as an instigator of the plot to abolish the French constitution and legislature.
>
> **PRIMARY SOURCE**
>
> The Council of Elders summoned me; I answered its appeal. A plan of general restoration had been devised by men whom the nation has been accustomed to regard as the defenders of liberty, equality, and property; this plan required an examination, calm, free, exempt from all influence and all fear. Accordingly, the Council of Elders resolved upon the removal of the Legislative Body to Saint-Cloud; it gave me the responsibility of disposing the force necessary for its independence. I believed it my duty to my fellow citizens, to the soldiers perishing in our armies, to the national glory acquired at the cost of their blood, to accept the command.
>
> —from Napoleon's account of his role in the coup, 1799

such as language and heritage. Earlier empires such as the Roman, Ming, Mughal, and Habsburg empires always included diverse peoples. However, the unity often ended when the empire fell. In the nation-states that formed in modern times, people began to see themselves as "Dutch," "French," or "English" and maintained this identity through changes in leadership. Today, a sense of nationalism and of belonging to a nation is common around the world.

BUILDING AN EMPIRE

Napoleon's military seemed unstoppable in what became known as the Napoleonic Wars. His troops swept through Italy and Spain, which also created conditions for independence in Latin America, which you will read about later. Napoleon's forces claimed control over the Netherlands, Switzerland, Poland, and the western half of Germany, and inflicted losses on the Austrians and the Prussians. However, Napoleon experienced challenges and losses as well. In 1798, his defeat in a disastrous expedition into Egypt dashed his plans to conquer lands in Africa. In 1803, Napoleon sold a huge parcel of North American land to the United States in an exchange known as the Louisiana Purchase, quite possibly to raise money for his military efforts.

The French invasions spread nationalism through Europe. At first, many Germans hoped the French would bring the Enlightenment principles of freedom and equality. But they were treated as conquered people with limited rights. Resistance to France's domination encouraged a sense of German nationalism. Likewise, people in the diverse kingdoms of the Italian Peninsula developed a common "Italian" identity to rally against French invaders.

NAPOLEON'S DOWNFALL

In the end, Napoleon's ambition caused his demise. In 1812, he mounted an attack on Russia. Napoleon and his troops trekked thousands of miles to reach Moscow only to find it abandoned and almost burned to the ground. Forced to retreat during the harsh Russian winter, the French suffered enormous losses. Fewer than 100,000 of the 700,000 troops returned home.

Anti-French forces across Europe banded together to form a coalition. The united front invaded France, made Napoleon abdicate, and restored the monarchy by placing Louis XVIII on the French throne. After being banished to the Mediterranean island of Elba, Napoleon escaped. He rebuilt his army and made a dramatic return to Paris before he was overpowered by British and Prussian forces at the Battle of Waterloo in 1815. After Napoleon's final loss, France finally became a constitutional monarchy.

Napoleon died in exile, but his global impact was substantial. His grouping of small western German states into the Confederation of the Rhine paved the way for German nationalism. Eventually, German-speaking people formed a centralized German nation-state. The people of the Italian Peninsula would also unite. Across the ocean, the United States expanded to twice its size as a result of the Louisiana Purchase. In contrast, Ottoman power was reduced when Ottoman armies lost control of the Nile to an ambitious new Egyptian dynasty.

The return of Louis XVIII to the French throne was a major sign that Europe's enthusiasm for revolutions had run out of steam as European elites worked to suppress reform. A series of meetings called the **Congress of Vienna** began in 1814 and restored the balance of power among Britain, France, Austria, Prussia, and

592 CHAPTER 21

In 1806, Napoleon commissioned a monument to be built in Paris to celebrate French victories during the Napoleonic Wars. The Arc de Triomphe de l'Étoile (Triumphal Arch of the Star)—known more simply as the Arc de Triomphe—is one of the most famous symbols of France.

Russia. The main goal of the aristocratic members of the congress was to return to a time when the upper class wielded power and to make sure that monarchies would continue as forms of government. The former French empire was taken apart and the monarchical government restored. However, no territory was taken from France itself, and the nation remained one of the great powers of Europe along with Britain, Austria, Prussia, and Russia.

The Concert of Europe was an informal agreement among the major European monarchies aimed at safeguarding peace in Europe. It was also meant to preserve the European **status quo**, or existing condition, and ensure that all the major monarchies would support and defend any monarchy threatened with upheaval. Europe enjoyed relative peace for almost a century. But demands for nationalism continued to grow stronger and stronger.

HISTORICAL THINKING

1. **READING CHECK** How did Napoleon rise to power, and what was his role in French government?

2. **DRAW CONCLUSIONS** How did growing nationalism in France help Napoleon achieve his goals?

3. **FORM AND SUPPORT OPINIONS** Do you think a European ruler today could gain the power Napoleon had? Use evidence in the text to support your answer.

4. **INTERPRET MAPS** What was the status of the cities of Berlin, Milan, Vienna, and London during the time period shown on the map?

Political Revolution 593

2.2 DOCUMENT-BASED QUESTION
Portraits of Power

During the 18th and 19th centuries, political leaders in the Americas and in Europe commissioned paintings of themselves to project images of power. The portraits were meant to inform people not only of the leaders' power but also of the type of power with which they were associated.

President George Washington of the United States and Emperor Napoleon Bonaparte of France were both aware of classical Greek and Roman models that signified power. Their respective portraitists Gilbert Stuart and Jean-Auguste-Dominique Ingres knew about these examples as well. Washington identified himself with the democratic tradition of Athens and the republican period of Rome. In contrast, Napoleon emphasized the imperial Roman tradition.

No portrait of Toussaint L'Ouverture was created during his lifetime. Many portraits made after his death exaggerated Toussaint's physical features. In 1877, Haitian artist Louis Rigaud used written eyewitness descriptions to present a realistic approximation of the revolutionary's appearance. Rigaud wanted viewers to think of Toussaint as a leader who adhered to the democratic tradition.

This marble statue—*Augustus of Prima Porta*—shows an idealized image of the Roman emperor Augustus. Recall that Augustus ended the Roman Republic but brought peace to the Roman Empire. Here, the sculptor portrays Augustus as a strong young military leader addressing his troops.

ARTIFACT ONE

Primary Source: Painting
George Washington by Gilbert Stuart, 1796

CONSTRUCTED RESPONSE Why do you think Stuart included the inkstand on the table and the books below it in Washington's portrait?

The stormy sky in the background might illustrate the difficult times that Washington and his comrades weathered, while the rainbow might symbolize their ultimate victory.

Washington wears no sign of military rank, holds a sheathed sword that points down, and offers his open hand. The impression is one of a man who seeks peace.

ARTIFACT TWO

Primary Source: Painting
Napoleon on His Imperial Throne by Jean-Auguste-Dominique Ingres, 1806

CONSTRUCTED RESPONSE Why do you think Ingres shows Napoleon wearing a crown?

Napoleon holds a scepter topped by a figure of Charlemagne, the early medieval emperor who ruled over most of Europe.

Unlike Washington's open right hand, Napoleon's right fist is clenched high on his scepter, adding to the contrast between the French emperor and Washington.

ARTIFACT THREE

Primary Source: Painting
Toussaint L'Ouverture by Louis Rigaud, 1877

CONSTRUCTED RESPONSE Why do you think Rigaud chose a simple background, without much adornment?

The portrait shows Toussaint in uniform because he is most remembered as a military leader. He was killed before he could rule Haiti in peacetime.

Rigaud references written and visual descriptions that emphasize Toussaint's good posture, determined expression, and care in dress.

SYNTHESIZE & WRITE

1. **REVIEW** Review what you have read and observed about revolutionary leaders and their portraits.
2. **RECALL** On your own paper, list two details you observed by looking at each portrait.
3. **CONSTRUCT** Construct a topic sentence that answers this question: How are the three portraits similar to and different from one another?
4. **WRITE** Using evidence from this chapter and the portraits, write an informative paragraph that supports your topic sentence in Step 3.

Political Revolution 595

2.3

MAIN IDEA The cultural movement now known as Romanticism put less emphasis on order and reason and embraced nature and emotion.

The Culture of Romanticism

Often, cultural movements are closely connected to historical events. The chaos of the French Revolution and the Age of Napoleon turned Europeans away from Enlightenment concepts of structure and restraint and aimed them toward the untamed wonders of nature and the imagination.

EMERGENCE OF ROMANTICISM

Writers, artists, and musicians of the Enlightenment practiced **neoclassicism**, a style based on Greek and Roman ideals. Neoclassic works usually showed symmetry and proportion, for example, in graceful images and buildings. In contrast, **Romanticism** emphasized emotions. Romantic writers, artists, and musicians introduced unpredictability into their creations, with possible surprises around every corner. Their work was subjective, or based on an individual's personal viewpoint. Nature was a way to connect to spirituality, and Romantic writers and artists addressed their topics in a sublime—or awe-inspiring—manner.

Romantics made seemingly insignificant objects appear grand or even terrifying. A simple Greek vase inspired the English poet John Keats to write "Beauty is truth, truth beauty,—that is all / Ye know on earth, and all ye need to know." Romantics believed works of true beauty could only come from the imagination. They tackled subjects such as imagined places, unusual locations, and the supernatural. However, Romantic artists also found inspiration in folktales and myths from the Middle Ages.

LITERATURE

In Britain, writers like **William Wordsworth**—considered the first Romantic writer—sought new poetic forms, innovative word choices, and passionate appeals. Long walks in nature provided inspiration for Wordsworth and other Romantic artists, and he claimed that "all good poetry is the spontaneous overflow of powerful feelings."

In Britain, George Gordon, best known by the title **Lord Byron**, wrote Romantic poetry as well. Byron was well known for his dashing good looks and daring lifestyle, which were similar to the main characters of many

---

The English Romantic poet **William Blake** composed songlike lyric poems, often with spiritual and supernatural overtones. He wrote political poems as well. His works—which were sometimes accompanied by images he drew himself—contained themes of freedom, innocence, and the dangers of commercialism.

PRIMARY SOURCE

Tyger Tyger, burning bright,
In the forests of the night;
What immortal hand or eye,
Could frame thy fearful symmetry?

In what distant deeps or skies
Burnt the fire of thine eyes?
On what wings dare he aspire?
What the hand, dare seize the fire?

And what shoulder, & what art,
Could twist the sinews of thy heart?
And when thy heart began to beat,
What dread hand? & what dread feet?

What the hammer? what the chain,
In what furnace was thy brain?
What the anvil? what dread grasp,
Dare its deadly terrors clasp!

When the stars threw down their spears
And water'd heaven with their tears:
Did he smile his work to see?
Did he who made the Lamb make thee?

Tyger Tyger burning bright,
In the forests of the night:
What immortal hand or eye,
Dare frame thy fearful symmetry?

—"The Tyger" by William Blake, 1789

Romanticism vs. Neoclassicism

In painting, neoclassicism is a simple, straightforward technique that uses distinct and purposeful lines. Jacques-Louis David, a leading French neoclassic painter, created works inspired by the styles of ancient Greece and Rome as well as their values of courage and honor. However, the lush and expressive Romantic movement that emerged from the calm, rational order of neoclassicism led to a distinct change in painting and portraiture. Many of Spanish artist Francisco de Goya's works feature visible, blurred brushstrokes, which are a visual representation of Romanticism's reaction against the established values of the time.

CRITICAL VIEWING Compare and contrast de Goya's Romantic *The Clothed Maja* (below) with David's neoclassic *Portrait of Madame de Verninac* (left).

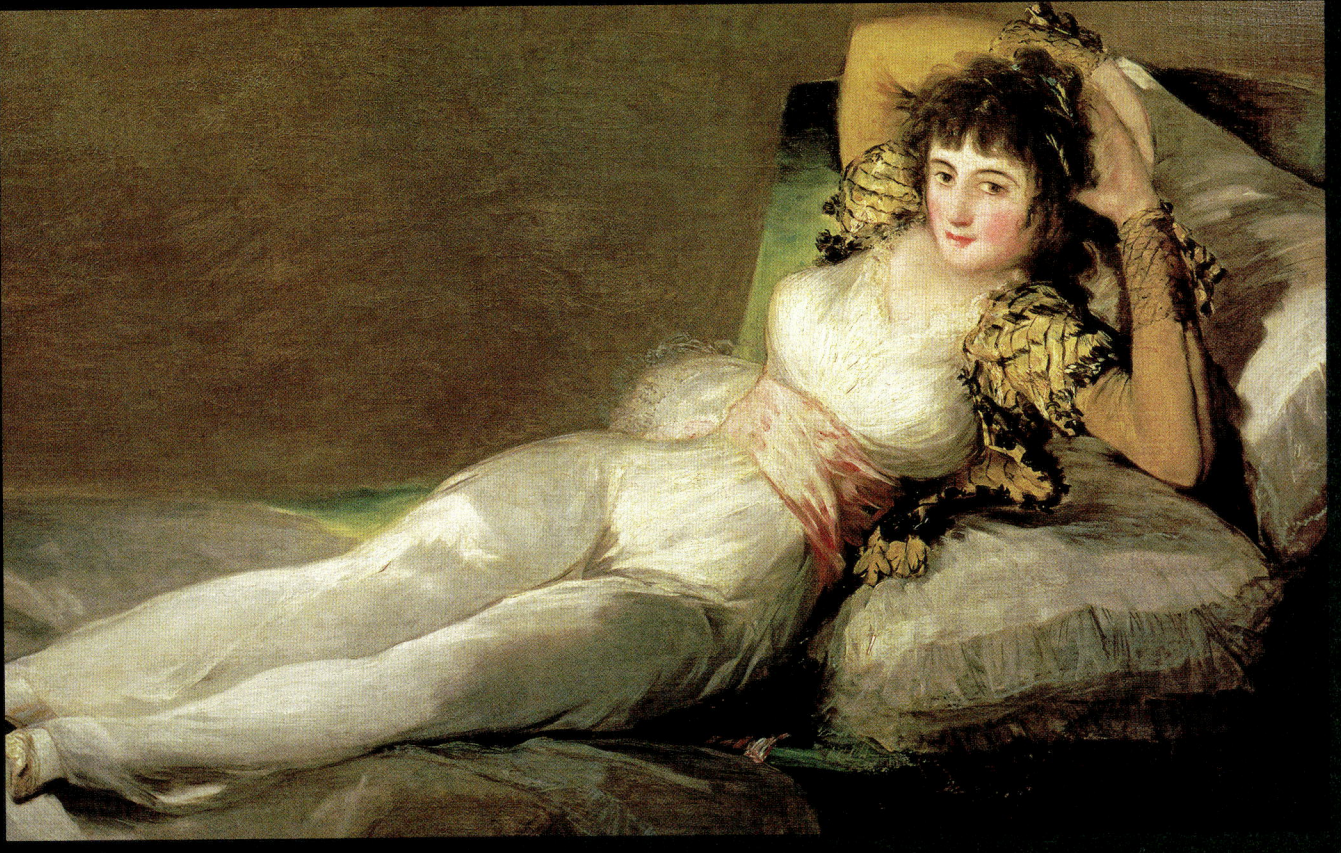

Political Revolution 597

literary works of the era. These fictional individuals were **archetypes**, or perfect examples, of a Romantic hero. Sometimes called a Byronic hero, this archetype was an unhappy, defiant figure who faced internal and external conflicts. Romantic heroes often came to tragic ends. One fellow aristocrat described Byron as "mad, bad, and dangerous to know."

Romanticism was not just a British cultural movement. In Germany, **Johannes Wolfgang von Goethe** (GUHR-tuh) wrote novels, plays, and poems. In his famous epic poem *Faust*, the main character signs a pact with the devil to exchange his soul for knowledge and power. Faust was presented as not only a Romantic figure but also a tragic one. Goethe was a strong supporter of both art and science. At his home, Goethe hosted a salon for the most important German artists and thinkers.

This cultural movement also included female authors from different European countries. The English writer **Mary Shelley** wrote her famous novel *Frankenstein* to address the Romantic themes of nature and human ambition. The story raised moral questions such as, "Was Dr. Frankenstein interfering with God and Nature by bringing his monstrous creation to life?"

VISUAL ART

Painters of the 1790s and early 1800s took the medium in dramatically new directions. Romantic artists captured on canvas the raging waters of Niagara Falls, torrential storms, and imposing cliffs. The English painter **J.M.W. Turner** and German painter Caspar David Friedrich showed the power of nature and instilled fear and awe in viewers. Yet some Romantic painters, such as John Constable, portrayed nature at peace.

Romanticism inspired artists to paint portraits to show what a person thought and felt rather than what that individual exactly looked like. Some painters illustrated the stories created by writers such as Lord Byron or Goethe. Recall that Blake often illustrated his own works. Nationalism, which you learned about earlier in this chapter, motivated artists to concentrate on local folklore and nature as well as victories in battle and the attainment of liberty, as demonstrated by the works of the French artist Eugène Delacroix (oo-ZHEHN deh-luh-KRWAH).

J.M.W. Turner's 1810 painting *The Wreck of a Transport Ship* exemplifies Romanticism's love of dramatic, emotional scenes of nature and natural events.

Richard Wagner drew on medieval German romances for the plot of his opera *Lohengrin*, which tells the tale of a mysterious knight in the 10th century. London's Royal Opera updated the setting to the 1930s in its 2018 production.

MUSIC

During the final years of the French Revolution, the German composer **Ludwig van Beethoven** worked on a piece of music to be titled "Bonaparte Symphony." However, he scratched out that dedication on the manuscript after Napoleon crowned himself emperor. Beethoven dedicated his Third Symphony, also called the *Eroica* Symphony, to a patron instead. First performed in 1804, this intricate symphony built on the neoclassical tradition of symmetry and proportion but added elements of surprise that provoke an emotional response. Beethoven's Ninth Symphony is often performed today to celebrate moments of human triumph over adversity.

The Austrian composer Franz Schubert blurred the line between classical and Romantic music styles like Beethoven did. Other musicians represented Romanticism more fully. The Hungarian pianist and composer Franz Liszt whipped audiences into excited frenzies with his musical originality, experimentation, focus on nature, and revolutionary zeal. In contrast, the Polish-French musician Frédéric Chopin simply expressed his creativity and individuality through his piano concertos. The Russian composer Peter Ilych Tchaikovsky (chy-KAWF-skee) appealed to listeners' emotions, heritage, and nationalistic desires in famous symphonies as well as in ballets such as *Swan Lake* and *The Nutcracker*. As the Prussian Romantic writer and composer E.T.A. Hoffmann rejoiced, "Music is the most Romantic of the arts."

The German **Richard Wagner** was an extremely ambitious composer, writing massive operas on mythological themes. Wagner created a specifically "German art" that clearly connects the concepts of Romanticism and nationalism. His works are still performed, although critics have been disturbed by Wagner's prejudice against Jews as well as the presence of anti-Semitism in his music.

HISTORICAL THINKING

1. **READING CHECK** What universal themes are expressed in the works of Romantic writers, artists, and musicians?
2. **ANALYZE CAUSE AND EFFECT** How did the distant and recent past influence the development of Romanticism?
3. **IDENTIFY MAIN IDEAS AND DETAILS** What was William Wordsworth's contribution to Romanticism?
4. **DESCRIBE** In what ways did musical composers of the time communicate the themes of Romanticism?

3.1

MAIN IDEA Simón Bolívar devoted most of his life to liberating the people of South America from Spain.

Simón Bolívar

Some people dedicate themselves to supporting causes such as helping animals, fighting injustice, or protecting the environment. History includes many individuals who took great risks for a cause they truly believed in. For Simón Bolívar, that goal was independence and unity for South America.

DEMOCRATIC IDEALS TAKE SHAPE

Simón Bolívar was born in South America in 1783, six years before the French Revolution. He was raised in a privileged household in Spanish-controlled Caracas, now the capital of Venezuela, but he witnessed firsthand the inequities in the South American social classes. Recall that the *peninsulares* (Spaniards born in Spain) dominated the affairs of church and state in the Spanish colonies. American-born Spaniards were known as *criollos* (cree-OH-yohs). Criollos were aware of Enlightenment calls for fairness and equality. They wanted more economic and political freedom, and the lack of it caused them to resent the Spanish.

As a young man, Bolívar became enthralled with the Enlightenment principles and the democratic ideals expressed during the American and French revolutions. Traveling to Madrid, Rome, and Paris during Napoleon's rule convinced Bolívar to play a part in winning liberty for South Americans. He vowed, "I swear before you, I swear by the God of my fathers, I swear on their graves, I swear by my Country that I will not rest body or soul until I have broken the chain binding us to the will of Spanish might!"

This oath changed not only Bolívar's life but also the course of South American history. Bolívar envisioned true liberation for South America. He did not want his homeland to experience a reign of terror or rule by a dictator like Napoleon. At the same time, he envied Napoleon's success and thought he could gain his own glory as a freedom fighter. Bolívar would dedicate all his time and energy to the struggle for South American independence. He wanted South America to equal or surpass the revolutionary success of the neighboring United States and Haiti.

BOLÍVAR IN ACTION

In 1808, Napoleon replaced Spain's king with his own brother. The South American elite did not believe that France had a rightful claim to South America, so its members set up **juntas** (HUN-tuhs)—military or political ruling groups who take power by force—to oversee local lands until Spain regained its authority. Bolívar, however, saw the transition to French rule as the perfect time for an attempt at independence.

Bolívar soon proved his brilliance as a military leader. To gain followers, he formed alliances and offered freedom to slaves who joined his army. He encouraged the spirit of revolution in indigenous peoples, Africans, and people of mixed descent as well. They made up the majority of Venezuela, so their support was critically needed. Bolívar gained the loyalty of his soldiers through his toughness

---

While in exile on the island of Jamaica in 1815, Simón Bolívar wrote a letter to the governor of Jamaica. It analyzes the state of the struggle for independence. In this excerpt, he explains why the people of South America desire independence.

PRIMARY SOURCE

Americans today, and perhaps to a greater extent than ever before, who live within the Spanish system occupy a position in society no better than that of serfs destined for labor. . . . Yet even this status is surrounded with galling restrictions, such as being forbidden to grow European crops, or to store products which are royal monopolies, or to establish factories of a type the Peninsula itself does not possess. . . . South Americans have made efforts to obtain liberty . . . doubtless out of that instinct to aspire to the greatest possible happiness, which common to all men, is bound to follow in civil societies founded on the principles of justice, liberty, and equality.

in battle and by enduring the same hardships. For example, he once spent a whole night immersed in a lake to avoid Spanish forces.

In 1813, Bolívar led his army to a successful takeover of Venezuela, but civil war soon broke out among Venezuela's social classes. Bolívar fled into exile. Then, in 1815, Napoleon's defeat at Waterloo resulted in the restoration of the Spanish monarchy. South Americans did not want to lose freedoms they had gained when Spain was under French control, and more and more of them lost their sense of loyalty to Spain.

Bolívar returned to Venezuela. By 1817, he made some progress and headed into Venezuela's interior to rebuild his army. Soon, the freedom fighter was recognized as the supreme commander of the various patriotic forces.

In 1819, Spain still held Caracas, but colonial delegates at the ongoing Congress of Angostura made plans for Venezuela's independence. Bolívar argued for a solid central government with effective executive powers because he thought a strong legislature would lead to instability and division. Fearing that the congress would not heed his advice, he developed a new plan. He would move his army south and attempt to liberate a larger area, where he could create a constitutional union called **Gran Colombia**. This union included present-day Venezuela, Colombia, Panama, Ecuador, and Peru.

Simón Bolívar, shown here, was nicknamed "the Liberator" of South America. His birthday, July 24, is a holiday that is celebrated in many Latin American countries.

Bolívar, sometimes called "the Liberator," started his military and political journey with high hopes founded in Enlightenment optimism, and he did help overthrow monarchical authority in South America. Still, turning independence from Spanish rule into true liberty for South Americans proved harder than he imagined. Even though he fought for freedom until his death, Bolívar never achieved his goal of a stable and united continent. His story, as one biographer explained, was one of "liberation and disappointment."

HISTORICAL THINKING

1. **READING CHECK** What were Simón Bolívar's goals for South America?
2. **COMPARE AND CONTRAST** How did differences in South American social classes both help and hurt the revolutionary cause?
3. **ANALYZE SOURCES** What evidence in Bolívar's letter to the governor of Jamaica suggests his belief in Enlightenment principles?

Political Revolution 601

3.2 **MAIN IDEA** In the early 1800s, the people of Latin American and Caribbean colonies fought for and won independence from the nations in Europe that controlled them.

Latin American Wars of Independence

Almost all of Latin America—Mexico, Central America, South America, and the islands of the Caribbean—was controlled by European powers at the beginning of the 19th century. Yet the people who lived there heard the call of liberty and were eager to answer it.

CRITICAL VIEWING In 1810, Father Miguel Hidalgo y Costilla rallied the common people of Mexico, especially mestizos and native peoples, under the banner of the Virgin of Guadalupe for independence from Spain. Based on this mural painted by David Leonardo in 1999, how do you think Mexicans remember Father Hidalgo?

A CONTINUING STRUGGLE

In late 1819, Simón Bolívar led his troops south, intent on liberating South America and establishing Gran Colombia. Even though Bolívar and his troops suffered greatly as they traveled into the frigid Andean Mountains, their morale remained high. The same was not true for the Spanish soldiers who realized that their generals' skills could not match those of the Liberator. Bolívar's army quickly won territory as far south as Ecuador. At the same time, another leader, **José de San Martín**, was successfully leading the fight for independence in central and southern South America. His military prowess allowed him to win freedom for Argentina and Chile. San Martín next moved north into Peru, where he claimed the capital, Lima.

Meanwhile, Bolívar continued his march south until he met up with San Martín, who stepped aside to enable the Liberator to win the final victory. Bolívar's soldiers engaged the Spanish in the Andes in 1824 at the Battle of Ayacucho in southern Peru. Their triumph finally freed South America from Spanish control.

MEXICO, BRAZIL, AND THE CARIBBEAN

In Mexico, indigenous peoples and mestizos led the way to independence. In 1810, a priest in the parish of Dolores named **Miguel Hidalgo y Costilla** rallied the poor with his speech now known as "Grito de Dolores," or "Cry of Dolores," which implored Mexicans to fight for freedom. However, criollo soldiers supporting the Spanish status quo crushed Hidalgo's troops and killed the priest. When Spain began to enact liberal reforms, however, Mexican criollos feared such changes would cause them to lose their power. Criollo military leader Agustín de Iturbide and his elite supporters fought for and won Mexico's freedom in 1821. Wealthy hacienda owners now controlled Mexico. This independence brought neither the social nor economic reform Father Hidalgo had hoped for.

Controlled by Portugal, Brazil followed its own distinct path to independence. In 1808, the Portuguese royal family sought refuge in Brazil to escape an invasion by Napoleon. The king returned to his home country in 1821, but his son Pedro remained in Brazil. Pedro then announced that he would support the cause of Brazilian independence, which was achieved in 1822. In 1824, Pedro I became the constitutional monarch of Brazil.

Women, such as Manuela Sáenz (shown here with Simón Bolívar), played an important role in Latin America's struggle for independence. Sáenz was an Ecuadorian noblewoman who saved Bolívar's life when political rivals tried to assassinate him in 1828.

Just as in the United States, Brazil became free without toppling the elite control of society and the economy. Also, the institution of slavery continued.

Meanwhile, in the Caribbean, enslaved Jamaicans revolted in 1831 and 1832, inspired by the abolitionist movement in Britain. They wanted to be paid for their labor and to be free to leave their plantations. Plantation owners put down the uprising, but it marked the last gasp of slavery in Jamaica. Two years later, Parliament freed all enslaved people in the British Empire.

Just south of Mexico, the people of Central America gained independence with little bloodshed. This region briefly became a territory of the newly independent Mexico. Then it broke away from foreign control in 1824 to become the United Provinces of Central America. The union soon disbanded, however, and Guatemala, Honduras, Nicaragua, El Salvador, and Costa Rica became independent republics.

HISTORICAL THINKING

1. **READING CHECK** In what different ways did countries of Latin America win independence?

2. **ANALYZE CAUSE AND EFFECT** What effect did José de San Martín's military actions have on South America's history?

3. **FORM AND SUPPORT OPINIONS** Did independence make life better or worse for the Mexican people? Explain.

3.3 MAIN IDEA: Enlightenment principles inspired revolutions in the United States, France, Haiti, and Latin America, with varying and lasting effects.

The Spread of Revolutionary Ideas

The revolutions of national independence and the search for liberty did not have the same results everywhere. Different circumstances, situations, and attitudes of the era influenced how and why successive events unfolded.

SPREAD OF DEMOCRATIC CONCEPTS

During the Enlightenment, philosophers and other educated individuals took part in what became informally known as the "republic of letters," sharing thoughts about topics such as medicine, science, religion, and government through their correspondence with one another. John Locke alone composed more than 3,000 letters.

In the revolutionary era, letters became an important way to transmit ideas and news of current events over the Atlantic Ocean. This transatlantic communication helped relay subversive ideas to other parts of the world. It also inspired people in the Americas to fight for liberty and independence. In addition to letters, visits from foreign leaders and printed books and pamphlets sowed the seeds of revolution. For example, American founder Benjamin Franklin lived in Europe for a significant amount of time and sent back letters before, during, and after the American Revolution.

REVOLUTIONARY OUTCOMES

The circulation of revolutionary ideas and experiences connected the Atlantic world. Clearly, knowledge of the struggles in the United States and France inspired the uprising in Saint-Domingue, which you know later became Haiti. Likewise, those revolutions and Haiti's success influenced Simón Bolívar's drive for South American independence. In the Americas, leaders hoped to bring liberty and equality to their people, and many succeeded in overthrowing monarchical authority. Yet by 1830, the outcomes of revolutions in Europe and the Americas proved to be vastly different.

In Europe, the excesses of French politics led to the revival of conservative ideas. Europe's revolutionary flame was quickly extinguished after the fall of Napoleon. European conservatives attempted to return to the age of strong monarchs, but they could not combat the surge of nationalism that would eventually lead regions such as Greece, Germany, and Italy to unite. In addition, many Europeans would not rest until a more equal distribution of wealth existed on their continent.

Benjamin Franklin (shown at right in a 1767 portrait) spent most of the American Revolution in France. In a 1782 letter from Paris, Franklin shares some concerns with Henry Laurens, an American who was tasked with negotiating peace with Great Britain.

PRIMARY SOURCE

I have never yet known of a Peace made that did not occasion a great deal of popular Discontent, Clamor, and Censure on both Sides. This is, perhaps, owing to the usual Management of the Ministers and Leaders of the contending Nations who, to keep up the Spirits of their People for continuing the War, generally represent the State of their own Affairs in a better Light and that of the Enemy in a worse than is consistent with the Truth. Hence the Populace on each Side expect better Terms than really can be obtained, and are apt to ascribe their Disappointment to Treachery.

In North America, the more privileged and educated had spearheaded the American Revolution. However, the doctrine of popular sovereignty required the leaders of the newly formed United States to look beyond their own self-interests to create a more just society. They increased access to political power—but only to white men with property. African Americans, Native Americans, and women did not gain any rights.

The United States set up a strong federal system based on popular sovereignty, constitutionalism, separation of powers, and checks and balances. It then focused on expansion; it doubled its size with the Louisiana Purchase in 1803 and claimed territory even farther west. European immigrants rushed to the new country, which promised opportunities for cheap land and good wages. Although the republic seemed to be flourishing, its relations with Native Americans were poor, and the institution of slavery caused division.

Independence in the Americas, 1804–1839

In Haiti, the shift from slave colony to free republic proved difficult. Former slaves fled plantations to establish small farms of their own. These changes led to a drop in crop production, which resulted in a decrease in government tax revenue. The greed of Haitian leaders and divisions between the mixed-race gens de couleur and Haitians of African heritage caused additional problems. The republic became a dictatorship that was run by corrupt leaders, and control by military dictators allied with wealthy landowners doomed democracy in the island nation.

In Latin America, Simón Bolívar's attempt at a united South America fell apart. Military commanders seized power, allying themselves with dominant landowners and church officials. By 1830, much of South America was ruled by self-interested military rulers called **caudillos** (cow-THEE-yohs), who gained power through violence. Criollos prospered following the exodus of peninsulares, but the other classes suffered. Africans, indigenous peoples, and people of mixed races had played an important role during the fight for freedom, but they did not reap the benefits. In general, the Catholic Church still sided with the wealthy and powerful instead of those who suffered in poverty.

Rebels around the world were unable to undertake a "complete revolution," or a top-to-bottom transformation of society. However, Enlightenment concepts were now a permanent part of the political conversation in many parts of the world.

HISTORICAL THINKING

1. **READING CHECK** In what ways were the consequences of the American Revolution unique compared to other revolutions that followed?

2. **IDENTIFY MAIN IDEAS AND DETAILS** What were positive and negative effects of independence for Haiti?

3. **MAKE CONNECTIONS** In what ways were the challenges faced by the rulers of newly independent nations similar?

Political Revolution 605

CHAPTER 21 POLITICAL REVOLUTION REVIEW

VOCABULARY

Complete each of the following sentences using one of the vocabulary words from the chapter.

1. Any government that places legal limits on its powers is practicing _____ .
2. The upper class in South America established violent _____ that supervised local lands.
3. Some people in France were _____ and wanted more rights.
4. Napoleon Bonaparte used _____ to manipulate French citizens to think and act in a particular way.
5. The rise of _____ gave the French a sense of their common identity.
6. The 18th-century cultural movement that emphasized emotion over reason is known as _____ .
7. Rebel fighters, or _____ , in Saint-Domingue followed Boukman as they fought for independence.
8. The people of Venezuela feared their _____ , a powerful leader.

READING STRATEGY
DRAW CONCLUSIONS

When you draw conclusions, you make a judgment based on what you have read. You analyze the facts, make inferences, and use your own experiences to form your judgment. Use a diagram like this one to draw conclusions about why people rebelled against their governments. Then answer the question.

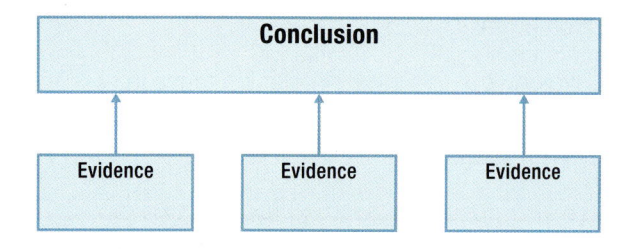

```
           Conclusion
    ↑         ↑         ↑
 Evidence  Evidence  Evidence
```

9. Why did people in Europe and the Americas rebel against their governments in the late 1700s and early 1800s?

MAIN IDEAS

Answer the following questions. Support your answers with evidence from the chapter.

10. How did Thomas Jefferson use Enlightenment ideas to justify the American colonists' break from Britain? **LESSON 1.1**
11. Who were the bourgeoisie in France, and what was their role in the French Revolution? **LESSON 1.2**
12. Why did most people in the French colony of Saint-Domingue want to rebel? **LESSON 1.3**
13. What actions did Napoleon take to assure that he would be well remembered throughout history? **LESSON 2.1**
14. What types of subject matter did Romantic writers address? **LESSON 2.3**
15. What led Simón Bolívar to seek independence for Latin America? **LESSON 3.1**
16. What was the role of Miguel Hidalgo y Costilla in Mexico's fight for freedom? **LESSON 3.2**
17. What new challenges did South American countries face following independence? **LESSON 3.3**

HISTORICAL THINKING

Answer the following questions. Support your answers with evidence from the chapter.

18. **MAKE CONNECTIONS** Why were American colonists so interested in John Locke's ideas of popular sovereignty and "consent of the governed"?
19. **COMPARE AND CONTRAST** In what ways were the American Revolution and the French Revolution similar and different?
20. **ANALYZE CAUSE AND EFFECT** What were the immediate effects and long-term effects of the revolution led by Toussaint L'Ouverture?
21. **DETERMINE CHRONOLOGY** What sequence of events illustrate the rise, rule, and fall of Napoleon Bonaparte?

22. **MAKE GENERALIZATIONS** Based on what you read, how important was Romanticism to society in the early 1800s?

23. **FORM AND SUPPORT OPINIONS** Do you agree with Simón Bolívar's viewpoint that South America needed a strong executive branch and a weak or nonexistent legislative branch? Explain.

24. **ANALYZE CAUSE AND EFFECT** What impact did Napoleon have on Latin America in the early 1800s?

25. **DRAW CONCLUSIONS** Why did European leaders want to revert to the past while American leaders preferred to focus on the future?

INTERPRET VISUALS

Caspar David Friedrich was a leading artist in the German Romantic movement. His painting *Wanderer Above the Sea of Fog* is one example of his extensive work. Study the painting and answer the question that follows.

26. In what ways does this painting represent the ideals of Romanticism?

ANALYZE SOURCES

Mercy Otis Warren was a political writer and propagandist who knew several key figures of the American Revolution. Read the following excerpt from a letter she wrote to the writer and historian Catharine Macaulay in 1787 and answer the questions.

> Our situation is truly delicate and critical. On the one hand we are in need of a strong federal government founded on principles that will support the prosperity and union of the colonies. On the other hand we have struggled for liberty and made lofty sacrifices at her shrine: and there are still many of us who revere her name too much to relinquish (beyond a certain medium) the rights of man for the dignity of government.

27. What Enlightenment political idea does the excerpt best support? Explain your answer.

28. The letter was written in 1787. How did events at that time influence the message conveyed in the excerpt?

CONNECT TO YOUR LIFE

29. **NARRATIVE** Choose a revolutionary movement from this chapter. Imagine you are living in the time and place of this revolution. The rebellion has ended, and you are writing a letter to a friend or relative in another country describing the events that happened during and after the revolution and whether you think the movement succeeded or failed.

    TIPS

    - Skim the chapter and choose a revolution that interests you.
    - Consider the leadership and initial goals of your chosen revolutionary movement, who participated in the revolution, expected or unexpected obstacles, and the outcomes of the revolutionary effort.
    - Develop your topic by discussing ways in which your own circumstances and attitudes changed or did not change.
    - Use vivid, descriptive language and two or three vocabulary terms from the chapter in your letter.
    - End your letter with a brief summary of how you feel at the current time.

NATIONAL GEOGRAPHIC CONNECTION

Jane Goodall: A Revolutionary Naturalist

BY TONY GERBER Adapted from "Becoming Jane" by Tony Gerber, *National Geographic*, October 2017

The basic narrative of Jane Goodall's life is instantly recognizable from the many times it's been written, broadcast, or otherwise sent into the world: *A young Englishwoman conducts chimpanzee research in Africa and winds up revolutionizing primate science.* But how did it happen? How did a woman with a passion for animals but no formal background in research navigate the male-dominated worlds of science and media to make enormous discoveries in her field and become a world-famous face of the conservation movement?

While conducting research at Gombe Stream Game Reserve in present-day Tanzania, Goodall withstood all manner of natural threats: malaria, parasites, snakes, storms. But in her dealings with the wider world, the challenges often required shrewd strategy and delicate diplomacy. Early in her career, Goodall had to contend with a primarily male science establishment that didn't take her seriously and with media executives whose support hinged on her willingness to be scripted and glamorized. Through it all, Goodall's philosophy seemed the same: She would endure slights, accommodate demands, tolerate fools, make sacrifices—if it served to sustain her work.

From the start, Goodall followed her instincts for conducting research. Not knowing that the established scientific practice was to use numbers to identify animals under study, she recorded observations of the chimps by names she concocted. She wrote about them as individuals with distinct traits and personalities.

At Gombe, Goodall made three discoveries that would turn established science on its head. First, she observed a chimp she named David Greybeard gnawing on the carcass of a small animal, which belied the prevailing belief that apes didn't eat meat. Her next discovery was truly game-changing. She saw the same chimp pick a blade of grass and poke it into a termite tunnel. When he pulled it out, it was covered with termites, which he slurped down. In another instance, Goodall saw David Greybeard pick a twig and strip it of leaves before using it to fish for termites.

In the early 1960s in what is now Tanzania, Jane Goodall touches chimpanzees Fifi and Flint as Flo, the chimps' mother, looks on. Physical contact with chimps in the wild is no longer deemed appropriate.

The chimp had exhibited both tool use and toolmaking—two things that previously only humans were believed capable of. In the wake of these discoveries, National Geographic gave Goodall a grant to continue her work.

But as Goodall began to publish her field research, she met with skepticism from the scientific community. In the spring of 1962, she gave a presentation at the Zoological Society of London's primate symposium. Although she impressed many people, she also faced derision. A society officer critiqued her work as making no "real contribution to science." An Associated Press report described Goodall as a "willowy blonde with more time for monkeys than men."

Over time, however, her findings sparked worldwide interest and upended conventional wisdom about humans. Since those early discoveries, Goodall has completed a Ph.D. at Cambridge University, authored dozens of books, mentored new generations of scientists, promoted conservation, and established several sanctuaries for chimps. Today, the Jane Goodall Institute's Roots & Shoots program operates in nearly a hundred countries, training young people to be conservation leaders.

And on her way to becoming a world-renowned naturalist, Goodall forever changed the way we think about our relatives, the apes. ∎

UNIT INQUIRY
UNIT 7 Plan a Revolution

Staging the Question

In this unit, you learned about various revolutions that brought dramatic changes to Western society. The Scientific Revolution introduced a new procedure for developing and testing ideas in science. The Enlightenment spread revolutionary ideas in philosophy, government, religion, economics, education, and other fields. These new ideas helped inspire political revolutions in Europe and the Americas. All these revolutions were sparked by individuals or groups who were able to change the way an entire society thought or acted. How does an individual change the thinking or actions of a whole culture?

ASSIGNMENT

Select three individuals who have initiated or contributed to revolutions in a particular field. You may choose people from this unit or from your own research.

Identify the kind of change that each person promoted and the reasons for it.

Describe the revolutions that resulted.

Based on your analysis of how individuals have sparked revolutions, plan a revolution of your own on a subject you care deeply about.

Supporting Questions: Begin by developing supporting questions to guide your thinking. For example: What topic are you passionate about? Perhaps you have ideas about revolutionizing education or changing social media. What changes would you like to see? How would you go about effecting those changes?

Summative Performance Task:
Use the answers to your questions to plan your revolution. Identify your goal and list specific actions to be taken to promote the changes you'd like to see. You might use a graphic organizer like this one to develop your plan.

Goal → Events → Outcome

Present: Share your revolution with the class. You might consider one of these options:

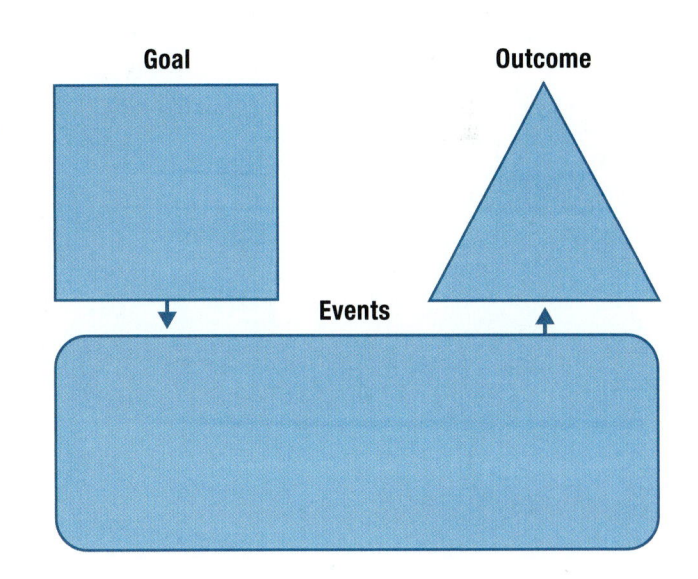

CREATE A FLYER
Write and illustrate a flyer that describes the changes you're promoting, the reasons for the changes, and their benefits. Use persuasive language or a personal story to engage readers and enlist them in your cause. Display the flyer in your classroom.

PREPARE A TALK
Record a short talk in which you promote your ideas. Include graphics, photos, or other visuals to support your ideas. You might search the Internet for an inspiring talk to serve as a model.

Take Informed Action:

UNDERSTAND Identify both the pros and the cons of your plan. Ask yourself who would be likely to oppose the plan and why.

ASSESS Revolutions seldom happen overnight; they occur over time. Assess how long it would likely take for your revolution to take hold.

ACT Choose one of the actions listed in your plan and start your revolution.

New Ideas and Revolution 609

UNIT 8

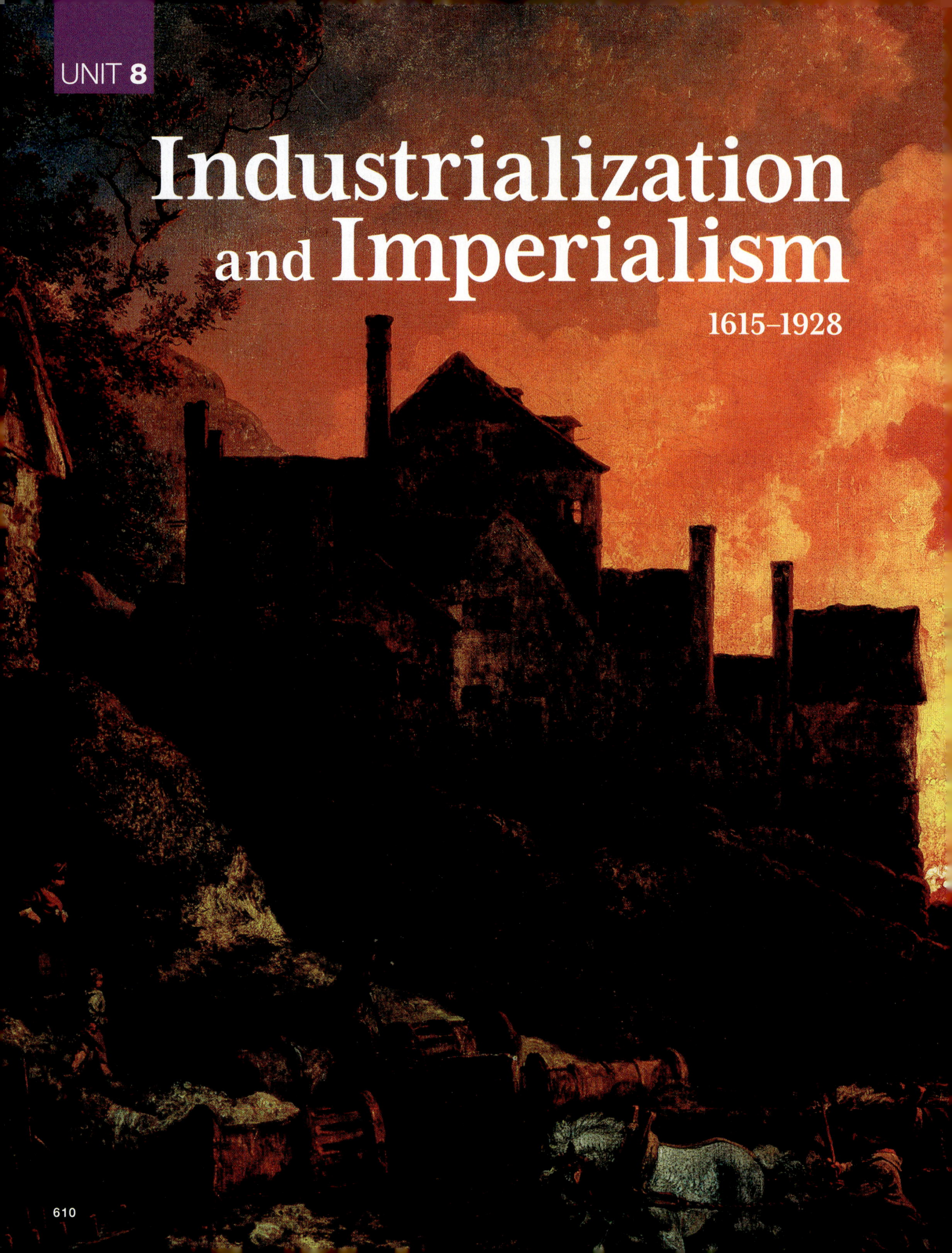

Industrialization and Imperialism
1615–1928

CRITICAL VIEWING
This 1801 painting by the artist Philip James de Loutherbourg depicts the Bedlam furnaces in Shropshire, England, which burned day and night to smelt iron. This area of England is often called the "cradle of the Industrial Revolution." What do you think life was like for the people who lived near the furnaces?

UNIT 8 Industrialization and Imperialism

WORLD EVENTS
1765–1912

1776 EUROPE Scottish philosopher Adam Smith publishes *The Wealth of Nations*, in which the idea of capitalism is described for the first time. *(portrait of Adam Smith, 1795)*

1839–1842 ASIA The First Opium War is fought between China and Britain after the Chinese government tries to stop the trade of opium in its country. *(painting of British ships destroying an enemy fleet off the coast of China)*

1831 AMERICAS American industrialist Cyrus McCormick develops a mechanical reaper that revolutionizes wheat harvesting.

| 1750 | 1775 | 1800 | 1825 |

1765 EUROPE Scottish inventor James Watt greatly improves the efficiency of the steam engine.

1836 AFRICA The Boers, farmers of Dutch, French, and German descent, undertake their "Great Trek" through southern Africa to escape British rule.

c. 1793 AMERICAS American inventor Eli Whitney invents the cotton gin, making it easier to remove cottonseeds from cotton fiber. *(patent model of Whitney's cotton gin)*

1838 EUROPE English writer Charles Dickens publishes *Oliver Twist*, which criticizes the workhouse system and exposes the conditions of the poor in Britain. *(title page of a serialized version of Oliver Twist)*

1848 EUROPE German philosophers Karl Marx and Friedrich Engels publish the pamphlet *The Manifesto of the Communist Party*, which calls for the creation of a workers' society that does away with class struggles and abolishes private property.

HISTORICAL THINKING

ANALYZE CAUSE AND EFFECT What earlier event might have helped promote the European race for territory in Africa?

1848 EUROPE Nationalism stirs unrest and revolution across Europe. *(portrait of Italian patriot Giuseppe Garibaldi)*

1858 ASIA France begins colonizing cities in Vietnam and eventually expands its control over Cambodia and Laos. *(presidential palace in Hanoi, once the home of the French governor of Indochina)*

1884–1885 AFRICA The Berlin Conference divides Africa among European powers and triggers a race for territory on the continent.

| 1850 | 1875 | 1900 | 1925 |

1856 EUROPE English engineer Henry Bessemer invents a process to manufacture steel inexpensively.

1859 EUROPE British naturalist Charles Darwin publishes *On the Origin of Species*, which some people use to justify inequality in human society as "survival of the fittest."

1869 AFRICA The completion of the Suez Canal in Egypt separates the continents of Africa and Asia and links the Mediterranean and Red seas. *(painting of the inauguration of the Suez Canal)*

1912 ASIA Two thousand years of imperial rule in China come to an end when revolutionary forces overthrow the Qing dynasty. *(Puyi, China's last emperor, in 1910)*

CHAPTER 22

Industrial Revolution
1615–1928

HISTORICAL THINKING How did the Industrial Revolution transform people's lives around the world?

SECTION 1 **Industry and Workers**
SECTION 2 **Global Context and Impact**
SECTION 3 **Asian Tensions in the Industrial Age**

CRITICAL VIEWING
A steam-powered locomotive chugs along through a snow-covered forest in Germany. In what way is the steam-powered locomotive symbolic of the Industrial Revolution?

Industrial Revolution

1.1

MAIN IDEA Scientific advancements in energy, agriculture, and technology caused the Industrial Revolution, which had a dramatic impact on human society.

Origins of Industrialization

Look around the room. How many objects around you were manufactured by machines? Now imagine how the room would look if every object had been made by hand. The way in which things were produced is one of the changes caused by the Industrial Revolution.

COAL, STEAM, AND IRON

In 1750, India and China made over half of the world's manufactured products. By 1860, this had changed. Using revolutionary techniques to expand production, western European nations were now in the lead role.

You have learned about the "practical science" of Britain in the 1800s. Now Britain, with a strong mercantile class and an aristocracy willing to provide capital, was becoming the most powerful nation in the world. It controlled the seas, had an extensive trading network, and ruled colonies around the globe that supplied low-paying and unpaid (slave) labor while also providing access to a huge variety of raw materials. Before 1780, sugar had been the most important import, along with cotton textiles from India. Profits from the earlier trade provided the money for British businessmen to invest in new machines and systems of working. With the rise of the factory system, raw cotton became the most significant import, especially from the expanding plantation system in the southern United States.

CRITICAL VIEWING This 19th-century painting shows a pithead, which is the top of a mining pit or coal shaft. What elements in the painting illustrate the ways people worked before the Industrial Revolution? What elements illustrate innovations that changed the way people worked?

In 1765, a Scotsman named **James Watt** introduced a machine he'd invented—the world's first workable steam engine. The machine was powered by coal, which heated water into steam that moved pistons and gears. With this machine the Industrial Revolution began.

It would be difficult to exaggerate the consequences of the Industrial Revolution. There had been no bigger revolution in human society since humans first began farming 12,000 years ago. Between 1750 and 1900, total global manufacturing production rose more than 400 percent. The centers of manufacturing shifted from India and China in the east to Europe and the United States in the west. So did the profits. Europe and the United States accounted for nearly three-quarters of production output by 1900. Global population doubled in the same time period.

The Industrial Revolution was also an energy revolution. The massive use of fossil fuels began at this time, unlocking the vast stored energy of coal—and later petroleum and natural gas. Less than 90 years after the introduction of Watt's machine, Britain's coal production had increased 10 times. This huge increase in power from fossil fuels led to further innovations in technology and in ways of organizing human labor. Almost every sphere of human activity was altered.

Coal provided more than just steam for the steam engine. It also provided the ability to create mass quantities of the iron needed to build the engine itself. For thousands of years, charcoal from wood had fueled smelting furnaces, which meant iron could only be produced in small batches. British forests could never supply the amount of wood needed for an industrial breakthrough, even with imports from North America. Improvements in technology, including the use of stronger vacuum pumps to remove water from coal mines, helped the British break through that energy barrier.

Around the same time that Watt unveiled his steam engine, English inventors learned to use coal more efficiently. A purified, concentrated form of coal called "coke" made it possible to produce low-cost, high-quality iron in large amounts. In 1856, the Industrial Revolution received another boost when **Henry Bessemer** invented a way to manufacture high-quality steel more cheaply. Steel is much stronger than iron and could be turned into track for railroads and beams and girders for skyscrapers.

Meanwhile, other changes were happening in manufacturing. In his book *The Wealth of Nations*, which you read about earlier, Adam Smith argued that **division of labor**, or a process that divides a task into separate parts with each completed by a different person or group, was a key to increased productivity. For example, a single shoemaker could make an excellent pair of shoes, but not as efficiently as a group of workers who each focused on a single step in the process. Smith was describing the new factory system of production.

The Luddites Many workers protested the changes brought about by new machines. In the late 18th and early 19th centuries, artisans organized secret societies and attacked the textile machines that threatened their way of life. Factory work required less training, and these skilled artisans resented the reduced quality and lower wages that occurred as a result. Those machine smashers were called "Luddites" after a fictional figure, shown here, named Ned Ludd, or General Ludd, who supposedly organized armies of machine smashers. In response to such incidents, Parliament made industrial sabotage, or deliberate destruction, a capital crime, and many Luddites were executed or exiled. Over time, however, the Luddites themselves became as mythological as their fictional leader, representing the desire of many to halt or slow the changes forced by new technology. Today, you might call anyone slow to adopt new technology a "Luddite."

TEXTILE MANUFACTURING

It was in the textile industry where division of labor and steam power combined to full potential. For a thousand years, India had been the world's largest producer of cotton textiles, and Indian calico cloth flooded the British market. This competition hurt the British wool industry, so in the early 18th century Parliament passed the Calico Acts, which limited the amount of cotton cloth that could be imported from India. The Calico Acts helped Britain's wool industry—more than a quarter of British exports for the next 80 years were woolen goods—and the British cotton cloth industry.

Prior to industrialization, British cotton textiles were a **cottage industry**. A merchant provided raw materials to a rural family. In a traditional division of labor, the women spun the cotton into thread, and the men wove the thread into cloth. These methods were slow. With the steam engine, cloth manufacturers could organize and speed up the process.

Spinning raw cotton into thread was the slowest part of the manufacturing process and was the first to be mechanized. Women were no longer needed to spin, but men still worked in their own homes to weave the thread. Within decades, though, the steam-driven loom took the entire process out of homes and into factories. As the production of cloth grew faster and more efficient, demand for raw cotton rose. Another new invention would meet that demand, shift the main source of raw cotton away from India, and change the course of U.S. history.

In the late 1700s, some observers thought that slavery was in the process of dying out in the United States. Then in 1793, the American inventor **Eli Whitney** invented the cotton gin, a machine that quickly separated seeds from cotton, a process that took a long time when done by hand. This new machine meant that cotton grown and processed through slave labor in the South could supply the growing demand for cheap cotton in Britain at a huge profit to plantation owners in North America. These profits created a powerful incentive to acquire land—at any cost—to establish cotton plantations. New and devastating policies removed native Cherokee and Creek people

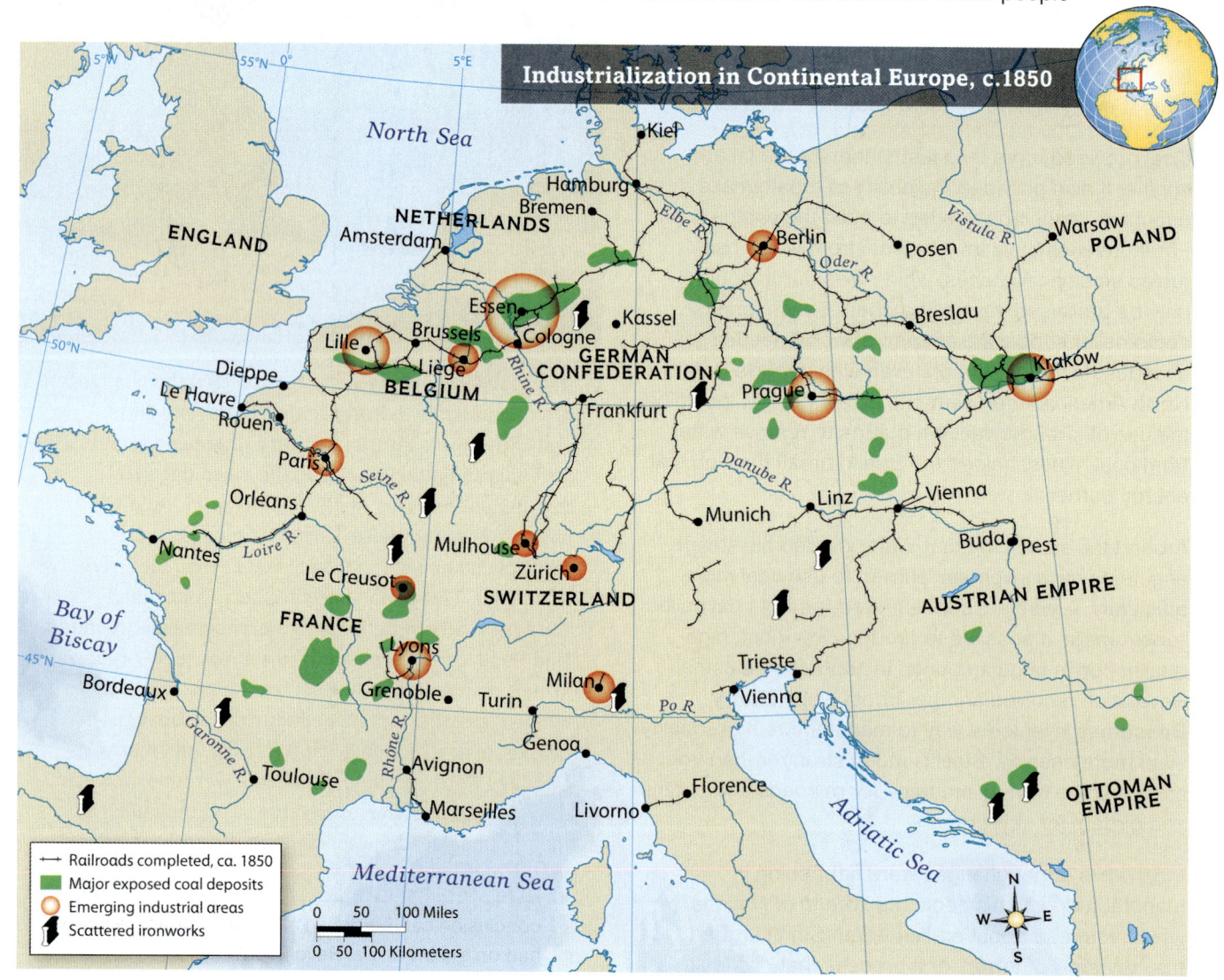

Industrialization in Continental Europe, c. 1850

Map legend:
- Railroads completed, ca. 1850
- Major exposed coal deposits
- Emerging industrial areas
- Scattered ironworks

618 CHAPTER 22

from the southeastern United States to Oklahoma. As plantations expanded, slavery increased in extent and barbarity, cotton production surged, and the southern United States became the largest source of cotton for British textile manufacturers. By the 1830s, cloth manufacturing was fully mechanized, and Britain was the world's leading textile manufacturer, with sources of raw cotton from India and Egypt in addition to the United States.

AGRICULTURAL AND TECHNOLOGICAL INNOVATIONS

As you read earlier, the use of scientific improvements such as crossbreeding of livestock and crop rotation provided more food in England. In addition, farmers were reclaiming land, especially marshlands in eastern England, so more was available for farming. At the same time, however, new enclosure laws passed in the 17th and 18th centuries allowed aristocrats and wealthy farmers to claim common lands as their own private property, cutting off access by the common people to grazing lands and hunting grounds. Furthermore, new inventions such as the seed drill, which planted seeds more quickly, meant fewer farm laborers were needed. The McCormick Reaper, invented by the American industrialist **Cyrus McCormick** in 1831, revolutionized wheat harvesting in England. With no access to common land and fewer jobs for farm laborers, many rural families moved to towns and cities and became the workforce for mines and factories.

In addition to new agricultural practices, there were innovations in technology, specifically in transportation and communication. Steam power and iron production created new types of transportation that shipped raw materials into and finished products out of factories at greater speeds and in greater quantities than ever before. In the 1820s, steamships began to increase the efficiency of water transport, especially regarding international trade. As important as the rise of the steamship was the advance of the railroad. As iron became easier and cheaper to produce, its price dropped, and so did the cost of railroad tracks.

Britain led the Industrial Revolution, but it was not the only nation to industrialize. Belgium had rich iron ore and coal deposits as well as a history of textile manufacturing, so it industrialized soon after Britain. France and Switzerland had fewer natural resources but became leaders in the production of specialty and luxury goods. France's industrial output came to equal Britain's. Germany and the northern United States developed later but both had the raw materials (coal and iron) needed to build powerful industrial economies. You'll read later about how North American and European industrial states turned to Africa, Asia, and Latin America as sources of raw materials and markets for manufactured goods.

STEAM ENGINE This sectional model, made in 1866, shows an 18th-century beam engine, a type of steam engine, invented by William Murdock, a Scottish inventor and engineer.

HISTORICAL THINKING

1. **READING CHECK** What was the Industrial Revolution?
2. **ANALYZE CAUSE AND EFFECT** How did mechanization in agriculture change life in Britain's cities and towns?
3. **MAKE CONNECTIONS** What was the relationship between the invention of a workable steam engine and the Industrial Revolution?
4. **INTERPRET MAPS** Based on details in the map, what conclusion can be drawn about the impact railroads had on the Industrial Revolution?

1.2 MAIN IDEA The Industrial Revolution dramatically changed the way people lived in Europe.

Daily Life Transformed

When you think of a revolution, you might think of crowds in the streets and breaking news reports. People in Europe experienced a revolution starting in the 1700s, but most of it took place in their homes and workplaces, not in the streets.

SOCIAL CHANGE

Daily life in Britain began to change drastically and rapidly in the 1700s compared to the small, slow changes of previous centuries. People moved from rural areas to live in cities and towns. In 1801, the population of Britain was about 9.3 million. Just 40 years later, it climbed 60 percent to 15.9 million. Manchester, England, a textile manufacturing center, grew by six times between 1771 and 1831.

The rapid social change of modern times disrupted many older ways of life. For example, in a traditional English village time was flexible, measured by the tasks that needed to be done that day and by the rhythm of the seasons. Now a worker's schedule was dominated by the blast of the factory whistle and the need to keep pace with ever faster machines.

Population growth outstripped the ability of urban areas to create housing and sanitation systems. As a result, cities became crowded and filthy. Air and water were polluted by factory smokestacks and manufacturing waste. The Romantic poet William Blake wrote of the "dark, Satanic mills" that created so much smog in some cities that people had to light candles in the middle of the day in order to see. Most workers lived in small houses with no yard, little natural light, and no toilet, bathing facilities, or running water. A typical block of homes might have 40 houses with nine people living in each house, and only six toilets for the entire block.

Disease spread rapidly in such neighborhoods, becoming even more deadly after increased contact with India brought cholera to England. In London alone, thousands died from infected water supplies. Even as some suffered from poverty, filth, and disease, however, the middle class was growing and consuming the merchandise being produced in the new factories. Better-off families moved to cleaner neighborhoods.

It was typical for everyone in a working-class household, including children, to work outside the home. Employers hired children to work many jobs because they could pay children a lower wage, and children could fit into tight spaces and were easier to control. Mine owners hired adult men but also relied on young women and adolescent boys and girls. Mining was dangerous work, and even those who survived the frequent accidents were likely to die early from lung disease. But conditions in factories weren't much better. Wages were low and working conditions were hazardous. The advances of the early Industrial Revolution might have improved life for the middle and upper classes, but not for the working class and poor. Even animals suffered for Britain's industrial progress—for example, the "pit ponies" who labored in the darkness of deeper and deeper coal mines.

POLITICAL CHANGE

Early in the Industrial Revolution, workers had almost no political rights. They could not vote, and Parliament made it illegal for them to form unions to increase their bargaining power. In 1819 in the city of Manchester, the British cavalry charged a crowd of about 60,000 that was demanding parliamentary representation. At least 15 demonstrators were killed. Finally in 1832, the Great Reform Act passed through Parliament, giving more seats to growing urban areas and the right to vote to more members of the middle class.

Reforms continued during the long reign of **Queen Victoria**, who ruled from 1837 to 1901. The popular queen supported social and political reforms, and Britain saw dramatic improvements in health conditions, wages, and political rights for the working class. Her belief in modesty, thrift, and hard work, as well as personal and social responsibility, informed the character of the entire era, known today as the Victorian Era.

CRITICAL VIEWING People gather in a courtyard on the Kensington High Street, London, in this photo taken around 1895. What details in the photo show what living conditions were like in urban homes and neighborhoods?

After a movement gathered one million signatures in support of greater voting rights, finally, by the 1880s, nearly all British men could vote. (Women would not get the vote until 1928, which you will read about later.) Representation in Parliament was changed to reflect the movement of much of the population from farms to towns and cities. To a small degree, new legislation protected the needs of the working poor over the profits of the gentry. Restrictions on trade unions were eased and the bargaining power of the working class increased. Laws regulated labor conditions and put some controls on the use of child labor.

Writers such as **Charles Dickens** and **Elizabeth Barrett Browning** sought change through **social criticism**, or a type of writing that tries to improve social conditions. For example, a government report, "The Condition and Treatment of the Children" about conditions in the mines, inspired both Dickens's famous story "A Christmas Carol" and Browning's poem "The Cry of the Children," in which she imagines children escaping from urban poverty to nature. Dickens himself grew up in poverty and became the most famous English author of the period, writing about the appalling living and working conditions of the poor. He wrote Oliver Twist in part as a criticism of the 1834 New Poor Law, which created the workhouse system that provided lodging for the poor in return for labor. He was such a popular author that his works made people all over the world aware of the conditions of the poor.

Scientists also contributed to reforms. For example, after **Louis Pasteur** discovered that microorganisms cause fermentation and disease in the 1860s, he developed a heating process to make milk safe to drink. This widely used process was named *pasteurization* after him. He also developed vaccines against anthrax and rabies. Joseph Lister applied Pasteur's discoveries to hospitals and surgery. His demands for cleanliness and the use of antiseptics to prevent infection saved countless lives.

The combination of economic success and relatively peaceful political reform made many Victorians extremely confident about their nation and optimistic about its future. Elsewhere, in Ireland and on the European continent, in contrast, many societies were rocked by famine, revolution, and changing national borders.

HISTORICAL THINKING

1. **READING CHECK** How did the Industrial Revolution change British society?
2. **IDENTIFY PROBLEMS AND SOLUTIONS** What were some of the problems created by the Industrial Revolution and how were they solved?
3. **DRAW CONCLUSIONS** How did writers such as Dickens and Browning influence reform in Britain?

1.3

MAIN IDEA Britain held an exhibition in 1851 to show the world the advancements of its Industrial Revolution.

London's Great Exhibition

Have you ever been excited to attend an exhibition of the latest comics, movies, and video games? In the mid-1800s, people were just that excited to go to an exhibition about what was new in the field of industry.

THE GREAT EXHIBITION

In 1851, Britain celebrated the Industrial Revolution with an event called the *Great Exhibition of the Works of Industry of All Nations*. Queen Victoria's husband, Prince Albert, was one of the main planners for the event. In a period of five months, over six million people—more than twice as many who lived in the city of London—came from around the world to see the Great Exhibition.

The exhibition building, called the Crystal Palace, was itself a work of art and a testament to industrial progress. A new process for manufacturing large, strong sheets of glass made this building possible and provided architects with the large panes necessary to give the building a "crystal" effect of clear walls and ceilings. The building measured 1,851 feet long (more than five football fields) and 128 feet (or about 12 stories) high. Over 10 miles of viewing space inside displayed 100,000 objects.

The main attractions were exhibits of the latest industrial technology. Queen Victoria wrote in her diary that "every conceivable invention" was on display. Visitors could examine the recently invented daguerreotype, an early type of photograph. A number of American inventions were introduced to the world at the exhibition, including Cyrus McCormick's reaper, which harvested crops more efficiently. The largest exhibit was a huge hydraulic press used for bridge building that included a series of enormous metal tubes, each weighing over 1,000 tons. A central area was the site of concerts, circuses, and tightrope walking. The world's largest organ provided music. The exhibition also provided the world's first public toilets, first just for men, then later for women as well.

Over half the exhibit space was used to display British products, with a special section showing colonial contributions. For example, the Great Exhibition featured the arts of India, including the world's largest diamond. In these galleries, visitors learned that Britain was now a great power in Asia.

INFLUENCE OF THE EXHIBITION

When the Great Exhibition ended, it had raised enough money through admission fees to fund the creation of Britain's Victoria and Albert and Natural History museums, both of which still stand near Hyde Park in London today. It also inspired other world fairs,

---

PRIMARY SOURCE

Of foreign contributions to the Exhibition, France will be the largest contributor; next to it will come the Zollverein [German states] and Austria; then Belgium. To these succeed Russia, Turkey, and Switzerland. Holland, its commercial importance considered, will occupy a very small space. The northern states of Germany not included in the Zollverein, Egypt, Spain, Portugal, the Brazils, and Mexico have confined themselves within still narrower limits; and China, Arabia, and Persia have the smallest. Of the British dependencies the East Indies claim the lion's share of room, and of the whole ground assigned to industrial products of the United Kingdom, nearly one-half has been appropriated to machinery. As far as possible, the different nations have been arranged in a manner corresponding to their distances from the equator; the products of tropical climates being brought nearest to the transept [central aisle], and those of colder regions being placed at the extremities of the building.

—Excerpt from "London Companion During the Great Exhibition" by R. Beasland, London, 1851

This engraving shows the exterior of the Crystal Palace, as seen from Kensington Gardens in 1851. Designed by Sir Joseph Paxton, the glass-and-iron exhibition hall included more than eight miles of display tables on the ground floor and galleries for the 14,000 exhibitors who participated.

or **expositions**. In a time before television or the Internet, these exhibitions were ways for countries to celebrate their power and accomplishments, often through a signature structure. A major Paris exhibition in 1889 included the monumental Eiffel Tower, and the Chicago World's Fair in 1893 introduced the world to the Ferris Wheel.

Far more important, however, was the way these exhibitions spread interest in and knowledge of technological advancements. An 1878 exhibition in Paris introduced the world to the Singer sewing machine, Alexander Graham Bell's telephone, and **Thomas Edison**'s microphone and phonograph. Edison displayed his other major invention, electric lighting, at an 1881 Paris exposition and a London exposition the following year. By the Chicago exposition in 1893, electricity had advanced enough that 120,000 electric lamps lit the exhibition halls at night. Other uses of electricity at that fair included an elevated railroad, electric boats, and a moving sidewalk. The 1964 New York World's Fair introduced the world to the first picture phone and computer modem. In 2010, the Shanghai World Exposition showed off China's economic and technological advances in the 21st century. For many years, these exhibitions have inspired, educated, and shown the world the future.

HISTORICAL THINKING

1. **READING CHECK** What was the main purpose of the Great Exhibition?

2. **DRAW CONCLUSIONS** What was the most important outcome of the Great Exhibition, and why?

3. **MAKE INFERENCES** Why do you think so many exhibitions included monumental architecture, such as the Crystal Palace or the Eiffel Tower?

2.1
MAIN IDEA The Industrial Revolution had a significant effect on the world economy and led to a shift in the global balance of power.

The World Economy Accelerates

From its beginning, the Industrial Revolution was a global process. Improvements in transportation and communication created a worldwide market. However, the entire world did not profit from it.

Because of a labor shortage on the Pacific coast of the United States, Chinese immigrants performed much of the work building the Transcontinental Railroad, which was completed in 1869. This photo, part of a series taken by Alfred A. Hart between 1865 and 1869, shows a Chinese camp and construction train in Nevada.

GLOBAL DIMENSIONS OF THE INDUSTRIAL REVOLUTION

Some historians point to the Industrial Revolution as one of the first examples of globalization. **Globalization** refers to the development of an increasingly integrated global economy marked especially by free trade and by the free flow of capital. The Industrial Revolution created a growing world economy that tightly connected producers and consumers around the world like never before. By the end of the 19th century, most of humankind was participating in the global commodity markets of industrial capitalism.

As the Industrial Revolution spread, steamships and railroads made the world a much smaller place. The first steam-powered crossing of the Atlantic took place in 1838 and of the Pacific in 1853. By the 1870s, steamships dramatically reduced transportation times and shipping costs. In the United States, large waterways like the Mississippi River transported people and goods over great distances. The **Suez Canal**, finished in 1869, linked the Mediterranean and Red Seas and reduced the travel time from Europe to South Asia from months to weeks. These advances enabled an increased European presence in Africa and Southeast Asia and the tightening of control over existing colonies, such as British India.

By midcentury, a dense network of railroads covered western Europe, increasing both urbanization and mobility. In North America, transcontinental railroads crossed the United States and Canada, linking the coasts and creating national identities. By 1880, railroads were spreading across Russia, British India, and Mexico.

Inventions in communication also increased the pace of global interactions. After **Samuel Morse** invented the telegraph, information moved even more quickly than people and goods. The first long-range telegraph message was sent in 1844. In 1869, an underwater cable was laid in the Atlantic Ocean. Telegraphs allowed traders to accurately compare prices instantaneously across continents. Shipping companies used the telegraph to lower their costs and increase global trade.

All of these advances led to more powerful European (and later, U.S., Russian, and Japanese) militaries. Railroads, steamships, and increasingly sophisticated weaponry moved soldiers quickly and made them deadlier than the people they set out to conquer or subdue.

Globalization through military conquest or trade had enormous cultural and intellectual effects. European tastes and ideas gained prominence, and as their power grew, Europeans came to view customs and cultures in many other parts of the world as inferior to their own.

FACTORS IN INDUSTRIAL GROWTH

Historians are still debating why the Industrial Revolution took off in Britain and not in the more developed regions of China. By 1750, the two countries had a great deal in common. They shared a high life expectancy. They were both consumer societies, and they both traded and had advanced national and international markets. Furthermore, they both faced the same ecological challenges, so were at the same disadvantage.

Some historians refer to the split that occurred between western Europe and Asia around 1750 as the Great Divergence. (*Divergence* means "a drawing apart or a separating.") Historians are still debating why it took place. Some emphasize cultural factors, such as the Protestant Reformation, which connected hard work with godliness, and the Scientific Revolution, which stimulated the spirit of invention. Other historians argue that material factors were more important. First, British coal fields lay close at hand, while in China the main coal areas were thousands of miles from the manufacturing regions. Second, the British could import timber from its colonies in North America, easing ecological limits to growth. Finally, workers' wages were higher in Britain than in China. That gave European businessmen an incentive to invest in machines to lower costs, leading to expanded markets and greater profits.

Some historians have also pointed out that a lot of British capital came from the huge profits of the Atlantic slave trade and the sugar plantations of the Caribbean. The unpaid labor of enslaved Africans was thus used to finance industry, even as the slave plantations of the southern United States provided much of the cotton for Britain's factory system.

British inventor and entrepreneur Charles Wheatstone invented the automatic telegraph transmitter in 1858.

HISTORICAL THINKING

1. **READING CHECK** How is the Industrial Revolution the first example of globalization?

2. **MAKE CONNECTIONS** Why did European tastes and ideas become more valued around the world during the Industrial Revolution?

3. **MAKE PREDICTIONS** What do you think will happen to the nations of Asia as a result of the Great Divergence?

2.2

MAIN IDEA The changes caused by the Industrial Revolution led to the development of various economic, political, and social philosophies.

Political Ideals

Is it better to focus on individual freedom or the collective good of society? Should the production of goods be controlled by the government or by the seller and consumer? The events of the Industrial Revolution led many people to ask these questions and to think and act to find answers.

PHILOSOPHY AND CHANGE

As you have read, the Industrial Revolution resulted in more efficient transportation and communication. However, it also resulted in unsanitary and unsafe working conditions, poverty, and overcrowded living spaces. Philosophers, politicians, and religious leaders looked at the changing world and began to question ideas about how humans should live. Latin Americans, Africans, and Asians, as well as Europeans, all discussed these key ideas.

In Victorian Britain, the rising ideals were those of classical **liberalism**, which stressed the virtues of freedom. Though the term has different meanings today, to 19th-century liberals, freedom of religion, freedom of trade, freedom of conscience, and freedom of expression were universal values. Following these ideals, Parliament agreed to remove restrictions on British Catholics, eliminate tariffs on imported grain, and allow workers the legal right to organize unions.

A major supporter of liberalism was the British philosopher **John Stuart Mill**. In his book *On Liberty*, Mill argued that liberty involved freedom not only from unnecessary government interference but also from "the tendency of society to impose . . . its own ideas and practices . . . on those who dissent from [disagree with] them." His emphasis on freedom from both political oppression and social conformity led Mill to opinions that were radical for the time. For example, he thought the vote should be extended not only to working men but also to women. British liberalism was a global inspiration for people seeking freedom. For example, Mill's liberal ideas spread to East Asia after the book was translated by a Japanese reformer.

CRITICAL VIEWING In 1848, demonstrators in Paris set up barricades and demanded a republican form of government. This painting by Horace Vernet captures the uprising. What ideas and emotions are conveyed in the painting?

626 CHAPTER 22

You've already read about capitalism, in which the means of production are owned by private individuals and the production, prices, and distribution of goods are determined by competition in a free market. This term was first used in the middle of the 19th century, but it describes an economic system that had been growing in Europe since the development of the cloth industry in the 16th and 17th centuries.

Industrialists across Europe wanted governments that supported capitalism; therefore, as industry became a more dominant force in daily life, so did capitalism. But some members of society did not benefit as much from capitalism as others. This led to the development of alternative economic philosophies, which challenged the idea of private ownership and a free market.

Debates about liberalism and capitalism became more intense in 1848 when political revolutions spread across Europe. Starting in Paris, the revolutionary spirit quickly sparked revolts in Rome, Berlin, Prague, and other capitals. By then, people were debating ideas of how industrial society might emphasize the greater good over individual interests. The most influential work resulting from the debate was *The Manifesto of the Communist Party*, published in 1848 by **Karl Marx** and **Friedrich Engels**. In the manifesto, Marx argued that economic forces—the way things are produced—shape society and that the social classes created by the economic forces come into conflict politically.

Marx believed that industrial society created two social classes in conflict: the property-owning bourgeoisie and the exploited industrial workers, whom he called the **proletariat**. He predicted that the clash between the bourgeoisie and the proletariat would inevitably lead to a violent overthrow of capitalism. At first, the workers would seize power, take property from the bourgeoisie, and use state ownership of factories to create a more equal and just society—an economic system known as **socialism**. Eventually, class divisions would disappear, and society would follow the motto "From each according to his abilities, to each according to his needs." This new economic and political system was known as **communism**.

Marx's theory wasn't the only socialist ideal. Welsh industrialist Robert Owen believed that factory owners themselves could reform the industrial system so that workers would lead better lives, with clean surroundings and education for their children. Owen tried out his ideas at New Lanark, Indiana, a utopian community built as a model to a brighter future. He lost all his money on this experiment and then became a leader in the early trade union movement.

Other socialists opposed Marx's idea of violent overthrow by arguing that liberalism and socialism could be combined. These moderate socialists argued that when workers gained the vote they could use the power of government for socialist reforms.

Apart from liberalism and socialism, the most important political philosophy of the period was nationalism. To Marx, the workers' true interests lay not with the rich and powerful who might speak the same language, but with workers across the world who share the same economic and social burdens. Nationalists, on the other hand, believed that bonds of culture and history unified people across class lines.

Germans were discussing all these ideals, and reformers hoped to combine liberalism and nationalism to create a modern, unified country. In 1848, the Frankfurt Assembly proposed to unify Germany as a constitutional monarchy. They offered the crown to the king of Prussia, but he refused to accept popular sovereignty or the separation of powers. Later, Germany would be unified not by liberalism but by the combination of military power and nationalism.

Meanwhile, in 1859, **Charles Darwin** published his groundbreaking book, *On the Origin of Species*, which put forward the theory of evolution. Some people applied Darwin's concepts of biological adaptation and natural selection to human society, with dangerous implications. **Social Darwinism** was the idea that differences in wealth and power could be explained by the superiority of some and the inferiority of others. Some Europeans and North Americans used it to justify social inequality and the idea that Europe's increasing global dominance was a natural result of racial superiority. Darwin himself did not draw such social and political conclusions, but many others did as they looked to science to justify their prejudices.

NATIONALISM AND A CHANGING EUROPE

As you have learned, 1848 was a turbulent year in Europe. For a while it seemed that the status quo of monarchs and aristocrats was coming to an end. However, in most countries conservatives won out over liberal and socialist reformers.

In early 1848, France was a constitutional monarchy, but only male property owners had the right to vote. In February, police in Paris fired on a crowd of demonstrators calling for a democratic form of government, and in response 1,500 barricades went up around the city. The king, Louis Philippe, gave up the throne and fled to England. A few weeks after the uprising in Paris, people in Vienna also took to the streets to demand new rights from the Austrian Empire. But unlike France, Austria was a multiethnic empire. Italians, Hungarians, Germans, Czechs, Croatians, and other subjects fought for their rights, which threatened the existence of the empire itself. The uprising spread to Italy, which at the time was a group of individually governed states. There the desire was not to break up an empire, but to create a new country.

The French uprising was the only one that was immediately successful. A moderate socialist government was created, but it was not popular with the rural majority. By summer, the tide was turning away from republicanism, and people turned to nationalism. Louis Napoleon, nephew of Napoleon Bonaparte, was elected president and then organized and won a national vote making him Napoleon III, Emperor of France. He represented, in his own words, "order, authority, religion, popular welfare at home, national dignity abroad." Once again, France had gone from monarchy, to republic, to empire.

Napoleon III ruled over France's Second Empire, a period of stability, prosperity, and expanding French power that lasted from 1852–1870. The government invested in infrastructure and supported industry. Although Napoleon III had absolute power, he respected the rule of law and basic civil liberties. Like his uncle, he gained support by appealing to French nationalism and by expanding the overseas French Empire.

In Austria, the rebellions were suppressed, but over the next 20 years the empire lost northern Italy and the northern German states. Other regions were in rebellion as well. In 1867, Emperor Franz Joseph II eased tensions in Hungary by proclaiming a dual monarchy under which he would be both emperor of Austria and king of Hungary, but Hungary would control its own state institutions. However, this did not solve the many other ethnic and national grievances within the empire.

The uprising in Italy was the beginning of a 20-year effort led by **Giuseppe Garibaldi** to unify the peninsula under a liberal, representative government. Garibaldi was a revolutionary who was condemned to death for leading an uprising in Genoa. He fled to Brazil, took part in an uprising there, and returned to Italy to lead a revolutionary army. By 1870, the Italian Peninsula was joined in a single constitutional monarchy with a limited electorate, a relatively weak legislature, and Rome as its capital. Sharp divisions remained, however. For many, the concept of being "Italian" was still something entirely new. The north, which had been under Austrian rule, had experienced industrialization and urbanization, while the south was still largely agricultural.

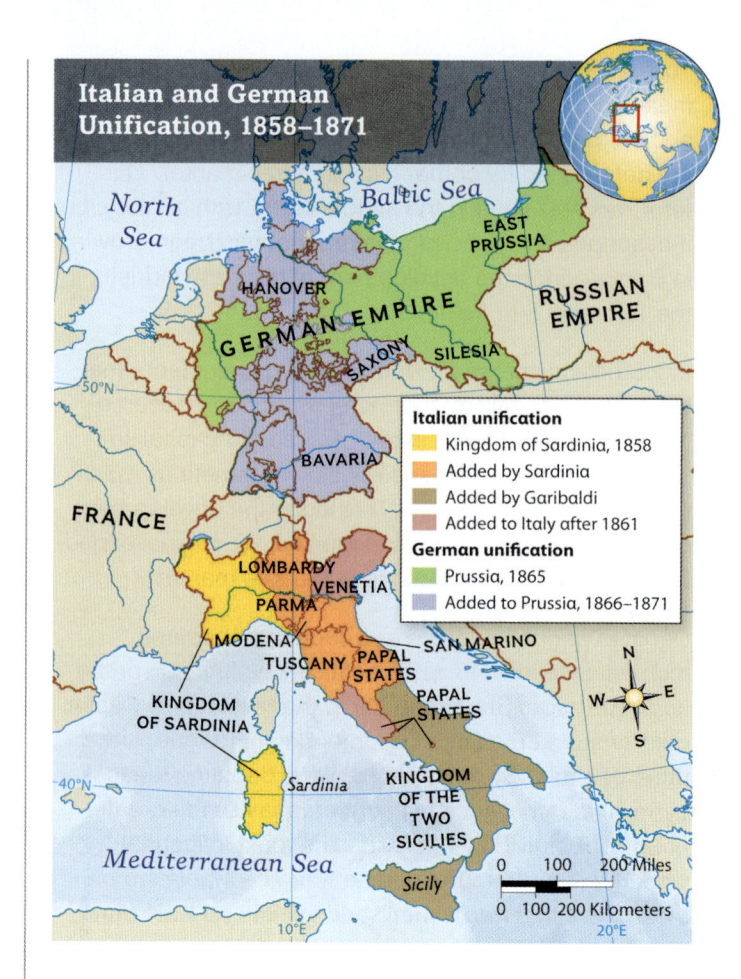

Italian and German Unification, 1858–1871

Germany also unified in the 1860s. Led by chancellor **Otto von Bismarck**, Prussia—the largest and most powerful German state—united the other states, captured territory from Austria, and won wars with both Denmark and France. In 1871 a new German state was founded under the leadership of the Prussian king, Kaiser Wilhelm II. The new Germany was based on nationalism and military power. Manufacturing boomed and the new state's gross national product doubled between 1870 and 1890.

Almost immediately, Germany became an important force in world affairs and significantly altered the balance of power. It became more aggressive in challenging the British Empire, leading to a competition for colonies in Africa and Asia. This military and economic power fed a nationalism that would have far-reaching consequences in the next century.

GLOBAL LABOR

The Industrial Revolution changed how people worked. Before that time, not many people supported themselves and their families by working for wages. In most places, peasants grew their own food, while nomads tended their herds. Capitalism now brought the very different idea that people would sell their labor to an employer and be paid wages set by the marketplace.

This transition was difficult for traditional farmers. Even those who remained in the countryside were affected by the spread of commodity markets, for example by growing more crops for export. The results were especially painful in Ireland. English landlords charged high rents that could only be paid for by exporting Irish crops. Local farmers became dependent on cheap potatoes for food, and in the 1840s many starved to death when a potato blight left them with nothing to eat. This period is known as the Irish Potato Famine.

Of course, spreading markets could also mean new opportunities. In Argentina, cheaper transport meant the growth of the beef industry. In the past, cattle had to be slaughtered very near the place of consumption. Then after 1870, refrigerated steamships allowed the export of fresh meat from South America to Europe. Livestock farmers grew rich.

In Asia, mines and plantations combined foreign investment with social labor. Instead of growing their own food, some people in Vietnam and Malaysia were now working for wages on rubber plantations or in tin mines. Much of the rice they ate came from increasing production in other parts of the region. As to be expected with globalization, economies were becoming more and more interconnected.

Just as financial investment went global, so did labor. The late 19th century saw massive movements of people in search of a better life. Migrants from the poorer parts of Europe came to the Americas looking for opportunity, joined by Chinese and Japanese immigrants crossing the Pacific. Many rural Jews left the Russian Empire to escape political oppression and poverty. Irish emigrants streamed toward the United States, Canada, and Australia. Vast new gold mines in South Africa attracted workers from across the region.

Abuses of migrant laborers were common. Many in British India were so desperate to escape village poverty that they signed up as indentured servants for very low pay and were taken to distant lands. Very often, immigrants were met with racism and discrimination. Still, these great population movements showed just how global the Industrial Revolution really was.

THE ANTHROPOCENE: A NEW GEOLOGICAL EPOCH Geologists, who study the history of Earth, employ much larger time frames than historians. In fact, most of the world history you've read about has taken place during a single geological epoch: the Holocene. This epoch extends back 11,700 years—since the end of the last ice age.

Now some geologists think it is time to insert a new benchmark: the Anthropocene ("human epoch"). They argue that the planet's physical features have been so strongly affected by the human species since 1800 that this new epoch better describes Earth systems in the very recent past. According to this view, the Anthropocene began about two centuries ago with the intensive use of fossil fuels during the Industrial Revolution.

An article published by the Royal Swedish Academy of Sciences used measurements of carbon dioxide in the atmosphere to track the impact of fossil fuels. The preindustrial level of 270–275 parts per million (ppm) had risen to 310 ppm by 1950. In 2014, carbon dioxide peaked at over 400 ppm. This "Great Acceleration," as the authors call it, "is reaching criticality. Whatever unfolds, the next few decades will surely be a tipping point in the evolution of the Anthropocene." That tipping point could mean catastrophic and irreversible global warming.

The International Union of Geological Sciences is currently considering a proposal that formally declares that the end of the Holocene was in 1800 and that the current epoch is the Anthropocene. That term, they state, "has emerged as a popular scientific term used by scientists, the scientifically engaged public, and the media to designate the period of Earth's history during which humans have had a decisive influence on the state, dynamics, and future of the Earth system."

Historians have long recognized that the Industrial Revolution was also an energy revolution. Now geologists are affirming that the global effects of those changes were even more revolutionary than previously thought.

HISTORICAL THINKING

1. **READING CHECK** What were the major political philosophies that arose as a result of the Industrial Revolution?
2. **COMPARE AND CONTRAST** What are the main differences between capitalism, communism, and socialism?
3. **INTERPRET MAPS** What do the unification of Germany and Italy have in common?
4. **DRAW CONCLUSIONS** How did nationalism influence changes in Europe during the Industrial Revolution?

3.1

MAIN IDEA During the Industrial Revolution, people everywhere had to decide how to balance traditional values and cultures with modern technology and industry.

How To Be Modern?

Imagine having to choose between something old that feels like it defines who you are and something new that would help you achieve who you want to become. That is what societies all over the world faced during the Industrial Revolution.

Taken in 1855 during the Crimean War, this photo shows rows of caissons, or chests, holding artillery ammunition and, in the background, British military tents. Britain and France joined the Ottomans to fight against the Russians during the war.

A SHIFTING BALANCE OF POWER

As you have read, the rise of modern nation-states and economies was disruptive of Europeans' social stability and traditional values. In the 19th century, that instability spread across the entire world. For Africans and Asians, and for indigenous peoples everywhere, that meant dealing with the rising influence of Europe.

The technological and financial costs of manufacturing steam-powered battleships and more powerful weapons were difficult, if not impossible, for other countries in other parts of the world to meet. Not even the mighty Russian military was able to keep up. The Industrial Revolution had given western Europe the advantage in finance, logistics, medical science, engineering, and many other areas, elevating European social, cultural, and political systems in the rest of the world as well. The question other nations faced was how to become a modern industrial society without losing their unique cultural identity.

THE CRIMEAN WAR

In the middle of the 19th century, the Russian and Ottoman empires were in a tense rivalry. In 1853, the Russian army crossed into Ottoman territory near the Danube River and the Ottomans declared war. Britain and France, fearing a stronger Russia, allied with the Ottomans. Named the **Crimean War** because it was mainly fought on the Crimean Peninsula, the war ended in a deadlock in 1856.

While neither country won, the Crimean War helped Russian and Ottoman leaders realize that modern wars could not be won without the development of industry. But how? Should they emulate western Europe or reject foreign influences and remain true to their own traditions?

Even before the war, Ottoman leaders recognized the need to modernize and, starting in 1839, instituted the Tanzimat Reforms. These ambitious reforms reshaped the government, as well as the Ottoman legal and educational systems, resulting in a more efficient administration, greater investment, and economic growth. But the reforms also increased divisions among more secular, European-oriented people in urban areas and more traditional, religiously oriented people in rural areas. After 1880, the traditional factions defeated liberal reformers and instituted policies based on the authority of the sultan and religious conservatives.

Russia came to reform later than the Ottomans, and even less successfully. At the time of the Crimean War, Russia had the world's largest army, a vast Eurasian empire, and yet was still overwhelmingly rural. It had a powerful aristocracy, a weak middle class, a huge underclass of serfs owned by the landowning nobility, and almost no modern industry. Serfs had so few rights that they could be traded in a game of cards. The country lacked a property-owning class willing to build factories and an urban labor force to work in them. The nobility profited from the old system, as did the government, which depended on serfs to populate Russia's huge army.

By the end of the Crimean War, **Tsar Alexander II** understood the need for change. In 1861, he attempted to reform the feudal system by freeing the serfs. But in an attempt to appease the nobility, he required serfs to pay for their own emancipation, which most could not afford. As with freed slaves in the southern United States, not much changed for most Russian serfs after their emancipation. Unpaid for their own labor, they did not have resources that would have allowed them to escape the poverty of their villages.

Alexander's efforts toward industrialization were more successful. He boosted railroad construction, which stimulated the coal and iron industries, and instituted tariffs on imports, which stimulated the establishment of some factories. As a result, by the 1880s Russian workers were living and working in the same dangerous and squalid conditions that marked the early industrial periods of western Europe.

At the same time, Russian intellectuals and artists were debating how deeply Russian society should change. Should Russia learn from and adopt western European cultural and constitutional models? If so, to what degree? "Westernizers" believed in looking to Europe, while "Slavophiles" declared that Russia should keep its own Slavic traditions. The debate produced a flowering of art in Russia, particularly in the field of music. Two composers in the Romantic tradition, represent the two sides. **Peter Ilyich Tchaikovsky** followed Western classical models to become Russia's best-known composer, while "Slavophiles" like **Nicolai Rimsky-Korsakov** emphasized Slavic and central Eurasian themes.

In 1881, Alexander II was assassinated, resulting in a backlash against reform and a crackdown on opposition. Reform initiated from above can be revoked from above, and Alexander's son and successor did just that. While the building of railroads and industrial development continued, modest steps toward representative government, even at the local level, stopped. The Westernizers lost and the Slavophile slogan "Orthodoxy, Autocracy, and Nationality" came to guide Russian policy.

FLORENCE NIGHTINGALE AND MARY SEACOLE Great advances in nursing were one result of the Crimean War. In 1854, a British nurse named Florence Nightingale (far left) arrived to find filthy and overcrowded hospitals. She and her team secured more supplies, cleaned the wards, and greatly improved the standard of care. Another nurse named Mary Seacole (left), who was originally from Jamaica, wanted to assist but was turned down by the British government. Instead, she set up her own "hotel" behind the battle lines and tended to soldiers. While Nightingale brought modern medical science to the battlefield, Seacole added emotional support and herbal medicines to her therapy.

Given to the British after defeat in the Opium Wars, Hong Kong was returned to China on July 1, 1997. The city, which continued to exercise political autonomy after its return, had its political freedom sharply curtailed by the Chinese government in 2020 after an increase in pro-democracy protests there.

THE OPIUM WARS

As Russia and the Ottoman Empire struggled to industrialize, China faced a different problem. In the 1600s, the British discovered Chinese tea and loved it. By the late 1700s, the drink was so popular that the average Londoner spent five percent of his or her income on tea. But the old problem for European merchants was that they did not have any goods that interested the Chinese. Opium solved that problem.

In the 1770s, European countries (mainly Britain) began to smuggle the highly addictive drug from India into China to trade it for tea, silk, and other goods. To build a market for the drug, traders gave out free samples. The plan worked: Opium use in China rose and the market grew. Many in Britain knew that the trade was morally wrong and even hypocritical. At the same time that opium was being smuggled into China, the British were trying to end opium addiction at home. However, the supporters of free trade and profit got their way.

By the 1820s, opium addiction had reached epidemic proportions and was causing great harm to China's society and economy. In 1839, the Qing government decided to fight back. An official named Lin Zezu was put in charge, and he wrote to Queen Victoria informing her that any foreigners caught importing opium would be put to death. In addition, Lin dumped large amounts of opium into the sea. Britain demanded to be compensated for its lost product, but China refused and the first Opium War began.

The Chinese were stunned by Britain's advanced ships and weapons. Ironclad British steamships simply blew the Chinese ships out of the water. Unlike the Qianlong emperor who had rejected British diplomacy five decades earlier, by 1842 Qing officials knew they had lost and agreed to the humiliating terms of the Treaty of Nanjing, which opened five "treaty ports" to unrestricted foreign trade and gave Hong Kong to the British. The treaty also promised British subjects **extraterritoriality**, or exemption from local laws in the treaty ports.

This was the first in a series of unequal treaties that eroded Chinese sovereignty. The following year, France and the United States signed similar treaties with the Qing. China's loss in the second Opium War (1856–1860) led to more open ports and the creation of "international settlements" in key Chinese cities. Only Europeans were allowed to live in these settlements, and they were ruled by European law. Foreigners were also given permission to travel, work as missionaries, and establish businesses anywhere in the country.

After losing the two Opium Wars, China was forced to face the same questions as the Russian and Ottoman empires: whether and how to become a modern industrial nation that could compete with western Europe. Some government officials recognized that things needed to change. Beginning with the loss of the first Opium War in 1842, these men advocated for reform. You will read more about these "self-strengthening" policies shortly.

JAPAN AND SIAM

You have already read about Tokugawa Japan and know that Japanese society in the early 19th century was strictly hierarchical and ruled by conservative shoguns who upheld conservative Confucian values, one of which was to disrespect commerce and the Japanese merchant class. Interaction with Europeans was still limited to a single Dutch trade mission every year.

Then, in 1853, the American commodore **Matthew Perry** came to Japan. He arrived with two steamships and two sailing ships. Perry's mission was to intimidate the Tokugawa government, force it to establish diplomatic relations, and open Japanese ports to foreign trade. Edo's (now Tokyo's) harbor was poorly defended. Aware of China's loss in the first Opium War, Japanese officials saw that isolation was no longer possible and decided to negotiate.

In 1858, the Japanese signed an unequal treaty with the United States and five European powers that—like the treaties with China—granted the Europeans access to treaty ports and rights of extraterritoriality. Daimyo lords were angered by the treaty, and some rebelled against the shogun. By the early 1860s, it was not clear whether the Tokugawa government would be able to maintain power. Japan faced the same decision as other societies that had been challenged by European industrial power: develop Western-style industry or reject the West and try to maintain a traditional society. Until 1868, the traditionalists held power, but then Japan took a different course. It adopted many Western institutions and technologies, adapting them to Japanese culture and creating a modern industrial society.

Like Japan, the kingdom of Siam (present-day Thailand) adopted Western technology while maintaining its culture and political independence. Two kings, **Mongkut** (MANG-koot) and **Chulalongkorn** (CHOO-luh-AWHN-korn), used internal reform and diplomatic engagement to achieve this balance. King Mongkut included Westerners among his advisors and opened Siam to foreign trade. His son, Chulalongkorn, who was educated by an English tutor, altered the legal system to protect private property and abolished slavery and debt peonage, expanded access to education, and encouraged development of telegraphs and railroads. At the same time, these Siamese kings balanced imported ideas with continued support for Buddhist temples and traditional artistic traditions.

Like his father, Chulalongkorn was a skilled diplomat who played Europeans off one another. Lacking a strong army, he gave up claims to parts of his empire to protect the core of his kingdom. Despite this, if the British or French had wanted to conquer Siam, they could have. But Siam sat—and served as a buffer—between the British in India and the French in the Southeast Asian region of Indochina. In 1896, the two powers agreed to recognize the independent kingdom of Siam.

CRITICAL VIEWING This Japanese woodblock print depicts the arrival of American commodore Matthew Perry to Japan in 1853. What details in the print express the point of view of the artist toward Perry's arrival?

HISTORICAL THINKING

1. **READING CHECK** How did Siam's kings balance Western ideas and local traditions?

2. **COMPARE AND CONTRAST** How were the Ottomans and Russians similar in their reactions to the Industrial Revolution?

3. **MAKE PREDICTIONS** How do you think opium addiction harmed China's economy and society?

4. **MAKE INFERENCES** Why is this lesson titled "How To Be Modern?"?

3.2

MAIN IDEA After establishing trading stations, the British slowly took over control of all of India and suppressed any attempts at rebellion.

British India and Indian Revolt

For centuries, invaders like the Mughals had crossed the Himalaya mountain passes into the Indian subcontinent. Arriving by sea, however, the British represented an entirely new threat. Starting from a base in Bengal, they would fill the power vacuum left by Mughal decline.

THE BRITISH EAST INDIA COMPANY

Unlike China and Japan, the Mughal Empire welcomed trade with Europe, and in the 17th century allowed European companies to open trading stations, or "factories." The most powerful was the British East India Company, which founded its first factory in 1615 at Surat on India's west coast. Another factory, founded by the company in 1690 in Calcutta (present-day Kolkata) in the province of Bengal, received permission in 1717 to trade tax-free, giving it a great advantage over both Indian and European competitors.

After an Iranian invasion in 1739, the Mughal Empire became less powerful. The expansion of British power in India was not planned, but the vacuum left by declining Mughal power eventually combined with greed and ambition to push British frontiers forward. The British East India Company let the Mughal emperor keep his throne while steadily extending the company's power, first by becoming the official tax collector, then by using the threat of military force to divide and conquer local rulers. Company employees abused their power and plundered Bengal and other areas. In 1769, the company's brutal treatment of Indians became crystal clear when a famine hit Bengal and killed one-third of its population. The company was accused of only feeding its own people, not even giving its surplus food to starving Bengalis while still demanding regular tax payments from them.

In an effort to end abuses such as the East India Company's actions during the famine, the British government took greater control in India with a plan to promote justice and fairness by keeping the roles of commercial traders and government officials separate. As the Mughal Empire continued to weaken, Britain expanded its control. In 1818, Britain defeated its last major resistance, the Maratha confederacy from the west coast of India. Without an initial plan of conquest, the British had gone from coastal factories devoted to trading to complete control of the Indian subcontinent.

Britain used its newfound power to drain India of its raw materials to feed British industry. One result was Indian deindustrialization, notably in textile manufacturing. As you have read, the British had been importing Indian cotton cloth, but with the development of factories in Britain, Britain began to import only raw cotton. By 1830, millions of unemployed Indian textile workers were forced to leave factory work for farming in a reversal of the industrial British rural-to-urban migration.

Technological advancements also caused shifts in British-Indian society. In the early days of the East India Company, many British employees adopted aspects of Indian culture and married into Indian families. After steamships, telegraphs, and the Suez Canal shortened the distance between Europe and India, British men brought their families from England with them. The British began to create a separate society in India. Indians—no matter how accomplished—were excluded, except as servants. Meanwhile, the British intruded more and more into Indian customs and culture. This intrusion provoked a powerful counterreaction, especially after an increase in the number of missionaries raised both Muslim and Hindu concerns that the British wanted to convert them to Christianity.

THE REBELLION OF 1857

Indians under British rule faced a dilemma: reject British customs, embrace them, or balance them with Indian traditions. The first of those choices inspired a major rebellion in 1857.

The immediate cause of the revolt was Britain's introduction of a new, faster-loading rifle. The loading

CRITICAL VIEWING This 1784 painting is based on an actual cockfight in the city of Lucknow. The fight had been arranged as an amusement by Colonel Mordaunt, the tall standing figure dressed in white. In 1857, Lucknow became the center of a massive revolt against British authority. What differences are there in the depiction of the Europeans and Indians in this painting?

procedure required the **sepoys**, or Indian soldiers under British command, to bite off the greased ends of the guns' ammunition cartridge casings. A rumor spread among Muslim troops that the cartridges had been greased with pig fat, while many Hindus believed that fat from cattle had been used. Since contact with pork was forbidden to Muslims and cattle were sacred to Hindus, both groups suspected that the British were trying to pollute them as part of a plot to convert them to Christianity. Some soldiers refused to use the new cartridges and were arrested. In response, other soldiers rebelled and killed their British officers.

Ultimately 200,000 sepoys joined the rebellion. They marched to Delhi and rallied support for the restoration of the Mughal emperor. The revolt quickly spread across northern and western India, where the queen of Jhansi, one of the Maratha kingdoms, rode into battle with her troops. The rebellion was very violent on both sides and many were killed.

However, in less than a year, Britain regained control. The British government disbanded the East India Company, destroyed all remaining Mughal authority, and took over the rule of India itself. In 1876, Queen Victoria added "Empress of India" to her titles, and British dominance of India was complete.

Even under the Mughals, India was one of the most ethnically diverse regions of the world, with more than a dozen major languages, multiple castes, and many different religions and ethnicities. While that diversity continued, after 1857 there was also a move toward greater unity. The British built an extensive transportation and communication infrastructure throughout the country, which put India's diverse peoples and regions in closer contact than ever before. Thus, the tools of industrialization provided the foothold for Indians to overthrow their colonizers. A growing middle class began to join together and develop a clear vision of India as a single, unified nation. In 1885, they organized a new political movement called the Indian National Congress.

HISTORICAL THINKING

1. **READING CHECK** How did the East India Company expand its control over India?
2. **MAKE CONNECTIONS** How did the Industrial Revolution in Britain lead to deindustrialization in India?
3. **MAKE INFERENCES** Why did the British improve railway and communications systems in India, and what was an unintended consequence of those improvements?

3.3

MAIN IDEA After the encroachment of Europeans into their affairs, the Chinese began to rebel, both against their Qing rulers and against British and other European powers.

Rebellions in China

In the 1700s, the Qing dynasty in China was at the top of its game. But by the end of the 1800s, the empire was devastated economically, socially, and politically. How did China fall so far, so fast?

THE TAIPING REBELLION

By the mid-19th century, in addition to the devastation of opium addiction, the Opium Wars, and the growing power of the Europeans, China also faced enormous internal stresses, mainly as a result of four centuries of success.

The main issue was high population growth. Food production and government services could not keep up. Some scholars estimate that by the early 1800s, one local magistrate might be responsible for as many as 250,000 people. As a result, corruption rose and local strongmen gained power. Rural farmers became poorer as revenues went down and taxes went up, leading to peasant revolts in different regions. By far the largest and most successful was the Taiping Rebellion, which began in 1850 in Guangdong province and then spread throughout southern China.

The leader of the rebellion was Hong Xiuquan (hoong shee-OH-chew-an), who proclaimed that he was the younger brother of Jesus Christ. Educated by missionaries, Hong mixed Christianity with a traditional Buddhist message of fairness and justice, which appealed to the poor and attracted hundreds of thousands of followers. Many at the center of the rebellion were, like Hong, from the Hakka ethnic group, which had been independent until the Ming era. As a result, they had not completely adopted Confucian ideas of hierarchy. Women had relatively independent roles, and Hakka men often refused to wear the long, braided ponytail (or queue) required as a sign of subservience by the Manchu ethnic group that founded the Qing dynasty.

During the Taiping Rebellion, Taiping forces broke through a strategic encirclement by the Qing army in Fucheng, as shown in this finely detailed painting.

In late 1850, Taiping rebels captured the city of Nanjing and killed tens of thousands of Manchu, but the rebels had difficulty maintaining a functional government. Their religious beliefs went against the Confucian ideals of scholar-officials on which the imperial system had long been based. Also, landowners and educated elites, who were threatened by the rebellion's ideas about equality, successfully resisted Taiping rule. By 1853, the rebellion was in trouble, and in the 1860s European interests began to support the very dynasty they had just finished fighting in the Opium Wars. In 1864, Qing forces, supported by European soldiers and arms, took Nanjing, and the Taiping Rebellion ended. A staggering 30 million people had been killed, and China's rulers were more indebted to European powers than ever before.

THE BOXER REBELLION

As you have read, in response to the loss of the Opium Wars, some Chinese began arguing for internal "Self-Strengthening" reforms. The movement's motto was "Confucian ethics, Western science." China, these reformers said, could acquire modern technology and scientific knowledge while keeping its Confucian traditions. Traditionalists, however, opposed the Self-Strengthening Movement. Like Muslim scholars who opposed reforms in the Ottoman Empire, Chinese scholar-officials got their power and prestige from training in a traditional body of knowledge. To accept foreign principles in education would give them less influence, and to emphasize military over scholarly pursuits would go against Confucianism.

The powerful regent **Empress Ci Xi** (kee SHEE) shared these traditional views. She resented the unequal treaties with European nations, and the arrogance of their representatives infuriated her. Ci Xi stopped funding modernization programs, such as railways and military improvements, and started funding projects like rebuilding the ruined summer palace destroyed earlier by European soldiers. She even spent from the naval budget on a marble boat to host tea parties in her garden.

This meant that China was unable to address internal crises. From 1876 to 1879, drought combined with overpopulation, resulting in one of the most brutal famines in the empire's history and claiming at least 9.5 million lives. Ten years later, another major famine hit the country, weakening it even more.

External pressures threatened China as well. From their base in Vietnam, the French had conquered most of Indochina by 1885, and the Korean Peninsula and Taiwan were lost to Japan in 1895. From 1895 to 1900, European aggression intensified. Germans seized the port city of Qingdao and claimed mineral and railway rights on its entire peninsula. The British and Russians expanded their control. Public anger toward the Qing grew in China.

In 1898, Ci Xi quickly charged some advocates of Self-Strengthening with conspiracy. Those who were not executed left the country or gave up and went silent. In the meantime, Empress Ci XI leant her support to an anti-foreign secret society, the "Society of Righteous and Harmonious Fists" (also known as the Boxers), which had been gaining power and influence. In 1898, the society attacked European missionaries and Chinese Christian converts, beginning the Boxer Rebellion.

To put down the Boxers, troops from different nations, including Russia, Britain, the United States, Austria-Hungary, and Italy, marched on Beijing and occupied the Forbidden City in the summer of 1900. Most humiliating to the Chinese were the Japanese soldiers proudly flying their flag in the heart of the Chinese capital. It seemed that this invasion of "barbarians" had turned the world upside down.

The Qing were required to pay 450 million ounces of silver (twice the country's annual revenue) to the occupying forces. In addition, the Confucian examination system was abolished, and plans were made to draw up a constitution with some degree of popular representation. But it was much too late. Just a few years later, in 1912, revolutionaries overthrew the decrepit Qing dynasty.

A court photographer took this official portrait of Empress Ci Xi, c. 1895.

HISTORICAL THINKING

1. **READING CHECK** Why was the 19th century a period of rebellion and unrest in China?

2. **ANALYZE CAUSE AND EFFECT** What effect did rejection of Confucian ideals have on the success of the Taiping Rebellion?

3. **DESCRIBE** How did the Qing dynasty react to attempts to adopt Western ideas and industry?

3.4 **MAIN IDEA** In response to aggression from Europe, Russia, and the United States, Japan industrialized and centralized state power while maintaining its social, cultural, and spiritual traditions.

The Meiji Restoration

If someone tries to force you to change, how do you respond? Perhaps you think some kind of change might be a good thing. Even so, you probably want to do things *your* way, not theirs.

MEIJI REFORMS

Both Tokugawa Japan and Qing China were divided between conservatives, who rejected Western influences, and reformers, who argued for modernization to strengthen the empire. In China, it was the opponents of change who won out, but Japan was able to borrow foreign ideas and adapt them to their own culture, achieving the "self-strengthening" that Chinese reformers had not.

In 1867, the army of the Tokugawa shogun faced off against supporters of the Japanese emperor. Inspired by the slogans "Revere the Emperor!" and "Expel the Barbarians!" the emperor's armies were successful, and in 1868 the Meiji (MAY-jee) Restoration brought the Meiji ("enlightened") teenage emperor into power.

Reformers dominated the new emperor's administration, and they began to transform Japan's closed, traditional society. Mainly men from middle- and lower-class samurai families who placed a strong emphasis on scholarship, the Meiji reformers dismantled the feudal system and declared all classes in society equal. Tax collection was centralized to solidify the government's economic control, and a modern army and national education system were created.

CRITICAL VIEWING From a series of prints called *Famous Places on the Tokaido: A Record of the Process of Reform*, this print showcases the new Tokyo-Yokohama railway, built in 1872. What message about Meiji reforms does the print express?

These reforms were met with some resistance, but any rebellions were quickly put down. And while Japan adopted a constitution in 1889, like the German constitution it copied, the emperor, rather than elected representatives, had the real power.

The Meiji reformers did not believe in a free-market economy, and free-trade economic ideas were never particularly strong in Japan as compared to Britain and the United States. Japanese leaders thought that economic planning would be more likely to lead to social harmony than market competition. And the Meiji government, like Germany but even more so, gave the state control over industrial development. The government constructed railroads, harbors, and telegraph lines and made direct investments in industry as well.

Ultimately, the government did begin to open industry to private companies and sold off some of its industrial assets. After 1880, Japanese industry was dominated by **zaibatsu**, large industrial conglomerates that worked closely with the government. (Some of the 19th-century zaibatsu, like Mitsubishi, still exist today.)

As in Europe, the rewards of increased industrial productivity were not equally distributed in Meiji Japan. Landowners benefited the most from advances in agriculture. Rice output increased 30 percent between 1870 and 1895, but peasants often paid half their crop in land rent and now had to pay taxes to the central government as well. To make ends meet, many rural families sent their daughters to work in factories.

Some reformers worked to bring education to girls as the first step toward greater equality. A 20-year-old woman named Kishida Toshiko went even further, speaking powerfully for women's rights in meetings across the country. Toshiko was arrested, fined, and silenced for speaking out. The men at the top of Meiji society chose the slogan "Good Wife, Wise Mother" to reinforce tradition, defining proper women as submissive, subservient, and legally inferior.

Women work in a Japanese silk factory at the beginning of the 20th century, boiling cocoons and spinning silk.

GROWING MILITARISM

During the late 19th century like many other industrialized countries around the world, Japan was moving toward **militarism**, a policy of continuous military development and readiness for war. Many in Japan embraced Social Darwinist concepts, promoting the idea that the Japanese were racially superior to other Asians and destined to lead the continent forward.

The first place Japan showed its true intentions was on the Korean Peninsula. As you have read, Japan gained control of the peninsula and Taiwan in 1895. In addition, the Meiji government forced the Qing to grant it access to China's treaty ports and rights of extraterritoriality, similar to those of the European powers. At the same time, Japan renegotiated its own treaties with Europe, this time demanding equality. In 1910, the Meiji government formally annexed Korea.

Next, in order to solidify its influence in northeastern Asia, the Meiji government decided to challenge Russian ambitions in Manchuria and Korea. In 1905, the Japanese navy won a great military victory over the Russian fleet. Japan's victory proved that European superiority was not inevitable and that Japan had to be counted among the world's great powers.

HISTORICAL THINKING

1. **READING CHECK** What were the major reforms of the Meiji Restoration?

2. **MAKE CONNECTIONS** How did women's lives change or not change in Japan during this period?

3. **MAKE PREDICTIONS** How might increasing nationalism affect Japan in the future?

CHAPTER 22 INDUSTRIAL REVOLUTION REVIEW

VOCABULARY

Use each of the following vocabulary words in a sentence that shows an understanding of the term's meaning.

1. division of labor
2. sabotage
3. exposition
4. globalization
5. liberalism
6. communism
7. socialism
8. extraterritoriality

READING STRATEGY
DETERMINE CHRONOLOGY

When you determine chronology, you place events in the order in which they occurred and note correlations between events. Use a time line like this one to order key events of the Industrial Revolution and analyze its impact.

Year	EVENTS
1750	Revolutionary uprisings across Europe
1775	Meiji Restoration
1800	Cotton gin
1825	Indian National Congress
1850	England controls India
1875	Steam engine
1900	China loses Opium War
	London's Great Exhibition
	Boxer Rebellion
	Abolition of British slave trade

9. Choose two of the events from your time line and describe the relationship between them.

MAIN IDEAS

Answer the following questions. Support your answers with evidence from the chapter.

10. What were two major changes in manufacturing that occurred as a result of the Industrial Revolution? **LESSON 1.1**

11. How did the Crystal Palace serve as an emblem of the advancements of the Industrial Revolution? **LESSON 1.2**

12. How did the Industrial Revolution lead to reform movements? **LESSON 1.3**

13. What do some historians mean by the term *Great Divergence*? **LESSON 2.1**

14. How are the Industrial Revolution and capitalism linked? **LESSON 2.2**

15. What were some dilemmas faced by non-Western countries in the 19th century? **LESSON 3.1**

16. What role did the British East India Company play in the British colonization of India? **LESSON 3.2**

17. What effect did the rebellions of the 19th century have on China and its development? **LESSON 3.3**

18. What effect did the Industrial Revolution have on Japan? **LESSON 3.4**

HISTORICAL THINKING

Answer the following questions. Support your answers with evidence from the chapter.

19. **ANALYZE CAUSE AND EFFECT** How did the Industrial Revolution affect the balance of power among the world's nations?

20. **FORM AND SUPPORT OPINIONS** Do you think life was better for most people before or after the Industrial Revolution? Explain.

21. **IDENTIFY PROBLEMS AND SOLUTIONS** What problems were communism, socialism, and utopian socialism trying to solve?

22. **MAKE CONNECTIONS** How did access to coal lead to the development of new technologies?

23. **SUMMARIZE** How did attitudes toward slavery change over the course of industrialization?

24. **HYPOTHESIZE** How might the world have been different if China had won the Opium Wars and decided to modernize?

25. **COMPARE AND CONTRAST** How did Siam and Japan react to Western power and influence?

26. **DRAW CONCLUSIONS** Why was the Industrial Revolution categorized as a "revolution"?

INTERPRET GRAPHS

Study the graph below, which shows the respective share of gross domestic product (GDP) among the world's most powerful countries.

Economic History of China and Other Major Powers
Share of world GDP

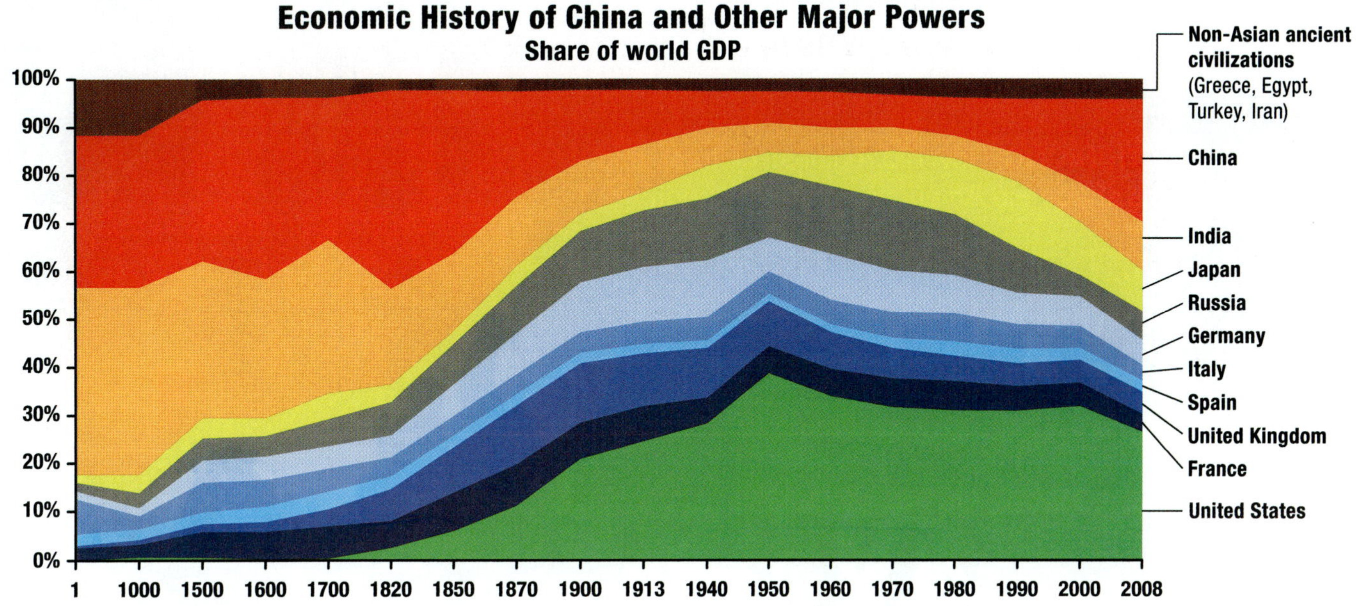

100%
90%
80%
70%
60%
50%
40%
30%
20%
10%
0%
1
1000
1500
1600
1700
1820
1850
1870
1900
1913
1940
1950
1960
1970
1980
1990
2000
2008
Non-Asian ancient civilizations (Greece, Egypt, Turkey, Iran)
China
India
Japan
Russia
Germany
Italy
Spain
United Kingdom
France
United States

Source: *Statistics on World Population, GRP, and Per Capita GDP, 1–2008 A.D.*, Angus Maddison, University of Groningen

27. Which countries had the largest share of the world's GDP in 1700?

28. According to this graph, which countries had the largest share in 1900? Based on the text, how would you explain this change?

ANALYZE SOURCES

In 1835, Andrew Ure wrote about the growing Industrial Revolution in *The Philosophy of Manufactures*.

> Steam-engines . . . create a vast demand for fuel; they call into employment multitudes of miners, engineers, shipbuilders, and sailors, and cause the construction of canals and railways. Thus therefore, in enabling these rich fields of industry to be cultivated to the utmost, they leave thousands of fine arable fields free for the production of food to man, which must have been otherwise allotted to the food of horses.

29. What is the author's argument on the benefits of steam engines?

30. How does this excerpt relate to the population increase that resulted from the Industrial Revolution?

CONNECT TO YOUR LIFE

31. **ARGUMENT** The British abolitionist movement used many tactics in its efforts to end slavery in the British Empire and beyond. One of these techniques was a boycott, or refusal to buy or use, sugar because sugar was produced with the labor of enslaved people. Have you ever taken part in or considered taking part in a boycott? Why did you or did you not participate? Do you think boycotts are effective? Write a paragraph in which you make an argument for or against taking part in a boycott.

TIPS

- Describe the boycott you want to argue for or against.
- Explain the goals of the boycott you are describing.
- Evaluate how effective the boycott is likely to be or was. Think in terms of both short- and long-term effects as well as direct and indirect effects.
- Address any counterarguments.
- Conclude your argument with a sentence summarizing your position.

CHAPTER 23

Changes in the Americas
1803–1924

HISTORICAL THINKING How did regional, cultural, and ethnic divisions shape the Americas in the 19th century?

SECTION 1 **North America After Industrialization**

SECTION 2 **Latin America After Independence**

SECTION 3 **Rebellion and Reform**

CRITICAL VIEWING
Many Europeans immigrated to the United States in the 19th century in search of greater economic opportunities and settled in big industrial cities, including New York, Chicago, Detroit, and Philadelphia. By the late 1800s, American cities were becoming the bustling places we know today. What modern aspects of a city do you recognize in this 1899 photo of a downtown street in New York?

Changes in the Americas 643

1.1

MAIN IDEA Economic and cultural differences between the North and the South in the United States led to a civil war that tore the country apart.

Civil War in the United States

Do you think regional differences could cause the United States to split into two countries today? It's happened before. In the 1860s, some states chose to break away and form their own government. A war would decide the nation's fate.

TENSIONS BETWEEN NORTH AND SOUTH

In the years following the American Revolution, the United States had steadily expanded westward. By 1850, the country had spread to the Pacific Ocean. But as each new state entered the Union, the question of whether it would allow slavery bitterly divided the nation. Those in the North thought the new territories should be admitted as free states, while the South called for new slave states. Northerners didn't want to strengthen the institution of slavery. And both sides feared that an imbalance in free and slave states would result in more political power for the other side. Congress tried to keep the total of free and slave states equal, but tensions between the two regions grew.

The North and the South began to establish separate identities, and people came to feel strong loyalty toward the part of the country in which they lived, a concept called **sectionalism**. Economic differences between the two regions helped drive sectionalism. The Industrial Revolution had spread to the United States, and factories sprang up in the North. Manufacturing boosted industries that supported the factory-based economy, including banking and improved transportation systems—roads, canals, and railroads—to transport goods. The South, on the other hand, remained an agrarian, or agricultural, society. Cotton was a major cash crop. And white plantation owners in the South relied heavily on slave labor to grow this crop and others.

Violent conflicts took place between proslavery and antislavery forces. For example, violent assaults by pro-slavery activists and armed retaliation by their enemies in Kansas further divided the nation. In 1854, the Republican Party was established. Its members dedicated themselves to stopping the spread of slavery. They opposed those in the Democratic Party, particularly southern Democrats, who supported slavery. The Republicans nominated **Abraham Lincoln** as their candidate in the presidential election of 1860. Lincoln won by carrying the western states and most of those in the North. He didn't even appear on the ballot in the South.

After Lincoln's election, several southern states **seceded**, or withdrew, from the Union. More states joined them and, in 1861, they established a new country called the Confederate States of America, also referred to as the **Confederacy**. That same year, Confederate soldiers bombarded Union soldiers inside Fort Sumter, a U.S. possession in South Carolina. The Union forces surrendered, but the attack sparked the Civil War.

WAR AND ITS AFTERMATH

The Union and the Confederacy quickly mobilized armies and prepared to fight. At the outset, the North held an advantage in terms of overall resources, including a more extensive system of roads and canals, greater industrial capacity, more food, and four times as many men eligible for military service. The South had an initial advantage in military leadership. In addition, Confederate soldiers were fighting to protect their homeland and way of life.

Union and Confederate forces clashed in bloody battles throughout the war. Advances in technology made the fighting deadlier than ever. A new and more precise kind of rifle replaced the muskets used in the American Revolution, and the repeating rifle allowed soldiers to fire several times before having to reload. During battles at sea, ironclad ships plated with thick metal withstood cannon and rifle fire. You have learned that, during the Crimean War, advances in nursing improved care for wounded soldiers. Unfortunately, medical technology had not kept pace with weapons technology. Effective treatments for infections, such as antibiotics, had not yet been discovered. When the Civil War ended with a Union victory in 1865, an estimated 620,000 men had died—the most American lives lost in any conflict to date.

CRITICAL VIEWING Throughout the Civil War, Mathew Brady and his team photographed its key players and battle scenes. Their images of the dead and wounded on the battlefield brought home the terrible reality of warfare. This photo was shot a couple of weeks after the Union victory at the one-day Battle of Antietam, which caused a total of about 23,000 casualties. President Lincoln stands in the center of the photo and is flanked on his right by Allan Pinkerton, the head of the newly formed Secret Service, and by General George McClellan on his left. Why would Lincoln travel to a battlefield after a victory?

At the beginning of the war, the Union fought to reunite the nation. In 1863, however, President Lincoln shifted the purpose to ending slavery. Just before the war ended, Congress passed the 13th Amendment, which abolished slavery. Over the next five years, two more amendments were passed: the 14th, which guaranteed citizenship and equal protection under the law to all persons born or naturalized in the United States; and the 15th, which prohibited federal and state governments from restricting the right to vote because of race, color, previous condition of servitude, or slavery.

On April 11, 1865, two days after the Confederacy surrendered, Lincoln announced a plan to rebuild the former Confederate states and integrate former slaves into the American republic. The plan became known as **Reconstruction**. But just a few days after his announcement, Lincoln was shot by an assassin's bullet and died. Reconstruction went forward, but it fell short of its goals. African Americans made some advances. For instance, they took part in the political process for the first time and had increased educational opportunities. But white southerners resisted Reconstruction and undermined efforts to promote African-American equality—sometimes violently. A secret society called the Ku Klux Klan became particularly powerful and used terrorism to deprive African Americans of their new constitutional rights.

Finally, in 1877, Republicans and Democrats agreed to end Reconstruction. Discrimination against black southerners continued in the South, where state legislatures enacted policies that enforced **segregation**, or the separation of races, in public places. African Americans were also deprived of their right to vote through violent intimidation and through laws that made registration almost impossible. Racial discrimination would become entrenched throughout the nation.

HISTORICAL THINKING

1. **READING CHECK** What factors contributed to the development of sectionalism in the United States?

2. **DRAW CONCLUSIONS** How did states in the South feel about the Republican Party?

3. **MAKE INFERENCES** Why do you think Lincoln shifted the war's purpose to ending slavery?

1.2 A Global Commodity: Cotton

In the 19th century, cotton was king in the southern United States. After 1793, Eli Whitney's cotton gin had greatly decreased the time required to process cotton crops. It also significantly increased the demand for enslaved people in the South. In the 1800s, southern plantations began to supply large quantities of cotton to textile industries at home and abroad—including Britain, where the manufacture of cotton cloth was its biggest industry.

After the outbreak of the American Civil War, the Confederacy tried—and failed—to pressure Britain into supporting its cause by threatening an **embargo**, or ban, on cotton sold to British manufacturers. As a result, exports of the commodity to Britain fell dramatically, eventually triggering a "cotton famine" there. But traders at the port of Liverpool, England, where most of the cotton arrived, had been stockpiling it in the months leading up to the war. In time, the traders began a lucrative business, exporting armaments to the South in exchange for more cotton. Meanwhile, British merchants found other sources of cotton in India, Egypt, and Brazil. King Cotton still reigned, but a thread of new global industrial networks had been spun.

Today, with the advent of the fast fashion industry, cheap cotton is still in high demand—resulting in unfair labor practices (especially forced or child labor) in some of the largest cotton-producing countries in the world, including Uzbekistan, India, China, and Egypt.

Why do commodities like cotton have the power to impact war?

IN HIGH COTTON

The fluff in this Texas field may look like cotton candy, but it's not edible. These cotton balls are likely to be woven into a lacy tablecloth or sturdy denim jeans. Cotton grows fairly quickly and produces an abundant harvest. A few months after the seeds are sown, green pods, called bolls, appear on the plants. Fibers inside the boll expand until they split it apart, and soft balls of cotton pop out. The expression "in high cotton," which refers to doing well or being successful, is a nod to the time when cotton was the main cash crop in the southern United States.

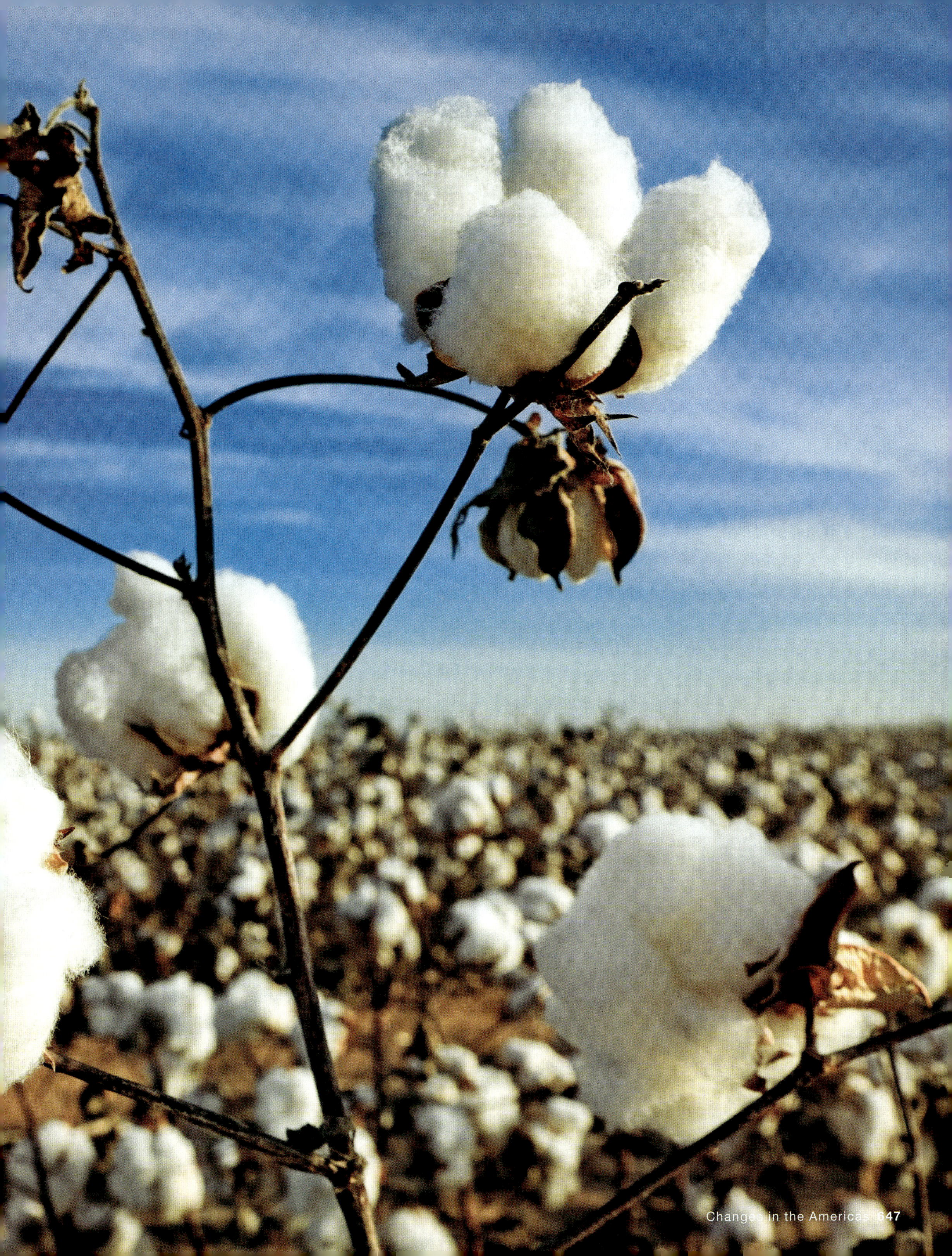

THE TRUE COST OF COTTON

Enslaved people of all ages, such as this family in Georgia, worked long hours picking cotton on southern plantations in the United States in the 19th century. Work began as soon as the sun came up and continued until it was too dark to see. And on nights when the moon was full, slaves often labored well into the night. Adult pickers carried baskets on their heads or bags over their shoulders and were expected to fill them with about 200 pounds of cotton every day. If they didn't, they were often punished.

USES	• Most cotton fiber is used to make clothing and household goods, such as sheets and towels.	• Cotton is used in the production of bandages, x-rays, coffee filters, and even bank notes.	• Livestock feed on cotton seeds, and cottonseed oil is used in cooking and in products such as soap.
PRODUCTION	• After a cotton plant flowers, farmers harvest the bolls, which contain cotton fibers.	• Modern cotton gins dry and clean the cotton and separate the fibers from the seeds.	• Textile mills weave the cotton fibers into yarn and then spin it into thread.
VALUE	• The value of the U.S. cotton crop rose from $150,000 to about $8 million 10 years after the cotton gin was introduced.	• New York City became the financial center of the United States because it controlled much of the cotton trade.	• In the first few years of the Civil War, the price of American cotton soared from 10 cents a pound to $1.89 a pound.
HISTORY	• Archaeologists in Mexico found the oldest fragments of cotton bolls and fibers, dating from around 5000 B.C.E.	• People in ancient India and Egypt had begun to grow, spin, and weave cotton into cloth by 3000 B.C.E.	• Arab traders introduced cotton cloth to Europe around 800 C.E.; cotton had spread worldwide by 1500.
ECONOMICS	• Cotton was the chief U.S. export between 1803 and 1937 and made the United States a major player in the global economy.	• From the early 1800s to the start of the Civil War, Britain obtained about 80 percent of its cotton from the United States.	• As a result of Britain's cotton famine, mills closed, workers lost their jobs, and many areas suffered widespread poverty.

COTTON HARVEST

In the United States, cotton is no longer picked by hand. Machines harvest the crops by either stripping the bolls off the plants or by using spindles to pick the cotton from the bolls. Once the cotton is loaded into bins like the ones in this photo of a California farm, it's packed and taken to be ginned. Modern cotton gins dry, clean, and separate the fiber from the seeds. The cotton fibers eventually go to textile mills, but nothing is wasted. Stems, leaves, and other debris picked out during the ginning process go to farms as livestock feed.

1.3

MAIN IDEA The Confederation of Canada was forged from a diverse population.

Confederation in Canada

Canada is the second largest country in the world today—and also one of the most sparsely populated. In the late 1700s, Canada seemed to have room for its diversity of immigrants and indigenous peoples alike. But would they all get along?

PEOPLE AND PROVINCES

As you've read, Britain acquired most of New France—the French colonies in North America—in 1763 after winning the French and Indian War. Britain called the territory Quebec. Many immigrants from Great Britain settled in the province after it came under British rule. People also arrived from the American colonies. When the American Revolution began, some colonists remained loyal to Britain. About 40,000 of these mostly Protestant Loyalists settled in Quebec and Nova Scotia after the war and lived separately from the largely Catholic French.

Nevertheless, religious and cultural differences between the English and French speakers led to conflict. In an attempt to resolve these issues, Britain divided Quebec into two provinces in 1791: a predominantly English-speaking Upper Canada and a predominantly French-speaking Lower Canada. Each province had its own elected legislature. The government in Upper Canada was based on English law, while the government in Lower Canada was based on French law and Catholicism.

Some parts of Canada remain as unspoiled as they were when the confederation was formed. In 1893, the Canadian government established the Algonquin Park, shown here, in the province of Ontario to protect the territory's forests and rivers. The huge park, which covers nearly 3,000 square miles today, is the oldest provincial park in Canada and can only be explored by foot or canoe.

You might remember that the French had conducted a profitable fur trade with Native Americans in New France. The British took over this trade and, at first, traded north and west of the Great Lakes. Eventually, trading posts were established in territory as far west as the present-day province of Manitoba. British merchants traded with many First Nations groups. The **Métis**, people of mixed European and indigenous descent, also took part in the trade.

UNION AND EXPANSION

Although the people of Upper and Lower Canada had been granted some say in their governments, real power remained in the hands of British officials. In time, people began to call for political and economic reforms. In 1830, rebellions in both provinces broke out. To remedy the situation, Britain reunited Upper and Lower Canada to form the province of Canada and allowed it to largely control its domestic matters. Canada would also welcome more British immigrants. Through these reforms, the British hoped to avoid another expensive war of independence in North America.

By the mid-1800s, many Canadians believed they needed a strong central government. Britain possessed several other colonies in Canada, including Nova Scotia, Prince Edward Island, and New Brunswick. Canadian politicians wanted to unite all of the British North American colonies and form a larger, stronger territory. They feared the United States might start eyeing the lands to its north and stage an attack. Moreover, Britain was getting tired of the expense and burden of governing its far-flung Canadian colonies.

In 1867, the union, or confederation, of the colonies finally took place. Canada was divided into two new provinces—Quebec and Ontario—and these united with Nova Scotia and New Brunswick to form the Dominion of Canada. As a **dominion**, Canada was self-governing but still part of the British Empire. Canada expanded to the west, and the confederation gained many new provinces. By 1871, Canada stretched to the Pacific Ocean. To connect the vast lands, the country's first prime minister, John Macdonald, had a transcontinental railway built. It was completed in 1885.

As the century ended, the railway and the country's increasing industrialization, mining, and agricultural enterprises caused a great crisis for the First Nations when they were displaced from their traditional lands. Meanwhile, the government emphasized the idea that Canada would be a bicultural land where English and French could live in peace with mutual tolerance. Although Canadians did not always live up to that ideal, a unique national identity took shape.

PAULINE JOHNSON-TEKAHIONWAKE
A popular Canadian poet and performer in the 19th century, Pauline Johnson-Tekahionwake (da-geh-EEON-wah-geh) was born in 1861 to an English mother and a father of Mohawk and European descent. Johnson-Tekahionwake traveled throughout Canada (and sometimes in the United States), reading her poetry. She often wore traditional Mohawk dress, as shown in the photo here, while reciting poems dealing with the racism and poverty indigenous peoples faced and then changed into western clothes to read her work about nature and love. As a loyal Canadian whose Mohawk ancestors had fought alongside the British, Johnson-Tekahionwake's poetry reflected her desire to find a balance between her English and Native American roots.

HISTORICAL THINKING

1. **READING CHECK** Why did Britain divide Quebec into Upper Canada and Lower Canada?

2. **DRAW CONCLUSIONS** Why weren't indigenous people included in the Canadian national identity envisioned by the government?

3. **MAKE INFERENCES** Why did Pauline Johnson-Tekahionwake wear different styles of clothing when she recited her poems?

1.4

MAIN IDEA In the late 19th century, industrialization drew millions of people to American cities where the disparity between rich and poor led many workers to demand their rights.

The Gilded Age

All that glitters is not gold. Toward the end of the 1800s, many cities in the United States glittered with new buildings, department stores, and streetcars. But beneath the surface, poor working-class people were struggling to get by.

URBANIZATION

Between 1870 and 1900, approximately 12 million people migrated to the United States, most of them from southern and eastern Europe, Asia, and Mexico. These immigrants came in search of a better life and greater job opportunities, particularly in the cities. Many Americans also flocked to urban areas seeking work in the factories and industries that emerged as a result of the Industrial Revolution. As the country's railroad transportation hub, Chicago experienced the most dramatic growth. In 1840, it had a population of just under 4,500 citizens. By 1890, it numbered more than one million.

But cities like Chicago and New York had trouble coping with the influx of both immigrants and American citizens. Housing couldn't keep up with the increased demand. So apartment buildings called tenements were quickly constructed to shelter the new residents. Most tenements were six- or seven-story multi-resident buildings designed to house as many people as possible. The tiny apartments were dark and narrow, and the space between two tenement buildings was so small that people could reach out a window and touch their neighbor next door. Diseases spread quickly in the tenements because of the poor ventilation and unsanitary conditions. And the overcrowding and shoddy construction made the structures prone to fire. By contrast, wealthy city residents lived in spacious apartment buildings and townhouses.

CRITICAL VIEWING Photographer Jacob Riis took this picture of an immigrant family crowded into a one-room apartment in New York around 1910. Riis, an immigrant from Denmark, photographed the living conditions of the urban poor in New York and published what he saw in his 1890 work *How the Other Half Lives*. How do you think the public reacted when they saw this image and others of crowded tenements?

As industry in the United States expanded over the last three decades of the 19th century, those who profited by it were mainly owners and stockholders, and they grew immensely rich. Many of them engaged in dishonest business practices to increase their wealth and power. Because of this greed and corruption, the era is called the Gilded Age. To gild something means to coat it with a thin layer of gold that can disguise what

652 CHAPTER 23

lies underneath. The term was coined by the American writers Mark Twain and Charles Dudley Warner in their novel *The Gilded Age* to draw attention to the way in which spectacular wealth masked the greed and corruption of industrialists and politicians.

WORKERS ORGANIZE

In reaction to the inequality between the industrialists and their employees, workers began to organize into labor unions. You may recall that British workers fought to form unions. Americans first started to unionize in the 1820s to call for better pay, safer working conditions, and other benefits. The effort gathered strength after the Civil War. Most union members then sought an 8-hour workday to replace the more typical 10- to 12-hour workday. They often used **strikes**, or work stoppages, as a tactic to achieve their demands when companies refused to negotiate with them. In 1877, about 100,000 railroad workers across the country took part in what came to be known as the Great Railroad Strike. Violence broke out at one point, resulting in the deaths of about 100 people. However, the strikers eventually succeeded in convincing management to negotiate with their union representatives.

Another violent episode occurred in 1886 after a striking union member at Chicago's McCormick Works, a harvesting machine factory, was killed by police. The next day, union leaders organized a peaceful rally in the city's Haymarket Square. However, the rally became chaotic when someone threw a bomb and police responded with gunfire. Several police officers and protesters died during the **Haymarket Riot**, as it came to be called. The police arrested eight protesters, whom they claimed were **anarchists**, people willing to use force to overthrow oppression. Four of those arrested were hanged, and one was sentenced to 15 years in prison. Their guilt was never adequately proven, however, and the remaining defendants were eventually pardoned. In much of the world, May 1, the anniversary of the Haymarket Riot, is celebrated as International Workers' Day.

In 1893, the United States suffered a severe economic depression, the worst in the nation's history up to that time. The collapse of a major railroad and a growing depression in Europe were among its causes. As panic gripped American financiers, banks closed, businesses failed, and the unemployment rate in the country climbed to about 20 percent. Many of those who remained employed were forced to take substantial pay cuts, causing workers all over the country to stage strikes and protests. The economy began to stabilize around 1897, and by 1900 the United States had become the world's largest economy. But the continuing social inequalities inspired even more people to call for workers' rights and social reforms.

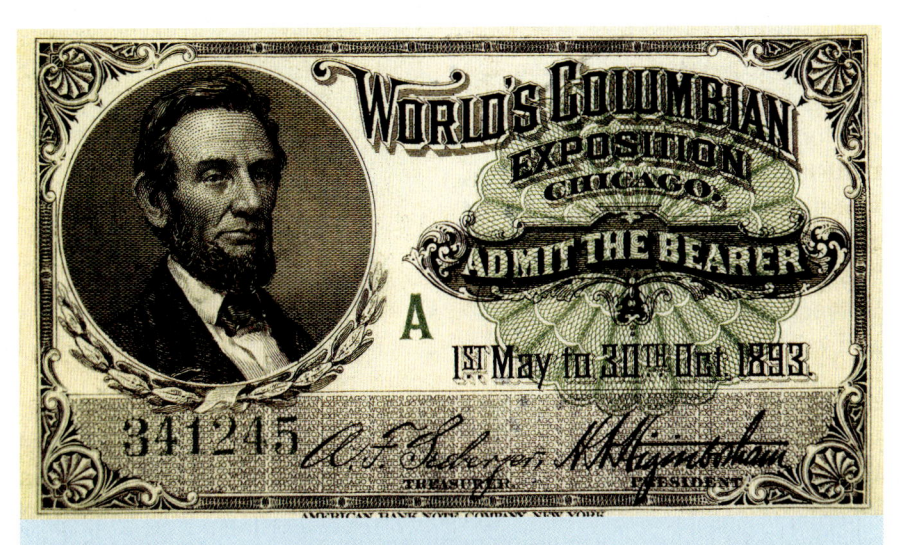

CHICAGO'S COLUMBIAN EXPOSITION In 1893, Chicago hosted the World's Columbian Exposition to celebrate the 400-year anniversary of Columbus's arrival in the Americas. The fair showcased the "progress of civilization" and trumpeted the country's rapid industrialization and the strength of its industries. Visitors enjoyed a ride on the world's first Ferris wheel, which rose 264 feet in the air, and marveled at the new inventions—especially electricity, which most Americans had never seen before. Hundreds of thousands of electric lights illuminated the fair at night, creating a magical setting. Those attending the exposition bought an admission ticket like the one shown above, featuring a photo of Abraham Lincoln, to gain entry.

HISTORICAL THINKING

1. **READING CHECK** How did some cities solve the problem of housing their growing populations?

2. **MAKE INFERENCES** Why do you think the police considered those they arrested at the Haymarket Riot to be anarchists?

3. **SYNTHESIZE** How did the Columbian Exposition symbolize the Gilded Age?

Changes in the Americas 653

2.1

MAIN IDEA After achieving independence, many Latin Americans suffered under economic and political systems that left them in poverty and without a voice.

Latin America in the Industrial Age

When a country wins its independence, the people celebrate their victory. But after the confetti is swept away, they're faced with the difficult task of building a new nation. In Latin American countries, the struggle to recover economically and politically was just as hard as the struggle for independence.

ECONOMIC DEPENDENCY

The economies of many Latin American countries didn't change after independence. Most people still worked on large farms that belonged to wealthy landowners. Workers had to use their wages to pay for the supplies they needed to do their jobs. And since wages were low and the price of the supplies was high, workers went into debt. In this system, called **debt peonage**, workers paid their debts with labor and were, in effect, reduced to the status of slaves.

Landowners, on the other hand, grew richer. Government leaders often seized lands that had belonged to native peoples or the Catholic Church and then sold them to the highest bidders. Only the wealthy could afford to buy this property, and as a result, the lands fell into the hands of a small percentage of the population. The unequal distribution of land ensured that the old rigid social order remained in place. The inequality increased when the owners of these *latifundia*, or very large farms, used their land to grow crops to sell internationally. The owners reaped the profits of global trade while rural workers lived in poverty.

After independence, Latin American countries were no longer limited to conducting trade with their colonizers. In time, Britain and the United States were among their major trading partners. However, Latin American countries produced mainly cash crops and mined raw materials and exchanged these for cheap goods, which harmed local industries. Just as in colonial times, they depended on exports from other countries to obtain manufactured goods. Consequently, landowners and businesspeople had little incentive to develop manufacturing industries.

CUBAN FREEDOM FIGHTER While other Latin American countries achieved sovereignty, Spain crushed Cuba's bid for independence in 1878. **José Martí**, a writer and an outspoken advocate for Cuban independence, was exiled and lived many years in New York City. While there, he helped organize an army to continue the fight and, in 1895, led his followers to Cuba to launch a second war for independence. Martí was killed early in the struggle, but the United States would eventually join Cuba's war for independence—with mixed results for the Cuban people. Today, Martí appears on Cuba's one-peso banknote.

The region did benefit in some ways from the Industrial Revolution. Railroads and steamships connected it with North America and the world beyond, and Latin America's exports grew. For example, gold mines and coffee plantations stimulated Brazil's economy, leading to the growth of cities and the arrival of new immigrants. However, most of the profits went to a small minority of privileged Brazilians, and slavery remained part of society until 1888.

Debt was often a problem in Latin America. Countries often came under the power of European nations and the United States after accepting large loans to help them develop transportation and communication networks. If the countries were unable to pay their debts, their lenders sometimes seized their industries. As you'll learn in the next chapter, foreign control over Latin American economies set the stage for this practice elsewhere.

POLITICAL DIVISIONS IN MEXICO

You probably remember reading that Latin American countries also experienced political challenges

CRITICAL VIEWING
After rule by a series of dictators, a liberal reformer named Benito Juárez rose to power and became Mexico's president in 1861. This 1948 mural by José Clemente Orozco, *Benito Juárez and La Reforma*, represents Juárez's triumph over Mexican emperor Ferdinand Maximilian Joseph, who had overthrown the president. Maximilian's shrouded corpse is carried on the shoulders of Mexican conservatives. How does the mural's portrayal of Juárez—the monumental head in the center—contrast with that of the conservatives?

following independence. Like other countries, Mexico's government fell into the hands of caudillos. Only those from the upper and middle classes who owned property and could read were allowed to vote, and caudillos supported their interests. And after colonial rule, most Mexicans were accustomed to dictatorship.

One of Mexico's military dictators, General **Antonio López de Santa Anna**, served as president four times between 1833 and 1855. Under his presidency and military leadership, Mexico lost Texas after that territory won its war for independence in 1836. And then, when the United States annexed Texas and invaded Mexico, Santa Anna and his troops fought and lost the Mexican-American War in 1848. In exchange for $15 million, Mexico gave up its northernmost territories to the United States, including present-day California, Nevada, and Utah, as well as parts of Arizona, New Mexico, Colorado, and Wyoming.

As Santa Anna's power declined, a Zapotec from Oaxaca named **Benito Juárez** became a strong force in Mexican politics. He started a reform movement called **La Reforma**, which called for the redistribution of lands, the separation of church and state, and greater educational opportunities for the poor. Conservatives in the country—mostly wealthy upper-class Mexicans—opposed Juárez's reforms, and a civil war erupted. The reformers won the war, and Juárez was elected president in 1861. But the conservatives in Mexico didn't give up. They enlisted the help of the French emperor Napoleon III, who overthrew Juárez. France occupied Mexico for five years but was under constant attack by those, including Juárez, who opposed French rule. Exhausted by the struggle, the French withdrew from Mexico in 1867.

Juárez was re-elected president that same year, and Mexico enjoyed a period of relative peace and progress. After his death, however, **Porfirio Díaz** came to power in 1876 and ruled as a dictator. Under his regime, railroads in Mexico expanded, the economy stabilized, and foreign investments grew. However, these measures mostly benefited wealthy landowners. The poor, meanwhile, grew poorer. Díaz remained in power until the early 1900s, when protesters called for reforms, and a revolution began to brew.

HISTORICAL THINKING

1. **READING CHECK** Why did farm workers in many Latin American countries fail to benefit economically after independence?

2. **DRAW CONCLUSIONS** What prevented Latin American countries from becoming world economic powers?

3. **MAKE INFERENCES** Why did the conservatives in Mexico oppose Juárez and his reforms?

2.2 DOCUMENT-BASED QUESTION
Labor and Profit in Latin America

Most Latin American countries gained independence while the Industrial Revolution was taking place in Europe. And, as you know, textile production under the factory system in the 1830s led to an expansion of slavery in the southern United States. Just as in Europe and the United States, economic growth in Latin America resulted in wealth for some and hard work with little reward for many.

The growth of international trade did have positive effects, however. For example, Britain, Germany, the United States, and other countries invested capital in Latin America, where much of the money was used to build railroads. Railroads and steamships with refrigerated compartments carried goods such as beef from Argentina, silver from Mexico, and coffee from Brazil to international markets. In return, manufactured goods and luxury items flowed back to Latin America. This relationship, in which Latin America exported relatively cheap products and depended on foreign markets for more expensive imports, is called "economic dependency."

Economic dependency caused two problems. First, governments often had to borrow money to build ports and railroads to support trade. These debts meant that the governments often put the interests of foreign investors above those of their own people. Second, this type of trading system concentrated wealth in only a few hands.

In Argentina and most other Latin American countries, this wealth was concentrated in less than 10 percent of the population—upper-class landowners and middle-class professionals. The lower-class majority lived in poverty. Slavery had been abolished in most Latin American countries by the late 19th century, but those who worked on farms and in mines, as you know, were no better off than slaves. The resulting inequality between the wealthy and the poor was mirrored by growing divisions between the "haves" and "have nots" in many of these societies. As governments ignored the condition of urban laborers, the workers began to strike and organize.

By the early 1900s, Argentina had greatly prospered from trade, although only those at the very top of society enjoyed the wealth. In this photo of the Argentine capital of Buenos Aires from that period, automobiles cruised along its spacious boulevards. The modernized city became known as "The Paris of South America."

DOCUMENT ONE

Primary Source: Travel Chronicle
from *Exploration of the Valley of the Amazon, 1851–1852*, by William Lewis Herndon

In 1851, U.S. Navy commander William Lewis Herndon led an expedition from Peru to Brazil to explore the Amazon Valley. He recorded his observations in narrative form in *Exploration of the Valley of the Amazon*. In this excerpt from the book, Herndon describes a rural area after visiting Lima, the capital of Peru.

CONSTRUCTED RESPONSE How do conditions in the rural area compare with those in Lima?

To the right were the green cane and alfalfa fields . . . but ahead all was barren, grim, and forbidding. . . . It was remarkable to see such poverty and squalid wretchedness at nine miles from the great city of Lima; it was like passing in a moment from the most luxurious civilization into savage barbarity . . . from the garden to the desert. . . . [Later the] superintendent of the mines . . . received us kindly. . . . His house was comfortably heated with a stove, and the chamber furnished with a large four-post bedstead and the biggest and heaviest bureau I had ever seen.

DOCUMENT TWO

Primary Source: Letter
from "A Letter to Striking Workers" by Matías Romero, 1892

As Minister of Finance under President Porfirio Díaz, Matías Romero strongly supported foreign investment. The following is an excerpt from a letter Romero wrote to striking workers after they requested his help.

CONSTRUCTED RESPONSE What does Romero say the government can do for the striking workers?

Given the institutions that govern us, it is unfeasible [impossible] to restrict freedom of hiring or to intervene directly in the improvement of basic working conditions. No legal document authorizes this, nor do any economic interests oblige the Government to dictate salaries, or prices, or working hours. . . . The Government can only contribute to improving labor conditions by indirect means such as keeping the peace, the promotion of industry, and the investment of both national and foreign capital in native elements of the country's wealth [such as plantations and mines], and thus ensure national credit.

DOCUMENT THREE

Primary Source: Political Pamphlet
from "First Electoral Manifesto of the Argentine Socialist Worker Party," 1896

In reaction to the inequality between Argentina's lower and upper classes, many laborers united to form the Argentine Socialist Worker Party. The unions that arose in many countries were often inspired by new ideologies of socialism, particularly the concept of conflict between capitalists and laborers. In this excerpt from their manifesto, the party takes aim at the treatment of workers in Argentina.

CONSTRUCTED RESPONSE According to the manifesto, what will happen as a result of the greed of Argentina's "rich class"?

All of the parties of Argentina's rich class are of one mind when it comes to increasing profits of capital at the cost of working people, even as it stupidly compromises the country's general development. . . . [T]hey have increased . . . the price of products and reduced wages. They have seized public lands, expelling primitive peoples, the only ones with a right to occupy them. . . . And to complete this barbaric system of exploitation [unfair treatment], they use taxes on consumption, internal taxes, and customs duties [taxes on imports] to take away a large share of what little workers earn.

SYNTHESIZE & WRITE

1. **REVIEW** Review what you have learned about the economic and political challenges Latin American countries faced after independence.

2. **RECALL** On your own paper, write down the main idea expressed in each document.

3. **CONSTRUCT** Construct a topic sentence that answers this question: How did the plight of workers and owners in 19th-century Latin America differ?

4. **WRITE** Using evidence from this chapter and the documents, write an informative paragraph that supports your topic sentence in Step 3.

3.1

MAIN IDEA In the 19th century, indigenous people in North America fought bravely but unsuccessfully to keep their land, culture, and identity intact.

Indigenous Societies Rebel

What would you do if the government seized your home and gave it to someone else? When that happened to indigenous people in North America, some of them chose to resist and fight back.

National Geographic photographer Anand Varma captured this scene overlooking a canyon in the Black Hills, a small mountain range that rises in South Dakota and extends into Wyoming. The Lakota have long considered the Black Hills their spiritual home. Ever since the U.S. government seized the mountain range from them, the Lakota have sought to get it back. Their efforts continue today, and they have refused monetary compensation for the land.

MAYA REVOLT

After the Spanish conquered Central America, many Maya continued to live on the Yucatán Peninsula where they grew maize and other crops. In 1846, Yucatán claimed **autonomy**, or independence, from Mexico and formed the Republic of Yucatán. But like Mexico, the republic was controlled by rich *peninsulares*, the descendants of Spanish-born settlers. The following year, Yucatán's government took control of Maya farms and sold them to plantation owners.

Soon, sugar plantations sprang up on former Maya cornfields in the southeastern part of the Yucatán Peninsula. Taxes also increased. In need of work, Maya farmers labored on the plantations, where they sometimes endured physical abuse. Similar to many other poor farmers in Latin America, the Maya became trapped in their jobs by debt peonage and worked to repay their employers.

Angered by their mistreatment and domination by white leaders, a group of Maya militants attacked government officials and landowners in 1847. By the spring of 1848, the Maya had taken over most of the Yucatán Peninsula in a conflict that came to be known as the **Yucatán Rebellion**. Because the rebellion was partly motivated by the Maya's resentment of the white leaders' ideology—their belief in their racial superiority—it is also called the Caste War of the Yucatán.

The Yucatán government offered to reunite with Mexico in exchange for help in putting down the rebellion. Mexico agreed. The country had extra funds due to the payment it had received from the United States for territory taken at the end of the Mexican-American War. Armed with new guns and joined by Mexican troops, the large landowners gradually regained control of the peninsula.

Scattered fighting continued until 1901, when Mexican forces overran the Maya rebels. About 50 percent of the Maya on the Yucatán Peninsula were killed during the long conflict, and many of their villages were destroyed. A group of Maya rebels retreated to the eastern part of the peninsula, where they established new villages and preserved their traditions and identity.

NATIVE AMERICAN RESISTANCE

Native Americans, such as the Creek and Choctaw, were also forced to leave their traditional lands in the southeastern United States. After gold was discovered in Georgia, southern states passed laws allowing farmers, miners, and other settlers to claim Native American lands for themselves. Then in 1830, President Andrew Jackson approved the Indian Removal Act, a law that relocated Native Americans to an area of land that includes present-day Oklahoma and parts of Kansas and Nebraska, and would be called Indian Territory. In time, the U.S. government also set aside specific areas of land for Native Americans called reservations. But some offered resistance to removal, including the Cherokee. Their forced march to Indian Territory in the late 1830s is known as the Trail of Tears.

In the Great Plains, the Lakota—part of the larger Sioux nation—had negotiated a treaty with the U.S. government that forbade white settlement in the Black Hills, which the Lakota considered sacred. The treaty was canceled, however, when gold was discovered there in 1874, and U.S. authorities demanded that all Lakota leave the Black Hills. Sitting Bull, the leader of the Lakota, refused to move, and troops arrived to force the relocation. Eventually, **Sitting Bull** moved his band to a camp in the valley of the Little Bighorn

Sitting Bull was imprisoned on a Dakota reservation in 1881, but he was allowed to join Buffalo Bill's Wild West Show in 1885. This traveling show used Native Americans, cowboys, sharpshooters, and bison to re-enact stories of the West—often inaccurately. Sitting Bull only appeared in the show's opening procession, but he gained international fame. He returned home after a single season and was eventually sent back to the reservation.

CRITICAL VIEWING The Apache children shown in these two photos taken by John Choate were sent to the Carlisle Indian Industrial School, a boarding school in Pennsylvania, to learn white values and culture. Choate took the photo on the left in November 1886, shortly after the children's arrival at the school. The photo on the right, showing the same children, was taken four months later. What does the children's physical appearance reveal about the ways in which they were changed by the school?

River in present-day Montana. He was joined there by the Cheyenne and other Native Americans who had abandoned their reservations.

In 1876, roughly 2,000 Native Americans clashed with about 200 U.S. troops led by Colonel George Custer at Sitting Bull's encampment. The Native Americans killed nearly all of the soldiers, including Colonel Custer, in the **Battle of the Little Bighorn**. However, the U.S. Army ultimately forced the Lakota to relocate to reservations, and the United States seized the Black Hills.

By the late 1880s, most Native Americans lived on reservations, but they were still defiant. Some Native Americans, including the Lakota, practiced the ==Ghost Dance==, a ceremony they believed would drive evil from the land, restore the bison, and allow them to return to lives of peace and prosperity. The U.S. government believed Sitting Bull had instigated the Ghost Dance, and authorities went to arrest him in 1890 at his reservation on Wounded Knee Creek in present-day South Dakota. Sitting Bull resisted and was fatally shot. Two weeks later, the U.S. Army confronted Lakota ghost dancers at Wounded Knee Creek and demanded they hand over their weapons. When an unknown person fired a shot, the U.S. troops opened fire in return, killing about 300 people. The **Wounded Knee Massacre** put an end to any further Native American resistance.

FIRST NATIONS AND THE MÉTIS REBELLION

Like other indigenous people in the Americas, the First Nations people in Canada endured racism and discrimination. In 1876, Canada passed the Indian Act, which aimed to assimilate, or integrate, First Nations people into the rest of Canadian society. By doing so, the Canadian government hoped to wipe out First Nations culture. The act also established reserves for First Nations people, lands set aside for their "use and benefit."

To further the assimilation process, later amendments to the act required First Nations children to attend residential, or boarding, schools. Students in these "industrial" schools wore Western-style clothing, spoke only English or French, and were pressured to convert to Christianity. Similar schools were established for Native American children in the United States. Another amendment to Canada's Indian Act outlawed certain religious ceremonies, including the potlatch, practiced by First Nations people in the Canadian province of British Columbia. The potlatch is a gift-giving feast used to mark important events and occasions.

The Métis, the people of mixed European and indigenous descent you've read about, took action to protect their culture and land rights just before Canada acquired Rupert's Land, a vast territory in northern and western Canada. The Métis, who lived in the territory, feared the Canadian government would take away their rights. As a result, they staged an uprising between 1869 and 1870 and formed a temporary government to negotiate terms for joining the Canadian Confederation.

Negotiations led to the creation of the province of Manitoba, where the Métis were granted rights to some land. The Métis also gained a new leader, **Louis Riel**, who emerged as a hero to the indigenous people. The Canadian government, however, considered him an outlaw. In 1870, British and Canadian troops marched into Manitoba, and Riel fled to the United States. Over the next decade, the Métis were increasingly pushed into the North-West Territories by European settlers from places like Germany and Sweden, and the Canadian government failed to honor its promise to protect indigenous land rights. The Métis way of life was disappearing and so were the bison, a major food source of the indigenous people.

Riel returned to Canada in 1884 to plead the Métis' case, but the government ignored his petition. The following year, Riel organized an army and formed alliances with First Nations peoples. Their goal was to establish a nation independent of the Dominion of Canada, but they were no match for the Canadian soldiers. After a series of battles, the indigenous people lost the **North-West Rebellion** within about three months. Riel was arrested, convicted of treason, and hanged.

The struggle for indigenous rights continued for decades in North America. Pauline Johnson-Tekahionwake expressed the sadness of all indigenous people in her poem "A Cry from an Indian Wife." She asks how white settlers would feel "If some great nation came from far away, / Wresting [seizing] their country from their hapless braves [unfortunate warriors], / Giving what they gave us—but war and graves."

NATIONAL GEOGRAPHIC EXPLORERS
JON WATERHOUSE AND MARY MARSHALL

Capturing Indigenous Voices

National Geographic Explorer Jon Waterhouse and photographer Mary Marshall share a remarkable mission and passion—giving voice to indigenous peoples, specifically empowering them to communicate their knowledge of the natural world. As a person of S'Skallam, Chippewa, and Cree descent, Waterhouse believes we must blend indigenous knowledge with contemporary science to fully understand our planet. In 2007, he collected scientific readings of water quality on the Yukon River while also gathering traditional knowledge about respecting and protecting the environment from people living there. Since then, Waterhouse and Marshall have partnered with people in remote regions to study their local water and environmental health and digitally record aspects of their cultures. For the explorers, environmental stewardship involves listening to native voices. As Waterhouse says, indigenous people "are witnesses to significant environmental changes from place-based people." Marshall took the above photo of Waterhouse (on the left) giving final instructions to his team before they canoed down the Tanana River in Alaska to collect water-quality data.

HISTORICAL THINKING

1. **READING CHECK** Why did the Maya who lived on the Yucatán Peninsula rebel?

2. **DRAW CONCLUSIONS** Why did the U.S. government want to put a stop to the Ghost Dance ceremony?

3. **MAKE INFERENCES** What impact do you think the residential schools in North America had on indigenous families?

4. **MAKE CONNECTIONS** How do Pauline Johnson-Tekahionwake's words reflect the experience of all indigenous peoples in the Americas?

Changes in the Americas 661

MAIN IDEA Near the turn of the 20th century, people of color in the United States often faced discrimination, but reformers worked to make life better for all Americans.

Inequality and Reform

Immigrants arrived in the United States full of hope, but they did not always feel welcome. Like African Americans and others outside of the white majority, they were often met with resentment and distrust.

SEPARATE BUT EQUAL

The millions of immigrants who came to the United States in the late 19th and early 20th centuries encountered not only difficult living and working conditions but also discrimination. Asian immigrants were frequent targets of racial hostility. Anti-Chinese sentiment led the federal government to pass the **Chinese Exclusion Act** in 1882 to prevent Chinese immigrants from working in the United States. And, while Mexican immigrants in the West and Southwest were welcomed as workers, they were often the victims of violence.

As you know, racism against African Americans continued after the Civil War and Reconstruction. Southern politicians stripped away the rights African Americans had gained by passing so-called Jim Crow laws, named for a form of entertainment in the early 1800s that mocked people of African descent. These laws established separate schools for African Americans and prohibited them from using the same restrooms, restaurants, theaters, and parks as white people. Since African Americans were often prevented from voting, they could not use democracy to protect their constitutional rights.

In 1891, a man named Homer Plessy, who was one-eighth African American, tested a law that separated whites and African Americans on public transportation by sitting in a railway car reserved for whites. He was arrested, and his case eventually came before the U.S. Supreme Court. His lawyers argued in ***Plessy v. Ferguson*** that the legalized segregation on trains violated the 14th Amendment, which guaranteed "equal protection of the laws" to all American citizens. However, in 1896, the court upheld the segregation, stating that the accommodations on the train were the same for whites and African Americans (they weren't), even if they were separate. The ruling allowed governments, businesses, and institutions to enact "separate but equal" policies for decades to come.

CRITICAL VIEWING This political cartoon appeared in a humor magazine called *Puck* in February 1913. The cartoon satirizes the "separate but equal" policy enforced in the southern United States with this airplane and its segregated accommodations for white and African-American passengers. How does the cartoon convey the inherent inequality of segregated accommodations?

MUCKRAKERS AND REFORMERS

You've read that American industrial workers formed unions to protect their rights. In 1886, a British immigrant named Samuel L. Gompers brought many small unions of skilled industrial workers together to form the **American Federation of Labor (AFL)**. The AFL did not focus on political issues but rather used collective bargaining to fight for higher wages, shorter hours, and improved working conditions for its members.

662 CHAPTER 23

The causes championed by unions were sometimes brought to the attention of the public by journalists known as **muckrakers**, who investigated and exposed corruption and poor social and working conditions. One of the first muckrakers, **Ida Tarbell**, wrote about the secret deals and unethical practices of John D. Rockefeller, the founder of the Standard Oil Company. Largely as a result of her articles, the Supreme Court decided in 1911 that Standard Oil was an illegal **monopoly**, or a company that has complete control of an industry, and ordered it broken into 34 separate companies. Many Americans supported this antitrust legislation because they wanted to prevent such monopolies from forming again.

Muckraker **Upton Sinclair** investigated the working conditions in the meatpacking industry and wrote about what he saw in his 1906 novel *The Jungle*. Sinclair's description of the industry's unsanitary conditions led Congress to pass the Pure Food and Drug Act and the Meat Inspection Act. Like the British in the 19th century, Americans came to expect their government to play a positive role in making life better by preventing dangerous food from reaching the market or by limiting child labor and other abuses.

Private citizens such as **Jane Addams** also worked to address social problems. She founded a community center in Chicago called Hull House that provided services for immigrants in the neighborhood, including a kindergarten, day care, and classes and activities for adults. The Salvation Army and the YMCA, which spread to the United States from Britain, also supported aid for the poor. Members in both countries were motivated by their Christian faith to work with the poor and the vulnerable.

Another powerful voice for change was Emma Goldman, an immigrant who spoke only Russian and Yiddish when she arrived in New York. After working to bring medical care to immigrant women, she became a prominent public speaker, supporting the rights of working women from all backgrounds.

WOMEN'S RIGHTS

Women worked alongside men in the fight for social and political reform. They also demanded their own right to full U.S. citizenship. Women took a major step toward this goal in 1848 at the **Seneca Falls Convention** in New York, the first women's rights convention held in the United States. There, organizers Elizabeth Cady Stanton and Lucretia Mott read their "Declaration of Sentiments and Resolutions," modeled after the U.S. Declaration of Independence, and asserted that "all men and women are created equal."

One of the first programs Jane Addams set up at Hull House was a nursery school, where she often read to and taught young children. Addams also fought for women's suffrage in the late 1800s.

Daringly, Stanton and Mott even called for women's **suffrage**, or the right to vote, a demand that was met with anger even by some who supported other rights for women. Later reformers would continue the fight, but women's suffrage wouldn't be granted until 1920 with the passage of the 19th Amendment. Still, some states were ahead of the federal government. Wyoming gave women the vote in 1890, and Colorado followed in 1893.

The move toward women's rights was global. In 1893, New Zealand became the first nation to give women the vote. By 1900, women in Mexico, Brazil, and Canada were also fighting to achieve legal equality and voting rights. Historians call this movement "first-wave feminism." Later in the 20th century, as you will learn, "second-wave feminism" would spread even more widely, expanding women's demands to include equal rights in education and employment.

HISTORICAL THINKING

1. **READING CHECK** How did the Supreme Court uphold the segregation of whites and African Americans on public transportation?

2. **ANALYZE CAUSE AND EFFECT** What effect did the work of the Muckrakers have on the poor business practices of the era?

3. **MAKE INFERENCES** Why do you think it took so long for women to gain the right to vote in the United States?

CHAPTER 23 CHANGES IN THE AMERICAS REVIEW

VOCABULARY

Use each of the following vocabulary words in a sentence that shows an understanding of the term's meaning.

1. secede
2. suffrage
3. tenement
4. debt peonage
5. monopoly
6. autonomy
7. segregation
8. muckraker

READING STRATEGY
DRAW CONCLUSIONS

Use a cluster diagram like the one below to draw conclusions about the changes that occurred in the Americas during the late 19th and early 20th centuries. Then answer the questions.

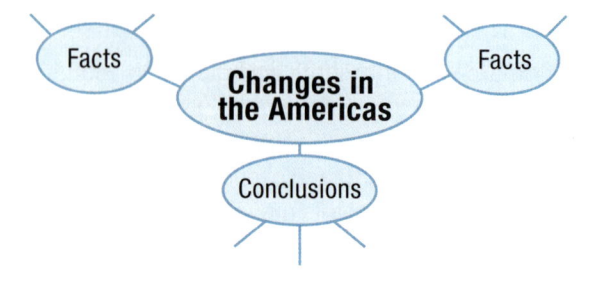

9. Who benefited most from industrialization in the Americas in the late 1800s and early 1900s?

10. What role did racism play in the plans of the U.S. and Canadian governments to forcibly assimilate indigenous people into their societies?

MAIN IDEAS

Answer the following questions. Support your answers with evidence from the chapter.

11. How did advances in weapons technology affect soldiers fighting the U.S. Civil War? **LESSON 1.1**

12. What impact did Canada's transcontinental railway have on indigenous people? **LESSON 1.3**

13. What tactics did union members sometimes use to achieve their demands? **LESSON 1.4**

14. In what ways did Latin Americans benefit from the Industrial Revolution? **LESSON 2.1**

15. Why did the U.S. government want the Lakota to leave the Black Hills? **LESSON 3.1**

16. What issues did American women fight for in the late 1800s? **LESSON 3.2**

HISTORICAL THINKING

Answer the following questions. Support your answers with evidence from the chapter.

17. **MAKE INFERENCES** Why do you think Abraham Lincoln's name didn't appear on the ballot in southern states in the U.S. presidential election of 1860?

18. **EVALUATE** How would you describe Canada's road to independence?

19. **COMPARE AND CONTRAST** How did the lives of rich industrial owners and their employees differ during the Gilded Age in the United States?

20. **DRAW CONCLUSIONS** After achieving independence, why did many government leaders in Latin America seize lands and sell them to the highest bidders?

21. **ANALYZE CAUSE AND EFFECT** What impact did the close of the Mexican War have on events in the Yucatán?

22. **MAKE CONNECTIONS** Why did Elizabeth Cady Stanton and Lucretia Mott assert that "all men and women are created equal" in their "Declaration of Sentiments and Resolutions"?

23. **SYNTHESIZE** What role did railroads play in the U.S. Civil War, the Confederation of Canada, and the economies of Latin America?

INTERPRET VISUALS

In this 1900 political cartoon called "What a Funny Little Government," Standard Oil Company founder John D. Rockefeller holds the White House in his hand and peers at it through a magnifying glass. Illustrator Horace Taylor has turned the Capitol Building and Treasury Department in the background into oil refineries, with thick smoke pouring out of their smokestacks. Study the political cartoon. Then answer the questions that follow.

24. How are the officials in the White House portrayed and what are they giving to Rockefeller?

25. What does the cartoon suggest about the relationship between industries like Rockefeller's and government?

ANALYZE SOURCES

In 1858, Abraham Lincoln ran for a U.S. Senate seat in Illinois. After accepting his party's nomination, he delivered what is known as the "House Divided" speech at the Republican Convention. In this excerpt from the speech, Lincoln uses a Bible quotation and metaphor to compare the nation to a house. Read the excerpt and then answer the following question.

> "A house divided against itself cannot stand." I believe this government cannot endure permanently half slave and half free. I do not expect the Union to be dissolved; I do not expect the house to fall; but I do expect it will cease to be divided. It will become all one thing, or all the other.

26. How does the excerpt foreshadow what would occur in the country?

CONNECT TO YOUR LIFE

27. **INFORMATIVE** In this chapter, you've read about many groups and individuals who fought for their rights or worked to reform social problems. What right or cause would you like to champion? Perhaps you'd like to address an injustice in your school or provide a service to help the homeless in your community. Choose a problem that interests you and write a brief essay about how you would try to solve it.

TIPS

- Review what you've read about the indigenous people and reformers in this chapter who fought for themselves and for others.
- Consider how you might use their example to effect change of your own.
- Use two or three vocabulary terms from the chapter in your essay.
- Provide a concluding statement in which you compare your goals and methods with those of the fighters and reformers in the chapter.

CHAPTER 24

The New Imperialism
1850–1914

HISTORICAL THINKING How did imperialism affect the economic, political, and cultural life of subjugated peoples?

SECTION 1 **Dividing and Dominating**
SECTION 2 **Targeting the Pacific**

CRITICAL VIEWING
With a depth of approximately 700 feet, the Big Hole in Kimberley, South Africa, is the largest hand-dug excavation in the world. More than 13.6 million carats of diamonds were mined from the site, which was owned by the De Beers Mining Company, between 1871 and 1914. Today, the hole serves as a reminder of the exploitation of Africa's resources and people by Europeans. Based on the details in the photograph, how would you describe the impact of the mining process on the land?

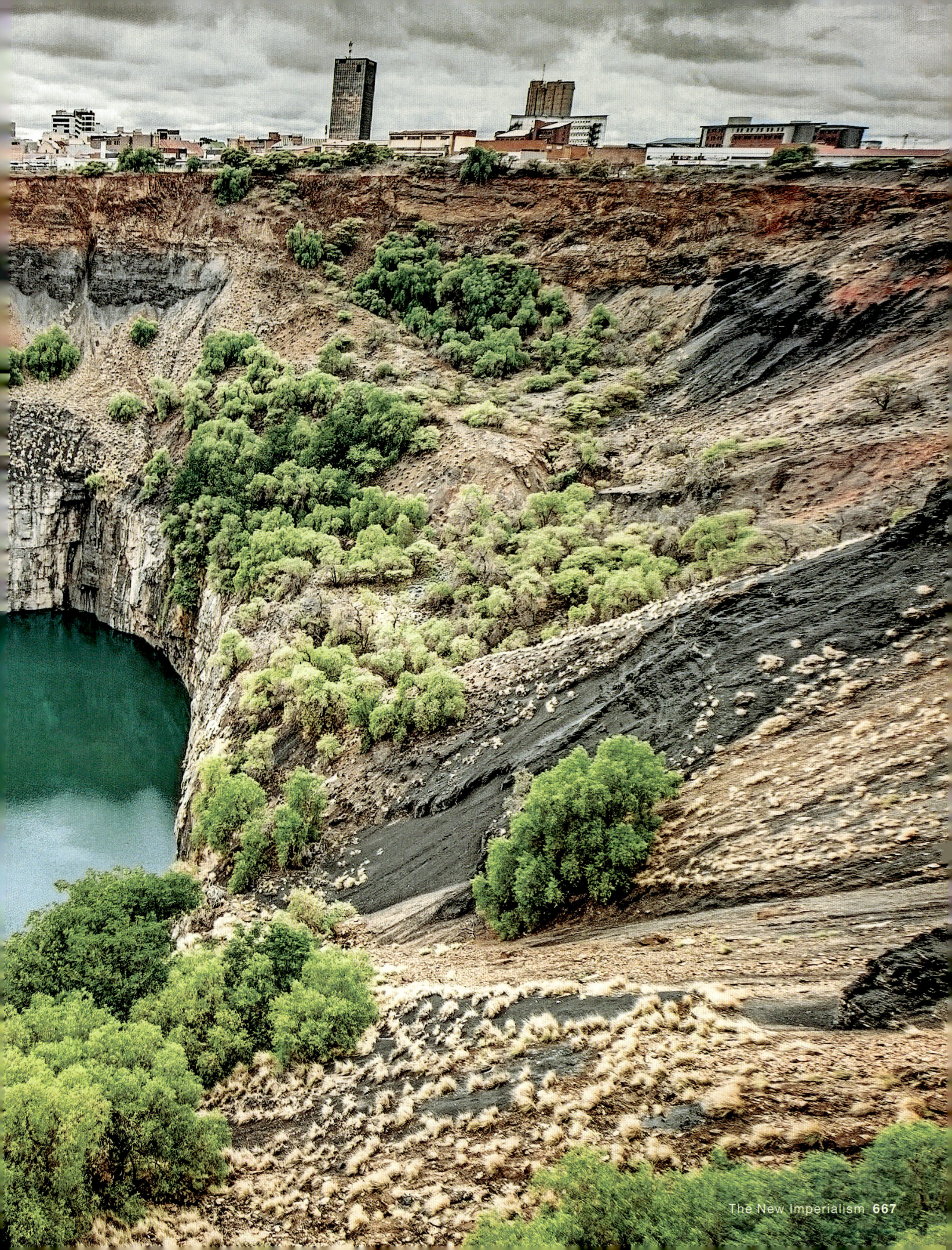

1.1

MAIN IDEA After Europeans flooded into their lands in Africa, King Khama and neighboring kings set out on a journey to protect their land and people.

Traveler: King Khama III
Mission of Diplomacy c. 1837–1923

Who would you go to if people were invading your country? For King Khama and his neighboring kings, the only option seemed to be to go to the home of the invaders and to appeal to their neighbors for help.

A FLOOD OF INVADERS

During his lifetime, King Khama III of the Bangwato people of southern Africa witnessed great challenges as European empires advanced. As a child, he had been familiar with the occasional European hunter or missionary crossing the kingdom. As a king, however, he decided to take drastic action to prevent the complete **subjugation**, or conquest, of his society.

In the short space of 20 years, European powers had drawn colonial boundaries on maps of Africa without the consent or knowledge of those they planned to rule. In many places, Africans resisted, but the Europeans' technological superiority was impossible to overcome.

A DIPLOMATIC MISSION

In 1895, King Khama III and two neighboring kings began a long diplomatic mission. They were in a difficult position. White settlement had already been established in South Africa, but now it was moving northward. The discovery of diamonds and gold had added momentum to that expansion. The kings hoped to convince the British government to declare the Bangwato lands as a protectorate of Great Britain. In this way, the Bangwato people would retain their farming and grazing lands and at least keep some control over their own affairs.

Khama and his companions had converted to Christianity years earlier. So they sought out evangelical groups in London and appealed to Christians' sense of morality. After hearing their appeals, many British Christians supported the kings. The colonial secretary argued in their favor, too. They even met with Queen Victoria. Thanks in large part to the kings' effort and skill, the Bechuanaland protectorate was established.

King Khama went on to establish schools and a trading company in the 20th century. Today, the people of Botswana live in a peaceful and relatively prosperous state. Because they were not ruled by South Africa, they avoided the terrible violence resulting from a system of segregation and discrimination that separated black Africans from white settlers who occupied the land.

Still, measured against the great events of the time, Khama's success was a small victory. African societies could not escape the forces taking over the continent. Technological advances and economic demand for commodities and markets powered what became known as the New Imperialism. **Imperialism** is a practice in which a country increases its power by gaining control over other areas of the world. In Africa and Southeast Asia, local leaders were able to resist only by manipulating European rivalries for their own ends. However, even the most independent states eventually succumbed to imperialism. Indigenous leaders around the world shared King Khama's predicament. But many did not achieve as positive an outcome.

PRIMARY SOURCE

At first we saw the white people pass, and we said, "They are going to hunt for elephant-tusks and ostrich-feathers, and then they will return where they came from." . . . But now when we see white men we say "Jah! Jah!" ["Oh Dear!"]. And now we think of the white people like rain, for they come down as a flood. When it rains too much, it puts a stop to us all. . . . It is not good for the black people that there should be a multitude of white men.

—King Khama III

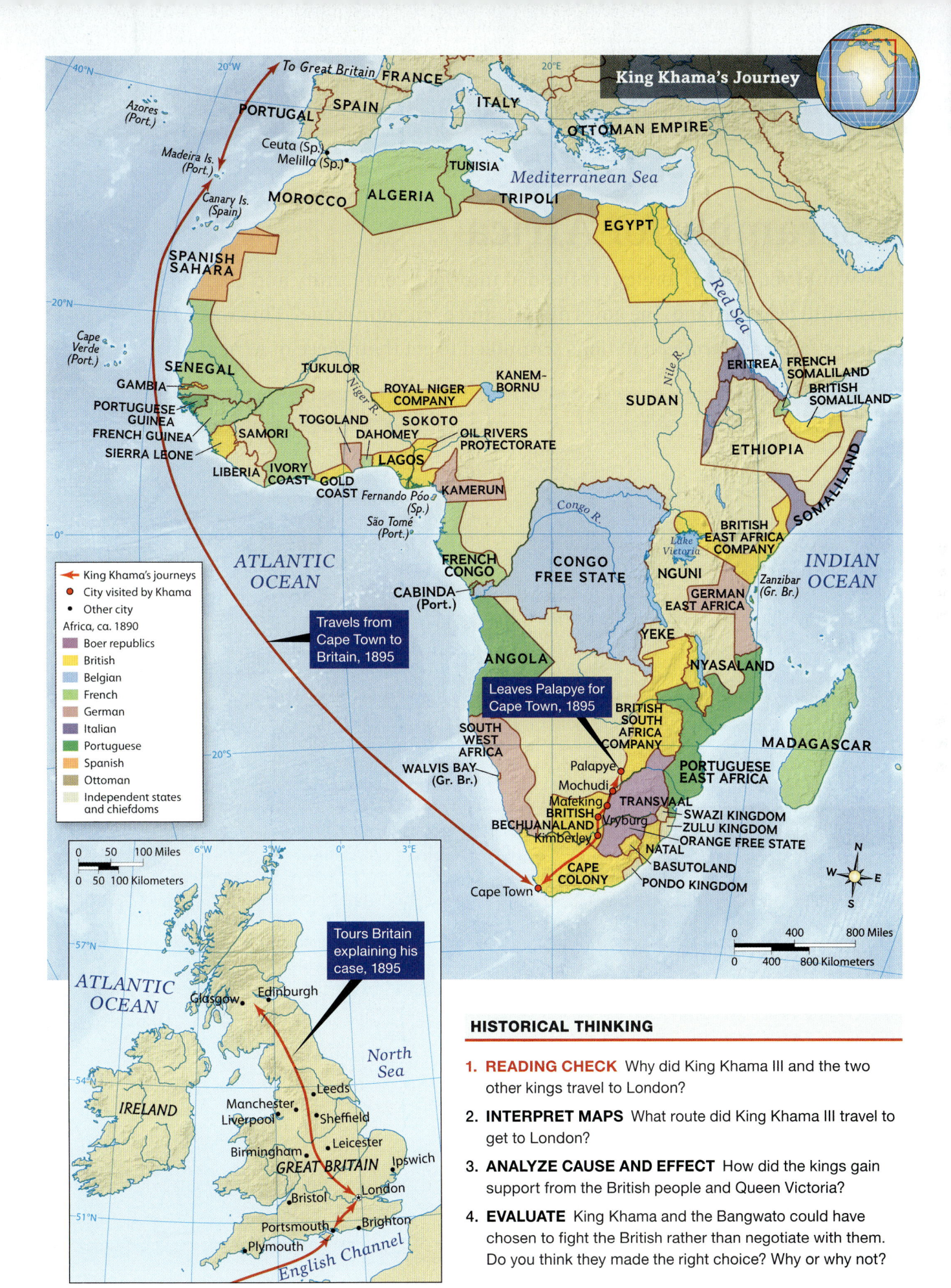

King Khama's Journey

Map Legend:
- King Khama's journeys
- ○ City visited by Khama
- • Other city

Africa, ca. 1890
- Boer republics
- British
- Belgian
- French
- German
- Italian
- Portuguese
- Spanish
- Ottoman
- Independent states and chiefdoms

Travels from Cape Town to Britain, 1895

Leaves Palapye for Cape Town, 1895

Tours Britain explaining his case, 1895

HISTORICAL THINKING

1. **READING CHECK** Why did King Khama III and the two other kings travel to London?

2. **INTERPRET MAPS** What route did King Khama III travel to get to London?

3. **ANALYZE CAUSE AND EFFECT** How did the kings gain support from the British people and Queen Victoria?

4. **EVALUATE** King Khama and the Bangwato could have chosen to fight the British rather than negotiate with them. Do you think they made the right choice? Why or why not?

The New Imperialism 669

1.2 **MAIN IDEA** European competition fueled an all-out scramble for control of Africa. Many Africans resisted but could not compete with European technology such as machine guns.

A Scramble for Africa

How would you react if foreigners flooded into your community and claimed ownership over the land, the government, and even your home? This was what Africans faced as European nations scrambled to get their piece of Africa.

Colonial Presence in Africa, 1914

Legend:
- Belgian
- British
- French
- German
- Italian
- Portuguese
- Spanish
- ★ Site of African resistance to European occupation

Colonial Presence in Africa, 1878

Legend:
- British
- French
- Portuguese
- Spanish

670 CHAPTER 24

THE NEW IMPERIALISM

As King Khama witnessed, after 1870 Africans suddenly confronted large numbers of Europeans. The era of the New Imperialism had begun. Industrialized countries were engaged in heavy competition for African resources, and the British were determined not to lose their earlier dominance of Africa. But the newly united Germany was the fastest growing industrial economy, and Germans were eager to gain equality with Britain. The French had just been defeated by Germany, and they were itching to restore their international standing. The Americans and Japanese had also joined the imperial club and were gaining military power in Asia.

Competition was fueled by technology and industrial capitalism. Refinements for processing chemicals and metals were brought on by the Industrial Revolution. To compete economically, countries developed more sophisticated production techniques and much larger industrial corporations, which required secure access to raw materials from around the world.

As you have learned, in Latin America this search for raw materials could lead to economic growth but also to violence and inequality. The same was true in Africa, and a good example is rubber. Factories required rubber for conveyor belts, and the invention of bicycles and cars led to even greater demand. There were only two places where wild rubber grew in abundance: the Amazon region of South America and the Congo region of Central Africa. In both places, ruthless exploitation of indigenous lands and labor made a small number of outsiders very wealthy, while local peoples suffered from violence and even death.

Before that time, the interior of most of Africa had been "off-limits" to Europeans. For example, European slave traders faced death from malaria, a blood disease transmitted by mosquito bites, if they ventured far into Africa. However, the discovery of the medicine quinine in the 1840s provided protection against malaria, opening access to Africa's interior. With this medical advance, European exploration and exploitation in the tropics became possible.

Politicians used patriotic appeals to gain support for their imperialist endeavors. Leaders of the French Third Republic appealed to "national honor" in extending their colonial frontiers, and candidates of the Conservative Party in Britain used appeals to pride in global dominance to win elections. In Germany, Kaiser Wilhelm focused on military glory and imperial expansion to strengthen German unity.

Europeans also used humanitarian and religious appeals to justify imperialism. Many considered their mission to be one of "civilizing the savages." Missionaries believed they were "saving" African souls. David Livingstone, one of the most famous missionaries, believed that Africans who converted to Christianity would uplift the continent spiritually and materially. He spent the better part of his life exploring the continent and preaching Christianity. However, when the British lost contact with Livingstone, they feared he was lost in Central Africa. They sent explorer Henry Morton Stanley to find him. Unlike Livingstone, Stanley treated Africans harshly. After the British government condemned him, Stanley formed an alliance with King Leopold II of Belgium who was convinced he could gain great wealth in Africa. Joining in the imperial scramble, King Leopold declared, "I must have my share of this magnificent African cake!"

A group of men sit atop a pile of ivory tusks on the island of Zanzibar off the coast of Africa. Ivory became one of the primary materials exploited by Europeans, decimating the elephant population.

Afraid that King Leopold would destabilize the balance of power, Germany's Otto von Bismarck organized the Berlin Conference in 1884. Thirteen European nations met in Berlin to divide up the continent and determine **spheres of influence**, or areas in which colonial powers recognized one another's claims to dominance. No Africans were invited to attend, nor did European representatives pay any attention to traditional ethnic or cultural boundaries. According to the rules of the conference, nations in attendance could claim any unclaimed area of Africa as long as they occupied and administered it. For Africans, this decision meant 20 years of warfare and instability as European governments launched waves of invasions to secure their claims. Millions of Africans died in this "scramble for Africa."

Some of the worst violence occurred in the Congo, which King Leopold claimed as his own personal property. While claiming to be spreading Christianity and "civilization," Leopold's agents brutalized the indigenous people, using armed force and torture to increase supplies of ivory and rubber. African women were held captive until their husbands brought enough rubber to free them. Famine spread as farmers were forced to ignore their own crops.

The Polish-English writer Joseph Conrad witnessed this brutality. In his novella *Heart of Darkness*, he tells the story of an Englishman who travels up the Congo River as he searches for a successful but mysterious European merchant. When he finally reaches the remote camp, he finds that the man has gone insane with greed. The merchant's final words, "The horror! The horror!" reflect the darkness that had come with European imperialism.

AFRICAN RESPONSES

Before 1878, European colonial presence was largely limited to coastal areas. The all-out scramble for control of Africa was something new. Telegraphs provided an important source of communication, and steamships allowed Europeans to venture farther up African rivers. The suddenness of the onslaught caught Africans off guard. Should they fight back? Seek diplomatic options? Ally themselves with the intruders? African leaders tried all of these options with little success. When Africans rose up to defend their lands and traditions, the Europeans came in with machine guns and field cannons.

The Industrial Revolution was changing the balance of power, as witnessed in the 19th-century Anglo-Asante (ah-SAHN-tee) Wars. The powerful Asante Empire in the West African forest resented British attempts to use their coastal settlement to dominate trade. In 1824, this competition led to warfare, and the Asante easily won. But by 1896, the British had much better technology, including rifles, and now easily conquered the Asante. The Asante king, known for his wealth in gold, was sent into exile.

This African salt cellar, or salt container, is carved out of an ivory elephant tusk. The carvings on the salt cellar depict European men with long hair and beards.

Many Asante people felt humiliated, and a queen mother, **Yaa Asantewaa**, spoke up to motivate her people: "[If] you the men of Asante will not go forward, then we . . . the women will. I shall call upon my fellow women. We will fight the white men. We will fight till the last of us falls in the battlefields." The British defeated the Asante. But Yaa Asantewaa's passion caused the British governors to treat the royal family and Asante traditions with greater respect.

The British were competing with the French for control in West Africa, and that is why they moved to occupy the area of today's northern Nigeria. The region had been dominated by the Sokoto (SOH-kuh-toh) caliphate, but after its leader's death, it had split into a number of separate states. The lack of a unified army made British occupation easier. Some leaders fought, but their cavalry forces on horseback were no match for machine guns, and British cannons easily blew holes in their palace walls.

The British and the Germans scrambled for territory in East Africa. The lands the Germans conquered did not have any obvious sources of wealth, however. To make their East African colony pay, the Germans forced East Africans to grow cotton. It was hard work, enforced by the whip, and cotton ruined the soil with no benefit to local farmers. As a result, in 1905 the religious prophet, Kinjeketile (kin-JEK-eh-tayl), led the Maji Maji Revolt. The Germans easily overpowered Kinjeketile's followers who believed they would be spared by bathing in a stream of *Maji Maji*, meaning "powerful water." The rebellion was not completely futile, though. After the revolt, the Germans no longer imposed such heavy restrictions on the African people under their control.

Egypt became another area of resistance. You already read that in 1869 the French designed and built the Suez Canal to create a shipping route between Europe and Asia. The Egyptian leader believed that revenue from the canal would allow Egypt to maintain its independence. However, economic hardships forced the Egyptians to sell their shares in the canal to the British. Taking control of more than the canal, the British imposed their own officers on Egypt's military. Nationalist Egyptian military officers rebelled, but the British quickly suppressed the rebellion.

THINGS FALL APART In 1958, a young Nigerian writer named Chinua Achebe imagined what the "scramble for Africa" would have felt like for his own ancestors. Achebe was an Igbo, a society with a complex culture where status came from achievement rather than inherited status. The main character in Achebe's novel, *Things Fall Apart*, is Okonkwo, a man who received nothing from his father but had a burning ambition to earn the "titles" that would mark him as a great man. Unfortunately, the British arrived and changed the rules of success. Okonkwo's community became divided between Christian converts, including his own son, and those who, like Okonkwo, stuck to the old ways. Says one character in the course of the novel, "They have put the knife on the things that held us together, and we have fallen apart." For many years, Achebe's great novel has helped readers understand the human side of this tragic period in Africa's long history.

Once in control of Egypt, the British needed to control the Upper Nile Valley as well. First in the 1880s and again in the 1890s, the British fought Sudanese resistance to take control of the Nile Valley. The Battle of Omdurman (ohm-der-MAHN) in 1898 was the bloodiest battle between European and African forces during the entire period. The Sudanese forces were fighting on behalf of a Muslim religious prophet who said he had come to declare the end of days and the victory of the righteous. The battle was one of the most lopsided in history. The British, armed with machine guns invented in 1884, lost 47 soldiers. Over 10,000 Sudanese forces were killed.

The British also faced stiff resistance in the southern African kingdom of the Ndebele (endeh-BEE-lee). The Ndebele were militarily formidable, but they were no match for the British. The Ndebele king tried to protect his people by signing a treaty granting the British mineral rights while retaining his own authority. He feared the British would not keep their promises, and sure enough, the kingdom fell to the British colony of Rhodesia (roh-DEE-zhuh) after losing two wars of resistance in the 1890s.

HISTORICAL THINKING

1. **READING CHECK** What political, economic, and social motivations influenced European imperialism in Africa?

2. **IDENTIFY** How did military technology, communications technology, and medical advancements help initiate and advance imperialism in Africa?

3. **INTERPRET MAPS** According to the information in the map, which European country's occupation was met with the most resistance movements?

1.3

MAIN IDEA Imperial interests in South Africa led to war between European colonists.

The South African War

Wars usually end with one side winning and another losing, right? In South Africa, the white warring parties ended up with a compromise that benefited both sides while resulting in a brutal loss for indigenous Africans.

Boer families were placed by British soldiers in concentration camps like this one in Eshowe, Zululand, during the second Boer War.

CLASHING INTERESTS IN SOUTH AFRICA

The European presence in Africa increased greatly after 1870, but some countries had begun exploring the continent even earlier. As you have learned, the Dutch East India Company had established a trade center in Cape Town in present-day South Africa as early as 1652. Later, settlers known as **Boers**, or farmers, moved to the interior. There was no malaria here to block European movement. Also, the indigenous people were unable to resist as they were hunter-gatherers with no metal weapons and no resistance to the smallpox brought by the settlers. By the time of the New Imperialism, the Boers, who are now known as Afrikaners, had lived in the Cape area for 200 years.

On the other side of South Africa, the Boers were challenged by entirely different African societies with great herds of cattle, powerful chiefs, and iron weapons. These were the descendants of the Bantu-speaking migrants you already learned about. In the late 18th century, drought had caused these chiefdoms to compete for water resources, and one group rose to dominate the others. This was the Zulu Empire under the great warrior **King Shaka**, who grew in power as he brought the young men of conquered chiefdoms into his own regiments. Other societies abandoned their lands to escape the violence.

At the same time, the Boers were expanding. They moved into territories that had been abandoned in the wake of Zulu warfare. However, they were unable to overpower Zulu resistance, and the Zulu and other African societies retained their sovereignty into the 1870s.

Earlier, the British had taken Cape Town from the Dutch during the wars with Napoleon. Initially, the British focused their attention on maritime trade. But when diamonds were discovered in 1868, the British looked to conquer the interior. That led to conflict with the Zulu kingdom. In 1879, British authorities demanded that the Zulu disband their regiments, but the Zulu king refused. The Zulu warriors attacked and defeated the British at the Battle of Isandhlwana (ee-san-DLWAH-nah). Enraged by their defeat, the British sacked the Zulu capital and sent the king into exile.

Meanwhile, as many Africans sought safety in the mountains, the Boers took advantage by settling much of the interior. But the republics they founded there were also challenged by the British Empire, especially after gold was discovered in 1884. The city of Johannesburg rose almost overnight, and the clash between Boer and British aspirations led to the South African War.

WAR AND AFTERMATH

During the war, which lasted from 1899 to 1902, the British took control of towns and railway lines while Boer combatants blended into civilian populations and engaged in **guerrilla warfare**, or small-scale surprise attacks, against the British. To separate civilians from soldiers, the British sent Boer civilians to **concentration camps**, where they were confined under armed guard. Over 20,000 Boers, many of them women and children, died of illness in the camps. Though the South African War was between the British and the Boers, tens of thousands of Africans also died.

The British won the war, but less than a decade later they developed a compromise with the Boers. They created the Union of South Africa to combine British colonies with Boer republics under the British flag. This 1910 compromise secured both groups' common interest: cheap African labor for mining and agriculture.

In 1913, the all-white South African parliament passed the Native Land Act. The law limited Africans to "native reserves" that included only a tiny portion of their traditional land. The goal was to strip indigenous communities of their ability to grow their own food and to force them to work in mines and white farms at the lowest possible pay.

In response to the injustice of the Native Land Act, a group of educated African leaders banded together to form the **African National Congress (ANC)**. At first the ANC had no success challenging white domination of South Africa. But much later, as you will learn, the ANC would finally win its battle for democracy and greater racial equality.

GENOCIDE IN GERMAN SOUTHWEST AFRICA

As the British and Boers ended their war in South Africa, another chilling event was underway in neighboring German Southwest Africa (present-day Namibia). After the Germans claimed the territory, they took more and more land from the Herero people. In 1904, the Herero rebelled, but the Germans suppressed the rebellion and drove the Herero into the Kalahari Desert. Prevented from returning, tens of thousands of Herero died. Those who survived were sent to concentration camps and forced to perform hard labor. Harsh labor conditions killed half of the people in the camps. All in all, about 75 percent of the Herero population died. This was the 20th century's first **genocide**, or attempt to destroy an entire people and their culture.

THE RHODES COLOSSUS

CECIL RHODES The main figure of the New Imperialism in southern Africa was the mining **magnate**, or wealthy and powerful businessperson, Cecil Rhodes (shown above). He dreamed of British imperial control of eastern and southern Africa "from Cape to Cairo." Combining political and economic clout, Rhodes was prime minister of the Cape Colony, owner of some of the world's richest gold and diamond mines, and head of the British South Africa Company (BSAC). Through the BSAC, Rhodes even had his own army, which he used to conquer the territory later named Rhodesia. Once Africans regained their independence, they dropped Rhodesia and proudly called their country Zimbabwe, after the great early kingdom of their ancestors.

HISTORICAL THINKING

1. **READING CHECK** What interests led the Boers and the British to fight the South African War?

2. **COMPARE AND CONTRAST** How did British colonialism differ in the Asante Kingdom and South Africa?

3. **ANALYZE CAUSE AND EFFECT** How did the compromise between the British and the Boers affect black South Africans?

The New Imperialism 675

2.1

MAIN IDEA The continued pursuit of raw materials led European and industrial powers to take control of Southeast Asia, Austronesia, and the Pacific.

Southeast Asia and Austronesia

Have you ever heard people say they must "keep up with the Joneses"? The idiom refers to the need to compete with one's neighbors for social status. During the New Imperialism, imperialist nations were not content to just take over Africa and South America. They also swept up lands in Asia and the Pacific. After all, they had to keep up with their neighbors.

SOUTHEAST ASIA

As in Africa, Europeans competed for access to trade in Southeast Asia well before the 19th century. But the same motives that drove the New Imperialism in Africa motivated industrial powers to clamor for control of Southeast Asia and Austronesia, or the islands of the southern Pacific Ocean. By the end of the 19th century, Western domination was nearly complete.

In 1802, the French aided the Nguyen family in establishing a new dynasty in Vietnam. As a result, French missionaries were allowed to preach there. However, Nguyen tolerance toward Catholicism declined, leading to the execution of a missionary. In 1858, the French emperor Napoleon III invaded Vietnam, citing as justification the persecution of missionaries, increased interest in trade in Southeast Asia, and the belief that the British would take Vietnam if the French didn't. Finally, the besieged Nguyen ruler ceded the commercial center of Saigon to France, opened three "treaty ports" to European trade, and gave the French free passage up the Mekong River.

Adding to their territory, the French conquered the neighboring kingdom of Cambodia. An agreement with the kingdom of Siam also gave Laos to the French. In 1887, they combined the three territories into the Federation of Indochina, or simply **French Indochina**. French authorities took over vast estates and grew rubber and rice, which they exported. The profits went almost entirely to the French.

Like the French in Indochina, the British took Burma into their empire in stages. By the 1870s, Britain controlled the south. In 1886, British forces from India invaded Burma and took Mandalay, the capital. They suppressed a number of rebellions and began building railroads. Their goal was to access the rich timber resources of the Burmese jungles.

Singapore had been Britain's most valuable possession in Southeast Asia since 1819. Initially, the British were content to control the port and grow rich on the trade between the Indian Ocean and the South China Sea. But after the completion of the Suez Canal in

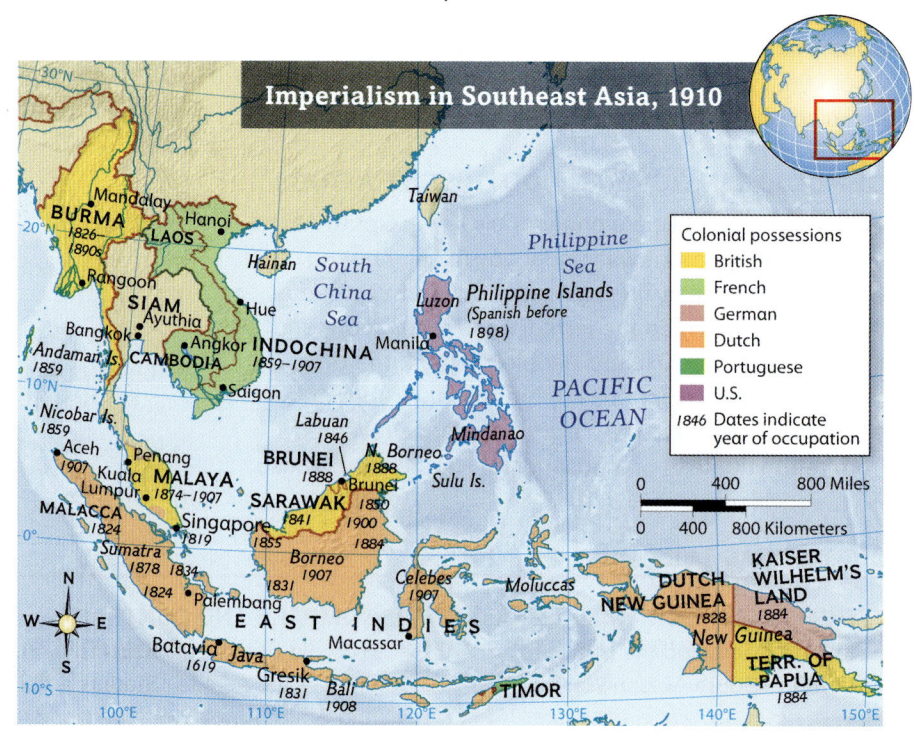

Imperialism in Southeast Asia, 1910

Colonial possessions:
- British
- French
- German
- Dutch
- Portuguese
- U.S.

1846 Dates indicate year of occupation

676 CHAPTER 24

Workers in Myanmar use elephants to help them haul teak wood. Teak, which is a preferred wood for boats and furniture, has been a main export from Myanmar (once known as Burma) since the New Imperialism.

Egypt, British merchants became anxious to exploit the rich tin resources of the Malay Peninsula.

The British started their conquest of Malaya by making alliances with local Muslim leaders. When some of those leaders refused British demands, the fighting started, and British firepower dominated. Once in control, the British expanded plantations of commercial crops such as pepper, palm oil, and rubber.

The Dutch had been the dominant European presence in the islands of Southeast Asia since the 17th century. During the 19th century, authorities asserted more and more formal control over Java and Sumatra, where individual sultans had previously been left in charge of local affairs. At the same time, the increasing presence of other European powers motivated the Dutch to seek control of hundreds of other islands. Under the New Imperialism, the Dutch significantly expanded their power over the Indonesian archipelago.

THE PACIFIC AND AUSTRONESIA

While European powers vied for control of Southeast Asia, the United States claimed a direct territorial stake in the Pacific by annexing the Hawaiian Islands in 1898. The further extension of American imperialism to the Philippines came as a result of the Spanish–American War from 1898 to 1900. That war initially centered in Cuba. It then spread to include the Philippines, which Spain had ruled since the founding of Manila in 1571.

As you have learned, British involvement in Australia and New Zealand predated the New Imperialism. By the 1870s, in fact, the Australian economy was booming as a result of wool exports and the discovery of gold. However, the boom had been at the expense of the Aboriginals. White immigrants reduced them to a defeated and subservient people. In New Zealand, however, British settlers faced tough resistance from the Polynesian-speaking Maori. An 1840 treaty created the framework for British-Maori coexistence. The treaty guaranteed land rights and status as British subjects to the Maori. But by the 1860s, war had broken out. A British victory followed, and by 1890 indigenous Maori, like the people of Hawaii, had lost nearly all of their land. That was the same year as the massacre of the Lakota Sioux at Wounded Knee, which you read about earlier. By then, indigenous people had lost their sovereignty all across the world.

HISTORICAL THINKING

1. **READING CHECK** What were some of the raw materials that Europeans sought in Southeast Asia and Austronesia?

2. **INTERPRET MAPS** Who controlled the most land as colonial possessions in the Pacific?

3. **IDENTIFY SUPPORTING DETAILS** How did the United States participate in the New Imperialism in these areas of the world?

2.2

MAIN IDEA Imperial powers used a number of tactics to control their colonies but not without controversy at home.

Imperialist Tactics

What would you do if your country took over another country and used violent tactics to control the people there? Would you support your country, or would you try to persuade your government to change its ways? This was the situation Americans and Europeans faced when their countries took control of other lands.

IMPERIALIST TACTICS

Taking control of Southeast Asia, the Pacific, and Austronesia wasn't always easy. Guerrilla warriors took up arms against the French in Indochina. The Maori fought a war against the British in New Zealand. Farmers in the islands of Southeast Asia rebelled against Dutch demands, and Filipino revolutionaries struggled for independence from the United States. To subdue these groups, imperialists developed a series of tactics.

Resistance to foreign occupation was a constant theme in Vietnamese history, first with imperial China and then with the French. The Vietnamese people were not willing to simply hand their country over to the French. Guerrilla fighters rose up from rural villages across the country. To fight guerrilla resistance, French authorities started a campaign of "pacification." This tactic was to subdue and calm the resisters. French authorities sought to win the hearts of the Vietnamese by building roads, opening schools, and providing health care. At the same time, they forcibly suppressed rebels, killing anyone who appeared to be hostile to their control.

The British took a different tactic. In Malaya, as in Africa, the British supported a policy of "divide and conquer," creating and playing off local rivalries. British "residents" gave local Malaya rulers "advice" on the governance of their sultanates. If a sultan refused to follow their advice, the British simply recognized another ambitious man as ruler and worked through him. In this way, the British could claim that indigenous rulers remained in place, but power was squarely in the hands of Europeans.

The Dutch used **coercion**, or force. Farmers in Java had long grown rice for self-sufficiency. But in 1830, Dutch authorities forced rice farmers to convert to

Queen Liliuokalani was the last sovereign ruler of the Kamehameha dynasty of the Hawaiian kingdom.

sugar production. One Dutch official declared that "they must be taught to work, and if they were unwilling out of ignorance, they must be ordered to work." Through such coercion, the Dutch could buy sugar at low prices and then sell it for a large profit on world markets. The Europeans demanded cash taxes, but the only way local people could obtain colonial currency was by working for Europeans or by growing cash crops for export. Thus, peasants became dependent on the sale of crops like sugar and coffee. Those who resisted, such as rebels on the Hindu-ruled island of Bali, were killed or sent into exile.

Meanwhile, the tactic of the United States was occupation. Hawaii was a monarchy with a constitution that blended indigenous elements with imported ones, such as an elected legislature and limits on executive power. Americans with business interests in Hawaii such as Sanford B. Dole, a pineapple planter, worked with missionaries to lead a coup against Hawaii's **Queen Liliuokalani** (leelee-ookah-LAHNI). President Benjamin Harrison justified the overthrow of the queen saying, "It is quite evident that the monarchy had become effete [ineffective] and the Queen's Government so weak and inadequate as to be the prey of . . . unscrupulous [immoral] persons." He claimed that annexing Hawaii was "highly promotive of the best interests of the Hawaiian people" and was the only way to "adequately secure the interests of the United States." Writing from the Iolani Palace in Honolulu, where she was kept under house arrest, Queen Liliuokalani wrote: "It was the intention of the officers of the government to humiliate me by imprisoning me, but my spirit rose above that. I was a martyr to the cause of my people and was proud of it."

As you have read, the United States occupied the Philippines after the Spanish–American War. Initially, the Filipinos believed that the United States would grant them independence. However, when that did not happen, Filipino revolutionaries led by **Emilio Aguinaldo** took up arms in a guerrilla war against the U.S. Army. Over 20,000 Filipino combatants were killed and 200,000 Filipino civilians died from violence, disease, or famine.

DEBATE OVER IMPERIAL AMBITIONS

Some Americans protested that waging war against people who were fighting for independence was contrary to American principles. The writer Mark Twain joined the Anti-Imperialist League, declaring that American involvement in the Philippines was impure and motivated by economic greed. Commenting on the Americans' use of torture against Filipinos, the American journalist and explorer George Kennan wrote: ". . . to resort to inquisitorial methods [torture], and use them without discrimination, is unworthy of us and will recoil [backfire] on us as a nation."

Observing the debate in America, the British poet Rudyard Kipling urged the United States to shoulder its imperial responsibilities after it took over the Philippines. He worried that the British Empire was in decline and that only an imperialistic United States could save the world for "Anglo-Saxon civilization."

PRIMARY SOURCE

American author Mark Twain and British author Rudyard Kipling were on opposite sides of the debate as to the motivations behind imperialism. Twain wondered what the United States' true purpose was. Kipling felt the Americans had a duty to continue the spread of "civilization."

[I] have seen that we do not intend to free, but to subjugate the people of the Philippines. We have gone there to conquer, not to redeem. . .

It should, it seems to me, be our pleasure and duty to make those people free and let them deal with their own domestic questions in their own way.

—Mark Twain, from the *New York Herald*, October 15, 1900

Take up the White Man's burden—
Send forth the best ye breed—
Go bind your sons to exile
To serve your captives' need;
To wait in heavy harness,
On fluttered folk and wild—
Your new-caught sullen peoples,
Half-devil and half-child.

—Rudyard Kipling, from "The White Man's Burden," 1899

HISTORICAL THINKING

1. **READING CHECK** Describe some of the tactics that Europeans used to suppress resistance to their control of Southeast Asia.

2. **EVALUATE** How effective do you think the French tactic of pacification was in winning support in French Indochina?

3. **ANALYZE POINTS OF VIEW** What different viewpoints did Twain and Kipling have regarding the occupation of the Philippines? How do you think the Filipinos felt about the occupation?

2.3 A Global Commodity: Rubber

European explorers brought samples of rubber back from the Americas after marveling at the elastic balls Native American players bounced off their hips in a ritual game. The ancient Olmec of Mesoamerica—sometimes called "the rubber people"—were probably the first to make rubber using latex, a sticky, milky sap found in some plants and trees, more than 3,000 years ago. The substance was dubbed *rubber* in 1770 by British scientist Joseph Priestly after he discovered it could be used as an eraser to rub out pencil marks on paper.

In the 1840s, the American chemist Charles Goodyear found that heating rubber, in a process he called *vulcanization*, allowed it to remain elastic in extreme temperatures. His discovery helped fuel the new industrial age, with rubber in great demand for tires. So-called rubber barons in Brazil, the main source of rubber at that time, stepped up production by making indigenous peoples toil in the Amazon jungles. But Brazil's rubber boom would be short-lived. In the early 1900s, Southeast Asia, with its cheaper supplies of rubber, came to dominate the market.

How did rubber help promote imperialism?

WHERE THE RUBBER MEETS THE ROAD

From rubber bands to wetsuits to tires, rubber is an incredibly useful commodity. Natural rubber starts with latex, the white sap you can see in this photo. Workers harvest latex by cutting slits in the bark of a rubber tree and collecting the sap in cups. The chemicals in latex allow the substance to stretch and snap back. About 99 percent of natural rubber is obtained from a tree called *Hevea braziliensis*, commonly known as the rubber tree. Other plants, including dandelions, produce latex, but you'd need to grow an awful lot of the weeds to satisfy the world's demand for rubber.

RUBBER FACTORY

Workers at a rubber factory in Africa's Ivory Coast select dried latex to use in the production of finished rubber products. The latex has been set in a heated mold, which helps vulcanize the material. Charles Goodyear named the process after Vulcan, the ancient Roman god of fire. Ivory Coast was the first African country to grow rubber and is the continent's top producer of the commodity. However, since 2011, falling natural rubber prices have sharply reduced the profits for many Ivory Coast rubber farmers.

RUBBER AT A GLANCE

USES	• More than half of all natural and synthetic rubber is used in tires for cars and other vehicles	• Rubber goes into industrial parts, including tubes, hoses, belts, and gaskets.	• Consumer goods, such as toys, shoes, furniture, and medical gloves, contain rubber.
PRODUCTION	• Natural rubber is most often harvested by tapping rubber trees and extracting their latex.	• To produce commercial rubber, the latex is dried, rolled, mixed with chemicals, and vulcanized.	• To produce synthetic rubber, oil is first processed in a refinery and then treated in a rubber plant.
HISTORY	• In 1876, English explorer Henry Wickham collected thousands of rubber tree seeds in Brazil to cultivate and plant in Southeast Asia.	• In the 1890s, Leopold II of Belgium forced Africans in the Congo Free State to harvest rubber, resulting in the deaths of 10 million people.	• During World War II, the demand for rubber led scientists to develop synthetic rubber that could be produced cost-effectively.
VALUE	• Wickham was paid about $1,000 for the Brazilian rubber tree seeds he took—some say stole—from Brazil.	• The price of rubber fell sharply after the low-cost rubber from plantations in Southeast Asia flooded world markets.	• By 2017, big increases in rubber supplies caused the price of rubber to drop to less than one U.S. dollar per pound.
ECONOMICS	• During the rubber boom in the late 1800s, Manaus, Brazil, grew from a small Amazon River town to a wealthy center of commerce.	• In 1855, Brazil exported about 2,100 tons of rubber; by 1879, Brazilian exports of rubber rose to about 10,000 tons.	• Synthetic rubber came to dominate the U.S. rubber market until an oil embargo in 1973 doubled its price.

RUBBER TIRES

Most rubber today—both natural and synthetic—is used in the production of tires. But manufacturers made tires for bicycles first. Before rubber, bike tires were wooden and covered by bands of leather or metal. Scotsman John Dunlop developed the first type of rubber tire. After World War II cut off U.S. access to most of the rubber supply from Southeast Asia, Americans held rubber drives to support the war effort. People brought items such as old tires, boots, and raincoats to the drives and received a penny per pound.

2.4

MAIN IDEA Through diplomatic skill and reform, the rulers of Ethiopia and Siam were able to maintain independence while imperialist powers occupied even more areas of the world.

Adaptation and Resistance to Empire

Would you believe a peace treaty if it were written in another language? What if it were translated to your language, too? The Ethiopians believed the Italians had accurately translated the articles of a treaty, only to learn that their translation did not match the Italian treaty.

ENDURING MONARCHIES

While European countries used their overwhelming strength to exert domination over Africa and Southeast Asia, Ethiopia and Siam retained their independence. Both countries used skillful diplomatic maneuvering to take advantage of inter-European rivalries.

You have read about the ancient Christian kingdom of Ethiopia. It first met modern European firepower in 1868 when a British relief team rescued several British subjects held hostage by the Ethiopian king. The British easily crushed the African army but did not stay to occupy the land. The "scramble for Africa" had not yet begun.

King **Menelik II** desired to strengthen his state against further attack. He consolidated power at the imperial court, created his own standing army, and imported the latest firearms from Europe. Through military conquests, he doubled the size of Ethiopia and moved the capital to new lands in the south. He also introduced land reforms allowing males and females of any social class the right to inherit land.

In 1896, Italy attacked Ethiopia at the Battle of Adowa. Although Italy took the region of Eritrea on the Red Sea, the Ethiopians held out against the Italians. As a Christian, Menelik was able to gain diplomatic influence in Europe. He also played European powers against one another to Ethiopia's advantage. Menelik convinced Britain, the dominant power in northeastern Africa, that Ethiopia would provide security along the Egyptian border and allow European traders free access into Ethiopia. Permitting Menelik to retain his reign was a cheaper solution than occupying Ethiopia by force. Instead, the British and the French sponsored the development of banks and railroads in Ethiopia.

Simultaneously, the kings of Siam also faced the danger of European imperialism. The British expanded from India in the west and the French threatened from Indochina in the east. But two kings whom you read about earlier, Mongkut and his son Chulalongkorn, secured Siam's independence using internal reform and diplomatic engagement.

King Menelik II used diplomacy and military reorganization to retain Ethiopian independence, defeating an Italian army at the Battle of Adowa in 1896.

You may recall that, Mongkut invited Westerners to his capital and installed them as advisors. Though he favored the British, he had French and Dutch advisors, too. He also opened Siam to foreign trade, giving merchants from various countries a stake in his system.

When Chulalongkorn came to power in 1868, he appointed Siamese advisors who understood that their independence depended on reforms and diplomacy. As you already learned, Chulalongkorn gave up Laos to the French to protect his core kingdom. This action satisfied the French and the British, who understood that Siam would continue to welcome Europeans and provide security. In 1896, the French and British agreed to recognize the independence of Siam.

IDEAS FOR AND AGAINST EMPIRE

The territorial acquisitions of the New Imperialism continued into the Pacific. Japan annexed Okinawa in 1879. Germany took New Guinea in 1899, and in the same year Samoa was divided between Germany and the United States. In 1900, the French combined their island claims in the Pacific to establish French Polynesia. By 1900, there were no more unclaimed territories on which to plant the flag of empire.

The continuation of imperialism was driven by Social Darwinism, which you learned is the idea that racial groups are naturally arranged along a hierarchy and that white people sit on top of that hierarchy. This philosophy (since rejected) had become conventional wisdom in Europe, something that people simply believed without question, fueling colonial expansion as part of the natural order of things.

Meanwhile, nationalist movements among colonized people were growing all across Africa and Asia. Wealthy, Western-educated Indians formed the **Indian National Congress** to organize for self-rule under the British Empire. Other Indian nationalists called for an end to British rule altogether.

In Africa, religion often played a role in anti-colonial resistance. As you know, in the Sahel region of West Africa, Islam was well-established. Here guerrilla leader Samori Toure (sam-or-REE too-RAY) used the doctrine of jihad—"struggle"—to organize a long resistance to French invasion. Resistance to empire could also be found among the many Africans who converted to Christianity at this time. Some rejected European religious authority, breaking away from missionary groups and founding their own Protestant denominations, often blending African culture into their Christian worship.

Chulalongkorn, shown here with his son in 1890, used diplomacy to maintain the independence of Siam during the height of the European scramble for colonial territory.

Nationalist movements grew in Africa when educated and highly trained Africans were denied leading positions due to colonial racism. Some organized for greater rights within their own colonies, while others joined with people of African descent from around the world to support **Pan-Africanism**, which stressed the need for solidarity to overcome the inequalities in treatment of black people everywhere.

As anti-colonial nationalism campaigns grew, the flags of empire crowded against each other across the world. As you will read, inter-European competition led the colonial powers to turn their deadly weapons against one another, simultaneously drawing the world's peoples into their devastating conflicts.

HISTORICAL THINKING

1. **READING CHECK** How did Ethiopia and Siam retain their independence?

2. **COMPARE AND CONTRAST** How were the actions of Menelik II and the kings of Siam similar? How were they different?

3. **MAKE PREDICTIONS** What problems will following the ideas of Social Darwinism create for the future of the people during this time period?

CHAPTER 24 THE NEW IMPERIALISM

REVIEW

VOCABULARY

Match each vocabulary word with its definition.

1. coercion
2. imperialism
3. genocide
4. magnate
5. sphere of influence
6. Boer
7. concentration camp
8. subjugation
9. guerrilla warfare
10. Pan-Africanism

a. a Dutch or French settler in South Africa
b. the practice by which a country gains control over other areas of the world
c. the idea that people of African descent should be unified
d. small-scale surprise attacks
e. the state of being under control or governance
f. a place where large numbers of people are imprisoned
g. the systematic destruction of a racial or cultural group
h. an area in which the dominance of one power is recognized above all others
i. the use of force or threats
j. a wealthy, powerful, and influential businessperson

READING STRATEGY
SYNTHESIZE

When you synthesize, you use evidence and explanations from the text along with prior knowledge to form an overall understanding. Use the chart below to help you synthesize the information presented in this chapter. Then answer the question.

The New Imperialism

Evidence:	Supporting Explanation:	Synthesis:

11. What were the motives that drove the New Imperialism?

MAIN IDEAS

Answer the following questions. Support your answers with evidence from the chapter.

12. What motivated King Khama and his neighboring kings to travel to London? **LESSON 1.1**

13. Why were Europeans so successful in colonizing Africa? **LESSON 1.2**

14. Which two groups of people fought in the South African War? **LESSON 1.3**

15. Which European countries colonized Southeast Asia? **LESSON 2.1**

16. What controversy did the United States face when it took control of the Philippines? **LESSON 2.2**

17. What skills did Emperor Menelik II and kings Mongkut and Chulalongkorn employ to keep their countries free of imperialist control? **LESSON 2.4**

HISTORICAL THINKING

Answer the following questions. Support your answers with evidence from the chapter.

18. **ANALYZE POINT OF VIEW** How did Europeans' opinions of their own cultures and religions, and those of Africa and Asia contribute to imperialism?

19. **SYNTHESIZE** What was the role of transportation technology in initiating and advancing imperialism in Africa, Latin America, and Southeast Asia?

20. **ANALYZE CAUSE AND EFFECTS** Analyze the causes of the New Imperialism and its effects on indigenous peoples.

21. **MAKE PREDICTIONS** What effect will imperialism have on the world into the 20th and 21st centuries?

686 CHAPTER 24

INTERPRET VISUALS

Study the 1884 French political cartoon at right, which shows Otto von Bismarck of Germany preparing to cut into a cake. Then answer the questions that follow.

22. What event does this political cartoon depict?

23. What do the expressions of the men at the table convey about what is happening?

ANALYZE SOURCES

In 1897, the king of Ethiopia, Menelik II, wrote a letter to his neighbor, the caliph of Sudan. Read the excerpt below from that letter and answer the questions.

> This is to inform you that the Europeans who are present round the White Nile with the English . . . intended to enter between my country and yours and to separate and divide us. . . . I have ordered my troops to advance towards the White Nile. . . . And you look to yourself, and do not let the Europeans enter between us. Be strong, lest if the Europeans enter our midst a great disaster befall us and our children have no rest. And if one of the Europeans comes to you as a traveler, do your utmost to send him away in peace; and do not listen to rumors against me. All my intention is to increase my friendship with you, and that our countries may be protected from enemies.

24. What is King Menelik's opinion of Europeans?

25. What is his purpose for writing this letter?

CONNECT TO YOUR LIFE

26. **EXPLANATORY** Nationalism, or the belief that people are bound through identification with a certain nation, was a driver of imperialism as well as of resistance to imperialism and growing independence movements. Write a short paragraph describing how you see nationalism affecting the world or a part of the world today. Do you think nationalism is a positive force? Explain why or why not.

TIPS

- List examples of nationalism you see in today's world. Do additional online research if you need to understand the causes and effects of the examples you think of.

- Decide whether the examples you've chosen have a positive or negative impact by evaluating the ways in which they affect those who are part of the nationalist movement and those who are not part of it.

- State your main idea at the beginning of the paragraph.

- Provide a concluding sentence that summarizes your views about nationalism and its impact.

NATIONAL GEOGRAPHIC | CONNECTION

Awash in Plastic

BY LAURA PARKER Adapted from "Plastic" by Laura Parker, *National Geographic,* June 2018

We made it. We depend on it. Now we're drowning in it.

Although plastic was invented in the late 19th century, its production really only took off around 1950. A *Life* magazine article in 1955 celebrated the dawn of "Throwaway Living," in which American housewives would be liberated from drudgery, thanks in large part to disposable plastics. While single-use plastics have brought great convenience to people around the world, they also make up a big part of the plastic waste that's now choking our oceans. The growth of plastic production has far outstripped the ability of waste management to keep up, which is why the oceans are under assault. In 2013, a group of scientists, writing in *Nature* magazine, declared that disposable plastic should be classified not as a housewife's friend but as a hazardous material.

A Bangladeshi family removes labels from plastic bottles, sorting green from clear ones to sell to a scrap dealer.

No one knows how much unrecycled plastic waste ends up in the ocean, Earth's last sink. In 2015, Jenna Jambeck, a University of Georgia engineering professor, caught everyone's attention with a rough estimate: between 5.3 million and 14 million tons each year just from coastal regions. Most of it isn't thrown off ships, she and her colleagues say, but is dumped carelessly on land or in rivers, mostly in Asia. It's then blown or washed into the sea. Imagine five plastic grocery bags stuffed with plastic trash, Jambeck says, sitting on every foot of coastline around the world—that would correspond to about 8.8 million tons, her middle-of-the-road estimate of what the ocean gets from us annually. It's unclear how long it will take for that plastic to completely biodegrade into its constituent molecules. Estimates range from 450 years to never.

Meanwhile, ocean plastic is estimated to kill millions of marine animals every year. Nearly 700 species, including endangered ones, are known to have been affected by it. Some are harmed visibly—strangled by abandoned fishing nets or discarded six-pack rings. Many more are probably harmed invisibly. Marine species of all sizes, from zooplankton to whales, now eat microplastics, the bits smaller than one-fifth of an inch across. On Hawaii's Big Island, on a beach that seemingly should have been pristine—no paved roads lead to it—I walked ankle-deep through microplastics. They crunched like Rice Krispies under my feet. After that, I could understand why some people see ocean plastic as a looming catastrophe, worth mentioning in the same breath as climate change.

And yet there's a key difference: Ocean plastic is not as complicated as climate change. There are no ocean trash deniers, at least so far. To do something about it, we don't have to remake our planet's entire energy system.

"This isn't a problem where we don't know what the solution is," says Ted Siegler, a Vermont resource economist who has spent more than 25 years working with developing nations on garbage. "We know how to pick up garbage. Anyone can do it. We know how to dispose of it. We know how to recycle." It's a matter of building the necessary institutions and systems, he says—ideally before the ocean turns, irretrievably and for centuries to come, into a thin soup of plastic. ■

UNIT INQUIRY
UNIT 8: Create a Sustainable Living Plan

Staging the Question

In this unit, you learned about the widespread changes that the Industrial Revolution brought to people's lives. With the increased production and consumption of manufactured goods, the Industrial Revolution brought a higher standard of living for many people. But it also introduced a host of environmental problems, including air pollution, water pollution, habitat destruction—and eventually climate change and a massive amount of plastic waste. The long-term impact of the Industrial Revolution can be seen around the world, from our crowded cities to the most remote ocean beaches. How can individuals today reduce the negative impact of the Industrial Revolution on our planet?

> **ASSIGNMENT**
>
> **Identify** some current environmental problems that stem from the Industrial Revolution.
>
> **Analyze** the causes of these environmental problems.
>
> **Think** of ways that individuals could help solve these problems by making changes in their lifestyles.
>
> Create a plan identifying lifestyle changes that individuals today could make to help solve serious environmental problems.

Supporting Questions: Begin by developing supporting questions to guide your thinking. For example: What aspects of the way I live and act have a negative impact on the environment? What is the negative effect of each action?

Summative Performance Task: Use the answers to your questions to create a sustainable living plan that identifies at least 10 actions individuals can take to help protect the environment. Describe each action to be taken and the positive effect it will have. You might use a graphic organizer like this one to develop your plan.

Action	Effect

Present: Share your plan with the class. You might consider one of these options:

DISCUSS IN GROUPS

Form small groups and share your ideas. Then compile your group's ideas with those of other groups to create a master plan. Post the composite plan in the classroom.

MAKE A PODCAST

Work with classmates to create a podcast in which everyone shares their ideas on sustainable living. You might incorporate such elements as music, interviews, research, and storytelling.

Take Informed Action:

UNDERSTAND Recognize that people act out of habit much of the time but may change their habits for important reasons.

ASSESS Think about the reasons for protecting and preserving our natural resources. Ultimately, our lives and the lives of those who come after us depend on it.

ACT Choose at least one of the actions in your plan and incorporate it into your daily life. Then gradually make other changes.

UNIT 9

The World Wars
1870–1945

CRITICAL VIEWING

A wave of ceramic poppy flowers appears to tumble into the dry moat of England's Tower of London as part of an art installation created in 2014 to commemorate World War I. Flowers were added over a four-month period until they numbered 888,246, one for each British fatality in the conflict. The poppy, which grew in many of the war's battlefields, became a symbol of the sacrifice made by the soldiers. What emotions did this installation probably inspire?

UNIT 9 The World Wars

WORLD EVENTS 1914–1945

1914 EUROPE The assassination of Archduke Franz Ferdinand of Austria-Hungary sets off a chain of events leading directly to World War I. *(Italian newspaper artwork depicting the assassination)*

1917 EUROPE The Russian Revolution begins as revolutionaries overthrow the tsar and the Bolsheviks take control of the government. *(Soviet propaganda poster featuring Vladimir Lenin)*

1917 AMERICAS On April 6, the United States enters World War I after German U-boats sink three U.S. ships in one month.

1918 EUROPE On November 11, Germany signs the Armistice, ending World War I.

1929 AMERICAS The stock market crashes in October, marking the start of the Great Depression. *(unemployed men lined up outside a soup kitchen in Chicago in 1931)*

HISTORICAL THINKING

COMPARE AND CONTRAST What was similar about the decisions by the United States to enter the two world wars?

1945 ASIA In early August, the United States drops atomic bombs on Hiroshima and Nagasaki in Japan. *(replica of the "Little Boy" atomic bomb that dropped over Hiroshima)*

1938 EUROPE On *Kristallnacht*, Nazis destroy Jewish homes, businesses, and synagogues and force Jews into segregated ghettos. *(Jewish-owned shoe store destroyed by Nazis in Vienna, Austria)*

1939 EUROPE Germany invades Poland, causing Britain and France to declare war on Germany, beginning World War II.

1942 ASIA The United States wins an important victory over Japan at the Battle of Midway.

1945 EUROPE Germany surrenders on May 8, a day that becomes known as V-E Day. *(German military officials signing the document of surrender in Reims, France)*

1933 EUROPE Adolf Hitler becomes chancellor of Germany.

1945 ASIA On September 2 (V-J Day) Japan officially surrenders, ending World War II. *(people celebrating V-J Day in Times Square in New York City)*

1944 EUROPE Germany launches its last major offensive of the war in the Battle of the Bulge but is forced to retreat.

1944 EUROPE On June 6 (D-Day), American, British, and Canadian troops storm German-occupied beaches at Normandy on the coast of France.

1941 AMERICAS On December 7, the Japanese attack Pearl Harbor, drawing the United States into the war. *(front page of a special edition of the Honolulu Star Bulletin on December 7, 1941)*

CHAPTER 25

The First World War and 20th-Century Revolutions
1870–1935

HISTORICAL THINKING How did the Great War affect the world politically, socially, and economically?

SECTION 1 **Total War and Its Causes**
SECTION 2 **The Great War's Consequences**
SECTION 3 **Revolutions in Russia and China**
SECTION 4 **Revolution in Mexico**

CRITICAL VIEWING

Munitions workers inspect weapons in a storage warehouse in Chilwell, Nottinghamshire, in 1917. National Shell Filling Factory No. 6 was one of the largest shell factories in Britain. What details in this photo convey the magnitude of the war?

1.1 Rivalries, Assassination, Propaganda

MAIN IDEA After the death of an aristocrat in the Balkans in 1914, the complicated agreements and entanglements between the European powers triggered the Great War.

Over several generations, regional and global conflicts and wars increased simmering tensions throughout Europe. People of the early 20th century could not have predicted that what came to be known as World War I would be the deadliest conflict ever recorded at the time.

TURMOIL IN THE BALKANS

By the early 1900s, the dominant European nations known as the Great Powers were Britain, France, Russia, Italy, Germany, and Austria-Hungary. Britain and France presided over immense global empires. Russia led the world's largest military, and Germany had the fastest-growing industrial economy. Italy and Austria-Hungary were both eager to extend their territories. All six nations viewed one another as rivals. The competition for economic and political dominance would, in 1914, lead these powerful countries into the Great War—later known as the First World War or World War I.

In the late 19th century, tensions between the Great Powers had found an outlet in competition for colonies outside of Europe. By 1900, however, European empires had seized large swaths of territory in Africa, Asia, and the Pacific. No unclaimed lands remained. Instead, the Great Powers chose to focus their attentions much closer to home—the Balkan Peninsula in southeastern Europe.

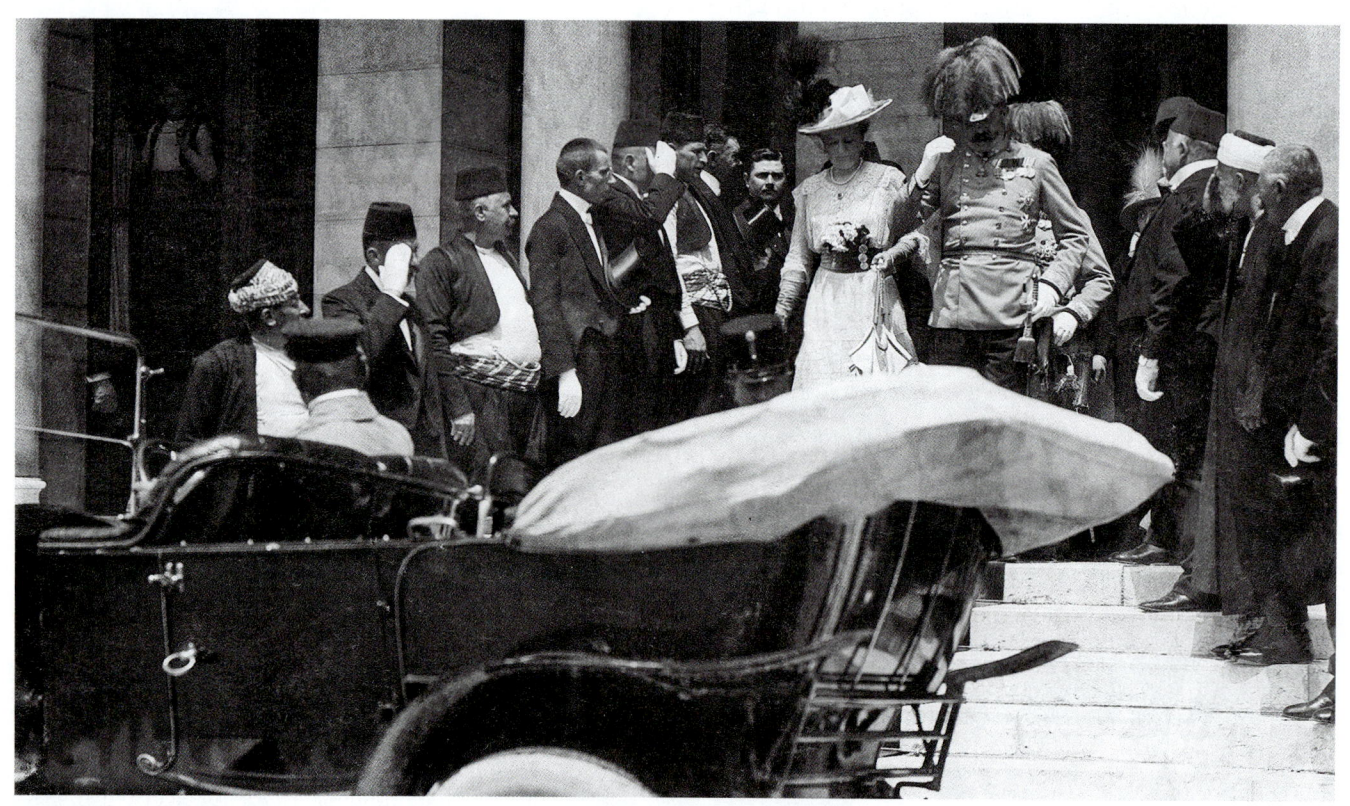

Archduke Francis Ferdinand and his wife, Sophie, leave City Hall in Sarajevo on June 28, 1914. The archduke was heir to the Austro-Hungarian throne. Minutes later, the couple was assassinated by a Serb nationalist, sparking the beginning of the First World War.

The Balkans included Greece, Serbia, Bulgaria, and a few other states. In the early 1800s, the Ottoman Empire ruled this territory as well as areas in North Africa and Southwest Asia. By 1900, however, the Ottoman Empire was losing territory, including to an independent nationalist government in Serbia. In spite of that setback, the Ottomans managed to retain several Balkan provinces. But an alliance of Balkan states backed by Russia stripped away these lands in the First Balkan War between 1912 and 1913. A brief Second Balkan War between the Balkan allies resulted in a substantial expansion of Serbia's territory.

The powerful empire of Austria-Hungary took advantage of Ottoman weakness. In 1908, the empire **annexed**, or incorporated into its territory, Bosnia and Herzegovina, a land populated by Catholic Croatians, Orthodox Serbians, and Muslim Bosnians. Orthodox nationalists were outraged by the intrusion of rulers from Vienna and called upon Serbia and Russia for support. Bosnian Muslims with ties to the Ottoman Empire were also concerned. The stage for conflict was now set.

RISING TENSIONS

Historic rivalries created long-lasting friction between some of the Great Powers. The treaty ending the Franco-Prussian War of 1870 transferred the French territory Alsace-Lorraine to Germany. This loss created anti-German feelings among the French. Russia and Austria-Hungary both continued to compete for control of former Ottoman territories in the Balkans.

In search of greater security, some Great Powers formed alliances. In 1879, Germany and Austria-Hungary signed a treaty promising mutual support. In 1894, France and Russia pledged to assist each other if Germany ever attacked either country. This partnership made Germany nervous—now it had potential enemies to the east and west.

In the early 1900s, the alliance system solidified into two opposing blocs. France and Russia added Britain to their existing alliance to form the **Triple Entente**. Germany, Austria-Hungary, and Italy established the **Triple Alliance** in response. Treaties signed by these nations obligated each country to come to the aid of any ally who was attacked. Members of both groups felt more secure, but the very nature of their alliances could cause a minor dispute to turn into a major conflict.

The Russian rivalry with Austria-Hungary was a prime example. The growing strength of Serbia threatened Austria-Hungary's quest to dominate the Balkans. Austria-Hungary anticipated that one day it might go to war against Serbia. Austria-Hungary and its ally Germany realized that Russian support for the Serbs could draw all of the Great Powers into conflict.

If war should break out, however, Germany was ready. In 1890, **Wilhelm II**, Germany's emperor, had dismissed his chancellor, Otto von Bismarck. Wilhelm abandoned Bismarck's cautious foreign policy and instead pursued militarism. By 1914, the German army had grown to more than 600,000 men.

The other Great Powers decided to respond in kind to Germany's aggressiveness. As imperialist nations, they already had the strong armies and navies needed to establish and maintain control of their colonial resources and markets. Now they took stock of their armed forces and made improvements where needed. Should war happen, they all intended to be prepared.

Britain, known for its centuries of seafaring prowess, boosted its construction of warships to match Germany's naval buildup. Russia, still reeling from its loss to Japan in the Russo-Japanese War of 1905,

The First World War and 20th-Century Revolutions **697**

The Great Powers of World War I

Country	Leader	Title	Reason for Going to War
Britain	Herbert Henry Asquith	Prime Minister	To secure the freedom of Belgium and France after Germany had invaded both countries
Germany	Theobald von Bethmann Hollweg	Chancellor	To support its ally Austria-Hungary and to crush historical enemies (and neighbors) France and Russia before they built up their militaries
France	Raymond Poincaré	President	To restore French control over the region of Alsace-Lorraine, lost to German states in the Franco-Prussian War
Austria-Hungary	Franz Joseph II	Emperor	To avenge the assassination of Archduke Franz Ferdinand
Russia	Nicholas II	Tsar	To protect Serbia from the threat of invasion by Austria-Hungary
Ottoman Empire	Ismail Enver	Minister of War	To end its steady decline and strengthen itself by allying with Germany, a military powerhouse
Italy	Antonio Salandra	Prime Minister	To gain control of Austro-Hungarian and Ottoman territory it had long wanted

believed it could field some 800,000 soldiers. France set a goal of 1.3 million regular troops and reserves. Besides expanding its regular army, Austria-Hungary moved 200,000 reserves into Bosnia and Herzegovina. All allies on both sides made detailed plans for war.

The growing militarism, the rivalries between the Great Powers, and the alliance system all seemed to edge Europe closer to war. However, in 1899 and again in 1907, representatives of more than 40 countries met in the Dutch city of The Hague, Netherlands. There, they established rules for land warfare and a court for the peaceful settlement of international disputes. All Great Powers signed what became known as the Hague Convention. In 1912 and 1913, the same nations met again, this time at the London Peace Conference. They worked together to resolve disputes among the states involved in the First Balkan War. The forces of peace still seemed to hold the upper hand.

THE SPARK: ASSASSINATION

As you have read, Austria-Hungary was a multiethnic empire ruled by Franz Joseph II. Within its borders lived Germans, Magyars (Hungarians), and Slavs. Slavic groups included Czechs and Poles as well as Serbs and Croats. Even though Slavs accounted for more than 60 percent of the population, they had little power. The Germans controlled the Austrian half of the empire, and the Magyars controlled the Hungarian half.

Ethnic difficulties plagued Austria-Hungary. The Czechs, who inhabited a large area in the northwest of the empire, wanted greater self-government. Their demands awakened nationalistic feelings in the empire's other Slavic peoples, including the Serbs, Croats, and Bosnians. In the years following the annexation of Bosnia and Herzegovina in 1908, nationalist movements in the Balkans grew stronger. Activists talked of rebelling against Austro-Hungarian rule and forming an independent Slavic state.

On June 28, 1914, Bosnian Serb nationalist Gavrilo Princip saw an opportunity to advance the Slavic cause. **Archduke Franz Ferdinand**, heir to the Austro-Hungarian throne, had traveled to Bosnia and Herzegovina on an official visit. As the archduke rode through the streets in an open car, Princip shot and killed him and his wife. This assassination kindled a series of events that drew all the Great Powers into war.

Austria-Hungary blamed its longtime rival Serbia for the assassination, and it threatened Serbia with war if Serbia did not comply with a set of humiliating demands. Serbia refused. Nobody at the time thought a war between these adversaries would affect other nations, but the alliance system soon took effect. The Serbs appealed to Russia for help, and the Germans backed Austria-Hungary. The Russian army started to **mobilize**, or assemble and prepare for war. Throughout July, many European leaders searched for a diplomatic way to end the crisis. They failed.

On July 28, Austria-Hungary declared war on Serbia. Two days later, Germany began to mobilize its army, and the next day Austria-Hungary did the same. Then, on August 1, Germany declared war on Russia. On August 3, Germany declared war on France and immediately sent soldiers toward the French border. These German troops first crossed into Belgium. A British security agreement with neutral Belgium led Britain to declare war on Germany on August 5. That same day, Austria-Hungary declared war on Russia, and a week later Britain and France officially declared war on Austria-Hungary. Any hopes for peace evaporated.

The Ottoman Empire, weak as it was, allied itself with Germany and Austria-Hungary. They became known as the **Central Powers**. After a period of indecision, Italy joined Britain, France, and Russia, and the four nations became known as the **Allies**. All the European powers plunged into war.

PREPARING FOR WAR

How did Europe find itself engulfed in this conflict? Historians believe that imperialism, militarism, ethnic unrest, and nationalism all played a role. The assassination of Archduke Franz Ferdinand provided the spark that set Europe alight, propelling the Great Powers toward full-scale war.

Whatever the causes, Europeans did not express alarm at the declarations of war. They seemed to think this contest would be quick and conclusive and that their side would win. The press created war fever to sell newspapers, and the public responded with patriotic demonstrations. Europeans simply could not conceive of the horrors of modern industrialized warfare.

The leaders of the main combatants may have known better. In addition to mobilizing their armies, they set out to rally the civilian population. Governments expected everyone to contribute to the war effort. They clarified this point through posters, songs, newspapers, and other propaganda. Both the Allies and the Central Powers sought to persuade their citizens that the war was a just war. They also used propaganda to provoke nationalistic feelings and hatred of the enemy.

As the war progressed, some nations appealed more to ideology. Britain and France encouraged their citizens to think of the war as a battle to preserve liberty, democracy, and the rule of law. Meanwhile, Germany told its people that the British and French colonial powers were trying to deny the German nation the global stature it deserved.

This was a **total war**. It required the complete mobilization of all resources, including human resources. Men marched off to battle. Some women served as nurses in the war zones, while others joined the labor force at home. Factories had to drastically increase their production of war materials—from guns and bombs to wagons and ships. Sources of oil, coal, and iron needed to be secured. To manage all this, governments assumed controls over the economy and society that they had not had before.

Total war also required access to global reserves. European imperial powers looked to their colonies for manpower and raw materials. Because of their huge empires, Britain and France benefited more from their colonial resources than other nations engaged in the war. Their empires also ensured that the war would not be limited to Europe.

CRITICAL VIEWING The title of this German propaganda poster translates to "Who Is a Militarist?" The size of the soldiers reflects the amount of military spending in Britain, Germany, and France. What message was the German government trying to communicate with this poster?

HISTORICAL THINKING

1. **READING CHECK** How did ethnic conflict and nationalism lead to the assassination of Archduke Franz Ferdinand?
2. **MAKE INFERENCES** Why did the Ottoman Empire ally with Germany and Austria-Hungary in 1914?
3. **DRAW CONCLUSIONS** Do you think the Great Powers wanted to engage in a major war? Why or why not?
4. **EXPLAIN** How did propaganda support a nation's ability to engage in total war?

1.2

MAIN IDEA During the early weeks and months of the Great War, members of the two opposing military alliances battled one another in many different parts of the world.

War on Many Fronts

Hundreds of thousands of soldiers fighting in World War I were teenagers—some as young as 14. Many of them joined the army for patriotic reasons, often lying about their age, and others thought the war would be an amusing adventure. Imagine how quickly their minds changed once they leaped headfirst into a muddy hole in the ground to escape a burst of deadly machine-gun fire.

STALEMATE IN THE WEST

From the start of the war, geography put Germany in an awkward position. Germany would have to face the Russian army to the east and the French army to the west, but this position was not a surprise to the military-minded Germans. Years earlier, they had established a plan to handle a war on two fronts—zones of combat between two opposing forces. The Germans knew that the Russians, who were not fully mobilized, would be slower than the French to form an invasion force. Germany's strategy was to attack France first.

The French fully expected a German invasion; they had established defensive fortifications along the German border. After the German army's initial push through Belgium in early August 1914, French and German forces battled along France's eastern border.

In early September, the Germans broke through French defenses and moved toward Paris. The French, aided by a British force, counterattacked. Their success at the First Battle of the Marne forced the Germans to withdraw. More attacks and counterattacks followed. By the end of 1914, each side had seen hundreds of thousands of soldiers killed and even more wounded.

The First Battle of the Marne is considered a turning point in the war. After the French victory in northern France, the Western Front settled into a **stalemate**, a situation in which neither side can defeat the other. The opposing armies dug in—literally. They sought protection from opponents' gunfire by concealing themselves in trenches, or long ditches in the ground, that were fortified with barbed wire. What followed became known as **trench warfare**.

Soldiers were constantly miserable, eating and sleeping in the muddy trenches as they fought a nonstop battle

German soldiers in a trench in Ypres, Belgium, take advantage of a break during the fighting to read newspapers.

against rats and lice and suffered from boredom and disease. As the war continued, troops dug deeper trenches and linked them into networks that included supply posts, kitchens, and first-aid stations.

Battle lines established during this time in Belgium and northern France hardly shifted as the war continued, but not for lack of trying. Soldiers were regularly ordered to climb "over the top" of trenches and charge enemy positions. Their chances of breaking through the battlefront were small, and their chances of dying were high.

Charging troops faced rapid-firing machine guns and **artillery**, large field guns that fire high-explosive shells. They were also often bombarded with chemical weapons. Clouds of chlorine gas and a much deadlier chemical, phosgene, attacked victims' lungs, and mustard gas blistered people's skin. And in spite of soldiers' heroic efforts, neither side made much progress.

Trench warfare had many victims. In the 19th century, cavalry units led by officers on horses were the pride of European armies. But animals had no place in industrialized warfare. Like thousands of men that they served, millions of horses were killed by barbed wire, artillery, and poison gas.

A GLOBAL CONFLICT

In 1914, while fighting raged on the Western Front, Austria-Hungary launched an invasion north into Russia's Polish provinces. The Russian army forced the Austro-Hungarian army to retreat and then threatened to invade Germany's heavily industrialized northeast. The Germans beat the Russian troops back. Russia lost many men in these early battles, and by the end of September 1914 it had suffered some 250,000 casualties—soldiers captured, wounded, or killed. The Eastern Front later expanded farther into Russia.

Austria-Hungary invaded Serbia in late August 1914. Their two armies clashed for months, but neither side could gain a complete victory. By the end of the year, the Serbs had driven enemy forces from their country. Warfare on the Balkan Front, however, resumed in 1915.

Other regions experienced a similar series of battles. In 1915, an Italian army invaded Austria-Hungary in hopes of seizing lands it claimed belonged to Italy. Fighting on the Italian Front would continue into 1917. Also in 1915, a British naval force opened the Southern Front by attacking the Ottoman Empire. The Ottomans had joined the Central Powers in October 1914 partly because, in the late 19th century, German banks, businesses, and manufacturers had invested heavily in the Ottoman economy. Ottoman leaders saw an alliance with Germany as protection against the French, British, and Russians. You will learn more about how the opening of this Southern Front brought the peoples of Egypt, Syria, and India into World War I.

Another alliance carried the Great War to East Asia. In 1902, Japan had sought support against Russian aggression by allying itself with Britain. After World War I began, Japan sided with the Allies and declared war against Germany. Japan, however, did not play a major role in the war beyond seizing German colonial holdings in China and occupying German islands in the Pacific.

German colonies in Africa also came under attack. In 1915, soldiers from the Union of South Africa captured German South West Africa, present-day Namibia. In East Africa, a German general led his African troops on raids against invading British forces, which were largely composed of soldiers from India. Local Africans were forced to carry loads for the European armies, and many died when famine spread in the wake of war.

Troops from Australia, New Zealand, India, Canada, and other nations with links to Britain fought for the Allies. One former British colony joined the Allies in April 1917. That nation, the United States, would play a major role in the remainder of the war.

HISTORICAL THINKING

1. **READING CHECK** Why was the Great War a worldwide struggle?

2. **MAKE INFERENCES** Based on what you have read, what can you infer about the effectiveness of trench warfare?

3. **INTERPRET MAPS** How did Germany's geographic location affect its strategy for fighting the Great War?

1.3

MAIN IDEA The Great War's new weapons technologies, military strategies, and civilian involvement set off the deadliest war yet.

The Course to the End

Although industrialization brought many new and helpful technologies to Europe, it also led to the development of destructive advancements. Powerful new military weapons would add to the horror and devastation of warfare.

German sailors crowd together in the engine room of an oil-burning submarine.

WEAPONS OF WAR

During the First World War, the goal of the Allies and the Central Powers was the same: win at all costs. This contest was, after all, a total war. As a result of this approach, millions of people—soldiers and civilians—died. The weapons used in this armed conflict contributed greatly to the enormous number of killed and wounded.

Europeans dominated many areas of the world in part because of their innovations in firearms technology. Soldiers carried semiautomatic pistols that had higher rates of fire than older revolvers, and artillery pieces fired faster as well. The heavy, single-barrel machine guns used in colonial warfare during the 1890s were made lighter and more mobile by the time of World War I.

These new technologies and other improvements came into play during the Battle of Verdun, on the Western Front in France. In February 1916, the Germans attacked the fortress of Verdun with artillery and machine guns, and the French defended their positions with the same deadly weapons. The Germans also lobbed more

702 CHAPTER 25

than 100,000 shells of poison phosgene gas at their enemy, although another piece of modern technology—the gas mask—prevented mass French casualties.

To monitor the progress of its soldiers on the ground, the Germans took to the air. They employed 168 airplanes, 14 observation balloons, and 4 airships known as zeppelins. At first, the aircraft mainly tracked troop movements. Later in the conflict, German and French pilots engaged in "dogfights" over Verdun. In these close-range aerial battles, pilots often fired pistols at their opponents.

The Battle of Verdun lasted until December 1916, when the Germans had to retreat for lack of resources. After 10 months of fighting, neither side had taken much territory. Casualties were fairly equal too—337,000 Germans killed or wounded and somewhat more for the French. Like much of the area throughout the Western Front, the environment surrounding Verdun had been pulverized. Trenches and huge craters left by artillery shells dotted the landscape. A forest of oak and chestnut trees lay shattered. At least one nearby village was completely destroyed.

In 1916, Britain introduced a new and menacing weapon: the tank. The British first used this technology in September at the Battle of the Somme in France. As one German soldier remarked, the tanks "advanced relentlessly. . . . Holes, hills, rocks, even barbed wire meant nothing." From inside the vehicle, the crew fired machine guns at enemy positions.

THE WAR AT SEA

Much of the Great War was fought at sea. Germany and Britain had engaged in a naval arms race dating from about 1900. In 1906,

THROUGH THE LENS JEFF GUSKY

The Hidden World of the Great War

Descriptions of conditions on the Western Front usually paint a picture of dejected soldiers crouched in a muddy ditch, bullets whizzing overhead. National Geographic Explorer Jeff Gusky, who is a photographer and also an emergency medicine physician, took his camera underground to document a less hostile side of trench warfare.

In northern France, deep below Earth's surface, Gusky entered a network of ancient limestone rock quarries. During the First World War, the quarries were transformed into underground cities that had electric lights, telephones, housing, offices, hospitals, and a rail line. In this hidden world, troops from both sides of the war found refuge from the mud, noise, and terror of the battlefield.

These soldiers realized that the limestone could be carved, and many of them left their names and addresses in the stone walls. Others chiseled images that represented their families, their homes, their religious views, or their states of mind. Gusky first captured these carvings in a series of black-and-white photographs, and a Smithsonian Channel 2017 documentary shows his further examinations of this underground world. According to Gusky's website, he wants "to inspire belief in a future where we find hope in the human decency and courage of ordinary people and safety in seeing human nature for what it is . . . permanently imperfect."

This underground chapel, tucked away from a French hospital in a limestone quarry, offered a place for World War I soldiers to seek solace and temporarily escape the horrors of the battle above.

the British unveiled a newly designed battleship—the H.M.S. *Dreadnought*—that was bigger, faster, and more powerful than any existing warship. By 1914, Britain had built 30 more *Dreadnought*-style ships.

The Germans were determined to keep up with the British, long considered "masters of the sea." German engineers produced their own version of the new British battleship. When World War I broke out, Germany had 13 of its own large, formidable warships. The navies of both nations were prepared for battle.

After the war was underway, the British used their superior naval resources to prevent merchant ships from entering the North Sea and German ports. Britain sharply limited German imports of food and raw materials from overseas, and Germany intended to break this blockade. In 1916, German battleships faced off against British battleships in the North Sea off Jutland, or mainland Denmark.

At the Battle of Jutland, the two fleets clashed from May 31 to June 2, their big guns blazing. Both countries lost many sailors, and their ships were heavily damaged. Even though both sides claimed victory, the blockade continued. Jutland was the last major sea battle of the war that did not include airplanes or another development in military technology: the submarine.

France designed and built the first submarines in the late 19th century. By 1914, France, Britain, Russia, and Germany each had at least three dozen submarines. The Germans had the fewest, but they saw the value of U-boats (short for *unterseeboot*, or "undersea boat") to their war effort. As the war persisted, technologically advanced German U-boats continually launched torpedo attacks against Allied merchant and military ships.

ON THE HOME FRONT

Soldiers fighting on the various military fronts relied on their home country's resources—human and material—to support them. The term *home front*, used to describe the activities of civilians in support of the troops, reflects the nature of the First World War as a total war. Everyone had to participate to keep the war machine running.

Governments expanded their powers to mobilize their economies and keep them strong. In Germany, state agencies assumed control of production, labor, wages, and prices, while other European powers established some form of national economic planning as well. As a result, the free market was restricted. To blunt opposition to their policies, governments also often limited civil liberties such as freedom of speech and freedom of assembly.

For European women, the war brought opportunities. The nursing profession expanded, and women took on greater responsibilities in factories and on family farms. However, women also paid a high price. They toiled long hours on extra shifts in factories, often in dangerous conditions, to make up for the labor shortage. They raised their children on their own, and they feared for their husbands, brothers, and sons in combat zones.

Total war also brought the violence of the battlefield to the home front. Many civilians living in or near an area of conflict were killed unintentionally, but in January 1915, for the first time, civilians were specifically targeted in war. With the Western Front at an impasse, the Germans sent two zeppelins across the North Sea to Britain. There, the airships dropped bombs on two coastal towns, killing several people.

Nations also engaged in economic warfare. Britain's blockade of the North Sea deprived Germans of food and other resources, and similar blockades had similar effects. German U-boats prowling the Mediterranean Sea regularly sunk Allied supply ships headed for the Balkan Front or the Southern Front. The French barricaded Ottoman territory in the eastern Mediterranean.

Britain managed to maintain its troop strength through volunteers. Other governments relied on conscription, which you learned is forced enrollment in the armed services. Universal military service was the rule in Germany, and every French man was expected to serve his country.

Russian conscripts were mainly peasants, and morale among them was poor; they did not want to fight and die for the tsar. Sometimes they just dropped their weapons on the battlefield and walked home. Life for Russian civilians was no better. The disruption of food production led to famine, and factories shut down for lack of capital. In March 1917, Russian revolutionaries overthrew the tsar, and a year later, Russia signed a peace treaty with Germany. You will learn more about the Russian Revolution later in this chapter.

AMERICAN ENTRY INTO THE WAR

With the Eastern Front stabilized, Germany could move its forces from Russia to the Western Front, end the stalemate there, and achieve victory. France and Britain needed help. It came from the United States.

When the Great War started in 1914, the United States had only a small army. Americans at the time tended

The May 8, 1915, edition of the *New York Times* reported details of the *Lusitania* attack on its front page.

to agree with the viewpoint that George Washington held more than a century earlier. He believed that the republic should not "entangle our peace and prosperity in the toils of European ambition." U.S. neutrality in the war had brought the nation benefits, including profitable exports to Britain and France that boosted U.S. industry without any military cost.

The United States entered the war largely in response to Germany's submarine warfare. In 1915, a German U-boat sank the R.M.S. *Lusitania*, a privately owned British passenger ship that had many Americans onboard. After U.S. president **Woodrow Wilson** protested the unprovoked action, Germany promised to stop attacking ships without warning them first.

In January 1917, Germany foreign secretary Arthur Zimmermann, a backer of unregulated submarine attacks, sent a coded telegram to the Mexican president. He proposed that, in return for financial support, Mexico ally itself with Germany and "reconquer the lost territory in Texas, New Mexico, and Arizona." Britain intercepted the **Zimmermann Telegram**, translated it, and forwarded it to the United States in February.

That same month, Germany restored its policy of unrestricted submarine warfare against all shipping by any nation and sank three U.S. ships in March. President Wilson then asked Congress to declare war, proclaiming that "the world must be made safe for democracy." Congress complied with his request on April 6, 1917. The arrival of a million-strong U.S. force in Europe was the turning point in favor of the Allied cause. On November 11, 1918, the Germans signed an **armistice**, an agreement to end hostilities. The war was over.

HISTORICAL THINKING

1. **READING CHECK** How did new technology influence the Great War?

2. **MAKE GENERALIZATIONS** How did the Battle of Verdun echo the general experience of the armies fighting on the Western Front?

3. **ANALYZE CAUSE AND EFFECT** Why do you think governments limited freedom of speech and assembly during the war?

4. **FORM AND SUPPORT OPINIONS** Do you think that the United States should have remained neutral instead of involving itself in European affairs? Explain your response.

The First World War and 20th-Century Revolutions

1.4

MAIN IDEA The recruitment by Britain and France of soldiers from throughout their colonial empires reflected the global nature of the Great War.

Global Dimensions of Total War

In the past, historians writing about the First World War generally focused on the Western Front and on the Europeans who fought there, which left a lot of the story uncovered. They now have a better idea of the worldwide range of this conflict.

GALLIPOLI: AN EXAMPLE OF GLOBAL WAR

By the time the United States joined the Allies in 1917, the Great War was truly a world war. Battles took place in various regions of Europe, Asia, and Africa. The theaters of war—areas of land, sea, or air directly involved in military operations—also included the North Sea, Mediterranean Sea, and Atlantic and Pacific oceans.

In 1915, with the Western Front in stalemate, Allied military leaders looked for a major victory elsewhere. They decided that the Ottoman Empire, the weakest of the Central Powers, could be defeated fairly quickly. They were wrong.

The Allies' Ottoman strategy called for taking the Dardanelles. This narrow strait is part of a waterway that leads from the Mediterranean Sea to the Black Sea. The Ottoman capital, Constantinople, was located between these two bodies of water, along the Sea of Marmara. Controlling the Dardanelles and then capturing Constantinople would open up the waterway as a badly needed Allied supply route to Russia. This defeat would also likely knock the Ottoman Empire out of the war.

In February 1915, fully armed British and French battleships tried to force their way through the thin channel. Ottoman artillery, fired from the heights above the port of Gallipoli, pushed them back. The Allies shifted to a new strategy.

In April, Britain and France attacked the heavily fortified high ground. These ground troops included soldiers from Australia, New Zealand, Ireland, India, Arabia, and Senegal. The Ottomans fiercely defended their positions. The Allies resorted to trench warfare, but they were overmatched. In January 1916, having experienced 250,000 casualties, they withdrew.

This Senegalese Sharpshooter fighting for "the greater glory of France" is most likely a West African Muslim. He wears several German helmets atop his head.

MOBILIZATION OF COLONIAL SUBJECTS

In the wake of their losses at Gallipoli, British leaders decided they could no longer spare men or war materials from their home islands to fight on the Southern Front. Instead, they relied on army units from their African and Asian colonies.

The British army sent Jamaican soldiers from its West Indian Regiment against the Ottomans in Palestine. The majority of troops in that theater were Egyptian soldiers under British command. Meanwhile, Indian soldiers engaged Ottoman forces in Mesopotamia. India also supplied troops to fight on the Western Front, and by the end of the war, Britain had mobilized some 1.5 million Indians.

To help their effort against the Ottomans, the British formed an alliance with Arab leaders eager to overthrow Turkish rule. Having been promised an independent Arab kingdom after the war, Arab fighters conducted guerrilla strikes against Ottoman positions. Elsewhere, Egyptian forces helped the British take Jerusalem, and Indian troops captured Baghdad. Many of these allied soldiers were Muslims.

France, who did little fighting outside of Europe, also looked to its empire for support. At the start of the war, colonial French troops numbered around 90,000. The most famous regiment was the Senegalese Sharpshooters, who were mostly young Muslims. Of the 130,000 of these highly disciplined soldiers sent to the Western Front, around 30,000 died and many more were wounded.

When the number of volunteers from its imperial possessions in Africa did not meet wartime demand, France turned to conscription. French officials pressured local African leaders to supply troops for the French army. France ended up recruiting more than 400,000 men from its African colonies. Most of them served in Africa as laborers or as porters, carrying supplies for the army.

In Southeast Asia, the French recruited young Vietnamese men for the Indochinese Labor Corps. These young conscripts worked on the Western Front, behind the battle lines. They performed tedious tasks such as digging fortifications and maintaining roads, which allowed the French army to concentrate more troops on the front line. At the same time, rice and rubber from Indochina were exported to France to further support the war effort.

The Indians, West Africans, and Vietnamese who served as volunteers or conscripts contributed greatly to the Allied victory in the war, as did the civilians in colonial territories who produced coffee, rubber, tin, and many other goods for imperial forces. However, they received little in return. Later, anti-colonial nationalists would base their claims to greater self-government or independence on the sacrifices they made during World War I.

Members of an Indian cavalry march near the Franco-Belgian border in 1915.

The Allied troops entrenched at Gallipoli suffered through trying environmental conditions. The heat, poor sanitation, and intestinal diseases all served to sap soldiers' strength. One British soldier still remembered the flies, long after the Gallipoli campaign had ended.

PRIMARY SOURCE

One of the biggest curses was the flies. There was millions and millions and millions of flies. The whole of the side of the trench used to be one black swarming mass. Anything you opened, if you opened a tin of bully [canned beef] or went to eat a biscuit [cookie], next minute it would be swarming with flies. They were all around your mouth and on any cuts or sores that you'd got. . . . It was a curse, really, it really was.

—from an oral history by British private Harold Boughton, 1984

HISTORICAL THINKING

1. **READING CHECK** What two strategies did the Allies employ to attack the Ottoman Empire between 1915 and 1916?
2. **MAKE INFERENCES** Why do you think it was so important to the Allies to "knock the Ottoman Empire out of the war"?
3. **DRAW CONCLUSIONS** How did colonial conscripts feel about fighting for France?

2.1

MAIN IDEA The Treaty of Versailles officially ended the Great War but failed to bring stability and security to Germany, Eastern Europe, or Southwest Asia.

Postwar Treaties and Conflicts

After the First World War, the victors had an opportunity to put world affairs on a new, more stable, and peaceful path. Would their decisions ensure a better future for themselves as well as for those they defeated?

POSTWAR SETTLEMENTS

Recall that the entry of the United States into World War I tipped the balance toward the Allies, which put the United States in a position to influence the peace talks that followed the armistice. Those meetings took place in Versailles, just outside Paris, in 1919. The Central Powers were excluded from the Paris Peace Conference, as were Asians and Africans whose fates were also to be determined.

As diplomats headed to the conference, a lethal outbreak of influenza was racing around the world. Between 1918 and 1920, as many as 50 million people died from it, far more than those who had lost their lives during the war itself. This **pandemic**, or worldwide outbreak of infectious disease, further deepened the global distress resulting from the Great War. The world seemed changed in some fundamental way, leaving people uncertain about the future.

In this charged atmosphere, representatives of the Allies gathered in Versailles. They faced the enormous challenge of reincorporating a defeated Germany into Europe as well as addressing the postwar collapse of the Austro-Hungarian and Ottoman empires. Their declines left entire regions of central Europe and Southwest Asia in need of new political systems.

U.S. president Wilson presented a plan known as the Fourteen Points in a speech to Congress months before the war ended. The plan contained recommendations based on a few clear principles. Wilson called for freedom of navigation on the seas and progress toward free trade, and he spoke against treaties drawn up in secret. He supported the right of people to engage in **self-determination**—the process by which a people forms its own state and chooses its own government. He also proposed the creation of a permanent international assembly to safeguard against future wars.

The other Allies, however, had their own agendas. The British wanted to safeguard their imperial interests. The French priority was to penalize Germany. And the Italians wanted some of Austria-Hungary's territory.

In the end, the **Treaty of Versailles**, signed in June 1919, fell far short of Wilson's goals. Britain and France held to their imperialist ambitions, refusing to encourage self-determination in their colonies. France insisted on punishing Germany. The Germans had to hand over all of their colonial possessions and about 10 percent of their territory, which included the return of Alsace-Lorraine to France.

The Allies forced Germany and Austria-Hungary to take the blame for starting the war, in what is known as the "war-guilt" clause of the treaty. Germany also had to agree to provide **reparations**—money or goods paid to cover wartime damages—totaling some $33 billion. To keep Germany from starting another conflict, the Allies limited the size of its army and banned it from producing tanks, submarines, and other weapons of war.

The Allies did not ignore all of Wilson's ideas. They accepted his plan for a **League of Nations**, the assembly of sovereign states that intended to provide a permanent diplomatic forum in hopes of avoiding future conflict. However, the U.S. Senate rejected membership in the league and refused to ratify the Treaty of Versailles, thus returning to the United States' prewar position of avoiding entanglement in European affairs.

NATION-BUILDING IN EUROPE

The German Empire ended in November 1918, when Wilhelm II abdicated. In 1919, as peace talks took place in France, the German assembly established a liberal, democratic constitution and a government known as the **Weimar Republic**. The new government faced enormous challenges. At the war's end, the German people were hungry, cold, and dejected. The treaty's

708 CHAPTER 25

Territorial Changes in Europe After World War I

Legend:
- Boundaries of German, Russian, and Austro-Hungarian empires in 1914
- Areas lost by Austro-Hungarian Empire
- Areas lost by German Empire
- Areas lost by Russian Empire
- Areas lost by Bulgaria
- Demilitarized Zones

huge reparation payments undermined Germany's recovery, and its military and territorial reductions wounded the people's national pride.

German centrists in the government tried to promote the liberal political culture needed to sustain a free society. Other and more radical elements opposed them, leading to uprisings, an attempt to seize power, and general instability. By 1923, the republic was struggling. It could not pay reparations. The government printed more money, but that caused inflation to spiral out of control. By 1925, the situation began to improve. International agreements eased Germany's reparations payments, the economy returned to prewar levels, and Germany was offered membership in the League of Nations.

Postwar diplomacy created new nations in eastern, central, and southeastern Europe, but nearly all of them proved to be unstable. They were prone to **authoritarianism**, a political system characterized by a powerful leader and limited individual freedoms. The complex mix of ethnic, linguistic, and religious groups in these regions made democratic government difficult, especially when leaders targeted minority groups.

The slide toward authoritarian rule arose mainly from a conflict between two ideologies. Nationalism, you may recall, stresses loyalty to the nation-state, while liberalism focuses on the rights of individuals within the state. Nationalists also had an "us versus them" view of the world. They tended to restrict the rights of minorities rather than follow the liberal philosophy of protecting the individual rights of all people, regardless of their ethnic background. The problem was particularly acute for groups such as Europe's Jews and Roma (formerly called Gypsies), neither of whom had an official state of their own to protect them.

HISTORICAL THINKING

1. **READING CHECK** What key goals kept the British and French from supporting Wilson's Fourteen Points?

2. **IDENTIFY PROBLEMS AND SOLUTIONS** Why did the representatives at the peace talks near Paris agree to form the League of Nations?

3. **MAKE INFERENCES** How did the reparations clause of the Treaty of Versailles stifle Germany's economic recovery?

The First World War and 20th-Century Revolutions

2.2 DOCUMENT-BASED QUESTION
The Paris Peace Conference

How would you feel if you could not determine your own future and, instead, a group of powerful people determined it for you? At the Paris Peace Conference in 1919, four countries—Britain, France, Italy, and the United States—made decisions that affected the political and economic future of much of the world.

In 1919, delegates from the victorious nations traveled to France for the Paris Peace Conference. Concerned about the outcome of those negotiations, representatives from defeated nations like Germany and spokespeople for African, Southeast Asian, and Arab societies entangled in European empires also came to Paris, but they were not allowed to participate in peace talks. They could only wait to see what the Allies would decide for them.

Syrian nationalists had sided with Britain against the Ottoman Empire during the war, and after the fighting ceased Syria wanted independence. Influenced by Woodrow Wilson's Fourteen Points, a young nationalist named Nguyen Ai Quoc (later known as Ho Chi Minh) sought greater autonomy for Vietnam. And the Pan-African Congress demanded an end to colonial rule.

W.E.B. Du Bois (doo BOYS)—an African-American scholar, journalist, and social reformer—helped organize the first formal Pan-African Congress in 1919 in Paris. Nearly 60 representatives from 15 nations joined Du Bois in France to ask the Allies and their associates to "establish a code of laws for the international protection of the natives of Africa."

DOCUMENT ONE

Primary Source: Resolution from the "Congress of Damascus Resolution" by the General Syrian Congress of Damascus, July 2, 1919

Article 22 of the Covenant, or formal agreement, of the League of Nations classified Syria as one of the territories "not yet able to stand by themselves under the strenuous conditions of the modern world." France was assigned to provide advice and assistance until Syria was "able to stand alone." The Syrian Congress passed a resolution that attempted to stop France from applying Article 22.

CONSTRUCTED RESPONSE Why would an independent Syrian government, as described in the excerpt, appeal to the expressed democratic ideals of France, Britain, and the United States?

We ask that the Government of this Syrian country should be a democratic civil constitutional Monarchy on broad decentralization principles, safeguarding the rights of minorities. . . .

Considering the fact that the Arabs inhabiting the Syrian area are not naturally less [capable] than other more advanced races . . . we protest against Article 22 of the Covenant of the League of Nations, placing us among the nations in their middle stage of development which stand in need of a mandatory power. . . .

We do not acknowledge any right claimed by the French Government in any part whatever of our Syrian country.

DOCUMENT TWO

Primary Source: Petition from "Eight Points" by Nguyen Ai Quoc, 1919

Nguyen Ai Quoc drafted and submitted an eight-point petition to the Paris Peace Conference. His demands reflected Wilson's call for self-determination as well as Thomas Jefferson's ideas about equality and rights. Nguyen aimed his requests at "the governments of the Allied Powers in general, and the French government in particular."

CONSTRUCTED RESPONSE According to the petition, did Nguyen demand independence for Vietnam? Explain your response.

1. General amnesty for all Vietnamese political prisoners.
2. Equal rights for Vietnamese and French in Indochina, suppression of the Criminal Commissions which are instruments of terrorism aimed at Vietnamese patriots.
3. Freedom of press and opinion.
4. Freedom of association and assembly.
5. Freedom to travel at home and abroad.
6. Freedom to study and the opening of technical and professional schools for natives of the colonies.
7. Substitute rule of law for government by decree.
8. Appointment of a Vietnamese delegation alongside that of the French government to settle questions related to Vietnamese interests.

DOCUMENT THREE

Primary Source: Manifesto from "To the World" by the Second Pan-African Congress, 1921

In 1921, the Second Pan-African Congress met in London, Brussels, and Paris. Delegates came from Africa, the Caribbean, Europe, and the United States. These representatives produced a manifesto in hopes of persuading the Allied powers to encourage and support self-determination in Africa and around the world.

CONSTRUCTED RESPONSE What political demands did the Second Pan-African Congress delegates make in their manifesto?

The absolute equality of races, physical, political, and social, is the founding stone of world peace and human advancement. . . . The beginning of wisdom in interracial contact is the establishment of political institutions among suppressed [conquered] peoples. The habit of democracy must be made to encircle the earth. . . . Local self-government with a minimum of help and oversight can be established tomorrow in Asia, in Africa, in America and in the Isles of the Sea.

SYNTHESIZE & WRITE

1. **REVIEW** Review what you have learned about the political desires of colonial peoples after the Great War.
2. **RECALL** On your own paper, list two details about the person or organization that produced one of the excerpts and two details about the excerpt itself.
3. **CONSTRUCT** Construct a topic sentence that answers this question: What kind of political system did colonial peoples favor?
4. **WRITE** Using evidence from the documents, write a paragraph that supports your topic sentence in Step 3.

2.3

MAIN IDEA In 1915, the Ottoman government expelled its Armenian population in a forced relocation that killed over a million people, an action that most historians consider genocide.

The Armenian Genocide

Imagine being told by government officials that you must leave your home. They give you barely any time to sell your possessions and pack your things. Armed guards march you, your family, and all your neighbors out of your village. You have no idea where they will take you. Many Armenians faced this exact fate in the Ottoman Empire.

CRITICAL VIEWING Yepraksia Gevorgyan (seated) and her family escaped the Armenian genocide by crossing the Akhurian River, pictured in the large photographic panel behind her, in 1915. She remembers the river, now bordering Armenia and Turkey, as "red, full of blood" after the Ottomans threw dead Armenians into the water. What does the panel add to this portrait of Gevorgyan?

NATIONALISM, REBELLION, AND WAR

Anatolia (present-day Turkey) was the core territory of the Ottoman Empire. Most Armenians in the empire lived as peasant farmers in eastern Anatolia. They considered this mountainous region their homeland, although they remained a minority within it. Armenians also lived just across Anatolia's northeastern border in the Caucasus region of southern Russia.

For centuries, Armenian Christians had flourished in the Ottoman Empire. But rising Turkish nationalism made their situation less comfortable, and by the 1880s, some Armenian leaders began to call for a nation of their own. Ottoman leaders refused to listen to Armenian demands because Armenian self-determination could lead to the breakup of their empire.

During World War I, the Ottomans faced an invasion by Russia across their northeastern border. Some Armenian revolutionaries fought alongside the Russians and otherwise aided the Russian army against the Ottoman troops. Pressured by events on the Eastern Front, Russia chose to pull its forces out of Ottoman territory.

DEPORTATIONS AND DEATH

Ottoman leaders decided that because some Armenians were aiding enemy Russians, the leaders were justified in taking radical steps against them. In the first few months of 1915, government orders led to the murder of many Armenian leaders and soldiers as well as Armenian villagers thought to support Russia. These human rights violations were just the beginning of the retaliations. Mehmed Talaat Pasha (meh-MEHT tah-LAHT pah-SHAH), a top Ottoman leader, ordered a series of mass **deportations**, or removals, of Armenians from eastern Anatolia and other areas.

From the spring through the fall of 1915, entire Armenian villages were emptied. Able-bodied men were killed. Women, children, and the elderly were forced to march southward through the mountainous terrain of eastern Anatolia. Most Armenians who survived this trek ended up in camps in the Syrian Desert. Others were sent farther east into an arid, hostile region of Mesopotamia. Often left without food or shelter, many died of starvation or exposure to the desert environment.

> Henry Morgenthau wrote a book at the end of the First World War. In it, he cites a conversation with Talaat Pasha in which the Ottoman leader clarifies why his government began deporting Armenians in August 1915. Talaat Pasha was assassinated in 1921 in Berlin by an Armenian nationalist.
>
> **PRIMARY SOURCE**
>
> "I have asked you to come to-day," began Talaat, "so that I can explain our position on the whole Armenian subject. We base our objections to the Armenians on three distinct grounds. In the first place, they have enriched themselves at the expense of the Turks. In the second place, they are determined to domineer over us and to establish a separate state. In the third place, they have openly encouraged our enemies. They have assisted the Russians in the Caucasus and our failure there is largely explained by their actions. We have therefore come to the irrevocable decision that we shall make them powerless before this war is ended."
>
> —from *Ambassador Morgenthau's Story* by Henry Morgenthau, 1918

As U.S. ambassador to the Ottoman Empire from 1913 to 1916, Henry Morgenthau had access to information about the mass Armenian deportations. On July 16, 1915, he wrote a telegram to the U.S. secretary of state describing what he had learned. "Deportation of and excesses against peaceful Armenians is increasing," he explained, "and from harrowing reports of eyewitnesses it appears that a campaign of race extermination is in progress under a pretext of reprisal against rebellion." In spite of his report, the U.S. government failed to act. Since the United States had not officially declared war on the Ottoman Empire and no American rights had been violated, President Wilson did not encourage intervention.

Historians generally agree that what Morgenthau called "race extermination" amounted to an Armenian genocide. Hundreds of thousands of Armenians— perhaps as many as 1.5 million—died during the deportation period. Many others escaped into neighboring countries, where relief organizations such as the International Red Cross supplied desperately needed aid to the survivors. Most Armenians would never return to their homes. They had lost their property, their possessions, and for many, their families.

HISTORICAL THINKING

1. **READING CHECK** Why did some Armenians clash with Ottoman leadership?
2. **DRAW CONCLUSIONS** Why do you think the U.S. government did not take action to stop the deportations?
3. **ANALYZE SOURCES** What reasons did Mehmed Talaat Pasha give the U.S. ambassador for the Ottoman government's deportation of the Armenians?

2.4

MAIN IDEA After World War I, members of the League of Nations set up a Mandate System by which Allies—mainly Britain and France—took charge of former German colonies and Ottoman provinces.

Expanding European Imperialism

The triumphant Allied powers viewed the former colonies and provinces of the German and Ottoman empires as weak regions that needed authority figures to oversee them. This paternalistic attitude reinforced the victors' greed to exploit their new territories.

THE MANDATE SYSTEM

After the war, the fate of former German colonies and Ottoman provinces lay with the Allies. To govern those peoples, the Allies devised the **Mandate System**, which was authorized by Article 22 of the League of Nations Covenant. The covenant mandated, or empowered, "advanced nations" to rule over certain territories until the "advanced" leaders felt that the peoples in those areas were ready to govern themselves. Race was the unspoken but key factor in determining which colonies and provinces were considered capable of self-rule.

In Africa, the Mandate System allowed the French, British, Belgian, and South African governments to take over former German colonies. Britain added German East Africa (present-day Tanzania) to its assets, France expanded its West African holdings, and Belgium enlarged its Central African empire. The Mandate System required reports to the League of Nations from each European nation showing that they were furthering "native rights." Instead, European nations ruled the mandated territories like traditional colonies. They did little or nothing to prepare people in these regions for eventual self-determination.

Still, the ideal of national self-rule inspired a new generation of African nationalists. In South Africa, leaders of the African National Congress called for greater rights. In West Africa, returning war veterans promoted an awareness of Africa's role in the wider world. More African students left to study in Europe and the United States and returned to their home countries questioning the concept of colonial rule.

THE BALFOUR DECLARATION

Many of today's complications in Southwest Asia can be traced to several contradictory promises made by the British during World War I. First, to secure Arab help in defeating the Ottomans, the British pledged to support an independent Arab state. At the same time, Britain and France secretly agreed to divide Ottoman provinces—including Arab lands—between them after the war. Finally, Britain backed the Zionists, or Jewish nationalists, and their dream for a Jewish homeland.

In the **Balfour Declaration**, the British government agreed to help create a "national home" for the Jewish people in what was then Ottoman Palestine. Zionists hoped to establish their own state on the site of the ancient Hebrew kingdoms. Zionism had originated in the later 19th century among European Jews who were alarmed by persistent anti-Semitism. Zionists argued that a nation-state was necessary to the security of Jews and to represent their interests in the world.

At the end of the war, the British occupied Palestine. In 1920, they began permitting Jews to settle there. By 1922, when the League of Nations approved a British mandate in Palestine, Jewish immigration was steadily increasing. However, more than 80 percent of the people living in Palestine were Muslim or Christian Arabs. Palestine was their traditional homeland, and massive Arab demonstrations erupted. When the British responded by cutting back Jewish immigration, Zionist leaders were furious. Political tensions in the territory remained high.

SYRIA AND IRAQ

In 1920, Britain assumed a proposed mandate over three Ottoman provinces. The British stitched those provinces together into a new entity they called Iraq. In 1923, the League of Nations assigned a mandate over Syria and Lebanon to France. Lebanon, a mix of Christians and Muslims, fairly quickly accepted French oversight. Stability was far more difficult to achieve in Syria.

As you have read, the Syrian Congress of Damascus refused to accept French authority over their country. In March 1920, the Syrian Congress declared Faisal al-Hashemi king of Syria. When Faisal rejected French authority, France imposed it by force. Faisal, a Sunni Muslim, then fled to Baghdad, where the British agreed to install him as king of Iraq.

Iraq was unstable at the start. An artificial creation, it was divided among the Shiite majority in the south, a Sunni minority in the center, and a Kurdish-dominated region in the north. Britain's installation of Faisal as king caused friction because Shiite Iraqis resented the Sunnis' rise to political power. Nationalist opposition to British control and a shared goal of establishing an Arab state, however, helped foster unity between the Sunni and Shiite populations.

British and French leaders viewed their mandated territories as spoils of war—profits they were entitled to as victors. Both countries assumed they would retain their global empires after the war. But the world had changed. Britain had been forced to cash in many foreign investments to pay for the war, and it also took on significant debts, especially to the United States. Western European global economic supremacy was declining. Simultaneously, the forces of anti-colonial nationalism were on the rise through Africa and Asia. The British and French could not know it, but the age of European empires would soon come to an end.

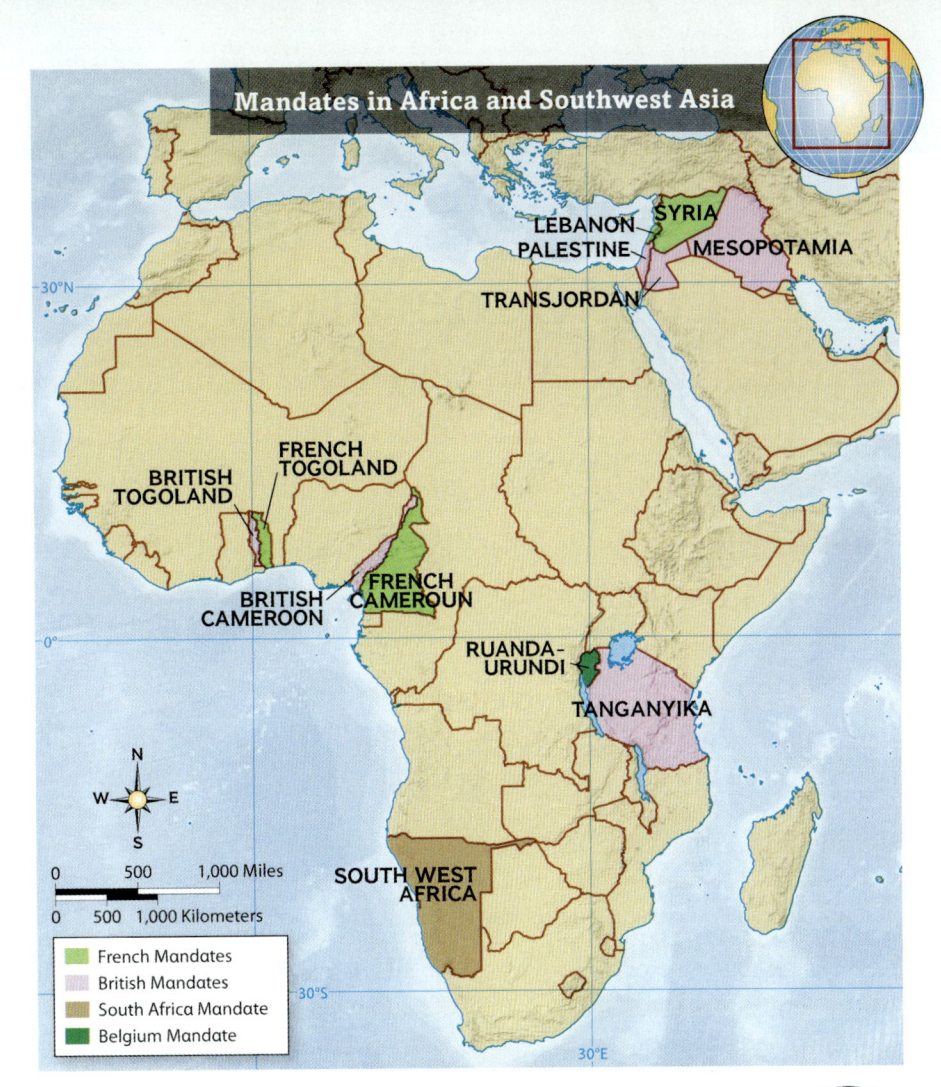

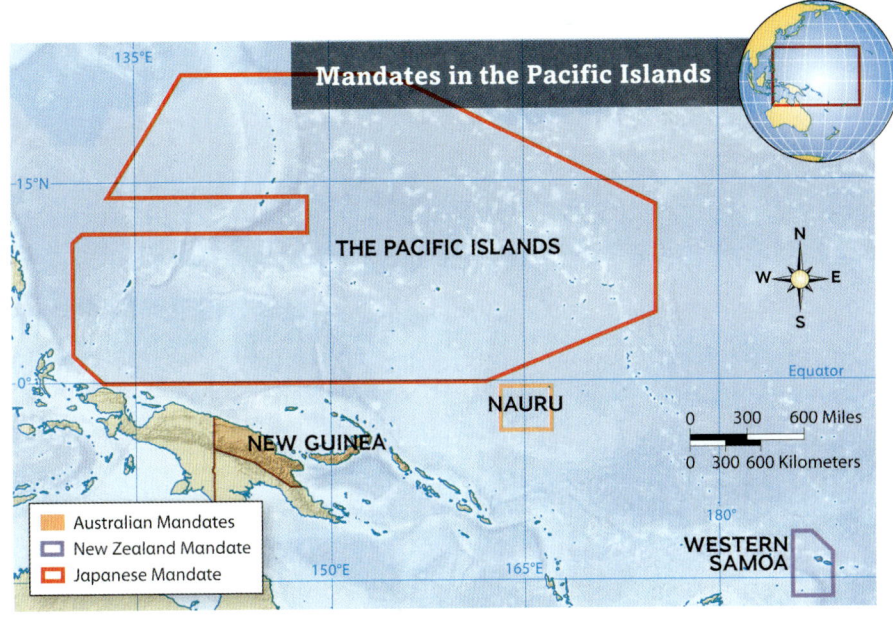

HISTORICAL THINKING

1. **READING CHECK** Why did the mandated territory of Iraq suffer from instability?

2. **MAKE CONNECTIONS** Why were Britain and France the main beneficiaries of the Mandate System?

3. **INTERPRET MAPS** What do you notice about the British and French mandates in Africa and Southwest Asia?

2.5

MAIN IDEA The Great War had an enormous impact on people, society, and the environment for years after the conflict.

The "Lost Generation"

A thunderstorm can be a frightening thing. First comes a bright flash of lightning, followed by a loud crack of thunder. Even indoors, out of danger, the noise can be startling. Soldiers in trenches on World War I battlefields had a similar—but much more terrifying—experience with the thunderous explosions of artillery shells, which haunted them for years to come.

THE GREAT WAR'S LASTING EFFECTS

During and after the First World War, people had to adjust to the harsh realities of existence during a time of total war. Around nine million soldiers, sailors, and airmen died, leaving women without husbands, children without fathers, and parents without sons. In addition, at least five million civilian deaths can be blamed on bombings, famine, and other war-related causes.

The millions of young adults in their teens and twenties who died in the conflict comprise a "**Lost Generation**." Along with their lives, the war wiped away their potential contributions to the world—as leaders, teachers, artists, or scientists. The term, which originally referred to a particular group of writers but is now used generally, applies not just to those who lost their lives but also to everyone who lost their faith in traditional values as a result of the war.

The Great War had a devastating effect on the environment as well. Artillery did the most damage; an array of these field guns could spray projectile bombs, or shells, over a wide expanse. The resulting explosions smashed buildings, roads, trees, and everything else in the area. By the end of the war, the Western Front was largely a wasteland.

CRITICAL VIEWING One hundred years after the Battle of the Somme, morning mist rises from the Beaumont-Hamel Newfoundland Memorial in France. The clash on these grounds began on July 1, 1916, and ended four-and-a-half months later. It is considered one of the bloodiest battles in history: more than one million people were wounded or killed. Why do you think the French chose to preserve the battlefield in this way?

During the five days of the First Battle of the Marne in 1914, the opposing armies fired some 432,000 artillery shells at one another. Artillery shells easily destroyed shallow trenches, and they could also cause deeper trenches to collapse. Soldiers in the trenches could hear the "loud singing, wailing noise" of an incoming shell and knew it could mean death if the shell landed nearby. A German soldier later described how soldiers felt during the shelling: "You cower in a heap alone in a hole," he wrote, "and feel yourself the victim of a pitiless thirst for destruction."

Many who survived the unceasing barrage of rifle, machine-gun, and artillery fire experienced trembling, dizziness, confusion, loss of memory, and sleeplessness. This set of symptoms indicated a condition doctors called **shell shock**, a mental health condition that would later be referred to as combat fatigue or post-traumatic stress disorder (PTSD). Doctors in field hospitals near the front lines had limited means to treat shell-shocked troops. They could, however, save many soldiers whose physical injuries might have killed them in an earlier conflict, such as the U.S. Civil War. Advances in the understanding of infections improved survival rates. So did the use of blood transfusions—transfers of blood from healthy soldiers to patients.

The scientist **Marie Curie**, a winner of the Nobel Prize for physics in 1903 and then for chemistry in 1911, believed that radium, the element she discovered in 1898, had value as a medicine. She also promoted the use of x-rays to diagnose injuries. In France during the Great War, she rode to field hospitals in an ambulance equipped with an x-ray machine.

Soldiers returning home from the battlefield with mental or physical conditions needed care. Hospitals excelled at healing physical wounds, but doctors had no standard way to treat those suffering from severe emotional wounds. Families of shell-shocked soldiers often bore the main burden of care—one more expectation of those on the home front.

The war also disrupted the global economy. Before World War I, living standards were rising rapidly, people were free to migrate across borders, and international trade was booming. After the war, the increase in living standards slowed, nations put up barriers to migration, and tariffs blunted trade. Also, as you have read, governments expanded their powers during the war.

> Ernest Hemingway served as an ambulance driver in World War I. His novels *A Farewell to Arms* and *For Whom the Bell Tolls* reflect that experience. In this brief excerpt from one of his essays, he pointedly expresses his disgust for war.
>
> **PRIMARY SOURCE**
>
> They wrote in the old days that it is sweet and fitting to die for one's country. But in modern war there is nothing sweet nor fitting in your dying. You will die a dog for no good reason.
>
> —from "Notes on the Next War: A Serious Topical Letter" by Ernest Hemingway, 1935

Afterward, especially in Europe and the United States, they used business regulations and income taxes to continue to exert control over the economy.

THE "LOST GENERATION" IN PARIS

The American writer **Gertrude Stein** was an **expatriate**, or person who chooses to live outside his or her home country, who settled in Europe in the early 20th century. A respected art critic, she collected works by **Pablo Picasso** and other artists whose experimental paintings expanded the definition of modern art.

In the 1920s, Stein befriended American novelists **Ernest Hemingway**, F. Scott Fitzgerald, and John Dos Passos, as well as poets Hart Crane and E.E. Cummings. The First World War had left these men feeling disillusioned. They thought the social values they believed in before the war were an illusion and no longer applied to postwar society. Stein hosted a literary salon in Paris that gave them a place to share ideas. Reportedly, she was the first to call these writers the Lost Generation. The label stuck.

Like many postwar artists, the Lost Generation writers created **countercultural** art movements that challenged or rejected existing styles and traditions. Their ways of looking at the world contradicted those of mainstream society. The war, they believed, had radically changed society, and their writings reflected that change.

HISTORICAL THINKING

1. **READING CHECK** What medical advances helped doctors at the battlefront treat soldiers' physical injuries?
2. **IDENTIFY MAIN IDEAS** What was the main cause of shell shock?
3. **MAKE PREDICTIONS** How do you think older members of mainstream society might have reacted to the works of the Lost Generation writers, and why?

3.1 MAIN IDEA A series of revolutions that toppled the monarchy in Russia transformed the country into a communist dictatorship led by Vladimir Lenin.

Lenin and the Bolshevik Revolution

In 1905 and in 1917, people rebelled in Russia because of poor leadership, food shortages, and a war that would not end. The final chapter of the Russian Revolution tells the story of how a group of political radicals forced their way into power.

LENIN THE REVOLUTIONARY

In 1905, the Russian navy was reeling from its humiliating loss to Japan, and Russians had grown disillusioned with their all-powerful tsar, Nicholas II. Worker strikes, student riots, and a general uprising forced the tsar to accept a set of reforms. They included the establishment of the Duma, a representative assembly. Although Russia became, for the first time, a constitutional monarchy, Nicholas and his ministers retained most of the power over the government and the military.

The main Russian revolutionary group at the time, the Social-Democratic Workers' Party, consisted of two socialist factions with opposing plans for Russia: the Mensheviks and the Bolsheviks. The Mensheviks were traditional Marxists. Recall that Karl Marx's ultimate goal was communism, an economic and political system in which all property is public and owned by the central state and in which goods are distributed to everyone according to their needs. Mensheviks believed that a modern industrial economy would have to be built before the workers would be strong enough to seize power.

The Bolsheviks, led by **Vladimir Lenin**, were Marxists who had a more radical ideology. They argued that a small group of revolutionaries

CRITICAL VIEWING The title of this propaganda poster from 1929 translates to "Long Live the First of May." A working man stands on a globe, breaking chains and waving a flag with Vladimir Lenin's profile on it. Based on details from the poster, what inference can you make about the importance of Lenin and the Russian Revolution?

should seize power first and establish a "dictatorship of the proletariat." In communism, the proletariat is the industrial working class, or factory workers. Public outrage over the failures of Russia in the Great War as well as the lack of food and other problems would offer the Bolsheviks the chance to put their beliefs into practice.

In September 1915, a year after World War I began, Nicholas took command of the Russian army. The tsar was an incompetent general, and when the army failed to stop the German invaders, the people blamed him. By early 1917, Russian soldiers were abandoning their posts in droves. The Russian masses, angered by factory closings and the scarcity of food, rioted in the streets of the capital, Petrograd (present-day St. Petersburg). The local military unit supported the people of Petrograd in what they called the February Revolution. This was the first of two uprisings in 1917 that, together, became known as the Russian Revolution. Nicholas was forced to abdicate, which ended the monarchy in Russia.

That summer, the moderate Provisional Government that replaced Nicholas decided to continue fighting against the Central Powers. At that point, though, the Russian people were simply tired of war. Throughout the country, they had begun setting up a new form of social and political organization: the soviet (Russian for "committee"). The soviets were local councils of workers, urban residents, soldiers, and sailors, and anyone could vote for representatives to the councils. A radical form of democracy, the soviets passed laws through public discussion and agreement.

In the capital, the Petrograd Soviet challenged the authority of the Provisional Government. Leon Trotsky, a prominent Bolshevik, gave fiery speeches and organized tirelessly to advance the communist cause. By the fall of 1917, the Bolsheviks, demanding "peace, land, and bread," controlled the Petrograd Soviet.

Lenin and the Bolsheviks made their move, executing a coup and overthrowing the Provisional Government in what is called the October Revolution. Bolshevik forces faced only minimal resistance. Lenin quickly disbanded the Duma and took charge of the government. In just two days, he and the Bolsheviks successfully completed the Russian Revolution.

CIVIL WAR IN RUSSIA

For the Bolsheviks, securing the government was its first goal. In November 1917, they decreed that Russia would withdraw from the Great War. Four months later, in March 1918, the Bolsheviks signed a treaty with Germany officially ending Russian participation in the war. Russia relinquished large swaths of its western territory—including Ukraine, Poland, and Finland—to Germany. Those lands contained at least one-fourth of Russia's citizens and much of Russia's industrial, agricultural, and mineral resources. The Bolsheviks believed that a communist uprising in Germany would return all that land to them.

That same month, the Bolsheviks changed their name to the Russian Communist Party and moved the capital from Petrograd to Moscow. The communists soon found themselves contending with powerful counterrevolutionary forces. Once Russia pulled out of World War I, aristocratic generals turned their attention from fighting the Germans to undoing the revolution.

The Russian Civil War broke out by June 1918. It pitted the communist Red Army against the volunteers of the White Army, a variety of groups that united to oppose the Bolsheviks. The Reds' control of the major cities and their industries gave them an advantage, and so did their army of peasants and workers. The western Allies sent around 60,000 soldiers to help the White Army but limited Allied troops mainly to support roles away from the battlefields.

Lenin took steps to ensure the survival of his new government. In July 1918, fearing that opponents might rally around the tsar, Lenin had Nicholas and the rest of the royal family brutally murdered. In the past, the Romanovs had employed secret police and Siberian prison camps to identify and punish their enemies. Lenin and the Bolsheviks greatly expanded both systems. Through the secret police, the government weaponized terror.

In November 1920, the Russian Civil War ended with a communist victory. The Bolsheviks had already secured control of the government by expelling non-Bolshevik socialists from the soviets. The democratic nature of rule by the soviets gave way to an authoritarian, communist dictatorship with Lenin in charge.

HISTORICAL THINKING

1. **READING CHECK** How did the Mensheviks' plan for seizing power differ from the Bolsheviks' plan?

2. **SEQUENCE EVENTS** Put the following events in the order in which they occurred: February Revolution, Russian Civil War, 1905 uprising, October Revolution.

3. **DRAW CONCLUSIONS** Why do you think the communist Reds won the Russian Civil War?

3.2

MAIN IDEA After their revolution, Lenin and the Bolsheviks created a communist economic system, restored much of the former Russian Empire, and rid the new nation of their political opponents.

Communist Policy in the New U.S.S.R.

In *The Manifesto of the Communist Party* and other writings, Karl Marx introduced the idea of a complex, revolutionary economic system that inspired Vladimir Lenin and the Bolsheviks decades later. Marx could hardly have predicted how his theory would play out in the real world.

NEW ECONOMIC POLICY

Lenin ruled with an iron hand. He made sure that all political parties and social organizations either accepted Communist Party rule or were destroyed. He expected the proletariat to demonstrate discipline, which he defined as "unity of action, freedom of discussion and criticism." Even within the Communist Party Central Committee—the core group of Bolshevik decision-makers—Lenin allowed only limited debate.

After the October Revolution, the Bolsheviks **nationalized**, or seized for the state, most privately owned industries and railroads. They established a centrally planned economy for Russia, meaning that the communist government would do the planning.

The Bolsheviks also struck a blow against large landowners and in favor of the peasants, who historically did not own the land they cultivated. In the early 1900s, new laws had allowed peasants to establish their own farms. By the time of the Russian Revolution, peasants owned much of the available farmland or rented it from large landowners. A 1918 decree broke up Russia's remaining large estates into small holdings. The government distributed these state-owned properties only to peasants willing to cultivate the land themselves.

Lenin speaks to Soviet soldiers in Sverdlov Square in Moscow in 1920. Even though this image implies that Lenin was a passionate orator, he was not as good a public speaker as Leon Trotsky, who stands to the right of the podium. A similar photograph from this speech was reproduced around the world.

During the civil war, however, Lenin took a radical step to supply the Red Army and people in the cities with food. He ordered peasants to give all their surplus grain to the government. In return, the government would provide peasants with any needed factory goods. Lenin justified this action as reflecting the socialist principle that basic resources are to be distributed equally. However, the peasants defied Lenin's order and instead grew less grain. This reaction resulted in widespread famine that led to an estimated five million deaths in 1921 and 1922. At the same time, peasant rebellions broke out in the countryside.

Lenin knew that the Communist Party could not stay in power without the support of the peasants—and the food that they produced. In 1921, in the midst of the famine, he instituted the New Economic Policy. This policy stopped forcing peasants to surrender their grain, gave them long-term leases on their land, and allowed them to sell food on the open market. It also returned small-scale businesses to private hands. However, the government maintained firm control of heavy industry, transportation, and banking.

Labor camp inmates haul rocks to build the Belomorkanal, or the White Sea–Baltic Canal. Between 12,000 and 24,000 workers died during its construction from 1931 to 1933.

FIRST YEARS OF THE U.S.S.R.

For the rest of the 1920s, the country experienced a period of relative peace. The New Economic Policy reenergized the peasants and stimulated the economy. Industry bounced back, and more private enterprises emerged. An improved economy helped Lenin and the Bolsheviks solidify their rule. They were able to assert their claim to power not only in Russia but also across much of the former Russian Empire. They restored to Russia the rich farmlands of Ukraine. They exerted control over Central Asia and the Caucasus to the south and the vast territory of Siberia to the east.

In 1922, Russia and the regions it controlled formed the **Union of Soviet Socialist Republics (U.S.S.R.)**, also known as the Soviet Union. Officially a federal republic, the Soviet Union was in reality a dictatorship, dominated by Russia and ruled from Moscow by the Bolsheviks. The Soviet government continued a practice employed by the Russian Empire that sent citizens to distant prison camps where they had to complete physically demanding tasks in brutal conditions. In 1923, Lenin's secret police opened the first Bolshevik forced-labor camp on a remote island off the nation's northern coast.

The people sent to these remote detention locations were political prisoners—opponents of Lenin and the Bolsheviks. They worked as slave laborers at various jobs, such as logging, fishing, and construction. Besides being forced to work, prisoners were often tortured; sometimes, they were killed in mass executions. In the years that followed, many additional sites were built. The Soviets called this system of labor camps the **Gulag** (GOO-lahg).

Lenin, the founder of the Communist Party and its undisputed leader, had a stroke in 1922 that left him partially paralyzed. As a result, he began to cut back his activities. At the same time, **Joseph Stalin**—someone Lenin did not like or trust—began exerting greater influence over party matters. In January 1924, after two more strokes, Lenin died. Stalin used his position as General Secretary of the Central Committee to seize the leadership of the Soviet Union. Stalin was impatient with the New Economic Policy and began radical changes to create a highly centralized, fast-growing industrial economy.

HISTORICAL THINKING

1. **READING CHECK** How did Lenin's order to peasants to supply food for the Red Army and the urban population affect the entire nation?

2. **DRAW CONCLUSIONS** Did the New Economic Policy end the policy of nationalization? Explain your response.

3. **COMPARE AND CONTRAST** How did Soviet forced-labor camps differ from traditional prisons?

China's Republic and Mao's Goals

MAIN IDEA The revolution that ended China's Qing dynasty led to the establishment of a republic, but the weak new government could not keep the country unified.

Does your local government accomplish its goals? Efficient governments include honest and skillful leadership, sound policies and programs, and broad popular support. After the collapse of the Qing dynasty, the Chinese people struggled to establish an effective national government.

END OF THE QING DYNASTY

The Boxer Rebellion of 1899–1901 did little to halt the spread of Western and Japanese influence in Qing China. The country desperately needed a government that could unify the Chinese people and defend them against foreign aggression. Some Chinese pushed for reforms, while others argued that only a revolution would bring about the needed changes.

In October 1911, a mutiny by troops in southeastern China triggered an uprising. Frustration with Qing rule helped the insurrection spread. By the end of the year, more than a dozen provinces and numerous army units had joined the Chinese revolution. The rebels set up a provisional republic in the city of Nanjing. They chose respected revolutionary **Sun Yat-sen** to lead it.

Sun was a nationalist who envisioned a strong, unified, and modernized China. As head of a political movement known as the Revolutionary Alliance, he had spent much of his time outside China, trying to raise money and support. Now he hoped to help China take its rightful place among the world's great powers.

In February 1912, the Qing emperor—just six years old—abdicated. After more than 2,000 years of imperial rule, the Chinese empire quietly came to an end. In its place arose the Republic of China, with a new constitution and an elected assembly, in which Sun's newly formed Nationalist Party held a majority of seats.

For the sake of peace and unity, Sun yielded the presidency of the new republic to a leading military official who ruled from Beijing. But instead of governing according to the constitution, the president tried to make himself emperor, and in 1916 he was overthrown. A period of disorder followed. Local warlords reigned over large parts of the country, backed by private armies. China was no longer a unified state.

In the southern port city of Guangzhou (gwahng-joh), Sun tried to establish a government separate from the weakened government in Beijing, and a hundred or so members of the national assembly joined him there. They tried but failed to gain recognition by Western nations as the legitimate Chinese government.

During the First World War, China and Japan both supported the Allies. After the war, the Chinese expected the return of German-held territory on the Shandong Peninsula in eastern China. Instead, the Treaty of Versailles gave the territory to Japan. Japan, as you read earlier, had already acquired Taiwan and Manchuria, in northeastern China, in previous wars.

On May 4, 1919, some 3,000 university students held a demonstration in Tiananmen Square in Beijing to oppose the plan to give additional Chinese territory to Japan. They appealed to the government to restore Chinese dignity in the face of Japanese aggression. Their **May Fourth Movement** led to labor strikes, mass meetings, and a boycott of Japanese goods. As a result of these widespread protests, China refused to sign the Treaty of Versailles. Chinese nationalism was on the rise.

COMMUNISM IN CHINA

The activist spirit generated by the May Fourth Movement increased membership in Sun Yat-sen's Nationalist Party. The Western powers had no interest in helping Sun, so he turned to the new communist government in Russia for support. Lenin's Bolsheviks offered to help Sun strengthen the Nationalist Party. They told Sun that they would provide him political guidance, guns, and money if he agreed to cooperate with the Chinese communists. He conceded. He also agreed to modify his ideology with a shift from nationalism and economic security to anti-imperialism and socialism.

A statue of young Mao Zedong towers to a height of more than 100 feet on Orange Isle in Changsha, China. The sculpture was unveiled in 2009.

After Sun died in 1925, his brother-in-law Jiang Jieshi, known in the West as **Chiang Kai-shek**, gained control of the Nationalist Party. After defeating the warlords to take control of China, Chiang turned against the communists in 1927. His National Party forces killed thousands of communists in the coastal cities, forcing the survivors to flee to the countryside.

These communists were now guided by **Mao Zedong** (mow dzuh-dahng), who had participated in the May Fourth Movement while he attended university. Mao proved to be a brilliant military strategist, shifting the Chinese communist emphasis from industrial workers toward an alliance with the rural poor, the peasant class who made up the vast majority of China's population. Mao became the leader of the Chinese Communist Party in 1935.

Unlike Marx and Lenin, Mao believed it would be the peasants—not industrial workers—who would lead the way to socialism in China.

PRIMARY SOURCE

In a very short time, in China's central, southern and northern provinces, several hundred million peasants will rise like a mighty storm, like a hurricane, a force so swift and violent that no power, however great, will be able to hold it back. They will smash all the trammels [shackles; restraints] that bind them and rush forward along the road to liberation. They will sweep all the imperialists, warlords, corrupt officials, local tyrants and evil gentry into their graves.

—from "Report on an Investigation of the Peasant Movement in Hunan" by Mao Zedong, March 1927

HISTORICAL THINKING

1. **READING CHECK** What group started the May Fourth Movement, and what effects did it have on Chinese society?

2. **DRAW CONCLUSIONS** Based on what you have read earlier, why do you think warlords arose in a country like China in the early 1900s?

3. **MAKE PREDICTIONS** Who do you think will be involved in a future conflict over the right to govern China, and why?

The First World War and 20th-Century Revolutions

4.1

MAIN IDEA The Mexican Revolution involved a decade of violent conflict over increasing the political rights of the people and meeting their demands for social reform.

Instability and Revolt

Have you ever taken part in a public demonstration? If so, what motivated you? If not, what would it take for you to personally commit to a cause? The main force propelling the Mexican Revolution was peasants who were willing to stand up and fight for their rights.

THE MEXICAN REVOLUTION

From 1870 to 1911, Porfirio Díaz ruled Mexico for all but four years. He held the title of president, but in reality he was a dictator. He won elections, but they were rigged. By the early 1900s, many middle-class Mexicans no longer accepted Díaz's political monopoly. Mexican peasants were angry that farming policies favored wealthy landlords producing commodities for distant markets. Instead, the peasants, mainly mestizos and indigenous peoples, wanted control of their own land and labor.

Francisco Madero, son of a prosperous merchant and landowner, ran against Díaz in the presidential election of 1910. Madero's campaign slogan—"Effective Suffrage and No Re-election"—reflected the desire of many Mexicans for voting rights and an end to Díaz's six-term presidency. Díaz, fearing he might lose, had Madero arrested. He ran unopposed in June and claimed victory.

Released from prison after the election, Madero fled to Texas. There, in October 1910, he published a plan in which he proclaimed himself president of Mexico, argued for a single-term presidency, and supported land reform. He also called on Mexicans to revolt on November 20, which came and went without any unrest. Madero did, however, inspire several groups to organize against the Díaz regime. The Mexican Revolution had begun.

When Madero returned to Mexico in February 1911, he participated in some of the fighting but mainly focused on persuading Díaz to leave office. Finally, in May, Díaz resigned and went into exile in France. In new elections that June, Madero won the presidency of Mexico. However, this achievement did not mark the end of the revolution. Motivated peasants kept fighting for their land rights.

Francisco Madero was declared president in 1911 at the beginning of the Mexican Revolution.

POLITICAL DISORDER

As president, Madero failed to please either his revolutionary supporters or government officials who had retained their positions after the fall of the Díaz government. In 1913, Madero's army chief of staff, Victoriano Huerta, joined a rebellion of army soldiers and arrested Madero, who was later executed. Huerta became a military dictator—but he did not rule for long.

In 1914, rebels from the countryside led by **Venustiano Carranza**—and aided by U.S. troops—forced Huerta to flee the country. For two years, Mexico had an interim, or temporary, president. Carranza and other reformers, including **Álvaro Obregón**, gathered armies, formed alliances, and fought for control of the nation. When this civil war ended in 1917, Carranza's forces controlled all but two of Mexico's 28 states.

Carranza, a nationalist, had not wanted the U.S. Army's help in ousting Huerta from office. After he was elected president in 1917, Carranza tried to nationalize Mexico's oil industry, prompting loud protests from the United States because three-quarters of Mexico's oil wells were American-owned.

As president, Carranza helped draft a new constitution. A constitutional assembly that included a mix of conservative and liberal delegates drafted a document that gave Carranza significant powers but also included articles that responded to the demands of middle-class Mexicans and peasants. One of those articles supported land reform. All lands taken from the peasants during the Díaz regime were to be returned to them. Another article established free, compulsory education and completely separated the church from the state.

The constitution also provided for an eight-hour workday, a minimum wage, and the right of workers to strike. However, Carranza did not enforce the social reforms built into the constitution, and peasants continued to attack government positions in the north and south. The revolution moved forward.

Obregón stayed out of the fight until 1920, when Carranza threatened to use federal troops to break a strike by rail workers in Obregón's home state of Sonora. In April, Obregón joined an uprising that pushed Carranza out of office, and that November, Obregón was elected president. More realist than revolutionary, Obregón enforced constitutional reforms but also encouraged Mexican capitalists. In this way, he brought a measure of peace and unity to Mexico.

The Mayo people joined Obregón's forces during the Mexican Revolution. Many of them brought bows and arrows into battles.

HISTORICAL THINKING

1. **READING CHECK** Which of the many Mexican presidents during the revolutionary era accomplished the most in terms of social reform?

2. **CATEGORIZE** Would you label Francisco Madero a revolutionary? Why or why not?

3. **MAKE INFERENCES** Why did Venustiano Carranza's presidency fail to end the revolution?

The First World War and 20th-Century Revolutions 725

4.2

MAIN IDEA Emiliano Zapata and Pancho Villa led armies of peasants, cattle herders, and other dispossessed groups in a quest for land reform in Mexico.

The Campesinos, Zapata, and Villa

When people choose leaders, they often favor those who are like them and who they think will understand their needs. The main military leaders of the Mexican Revolution were, like most of their followers, peasants.

DEMANDING LAND REFORM

During the Mexican Revolution, the government in Mexico City changed hands a number of times. In the countryside, peasants and their leaders carried the revolution forward. Their main goals related to land reform. The most valuable farmland in the nation was located in south-central Mexico, where most Mexicans lived. Historically, the indigenous peoples of this region cultivated communal lands: lands that they held in common, not privately or individually.

Policies put forth by Porfirio Díaz established a market-based approach to land ownership. Encouraged by these protocols, wealthy landowners bought or seized more and more agricultural land and the villages linked to it. As a result, the **campesinos**—rural villagers and small farmers—lost control of their communal lands. To survive, they were forced to work for low wages on haciendas, or vast privately owned agricultural estates.

Mexico's arid and mountainous north had a much smaller population. A rural middle class of cattle ranchers controlled much of the land. They hired many **vaqueros** (vah-KEHR-ohs), or cowboys and cattle herders, to work as ranch hands on their relatively small haciendas. Other poor laborers in this region included peasants, miners, and railroad workers.

By 1910, haciendas had consumed around 80 percent of all local communities in Mexico. Two key leaders of the Mexican Revolution, **Emiliano Zapata** and **Pancho Villa** (VEE-yuh), organized armies of peasants who had been evicted from their homes as well as other poor Mexicans. They engaged in guerrilla warfare against Mexican army posts. Zapata and Villa vowed to fight for the return of their followers' lost land and independent way of life.

Zapata was born into a peasant family in 1879 in the state of Morelos, just south of Mexico City. The economy of this agricultural state was based on growing and processing sugar. Expanding haciendas claimed land and water rights at the expense of peasants and others in the region. As a teenager, Zapata took part in a protest against a hacienda that sought to take over his village. In 1909, after briefly serving in the army, he led a group of villagers that reclaimed, by force, the hacienda land.

This photograph from 1915 shows Pancho Villa (left, sitting on the presidential throne in the National Palace) with Emiliano Zapata (right) at his side, Zapata's trademark hat on his knee. Forces loyal to Venustiano Carranza soon chased the two revolutionaries from Mexico.

726 CHAPTER 25

Villa, who like Zapata was a peasant, worked on a hacienda in the state of Durango in northern Mexico. In 1894, at the age of 16, Villa shot and killed a hacienda owner who had attacked his sister. Villa fled to the mountains, where he joined and later led a group of bandits. These outlaws survived mainly by stealing cattle from wealthy ranchers.

ARMIES OF THE SOUTH AND NORTH

In February 1911, when Francisco Madero returned to Mexico, Villa and his followers joined him. Together, they gathered an army of peasants and other rural poor and fought their way toward Mexico City. In March, Zapata led a small force northward from his village. They seized a town and blockaded the road to Mexico City. The revolutionaries forced Díaz to give up the presidency. When Madero failed to support land reform as president, Zapata issued the Plan of Ayala, which declared that Madero had betrayed the revolution. Zapata vowed to "end the tyranny which oppresses us."

In the mountains of the southwest, Zapata organized a band of peasants to "sustain and carry out the promises" of the revolution. This group, which grew to number some 25,000 soldiers, became known as the Liberation Army of the South. With Zapata in command, the army quickly took control of the haciendas in his home state of Morelos and redistributed the land to peasants. These revolutionaries adopted the slogan "¡Justicia, Tierra, y Libertad!—Justice, Land and Liberty!"

Zapata and his Liberation Army helped overthrow Madero and Victoriano Huerta. However, his opposition to Mexico's next president, Venustiano Carranza, ended badly for Zapata. In 1919, Carranza's troops ambushed Zapata and killed him.

Meanwhile, Villa gathered and trained peasants, small ranchers, vaqueros, and railroad workers. This army became known as the Division of the North. Villa used his soldiers' skills to advantage. He and his horse-riding vaqueros made cavalry charges against federal soldiers, and his railroad workers took over trains and used them to transport men, weapons, and supplies.

In March 1916, Villa crossed into U.S. territory. His army raided Columbus, New Mexico, leaving 18 Americans—including 10 civilians—dead. Backed by machine guns, U.S. soldiers retaliated and killed more than 100 of Villa's troops. The United States, which supported Carranza over Villa in the civil war, sent a force of some 12,000 soldiers into Mexico to punish Villa, but the former bandit and his guerrillas had vanished.

A *soldadera*, or female soldier, looks down the Buenavista station train platform in Mexico City.

Smaller revolutionary forces also emerged in Mexico. In the south, the Mayo people fought for land reform. In the north, the Yaqui and Ocuila (oh-KWEE-luh) did the same. Women joined some of the revolutionary armies, and a few led their own. Margarita Neri, a former landowner, formed an army that looted haciendas in southern Mexico until she was caught and executed. Other women rose to high positions in existing armies.

Villa and his army continued guerrilla raids against haciendas and Carranza's forces in the north. Only after Carranza was driven out of the presidency in 1920 did Villa put down his weapons. The struggle for peasants' land rights would endure for more than a decade. Finally, in the late 1930s, Lázaro Cárdenas (KAHR-duh-nahs), a progressive president, redistributed land to peasants and enacted other policies that supported the goals of the Mexican Revolution.

HISTORICAL THINKING

1. **READING CHECK** Why did Emiliano Zapata and Pancho Villa focus on attacking haciendas?

2. **IDENTIFY MAIN IDEAS AND DETAILS** Why did Zapata issue the Plan of Ayala?

3. **IDENTIFY PROBLEMS AND SOLUTIONS** Why do you think Zapata and Villa joined forces to pursue change in Mexico?

4.3 DOCUMENT-BASED QUESTION
The Revolution in Murals

How important is it for people to have a positive image of themselves, of their nation, and of their culture? The Mexican Revolution focused on the rights of peasants, mainly people of native or mixed descent. In a sense, the revolution began a period in which Mexicans incorporated their ancient, indigenous past into their present sense of who they were. Mexican artists and their murals influenced how Mexicans saw—and still see—themselves.

Mexican muralists Diego Rivera, David Alfaro Siqueiros, and José Clemente Orozco emerged in the years following the Mexican Revolution. The revolution inspired all three men, not only as a subject for their art but as motivation to examine Mexico's heritage.

Rivera took part in the Mexican Revolution as an artist, not a fighter. In 1910, at age 23, he designed a poster backing Francisco Madero's call for a peasant rebellion. In 1922, Rivera began his first mural work, mixing European and Mexican folk-art styles. He subsequently created murals in public buildings across Mexico and in major U.S. cities. His mural *History of Mexico* is in the National Palace in Mexico City, home to the executive branch of the federal government. It includes a slogan of the Zapatistas, or followers of Emiliano Zapata: "Tierra y Libertad," which means "Land and Liberty."

Siqueiros earned a scholarship to study art in Paris. There, in 1919, he met Rivera, who urged him to pursue mural painting, which Siqueiros did with a passion. At first, Siqueiros worked in the fresco style, but he later shifted to an experimental, modernist approach. He sometimes dripped or splattered paint on a wall or used an airbrush to apply it.

As a young man, Orozco had a job preparing architectural drawings. He later applied his drawing and mathematics skills to his art. In the 1920s, the Mexican government commissioned him, along with Rivera and Siqueiros, to paint murals aimed at educating and unifying the people. Orozco's murals, created using the traditional fresco technique, are known for their vivid colors.

Diego Rivera studied art for eight years in Europe, where he learned the traditional fresco technique of painting with watercolors on moist plaster that he used to create his murals.

ARTIFACT ONE

Primary Source: Mural (detail)
from *From the Dictatorship of Porfirio Díaz to the Revolution* by David Alfaro Siqueiros, 1957–1966

Siqueiros fought in the Mexican Revolution, joining the army of Venustiano Carranza at the age of 16. Siqueiros's military experience may have contributed to the emotional intensity of his murals. This detail is from a much larger work that covers several walls in Mexico's National Museum of History. The entire mural—not a fresco but acrylic paint on plywood—portrays the politicians and revolutionaries, as well as the peasants, who made history during this era. The way the soldiers are dressed suggests they are Zapatistas.

CONSTRUCTED RESPONSE What gives this image its emotional intensity?

ARTIFACT TWO

Primary Source: Mural
Zapatistas by José Clemente Orozco, 1916

At age 17, Orozco lost his left hand in a school laboratory accident, so he did not fight in the Mexican Revolution. In 1914, however, when the revolution turned into a civil war, Orozco joined the staff of a revolutionary newspaper. He worked as a political cartoonist for the paper, which supported Carranza. Unlike Rivera and Siqueiros, Orozco did not glorify the revolution in his murals; he tried to present a realistic view, one that often revealed the horrors of war. His mural *Zapatistas* offers a somber look at the lives of peasants on the march.

CONSTRUCTED RESPONSE How is Orozco's vision of the revolution in his *Zapatistas* mural similar to and different from Siqueiros's depiction in *From the Dictatorship of Porfirio Díaz to the Revolution*?

SYNTHESIZE & WRITE

1. **REVIEW** Review what you have learned about the three Mexican muralists, their styles, and their subjects.

2. **RECALL** On your own paper, list two details about one artist and two details about that artist's mural.

3. **CONSTRUCT** Construct a topic sentence that answers this question: Which muralist best represents the Mexican Revolution, its goals, and its participants?

4. **WRITE** Using evidence from this chapter and the images, write an informative paragraph that supports your topic sentence in Step 3.

CHAPTER 25 REVIEW
THE FIRST WORLD WAR AND 20TH-CENTURY REVOLUTIONS

VOCABULARY
Complete each of the following sentences using one of the vocabulary words from the chapter.

1. Russia began to _____ its armed forces in case the country was drawn into war.
2. Many historians consider the Ottoman Empire's _____ of Armenians to be genocide.
3. After World War I, the Germans agreed to pay _____ to the Allies to cover wartime damages.
4. Many of Pancho Villa's soldiers were cowboys and cattle herders, known in Mexico as _____.
5. After the Russian Revolution, the Bolsheviks decided to _____ many industries.
6. Many _____ settled in Paris after World War I.
7. Imperialists often add to their empires by _____ smaller countries or territories.
8. The war on the Western Front settled into a _____ in which neither side could win.

READING STRATEGY
COMPARE AND CONTRAST
Making a chart can help you understand events in history. List details about the Russian, Chinese, and Mexican revolutions. Then answer the question.

Compare Revolutions

	Russian	Chinese	Mexican
Starting Date			
Goals			
Major Figures			
Significant Events			

9. Why is it difficult to identify the point at which a revolution ends?

MAIN IDEAS
Answer the following questions. Support your answers with evidence from the chapter.

10. Why is the Great War considered to have been a total war? **LESSON 1.1**
11. How did imperialism prepare European powers to immediately engage in battle? **LESSON 1.2**
12. What role did German U-boats play in the First World War? **LESSON 1.3**
13. What was the result of the Allies' attempt to secure the Dardanelles in 1915? **LESSON 1.4**
14. Which agreement from the Paris Peace Conference established new borders in Europe? **LESSON 2.1**
15. How did Ottoman authorities justify their decision to remove the Armenian population? **LESSON 2.3**
16. For which people did the Balfour Declaration create a "national home"? **LESSON 2.4**
17. What political party did Vladimir Lenin and the Bolsheviks establish in 1918? **LESSON 3.1**
18. How did the New Economic Policy help stimulate the Soviet market? **LESSON 3.2**
19. Why did Sun Yat-sen agree to cooperate with the Chinese communists? **LESSON 3.3**
20. Why did Mexican peasants dislike Porfirio Díaz's market-based land policies? **LESSON 4.2**

HISTORICAL THINKING
Answer the following questions. Support your answers with evidence from the chapter.

21. **ANALYZE CAUSE AND EFFECT** What was the main cause of the Great War? Explain.
22. **EXPLAIN** Why did the First World War result in so many casualties?
23. **DRAW CONCLUSIONS** What limited the role of airplanes in World War I?
24. **MAKE INFERENCES** Why do you think that the Weimar Republic failed in Germany?
25. **IDENTIFY PROBLEMS AND SOLUTIONS** Why did Lenin and the Bolsheviks send their political opponents to the Gulag?
26. **EVALUATE** Did the tactic of guerrilla warfare benefit the Mexican revolutionaries? Explain.

INTERPRET VISUALS

Study the table at right, which shows the casualties suffered by each of the main powers in the Great War. Then answer the questions that follow.

27. Which country suffered the greatest number of casualties?

28. Why are U.S. casualties so much lower than those of the other countries?

Casualties in the Great War

Country	Killed and Died	Wounded	Prisoners and Missing	Total Casualties
Allies				
Russia	1,700,000	4,950,000	2,500,000	9,150,000
France	1,357,800	4,266,000	537,000	6,160,800
Britain	908,371	2,090,212	191,652	3,190,235
Italy	947,000	650,000	600,000	2,197,000
United States	116,516	204,002	4,500	325,018
Central Powers				
Germany	1,773,700	4,216,058	1,152,800	7,142,558
Austria-Hungary	1,200,000	3,620,000	2,200,000	7,020,000
Ottoman Empire	325,000	400,000	250,000	975,000

Sources: U.S. War Department in February 1924. U.S. casualties as amended by the Statistical Services Center, Office of the Secretary of Defense, Nov. 7, 1957

ANALYZE SOURCES

In 1917, Lenin and the Bolsheviks hoped to seize power and establish a "dictatorship of the proletariat." Read the excerpt from an essay by Lenin that first appeared in a Russian magazine less than two weeks before the Bolshevik victory in the October Revolution. Then answer the question that follows.

> We have already seen the strength of the capitalists' resistance. . . . *We have not yet seen*, however, the strength of resistance of the proletarians and poor peasants, for this strength will become fully apparent only when power is in the hands of the proletariat, when tens of millions of people who have been crushed by want and capitalist slavery see from experience and *feel* that state power has passed into the hands of the oppressed classes, that the state is helping the poor to fight the landowners and capitalists, is *breaking* their resistance.

29. According to Lenin, what groups in Russian society are the enemies of the "proletarians and poor peasants"?

CONNECT TO YOUR LIFE

30. **NARRATIVE** You have read about the aftermath of the Great War and its lasting effects on ordinary citizens. Write a story in which you are a main character and explore what you may have thought or done in the aftermath of the Great War.

TIPS

- Skim the chapter for a person who appeals to you, such as a soldier, someone on the home front, a colonial subject, or a member of the Lost Generation. Use that person as a basis for your character.

- Identify when and where your story takes place and your character's thoughts and feelings about events.

- Use vivid language to describe the location of your story, what is occurring, and how your character reacts.

- Include realistic dialogue in your story.

- Use two or three vocabulary terms from the chapter in your narrative.

- End your narrative by describing what you think one or more of the characters will do in the future.

CHAPTER 26

Economic Depression and Authoritarian Regimes
1908–1939

HISTORICAL THINKING Is it better to have security or freedom?

SECTION 1 **The Twenties**
SECTION 2 **Dictatorships**
SECTION 3 **Nationalism and Colonial Resistance**
SECTION 4 **The Road to War**

CRITICAL VIEWING

In 1936, during a Nazi Party rally in Nuremberg, Germany, soldiers in combat gear stand at attention, listening to a speech by Adolf Hitler. Based on details in the photo, what can you infer about the purpose of the rally? What message do the Nazis want to convey to the world?

1.1

MAIN IDEA In the early 20th century, the airplane and the radio transformed transportation and communication technologies around the world.

Over the Air

Many people today want to get their hands on the latest smartphone or other communication technology. Likewise, in the 1920s, people were thrilled by the chance to listen to a popular radio program or the possibility of traveling by air.

AVIATION TAKES FLIGHT

The early years of the 20th century introduced the age of aviation, or the use of aircraft. **Orville and Wilbur Wright** attained a remarkable achievement when their *Flyer I* briefly rose off the ground in Kitty Hawk, North Carolina. For the first time, a powered vehicle had lifted off the ground and successfully taken flight. In 1908, the brothers brought their invention to Europe. Soon, people around the globe became captivated by air flight and the speed at which people and goods could travel.

Aviation innovations increased during World War I as fighting nations looked to use the new technology to their advantage. The first war planes were used simply to observe the position and movement of enemy forces, but later airplanes were fitted with machine guns and engaged in battle. In another military advancement, grenades were tossed from airplanes called bombers. Civilians were enthralled by tales of dogfights, or conflicts between fighter planes. The daring exploits of flying aces—such as the German Red Baron (Manfred

On the morning of December 17, 1903, Orville Wright makes the historic first powered airplane flight, as his brother Wilbur runs alongside the wingtip of *Flyer I* in Kitty Hawk, North Carolina. On this first successful flight, which lasted 12 seconds, Wright flew the airplane 120 feet.

This photo of Bessie Coleman was taken in the 1920s. Discrimination kept Coleman from entering aviation schools in the United States. However, that didn't stop her from fulfilling her dream to fly. Coleman learned French and was accepted at an aviation school in France. In 1921, she became the first American woman to receive an international pilot's license.

von Richthofen), American Eddie Rickenbacker, France's Georges Guynemer, and Britain's Albert Ball—were used as propaganda tools in the war. In reality, aircraft and air battles did not play a major role in the war's outcome, but aviation proved it could be important in future wars.

Aviation advances and enthusiasm did not stop after World War I. In 1927, pilot Charles Lindbergh impressed the world with his solo, nonstop transatlantic voyage in the airplane *Spirit of St Louis*. Bessie Coleman, the first African-American pilot, used her aviation skills to demonstrate that the skies were open to all. Amelia Earhart served as a role model for other women to become pilots. The achievements of such pilots help explain why the period following World War I is remembered as the "Golden Age of Flight." At this time, the first permanent commercial airports were built in such locations as the United States, Australia, France, Britain, Germany, and Thailand. The growing demand for the movement of passengers and freight caused even more aviation innovation.

TUNING INTO THE RADIO

Alexander Graham Bell's telephone had shown that spoken words could travel long distances by wire. But could words travel over the air without wires? In

1902, **Guglielmo Marconi** showed that they could by using his new invention—the radio—to send a wireless message across the Atlantic Ocean.

As it did for aviation, World War I brought improvements and refinements to the radio. Military radio operators used the new technology to warn soldiers of attacks and relay orders. The portability of the radio provided fighters with a way to communicate no matter their location. As technology improved, the radio allowed battleships and warplanes to communicate with one another through Morse code, a series of dots and dashes that could be transcribed into letters.

After the war, the radio became an important source of entertainment for the war-weary. Listeners in the United States tuned into the news, musical presentations, political speeches, weather reports, comedy and adventure shows, and soap operas. In Europe and Asia, the radio was used at first primarily for public service purposes, such as the first broadcasts of the British Broadcasting Corporation, or BBC.

Never before had so many people had such quick and convenient access to the same information and entertainment at the same time. Radio, along with newspapers and magazines, became an early form of ==mass media==, or means of communication meant to reach many people. These mass media influenced the ==popular culture==, or the shared experiences and interests of everyday people. Popular culture in the United States at the time included a love of jazz, baseball, and the Charleston dance. Some people say that mass media caused the formation of a ==mass society==, in which large numbers of people share the same experiences without actually having to meet.

The radio was not the only new technology that fascinated people in the world's more advanced consumer societies. They were happy to replace their old iceboxes with electric refrigerators. Movies with sound provided hours of entertainment. Where mass-produced and less-expensive automobiles were available, people could explore beyond their region and gain more freedom—especially women.

A German family gathers around a radio in their home in 1933. Radios became popular consumer items and offered in-home entertainment.

MASS SOCIETY AND GLOBAL CULTURE

New forms of communication and transportation allowed greater cultural exchange around the early 20th-century world. Both radio and early films, for example, made possible the global popularity of jazz music. Jazz originated with African-American musicians combining African rhythmic traditions with sparkling new melodies. Radio listeners from Miami to Berlin and Cape Town to Shanghai tapped their toes to jazz rhythms.

Apart from radio, new phonograph technology played a role, helping the jazz trumpeter and vocalist Louis Armstrong make his way from childhood poverty in New Orleans to international fame. The voice of Italian opera singer Enrico Caruso could be heard in living rooms around the world. Mass magazines also played a role, for example, spreading the word about the glamorous cabaret star Josephine Baker, who escaped a tough childhood in East St. Louis and found stardom in Harlem. She then left New York City for Paris, opening her own nightclub and becoming one of Europe's wealthiest performers.

This photograph of American trumpeter and singer Louis Armstrong was taken around 1930. Armstrong, who excelled at the art of improvisation, became one of jazz's legendary greats.

Women's fashions were also affected. In cities everywhere you could find the controversial figure of the "modern girl." Whether in Dallas, Istanbul, or Mexico City, these young women pushed back against traditional ideas of how they should dress and behave, wearing elegant clothing and using cosmetics that showed cosmopolitan influences from fashion centers like Paris. Their idea of being free to express themselves as individuals and not limited to roles as daughters and wives was a very bold one at that time.

Sports also showed the influence of mass society. In the United States and much of Latin America and the Caribbean, fans could now follow their team's games play-by-play, and the best players, like the Yankees' Babe Ruth, became international stars. In most of the world, football—or soccer—held center stage. The modern Olympics were first held in Athens, Greece, in 1896. Before long, millions would listen and watch as the world's best athletes represented their nations, giving people both a sense of national pride and a greater awareness of the wider world.

HISTORICAL THINKING

1. **READING CHECK** How did the inventions of the airplane and radio change people's lives?

2. **DRAW CONCLUSIONS** How do times of peace and war affect the development of technology differently?

3. **COMPARE AND CONTRAST** How did new technologies affect music and fashion around the world?

1.2 NATIONAL GEOGRAPHIC EXPLORER AMELIA EARHART

Daring to Fly

"As soon as we left the ground, I knew I myself had to fly."
—Amelia Earhart, after her first plane ride

A crowd of people enthusiastically greet Amelia Earhart after her transatlantic crossing from Newfoundland in 1932.

WHERE IS AMELIA EARHART? On July 2, 1937, Amelia Earhart and her navigator, Fred Noonan, took off from Lae, Papua New Guinea, bound for Howland Island, one of the last stops on their 29,000-mile flight around the world. They disappeared somewhere over the Pacific, spawning multiple theories about their fate.

— Flight path   --- Intended flight path

738 CHAPTER 26

MAIN IDEA Pioneer pilot Amelia Earhart set numerous aviation records and championed women's rights and abilities.

Amelia Earhart fell in love with flight on her first airplane ride in 1920, when she was just 23 years old and aviation was still in its infancy. Within a year, Earhart was flying solo. The next year, she set a record, flying at an altitude of 14,000 feet—higher than any woman had flown before. Earhart went on to set numerous aviation records, and in the process she challenged people's notions about women's limitations. Adventurous and independent from childhood on, Earhart encouraged women to dare to fly—not only in airplanes but in their personal lives as well. She challenged herself and other women to explore the frontiers of what a woman could achieve.

SETTING RECORDS

Amelia Earhart first made worldwide headlines for a flight on which she was only a passenger. In 1928, she became the first woman to cross the Atlantic Ocean in an airplane piloted by two men. Although Charles Lindbergh had completed a nonstop, solo flight from New York to Paris in 1927, transatlantic flights were still risky. Others had died trying to fly nonstop across the Atlantic Ocean. Treated to a ticker-tape parade in New York and a reception at the White House, Earhart became an international celebrity.

By 1932, Earhart was ready to attempt the transatlantic flight by herself. Piloting her red Lockheed Vega 5B, she set a record as the first woman to make a solo, nonstop flight across the Atlantic Ocean. Moreover, she overcame mechanical problems, strong winds, and icy conditions to complete the flight in record time: 14 hours, 56 minutes. She was the first person since Charles Lindbergh to accomplish the feat. The National Geographic Society awarded her its Gold Medal, given for notable geographic achievement. Earhart was the first woman to receive the prestigious medal.

In addition to "first woman" records, Earhart also set "first person" records. In 1935, she made the first solo flight from Hawaii to California, a hazardous trip that was longer in distance than the flight from the United States to Europe. Later that year, she became the first person to fly alone from Los Angeles to Mexico City.

One of the most celebrated aviators of her time, Earhart wrote three books about her flights as well as articles for *National Geographic* and other magazines. She used her fame to promote opportunities for women in aviation and other fields. She supported women's issues and encouraged women to assert their independence and gain control of their lives. Earhart described her own marriage to George Putnam, a publisher, as a "partnership" with "dual control."

THE LAST FLIGHT

In 1937, nearing the age of 40, Earhart was determined to become the first woman to fly around the world. She declared, "I have a feeling that there is just one more flight in my system." On June 1, Earhart and navigator Fred Noonan left Miami for the 29,000-mile trip. Over the next few weeks, they stopped a number of times to refuel before landing at Lae, New Guinea, on June 29. By then, they had covered 22,000 miles—more than three-fourths of the distance.

On July 2, Earhart and Noonan took off for Howland Island, located about 2,600 miles away in the Pacific Ocean. Earhart knew that the tiny island would be difficult to spot in the vast Pacific. During the flight, she maintained intermittent radio contact with a U.S. Coast Guard boat situated nearby. Late in the journey, Earhart radioed that she and Noonan must be near the island, but they couldn't see it and were running low on fuel. One more radio message arrived . . . and then silence.

In a rescue attempt, the U.S. government launched the largest air and sea search in naval history, involving 3,000 people, 10 ships, and about 65 planes. No sign of Earhart, Noonan, or their plane was discovered, and the search ended on July 19. The U.S. government concluded that Earhart's plane had run out of fuel and crashed into the Pacific.

Over the years, other theories about Earhart's fate have circulated. Many groups searched for traces of Earhart, Noonan, and the plane. In August 2019, National Geographic sponsored an expedition to the tiny island of Nikumaroro based on a theory that Earhart landed the plane there after she couldn't locate Howland Island. However, the expedition, led by National Geographic Explorer Robert Ballard, found no evidence of the plane. After nearly a century, people are still transfixed by this trailblazing woman who dared to explore the frontiers of flight.

HISTORICAL THINKING

1. **READING CHECK** What are some of the aviation records that Amelia Earhart set?

2. **EVALUATE** Why was Amelia Earhart an unusual woman for her time?

1.3

MAIN IDEA A falling stock market in the United States brought about a global economic depression that lasted throughout the 1930s.

The Great Depression

The economies of countries around the world have ups and downs all the time. When a country's economy declines over a period of time, that country is experiencing a recession. If the country's economy dips far lower, then it enters into a depression, or an extremely difficult economic time. That's just what happened around the world in the 1930s.

GLOBAL IMPACT OF U.S. ECONOMIC WOES

By the mid-1920s, the global economy had recovered from World War I, and international trade and investment were once again on the rise. No one was prepared for the shock that came next. In October 1929, prices on the New York Stock Exchange plunged so low that the stock market crashed. Within two months, stocks lost half their value. Bank failures across Europe and the Americas brought about the **Great Depression**, a time of intense financial hardship that lasted throughout the 1930s. Today, historians still discuss and debate the multiple causes of the global economic depression.

Just a few years earlier, many people in the United States were living a good life, buying homes, automobiles, and shares of stock. Many people thought that investing in the stock market was the key to gaining wealth. They were so intent on becoming stockholders that they bought shares on **speculation**, or the taking of huge risks to gain great rewards. Speculators low on cash borrowed money from banks to buy shares. They falsely believed that markets would endlessly increase in value and did not realize speculation would cause problems.

Worried that their stocks were overvalued, some investors sold them. This caused other investors to panic and sell as well, sending stock prices down. Many Americans lost all their money and could not buy products, causing factories to close. By 1932, one-fourth of workers in the United States were unemployed.

The Great Depression soon revealed problems with the international financial system. Following World War I, many European governments were deeply in debt to American banks. In fact, they had acquired more debt than they could repay. Germany was particularly affected because it owed $33 billion in reparations, payments to France required by the Versailles Treaty. It had turned to American banks for loans to repay these reparations. After the stock market crash, the U.S. banks called in their loans to German banks, leading to the collapse of the financial system.

The Great Depression also had a devastating effect on people in countries that depended on the export of minerals and agricultural commodities. Prices for crops fell sharply because of a drop in demand. Hard-hit farmers tried producing more, but this lowered prices even further. In Africa, a huge drop in cocoa and coffee prices meant farmers could not pay their debts or taxes to colonial governments. In Southeast Asia, a decline in automobile and bicycle production caused rubber

People gather on Wall Street by the New York Stock Exchange on October 24, 1929.

prices to crash and unemployment to soar. In India, desperate peasant families were forced to sell gold jewelry they were saving for their daughters' weddings. Throughout the nonindustrial world, people could no longer purchase the manufactured products industrial nations depended on them to buy.

GOVERNMENTS RESPOND

Around the world, people expected their governments to solve economic problems, no longer believing that free markets were the answer. British economist John Maynard Keynes developed a theory supporting the idea of greater government involvement. Keynes argued that during a severe downturn government should increase the money supply and borrow money for investment to stimulate the economy and lead to the return of economic growth. Once the economy was healthy again, governments should pay down the debt they had taken on.

Governments in France, Britain, and the United States took a more active role in their economies. U.S. president **Franklin Delano Roosevelt** responded to the depression by implementing his New Deal programs. Social Security, one of these programs, created a "safety net" for many of the nation's elderly. The Works Progress Administration (WPA) put many unemployed people to work on roadbuilding and construction projects and employed writers, artists, and actors in cultural programs. Price subsidies helped stabilize prices. France and Britain undertook similar measures. Sweden, Norway, and Denmark used a different approach. These nations promised to protect their citizens through comprehensive education, health care, housing subsidies, and unemployment insurance.

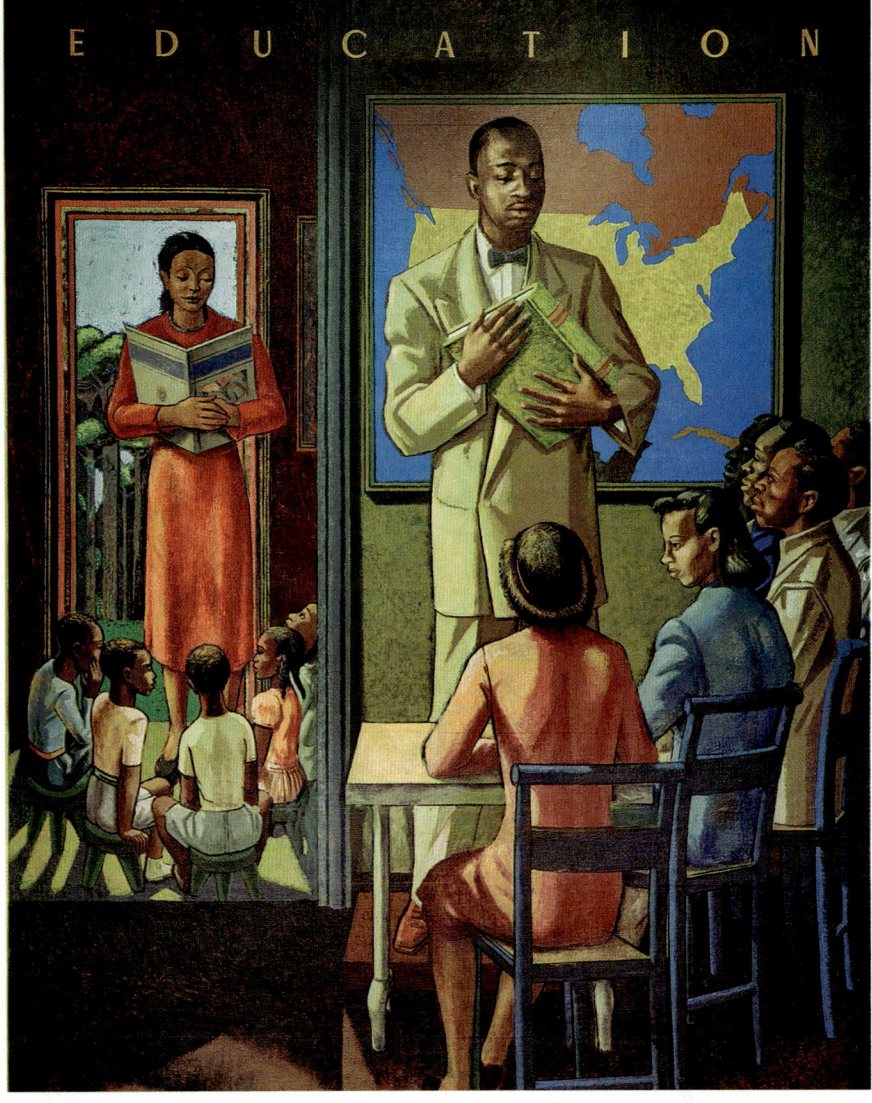

A WPA project, this mural was painted by Millard Owen Sheets in 1939.

One common response was economic nationalism. Many countries, including the United States, raised their tariffs. The idea was for each nation to protect its own producers from competition, but international trade declined even further as a result, making most people even poorer. In Latin America, some leaders took up economic nationalization, or the claiming of ownership of private business or industry by a government. In the late 1930s, Mexico's president, Lázaro Cárdenas, nationalized the country's petroleum industry. He argued that oil profits should benefit the Mexican people, not foreign companies.

HISTORICAL THINKING

1. **READING CHECK** How did the results of World War I contribute to the global economic collapse?

2. **ANALYZE CAUSE AND EFFECT** What were the two most important causes of the Great Depression? Explain.

3. **COMPARE AND CONTRAST** What did the economic relief efforts of various political leaders have in common?

2.1

MAIN IDEA The uncertainties of modern life in Italy paved the way for Benito Mussolini to gain absolute power as the world's first fascist dictator.

The Rise of Mussolini

You've probably heard the expression "desperate times call for desperate measures." The tough conditions of World War I, followed by the desperate times of the Great Depression, caused people in Italy and other countries to take desperate steps to reverse their dismal economies.

FASCISM GAINS MOMENTUM

Before World War I, many people saw a promising future in liberal democracy, with fair elections, protection of individual rights, and free market economies spreading around the world. During and after the war, some began to lose faith in liberal democracy. On the far political left were the communists who argued for a "dictatorship of the proletariat." On the far right were fascists who believed that the interests of the nation are more important than individual rights.

By the early 1920s, fascists in Italy and Germany were arguing that inefficient and corrupt politicians needed to be replaced by stern, disciplined leaders. The crisis of the Great Depression made this idea even more appealing. **Fascism** then developed as

Benito Mussolini, the founder of the fascist movement in Italy, speaks to a large crowd gathered at the Colosseum in Rome on November 2, 1920.

a way of governing based on extreme nationalism, racism, and suppression of opposition. Fascists opposed democracies that placed a high value on individual liberty and leaders who yielded to the will of the people. In contrast, they supported strong leaders who promised national greatness and put the needs of the nation as a whole over those of minority groups. To fascists, pursuing a united national purpose and the goals of the state was more important than individual rights.

Fascism, like communism, is a political philosophy that establishes a **totalitarian** political system to exert total control over a society, often violently. However, communism stressed class solidarity over national unity. Fascists and communists despised each other, but they loathed even more the compromises that marked liberal democratic government and the limits that legislatures placed on executive power.

MUSSOLINI TAKES CONTROL OF ITALY

Uncertain times in Italy led to the rise of **Benito Mussolini**. For Mussolini, the state bound the people together: "Everything for the state, nothing against the state, no one outside the state." To kickstart his political rise, Mussolini organized military-like groups made up of former soldiers called **Blackshirts**. The main purpose of these groups was to crush those Mussolini opposed, such as socialists and communists. Soon Mussolini's supporters began calling him *Il Duce* (ihl DOO-chay), or "the leader." Mussolini proved to be an electrifying and charismatic speaker who confidently relayed his plans for solving Italy's problems. He presented a strong case for order, discipline, and unity in the form of extreme nationalism. He also advocated replacing local dialects and cultural traditions with a united Italian identity. Soon he won the financial support of landowners and industrialists, who hired the Blackshirts to attack striking automobile workers in the north and put down protests by rural tenants on large farms in the south. In return, Mussolini gained support from wealthy Italians.

In 1922, Mussolini organized dissatisfied war veterans to march on Rome. Italy's elected government tried to put down Mussolini's play for power. However, the support of the elite allowed Mussolini to bully his way into the prime minister's position. To solidify his control, he had his opponents arrested or killed and outlawed competing political parties. After 1926, Mussolini ruled as dictator, and after the economic crash of 1929, he centralized power even more.

As Italy's absolute ruler, Mussolini made changes that conflicted with democratic ideals. For example, he denied citizens the right to meet freely in groups of their own choosing. Instead, he formed "corporations" that forcibly organized all citizens who shared a similar undertaking. In this way, labor unions and youth groups came under state influence. Yet despite Mussolini's efforts, he could not gain complete control of society. Most Italians remained loyal to the church, community, and family.

In the past, Italy's parliamentary democracy had made decisions through discussion and compromise. Mussolini relied instead on theatrical politics that involved singing, flag waving, marching, propaganda, and stirring speeches. Mussolini often alluded to Rome's imperial past and promised to make Rome the center of a mighty Italian empire once again. He began his efforts by invading Ethiopia in 1935 as payback for Italy's 1896 defeat by King Menelik II's army. In May 1936, after a brutal campaign of bombing the Ethiopian people, Mussolini proudly announced his success to a crowd of 400,000 people. Rousing patriotism in the cause of empire building allowed Mussolini to firmly unite the Italian people.

Some Italians willingly traded their liberty for security and a sense of national pride. Others, especially communists, paid for their opposition to Mussolini with their lives. Most Italians did not seem to care about politics and simply went on with their lives.

The Italian socialist writer Antonio Gramsci wrote about the situation in Italy before he was imprisoned for most of the rest of his life by fascist forces.

PRIMARY SOURCE

Indifference is actually the mainspring of history. . . . What comes to pass does so not as much because a few people want it to happen, as because the mass of citizens abdicate their responsibility and let things be.

—from *Avanti!* (an Italian newspaper), August 1916

HISTORICAL THINKING

1. **READING CHECK** What were three reasons Benito Mussolini and his fascist regime rose to power in Italy?

2. **MAKE CONNECTIONS** How did Mussolini's rise to power reflect political trends of the times?

3. **ANALYZE POINT OF VIEW** Why do you think some people opposed Mussolini's tactics while others embraced them?

Economic Depression and Authoritarian Regimes

2.2

MAIN IDEA Adolf Hitler solidified his position as the totalitarian leader of Germany through the use of scapegoats, extreme nationalism, violence, and centralized economic policy.

Hitler's Scapegoats

Like the Italians, Germans suffered from the postwar settlements and the effects of the Great Depression. In spite of the democracy of the Weimar Republic, many of them became disillusioned and were ready for new solutions.

REASONS FOR HITLER'S RISE

As you've read, Germany was both humiliated and financially devastated after World War I. The Weimar Republic had brought liberal democracy to Germany in the 1920s, but the Great Depression left Germans once again desperate for solutions. Weimar leaders believed in Enlightenment ideas as a means of achieving a just and stable social order. However, for many Germans, the war had called that belief into question.

During what some historians have called an "age of anxiety," artists explored darker emotions, as with the nightmarish images painted by German Expressionists. New scholarly ideas added more uncertainty. Austrian **Sigmund Freud** introduced a new view of human psychology in his unsettling theory that powerful subconscious urges challenged the reason of the conscious mind. Meanwhile, in physics, German astrophysicist **Albert Einstein** announced his special theory of relativity. He discarded Newton's idea of a constant relationship between time and space, stating that the location of the observer could affect the relationship between these dimensions. Thus science, along with artistic modernism and psychology, reinforced the climate of uncertainty.

The Great Depression made everything worse for the German people. Into this time of uncertainty stepped **Adolf Hitler** and the National Socialist German Workers, or Nazi, Party. Hitler promised to restore greatness, confidence, and order to Germany, just as Mussolini had promised in Italy. Hitler denounced modern painting as "degenerate art" and ranted against "Jewish science." Feeling harassed, Einstein and many other Jews who were able to do so fled Germany.

Already in 1925, Hitler had written about Germany's Jews, saying that "the personification of the devil as the symbol of all evil assumes the living shape of the Jew." Needing a scapegoat to blame for the country's problems, Hitler tapped into the centuries-old practice of anti-Semitism, or hostility and discrimination against Jews. German Jews had been assimilated into the national culture, but now their differences were highlighted. Step by step, Hitler led Germans toward his "final solution": the mass murder of European Jews.

Hitler's attack on the Jews was based on his claim that people of "pure" German descent were a superior race, and that mixing with Jews threatened that "purity." According to Hitler's views, which became known as Nazism, anyone who did not live up to the ideal of racial purity needed to be excluded from society. In this way, Germany could create a "master race." Apart from Jews, the Nazis targeted Germans with disabilities as "degrading" their "superior" race, performing horrible experiments and forced sterilizations in the name of "racial science."

The Nazis' other targets included communists because they divided the nation by dividing the rich and the poor. Jehovah's Witnesses were targets because they believe that only God can be worshiped, and they refused to salute Hitler or his flag. Homosexuals were hunted down and sent to concentration camps since they did not conform to the Nazi idea of the "proper family." The Nazis saw Germany's Roma minority like they did the Jews—as needing to be wiped out.

Support for the Nazi Party rose as the Great Depression increased fear and anxiety. Its share of the vote jumped from 2.6 to 37.6 percent between 1928 and 1932. By 1932, Hitler's supporters controlled more than a third of the seats in the Reichstag, or German legislature.

The nation's newly elected president needed Hitler's support to form a conservative governing coalition, supported by industrial and military leaders who feared rising support for socialists and communists on the left. Hitler agreed to join the coalition, on the condition that he be made Germany's chancellor.

HITLER'S EXTREME TACTICS FOR CONTROL

After becoming chancellor in 1933, Hitler ordered elected Communist Party legislators arrested and sent to concentration camps, where they could be brutally mistreated without ever being charged with a crime. More moderate socialist legislators saw the danger and boycotted the legislature. Then Hitler seized his chance. He said that a fire in the Reichstag building showed the communist danger, and in 1933 the remaining Reichstag members passed a "temporary" law giving Hitler dictatorial powers. He never gave those powers back.

Hitler then took command of Germany as dictator and made extreme changes to society. The state took over all responsibility for the national economy and most other aspects of life. To eliminate dissent, the Nazis outlawed other political parties and jailed their opponents. They also restricted the authority of religious leaders. Even so, most people did not speak out in protest of Hitler's policies.

The Nuremberg Laws of 1935 deprived Jews of all civil rights and forbade intermarriage with other Germans. Some Jews emigrated, but others could not bring themselves to leave their homes, businesses, friends, and extended families. Then, on November 9 and 10, 1938, the Nazis attacked Jewish homes, businesses, and synagogues across Germany and Austria during **Kristallnacht**, or "Night of Broken Glass." More Jews fled. Those who stayed were forced into segregated ghettos, their property taken over by their former neighbors.

German citizens' wish to pin their problems on others was one reason why Hitler's tactics gained traction. Another reason was the sharp drop in unemployment because of Hitler's intervention in the German economy. Huge public works projects, such as the world's first superhighways, and a large military re-armament put Germans back to work.

Leipzig Street with Electric Tram is a painting created in 1914 by Ernst Ludwig Kirchner. Kirchner was one of the founders of an artists' group called "The Bridge," which is now considered to be the birth of German Expressionism. In Kirchner's words, the Expressionists sought to express themselves "directly and authentically" in their art.

Hitler promised the return of the traditional values of courage, order, and discipline. He imposed new social hierarchies to do this. In Hitler's new social order, non-Germans fell to the bottom of society, and the roles of men and women grew further apart. To Hitler, women's highest calling was raising purebred German children. To cement their control, the Nazis held ultra-patriotic rallies, with in-step marching, flag waving, and rousing speeches. Such events gave ordinary Germans a sense of being part of something larger than themselves. Propaganda-filled radio broadcasts and films further spread excitement. Most Germans did not seem to mind new limitations on individual rights and were content with their country's order and economic success.

HISTORICAL THINKING

1. **READING CHECK** Why did Hitler and the Nazis rise to power? Why did the German people support them?

2. **FORM AND SUPPORT OPINIONS** Do you think Hitler could have risen to power if the Great Depression had not taken place? Explain your response.

3. **DRAW CONCLUSIONS** How did *Kristallnacht* gain its name?

2.3
MAIN IDEA Joseph Stalin exerted absolute control over the Soviet Union as he instituted campaigns to reorganize its economy and society and eliminate opposition.

Stalin's Dictatorship and Purges

Think about how well you adapt to change. How would you feel if your country's leader was determined to alter every aspect of your life, including how and what you learn, the kind of work you do, and even what you think? Joseph Stalin attempted to do that in the Soviet Union during the later 1920s through the early 1950s.

RISE TO POWER
Following Lenin's death in 1924, **Joseph Stalin** vied for leadership with other communists, including Leon Trotsky. Trotsky believed that socialism in Russia could only be advanced through worldwide uprisings of the proletariat. In contrast, Stalin supported the idea that the Soviet Union could go it alone with a policy of "Socialism in One Country." He also thought that Soviet socialism must be built through top-down government control of every aspect of life. Even Lenin had allowed peasants to have some control over their own lives, including owning land. By 1926, Stalin had become the sole Soviet leader, had forced Trotsky into exile, and had begun totally transforming his country into a communist totalitarian state.

In 1928, Stalin launched his first **Five-Year Plan**. Stalin's goal was to catapult the backward Soviet Union into an industrial powerhouse and a true global power. Noting that Russia was far behind more advanced economies, Stalin said, "We must make good this lag in ten years . . . or we will be crushed." However, the dictator was determined to follow a state-controlled Marxist model rather than a capitalist structure. Stalin explained why the country needed to industrialize in this way: ". . . we are

This communist propaganda poster from the Soviet Union proclaims, "Long live Stalin!" A profile of Lenin appears behind the image of Stalin.

still the only country of the proletarian dictatorship and are surrounded by capitalist countries, many of which are far in advance of us technically and economically." To meet his goal, Stalin nationalized all industries and quickly made them more productive. The drive for industrialization focused on such industries as oil, steel, and electricity at the expense of consumer-oriented industries. The Soviet people were subjected to low wages and harsh working conditions in the new factories.

Stalin's methods were harsh, but they did produce results. While the capitalist economies fell into economic depression in the 1930s, the Soviet Union became the world's fastest-growing industrial economy.

Workers on a Soviet collective farm break for lunch during the harvest of August 1936.

Stalin next applied his policy of "Socialism in One Country" to rural areas. Unlike Lenin, Stalin rejected private ownership, requiring farmers to give up their small plots of land. He ordered **collectivization**, or the replacement of privately owned peasant farms with state-run collective farms. On a collective farm, farmers work together and do not gain individual profits. Unwilling peasants were marched at gunpoint onto the collective farms. Stalin claimed that violence was necessary to overcome the resistance of **kulaks** (koo-LAHKs), the most prosperous peasants. In fact, Stalin used the Red Army to wage war on his own people, murdering many while forcing villagers onto collective farms. A famine that resulted from the attempt at collectivization killed two million people between 1932 and 1933. The Ukrainian people were hit especially hard during this Terror Famine, as starving peasants there had to surrender to the state any food they managed to grow.

Meanwhile, industrialization of the Soviet Union continued at a frantic pace. The Communist Party bureaucracy made use of non-Russian parts of the Soviet Union mainly as a source of raw materials as if they were colonial territories. Their resources were transported into the Russian heartland for industrial use. The Soviets required all citizens to work but offered low wages so they could pour money into industry. The government established a system of Gulag labor camps in the Soviet Union and Siberia. Slave labor at these camps also boosted Soviet productivity. One survivor, author Aleksandr Solzhenitsyn (sohl-zhuh-NEET-suhn), wrote about the hardships endured at a slave-labor camp in his nonfiction book *The Gulag Archipelago*.

THE GREAT PURGES

As Soviet leader, Stalin expanded the Gulag system, using it to imprison all those who opposed him, targeting Jews, leaders of non-Russian minority groups, and dissident communists. Stalin was paranoid about plots against him, which led him to initiate the **Great Purges**, the execution of those who had served under Lenin. Stalin feared these Old Bolsheviks might threaten his rule. He also ordered the rounding up of artists, intellectuals, writers, army officers, engineers, and scientists who he believed would undermine him. Stalin staged show trials, in which the accused were forced to confess and predetermined verdicts were announced.

Stalin worked hard to achieve what is known as a **cult of personality**, presenting himself as a great person to be admired through the use of propaganda. For example, he ordered reporters to write glowing articles about him and eliminated a free press that could report on the problems of his regime. Yet Soviet citizens lived in a constant state of terror. One wrong word or glance could lead to a trip to the Gulag. As Stalin said, "The easiest way to gain control of the population is to carry out acts of terror."

HISTORICAL THINKING

1. **READING CHECK** How did Joseph Stalin transform the Soviet Union?

2. **DRAW CONCLUSIONS** Why do you think peasants in the Soviet Union objected to collectivization?

3. **MAKE INFERENCES** Why did Stalin expand the Gulag system?

Totalitarianism in Asia and Latin America

2.4 MAIN IDEA Uncertain times in the early 20th century also led to the rise of totalitarian governments in parts of Asia and Latin America.

Living in a democracy, you may not understand how anyone would accept another system of government. Yet when faced with crises in the 1920s and 1930s, people in much of Asia and Latin America, as in Germany and Italy, turned to totalitarian leaders who promised relief from economic hardship and growing uncertainty.

INTENSE NATIONALISM IN JAPAN

In the 1920s, Japan had shown signs of heading in a more democratic direction. It had become a constitutional monarchy, with an emperor whose role was mainly ceremonial. Yet, Japan's large industrial businesses, the zaibatsu, exerted much power over the government and the influence of the military was increasing. Like Mussolini in Italy, Japan's military leaders emphasized national glory over individual liberty. When the emperor **Hirohito** rose to the throne in 1926, these **ultranationalists**, or extreme nationalists, saw a chance to expand their powers. After the market collapse of 1929 and the onset of the Great Depression, support for the military grew among the many farm families whose sons made up most of the empire's armies.

The Japanese had begun to build an empire by claiming Korea, Taiwan, and China's Shandong Province across the Yellow Sea from Korea. The ultranationalists believed that Japan's only avenue for gaining economic strength was through expansion, and they wanted to make use of East and Southeast Asia's resources and cheap labor. To accomplish this, they invaded Manchuria, a province in China north of Korea, in 1931. The Japanese military blew up some railroad tracks there and then blamed Chinese nationalists. Western nations condemned the action. The Japanese people, however, became enraged by the outside criticism, feeling more enthralled with the Japanese military and increasingly supportive of imperial expansion. As imperial fever grew, elected politicians lost control of the military. As in Italy and Germany, militarization strengthened the economy, and rising employment caused the working class to rally behind the ultranationalists.

RISE OF MODERN TURKEY

Meanwhile, in Southwest Asia, the new nation of Turkey emerged from the violent collapse of the Ottoman Empire. The leadership of **Mustafa Kemal** prevented Turkey from being divided by victorious Allies after World War I. With the success of Kemal's armies, by 1923 the Great Powers agreed to recognize a sovereign Turkish republic. For his role, Kemal earned the name *Atatürk*, or "Father Turk." The new country was a result of Turkish nationalism, so the needs of other ethnic groups, such as the Armenians, Greeks, and Kurds, were largely ignored. Thousands of Greeks were forced to flee Turkey

In promoting modernization, Turkish leader Mustafa Kemal launched an alphabet reform initiative. Arabic script was replaced by a new alphabet to reflect the sounds of spoken Turkish. Kemal toured the country, explaining the new writing system.

748 CHAPTER 26

for their homeland and many Turks were expelled from Greece in a population exchange between the two countries. Such mass movements provide evidence of how hard it can be to organize national boundaries along ethnic lines.

From the start, Atatürk made it clear that he intended to be the unchallenged ruler of Turkey. He ordered rapid modernization so that Turkey might rival the economy and military power of European countries. Atatürk believed that adopting Western ways would bring his country success, so he imposed a secular constitution with strict separation between Islam and government. His drive to remove religion from politics included laws to improve the status of women. He also granted girls the right to an education and extended suffrage to women. At the same time, he banned the wearing of veils in public.

Wanting immediate change rather than gradual reform, the totalitarian leader imposed his own will on the nation. Atatürk died in 1938, but an authoritarian government continued in Turkey with the military playing a strong role.

BRAZIL'S "NEW STATE"

Latin American nations also experienced the growth of totalitarianism to combat the economic problems brought on by the global Great Depression. Brazil came closest to following the European models of fascism. **Getúlio Vargas** (jay-TOO-lee-oh VAHR-guhs) assumed power in 1930 and soon began strengthening the economy through government involvement, such as nationalizing natural resources.

In 1937, Vargas made a bold political move by suspending the Brazilian constitution and announcing the beginning of his *Estado Novo*, or "New State." According to Vargas, the goal of the *Estado Novo* was to stimulate Brazil's weak economy. He swore to "crisscross the nation with railroads, highways, and airlines; to increase production; to provide for the laborer." He also pledged to bring about unity in Brazil by eliminating regional competition. His stated goal was "to organize public opinion so that there is, body and soul, one Brazilian thought." That one thought would be his own.

Brazil had something in common with Turkey, Japan, Italy, Germany, the Soviet Union, and other countries that abandoned democracy and free markets for more centralized political and economic systems. Would the values of liberal democracy—such as divided government, free enterprise, and the rule of law—be able to make a comeback?

By 1932, the world market price for coffee had plunged so dramatically that Brazil, the world's leading producer, destroyed tens of thousands of tons of coffee by burning it or shoveling it into the sea.

HISTORICAL THINKING

1. **READING CHECK** What was the connection between totalitarianism and economic conditions in the 1930s?

2. **COMPARE AND CONTRAST** How was the rise of totalitarianism in Germany similar to and different from that in Japan?

3. **DRAW CONCLUSIONS** Why might someone living in Turkey have opposed Mustafa Kemal?

3.1

MAIN IDEA Mohandas Gandhi encouraged the use of nonviolent protest in the effort to achieve self-rule in India.

Gandhi and India

While nationalism in Europe led people to yield to totalitarian control, it had a different effect on people in South Asia. India had long been subjected to imperialism under British rule. Now its people were ready for change, leading to the rise of anti-colonial nationalism on the Indian subcontinent.

INDIANS CALL FOR MORE RIGHTS

India's rich natural resources and large workforce made it the "Jewel in the Crown" of the British Empire. Yet the people of India were growing discontented with their lack of rights. More than a million Indians had risked their lives for Britain in World War I, and they believed they deserved a greater voice in government in return.

CRITICAL VIEWING Mohandas Gandhi sits and spins cotton in Ceylon in November 1927. He was committed to traditional ways of making cloth in part to boycott British-made goods. What details in the photo express Gandhi's commitment to the Indian people?

At first, the Indian National Congress simply worked for reforms and better treatment, but the British only slightly increased Indian participation in government.

Then in 1919, the **Amritsar Massacre** shocked the Indian people. An unarmed crowd had gathered in a garden area for a religious ceremony, unaware that the British had banned public meetings. A British officer ordered his Indian troops to fire directly into the crowd. This horrible display of violence left 400 dead and 1,200 wounded and caused the Indian National Congress to stop cooperating with the British and confront them instead. In 1920, the Indian National Congress launched its first mass public protest to gain **Hind Swaraj**, Indian self-rule.

GANDHI AND NONVIOLENCE

At about this time, the young Western-educated lawyer **Mohandas K. Gandhi** became a leader of the Indian National Congress. To show his commitment to the Indian people, Gandhi discarded European dress for the spare clothing of a Hindu holy man. Yet his philosophy was inspired by both Western and Indian traditions. Western ideals of equality affected his view that the **Dalits**, those lowest in the Hindu caste hierarchy, were entitled to more rights. But Gandhi acquired two main moral principles from South Asian tradition. He strongly believed in **ahimsa** (uh-HIHM-sah), or absolute nonviolence, and **satyagraha** (suh-TYAH-gruh-huh)—or "soul force"—the application of nonviolence to politics. Gandhi's idea that violence should never counter violence earned him the title *Mahatma*, or "Great Soul."

Gandhi implored the Indian people to engage in **civil disobedience**, or the refusal to follow unjust laws, in a peaceful way. In 1920, the British threw Gandhi and other congress leaders in jail for encouraging dissent. Acts of violence that followed caused Gandhi

THE SALT MARCH Salt was readily available along the long ocean shores of India. However, the British required that all purchases of salt be made through them. Indians had objected to this policy for many decades because most of them could not afford the expensive, heavily taxed salt. Protesting this situation, Gandhi began his 240-mile walk to the sea that became known as the Salt March, along with several dozen supporters. Dressed in traditional Indian clothing using a walking stick, Gandhi gained the world's attention. Newspapers everywhere printed stories and published photographs of the 24-day journey.

Every day, Gandhi was joined by many more marchers, and many others gathered in crowds along the route to hear him speak. Once at the coast, Gandhi and the other marchers symbolically gathered salt deposits lying on the beach. His march had made clear the injustices that Indians faced under British rule, as people around the world saw films and photographs of Gandhi's protest.

to determine that the Indian people were not ready for self-rule through satyagraha. He then retreated to his *ashram* (AHSH-ruhm), a communal rural home, where he enjoyed the simple rural life that he believed was the ideal existence. He spent hours sitting at a wheel spinning cotton, and the gentle clicking of the wheel helped him meditate. It also symbolized the rejection of British textiles and the exploiting of the Indian workforce. Without Gandhi, a new generation of congress leaders emerged in India, including British-educated **Jawaharlal Nehru** (juh-WAH-hur-lahl NAY-roo), who would later win election as the party's president in 1929.

In 1930, Gandhi re-emerged to lead a new campaign of civil disobedience. He led strikes as well as boycotts of British products. His best-known act of mass disobedience was the Salt March to protest a British law that forbade Indians from making their own salt. The march kicked off a movement that led to the arrests of some 60,000 people for nonviolent civil disobedience by the end of 1930.

Initially, the British responded by jailing congress leaders, but then they compromised by issuing the Government of India Act of 1935. This act called for the election of semi-representative regional assemblies. The congress complained that this action was inadequate, but it took part in the elections anyway, scoring huge victories.

Gandhi and Nehru agreed that the Indian National Congress should embrace members of all faiths. This did not appease, or satisfy, leaders of the new **Muslim League** in India. They feared that under Indian self-rule they would be oppressed by the Hindu majority. Distrust grew between the two religious communities. Muslim League leaders began to call for the creation of a separate Muslim state called Pakistan. Gandhi did his best to reassure the Muslim community, and Nehru envisioned a secular nation. The British insisted that only through their continued control could the diverse people of India live in peace.

HISTORICAL THINKING

1. **READING CHECK** Why did Gandhi undertake the Salt March?

2. **MAKE PREDICTIONS** How might events have been different if the British had met the early demands of the Indian National Congress?

3. **EVALUATE** How effective was Gandhi as a leader?

3.2 On Progress and Civilization

DOCUMENT-BASED QUESTION

Which would you prefer, living in the city and working in an office or living in the countryside and working outdoors? Your answer may depend on your past experiences and how they have shaped your way of thinking. Like other people, whether in the past or present, you have developed a frame of reference that is based at least partially on where, when, and how you live your life.

Nehru and Gandhi discuss ideas at a meeting of the Indian National Congress in 1936.

Mohandas K. Gandhi and Jawaharlal Nehru were the two most influential Indian leaders of the 20th century. Born 20 years apart, they represented different generations in the Indian National Congress. Gandhi was the main force behind Indian resistance to British colonialism in the 1920s and 1930s. In contrast, Nehru served as the first prime minister of the independent Indian republic from 1947 to 1964.

Both men were influenced by the time they spent in Britain. Living there as a law student in the late 1800s, Gandhi met British idealists and rebels who valued intuition over reason and rejected the mainstream values of an industrial society.

Nehru's British experience was quite different from Gandhi's. Nehru's wealthy background allowed him to mingle with Britain's elite. He was also strongly influenced by the reformist socialist movement of the early 1900s. These socialists accepted the economic development that came with capitalist industrialism, but they wanted fairer distribution of wealth. Gandhi and Nehru's varying experiences would shape the two leaders' visions for an independent India.

DOCUMENT ONE

Primary Source: Book
from *Hind Swaraj* by Mohandas K. Gandhi, 1909

Born in 1869 in the western Indian state of Gujarat, Mohandas Gandhi grew up under modest circumstances in a deeply religious Hindu family. Gandhi's time in London for legal studies confirmed his belief that industrialism negatively affected society. Gandhi would later describe the ills of society as well as possible solutions in his book *Hind Swaraj*. Written over the course of a voyage from London to South Africa, the book is a condemnation of "modern civilization." In it, Gandhi argues that Indian self-rule will make little difference in the lives of the Indian people if the new leaders govern by the same principles and commitment to industrialization as their English oppressors. In this excerpt, Gandhi questions characteristics of "civilization" and wonders if they really do make people happier.

CONSTRUCTED RESPONSE Based on this excerpt, what are the evils of civilization?

Let us first consider what state of things is described by the word "civilization." . . . Formerly, in Europe, people ploughed their lands mainly by manual labor. Now one man can plough a vast tract by means of steam engines and can thus amass great wealth. This is called a sign of civilization. . . . Formerly, men worked in the open air only as much as they liked. Now thousands of workmen meet together and for the sake of maintenance work in factories or mines. Their condition is worse than that of beasts. They are obliged to work, at the risk of their lives, at most dangerous occupations, for the sake of millionaires. Formerly, men were made slaves under physical compulsion. Now they are enslaved by temptation of money and of the luxuries that money can buy. . . . This civilization takes note neither of morality nor of religion. . . . This civilization . . . has taken such a hold on the people in Europe that those who are in it appear to be half mad. They lack real physical strength or courage. . . . They can hardly be happy in solitude.

DOCUMENT TWO

Primary Source: Book
from *Jawaharlal Nehru, An Autobiography*, 1936

The future prime minister was born into the highest class of Hindu society in 1889, making him 20 years younger than Gandhi. Nehru earned a degree from Britain's Cambridge University and then became a lawyer, but he was more interested in politics and helping India win independence than in practicing law. Nehru describes his close relationship with fellow freedom seeker Gandhi in his autobiography; however, the two men did not see eye to eye on everything. While many Indians have been strongly influenced by Gandhi's philosophy, Nehru's attitude has been much more evident in Indian government policy since the country achieved independence in 1947.

CONSTRUCTED RESPONSE According to the excerpt, why is it best to accept the existence of civilization?

Personally I dislike the praise of poverty and suffering. . . . Nor do I appreciate in the least the idealization of the "simple peasant life." I have almost a horror of it, and instead of submitting to it myself I want to drag out even the peasantry from it. . . . What is there in "The Man with the Hoe" to idealize over? Crushed and exploited for innumerable generations, he is only little removed from the animals who keep him company. . . . The desire to get away from the mind of man to primitive conditions where mind does not count, seems to me quite incomprehensible. . . . Present-day civilization is full of evils, but it is also full of good; and it has the capacity to rid itself of those evils. To destroy it root and branch is to remove that capacity from it and revert to a dull, senseless, and miserable existence. But even if that were desirable it is an impossible undertaking. We cannot stop the river of change or cut ourselves adrift from it, and psychologically we who have eaten of the apple of Eden cannot forget that taste and go back to primitiveness.

SYNTHESIZE & WRITE

1. **REVIEW** Review what you have read and observed about the two viewpoints regarding civilization.

2. **RECALL** On your own paper, list two details about the writer of one of the excerpts and two opinions expressed in the excerpt from that writer.

3. **CONSTRUCT** Construct a topic sentence that answers this question: How and why are the two leaders' opinions about civilization both similar and different?

4. **WRITE** Using evidence from this chapter and the documents, write an informative paragraph that supports your topic sentence in Step 3.

3.3 Global Resistance to Colonialism

MAIN IDEA Living under harsh colonial rule, the peoples of Africa, the Caribbean region, and Southeast Asia increased their protests against outside domination.

Thinking only of one's self-interest can have devastating effects on others. That's just what happened in Africa, the Caribbean, and Southeast Asia. The people in these locations suffered at the hands of imperialist powers that profited at their expense. The oppressed people longed for self-rule.

COLONIAL RULE CONTINUES

As in South Asia, nationalist movements developed in Africa, the Caribbean, and Southeast Asia. Many colonized people believed they deserved freedom for their help in fighting World War I, but European powers continued to rule. One way they maintained control was by enlisting indigenous allies—native people who helped control and administer the colonial territory. The native workers were educated so they could perform their jobs as clerks, nurses, and primary school teachers. Along the way, however, they also learned about Western revolutions and began to envision freedom for their own nations.

Nnamdi Azikiwe smiles in response to greetings from crowds of Nigerians at Euston Station in London, where he was attending the Nigerian constitutional conference in 1958. In 1963, Azikiwe would become the first president of independent Nigeria.

French assimilation policies promised that Asians and Africans could become French in language and culture. Despite this, they would always be perceived as inferior because of the racist ideas of the colonialists. The British did not believe in assimilation, so there the distinction between the rulers and the ruled was even clearer. The British employed what they called "indirect rule," relying on "native authorities" to carry out day-to-day administrative tasks such as collecting taxes. Yet in no way were these authorities considered British.

AFRICA

In Africa, chiefs were made "native authorities," supposedly to show that the British respected local customs. In reality, the colonialists simply wanted the local leaders to work at the bottom rungs of their administration. By the 1930s, many nationalists viewed this practice as hurtful to their cause. One such leader was Western-educated Nigerian nationalist **Nnamdi Azikiwe** (NAHM-dee ah-zee-KEE-way). He believed that Nigerians of varying backgrounds needed to join together to work for self-rule and founded the Nigerian Youth Movement as one way to achieve unity. Azikiwe also created a sports association focused on Nigerians' love of soccer to encourage nationalist feeling.

At the same time, occasional uprisings took place in response to colonial tax, trade, and land policies. In the 1929 Igbo Women's War, women in southeastern Nigeria protested colonial interference in household and village affairs. They gathered in large numbers, wore symbolic costumes, and sang songs mocking chiefs who followed British orders. The British changed their tax system slightly after this, but the local uprising did not threaten colonial rule.

Tensions were greatest in places where Europeans came to Africa not just as rulers but also as settlers. In South Africa and Kenya, Africans not only lost their sovereignty but also their best lands. Because of this, a mass protest movement arose in Kenya in the 1920s. Again, local protest was not enough to bring immediate and major reforms, but the groundwork was being laid. While Europe prepared for yet another deadly war, young Africans such as **Jomo Kenyatta** studied abroad, preparing for their roles as future leaders of nationalist movements. Kenyatta's book *Facing Mt. Kenya* was one of the first to explain African history and culture from an African point of view.

THE CARIBBEAN

Mass nationalism developed more rapidly in the British West Indies than in Africa. By the 1920s, Jamaican-born **Marcus Garvey** had gained a huge following for his United Negro Improvement Association (UNIA). His "back-to-Africa" philosophy called on all people of African heritage to band together. In this way, he believed they could gain dignity and improve their economic situation. In the United States, the National Association for the Advancement of Colored People (NAACP) continued to agitate for equal rights, with W.E.B. Du Bois writing on international affairs in the NAACP journal, *The Crisis*.

Meanwhile, the Great Depression made the conditions even worse in the Caribbean as well as in African colonies. Colonial powers were desperate for cheap goods to prop up their own weak economies. In the British West Indies, falling prices and depressed wages led to unrest. Across the ocean in **equatorial** Africa, the French made farmers keep planting, weeding, and harvesting cotton despite falling prices. The British imposed a "grow more crops" campaign in East Africa, where peasants were required to keep growing coffee for export despite losses from doing so. This meant that farmers did not have time or land for the subsistence farming that fed their families.

SOUTHEAST ASIA

After 1929, a drop in automobile manufacturing depressed the world market for rubber. Unemployment

Many civil rights groups adopted Marcus Garvey's message that urban blacks should unite to gain political and economic power. This 1920 photo portrays the charismatic Garvey riding in a Harlem parade at what he called the "First International Convention of the Negro Peoples of the World."

jumped in the Southeast Asian lands of Malaya, Vietnam, and the Dutch West Indies. Some farmers stopped growing export crops to raise food for themselves and their families, but the French still required them to pay taxes in cash. Those who objected were forced to work on government projects and French-owned plantations.

The people of French Indochina were not organized enough to resist the colonialists, but their continued oppression would change that over time. In 1930, the Vietnam National Party was punished for a failed rebellion. The group's leader stated at his execution: "If France does not want to have increasing trouble with revolutionary movements, she should immediately modify the cruel and inhuman policy now practiced in Indochina."

Across the colonies, nationalist leaders were laying the foundation for change. Mass nationalism would emerge following the new worldwide military conflict soon to erupt.

HISTORICAL THINKING

1. **READING CHECK** What was the effect of the Great Depression on colonized peoples?

2. **EXPLAIN** Why did tensions increase between colonized peoples and European colonizers following World War I?

3. **MAKE PREDICTIONS** What might cause colonial independence movements to gain traction in the coming years?

4.1

MAIN IDEA Land grabs by both Japan and Italy set the stage for world conflict in what would become known as World War II.

Japanese Aggression, Italian Invasion

War does not sneak up on anyone. Usually, there are warning signs even if they are not fully recognized at the time. Prior to World War II, aggressive acts by Japan toward China and by Italy toward Ethiopia heralded a coming conflict.

Chinese students light candles during a memorial service on December 13, 2007, to mark the 70th anniversary of the Rape of Nanjing and to remember those killed by Japanese soldiers.

JAPAN ON THE OFFENSIVE

As Japan's military attempted to expand its empire, it found China vulnerable to conquest. China was in a state of internal conflict between the nationalist government of Chiang Kai-shek and communist revolutionaries led by Mao Zedong. A nationalist attack in 1927 forced the communists to retreat to China's interior. During the Long March of 1934–1937, the communists walked about 7,500 miles across deserts and mountains to regroup in the northeast.

The Japanese had already defied the League of Nations with the occupation of Manchuria. In 1937, they launched a savage attack on coastal China in what become known as the Second Sino-Japanese War. Chiang and Mao agreed to put aside their differences to fight the common enemy, but they never combined forces or coordinated their efforts.

Convinced of their ethnic superiority, the Japanese cruelly mistreated the Chinese in their path. Japanese soldiers killed hundreds of thousands of civilians during the **Rape of Nanjing**. They viciously attacked women and disfigured children to spread terror among the population. Their complete disregard of the difference between soldiers and civilians took total war to a new level. About 300,000 noncombatants died. The Japanese then headed west and farther south through China. Other nations seemed unable or unwilling to stop Japanese aggression and atrocities.

MUSSOLINI STRIKES

Like Japanese leaders, Benito Mussolini of Italy did not listen when world leaders criticized his military aggression, and he ordered the invasion of Ethiopia in 1935. The Ethiopians put up a strong fight to defend their independent kingdom. But Mussolini was willing to bring total war to Africa, for example, by ordering Italian planes to drop poison gas on Ethiopian villagers. Such use of new, highly destructive technology gave the Ethiopians little hope.

The Ethiopian emperor **Hailie Selassie** went to Geneva to beg the League of Nations for help. He warned that no small nation would ever be safe if the international community did not take action now. The League of Nations placed economic **sanctions**, or trade restrictions, on Mussolini but went no further. Italy had access to colonial resources such as Libyan oil and received aid from Germany, so the League's economic sanctions had little effect. Also, most European nations seemed uninterested in assisting African people. Little did they realize that Italy's aggressive action put the entire world at risk.

Ethiopian emperor Hailie Selassie addresses the League of Nations in 1936, urging members to take action to protect his country from Italian invasion: "I ask the 52 nations, who have given the Ethiopian people a promise to help them in their resistance to the aggressor, what are they willing to do for Ethiopia? . . . What reply shall I have to take back to my people?"

HISTORICAL THINKING

1. **READING CHECK** What made China vulnerable to Japanese attacks in the 1930s?

2. **COMPARE AND CONTRAST** How were the plights of the Chinese and Ethiopian people similar? How were they different?

3. **DRAW CONCLUSIONS** What did Mussolini's attack on Ethiopia reveal about the League of Nations? How did this affect the League?

4.2

MAIN IDEA With the support of Italy and Germany, fascist leader Francisco Franco fought for and won complete control of Spain during a time of civil war.

Franco and the Spanish Civil War

What sparks creativity? Often it can be the desire to bring beauty into the world. Or it can be to express an important idea or message. During a time of turbulence in Spain, artists, photographers, and writers found new ways to portray the evils of war and fascism.

FRANCO GAINS POWER

A warning bell was tolling across the world in the late 1930s. Japanese, Italian, and German aggression hinted that another war was imminent. The Paris Peace Conference that ended World War I had left a bitter taste for those penalized by it, and as you have read, the Great Depression led many to lose interest in liberal democracy and capitalism. In Europe, far-right fascism competed for influence with far-left communism. Intent on maintaining peace, liberal democracies ignored the warnings against authoritarianism.

Spain became a battleground in the struggle for power between right and left. Spain's monarchy had come to a crashing end in 1931, and a democratic government took its place. But some Spanish citizens were unhappy with the government's socialist approach to combating the Great Depression. By this time, the fascist movement had spread from Italy and Germany to Spain. Spanish conservatives, intrigued with fascism, took up arms under General **Francisco Franco** to seize power in Spain in 1936.

THE SPANISH CIVIL WAR

Francisco Franco's attempted coup divided the nation, leading to the Spanish Civil War. On one side were the conservative national forces, or Nationalists, led by Franco and backed by Germany and Italy. On the other side were the Republican forces, or the Loyalists, backed by the Soviet Union. Both sides depended on external support for war supplies. Eager to spread fascism in Europe, Germany offered Spain not only soldiers but also tanks, rifles, and airplanes. Germany

CRITICAL VIEWING After the Germans bombed Guernica, Spain, the artist Pablo Picasso created what would become one of his most famous works, *Guernica*. A powerful political statement, Picasso painted it as an immediate reaction to the inhumanity of the attack and to show the world the suffering of the Spanish people. What images in the painting help convey suffering and inhumanity?

© 2019 Estate of Pablo Picasso/Artists Right Society (ARS), New York saw the conflict in Spain as a chance to try out its newest military technology. Noticeably absent from involvement in the Spanish Civil War were Britain, France, and the United States. Yet some of their citizens fought alongside the Republicans. Anti-fascist volunteers from the United States organized themselves in "Lincoln Brigades" to fight for Spanish democracy.

The Nationalists began a concentrated advance on Republican territory. Unsuccessful in capturing Madrid outright, they began a 28-month siege on the capital city. They also attacked northern Spain, home of the Basque people and a center of Republican support. Soon Nationalist troops occupied the entire northern coast of Spain. Catalonia, the last holdout, eventually fell as well. The Republicans had been largely defeated, and many fled the country. The Nationalists claimed Madrid and all government power in 1939. In all, almost one million people died as a result of the war.

Both sides committed horrendous acts, but those inflicted by the Nationalists were more deliberate and intense. One especially cruel event was the **carpet-bombing**, or dropping of a large number of bombs, of the Basque town of Guernica in 1937. The plan was to

For Whom the Bell Tolls The writer Ernest Hemingway believed that the United States should do more to stop fascism. His novel *For Whom the Bell Tolls* follows a young American volunteer in the Lincoln Brigade as he risks his life for the cause of Spanish democracy. Hemingway borrowed the title from an English poet, who had written: "No man is an Island, entire of itself. . . any man's death diminishes me, because I am involved in Mankind; and therefore never send to know for whom the bell tolls; It tolls for thee." For Hemingway, the Spanish Civil War was a warning bell for democracy everywhere.

kill as many civilians as possible rather than hit military targets. Through his painting *Guernica*, Pablo Picasso hoped to alert the world to the attack's inhumanity and sway public opinion against the fascists. Other artists and writers used the Spanish Civil War as subject matter as well. Photographers Robert Capa and Gerda Taro documented the war in their photographs. Ernest Hemingway's experiences while reporting the war led him to write the novel *For Whom the Bell Tolls*. Fellow writer George Orwell fought on the Republican side and described his experience in his *Homage to Catalonia*.

The war's end left Franco firmly in control of Spain. He then launched a campaign to eliminate or imprison any Republicans still in the country. He also imposed harsh restrictions on Spain's population, such as outlawing labor unions and curtailing the rights of the Basques. The war left Spain in rough economic shape. Franco supported the fascist cause but would not be a major player in the upcoming world conflict.

HISTORICAL THINKING

1. **READING CHECK** How did Francisco Franco become Spain's dictator?
2. **DRAW CONCLUSIONS** Why do you think the bombing of Guernica targeted civilians?
3. **FORM AND SUPPORT OPINIONS** What do you think rule under the Republicans would have been like had they been victorious in Spain? Why?

4.3 **MAIN IDEA** Western democracies accommodated Adolf Hitler's aggression until the German leader invaded Poland, which caused Britain and France to declare war on Germany.

The Hitler-Stalin Pact

Throughout history, people have encroached on the rights and land of others. Sometimes, the encroachment is simply accepted, but often the affected people or others step up to take immediate action. However, like in Spain, Western democracies were well aware of Adolf Hitler's escalating aggression in the 1930s, but they did little to stop it.

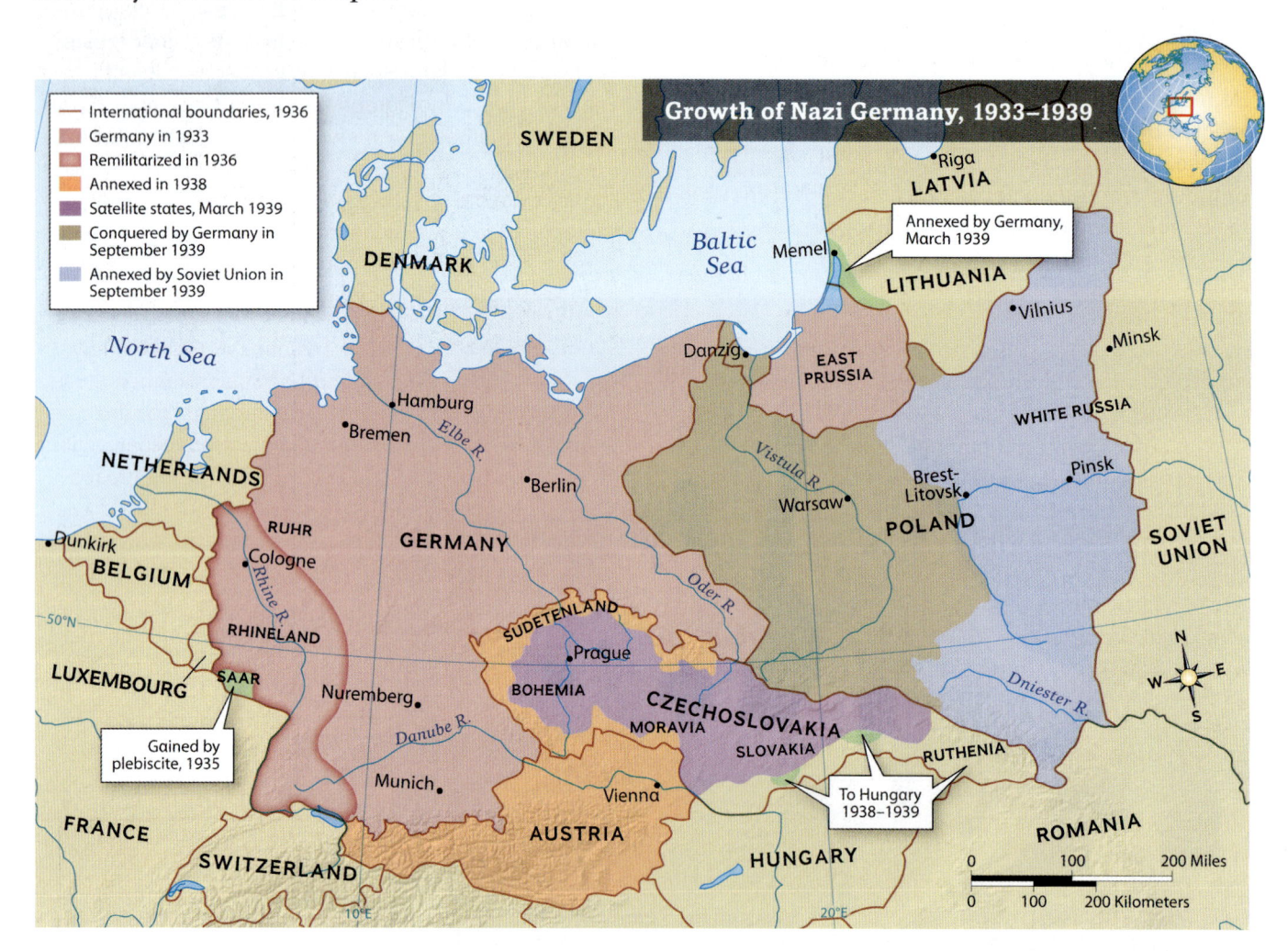

Growth of Nazi Germany, 1933–1939

Map legend:
- International boundaries, 1936
- Germany in 1933
- Remilitarized in 1936
- Annexed in 1938
- Satellite states, March 1939
- Conquered by Germany in September 1939
- Annexed by Soviet Union in September 1939

GERMAN ENCROACHMENTS

Before World War I, the Rhineland, which abutted France, had belonged to Germany. The Treaty of Versailles gave some of that land to France and also specified that the rest be demilitarized to ensure France's safety. Hitler was furious about this and other clauses in the treaty. In 1936, he built up German military forces and ordered them into the Rhineland region. This **remilitarization**, or rearming, and reoccupation of land both violated the Treaty of Versailles. The Western democracies complained but did not take any action. Their policy of **nonintervention**, or not getting involved, made Hitler even bolder.

760 CHAPTER 26

Hitler had long declared that the Germans needed *Lebensraum* (LAY-buhns-rowm), or "living space" and that Germans in countries to the east needed to be reunited with their homeland. Hitler believed that Germans could pursue their racial destiny only by gaining more land and imagined vast eastern spaces cleared of Jews. The Slavic peoples, whom he considered inferior to Germans, would provide slave labor under German command. The Nazi leader's plan carried the Social Darwinist idea of a racial "struggle for existence" to the extreme. Joseph Stalin took Hitler's expansion threat seriously, but Western leaders were more worried about their own domestic issues. In fact, some Westerners agreed with Hitler's anti-Semitic and anti-communist views.

Encouraged by the lack of response to his remilitarization of the Rhineland, Hitler annexed neighboring Austria. Next, Hitler moved to annex the Sudetenland, a province in Czechoslovakia. One member of the British Parliament, **Winston Churchill**, urged quick action against German aggression. But Churchill, who would become Britain's great wartime leader, was unable to get the British people to take a firm stand and thus risk war.

APPEASEMENT AND ISOLATIONISM

Instead of taking military action, British prime minister **Neville Chamberlain** flew to Munich to negotiate with Hitler through **appeasement**, or the giving of concessions to keep the peace. Chamberlain did not trust Hitler, but he was willing to appease Hitler to avoid the horrors of another total war. Still dazed from World War I, the British public largely supported Chamberlain's quest for "peace for our time." Because of this, Germany occupied the Sudetenland unchecked. Ever since, the term *appeasement* has meant the failure to stop an aggressor in time.

The lack of resolve on the part of Western nations alarmed Joseph Stalin. He came to believe that only through Western support could his Soviet army withstand a German attack. Without the promise of such support, Stalin decided to deal with Hitler directly. Even though the two leaders hated and distrusted each other, they signed a nonaggression agreement that became known as the Hitler-Stalin Pact in 1939.

British Prime Minister Neville Chamberlain returns to London in September 1938, claiming "peace for our time" after negotiating with Hitler.

A secret addition to this nonaggression agreement divided Poland and other parts of eastern Europe into Soviet and German spheres of influence. Neither man was a trustworthy negotiator, however. Hitler was merely delaying his planned attack on Russia, while Stalin was stalling for time to prepare his country for war.

Hitler's invasion of Poland on September 1, 1939, caused Britain and France to immediately declare war on Germany. However, they took no active steps to confront the German army. Meanwhile, public opinion in the United States remained opposed to getting involved in European affairs. Thus, the United States chose **isolationism**, meaning it intended to stay out of foreign politics. Soon, however, peoples across Europe, Africa, Asia, and the Americas would be embroiled in total war. This world conflict would be unlike anything humanity had seen before.

HISTORICAL THINKING

1. **READING CHECK** What were two early acts of aggression by Adolf Hitler?

2. **MAKE CONNECTIONS** Why did nonintervention by Western democracies following Hitler's early aggression make the German leader bolder?

3. **ANALYZE CAUSE AND EFFECT** What event caused Great Britain to end its policy of appeasement toward Hitler? Why did this event spark Great Britain to abandon appeasement?

CHAPTER 26
ECONOMIC DEPRESSION AND AUTHORITARIAN REGIMES
REVIEW

VOCABULARY

Write one or more sentences that explains the connection between each pair of words.

1. mass media; popular culture
2. Great Depression; speculation
3. fascism; totalitarianism
4. collectivization; kulak
5. Hind Swaraj; civil disobedience
6. ahimsa; satyagraha
7. remilitarization; nonintervention
8. appeasement; isolationism

READING STRATEGY
COMPARE AND CONTRAST

Comparing and contrasting can help you form a deeper understanding of concepts. Complete a Venn diagram to compare and contrast the totalitarian leaders of Nazi Germany and the Soviet Union.

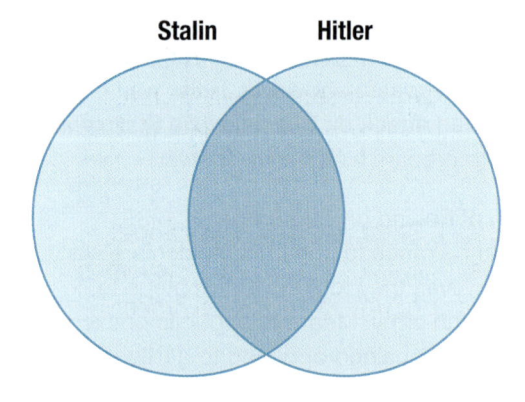

Stalin   Hitler

9. What was the greatest similarity between the two leaders? What was the greatest difference?

MAIN IDEAS

Answer the following questions. Support your answers with evidence from the chapter.

10. What made radio technology so useful during World War I? **LESSON 1.1**
11. What was a political cause of Germany's suffering during the Great Depression? **LESSON 1.3**
12. What is the main characteristic of totalitarianism? **LESSON 2.1**
13. Why did Hitler believe that Germans should dominate the world? **LESSON 2.2**
14. Why did Stalin introduce collectivization in the Soviet Union? **LESSON 2.3**
15. Why did the Japanese launch an invasion of the Manchurian province of China? **LESSON 2.4**
16. What was the goal of Gandhi's Salt March and what were the effects? **LESSON 3.1**
17. How did Nnamdi Azikiwe think independence could be achieved for Nigeria? **LESSON 3.3**
18. How did technology give the Italians an advantage over the Ethiopians? **LESSON 4.1**
19. What caused the Spanish Civil War, who were the opponents, and how did it end? **LESSON 4.2**
20. How did the political views of Winston Churchill and Neville Chamberlain differ? **LESSON 4.3**

HISTORICAL THINKING

Answer the following questions. Support your answers with evidence from the chapter.

21. **EVALUATE** How important was aviation technology to the winning of World War I?
22. **ANALYZE POINT OF VIEW** Why might Americans have had differing views about the government's response to the Great Depression?
23. **FORM AND SUPPORT OPINIONS** Do you think a leader like Mussolini could rise again? Explain.
24. **DRAW CONCLUSIONS** What was Hitler's rationale for excluding certain groups of people from society?
25. **DESCRIBE** How might you describe the government of Japan during the 1930s?
26. **COMPARE AND CONTRAST** How were the rise and aggression of Hitler, Mussolini, and Stalin alike and different?

INTERPRET VISUALS

Study the table, which shows unemployment rates for various countries in the years 1929–1934. Then answer the questions below.

27. Which country had the highest unemployment rate in 1929? Why do you think this was so?

28. What might have caused the sharp drop in Germany's unemployment rate in 1934?

Unemployment Rates, 1929–1934

	Great Britain	Germany	Belgium	Sweden	United States
1929	10.4	13.3	1.3	10.2	3.2
1930	16.1	22.7	3.6	11.9	8.7
1931	21.3	34.3	10.9	16.8	15.9
1932	22.1	43.8	19.0	22.4	23.6
1933	19.9	36.2	16.9	23.3	24.9
1934	16.7	20.5	18.9	18.0	21.7

Source: Walter Galenson and Arnold Zellner, "International Comparison of Unemployment Rates," *The Measurement and Behavior of Unemployment* (National Bureau of Economic Research, 1957)

ANALYZE SOURCES

In the 1930s, the Japanese began a policy of expansion to solve their overcrowding problem and improve their economy. In this excerpt from a 1939 speech, military leader Hashimoto Kingoro offers a justification for why Japan chose this path for growth. Read the excerpt and answer the question that follows.

> We are like a great crowd of people packed into a small and narrow room, and there are only three doors through which we might escape, namely emigration, advance into world markets, and expansion of territory. The first door has been barred to us by the anti-Japanese immigration policies of other countries. The second is being pushed shut by tariff barriers. . . . It is quite natural that Japan should rush upon the last remaining door . . . of territorial expansion.

29. What does the primary source tell you about why Japan concentrated on expansion to meet its needs?

CONNECT TO YOUR LIFE

30. **EXPLANATORY** Think about how Mahatma Gandhi's and Jawaharlal Nehru's different views made them both great leaders of India's independence movement. Then think about movements you care about today. Can you identify two leaders who exemplify the inspirational and practical roles for this movement? Do you think one role is more important than the other, or are both roles needed? Write a short essay to express your views, using examples from movements you know of today.

TIPS

- Use a T-Chart to make notes about Gandhi's and Nehru's views and their roles. Conduct additional Internet or library research if necessary.

- Use another T-Chart to make notes about the views and roles of leaders of a movement today, again conducting additional research as necessary.

- Draft an essay describing the two leaders you've chosen, explaining their roles and evaluating the importance of those roles.

- Use two or three vocabulary terms from the chapter in your essay.

- End your essay with a generalization explaining why different types of leaders are needed in different situations.

CHAPTER 27

The Second World War
1939–1945

HISTORICAL THINKING How was World War II a total war?

SECTION 1 **The Allied and Axis Powers**

SECTION 2 **Total War**

SECTION 3 **The Holocaust and the Legacy of War**

CRITICAL VIEWING

On June 6, 1944, Allied British, American, and Canadian forces invaded western Europe to free the region from German occupation during World War II. The Allies began the operation by landing on the beaches of the French province of Normandy. In this photo, U.S. soldiers jump off their landing craft and prepare for battle on what came to be known as D-Day. What might have been some of the challenges and dangers the soldiers faced once they jumped into the water?

The Second World War 765

1.1 **MAIN IDEA** In the first two years of World War II, Germany's powerful military overran much of western Europe.

Germany's Military Might

You can't always reason with a bully. Britain tried to keep the peace with Germany, but then the Nazis bullied their way into Poland. In the end, Britain and other European nations decided they had no choice but to fight.

German Advances, 1938–1941

Map legend:
- Allied territory
- Axis powers
- Axis satellite
- Axis-controlled by 1940
- Soviet territory
- Neutral nation
- German troop movements
- Battle of Britain and the Blitz, 1940–1941

GERMAN OFFENSIVE

The German army was ready for war. By the time Adolf Hitler's forces invaded Poland on September 1, 1939, Germany had mobilized 100 infantry divisions, with between 12,000–25,000 soldiers in each one. The army also boasted six armored divisions, which included its superior fleet of thickly armored tanks known as *panzers*. In the early years of the war, German soldiers used a tactic called the **blitzkrieg** (BLIHTS-kreeg), or "lightning war." This tactic employed speed, surprise, and the combined firepower of tanks, bombers, and ground forces. All of these elements were set into motion before the enemy could organize a defense. The blitzkrieg was used to overwhelm Poland.

As you've read, Britain and France declared war on Germany after the invasion, marking the beginning of World War II. The two countries—and others that would later oppose Germany—were called the **Allied Powers**. Germany, Italy, and Japan would form the principal partners of the **Axis Powers**. After declaring war, France and Britain moved troops to the Maginot Line, a series of fortifications built after World War I along the French-German border. But for the next six months, no major battles took place. For that reason, some journalists referred to the period as the "Phony War."

Unfortunately, the war would soon become all too real. In April 1940, German forces swept through Denmark and Norway, quickly conquering both countries. Following this act of German aggression, British prime minister Neville Chamberlain resigned from office, and Winston Churchill took his place. Then in May, Germany invaded Luxembourg, the Netherlands, and Belgium. Luxembourg and the Netherlands surrendered within days. Meanwhile, Britain and France sent troops north to Belgium and fell into a trap. Germany invaded the country from the south and surrounded the British and French forces.

The Allies were cornered in the port of Dunkirk on the northern coast of France. Convinced it was his only option, Churchill ordered the evacuation of the Allied troops. While German planes bombed the port, British naval ships and even private vessels owned by British civilians came to rescue the soldiers and carry them across the English Channel. Nearly 350,000 British and French troops were saved. Although they had been driven from the European continent, the British resolve to fight was strengthened by their effort at Dunkirk.

BRITISH RESOLVE

After the evacuation, the German army swept through France, defeating the remaining French forces. The Germans entered Paris on June 14, and about a week later, France signed an armistice with Germany. Under its terms, German troops occupied northern France and a strip of western France along the Atlantic coast. Southern France remained under French control, and the town of Vichy (VIH-shee) became the capital of this unoccupied part of France. The government of Vichy France largely cooperated with the Germans. Nevertheless, some of the French continued their fight against the Nazis. French general **Charles de Gaulle** set up headquarters in Britain to allow "Free French" forces to continue fighting as a resistance force. De Gaulle had the support of many French citizens who saw Vichy leaders as Nazi puppets, but he had few troops or bases. As a result, Britain was left largely isolated.

In control of continental Europe, Hitler targeted Britain next. Germany began the **Battle of Britain** in July, which pitted Britain's Royal Air Force (RAF) against the German air force, the Luftwaffe. While the Luftwaffe inflicted heavy damage on British cities, the RAF put up stiff resistance and eventually forced Germany's air force to retreat. The Luftwaffe then began to bomb London and other British cities in September. These air raids, known as the Blitz, continued nearly every night until May 1941. The Blitz left much of London in ruins and killed about 43,000 British civilians.

Although the United States maintained a neutral position in the war, President Franklin Roosevelt began to provide military supplies and other aid to Britain in March 1941. By doing so, Roosevelt claimed the United States would become "the arsenal of democracy." The American president also agreed to issue the **Atlantic Charter** jointly with Churchill in August. Under the eight-point charter, the two leaders agreed to such principles as freedom of the seas, greater trade among nations, and the right of people to choose the kind of government they desired. Very soon, Roosevelt would take more substantial action to protect these principles.

After the retreating Allied soldiers made it safely across the English Channel from Dunkirk, Winston Churchill spoke before the House of Commons. In this excerpt from the House of Commons speech, the prime minister seeks to rally the British to fight on against Germany.

PRIMARY SOURCE

[W]e shall not flag [tire] or fail. We shall go on to the end, we shall fight in France, we shall fight on the seas and oceans, . . . we shall defend our island, whatever the cost may be, we shall fight on the beaches, we shall fight on the landing grounds, we shall fight in the fields and in the streets, we shall fight in the hills; we shall never surrender.

—from a speech before the House of Commons by Winston Churchill, June 4, 1940

HISTORICAL THINKING

1. **READING CHECK** What made the German army a formidable fighting force?

2. **INTERPRET MAPS** Why was it important for Germany to occupy France before targeting Britain?

3. **DRAW CONCLUSIONS** How did Hitler underestimate Britain and the British people?

1.2 MAIN IDEA Japan's attack on Pearl Harbor triggered U.S. entry into World War II.

Japan's Rising Sun

On December 7, 1941, the unthinkable happened. Flying its flag, the "Rising Sun," Japan launched an unprovoked attack on the U.S. Navy, forcing the Americans to go to war.

A DAY OF INFAMY

President Franklin Roosevelt had watched Japan's aggression and expansion into China under its emperor, Hirohito, and prime minister, **Tojo Hideki**, with alarm. Tojo would go on to direct many of Japan's battles and essentially seize control of the country's government. Roosevelt's concern over Japanese expansionism increased after Japan joined Germany and Italy in the war.

In response, the president froze Japanese business assets in the United States in 1941. Roosevelt also placed an embargo on essential goods, such as oil, to Japan. A country of limited natural resources, Japan needed oil to ensure the continued growth of its industries and military. Many people believed war between the United States and Japan would erupt soon. But no one guessed the Japanese would be bold enough to strike Pearl Harbor, Hawaii, where the U.S. Pacific Fleet was headquartered.

Japan's military saw American power in the Pacific as an obstacle to its imperial designs and had planned the attack for months. On December 7, 1941, a large convoy of Japanese battleships, destroyers, aircraft carriers, and cruisers was within 200 miles of Pearl Harbor. Early that morning, Japanese bomber planes took off from the aircraft carriers. When military personnel at the U.S. naval base at Pearl Harbor detected the planes on their radar, they thought the bombers were American aircraft. And the Japanese had deliberately chosen a Sunday for their attack, when they believed security would be more relaxed.

Japanese soldiers charge into battle under the banner of the Rising Sun flag. The flag was first used by feudal Japanese warlords in the 1600s. Since Japan is often referred to as "the land of the rising sun," many Japanese view the flag as a symbol of their country.

The assault came in two waves as Japanese planes rained their bombs and bullets down on U.S. battleships and military aircraft. Nearly 20 American warships and about 200 planes were demolished or damaged. And more than 2,300 Americans were killed. The Japanese lost fewer than 100 men.

The next day, President Roosevelt addressed Congress and the American people by radio, saying, "Yesterday, December 7, 1941—a date which will live in infamy—the United States of America was suddenly and deliberately attacked by naval and air forces of the Empire of Japan." **Infamy** refers to an extremely shameful or evil act. Roosevelt called for a declaration of war, and Congress agreed. On December 8, Congress declared war on Japan. Three days later, Germany and Italy declared war on the United States. The United States joined the other Allied Powers in the fight against the Axis.

JAPANESE VICTORIES AND DEFEATS

Just hours after the attack on Pearl Harbor, Japan struck the Philippines, a U.S. territory at that time. Under the command of American general **Douglas MacArthur**, the U.S. Armed Forces in the Far East (USAFFE), which included many Filipino troops, had mobilized but were unprepared for a full-scale attack. The Japanese struck the Philippines by air and on land. By January 2, 1942, they had taken Manila, the country's capital. Unable to defend the territory, the USAFFE retreated to the jungles of the Bataan Peninsula. The crippled U.S. Navy was unable to provide backup. Eventually, 75,000 Filipino and American troops surrendered to the Japanese.

Allied soldiers captured by the Japanese were often horribly mistreated. After the USAFFE troops surrendered in the Philippines, the Japanese forced them to march about 60 miles to a prison camp with very little food or water. Those who fell, tried to escape, or stopped to drink from a puddle along the way were beaten, bayoneted, or shot. About 10,000 Filipinos and 750 Americans died in what became known as the **Bataan Death March**.

Meanwhile, Japan's Imperial forces were expanding their control of the Pacific. By 1942, Japan had seized Korea, Taiwan, Hong Kong, French Indochina, Singapore, and the Dutch East Indies. The Japanese claimed they were liberating the European colonies. But economic reasons and imperialist ambitions were the real motivating factors.

In the summer of 1942, the Allies finally handed the Japanese a couple of major setbacks. Japanese forces wanted to take control of the sea route north of Australia so they could destroy U.S. naval bases along the nation's eastern coast. However, Allied code breakers had uncovered the plan and alerted U.S. officials. The Allies launched a preemptive strike and battled the Japanese by air and sea off the coast of New Guinea for several days in May during the Battle of the Coral Sea. Eventually, the Japanese fighters turned back.

Next, Japan intended to seize Midway Island, located 1,400 miles west of Hawaii, and destroy a U.S. carrier stationed there. Yet once again, code breakers discovered Japan's battle plans. The intelligence allowed the Allies to stay one step ahead of the Japanese. On June 3, U.S. bombers attacked the Japanese fleet when it was still 500 miles from Midway. Japan attacked Midway the following morning. The three-day-long **Battle of Midway** that ensued greatly reduced Japan's naval forces. The Allied victory marked a major turning point of the war in the Pacific.

NATIONAL GEOGRAPHIC EXPLORER
ROBERT BALLARD

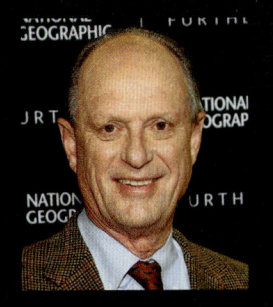

Discovery on the Sea Floor

National Geographic Explorer Robert Ballard, shown here, is best known for his 1985 discovery of the R.M.S. *Titanic*, a British ocean liner that sank in the North Atlantic in 1912. In May 1998, he also found the wreckage of the U.S.S. *Yorktown* in the Pacific Ocean. Japanese forces sank the aircraft carrier on June 7, 1942, during the Battle of Midway. When Ballard and his team found the ship 56 years later, it was resting almost 17,000 feet beneath the surface of the ocean. Surprisingly, the stainless-steel surfaces of the *Yorktown* were still shiny, and the ship's guns were still pointing skyward, as you can see in the photo below. The expedition crew left a memorial plaque by the ship, but the site remains a secret. "There is a big difference between the *Yorktown* and the *Titanic*," Ballard points out. "A warship is forever the property of the country."

HISTORICAL THINKING

1. **READING CHECK** What happened on December 7, 1941?
2. **MAKE PREDICTIONS** What might have happened if Allied code breakers hadn't uncovered Japan's plan to seize Midway Island?
3. **DRAW CONCLUSIONS** Why was the victory at the Battle of Midway a major turning point of the war in the Pacific?

1.3 MAIN IDEA Allied victories in Europe, Africa, and Asia finally brought World War II to an end.

Allied Momentum

When Napoleon invaded Russia in 1812, the campaign ended in disaster. Adolf Hitler hoped for a different outcome when his powerful German army marched into the Soviet Union. He didn't get one.

INVASION OF THE SOVIET UNION

As you've read, Adolf Hitler and Soviet leader Joseph Stalin signed a nonaggression pact in 1939. Hitler ended the pact between the two nations in June 1941, however, when his army invaded the Soviet Union. Stalin had asked the Allies to establish a front in western Europe to help his soldiers combat the Germans, but the Allies refused. The Soviet Union would bear the brunt of the German army alone.

More than three million German soldiers and 3,000 panzers plunged deep into Soviet territory at the beginning of the invasion known as Operation Barbarossa. But the Soviet forces, or Red Army, used a "scorched-earth" strategy as it retreated, destroying crops, bridges, and railroad cars. This meant that advancing German troops were left without shelter or additional food supplies as they advanced. Nonetheless, Hitler's soldiers pushed on. By mid-July, they were within a couple hundred miles of Moscow.

Over the next few months, an early and severe winter settled across the Soviet Union. Because they were running short of fuel, German commanders abandoned their plan to take Moscow and moved their troops south toward Soviet oil fields. As the German army pressed on, the troops suffered in the cold. By November 1941, about 700,000 Germans had died. Still, the German army continued to fight and managed to hold onto most of the ground it had captured earlier in the year. By the summer of 1942, Soviet casualties stood at about four million. The number of Germans who died or were wounded was high but not nearly as staggering.

The Soviets finally put an end to the German advance at the **Battle of Stalingrad**. (Stalingrad is now known as Volgograd.) About two million soldiers fought for nearly six months in the Soviet city. The two armies fought in the streets, causing high numbers of civilian casualties. When the German troops finally surrendered at the end of January 1943, the momentum of the entire European war shifted. Most historians regard the Battle of Stalingrad as the single most important Allied victory of World War II.

CAMPAIGNS IN NORTH AFRICA AND ITALY

While German forces were on the offensive in 1940 and 1941, Italy's Benito Mussolini was having a difficult time in the Mediterranean. Italy invaded Greece in October 1940, but the German army had to come to the aid of their fascist ally in 1941 when Greek partisans strongly resisted Italian forces. In Africa, Mussolini used his control over Libya and Ethiopia to invade British-controlled Egypt in 1940. After the British repelled that incursion, the Germans once again intervened the following year. However, the British beat the German army in Egypt at the Second Battle of El-Alamein in the fall of 1942. The victory marked the beginning of the end for the Axis Powers in North Africa and was another turning point for the Allies.

The United States now entered the North African theater when U.S. general **Dwight D. Eisenhower** led the Allied forces there in an invasion called Operation Torch in November 1942. By May 1943, American and British forces had recaptured Morocco and Algeria and defeated the German army. Vichy collaborators were replaced in North Africa by French officials loyal to Charles de Gaulle. As a result, his Free French army was now bolstered with North African recruits.

Once they were firmly established in North Africa, the Allied forces used it as a base of operations against Italy. In July 1943, the Allies began the Italian campaign by invading the island of Sicily and conquering it within about a month. As Italian troops fell back, the government in Rome arrested Mussolini. He managed to escape with German support but was eventually captured and executed by communist partisans. Fascism in Italy was over.

D-DAY AND THE BATTLE OF THE BULGE

Following these victories, the Allies were in a very strong position. At the end of 1943, Roosevelt, Churchill, and Stalin met in Tehran, Iran, to discuss plans to invade western Europe and take back France. British and Soviet troops had seized Iran in August 1941 in large part because the overland resupply routes there were critical to the war effort. After months of strategizing, General Eisenhower led an Allied invasion of the French coastal province of Normandy. On June 6, 1944, a fleet of warships and thousands of airplanes and naval vessels, called amphibious landing craft, headed toward five Normandy beaches. By sundown that day, which came to be known as **D-Day**, about 150,000 American, British, and Canadian troops had stormed the beaches.

Many troops drowned during the landing, and others were struck by German machine-gun fire as they set foot on the beaches. But Allied forces soon began to move inland. On August 19, Parisians, who were aware that the Allies would soon reach them, rose up against the occupying Germans. When the Allies arrived in Paris on August 25, the Nazis were ready to surrender.

In early September, the Allies advanced from northern France and recaptured Antwerp, Belgium. From there, they set off for the German border. But German forces had strengthened. In mid-December, more than 200,000 German soldiers advanced into southern Belgium, greatly outnumbering the Allied troops there, and broke through the Allied front line. This break in the front created a "bulge," which gave the battle its name: the **Battle of the Bulge**. Eisenhower called in reinforcements, and on December 26, the soldiers broke through German lines and captured the strategic Belgian town of Bastogne. Then in January 1945, thousands of Allied aircraft bombed the Germans and their supply lines, forcing the Nazis to withdraw.

The Second World War

Meanwhile, Soviet troops had moved across Poland toward Germany. Other Allied forces pressed east from France and Belgium, while those on the Italian Peninsula continued to push German troops north. To prepare for the ground-force invasion of Germany, the Allies intensified the aerial bombing of the country in February, targeting both industrial and civilian areas.

Soviet troops reached Berlin around mid-April. As they closed in on the underground bunker where Hitler was hiding, he committed suicide on April 30. Germany surrendered on May 8, 1945. The war in Europe was over. However, the war in the Pacific dragged on.

ISLAND HOPPING

After their victory at the Battle of Midway, the Allies went on the offensive to gain control of the Pacific. They used a two-pronged approach. Admiral Chester Nimitz of the U.S. Navy would travel west from Hawaii, and General Douglas MacArthur would travel north from Australia, both carrying out a campaign of **island hopping**. This strategy was designed to capture and control islands in the Pacific one by one. The Allies planned to establish bases on the islands to create a path to the Japanese homeland in preparation for an Allied attack on Japan.

The offensive began with an invasion of U.S. Marines on the island of Guadalcanal, where the Japanese were building an air base. By late 1942, each side had more than 20,000 troops engaged in battle on the small island. After six months of grueling combat, the Americans finally held Guadalcanal.

More Pacific victories soon followed for the Allies. By early 1944, Nimitz and MacArthur had taken control of the Marshall Islands and Guam. From there, the two commanders set their sights on the islands of Japan, only about 1,200 miles away.

By March 1945, the United States had reconquered the Philippines. The Japanese suffered heavy losses in the fighting, largely due to the use of suicide bomber pilots called **kamikaze**, meaning "divine wind." These Japanese pilots volunteered to crash their planes, loaded with explosives, into Allied ships. From October 1944 to the end of the war, the kamikaze destroyed 34 ships, but about 2,800 pilots died in the process.

The Allies were getting closer and closer to Japan. During the **Battle of Iwo Jima**, U.S. Marines were surprised by the fierce resistance of the Japanese soldiers, who fought from hidden caves and tunnels. In the American counterattack, nearly every Japanese soldier and civilian on the island perished. Fierce Japanese resistance also took place during the Battle of Okinawa, just 400 miles from Tokyo. Despite kamikaze air raids and artillery fire from Japanese troops deeply entrenched in concrete bunkers, the Allies prevailed.

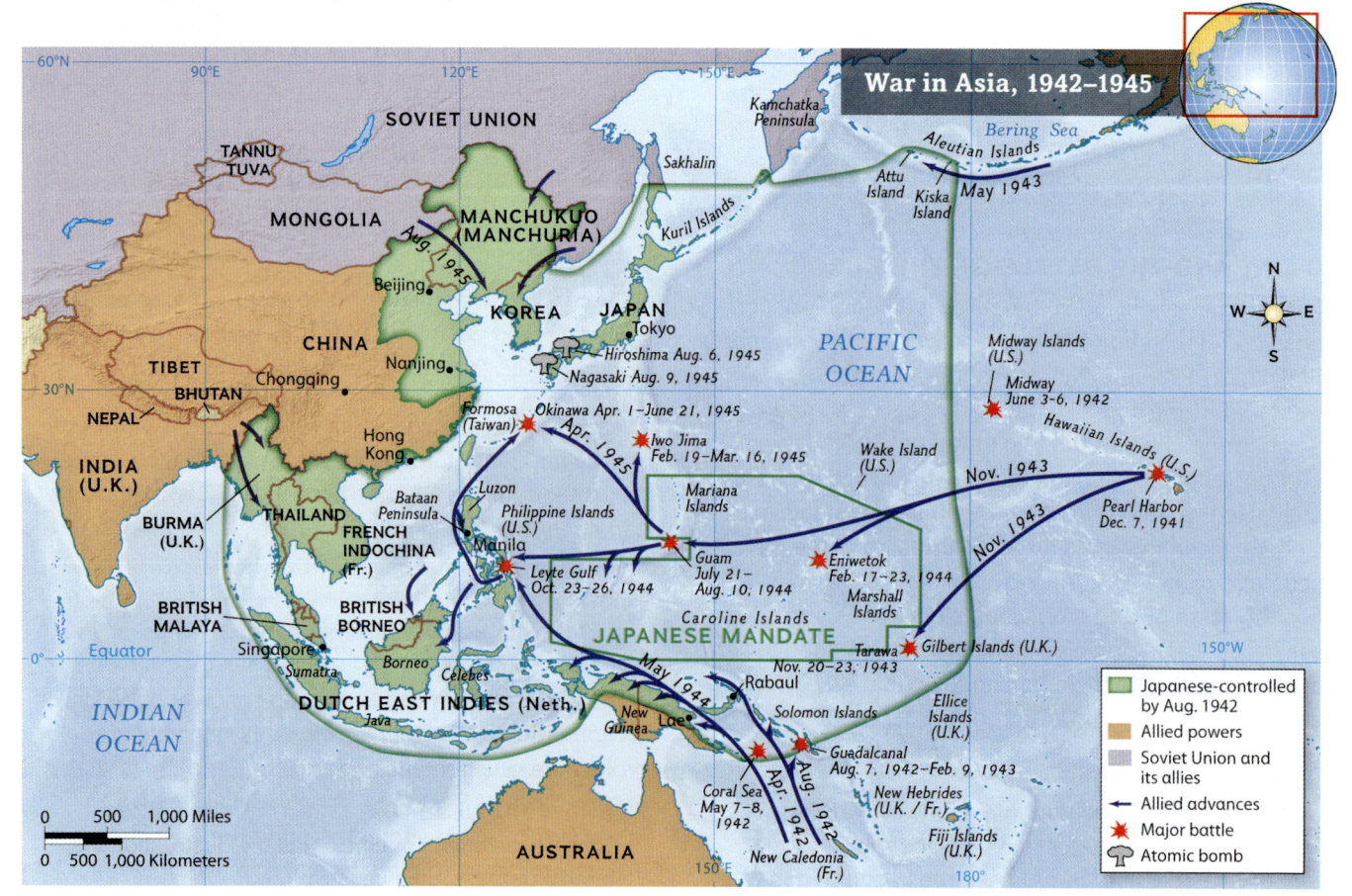

VICTORY OVER JAPAN

Now Japan lay open to invasion. But an alternative plan presented itself to **Harry S. Truman**, who became president after Franklin Roosevelt's death in April 1945. Soon after taking office, Truman learned that Roosevelt had decided to have an atomic bomb built after he was advised the Nazis were building one themselves. An **atomic bomb** is a type of nuclear bomb whose violent explosion is triggered by splitting atoms and that releases intense heat and radioactivity. Truman was prepared to deploy it.

The American president warned Japan about the disaster that would befall if the nation refused to surrender. But for the Japanese, any surrender would be a great dishonor to their country. Finally, Truman decided that, although using atomic weapons would cause horrendous loss of life, it would also end the war more quickly and thereby save more lives in the long run. He had two Japanese cities bombed, Hiroshima on August 6, and Nagasaki on August 9. More than 200,000 people were killed in the bombings.

On August 15, Japan accepted the terms of surrender, and the war officially ended on September 2. The Allies occupied Japan, but Hirohito was allowed to remain in power to restore order. Tojo was not so fortunate—he was executed in 1948. World War II was over, and the Allies had won, but the human toll and destruction caused by the conflict were immense.

CRITICAL VIEWING Japanese pilots salute their commander before they take part in suicide attacks during the fighting in the Philippines. These pilots—and many others—had volunteered to crash their aircraft into enemy ships, mainly aircraft carriers. The tactic reflects the Japanese tradition of choosing death over defeat or capture. How do the pilots in the photo seem to be facing their imminent death?

An atomic bomb explodes over Nagasaki, Japan, on August 9, 1945. In addition to the deaths caused by the explosions in both Nagasaki and Hiroshima, tens of thousands more Japanese died from radiation sickness.

HISTORICAL THINKING

1. **READING CHECK** How did the Soviet army's scorched-earth strategy impact the German offensive?
2. **INTERPRET MAPS** Why was North Africa a logical choice as a base of operations against Italy?
3. **IDENTIFY MAIN IDEAS AND DETAILS** What was the ultimate goal of island hopping?
4. **DRAW CONCLUSIONS** Why did President Truman warn Japan ahead of time about the destruction the atomic bombs would cause?

The Second World War

2.1

MAIN IDEA Nancy Wake and Josephine Baker worked as agents to free France and fight against Nazi Germany.

Travelers: Nancy Wake 1912–2011 and Josephine Baker 1906–1975
French Resistance Fighters

War can produce unlikely heroes. Before World War II, Nancy Wake and Josephine Baker moved to France looking for adventure, fame, and fun. After the war started, they risked their lives to spy for the Allies.

THE WHITE MOUSE

Earlier in this chapter, you read about French general Charles de Gaulle, who left German-occupied France and established a resistance force in London. From this base, de Gaulle recruited an army of volunteers to liberate France. His resistance movement and other anti-German movements that operated underground in France are often collectively referred to as the French Resistance.

Australian Nancy Wake did not set out to be a resistance fighter. As a child, she dreamed of seeing the world. When she settled in Paris as a journalist in 1934, Wake was more interested in parties than politics. However, her attitude changed during a trip to Vienna, Austria, when she witnessed Jews being publicly beaten by a group of Nazis. After that episode, she resolved to "do anything, however big or small, stupid or dangerous" to oppose the Nazi Party. In 1939, Wake married a wealthy French businessman and continued to enjoy her life in France. But she and many of her friends believed war with Germany was inevitable.

The German invasion of Poland in 1939 confirmed their fears. Six months after the invasion of France in 1940, Wake joined the resistance. She began serving as a courier, passing messages and helping resistance fighters escape from the Nazis and French collaborators, or traitors. Wake also assisted in the escape of Allied soldiers and Jewish refugees from France into neutral Spain. Nazi Germany's secret police, the *Gestapo*, called her "the White Mouse" for her ability to evade capture.

Nancy Wake wrote about her experiences as a resistance agent in *The Autobiography of the Woman the Gestapo Called the White Mouse*. In this excerpt from the book, Wake describes her appearance and her feelings just before she parachutes into France.

PRIMARY SOURCE

Huddled in the belly of the bomber, airsick and vomiting, I was hardly Hollywood's idea of a glamorous spy. I probably looked grotesque. Over civilian clothes, silk-stockinged and high-heeled, I wore overalls, [and] carried revolvers in the pockets. . . . Even more incongruous [odd] was the matronly handbag [a large, plain purse], full of cash and secret instructions for D-Day. . . . But I'd spent years in France working as an escape courier . . . and I was desperate to return to France and continue working against Hitler. Neither airsickness nor looking like a clumsily wrapped parcel was going to deter me.

—from *The Autobiography of the Woman the Gestapo Called the White Mouse* by Nancy Wake, 1985

As pressure from the Gestapo mounted, Wake hiked over the Pyrenees Mountains into Spain in 1943. From there she traveled to England where she was trained in special intelligence operations. In April 1944, along with other resistance agents, Wake parachuted into central France behind German lines to help with preparations for D-Day. Among other tasks, she hid weapons and ammunition dropped by parachute for the advancing Allied armies. Wake reached Paris just as Allied forces liberated the city on August 25.

After World War II ended, Wake became the most decorated woman of the war. From Britain, she received the George Medal; from France, the Legion of Honor, the Croix de Guerre (War Cross), and the Resistance Medal; and from the United States, the Medal of Freedom.

774 CHAPTER 27

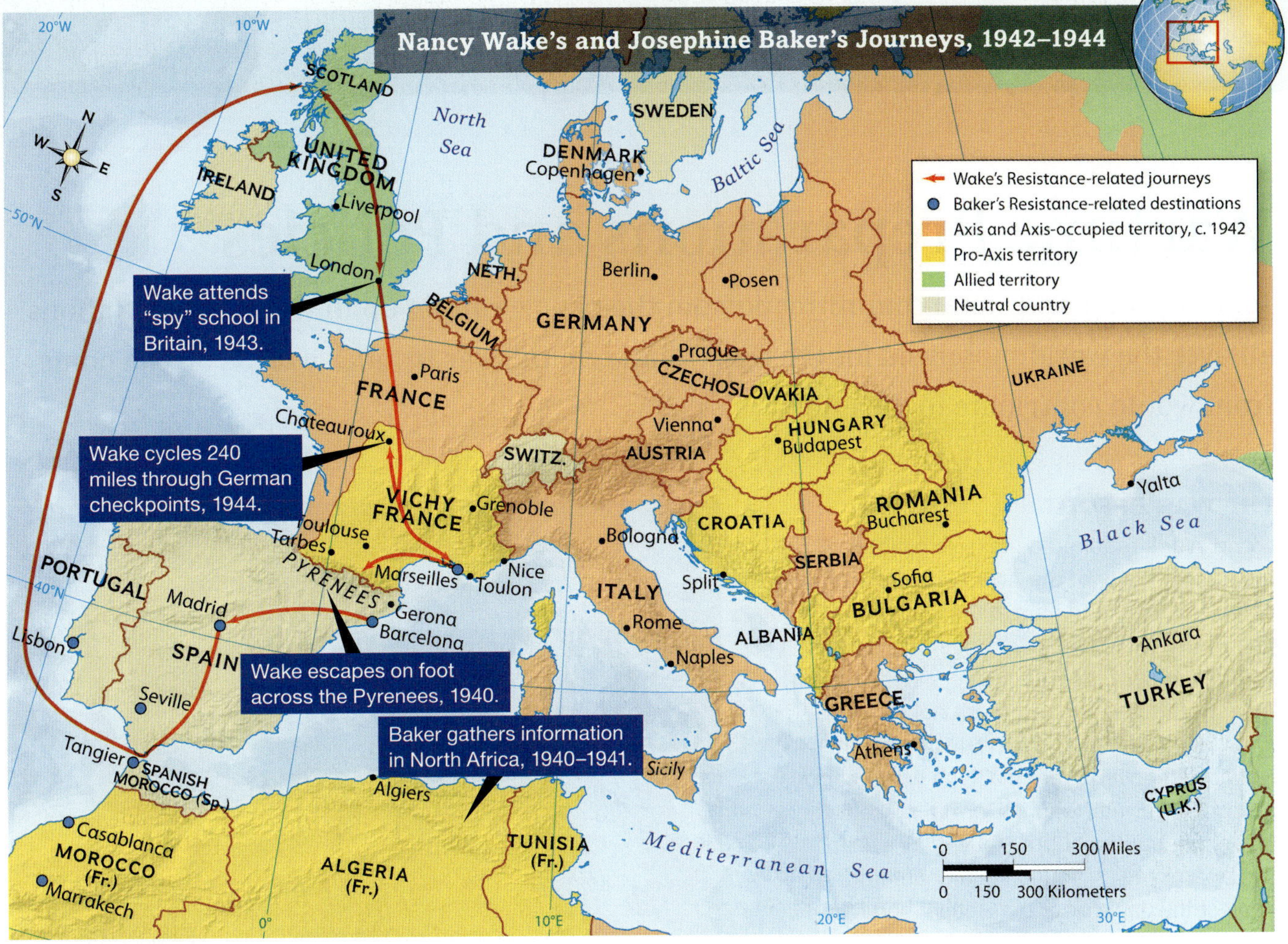

Nancy Wake's and Josephine Baker's Journeys, 1942–1944
Wake's Resistance-related journeys
Baker's Resistance-related destinations
Axis and Axis-occupied territory, c. 1942
Pro-Axis territory
Allied territory
Neutral country
Wake attends "spy" school in Britain, 1943.
Wake cycles 240 miles through German checkpoints, 1944.
Wake escapes on foot across the Pyrenees, 1940.
Baker gathers information in North Africa, 1940–1941.
SCOTLAND
UNITED KINGDOM
IRELAND
Liverpool
London
North Sea
DENMARK
Copenhagen
SWEDEN
Baltic Sea
NETH.
BELGIUM
Berlin
Posen
GERMANY
Prague
CZECHOSLOVAKIA
UKRAINE
Paris
FRANCE
Chateauroux
Vienna
AUSTRIA
HUNGARY
Budapest
SWITZ.
VICHY FRANCE
Grenoble
ROMANIA
Bucharest
Yalta
Black Sea
Toulouse
Tarbes
Marseilles
Nice
Toulon
Bologna
CROATIA
SERBIA
Split
ITALY
Sofia
BULGARIA
PYRENEES
Gerona
Barcelona
PORTUGAL
Madrid
Lisbon
SPAIN
Rome
Naples
ALBANIA
Ankara
TURKEY
Seville
GREECE
Athens
Tangier
SPANISH MOROCCO (Sp.)
Algiers
Sicily
CYPRUS (U.K.)
Casablanca
MOROCCO (Fr.)
Marrakech
ALGERIA (Fr.)
TUNISIA (Fr.)
Mediterranean Sea
0 150 300 Miles
0 150 300 Kilometers
20°W
10°W
50°N
40°N
0°
10°E
20°E
30°E
N
S
E
W

DANCER, SINGER, SOLDIER, SPY

Like Wake, American Josephine Baker moved to Paris when she was a young woman. She moved, in part, to escape the racism she had experienced as an African American. Baker was already a well-known dancer in the United States, but in 1925, she was offered twice as much money to perform in Paris. Her singing, dancing, and outrageous costumes soon made her one of the most popular entertainers in France. In 1937, she became a French citizen.

After World War II began and Germany occupied France, Baker added to her accomplishments. She worked for the Red Cross, where she aided Belgian refugees, and served as a sub-lieutenant in the French Women's Auxiliary Air Force. Baker also became a spy for the French Resistance. As a celebrity, Baker was often invited to perform at embassy parties attended by high-ranking Axis officials and diplomats. Always charming, she coaxed secret military information from the guests and then passed it along to leaders of the resistance.

Because Nazi authorities considered Baker to be a harmless entertainer, she was allowed to travel outside of France to entertain troops in its colonies in North Africa. She also traveled in other parts of Europe where she met with Allied agents and passed them notes describing Nazi activities in France. The notes were written on her sheet music—in invisible ink. Sometimes Baker also smuggled photos of German military installations out of France by pinning them to her underwear.

At the end of the war, General de Gaulle awarded Baker the Croix de Guerre and the Legion of Honor with the Resistance Medal. She was the first American-born woman to receive these honors.

HISTORICAL THINKING

1. **READING CHECK** What did Nancy Wake do soon after Germany invaded France?
2. **ANALYZE SOURCES** Why do you think Wake was wearing civilian clothes and high-heeled shoes and carrying a purse when she parachuted into France?
3. **COMPARE AND CONTRAST** How were the lives of Nancy Wake and Josephine Baker similar?

2.2 MAIN IDEA People of all nations took part in the war effort, sometimes at the expense of their civil liberties.

Wartime Preparations and Policies

Total war demands total commitment from the people caught up in the conflict. Nations all over the world mobilized for the fight. Those on the war front as well as on the home front would contribute to the effort.

THE WAR EFFORT

World War II required a massive buildup of resources. Many of the Allied Powers drafted colonial subjects to help in the war effort. The British mobilized over two million Indian soldiers to fight the Axis Powers in Europe and Asia. But these numbers were not enough. The United States and Britain supplied the Nationalist government of China with weapons along the Burma Road in Burma, present-day Myanmar, but the supply route was seized by Japan in 1942. To launch a counterattack against the Japanese, the British recruited soldiers from their African colonies, including Nigeria and Kenya, and sent them to fight in the jungles of Burma. By defending Burma, the British were also seeking to secure the borders of nearby India. The Burma Road was finally reopened in early 1945.

As you know, France had a long history of recruiting African soldiers into its armies. When France came under the control of the Germans and the Vichy government, the first Free French outpost was established in French Equatorial Africa. After the Allies took North Africa back from Germany, African troops were once again conscripted in large numbers. In fact, almost half of the Allied soldiers who liberated France in 1943 and 1944 came from French colonies such as Morocco, Algeria, and Senegal.

Millions of men volunteered for military service in the United States, including many from minority groups. These soldiers were placed in segregated troops. Nevertheless, they served with valor and distinction. The Tuskegee Airmen, a squadron of African-American pilots, shot down a dozen Nazi planes during an invasion in Italy in 1943. The 442nd Regimental

Total war required the complete mobilization of civilian populations beyond a nation's military. Traditional gender roles were transformed as female factory workers replaced departed servicemen. In this photo, a British worker finalizes the assembly of the nose cone of a bomber in 1943.

776 CHAPTER 27

Combat Team, a military unit that consisted entirely of Japanese Americans, fought in Europe in 1944 and rescued a regiment of Texas soldiers surrounded by German forces.

People at home also contributed to the war effort. When men in the United States and Britain left their jobs to fight in the war, for instance, women filled their places in factories and offices. And many of these women worked in the defense industries to produce airplanes, weapons, and ammunition. In the Soviet Union, women not only worked on the home front but some also took up arms to resist the Nazi invasion.

To help pay for the high cost of war, free markets were often controlled. In Britain, the government took over the economy and allocated resources for the military. Few consumer goods were produced, and a rationing system limited each family's supply of bread, milk, eggs, sugar, and meat. Still, the British largely accepted such sacrifices as a necessary price to defeat Hitler.

LIMITED FREEDOMS

You may recall that many governments put restraints on civil liberties during World War I. The same thing happened in World War II. In the United States, thousands of Japanese Americans were relocated and sent to internment camps in military zones, where they lived in prison-like surroundings until the war's end. In the Soviet Union, Joseph Stalin squashed whatever freedom his people had enjoyed before the war. Still, during the Great Patriotic Fatherland War, as they called World War II, the Soviet people banded together as never before and conferred on Stalin a near god-like status.

Britain also curtailed the freedom of local governments in colonial countries. Although Egypt had been given the basic right to govern itself, Britain still had troops stationed there, including in the Suez Canal zone. The British used those forces to defend Egypt from Italian invasion. However, they did not clear these actions with the Egyptian government first. Offended Egyptian protesters filled the streets of Cairo.

The wartime situation was equally tense in India. As you've read, millions of Indian soldiers aided the Allied cause, but the Indian National Congress refused to

Indian army troops march in formation in 1942.

cooperate. As in Egypt, the British had declared war against the Axis on behalf of India without consulting Indian political leaders. Indian activist Mohandas Gandhi responded with a "Quit India" campaign, calling for the British to leave India.

In Italy and Germany, Mussolini and Hitler eliminated independent social organizations. Strict controls were placed on Catholic and Protestant churches to make sure they adhered to fascist policy. While some Christians obeyed, others remained defiant and held fast to their principles. Some European Jews owed their lives to the courageous help of their Christian neighbors.

Both Allied and Axis powers tried to control public opinion through propaganda and media censorship. Racist imagery was often used to justify military policy. Americans saw stereotypical images of the Japanese, while Japanese children were told they were racially superior to all other Asians. Nazi propaganda focused on the "decadence" of the United States and its racial diversity, which was seen as a weakness.

HISTORICAL THINKING

1. **READING CHECK** How did people in British and French colonies help the Allied war effort?

2. **MAKE INFERENCES** Why do you think Japanese Americans wanted to fight in World War II?

3. **DRAW CONCLUSIONS** Why did the Indian and Egyptian people object when Britain declared war against the Axis on their behalf without consulting their leaders?

2.3

MAIN IDEA Attacks on civilians and the machinery of war exacted a high price on the global population.

Civilians, Technology, and the War's Toll

Soldiers aren't the only casualties of war. Civilians, caught in the crossfire, have always died in conflicts. But World War II introduced a whole new dimension to this killing. New weapons and technology allowed both sides to inflict severe tolls on civilian populations.

TARGETING CIVILIANS

The targeting of civilians was a tactic adopted by both Axis and Allied powers. One of the worst examples was the Siege of Leningrad in the Soviet Union. Between 1941 and 1944, the German army surrounded the city and prevented supplies from reaching the starving residents. An estimated one million people died before the city was liberated.

Both Japan and Germany used slave labor. The Japanese forced hundreds of thousands of Koreans to toil in terrible conditions. In Vietnam, the Japanese occupiers worked the local population so hard and left them with so little food that as many as one million people died during a famine in 1945. Of course, the Nazis were notorious for their harsh treatment. With many of their men off to fight, they forced Poles and Russians to perform menial work.

As you know, Germany mainly targeted British civilians during the Blitz. Later on, the Allies used their bombers to attack Japanese and German cities. First, Allied bombers focused on military and industrial targets. Then in 1945, the Allies used napalm firebombs against Japan. **Napalm** is a highly flammable, jelly-like substance that sticks to targets and generates extreme heat. The first of these firebombs was dropped on Tokyo and destroyed 25 percent of the city's buildings and killed tens of thousands of its people. Around the same time, the Allies also used napalm in the firebombing of Dresden, Germany, in which an estimated 25,000–35,000 civilians died.

In the Pacific war, the Allies used several Native American languages as wartime codes. Recruits speaking the Navajo language, like those in this photo, were the largest group of Code Talkers, as they came to be called.

TECHNOLOGY OF WAR

After the United States entered World War II, President Franklin Roosevelt stated, "This war is a new kind of war. . . . It is warfare in terms of every continent, every island, every sea, every air lane in the world." From the beginning, technology developed to meet the demands of the war. Soldiers used tanks, airplanes, and submarines more extensively than in World War I.

While the tanks used by the Allied and German forces in Europe and North Africa often determined the outcome of land battles, success at sea depended on new technology such as **depth charges**, underwater bombs that are programmed to explode at certain depths. By mid-1943, the German submarine threat in the Atlantic had been neutralized.

Knowledge of the enemy's position was key in battle. The Allies used radar to locate German and Japanese ships and airplanes. They also tried to decode

778 CHAPTER 27

enemy intelligence. The Germans sent coded naval communications—on a device called the Enigma machine—about the movements of their submarines. If the Allies could understand these messages, they could direct their fleets away from German torpedoes. By 1940, a British mathematician named **Alan Turing** had designed a machine called the Bombe that could crack the code used in messages sent by the Enigma machine. The Bombe would help decode intercepted enemy messages for the remainder of the war.

The Allies devised codes of their own. In 1942, the U.S. Marines began using a secret code that relied on speakers of the Navajo language. Code Talkers sent and received messages rapidly over open radio channels. Enemy listeners could hear them, but they could not decode the language. In the Pacific, the Navajo Code Talkers were instrumental in several Allied victories.

THE HUMAN TOLL

Overall, historians estimate that 60 million, or three percent of the world's population, died as a result of the war. This toll includes a large casualty rate among civilians. The Soviet Union is believed to have suffered the most civilian deaths at an estimated 19 million, followed by China, with as many as 10 million. A total of about 17 million soldiers died in World War II.

The war also inflicted terrible damage on cities, particularly in Japan and Germany, where houses, factories, and transportation and communication systems were destroyed by bombs. After the war, millions of starving and homeless people were left to wander through the ruins. The financial cost of the war was immense. Economists estimate that it reached approximately $1 trillion in 1945 dollars, with the United States spending the most at about $300 billion.

As terrible as the death toll of World War II was, even more deaths remained to be discovered. Toward the close of the war, the Allies confronted murder of civilians on a scale never seen before.

COMFORT WOMEN The Japanese forced some female civilians to live under conditions of sexual slavery during the war. Known as "comfort women," these women provided sexual services to improve the morale of Japanese troops. At least 200,000 women—mostly from Korea, Taiwan, and the Philippines—were held against their will in so-called comfort stations located in Japan and all Japanese-occupied areas. Women who resisted were often beaten or murdered.

NATIONAL GEOGRAPHIC EXPLORER
ARI BESER

The Survivors' Side of the Story

National Geographic Explorer Ari Beser has a unique connection to the bombs that fell on Hiroshima and Nagasaki. His grandfather was the only U.S. serviceman to fly on both bombing missions. Beser's research began in 2011 but culminated in a 2015 Fulbright-National Geographic Storytelling Fellowship that allowed him to travel to Japan and visit with some of those who survived the bombings. The experience helped him understand that all stories have more than one point of view. Ever since, he has been sharing both American and Japanese stories of the bombings to promote reconciliation and nuclear disarmament. As Beser says, "I believe it is crucial to our understanding and our future as a functioning society that we take a step back and look objectively at each side." In the photo above, Ari Beser (far left) poses with Clifton Truman Daniel (far right), grandson of President Truman. They are joined by survivors of the bombs and their family members in Hiroshima.

HISTORICAL THINKING

1. **READING CHECK** What happened at the Siege of Leningrad?
2. **MAKE INFERENCES** Why do you think more soldiers and civilians were killed in the Soviet Union than in any other country?
3. **SYNTHESIZE** Why was the death toll so high in World War II?

3.1

MAIN IDEA The Nazis persecuted Jews and planned their mass killing.

"The Final Solution"

People in the Allied nations knew about Adolf Hitler's hatred of the Jews, but few grasped the full extent of his anti-Semitic fervor. After the war in Europe was over, the world learned what the Nazis were capable of.

CRITICAL VIEWING The Nazi plan for the mass killing of Jews included imprisoning them in concentration camps. This 2004 photo shows the train tracks leading to Auschwitz, the most notorious camp. Zyklon B, the poison gas used to murder Jews, was first tested there. Why do you think the Nazis built this concentration camp in such an isolated area?

PERSECUTION OF THE JEWS

When the Allies invaded Germany and Poland in the spring of 1945, they encountered scenes of horror: concentration camps full of starving and dying prisoners. Most were Jews, but there were also non-Jewish Poles, Roma, homosexuals, Jehovah's Witnesses, and political dissidents who opposed the policies of the Nazi Party.

Europe had a long tradition of anti-Semitism. Jews had been persecuted and confined in ghettos for centuries. In the 19th century, the idea that people within a nation were bound by race and common values and characteristics took hold. Those who belonged to a different race and shared different values were often considered inferior and even subhuman. A movement called eugenics also arose in the 1800s, which promoted the idea that traits from "only the more suitable races" should be passed down to future generations.

As you've learned, Hitler believed in racial "purity" and in the superiority of what he called the Aryan race. The Jews, he asserted, belonged to an inferior race. Nazi dehumanization of the Jews and other victims began after Hitler became Germany's chancellor in 1933. On his command, the Nazis began to systematically restrict the civil and political rights of Jews. They removed Jews from German schools and universities and banned them from many public areas. Businesses were taken away from their Jewish owners, and Jewish doctors and lawyers were not allowed to practice their vocations. In time, the Jewish people lost their right to vote. Nazi persecution of the Jews escalated with Kristallnacht on November 9, 1938, when, as you have read, rioters attacked and killed about 100 Jews and destroyed Jewish shops and synagogues.

Remember reading about the Armenian genocide carried out by the Ottoman Turks during World War I? On the eve of the invasion of Poland in 1939, Hitler said to his generals, "Who, after all, speaks today of the annihilation [massacre] of the Armenians?" Numerous German military officers who had been stationed in Turkey during World War I had been aware of the Ottoman regime's plan to destroy the Armenians, and some of them even issued orders for the deportation of Armenians. A few of these officers later became leaders in the Nazi military apparatus that would carry out the systematic murder of Jews. Hitler thought that, like the Armenian genocide, the execution of Jews could be accomplished without penalty.

After the invasion of Poland, German authorities required Polish Jews over the age of 10 to wear a yellow Star of David, a symbol of Judaism. Eventually, all Jews six years of age or older in many German-occupied territories were ordered to wear the star with *Jew* written on it in the local language. The Germans also created about 1,000 ghettos in Poland, Hungary, and the Soviet Union. Huge numbers of Jews were forced to live in these ghettos, which were isolated from non-Jewish populations and surrounded by barbed wire, thick walls, and armed guards. In 1941, the Nazis rounded up others they had imprisoned as "undesirables" and sent them to the ghettos. But these enclosed districts were just holding places until the Nazis came up with a plan to solve what they called "the Jewish question."

THE WANNSEE CONFERENCE

Hitler thought the answer to the question was the extermination of the Jews. This had been his goal since at least 1919 when he wrote in a letter that the final objective of anti-Semitism "must unswervingly [without fail] be the removal of Jews altogether." "Final solution" was code for the plan to murder all the Jews in Europe—approximately 11 million in all.

In January 1942, **Reinhard Heydrich**, the head of the Gestapo, called a meeting of high-ranking Nazis in Wannsee, a suburb of Berlin. Heydrich gathered the men together at the **Wannsee Conference** to explain how the "final solution" would be carried out. Heydrich told the men that concentration camps would be constructed in eastern Europe. Jews would be sent to the camps, where those strong enough would build roads and work in factories to support Germany's economy. However, the work would be so hard that many Jews would die due to "natural reduction." Those who resisted or refused to work would be killed.

Actually, the real purpose of the camps was genocide. A major step toward this objective had been taken in 1941 when Germany invaded the Soviet Union. Special military forces known as mobile killing units accompanied the German army during the invasion. These groups were mostly composed of special officers of the SS, or *Schutzstaffel* (SHOOT-stah-fuhl), meaning "Protection Guards." The SS were the "political soldiers" of the Nazi Party. Their task in 1941 was to kill Jews, Roma, and Soviet political leaders. By 1943, they had executed an estimated one million Jews. As the war continued, it took thousands of ordinary Germans to operate the machinery of death. The German military, infrastructure, and even the economy would be mobilized to carry out the mass killings.

Jews in Germany were forced to wear a yellow badge, like this one, with the German word *Jude*, meaning "Jew," written on it. Any Jew who refused to wear the badge faced severe punishment or even death.

HISTORICAL THINKING

1. **READING CHECK** What did the Allies find when they invaded Germany and Poland in the spring of 1945?

2. **MAKE INFERENCES** Why do you think the Nazis forced Jews to wear the Star of David badges?

3. **IDENTIFY MAIN IDEAS AND DETAILS** What was the "final solution"?

3.2

MAIN IDEA European Jews confined in ghettos resisted their captivity, but most were shot or sent to death camps.

The Holocaust

Life in the ghettos was miserable. In the crowded quarters, food was scarce, and disease spread quickly. There was little the Jews could do to fight back against the Nazis. But some still tried.

WARSAW GHETTO UPRISING

Even though they risked their lives by doing so, many Jews in the ghettos put up some resistance. They smuggled in food, medicine, and weapons. Others set up secret schools or organized musical performances. And some brave ghetto dwellers even tried to escape. Those who succeeded often joined local resistance fighters who carried out surprise attacks on German army units.

The most famous example of resistance took place in the Polish ghetto of Warsaw. This ghetto in Poland's capital was the largest in the country. More than 400,000 Jews were crowded into the ghetto, which covered an area of only about 1.3 square miles. In 1942, the Nazis had begun rounding up millions of Jews all across Europe. They were then packed into trains for "deportation," or transport, to the death camps, where Jews and other enemies of the Nazis were murdered. The Germans removed about 265,000 Jews from the Warsaw ghetto for transport and killed another 35,000. Only about 60,000 Jews remained.

In 1943, most of the remaining residents decided to fight back. On April 19, SS and police units entered the ghetto and found the streets deserted. The Jews were hiding, some of them in underground bunkers they'd built in preparation for a battle with the Nazis. Suddenly, armed with weapons they had snuck into the ghetto, the Warsaw Jews fired on the Germans, forcing them to retreat. On the third day of fighting, the Germans began burning down all the buildings in the ghetto to drive the Jews from their hiding places. Jewish fighters held off the Nazis for almost a month during the **Warsaw Ghetto Uprising** but finally surrendered on May 16. About 7,000 of those in the Warsaw ghetto were shot immediately. The rest—about 50,000—were sent to the death camps.

When he was a teenager, Romanian-born Elie Wiesel was transported with his parents and sisters to Auschwitz in 1944. His mother, father, and little sister died, but Wiesel survived. After U.S. forces arrived in April 1945 at Buchenwald, the concentration camp to which Wiesel had been transferred, they photographed the survivors, including Wiesel. In the photo below, he is seventh from the left in the second row of bunks from the bottom. In 1958, Wiesel published *Night*, a memoir of his experiences in the camps. In this excerpt from the book, he describes the horrors he witnessed the day he arrived at Auschwitz.

PRIMARY SOURCE

Never shall I forget that night, the first night in camp, that turned my life into one long night seven times sealed. Never shall I forget that smoke. Never shall I forget the small faces of the children, whose bodies I saw transformed into smoke under a silent blue sky.

—from *Night* by Elie Wiesel, 1958

In 1943, the Jews in Poland's Warsaw ghetto fought back against the Nazis but were eventually forced to surrender. An SS general placed photos like this one in his report to his commanding officer. After the war ended, the report was used as evidence to convict the general of war crimes, and he was hanged.

DEATH CAMPS

The major death camps were located in Poland and included Chelmno, Treblinka, and Auschwitz (OWSH-vits), the largest of the camps. The Auschwitz complex consisted of three main camps. All were labor camps, and one included a killing center. Because Auschwitz was at a junction where several railways converged, the camp served as a convenient place for the Nazis to transport prisoners from all across Europe. In 1944, for example, Nazis transferred more than 400,000 Hungarian Jews there.

The train cars that brought the Jews to the death camps were overcrowded and hot in the summer and freezing in the winter. Passengers did not receive food or water during the journey. Some died before they reached their destination. Those who survived were inspected by a doctor upon arrival. The doctor sent certain groups of people to their death, including pregnant women, young children, the elderly, the disabled, and the ill. Most of these people were killed immediately in specially prepared gas chambers, where they were told they would simply be taking a shower. Then the victims' bodies were burned in **crematoria**, or ovens.

As you've read, those who were in good physical shape were put to work, often in factories in the area. When the laborers could no longer work due to malnutrition, illness, or exhaustion, the Nazis sent them to the gas chambers. An estimated 1.1 million Jews died at Auschwitz alone, including those who had been subjected to terrible medical "experiments" performed by the camp's chief doctor, Josef Mengele.

Even when the end of the war in Europe—and the end of Nazi Germany—was in sight, the killings at Auschwitz and other death camps continued. But as the Soviets and other Allies advanced across eastern Europe, the Nazis who ran the camps tried to destroy any evidence of what had happened there before they fled. They dismantled the barracks where prisoners had lived, burned down buildings that housed crematoria, and destroyed warehouses containing prisoners' clothing and personal items. Nonetheless, plenty of evidence remained of the murders that had taken place in the camps. In all, about six million Jews died in the Holocaust, which is what the systematic genocide carried out by the Nazis came to be called. Jews often use the word *Shoah*, a Hebrew word meaning "catastrophe," to refer to the Holocaust.

HISTORICAL THINKING

1. **READING CHECK** What happened in the Warsaw Ghetto Uprising?

2. **DRAW CONCLUSIONS** Why did the Nazis try to destroy evidence of what they'd done in the death camps?

3. **ANALYZE SOURCES** Why do you think Wiesel repeats "Never shall I forget" several times in the passage?

3.3 Preserving Cultural Heritage

SAVING THE PAST

In 1943, President Roosevelt established the Roberts Commission to promote the preservation of cultural properties during war. This commission provided the military with lists and reports of valuable works of art, and they established the Allies' Monuments, Fine Arts, and Archives (MFAA) program.

The MFAA—or the Monuments Men—was a small corps of men and women who found and recovered priceless artwork damaged or stolen by the Nazis during World War II. The men and women who served in the MFAA were not soldiers. Most of the group consisted of historians, art conservators, architects, museum curators, archivists, and professors.

Hitler had a mission to culturally dominate the world and set out to create his own museum filled with Europe's great works of art. The Nazis stole valuable artwork from wealthy Jewish families to stockpile Hitler's collection. The Monuments Men set out to recover the countless pieces of art hidden away. With limited resources and virtually no crew, the Monuments Men used German sheepskin coats and gas masks as packing material and enlisted local prisoners to pack and load the art for safe transport.

This group of committed men and women risked their lives to recover, restore, and return approximately five million pieces of priceless art and artifacts. Without their determination and tireless action, important pieces of cultural heritage would have been erased forever.

HISTORICAL THINKING

MAKE INFERENCES Why would restoring a country's art and artifacts be important?

MONUMENTS MAN Harry Ettlinger stands in front of Rembrandt's *Self-Portrait*. The painting had been removed legally from a museum in Karlsruhe during World War II and stored in a crate in a German mine. A Jew born in Karlsruhe, Ettlinger had fled Germany with his family in 1938 and settled in the United States. Nazis prohibited Jews from entering museums. As a result, Ettlinger saw the painting for the first time when he opened the crate where it had been placed for safekeeping.

GERMANY

In this 1945 photo, an American soldier stands guard over artwork and other items stored by the Nazis in a German church during World War II. As Nazi soldiers stormed through Europe, they stole valuable paintings from private and public collections. Many pieces of art were looted from the homes of Jews who were rounded up and transported to concentration camps.

3.4

MAIN IDEA After World War II, the Nazis were tried for their crimes, and the world took steps to prevent further genocide.

Justice and Remembrance

Following the war, the Allies had to decide how to deal with the Nazis who had carried out the most monstrous crimes, particularly in the Holocaust. Rather than simply execute them, the Allies chose to bring them to trial.

THE NUREMBERG TRIALS

The world learned about the extent of Nazi **atrocities**, or extremely cruel and shocking acts of violence, when the International Military Tribunal charged and tried former Nazi officials, military officers, industrialists, and others as war criminals. A **tribunal** is a court with authority over a specific matter. The series of trials, known as the **Nuremberg trials**, took place in Nuremberg, Germany, beginning in 1945.

The tribunal determined that defendants could be charged with any of the following: crimes against peace, for having waged a war of aggression; crimes against humanity, for having exterminated groups of people; and war crimes, for having violated common and agreed-upon laws of war. Members of the tribunal represented the United States, Britain, France, and the Soviet Union and had the authority to determine the guilt of any individual or group. As evidence, the prosecution presented Nazi propaganda films, footage taken by Allied troops at concentration camps, and ghastly artifacts taken from the camps. Survivors of the camps also described what they had witnessed and experienced.

Trials for 22 major Nazi war criminals were held in 1945 and 1946. Several of the leading figures in the party could not be tried, however. Hitler and two of his top officers, Heinrich Himmler, the head of the SS, and Joseph Goebbels, the minister of Nazi propaganda, committed suicide before they could be brought to justice. Most of those charged did not deny or apologize for their actions. In their defense, many said they were "just following orders."

On October 1, 1946, the tribunals issued their verdicts, acquitting some of those charged with war crimes and sending others to prison. They also sentenced 12 to death by hanging, including Hermann Goering, whom Hitler had designated as his successor. However, Goering evaded execution by taking poison.

NEVER AGAIN

Nazi officials weren't the only ones complicit in the Holocaust. Ordinary German citizens often turned on their Jewish neighbors. Some operated the trains that carried Jews to death camps. Others processed the documents authorizing the deportation of the Jews. Still others served as guards in the concentration camps.

Before the death camps were built, thousands of Jewish refugees fled Europe. Some were able to move to Britain or the United States, but poorer Jews were often turned away. Anti-Semitism and racially discriminatory immigration policies meant that ships full of Jewish refugees were turned back from both New York and British-controlled Palestine.

Robert Jackson, a public prosecutor and the Chief of Counsel for the United States at Nuremberg, delivered the opening statement at the International Military Tribunal. In these first words from his statement, Jackson explains why Nazi atrocities had to be punished.

PRIMARY SOURCE

The privilege of opening the first trial in history for crimes against the peace of the world imposes a grave responsibility. The wrongs which we seek to condemn and punish have been so calculated, so malignant [evil], and so devastating, that civilization cannot tolerate their being ignored, because it cannot survive their being repeated. That four great nations, flushed with victory and stung with injury stay the hand of vengeance and voluntarily submit their captive enemies to the judgment of the law is one of the most significant tributes that Power has ever paid to Reason.

—from the Opening Statement before the International Military Tribunal by Robert H. Jackson, Nuremberg, November 21, 1945

Shoes that belonged to people deported to Auschwitz are displayed at the Auschwitz-Birkenau Memorial and Museum, located in the former German death camp. The shoes in the photo number about 25,000 and were collected in one day, at the height of the gassing. This is one of several such exhibits that appear in Holocaust memorials and museums around the world.

Even Allied leaders did not do all they could to stop the genocide. In 1942, Roosevelt, Churchill, and Stalin officially recognized the mass murder of European Jews. Still, the Allies did not make bombing death camps and the railroad tracks that led to them a priority. In 1944, Roosevelt created the War Refugee Board, but by then millions of Jews had been killed.

Immediately after the war, genocide was established as a crime under international law through the development of the **United Nations**. This international organization was founded in 1945 by 51 countries committed to maintaining international peace and security and preventing future wars.

For the rest of their lives, the Jews who survived the Holocaust were haunted by their experiences, but they did not want the world to forget that the Nazis had tried to exterminate them and their culture. The phrase "never again" became a call to action when those in power threatened any group of people with destruction. Holocaust museums created after World War II document the experiences of those victimized by genocide. By telling the stories of the victims and survivors, these museums show that those affected were not numbers but real people. The museums also stress the responsibility of citizens to speak out against hatred and prejudice to help prevent genocide from happening again.

HISTORICAL THINKING

1. **READING CHECK** What was the purpose of the Nuremberg trials?

2. **ANALYZE SOURCES** Why do you think the Allies chose not to seek vengeance against the Nazis?

3. **DRAW CONCLUSIONS** How does telling the stories of victims in Holocaust museums help visitors understand that the victims were not just numbers?

CHAPTER 27 — THE SECOND WORLD WAR
REVIEW

VOCABULARY

Use each of the following vocabulary words in a sentence that shows an understanding of the term's meaning.

1. blitzkrieg
2. infamy
3. island hopping
4. kamikaze
5. tribunal

READING STRATEGY
IDENTIFY MAIN IDEAS AND DETAILS

Use a diagram like the one below to list details about the ways in which Germany mobilized its forces to carry out the Holocaust. Then answer the questions that follow.

Main Idea: Germany mobilized all its resources to operate its machinery of death during the Holocaust.

Detail
Detail
Detail
Detail

6. How was Germany's economy mobilized to carry out the murder of the Jewish people?
7. What role did some ordinary German citizens play in the Holocaust?

MAIN IDEAS

Answer the following questions. Support your answers with evidence from the chapter.

8. What happened at Dunkirk? **LESSON 1.1**
9. How did code breakers help secure an Allied victory at the Battle of Midway? **LESSON 1.2**
10. What was the objective of the D-Day invasion? **LESSON 1.3**
11. What strategy finally brought an end to World War II? **LESSON 1.3**
12. How did both Allied and Axis powers try to control public opinion during the war? **LESSON 2.2**
13. Why did the Navajo language serve as an effective code? **LESSON 2.3**
14. How did the Nazis isolate the Jewish ghettos? **LESSON 3.1**
15. What were conditions like on the trains that brought the Jews to the death camps? **LESSON 3.2**
16. Which four Allied nations were represented at the Nuremberg trials? **LESSON 3.4**

HISTORICAL THINKING

Answer the following questions. Support your answers with evidence from the chapter.

17. **EVALUATE** What do you think President Roosevelt meant when he said that, through the Lend-Lease Act, the United States would become "the arsenal of democracy"?
18. **DRAW CONCLUSIONS** What were the key goals of the Axis and Allied powers?
19. **SYNTHESIZE** How did technology affect World War II?
20. **COMPARE AND CONTRAST** How did World War II's actors, goals, and strategies compare with those of World War I?
21. **IDENTIFY MAIN IDEAS AND DETAILS** How was the war mobilized on different fronts?
22. **DESCRIBE** What characteristics do you think Nancy Wake and Josephine Baker possessed to become resistance fighters?
23. **DRAW CONCLUSIONS** Why was it important to the Allies to take back France?
24. **MAKE INFERENCES** Why do you think so many German citizens were complicit in the Holocaust?

INTERPRET VISUALS

When the United States entered the war, the government mobilized its civilians to combat the Axis Powers. Americans were urged to hold metal and rubber drives to collect scrap for the war effort. Posters like the one shown here were created to stir the public to action. Study the poster. Then answer the questions below.

25. What does the poster suggest is being produced from scrap metal?

26. Why is the poster effective?

ANALYZE SOURCES

President Roosevelt's annual address to Congress in January 1941, in which he discussed "four essential human freedoms," became known as the "Four Freedoms" Speech. He used his speech to frame the war as a conflict about fundamental values. This excerpt from Roosevelt's address details the four freedoms. Read the excerpt and answer the question that follows.

> The first is freedom of speech and expression—everywhere in the world.
>
> The second is freedom of every person to worship God in his own way—everywhere in the world.
>
> The third is freedom from want—which, translated into world terms, means economic understandings which will secure to every nation a healthy peacetime life for its inhabitants—everywhere in the world.
>
> The fourth is freedom from fear—which, translated into world terms, means a worldwide reduction of armaments to such a point and in such a thorough fashion that no nation will be in a position to commit an act of physical aggression against any neighbor—anywhere in the world.

27. How does Roosevelt frame his speech on both a personal and an international level?

CONNECT TO YOUR LIFE

28. **INFORMATIVE** Think about the causes and effects of President Truman's decision to drop the atomic bombs on Japan. Do a little research to find more information on the effects of the bombs and learn what historians say today about Truman's decision. Then consider whether Truman's actions were justified. Write an essay in which you discuss the causes and effects of the bombings and indicate whether you believe Truman's decision was the right one.

TIPS

- Review what you've learned about what led Truman to drop the bombs and what happened as a result of the bombings.
- Conduct research to find out more about the effects of the bombings, including the long-term impact of radiation in Japan.
- Study the opinions of historians today regarding Truman's decision.
- Use two or three vocabulary words from the chapter in your essay.
- Provide a concluding statement in which you explain whether you think Truman's actions were justified.

NATIONAL GEOGRAPHIC CONNECTION

The Science of Good and Evil

BY YUDHIJIT BHATTACHARJEE Adapted from "The Science of Good and Evil" by Yudhijit Bhattacharjee, *National Geographic*, January 2018

For centuries, the question of how good and evil originate was a matter of philosophical or religious debate. But in recent decades, researchers have made advances toward understanding the science of what drives good and evil. Both seem to be linked to empathy, an intrinsic ability of the brain to experience how another person is feeling. Researchers have found that empathy is the kindling that fires compassion, impelling us to help others in distress. Studies have traced violent, psychopathic behaviors to a lack of empathy, which appears to stem from impaired circuits in the brain.

Most individuals do not ordinarily commit violent acts against one another. And yet, there are genocides, which require the complicity and passivity of large numbers of people. Time and again, social groups organized along ethnic, national, racial, or religious lines have savaged other groups. Nazi Germany's gas chambers extinguished millions of Jews, the Communist Khmer Rouge slaughtered fellow Cambodians, and Hutu extremists in Rwanda killed several hundred thousand Tutsis and moderate Hutus. Events such as these provide evidence that evil can hold entire communities in its grip.

How the voice of conscience is silenced in a genocide can be partly understood through the prism of the well-known experiments conducted in the 1960s by the psychologist Stanley Milgram at Yale University. In those studies, subjects were asked to deliver electric shocks to a person in another room for failing to answer questions correctly, increasing the voltage with every wrong answer. At the prodding of a person who played the role of a researcher, the subjects often dialed up the shocks to dangerously high voltage levels. The shocks weren't real and the cries of pain were prerecorded, but the subjects only found that out afterward. The studies demonstrated what Milgram described as "the extreme willingness of adults to go to almost any lengths on the command of an authority."

Gregory Stanton, founder of Genocide Watch, a nonprofit that works to prevent mass murder, has identified the stages that can lead otherwise decent people to commit murder. It starts when demagogic leaders define a target group as "the other" and claim it is a threat. Discrimination follows, and soon the leaders characterize their targets as subhuman, eroding the in-group's empathy for "the other."

Next, society becomes polarized. "Those planning the genocide say, 'You are either with us or against us,'" says Stanton. This is followed by a phase of preparation, with the architects of the genocide drawing up death lists, stocking weapons, and planning how the rank and file are to execute the killings. Members of the out-group are sometimes forced to move into ghettos or concentration camps. Then the massacres begin.

Many perpetrators show no remorse because they find ways to rationalize the killings. James Waller, a genocide scholar at Keene State College in New Hampshire, says he got a glimpse of this "incredible capacity of the human mind to make sense of and to justify the worst of actions" when he interviewed Hutu men convicted or accused of atrocities during the Rwandan genocide. Some had killed children. Their rationale, according to Waller, was: "If I didn't do this, those children would have grown up to come back to kill me. This was something that was a necessity for my people . . . to survive."

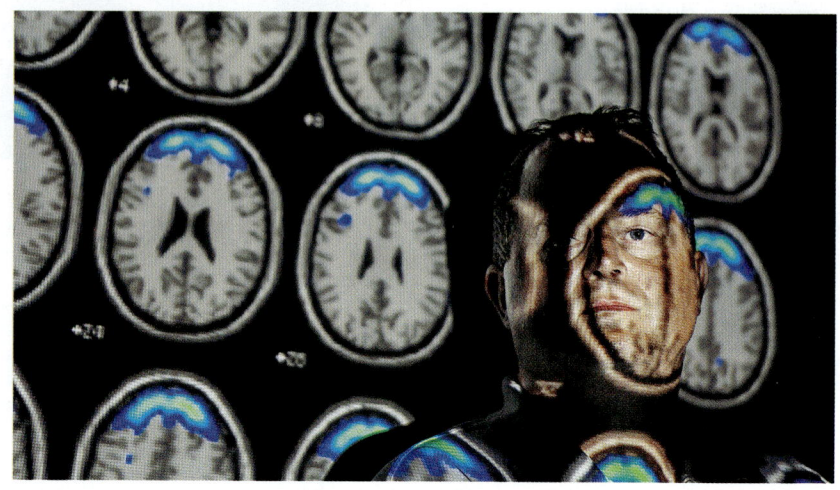

Neuroscientist Kent Kiehl, shown here, has taken brain scans of more than 4,000 prison inmates to measure brain activity and size in different regions of the organ. According to Kiehl, psychopaths have impairments in the part of the brain that helps process emotions.

UNIT 9 Nominate a Candidate

Staging the Question

In this unit, you learned about two world wars and a worldwide economic depression, all of which occurred in the first half of the 20th century. These events resulted in horrific suffering for people in many parts of the world and included some shocking examples of human behavior at its worst. Amid all the suffering and brutality, where did people find hope? How did people manage to maintain their human decency in the face of so much horror? What lessons can we learn from this period in history?

ASSIGNMENT

Research primary and secondary sources to find examples of people—whether famous leaders or average citizens—who acted honorably or compassionately during these trying times. You might choose examples from this unit or from your own research.

Select one of the people or groups of people to focus on. Conduct additional research to learn as much as you can about the situation and the actions of the person or people involved.

Analyze what lessons might be learned from the actions of the person or people you've chosen.

Write a letter of recommendation nominating the person or people you have chosen for a humanitarian award. Explain the circumstances behind your candidate's actions.

Supporting Questions: Begin by developing supporting questions to guide your thinking. For example: What was admirable about this person or group's actions in this situation?

Summative Performance Task: Write a letter nominating your candidate for a humanitarian award. You might use a graphic organizer like this one to explain the situation behind the person or people's heroic actions.

Who?
What?
Where?
When?
Why?

Present: Share your nomination letter with the class. You might consider one of the following options.

DELIVER A NOMINATION SPEECH

Practice your speech before delivering it to the class. Invite the class to comment on what they can learn from the nominee's actions. Your class might compile a list of lessons gained from all the nomination speeches.

PRODUCE A NOMINATION VIDEO

Instead of delivering your speech live, you might record it as part of a nomination video. This option allows you to incorporate other media to help you present your choice for nominee.

Take Informed Action:

UNDERSTAND In one or two sentences, write the lesson to be learned from the person or people you chose.

ASSESS Think about how you might apply that lesson in your own life and who you might share it with.

ACT Share the lesson with others and implement it in your life if possible.

UNIT 10

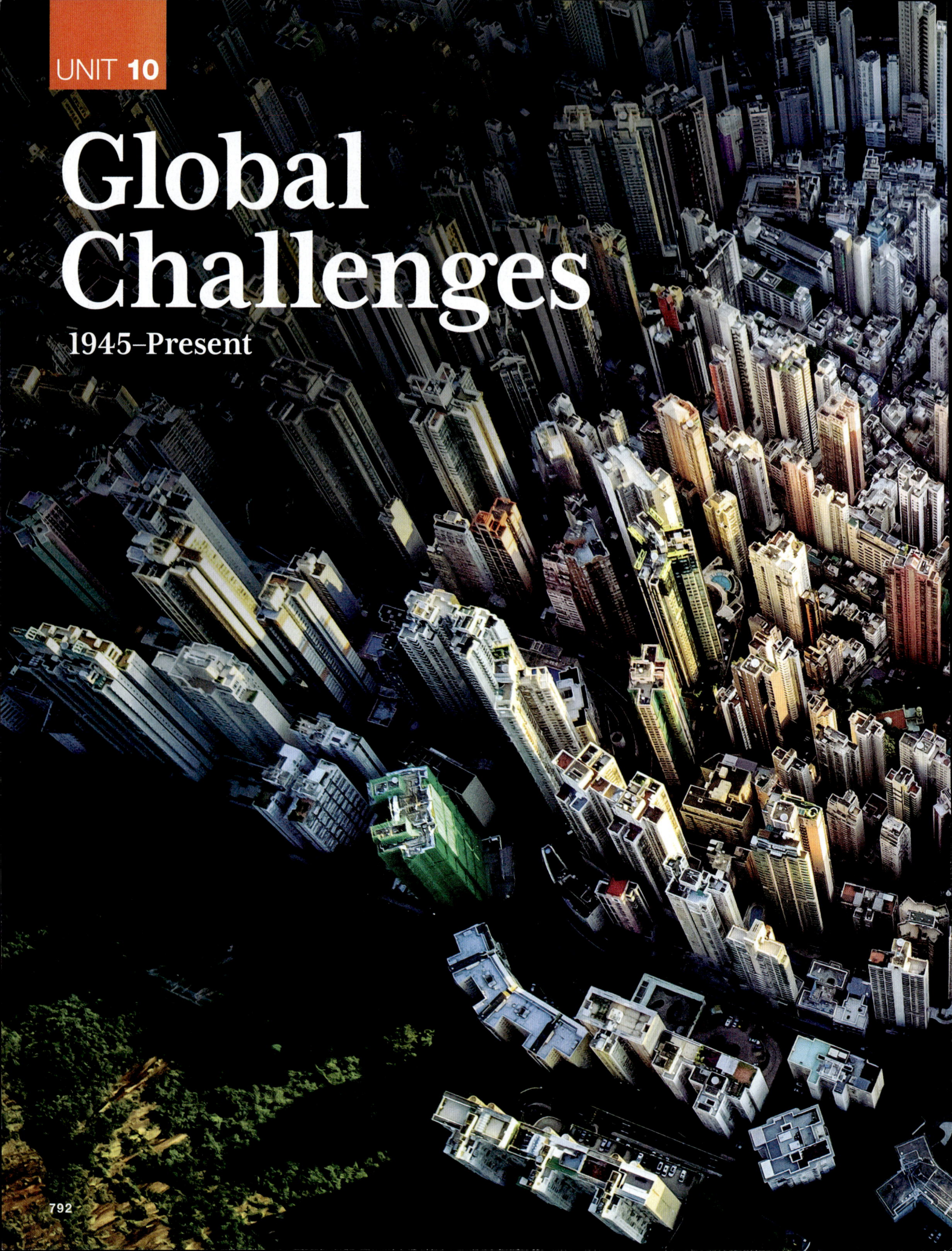

Global Challenges
1945–Present

CRITICAL VIEWING

Hong Kong, shown in this aerial photo, is one of the most densely populated places in the world. What details in the photo help convey the city's overcrowding?

UNIT 10 Global Challenges

WORLD EVENTS 1945–PRESENT

1947 AMERICAS The Truman Doctrine promises U.S. support for countries threatened by communism.

1948 ASIA Israel declares independence as a Jewish state; Arab nations respond by declaring war and invading the country. *(Jewish immigrants with the flag of Israel)*

1949 ASIA In China, Mao Zedong and his Communist Party defeat nationalist forces and establish the People's Republic of China. *(portrait of Mao Zedong at the Forbidden City in Beijing)*

1950 ASIA North Korea invades South Korea, starting the Korean War.

1952 AFRICA Mau Mau rebels in Kenya revolt against British rule. *(Mau Mau soldiers at their military camp)*

1959 AMERICAS Fidel Castro leads the Cuban Revolution, overthrowing the regime of dictator Batista and establishing a communist government in Cuba.

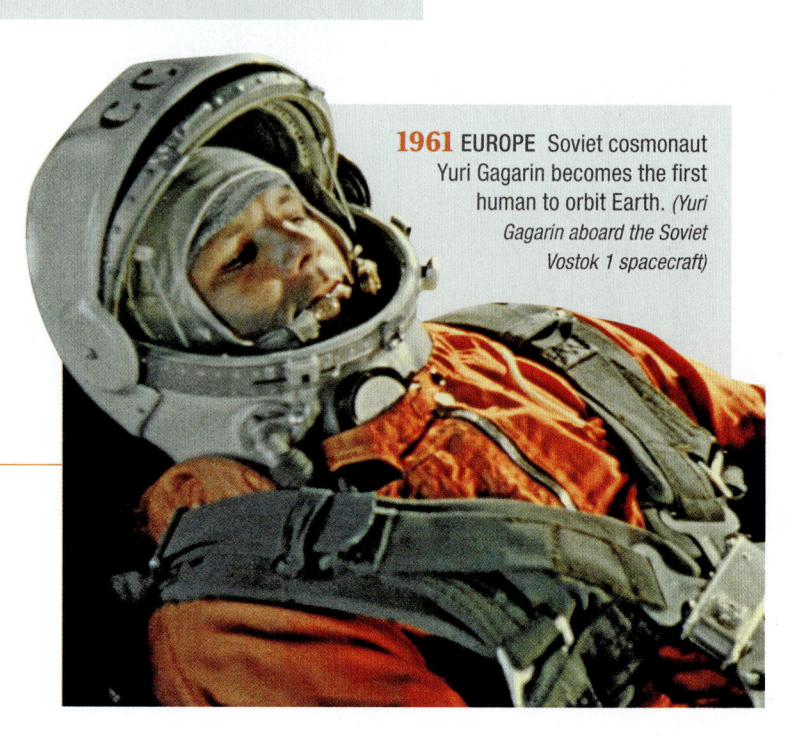

1961 EUROPE Soviet cosmonaut Yuri Gagarin becomes the first human to orbit Earth. *(Yuri Gagarin aboard the Soviet Vostok 1 spacecraft)*

1962 AMERICAS During the Cuban Missile Crisis, the United States prevents the Soviet Union from placing nuclear missiles in Cuba. *(The New York Times front page on Tuesday, October 23, 1962)*

2018 THE WORLD A refugee crisis occurs around the world as people flee religious persecution, war, poverty, and climate change. *(Honduran migrant caravan heading through Mexico to the United States)*

HISTORICAL THINKING

ANALYZE CAUSE AND EFFECT What effect do you think the Truman Doctrine might have had on conflicts that arose in the second half of the 20th century?

1989 EUROPE The Berlin Wall comes down, leading to the reunification of Germany.

2008 AMERICAS The crash of the New York Stock Exchange and the housing market cause the Great Recession, which spreads across the globe.

1965 ASIA President Lyndon Johnson sends U.S. combat troops to Vietnam. *(American soldiers with transport helicopter, 1966)*

1994 AFRICA Three years after the end of apartheid, voters elect Nelson Mandela president in South Africa's first democratic election. *(Nelson Mandela's inauguration)*

1985 EUROPE Soviet leader Mikhail Gorbachev introduces reform programs called glasnost and perestroika to encourage more openness and freedom within the Soviet Union. *(Mikhail Gorbachev speaking to the press)*

CHAPTER 28

Cold War and Global Upheavals
1945–1979

HISTORICAL THINKING How do countries maintain their independence and security?

SECTION 1 **Superpowers in an Arms Race**
SECTION 2 **Communism**
SECTION 3 **Colonies Seek Independence**
SECTION 4 **Wars in Asia and Global Crises**

CRITICAL VIEWING
Antiaircraft tanks parade in Red Square in Moscow in 1958 past a portrait of Vladimir Lenin, the founder of the Russian Communist Party. What does such a parade suggest about the Soviet Union at this time?

1.1 MAIN IDEA As World War II came to an end, a split developed between the United States and the Soviet Union over plans for Europe.

The Yalta Conference and Shifts in Power

Have you ever heard the saying "The enemy of my enemy is my friend"? The alliance between the United States and the Soviet Union during World War II was built on the basis of a common enemy. It fell apart soon after the Axis powers no longer posed a threat.

CAUSES OF THE COLD WAR

Just before the end of World War II, in February 1945, the Allied Powers met at Yalta, a Black Sea port on Ukraine's Crimean Peninsula, to plan Germany's unconditional surrender and the war's aftermath. President Franklin Roosevelt's priority for the meeting, called the **Yalta Conference**, was to get Joseph Stalin to cooperate in founding the United Nations (UN). Roosevelt achieved that goal.

The chief purpose of the UN was to maintain international peace and security through diplomacy. All the main bodies of the UN that exist today were established in 1945. They include the General Assembly, a policymaking body composed of all member nations, and the Security Council, a body originally composed of the major war allies: Great Britain, China, France, the Soviet Union, and the United States. Each member of the Security Council has veto power, which means that decisions can only be reached through consensus. The UN also includes the International Court of Justice, which settles legal disputes, and the Secretariat, which carries out the organization's day-to-day work. The Allies believed that the design of the UN would make it more effective than the League of Nations had been.

Another goal of the Yalta Conference was to create a plan for the countries of Eastern Europe that had been liberated from Nazi rule. The British and Americans had

At the Yalta Conference on the Crimean Peninsula in 1945, Prime Minister Winston Churchill of Great Britain, President Franklin Roosevelt of the United States, and Premier Joseph Stalin of the Soviet Union (seated left to right) met to plan the end of World War II and its aftermath.

promised that Poland would have free elections after the war. However, Stalin was not willing to give up Soviet control—he knew that any Polish government chosen through free elections would be hostile to the Soviet Union. As soon as the war was over, it became clear that Stalin would continue to occupy Poland and install a communist government there.

The Allied Powers met again six months later in Potsdam, Germany. By this time, the Soviets had occupied all of Eastern Europe, and Roosevelt had died and been replaced as U.S. president by Harry Truman. The Allies agreed to reduce the size of Germany, hold trials of Nazi war criminals in an international court, and dismantle Germany's military. They couldn't agree on

798 CHAPTER 28

the fate of Europe, however. Truman insisted that the people of Europe had the right to free elections. Stalin responded, "Everyone imposes his own system as far as his army can reach."

In some Eastern European countries, local communists had strong political influence since they had played an important role in resisting the Nazis. In elections held in Czechoslovakia after the war, the Communist Party won enough seats in parliament to join a coalition government along with other parties. But Stalin wanted complete control and unquestioned loyalty. He used the Soviet army to establish loyal communist governments in Eastern European countries. A major reason that Stalin wanted to control Eastern Europe was to provide a buffer against any future invasion of Soviet territory from the west. Russia, after all, had just suffered its second 20th-century invasion by Germany.

By 1948, the countries of Europe had been divided into two opposing camps, one aligned with the United States and the other aligned with the Soviet Union. The United States and the Soviet Union, two superpowers, were now bitter enemies rather than allies. The Cold War division of Europe became economic as well as political and military. Countries aligned with the United States had market-based, capitalist economies. Those aligned with the Soviet Union had socialist economies with centralized government planning.

RECONSTRUCTION, NOT REPARATIONS

At both the Yalta and Potsdam conferences, the Allies discussed requiring reparations from Germany. However, Truman knew that the harsh reparations imposed on Germany following World War I had led to the rise of the Nazis. Instead, he proposed the **Marshall Plan** to assist in the rebuilding of war-ravaged countries. The plan was named after U.S. secretary of state George C. Marshall. In early 1948, the United States announced that $13 billion would be available to rebuild Europe's postwar economies and restore prosperity.

The Marshall Plan worked in conjunction with two international institutions formed earlier: the World Bank and the International Monetary Fund. The World Bank loaned money to nations in need of a jumpstart. The International Monetary Fund provided emergency loans to nations in danger of insolvency, or bankruptcy.

Because the Marshall Plan was designed to enhance the stability of free-market economies, the Soviet Union and its Eastern European satellite states refused to participate. A satellite state is a country that is formally independent but under the control or influence of another country. Instead of joining the Marshall Plan, the Soviet Union focused on rebuilding itself with resources from Eastern Europe. Entire factories were moved from eastern Germany to the Soviet Union.

Like Germany, Japan was also in need of rebuilding. After Japan surrendered, the Allies occupied the country and initiated a series of reforms. The occupation and reconstruction was completed in three phases. In Phase 1 (1945–1947), war criminals were tried in Tokyo, the Japanese army was dismantled, and military officials were banned from political leadership. In Phase 2 (1947–1950), Allied advisors drafted a new constitution to reduce the emperor's power, empower parliament, advance the rights of women, and abolish Japan's right to wage war. Economic reforms included the redistribution of land and the breakup of monopolies. In Phase 3 (1950–1951), a formal peace treaty ensured Japan's continued security while allowing the United States to keep military bases in Japan as protection against communist incursion in the area.

THE BERLIN AIRLIFT After the Potsdam Conference, collaboration between the Soviets and the Western powers broke down, and no conclusive agreement was reached on Germany's future. The Soviets occupied the eastern part of the country, and the British, Americans, and French occupied the western part. The capital city of Berlin was divided into four sections: British, American, French, and Soviet. Tensions escalated in 1948 when the Soviets cut off rail, road, and water access to Berlin. The United States and the United Kingdom responded by sending supplies to West Berlin by air. The Berlin Airlift was successful; supplies were delivered efficiently to the war-torn city and eventually the Soviets lifted the blockade. But the crisis led to the creation of two separate states: the Federal Republic of Germany (West Germany) and the German Democratic Republic (East Germany). This division became the symbolic battle line of the Cold War.

HISTORICAL THINKING

1. **READING CHECK** How did the outcome of World War II contribute to the development of the Cold War?

2. **DRAW CONCLUSIONS** At the Yalta Conference, why was Roosevelt eager to form the United Nations?

3. **COMPARE AND CONTRAST** How did the Marshall Plan in Europe compare with economic reforms in Japan?

1.2

MAIN IDEA As the Soviet Union established communist governments throughout Eastern Europe, the Western powers worked together to contain the spread of communism.

American Alliances vs. the Soviet Bloc

Have you ever lined up dominoes in a row so that when you push on one at the end, the others all topple over? As the Soviet Union took control of Eastern Europe, American leaders envisioned one country after another falling to communism, just like a row of dominoes.

CONTAINING THE SPREAD OF COMMUNISM

Throughout the Cold War years, the term **Iron Curtain** would be used to describe the political and military barrier created by the Soviets to keep the people of Eastern Europe and the Soviet Union from having contact with the West.

Western leaders began to fear a **domino effect**, by which one country after another would fall to communism like a row of dominoes. Hoping to stop the spread of communism, President Truman issued the **Truman Doctrine** in 1947, declaring that the United States would aid countries threatened by communism. Truman's declaration came as communists in Greece fought to establish a socialist government there. Truman promised American aid to suppress the rebellion.

The Truman Doctrine advanced the **containment policy**, providing military and economic aid to protect countries from communist takeover. In reality, however, Stalin had already conceded Greece to Western control. And despite Truman's strong language, the United States did nothing to stop the Soviet takeover of Czechoslovakia.

SPHERES OF INFLUENCE

As hostilities increased between the Soviets and the Western powers, the United States allied with Canada and the European democracies to form the **North Atlantic Treaty Organization (NATO)**. The member nations agreed to a collective defense, stating "an armed attack against one or more of them in Europe or North America shall be considered an attack against them all." When West Germany was accepted as a member of NATO, the Soviet Union responded by forming the **Warsaw Pact**, an alliance with Eastern European nations under its sway.

Both superpowers presented themselves as champions of freedom. The Soviets identified colonialism and imperialism as the main barriers to liberation. They supported nationalists and socialists fighting European or American domination. But Moscow did not tolerate liberation movements within the **Soviet bloc**, the group of nations under its control. Secret police networks kept people from openly expressing anti-communist or anti-Soviet views. East Germany, for example, had a spy network called the *Stasi* that planted informers at all levels of society and encouraged neighbors to spy on one another. Still, in June 1953 East Germans rose up in large demonstrations to protest against low wages and bad working conditions. The communist

---

The term *Iron Curtain* originated in a speech given in 1946 by former British prime minister Winston Churchill in which he described the division of Europe into two opposing camps.

PRIMARY SOURCE

From Stettin in the Baltic to Trieste in the Adriatic, an iron curtain has descended across the Continent. Behind that line lie all the capitals of the ancient states of Central and Eastern Europe. . . . [A]nd the populations around them . . . are subject in one form or another, not only to Soviet influence but to a very high and, in many cases, increasing measure of control from Moscow.

—Winston Churchill, former British prime minister, March 5, 1946

Division of Europe During the Cold War, 1960

Legend:
- NATO nation
- Warsaw Pact nation
- Non-aligned nation
- Iron Curtain

government violently put down the protests with the aid of Soviet tanks.

Americans were quick to point out that the Soviet Union suppressed individual freedoms. But by the 1950s, paranoia about communism led to practices that contradicted American ideals in the United States. In Congress, Senator Joseph McCarthy from Wisconsin stoked public fear by making unproven charges of communist infiltration in the government. As a result, many Americans accused of communist leanings lost their jobs and reputations.

The United States also backed authoritarian dictatorships around the world simply because they opposed communism. Guatemala was a democratic country with an elected president who wanted to redistribute land to aid the country's poor. That policy was opposed by the powerful United Fruit Company, which convinced the U.S. government to secretly intervene to overthrow the elected government and replace it with an authoritarian one. Democracy was overthrown in Guatemala in the name of anti-communism.

THE ORGANIZATION OF AMERICAN STATES In 1948, a year before the formation of NATO, the Organization of American States (OAS) was formed at the urging of the United States to fight communism in the Americas and to maintain peace among the North and South American states. Initially, the OAS had 21 member countries, including the United States. Today, it includes all 35 independent states of the Americas. The OAS works to promote democracy, defend human rights, ensure security, and foster development and prosperity.

HISTORICAL THINKING

1. **READING CHECK** How did Western nations work together to keep the Soviets from expanding into Western Europe?

2. **IDENTIFY PROBLEMS AND SOLUTIONS** What problem did the Truman Doctrine seek to address?

3. **INTERPRET MAPS** What European countries were aligned with the Soviet Union during the Cold War?

1.3

MAIN IDEA Rivalry between the Soviet Union and the United States led to a competition to build the most powerful arsenal of weapons and to lead in space exploration.

The Arms and Space Races

In 1969, more than half a billion people around the world watched an awe-inspiring event on TV: American astronauts walking on the moon. They also saw a clear view of the entire Earth, maybe sensing the common destiny of all those living on that fragile sphere.

CAUSES AND EFFECTS OF THE ARMS RACE

As you've read, the United States and the Soviet Union had become bitter enemies by 1948. The two superpowers engaged in a global struggle for power, seeking to draw more countries into their orbits. But full-scale war between them never developed. The threat of nuclear weapons raised the stakes of total war too high. Fearful of nuclear annihilation, they never engaged in direct combat with each other. Instead, the Cold War turned hot in **proxy wars** around the world. In a proxy war, one or both sides are supported by, and serve the interests of, another country. The Cold War featured proxy wars in such countries as Greece, Korea, the Democratic Republic of the Congo, and Vietnam.

Seeking military superiority, the United States and the Soviet Union competed in an arms race from the late 1940s to the early 1990s. They spent billions of dollars building up their military strength and amassed nuclear weapons many times more powerful than those dropped on Hiroshima and Nagasaki. At the height of the arms race in 1986, each superpower possessed the ability to destroy the planet several times over.

People in both countries lived with the fear of a nuclear war. In the United States, school children practiced "duck and cover" drills, in which they ducked under their desks and covered their heads. Families built bomb shelters behind their homes where they hoped to hide in the event of a nuclear explosion. But most people realized that a nuclear war would result in the destruction of both countries and much of the world.

In 1972 and 1979, leaders of the two governments met to discuss how to limit nuclear weapons. These **Strategic Arms Limitation Talks (SALT)** had little success, but during the 1970s, both sides agreed to nuclear test ban treaties and limits on weapons production. Talks broke down, however, in 1979 when the Soviet Union invaded Afghanistan. By the time the Cold War ended in 1991, the cost of the arms race had overwhelmed the Soviet Union, contributing to its demise.

Both sides also expanded their intelligence operations during the Cold War. The Soviet spy agency, known as the KGB, worked through local proxy agencies, such as the East German Stasi, to maintain tight control over its satellite states while trying to infiltrate Western political, military, and intelligence communities. The United States formed the Central Intelligence Agency (CIA), which greatly expanded its operations during the 1950s to counter Soviet influence. The agency was involved in the overthrow of elected leaders in Guatemala, Iran, and the Democratic Republic of the Congo.

THE SPACE RACE

As the Soviets and Americans built rockets to transport long-range weapons, they realized that rockets could also be used to transport people into outer space. Thus began the space race, the competition between the United States and the Soviet Union to lead in space exploration. Getting to outer space first became a matter of national pride. In 1957, the Soviets launched Sputnik I, a satellite that successfully orbited Earth. Americans were humiliated and enraged that the Soviets had beat them, so the Eisenhower administration responded by creating the **National Aeronautics and Space Administration (NASA)** in 1958.

The American public eagerly followed news of the space race, and many Americans became obsessed with space exploration. The Soviet government, on the other hand, didn't announce its launches in advance. But its successes were highly publicized. The Soviets followed the launching of the first satellite in 1957 by sending the

NATIONAL GEOGRAPHIC EXPLORER BUZZ ALDRIN

Beyond the Moon

On July 20, 1969, Buzz Aldrin and Neil Armstrong became the first two people to walk on the moon. Following that Apollo 11 mission, Aldrin and his fellow crew members were awarded the Presidential Medal of Freedom and the Congressional Gold Medal.

While Aldrin is most famous for the moon landing, he has had many other accomplishments. Born in 1930, Aldrin was raised in New Jersey and graduated third in his class at the United States Military Academy at West Point. He earned his doctorate in astronautics from the Massachusetts Institute of Technology (MIT) and flew a jet fighter in the Korean War. In 1963, he was selected by NASA to be a member of the third group of astronauts.

Aldrin retired from NASA in 1971, but he has dedicated his life to promoting space exploration. He has written nine books, made speeches around the world, and appeared on numerous TV shows to advance education in space research and exploration.

Astronaut Buzz Aldrin (shown here inside the Apollo 11 lunar module and above walking on the moon near a leg of the lunar module) famously described the lunar landscape as "magnificent desolation."

---

first dog, Laika, into space later the same year. Soviet cosmonaut Yuri Gagarin became the first man to orbit Earth in 1961, and two years later cosmonaut Valentina Tereshkova became the first woman to do so. By 1966, the Soviets had achieved the first spacewalk and had orbited the moon for the first time.

In 1961, U.S. president John F. Kennedy challenged NASA to put an American on the moon by the end of the decade. That ambitious goal became a reality in 1969 when U.S. astronaut Neil Armstrong became the first human to set foot on the moon.

HISTORICAL THINKING

1. **READING CHECK** What prevented the Soviet Union and the United States from actually fighting a war against each other?

2. **ANALYZE CAUSE AND EFFECT** How did the arms race contribute to the eventual demise of the Soviet Union?

3. **SEQUENCE EVENTS** When did the United States and the Soviet Union begin to work toward denuclearization—before or after the main events of the space race?

2.1

MAIN IDEA Cold War conflicts increased in the Americas as Cuba formed ties with the Soviet Union.

Cuba and Castro

For 13 days in October 1962, people around the world waited in fear as the two superpowers hovered on the brink of nuclear war. The Americans and Soviets both stood their ground in a showdown over Cuba.

THE CUBAN REVOLUTION

In the 1950s, Cuba was an island of contrasts. Its capital, Havana, was famous for its beaches and nightclubs. But Cuba's wealthy economy, based on luxury hotels and tourism, obscured a darker underside of corruption. The American Mafia, an organization of criminals, controlled Havana's casinos, and American business interests supported the country's corrupt dictator, Fulgencio Batista (fool-HEHN-see-oh buh-TEE-stuh). Most Cubans lived in poverty, without democratic freedoms or access to good jobs, health care, or education.

Cuban revolutionary leader Fidel Castro, shown with his arm raised, and his fellow rebels enter Havana, Cuba, on January 8, 1959, after overthrowing the dictatorship of Fulgencio Batista.

An idealistic young Cuban named **Fidel Castro** renounced middle-class privilege and promoted ==populism==, or support for the concerns of ordinary people, as he started the Cuban Revolution to end Batista's rule. Castro led an attack on an army barracks and was imprisoned in 1953. After his release, he fled to Mexico, where he formed a small band of rebels determined to overthrow the Cuban dictator. One of Castro's revolutionary friends was the Argentinian **Ernesto "Che" Guevara**. Guevara was in Guatemala during the U.S. overthrow of its government, fled to Mexico, and then went on to Cuba.

In 1956, when Castro and Guevara and other revolutionaries returned to Cuba, they recruited more rebels from the local population and stockpiled ammunition. They used guerrilla tactics, such as quick raids and surprise ambushes, to fight the Cuban army. On New Year's Day 1959, Batista fled to the Dominican Republic, and Castro's forces entered Havana a few days later.

RELATIONS WITH THE SUPERPOWERS

As the new leader of Cuba, Castro sought support from the United States. But relations with the United States deteriorated after Cuba passed a law that nationalized land owned by American corporations. Soon corporate lobbyists and Cold War hawks, who supported an aggressive foreign policy, portrayed Castro as a Soviet threat. Pro-Batista forces in the United States, who were mostly Cuban exiles, lobbied for an American-backed invasion.

In the spring of 1961, a U.S.-sponsored group of Cuban exiles stormed Cuba's Bay of Pigs. Castro's forces crushed the invasion, but Castro's distrust of the United States increased. Meanwhile, the United States placed

THROUGH THE LENS DAVID GUTTENFELDER

This photograph, taken by National Geographic photographer David Guttenfelder, shows people lining the streets of the town of Las Tunas, Cuba, as Fidel Castro's funeral procession passes by. Guttenfelder rented a blue 1958 Buick and followed the multi-day funeral cortege from Havana to Santiago de Cuba.

"All along the way, on the edge of the highway, with their horses in sugarcane fields, on the streets of every village and town," says Guttenfelder, "people came out to line the road—millions of people, whole communities—standing in silent attention, some weeping, to witness the end of an era."

an economic **embargo**, or trade ban, on Cuba, making diplomacy and compromise all but impossible.

Tensions between the United States and Cuba culminated in the **Cuban Missile Crisis** of 1962. Castro was convinced that the United States would never let his socialist changes in Cuba proceed in peace, so he developed closer ties with the Soviet Union. **Nikita Khrushchev** (nuh-KEE-tuh krush-AWF), the Soviet premier, took advantage of the situation and secretly shipped nuclear missiles to Cuba. When American surveillance aircraft detected the missiles, President Kennedy demanded their removal. Khrushchev refused, and Kennedy ordered a naval quarantine to prevent Soviet ships from reaching Cuba. For 13 days, the people of the world held their breath as the two countries moved closer to war. Then both sides backed down. Khrushchev removed the Soviet missiles from Cuba, and Kennedy removed U.S. missiles from Turkey and promised not to invade Cuba.

To help Cuba withstand the American embargo, the Soviets bought the island's entire sugar crop at above-market prices and provided subsidized fuel and agricultural machinery. By the mid-1960s, Cubans were better fed and better housed than they had been before the revolution. Basic healthcare and education became free for all. But as Castro transformed Cuba into a communist country, underlying economic problems remained. Cuba depended on the Soviet Union in the same way Latin American countries had depended on colonial powers in the past, exporting agricultural products while importing higher-valued industrial goods. In time, Cuban workers complained of low wages and shortages of basic goods. Castro's government viewed all opposition to its policies as being promoted by the United States and its community of Cuban exiles in Florida. Cubans who publicly complained might be denied jobs, arrested, sent to labor camps, or even executed.

HISTORICAL THINKING

1. **READING CHECK** What conditions in Cuba motivated Fidel Castro and other rebels to start the Cuban Revolution?
2. **MAKE INFERENCES** Why did American troops invade Cuba at the Bay of Pigs?
3. **DESCRIBE** Explain what happened during the Cuban Missile Crisis.

Cold War and Global Upheavals 805

2.2 Preserving Cultural Heritage

FORGOTTEN ART SCHOOLS

The Cuban Revolution brought a spirit of optimism to life in Cuba. The oppressive Batista regime was in the past, and the future seemed to hold great possibilities. In 1961, Fidel Castro and Argentine revolutionary leader Che Guevara enthusiastically proposed five tuition-free schools where students from around the world could study ballet, modern dance, music, art, and theater in a creative environment.

A trio of architects developed a different design for each of the five schools. But all the designs incorporated the natural landscape, common architectural structures, and Cuban-made bricks and terra-cotta tiles. For four years, the schools buzzed with activity as students danced through curved colonnades and construction continued on domed pavilions and concert halls.

Following the Cuban Missile Crisis in 1962, national security became Cuba's top priority and Soviet ideology took precedence over artistic endeavors. The project came to a dramatic halt in 1965. The schools' three architects were accused of valuing material goods rather than revolutionary ideals. One architect was imprisoned; the other two fled the country. Over the next 40 years, the unfinished schools fell into ruin, though students continued to study at several of the neglected campuses.

In the 1990s, Castro invited the original architects to restore the school buildings. Cuba's National Council of Cultural Heritage recognized the schools as a national monument in 2011. Today, the National Art Schools are considered the most important architectural achievement of the Cuban Revolution.

HISTORICAL THINKING

ANALYZE VISUALS How do the photos and history of Cuba's National Art Schools reflect the country's own history?

HAVANA, CUBA

The National Art Schools were added to the 2016 World Monuments Watch, which lists sites around the world "that are at risk from the forces of nature and the impact of social, political, and economic change."

The unifying design element of the National Art Schools was a ceiling made by a technique called *Catalan vault*. Using this technique, a builder places bricks lengthwise over parallel wooden beams to form an arch-shaped ceiling. The Catalan vaults increased the structural strength of ceilings and allowed builders to use materials readily available in Cuba.

This unfinished hallway is part of the School of Music.

Cold War and Global Upheavals

2.3

MAIN IDEA Mao Zedong's Communist Party took power in China in 1949, but it soon split with the Soviet Union to create its own version of communism.

Mao Zedong and the People's Republic of China

Have you ever asked your friends for their opinions, only to have them tell you something you really didn't want to hear? That's what happened in China. The leader of the Chinese Communist Party got such negative feedback that he punished all the people who spoke out, along with anybody associated with them.

THE CHINESE CIVIL WAR

As a young man, **Mao Zedong**, the future ruler of China, studied various political philosophies before embracing communism. He believed revolution in China would start with the peasants, and beginning in the 1920s, he spent many years politically organizing the peasants in China's countryside. Meanwhile, **Chiang Kai-shek** became the head of the Nationalist government in China in 1928. The Nationalists fought the Communists intermittently for years until the two groups united in 1937 to fight the Japanese, who had invaded China.

After Japan's defeat in World War II in 1945, Mao and Chiang resumed the Chinese Civil War. Chiang's Nationalists had a large army, the support of Western powers, and control of China's largest cities. But Mao had the support of Chinese peasants who had waged guerrilla warfare against the Japanese invaders. After World War II, Mao's People's Liberation Army joined with peasants in waging guerrilla warfare against the Nationalists.

In 1949, Mao Zedong and his Communist Party emerged victorious in the civil war and established the People's Republic of China on the mainland. Chiang Kai-shek and his Nationalist followers fled to the island of Taiwan, where they established the Republic of China.

Once in power, the Communists revolutionized China from the bottom up. They organized peasants into agricultural working groups called cooperatives, expanded educational opportunities, formed youth organizations, and enrolled workers in state-sponsored unions. Within the youth organizations, unions, and other groups, citizens were **indoctrinated**, or rigidly trained, in "Mao Zedong Thought." Those who expressed ideas that deviated from Mao's ideology were shamed and forced to publicly confess their "errors."

This photograph shows Chinese Communist leader Mao Zedong (far left) talking with peasants in a northern province of China. The photo dates to the time of the war between the Chinese and the Japanese that lasted from 1937 to 1945.

The People's Republic of China and Taiwan, 1949

Nationalist retreat, 1948–1949

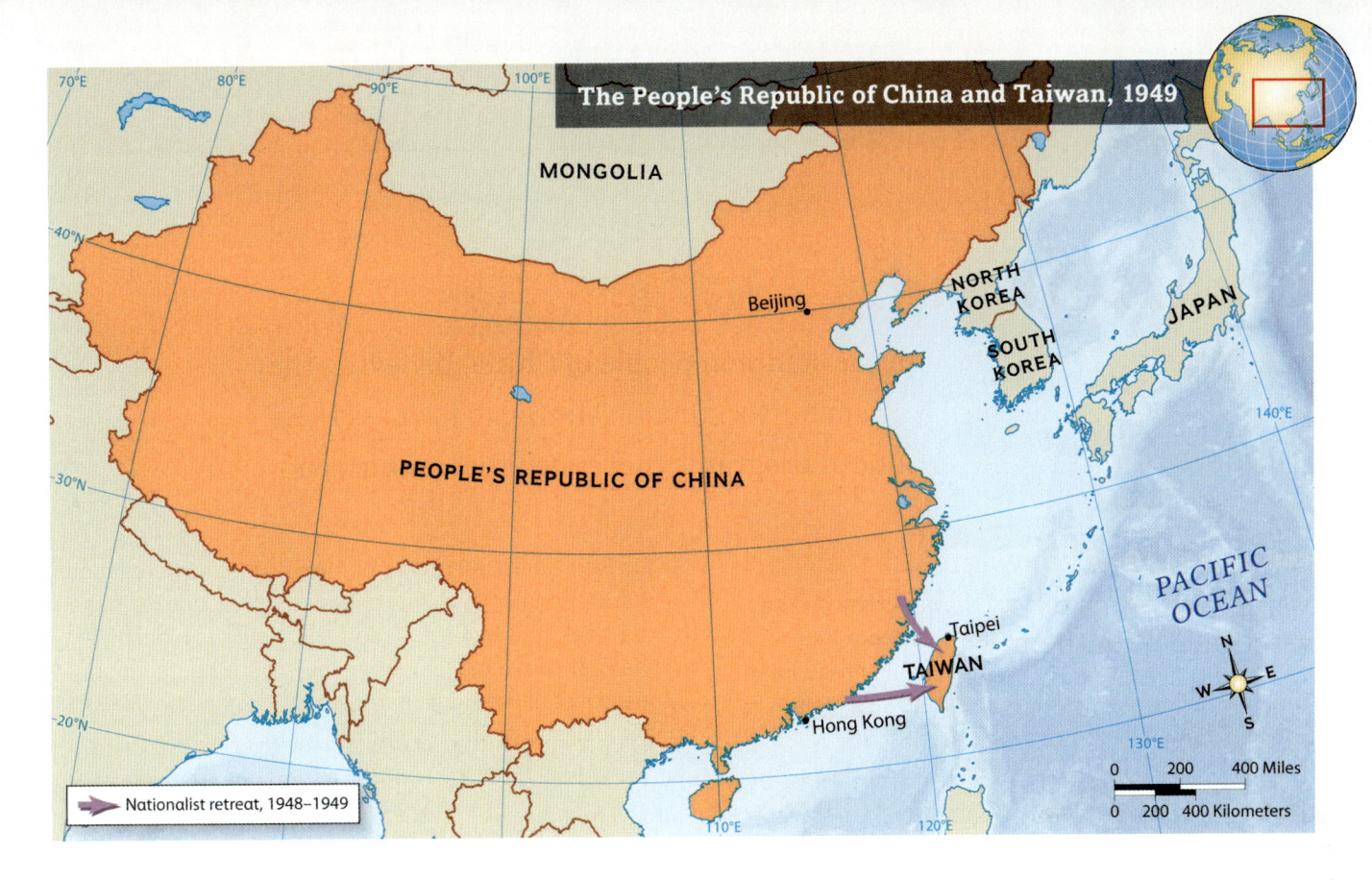

THE CHINESE AND SOVIETS SPLIT

Initially, the People's Republic of China followed Soviet-style economic policies of state-run industries and collective farms, which were cooperative associations of farmers who worked land owned by the government. The Chinese sent engineers and state planners to the Soviet Union for training. Mao hoped to stimulate rapid economic growth, but the results were disappointing. The growth of industrial and agricultural production was slower than Mao expected, and new leadership in the Soviet Union didn't suit Mao's ideology. Soviet Premier Khrushchev criticized his predecessor—Stalin—for fostering a cult of personality, in which a public figure is idolized. Mao had admired Stalin, and he had modeled his own cult of personality after Stalin's. Khrushchev also implemented political reforms, such as relaxing censorship and easing tensions with the West. Mao considered Khrushchev's approach weak and **revisionist**, or straying from the revolutionary spirit of Marxist doctrine. Mao continued to use strong anti-capitalist and anti-imperialist rhetoric against the West.

Mao broke ties with the Soviets and sought a solution to China's slow advancement. To inspire new ideas, he launched a program that became known as the Hundred Flowers Campaign. The program encouraged people to speak freely and offer suggestions. China's intellectuals responded with open criticism of the Communist Party and Mao's leadership. In 1957, Mao had the intellectuals arrested, imprisoned, and exiled.

After purging the intellectual "rightists," Mao began to describe the Communist Party as being divided into two factions, which he labeled "expert" and "red." According to Mao, the "experts," who managed collectivization and industrial development, were becoming a technical elite, or upper class, cut off from the "masses," or common people. Mao believed the "reds," leaders who emphasized socialist willpower rather than technical ability, would rapidly bring about socialist prosperity by unleashing the true revolutionary potential of China's peasants and workers. Basically, Mao believed people would work harder because of their deeply held socialist beliefs. In Mao's thinking, the people working collectively could literally move mountains.

HISTORICAL THINKING

1. **READING CHECK** What led Mao Zedong to break away from Soviet communism?

2. **ANALYZE CAUSES AND EFFECTS** What factors contributed to the Communists' victory in the Chinese Civil War?

3. **INTEGRATE VISUALS** How did the Republic of China, established by Chiang Kai-Shek, compare in size with the People's Republic of China?

Cold War and Global Upheavals

2.4

MAIN IDEA Mao Zedong initiated economic and social programs that caused massive turmoil in China.

Communes and Chaos

Mao Zedong had great faith in the common people of China, believing they had an "inexhaustible enthusiasm for socialism." Aiming to harness their revolutionary spirit, he introduced programs that tested that enthusiasm.

THE GREAT LEAP FORWARD

Hoping to harness the zeal and power of the masses, Mao launched a campaign called the **Great Leap Forward** in 1958 to stimulate rapid industrialization. The peasants were now organized into **people's communes**, which combined a number of collective farms. Unlike the former collective farms, in which people engaged exclusively in agricultural activities, the people's communes were multipurpose. The communes pooled the labor of thousands of peasants from different villages to increase agricultural production and to engage in local industrial production. Small furnaces were set up across the country to produce steel, for example.

On the communes, the people were organized into communal, or shared, living areas as well as work units. Communal kitchens replaced private kitchens, and a team of people cooked for the community, whose members ate together. Meanwhile, property rights were restricted, and peasants lost access to the small plots they had formerly relied on to feed their families. Mao directed the masses to pour all their energy and enthusiasm into communal production.

The Great Leap Forward was disastrous. The steel produced in small communal furnaces was of poor quality, and food production declined. As many as 30 million people died in the famine that followed. Recognizing the catastrophic failure of the plan, the Communist Party secretly reduced Mao's authority. But party leaders disagreed on the cause of the failure. Some claimed it was poor management and overzealous policies. Others blamed the lack of expertise and material incentives.

THE CULTURAL REVOLUTION

In an effort to reassert his authority and silence his critics, Mao launched a movement in 1966 to instill his thinking into Chinese society. In the **Cultural Revolution**, Mao organized young people into militant groups called the Red Guard. Members of the Red Guard were taught that Mao himself was the source of all wisdom. A "little red book" of Mao's quotations became the bible of the Red Guard movement. At large public gatherings, members of the Red Guard would wave the book enthusiastically in the air to pay homage to their leader.

Mao used the Red Guard to attack his enemies within the Communist Party, the "rightists" and "experts" who had reduced Mao's power following the Great Leap Forward. The Red Guard attacked party officials and publicly humiliated schoolteachers. They destroyed cultural artifacts that linked China to its past and harassed anyone they thought needed "re-education." Educated people were sent to farms or factories to humble themselves and to absorb the revolutionary spirit of the masses. Many died.

CRITICAL VIEWING Members of the Red Guard wave the "little red book" of quotations by Mao Zedong in the air to honor their leader. What details about these Red Guard members stand out?

CRITICAL VIEWING This poster promotes the Great Leap Forward, a campaign that Mao Zedong launched in 1958 to increase industrial and agricultural production in China. What kind of image of Chinese society does the poster convey?

By 1968, the Cultural Revolution had reduced the country to chaos. Schools had closed, and the economy was at a standstill. Communist leaders who had a pragmatic, or practical, approach to politics finally convinced Mao to allow the People's Liberation Army to restore governmental authority. Now the Red Guard themselves were sent to remote villages and labor camps. Still, a bitter power struggle continued behind the scenes. A radical faction called the "Gang of Four," led by Mao's wife, Jiang Qing (jahng CHIHNG), plotted to restore the Cultural Revolution. On the other side were pragmatists like Deng Xiaoping (DEHNG shah-oh-PIHNG), an "expert" who was struggling to regain his influence. By this time, Mao was no longer in complete command, so Deng and the "expert" faction reasserted themselves.

In 1972, the pragmatists scored a victory when U.S. president Richard Nixon came to Beijing to re-establish relations with China. Armed confrontation had recently taken place along China's border with the Soviet Union. The Chinese were worried about the Soviets and so welcomed the possibility of closer ties with the Americans. Although Nixon was a die-hard anti-communist, he hoped that better relations with China would increase his bargaining power with the Soviet Union and might help the United States get out of Vietnam, a conflict you'll read about later in this chapter.

While the shadow of the Cultural Revolution still hung over China at the time of Mao's death in 1976, the eventual victory of Deng Xiaoping over the Gang of Four carried the People's Republic of China into an entirely new, market-oriented direction. But the people of China had paid a terrible price for Mao's political adventures: the Great Leap Forward and the Cultural Revolution had killed tens of millions.

HISTORICAL THINKING

1. **READING CHECK** What were the purpose and the result of the Great Leap Forward?

2. **IDENTIFY PROBLEMS AND SOLUTIONS** What problems did the Cultural Revolution produce?

3. **EVALUATE** How effective was Mao as a leader? Support your evaluation with evidence from the text.

Cold War and Global Upheavals 811

3.1

MAIN IDEA Following World War II, African colonies sought independence from European rule, but many remained economically tied to their former colonial rulers.

Decolonization in Africa

Look at a map showing Africa in 1945, and you'll see only four self-governing countries: Egypt, Ethiopia, Liberia, and South Africa. European colonial powers controlled the rest of the continent. Three decades later, just a few colonies remained.

AFRICAN INDEPENDENCE MOVEMENTS

After supporting the Allies during World War II, Africans thought the time had come for the end of colonialism, and nationalist movements grew throughout Africa. Entering the 1950s, the French, British, and Belgians failed to recognize the change in African attitudes. Over the next three decades, however, these colonial powers would confront a wave of independence movements that would engulf the continent, creating many new nations.

The people of Ghana led the effort, gaining their independence in 1957. Their leader was **Kwame Nkrumah**, who returned to Africa after studying in the United States and Britain. He became Ghana's first prime minister and an international symbol of African liberation and Pan-Africanism. But the economic structures of colonialism remained in most nations, making true independence difficult. The new nations lacked the capital and expertise to develop their economies. They borrowed money from European nations, which led to **neocolonialism**, the continuation of dependence on, and domination by, a colonial power.

Achieving Independence in Africa, 1847–1993

Colonial Rulers:
- Great Britain
- France
- Italy
- Belgium
- Portugal
- Spain
- Other

1960 Year independence achieved

- MOROCCO 1956
- TUNISIA 1957
- ALGERIA 1962
- LIBYA 1951
- EGYPT 1922
- WESTERN SAHARA (MOROCCO)
- MAURITANIA 1960
- MALI 1960
- NIGER 1960
- SUDAN 1956
- ERITREA (from ETHIOPIA) 1993
- SENEGAL 1960
- GAMBIA 1965
- GUINEA-BISSAU 1974
- BURKINA FASO 1960
- CHAD 1960
- DJIBOUTI 1977
- GUINEA 1958
- BENIN 1960
- NIGERIA 1960
- CENTRAL AFRICAN REPUBLIC 1960
- SOUTH SUDAN (from SUDAN) 2011
- ETHIOPIA
- SIERRA LEONE 1961
- LIBERIA
- CÔTE D'IVOIRE 1960
- GHANA 1957
- TOGO 1960
- CAMEROON 1960
- UGANDA 1962
- KENYA 1963
- SOMALIA 1960
- GABON 1960
- DEM. REP. OF CONGO 1960
- RWANDA 1962
- EQUATORIAL GUINEA 1968
- CONGO 1960
- BURUNDI 1962
- TANZANIA 1964
- MALAWI 1964
- ANGOLA 1975
- ZAMBIA 1964
- MOZAMBIQUE 1974
- ZIMBABWE 1980
- MADAGASCAR 1960
- NAMIBIA (from SOUTH AFRICA) 1990
- BOTSWANA 1966
- ESWATINI 1968
- SOUTH AFRICA (Republic 1961)
- LESOTHO 1966

Even before talk of independence, France had laid the foundations for neocolonial control of its African colonies. The French promised citizenship to educated Africans, creating an African elite that strongly identified with French culture. Appealing to these French Africans, French President Charles de Gaulle announced a **referendum** on the question of independence to be held across French Africa. A referendum is a public vote on a single political question. A "yes" vote would allow former French colonies to control their own internal affairs, while the French would retain control over their economic policy, foreign affairs, and military. A "no" vote meant complete and immediate independence, with all ties to France severed.

All but one colony voted to retain ties with France. The exception was Guinea, where the vote for complete independence prompted the French government to stop economic aid and withdraw its administrators overnight. The French ripped telephones from the walls as they vacated their offices. The result was an economic crisis and the rise of an authoritarian regime. Other African leaders heeded the French message and cooperated with France.

In some colonies, especially those in which many Europeans had settled, Africans took up arms to liberate themselves. For instance, over a million Europeans lived in Algeria, and after World War II, Algerian nationalists demanded rights equal to those of the white settlers. To gain a voice in their own governance, they began an armed struggle in 1954. It became a brutal war. Some Algerians launched terrorist attacks on French civilians, and the French military tortured Algerian resistance fighters. Over time, French public opinion soured on the violence, and in 1962, the French agreed to recognize Algerian independence.

Like Algeria, Kenya had a large population of European settlers. The Kenyan activist Jomo Kenyatta had met with other African nationalist leaders in England at a Pan-African Congress in 1946, hoping to develop a large organization to force the British into negotiations. But an impatient group of Kenyan rebels took a more militant stand. They formed a secret society, stole arms from police stations, and assassinated a chief who collaborated with the colonists. The British called the rebels the Mau Mau and depicted them as "savages."

Outgunned by colonial forces, the rebels carried on their guerrilla fight by relying on their knowledge of the forest and the support of the local population. The government moved the rural population into barbed-wire villages to cut them off from the rebels. By the late 1950s, the rebellion was contained, but publicity of British military abuses embarrassed the British, leading them to compromise with more moderate African nationalists. In 1963, Jomo Kenyatta became prime minister of an independent Kenya.

PROXY WAR IN THE CONGO

Although Britain and France negotiated independence for their African colonies without superpower intervention, Belgium did not. A former Belgian colony, the new Democratic Republic of the Congo became the site of a proxy war between the United States and the Soviet Union.

The Belgian administration did little to prepare Africans in the Congo for independence. But with the Congo caught up in the nationalist fever spreading across the continent, the Belgians made hasty plans for independence. At the independence ceremony in 1960, the Belgian king gave a patronizing speech praising his country's "civilizing mission" in Africa. **Patrice Lumumba**, the country's new prime minister, responded with a list of Belgian crimes against Africans. The speech made Lumumba a hero to African nationalists, but Belgium and the United States regarded him as a dangerous radical.

Although the Democratic Republic of the Congo was rich in natural resources, including gold, copper, diamonds, cobalt, uranium, and oil, Lumumba faced immediate challenges. African soldiers mutinied against their Belgian officers, and the mineral-rich province of Katanga seceded. The United Nations sent in peacekeeping forces, but Lumumba also turned to the Soviet Union for military aid. Branding Lumumba a "communist," the CIA cooperated in his capture and execution. Rebel armies arose in several provinces. Finally, **Joseph Mobutu**, an army officer long on the CIA payroll, seized power in late 1960. Its relationship with Mobutu allowed the United States to become the main power broker in Central Africa and to secure the mineral riches of the Congo. Some of these minerals were vital to the defense and aerospace industries.

HISTORICAL THINKING

1. **READING CHECK** Why did many newly independent African countries choose to maintain ties with their European colonizers?

2. **INTERPRET MAPS** Which two European countries had the largest number of colonies in Africa?

3. **ANALYZE CAUSE AND EFFECT** Why did the United States and the Soviet Union get involved in the Democratic Republic of the Congo?

3.2

MAIN IDEA As nationalism spread across Africa, the white minority rulers of South Africa imposed strict racial segregation and limited the rights of black South Africans.

Apartheid in South Africa

After World War II, most Africans began gaining their freedom and independence from European rule. But those in South Africa were losing more of their rights. A white minority controlled the government of South Africa and refused to share power with the country's black majority.

RACIAL SEGREGATION IN SOUTH AFRICA

As you have already learned, the discovery of diamonds and gold in southern Africa in the late 1800s led to a struggle between the Dutch settlers called Boers and British imperialists for control of the region. The British won the war that resulted, known as the South African War, in 1902. The British and the Dutch then formed the Union of South Africa in 1910. They ruled together, united by their shared desire for cheap African labor. In 1961, South Africa became a republic, controlled by a white minority.

After World War II, white minority rulers in South Africa solidified their power over the African majority, as well as mixed-race South Africans known as "coloreds" and the country's Indian minority. In 1948, the older system of racial segregation grew even more extreme when the National Party came to power and instituted **apartheid** (uh-PAHR-tayt), which means "separateness." This system of racial segregation and discrimination lasted until the early 1990s. The system dictated where black and brown people could live and work, what they could and could not study, and who they could date and marry. Nonwhites were denied the right to vote and other basic rights.

Less than 10 percent of South Africa's population was white, but white people owned and controlled 90 percent of the land and resources. People classified as "black" or "colored" could not even live in the same town with white people unless they were working for a white-owned business. Their families had to live elsewhere.

RESISTANCE TO APARTHEID

During the early years of the Cold War, British and American governments overlooked the repressive policies in South Africa because the country's leaders were adamantly anti-communist. In 1952, an organization called the **African National Congress (ANC)** began a "defiance campaign" based on nonviolent resistance. Led by South African activist **Nelson Mandela**, the campaign followed Gandhi's method of drawing attention to repressive laws by having large numbers of people openly violate them. The hope was that as the police arrested lawbreakers, the prisons would overflow, forcing

TREVOR NOAH Growing up in apartheid South Africa, comedian Trevor Noah was literally "born a crime." His white European father and his Xhosa African mother were not allowed to be together. Walking in the park, Noah had to be careful not to shout "Papa" to his father—since Noah was an illegal child, police could take him away from his parents at any time. With the sacrifice and support of his mother, Noah overcame the tough street life of the segregated black townships, got a good education, and found success as an international television star.

814 CHAPTER 28

the government to abolish the laws. However, the police responded with brutality, and instead of abolishing laws, the government intensified the repression.

In 1960, about 20,000 people assembled before a police station in the black township of Sharpeville to protest the "pass laws," which restricted the movements of black Africans. The police shot into the crowd, killing 69 protesters and wounding another 180. This event, which became known as the Sharpeville massacre, sparked international criticism of apartheid.

Mandela and the ANC then turned to a sabotage campaign, in which they deliberately bombed pass offices and other targets. Mandela and other organizers were arrested. Mandela was tried for treason, and in 1964, he was sentenced to life in prison.

With the imprisonment of Mandela, hopes for transforming South Africa were at an all-time low. The government invested heavily in defense in the 1970s to suppress domestic and outside resistance to apartheid. However, the resistance continued. The Black Consciousness Movement led by **Steve Biko** inspired young people to overcome the sense of inferiority they had been given by apartheid, to be proud and confidant in themselves as Africans.

Although Biko was murdered by apartheid police, his influence was shown in 1976 when thousands of children in Soweto, a black township, rose up to protest their inferior education. As protesters marched to a rally, police shot into the crowd. The event caused a national uprising and a series of protests, during which the police killed more than 500 people. The UN Security Council voted unanimously to ban sales of arms to South Africa.

As images of police violence in South Africa spread around the world, more leaders and groups in the global community condemned apartheid. Many countries levied economic and cultural sanctions against the regime. In the 1970s, students at historically black U.S. colleges and universities such as Spelman, Morehouse, and Howard launched a series of protests. They called for their schools to divest, or remove their investments, from South Africa. Protests spread to other universities, including Occidental College in California, where a young student named Barack Obama gave his first public speech, denouncing apartheid. Obama later became president of the United States.

Continued domestic resistance and economic sanctions made governance increasingly difficult for the ruling National Party. In 1990, South Africa's newly elected moderate president, **F.W. de Klerk**, released Nelson Mandela from prison. De Klerk legalized the ANC and prepared the way for democratic, multiracial elections. You will read more about Nelson Mandela and the changes in South Africa in the next chapter.

South Africa's system of strict racial segregation applied to public restrooms and other facilities. Bold letters in English, Afrikaans, and Tswana indicated who could use this restroom in Soweto, a township on the outskirts of Johannesburg, South Africa.

HISTORICAL THINKING

1. **READING CHECK** How did apartheid affect the lives of South Africans?

2. **ANALYZE CAUSE AND EFFECT** How did the international reaction to apartheid change over time, and what effect did it have?

3. **DESCRIBE** What were some of the successes and failures of the resistance movement in South Africa?

Cold War and Global Upheavals 815

3.3

MAIN IDEA Many newly independent African and Asian countries tried to remain neutral as the United States and the Soviet Union pushed them to take sides in the Cold War.

The Bandung Generation

Voters sometimes find it difficult to embrace either candidate in a major election because the flaws of both are obvious. That was the situation many Asian and African countries faced in the Cold War as they were pressured to align with either the United States or the Soviet Union.

THE BANDUNG CONFERENCE

In 1955, the leaders of 29 former colonial states met in Bandung, Indonesia, for the first Asian-African Conference, also called the Bandung Conference. They discussed strategies to avoid both neocolonialism and superpower intervention and to promote economic and cultural cooperation. The participating countries unanimously agreed to the following goals:

- abolish colonialism and the subjugation, domination, and exploitation of people;
- support human rights and self-determination;
- promote world peace and international cooperation;
- work to abolish nuclear weapons;
- cooperate in promoting economic development; and
- promote cultural understanding, education, and information exchange.

The Bandung Conference formed the basis of a general movement toward **nonalignment**, in which leaders of developing countries joined together in remaining neutral in the Cold War. The participants in the Bandung Conference later were called the Bandung Generation. The term **Third World** was used to describe economically developing countries that did not align with either the United States or the Soviet Union.

The United States did not participate in the Bandung Conference. American leaders were suspicious of the gathering, fearing it would issue a general condemnation of the West. The Americans supported decolonization and self-determination in theory, but in practice they usually supported the British, Dutch, French, and Portuguese colonizers who were close allies in the fight against communism.

DIFFICULTIES WITH NONALIGNMENT

Many developing countries found it difficult to remain nonaligned with either the United States or the Soviet Union during the Cold War. The careers of two leaders at the Bandung Conference—one Indonesian and one Indian—illustrate the difficulties.

Many Muslims fled India after the British divided the Indian colony into two states based on religion in 1947. In this photograph, Muslim refugees crowd onto the roof of a train near New Delhi as they try to reach Pakistan.

In 1945, Indonesian nationalist **Ahmed Sukarno** and his party declared Indonesia's freedom from both the Dutch and the Japanese. Indonesia had been a colony of the Netherlands when the Japanese invaded during World War II. After the war, Indonesia had to fight Dutch reoccupation forces for five years. In 1950, the hundreds of diverse islands that formed the colony joined together to create the independent nation of Indonesia. Today, Indonesia is the world's fourth most populous nation and the largest Muslim majority country. To unify the country's scattered islands, Sukarno sponsored the development of a common language with a simplified grammar.

Sukarno was popular at first, but he had no experience running a country. In 1963, he declared himself "president for life," and his popularity waned. A powerful communist insurgency developed. The Indonesian military suspected that Sukarno was either sympathetic to communism or too weak to fight it and so carried out a murderous crackdown in 1964.

The United States also considered Sukarno too weak to battle communism. In 1967, the United States backed a corrupt, authoritarian general named Suharto in ousting Sukarno. American leaders turned a blind eye when Suharto suspended the constitution. Having a dependable ally in the struggle against communism took precedence over the civil rights of Indonesians.

India's prime minister, Jawaharlal Nehru (whom you read about earlier), was more successful in remaining neutral in the Cold War. However, like other leaders of newly independent nations, he faced tremendous problems. In 1947, the British divided the Indian colony into two separate states based on religious differences in their populations: India, with a Hindu majority, and Pakistan, with a Muslim majority. However, a substantial Hindu minority lived in Pakistan, and an even larger Muslim minority lived in India. Fearing religious persecution, millions of people tried desperately to cross to the country of their religion after the ==partition==, or division. Violence followed. As many as 10 million people were dislocated, perhaps 75,000 women were abducted, and more than 1 million people were killed.

Nehru also faced military tensions along India's borders with Pakistan and China. To maintain neutrality, Nehru purchased military equipment from both the United States and the Soviet Union. Despite India's nonalignment, the United States was concerned about its military ties to the Soviet Union. In 1958, the United States entered into a defense agreement with India's neighbor—and enemy—Pakistan. This agreement gave the United States a reliably anti-communist ally in the region and pulled South Asia into Cold War politics.

MOTHER TERESA'S WORK IN INDIA

Along with international problems, India faced the domestic challenges of poverty and illiteracy. Mother Teresa, a Catholic nun from Albania, went to India in 1929 to serve as a teacher. She taught for 17 years before she realized that her true calling was working with India's poor and sick. To fulfill her calling, she moved to the slums of Calcutta (now Kolkata), where she founded the Order of the Missionaries of Charity. The photograph above shows Mother Teresa with children at her mission in Calcutta.

Mother Teresa eventually became an Indian citizen and established a hospice for India's terminally ill, centers for blind and disabled people, and a colony for people suffering from leprosy. Mother Teresa's work later extended beyond India. Beginning in the 1960s, she opened houses for the poor in Venezuela, in Tanzania, and in communist countries, including her childhood home, Albania.

Mother Teresa was honored with numerous awards for her humanitarian work, including the Nobel Peace Prize in 1979. In 2016, nearly 20 years after her death, Mother Teresa was canonized, or declared, a saint in the Roman Catholic Church.

HISTORICAL THINKING

1. **READING CHECK** What was the purpose of the Bandung Conference?
2. **SYNTHESIZE** How did the threat of the spread of communism affect American foreign policy in Africa and Asia?
3. **IDENTIFY PROBLEMS AND SOLUTIONS** What problems did Nehru face as he formed an independent government in India?

Cold War and Global Upheavals

3.4

MAIN IDEA An international crisis occurred during the Cold War when the Egyptians seized the Suez Canal and the British, French, and Israelis responded by invading Egypt.

The Suez Crisis

Have you ever had a trusted friend you thought would always have your back? That is what Britain thought about the United States. But when Egypt resisted Britain's attempts to retain control of the Suez Canal, the United States refused to support Britain's military aggression.

EGYPT NATIONALIZES THE SUEZ CANAL

One of the prominent leaders at the Bandung Conference in 1955 was **Gamal Abdel Nasser**, prime minister of Egypt. Nasser believed that Arabs should unite against European neocolonialism and American imperialism. Rejecting religion as a basis for politics, he embraced secular, or nonreligious, Arab nationalism. He banned the Muslim Brotherhood, a political organization that promoted Islam as a guiding philosophy for government. Instead, he elevated the military as a political force.

Nasser had plans for building a giant dam on the Nile River to provide electricity for industrialization. However, Egypt could not fund the dam's construction without aid,

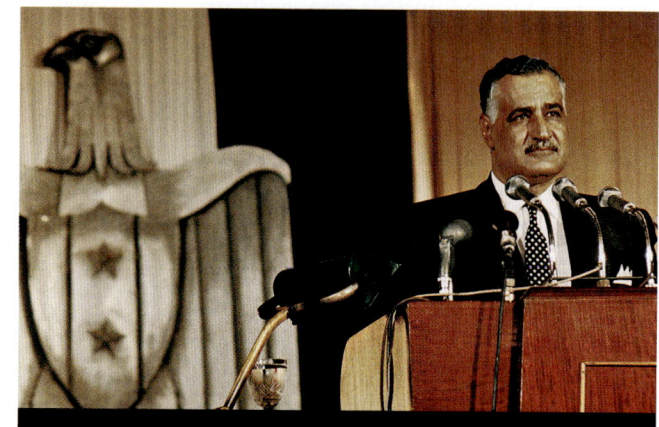

Gamal Abdel Nasser became a hero in the Arab world for confronting Western powers in the Suez Crisis of 1956. Nasser served as prime minister of Egypt from 1954 to 1956 and then as president from 1956 to 1970.

The Suez Canal in Egypt, completed in 1869, provides the shortest sea route between Europe and countries bordering the Indian and Pacific oceans. This photograph shows a container ship passing through the canal in the present day.

so Nasser approached the British and the Americans for financial assistance. They agreed to provide $270 million for the first stage of the project. However, as a precondition, they insisted that Nasser join an anti-Soviet alliance. Nasser was committed to nonalignment after the Bandung Conference and so refused. Instead, he nationalized the Suez Canal, which passed through Egyptian territory. He believed that Egypt could pay for the dam by collecting tolls from ships traveling through the canal. At the time, the Suez Canal Company, a joint British-French enterprise that owned and operated the canal, made a yearly profit of approximately $31 million.

Egypt's nationalization of the canal, legal under international law, was a humiliation for the British, who saw their once great empire in rapid decline. For standing up to them, Nasser became a great hero not only to Egyptians and Arabs but to anti-colonial nationalists around the world.

INTERNATIONAL REACTION

Outraged at Egypt's action, the British secretly met with the French and Israelis on October 24, 1956, to plan an attack. The Israelis and Egyptians had been in conflict since the establishment of the state of Israel in 1948, and Egypt had blocked the Israelis from accessing the Suez Canal. The Israelis were eager to gain support in their conflict with Egypt, and they invaded Egypt's Sinai Peninsula on October 29. Under the pretext of protecting the canal from both the Egyptians and the Israelis, the French and British followed two days later. They bombed Egyptian air bases and occupied the Canal Zone.

The Egyptian military responded by blockading the canal, preventing Britain from gaining access to the Middle Eastern oil on which it depended. Meanwhile, Egyptian civilians took up arms to protect their country from the foreign invaders. The international community was critical of the occupation, and the United States quickly condemned the action.

At the time of the Suez Crisis, the Soviet Union was involved in a violent suppression of an uprising in Hungary. To distract from the Soviets' own brutality, Soviet premier Nikita Khrushchev strongly criticized the British for occupying Egypt. He threatened to use nuclear weapons against the British and French. Faced with the threat of nuclear war, the United Nations sent an emergency peacekeeping force to Egypt on November 21. The French, British, and Israelis then withdrew all their troops.

The Suez Canal remained in the hands of the Egyptians, who formed a military alliance with the Soviet Union. The Soviets then funded the building of the Aswan Dam. True "non-alignment" was difficult to achieve.

In an address to the House of Commons, British prime minister Anthony Eden explained the reasons for the military action taken by the Israelis, French, and British in the Suez Crisis. That same day, U.S. president Dwight D. Eisenhower spoke about the Suez Crisis in a radio and television address to the American people.

PRIMARY SOURCE

It is really not tolerable that the greatest sea highway in the world, one on which our Western life so largely depends, should be subject to the dangers of an explosive situation in the Middle East, which it must be admitted has been largely created by the Egyptian government. . . . [W]e have witnessed, all of us, the growth of a specific Egyptian threat to the peace of the Middle East. Everybody knows that to be true. In the actions we have now taken, we are not concerned to stop Egypt, but to stop war. Nonetheless, it is a fact that there is no Middle Eastern problem at present which could not have been settled or bettered but for the hostile and irresponsible policies of Egypt in recent years.

—Anthony Eden, British prime minister, October 31, 1956

As it is the manifest right of any of these nations to take such decisions and actions, it is likewise our right—if our judgment so dictates—to dissent. We believe these actions to have been taken in error. For we do not accept the use of force as a wise or proper instrument for the settlement of international disputes. To say this—in this particular instance—is in no way to minimize our friendship with these nations—nor our determination to maintain those friendships. . . . In the circumstances I have described, there will be no United States involvement in these present hostilities.

—Dwight D. Eisenhower, president of the United States, October 31, 1956

HISTORICAL THINKING

1. **READING CHECK** Why did Egyptian prime minister Nasser nationalize the Suez Canal?

2. **EXPLAIN** Why was the Suez Canal so important to Britain and France?

3. **DRAW CONCLUSIONS** Was the resolution of the Suez Crisis a victory for the Americans or the Soviets in the Cold War? Explain your response.

Cold War and Global Upheavals 819

4.1

MAIN IDEA The Cold War broke out in combat when the communists of North Korea, backed by the Soviet Union, attacked South Korea, a U.S. ally.

The Korean War

After living through the fear, pain, and horror of World War II, Americans hoped to avoid any more war in their lifetimes. But just five years later, American parents were sending their young sons to fight and die in the Korean War, the first major conflict of the Cold War.

DIVISION OF THE KOREAN PENINSULA

The Koreans are a proud people who, as you have learned, borrowed a great deal from Chinese civilization while retaining their independence. It was a great shock when, in 1910, the country was annexed by Japan. People resented the arrogance of their colonial rulers, who forced Korean schoolchildren to adopt Japanese names and sing the praises of the Japanese emperor. The peninsula suffered under Japanese control into World War II.

The Allies agreed that Korea should one day be free and independent. With that goal in mind, the Soviets attacked the Japanese from the north in the last year of the war, and the Americans attacked from the south. The Japanese surrendered to either the Soviets or the Americans depending on their location.

At the Potsdam Conference in 1945, the Allies agreed that Korea would be temporarily divided at the 38th parallel, or latitude 38 degrees north of the equator. The Soviets would occupy the north, and the Americans would occupy the south in a five-year **trusteeship**, in which they would have administrative control. The Allies hoped to develop a plan for unification of the peninsula over the course of the five years.

In 1947, the new United Nations took over responsibility for Korea. The UN recognized the democratic Republic of Korea, also called South Korea. Anti-communist leader Syngman Rhee became president. At the same time, communist leader **Kim Il-sung** had taken control of North Korea and began to strengthen its military. By 1950, he had built a strong military with armaments supplied by the Soviet Union. He sought to unite the two Koreas by force.

WAR BREAKS OUT

With the backing of the Soviets, North Korean soldiers invaded South Korea on June 25, 1950. South Korea's military was unprepared and poorly trained, so the United Nations came to the country's assistance. The United States provided the largest number of troops, who fought under the leadership of U.S. general Douglas MacArthur. The United States considered the Korean War an application of the Truman Doctrine, providing military aid to prevent the spread of communism.

UN troops recaptured Seoul and South Korea in September 1950. They drove the communists north in an attempt to control the entire peninsula. Kim Il-sung requested military aid from the Chinese, who feared that the United States intended to attack them as well. With

Division of Korea, 1953

CRITICAL VIEWING The Joint Security Area in Korea was the site of peace talks during the Korean War and has since hosted many diplomatic conferences. It is the only part of the Demilitarized Zone (DMZ) where North and South Korean forces directly face each other. This photograph shows North Korean guards standing near the blue buildings. In the background is Freedom House in South Korea. How would you describe the level of fortification in this section of the DMZ?

a commitment from the Soviets to provide air power, the Chinese sent in ground forces to support North Korea. With Soviet and Chinese support, North Korea pushed its enemies back below the 38th parallel.

Some military leaders urged President Truman to strike China with nuclear weapons, believing such force was necessary to win the war. President Truman refused, fearing the use of nuclear weapons would provoke a larger, more deadly war. Acting on his own, General MacArthur threatened to attack Chinese territory. Truman then replaced the general.

In July 1953, after three years and more than three million deaths, the two sides signed a truce that stopped the fighting without formally ending the war. The truce called for both sides to pull back from the battle line. It designated the space between them along the 38th parallel as a **demilitarized zone**, an area where weapons and military forces are forbidden. This neutral area separated the communist regime in North Korea from the authoritarian regime that Rhee had established in South Korea. The stalemate between the two sides has continued into the 21st century.

SOUTHEAST ASIA TREATY ORGANIZATION After the Korean War, the United States and its allies were concerned that communism might spread throughout Southeast Asia. To prevent such communist expansion, representatives from Australia, France, Great Britain, New Zealand, Pakistan, the Philippines, Thailand, and the United States came together in 1954 to form the Southeast Asia Treaty Organization (SEATO). Like NATO, SEATO was intended to provide nations in the region with advice on self-defense, to prevent or thwart subversive activities, and to promote economic and social progress. Before long, the United States would use the provisions of SEATO as justification for its involvement in Vietnam.

HISTORICAL THINKING

1. **READING CHECK** Why did the Americans, Soviets, and Chinese all get involved in the Korean War?

2. **FORM AND SUPPORT OPINIONS** In your opinion, did Truman make the right decision about the use of nuclear weapons in the Korean War? Why or why not?

3. **INTERPRET MAPS** Why do you think the 38th parallel was chosen as the dividing line between North and South Korea?

Cold War and Global Upheavals 821

4.2

MAIN IDEA To gain independence for their country, Vietnamese communists fought off the Japanese, the French, and the Americans.

Two Wars in Vietnam

How did an Asian country 30 times smaller than the United States become the site of the longest and "hottest" war in the Cold War? For many Vietnamese, the war was about independence from 80 years of colonialism. For many Americans, it was about containing the spread of communism.

VIETNAM FIGHTS FRENCH COLONIALISM

For most of their history, the Vietnamese had lived in the shadow of imperial China and often had to fight for their independence from their northern neighbors. Then in the 1800s, the French were a new threat when they colonized Indochina, which included Cambodia, Laos, and Vietnam.

As you have learned, during World War II the Germans conquered France and found collaborators in the French Vichy regime. The Vichy government agreed to let Japan, Germany's ally, send troops to occupy Vietnam and use its airports. **Ho Chi Minh**, a revolutionary Marxist who had sought Vietnam's independence from France before World War II, cooperated with the Allied powers. He led military campaigns against the Japanese during the war. With the defeat of Germany and Japan in 1945, Ho Chi Minh declared an independent Democratic Republic of Vietnam, referring to the American Declaration of Independence as inspiration.

France ignored Ho's declaration and sent forces into Vietnam to re-establish colonial control. But French forces were simultaneously fighting to hold on to Algeria, France's colony in north Africa. Since Algeria was home to a million French citizens, it became the priority. In 1954, the Vietnamese defeated the French, ending 80 years of French colonial rule in Vietnam.

The U.S. military helps South Vietnamese citizens flee the capital city of Saigon during the North Vietnamese invasion in April 1975. American involvement in the Vietnam War came to an end with the fall of Saigon.

822 CHAPTER 28

THE UNITED STATES INTERVENES

A peace agreement in 1954 called for temporarily partitioning Vietnam into northern and southern regions with a plan to reunite the country after elections there. But the United States feared that Ho Chi Minh would win the elections and communism would spread throughout Southeast Asia. To prevent such an occurrence, the United States supported the formation of a separate anti-communist government in South Vietnam.

Conflict between the two Vietnams intensified as the United States supplied the south with weapons and military training, while the communist government in the north sponsored a rebel army in the south. The rebel army was called the National Front for the Liberation of South Vietnam, or the **Vietcong**.

In 1964, U.S. president Lyndon Johnson began to escalate the war against North Vietnam. By the next year, 200,000 American troops had been deployed to Southeast Asia. Despite massive U.S. bombing attacks on North Vietnam, the Vietcong grew in strength and gained support among the Vietnamese people. American soldiers were often unable to distinguish between guerrilla soldiers and civilians. In this first "televised war," gruesome images of death and destruction were transmitted around the world. Protests against the war grew in the United States and in other countries as people witnessed the slaughter of villagers and the spread of napalm and poisonous chemicals across the Vietnamese countryside by U.S. forces. Anti-American sentiment increased in countries throughout the world.

On January 31, 1968, the Vietcong launched attacks on South Vietnam's capital of Saigon and over 100 other cities and airfields during *Tet*, the Lunar New Year festival in Vietnam. Television coverage of the widespread attacks, called the Tet Offensive, showed the American public that the war was not proceeding as successfully as the government had reported. Opposition to U.S. military action intensified, and anti-war protests spread across American college campuses and among young people all across the world. Church groups and American veterans joined the anti-war efforts.

Having replaced Johnson as U.S. president in 1969, Richard Nixon promised to achieve "peace with honor." He intensified the bombing of North Vietnam and began replacing American ground troops with South Vietnamese forces. But after the United States withdrew its last ground troops, communist forces overtook Saigon on April 30, 1975. They renamed it Ho Chi Minh City and reunified the country under communist rule.

Ho Chi Minh led the Vietnamese nationalist movement for almost 30 years. He became president of North Vietnam in 1945. He died in 1969, before Vietnam was united under communist rule.

HISTORICAL THINKING

1. **READING CHECK** Why did the Vietnamese support Ho Chi Minh?

2. **IDENTIFY PROBLEMS AND SOLUTIONS** What were some problems the American government faced in Vietnam and at home during the years of the Vietnam War?

3. **INTERPRET MAPS** How would you describe the physical shape of Vietnam before its partition?

Cold War and Global Upheavals 823

4.3

MAIN IDEA The United States and the Soviet Union became involved in conflicts around the world during the Cold War.

Strife Around the Globe

Although the armed forces of the United States and the Soviet Union never directly battled each other during the Cold War, they were busy nonetheless. Both countries sent their troops or provided military aid to other countries in attempts to control the outcome of conflicts that spanned the globe.

POLAND AND EASTERN EUROPE

Like the United States, the Soviet Union sometimes faced strong opposition to its interference in the affairs of other nations. You've read that the Soviets did not tolerate liberation movements within the Soviet bloc. Opposition to Soviet control sprang up in Poland, Hungary, and Czechoslovakia.

The predominantly Catholic people of Poland detested the policies of the pro-Moscow government imposed on them by Stalin, especially the official **atheism** of the communist state. Atheism is the belief that there is no God. In June 1956, a religious gathering attended by many Poles turned into an anti-government demonstration. Rather than cracking down on the protest, the Soviets compromised and allowed some religious freedom. However, they made it clear that any attempt to weaken Poland's ties to the Soviet Union would not be tolerated.

Later in 1956 in Hungary, students, factory workers, and middle-class professionals rose up to protest the country's Soviet-imposed communist dictatorship. The protest became known as the Hungarian Uprising. The Hungarian government collapsed. Leaders of the new provisional government feared a Soviet invasion, but they expected support from the Western democracies. While the Americans encouraged the rebellion, they did not intervene because they considered the danger of nuclear confrontation with the Soviets too great. Soviet tanks rolled in and crushed the Hungarian revolt with mass arrests and executions.

More than a decade after the Polish and Hungarian uprisings, workers and students in Czechoslovakia organized strikes and protests against Soviet-imposed communism. They forced hardline communist leaders to resign. In early 1968, political leader Alexander Dubček became the new head of the Czechoslovak Communist Party. He promised "socialism with a human face" and granted greater freedom of speech and more market-oriented economic policies. The people of Czechoslovakia enthusiastically supported Dubček's reforms, known as the **Prague Spring**. But the Soviets, fearing the reform movement would spread, sent troops into Czechoslovakia. They believed they could remove Dubček from power and quell any resistance within a few days. But a nonviolent resistance movement rose up. For eight months, people defied curfews, moved street signs to confuse invading troops, and even set themselves on fire in protest. In the end, however, the Soviets succeeded in removing Dubček and returning hardline communists to power.

GLOBAL HOT SPOTS

From the 1950s through the 1970s, the Cold War played out in hot spots around the world. These hot spots included Iran, Haiti, Angola, Afghanistan, and Cambodia.

In the early 1950s, Iran had a parliament led by democratically elected prime minister Mohammad Mosaddegh (MOH-sah-dehk). Tensions rose in Iran when **Mohammad Reza Shah Pahlavi** (rih-ZAH shah PAH-luh-vee), the shah, or king, of Iran and an ardent anti-communist, fostered a close alliance with the administration of U.S. president Dwight Eisenhower.

Hoping that Iran could earn more money from its rich oil fields, Prime Minister Mosaddegh tried to renegotiate Iran's contracts with multinational petroleum companies. When negotiations failed, he threatened to nationalize the entire oil industry. Fearing that the Soviet Union would gain control of Iran's oil, the United States supported the Iranian military in arresting the popular prime minister and expanding Shah Pahlavi's power. Many Iranians considered the shah to be an American puppet.

In Haiti, **Francois Duvalier**, also known as "Papa Doc," was elected president in 1957. He became an authoritarian dictator. He amassed power by removing Haiti's Supreme Court, reducing the size of the military, and forming a secret army that terrorized the population. Duvalier gained U.S. aid with the claim that Haiti was likely to fall to communism unless the United States backed his presidency.

After gaining independence from Portugal in 1975, Angola became another Cold War battleground. Civil war broke out among three groups: the National Front for the Liberation of Angola (FNLA), the National Union for the Total Independence of Angola (UNITA), and the Popular Movement for the Liberation of Angola (MPLA). The United States backed both the FNLA and UNITA, the Soviet Union and Cuba supported the MPLA, and China assisted the FNLA. The Angolan civil war heightened tensions between the United States and the Soviet Union just as they were trying to improve relations through arms control and trade agreements in the late 1960s and the 1970s. The discovery of massive oil reserves made Angola even more valuable as a Cold War prize.

Perhaps the most aggressive Soviet intervention came in 1978 when the Soviet Union supported Afghan communists in seizing power. The Soviet occupation of Afghanistan faced tough resistance from Islamic guerrilla fighters known as the **mujahideen** (moo-ja-hih-DEEN). The United States and neighboring Pakistan responded by aiding the mujahideen, whose familiarity with the land and the people proved to be an advantage. As death tolls increased, the Soviets grew weary of the war, but their occupation lasted almost 10 years. The Soviets finally withdrew from Afghanistan in 1988.

In 1956, Hungarians revolted against the Soviet-imposed communist dictatorship that ruled the country. The Soviets sent tanks and troops and brutally crushed the rebellion. This photograph shows Hungarian patriots on top of a Soviet tank in Budapest during the uprising.

In Cambodia in 1975, radical communist forces called the **Khmer Rouge** replaced the existing government, which had been supported by France and the United States. The Khmer Rouge began a campaign of genocide. Hoping to create a classless society, they murdered former government officials, intellectuals, and monks. Then they emptied out cities and marched people to the countryside, where they forced them to work in what were called "the killing fields" in a film about the Khmer Rouge regime. Between 1975 and 1979, more than two million Cambodians died from mistreatment, starvation, disease, or execution. The United States refrained from getting involved, having just experienced a disastrous defeat in Vietnam. The brutal regime came to an end after the Vietnamese, backed by the Soviet Union, invaded Cambodia in 1979.

HISTORICAL THINKING

1. **READING CHECK** Why did the United States and the Soviet Union engage in conflicts around the world during the Cold War?

2. **SYNTHESIZE** Why would people in Eastern Europe have expected the United States to help them if they resisted their communist governments?

3. **EXPLAIN** Why might less powerful countries have mistrusted both the United States and the Soviet Union during the Cold War?

Cold War and Global Upheavals

4.4 State of the World

1968 C.E.

A TURBULENT YEAR

Some historians have said there has never been a year like 1968. Countries throughout the world witnessed political, social, and cultural upheaval. In Czechoslovakia, the communist country's new leader, Alexander Dubček, proposed plans to grant the people greater civil liberties and offered "socialism with a human face." By June, during a period that came to be known as the Prague Spring, Czechs were calling for further strides toward democratization. But all hope for a more democratic state was crushed by the Soviet Union in August. Soviet forces invaded the country, removed Dubček from office, and limited the reforms.

Students often spearheaded the call for change in 1968. In May, French university students staged protests, demanding educational reform. Officials responded by closing several universities. About 40,000 students then took to the streets of Paris, resulting in a bloody confrontation with police. The student movement gained more followers and soon spread all over France. Factory workers went on strike in support of the students and demanded their own economic reforms. Eventually the movement lost momentum, but it did liberalize France's conservative society.

Protests across Japan were also sparked by students. In January, they demonstrated their opposition to nuclear weapons and the Vietnam War when the nuclear-powered U.S.S. *Enterprise* was due to visit a U.S. naval base in Japan before going on to Vietnam. Armed students clashed with police outside the base. In the wake of the Paris riots in May, Japanese students also called for reform in university administration and the right to engage in negotiations for change.

Martin Luther King, Memphis, U.S.

Summer Olympic Games, Mexico City, Mexico

FIVE LARGEST CITIES

1 Tokyo	2 New York	3 Osaka	4 Mexico City	5 Buenos Aires
23.3	16.2	15.3	8.8	8.4

*Population in millions (approximately)

WORLD POPULATION

7 billion

1968
3.55 billion

2010

826 CHAPTER 28

Prague Spring Prague, Czechoslovakia

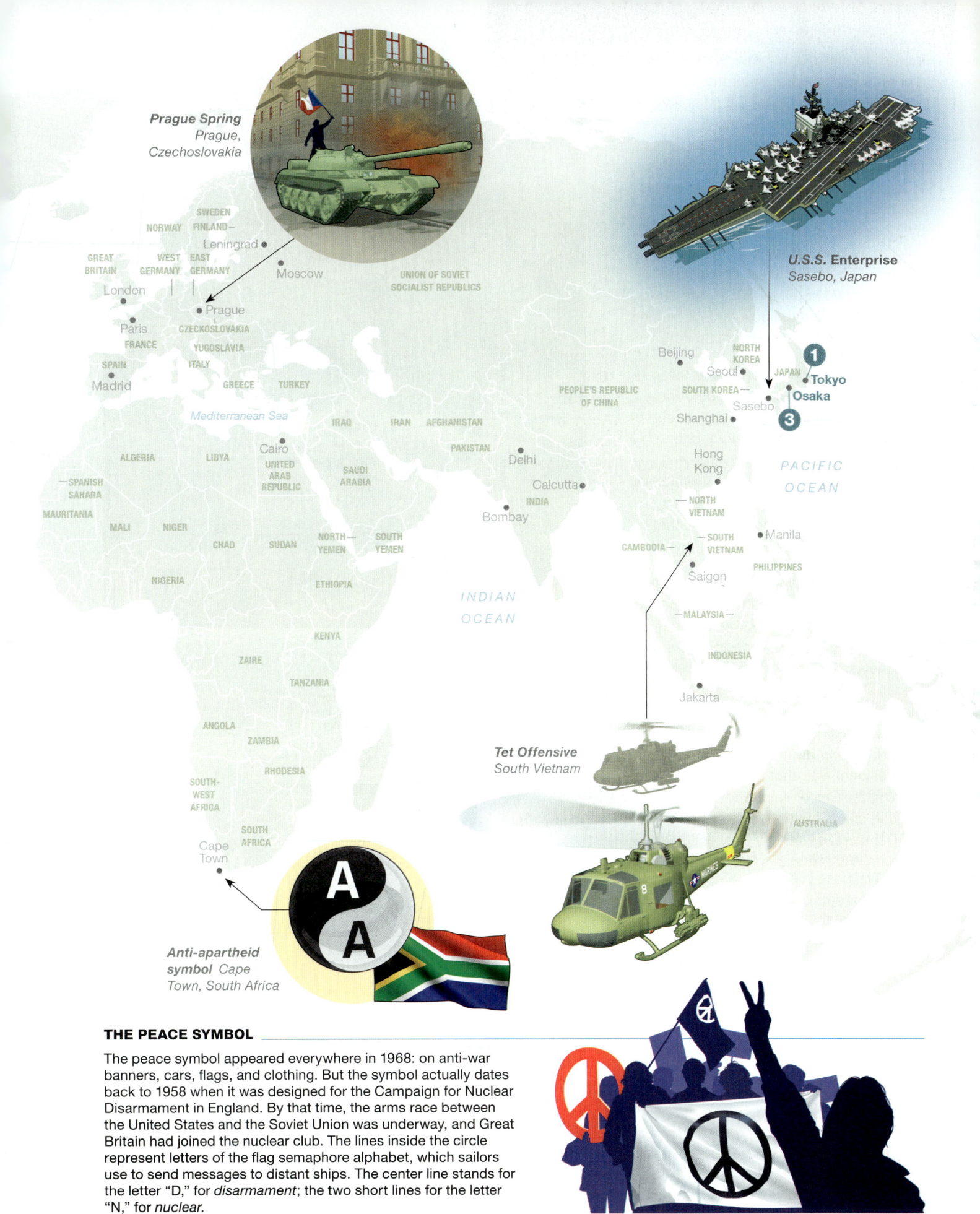

U.S.S. Enterprise Sasebo, Japan

Tet Offensive South Vietnam

Anti-apartheid symbol Cape Town, South Africa

THE PEACE SYMBOL

The peace symbol appeared everywhere in 1968: on anti-war banners, cars, flags, and clothing. But the symbol actually dates back to 1958 when it was designed for the Campaign for Nuclear Disarmament in England. By that time, the arms race between the United States and the Soviet Union was underway, and Great Britain had joined the nuclear club. The lines inside the circle represent letters of the flag semaphore alphabet, which sailors use to send messages to distant ships. The center line stands for the letter "D," for *disarmament*; the two short lines for the letter "N," for *nuclear*.

Cold War and Global Upheavals 827

In Mexico City, a fight between high school students led to unrest. After the government called out the army to stop the fighting, the soldiers killed some of the students. Over the next few months, university students in the city organized protests and rallies to demonstrate against the government's use of violence. At a meeting attended by thousands of the students in October, soldiers arrived to arrest the movement's leaders. Gunfire broke out and lasted for almost two hours. An estimated 300 civilians died, and the government blamed the deaths on the students' actions.

Students challenged apartheid at the University of Cape Town in South Africa. The university had offered employment to a black lecturer but was forced to withdraw the offer by the government. Students staged a sit-in at the university's administration building but, bowing to pressure from the government and the university, ended it after 10 days.

Perhaps no country was roiled more by the turmoil of 1968 than the United States. Throughout the year, anti-war protests took place on many college campuses. And the assassination in April of civil rights leader Martin Luther King, Jr., triggered racial violence across the country. Another assassination took place in June when Robert F. Kennedy, a Democratic candidate for president was shot and killed after winning the California primary. Then in August, chaos erupted in Chicago during the Democratic National Convention as Vietnam War protesters battled police in the streets.

At the end of the year, the U.S. crew of Apollo 8, the first manned spacecraft to orbit the moon, sent a note of hope from space. On Christmas Eve, they read a message wishing everyone on Earth "good night, good luck." Still, the aftershocks of 1968 continue to be felt worldwide more than 50 years later.

HISTORICAL THINKING

INTERPRET VISUALS Based on the images and the map, what words best describe the world in 1968?

Smoke billows from the remains of the U.S. Army 8th Division headquarters in Saigon after an attack by the Vietcong on January 31.

Martin Luther King, Jr., lies at the feet of his associates on the balcony of the Lorraine Motel in Memphis, Tennessee, on April 4.

Students and workers march through the streets of Paris on May 13 to demand educational and economic reform.

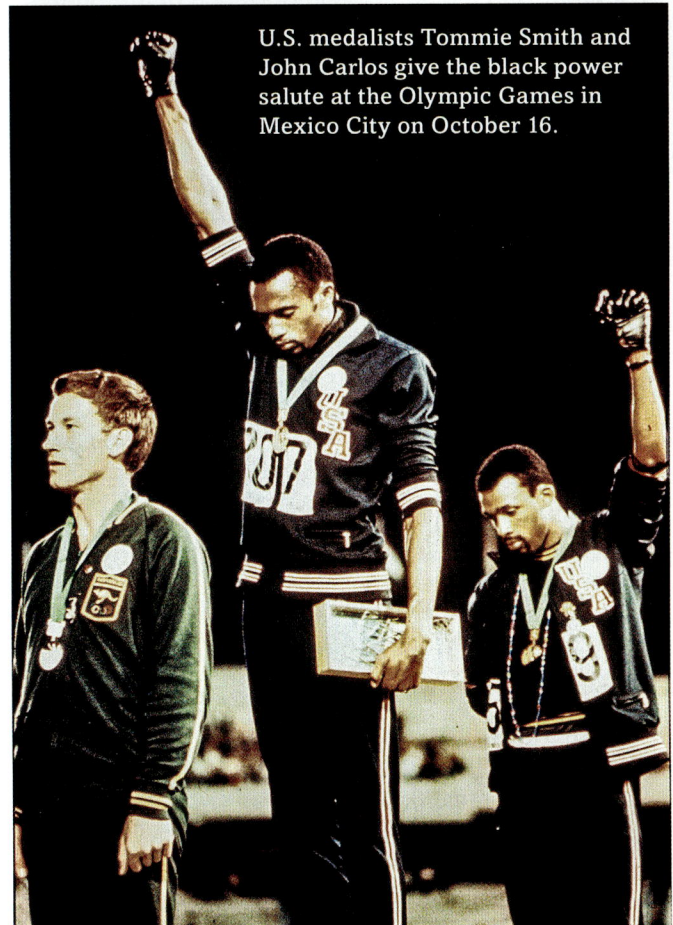

U.S. medalists Tommie Smith and John Carlos give the black power salute at the Olympic Games in Mexico City on October 16.

U.S. astronaut Bill Anders took this photo of Earth rising above the moon's surface on December 24.

Cold War and Global Upheavals **829**

CHAPTER 28 REVIEW
COLD WAR AND GLOBAL UPHEAVALS

VOCABULARY

Match each vocabulary word below with its definition.

VOCABULARY WORDS

1. proxy war
2. populism
3. apartheid
4. indoctrinate
5. domino effect
6. neocolonialism
7. nonalignment
8. satellite state
9. nationalize

DEFINITIONS

a. a policy of not allying with other countries

b. an independent country under the control of a stronger country

c. the theory that the fall of one country to communism will result in neighboring countries falling to communism

d. a former system of racial segregation and discrimination against nonwhites in South Africa

e. to transfer from private to government ownership

f. a war in which one or both sides are serving the interests of another country

g. the domination of less-developed countries by former colonial powers

h. to train a person to accept a certain doctrine

i. political philosophy that emphasizes support for the concerns of ordinary people

READING STRATEGY
DETERMINE CHRONOLOGY

Use a time line like the one below to organize the major events of the Cold War. Include dates and notes on the events and add boxes if necessary. Then answer the question.

Major Events of the Cold War

1945 — Yalta Conference—Allies win Stalin's support for UN and begin planning for post-war Europe

10. What was the most significant event of the Cold War? Explain your choice.

MAIN IDEAS

Answer the following questions. Support your answers with evidence from the chapter.

11. What was the purpose of the Marshall Plan? **LESSON 1.1**

12. How did the arms race affect direct hostility between the Soviet Union and the United States? **LESSON 1.3**

13. Why did Fidel Castro seek a closer relationship with the Soviet Union? **LESSON 2.1**

14. What were the outcomes of the Great Leap Forward and the Cultural Revolution? **LESSON 2.4**

15. How did France foster neocolonial control of its former African colonies? **LESSON 3.1**

16. What was the main result of the Bandung Conference in 1955? **LESSON 3.3**

17. What was the strategic importance of the Suez Canal? **LESSON 3.4**

18. What was the cause of the Korean War? **LESSON 4.1**

19. What led the United States to support the formation of South Vietnam? **LESSON 4.2**

HISTORICAL THINKING

Answer the following questions. Support your answers with evidence from the chapter.

20. **ANALYZE CAUSE AND EFFECT** How did power shifts resulting from World War II lead to Soviet control over Eastern Europe and economic recoveries in Germany and Japan?

21. **DESCRIBE** Explain the purpose of the UN, NATO, the Warsaw Pact, SEATO, and OAS.

22. **DRAW CONCLUSIONS** Choose one of these nationalist leaders mentioned in the chapter. What was the leader's impact on the country?

23. **COMPARE** How and why was the U.S. response to policies in South Africa similar to its response to the Democratic Republic of the Congo?

INTERPRET VISUALS

This political cartoon by Edmund Valtman entitled "This hurts me more than it hurts you!" was published in 1962 following the Cuban Missile Crisis. Study the cartoon and answer the questions that follow.

24. The man with the pliers represents Soviet premier Nikita Khrushchev. Who does the man with the open mouth represent?

25. What is Khrushchev pulling out of the man's open mouth?

26. What message does the cartoon convey about the results of the Cuban Missile Crisis?

ANALYZE SOURCES

In April 1961, President Kennedy of the United States and Premier Khrushchev of the Soviet Union exchanged letters regarding the political situation in Cuba. Read the following excerpts from their letters and answer the question that follows.

> You are under serious misapprehension in regard to events in Cuba. For months there has been evident and growing resistance to the Cuban dictatorship. More than 100,000 refugees have recently fled from Cuba into neighboring countries. . . . These are unmistakable signs that Cubans find intolerable the denial of democratic liberties. . . .
>
> —John F. Kennedy, U.S. president, letter to Nikita Khrushchev, 1961
>
> In the present case, apparently, the United States Government is seeking to restore to Cuba that "freedom" under which Cuba would dance to the tune of her more powerful neighbor and foreign monopolies would again be able to plunder the country's national wealth, to wax rich on the sweat and blood of the Cuban people.
>
> —Nikita Khrushchev, Soviet premier, reply to John Kennedy's letter, 1961

27. How did the two world leaders differ in their view of the political situation in Cuba?

CONNECT TO YOUR LIFE

28. **ARGUMENT** During the Vietnam War, American men between the ages of 18 and 25 were drafted to fill vacancies in the armed forces. Opposition to both the draft and the war fueled protests on college campuses. Put yourself in the place of a young college student eligible for the draft. How would you feel about being drafted to fight in a war? Would you agree to serve your nation or protest against the war? Write an essay stating your position and explaining your reasons.

TIPS

- Review the discussion of the Vietnam War in the chapter. If necessary, conduct research to learn more about the military draft. Based on what you learn, form an opinion.

- Write an introductory paragraph that provides the context for your essay and includes a topic sentence that clearly states your position on the war and the draft.

- In the body of your essay, explain the reasons for your position. If appropriate, use two or three vocabulary words from the chapter in your argument.

- Conclude your essay by summarizing your position.

CHAPTER 29

Conflicts and Transformations
1947–2000

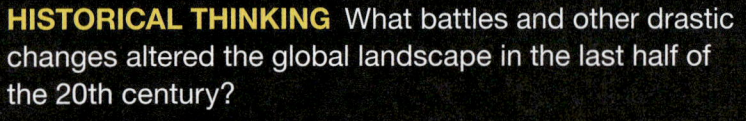

HISTORICAL THINKING What battles and other drastic changes altered the global landscape in the last half of the 20th century?

SECTION 1 **Soviet Collapse**

SECTION 2 **Global Democratic Possibilities**

SECTION 3 **The Middle East**

SECTION 4 **Promises and Challenges of Globalization**

CRITICAL VIEWING

In East Germany, people gather at the Berlin Wall near the Brandenburg Gate after it was opened in November 1989. The sign translates to "Caution! You are now leaving West Berlin" in English. Why was the collapse of this structure such an important moment?

Conflicts and Transformations 833

1.1

MAIN IDEA Liberal reform policies in the Soviet Union triggered nationalist movements and calls for more freedom and self-government in the Soviet bloc.

Glasnost to the Fall of the Berlin Wall

Imagine a crack in a dam splitting open as the pent-up water rushes through. During the 1980s, cracks began to appear in the political structure of the Soviet Union. Borders opened, a wall fell, and many people who had suffered under Soviet rule for decades rushed toward freedom.

GORBACHEV'S REFORMS

By 1980, after the communist victory in Vietnam, the Soviet Union was seen as advancing on the world stage, while the United States was in retreat. An earlier policy of eased tensions between the two countries, known as **détente**, had also come to an end with the Soviet invasion of Afghanistan in 1979.

The new U.S. president, **Ronald Reagan**, set out to restore America's global power and influence. During his first term in office (1981–1985), he sharply increased defense spending to strengthen the U.S. military and modernize its nuclear arsenal. Calling the Soviet Union an "evil empire," he vowed to destroy communism. **Margaret Thatcher**, Britain's prime minister from 1979 to 1990, fully supported Reagan's anti-communist stance and arms buildup.

In 1985, a new leader emerged in the Soviet Union. **Mikhail Gorbachev** (mih-KYL GOR-buh-chof), unlike previous Soviet leaders, was a reformer. He believed the Soviet system needed major changes to better serve the Soviet people and to achieve the economic success of the United States and the rest of the Western world. Gorbachev introduced two major reforms: **glasnost**, or "openness," and **perestroika** (pehr-uh-STROY-kuh), or economic restructuring.

A Soviet woman waiting in line displays a ration coupon for sugar in a state-owned store in St. Petersburg.

Through his policy of glasnost, Gorbachev encouraged an unrestricted discussion of political and social issues and greater freedom of the press. Honesty, he promised, would replace the lies and cover-ups that marked earlier Soviet administrations. For the first time since the earliest days of the Russian Revolution, the Soviet people were free to speak their minds and publish their opinions without repercussions.

Gorbachev's new openness was soon put to the test. In April 1986, Soviet officials tried to cover up a disastrous explosion at the Chernobyl nuclear power plant in Ukraine. It was the worst nuclear accident in history up to that time, and it contaminated a wide area around the plant. Three weeks after the explosion, Gorbachev gave a speech explaining how the accident had happened and what Soviet officials were doing to protect people. He also took the opportunity to call for a ban on nuclear weapons testing.

Through his policy of perestroika, Gorbachev sought to reform the Soviet economy. The state would still dominate, but industry would respond to market signals rather than economic commands issued by government planners. However, perestroika did not have the hoped-for effect on the economy. Soviet citizens still faced their dreary daily routine of standing in long lines for basic staples like milk, bread, and eggs. The only difference was that citizens were free to voice their displeasure about the lack of food and other goods.

Gorbachev recognized that massive military spending was a drain on the struggling Soviet economy. The arms race with the United States and the ongoing war in Afghanistan were both major drains on the Soviet treasury. Meeting with Reagan in 1988, Gorbachev agreed to an arms-control treaty eliminating many land-based missiles. In 1989, he withdrew Soviet troops from Afghanistan.

MARGARET THATCHER Margaret Thatcher (shown here with U.S. president Ronald Reagan at the White House in 1983) served as Britain's first woman prime minister from 1979 to 1990. She advocated for the independence of the individual from the state and less government interference in the economy. Her conservative approach focused on privatization and deregulation. During her first term, unemployment increased dramatically and inflation doubled in just over one year, drastically reducing her popularity. This unpopularity would have guaranteed her defeat in the 1983 election but for two factors: the Falkland Islands War and division within the opposing Labour Party. Her leadership during the Falkland Islands War in 1982 led to Britain reclaiming the islands, which rallied much of the British population around her. Thatcher also made gains in international relationships, condemning communism and supporting NATO. However, against much opposition, she also reduced Britain's contribution to the European Community's (EC's) budget. This action instigated discord in her traditionally pro-Europe party. Her implementation of a poll tax in 1989 met with public disapproval and alarmed her already divided Conservative Party. Without majority support from her party, Thatcher announced her resignation in November 1990.

The effectiveness of glasnost was not all positive for the Soviet Union. The policy allowed discontented ethnic groups to publicly vent their negative feelings about Russian domination of the U.S.S.R. In the late 1980s, those objections expanded into outbursts of nationalism in several non-Russian Soviet republics. For example, demonstrators in Georgia demanded greater self-government. Each Baltic state—Latvia, Lithuania, and Estonia—replaced Russian with its home language as the official "state language."

Rising Russian nationalism also undermined Soviet unity. After glasnost increased free speech, old prejudices reappeared, including anti-Semitism and negative stereotypes of ethnic groups from the largely Muslim regions to the south.

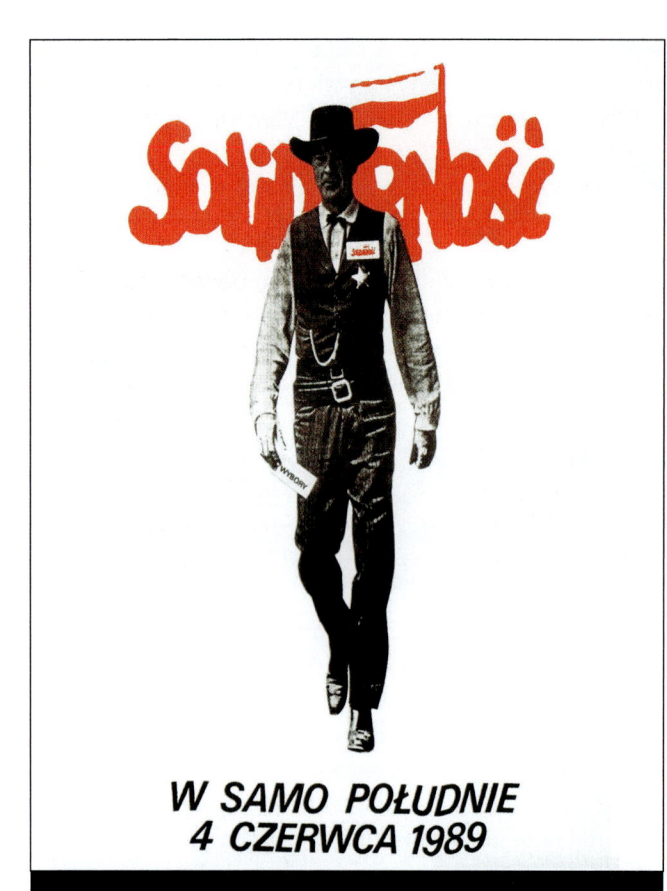

CRITICAL VIEWING A Solidarity movement poster shows actor Gary Cooper in his role as a U.S. marshal in the western film *High Noon*. The artist added a Solidarity badge on Cooper's chest and ballot in his hand. The text translates to "High Noon, June 4, 1989" in English. Why do you think members of Solidarity chose this image and slogan for their 1989 campaign?

REVOLUTIONS IN EASTERN EUROPE

In Poland, discontent with the communist regime led to radical political change. In 1980, Polish workers led by **Lech Wałęsa** (LEHK vuh-WEHN-suh) formed **Solidarity**, the first independent trade union in the Soviet bloc. In a direct challenge to the authority of the Communist Party, nearly one-third of Poland's population joined Solidarity. Pope **John Paul II**, a native of Poland, supported Wałęsa, helped keep Solidarity a nonviolent movement, and discussed relevant issues with Soviet and Polish Communist officials. Meanwhile, in 1988, the Polish people demanded greater self-government. Faced with increasing unrest and nationwide strikes, the government agreed to hold free elections in August 1989. Solidarity won a huge victory and took control of the government, and a year later, Wałęsa became Poland's first directly elected president.

Challenges to Soviet domination also occurred elsewhere in Eastern Europe. In January 1989, Hungary's parliament voted to allow noncommunist political parties. Soviet control was further weakened when, in September, Hungary opened its border with the democratic republic of Austria. East Germans by the tens of thousands fled into Hungary, crossed the open border into Austria, and moved from there into West Germany—and to freedom.

The imaginary Iron Curtain surrounding the Soviet empire had begun showing its cracks. But in Berlin, Germany, a very real wall was about to crumble.

THE WALL: A SYMBOL OF OPPRESSION

Berlin, a city divided between West and East, was located completely inside communist East Germany. Residents of East Berlin could cross fairly easily into West Berlin—and they did, by the thousands each month. After World War II, many East Berliners left their communist-controlled city for the freedom in West Berlin and beyond. Worried about the large numbers of skilled and educated workers moving west for higher pay, East German and Soviet leaders vowed to block the flow of escaping citizens. In 1961, with Soviet backing, East Germany built a tall wall of brick and concrete that separated East Berlin from West Berlin and also sealed off the rest of West Berlin with walls and fences. Workers placed minefields and guard towers along the border. For the next 28 years, few East Germans managed to escape to the West.

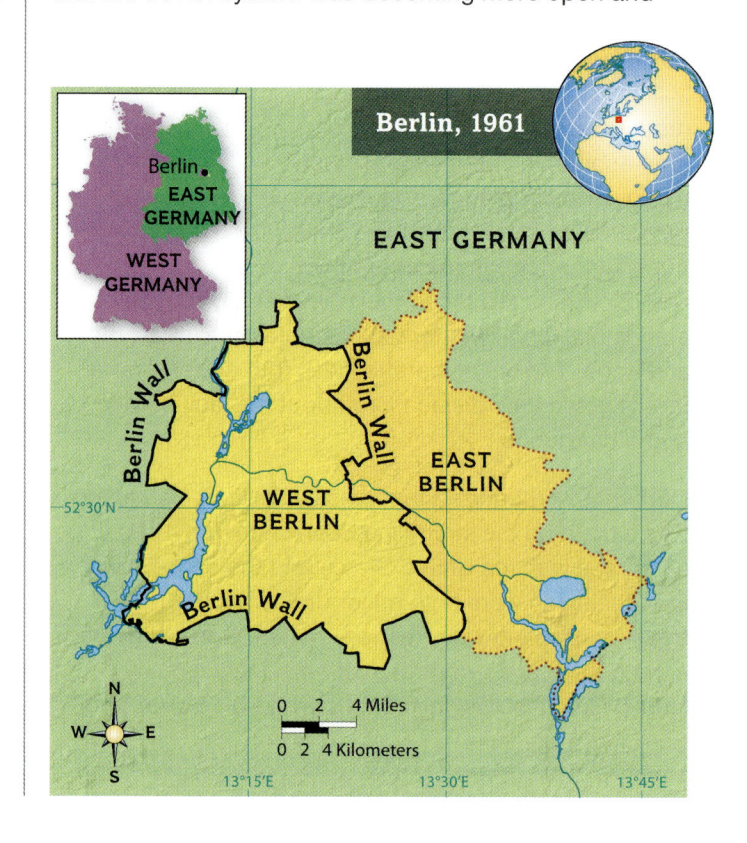

In 1987, President Reagan visited West Berlin. Standing before the Berlin Wall, he spoke in general terms about Gorbachev's liberal policies, expressing hope that the Soviet system was becoming more open and free. However, Reagan suggested that the wall was a barrier to tolerance and independence. Partway through his speech, he challenged the Soviet leader. "Mr. Gorbachev," he called out, "tear down this wall!"

After Hungary opened its border to Austria in September 1989, East German demonstrators pressured their government to allow freer transit to the West. On November 9, as huge crowds gathered at the wall, a single gate unexpectedly opened, and a flood of East Berliners streamed through into West Berlin. Soon, jubilant residents of East Berlin and West Berlin began demolishing the wall. The fall of the Berlin Wall, the most visible symbol of communist oppression, signaled the coming collapse of the entire Soviet empire.

MORE POLITICAL UPRISINGS

In the days and weeks that followed, the Soviet bloc continued to splinter. On November 10, a communist reform politician ousted Bulgaria's authoritarian party leader. On December 3, the East German government resigned. Three weeks later, **Nicolae Ceauşescu** (NIHK-oh-ly chow-SHEHS-koo), Romania's hated leader, ordered troops to fire on antigovernment demonstrators. Instead, the troops joined the protesters, overthrew Ceauşescu, and executed him.

The revolution in Czechoslovakia happened less violently. Anti-communist reformers had long pushed for a new constitution. Nationwide demonstrations starting in mid-November 1989 brought a police crackdown, but this time—unlike during the Prague Spring of 1968—no Soviet forces arrived to support them. The reformers in Czechoslovakia, like those in much of Eastern Europe, triumphed. The Czech people elected a noncommunist government on December 10, and on December 25, **Václav Havel** (VAHT-slav HAH-vehl) became the first democratically elected president of the country. Communism's fall went so smoothly in Czechoslovakia that it has been called the "Velvet Revolution."

During the revolution in Romania, some protesters cut out the communist symbol in the center of the Romanian national flag.

HISTORICAL THINKING

1. **READING CHECK** How did Gorbachev's policies change Soviet economic, social, and cultural life?

2. **IDENTIFY MAIN IDEAS AND DETAILS** What factors helped Margaret Thatcher keep her position as British prime minister in 1983?

3. **ANALYZE CAUSE AND EFFECT** Why did so many citizens of East Germany want to flee to the West?

4. **MAKE CONNECTIONS** How did Poland's Solidarity movement connect with the series of political revolutions that took place in the Soviet bloc?

Conflicts and Transformations 837

1.2 Through The Lens

GERD LUDWIG

National Geographic photographer Gerd Ludwig has covered a variety of subjects related to the post–Cold War era, including the reunification of Germany in 1990 and the changes that occurred in the former Soviet Union after its dissolution in 1991. He is best known for his photos of the aftermath of the Chernobyl nuclear disaster, which he turned into an award-winning book, The Long Shadow of Chernobyl, in 2014.

In 2015, Ludwig shot a series of photos of Berlin to accompany a National Geographic magazine story about how the city had transformed itself after the fall of the Berlin Wall over 25 years earlier. Growing up in Germany during the Cold War, Ludwig had a personal connection to the assignment, which he says always helps shape his approach: "As a documentary photographer I have the obligation to show what is out there, but I also show it from a very personal point of view. And that personal point of view is determined by my life experience."

How do the buildings and monuments shown in these images reflect both Germany's past and present?

BERLIN, GERMANY

A Slovakian street artist (above) poses as an East German border guard in front of the Brandenburg Gate. Once a symbol of Cold War oppression, Berlin is now a city of opportunity that attracts people from all over the world. The face of Dieter Weckeiser (top, opposite page), who was killed in 1968 while attempting to swim to freedom across the Spree River to West Berlin, forms part of a memorial where a stretch of the wall has been preserved. Young professionals (opposite page, bottom) go about their daily business outside the St. Oberholz cafe. Located in a 19th-century building that once housed a restaurant for the working class, the cafe provides specialty coffee and trendy coworking spaces. The sign on the wall of the cafe reads: "Das Leben ist kein Ponyhof"—life isn't easy.

Conflicts and Transformations 839

1.3

MAIN IDEA The weakening and eventual collapse of the Soviet Union resulted in the formation of many new countries.

Post-Soviet Transitions

Changing a lifelong habit is rarely easy, even if you know it will improve your life. Trying to get others to change is even more challenging. When Mikhail Gorbachev set out to reshape the Soviet political system, he discovered just how difficult the process of change can be.

TURMOIL IN THE SOVIET UNION

As Soviet power over its empire eroded in the fall of 1989, Mikhail Gorbachev continued moving the U.S.S.R. closer to representative democracy. In February 1990, the Congress of People's Deputies, or Soviet parliament, accepted Gorbachev's plan to eliminate the Communist Party's monopoly on political power and allow the formation of competing political parties. The parliament also elected Gorbachev president of the Soviet Union.

Gorbachev's ongoing reforms provided further challenges to Soviet domination. In March 1990, Lithuania declared its independence. Gorbachev initially threatened military action, but he decided against it. Two months later, the other two Baltic republics—Latvia and Estonia—also declared independence. As Poland, Hungary, and Czechoslovakia continued toward democratic rule, Gorbachev quietly accepted their noncommunist governments.

The future of East Germany, however, had not yet been settled. Gorbachev wanted to keep East Germany within the Soviet bloc, at least for a while, but pressure for the speedy restoration of a united Germany came from the West German government as well as from vocal groups within East Germany. Gorbachev finally conceded. East Germany and West Germany were officially reunified as Germany in October 1990.

By the summer of 1991, Soviet-bloc countries and individual republics were steadily moving beyond the control of the U.S.S.R. In July, Warsaw Pact leaders canceled their mutual-defense treaty, and Gorbachev began to withdraw Soviet troops from Eastern Europe. It was clear that the Soviet communist system was breaking down.

However, a group of communist hard-liners—people who remained stubbornly loyal to Soviet ideology—would not give up. In August, this group launched a coup to try to restore central control and remove Gorbachev from power. In Moscow, the popular president of the Russian Republic, **Boris Yeltsin**, led protests against the coup, which ended when the army refused to attack the Russian parliament building.

840 CHAPTER 29

COMMONWEALTH OF INDEPENDENT STATES

After the coup attempt, Gorbachev left the Communist Party. Then he banned the party completely. In September 1991, he and leaders of 10 of the republics agreed to shift their authority to an emergency State Council.

In December, Russia, Ukraine, and Belarus formed a loose association of equals known as the **Commonwealth of Independent States (CIS)**. Eight additional republics soon joined the CIS. Each member of the commonwealth participated as a sovereign nation. The Soviet Union was dissolved, and Gorbachev resigned his presidency.

Boris Yeltsin (left) stands on top of a tank, rallying the people of Moscow in defense of their new democratic institutions. This image was shown on state television and became a uniting point for further defense of democracy.

STRUGGLES FOR PROSPERITY AND DEMOCRACY

The failure of the coup and Gorbachev's resignation put Russian president Yeltsin in a position to define a new path for his country—by far the strongest state in the CIS. U.S. economists advised him that free markets would bring prosperity. Following their advice, Yeltsin instituted bold economic reforms.

The immediate results were disappointing. The transition to a market economy caused many Russians to suffer. The Soviet system had provided free education and health care, guaranteed jobs, and old-age pensions. The new market system did not instantly make up for these losses. Stores filled with imported consumer products, but few Russians had the means to purchase them. By the end of the 1990s, too many Russians were hungry and cold.

The former Central Asian republics faced equally difficult transitions. Kazakhstan and Uzbekistan were typical, run by former Communist officials who paid lip service to democracy, holding tight to power and exploiting the region's plentiful natural resources.

In 1999, an ailing Yeltsin handed power to **Vladimir Putin**, a former intelligence officer for the KGB, the Soviet spy agency. Putin won the presidency of Russia in 2000 by appealing to voters eager for a strong leader. As president, he reined in capitalism by reestablishing state authority over the economy and the media, and he used his control of oil revenues and television as bases of power. He stood up to the United States on the global stage and restored order at home. Putin managed to achieve stability at the expense of democracy and civil rights.

In general, the countries of Eastern Europe enjoyed a smoother transition to liberal governance and market economics than Russia did. Poland and Estonia made steady political and economic progress in the 1990s, with the formation of the free associations that characterize a democratic society. Czechoslovakia split peacefully into the Czech Republic and Slovakia in 1993. Yugoslavia, as you will learn, was a different story, with ethnic differences tearing the nation apart.

The reunification of Germany proved difficult as well. East Germans were much poorer than West Germans, and many East Germans lacked competitive job skills. They gained freedom and opportunity but also faced unemployment and insecurity. Still, a unified Germany became a global leader in science, technology, and manufacturing.

HISTORICAL THINKING

1. **READING CHECK** Why was the reunification of Germany such a challenge?

2. **DRAW CONCLUSIONS** Do you think Gorbachev planned to dissolve the Soviet Union? Explain.

3. **COMPARE AND CONTRAST** How did the Commonwealth of Independent States differ from the Soviet Union?

1.4

MAIN IDEA Pro-democracy demonstrations in Beijing, China, in which students demanded political freedoms to match growing economic freedoms, ended in a massacre.

Unrest in Beijing

Like the Soviet Union, China struggled to make its communist economic and political systems work. When Chinese students and workers gathered peacefully in a public square to protest against their government, leaders ordered the Red Army to attack.

CHINA'S ECONOMIC REBOUND

In 1800, China produced one-third of the world's manufactured goods. But the Industrial Revolution bypassed China, and Europe dominated the world's economy. By 1949, the country produced just three percent of the world's total industrial output, and the following years under communist rule saw little improvement. Recall that in 1958, Mao Zedong aimed to fix the economy with his Great Leap Forward. As you learned, it proved to be a disaster.

By the last two decades of the 20th century, however, China was experiencing astonishing economic growth. More people were lifted out of poverty than at any previous stage in human history. That turnabout resulted from the policies of **Deng Xiaoping**, who rose to power in the late 1970s, after Mao's death. (You first read about Deng in the previous chapter.)

Deng put China on a new economic path by adopting market incentives. His first step was to grant peasants their own farm plots for private cultivation, and Deng allowed them to sell their surplus crops in free markets. Food production surged. Deng became a hero to millions of Chinese farming families, who could now afford small luxuries for the first time. When asked how he, a lifelong communist, justified adopting capitalist principles, Deng replied, "It does not matter whether the cat is black or white, as long as she catches mice." He added, "To get rich is glorious."

The second stage in Deng's reforms was development of China's industrial sector. Deng invited foreign investors to build manufacturing plants in Guangzhou (gwahng-joh), a region of southern China near the British-controlled territory of Hong Kong. Deng's embrace of international capitalism would have been unthinkable under Mao. Cheap Chinese labor drew many corporations to Guangzhou.

As manufacturing spread from Guangzhou throughout eastern and central China, a vast stream of finished goods crossed the Pacific to reach American markets. China's cities experienced a huge construction boom, attracting millions of rural migrants. The coastal city of Shanghai became a glittering cosmopolitan center, with soaring skyscrapers and a rapid-transit system.

By the 1990s, China's economic transformation was generating challenges for the government. Environmental problems multiplied. The gap between rich and poor increased, as did imbalances between wealthier coastal regions and China's interior. Money brought corruption, which triggered protests among the same rural population that Mao had made the center of his revolution. Still, Deng's economic policies raised the standard of living, linked the nation to the global economy, and allowed China to achieve the status of a great world power. Many Chinese believed their country had returned to its proper place after two centuries of humiliation by Western imperialists and Japan.

PROTESTS IN TIANANMEN SQUARE

A big test of Deng's leadership came in the spring of 1989. University students organized an anti-government rally in Tiananmen Square, a large public plaza in the center of Beijing. They called for liberal political reforms—including freedom of speech and assembly—to match the economic reforms established in the preceding decade. They also criticized corruption among officials and the widening income gap.

The first student protests at Tiananmen Square took place on April 17. Word spread quickly. On April 22, tens

This photograph was taken with a long-range lens from a Beijing hotel room. The lone figure trying to stop a line of surging tanks (which eventually went around him) along the Avenue of Eternal Peace in Beijing sums up both the heroism and the futility of the Tiananmen protests. This individual has never been identified.

of thousands of students gathered in Beijing as well as in other cities all over China. The government began to notice. On April 26, a front-page editorial in the *People's Daily*, the Beijing newspaper controlled by the Chinese Communist Party, accused student activists of causing turmoil and undermining political stability.

Peaceful protests of varying sizes continued for the next few weeks. In mid-May, some participants began a weeklong hunger strike. Around the same time, student leaders presented their demands at a meeting with officials and later with China's premier, Li Peng. But the talks failed to end the demonstrations. Thousands of protesters remained in Tiananmen Square through the end of May, their spirits raised after art students built the 33-foot-high statue that became known as the Goddess of Democracy out of foam, papier mâché, and plaster. While the statue began as the figure of a man holding a pole, during construction it was transformed into a woman holding a torch.

During this time, government and party officials debated how they should respond. Some advocated negotiating with the students, but hard-liners argued in favor of crushing the demonstrations. They were aware of how Gorbachev's glasnost policy was undermining Soviet power, and they did not intend to make the same mistake. Ultimately, the decision was up to Deng, who remembered the chaos caused by student rebels during the Cultural Revolution, which you read about earlier. On the night of June 3–4, 1989, tanks and armored personnel carriers rolled into Tiananmen Square, and troops opened fire on the demonstrators. Hundreds, perhaps thousands, of student activists were killed in the **Tiananmen Square Massacre**. Thousands more were wounded. A widespread crackdown on dissidents led to thousands of arrests.

A year and a half after the bloodshed at Tiananmen Square, Chai Ling, one of the main leaders of the pro-democracy movement, recalled why students protested. "The key issue for the demonstrators," she told a reporter for the *New York Times*, "was that people were used to being treated like slaves, and the people naturally wanted to become human beings, have equality, dignity, and freedom."

HISTORICAL THINKING

1. **READING CHECK** What policy put in place by Deng Xiaoping led to a surge in food production?
2. **IDENTIFY MAIN IDEAS AND DETAILS** What allowed for the growing presence of corporations in China?
3. **MAKE CONNECTIONS** Were the Tiananmen Square demonstrators influenced by the political ideals of the United States? Explain.

2.1

MAIN IDEA Though they faced economic challenges and some dictatorships, many Latin Americans experienced increased prosperity and freedom by the end of the 20th century.

Toward Democracy in Latin America

After a rough period, a fresh start can be quite welcome. That was Latin America after the Cold War, which had promoted divisions and justified dictatorships. Though challenges remained, many Latin Americans were on the path toward democracy.

POLITICS IN SOUTH AMERICA AND MEXICO

By the late 1990s, military rule and dictatorships were disappearing throughout Latin America as trends moved toward democracy and civilian rule. The end of the Cold War opened the door to new democratic possibilities. In Argentina, defeat in 1982's Falklands War against Britain showed the incompetence of Argentine generals and brought about calls for change. Elections swept the military from power in Brazil as well. Even in Chile, where the Pinochet regime was deeply entrenched, pressures mounted for a free election. In 1988, Chilean voters turned down Pinochet's continued dictatorship.

The democratization of Latin American nations paralleled the liberation of Eastern Europe. But where countries like Poland had escaped from Soviet domination, nations like Chile had freed themselves from dictatorships allied with the United States.

In Mexico, the problem was neither military governments nor Cold War alignments but the political monopoly of the Institutional Revolutionary Party (PRI). The PRI had ruled Mexico since 1929—when the party brought peace and stability to the country after the chaos of the Mexican Revolution. After World War II, Mexico prospered thanks in part to a flourishing oil industry. But because the PRI had a political monopoly, elections were little more than a joke. Economic growth mostly benefited PRI's leadership, and corruption was everywhere. Lacking opportunity at home, many Mexicans crossed into the United States in search of a better life.

By the 1990s, Mexicans grew tired of the PRI's corruption and incompetence. Helped by PRI-backed electoral reforms, opposition parties began to win elections at the local, state, and national levels. In 2000, the National Action Party (PAN) finally broke the PRI's 71-year grip on power when its candidate won the presidency. Mexico—like much of Latin America—does not have many liberal institutions, but it is still working toward establishing a strong democratic culture.

CRITICAL VIEWING Salvadorans participate in a commemorative march 38 years after Archbishop Oscar Romero's assassination in 1980. Which details in the banner connect to Romero and what he represents?

CONFLICT IN CENTRAL AMERICA

A key goal for the United States during the Cold War was to contain the Soviet Union and block its efforts to spread communism around the world. In the 1970s and 1980s, Central America was a principal battleground between **leftist** rebels and military forces backed by the United States. (Leftists generally fight for radical economic and social changes, including an end to inequality and poverty.)

Nicaragua had long been ruled by members of the Somoza family, dictators whose anti-communism brought them strong U.S. support, even though they stole millions of dollars earmarked for relief aid. Resistance to the Somoza dictatorship was organized by the Sandinista National Liberation Front. The Sandinistas ousted the regime in 1979. The newly formed government seized the Somoza family's landholdings and nationalized major industries.

Soldiers loyal to Somoza leadership aimed to take back political control. These counterrevolutionaries—known as contras—received support from U.S. president Reagan after he took office in 1981. Reagan illegally evaded a congressional ban on military aid to the contras by selling arms to Iran. He then used the resulting funds to finance the contras. The Sandinistas relied on support from the Soviet Union and Cuba and clamped down on civil liberties.

The end of the Cold War brought a solution. The collapse of the Soviet Union led Mikhail Gorbachev to sharply reduce aid to Cuba. Cuba could no longer support the Sandinistas, and U.S. leaders no longer saw the contras as necessary allies. Nicaragua held free elections in 1989. The defeated Sandinistas handed over power peacefully, a major step forward.

Violence also marred Guatemalan society in the 1980s. Semiofficial "death squads" linked to the military government targeted villagers, mostly indigenous Maya people, suspected of aiding rebel guerrillas. As many as one million Guatemalans fled from their mountain homes to the cities or across the border to Mexico.

After the Cold War, the United States helped work out a peace deal in Guatemala. In 1996, the rebels laid down their arms in exchange for land. Guatemalans voted in free elections for the first time since 1952. In 1999, a special commission determined that the army had committed the majority of the human-rights abuses during the long civil war.

Nicaragua's Sandinistas modeled themselves on Cuban revolutionary heroes; the soldier on the right wears a red-starred beret like that of Che Guevara.

These conflict resolutions allowed the people of Nicaragua and Guatemala to begin the process of **nation-building**—establishing order and a functioning government in a country that has been plagued by violence and instability.

Latin America was largely Roman Catholic, and the church played an influential role in everyday society. In El Salvador, where the military had seized power, the Catholic Church suffered two major tragedies in 1980. In March, Archbishop **Oscar Romero**, long a voice for poor Salvadorans, was assassinated while offering Mass. Later that year, El Salvador's National Guard murdered three American nuns and a lay missionary who worked with the poor.

Although El Salvador held elections in 1992 after the end of its 12-year civil war, gangs took over much of the country, trading drugs for guns easily available in the United States. Threatened by both poverty and gang violence, many Salvadorans left their homes in search of a better life for themselves and their children.

HISTORICAL THINKING

1. **READING CHECK** Why did the United States support military dictatorships in Latin America during the Cold War?

2. **DRAW CONCLUSIONS** Under what circumstances would an election be free but not fair?

3. **MAKE CONNECTIONS** What effect do you think the end of the Cold War had on the level of conflict in Central America? Explain.

2.2

MAIN IDEA Nelson Mandela's courageous struggle to end discrimination and segregation in South Africa ended with his election to the presidency.

Traveler: Nelson Mandela
Anti-Apartheid Activist 1918–2013

Nelson Mandela devoted his life to fighting South Africa's apartheid policies. He paid a price for his activism—27 years in prison. But in the end, he led the way to the destruction of one of the world's most oppressive governments.

FIGHTING FOR DEMOCRACY AND FREEDOM

You've read that apartheid was a system in South Africa that separated black Africans from their white rulers. Throughout the 1950s, Nelson Mandela campaigned against apartheid in South Africa. As a leader of the African National Congress (ANC), he sought racial justice and democracy. Forced underground in 1961 when the South African government banned the ANC, Mandela traveled across Africa seeking support for a guerrilla army. After returning to South Africa in 1962, he was captured and charged with treason. In 1964, he was sentenced to life in prison.

Finally, in early 1990, after decades of repression and violence in South Africa, the nation's white leaders responded to massive South African protests and international calls for Mandela's release. A few hours after Mandela walked through the prison gates, he spoke before a large crowd in Cape Town and before a global television audience.

RISE TO THE PRESIDENCY

Mandela was born and grew up in the Transkei region of eastern South Africa. As a youth, he received an education in the history of his own Tembu people and in the protocols of the chief's court. He also attended an English-language primary school, where Mandela's teacher changed his name to Nelson, a "proper" English name. Before that, Mandela was called Rolihlahla ("pulling the branch of a tree" or "troublemaker"). He would live up to his African name.

To avoid an arranged marriage, Mandela fled to Johannesburg in 1941. There, he earned his college degree, studied law, and became one of South Africa's few black lawyers. He combined his practice of law with a passion for politics. In 1942, he joined the ANC—the political party that had worked for racial equality in South Africa since 1912—and soon rose to a leadership position.

During World War II, many Africans supported the Allies and applauded ideals expressed by Franklin Roosevelt and Winston Churchill in the Atlantic Charter: freedom and national self-determination. Members of the ANC invoked the Atlantic Charter in their call to end racial segregation and discrimination. Mandela praised the British and U.S. political systems. He later cited as additional influences the Magna Carta, the British Petition of Right, and the Bill of Rights.

As you have read, in the early 1950s, the ANC began to organize nonviolent demonstrations against South Africa's apartheid policies. Its program of **passive resistance**, or nonviolent opposition to authority,

> ### PRIMARY SOURCE
>
> Today, the majority of South Africans, black and white, recognize that apartheid has no future. . . . Negotiations on the dismantling of apartheid will have to address the overwhelming demands of our people for a democratic, nonracial, and unitary South Africa. There must be an end to white monopoly on political power, and a fundamental restructuring of our political and economic systems to ensure that the inequalities of apartheid are addressed and our society thoroughly democratized. . . . I wish to quote my own words during my trial in 1964. They are as true today as they were then: "I have fought against white domination and I have fought against black domination. I have cherished the ideal of a democratic and free society in which all persons live together in harmony and with equal opportunities. It is an ideal which I hope to live for and to achieve. But, if needs be, it is an ideal for which I am prepared to die."
>
> —from "Nelson Mandela's Address to Rally in Cape Town on His Release from Prison," February 11, 1990

Nelson Mandela's Journeys

Accepts Nobel Peace Prize, with de Klerk, 1993

Tours North America after imprisonment, 1990

Mandela honors Gandhi's legacy, 1995.

Travels to seek support for a liberation army, 1962

Imprisoned in several locations in and near Cape Town, 1964–1990

Travels to promote ANC, 1955

The Travels of Nelson Mandela
- Nelson Mandela's pre-imprisonment journeys
- Nelson Mandela's post-imprisonment journeys
- City visited by Mandela
- Other city

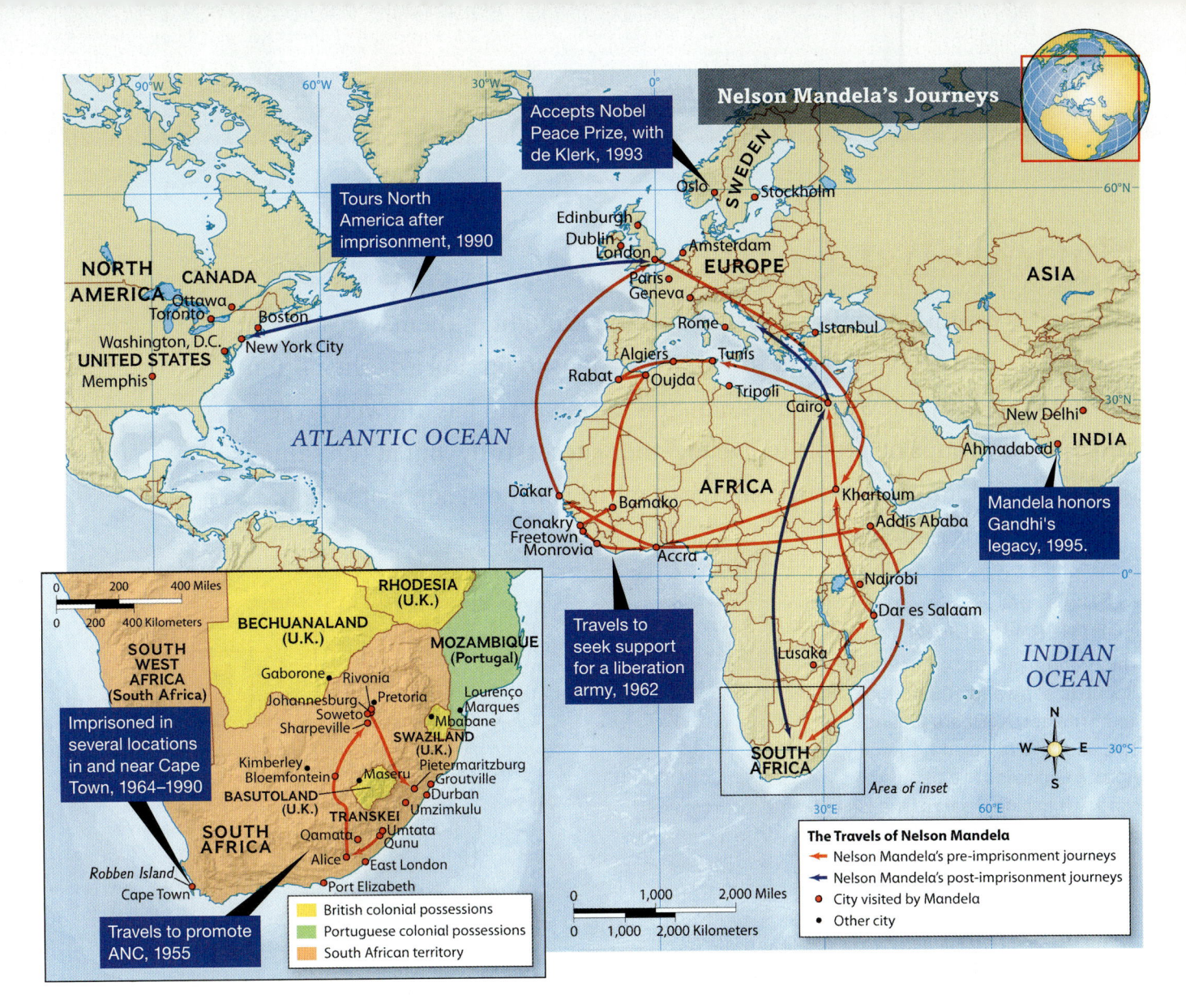

included refusing to obey unjust laws, such as one that required African men to carry passes that restricted their freedom of movement. Passive resistance also involved strikes and boycotts. But after the brutal police response to what became known as the Sharpeville Massacre in 1960, Mandela and the ANC began using sabotage, or the intentional destruction of property or disruption of transportation, communication, or government systems. After Mandela was imprisoned in 1964, South Africans from several racial groups continued the struggle against apartheid.

One of them, the Anglican archbishop **Desmond Tutu**, also promoted nonviolent protest and encouraged the United States and other countries to impose sanctions, or economic restrictions, on South Africa. In 1984, Tutu won the Nobel Peace Prize for his efforts. Mandela was released from prison in 1990, and by 1991, South Africa had gradually dismantled its apartheid policies. In 1993, Mandela was awarded the Nobel Peace Prize for his accomplishments.

Mandela ran for president in the 1994 election, the first election in which all South African citizens age 18 or older could vote. He won easily, and the ANC became the dominant political force in a new South Africa. True to the words he had spoken at his trial in 1964, Mandela emphasized inclusiveness in his government. He also worked to resolve the lingering tensions and anger of the apartheid era. Without Nelson Mandela, it is doubtful whether South Africa could have navigated the post-apartheid era as safely and successfully as it did.

HISTORICAL THINKING

1. **READING CHECK** How did the Sharpeville Massacre change the ANC's tactics?

2. **MAKE INFERENCES** How did Mandela "live up to his African name"?

3. **DRAW CONCLUSIONS** What did Mandela's election victory suggest about black South Africans' readiness to participate in political life?

Conflicts and Transformations **847**

2.3

MAIN IDEA In several parts of the modern world, nationalists and their opponents have engaged in decades of conflict.

Nationalist Conflicts

Until fairly recently in human history, people thought of themselves as belonging to large extended families—or perhaps to territories. The notion of a nation is only a few centuries old, and nationalism has allowed large and diverse groups of people to live together successfully. But at the same time, nationalism has been the source of many conflicts, some of which continue to this day.

NORTHERN IRELAND

The island of Ireland contains the Republic of Ireland and, to the far northeast, Northern Ireland. The Republic of Ireland is largely Roman Catholic. The people of Northern Ireland—part of the United Kingdom, which includes Britain—are a fairly even mix of Protestants and Catholics. Historically, however, Protestants have dominated Northern Ireland politically.

Since 1922, Protestant unionists (who want to remain in the United Kingdom) and Catholic nationalists (who want to join the Republic of Ireland instead) have regularly clashed. The level of conflict escalated in 1968, when Catholics marching in protest against discrimination were confronted by Protestant counterprotesters. In the 30 years that followed, during a period known as the "Troubles," British security forces tried to keep the peace between violent nationalist and unionist paramilitary forces. But armed battles and bombings continued, resulting in more than 3,600 deaths.

In 1985, Britain and the Republic of Ireland reached an agreement by which Irish government officials would serve as advisors in Northern Ireland. Paramilitary groups on both sides largely rejected this agreement. But by the 1990s, the adversaries began to realize that nobody could win this struggle militarily. In 1998, all sides signed the Good Friday Agreement, which stated that Northern Ireland would remain in the United Kingdom unless majorities in Ireland and Northern Ireland voted otherwise. Twenty years later, the agreement was still in place.

Local residents of Derry, Northern Ireland, watch as troops from the British Army dismantle barricades that had been erected against the unionists during what became known as the Battle of the Bogside. During this conflict, Catholic nationalists clashed with Protestants from August 12–14, 1969. The three-day riot led to similar violent outbreaks in other parts of Northern Ireland.

YUGOSLAVIA AND ETHNIC CLEANSING

You learned about religious and ethnic conflict in the Balkans region prior to World War I and similar hostilities during Nazi rule. After 1945, Yugoslavia finally became stable under the leadership of Josip Broz, commonly known as Marshal Tito. Although he was an authoritarian communist, Tito remained independent

848 CHAPTER 29

Bosnian Muslims in a UN refugee camp watch the trial of former Yugoslavian president Slobodan Milosevic on television in 2002. Milosevic was charged with crimes against humanity and genocide in the ethnic wars that broke out in the former Yugoslavia in the 1990s.

from the Soviet Union and treated all Yugoslavs equally. The successful Winter Olympics in 1984 showcased Yugoslavia as a modern, prosperous European republic.

After Tito's death and instability in the Soviet Union, Serbian nationalists were inspired to fight for their vision of a "Greater Serbia." Because the populations were so mixed, Serbian commanders ordered campaigns of "ethnic cleansing." The leaders' intention was to drive Catholic Croatians and Muslim Bosnians out of villages where they had formerly lived with Orthodox Serbs. During the Srebrenica massacre in the summer of 1995, more than 8,000 Bosnian Muslims were systematically murdered by Serbian militiamen. Ethnic cleansing became another term for genocide.

Fortunately, Western leaders were able to use international institutions to end the conflict. Through the North Atlantic Treaty Organization (NATO), the United States and its European allies launched a military intervention and then sponsored negotiations that led to the breakup of Yugoslavia. The former nation was divided into six republics and two provinces.

KASHMIR

Across Tibet's western border lies Kashmir, a mountainous territory claimed by India and Pakistan, which were separated into two nations in 1947. India declared that an Indian prince transferred the region to India as part of this partition. Pakistan based its case on Kashmir's large Muslim population. Soon after the split, India and Pakistan went to war to gain control of Kashmir.

The United Nations negotiated a cease-fire in January 1949 but could not persuade both sides to withdraw their troops from Kashmir. Later that year, India and Pakistan established a temporary cease-fire line. It ended up being a permanent boundary that split control of the territory between the two countries. Hostilities continued, with armed conflict breaking out in 1965 and again in 1971.

Starting in the late 1980s, pro-independence groups from the Pakistani side of the cease-fire line launched attacks against Indian troops. In 1999, their actions led to yet another war between Pakistan and India,

Conflicts and Transformations

two states with nuclear weapons. Ongoing violence, including renewed attacks by Pakistani nationalists as well as Indian assaults on Pakistani demonstrators, have kept tensions high in Kashmir well into the 21st century. Peace talks continue as well, but there is still little hope of settling the dispute.

CYPRUS

Greeks first immigrated to Cyprus, a large island in the eastern Mediterranean Sea, during the 1200s B.C.E. A number of Mediterranean empires controlled the island during the centuries that followed. In the 1570s C.E., the Ottoman Empire seized the island, beginning 300 years of Turkish rule. By the 20th century, the island's population consisted mainly of Greeks and Turks.

During World War I, Britain annexed the island, and in 1925, Cyprus officially became a British colony. The Greek Cypriots, or Greek inhabitants of Cyprus, demanded that Cyprus become part of Greece. But Britain and Greece could not agree on how to accomplish that task. In 1955, Greek Cypriot nationalists launched a campaign for unification with Greece that included the bombing of government buildings. Turkish Cypriots staunchly opposed union with Greece. Armed conflict began between the two Cypriot communities.

In 1960, prodded by Greece, Turkey, and Britain, Greek and Turkish Cypriots agreed to the creation of an independent republic of Cyprus. The two communities would share the governing, although the Greek Cypriots, by far the majority of the population, were to have greater political representation. After fighting erupted again, Turkish Cypriots largely withdrew to the northern third of the island, and Greek Cypriots took control of the rest.

Not much changed in the decades that followed. In 1981, the Turkish Republic of Northern Cyprus proclaimed its independence, but it did not receive international recognition. UN-sponsored talks aimed at reuniting the two Cypriot communities had, as late as 2017, all failed.

In the Kashmir Himalaya, a Changpa nomad and her herd of goats cross a stream. The area is claimed by both India and Pakistan.

The Dalai Lama speaks to a crowd in Central Park in New York City on September 21, 2003. This Tibetan religious leader continues to speak against Chinese dominion over his home region, where he has not lived for decades.

TIBET

Tibet is a region in Central Asia located largely on a plateau that averages 16,500 feet above sea level. The Himalaya form its western and southern borders, and the Kunlun Mountains rise to the north. For these reasons, Tibet is often called "the roof of the world."

From the late 1400s until the 1950s, Tibet was ruled by a Buddhist holy man known as the **Dalai Lama**. In 1950, a communist Chinese force invaded eastern Tibet and swiftly subdued Tibetan troops. Chinese emperors had long claimed the right to station troops in Tibet and oversee its politics. In reality, however, Tibetans had mostly looked after their own affairs. The Chinese communists in the 1950s wanted to expand their authority, and their invasion stirred Tibetan nationalism.

In 1959, Chinese troops quickly put down an anti-Chinese uprising centered in the Tibetan capital of Lhasa, and the reigning Dalai Lama fled to India. In 1965, China officially revoked Tibet's independent status, making Tibet an autonomous, or self-governing, region of China. In the years that followed, China's Cultural Revolution—which you read about earlier—led to the repression of Tibetans and attacks on their Buddhist culture.

Economic growth after the 1980s put even greater pressure on Tibet. Tibetan resources helped build the Chinese economy and increased immigration by Han Chinese onto the plateau. Government promises of autonomy were contradicted by authoritarian policies coming from Beijing.

Some Tibetan nationalists will settle only for complete independence. Others are willing to compromise in the direction of true "autonomy," in which Tibetan language and cultural rights, freedom of religious worship, and the development of the economy to meet Tibetan needs will be guaranteed. The Dalai Lama continues his nonviolent campaign for Tibetan rights. Like Desmond Tutu and Nelson Mandela, he too won the Nobel Peace Prize.

HISTORICAL THINKING

1. **READING CHECK** What action played a major role in most of these nationalist conflicts?
2. **MAKE CONNECTIONS** How did the "ethnic cleansing" in Yugoslavia in the 1990s build on pre-World War I conflicts in the Balkans?
3. **ANALYZE CAUSE AND EFFECT** How did China's rapid economic growth affect the fate of Tibet?
4. **FORM AND SUPPORT OPINIONS** Which region do you think has the best prospect for lasting peace? Why?

3.1

MAIN IDEA In 1947, a group of Jewish people living in what was then Palestine declared the establishment of an independent state: Israel.

The State of Israel

Since the late 1800s, Jews around the world have felt inspired to make Aliyah, to immigrate to Israel. Following World War II and the Holocaust, many Jewish people moved to Palestine for safety and to work for the creation of an independent Israel.

CALLS FOR A JEWISH STATE

You learned that in the Balfour Declaration of 1917, Britain promised Jewish independence and a "national home" for Jews on the lands of the ancient Hebrew kingdoms. This area, known at the time as Palestine, consisted of what is now Jordan, Israel, the West Bank, and the Gaza Strip. At first, the British allowed Jews to settle in Palestine freely. However, Britain also faced competing pleas from Arabs to protect the Arab majority of Palestine. Growing Arab protests caused Britain to limit Jewish immigration to Palestine. But many Jews still found ways to enter what they believed to be their promised land.

In June 1969, Israeli prime minister Golda Meir (center) meets with politicians—including British prime minister Harold Wilson (left) and West German minister for foreign affairs Willy Brandt (right)—at a Socialist International Congress meeting in Eastbourne, England.

By 1945, more than 660,000 Jews lived in Palestine, and Zionists—people who supported the formation of a Jewish nation—increased calls for independence. Other Southwest Asian countries, including Iraq, Lebanon, Syria, and Jordan, had all gained independence before, during, or shortly after World War II. The horrors of the Holocaust had also convinced many people of the need for a Jewish state. Jews who had survived the Holocaust moved to Palestine, and other Zionists from around the world who wanted to help build a Jewish nation joined them.

Frustrated by the growing conflicts between Arabs and Jews, Britain gave up its mandate in 1947 and transferred the land to the fledgling United Nations. The UN planned to partition Palestine into separate Jewish and Arab states. But when fighting broke out between Arabs and Jews, UN plans for a **two-state solution** were dashed.

ISRAELI INDEPENDENCE

In 1948, the Zionist leader **David Ben-Gurion** declared the independence of Israel. Ben-Gurion, a Polish immigrant, would become the new nation's first prime minister. Egypt, Lebanon, Iraq, Syria, Jordan, and Iraq immediately declared war, intending a quick end to the newly declared republic. During the 1948 conflict, at least 600,000 Arab refugees and perhaps as many as one million people fled the fighting in an event known as *al-nakbah*, or "the catastrophe," by Palestinians. Israelis routed the Arab armies and then expanded Israel's borders beyond what the UN planners had envisioned. Meanwhile, Egypt claimed the Gaza Strip, and Jordan occupied the West Bank and East Jerusalem. Arabs were angry that many Palestinian Arabs had been displaced and that a Palestinian state was never established. To this day, the quarrel between Arabs and Israelis has had a major effect on world affairs.

NATAN SHARANSKY Natan Sharansky (shown here) was born in Soviet-controlled Ukraine not long after Israel gained independence. As a young man, Sharansky spoke out against Soviet human-rights violations against the Jewish people. In 1973, he sought permission to emigrate to Israel, but the government would not let him leave. Sharansky voiced his opposition to the unfair treatment he and other *refuseniks*, as Soviet dissidents were called, received. The Soviet government accused him of treason and imprisoned him in a labor camp in Siberia in 1977. In time, the pleas of his wife prompted international protests. The Soviets finally released Sharansky in 1986, and he left the Soviet Union to make a new home in Israel. In 2018, he was awarded an Israel Prize—the highest award given annually by the Israeli government to those who make significant contributions to Israeli culture—for his efforts to guarantee human rights to all.

Following the war, Israeli leaders created a government, including a legislative body eventually known as the Knesset. One of these leaders was **Golda Meir**. Born in Kiev, Ukraine, Meir immigrated to Milwaukee, Wisconsin, with her family when she was a young girl. After she graduated from college, she moved with her husband to what was then Palestine in 1921. During World War II, she became a powerful spokesperson for the Zionist cause. She signed Israel's independence declaration in 1948 and served Israel as minister of labor (1949–1956), as foreign minister (1956–1966), and ultimately as its first woman prime minister (1969–1974). Meir died in 1978 after a 12-year battle with leukemia.

Israel won financial support from other nations, such as the United States and West Germany. Its leaders looked for ways to blend Jews of different ethnic backgrounds into one culture. The use of Hebrew helped unify Jews who arrived in Israel speaking different languages. Today, Israel is an economically successful and predominantly secular state. It is plagued, however, by pockets of religious extremism and the unresolved conflicts with Palestinians. You will learn more about these disputes in the next lesson.

HISTORICAL THINKING

1. **READING CHECK** What events led to the declaration of Israeli independence?

2. **DRAW CONCLUSIONS** Why do you think Jews around the world supported the establishment of an independent Israel even if they did not plan to live there?

3. **ANALYZE CAUSE AND EFFECT** Why did Israel's declaration of independence cause neighboring countries to immediately declare war?

Conflicts and Transformations 853

3.2

MAIN IDEA Territorial disputes in Southwest Asia and North Africa led to continuing conflicts between Israelis and Palestinians and their Arab allies during the mid-to-late 20th century.

Arab-Israeli Conflicts

Close proximity can bring about cooperation, conflict, or both. For example, people might decide to share resources with an ally or to wage battle against a foe. In Southwest Asia and North Africa, confrontations over contested territory seemed to be the rule.

THE SIX-DAY WAR AND AFTERMATH

Arab states neighboring Israel remained bitter about Israeli independence. Hundreds of thousands of Palestinians remained displaced, with the majority relocating to the West Bank. As many as 800,000 Jews left Muslim countries to resettle in Israel or elsewhere. Unlike the Jewish people, however, the Palestinians had not gained their own independent state. Although Jews from all nations have a right to settle in Israel, Palestinian families that became refugees in the war of 1948 are prevented from returning.

In 1967, Israel learned that Egyptian president Gamal Abdel Nasser was preparing for battle. Israel decided to **preempt**—or prevent from happening—Arab strikes by attacking Egypt first in what became known as the **Six-Day War**. Israeli planes eliminated much of the Egyptian air force and then occupied Egypt's Sinai Desert and Gaza, Syria's Golan Heights, and Jordan's West Bank and East Jerusalem. After the Arab League, a regional organization of Arab states in North Africa and Southwest Asia, made it clear it would never accept Israel's existence, Israel pledged to hold these lands as a security measure. When the conservative Likud Party gained power in Israel's Knesset, its members went further, claiming that the captured Arab lands were part of Israel itself. The Likud government sponsored Jewish settlements on the West Bank, in violation of international laws that prevent the colonization of land taken in war.

The Palestine Liberation Organization (PLO) headed by **Yasir Arafat** (YAH-ser AHR-uh-faht) dedicated itself to regaining lost Palestinian land and creating a Palestinian state. It used a variety of tactics, including terrorist attacks on civilians. Groups such as the Iranian-supported Hezbollah and the Palestinian Hamas also

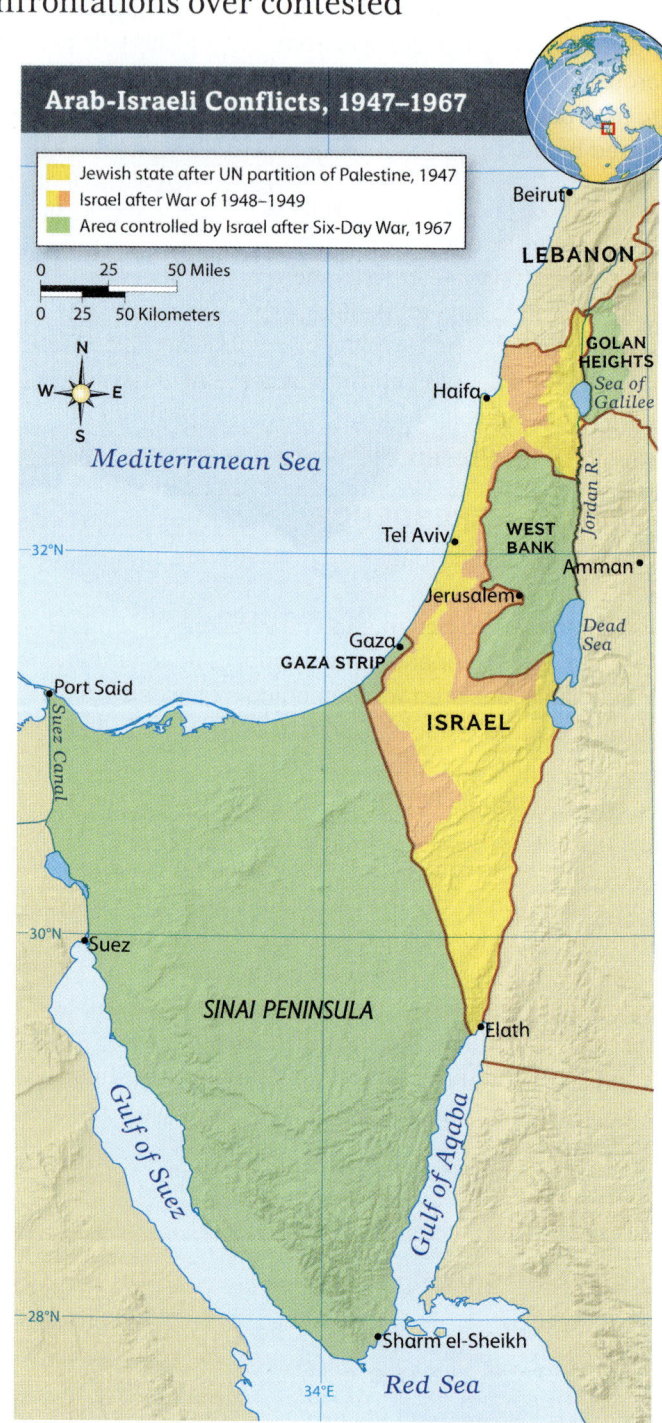

Arab-Israeli Conflicts, 1947–1967

- Jewish state after UN partition of Palestine, 1947
- Israel after War of 1948–1949
- Area controlled by Israel after Six-Day War, 1967

854 CHAPTER 29

This 1993 handshake between Israeli prime minister Yitzhak Rabin and PLO leader Yasir Arafat gave the world hope for peace in the Middle East. However, negotiations for a peace accord mediated by U.S. president Bill Clinton proved unsuccessful.

pursued the cause of a Palestinian state, though not always in agreement with one another.

Meanwhile, U.S. president **Jimmy Carter** encouraged Israeli prime minister **Menachem Begin** and Egyptian president **Anwar Sadat** to hold peace talks. The Camp David Accords of 1978 led to the Israel-Egypt Peace Treaty. Israel returned the Sinai Peninsula to Egypt in exchange for Egypt's acknowledgement of Israel's right to exist. Both Begin and Sadat were awarded the Nobel Peace Prize for their contributions to the agreements.

In 1987, Palestinians began the first intifada, or "ceaseless struggle," against Israeli occupation of Gaza and the West Bank. Israel responded by restricting the movement of Palestinians. However, while tensions increased on the ground, acts of diplomacy were also bearing fruit.

THE OSLO ACCORDS

In 1991, the United States and several European nations arranged for Israeli and Palestinian diplomats to meet. In 1993, the two sides signed the Oslo Accords. This peace agreement laid out a "road map" for peace based on the idea of two separate and secure nations side by side. U.S. president **Bill Clinton** invited Arafat and Israeli prime minister **Yitzhak Rabin** (YIHT-shak rah-BEEN) to Washington. But the talks soon broke down. Arafat refused to accept a land-for-peace offer more generous than any previous proposal. Israel still would not allow Palestinian refugees to return to their former homes. Also, the two sides could not agree on the status of Jerusalem, which both Israelis and Palestinians claim as their capital. The so-called road map had led nowhere. Rabin was later assassinated by an Israeli extremist angry with the prime minister's peaceful approach.

HISTORICAL THINKING

1. **READING CHECK** Following the Six-Day War, what did each side in the Arab-Israeli conflict want?

2. **DRAW CONCLUSIONS** Why was it difficult for the Israelis to give up occupied territory?

3. **INTERPRET MAPS** What impact did Israel's location have on Israel in the 20th century?

Conflicts and Transformations 855

3.3 **MAIN IDEA** Desire for the resource of oil and differing religious viewpoints caused clashes among the diverse nations in Southwest Asia.

Revolution and Turmoil

The Israelis and the Palestinians were not the only groups feuding in Southwest Asia in the mid-to-late 20th century. Other ethnic and religious rivalries also created divisions. By the 1970s, the strategic importance of the region as a source of oil added more turmoil.

Iranian nationalists, suspicious of both the United States and the Soviet Union, flocked to the banner of Ayatollah Khomeini to establish an Islamic republic in 1979. Khomeini returned from exile in France as their spiritual and political leader.

IRAN VERSUS IRAQ

The uneven distribution of oil has been a continuing source of worldwide conflict. Many nations depend on Southwest Asia's oil. In the 1960s, oil-producing nations such as Iran, Iraq, Kuwait, and Saudi Arabia formed the **Organization of the Petroleum Exporting Countries (OPEC)**. They banded together to topple the control Western oil companies had on oil prices. In 1973, OPEC suspended oil exports to the United States because of U.S. military aid to Israel. Increased oil and energy prices and a global economic slowdown followed.

In 1979, the world focused its attention on the Iranian Revolution. For the first time, a modern state would be expressly ruled by sharia, which you learned is Islamic law. Recall that Sunni and Shiite Muslims had many ideological differences. Yet both groups were increasingly influenced by Islamists who believe that laws and constitutions should be guided by Islamic principles and that religious authorities should be directly involved in the government. Islamists promised social and economic success by returning to the core religious values of Islam.

Islamism threatened secular Arab nations such as Egypt, Syria, Iraq, and Jordan, which were all ruled by secular, nationalist regimes. The United States had long supported Iran's authoritarian shah, Mohammed Reza Pahlavi. Pahlavi industrialized Iran and granted new freedoms to women, but he repressed any opposition. Conservative religious leaders claimed the shah supported decadent Western values. Spreading demonstrations against him led Pahlavi to flee to the United States in 1979.

Religious leader **Ayatollah Khomeini** gained control of Shiite-dominated Iran. He promised to reject Western influences and introduce more religious authority to his Islamic republic. For example, he wanted women to return to their earlier, more traditional roles. A growing sense of nationalism caused many Iranians to support the new government.

In neighboring Iraq, a Sunni minority ruled over a Shiite majority, and Iraqi leader **Saddam Hussein** felt threatened by the Iranian revolution. His brutal invasion of Iran in 1980 led to more than one million deaths. Iranians suffered terribly from the Iraqi army's use of chemical weapons, and the war ended eight years later in a stalemate.

Then, in 1990, Hussein invaded Kuwait, a small oil-rich state on the Persian Gulf. In response, U.S. president **George H.W. Bush** formed an international coalition against Iraq. The **Persian Gulf War** began in 1991 with the devastating U.S. bombing of Baghdad and quickly concluded with liberation for Kuwait. To maintain a balance of power between Iraq and Iran—and between Sunnis and Shiites—Bush decided not to oust Hussein from his position as president. Hussein then brutally crushed a rebellion in Iraq's Shiite south.

AFGHANISTAN AND SAUDI ARABIA

In 1993, U.S. president Clinton turned his attention toward Afghanistan. After the Soviet Union withdrew its forces, Afghanistan fell under the control of the **Taliban**. This group of Sunni Islamists supported ==fundamentalism==, or the belief that laws and social practices should be guided by strict principles, often religious ones. Women's freedoms were severely curtailed under Taliban control, and education for girls was eliminated.

The mujahideen, guerrilla fighters backed by the United States in the war to drive out the Soviets, supported the Taliban. Among them was **Osama bin Laden**, a son of a wealthy Saudi Arabian builder. He despised the United States for its aid to Israel and claimed that the United States supported corrupt regimes. Bin Laden and his followers in the terrorist group **al Qaeda** (ahl KY-dah) carried out truck bomb attacks on U.S. embassies in Africa in 1998.

Meanwhile, the United States maintained a close relationship with Saudi Arabia. It exchanged military aid for the right to import oil from Saudi Arabia's vast oil fields. The wealth derived from oil sales allowed the Saudis to improve their system of education, modernize industries, and expand urban centers. Yet many other nations were dismayed by Saudi Arabia's denial of rights to women, its suppression of opposing viewpoints, and the role that the Saudis played in sponsoring radical religious fundamentalism across Asia and Africa.

Members of the Taliban pose on top of a tank in Kabul, Afghanistan.

HISTORICAL THINKING

1. **READING CHECK** In what important way are nations of Southwest Asia vital to the interconnected world economy?

2. **ANALYZE CAUSE AND EFFECT** Why did radical Islamic fundamentalism develop in Southwest Asia, and what effect did it have?

3. **MAKE INFERENCES** Why is the Persian Gulf critical to the exportation of oil in Southwest Asia?

Conflicts and Transformations 857

4.1

MAIN IDEA The second half of the 20th century saw increased concern for human rights on the part of governments and organizations—even as abuses continued.

Global Human Rights

The horrors of the Holocaust and devastation caused by other wars pushed the issue of human rights into the global spotlight. The fascist affronts to humanity during World War II had been stopped. But the now closely connected global population knew action was needed to halt human rights abuses throughout the world.

HUMAN RIGHTS AND THE UNITED NATIONS

As you learned, 51 of the world's nations formed the United Nations in 1945. This international organization was established as a forum, or public meeting place, to maintain worldwide peace and security and prevent future wars. Protecting human rights across the globe was a top priority.

In 1946, the UN formed the Commission on Human Rights, which sought to protect all people. Former U.S. first lady Eleanor Roosevelt led the commission in the creation of a set of international standards for ensuring people's basic rights called the **Universal Declaration of Human Rights**. This document was approved by the UN in 1948. The standards include "all the rights and freedoms set forth . . . without distinction of any kind, such as race, color, sex, language, religion, political or other opinion, national or social origin, property, birth or other status." When **Kofi Annan** of Ghana became UN secretary general in 1997, he worked to widen awareness of war crimes, genocide, and crimes against humanity.

In 1979, a UN women's convention, or treaty, declared that women are entitled to voting rights, fair employment, and protection from sex trafficking. The 1989 UN Convention on the Rights of the Child declared that children should be protected from physical abuse and poor health. Yet as industrialized nations turned to developing nations for cheap labor, children faced dangerous working conditions in factories, farms, and mines. Sadly, children in some regions are forced to traffic drugs or serve as soldiers.

More than 15 years later, the UN established the Human Rights Council, a group of 47 countries elected for three-year terms. This council has been criticized, however, for its perceived unfair treatment of Israel as well as its inclusion of nations said to abuse human rights. Even so, most people around the world seem pledged to continue to protest human rights violations.

HUMAN RIGHTS AROUND THE WORLD

Some **nongovernmental organizations** (NGOs), nonprofit groups that support a particular cause, specialize in protecting human rights. NGOs

---

PRIMARY SOURCE

Article 4: No one shall be held in slavery or servitude; slavery and the slave trade shall be prohibited in all their forms.

Article 5: No one shall be subjected to torture or to cruel, inhuman or degrading treatment or punishment. . . .

Article 8: Everyone has the right to an effective remedy by the competent national tribunals for acts violating the fundamental rights granted him by the constitution or by law. . . .

Article 15: (1) Everyone has the right to a nationality. (2) No one shall be arbitrarily deprived of his nationality nor denied the right to change his nationality. . . .

Article 25: (1) Everyone has the right to a standard of living adequate for the health and well-being of himself and of his family, including food, clothing, housing and medical care and necessary social services, and the right to security in the event of unemployment, sickness, disability, widowhood, old age or other lack of livelihood in circumstances beyond his control. . . .

Article 26: (1) Everyone has the right to education. Education shall be free, at least in the elementary and fundamental stages. Elementary education shall be compulsory. Technical and professional education shall be made generally available and higher education shall be equally accessible to all on the basis of merit. . . .

—from the Universal Declaration of Human Rights by the United Nations, 1948

Members of the United Nations Human Rights Council listen to a report presented by the Commission of Inquiry on Syria, on March 13, 2018 in Geneva, Switzerland.

with this mission include Amnesty International, Human Rights Watch, Freedom House, and Médecins Sans Frontières (Doctors Without Borders). Others, such as the Human Rights Education Associates (HREA), provide educational material about humanitarian law.

Improved communications technology, such as satellite broadcasting and videos recorded on smartphones, made it more difficult to hide human rights abuses. Cold War tensions also played a part in exposing mistreatment. Western democracies criticized the Soviet Union for its cruelties, and many nations began to consider human rights when developing their foreign policy. However, NGOs also pointed to issues in Western nations, such as overcrowding in prisons and the use of the death penalty.

In the late 20th century, many countries employed diplomatic pressure and sanctions to convince South Africa to abandon apartheid. In the 1990s, indignation at ethnic cleansing in Bosnia led to a 1999 UN war crimes tribunal. The 1990s also saw the genocide of Rwanda's Tutsi people at the hands of the rival Hutu until growing world outrage brought an end to the slaughter and the guilty were put on trial.

THE INTERNATIONAL CRIMINAL COURT

Today, some of the most blatant cases of human rights abuses are tried at the International Criminal Court (ICC) at The Hague in the Netherlands. The ICC was founded in 1998 by the Rome Statute—an international treaty—and established in 2002 after 60 states ratified the agreement. The court works closely with the United Nations but is independent from it. The ICC prosecutes individuals, not nations or organizations, for genocide, war crimes, and crimes against humanity. In 2019, 123 nations have ratified the Rome Statute. The United States, Russia, Israel, and China are among the countries that do not recognize the ICC.

HISTORICAL THINKING

1. **READING CHECK** How did globalization affect human rights both positively and negatively in the 20th century?

2. **DRAW CONCLUSIONS** Why do racial- and ethnic-based human rights abuses take place, and why might other nations be slow or quick to try to stop them?

3. **FORM AND SUPPORT OPINIONS** Do you think some nations were right to criticize the UN's Human Rights Council? Explain.

4.2 DOCUMENT-BASED QUESTION
On Nonviolence

You probably know several methods of nonviolent conflict resolution. Until the middle of the 20th century, most people assumed that the most successful way to overcome oppression and settle conflict was through violence. However, as the century progressed, people began to realize that peaceful methods often worked better than physical aggression in achieving their goals.

CRITICAL VIEWING Images can often allow viewers to see the concern or anguish as well as the actions of the participants. What tools of nonviolent protest are the female protesters at Plaza de Mayo using in this photograph?

You have already learned that Mohandas K. Gandhi showed the world the effectiveness of nonviolent protest. His actions inspired **Dr. Martin Luther King, Jr.,** to organize African Americans in nonaggressive acts to gain civil rights in the United States. King's methods included boycotts and protest marches. Gandhi, King, and other participants of nonviolent direct action have motivated many other people around the world, including pacifists, people with a religious or philosophical objection to violence.

In 1977, Argentinian mothers, or *madres*, began weekly nonviolent demonstrations near Buenos Aires's Presidential Palace. They became known as Las Madres de la Plaza de Mayo, named for the place where they gathered every Thursday in silent protest. They sought information about the fate of their missing children: union-affiliated workers, intellectuals, and dissidents. These offspring had been made to "disappear" by the right-wing authoritarian government of Argentina in the late 1970s and early 1980s.

But Argentina led the way toward democracy in 1982, when its generals were overthrown and replaced by an elected government. Other nations followed that example over the next ten years, as corrupt dictatorships and authoritarian governments were pushed aside in countries such as Czechoslovakia, South Korea, East Germany, and Chile.

For decades, it seemed as if there were only two choices for deposing bad rulers: either a bloody revolution—as in Russia, Mexico, China, and Cuba—or the military replacing a corrupt government. But in the 1980s, the new option of "people's power" spread around the world. Demonstrators flooded the streets, stood up to tyrants and dictators, and demanded fundamental change. Their successes increased optimism about the future of democracy.

DOCUMENT ONE

Primary Source: Article
from "Guidelines on Christian Conduct during Elections" by Cardinal Jaime Sin, 1985

The leader of the Catholic Church in Manila, Cardinal Jaime Sin, played a central role in guiding the Philippines toward nonviolent, democratic change. Sin was instrumental in the 1986 People Power Revolution that overthrew the corrupt regime of Ferdinand Marcos and elected Corazon Aquino president.

CONSTRUCTED RESPONSE Based on this excerpt, how does the cardinal urge Christians to conduct themselves during the elections, and why?

> We all know how important these elections are. They are so decisive that their failure may plunge our country into even greater instability and violence. It is thus of the utmost importance that every voting Filipino does all in his power: 1) to vote in this election; 2) to assure that it is peaceful and honest in its conduct; and 3) to ensure that it becomes really an expression of the people's sovereign will. . . . By our vigilance and Christian involvement in the February 7 elections, let us prove . . . that there is an effective nonviolent way to change the structures in our society. May the Lord God of history lead us all to a better future through the expression of, and respect for, the people's sovereign will.

DOCUMENT TWO

Primary Source: Letter
from "Letter from the Gdańsk Prison" by Adam Michnik, 1985

In the 1980s, activist journalist Adam Michnik was jailed for his reform activities in communist Poland. While in prison, he wrote letters and articles about the situation in Poland and Solidarity's belief in nonviolence. Since Poland's independence, Michnik has continued his work as a journalist and has won a number of awards for his writing.

CONSTRUCTED RESPONSE According to the excerpt, what would be the consequence of Solidarity taking up arms?

> Why did Solidarity renounce violence? . . . People who claim that the use of force in the struggle for freedom is necessary must first prove that, in a given situation, it will be effective, and that force, when it is used, will not transform the idea of liberty into its opposite.
>
> No one in Poland is able to prove today that violence will help us to dislodge Soviet troops from Poland and to remove Communists from power. The U.S.S.R. has such enormous military power that confrontation is simply unthinkable. In other words: we have no guns.

DOCUMENT THREE

Primary Source: Article
from "Purple Reign" by Alison Ozinsky, 1989

In September 1988, local leaders in Cape Town organized massive protests against elections in which blacks could not vote. Police sprayed the demonstrators with purple dye so that authorities would be able to identify and arrest the protesters. Instead, the purple stains became a rallying symbol for further resistance.

CONSTRUCTED RESPONSE Based on this excerpt, how were these nonviolent actions effective?

> The marchers brace themselves. Somewhere a critical button is pushed and a sharp jet of water bursts forth, changing in mid-stream to lurid purple. Some are hit head on, full in the face. Some are knocked off their knees. . . . Then it stops. A lone protester has climbed on top of the truck and is diverting the nozzle away from the people. . . . The crowd stares for a moment in disbelief—then goes wild, cheering, shouting, and leaping in the air with delight for this brave young man. . . . By Monday morning an efficient graffiti artist has said it all for all of us. "The purple shall govern." I can believe it.

SYNTHESIZE & WRITE

1. **REVIEW** Review what you have read and observed about the three viewpoints about nonviolence in the 20th century.

2. **RECALL** On your own paper, list two details about the writer of one of the excerpts and two details about the excerpt from that writer.

3. **CONSTRUCT** Construct a topic sentence that answers this question: How, why, and when was nonviolent protest used in the 20th century?

4. **WRITE** Using evidence from this chapter and the documents, write an informative paragraph that supports your topic sentence in Step 3.

4.3

MAIN IDEA Increased economic globalization following World War II had enormous effects on the world's people, nations, and capital.

Economic Challenges

In the late 20th century, extensive financial integration moved front and center on the world stage. Expanding global trade led to unprecedented growth and international fiscal connections for many nations.

Development of the European Union

Legend:
- Founding member state, 1957–1967 (European Economic Community)
- Countries added 1967–1991 (European Community)
- Countries added 1991–2013 (European Union)
- Countries leaving EU, 2020

862 CHAPTER 29

GLOBALIZATION AND ECONOMIC CHANGE

At the end of the 20th century, countries once at conflict partnered to boost their economies. **Neoliberalism**—an economic approach that emphasizes free markets and international trade—was adopted by many governments. **Multinational corporations**, or companies with ownership and management teams from more than one nation, flourished with branches located in various countries.

International organizations formed after World War II played a greater role in the global economy. The World Bank and the International Monetary Fund, for example, loaned money to developing nations. In 1947, many nations signed the General Agreement on Tariffs and Trade (GATT), which encouraged free trade. In 1995, the World Trade Organization (WTO) replaced GATT. It established rules for international trade, with an emphasis on lowering tariffs and other barriers to the free movement of goods.

Economic globalization was not a new concept. But in the 1970s, new communications technology enabled rapid transmission of financial data and funds throughout the world. Lower transportation costs led to increased movement of goods. Advertisers could promote products worldwide. Radio and television commercials encouraged a homogenized world culture.

Asian economies in particular surged after World War II. Production of high-quality and well-priced products allowed Japan to rebuild its economy. However, by 1989 the bubble had burst. In contrast, China's economy soared in the last two decades of the 20th century because of the policies of its leader Deng Xiaoping.

FREE TRADE BLOCS

In the 1990s, neoliberalism led to the creation of free trade blocs. In 1992, the creation of the **European Union (EU)** increased the economic clout of Western European nations. It limited the debt new members could hold, created a European Central Bank to set monetary policy, and established the euro as the common currency. The EU accounted for more than 18 percent of global exports by the century's end.

In 1994, Canada, the United States, and Mexico created the **North American Free Trade Agreement (NAFTA)** to increase North American trade. NAFTA was controversial from the start. Critics in the United States warned that NAFTA might mean the loss of high-paying jobs as manufacturers seeking to pay lower wages moved south of the U.S. border. Some Mexican farmers worried about whether they could compete with U.S. farmers, who received government subsidies.

Debate still rages about whether free trade helps or hurts an economy. It leads to loss of high-paying factory jobs, and companies may be unable to compete on pricing. Consumers benefit because of increased purchasing power. Export companies may make gains as well, since they can expand their markets. Individual companies can see how free trade affects them by conducting a **cost-benefit analysis**, or comparison of the positive and negative effects, of free trade on their business. Free trade affected people in different ways, creating opportunity for some and insecurity for others.

Economic globalization brought greater financial security to much of the world, but it also increased inequality. More money flowed into the hands of business owners than into the pockets of workers. Foreign business owners increased profits by paying workers in developing nations low wages. The policy of **outsourcing**, or the use of people in lower-wage countries to do work once carried out in industrialized nations, means greater unemployment among former high-wage workers.

No matter if the expansion of free trade was cheered or jeered, one thing seemed certain: capitalism became the main player in the global economy.

"ASIAN TIGERS" The economies of other Asian nations grew enormously over the last half of the 20th century as well. South Korea, Taiwan, and Singapore were known as the "Asian Tigers." South Korea succeeded financially because of the close relationships between its government and large companies such as Samsung and Hyundai. Taiwan owed the growth of its trade to the now market-oriented Chinese mainland. Singapore's wealth soared because of its government's single-minded determination to attract foreign investment and build a world-class economy.

HISTORICAL THINKING

1. **READING CHECK** What was the impact of economic globalization in the late 20th century?

2. **MAKE PREDICTIONS** How do you think increased economic globalization will affect life in the early 21st century? in the next 30 years?

3. **INTERPRET MAPS** Study the map. Which nations were the original members of what became the European Union?

1000—the global population was 254–345 million people. A thousand years later, in a symbolic gesture, the United Nations declared October 12, 1999, as the Day of Six Billion, or D6B: the date when the planet's human population reached six billion. In actuality, this milestone was probably reached earlier that year. In the year 2000, about 6.1 billion people were alive on Earth. Globalization and technological advances linked humanity on a worldwide scale as never before in history. Personal computers, cellular phones, and the Internet allowed people from around the world to communicate directly. These connections meant that people were both spreading facets of their own cultures and embracing aspects of others. Different characteristics influenced everything from architecture to music to art.

e-Commerce Electric commerce, or e-commerce, dates to the 1940s. But with the birth of the World Wide Web in 1993, goods and services became available to a much wider audience. In 1994, Jeff Bezos started selling books online at Amazon.com, and the company soon branched out to include other merchandise. The online site now known as eBay launched in 1995. Its business model relied on auctions and trade, and eBay's millionth item was sold only two years later. PayPal, a company primarily used for Internet monetary transactions, emerged in 2000 (and was purchased by eBay in 2002). By 2000, 400 million people around the globe were able to buy and sell goods and services on the Internet. The Amazon fulfillment center in Swansea, Wales, (shown above) covers more than 800,000 square feet.

Mars Exploration On July 4, 1997, the Mars Pathfinder spacecraft—which included a rover named after Sojourner Truth—landed on the red planet. Sojourner spent 2.5 months collecting data, hoping to find evidence of life or circumstances that could support it. The Mars Polar Lander/Deep Space 2 mission, launched in 1999, aimed to dig for water, but the lander and its probes crashed to the surface. NASA exploration rovers Spirit (shown at left) and Opportunity landed on Mars in 2004. Their main goal was to search for evidence of past water activity.

Growth in Dubai By the end of the millennium, Dubai—a city-state in the United Arab Emirates—had started to transform itself from a small fishing and trading community into a luxurious international hot spot. In the 1980s, the government made a deliberate economic shift toward high-end tourism, finance, and communications. Dubai is also home to the tallest building in the world, Burj Khalifa, which was completed in 2010 and stands at 2,723 feet—that's more than half a mile!

▲ **Hip-Hop** Hip-hop—which includes deejaying, rapping, painting graffiti, and dancing—moved to the center of the U.S. stage in the 1980s and 1990s. Run D.M.C. (above) were the first rappers to have a gold album and the first to have a video air on MTV. Other notable hip-hop artists of the era were Public Enemy, Queen Latifah, N.W.A., Salt-N-Pepa, Notorious B.I.G., and Tupac Shakur. By the late 1990s, hip hop was the largest selling genre of music in the United States, and its style and influence began to dominate global pop culture.

▶ **The Latin Explosion** At the 1999 Grammy Awards, Puerto Rican Ricky Martin kicked off what later became known as "The Latin Explosion." Singing in English—and then in Spanish—Martin's dynamic performance of "La Copa de La Vida" (The Cup of Life) led to his mainstream success. Other Latino artists, including Marc Anthony, Enrique Iglesias, and Jennifer Lopez, followed. Lopez had portrayed Tejano singer Selena (right) in a biopic, bringing her story to a wider audience. Selena, who sang in Spanish but was working on an English album, was shot and killed by a former employee in 1995.

Afrofuturism In the early 1990s, academic Mark Dery coined the term *Afrofuturism* in the essay "Black to the Future." The concept had already been around for decades, but Dery gave a name to the intersection of black culture, including the African Diaspora, with technology and science fiction. He asked, "Can a community whose past has been deliberately rubbed out, and whose energies have subsequently been consumed by the search for legible traces of its history, imagine possible futures?"

Afrofuturism reached the global mainstream more recently in 2018's blockbuster film *Black Panther*. It was the highest-grossing movie that year. The fictional, never-colonized African nation of Wakanda disguises itself—and hides its highly advanced technology—to the rest of the world. But its new king, T'Challa, wonders if he should open up Wakanda's borders. Production designer Hannah Beachler and costume designer Ruth E. Carter both won Academy Awards for their work on the movie. They also made history by being the first African Americans to receive Oscars in their respective categories. Carter researched many cultures in Africa and then put her own modern twist on the clothing she produced. "This futuristic African film that's based on indigenous tribes connects the beginning and the future," she says.

Black Panther first appeared in a July 1966 comic book but was then sidelined. In 1998, Christopher Priest—the first black writer and editor in comics—reintroduced the character in a series.

According to *Black Panther* costume designer Ruth E. Carter, the spy Nakia's traditional costume (shown above) "is inspired by the Surma and the Suri people of Africa." Carter used a green color palate to connect all of the character's many outfits.

HISTORICAL THINKING

1. **READING CHECK** What two innovations linked people at the end of the second millennium on a scale never before seen in history?

2. **COMPARE AND CONTRAST** How do the examples of Afrofuturism you've read about differ, and how are they alike?

3. **MAKE PREDICTIONS** How do you think Afrofuturism will evolve in the future?

CHAPTER 29 CONFLICTS AND TRANSFORMATIONS
REVIEW

VOCABULARY

Complete each of the following sentences using one of the vocabulary words from the chapter.

1. Sit-ins, protest marches, and boycotts are all examples of _____.

2. Through his policy of _____, Mikhail Gorbachev encouraged an open discussion of political issues.

3. Several nonprofit groups, or _____, work to protect human rights all over the world.

4. A formerly unstable country begins the process of _____ to establish a functioning government.

5. The embrace of _____ led to the formation of many free-trade blocs.

6. In 1987, Palestinians began a multiyear _____ to protest Israel's presence in Gaza and the West Bank.

7. Companies that have ownership and management teams in more than one country are _____.

8. Moving a U.S. company's technology helpdesk to India is an example of _____.

READING STRATEGY
ANALYZE CAUSE AND EFFECT

When you identify causes and effects, you can examine and determine what different events might have in common. Complete the following chart to identify causes and effects related to major political transformations of the late 20th century. Then answer the question that follows.

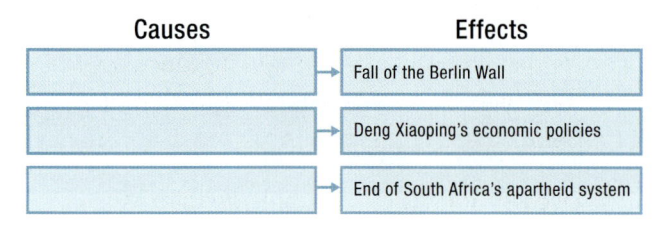

Causes	Effects
	Fall of the Berlin Wall
	Deng Xiaoping's economic policies
	End of South Africa's apartheid system

9. Describe ways in which ordinary people, as opposed to government officials, brought about one or more of the major transformations listed in the chart.

MAIN IDEAS

Answer the following questions. Support your answers with evidence from the chapter.

10. What changes in the late 1980s weakened Soviet control in Hungary? **LESSON 1.1**

11. What role did Boris Yeltsin play in the coup launched against Gorbachev? **LESSON 1.3**

12. What challenges did China's economic transformation present to the Chinese government? **LESSON 1.4**

13. Why were elections considered unfair during the period in which the Institutional Revolutionary Party (PRI) ruled Mexico? **LESSON 2.1**

14. Which two nations both claim Kashmir as their territory? **LESSON 2.3**

15. Which events from the 20th century explain the ongoing conflict between Palestinians and Israelis? **LESSON 3.2**

16. What role did Osama bin Laden play in the development of radical Islamic fundamentalism? **LESSON 3.3**

17. What are three ways in which the United Nations helped the cause of human rights in the 20th century? **LESSON 4.1**

HISTORICAL THINKING

Answer the following questions. Support your answers with evidence from the chapter.

18. **IDENTIFY SUPPORTING DETAILS** How did Ronald Reagan put pressure on the Soviet Union?

19. **DRAW CONCLUSIONS** When Lithuania declared its independence, why did Gorbachev decline to take military action against the new republic?

20. **MAKE CONNECTIONS** How did the United States apply Harry Truman's policy of containment in Central America?

21. **SUMMARIZE** How did Golda Meir influence the world in the 20th century?

22. **COMPARE AND CONTRAST** How was life in Iran different under Shah Mohammed Reza Pahlavi than under Ayatollah Khomeini?

23. **FORM AND SUPPORT OPINIONS** Do you think children in developing countries benefited more or suffered more because of 20th-century globalization? Explain.

INTERPRET MAPS

Study the map below, which shows the British Isles and the countries on each island.

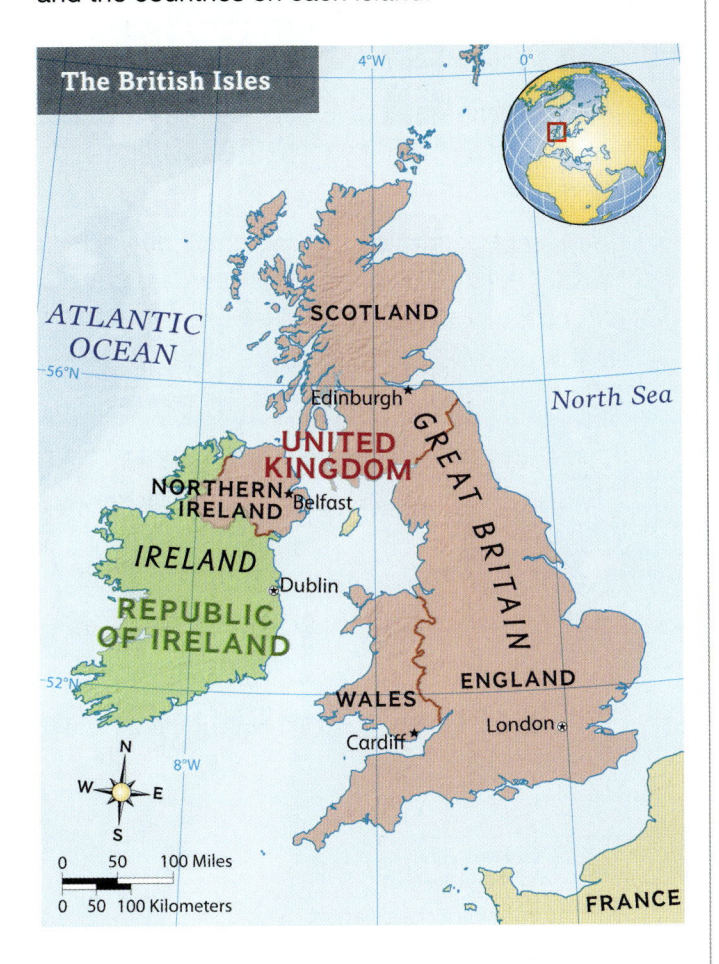

24. Northern Ireland is a part of what country?

25. How did geography contribute to the political conflict that plagued Northern Ireland?

ANALYZE SOURCES

Boutros Boutros-Ghali served as secretary-general of the United Nations from 1992 to 1996. In this excerpt from a 1996 speech, he describes the benefits and costs of economic globalization. Read the excerpt and answer the question that follows.

> The global economy is now a fact of life. In the economic field, large companies are feeling the impact of technological progress and new production methods. . . . Globalization brings progress. It should be encouraged. But dangers remain. The global economy can be hard on those unable to benefit from its opportunities. Traditional ties of community and solidarity can be undermined. Whole countries and regions can become marginalized. So the gap between rich and poor grows even wider.

26. Based on the excerpt, what are the advantages and disadvantages of globalization?

CONNECT TO YOUR LIFE

27. **INFORMATIVE** The costs and benefits of NAFTA depended on one's role. Write a short speech that you would deliver to a U.S. congressional hearing on this trade agreement. Choose the perspective of an American, Canadian, or Mexican business owner, farmer, or industrial worker.

TIPS

- Review the section about NAFTA in the text, taking note of who benefited and who lost ground under NAFTA.

- Decide which role you want to take. Make a list of ways in which NAFTA benefited you and ways in which it hurt you. Remember that NAFTA may affect the same person in different ways. For example, workers are also consumers.

- Prepare your speech. Be sure to identify your role. Use language appropriate to a hearing before the U.S. Congress.

- Use key vocabulary from the chapter in your speech.

- Conclude your speech with a clear statement that summarizes the costs and benefits.

Conflicts and Transformations 869

CHAPTER 30

A Global 21st Century
2000–Present

HISTORICAL THINKING What challenges does the world face in the 21st century?

SECTION 1 **The Political Picture**
SECTION 2 **The Economic Picture**
SECTION 3 **Science and Technology**
SECTION 4 **Visions for the Future**

CRITICAL VIEWING
Double-decker buses, taxis, shoppers, and tourists are a constant presence in London's Piccadilly Square. With a population of 8.8 million, London isn't the largest city in the world—that honor goes to Shanghai, China—but it is one of the most ethnically diverse. What challenges might a city like London face on a daily basis?

A Global 21st Century

1.1

MAIN IDEA The attacks of September 11 led the United States to take military action to combat terrorism, which had a great impact on the countries of Afghanistan and Iraq.

September 11 and Aftermath

Most people never forget tragic events that took place in their lifetimes. Events such as the assassination of President John F. Kennedy or the explosion of the space shuttle *Challenger* were etched into the minds of people of the times. Relatives older than you likely remember exactly what they were doing when terrorists struck on September 11, 2001.

Firefighters walk among the smoldering rubble of the World Trade Center following the September 11 terrorist attack.

A TRAGIC DAY

As the 21st century dawned, dreams that peace could finally triumph over conflict quickly ended on September 11, 2001. Nineteen **extremists**, people with radical views, hijacked four airplanes in the United States. They then turned them into weapons of destruction.

The terrorists crashed two planes into the twin towers of the World Trade Center—the tallest buildings in New York City. A third plane hit the Pentagon just outside Washington, D.C., while the fourth crashed into a Pennsylvania field. In all, almost 3,000 civilians were killed. The terrorist group al Qaeda had planned the attack. As you have already learned, one of the leaders of al Qaeda was Osama bin Laden, a former U.S. ally in the fight against the Soviet Union in Afghanistan. Embittered by U.S. support for "moderate" Arab regimes and Israel and seeking revenge for the oppression they thought was faced by Muslims across the world, bin Laden and al Qaeda intended the attack as a warning to the United States.

A "WAR ON TERROR"

In response to the September 11 attacks, U.S. president George W. Bush declared a "war on terror." In October 2001, he sent U.S. forces to Afghanistan to defeat the

Taliban, who had aided al Qaeda. An international coalition joined in the attack. Though battered, al Qaeda and Taliban fighters avoided capture. Since then, the Taliban has continued its fight to oust Afghanistan's internationally recognized government. Bin Laden continued to assail Western ideas, staging terrorist attacks in Yemen, Kenya, Saudi Arabia, Spain, and Britain. His reign of terror would end with his capture and killing by U.S. Navy Seals in 2011.

In 2003, President Bush carried his fight against terrorism to Saddam Hussein's Iraq, claiming that Hussein had stockpiled **weapons of mass destruction** (WMDs) that could destroy large areas. But many people believed that Iraq had no connection to al Qaeda or the events of September 11, and the WMDs were never found. With the British as their only ally, U.S. forces removed Saddam Hussein from power. The despotic leader was later tried and executed by the Iraqi people in 2006. The war in Iraq continued until 2011 as U.S. and British forces tried to quell insurgents in revolt against the new Iraqi republic. They faced Shiite militias funded by neighboring Iran as well as Sunni terrorists backed by al Qaeda. The United States had shifted the balance between Sunni and Shiite Muslims in the region by removing the Sunni leader of Iraq and allowing greater Shiite influence in the region, strengthening Iran. Meanwhile, in the north, Kurdish forces tried to establish their own autonomous area.

To combat terrorism, the United States and other nations strengthened airport security. The United States also created a new cabinet department called the Department of Homeland Security. In addition, nations refined their intelligence-gathering operations to prevent terrorist acts. In doing so, they made greater use of **surveillance**, methods for observing and tracking a person or group, a practice that many believe violates the right to privacy.

CRITICAL VIEWING Iraqis attempt to pull down a statue of Saddam Hussein in central Baghdad in April 2003. Why might citizens want to take down statues of their former leader?

THE RISE OF ISIS

By 2014, the U.S. withdrawal from Iraq left a power vacuum that the extremist group **Islamic State of Iraq and Syria (ISIS)**, also known as the Islamic State of Iraq and the Levant (ISIL), attempted to fill. It took advantage of instability in the region to try to create a new caliphate, a global center for Sunni Muslim power like the old Abbasid caliphate centered in Baghdad, which you learned about in an earlier chapter. ISIS fighters set to work gaining strongholds in parts of Iraq. The United States was reluctant to return troops to Iraq to halt their advance.

Terrorism continued to spread. Al Qaeda-backed gunmen killed 67 people in a siege on a Kenyan mall in 2013. Then in 2015, two gunmen shouting *"Allahu Akbar!" (God is Great!)* struck Paris. They opened fire in the offices of a French satire magazine, killing 12 people and wounding 11 others. The magazine had published cartoons of the Prophet Muhammad mocking Islamic terrorists. As of early 2019, ISIS had been driven out of many of its prior strongholds in Syria, but military intelligence indicates that many fighters simply fled to other parts of Syria, Turkey, and Iraq.

HISTORICAL THINKING

1. **READING CHECK** What action did the United States take to respond to the September 11 terrorist attack?

2. **FORM AND SUPPORT OPINIONS** Was George W. Bush's decision to invade Iraq in 2003 helpful or hurtful to the war on terrorism? Explain your response.

3. **DRAW CONCLUSIONS** What are the main stumbling blocks preventing the formation of a stable and democratic Iraqi government?

A Global 21st Century

1.2

MAIN IDEA Citizens of Arab countries sought democratic reform during what has become known as the Arab Spring, but few advances were achieved.

Arab Spring, Syrian Crisis

In the 21st century, social media plays a major role in connecting people around the world. In 2011, it even contributed to a time of revolution across the Arab world.

AN ARAB SPRING

Citizen outrage at autocratic leadership was slow to come to Muslim countries in Asia and Africa. However, in 2009 Iranians took to the streets of Tehran to protest a presidential election they considered fixed. Then in December 2010, a frustrated produce seller in rural Tunisia publicly set himself on fire in protest of harsh police action against him. This individual action inspired citizens throughout Tunisia to gather in mass protest against its government. Less than a month later, before the end of January 2011, Tunisia's president of 23 years resigned.

The success in Tunisia ignited citizen revolutions known as the **Arab Spring** across North Africa and Southwest Asia. The protesters, many of them young, turned out to agitate for **social justice**, or equal rights for all under the law. In Egypt, throngs of protesters in Cairo's Tahrir Square rose up against President Hosni Mubarak, eventually gaining the support of the military. A revolt by the citizens of Libya against their totalitarian leader, Muammar Qaddafi, led to armed conflict. In both cases, the end result was the overthrow of an autocratic leader. Other countries such as Yemen, Bahrain, and Syria also saw protests against authoritarian rulers.

Internet-based social media was a driving force in the Arab Spring. Young Arab bloggers spread news of injustices committed by repressive governments. Organizers spread word on Twitter of when and where

Egyptians rally in Cairo's Tahrir Square in February 2011 in hopes of pressuring President Hosni Mubarak to step down.

protests would take place. Activists posted cell-phone images and videos of mass demonstrations and of violence against protesters on social media.

Yet revolutions are not completed overnight, as you have seen in earlier efforts, and the optimism of the Arab Spring turned to disappointment. In Egypt, military and political elites regained control of the nation. In Libya, citizens continue to suffer as rival militias battle it out. Syria also remains mired in conflict.

PROBLEMS IN SYRIA

Despite calls for his resignation by hundreds of thousands of protesters, Syrian president **Bashir Al-Assad** refused to step down. Rebel groups formed to

A Kurdish refugee mother and her son walk beside their tent in a refugee camp on the Turkish-Syrian border in 2014. Many Syrian Kurds fled to Turkey to escape ISIS militants during the ongoing civil war in Syria.

battle with Assad and his Syria Arab Army in a civil war. ISIS fighters also joined the fray, as did Kurdish fighters who hoped for independence. By 2018, more than 400,000 Syrians had died in the fighting. Assad has been accused of using chemical weapons against rebels and civilians. Other charges against him include the targeting of civilians, torture, and the turning away of humanitarian assistance. The civil war entered a new phase with the use of **drones**, pilotless aircraft, to bomb enemy sites.

Syria's conflict has created tensions around the world. Rebel forces have the support of the United States, Britain, and France. Turkey, Saudi Arabia, and Jordan also support the rebel cause. Russia and Iran, on the other hand, back Assad financially and militarily. Yet Russia has joined with Western nations to force ISIS from the region. The militant group Hezbollah has provided military help to the Syrian government.

The war has caused many Syrian civilians to be **displaced**, or forced from their homes. More than six million refugees, mostly women and children, have moved elsewhere in Syria. Another nearly five million have sought refuge in other countries. Some of these now make their homes in refugee camps in countries such as Turkey and Jordan.

A stream of refugees from Syria and other troubled countries have sought **asylum**, or a place of safety, in Europe. While some countries have opened their borders to refugees, others have closed them. Hungary even erected a razor wire fence on much of its southern border to prevent refugees from crossing through the country on their way to Germany, which had a much more welcoming policy. In some countries, people fear that refugees may put a strain on their resources. **Xenophobia**, or fear of foreigners, also encourages anti-immigrant propaganda and support for far-right politicians and candidates who would deny human rights to refugees. Far-right politicians have won seats in the legislatures of such countries as Italy, Poland, Denmark, and Hungary.

HISTORICAL THINKING

1. **READING CHECK** How are the Arab Spring and the Syrian crisis related?

2. **EVALUATE** Explain how you would rate the success of the Arab Spring.

3. **MAKE PREDICTIONS** What do you think the situation will be like in Syria in five years? Explain your answer.

A Global 21st Century

1.3

MAIN IDEA Instability and ongoing conflicts have rocked Southwest Asia for years, but many people, including several National Geographic Explorers, are working to bring peace and stability to the region.

The Future of Southwest Asia

"The cradle of civilization," "the birthplace of three religions," "a trading crossroads" . . . Southwest Asia has long been a source of opportunity—and challenges. With ongoing conflicts and transitions throughout the region, the world watches to see what the future will bring.

DEFINING THE MIDDLE EAST

You have probably heard the region of Southwest Asia more commonly referred to as the "Middle East." However, people who live there do not call it that. That terminology is a Western construct that came about after World War I. Prior to the First World War, most of Southwest Asia was part of the Ottoman Empire. After the war and the decline of the empire, many people in that region hoped for their own independent states. Instead, as you may recall, Britain and France divided the area into states that they controlled, which they then called the Middle East. After the end of British and French colonialism, Westerners continued to use the term.

There is also no standard definition of the Middle East—though it is generally considered to consist of the countries of the Arabian Peninsula, Cyprus, Egypt, Iraq, Iran, Israel, Jordan, Lebanon, the Palestinian territories, Syria, and Turkey. At times, Afghanistan, Pakistan, and North African nations west of Egypt are also included.

As you've learned, this area has a rich history of trade and culture that continues to the present day. Two-thirds of the world's oil supply comes from this region, and nations that are the largest consumers of oil depend on that supply. The demand for oil brings wealth and power—as well as conflict—to the countries that produce it. But oil is not the only source of discord. Claims over disputed territory, ethnic and religious differences, and competition over other resources continue to create conflict in the region.

PRESERVING THE PAST TO BUILD THE FUTURE

According to the United Nations, the preservation of cultural heritage and identity is key to promoting stability in the Middle East. As you have seen in some of the Preserving Cultural Heritage lessons in this text,

876 CHAPTER 30

violent extremists often target sites of cultural importance along with human lives to destroy anything that doesn't fit within their system of beliefs. In addition to destruction by terrorism or extremism, cultural heritage sites are also falling victim to companies that want to extract valuable resources from their locations.

What does the future hold for this region? While no one can know for sure, many people are striving for peace and stability and working to preserve its culture for future generations. National Geographic is working with some of those people—educators, paleoanthropologists, archaeologists, peace activists—toward a brighter future.

BUILDING BRIDGES

As the Israeli-Palestinian conflict continues, we often hear stories of destruction and loss. However, there are also positive tales. And National Geographic Explorer Aziz Abu Sarah is helping people tell them. A cultural educator and peace activist, Abu Sarah works to help people find common ground through personal stories and cross-cultural learning in an attempt to bring peace to the region.

As a Palestinian and a native of Jerusalem, Abu Sarah has experienced firsthand the devastating damage from disputes in the region. When he was a young boy, his older brother, Tayseer, was arrested for suspicion of throwing stones. While in custody, Tayseer was beaten and later died from his injuries. Angered by Tayseer's death, Abu Sarah wanted revenge and was motivated to strike back. He became politically active, and by age 16 he was leading and organizing protests and writing political articles.

After high school, he realized that to live in Jerusalem he needed to learn Hebrew, something he had refused to do growing up. He went to an Israeli school to study the language. For the first time, he met Israelis who were not soldiers. As the only Palestinian in the class,

NATIONAL GEOGRAPHIC EXPLORER AZIZ ABU SARAH

Connecting Cultures

Palestinian Aziz Abu Sarah spent several years in the resistance movement against Israel. But he is now committed to fostering mutual understanding and improving relationships between people from different backgrounds. "I decided to dedicate my life to bringing down the walls that separate people," explains Abu Sarah.

he kept to himself at first but soon started talking to the other students. And at this point, things changed for Abu Sarah.

Through his conversations with Jewish classmates, Abu Sarah became aware of things that they had in common, such as a love of country music. He realized that what separates people isn't politics or the land but an emotional wall—a wall built of anger, fear, and ignorance. As he got to know his fellow students, those fearful preconceptions disappeared. "When that wall goes away, it's amazing how you can come together," says Abu Sarah.

From that point, he decided to take a different form of action. Instead of protesting, Abu Sarah committed himself to creating cracks in the metaphorical walls that divide Israelis and Palestinians. Today, he creates opportunities for dialogue among people on opposite sides of the conflict through education, tours, and personal narratives. He started a company called Mejdi Tours to foster peace by bringing tourists to Jerusalem with two guides—one Jewish and one Palestinian—so that people can learn about the history and narrative of the city from different perspectives.

And Abu Sarah isn't stopping with the Israelis and Palestinians; he has added tours to Iran, Turkey, and other regions with cultural and political struggles. His goal is international conflict resolution.

BRINGING LIGHT INTO THE DARK

Science and comedy may not seem like they go together. But to paleoanthropologist and archaeologist—and stand-up comic—Ella Al-Shamahi, comedy is a great tool for presenting scientific research. Al-Shamahi specializes in Neanderthals, studying their evolution and migration. She's searching for the origins of humanity. (You read that a Neanderthal is a member of an extinct species of early humans.)

Al-Shamahi is passionate about Neanderthals, and it's her mission to change our impressions of them. As the host and producer of the BBC/PBS two-part documentary, *Neanderthals: Meet Your Ancestors*, she worked with actor Andy Serkis to shed light on just what kind of people these early humans were. Even though the title of the series names Neanderthals as our "ancestors," modern-day people are not directly descended from this species. But recall that some individuals who have some European or Asian ancestry may have inherited Neanderthal DNA.

Al-Shamahi's work has taken her into conflict zones in Yemen and Iraq, underexplored areas that have much to offer in terms of early human history and culture.

In Yemen, her search for fossils is to test a theory that early humans may have migrated out of Africa via land bridges between East Africa and Yemen. Yemen has been in a state of civil war since 2015, so Al-Shamahi had to cut back her fieldwork there. The fighting has destroyed many cultural sites, including UNESCO World Heritage Sites. Today, along with digging for fossils, Al-Shamahi is trying to bring awareness to the destruction of Yemeni heritage and is working to preserve these historic sites.

Working in unstable places can take its toll, however, so Al-Shamahi uses comedy to brighten dark situations. She notes, "I'm the stereotype of the comic who does comedy because she needs to laugh." She also finds that comedy provides a way to engage people in science. When she's not excavating ancient remains or safeguarding cultural treasures, she's performing her comedy in London and internationally.

NATIONAL GEOGRAPHIC EXPLORER ELLA AL-SHAMAHI

Funny Bones

Ella Al-Shamahi contemplates a cast of a Neanderthal skull in her lab at the Anthropology Department of University College London. She uses humor to relieve stress, as her work often takes her to dangerous areas torn by strife. Al-Shamahi believes that these places "deserve narratives of hope, and science and exploration can be a part of that."

As the war continues in Yemen, the country's future seems dim. But Al-Shamahi believes preservation of Yemen's historic sites provides some hope. She says that Yemenis are proud of their heritage and know the importance of protecting those cultural places. "When you see devastation to our sites, you see Yemenis kick up a fuss about it." By giving its people the tools and solutions to preserve their culture, Yemen can gain strength.

SAVING OUR HERITAGE

As you have already learned, war causes destruction and robs a country of its heritage. Since the war began in Syria in 2011, countless historic sites and treasures have been destroyed. About 90 percent of Syria's cultural sites are located in areas of fighting and civil unrest. Syrian-born archaeologist Salam Al Kuntar has made it her mission to preserve not only the past but also the future of her war-torn homeland's heritage.

Before the war, Al Kuntar lived in Damascus and worked as the codirector of excavations at the Chalcolithic/Bronze Age site of Hamoukar. But the constant threat of bombings during the war meant she would not be safe doing her work in that area. So Al Kuntar accepted a position as a research scholar at the Penn Museum of the University of Pennsylvania.

Her work with Syria didn't end after she arrived in the United States. In response to the destruction of archaeological sites in her homeland, she helped design and implement a training program for the emergency preservation of Syrian artifacts. Collaborating with the Smithsonian Institution and a network of Syrian scholars in Europe along with a group of heritage professionals inside Syria, she and her colleagues have been able to provide much-needed emergency preservation work and conservation materials and training to salvage damaged collections and sites during the conflict.

Today, Al Kuntar is an assistant professor of archaeology at Rutgers University in New Jersey and a cofounder and board member of Syrians for Heritage (SIMAT), an organization striving to preserve Syrian heritage for all Syrians and for the rest of the world.

NATIONAL GEOGRAPHIC EXPLORER SALAM AL KUNTAR

Protecting Traditions

Salam Al Kuntar wants to make sure that Syrian customs and items will survive a brutal war that has been raging in the country since 2011. The unrest caused her to move to the United States, where she continues to advocate for the preservation of valuable sites and artifacts. "For me," Al Kuntar says, "keeping that connection alive and building on it to preserve the spirit of the people is important."

PHOTOGRAPHING SHARBAT GULA

For more than 30 years, National Geographic photographer Steve McCurry has been capturing the spirit of human struggle and joy all over the world with his compelling color photography. In 1984, he documented the plight of Afghan refugees who fled Afghanistan during the Soviet invasion. His work took him to a refugee tent camp in Pakistan, where he took pictures of young students in the school tent. The last photo he took was of a 12-year-old girl with piercing sea green eyes. This single haunting look came to represent the story of millions of refugees—and the tragedy of war.

The iconic photograph of the Afghan girl, as the photo came to be known, ran on the June 1985 cover of *National Geographic* magazine and became one of the

NATIONAL GEOGRAPHIC PHOTOGRAPHER STEVE MCCURRY

Solving A Mystery

The identity of the refugee in Steve McCurry's famous image was unknown for nearly two decades. McCurry found her in 2002 and was able to add a name to the face: Sharbat Gula. "She's as striking as the young girl I photographed 17 years ago," says McCurry.

most widely recognized photographs in the world. And although the photograph was well known, the young girl's name was not.

In 2002, after 17 years, National Geographic and McCurry returned to the same refugee camp in Pakistan to search for her. A local man recognized her photograph, and McCurry tracked her down in a small village in the mountains of the Afghanistan-Pakistan border. McCurry instantly knew the woman he met was her—she had the same eyes. And at long last, McCurry learned her name: Sharbat Gula.

For more than 30 years, Gula lived in Pakistan, surviving the wars and refugee camps. But in 2016, as an unregistered refugee, she was forced to return to Afghanistan. The Afghan government welcomed her back with a deed to her own home. Gula is one of the small percentage of women homeowners in the country. As someone recognized around the world, she has become a symbol again for the hundreds of thousands of refugees returning to Afghanistan.

RESCUING MES AYNAK

Conflict and war aren't the only threats to preserving Southwest Asia's cultural heritage. Mes Aynak, a 5,000-year-old Buddhist city in Afghanistan, is home to one of the most important archaeological finds in the region. It's also home to a large supply of copper ore that promises to bring a lot of business to a country greatly in need of an economic boost.

In 2007, the Afghan government granted China permission to extract copper from the site on a 30-

year lease. China bid three billion dollars and promised to provide infrastructure for the undeveloped region. Afghanistan would not only have much-needed revenue but better roads, railways, and electric grids.

While there were several challenges to getting the copper, the main issue was the preservation of many treasures and artifacts found at Mes Aynak. In a nation torn apart by successive wars, preserving any remnants of the rich history there is critical. Cultural heritage advocates lobbied to excavate the site's treasures and record them before any mining began—which was no easy task.

With time running out before the mining project began, archaeologists and conservationists worked to collect the artifacts before they disappeared. They also faced the risk of land mines left by the Soviets in the 1980s, explosive devices left by al Qaeda, and rocket attacks by the Taliban in 2012 and 2013.

Then the archaeologists got a lucky break. Scheduled to start in 2012, the mining project was suspended, due to logistical challenges. A lack of water and the lack of a railroad to transport the copper out of the region created major obstacles.

The delay wasn't good for business, but it gave the archaeologists more time to excavate. Today, decisions are still being made as to whether to allow the copper extraction to continue, which leaves the fate of Mes Aynak undetermined.

An Afghan worker walks through an ancient monastery at the Mes Aynak site in Afghanistan in this 2010 photo.

HISTORICAL THINKING

1. **READING CHECK** What is the current state of Southwest Asia?

2. **EVALUATE** What are the greatest challenges facing the region?

3. **FORM AND SUPPORT OPNIONS** What do you think are the best ways to preserve a culture and build for its future? Explain your response.

4. **EXPLAIN** Which of the explorers featured in the lesson do you find most interesting? Why?

A Global 21st Century 881

1.4

MAIN IDEA Enduring conflicts, support for authoritarian leaders, and opposing viewpoints have all influenced 21st-century events.

Breakdowns and Breakthroughs

Up to now, you've read about the distant and recent past. But events of today become history tomorrow. This lesson presents some of the history that has taken place during your lifetime.

ENDURING CONFLICTS AND RESOLUTION

Conflicts that stem from events long ago still present challenges in different parts of the world, but there has also been progress toward peace. For much of the 20th century, Ukraine was a part of the U.S.S.R. It gained independence as a democratic republic following the breakup of the Soviet Union. In 2013, as the fledgling democracy prepared to form an association with the European Union, the Russian-speaking minority backed a president whose plan was to align the country with Russia instead. Pro-democracy protesters thronged the Ukrainian capital of Kiev, eventually winning the corrupt president's ouster. Almost immediately, the eastern Ukrainian province of Crimea announced its secession, and Russia quickly annexed it. Fighting intensified between pro-Russian separatists and Ukrainian soldiers. A 2015 ceasefire did little to end the conflict. To date, the death toll has exceeded 10,000 people, many of whom were civilians not involved in the war. Then, in May 2019, the Ukrainians surprised the world by electing **Volodymyr Zelensky** president. Zelensky, a young comedian of Jewish heritage, had no ties to the old political system. By electing an outsider, the Ukrainians were gambling on a fresh start.

With the exception of the conflict between Russia and Ukraine, 21st-century foreign relations demonstrate that the Cold War is over for many countries. A number of former Soviet-satellite nations are members of the European Union, including Bulgaria, Estonia, Hungary, Lithuania, and Poland. Cuba began to reestablish economic ties with the United States in 2014. Vietnam, which remains communist, is on good diplomatic terms with Western countries. North Korea, however, is not part of this trend. For much of his time in office, North Korean leader **Kim Jong-un** has been belligerent toward democratic nations, and he has done little to ensure human rights or remove nuclear threats. In 2018, Kim Jong-un met with U.S. president Donald Trump and South Korean president Moon Jae-in, but future plans for closer ties seem uncertain.

Unmarked soldiers in full body armor and armed with assault rifles march away from a besieged Ukrainian military base in Crimea. The Russian government claimed the soldiers were members of locally organized self-defense groups protecting the residents of Crimea instead of Russian forces deployed to occupy the region.

Elsewhere in Asia, the Indian subcontinent's disputed region of Kashmir reflects the lasting effects of colonialism. As you have read, the question of who should control this far-northern region arose in 1947 when Britain partitioned its colony between India and Pakistan. After fighting for control of Kashmir, the two countries agreed to divide it. Since then, simmering tensions have periodically led to violence. Both nations have nuclear capabilities, so future war could be catastrophic. China's claim to parts of northern Kashmir also puts the region in peril. Given a choice, most Kashmir residents would prefer independence. However, in 2019, the Indian government revoked the region's decades-long special status as an autonomous region, creating a new conflict with Pakistan.

Continuing ethnic conflicts on the African continent also stem from European colonialism. You've already learned about the end of apartheid in South Africa and the Rwandan genocide at the end of the 20th century. In Sudan, civil war between the government and southern rebels carried over into the 21st century until a 2005 peace agreement led to the independence of South Sudan in 2011. But competition for oil meant that border skirmishes continued. Meanwhile, the world was shocked by another genocide, this time in Sudan's western region of **Darfur**. Sudan's longtime president, **Omar al-Bashir**, was indicted by the International Criminal Court for crimes against humanity, but he remained in power until ousted by a popular uprising in 2019. Elsewhere in Africa, Nigeria's Islamist militant group Boko Haram has ruthlessly fought for control of much of the countryside. Civil wars rage in Libya, Somalia, and the Central African Republic, and the International Criminal Court has launched an investigation into crimes against humanity in Burundi.

CHALLENGES TO DEMOCRACY

In the 20th century, millions of people worldwide yearned for democracy, but far fewer seem to be working toward this goal in the 21st century. This reality has caused the democratic system of government to become fragile. Often, citizens are unwilling or unable to prevent autocrats from usurping their rights. In Thailand, General Prayuth Chan-ocha and his military junta keep tight control of the government but promise a return to democracy. In Venezuela, the autocratic government of **Nicolas Maduro** has done little to solve such problems as crime, poverty, and a lack of food and electricity, and now there is a growing effort by opposition leaders to unseat him. This is unlikely as long as Maduro retains the support of the military. Myanmar's military government seemed to be improving its record on human rights, but in 2017 it began committing atrocities against a minority ethnic group, the Rohingya Muslims.

While Pakistan officially became an Islamic republic in 1956, it has alternated between civilian and military rule over the years. In 2001, ruling Pakistani general Pervez Musharraf claimed the presidency of his country. Shortly afterwards, Pakistan was drawn into the "War on Terror" launched by President George W. Bush in response to the 9/11 attacks. Hoping to maintain ties to the United States, Pakistan pledged to hunt out members of the Taliban and al Qaeda. However, Islamist sentiment remained strong in northwestern Pakistan near Afghanistan. The 2007 assassination of former prime minister Benazir Bhutto showed the extent of contention in Pakistani politics. Today, the country faces poverty, an unstable economy, internal ethnic conflicts, political corruption, terrorist attacks, and a tense political situation. Yet history was made in Pakistan in 2018 when a Hindu candidate defeated Muslim candidates for a seat in the previously all-Muslim legislature.

Turkey had long been a secular representative democracy, but the military frequently staged coups to gain control of government. In 2003, **Recep Tayyip Erdogan** (reh-JEHP ty-YEHP UR-doh-wahn) won election as Turkey's prime minister. As prime minister, he supported greater integration of Islam into government at the cost of secularism. Over time, Erdogan became more authoritarian in his rule, crushing opposition and limiting human rights. However, in 2010, he supported the passage of 26 constitutional amendments favoring democracy in a successful attempt to gain Turkey's entry into the European Union. Term limits on the office of prime minister led Erdogan to become Turkey's president, a less important office, in 2014. Two years later, he conducted a major purge of government following an unsuccessful coup attempt. In 2018, constitutional amendments strengthened the role of president.

Vladimir Putin has dominated Russia's politics for the entire 21st century, serving as president most of that time. Putin supported the U.S. "War on Terror" but otherwise has had a strained relationship with the United States and other democratic nations. In 2013, Putin angered the United States by providing refuge to classified document leaker Edward Snowden. To the dismay of many, he also initiated harsh laws against gays and lesbians and ordered cruel treatment of dissidents. Assistance to Iran, the Syrian government, and Crimean separatists have also placed Russia under fire. A U.S. investigation took place to determine whether Putin and other Russians interfered in the 2016 U.S. presidential elections. In 2018, Russian voters elected him to a fourth term as president, and in early 2020 he backed a proposed constitutional amendment that would allow him to run for two additional terms.

One beacon of democracy is Ethiopia, where the early 2000s saw rapid economic growth under an authoritarian government. Hopes for a more liberal political direction were raised in 2018 when a new prime minister, **Abiy Ahmed**, released imprisoned journalists, formed a government with more balanced regional representation, appointed women to more than half of

Rohingya refugees arrive on homemade rafts at an island off the coast of Bangladesh. Nearly 700,000 refugees have fled from Myanmar to neighboring Bangladesh since August 2017.

his cabinet positions, and extended a peace initiative to the country's long-time rival, neighboring Eritrea. Progress for Ethiopia, a U.S. ally with the largest military in Africa, will be a positive sign for the entire region.

You may wonder why democracy has become so fragile. Some experts point to 2008's Great Recession as a turning point for losing faith in democracy. (You will learn more about the causes and effects of this recession in the next lesson.) Others say that people began to believe that economic success is not contingent on democracy, citing China as proof.

RESPONSES TO GLOBALIZATION

As you have already learned, nation-states were created to unite people who share a language, culture, and religion. A unified government gave citizens a sense of identity and a source for solving conflicts and better meeting economic needs. Today, however, globalization has created challenges for nation-states. Issues such as protecting the environment or avoiding nuclear war cannot be solved by any one country alone. So organizations such as the United Nations have emerged, but they are not governments. This means there is no clear decision-maker for solving international problems. Nation-states are also challenged by non-state actors such as multinational corporations, offshore banks, and NGOs usually working on the ground to help poor communities. These private entities may have more influence on a nation's people than the nation itself.

Another problem is ethnic rivalry in a country that might tear it apart. The refugee crisis has also lessened loyalty to nation-states. In addition, mass media, especially social media, now unite people beyond their nation-states. For these reasons, nation-states no longer enjoy the autonomy they once had.

Perhaps as a response to increasing globalization, the early 2000s saw the rise of populism, which you learned is a movement that claims to represent the ordinary people over the established elite, in Europe and the United States. People have voted in favor of nationalism and expressed distrust for international groups. For example, citizens of the United Kingdom have voted for **Brexit**, or a British exit from the European Union. Populists generally oppose mass immigration; some are motivated by racism. Populist voters are often willing to accept authoritarian leaders who promise employment and economic growth at the expense of ==civil liberties==, or basic freedoms, and authoritarian leaders try to build support with propaganda about the opposition and condemnations of the free press. Some fear that such politicians herald a return to fascism.

In 2016, **Donald Trump**, running as a Republican on a populist platform, surprised much of the world with his victory over Democrat Hillary Clinton to become the 45th president of the United States. Clinton received almost three million votes more than Trump, but Trump won the Electoral College vote 306 to 232. Trump had promised to "Make America Great Again" by cutting taxes, renegotiating trade deals, curtailing Muslim immigration, and removing all illegal immigrants. He also pledged to reshape the U.S. Supreme Court, and so far he has had the opportunity to appoint two conservative justices. The passage of a Congressional tax package in 2017, that many say favors the rich, met an important economic goal. His administration has faced criticism for many actions, including its 2018 decision to separate newly arrived immigrant children from their parents. It is too early to tell whether Trump's 2018 trade tariffs on imports from other countries will positively or negatively affect the U.S. economy.

Trump's plan for a renegotiation of NAFTA, which opened Mexico to globalization, is one of many factors affecting the United States' neighbor to the south. Illegal immigration of Mexicans and refugees fleeing from Central America through Mexico to get to the United States is also an area of concern. Mexicans are pushed from their country for such reasons as unemployment, poverty, crime, and poor health care. They are pulled to the United States because of the perceived availability of jobs, the desire to reunite with family, and educational opportunities. Trump has promised his supporters that he will build a border wall to stop illegal entry.

Another problem for Mexico is the drug trade, which not only encourages violence but also government corruption. Extreme poverty is also a major issue in some Mexican states, such as Chiapas. Yet, starting in 2009, the number of Mexicans leaving the United States was greater than the number entering the country. The reasons for this shift may include a worsening U.S. economy and stricter border enforcement. In the meantime, however, the number of immigrants from Honduras, Guatemala, and El Salvador has increased, with those applying for refugee status citing widespread violence as a push factor and jobs as a pull factor in their decision to immigrate to the United States.

Another challenge to nation-states is a rebound of **religiosity**, or strong religious belief, in the 21st century. Religion now flourishes in Eastern Europe's formerly communist countries where atheism was once the rule. India was formed as a secular nation, but under the premiership of **Narendra Modi** the government has emphasized the country's essentially Hindu nature.

Western Europe and China may seem to be exceptions to the trend toward increased religiosity. But in many European countries, even many non-religious populists claim that their anti-immigration proposals are a defense of "Christian Europe." In China, attacks on religion have greatly increased in recent years. Christian churches have been closed, and in the far west as many as one million Muslims have been forced into concentration camps.

In many countries, debates rage between the religiously orthodox and secularists. In both Istanbul and Paris, people debate the issue of allowing women to wear headscarves. People in the United States are divided about the extent to which laws should be guided by conservative Christian beliefs. In Israel, ultra-orthodox rabbis work to impose their strict rules on more secular Jews. It is clear that religious belief will play a role in shaping political action in the coming years.

Supporters throw flower petals as Narendra Modi, leader of India's Bharatiya Janata Party (BJP), in 2014. The BJP, which has historically reflected Hindu nationalist positions, was part of a coalition that won a majority of seats in India's general election in 2014. Modi subsequently became prime minister.

HISTORICAL THINKING

1. **READING CHECK** What issues have caused problems for people throughout the world in the 21st century?

2. **DRAW CONCLUSIONS** Why is it important that such countries as Bulgaria, Estonia, Hungary, Lithuania, and Poland have joined the EU?

3. **MAKE PREDICTIONS** How do you think people will be united in the future?

A Global 21st Century 885

2.1

MAIN IDEA Economic globalization brought about a worldwide recession beginning in 2008.

Global Financial Crisis

Imagine scrimping and saving money for your future only to find that your savings are suddenly worth much less than you thought. Millions of people experienced this unfortunate situation during a major economic recession that began in 2008.

A TIME OF RECESSION

The interconnected world financial markets that resulted from globalization seemed strong as the 21st century began. In the United States, consumers eagerly bought new houses, and banks readily offered mortgages that kept payments low. **Subprime mortgages**, or loans to people with poor credit, encouraged people to buy more expensive homes even as the price of real estate increased due to all this activity. When home prices fell, many homeowners found they owed more than the value of their houses. The faltering economy left many people unemployed, and they could not pay their mortgages. Banks foreclosed, or took possession of these homes, leaving people with huge debts and nowhere to live. An economic domino effect caused stock exchanges around the world to drop. The New York Stock Exchange lost 22 percent of its value in a single week.

This period became known as the **Great Recession**. A **recession** is a period of reduced economic activity. Not since the Great Depression had the economy seen such a crisis. Panic spread across world financial markets as people faced the possibility of a collapse of the interconnected global banking and stock market systems. Banks and other financial institutions began to close.

Economists and world leaders decided that government intervention was needed to save more financial institutions from bankruptcy. U.S. president George W. Bush proposed a program that made $700 billion available to help financial institutions in the belief that they were "too big to fail"—in other words, their failure would bring down the whole economy. The United Kingdom organized a similar recovery operation. Some citizens voiced objection to the **bailout**, or financial rescue, of companies that made risky business decisions, but the infusion of cash kept many banks and investment houses in business.

Still, the world felt the effects of the recession. The United States and Europe faced high unemployment, and global markets shrank. The countries of the world had to make tough decisions. To recover, they could incur debt by borrowing money and cutting taxes. Or they could practice **fiscal austerity**, a debt-avoidance measure, by cutting spending and raising taxes.

GOVERNMENTS RESPOND

Under newly elected president Barack Obama, the United States provided a $787 billion **stimulus**, or incentive, package to strengthen the economy, an approach that had been advocated by British economist John Maynard Keynes during the Great Depression. The United Kingdom, by contrast, slashed spending and cut government services to avoid high debt. France offered a modest stimulus, and Ireland made harsh spending cuts. Greece was already deeply in debt, and a default on its debt would negatively affect all of Europe. Amid controversy, European Union members agreed to loan Greece money if it made deep spending cuts. Later, the EU would provide money to other struggling nations such as Spain and Italy. Meanwhile, members of the eurozone, EU nations using the euro, struggled to strengthen their currency.

The Great Recession had a huge effect on developing countries because they were highly dependent on imports for income. Financial disaster struck both Ireland and Iceland hard, leading to the failure of major banks. But Iceland emerged in better financial shape for several reasons. First, Ireland bailed out its banks, while Iceland let its banks collapse. Second, having its own currency (the króna) helped Iceland. The króna lost more value than Ireland's euro did, so Iceland gained

886 CHAPTER 30

Two employees of Christie's Auction House in London transport a corporate sign of Lehman Brothers, an investment bank. Lehman Brothers filed for the largest bankruptcy in U.S. history in September 2008, causing a ripple effect through global financial markets.

more purchasing power. Because of the devalued króna, Icelandic companies that chose to keep salaries the same actually lowered their employees' wages. However, this decision allowed the island nation to avoid the rising unemployment that affected other areas.

The financial crisis was not limited to North America and Western Europe. China was drawn into the recession because its exports to affected countries dropped severely. Highly dependent on trade with the West, Japan's economy sank dramatically as well. Developing countries found that their export products now sold for lower prices.

At the same time, the tremendous financial reserves that China had built up since the 1980s helped stabilize a global economy that now had multiple points of growth in Asia and Latin America. Though there was plenty of pain, there was no complete breakdown of international markets like the world had seen in the 1930s.

By 2015, the economic crisis had eased in some parts of the world. Europe, though, remained in a critical situation. Some displaced Europeans sought changes in government to address the situation. For example, Greek people were unhappy with the austerity measures foisted on them and voted out their government. The youth unemployment rate in Europe, especially in the southern part of the continent, remained high; in Italy, it was almost 32 percent in 2018. Throughout the world, a shift in wealth has taken place since the financial crisis. Today, the richest 1 percent of the world's population controls close to 50 percent of its wealth, and in 2017 the world's eight wealthiest families owned as much as the bottom 50 percent of the human population.

HISTORICAL THINKING

1. **READING CHECK** What did the 2008 financial crisis reveal about the world's economies?

2. **MAKE GENERALIZATIONS** Why did Europeans have such varied opinions about how to handle the financial crisis?

3. **CATEGORIZE** Why might the 2008 financial crisis not only be categorized as an economic challenge but also as a political challenge and a social challenge?

2.2 MAIN IDEA Globalization has affected people, nations, and capital in positive and negative ways.

The Impact of Globalization

For much of modern history, European countries and then the United States dominated the world's economy. Now the "rise of the rest" is leading to a world with multiple centers of economic power, such as in Asia.

EMERGING ECONOMIC PLAYERS

Despite the economic downturn that began in 2008, the global economic growth rate is now about three percent a year. Globalization has not only increased the world's overall wealth but also shifted it. Economic power is now more diversified, or balanced among countries.

The world economic shift stems from changes in world demographics. As the population soars in Asia, China—the world's most populous country, with over 1.4 billion people in 2018—is poised to have the largest economy of any nation by 2050. The market-oriented policies initiated by Deng Xiaoping have led China's economy to grow at nearly 10 percent a year. Yet this growth has come at the cost of damage to the environment and the spread of corruption. Thirty years after the Tiananmen Square Massacre, it was still unclear whether economic growth might lead to more liberal policies in China, but in the short run, the communist state was becoming more repressive than ever.

India's population of 1.35 billion in 2018 may well overtake China's by the early 2020s. India has used its huge present-day labor force to grow its economy through the production of high-tech and domestic goods. Add in modest growth in established economies, such as Japan, South Korea, and Taiwan, and dynamic growth in emerging economies, such as Vietnam, Malaysia, and Indonesia, and the future of Asia as an economic giant seems clear. Less certain is whether China's authoritarian government or India's democracy will be more successful.

The United States remains the world's economic leader but faces problems maintaining this position. Its aging population, shrinking workforce, and welfare and social security programs may stress its economy. Also, wage inequality, budgetary and trade deficits, and large amounts of money owed to foreign investors have all increased. Yet after the shock of 2008, the country's economy recovered, with GDP growing and unemployment falling by over half from 2012 to 2018.

By then, global trade had regained momentum lost through the economic recession. But problems loomed because of issues such as Brexit, a possible renegotiation of NAFTA, and the threat of tariffs—situations that might cause trade wars that would have a negative effect on economic growth. In the 21st century, it is growing more difficult to predict future winners in the race for economic success. Changes in leadership, loss of trade partners, and strikes or natural disasters can quickly turn an economy upside down.

ISSUES RELATED TO GLOBALIZATION

You have learned that globalization has affected the world in both positive and negative ways. Many people credit it with modernizing societies, but others say it has stripped them of their traditional cultures. Globalization

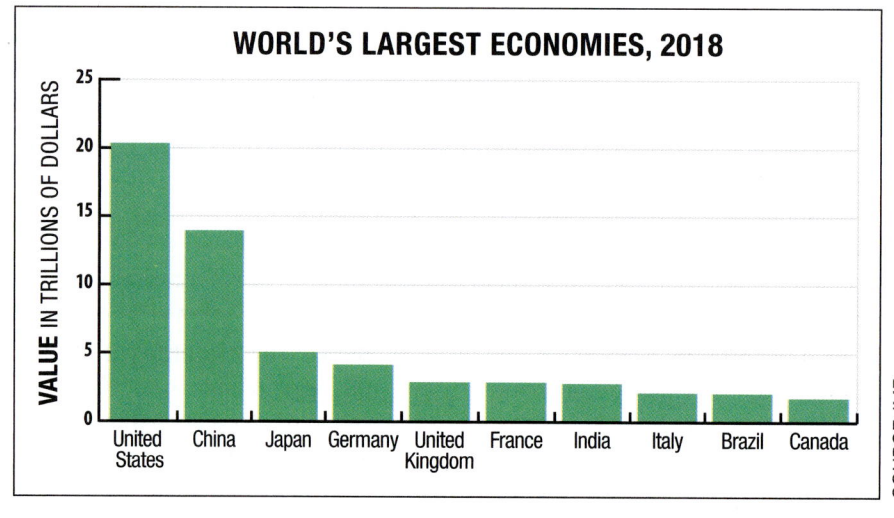

WORLD'S LARGEST ECONOMIES, 2018

Country	Value in Trillions of Dollars
United States	~20.5
China	~14
Japan	~5
Germany	~4
United Kingdom	~2.8
France	~2.7
India	~2.6
Italy	~2
Brazil	~2
Canada	~1.7

SOURCE: IMF

CRITICAL VIEWING A woman sews garments in Dhaka, the largest city and capital of Bangladesh. What can you infer about the job and its working conditions based on the details in the photograph?

has led to transnational organizations such as Amnesty International and Greenpeace that work to better the world. But it has also allowed the growth of both criminal and terrorist groups that want to advance their own interests at the expense of the rest of the world. International crimes include the illegal transport of drugs and weapons, human trafficking, and unlawful Internet activities. Terrorist groups commit violent acts against symbolic targets around the globe and use social media to gain new followers worldwide. However, Internet cooperation can also help prevent terrorist attacks.

People also disagree about the costs and benefits of multinational corporations. On the plus side, corporations bring jobs to various parts of the world. For example, workers in the United States, China, Taiwan, South Korea, and other nations contribute to manufacturing cell phones. People in developing countries may learn new skills in careers they never imagined. Their countries benefit from the infusion of money. In all these ways, the standard of living in developing nations improves.

On the minus side, many people claim that the corporations exploit the workers and natural resources of developing countries. These critics say that the corporations are more concerned about profits than about environmental deterioration and human rights abuses in the countries in which they do business. They also claim that foreign workers must adapt to the home country of multinational corporations. For example, workers in India might have to work through the night to be at their desks at the same time as their American counterparts.

HISTORICAL THINKING

1. **READING CHECK** What evidence supports the prediction that Asia will become an economic powerhouse by the mid-21st century?

2. **DRAW CONCLUSIONS** Why might U.S. budgetary and trade deficits become problems for the economy of the United States?

3. **FORM AND SUPPORT OPINIONS** Which country do you think has the best chance of solving such problems as violence, corruption, and instability—China or India? Explain your response.

A Global 21st Century

2.3 DOCUMENT-BASED QUESTION
Income Inequality

A trip to India can provide a crash course on income inequality. In the large city of Mumbai, you can marvel at how an emphasis on high technology has transformed the country economically. For example, many Indians use electric trains to get to their information processing jobs. Yet you will see a stark contrast between the wealthy and the poor. High walls protect glistening new suburbs from the noise and filth of overcrowded slums. And in rural areas, hundreds of millions of Indians live without clean water or basic sanitation.

Globalization has generated economic growth, but it has also caused rising income inequality. Money and goods move freely around the world, but workers do not have a similar mobility. They must try to eke out a living wherever they are, which is often where they were born. Many companies based in industrialized countries have moved their manufacturing plants to developing nations. These business decisions mean that some jobs are exported at a cost to workers in the industrialized nations. And workers in the developing countries have few choices but to accept the low wages offered. In many cases, children have to work to help their families survive.

You may have heard the expression "The rich get richer and the poor get poorer." The French economist Thomas Piketty concludes that structures of capitalism trend toward increasing inequality over time, which supports the saying. In his book *Capital in the Twenty-First Century*, he says that people with inherited money and property will always earn more income than people who can only offer labor and that market economies result in a gap between the "haves" and "have-nots" that grows bigger over time. So without corrective action, a disparity between rich and poor will continue within and among countries.

DOCUMENT ONE

Primary Source: Chart
Richest and Poorest Countries by Income

The extent of income inequality among nations is determined by examining various factors, including the use of economic measurement tools. One measure is the GDP (gross domestic product) per capita of a nation, which tells how much an individual would earn if the GDP of a country was divided evenly among everyone who lived in the country. Of course, people do not share equally in a nation's wealth, but comparing different countries' GDP per capita informs people of the extent of income inequality between nations.

CONSTRUCTED RESPONSE Based on the chart, what generalizations can you make about the countries with the lowest GDPs per capita?

Sampling of Richest and Poorest Countries by Income

HIGH GDP PER CAPITA		LOW GDP PER CAPITA	
Country	GDP Per Capita	Country	GDP Per Capita
Qatar	$124,500	Burundi	$700
Monaco	$115,700	Mozambique	$1,200
Singapore	$93,900	Malawi	$1,200
Brunei	$78,200	Yemen	$1,300
Norway	$71,800	South Sudan	$1,500
United States	$59,500	North Korea	$1,700
Saudi Arabia	$54,800	Afghanistan	$2,000
Germany	$50,400	Rwanda	$2,100
Australia	$50,300	Uganda	$2,400
Japan	$42,800	Kenya	$3,500

Latest available year per country **Source:** https://www.cia.gov/library/publications/the-world-factbook/rankorder/2004rank.html

DOCUMENT TWO

Primary Source: Chart
Greatest and Least Income Inequality Within a Country

The Gini coefficient (named for the Italian social scientist who invented it) examines the extent of income inequality within a country. This tool measures the distribution of income within a country by comparing the country's income distribution to that of an imagined country with equal income distribution. The result is a ratio that is often represented as a percentage, such as 59.7 percent. The higher the ratio (or percentage), the greater the income inequality in a country. Note, however, that even a country with little income inequality isn't necessarily wealthy. It may have a low GDP per capita, which means nearly everyone in the country has very little income.

CONSTRUCTED RESPONSE According to the chart, how does the income inequality of Guatemala compare to that of Botswana and Slovenia?

Greatest and Least Income Inequality Within a Country

GREATEST INCOME INEQUALITY		LEAST INCOME INEQUALITY	
Country	Gini Ratio	Country	Gini Ratio
Lesotho	63.2	Kosovo	23.2
South Africa	62.5	Slovakia	23.7
Micronesia	61.1	Slovenia	24.4
Haiti	60.8	Sweden	24.9
Botswana	60.5	Ukraine	25.5
Namibia	59.7	Belgium	25.9
Zambia	57.5	Kazakhstan	26.3
Comoros	55.9	Belarus	26.5
Guatemala	53	Norway	26.8
Paraguay	51.7	Moldova	26.8

Latest available year per country

Source: https://www.cia.gov/library/publications/the-world-factbook/rankorder/2172rank.html

---

DOCUMENT THREE

Primary Source: Chart
Countries with Highest and Lowest Happiness Index

Have you ever heard the expression, "Money can't buy happiness"? The Happiness Index is a tool that measures the extent of happiness within countries. It averages the responses of citizens in various countries to how they would rank the quality of their life on a scale from 0 to 10. And indeed, the countries with the happiest people are not necessarily the wealthiest. Experts on the topic find that the keys to happiness are livable income, healthy life expectancy, adequate social support, freedom, trust, and generosity. Causes for unhappiness include unfair treatment by the government, poverty, conflict in region, and prevalence of disease.

CONSTRUCTED RESPONSE What do most of the countries listed in the Low column of the chart have in common?

Countries with Highest and Lowest Happiness Index

HIGH HAPPINESS INDEX		LOW HAPPINESS INDEX	
Country	Happiness Index	Country	Happiness Index
Finland	7.632	Malawi	3.587
Norway	7.594	Haiti	3.582
Denmark	7.555	Liberia	3.495
Iceland	7.495	Syria	3.462
Switzerland	7.487	Rwanda	3.408
Netherlands	7.441	Yemen	3.355
Canada	7.328	Tanzania	3.303
New Zealand	7.324	South Sudan	3.254
Sweden	7.328	Central African Republic	3.083
Australia	7.272	Burundi	2.905

Latest available year per country

Source: https://countryeconomy.com/demography/world-happiness-index

---

SYNTHESIZE & WRITE

1. **REVIEW** Review what you have read and observed about income inequality in the 21st century.

2. **RECALL** On your own paper, list two details about one of the measurement tools and two details about the chart relating to it.

3. **CONSTRUCT** Construct a topic sentence that answers this question: How are people around the world affected differently by income inequality?

4. **WRITE** Using evidence from this chapter and the documents, write an informative paragraph that supports your topic sentence in Step 3.

3.1

MAIN IDEA The consequences of using fossil fuels for energy has led to interest in alternative energy sources.

New and Old Energy Sources

What's the best source of energy for the world's growing population? Decades ago, there weren't many choices. But today, we consider issues like pollution, climate change, environmental impact, cost, and safety as the world tries to meet its energy needs.

SEARCHING FOR ENERGY SOLUTIONS

You learned that scientists now use the term *Anthropocene* to describe the changed global ecology of the past 200 years—since the Industrial Revolution brought about the large-scale use of fossil fuels. Today, widely used fossil fuels such as oil and coal raise concerns about environmental harm.

Fossil fuels can not only cause air pollution when burned but also water and soil pollution when spilled during transport or drilling. In 2010, a huge spill fouled the Gulf of Mexico following an explosion on the Deepwater Horizon oil rig. **Fracking**, the process of drilling into the earth and applying water pressure to force out natural gases by breaking up rock, is also harmful to the environment.

Fossil fuels are nonrenewable resources. Once depleted they are gone forever. Nonrenewable resources do not provide a **sustainable**, or unceasing, source of energy. This fact has led companies and governments to explore renewable resources as sources of energy. Wind farms, some containing thousands of wind turbines, have become an important source for renewable energy.

The Gansu Wind Farm in China is huge, with 7,000 turbines, but an even bigger offshore wind farm is planned for the United Kingdom. At more than 150 square miles, this wind farm, slated for completion in 2022, will provide power to one million homes. While wind farms harness a renewable resource, they take up a lot of land, are expensive, and cause harm to birds.

Solar energy uses heat from the sun's rays to generate electricity. But it too faces hurdles in becoming a widely used energy source. Problems include resistance from fossil fuel suppliers, toxic materials in solar cells, the cost of switching to solar panels, and flaws in reliability. In some cases, governments have been slow to encourage the use of solar energy. In some areas, governments offer tax incentives to producers of solar panels and tax credits to individuals who install them. Governments can also stimulate use by allowing consumers to sell excess solar energy back to utilities.

Geothermal energy, derived from Earth's heat, is another source of sustainable energy. Renewable and clean, geothermal energy is ideal for heating and cooling. Hot water or steam from underground sources can also be used to turn turbines to create electricity. Large thermal power plants are located in California as well as in Italy, Mexico, Iceland, and Indonesia.

The most immediate alternative to fossil fuels is nuclear power. Nuclear power plants in 30 different countries produce more than 10 percent of the world's electricity. However, many people remain wary of its health and environmental consequences.

In 2011, an earthquake in Japan caused a tsunami that led to the release of radiation from the Fukushima electricity plant. The death toll was more than a thousand, but the deaths resulted from the evacuation process rather than radiation exposure. Even so, several nuclear reactors were damaged beyond use, and the vast majority of the area's former residents have decided not to return home. This disaster contributed to Germany's decision to shut down its nuclear energy program. However, France has decided to maintain its nuclear program, which provides 75 percent of the country's electricity.

Developing countries face special challenges in providing energy. China and India depend on burning coal for economic growth. They believe that this is the only way to fully develop their economies. Their leaders also realize the damage that fossil fuels inflict on people's health as the air becomes almost unbreathable in cities such as Beijing and New Delhi. Still, the challenge remains since more than one billion people worldwide do not have electricity.

A floating solar energy farm in the village of Chunjiangyuan in China's Zhejiang province provides 20 million kilowatt-hours each year through a power station. Though nearly two-thirds of the country's electricity still comes from burning air-polluting coal, demand for solar power is growing.

CONSERVING RESOURCES

Consumption of natural resources has increased since the Industrial Revolution. Environmentalists encourage the **conservation**, or careful protection, of natural resources. They stress reducing, reusing, and recycling. They also encourage **green building**, or designing and building structures with the environment in mind. Green builders make efficient use of natural resources such as water, minerals, and fuel sources to create buildings that are safe for humans and the environment. Examples of green buildings are Shanghai Tower in China and the Manitoba Hydro Place in Canada.

Obtaining food and water for survival can be hard in developing nations. The "green revolution" of the mid-20th century transformed the way in which rice, wheat, and other grains were grown and harvested. New seed varieties, advanced farm equipment, and chemical fertilizers allowed commercial farms to produce more crops and charge lower prices for them. However, the increased use of fertilizers and pesticides raised concerns about costs and environmental and human effects. In addition, some farmers could not afford the fertilizers and pesticides, so they did not obtain the promised results. Even so, the new methods are estimated to have saved as many as one billion people from starvation.

The challenge is great, but the story of the ozone layer provides hope that environmental progress is possible. In the 1980s, scientists became concerned that the ozone layer, which shields us from the sun's ultraviolet radiation, was disappearing. They traced the cause to the use of chemical compounds called chlorofluorocarbons (CFCs) in aerosol sprays. Since those compounds were banned by international agreement, the hole in the ozone layer has been steadily shrinking.

HISTORICAL THINKING

1. **READING CHECK** Classify the energy resources in this lesson as old energy or new energy, and then list important distinctions between the two types.

2. **FORM AND SUPPORT OPINIONS** Which new energy source do you think has the most potential for use in homes, and what roadblocks stand in the way? Explain your response.

3. **IDENTIFY** How does green building protect the environment?

3.2 NATIONAL GEOGRAPHIC EXPLORERS
LESLIE DEWAN AND ANDRÉS RUZO

Reinventing Clean Energy

"I think I can save the world with nuclear power."
—Leslie Dewan

CRITICAL VIEWING Leslie Dewan is determined to use nuclear power to provide energy for people all over the world. "I'm doing this because I think nuclear power is the best way of producing large amounts of carbon-free electricity," she says.

"The idea of an energy source that never turns off, and the concept of volcanoes leading us into a green energy future, blew my mind and became my passion." —Andrés Ruzo

Even with green energy projects, there is a responsible way and an irresponsible way of doing things. When he started his Ph.D. research, Andrés Ruzo's dream was to find a powerful geothermal feature to harness, and, by doing so, help Peru establish its first geothermal power plant. However, when Ruzo came face-to-face with the sacred Boiling River of the Amazon, it was clear to him that this place should not be developed and deserves legal protection.

Scores of scientific studies tell us that the primary cause of climate change on Earth is the burning of fossil fuels for energy. Scientists know it is of the utmost importance to protect our resources and develop clean energy options that are commercially viable, economically sustainable, and safe. Two visionary explorers are making clean energy their business.

> **MAIN IDEA** National Geographic Explorers Leslie Dewan and Andrés Ruzo analyze how clean energy sources can be economically sustainable.

SAFER, MORE EFFICIENT NUCLEAR REACTORS

Nuclear engineer Leslie Dewan is determined to develop a cleaner, more efficient form of nuclear power that will reinvent the definition of clean energy. She believes that with safer nuclear reactors that produce less waste, we can power the entire world with carbon-free energy.

One concern about nuclear power is the disposal of nuclear waste. Compared to the amount of waste created by fossil fuel plants, the amount of nuclear waste generated by nuclear power plants is small. However, spent nuclear fuel is highly radioactive and must be permanently stored somewhere safe and secure, usually deep underground.

That's where Dewan comes in. She and her colleague Mark Massie developed a new design for a molten salt reactor as a more secure, more economical alternative to today's nuclear reactors. In 2011, Dewan and Massie established Transatomic Power, intending to develop their reactor on a commercial scale.

They initially thought that their reactor would be able to consume nuclear waste directly, which would have helped solve one of the biggest problems with nuclear power. However, as they continued to develop their design and talked with other scientists about their work, they realized this was not possible with their reactor. Their design still has benefits—it uses half the fuel and produces less than half the waste of a conventional nuclear power plant—but it can't solve the nuclear waste problem on its own.

Dewan shut down her company in late 2018. At the same time, she made the decision to open-source its patents, reactor plans, and design. "We wanted to bring it out into the world," she says, "so that everyone could use it." She firmly believes in collaboration in the scientific community.

Dewan thinks that other new nuclear reactor designs will be able to consume nuclear waste. She is currently advising other companies that are developing these designs. Dewan also works with other experts at National Geographic Labs to use "satellite imagery to monitor nuclear facilities worldwide to make sure that they are safe and are not hurting the environment," continuing her aims of nuclear safety and scientific cooperation.

AN UNSTOPPABLE SOURCE OF CLEAN ENERGY

As a child growing up in Peru, geoscientist Andrés Ruzo played among fumaroles, the steaming openings found in or near volcanoes that emit hot, sulfurous gases. He also heard legends of a boiling river deep in the Peruvian Amazon. These experiences ignited a passion in Ruzo, and he pursued it by studying geologic wonders around the world. His fieldwork in the United States involved improving mapping methods to highlight geothermal energy potential within the country. In Peru, Ruzo proved the existence of the Boiling River of the Peruvian Amazon. "It's an anomalously large geothermal feature, which basically means it's freaking big," Ruzo explains. And although it is located far from any active volcano, the river can reach a temperature of more than 200°F.

As Ruzo solves this mystery, he continues to explore geothermal regions. Naturally, he visited Iceland, a geothermal paradise that provides a successful example of geothermal energy's commercial success. Ruzo applies what he learns to his own business-related work, which focuses on building maintainable economic systems to promote conservation and clean energy.

As a geothermal scientist, conservationist, science communicator, and educator, Ruzo anchors the many things that he does on the belief that environmentalism and economic prosperity can work together. And his enthusiasm for what he does is contagious. His oral and written storytelling inspires people to explore our world and consider how we can integrate clean energy and conservation into our lives.

HISTORICAL THINKING

1. **READING CHECK** What problems is Dewan attempting to solve with her development of new nuclear reactor technology?

2. **ANALYZE POINT OF VIEW** Why does Ruzo think geothermal activity could lead to a green energy future, and how is he trying to apply that belief?

3. **DRAW CONCLUSIONS** How might successful clean energy businesses help reduce the number of businesses that burn fossil fuels?

3.3 A Global Commodity: Conflict Minerals

Computers and handheld gadgets have revolutionized how people connect with each other and access information, but the technology has exacted a high price. Some of the commodities needed to produce these electronic devices, including gold; tin; tungsten; and tantalum, a hard, blue-gray metal that resists corrosion, are plentiful in the eastern regions of the Democratic Republic of the Congo (DRC). The sale of these natural resources—known as conflict minerals and often referred to as 3TG—have helped fund the fierce fighting that has embroiled the eastern DRC since the 1990s and killed an estimated six million people.

Armed militias have gained control of many of the DRC's rich mineral mines and employed local men and children to work them. Laborers use shovels and their bare hands to extract minerals that will be exchanged for weapons and ammunition. In 2010, Congress passed the Dodd-Frank Act, which included legislation requiring companies to disclose their sources of conflict minerals. Opponents of the law claimed it would result in the loss of mining jobs. Congress sought to repeal the conflict minerals rule in 2017, but the law's fate remains unclear.

In addition to conflict minerals, what other commodities traded throughout history have raised ethical issues?

GOLD
Congolese gold miners dig in an open pit and use a human chain to remove the red mud. Most of the gold produced by small-scale mines like this one is smuggled out of the Congo. And armed groups supervise about half of these artisanal mines. Miners are only paid when they find gold. Any amount found is usually so small that it is weighed against a matchstick.

A Global 21st Century 897

3.4

MAIN IDEA Advanced technology has improved world communication, transportation, and productivity but has also created new problems.

The Digital Era in the Balance

By definition, a revolution results in drastic change, and many times this change is positive. It is certainly true that the technology revolution of the late 20th and early 21st centuries has enhanced the modern world economy and society. But this transformation has also created new challenges.

REVOLUTIONS IN TECHNOLOGY

The 20th-century invention of computers and later the microchip that increased their speed and reduced their size and cost transformed the way the world works, communicates, and transports goods and people. New technology has improved world **connectivity**, the state of being connected to others. People today use computers to manage their finances, buy products and services, keep up with the news, and do their jobs from different places. These activities are accomplished via the Internet with the help of artificial satellites, which can also use Global Positioning Systems (GPS) to find exact locations. You use advanced technology every time you post a photo or an emoji on social media. Astronauts and physicists use some of this technology in modern space exploration, including the International Space Station, planet rovers, and space probes.

Advanced technology has given us new capabilities, but it has also created never-before-dreamed-of problems. The Internet allows quick transmission of information, but many people, businesses, and even governments want access to that information for personal gain or control. Cloud computing, or the storage of information through the Internet, has increased the risk of information falling into the wrong hands. **Hackers** are individuals who illegally gain access to electronic information. Some commit cybercrimes, or illegal activity committed online. For example, Russian hackers have been accused of using technology to interfere with the 2016 U.S. presidential election. Other hacking crimes include phishing, which is a type of Internet scam that tricks people into providing personal information, and the use of malware, software that makes computers unusable.

Other cyber criminals commit electronic espionage, or spying to gain information from businesses or government. The posting of classified U.S. documents

Selected Breakthroughs in Computer Technology

1946	ENIAC, the first programmable general-purpose electronic digital computer, is completed in Philadelphia, Pennsylvania. It takes up a 1,500-square-foot room.
1969	ARPANET—a forerunner of the Internet—is established as the first computer network.
1971	Intel introduces its first microchip, for memory storage, and microprocessor, for computation.
1972	The release of PONG jumpstarts the new industry of arcade video games.
1976	Steve Wozniak joins with partner Steve Jobs to market his Apple-1 computer.
1981	The market for personal computers booms after IBM introduces its PC with its MS-DOS operating system. The PC is widely cloned by companies such as Compaq.
1984	Apple introduces the Macintosh, developing a reputation not just for computer strength but also for innovative design.
1990	Microsoft introduces the Windows 3.0 operating system, bundling it with Word and Excel software programs.
1991	The U.S. Congress passes the High Performance Computing and Communication Act, providing massive financial support for Internet connectivity.
1998	Google launches its search engine.
2000	The camera phone, the USB flash drive, and Sony's PlayStation 2 are introduced to the market.
2003	MySpace is founded, spreading the popularity of social networks, followed by Facebook in 2004.
2006	Amazon introduces cloud-based computing services.
2007	Apple releases the iPhone, ushering in the age of the smartphone.
2011	Netflix transitions from a DVD-by-mail service to a streaming video service.
2015	Apple releases the Apple Watch.

A 2019 study suggests that the glacial ice sheet that covers Greenland is melting four times faster than scientists originally thought, with the loss of approximately 280 billion tons of ice per year between 2002 and 2016.

by the group WikiLeaks raised debate about the concept of treason versus free speech. Electronic sabotage—or destruction of property such as a company, political party, or government website—is a crime, too. Computer engineers continue to explore the use of **cryptography**, secret codes and scrambling of data, to keep electronic information safe. Other problems include lack of privacy, addiction to the Internet, and disrespectful social network messages. Those who post offensive or threatening messages are known as **trolls**. People also wonder whether workers will lose their jobs to robotic equipment in the near future.

ENVIRONMENTAL CHALLENGES

Today, Earth is warming at an alarming rate as a result of **climate change**, or changes to global weather patterns. Melting polar ice caps may cause extreme flooding in some places. For example, 55 million people living in Bangladesh's coastal lands would be displaced by a slight rise in sea levels. Elsewhere, global warming causes severe droughts. Most scientists believe current climate change is the effect of burning carbon-emitting fossil fuels, which create greenhouse gases. These gases trap heat in the atmosphere and speed global warming.

Climate change can disrupt economies and governments. You read about the theory that food shortages due to climate change contributed to wars and other hostilities around the world during the 17th century. Both floods and droughts may cause food shortages, which lead to higher food prices. Regional conflicts might erupt due to scarcity not only of food but also of water. Human migration patterns might change as people in affected locations try to move to safer places, causing overpopulation or tension over immigration policies. And disease flourishes in areas hit by natural disasters.

Some nations have made significant investments in renewable energy sources to replace fossil fuels. Germany developed a plan to rely primarily on renewable fuel sources by 2020. A 2015 meeting resulted in the UN-sponsored Paris Agreement on climate change, in which 195 nations pledged to limit greenhouse gas emissions. However in 2017, President Donald Trump announced that the United States would withdraw from the accord.

HISTORICAL THINKING

1. **READING CHECK** What are three benefits of communication technology?

2. **FORM AND SUPPORT OPINIONS** Which event from the time line of computer history do you think had the greatest impact on society? Explain.

3. **MAKE CONNECTIONS** How might climate change affect the region where you live?

4.1

MAIN IDEA Artist Ai Weiwei provoked a backlash from China's communist government by using his art to critique its corrupt and authoritarian bureaucracy.

Traveler: Ai Weiwei
A Creative Force in China B. 1957

Chinese artist Ai Weiwei uses his art to challenge the status quo, forcing us to take a critical look at the world around us. His works transcend the present day to convey universal themes, such as individuals in society. His conceptual art can make us uncomfortable, forcing us to think rather than merely consume.

HIS LIFE

Ai Weiwei grew up in poverty in the desert camp where his father, once a famous poet, was sent during one of Mao Zedong's purges. But he persisted in his quest to be an artist. As a young man, he traveled to New York City with a camera but almost no money. In 1993, he returned to China, finding success and impressing the world with his design for Beijing's Bird's Nest Stadium for the 2008 Summer Olympics.

However, Ai's work was often subversive of government authority, as when he investigated the 2008 Sichuan earthquake and exposed government lies by using his

Remembering (top right): This installation commemorates the children lost in a 2008 Sichuan earthquake because poorly constructed buildings collapsed. The Chinese government tried to keep this information secret, but Ai wanted the world to know.
Forever Bicycles (right): This dazzling installation of more than 1,200 Chinese bikes went on display in Austin, Texas, in 2017. Ai's work laments that bikes—a long-time important means of transportation for the Chinese people—are being replaced by cars.

900 CHAPTER 30

Ai Weiwei's Journeys

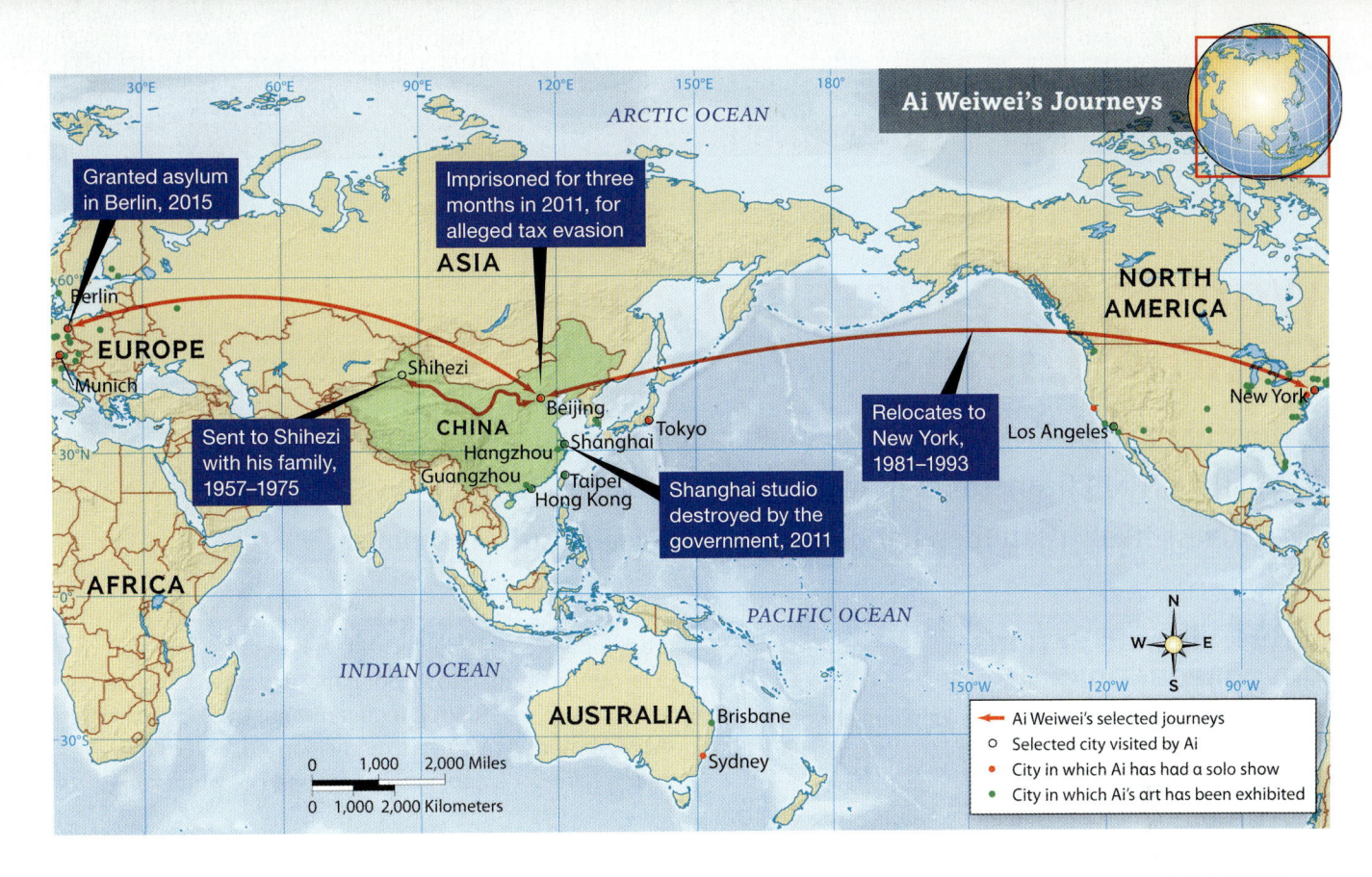

Map labels:
- Granted asylum in Berlin, 2015
- Imprisoned for three months in 2011, for alleged tax evasion
- Sent to Shihezi with his family, 1957–1975
- Shanghai studio destroyed by the government, 2011
- Relocates to New York, 1981–1993

Legend:
- Ai Weiwei's selected journeys
- Selected city visited by Ai
- City in which Ai has had a solo show
- City in which Ai's art has been exhibited

website to publish the names of all the children who were killed. To silence him, the Chinese government shut down his blog, put him under police surveillance, severely damaged his Shanghai studio, detained him for several months, and placed him under house arrest. When the government confiscated Ai's passport, his response was characteristically creative. As he explained, "Every morning I am putting a bouquet of flowers in the basket of a bicycle outside the front door." No longer allowed to post on his blog, he turned to Twitter to relay messages. Although he was allowed to travel again in 2015, China's harassment of Ai continues. His studio was destroyed again in 2018. Even so, he is determined not to give up his rights to freedom of expression and freedom of speech.

HIS WORK

Ai Weiwei mainly expresses himself through sculpture and art installations, which consist of many items made with mixed media displayed in a large area. Even when Ai was not allowed to travel, his exhibitions could. In 2014, an exhibit exploring the theme of incarceration went on display at the former Alcatraz Prison in San Francisco. In 2017, Ai created a documentary film called *Human Flow*, described as "a heartbreaking exploration into the global refugee crisis." At about the same time, his New York City public art project *Good Fences Make Good Neighbors* invited immigrants to share their own stories and those of their families.

On August 3, 2018, without warning, Chinese authorities began demolishing Ai Weiwei's studio in Beijing to make room for redevelopment. Ai's staff scrambled to remove artworks before they were destroyed. In the following excerpt from an interview with National Public Radio, Ai discusses the status of the art community in China.

PRIMARY SOURCE

Free speech and free expression have simply never existed in China or in its artist communities. Those who do not belong to the establishment, including artists, are always the first to be discriminated against and sacrificed. Often, the authorities face no consequences in doing so.

—Ai Weiwei, 2018

HISTORICAL THINKING

1. **READING CHECK** What three issues are important to Ai Weiwei?
2. **INTERPRET MAPS** Where has Ai's art been exhibited the most? Why?
3. **MAKE INFERENCES** What was the significance of Ai's putting flowers in a bicycle basket daily while he was denied his passport?
4. **ANALYZE VISUALS** Choose one of Ai's works. What universal themes are addressed in this work?

4.2

MAIN IDEA Women's leadership and gender rights have made progress in the 21st century, but there is still a long way to go for full equality.

Women's Leadership and Gender Rights

History has had no lack of powerful and notable women leaders, from Cleopatra VII to Elizabeth I. But while "women hold up half the sky," they are still less likely than men to hold positions of leadership and power.

WOMEN LEADING NATIONS AND CORPORATIONS

You have already learned about two influential women leaders in the 20th century—Golda Meir of Israel and Margaret Thatcher of the United Kingdom. Since their time in office, the number of women heads of state has grown—albeit slowly. According to the United Nations, as of January 2019 there are 10 women currently serving as head of state and 10 women serving as head of government.

The most recent of these leaders is **Sahle-Work Zewde** of Ethiopia, who was elected as the country's first female president in October 2018. While the role of president is traditionally a ceremonial role, her election was part of a larger movement to appoint more women to influential positions in the Ethiopian government by Prime Minister Abiy Ahmed. As you've already learned, half of the prime minister's cabinet is composed of women.

The world's youngest female head of government is **Jacinda Ardern** of New Zealand. She became prime minister in 2017 at the age of 37. In addition to promoting the progressive agenda of her Labour Party, including the passage of housing affordability measures and tax credits for new parents and vulnerable families, Ardern also gave birth to her first child, becoming the first leader of a country in nearly 30 years to give birth while in office.

CRITICAL VIEWING
New Zealand prime minister Jacinda Ardern consoles members of the Muslim community at a refugee center the day after a right-wing extremist terrorized two mosques in the city of Christchurch, killing 50 worshipers. Based on the details in the photo, how would you characterize Ardern as a leader?

In March 2019, attacks on two mosques in New Zealand left 50 dead and approximately 50 injured. Ardern was praised around the world for her response to the tragedy. Calling the assaults a "terrorist attack" and one of the "darkest days" in her country's history, she led the charge for changes to New Zealand's gun laws while showing empathy toward the victims and denouncing white nationalism. In 2020, Ardern was also praised for her response to the COVID-19 pandemic.

In addition to government and politics, women have also made strides as leaders of large corporations and international organizations. One of the most powerful women in the financial world is France's **Christine Lagarde**, who has served as managing director of the International Monetary Fund (IMF) since 2011—the first woman to do so. As a strong advocate of female economic empowerment, Lagarde believes it is key to the strength of the world economy. She also believes a greater presence of women in senior leadership positions in the financial industry would lead to less risk and speculation. After the 2008 financial crisis, she noted that "if it had been Lehman Sisters rather than Lehman Brothers, the world might well look a lot different today."

The "civilizing" presence of women in leadership positions also holds true in the corporate world. As CEO of PepsiCo, Indian-born **Indra Nooyi** guided the company through the Great Recession, creating a rise in shareholder returns and a growth in net revenue. She also steered the company toward selling more nutritious options such as hummus, juices, and kombucha. PepsiCo celebrated Nooyi as a new type of business leader who tried to "do well by doing good."

Even with these successes, there is still a long way to go. When Nooyi stepped down as CEO in 2018, she was replaced by a man. Today, the percentage of woman CEOs at Fortune 500 companies is 6.6 percent. In government, only 24 percent of all national legislative bodies around the world are women. And even though 39 percent of the global workforce consists of women, as of 2018, women are still paid only 68 percent of what men earn for the same jobs.

Malala Yousafzai gives a speech as she unveils her official portrait at the Barber Institute of Fine Arts in Birmingham, England, in 2015. The event occurred three years after she was shot and seriously wounded by Taliban fighters for speaking out against restrictions to women's education.

WOMEN LEADING CAUSES

Women's leadership isn't limited to political or business roles. Women have led social movements, taking a stand and improving not only women's rights but also human rights. From the fight for the right to vote to access to education to the fight for basic freedoms, women around the world have led the way in causes for social and economic advancement. The path has not been easy and those who have fought for women's rights have done so at great risk. Even so, their commitment and courage is unwavering.

In 2011, the Nobel Committee awarded the Nobel Peace Prize to Yemeni activist **Tawakkol Karman**, founder of Women Journalists Without Chains—an organization dedicated to women's rights, civil rights, and freedom of expression. She also became a leader of the Arab Spring in Yemen, organizing peaceful protests for which she was arrested and imprisoned several times. Today, she continues to speak out against the ongoing civil conflict that is tearing her country apart and creating a humanitarian crisis.

Another Nobel Laureate (2014), **Malala Yousafzai** of Pakistan, has led the way for young girls to demand equal education. When she was 11 years old, she began blogging about life under the Islamist Taliban, whose severe form of Islamic law restricted education for girls. As Yousafzai spoke out against the restrictions, she gained international prominence but also incited revenge from the Taliban. On her way home from school one day in 2012, Taliban fighters stopped her school bus and shot her in the head. After undergoing surgery and rehabilitation in Britain, Yousafzai launched the Malala Fund, an organization that supports leadership and learning for girls.

In Saudi Arabia, women have been fighting for decades for their rights, including their right to drive. In 2018, the country lifted the ban on women driving, but that progress came with a price. Weeks prior to the end of the ban, the Saudi government arrested several women's rights activists who challenged the driving ban and made peaceful calls for reform. Charged with harming national interests, the women were held in prison for nearly a year without a trial. In early 2019, some women faced trial and some women were released, but others remain in prison, where they have undergone torture and harassment.

GENDER RIGHTS FOR LGBTQ PEOPLE

In June 2015, the U.S. Supreme Court ruled that same-sex couples could marry nationwide. The court's ruling was a long-awaited step forward for the gay community. These rights aren't limited to the United States. In May 2019, Taiwan also made history by becoming the first country in Asia to legalize same-sex marriage. As of 2019, more than 25 countries in the world have laws protecting the right of same-sex couples to marry.

As support for LGBTQ (lesbian, gay, bisexual, transgender, and questioning or queer) rights seems to be increasing around the world, gender rights continue to be an issue. Many LGBTQ people have suffered from discrimination and violence because of their sexual orientation or gender identity. Many countries still criminalize same-sex relations—with some even applying the death penalty as punishment. In Russia, a 2013 law defined advocating for the human rights of LGBTQ people as "propaganda" and stated that anyone supporting LGBTQ rights could be arrested. In 2019 in

---

NATIONAL GEOGRAPHIC EXPLORER   KAKENYA NTAIYA

Empowering Kenya's Girls

Kakenya Ntaiya (shown here with her students) grew up in Enoosaen, Kenya, a rural community about 250 miles from Nairobi. Engaged to a neighbor boy at the age of five, Ntaiya was expected to marry him when she turned 12. Tradition required her to drop out of school at this time, but Ntaiya bargained with her father to let her finish high school and remain unmarried. He agreed. Ntaiya bucked tradition again when she won a scholarship to a U.S. college. The village elders eventually agreed to support her education after she promised to return to Kenya. Her dream? To build a school for girls. Ntaiya established the Kakenya Center for Excellence boarding school in Kenya in 2009 with 30 students, and today, it boasts several hundred success stories. "We've created a model for rural communities to empower and create leaders," Ntaiya says. "The goal is to plant women in leadership positions so they can make a difference." The families of girls who attend the school must promise that their children will remain unmarried while in school. "In the process, I learned something much bigger," Ntaiya notes. "When you empower a girl, you transform a community. School is just a start."

Supporters of same-sex marriage participate in a rally outside the parliament building in Taipei, Taiwan, as lawmakers discuss three different draft bills of a same-sex marriage law.

response to a global backlash, however, the government of Brunei backtracked on enforcing laws that would have made same-sex relationships punishable by stoning to death.

Progress has also been made related to transgender rights in some countries. Denmark became the first European nation to allow for legal documents reflecting the gender identity of transgender people. In 2014, India's Supreme Court officially recognized transgender people as a legal third gender. Third gender is a category for individuals defined by either themselves or by society as neither man nor woman. It is a category in societies that recognize three or more genders.

In 2017, National Geographic magazine dedicated an entire issue to the topic of gender. One of the topics covered in the issue was the complexity of gender and how it is an amalgamation of several elements, including chromosomes, anatomy, hormones, psychology, and culture. The magazine also profiled cultures where a third gender is the norm, such as the fa'afafine of Samoa.

With each step forward for gender rights for LGBTQ and third gender people, pioneering activists and lawmakers around the world are slowly making progress and creating hope for the future.

HISTORICAL THINKING

1. **READING CHECK** What are some key issues that women's rights activists around the world are fighting for?

2. **MAKE INFERENCES** Why do you think the growth in the number of women in political leadership positions has been slow to progress?

3. **ANALYZE LANGUAGE USE** What do you think Christine Lagarde meant when she said, "If it had been Lehman Sisters rather than Lehman Brothers, the world might well look a lot different today"?

4. **DRAW CONCLUSIONS** What conclusions can you draw about the attitude of groups like the Taliban and the government of Saudi Arabia toward women?

THROUGH THE LENS LYNSEY ADDARIO

A Different Dynamic

National Geographic photojournalist Lynsey Addario specializes in covering conflict zones. She has documented conflict and humanitarian issues in Afghanistan, Iraq, Lebanon, Darfur, Saudi Arabia, and Libya. She often focuses on refugees, women, and children, such as the images of Saudi women shown here. In societies segregated by gender, Addario can move more comfortably in spaces that are off-limits to her male colleagues. "Men and women have different access, we relate to people on different levels, and people respond to us differently," she notes. "So certainly that will create a different dynamic with a camera."

SAUDI ARABIA

ABOVE A girls basketball team holds practice at an outdoor court in Jeddah, Saudi Arabia. The team is one of the few athletic teams for women in the country and was founded in 2006. **TOP RIGHT** Saudi women and their children have a winter picnic in the desert outside Riyadh, Saudi Arabia. The women are wearing abayas—the ankle-length garment women must wear when out in public. **BOTTOM RIGHT** Women sit in a class at Yamamah University in Riyadh. Because the professor is a man, the women have to sit behind a barrier so they are in a separate room. Single men and women who are not related have to be kept separate according to Saudi law and custom.

A Global 21st Century 907

4.3

MAIN IDEA Globalism has led both to a growth of pandemics and the improved treatment of diseases worldwide.

The State of Global Health

Throughout history, the movement of diseases has accompanied the movement of people. At the end of 2019, a novel, or new, coronavirus was identified in Wuhan, China. The virus, which causes a serious respiratory illness called COVID-19, quickly spread around the world, leading to unprecedented social and economic disruptions as countries raced to contain outbreaks.

TODAY'S HEALTH CONCERNS

As you have witnessed with COVID-19, international mobility has increased the risk of pandemics around the world. Related illnesses, such as MERS and SARS, spread among countries through contact with infected foreign visitors. New strains of malaria hop from continent to continent by way of mosquito hosts carried on airplanes. Another species of mosquito spreads the Zika virus in a similar manner. And an overreliance on antibiotics has allowed the growth of new strains of bacteria that are resistant to treatment. Such developments overtax health care systems around the world.

Students return to class at a school in Hebei Province, China, for the first time in five months after schools were closed due to the COVID-19 pandemic.

Over the years, more than 35 million people worldwide have lost their lives to HIV/AIDS, which spreads through human contact. About 37 million people—two-thirds of them in Africa—currently live with the disease. It strikes people at the prime of their productive and reproductive lives, so it can have devastating effects on society. Infection rates have stabilized in wealthier nations but not in developing ones. In India, where hundreds of millions of people lack basic health care, the number of people with HIV/AIDS has soared past 2.5 million.

The social and economic impacts of pandemics can be catastrophic. Infected people are removed from the workforce, causing economic setbacks. Social interaction becomes limited as individuals avoid public places for fear of contracting the disease. Businesses may be forced to close for weeks or even months, creating a dip in a nation's revenue. A decline in tourism can cause monetary loss as well. Also, countries with pandemics must devote large sums to fighting them that might otherwise go to infrastructure improvements.

Diseases and health-related fatalities are more common among some populations than others. In high-poverty areas, people cannot afford medical attention, and any they receive may be inadequate. Proper health care may be unavailable in places torn apart by war, experiencing a natural disaster, lacking electricity, or located far from a city. The shortage of medical facilities in such places prevents adequate disease surveillance. Even in a country with advanced medical facilities, such as the United States, poorer people often suffer from medical conditions that might easily be treated.

Other causes for the spread of disease include food scarcity, overcrowding, and poor sanitary conditions. Groups such as the World Health Organization (WHO) work to solve health challenges. So do NGOs such as Doctors Without Borders, Partners in Health, and Project HOPE. These NGOs supply health resources such as medicines, vaccines, and dietary guidance.

While much of the work of NGOs is geared toward solving health problems in high-poverty nations, more affluent nations are not exempt from experiencing health issues. In this case, one crisis may be linked to too much food rather than too little. In wealthier countries, obesity and inactivity lead to heart disease, type 2 diabetes, and other deadly conditions.

HEALTH ADVANCES

Despite increasing the spread of disease, globalization has contributed to improved health throughout the world. Breakthroughs have led to positive advances worldwide. Surgeon Charles R. Drew developed a way to store blood plasma in blood banks for future transfusion: an innovation that saved many lives worldwide. Mass vaccination resulted in the eradication of smallpox and has mostly eliminated polio. However, a recent increase in vaccine hesitancy has led to a resurgence of diseases that were once considered extinct around the world, such as measles and whooping cough. Later innovations included open-heart surgery, organ transplants, and the pacemaker. All these medical advances have helped many people survive.

By the year 2000, a breakthrough had been made in knowledge of the genome—the **Human Genome Project** had successfully mapped DNA. Solving this puzzle paved the way for new medical improvements. Also, the new century witnessed many innovations ranging from bionic prosthetics to targeted disease therapy. Many breakthroughs have been made in the field of **biotechnology**, the use of biological organisms or processes to create new products that improve life. One result is increased **longevity**, or increased lifespan, of individuals around the globe.

HISTORICAL THINKING

1. **READING CHECK** What causes diseases to spread from their point of origin to other places around the world?
2. **DRAW CONCLUSIONS** Why might a country like Syria be prone to pandemics?
3. **POSE AND ANSWER QUESTIONS** What three questions would you ask a scientist about biotechnology and the world's food supply?

NATIONAL GEOGRAPHIC EXPLORER
HAYAT SINDI

A Paper Medical Lab

For a girl growing up in Saudi Arabia, a country in which it was recently illegal for women to drive, becoming an expert in biotechnology seemed almost impossible. But Hayat Sindi beat the odds. A National Geographic Explorer, doctor, and scientist, she sums up her exciting career in one sentence: "My mission is to find simple, inexpensive ways to monitor health that are specifically designed for remote places and harsh conditions." And Sindi did just that when she created a low-cost disease detector from a small piece of paper. An individual only has to spit on the chemical-laced paper. Almost instantly, a dot on the paper changes color to reveal any liver damage in the patient. Sindi's invention allows people in remote rural areas to receive the medical attention they need to survive.

NATIONAL GEOGRAPHIC EXPLORER
JACK ANDRAKA

A Science Fair Discovery

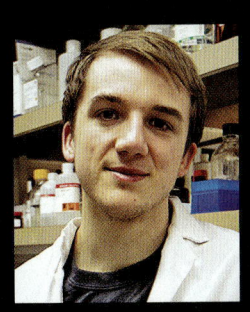

In 2012, 15-year-old Jack Andraka was grieving for a friend he had lost to pancreatic cancer. He was also thinking about what to do for a science fair project. Andraka ended up creating a blood-test strip that costs just pennies to produce but accurately identifies signs of pancreatic cancer. For his efforts, Andraka won the top prize at the 2012 Intel International Science and Engineering Fair. The youthful innovator majored in electrical engineering and anthropology at Stanford University and founded his own company. His dream is to find solutions to health-care deficiencies in the developing world.

4.4

MAIN IDEA Millions of people lack reliable access to nutritious food, but scientists and advocates are working to solve the problem of global food security.

Food Security

When you see an image of a vast field in Iowa or Nebraska—America's famed "amber waves of grain"—it probably doesn't occur to you that you're looking at the planet's largest ecosystem. Worldwide, agriculture covers more land than any other type of ecosystem. And yet, in many parts of the world, people struggle to get enough to eat.

A WORLD OF MOUTHS TO FEED

Food security means more than obtaining the minimum number of calories needed to stay alive. In the *Economist's* annual report on the state of global food security, the magazine defines it as "the state in which people at all times have physical, social and economic access to sufficient and nutritious food that meets their dietary needs for a healthy and active life."

Achieving food security is not simply a matter of quantity. When evaluating a region's food security, experts look at the availability of food, but they also consider affordability, quality, and safety. The Irish Potato Famine of 1845–1849 illustrates several of these issues. Irish people were starving because their diet relied on a potato crop that failed repeatedly, while Ireland under British rule was growing enough other crops to export. Food was being produced, but it was not available to a large part of the population. Or, when accessible, it was not affordable. Ireland's famine also illustrates a dimension of food security that many researchers are studying today—resilience in the face of shocks such as drought or natural disasters. Around one million people died because the potatoes they relied on for most of their nutrition were wiped out by a single disease.

CRITICAL VIEWING Small, individually owned farms border a giant corporate-owned banana farm outside the city of Maputo in the sub-Saharan African country of Mozambique. Once torn apart by civil war, the country is now a major producer of agricultural exports. How might the increased presence of corporate farms impact the owners of smaller farms?

Members of the Venezuelan military under the authority of President Nicolas Maduro guard the border between Venezuela and Colombia in an attempt to block humanitarian aid requested by opposition leader Juan Guaidó. The conflict between the two leaders had caused widespread food insecurity within the country.

Food security benefits not only individuals but society in general. You read that malnutrition contributes to rates of disease in a region. It also leads to stunted growth in children and can harm brain development. One study has found that undernutrition depresses the global gross domestic product of Asia and Africa by 11 percent.

THREATS TO FOOD SECURITY

Lack of food security remains a clear and persistent threat. A 2016 study estimated that 795 million people faced hunger every day. Additionally, more than two billion people were lacking nutrients such as zinc, iron, and vitamin A, which are essential to health and proper growth.

The origins of hunger are complex and varied. As you have learned, key forces such as globalization, technology, power, and conflict have been at work throughout human history, and food security is braided through all of them. For example, one theory claims that food shortages contributed to the French Revolution. Power and conflict also played a defining role in the Irish Potato Famine, as the British government prevented the Irish people from accessing other food sources. In the present day, the efforts of Venezuela's rulers to stay in power have led to profound food insecurity and open conflict in that nation.

In recent times, globalization and technology have supported advances in food security, making it easier to export food to regions experiencing hunger and helping make agricultural lands more productive. However, globalization becomes a disadvantage when prices rise and a region that relies on food imports can no longer afford them. Technology has also caused problems at times. In parts of India, for example, crops developed in labs to combat hunger eventually dried out and depleted the soil in which they were planted.

Looking to the future, many researchers view population growth and climate change as the greatest threats to food security. According to one estimate, if current population trends continue, farmers will need 120 percent more water and 42 percent more cropland to meet humanity's needs in 2050. It is highly doubtful that the planet can provide these resources.

Climate change, meanwhile, has already begun affecting food production. Rising temperatures have disrupted the regular climate patterns across Earth. Destructive events such as intense droughts, powerful storms, and cold snaps are becoming more common. Ironically, agriculture itself is part of the problem. It has been estimated that food production is responsible for one-third of all greenhouse gas emissions.

National Geographic Explorer T.H. Culhane stands in front of solar panels that help power his home in Florida.

NATIONAL GEOGRAPHIC EXPLORER T.H. CULHANE

Living Off the Grid

Being "off the grid" means generating one's own power rather than buying it from an electric or gas company. In many places where T.H. Culhane has lived and worked, people have no choice but to live off the grid, either because electricity is not available or because they cannot afford it. At his southern Florida home, Culhane can access electricity that he is able to pay for. And yet, he is living off the grid.

"After years of exploring ways to live off-grid around the world," he explains, "we've finally brought it all back to our home . . . without sacrificing any comforts at all." Indeed, he and his wife, Enas, live in a comfortable trailer home with familiar modern appliances, including a microwave, a dishwasher, a refrigerator, a big-screen TV, and computers. The electricity to operate these devices comes mainly from solar panels and biodigesters, which Culhane describes as "domestic fire-breathing dragons that turn all our food and toilet waste . . . into clean fuel and fertilizer." The fertilizer then feeds extensive gardens that grow a variety of produce.

What's the point of living like this when electricity is freely available and reasonably priced? Culhane believes in "life testing" the solutions he offers to other people, showing that his ideas work in the real world—and that the necessary technology is not difficult to build or buy. By living off the grid, he is showing the world that sustainable food and energy production is within everyone's reach.

Culhane demonstrates the effectiveness of using biogas to fuel a cookstove at the Mukuru Arts and Crafts Academy in Nairobi, Kenya. The school's cook (on the left) is amazed by how clean and odorless the fuel is.

Not all the food security news is bad, however. The *Economist* noted progress in several nations in its annual reports for 2015, 2016, and 2018. Some of these advances result from the hard work of researchers who use both global and local approaches to tackling problems surrounding food production. National Geographic Explorers T.H. Culhane and Jerry Glover are among the scientists working not only in labs and universities but also with groups and individuals worldwide to ensure a reliable, nutritious food supply for everyone.

THINK LOCAL . . .

T.H. Culhane travels the world with a garbage disposal in his suitcase. In Culhane's hands, however, a noisy machine that normally grinds up unwanted food and flushes it away becomes a tool for recycling resources and improving a community's food security. In places as diverse as Portugal and Florida, he has used an everyday disposal unit to shred all manner of waste. He then lets nature take over, watching as worms and bugs turn garbage into fertile soil. Giving people the tools to use all of their available resources is at the core of Culhane's mission.

Culhane's enlightened ideas about garbage were inspired in part by his work with the Zabaleen people in Cairo, Egypt, when he was earning his Ph.D. The name *Zabaleen* translates literally as "garbage people," and the Zabaleen make their living collecting and recycling the city's waste. "The Zabaleen view everything around them as useful for something," Culhane remarks. Building on this ethic, he introduced the Zabaleen to biogas digesters. These units convert kitchen scraps and other waste into gas that can be used for heating or generating electricity. He also helped families create roof gardens that allow them to grow their own food without using soil. Since his time in Egypt, Culhane has helped communities implement similar systems in Tanzania, Kenya, Brazil, and even refugee camps in Palestine.

These projects are possible, Culhane emphasizes, because they do not rely on advanced technology and are all based locally. Community members build their gardens and energy generators using basic plumbing supplies and easily available materials. More importantly, they bring their ingenuity and their hard-won knowledge of what works in their own environments. "The poor aren't a class of weak victims," Culhane insists. "They're millions of creative individuals."

When it comes to food security, Culhane sees opportunities in some of the most unlikely places. He points out, "Cities have not necessarily eliminated agricultural land. Instead, they've elevated it." In his view, building roofs and walls can be converted into productive spaces for growing food using techniques that do not require soil.

Cities as a whole have yet to take on the challenge of converting themselves into vertical, urban farm fields, but Culhane has faith in the power of individuals to create solutions for their own communities. And the best ideas, when they have been tested and shown to work, will make their way out into the world.

. . . THEN GO GLOBAL

When he's not on the road helping communities build energy and food solutions, Culhane lives in southern Florida. He is the Director of Climate Change and Sustainability at the University of South Florida's Patel College of Global Sustainability. He is also the founder of Solar CITIES, an organization that trains members of poor communities around the world to build biodigesters and food-growing systems. In addition, he is a founding member of the Rosebud Continuum, which serves as a testing ground for sustainable energy and food solutions. Rosebud invites students and community members to visit, learn, enjoy themselves, and—most enthusiastically—"try this at home."

While much of his focus is on intensely local, relatively low-tech projects, Culhane does not dismiss the advantages of globalization and advanced technology. At Rosebud, he has been experimenting with augmented and virtual reality to help visitors immerse themselves in a world of sustainable possibilities. Participants are encouraged to use this technology to advance their knowledge and spark their own ideas about producing food and energy. T.H. Culhane believes that all people can contribute to sustainable food security and that the globalization of good ideas benefits everyone.

ONE SIZE DOES NOT FIT ALL

Some commentators have remarked that Earth is capable of producing enough food for everyone. Jerry Glover is not so sure. "A good global food supply does not solve regional problems," he counters. An exceptional wheat harvest in Argentina does not translate to food security for a village in Malawi where farmers struggle with nutrient-poor soil. That's why Glover, like T.H Culhane, advocates for food security solutions that focus on local needs and conditions.

Jerry Glover is an agricultural ecologist who works with farming communities around the world to improve crop yields and local food security. His projects have taken him to parts of Africa where untold generations of

NATIONAL GEOGRAPHIC EXPLORER JERRY GLOVER

Women and Food Security

Often, the most effective way to introduce new farming techniques is to talk with women who live and work in the community. In Malawi and elsewhere in Africa, Jerry Glover noticed that training women in perennial planting techniques resulted in increased yields, greater nutrition for families, and crops that are better equipped to survive in harsh weather. Data supports these personal observations. A study by the University of Queensland, Australia, found that one of the surest predictors of crop yield was the level of education of the women in the household.

As Glover explains, agriculture is not simply a matter of food production. It is entwined with both the economics and culture of a community. Therefore, before approaching the women—or the men—in a village, it is important to understand their deeply ingrained traditions. "I've been in places where women were only allowed to speak to me through the men," he reports. The time and effort taken to understand the cultural dynamics and women's roles in a community reap an ample payoff when crops increase and families eat well.

In 2015, photographer Jim Richardson teamed up with National Geographic Explorer and agricultural ecologist Jerry Glover to create striking photographs of perennial prairie plants' deep roots.

farming have dried out the soil and depleted its nutrients. There, people often struggle to coax enough crops from their land to feed their families.

One strategy Glover uses to help farmers boost their yields is to introduce perennial plants into their fields. Perennials are plants that survive from year to year, in contrast to annual crops that are pulled from the ground after a growing season. Glover helped some farmers in Malawi plant "fertilizer trees" in their maize fields. The trees' roots draw water and nutrients from deep within the soil. When the trees drop their leaves, the leaves return the nutrients to the shallower layer of soil where the maize has its roots. One farmer in Malawi who planted fertilizer trees increased his yield by ten times in six years.

Glover and his colleagues are also attempting to cultivate perennial versions of familiar foods. These crops would be more resilient in the face of shocks related to climate change, and their deep roots would help stabilize the soil. They could also be bred so that they are adapted to local conditions. Promising perennial wheat and rice plants have been developed, but they have not yet been put into broader cultivation.

When working with farmers, Glover is mindful of their individual needs and concerns. Global solutions imposed by governments or large agricultural companies are doomed to fail, he says, because they ignore local conditions. "Farmers are not fools," he notes. "They make their decisions for logical reasons" based on their experiences, their culture, and the materials they have at hand. Successfully introducing new ideas means understanding where the old ones come from. It also means empowering farmers to make their own logical decisions based on the evidence presented to them.

Workers maneuver a boat around rows of algae that are being cultivated off the coast of the Philippines. This particular algae, known as carrageen, is used in both the food and pharmaceutical industries.

THE FUTURE OF FOOD

While Glover believes that improvements in agriculture can help feed today's hungry world, he sees the future of food security in new and different sources of nourishment. "We're working off a 19th-century vision of agriculture, trying to improve efficiency but still relying on the same group of crops we've had for years," he says.

Glover and many others believe that food producers need to explore new staples to put on our menu, including insects, algae, and meat grown in labs. With modern food-processing technology, these substances can be made into familiar dishes with no shock to the taste buds. "I've had pasta made from insects," he says, "and it tasted just like regular pasta." In fact, several food manufacturers have started to experiment with alternative ingredients. Crickets, for example, are high in protein and can be used to make chips, protein bars, and smoothie powders. At least two companies are already marketing popular burgers that taste remarkably like beef but are made from grains and vegetables, which take much fewer resources to grow than beef. Perhaps in the not-so-distant future, everyone will be joining Jerry Glover in a tasty meal made from sources we never imagined.

The pulled "pork" in this sandwich is actually jackfruit, a fruit that grows in the tropical areas of Southeast Asia, Brazil, and Africa. The fruit has the consistency of chicken or pork and is a popular meat replacement.

HISTORICAL THINKING

1. **READING CHECK** What factors contribute to food security?

2. **MAKE CONNECTIONS** How might efforts to slow climate change affect food security?

3. **COMPARE AND CONTRAST** How would you compare and contrast T.H. Culhane's and Jerry Glover's approaches to food security?

A Global 21st Century **915**

CHAPTER 30 A GLOBAL 21ST CENTURY REVIEW

VOCABULARY

Use each of the following vocabulary words in a sentence that shows an understanding of the term's meaning.

1. religiosity
2. displaced
3. xenophobia
4. bailout
5. conservation
6. connectivity
7. hacker
8. biotechnology

READING STRATEGY
MAKE INFERENCES

Use a chart like the one below to make inferences about the impact of globalization. Then answer the question.

Key Events	Impact	Inferences

9. How has globalization increased international cooperation? How has it increased international conflict? Offer one example of international cooperation and one of international conflict and explain your responses.

MAIN IDEAS

Answer the following questions. Support your answers with evidence from the chapter.

10. What event led to the rise of ISIS? **LESSON 1.1**
11. Why did citizens of many Arab nations participate in the Arab Spring protests? **LESSON 1.2**
12. How do foreign relations policies differ for the communist countries of Vietnam and North Korea? **LESSON 1.4**
13. Which banking policies caused the financial crisis that began in 2008? **LESSON 2.1**
14. How has globalization affected the world's wealth? **LESSON 2.2**
15. How are nonrenewable resources and renewable resources different? Provide an example of each. **LESSON 3.1**
16. How did Ai Weiwei resist the Chinese government's efforts to silence him? **LESSON 4.1**
17. How might you explain the term *biotechnology* to a younger student? **LESSON 4.3**

HISTORICAL THINKING

Answer the following questions. Support your answers with evidence from the chapter.

18. **DRAW CONCLUSIONS** Why do you think the September 11 terrorists picked the World Trade Center towers and the Pentagon as their targets?
19. **ANALYZE CAUSE AND EFFECT** How has civil war in Syria affected other countries?
20. **MAKE CONNECTIONS** How does a fast-growing population affect a nation's economy in positive and negative ways?
21. **FORM AND SUPPORT OPINIONS** Do you think the positive effects of multinational corporations outweigh the negative effects? Explain your response.
22. **MAKE PREDICTIONS** Is another world financial crisis likely in the next five years? Explain your response.
23. **SUMMARIZE** How has Ai Weiwei made a difference in the world?
24. **EVALUATE** Which 21st-century health advancement do you think is most important? Why?

INTERPRET GRAPHS

Study the graph at right, which shows the range of carbon dioxide levels through the centuries. Then answer the questions below.

25. By about how much has the carbon dioxide level risen since 1950?

26. This graph shows the naturally occurring ups and downs in carbon dioxide levels over many centuries. Why does this data alarm many scientists?

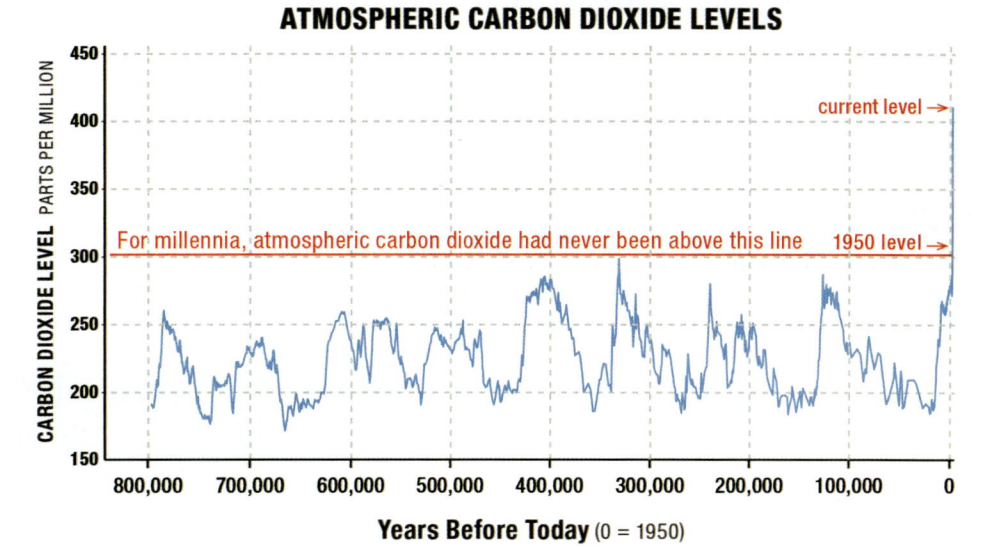

ATMOSPHERIC CARBON DIOXIDE LEVELS

For millennia, atmospheric carbon dioxide had never been above this line. 1950 level → current level →

Years Before Today (0 = 1950)

Source: Luthi, D., et al. 2008; Etheridge, D.M., et al. 2010; Vostok ice core data/J.R. Petit et al.; NOAA Mauna Loa CO_2 record

ANALYZE SOURCES

Some of the largest and most successful emerging economies—Brazil, Russia, India, China, and South Africa—have formed an economic bloc that is commonly referred to as BRICS. The bloc's main goal is to cooperate so that each member can continue to enjoy economic success. This excerpt is from a declaration issued at the 2017 BRICS Science, Technology & Innovation (STI) ministerial meeting. Read it and answer the question that follows.

> [We] agree to promote entrepreneurship and build platforms in BRICS countries and mainly collaborate in technology cooperation, technology transfer and translation, science and technology parks, youth innovation and entrepreneurship and in fostering strategic and long-term university-industry partnerships so as to build sound ecosystems for innovation and entrepreneurship.

27. What evidence in the excerpt shows that BRICS is looking to the future?

CONNECT TO YOUR LIFE

28. **INFORMATIVE** Talk to family members or other adults you know about the global refugee crisis. Ask them what they know about it and what they think should be done. Share your own views of the situation, including the ways in which an influx of refugees could change a country. Then write an essay about your conversation, describing ways in which you and the person or people you spoke with agreed and disagreed. Did anyone change their minds during the conversation? Explain why or why not.

TIPS

- Use information from the chapter to craft your questions before you conduct your interviews.

- Ask the people you interview for concrete details as they discuss what they know and what they think should be done.

- Maintain an open, curious, and respectful tone in your interview. Seek areas of agreement before you move to areas of disagreement.

- Be sure to thank people you interview for being willing to share their thoughts with you on an important topic.

- In writing about the views of others, try to find the logic in their position and also look for the emotional perspective. Ask yourself whether people are expressing fear, anger, compassion, or some other emotion in their response to the situation.

- Try to step outside your own position to see how it might appear to someone else. In writing your essay, assess areas of agreement and disagreement. Consider the ways in which your conversation might reflect areas of agreement or disagreement within the larger society.

NATIONAL GEOGRAPHIC | CONNECTION

Navigating the Anthropocene

BY OWEN GAFFNEY Adapted from "Walking the Anthropocene" by Owen Gaffney, Out of Eden Walk post, March 16, 2015

Throughout human history, major geological events have punctuated our journey. Just 11,700 years ago, a slight shift in Earth's orbit around the sun brought our planet out of a deep ice age. Earth's systems—ocean currents, ice sheets, biodiversity, and climate—settled into a new equilibrium, and we entered the epoch called the Holocene.

The Holocene was a "goldilocks" period for *Homo sapiens*: not too hot, not too cold. Preceded by an ice age, the Holocene's climate allowed agriculture to develop and flourish independently in the Middle East, China, and elsewhere. More complex social structures such as towns and cities arose, followed much more recently by enormous population growth and development. The Holocene is the only known epoch capable of supporting 7.2 billion people.

But what if Earth has moved out of the Holocene? What if the ship on which we sail has grown so large that its insatiable appetite and increasing effluence have radically altered all around it? Many of the world's top Earth-system scientists believe we have entered a new geological epoch shaped by people, called the Anthropocene. They debate when this new epoch began, however. Some argue that the Anthropocene began around 1800, with the Industrial Revolution.

Many others point to about 1950, when humanity's effect on Earth crossed a tipping point. Post–World War II production and consumption slipped into overdrive. We, the producers and consumers, moved onto a new, almost exponential trajectory fueled by use of Earth's natural resources. Incredibly, in a single human lifetime, changes in major planetary indicators started moving in accord with social and economic indicators of change, one force seemingly driving the other. A single species, ours, had come to dominate Earth's natural cycles.

Today we use an area the size of South America to grow our crops and an area the size of Africa to graze our livestock. We move more sediment and rock annually than all natural processes combined. And we are in the midst of Earth's sixth mass extinction, a result of human activity.

This nighttime image of Asia and Australia was assembled from data acquired by a satellite in 2012 and shows the regions' city lights. Scientists use images like this to track urban and suburban growth.

As we leave the Holocene behind, the human impact on the planet is growing, in what a team of Earth-system scientists has called the "Great Acceleration." To continue on this trajectory risks the stability of Earth's natural systems.

Two indicators of stability provide reason for hope, however. Following a ban on chlorofluorocarbons, the Antarctic ozone hole visibly stabilized. We also are on track for Earth's human population to stabilize soon.

But other indicators are worrisome. Marine fish captures are leveling off as we run out of fish to catch. Consumption and production continue to rise. From deforestation to fossil-fuel use, consumption is driving the most significant changes. With every passing year, we are degrading the only known safe operating space for our species.

While we—*Homo sapiens*—have traveled far, we did not travel together, nor take the same route. But we're all in the same boat now. ∎

UNIT INQUIRY
UNIT 10 Create an NGO

Staging the Question

In this unit, you learned about global challenges in the 20th and 21st centuries. Some, such as war and prejudice, are as old as humanity. Others, like human-caused climate change, are relatively recent. Still other forces, such as globalization and the digital revolution, remain ambiguous—do they hold the solutions to our problems, or will they ultimately cause more harm than good? In Units 9 and 10, you have also read about some NGOs (nongovernmental organizations) that confront today's challenges using both ages-old and cutting-edge methods. Which problem of today is the most urgent, and how can global citizens organize to solve it?

ASSIGNMENT

Identify the present-day global challenges described in this unit.

Choose the challenge you believe is the most urgent or that you feel most strongly about.

Analyze the problem and make a list of actions that individuals or organizations could take to help solve it.

Based on your analysis, make a plan for an NGO that focuses on the challenge you chose. You may work together with others who selected the same issue.

Supporting Questions: Begin by developing supporting questions to guide your thinking. For example: How have problems like this one been solved in the past? What resources can I use that did not exist in the past? Research the answers in this unit and in other sources. You might want to use a graphic organizer like this one to help you organize your ideas.

Summative Performance Task: Use the answers to your questions to help you envision a plan for an NGO that would work to overcome the challenge. Include a mission statement and specific actions for meeting your NGO's goals. For inspiration, you might research the websites of existing NGOs.

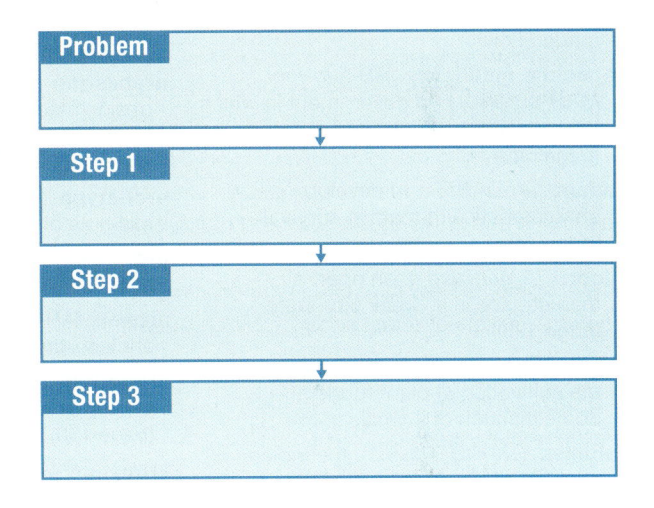

Problem
Step 1
Step 2
Step 3

Present: Share your NGO plan with the class. You might consider one of the following options:

CREATE A WEBSITE
Include pages that describe your NGO's message, mission, and goals. You may model your site on that of an existing organization. Include a page that tells readers what they can do to help.

MAKE A FUNDING PITCH
Present your NGO to the board of a company (your classmates) that is considering a big donation. Use presentation software to explain your NGO's goals and methods and to tell how you will effectively confront the challenge.

Take Informed Action:

UNDERSTAND Research existing NGOs that are working to solve the problem you chose.

ASSESS Compare and contrast the NGOs and choose the one you believe is the most effective and in line with your own beliefs.

ACT Contact the NGO and choose the way to participate in its activities that best suits you. Share with classmates why you support this organization.

STUDENT REFERENCES

English Glossary R1
Spanish Glossary R10
Index R18
Skills Index R34

AVAILABLE IN THE STUDENT eEDITION
Geography and the Environment Handbook
Primary and Secondary Source Handbook
Skills Handbook
Economics and Government Handbook
World Religions Handbook
National Geographic Atlas

GLOSSARY

A

abdicate *(AB-dih-kayt) v.* to formally give up something, such as a throne (page 203)

abolition *(a-buh-LIH-shuhn) n.* the movement to end slavery (page 519)

Aborigine *(a-buh-RIH-juh-nee) n.* an original inhabitant of Australia (page 554)

absolute monarchy *(AB-suh-loot MAH-nur-kee) n.* a government in which the monarch has unlimited authority (page 540)

adapt *(uh-DAPT) v.* to develop characteristics that aid in survival (page 14)

agora *(A-guh-ruh) n.* an open-air marketplace in a Greek city-state (page 128)

agriculture *(A-grih-kuhl-chur) n.* the cultivation of plant foods and domestication of animals (page 22)

ahimsa *(uh-HIHM-sah) n.* the Indian concept of absolute nonviolence (page 750)

alliance *(uh-LY-uhns) n.* a partnership (page 40)

alphabet *(AL-fuh-beht) n.* the group of letters that form the individual elements of a writing system (page 126)

amphitheater *(AM-fuh-thee-uh-tur) n.* a large, open-air theater (page 163)

amphora *(AM-fuh-ruh) n.* a large two-handled ceramic jar with a narrow neck (page 161)

anarchist *(A-nur-kihst) n.* a person who is willing to use force to overthrow authoritarian oppression (page 653)

anatomy *(uh-NA-tuh-mee) n.* the study of the interior and exterior structures of living things (page 418)

ancestor worship *(AN-sehs-tur WUR-shuhp) n.* the practice of contacting dead ancestors with the belief that they can intercede in human events on behalf of the living (page 83)

annex *(A-nehks) v.* to incorporate territory into an existing state (page 697)

anti-Semitism *(an-tee-SEH-meh-tih-zuhm) n.* hostility toward and discrimination against Jews (page 294)

apartheid *(uh-PAHR-tayt) n.* a system of racial segregation and discrimination against nonwhite South Africans that lasted until the early 1990s (page 814)

appeasement *(uh-PEEZ-muhnt) n.* the giving of concessions to keep the peace (page 761)

aqueduct *(A-kwuh-duhkt) n.* a stone channel that carried clean water from hilltops to cities (page 163)

arabesque *(a-ruh-BEHSK) n.* an abstract design made up of repeating patterns or flowers, leaves, vines, or geometric shapes (page 258)

archetype *(AHR-kih-typ) n.* a perfect example of something (page 598)

archipelago *(ahr-kuh-PEH-luh-goh) n.* a chain of islands (page 208)

archon *(AHR-kawn) n.* a chief ruler in ancient Athens (page 130)

aristocrat *(uh-RIHS-tuh-krat) n.* a person of wealth and high social rank (page 130)

armistice *(AHR-muh-stuhs) n.* an agreement between opposing sides to end hostilities (page 705)

artifact *(AHR-tih-fakt) n.* an object of historical value made by human beings (page 8)

artillery *(ahr-TIH-lur-ee) n.* large field guns that fire high-explosive shells (page 701)

ascetic *(uh-SEH-tihk) n.* one who chooses a life of poverty (page 72)

assimilate *(uh-SIH-muh-layt) v.* to merge into another culture (page 273)

astrolabe *(AS-truh-layb) n.* a sophisticated instrument that allowed users to calculate their location on Earth (page 259)

asylum *(uh-SY-luhm) n.* a place of safety (page 875)

atheism *(AY-thee-ih-zuhm) n.* the belief that God does not exist (page 824)

atomic bomb *(uh-TAH-mihk bahm) n.* a type of nuclear bomb whose violent explosion is triggered by splitting atoms and releases intense heat and radioactivity (page 773)

atrocity *(uh-TRAH-suh-tee) n.* an extremely cruel and shocking act of violence (page 786)

authoritarianism *(aw-thahr-uh-TEHR-ee-uh-nih-zuhm) n.* a political system characterized by a powerful leader and limited individual freedoms (page 709)

autonomous *(aw-TAH-nuh-muhs) adj.* self-governing (page 527)

autonomy *(aw-TAH-nuh-mee) n.* independence to self-govern (page 659)

B

bailout *(BAYL-owt) n.* a rescue from financial distress (page 886)

bioarchaeologist *(by-oh-AHR-kee-ah-luh-jihst) n.* a person who studies human remains to learn about archaeology (page 205)

biotechnology *(by-oh-tehk-NAH-luh-jee) n.* the use of biological organisms or processes to create new products that improve life (page 909)

Blackshirt *(blak-shurt) n.* a member of a militant group that attacked Mussolini's opponents (page 743)

blitzkrieg *(BLIHTS-kreeg) n.* a German battle tactic that used speed, surprise, and the combined firepower of tanks, bombers, and ground forces (page 766)

Boer *(bawr) n.* a Dutch or French settler in South Africa, also called an Afrikaner (page 674)

botany *(BAH-tuh-nee) n.* the study of plants and plant life (page 552)

bourgeoisie *(burzh-wah-ZEE) n.* the middle class (page 572)

bronze *(brahnz) n.* a mixture of the metals tin and copper (page 35)

bureaucracy *(byu-RAH-kruh-see) n.* a group of administrative government officials (page 88)

C

caliph *(KAY-luhf) n.* the title of a Muslim leader who was a successor of Muhammad (page 247)

calligraphy *(ka-LIH-gra-fee) n.* a form of elegant handwriting (page 258)

campesino *(kam-puh-SEE-noh) n.* a rural villager or small farmer in Latin America (page 726)

canonize *(KA-nuh-nyz) v.* to make someone a saint in the Catholic Church (page 441)

capital *(KA-puh-tuhl) n.* money or other assets that can be used to invest in business (page 277)

capitalism *(KA-puh-tuh-lihz-uhm) n.* a free-market economic system in which businesses are privately owned and exist for the purpose of making profits (page 492)

caravan *(KAIR-uh-van) n.* a group of people who travel together (page 367)

caravel *(KEHR-uh-vehl) n.* a small, fast ship used by Portuguese and Spanish explorers (page 482)

carpet-bombing *(KAHR-puht-bah-mihng) n.* the dropping of a large number of bombs on a designated area (page 726)

cartography *(kahr-TAH-gruh-fee) n.* the science or art of making maps (page 556)

caste system *(kast SIH-stuhm) n.* a rigid social hierarchy in ancient India that divided people into hereditary classes (page 71)

catacomb *(KA-tuh-kohm) n.* a hidden underground chamber where early Christians buried their dead (page 175)

cataract *(KA-tuh-rakt) n.* a steep, unnavigable rapid along the course of a river (page 42)

cathedral *(kuh-THEE-druhl) n.* the principal church of a district administered by a bishop (page 279)

caudillo *(cow-THEE-yoh) n.* a Latin American military dictator who gained power through violence (page 605)

cavalry *(KA-vuhl-ree) n.* a group of soldiers mounted on horseback (page 55)

celibate *(SEH-luh-buht) v.* to remain unmarried (page 204)

cenote *(sih-NOH-tee) n.* a large natural pool or open cave (page 391)

census *(SEHNT-suhs) n.* an official count of the population (page 204)

chinampa *(chuh-NAM-puh) n.* an artificial island created to raise crops (page 395)

chronicle *(KRAH-nih-kuhl) n.* a factual account or record (page 199)

circumnavigate *(sur-kuhm-NA-vuh-gayt) v.* to travel completely around the world (page 484)

city-state *(SIH-tee-STAYT) n.* a city whose ruler governs both the city and the surrounding countryside (page 37)

civil disobedience *(SIH-vuhl dihs-uh-BEE-dee-uhnts) n.* the refusal to follow unjust laws (page 750)

civil liberties *(SIH-vuhl LIH-bur-teez) n.* basic freedoms that cannot be regulated by the government, such as freedom of speech (page 884)

civilization *sih-vuh-luh-ZAY-shuhn n.* an advanced and complex society (page 34)

clan *(klan) n.* a group of people with a common ancestor (page 208)

clergy *(KLUR-jee) n.* people appointed to religious service by the church (page 278)

climate change *(KLY-muht chaynj) n.* changes to global weather patterns (page 899)

Clovis point *(KLOH-vuhs point) n.* a type of stone spear point used by prehistoric residents of North America (page 384)

coalition *(koh-uh-LIH-shuhn) n.* a temporary alliance (page 139)

codex *(KOH-dehks) n.* a folded book made of tree-bark paper (page 389)

coercion *(koh-UR-zhuhn) n.* the use of force or threats (page 678)

collectivization *(kuh-lehk-tih-vuh-ZAY-shuhn) n.* the replacement of privately owned peasant farms with state-run collective farms (page 747)

Columbian Exchange *(kuh-LUHM-bee-uhn ihks-CHAYNJ) n.* the exchange of plants, animals, microbes, people, and ideas between Europe and the Americas, following Columbus's first voyage to the Western Hemisphere (page 488)

commerce *(KAH-muhrs) n.* the large-scale buying and selling of goods (page 277)

commission *(kuh-MIH-shuhn) n.* a request for a specific art or design project, usually from the nobility (page 417)

commodity *(kuh-MAH-duh-tee) n.* a valuable trade good (page 134)

common law *(KAH-muhn law) n.* a set of laws determined by earlier court decisions (page 583)

communism *(KAHM-yuh-nih-zuhm) n.* an economic and political system where all property is public, owned by the central state, and goods are distributed to everyone according to their needs (page 627)

compulsory education *(kuhm-PUHLS-ree eh-juh-KAY-shuhn) n.* education required by law (page 395)

concentration camp *(kahnt-suhn-TRAY-shuhn kamp) n.* a place where large numbers of people are imprisoned under armed guard; especially the camps created by the Nazis to hold Jews and other prisoners during World War II (page 675)

Confederacy *(kuhn-FEH-duh-ruh-see) n.* the 11 southern states that seceded from the Union to form their own nation (page 644)

connectivity *(kah-nehk-TIH-vuh-tee) n.* the state of being connected to others, especially through a computer system (page 898)

conquistador *(kahn-KEE-stuh-dawr) n.* a Spanish explorer who conquered lands in the Americas (page 484)

conscription *(kuhn-SKRIHP-shuhn) n.* forced enrollment in the military (page 475)

conservation *(kahnt-sur-VAY-shuhn) n.* the careful protection and preservation of something (page 893)

consolidate *(kuhn-SAH-luh-dayt) v.* to unify and strengthen (page 299)

constitutional monarchy *(kahnt-stuh-TOO-shnuhl MAH-nur-kee) n.* a government in which the monarch's power is limited by a constitution (page 540)

constitutionalism *(kahnt-stuh-TOO-shuh-nuh-lih-zuhm) n.* the concept of governing based on a set of basic principles or laws called a constitution (page 583)

consumption *(kuhn-SUHMP-shuhn) n.* spending (page 468)

containment policy *(kuhn-TAYN-muhnt PAH-luh-see) n.* a U.S. Cold War policy of providing military and economic aid to protect countries from communist takeover (page 800)

cosmopolitan *(kahz-muh-PAH-luh-tuhn) adj.* diverse and having familiarity with people, ideas, and objects from many parts of the world (page 205)

cost-benefit analysis *(KAWST-BEH-nuh-fiht uh-NA-luh-suhs) n.* the process in which good and bad points are compared to see whether the benefits of something outweigh its cost (page 863)

cottage industry *(KAH-tihj IHN-duh-stree) n.* a type of industry in which a family unit or individual creates a product at home with their own equipment (page 618)

countercultural *(kown-tur-KUHLCH-ruhl) adj.* relating to styles and traditions that run counter to those of mainstream society (page 717)

coup *(koo) n.* a sudden overthrow of government (page 110)

covenant *(KUHV-nuhnt) n.* a religious agreement (page 59)

crematoria *(kree-muh-TAWR-ee-uh) n.* ovens, especially those used by the Nazis in World War II to burn the bodies of those they murdered (page 783)

GLOSSARY

Crusade (kroo-SAYD) *n.* a Christian military expedition to recover the land of Palestine from Muslim rule (page 290)

cryptography (krihp-TAH-gruh-fee) *n.* secret codes and scrambling of data to keep electronic information safe (page 899)

cult of personality (kuhlt uhv pur-suh-NA-luh-tee) *n.* the promotion of a public figure as a person to be revered (page 747)

cultural diffusion (KUHLCH-ruhl dih-FYOO-zhuhn) *n.* the process by which cultures interact and ideas spread from one area to another (page 81)

cultural heritage (KUHLCH-ruhl HEHR-uh-tihj) *n.* the attributes of a group or society inherited from past generations (page 56)

cuneiform (kyoo-NEE-uh-fawrm) *n.* the earliest form of writing, developed by the Sumerians (page 39)

currency (KUR-uhnt-see) *n.* money in circulation (page 311)

D

D-Day (DEE-day) *n.* a term used to refer to the Allied invasion of Normandy, France, during World War II (page 771)

daimyo (DY-mee-oh) *n.* a wealthy landowner in feudal Japan (page 317)

Dalit (DAL-iht) *n.* a member of the lowest Hindu caste in traditional Indian society (page 750)

debt peonage (deht PEE-uh-nihj) *n.* a system in which workers pay off their debt with labor (page 654)

deductive approach (dih-DUHK-tihv uh-PROHCH) *n.* an approach to scientific inquiry that involves moving from general principles to specific truths (page 549)

deism (DEE-ih-zuhm) *n.* a religious philosophy that supports the idea of natural religion, in which God does not interfere with natural laws (page 573)

deity (DEE-uh-tee) *n.* a god or goddess (page 133)

delegation (deh-lih-GAY-shuhn) *n.* a group of people chosen to represent others (page 198)

delta (DEHL-tuh) *n.* a triangular-shaped area of low, flat land at the mouth of a river (page 42)

demilitarized zone (dee-MIH-luh-tuh-ryzd zohn) *n.* an area where weapons and military forces are forbidden (page 821)

democracy (dih-MAH-kruh-see) *n.* a form of government in which common citizens have a voice in making decisions and choosing leaders (page 130)

demographics (deh-muh-GRA-fihks) *n.* the characteristics of a particular population (page 309)

deportation (dee-pawr-TAY-shuhn) *n.* the removal of a person from a nation (page 713)

depose (dih-POHZ) *v.* to remove from power (page 207)

depth charge (dehpth chahrj) *n.* an underwater bomb that is programmed to explode at a certain depth (page 778)

despotic (dehs-PAH-tihk) *adj.* tyrannical, having absolute power (page 340)

despotism (DEHS-puh-tih-zuhm) *n.* the oppressive rule by a leader with absolute power (page 587)

détente (day-TAHNT) *n.* the easing of tensions and an improvement in relations between nations (page 834)

dharma (DUR-muh) *n.* a Sanskrit term meaning the way of righteous conduct (page 71)

dhimmitude (DIH-muh-tood) *n.* the protected status of certain non-Muslims in the Muslim world (page 251)

dhow (dow) *n.* an early type of ship that carried trade goods across the Indian Ocean (page 375)

dialect (DY-uh-lehkt) *n.* a regional variation in language (page 309)

diaspora (dy-AS-puh-ruh) *n.* the migration of people from an ancestral homeland (page 17)

dictator (DIHK-tay-tuhr) *n.* a person who rules with total authority (page 153)

diplomacy (duh-PLOH-muh-see) *n.* negotiation between governments (page 48)

disenfranchised (dihs-ihn-FRAN-chyzd) *adj.* lacking rights or the ability to influence a government (page 584)

displaced (dihs-PLAYST) *adj.* forced from a place or home (page 875)

dissident (DIH-sih-duhnt) *n.* a person who is at odds with an established practice, such as a particular religion (page 442)

division of labor (duh-VIH-zhuhn uhv LAY-bur) *n.* a system in which people perform different jobs to meet the needs of a society; a process that divides a task into separate parts with each completed by a different person or group (pages 34 and 617)

doctrine (DAHK-truhn) *n.* an official belief (page 289)

domestication (duh-mehs-tih-KAY-shuhn) *n.* the taming of wild animals (page 23)

dominion (duh-MIH-nyuhn) *n.* a self-governing commonwealth within an empire (page 651)

domino effect (DAH-muh-noh ih-FEHKT) *n.* the belief that if one country becomes communist, its neighbors will fall to communism like a row of dominoes (page 800)

dowry (DOW-ree) *n.* property that a woman brings to her marriage (page 458)

drone (drohn) *n.* a pilotless airplane run by remote control (page 875)

duchy (DUH-chee) *n.* a territory ruled by a duke or duchess (page 271)

dynastic cycle (dy-NAS-tihk SY-kuhl) *n.* the pattern of the rise and fall of dynasties in ancient and early China (page 84)

dynasty (DY-nuh-stee) *n.* a series of rulers from the same family (page 44)

E

earthwork (URTH-wurk) *n.* a construction of soil and rocks (page 392)

economy (ih-KAH-nuh-mee) *n.* the system for producing and obtaining goods and services (page 24)

edict (EE-dihkt) *n.* an official proclamation (page 159)

embargo (ihm-BAHR-goh) *n.* a ban on engaging in commerce with specified countries (pages 646 and 805)

embellish (ihm-BEH-lihsh) *v.* to decorate with ornamental details (page 455)

empire (EHM-pyr) *n.* a group of nations or peoples ruled by a single person or government (page 39)

encomienda (ehn-koh-mee-EHN-duh) *n.* a legal system that allowed each settler in the Spanish Americas to exact tribute, mainly in labor, from a certain number of Native Americans (page 497)

enlightened despot (ihn-LY-tuhnd DEHS-puht) *n.* an absolute ruler who applied certain Enlightenment ideas (page 577)

enlightenment (ihn-LY-tuhn-muhnt) *n.* a state when someone obtains a deep understanding and sense of clarity (page 72)

entrepreneur (ahn-truh-pruh-NUR) *n.* a person who organizes and operates a business (page 465)

envoy (EHN-voy) *n.* a diplomatic representative (page 339)

epic (EH-pihk) *n.* a long narrative poem that relates the adventures of a legendary or historical hero (page 37)

epistle (ih-PIH-suhl) *n.* a letter (page 175)

equatorial (ee-kwuh-TAWR-ee-uhl) *adj.* located at or near the equator (page 755)

estate (ih-STAYT) *n.* one of three distinct social classes in prerevolutionary France—the First Estate (clergy); the Second Estate (nobility); and the Third Estate (commoners) (page 584)

ethnography (ehth-NAH-gruh-fee) *n.* the study of the linguistic and cultural relationships between peoples (page 554)

excommunication (ehk-skuh-myoo-nuh-KAY-shuhn) *n.* expulsion from the Christian Church (page 275)

exile (EHG-zyl) *n.* the forced removal from one's homeland (page 61)

expatriate (ehk-SPAY-tree-uht) *n.* a person who chooses to live outside of his or her home country (page 717)

exposition (ehk-spuh-ZIH-shuhn) *n.* a world fair or exhibition (page 623)

extraterritoriality (ehk-struh-tair-uh-tawr-ee-A-luh-tee) *n.* exemption from local law (page 632)

extremist (ihk-STREE-mihst) *n.* a person with a radical view (page 872)

F

famine (FA-muhn) *n.* an extreme shortage of food in a country or large geographic area (page 296)

fascism (FA-shih-zuhm) *n.* a way of governing based on extreme nationalism, racism, and suppression of opposition (page 742)

fauna (FAW-nuh) *n.* the animals of a specific place (page 554)

federal (FEH-duh-ruhl) *adj.* relating to a government where power is shared between the central, national government and that of states or provinces (page 583)

feudalism (FYOO-duh-lih-zuhm) *n.* a name given to the legal and social system in medieval Europe in which serfs worked the land and vassals performed military service for their lords in return for protection (page 276)

figurehead (FIH-gyur-hehd) *n.* a leader in name only (page 257)

filial piety (FIH-lee-uhl PY-uh-tee) *n.* respect for one's parents (page 86)

fiscal austerity (FIH-skuhl aw-STEHR-uh-tee) *n.* any measure to avoid debt, such as cutting spending or raising taxes (page 886)

flora (FLAWR-uh) *n.* the plants of a specific place (page 552)

food security (food sih-KYOOR-uh-tee) *n.* the assurance that food will be available to maintain health (page 552)

fracking (FRA-kihng) *n.* the process of drilling into the earth and applying water pressure to force out natural gases by breaking up rock (page 892)

fresco (FREH-skoh) *n.* a painting drawn on wet plaster (page 124)

fundamentalism (fuhn-duh-MEHN-tuh-lih-zuhm) *n.* a strict adherence to a set of basic principles, often relating to political or religious beliefs (page 857)

G

garrison town (GAIR-uh-suhn town) *n.* a town where soldiers of an empire were based (page 203)

genocide (JEH-nuh-syd) *n.* the systematic destruction of a racial or cultural group (page 675)

geocentric theory (jee-oh-SEHN-trihk THEE-uh-ree) *n.* the theory that the sun and planets revolve around Earth (page 546)

geoglyph (JEE-uh-glihf) *n.* a large geometric design or shape drawn on the ground, created by scraping away dark surface dirt and rocks to reveal lighter-colored soil (page 396)

geothermal energy (jee-oh-THUR-muhl EH-nur-jee) *n.* energy derived from heat released by Earth's interior (page 892)

ger (gur) *n.* a portable felt tent used by Mongol nomads (page 326)

ghazi (GAH-zee) *n.* a warrior for Islam (page 344)

ghetto (GEH-toh) *n.* a separate section of a city in which minority groups are forced to live (page 294)

Ghost Dance (gohst dahnts) *n.* a ceremonial dance performed by some Native Americans who believed the dance would summon a deliverer who would restore their world (page 680)

gladiator (GLA-dee-ay-tur) *n.* a man who battled wild animals or other men to entertain spectators (page 163)

glasnost (GLAZ-nohst) *n.* a government policy of open communication in the former Soviet Union (page 834)

globalization (gloh-buh-luh-ZAY-shuhn) *n.* the development of an increasingly integrated global economy marked especially by free trade, free flow of capital, and the tapping of cheaper foreign labor markets (page 624)

Great Depression (grayt dih-PREH-shuhn) *n.* a time of intense financial hardship that lasted throughout the 1930s (page 740)

green building (green BIHL-dihng) *n.* the act of designing and building structures with the environment in mind (page 893)

griot (GREE-oh) *n.* a West African storyteller who relates stories through the oral tradition (page 361)

guerrilla warfare (guh-RIH-luh WAWR-fair) *n.* small-scale surprise attacks (page 675)

guild (gihld) *n.* an association formed by artisans or merchants to improve their business (page 277)

guillotine (gee-yuh-TEEN) *n.* a machine with a sharp blade designed for beheading people (page 587)

Gulag (GOO-lahg) *n.* the Soviet system of forced-labor camps (page 721)

H

habeas corpus (HAY-bee-uhs KAWR-puhs) *n.* a legal procedure that prevents the government from holding a person indefinitely, without coming before a judge (page 283)

hacienda (hah-see-EHN-duh) *n.* a large plantation in a Spanish-speaking colony (page 497)

hacker (HA-kur) *n.* an individual who illegally gains access to electronic information (page 898)

hajj (haj) *n.* a Muslim pilgrimage to the holy city of Mecca (page 245)

heliocentric theory (hee-lee-oh-SEHN-trihk THEE-uh-ree) *n.* the theory that Earth and other planets revolve around the sun (page 547)

Hellenization (hehl-luh-nuh-ZAY-shuhn) *n.* the process by which Greek culture was spread throughout the Persian Empire (page 140)

helot (HEH-luht) *n.* a state-owned slave in ancient Sparta (page 129)

heretic (HEHR-uh-tihk) *n.* a church member who holds religious views contrary to official doctrine (page 294)

hieroglyph (HY-ruh-glihf) *n.* a picture representing an object, sound, or idea that was part of the ancient Egyptian writing system (page 46)

Hind Swaraj (hihnd swuh-RAHJ) *n.* the idea of self-rule in India (page 750)

Hindu-Arabic numerals (HIHN-doo-ehr-uh-bihk NOOM-ruhlz) *n.* the numerals 1, 2, 3 . . . etc. originally from India and brought to the West through Arab traders (page 195)

historiography (hih-stawr-ee-AH-gruh-fee) *n.* the art and science of creating a reliable and useful story from bits of information about the past (page 8)

holy war (HOH-lee wawr) *n.* warfare in defense of a religious faith (page 290)

hoplite (HAWP-lyt) *n.* a heavily armed soldier of ancient Greece (page 129)

human record (HYOO-muhn REH-kurd) *n.* the story of human life on Earth over the centuries (page 56)

humanism (HYOO-muh-nih-zuhm) *n.* an intellectual movement based on the works of classical Greek and Roman thinkers (page 424)

hunter-gatherer (HUHN-tuhr-GA-thur-ur) *n.* a person who survives by hunting game and gathering wild plants (page 13)

GLOSSARY **R4**

GLOSSARY

hypothesis (hy-PAH-thuh-suhs) n. an unproven theory that might answer a question and can be tested (page 549)

I

icon (EYE-kahn) n. a sacred or religious image (page 234)

iconoclast (eye-KAH-nuh-klast) n. a member of Byzantine society opposed to the use of icons; literally means "image breaker" (page 235)

ideology (eye-dee-AH-luh-jee) n. a system of ideas expressing a social or political philosophy about the world (page 591)

imperialism (ihm-PIHR-ee-uh-lih-zuhm) n. the practice by which a country increases its power by gaining control over other areas of the world (page 668)

indentured servant (ihn-DEHN-churd SUR-vuhnt) n. a person under contract to work, usually without pay, in exchange for free passage to the colonies (page 505)

indigenous (ihn-DIH-juh-nuhs) adj. native to a particular place (page 15)

indoctrinate (ihn-DAHK-truh-nayt) v. to rigidly train in a theory or doctrine (page 808)

inductive approach (ihn-DUHK-tihv uh-PROHCH) n. an approach to scientific research that involves working from carefully controlled observations to larger truths (page 549)

indulgence (ihn-DUHL-juhnts) n. a special prayer that could be purchased from the Roman Catholic Church to save a person's soul (page 434)

infamy (IHN-fuh-mee) n. an extremely shameful or evil act (page 768)

inflation (ihn-FLAY-shuhn) n. an increase in the price of goods and services compared to the value of money (page 455)

infrastructure (IHN-fruh-struhk-chur) n. networks for transportation, water, and other utilities (page 315)

Inquisition (ihn-kwuh-ZIH-shun) n. a special court formed by the Roman Catholic Church to hear charges against accused heretics (page 294)

insolvency (ihn-SAWL-vuhnt-see) n. the inability to pay debts; bankruptcy (page 799)

institution (ihn-stuh-TOO-shuhn) n. an organization that is established for a specific purpose and continues over time (page 35)

insurgent (in-SUR-juhnt) n. a rebel fighter (page 589)

intermediary (ihn-tur-MEE-dee-air-ee) n. a person who serves as a go-between in an exchange involving two other parties (page 362)

intifada (ihn-tuh-FAH-duh) n. a Palestinian uprising against Israel's occupation of the West Bank and Gaza (page 855)

iron (EYE-urn) n. a heavy metal that is used to make steel (page 54)

irrigation (ihr-uh-GAY-shuhn) n. a human-made system to transport water where it is needed (page 35)

Islamist (ihs-LAH-mihst) n. a Muslim who believes that laws and constitutions should be guided by Islamic principles and that religious authorities should be directly involved in the government (page 515)

island hopping (EYE-luhnd HAH-ping) n. a strategy designed by the Allies in World War II to capture and control islands in the Pacific one by one (page 772)

isolationism (eye-suh-LAY-shuh-nih-zuhm) n. a policy in which a nation refrains from alliances and other international political relations (page 761)

J

janissary (JA-nuh-sair-ee) n. a highly trained and disciplined soldier and slave in the Ottoman army (page 450)

Jim Crow Laws (jihm kroh lawz) n. laws established after Reconstruction that enforced racial segregation across the southern United States (page 662)

joint-stock company (joynt-stahk KUHM-puh-nee) n. a business enterprise funded by the sale of shares to multiple investors (page 492)

junta (HUN-tuh) n. a military or political ruling group who often take power by force (page 600)

K

kamikaze (kah-mih-KAH-zee) n. a Japanese suicide bomber pilot during World War II (page 772)

karma (KAHR-muh) n. the sum of a person's actions in life that determines his or her rebirth in the next life (page 71)

khanate (KAH-nayt) n. an area of the Mongol Empire ruled by a khan (page 328)

knight (nyt) n. a horse-riding warrior who served as a lord's vassal (page 276)

Kristallnacht (KRIH-stuhl-nahkt) n. the destruction of Jewish homes, businesses, and synagogues by the Nazis on the night of November 9, 1938 (page 745)

kulak (KOO-lak) n. a wealthy peasant in the Soviet Union of the early 20th century (page 747)

L

La Reforma (lah reh-FAWRM-uh) n. a reform movement in Mexico that called for the redistribution of land, the separation of church and state, and greater educational opportunities for the poor (page 655)

laissez-faire (LEH-say-FEHR) n. an economic system in which businesses and industries regulate their activities without government interference (page 569)

laity (LAY-uh-tee) n. members of the church who are not clergy (page 288)

lar (lahr) n. a Roman household god (page 157)

leftist (LEHF-tihst) n. a person who supports radical economic and social changes (page 845)

legionary (LEE-juh-nehr-ee) n. a paid professional soldier in the Roman army (page 162)

liberalism (LIH-buh-ruh-lih-zuhm) n. a belief system that argues that the liberty of the individual is the main concern of politics (page 626)

lineage (lih-NEE-ihj) n. a group of descendants from a common ancestor (page 361)

Linear B (LIH-nee-ur bee) n. the Mycenaean writing system, believed to be an early form of the Greek language (page 125)

linear perspective (LIH-nee-ur pur-SPEHK-tihv) n. an artistic technique in which the artist uses the placement and size of figures on a flat plane to make a scene appear three-dimensional (page 426)

liturgy (LIH-tur-jee) n. a form of worship (page 437)

loess (lehs) n. a type of fine, fertile, yellow silt that floats through the waters of the Huang He in China (page 83)

longevity (lahn-JEH-vuh-tee) n. an increased lifespan (page 909)

longitude (LAHN-juh-tood) n. an object's east-west position measured in degrees or difference in time (page 554)

M

magnate (MAG-nayt) n. a wealthy, powerful, and influential businessperson (page 675)

maize (mayz) n. a grain similar to corn (page 386)

Mandate of Heaven (MAN-dayt uhv HEH-vuhn) n. the ancient Chinese belief that Heaven, the generalized forces of the cosmos, chooses the rightful ruler who rules as long as Heaven believes he is worthy (page 84)

manorialism *(muh-NAWR-uh-lih-zuhm) n.* a medieval economic, social, and political system in which agricultural laborers were tied to the land they farmed and to the lord who owned the land (page 276)

mansa *(MAHNT-suh) n.* a West African king (page 362)

manumission *(man-yuh-MIH-shuhn) n.* the release of a person from slavery (page 518)

maritime *(MEHR-uh-tym) adj.* relating to the sea (page 200)

maroon community *(muh-ROON kuh-MYOO-nuh-tee) n.* one of the self-governing groups of escaped slaves common in the Caribbean and coastal areas of Central and South America beginning in the 1500s (page 527)

mass media *(mas MEE-dee-uh) n.* means of communication meant to reach many people (page 736)

mass society *(mas suh-SY-uh-tee) n.* a society in which large numbers of people share the same experience without actually having to meet (page 736)

mausoleum *(maw-suh-LEE-uhm) n.* a large tomb (page 459)

medieval *(mee-DEE-vuhl) adj.* referring to a period in European history from about 500 to 1500 C.E. (page 227)

mercantilism *(MUR-kuhn-tuh-lih-zuhm) n.* a system in which government protects and encourages trade, based on the theory that such businesses create wealth (page 483)

mercenary *(MUHR-suh-nehr-ee) n.* a soldier who is paid to fight (page 154)

meritocracy *(mehr-uh-TAH-kruh-see) n.* a system in which qualified people are chosen and promoted on the basis of their achievement rather than social position (page 88)

mestizo *(mehs-TEE-zoh) n.* person of mixed Spanish and Native American ancestry (page 497)

metallurgy *(MEH-tuhl-uhr-jee) n.* the science or technology of working with metals (page 195)

Métis *(may-TEES) n.* people of mixed European and indigenous descent (page 651)

Middle Passage *(MIH-duhl PA-sihj) n.* the journey by slave ships across the Atlantic from West Africa to the Americas (page 518)

migrate *(MY-grayt) v.* to move from one region to another (page 11)

militarism *(MIH-luh-tuh-rih-zuhm) n.* a government policy of continuous military development and readiness for war (page 639)

militia *(muh-LIH-shuh) n.* a volunteer army (page 582)

minaret *(mih-nuh-REHT) n.* a tall tower from which specially trained Muslims issue the call to prayer (page 252)

missionary *(MIH-shuh-nehr-ee) n.* a person sent out to convert others to a religion (page 175)

mitochondrial Eve *(my-tuh-KAHN-dree-uhl EEV) n.* a single human female ancestor common to all human beings (page 8)

mobilize *(MOH-buh-lyz) v.* to assemble and prepare for war (page 698)

monarchy *(MAH-nur-kee) n.* a government ruled by a single person, such as a king (page 44)

monastery *(MAH-nuh-stehr-ee) n.* a Christian religious community and center of learning, work, and worship (page 271)

monopoly *(muh-NAH-puh-lee) n.* sole control over something; the complete and exclusive control of an industry by one company (pages 362 and 663)

monotheism *(MAH-nuh-thee-ih-zuhm) n.* the belief in one God (page 59)

monsoon *(mahn-SOON) n.* a strong seasonal wind in South and Southeast Asia (page 81)

mosaic *(moh-ZAY-ihk) n.* a group of tiny colored stone cubes set in mortar to create a picture or design (page 239)

mosque *(mahsk) n.* a Muslim place of worship (page 247)

mother culture *(MUH-thur KUHL-chur) n.* a civilization that greatly influences other civilizations (page 387)

movable type *(MOO-vuh-buhl typ) n.* individual clay tablets that could be arranged to form text in an early form of printing (page 310)

muckraker *(MUHK-ray-kur) n.* an investigative journalist of the early 1900s who exposed misconduct by powerful organizations and people (page 663)

mujahideen *(moo-ja-hih-DEEN) n.* Islamic guerilla fighters (page 825)

multinational corporation *(muhl-tee-NASH-nuhl kawr-puh-RAY-shuhn) n.* a company with locations around the world that is owned and managed by teams from more than one nation (page 863)

mummy *(MUH-mee) n.* the preserved body of a pharaoh or other person in ancient Egypt (page 45)

mystic *(MIHS-tihk) n.* a person who seeks knowledge of God through devotion or meditation (page 279)

N

napalm *(NAY-pahm) n.* a highly flammable, jelly-like substance that sticks to targets and generates extreme heat (page 778)

nation-building *(NAY-shuhn BIHL-dihng) n.* the establishment of order and a functioning government in a country that has been plagued by violence and instability (page 845)

nation-state *(NAY-shuhn-STAYT) n.* a state made up of people of one nationality, sharing common traits (page 591)

nationalism *(NASH-nuh-lih-zuhm) n.* the belief that individuals are bound together by ties of language, culture, history, and often religion (page 591)

nationalize *(NASH-nuh-lyz) v.* to bring a private business or industry under the control of the national government (page 720)

nativism *(NAY-tih-vih-zuhm) n.* the practice of favoring ideas of the home country rather than those of immigrants or foreign countries (page 469)

natural rights *(NA-chuh-ruhl ryts) n.* inherent rights, such as life, liberty, and property (page 565)

naturalism *(NA-chuh-ruh-lih-zuhm) n.* an artistic style that strove for accurate depictions of people or the natural world (page 418)

Neanderthal *(nee-AN-dur-tawl) n.* a member of an extinct species of early humans (page 15)

nebula *(NEH-byuh-luh) n.* a cloud of gas and dust in outer space (page 551)

neoclassicism *(nee-oh-KLA-suh-sih-zuhm) n.* a creative style based on Greek and Roman ideals (page 596)

neocolonialism *(nee-oh-kuh-LOHN-yuh-lih-zuhm) n.* the continuation of dependence on, and domination by, a colonial power (page 812)

neoliberalism *(nee-oh-LIH-bruh-lih-zuhm) n.* an economic approach that emphasizes free markets and wide international trade (page 863)

Neolithic *(nee-uh-LIH-thihk) adj.* the term to describe people who use stone tools and practice agriculture; means "new stone age" (page 22)

nirvana *(nihr-VAH-nuh) n.* a state of blissful escape from suffering caused by the cycle of life and rebirth (page 72)

nomad *(NOH-mad) n.* a person who migrates from place to place (page 69)

nonalignment *(nahn-uh-LYN-muhnt) n.* a policy of not allying with other countries, specifically with either the communist or noncommunist countries during the Cold War (page 816)

nongovernmental organization (NGO) *(nahn-guh-vurn-MEHN-tuhl awr-guh-nuh-ZAY-shuhn) n.* a nonprofit group that supports a particular cause (page 858)

GLOSSARY

nonintervention *(nahn-ihn-tur-VEHNT-shuhn)* n. the policy of not getting involved in the affairs of other countries (page 760)

Northwest Passage *(nawrth-WEHST PA-sihj)* n. a sea route from the Atlantic Ocean to the Pacific along the northern coast of North America (page 493)

O

oasis *(oh-AY-suhs)* n. an isolated place in the desert with water where plants can grow (page 244)

oligarchy *(AW-luh-gawr-kee)* n. a form of government ruled by a few powerful citizens (page 129)

omnipotence *(ahm-NIH-puh-tuhnts)* n. unlimited power (pages 192 and 341)

optics *(AHP-tiks)* n. the study of light and vision (page 546)

oracle bone *(AWR-uh-kuhl bohn)* n. a bone used in ancient China to consult ancestors about the future; now known to be China's earliest surviving written records (page 83)

oral tradition *(AW-ruhl truh-DIH-shuhn)* n. a group of stories that take a standard form and are passed down through generations by people talking with one another (page 125)

oratory *(AWR-uh-tawr-ee)* n. the art of public speaking (page 184)

orthodoxy *(AWR-thuh-dahk-see)* n. established beliefs and practices (page 542)

outsourcing *(OWT-sawr-sihng)* n. the practice of sending work once done internally at a company to be done by people outside the company, usually for lower wages (page 863)

P

pacifist *(PA-suh-fihst)* n. a person with a religious or philosophical objection to violence (page 860)

Pan-Africanism *(pan-A-frih-kuh-nih-zuhm)* n. the idea that people of African descent have a common heritage and should be unified (page 685)

pandemic *(pan-DEH-mihk)* n. a worldwide outbreak of infectious disease (page 708)

pantheon *(PAN-thee-ahn)* n. a group of officially recognized gods and goddesses (page 157)

papyrus *(puh-PY-ruhs)* n. a paperlike material made from reeds (page 46)

Parliament *(PAHR-luh-muhnt)* n. the lawmaking body in England (page 283)

partition *(pahr-TIH-shuhn)* n. the division of a country (page 817)

passive resistance *(PA-sihv rih-ZIH-stuhnts)* n. nonviolent opposition to authority (page 846)

patriarchy *(PAY-tree-ahr-kee)* n. a society in which men have all the power (page 156)

patrician *(puh-TRIH-shuhn)* n. a wealthy landowner in Roman society (page 153)

patron *(PAY-truhn)* n. a person who gives artists financial support (page 415)

people's commune *(PEE-puhlz KAHM-yoon)* n. in China, a grouping of collective farms in which people lived and worked together to produce both crops and industrial goods (page 810)

perestroika *(pehr-uh-STROY-kuh)* n. a government policy of economic and government reform in the former Soviet Union (page 834)

petition *(puh-TIH-shuhn)* n. a formal written request (page 476)

phalanx *(FAY-langks)* n. a body of soldiers moving in close formation (page 114)

pharaoh *(FEHR-oh)* n. a king of ancient Egypt (page 43)

philosophe *(fee-luh-ZAWF)* n. one of the writers and thinkers of the European Enlightenment (page 568)

physiography *(fih-zee-AH-gruh-fee)* n. the physical geography of a place (page 316)

piety *(PY-uh-tee)* n. a strong belief in religion shown through worship (page 441)

pilgrimage *(PIHL-gruh-mihj)* n. a journey to a holy place (page 176)

plague *(playg)* n. a deadly epidemic disease (page 226)

plebeian *(plih-BEE-uhn)* n. a commoner in Rome (page 153)

pogrom *(puh-GRAHM)* n. an organized attack upon or massacre of a minority group (page 294)

polis *(PAW-luhs)* n. a Greek city-state (page 128)

polytheism *(PAH-lee-thee-ih-zuhm)* n. the belief in many gods (page 38)

popular culture *(PAH-pyuh-lur KUHL-chur)* n. the shared experiences and interests of everyday people (page 736)

popular sovereignty *(PAH-pyuh-lur SAH-vuh-ruhn-tee)* n. the belief that government arises from the people themselves (page 583)

populism *(PAH-pyuh-lih-zuhm)* n. a political movement that claims to support the concerns of common people (page 804)

preempt *(pree-EHMPT)* v. to prevent from happening (page 854)

principate *(PRIHN-suh-payt)* n. a type of monarchy in which some republican ideals are upheld (page 159)

proletariat *(proh-luh-TEHR-ee-uht)* n. the working class (page 627)

propaganda *(prah-puh-GAN-duh)* n. information used by a government to make people think or act in a particular way (page 591)

Protestant *(PRAH-tuh-stuhnt)* n. a person who protested against the Catholic Church and became part of a reformed church (page 436)

proxy war *(PRAHK-see WAWR)* n. a war in which one or both sides are supported by, and serve the interests of, another country (page 802)

public works *(PUH-blihk wurks)* n. government construction projects that benefit a community (page 40)

pull factor *(pul FAK-tur)* n. a factor or incentive that attracts people to move to a new country (page 477)

push factor *(push FAK-tur)* n. a factor or condition that causes people to leave their home countries (page 477)

pyramid *(PIHR-uh-mihd)* n. a large, four-sided monument built in ancient Egypt as a tomb for a pharaoh (page 44)

Q

qadi *(KAH-dee)* n. a Muslim judge (page 256)

quipu *(KEE-poo)* n. a series of knotted strings the Inca used to keep records (page 399)

quorum *(KWAWR-uhm)* n. a minimum number of people who must be present to conduct a group's business (page 131)

R

racism *(RAY-sih-zuhm)* n. the belief that the color of a person's skin makes them superior or inferior (page 521)

recession *(rih-SEH-shuhn)* n. a period of reduced economic activity (page 886)

Reconstruction *(ree-kuhn-STRUHK-shuhn)* n. the effort to rebuild and reunite the United States after the Civil War (page 645)

redistributive economy *(ree-duh-STRIH-byoo-tihv ih-KAH-nuh-mee)* n. a type of economy in which produce and other goods are stored in a central place and are then sorted and distributed to the population (page 124)

referendum *(reh-fuh-REHN-duhm)* n. a public vote on a single political question (page 813)

refugee *(reh-fyoo-JEE)* n. a person who is forced to leave his or her homeland because of war, persecution, or natural disaster (page 61)

regent *(ree-juhnt) n.* a person who rules when a monarch or emperor is unable to do so (page 209)

reincarnation *(ree-ihn-kahr-NAY-shuhn) n.* the rebirth of a soul in a different body over different life cycles (page 71)

relief *(rih-LEEF) n.* a type of sculpture in which three-dimensional elements rise from a flat background (page 56)

religiosity *(rih-lih-jee-AH-suh-tee) n.* a strong religious belief (page 885)

religious syncretism *(rih-LIH-juhs SING-kruh-tih-zuhm) n.* the blending of different belief systems (page 443)

religious tolerance *(rih-LIH-juhs TAH-luh-ruhnts) n.* the acceptance of the beliefs and practices of others (page 253)

remilitarization *(ree-mih-luh-tuh-ruh-ZAY-shuhn) n.* the process of rearming (page 760)

reparations *(reh-puh-RAY-shuhnz) n.* money or goods paid to cover wartime damages (page 708)

republic *(rih-PUH-blihk) n.* a form of government in which people choose officials to represent them instead of voting directly on laws and policies (page 153)

revenue *(REH-vuh-noo) n.* income for the government, such as taxes (page 458)

revisionist *(rih-VIH-zhuh-nihst) adj.* straying from the revolutionary spirit of Marxist doctrine (page 809)

Romanticism *(roh-MAN-tuh-sih-zuhm) n.* a cultural movement originating in the 18th century that emphasized emotions over reason (page 596)

S

sabotage *(SA-buh-tahzh) n.* a deliberate destruction (page 617)

Sahel *(SA-hihl) n.* a semidesert region south of the Sahara (page 360)

salon *(suh-LAHN) n.* a social gathering organized by Parisian women to discuss Enlightenment ideas (page 572)

sanction *(SANGK-shuhn) n.* a trade or financial restriction placed by one nation on another (page 757)

Sanskrit *(SAN-skriht) n.* a classical Indo-European language spoken by Indo-Aryan migrants to northern India around 1500–1000 B.C.E. (page 69)

satellite state *(SA-tuh-lyt STAYT) n.* a country that is formally independent but under the control or influence of another country (page 799)

satire *(SA-tyr) n.* humor and sarcasm used to expose or ridicule human foolishness or weakness (pages 133 and 425)

satrap *(SAY-trap) n.* a provincial governor (page 104)

satyagraha *(suh-TYAH-gruh-huh) n.* the application of nonviolence to politics, according to Indian belief (page 750)

savanna *(suh-VA-nuh) n.* an area of lush tropical grasslands (page 360)

scientific method *(sy-uhn-TIH-fihk MEH-thuhd) n.* a logical procedure for developing and testing scientific ideas (page 549)

scientific rationalism *(sy-uhn-TIH-fihk RASH-nuh-lih-zuhm) n.* a school of thought in which observation, experimentation, and mathematical reasoning replace ancient wisdom and church teachings as the source of scientific truths (page 549)

scribe *(skryb) n.* a professional writer who recorded official information in ancient societies (page 46)

script *(skrihpt) n.* a form of writing (page 153)

secede *(sih-SEED) v.* to formally withdraw from a nation (page 644)

sectionalism *(SEHK-shuh-nuh-lih-zuhm) n.* a loyalty to whichever section or region of the country one is from, rather than to the nation as a whole (page 644)

secular *(SEH-kyuh-lur) adj.* not belonging to a religious order (page 288)

segregation *(seh-grih-GAY-shuhn) n.* the separation of different groups of people, usually based on race (page 645)

self-determination *(sehlf-dih-tur-muh-NAY-shuhn) n.* the process by which a people forms its own state and chooses its own government (page 708)

Senate *(SEH-nuht) n.* the governing body in ancient Rome that advised the consuls and was initially made up of wealthy landowners (page 153)

sepoy *(SEE-poy) n.* an Indian soldier under British command (page 635)

serf *(suhrf) n.* a medieval agricultural worker who was tied to the land (page 276)

shah *(shaw) n.* a king in Iran (page 452)

sharia *(shuh-REE-uh) n.* Islamic law covering all aspects of life (page 246)

sheikh *(sheek) n.* the leader of a Bedouin clan (page 244)

shell shock *(shehl shahk) n.* a mental health condition resulting from exposure to warfare (page 717)

shogun *(SHOH-guhn) n.* a Japanese general who is the military ruler of the country (page 317)

silt *(silt) n.* especially fine and fertile soil (page 35)

slash-and-burn agriculture *(slash-uhnd-burn A-grih-kuhl-chur) n.* a method of clearing fields for planting (page 388)

slave narrative *(slayv NAIR-uh-tihv) n.* a written account of the life of a fugitive or former slave (page 518)

social class *(SOH-shuhl klas) n.* a system in which people are grouped according to rank and power (page 35)

social contract *(SOH-shuhl KAHN-trakt) n.* an agreement between rulers and the ruled to cooperate for mutual social benefits in pursuit of an ordered society, with clearly defined rights and responsibilities for each (page 565)

social criticism *(SOH-shuhl KRIH-tuh-sih-zuhm) n.* a type of writing that tries to improve social conditions (page 617)

Social Darwinism *(SOH-shuhl DAHR-wuh-nih-zuhm) n.* the idea that racial groups are naturally arranged along a hierarchy (page 627)

social justice *(SOH-shuhl JUH-stuhs) n.* equal rights for all under the law (page 874)

socialism *(SOH-shuh-lih-zuhm) n.* an economic system in which industry is collectively owned, private property is allowed, and people are paid based on their contribution to production (page 627)

sovereignty *(SAH-vuh-ruhn-tee) n.* freedom from external control (page 542)

Soviet bloc *(SOH-vee-eht BLAHK) n.* a group of nations under the control of the Soviet Union (page 800)

speculation *(speh-kyuh-LAY-shuhn) n.* the taking of huge risks to gain great rewards (page 740)

sphere of influence *(sfihr uhv IHN-floo-uhnts) n.* an area in which the dominance of one colonial power is recognized above all others (page 672)

stagnation *(stag-NAY-shuhn) n.* a lack of growth and development (page 227)

stalemate *(STAYL-mayt) n.* a situation in which neither side can defeat the other (page 700)

status quo *(STAY-tuhs-KWOH) n.* an existing condition (page 593)

stela *(STEE-luh) n.* a stone pillar used for the purpose of commemorating an important event or accomplishment (page 41)

steppe *(stehp) n.* a vast, grassy plain (page 326)

stimulus *(STIHM-yuh-luhs) n.* an incentive (page 886)

strike *(stryk) n.* a work stoppage used as a labor union tactic (page 653)

subjugation *(suhb-jih-GAY-shuhn) n.* the state of being under control or governance (page 668)

subprime mortgage *(SUHB-prym MAWR-gihj) n.* a home loan given to someone with poor credit (page 886)

GLOSSARY

succession *(suhk-SEH-shuhn) n.* the process by which a new leader is chosen to follow an outgoing leader (page 512)

suffrage *(SUH-frihj) n.* the right to vote (page 663)

sultan *(SUHL-tuhn) n.* a ruler of a Muslim state (page 345)

surplus *(SUR-pluhs) n.* a supply of goods and labor not needed for short-term survival (page 28)

surveillance *(sur-VAY-luhnts) n.* the act of watching over a person or group (page 873)

sustainable *(suh-STAY-nuh-buhl) adj.* unceasing, especially relating to a way of using a resource so it is not depleted (page 892)

synagogue *(SIH-nuh-gahg) n.* a Jewish house of worship (page 61)

T

taiga *(TY-guh) n.* land covered with scattered evergreen trees in the far north or subarctic area (page 470)

technology *(tehk-NAH-luh-jee) n.* the practical application of knowledge; any tool or technique that helps people accomplish tasks (page 35)

tenement *(TEH-nuh-muhnt) n.* a large apartment building that is usually overcrowded and badly maintained (page 652)

terrace *(TAIR-uhs) n.* a stepped platform (page 387)

tetrarchy *(TEH-trahr-kee) n.* a structure of government in which four persons rule jointly (page 180)

theocracy *(thee-AH-kruh-see) n.* a form of government in which the legal system is based on religious law (page 61)

tithe *(tyth) n.* ten percent of a person's income to be paid to the church (page 288)

total war *(TOH-tuhl wawr) n.* a war that requires assembling and preparing all national resources and engaging civilians as well as the military (page 699)

totalitarian *(toh-ta-luh-TAIR-ee-uhn) adj.* relating to a political system that exerts total control over a society often through violent means (page 743)

trans-Saharan trade network *(tran-suh-HAIR-uhn trayd NEHT-wurk) n.* a group of overland trade routes that carried goods between North Africa and sub-Saharan Africa (page 368)

treason *(TREE-zuhn) n.* the crime of betraying one's government or country (page 199)

trench warfare *(trehnch WAWR-fair) n.* a type of warfare in which soldiers fight from long ditches that are fortified by barbed wire (page 700)

triangular trade *(try-ANG-gyuh-lur trayd) n.* the transatlantic trade network connecting Europe, West Africa, and the Americas between the 1500s and the 1800s (page 520)

tribe *(tryb) n.* an extended family unit (page 60)

tribunal *(try-BYOO-nuhl) n.* a court with authority over a specific matter (page 786)

tribune *(TRIH-byoon) n.* an elected representative who protected the rights of ordinary citizens in Rome (page 153)

tribute *(TRIH-byoot) n.* a tax required of conquered people (page 194)

trireme *(try-REEM) n.* an ancient Greek warship with three banks of oars (page 115)

troll *(trohl) n.* a person who purposely posts offensive or threatening messages on the Internet (page 899)

truce *(troos) n.* a temporary halt of warfare (page 290)

trusteeship *(truh-STEE-shihp) n.* the administrative control over a territory by one or more countries (page 820)

tsar *(zahr) n.* the ruler of imperial Russia (page 471)

tundra *(TUHN-druh) n.* treeless arctic plains (page 470)

two-state solution *(too-stayt suh-LOO-shuhn) n.* a solution to the Israeli-Palestinian conflict that calls for an independent state of Palestine alongside the state of Israel (page 853)

tyranny *(TIHR-uh-nee) n.* a state of government in which rulers have unlimited power and use it unfairly (page 565)

U

ultranationalist *(uhl-truh-NASH-nuh-lihst) n.* an extreme nationalist (page 748)

V

vaquero *(vah-KEHR-oh) n.* a cowboy or cattle herder (page 726)

varna *(VAHR-nuh) n.* the four major social groups of ancient Indian society, ranked in order of purity (page 71)

vassal *(VA-suhl) n.* in medieval Europe, a person who gave military service and pledged loyalty to a lord in exchange for protection and land to live on (page 276)

Vedic *(VAY-dihk) adj.* associated with the society or religion of the Indo-Aryan migrants (page 70)

venerate *(VEH-nuh-rayt) v.* to honor or adore (page 234)

vernacular *(vuhr-NA-kyuh-lur) n.* the everyday language spoken by people (page 281)

veto *(VEE-toh) v.* to vote against (page 129)

viceroy *(VYS-roy) n.* a representative of the king in the Spanish Americas (page 497)

viceroyalty *(VYS-roy-uhl-tee) n.* a colony (page 497)

W

weapons of mass destruction *(WEH-puhnz uhv mas dih-STRUHK-shuhn) n.* weapons that can cause extreme destruction over a wide area (page 873)

X

xenophobia *(zeh-nuh-FOH-bee-uh) n.* a fear of foreigners (page 875)

Z

zaibatsu *(zy-BAHT-soo) n.* a powerful financial and industrial Japanese conglomerate (page 639)

ziggurat *(ZIH-gur-rat) n.* a large, stepped structure in a Sumerian temple (page 39)

GLOSARIO

A

abdicar *v.* renunciar formalmente a algo, como a la soberanía del trono (página 203)

abolición *s.* movimiento para acabar con la esclavitud (página 519)

aborigen *s.* habitante originario de Australia (página 554)

acueducto *s.* canal de piedra que transportaba agua limpia desde las colinas hasta las ciudades (página 163)

adaptarse *v.* desarrollar características que contribuyen a la supervivencia (página 14)

adoctrinar *v.* entrenar rígidamente en una teoría o doctrina (página 808)

adoración de los ancestros *s.* práctica de contactar a los antepasados muertos con la creencia de que pueden interceder en eventos humanos en nombre de los vivos (página 83)

ágora *s.* mercado al aire libre en una ciudad-estado griega (página 128)

agricultura *s.* cultivo de alimentos vegetales y la domesticación de animales (página 22)

agricultura de tala y quema *s.* método para despejar campos para plantar (página 388)

ahimsa *s.* concepto indio de la no violencia absoluta (página 750)

aislacionismo *s.* política en la que una nación se abstiene de alianzas y otras relaciones políticas internacionales (página 761)

alfabeto *s.* grupo de letras que forman los elementos individuales de un sistema de escritura (página 126)

alianza *s.* asociación (página 40)

alminar *s.* torre alta desde la cual musulmanes especialmente entrenados emiten el llamado a la oración (página 252)

análisis costo-beneficio *s.* proceso en el que se comparan los puntos buenos y malos para ver si los beneficios de algo superan su costo (página 863)

anarquista *s.* persona que está dispuesta a usar la fuerza para derrocar la opresión autoritaria (página 653)

anatomía *s.* estudio de las estructuras interiores y exteriores de los seres vivos (página 418)

anexar *v.* incorporar territorio a un estado existente (página 697)

anfiteatro *s.* teatro grande al aire libre (página 163)

ánfora *s.* gran jarrón de cerámica de dos asas con un cuello estrecho (página 161)

antisemitismo *s.* hostilidad y discriminación contra los judíos (página 294)

apaciguamiento *s.* proveer concesiones para mantener la paz (página 761)

apartheid *s.* sistema de segregación racial y discriminación contra sudafricanos no blancos que duró hasta principios de los años noventa. (página 814)

arabesco *s.* diseño abstracto compuesto por patrones repetitivos o flores, hojas, enredaderas o formas geométricas (página 258)

archipiélago *s.* cadena de islas (página 208)

arconte *s.* gobernante de importancia en la antigua Atenas (página 130)

aristócrata *s.* persona de riqueza y alto rango social (página 130)

armas de destrucción masiva *s.* armas que pueden causar destrucción extrema en un área amplia (página 873)

armisticio *s.* acuerdo entre las partes opuestas para poner fin a las hostilidades (página 705)

arquetipo *s.* ejemplo perfecto de algo (página 598)

artefacto *s.* objeto de valor histórico hecho por los seres humanos (página 8)

artillería *s.* grandes cañones de campaña que disparan proyectiles altamente explosivos (página 701)

asceta *s.* persona que elige una vida de pobreza (página 72)

asilo *s.* lugar seguro (página 875)

asimilar *v.* fusionarse con otra cultura (página 273)

astrolabio *s.* instrumento sofisticado que permitía a los usuarios calcular su ubicación en la Tierra (página 259)

ateísmo *s.* creencia de que Dios no existe (página 824)

atrocidad *s.* acto de violencia extremadamente cruel e impactante (página 786)

austeridad fiscal *s.* cualquier medida para evitar deudas, como recortar gastos o aumentar los impuestos (página 886)

autodeterminación *s.* proceso mediante el cual un pueblo forma su propio estado y elige a su propio gobierno (página 708)

autonomía *s.* independencia para autogobernarse (página 659)

autónomo *adj.* que se autogobierna (página 527)

autoritarismo *s.* sistema político caracterizado por un líder poderoso y libertades individuales limitadas (página 709)

B

bioarqueólogo *s.* persona que estudia restos humanos para aprender sobre arqueología (página 205)

biotecnología *s.* uso de organismos o procesos biológicos para crear nuevos productos que mejoren la vida (página 909)

Bloque soviético *s.* grupo de naciones bajo el control de la Unión Soviética (página 800)

bóer *s.* colono holandés o francés en Sudáfrica, también llamado Afrikaner (página 674)

bomba atómica *s.* tipo de bomba nuclear cuya explosión violenta se desencadena al dividir átomos y libera calor intenso y radiactividad (página 773)

bombardeo de saturación *s.* caída de una gran cantidad de bombas en un área designada (página 759)

botánica *s.* estudio de las plantas y la vida vegetal (página 552)

bronce *s.* mezcla de los metales estaño y cobre (página 35)

burguesía *s.* clase media (página 572)

burocracia *s.* grupo de funcionarios administrativos del gobierno (página 88)

C

caballería *s.* grupo de soldados montados a caballo (página 55)

caballero *s.* guerrero a caballo que servía como vasallo de un señor (página 276)

califa *s.* título de un líder musulmán que fue sucesor de Mahoma (página 247)

caligrafía *s.* forma de escritura elegante (página 258)

cambio climático *s.* cambios en los patrones climáticos globales (página 899)

Camisas negras *s.* miembros de un grupo militante que atacó a los oponentes de Mussolini (página 743)

campesino *s.* aldeano rural o agricultor menor en América Latina (página 726)

campo de concentración *s.* lugar donde un gran número de personas están encarceladas bajo una guardia armada; especialmente los campos creados por los nazis para retener a los judíos y a otros prisioneros durante la Segunda Guerra Mundial (página 675)

canonizar *v.* hacer de alguien un santo en la Iglesia Católica (página 441)

capital *s.* dinero u otros recursos que pueden usarse para invertir en negocios (página 277)

capitalismo *s.* sistema económico de libre mercado en el que las empresas son de propiedad privada y existen con el fin de obtener ganancias (página 492)

GLOSARIO **R10**

GLOSARIO

carabela *s.* barco pequeño y rápido utilizado por exploradores portugueses y españoles (página 482)

caravana *s.* grupo de personas que viajan juntas (página 367)

carga de profundidad *s.* bomba submarina que está programada para explotar a cierta profundidad (página 778)

cartografía *s.* la ciencia o el arte de hacer mapas (página 556)

catacumba *s.* cámara subterránea escondida donde los primeros cristianos enterraban a sus muertos (página 175)

catarata *s.* rápido empinado y no navegable a lo largo del curso de un río (página 42)

catedral *s.* iglesia principal de un distrito administrado por un obispo (página 279)

caudillo *s.* dictador militar latinoamericano que ganó poder a través de la violencia (página 605)

cazador-recolector *s.* persona que sobrevive mediante la caza de animales y la recolección de plantas silvestres (página 13)

celibato *s.* acto de permanecer soltero (página 204)

cenote *s.* piscina natural de gran tamaño o cueva abierta (página 391)

censo *s.* recuento oficial de la población. (página 204)

cha *s.* rey en Irán (página 452)

chinampa *s.* isla artificial creada para cultivar (página 395)

ciclo dinástico *s.* patrón del auge y caída de las dinastías en la antigua y temprana China (página 84)

cipayo *s.* soldado indio bajo mando británico (página 635)

circunnavegar *v.* viajar alrededor de todo el mundo (página 484)

ciudad de la guarnición *s.* ciudad donde se asentaban los soldados de un imperio (página 203)

ciudad-estado *s.* ciudad cuyo gobernador rige tanto la ciudad como las áreas circundantes (página 37)

civilización *s.* sociedad avanzada y compleja (página 34)

clan *s.* grupo de personas con un ancestro común (página 208)

clase social *s.* sistema en el que las personas se agrupan de acuerdo con el rango y el poder (página 35)

clero *s.* personas designadas para el servicio religioso por la iglesia (página 278)

coalición *s.* alianza temporal (página 139)

códice *s.* libro doblado hecho de papel de corteza de árbol (página 389)

coerción *s.* uso de la fuerza o amenazas (página 678)

colectivización *s.* reemplazo de granjas campesinas privadas con granjas colectivas estatales (página 747)

comercio *s.* compra y venta de bienes a gran escala (página 277)

comercio triangular *s.* red comercial transatlántica que conectaba Europa, África Occidental y América entre los años 1500 y 1800 (página 520)

comisión *s.* solicitud de un proyecto de arte o diseño específico, generalmente de la nobleza (página 417)

comuna popular *s.* en China, una agrupación de granjas colectivas en las que las personas vivían y trabajaban juntas para producir cultivos y bienes industriales (página 810)

comunidad granate *s.* uno de los grupos autónomos de esclavos que escaparon, común en el Caribe y las zonas costeras de América Central y del Sur a partir del siglo XVI (página 527)

comunismo *s.* sistema económico y político donde todas las propiedades son públicas, pertenecientes al estado central, y los bienes se distribuyen a todos de acuerdo con sus necesidades (página 627)

conectividad *s.* estado de estar conectado a otros, especialmente a través de un sistema informático (página 898)

Confederación *s.* los 11 estados del sur que se separaron de la Unión para formar su propia nación (página 644)

conquistador *s.* explorador español que conquistó tierras en las Américas (página 484)

conservación *s.* protección y preservación cuidadosa de algo (página 893)

consolidar *v.* unificar y fortalecer (página 299)

constitucionalismo *s.* concepto de gobernar basado en un conjunto de principios básicos o leyes llamadas constitución (página 583)

construcción nacional *s.* establecimiento del orden y de un gobierno en funcionamiento en un país que ha estado plagado de violencia e inestabilidad (página 845)

consumo *s.* gasto (página 468)

contracultural *adj.* relacionado con estilos y tradiciones que van en contra de los de la sociedad dominante (página 717)

contrato social *s.* acuerdo entre gobernantes y gobernados para cooperar en beneficio social mutuo en la búsqueda de una sociedad ordenada, con derechos y responsabilidades claramente definidos para cada uno (página 565)

conventillo *s.* edificio grande de apartamentos que generalmente está abarrotado y mal mantenido (página 652)

corporación multinacional *s.* empresa con ubicaciones en todo el mundo que es propiedad de y está administrada por equipos de más de una nación (página 863)

cosmopolita *adj.* diverso y familiarizado con personas, ideas y objetos de muchas partes del mundo (página 205)

crematorios *s.* hornos, especialmente aquellos utilizados por los nazis durante la Segunda Guerra Mundial para quemar los cuerpos de los asesinados (página 783)

criptografía *s.* códigos secretos y codificación de datos para mantener segura la información electrónica (página 899)

crítica social *s.* tipo de escrito que intenta mejorar las condiciones sociales (página 621)

crónica *s.* recuento o registro de hechos (página 199)

Cruzada *s.* expedición militar cristiana para recuperar la tierra de Palestina del dominio musulmán (página 290)

culto de personalidad *s.* promoción de una figura pública como persona que debe ser venerada (página 747)

cultura madre *s.* civilización que influye mucho en otras civilizaciones (página 387)

cultura popular *s.* experiencias e intereses compartidos de la gente común (página 736)

cuneiforme *s.* primera forma de escritura, desarrollada por los sumerios (página 39)

D

daimyo *s.* terrateniente rico en el Japón feudal (página 317)

Dalit *s.* miembro de la casta hindú más baja en la sociedad india tradicional (página 750)

Danza fantasma *s.* danza ceremonial realizada por ciertos pueblos nativoamericanos, quienes creían que la danza convocaría a un ente que restauraría su mundo (página 660)

Darwinismo social *s.* Idea de que los grupos raciales están naturalmente organizados a lo largo de una jerarquía. (página 627)

deidad *s.* dios o diosa (página 133)

deísmo *s.* filosofía religiosa que apoya la idea de la religión natural, en la que Dios no interfiere con las leyes naturales (página 573)

delegación *s.* grupo de personas elegidas para representar a otros (página 198)

delta *s.* área triangular de tierra baja y plana en la desembocadura de un río (página 42)

democracia *s.* forma de gobierno en la que los ciudadanos comunes tienen voz para tomar decisiones y elegir a sus líderes (página 130)

demografía *s.* características de una población particular (página 309)

deponer *v.* sacar del poder (página 207)

deportación *s.* remoción de una persona de una nación (página 713)

derechos naturales *s.* derechos inherentes, como la vida, la libertad y la propiedad (página 565)

desobediencia civil *s.* negativa a seguir leyes injustas (página 750)

déspota *adj.* tiránico, que tiene poder absoluto (página 340)

déspota ilustrado *s.* gobernante absoluto que aplicaba ciertas ideas de la Ilustración (página 577)

despotismo *s.* gobierno opresivo de un líder con poder absoluto (página 587)

desterrado *adj.* forzado a abandonar un lugar u hogar (página 875)

dharma *s.* término del sánscrito que significa el camino de la conducta justa (página 71)

dhimmitude *s.* estado protegido de ciertas personas no musulmanas en el mundo musulmán (página 251)

dhow *s.* primer tipo de barco que transportaba mercancías comerciales a través del océano Índico (página 375)

Día D *s.* término utilizado para referirse a la invasión aliada de Normandía, Francia, durante la Segunda Guerra Mundial (página 771)

dialecto *s.* variación regional de un idioma (página 309)

diáspora *s.* migración de personas desde su patria ancestral (página 17)

dictador *s.* persona que gobierna con total autoridad (página 153)

diezmo *s.* diez por ciento de los ingresos de una persona que se pagan a la iglesia (página 288)

difusión cultural *s.* el proceso mediante el cual las culturas interactúan y las ideas se difunden de un área a otra (página 81)

dinastía *s.* serie de gobernantes provenientes de una misma familia (página 44)

diplomacia *s.* negociación entre gobiernos (página 48)

director *s.* tipo de monarquía en la que se mantienen algunos ideales republicanos (página 159)

disidente *s.* persona que está en desacuerdo con una práctica establecida, como una religión en particular (página 442)

distensión *s.* el alivio de las tensiones y la mejora de las relaciones entre las naciones (página 834)

división del trabajo *s.* sistema en el que las personas realizan diferentes trabajos para satisfacer las necesidades de una sociedad (página 34)

división del trabajo *s.* proceso que divide una tarea en partes separadas, cada una completada por una persona o grupo diferente (página 617)

doctrina *s.* creencia oficial (página 289)

domesticación *s.* acción de domesticar animales salvajes (página 23)

dominio *s.* comunidad autónoma dentro de un imperio (página 651)

dote *s.* propiedad que una mujer aporta a su matrimonio (página 458)

dron *s.* avión sin piloto operado por control remoto (página 875)

ducado *s.* territorio gobernado por un duque o duquesa (página 271)

E

economía *s.* sistema para producir y obtener bienes y servicios (página 24)

economía redistributiva *s.* tipo de economía en la que los productos y otros bienes se almacenan en un lugar central y luego se clasifican y distribuyen a la población (página 124)

ecuatorial *s.* ubicado en o cerca del ecuador (página 755)

edicto *s.* proclamación oficial (página 159)

edificio verde *s.* acto de diseñar y construir estructuras teniendo en cuenta el medio ambiente.(página 893)

educación obligatoria *s.* educación requerida por ley (página 395)

efecto dominó *s.* creencia de que, si un país se vuelve comunista, sus vecinos sucumbirán al comunismo como una hilera de fichas de dominó (página 800)

embargo *s.* prohibición de participar en el comercio con países específicos (páginas 646 y 805)

embellecer *v.* decorar con detalles ornamentales (página 455)

empresario *s.* persona que organiza y opera un negocio (página 465)

encomienda *s.* sistema legal que permitió a cada colono en las Américas españolas extraer tributo, principalmente en trabajo, de un cierto número de indígenas americanos (página 497)

energía geotérmica *s.* energía derivada del calor liberado por el interior de la Tierra (página 892)

enfoque deductivo *s.* enfoque de la investigación científica que implica pasar de principios generales a verdades específicas (página 549)

enfoque inductivo *s.* enfoque para la investigación científica que implica trabajar desde observaciones cuidadosamente controladas hasta verdades más amplias (página 549)

enviado *s.* representante diplomático (página 339)

epístola *s.* carta (página 175)

escriba *s.* escritor profesional que registraba la información oficial en las sociedades antiguas (página 46)

esfera de influencia *s.* área en la que el dominio de una potencia colonial se reconoce por encima de todas las demás (página 672)

especulación *s.* asumir grandes riesgos para obtener grandes recompensas (página 740)

estado *s.* una de las tres clases sociales distintas en la Francia prerrevolucionaria: el primer estado (clero); el segundo estado (nobleza); y el tercer estado (plebeyos) (página 584)

estado satelital *s.* país que es formalmente independiente, pero que está bajo el control o influencia de otro país (página 799)

estancamiento *s.* falta de crecimiento y desarrollo (página 227)

estancamiento militar *s.* situación en la que ninguna de las partes puede vencer a la otra (página 700)

estela *s.* pilar de piedra utilizado para conmemorar un evento o logro importante (página 41)

estepa *s.* vasta llanura cubierta de hierba (página 326)

estímulo *s.* incentivo (página 886)

etnografía *s.* estudio de las relaciones lingüísticas y culturales entre los pueblos (página 554)

Eva mitocondrial *s.* un solo ancestro femenino humano común a todos los seres humanos (página 8)

excomunión *s.* expulsión de la Iglesia cristiana (página 275)

exilio *s.* expulsión forzada de la patria (página 61)

expatriado *s.* persona que elige vivir fuera de su país de origes (página 717)

exposición *s.* feria o exposición mundial (página 623)

extraterritorialidad *s.* exención de la ley local (página 632)

GLOSARIO **R12**

GLOSARIO

extremista *s.* persona con una visión radical (página 872)

F

faccionalismo *s.* lealtad a cualquier sección o región del país de la que provenga, en lugar de a la nación en su conjunto (página 644)

factor de atracción *s.* factor o incentivo que atrae a las personas a mudarse a un nuevo paí. (página 477)

factor de empuje *s.* factor o condición que hace que las personas abandonen sus países de origen (página 477)

falange *s.* cuerpo de soldados que avanzan en formación contigua (página 114)

faraón *s.* rey del antiguo Egipto (página 43)

fascismo *s.* forma de gobernar basada en el nacionalismo extremo, el racismo y la represión de la oposición (página 742)

fauna *s.* animales de un lugar específico (página 554)

federal *adj.* Relacionado con un gobierno donde el poder es compartido entre el gobierno central, nacional y el de los estados o provincias. (página 583)

feudalismo *s.* nombre dado al sistema legal y social en la Europa medieval en el que los siervos trabajaban la tierra y los vasallos realizaban el servicio militar para sus señores a cambio de protección (página 276)

fideicomiso *s.* control administrativo sobre un territorio por uno o más países (página 820)

figura insigne *s.* líder, pero solo de nombre (página 257)

filósofos *s.* escritores y pensadores de la Ilustración europea (página 568)

fisiografía *s.* geografía física de un lugar (página 316)

flora *s.* plantas de un lugar específico (página 552)

fracking *s.* roceso de perforar la tierra y aplicar presión de agua para liberar los gases naturales al romper la roca (página 892)

fresco *s.* pintura dibujada sobre yeso mojado (página 124)

fundamentalismo *s.* estricta adhesión a un conjunto de principios básicos, a menudo relacionados con creencias políticas o religiosas (página 857)

G

genocidio *s.* destrucción sistemática de un grupo racial o cultural (página 675)

geoglifo *s.* gran diseño geométrico o figura dibujada en el suelo, creada al rayar la tierra y las rocas de la superficie oscura para revelar un suelo de color más claro (página 396)

ger *s.* tienda de fieltro portátil utilizada por nómadas mongoles (página 326)

ghazi *s.* guerrero por el islam (página 344)

ghetto *s.* sección separada de una ciudad en la que los grupos minoritarios se ven obligados a vivir (página 294)

gladiador *s.* hombre que luchaba con animales salvajes u otros hombres para entretener a los espectadores (página 163)

glasnost *s.* política gubernamental de comunicación abierta en la antigua Unión Soviética (página 834)

globalización *s.* desarrollo de una economía global cada vez más integrada, marcada especialmente por el libre comercio, el libre flujo de capital y el aprovechamiento de mercados laborales extranjeros más baratos (página 624)

golpe *s.* derrocamiento repentino del gobierno (página 110)

Gran Depresión *s.* época de intensas dificultades financieras que duró toda la década de 1930 (página 740)

gremio *s.* asociación formada por artesanos o comerciantes para mejorar sus negocios (página 277)

griot *s.* narrador de historias de África Occidental que cuenta historias a través de la tradición oral (página 361)

guerra de guerrillas *s.* ataques sorpresa a pequeña escala (página 675)

guerra de poder *s.* guerra en la que uno o ambos bandos son apoyados y sirven a los intereses de otro país (página 802)

guerra de trincheras *s.* tipo de guerra en la que los soldados luchan desde largas zanjas fortificadas con alambre de púas (página 700)

guerra relámpago *s.* táctica de batalla alemana que usaba la velocidad, la sorpresa y la potencia combinada de fuego de tanques, bombarderos y fuerzas terrestres. (página 766)

guerra santa *s.* guerra en defensa de una fe religiosa (página 290)

guerra total *s.* guerra que requiere reunir y preparar todos los recursos nacionales e involucrar tanto a los civiles como a los militares (página 699)

guillotina *s.* máquina con una cuchilla afilada diseñada para decapitar personas (página 587)

guion *s.* forma de escritura (página 153)

Gulag *s.* sistema soviético de campos de trabajos forzados (página 721)

H

habeas corpus *s.* procedimiento legal que impide que el gobierno detenga a una persona indefinidamente sin presentarse ante un juez (página 283)

hacienda *s.* plantación de gran tamaño en una colonia de habla hispana (página 497)

hacker *s.* individuo que ilegalmente obtiene acceso a información electrónica (página 898)

hajj *s.* peregrinación musulmana a la ciudad sagrada de La Meca (página 245)

hambruna *s.* escasez extrema de alimentos en un país o área geográfica grande (página 296)

Helenización *s.* proceso mediante el cual la cultura griega se extendió por todo el Imperio persa (página 140)

hereje *s.* miembro de la iglesia que tiene opiniones religiosas contrarias a la doctrina oficial (página 294)

hierro *s.* metal pesado que se usa para fabricar acero (página 54)

Hind Swaraj *s.* idea del autogobierno en la india (página 750)

hipotecas de alto riesgo *s.* préstamo hipotecario otorgado a alguien con mal crédito (página 886)

hipótesis *s.* teoría no probada que puede responder una pregunta y puede ser probada (página 549)

historiografía *s.* el arte y la ciencia de crear una historia confiable y útil a partir de fragmentos de información sobre el pasado (página 8)

hoplita *s.* soldado poderosamente armado de la antigua Grecia (página 129)

huelga *s.* paro laboral utilizado como táctica sindical (página 653)

hueso oracular *s.* hueso usado en la antigua China para consultar a los antepasados sobre el futuro; ahora se sabe que son los primeros registros escritos que sobrevivieron en China (página 83)

humanismo *s.* movimiento intelectual basado en las obras de pensadores clásicos griegos y romanos (página 424)

I

ícono *s.* imagen sagrada o religiosa (página 234)

iconoclasta *s.* miembro de la sociedad bizantina opuesta al culto de íconos religiosos; literalmente significa "rompedor de imágenes" (página 235)

ideología *s.* sistema de ideas que expresan una filosofía social o política sobre el mundo (página 591)

ilota *s.* esclavo poseído por el estado en la antigua Esparta (página 129)

iluminación *s.* estado en el que alguien obtiene una comprensión profunda y un sentido de claridad (página 72)

imperialismo *s.* práctica mediante la cual un país aumenta su poder al obtener el control sobre otras áreas del mundo (página 668)

imperio *s.* grupo de naciones o pueblos gobernados por una sola persona o gobierno (página 39)

indemnización *s.* dinero o bienes pagados para cubrir los daños causados en tiempos de guerra (página 708)

indígena *adj.* que es originario de un lugar en particular (página 15)

indulgencia *s.* oración especial que se podía comprar de la Iglesia Católica Romana para salvar el alma de una persona (página 434)

industria artesanal *s.* tipo de industria en la que una unidad familiar o un individuo crea un producto en casa con sus propios equipos (página 618)

infamia *s.* acto extremadamente vergonzoso o malvado (página 768)

inflación *s.* aumento en el precio de los bienes y servicios en comparación con el valor del dinero (página 455)

infraestructura *s.* redes para el transporte, el agua y otros servicios públicos (página 315)

ingresos públicos *s.* entradas para el gobierno como, por ejemplo, los impuestos (página 458)

Inquisición *s.* tribunal especial formado por la Iglesia Católica Romana para escuchar los cargos contra los herejes acusados (página 294)

insolvencia *s.* incapacidad de pagar deudas; bancarrota (página 799)

institución *s.* organización establecida para un propósito específico y que continúa a lo largo del tiempo (página 35)

insurgente *s.* luchador rebelde (página 589)

intercambio colombino *s.* intercambio de plantas, animales, microbios, personas e ideas entre Europa y las Américas, luego del primer viaje de Colón al hemisferio occidental (página 488)

intermediario *s.* persona que sirve de intercesor en un intercambio que involucra a otras dos partes (página 362)

intifada *s.* levantamiento palestino contra la ocupación israelí de Cisjordania y Gaza (página 855)

irrigación *s.* sistema hecho por el hombre para transportar el agua hacia donde se necesita (página 35)

islamista *s.* musulmán que cree que las leyes y las constituciones deben guiarse por los principios islámicos y que las autoridades religiosas deben participar directamente en el gobierno (página 515)

izquierdista *s.* persona que apoya cambios económicos y sociales radicales (página 845)

J

jenízaro *s.* soldado y esclavo altamente entrenado y disciplinado en el ejército otomano (página 450)

jeque *s.* líder de un clan beduino (página 244)

jeroglífico *s.* imagen que representa un objeto, sonido o idea y que era parte del antiguo sistema de escritura egipcio (página 46)

junta *s.* grupo militar o político que a menudo toma el poder por la fuerza (página 600)

justicia social *s.* igualdad de derechos para todos bajo la ley (página 874)

K

kamikaze *s.* piloto suicida japonés durante la Segunda Guerra Mundial (página 772)

kanato *s.* área del Imperio mongol gobernada por un khan (página 328)

karma *s.* suma de las acciones de una persona en la vida que determina su renacer en una próxima vida (página 71)

Kristallnacht *s.* destrucción de hogares, negocios y sinagogas judías por los nazis en la noche del 9 de noviembre de 1938 (página 745)

kulak *s.* campesino rico de la Unión Soviética de principios del siglo XX (página 747)

L

La Reforma *s.* movimiento de reforma en México que pidió la redistribución de las tierras, la separación de la iglesia y el estado, y mayores oportunidades educativas para los pobres (página 655)

laicado *s.* miembros de la iglesia que no son clérigos (página 288)

laissez-faire *s.* sistema económico en el que las empresas y las industrias regulan sus actividades sin interferencia del gobierno (página 569)

lar *s.* dios de la casa romana (página 157)

legionario *s.* soldado profesional pagado del ejército romano (página 162)

ley común *s.* conjunto de leyes determinadas por decisiones judiciales anteriores (página 583)

Leyes de Jim Crow *s.* leyes establecidas después de la Reconstrucción que impusieron la segregación racial en todo el sur de los Estados Unidos (página 662)

liberalismo *s.* sistema de creencias que argumenta que la libertad del individuo es la principal preocupación de la política (página 626)

libertades civiles *s.* libertades básicas que no pueden ser reguladas por el gobierno, como la libertad de expresión (página 884)

limo *s.* suelo esencialmente fino y fértil (página 35)

linaje *s.* grupo de descendientes con un antepasado en común (página 361)

Lineal B *s.* sistema de escritura micénica, que se cree que es una forma temprana de la lengua griega (página 125)

liturgia *s.* forma de adoración (página 437)

loess *s.* tipo de limo fino, fértil y amarillo que flota a través de las aguas del Huang He en China. (página 83)

longevidad *s.* tener una larga vida útil (página 909)

longitud *s.* posición este-oeste de un objeto medida en grados o diferencia de tiempo (página 554)

M

magnate *s.* empresario rico, poderoso e influyente (página 675)

maíz indígena *s.* grano similar al maíz actual (página 386)

Mandato celestial *s.* la antigua creencia china de que el Cielo, las fuerzas generalizadas del cosmos, elige al gobernante legítimo que manda siempre y cuando el Cielo crea que es digno de hacerlo (página 84)

manorialismo *s.* sistema económico, social y político medieval en el que los trabajadores agrícolas estaban ligados a la tierra que cultivaban y al señor que poseía dicha tierra (página 276)

mansa *s.* rey de África occidental (página 362)

manumisión *s.* liberación de una persona de la esclavitud (página 518)

marítimo *adj.* relacionado con el mar (página 200)

mausoleo *s.* tumba de gran tamaño (página 459)

medieval *adj.* que se refiere a un período en la historia europea de aproximadamente 500 a 1500 e.c. (página 227)

medios de comunicación masivos *s.* medios de comunicación destinados a llegar a muchas personas (página 736)

mercancía *s.* bien comercial valioso (página 134)

GLOSARIO **R14**

GLOSARIO

mercantilismo *s.* sistema en el que el gobierno protege y fomenta el comercio, basado en la teoría de que tales negocios crean riqueza (página 483)

mercenario *s.* soldado al que se le paga por luchar (página 154)

meritocracia *s.* sistema en el que las personas calificadas son elegidas y promovidas en función de sus logros en lugar de su posición social (página 88)

mestizo *s.* persona de ascendencia mixta española y nativoamericana (página 497)

metalurgia *s.* ciencia o tecnología de trabajar con metales (página 195)

Métis *s.* personas de ascendencia mixta europea e indígena (página 651)

método científico *s.* procedimiento lógico para desarrollar y probar ideas científicas (página 549)

mezquita *s.* lugar de culto musulmán (página 247)

migrar *v.* mudarse de una región a otra (página 11)

milicia *s.* ejército voluntario (página 582)

militarismo *s.* política gubernamental de desarrollo militar continuo y preparación para la guerra (página 639)

misionero *s.* persona enviada para convertir a otros a una religión (página 175)

místico *s.* persona que busca el conocimiento de Dios a través de la devoción o la meditación (página 279)

momia *s.* cuerpo preservado de un faraón o de otra persona en el antiguo Egipto (página 45)

monarquía *s.* gobierno presidido por una sola persona como, por ejemplo, un rey (página 44)

monarquía absoluta *s.* gobierno en el que el monarca tiene autoridad ilimitada (página 540)

monarquía constitucional *s.* gobierno en el que el poder del monarca está limitado por una constitución (página 540)

monasterio *s.* comunidad religiosa cristiana y centro de aprendizaje, trabajo y adoración (página 271)

moneda *s.* dinero en circulación (página 311)

monopolio *s.* control exclusivo sobre algo; control completo y exclusivo de una industria por una sola empresa (páginas 362 y 663)

monoteísmo *s.* creencia en un Dios (página 59)

monzón *s.* fuertes vientos estacionales en el sur y sureste de Asia (página 81)

mosaico *s.* grupo de pequeños cubos de piedra de colores colocados en un mortero para crear una imagen o diseño (página 239)

movilizar *v.* armarse y prepararse para la guerra (página 698)

muckraker *s.* periodista de investigación de principios de 1900 que expuso la mala conducta de organizaciones y personas poderosas (página 663)

mujahideen *s.* guerrilleros islámicos (página 825)

N

nación-estado *s.* estado formado por personas de una nacionalidad, que comparten rasgos comunes (página 591)

nacionalismo *s.* creencia de que los individuos están unidos por lazos de idioma, cultura, historia y, a menudo, religión (página 591)

nacionalizar *v.* poner una empresa o industria privada bajo el control del gobierno nacional (página 720)

napalm *s.* sustancia gelatinosa altamente inflamable que se adhiere a los objetivos y genera calor extremo (página 778)

narrativa de esclavos *s.* relato escrito de la vida de un esclavo fugitivo o de un exesclavo (página 518)

nativismo *s.* la práctica de favorecer las ideas del país de origen en lugar de las de los inmigrantes o países extranjeros (página 469)

naturalismo *s.* estilo artístico que buscaba realizar representaciones precisas de personas o del mundo natural (página 418)

Neanderthal *s.* miembro de una especie extinta de humanos primitivos (página 15)

nebulosa *s.* nube de gas y polvo en el espacio exterior (página 551)

neoclasicismo *s.* estilo creativo basado en ideales griegos y romanos (página 596)

neocolonialismo *s.* continuación de la dependencia y el dominio de un poder colonial. (página 812)

neoliberalismo *s.* enfoque económico que enfatiza los mercados libres y el amplio comercio internacional (página 863)

Neolítico *adj.* término empleado para describir a las personas que usaban herramientas de piedra y practicaban la agricultura; significa "nueva edad de piedra" (página 22)

neurosis de guerra *s.* condición de salud mental resultante de la exposición a la guerra (página 717)

nirvana *s.* estado de gozoso escape del sufrimiento causado por el ciclo de la vida y el renacimiento (página 72)

no alineamiento *s.* política de no aliarse con otros países, específicamente con los países comunistas o no comunistas durante la Guerra Fría (página 816)

no intervención *s.* política de no involucrarse en los asuntos de otros países (página 760)

nómada *s.* persona que migra de un lugar a otro (página 69)

números hindúes-árabes *s.* los números 1, 2, 3 . . . etc., originarios de la India y traídos a Occidente a través de comerciantes árabes (página 195)

O

oasis *s.* lugar aislado en el desierto y con agua donde las plantas pueden crecer (página 244)

oligarquía *s.* forma de gobierno liderada por unos pocos ciudadanos poderosos (página 129)

omnipotencia *s.* poder ilimitado (páginas 192 y 341)

óptica *s.* estudio de la luz y la visión (página 546)

oratoria *s.* arte de hablar en público (página 184)

organización no gubernamental (ONG) *s.* grupo sin fines de lucro que apoya una causa particular (página 858)

ortodoxia *s.* creencias y prácticas establecidas (página 542)

outsourcing *s.* práctica de enviar trabajo una vez realizado internamente en una empresa a cargo de personas ajenas a la empresa, generalmente por salarios más bajos (página 863)

P

pacifista *s.* persona con una objeción religiosa o filosófica a la violencia (página 860)

pacto *s.* acuerdo religioso (página 59)

panafricanismo *s.* idea de que las personas de ascendencia africana tienen un patrimonio común y que deberían unificarse (página 685)

pandemia *s.* brote mundial de una enfermedad infecciosa (página 708)

panteón *s.* grupo de dioses y diosas oficialmente reconocidos (página 157)

papiro *s.* material hecho de cañas, parecido al papel (página 46)

Parlamento *s.* cuerpo legislativo en Inglaterra (página 283)

partición *v.* división de un país (página 817)

Pasaje del noroeste *s.* ruta marítima desde el océano Atlántico hasta el Pacífico a lo largo de la costa norte de América del Norte (página 493)

Pasaje Medio s. viaje en barco de esclavos a través del Atlántico desde África occidental hasta las Américas (página 518)

patriarcado s. sociedad en la cual los hombres tienen todo el poder (página 156)

patricio s. terrateniente rico en la sociedad romana (página 153)

patrimonio cultural s. atributos de un grupo o sociedad heredados de generaciones pasadas (página 56)

patrocinador s. persona que brinda apoyo financiero a artistas (página 415)

peonaje de la deuda s. sistema en el que los trabajadores pagan su deuda con la mano de obra (página 654)

peregrinaje s. viaje a un lugar sagrado (página 176)

perestroika s. política gubernamental de reforma económica y gubernamental en la antigua Unión Soviética (página 834)

perspectiva lineal s. técnica artística en la que el artista utiliza la colocación y el tamaño de las figuras en un plano para hacer que una escena parezca tridimensional (página 426)

petición s. solicitud formal por escrito (página 476)

piedad s. fuerte creencia en la religión que se muestra a través de la adoración (página 441)

piedad filial s. respeto por los propios padres (página 86)

pirámide s. gran monumento de cuatro lados construido en el antiguo Egipto como una tumba para un faraón (página 44)

plaga s. enfermedad epidémica mortal (página 226)

plebeyo s. persona que no era noble en Roma (página 153)

poema épico s. largo poema narrativo que relata las aventuras de un héroe legendario o histórico (página 37)

pogrom s. ataque organizado o masacre de un grupo minoritario. (página 294)

polis s. ciudad-estado griega (página 128)

politeísmo s. creencia en varios dioses (página 38)

política de contención s. política de la Guerra Fría de los Estados Unidos de proporcionar ayuda militar y económica para proteger a los países de la toma de poder comunista (página 800)

populismo s. movimiento político que apoya las preocupaciones de la gente común. (página 804)

prevenir s. evitar que algo suceda (página 854)

privado de sus derechos adj. despojado de sus derechos o de la capacidad de influir en un gobierno (página 584)

proletariado s. clase obrera (página 627)

propaganda s. información utilizada por un gobierno para hacer que las personas piensen o actúen de una manera particular (página 591)

protestante s. persona que protestó contra la Iglesia Católica y se convirtió en parte de una iglesia reformada (página 436)

Punto de Clovis s. tipo de punta de lanza de piedra utilizada por los habitantes prehistóricos de América del Norte (página 384)

Q

qadi s. juez musulmán (página 256)

quipu s. serie de cuerdas anudadas que los incas usaban para llevar registros (página 399)

quórum s. número mínimo de personas que deben estar presentes para llevar a cabo los negocios de un grupo (página 131)

R

racionalismo científico s. escuela de pensamiento en la que la observación, la experimentación y el razonamiento matemático reemplazan la sabiduría antigua y las enseñanzas de la iglesia como fuente de verdades científicas. (página 549)

racismo s. creencia de que el color de la piel de una persona la hace superior o inferior (página 521)

recesión s. período de actividad económica reducida (página 886)

reclutamiento s. inscripción forzada en el ejército (página 475)

Reconstrucción s. esfuerzo por reconstruir y reunir a los Estados Unidos después de la Guerra Civil (página 645)

red comercial transahariana s. grupo de rutas comerciales terrestres a través de las cuales se transportaban mercancías entre el norte de África y el África subsahariana (página 368)

reencarnación s. renacimiento de un alma en un cuerpo diferente a lo largo de diferentes ciclos de vida (página 71)

referéndum s. votación pública sobre una sola cuestión política (página 813)

refugiado s. persona que se ve obligada a abandonar su tierra natal debido a la guerra, la persecución o un desastre natural (página 61)

regente s. persona que gobierna cuando un monarca o emperador no puede hacerlo (página 209)

registro humano s. historia de la vida humana en la Tierra a lo largo de los siglos (página 56)

relieve s. tipo de escultura en la que elementos tridimensionales se elevan desde un fondo plano (página 56)

religiosidad s. fuerte creencia religiosa (página 885)

remilitarización s. proceso de rearme (página 760)

república s. forma de gobierno en la que las personas eligen a los funcionarios para que los representen en lugar de votar directamente sobre las leyes y políticas (página 153)

rescate financiero s. rescate de dificultades financieras (página 886)

resistencia pasiva s. oposición no violenta a la autoridad (página 846)

revisionista adj. que se desvía del espíritu revolucionario de la doctrina marxista (página 809)

Romanticismo s. movimiento cultural originario del siglo XVIII que enfatizaba las emociones sobre la razón (página 596)

S

sabana s. área de exuberantes praderas tropicales (página 360)

sabotaje s. destrucción deliberada (página 617)

Sáhel s. región semidesértica al sur del Sahara (página 360)

salón s. reunión social organizada por mujeres parisinas para discutir ideas de la Ilustración (página 572)

saltar entre islas s. estrategia diseñada por los Aliados durante la Segunda Guerra Mundial para capturar y controlar islas en el Pacífico una por una (página 772)

sanción s. restricción comercial o financiera impuesta por una nación a otra (página 757)

sánscrito s. idioma indoeuropeo clásico hablado por inmigrantes indoarios hacia el norte de la India alrededor de 1500–1000 A.E.C. (página 69)

sátira s. humor y sarcasmo utilizados para exponer o ridiculizar la tontería o debilidad humana (páginas 133 y 425)

sátrapa s. gobernador provincial (página 104)

satyagraha s. aplicación de la no violencia a la política, según la creencia india (página 750)

secular s. no perteneciente a una orden religiosa (página 288)

segregación s. separación de diferentes grupos de personas, generalmente basada en la raza (página 645)

GLOSARIO

seguridad alimentaria *s.* garantía de que habrá alimentos disponibles para mantener la salud (página 552)

Senado *s.* cuerpo gobernante en la antigua Roma que asesoraba a los cónsules y que inicialmente estaba compuesto por terratenientes ricos (página 153)

separarse *v.* retirarse formalmente de una nación (página 644)

sharia *s.* ley islámica que cubre todos los aspectos de la vida (página 246)

shogun *s.* general japonés que es el gobernante militar del país (página 317)

siervo *s.* trabajador agrícola medieval que estaba atado a una tierra (página 276)

sinagoga *s.* edificio dedicado al culto de la religión judía (página 61)

sincretismo religioso *s.* mezcla de diferentes sistemas de creencias (página 443)

sirviente por contrato *s.* persona bajo contrato para trabajar, generalmente sin paga, a cambio de un pasaje gratuito a las colonias (página 505)

sistema de castas *s.* rígida jerarquía social en la India antigua que dividía a las personas en clases hereditarias (página 71)

soberanía *s.* libertad del control externo (página 542)

soberanía popular *s.* creencia de que el gobierno surge de la gente misma (página 583)

socialismo *s.* sistema económico en el que la industria es de propiedad colectiva, se permite la propiedad privada y se paga a las personas en función de su contribución a la producción (página 627)

sociedad anónima *s.* empresa comercial financiada por la venta de acciones a múltiples inversores (página 492)

sociedad de masas *s.* sociedad en la que un gran número de personas comparten la misma experiencia sin tener que reunirse (página 736)

solución de dos estados *s.* solución al conflicto israelí-palestino que exige un estado independiente de Palestina junto con el estado de Israel (página 853)

sostenible *v.* incesante, especialmente en relación con una forma de utilizar un recurso para que no se agote (página 892)

status quo *s.* condición ya existente (página 593)

subyugación *s.* estado de estar bajo control o gobierno (página 668)

sucesión *s.* proceso mediante el cual se elige a un nuevo líder para suceder a un líder que deja su puesto (página 512)

sufragio *s.* derecho a votar (página 663)

sultán *s.* gobernante de un estado musulmán (página 345)

superávit *s.* oferta de bienes y mano de obra que no se necesita para la supervivencia a corto plazo (página 28)

T

taiga *s.* tierra cubierta de árboles de hoja perenne dispersos en el extremo norte o área subártica (página 470)

tecnología *s.* aplicación práctica del conocimiento; cualquier herramienta o técnica que ayuda a las personas a realizar tareas (página 35)

teocracia *s.* forma de gobierno en la que el sistema legal se basa en la ley religiosa (página 61)

teoría geocéntrica *s.* teoría que indica que el Sol y los planetas giran alrededor de la Tierra (página 546)

teoría heliocéntrica *s.* teoría que indica que la Tierra y otros planetas giran alrededor del Sol (página 547)

terraplén *s.* construcción de tierra y rocas (página 392)

terraza *s.* plataforma escalonada (página 387)

tetrarquía *s.* estructura de gobierno en la que cuatro personas gobiernan conjuntamente (página 180)

tipos móviles *s.* tabletas de arcilla individuales que podían organizarse para crear textos en una forma temprana de impresión (página 310)

tiranía *s.* estado de gobierno en el que los gobernantes tienen un poder ilimitado y lo usan injustamente (página 565)

tolerancia religiosa *s.* aceptación de las creencias y prácticas religiosas de los demás (página 253)

totalitario *adj.* relacionado con un sistema político que ejerce un control total sobre una sociedad, a menudo a través de medios violentos (página 743)

trabajos públicos *s.* proyectos de construcción impulsados por el gobierno que benefician a una comunidad (página 40)

tradición oral *s.* grupo de historias que toman una forma estándar y que son transmitidas de generación en generación por personas que se comunican entre sí (página 125)

traición *s.* delito de traicionar al gobierno o al propio país (página 199)

tregua *s.* alto temporal de la guerra (página 290)

tribu *s.* unidad familiar extendida (página 60)

tribuna *s.* representante electo que protegió los derechos de los ciudadanos comunes en Roma (página 153)

tribunal *s.* tribunal con autoridad sobre un asunto específico (página 786)

tributo *s.* impuesto requerido de los pueblos conquistados (página 194)

trirreme *s.* antiguo buque de guerra griego con tres bancos de remos (página 115)

troll *s.* persona que deliberadamente publica mensajes ofensivos o amenazantes en la Internet (página 899)

tundra *s.* llanuras árticas sin árboles (página 470)

U

ultranacionalista *s.* nacionalista extremo (página 748)

V

vaquero *s.* jinete o pastor de ganado (página 726)

varna *s.* los cuatro principales grupos sociales de la antigua sociedad india, clasificados en orden de pureza (página 71)

vasallo *s.* en la Europa medieval, una persona que prestaba servicios militares y prometía lealtad a un señor a cambio de protección y tierra para vivir (página 276)

védico *adj.* asociado con la sociedad o la religión de los inmigrantes indoarios (página 70)

venerar *v.* honrar o adorar (página 234)

vernáculo *s.* lenguaje cotidiano que hablan las personas (página 281)

vetar *v.* votar en contra de algo (página 129)

vigilancia *s.* acto de velar por una persona o grupo (página 873)

virreinato *s.* colonia (página 497)

virrey *s.* representante del rey en las Américas españolas (página 497)

X

xenofobia *s.* miedo a los extranjeros (página 875)

Z

zaibatsu *s.* poderoso conglomerado financiero e industrial japonés (página 639)

zar *s.* gobernante de la Rusia imperial (página 471)

zigurat *s.* gran estructura escalonada en un templo sumerio (página 39)

zona desmilitarizada *s.* área donde las armas y las fuerzas militares están prohibidas (página 821)

INDEX

A

Aachen Cathedral, 255v
abaya, 906–907v
Abbas I, 452–453, 477
Abbasids, 221v, 254–257, 332, 873
abbot, 288–289
Abiy Ahmed, 883–884, 902
abolition, 519, 572
Aborigines, 554–555, 677
Abraham, 59–60
absolute monarchy, 540–541, 565, 574, 576, 584
Abu Bakr, 247
Abu Sarah, Aziz, 877v
Achaemenids, 102–104, 113v, 114–115
Achebe, Chinua, 673
Acoma Pueblo, 431v
Acropolis, 120–121v, 131v
adaptation, 14
Addams, Jane, 663v
Addario, Lynsey, 906v–907
Adena, 392
Adowa, Battle of, 684
Adrianople, 345
Aeneid, 183
Aeschylus, 132
Afghanistan, 77v, 142–143, 802, 825, 834
　and September 11 attacks, 872–873
　Mes Aynak, 880–881v
　refugees from Soviet invasion, 879–880v
　Soviet withdrawal from, 835, 857
Africa, 358–381
　African origins of Egyptian civilization, 42–43
　African independence movements, 812–813
　Algeria, 812–813, 822
　Angola, 825
　Asante, 528
　Bangwato, 668–669
　Bantu-speaking peoples in, 510–511
　Bechuanaland, 668–669
　Berlin Conference, 613
　Botswana, 668
　British colonialism, 750–755
　British West Indies, 755
　Burundi, 883
　Cape of Good Hope, 490v, 493
　Cape Colony, 675
　Cape Town, 493, 674
　Congo, 672
　Congo Free State, 682
　Dahomey, 528–529
　Democratic Republic of the Congo, 406, 813, 896–897v
　diversity of, 510–511
　Eastern, 374v–375
　Eritrea, 684, 883–884
　Ethiopia, 375–377v, 684–685, 743, 757, 883–884, 902
　French Equatorial Africa, 776
　German South West Africa, 675
　Ghana, 362, 536v
　Great Lakes region of, 511
　Great Zimbabwe, 364–365v
　Guinea, 812
　Igbo, 511
　Igbo Women's War, 754–755
　imperialism in, 670–673
　Ivory Coast, 682
　Kenya, 755, 794v, 813, 906
　Kongo (kingdom), 346, 511, 528
　Libya, 757
　Mali (country), 516–517v
　Mali Empire, 364–365v, 508–509v
　Morocco, 9, 362, 515
　Mozambique, 910v
　Namibia, 675, 701
　Ndebele, 673
　Niger, 514
　Nigeria, 673, 754
　Pan-Africanism, 685
　Rhodesia, 673, 675
　Rwanda, 790, 859
　Senegal, 372–373v, 706
　slavery's impact on, 528–529
　Somalia, 883
　South Sudan, 883
　sub-Saharan Africa, 360–361
　Sudan, 673
　Swahili Coast, 378–379
　Tanzania, 608
　Tunisia, 874
　triangular trade, 520–521v
　Uganda, 370–371v
　Zanzibar, 671
　Zimbabwe, 675
　Zulu Empire, 674
　See also Egypt, South Africa
African diaspora, 867
African National Congress, 675, 714, 814–815, 846–847
Africatown, 529
Afrofuturism, 867v
afterlife, 43–45, 48, 71, 167v
Agamemnon, 136v
"age of anxiety," 744
Age of Exploration See European Age of Exploration
Age of Reason See Enlightenment
Agnesi, Maria Gaetana, 551
agnostic, 262
agora, 128, 131v
agriculture
　agricultural revolution, 552–553
　food security, 910–914
　history of, 22–25v, 68, 94
　in China, 83
　in Japan, 638
　in medieval Europe, 281, 283
　slash-and-burn, 388
　See also farming
Aguinaldo, Emilio, 679
ahimsa, 750
Ahmose-Nefertari, 53v
Ahmose, 48
Ai Weiwei, 900v–901
Ai-Khanoum, 142–143
AIDS, 908
Akbar I (the Great), 411, 456, 458–459v, 477
Akhenaten (Amenhotep IV), 47, 52
Akkadians, 39
Al Kuntar, Salam, 879v
al Qaeda, 857, 872–873, 883
Al-Assad, Bashir, 874–875
al-Bakri, Abu U'bayd, 362, 379
al-Bashir, Omar, 883
al-Din, Rashid, 331
Al-Idrisi, 558
al-Kamil, 416v
al-Khwarizmi, 259
al-Mamun, 221v, 259
al-nakbah, 853
al-Razi, 259
Al-Shamahi, Ella, 878v
al-Zahrawi of al-Andalus, 259
Albigensian Crusade, 295
Aldrin, Buzz, 803
Alepotrypa Cave, 122v–123
Alexander II (Russian tsar), 631
Alexander the Great, 98v, 115, 140v–141
Alexandria, 141, 166
Alexiad, 292
Alexius Comnenus, 290
algebra, 259
Algeria, 812–813, 822
Algonquin, 505
algorithm, 487
Alhambra, 221v
Aliyah, 852
alliances, 40, 697
Allied Powers, 767
Almoravid dynasty, 362
alphabet, 126–127, 144–145, 153, 183
　Cyrillic, 237
Alsace-Lorraine, 697, 708
Amaterasu, 208
Amazon (company), 864
Amenhotep III, 52v
American Federation of Labor (AFL), 662–663
American Revolution, 582–583, 587
Americas, 382–405
　Argentina, 656v, 657, 844
　Bahamian Archipelago, 403
　Bolivia, 497
　Chile, 384, 844
　early complex societies, 386v–387
　Gran Colombia, 601
　Guatemala, 801, 845
　Haiti, 537, 587–589, 605, 825
　indigenous peoples' struggles for rights, 658–661, 724, 726
　Jamaica, 603, 631, 706
　Jamestown, 411, 504v
　Mexico, 382–383v, 537, 654–655, 659
　Nicaragua, 845
　settling of, 384–385v
　Venezuela, 537, 600–601, 883
　See also Brazil, Canada, Caribbean island societies, Cuba, Mesoamerica, Mexico, Peru, North America, South America, United States
amphitheater, 163
amphora, 161
Amritsar Massacre, 750
Amun-Ra, 48, 52
Amundsen, Roald, 532
Anabaptists, 435
Analects, The, 86–87, 202
Analytical Institutions, 551
anarchist, 653
Anasazi, 356v, 393
Anatolia, 54–55, 102, 344–345, 713
anatomy, 418
ancestor worship, 83
Andean civilizations, 396–399v
Anders, Bill, 829
Andes, 385–386
Andraka, Jack, 909v
Angkor Thom, 210
Angkor Wat, 210–213
Anglo-Asante Wars, 672
Anglo-Saxons, 274–275
Angola, 825
Anguissola, Sofonisba, 421v
animals in art, 25–27v
Ankara, Battle of, 345
Anna Comnena, 290
Annals, The, 179
Annan, Kofi, 858
Anselm of Canterbury, 279
Anthropocene, 629, 892, 918
anti-colonial nationalism, 750–755, 812–813
anti-communism, 758–761, 823–825, 834
anti-fascism, 759
anti-imperialism, 722
Anti-Imperialist League, 679
Anti-Semitism, 294, 714, 744, 747, 761
　and refugees, 786–787
　and theft of art by Nazis, 784v–785v
　"Final Solution," 780–781
　Holocaust, 782–783
　in Soviet Union, 835
　in Vienna, 774
antipope, 299
Antoninus Pius, 180
Apache, 660v
apartheid, 795, 814–815, 846, 859
Apollo 8, 828
apostles, 175
appeasement, 761
Appian Way, 162–163
aqueduct, 163v, 187
Aquinas, Thomas, 279, 546
Aquino, Corazon, 861
Arab Spring, 874v, 903
Arab-Israeli conflicts, 854v–855
arabesque, 258, 455
Arabian Peninsula, 13, 109, 244–245, 375
　and Zheng He, 342v
　conquered by Muslims, 250–251
Arabic numerals, 185, 195
Arabs, 707, 711, 714, 852–853
Arafat, Yasir, 854–855v
Arawak, 403
Arc de Triomphe, 534–535v, 593v
Arch of Constantine, 186v
archaeology, 47, 56, 60, 69

INDEX R18

bioarchaeologist, 205
  in Afghanistan, 141–143
  in Cambodia, 210–213
  in China, 83, 90
  in Greece, 122v–123
  in Rome, 164v–165
  in Syria, 879
  in Yemen, 878–879
  of everyday objects, 108–109
  space archaeology, 273
Archimedes, 147
architecture
  Brunelleschi, Filippo, 414, 426
  Crystal Palace, 622–623v
  in Africa, 365, 378v
  in Anasazi culture, 393
  in China, 205, 341
  in Cuba, 806v–807v
  in Florence (building of dome), 414–415v
  in Greece, 144
  in Inca Empire, 398
  in India, 195
  in Japan, 209
  in Maya culture, 388
  in Muslim world, 242–243v, 252, 258–259
  in Ottoman court, 421
  in Rome, 162–163, 187, 434
  in Russia, 339, 472
  in Teotihuacán, 386v–387
  neoclassical, 562–563v
  of churches, 437v
  Taj Mahal, 446–447v, 460v–463v
archon, 130
Ardern, Jacinda, 902v–903
Argentina, 656v, 657, 844
Aristophanes, 133
Aristotle, 146, 546, 565
Armenian Church, 442–443
Armenian diaspora, 476–477
Armenian genocide, 712–713, 781
Armenians in Turkey, 748
armistice, 692, 705, 767
armor, 369v
arms race, 802, 835
Armstrong, Louis, 432v, 737v
Armstrong, Neil, 803
army
  Japanese, 317
  medieval, 298–299v
  Mongol, 327–328
  Muslim, 250
  Roman, 162–163, 183
art, history of, 20–21v
  and Angkor Wat, 210–211
  and protest, 900v–901
  cross-cultural exchanges, 339
  icons, 234–235v
  in China, 205
  in Greece, 144–145v
  in India, 194v–195
  in medieval Europe, 281
  in Ming Dynasty, 343
  in Mongol Empire, 339
  in Rome, 185–187
  Islamic art and architecture, 218–219v, 242–243v, 258–259

Minoan frescoes, 124v
  mosaics, 239v
Artemisia, 115
artifact, 8, 20–21, 249v
Aryabhata, 195
Asante Empire, 672–673
Ashikaga, 317
Ashkenazim, 476
Ashoka, 78–79
Asia
  "Asian Tigers," 863
  Bangladesh, 889v, 899
  Brunei, 905
  French Indochina, 676, 678, 822
  Hong Kong, 632v, 792–793v
  Indonesia, 406, 677, 817
  Java, 493, 494, 677, 678
  Korea, 206–207, 314, 558, 639
  Korean Peninsula, 266v
  Kuwait, 857
  Lebanon, 714
  Malaysia, 495, 629
  Mongol Empire, 326–334, 338–339, 344, 369
  Myanmar, 677v, 883
  Nepal, 76v
  North Korea, 820–821, 882
  Oman, 511
  Palestine, 290–295, 714, 852–853, 877
  Philippines, 439, 498, 677–679, 769, 915v
  South Korea, 820–821, 863
  Southeast Asia and Austronesia, 676–677
  Sumatra, 677
  Taiwan, 465, 722, 808, 863, 905v
  Uzbekistan, 334v–335, 841
  Yemen, 878–879, 903
  See also Afghanistan, China, India, Iran, Israel, Japan, Pakistan, Vietnam
Assyria, 54–56v, 61
Astell, Mary, 569
astrolabe, 259, 557v
astronaut, 803v
  See also cosmonaut
astronomy, 46, 216, 259
  in Germany, 551
  in India, 195
  in Maya culture, 389
Aswan Dam, 819
Atahualpa, 485
Atatürk (Mustafa Kamal), 748v–749
Aten, 48
atheists and atheism, 262, 824
Athena, 133v
Athens, 120–121v, 129–131, 138–139, 144
Atlantic Charter, 767, 846
Atlantic slave trade, 411, 518–519, 528, 531, 536
atlatl, 384
atomic bomb, 693v, 773
Augustine, 181
Augustus, 159v–160, 594v
Aurangzeb, 459
Auschwitz, 780, 783

Auschwitz-Birkenau Memorial and Museum, 785v
Australia, 554–555, 677, 772
Austria, 543, 577, 585, 627–628
  and border with Hungary, 836
Austria-Hungary, 692, 697, 698, 701
Austronesia, 676
authoritarianism, 709, 719, 801, 812, 825
  Arab Spring protests, 874v
  rule of Tito in Yugoslavia, 848–849
Autobiography of the Woman the Gestapo Called the White Mouse, The, 774
avatar, 192
Avesta, 104
aviation, 734v–735v, 738v–739
Avignon, 299
Axis Powers, 767
Ayacucho, Battle of, 603
Azikiwe, Nnamdi, 754
Aztec, 346, 357v, 394v–395, 443
  and Spanish, 484v–485

B

Babur, 456
Babylon, 40–41, 61, 556
  defeat by Cyrus II, 106–107
Bacon, Francis, 549, 561
Bacon, Roger, 283, 546
Baghdad, 256–257, 259, 333, 368–369, 451
  and Faisal al-Hashemi, 715
  and Persian Gulf War, 857
Bahamian Archipelago, 403
bailout, 886
Baker, Josephine, 737
Balamkú, 391
Balboa, Vasco Núñez, 484
Balfour Declaration, 714, 852
Balkans, 696–697v
Ball, Albert, 735
Ballard, Robert, 739, 769
Ban Zhao, 215
Bandung Generation, 816–817
Bangladesh, 889v, 899
Bangwato, 668–669
banking, 277, 591, 799, 863, 886–887
Banks, Joseph, 537, 554–555
Bantu, 360v, 510–511
Baptism, 181
Barbosa, Duarte, 379
Basho, Matsuo, 479
Basil (saint), 237v, 472
Basil I, 236
Basil II, 236, 241
Basques, 759
Bassi, Laura, 550–551
Bastien-Lepage, Jules, 302
Bastille, 585–586v
Bat (archaeological site), 109
Bataan Death March, 769
Batista, Fulgencio, 804
Battuta, Ibn, 357, 366–367, 381
Bay of Pigs, 804
Baybars, 293
Bayeux Tapestry, 274v
Bayezid, 345v

Beachler, Hannah, 867
Beaufort, Henry, 302
Bechuanaland, 668
Bedouin, 244
Beethoven, Ludwig van, 599
Begin, Menachem, 855
Beijing, 324–325v, 333, 341, 349
  and Boxer Rebellion, 637
  and Qing dynasty, 464
  Nixon visit, 811
Belgium, 671, 767, 771, 813
Belisarius, 220v, 226
Bell, Alexander Graham, 623
Ben-Gurion, David, 853
Benedictine Rule, 288–289
Beowulf, 281
Bergman, Ingrid, 303v
Beringia, 11, 14, 384
Berlin Airlift, 799
Berlin Conference, 613, 672
Berlin Wall, 795, 832–833v, 836–837
Berlin, 772
Bernard of Clairvaux, 279, 293
Bernini, Gian Lorenzo, 441
Beser, Ari, 779
Bessemer, Henry, 613, 617
Bezos, Jeff, 864
Bhagavad Gita, 70v–71
Bhattacharjee, Yudhijit, 790
Bi Sheng, 310
Bible, 59v, 62v–63, 106–107
  and graven images, 235
  King James translation, 541
  translation of, 237
Bhutto, Benazir, 883
Big Ben, 545
Big Hole, 666–667v
Biko, Steve, 815
biogas and biodigesters, 912–913
Bill of Rights (U.S. government), 583, 846
  See also English Bill of Rights and Declaration of the Rights of Man and the Citizen
bin Laden, Osama, 857, 872–873
bin Tughluq, Muhammad, 456
bioarchaeologist, 205
biotechnology, 909
Bismarck, Otto von, 628, 672, 687, 697
Black Consciousness Movement, 815
Black Death (bubonic plague), 297, 347v, 367
Black Hills, 658v–659
Black Seminoles, 528
Blackshirts, 743
Blackstone, William, 583
Blake, William, 596, 620
Blitz, 767
blitzkrieg, 766
Boers, 674v
Bogside, Battle of the, 848
Bohemond, 292
Boiling River, 895
Boko Haram, 883
Boleyn, Anne, 437
Bolívar, Simón, 537, 600–603, 605
Bolivia, 497
Bolsheviks, 718–719, 747

Bonaparte, Josephine, 590v
Bonaparte, Napoleon *See* Napoleon I
Book of Common Prayer, 437
Book of Duarte Barbosa, 379
Book of Highways and of Kingdoms, 379
Book of Travels, 449
Borobudur Temple, 255v
Bosnia and Herzegovina, 697, 698, 849
Bosporus, 225v, 349, 421
botany, 552–553
Botswana, 668
Boudicca, 161v
Boughton, Harold, 707
Boukman, 589
bourgeoisie, 572, 584
Boutros-Ghali, Boutros, 869
Boxer Rebellion, 637
Boyle, Robert, 550
Bradford, Sarah H., 527
Brady, Mathew, 645
Brahman, 192
branches of government, 568–569, 583
Brandt, Willy, 852v
Brazil, 483, 502 522–523v, 527–528
    economy of, 654, 749
    independence of, 603
    "New State," 749
    rubber and, 680, 682
Brexit, 884, 888
Brihadisvara Temple at Thanjavur, 197v
Britain
    and African colonization, 668–669
    and Cyprus, 850
    and Egypt, 818–819
    and Industrial Revolution, 616–617, 620–621
    and Qing dynasty, 465
    and World War I, 698
    Anglo-Asante Wars, 672
    Brexit, 884, 888
    British Empire and inequality, 552–553
    Great Exhibition (of London), 622–623
    in Roman times, 161
    union with Scotland, 566
Britain, Battle of, 767
British East India Company, 634–635
bronze, 35, 85, 396
Browning, Elizabeth Barrett, 621
Bruegel, Pieter, 296
Brunei, 905
Brunelleschi, Filippo, 414
Buddha, 72–77, 167v
Buddhism, 72–77, 78–81, 167v, 254–255
    and Angkor Wat, 210–211, 213
    divisions within, 442
    in China, 204–205
    in Japan, 209, 317, 320v
    in Korea, 207, 314
    in Vietnam, 207, 315
    on Silk Roads, 201
    Zen Buddhism, 317–318

Buenos Aires, 656v
Bulgaria, 837
Bulgars, 471
Bulge, Battle of the, 693, 771
Bullard, Gabe, 262
bureaucracy, 88, 256, 310
    in Ming dynasty, 341
    in Songhai Empire, 515
    in Yuan dynasty, 333
Burj Khalifa, 864v
Burma, 676, 776
Burundi, 883
Bush, George H.W., 857
Bush, George W., 872–873, 883, 886
bushido, 317
Buyids, 257
Byron, Lord George Gordon, 596–598
Byzantine Empire (Eastern Roman Empire), 180, 183, 224–225v
    and Crusades, 290–295
    and Russia, 471
    and Seljuks, 344
    growth and decline of, 236–237v
    influence of, 238–239v
Byzantium, 180

C

Cabral, Pedro Álvares, 502
Caesar, Julius, 53, 158–160
Cahokia, 356v, 392
Cairo, 369, 874v
Calais, 298
calculator, 550
calendar, 46, 167v, 248v–249v
    in Inca culture, 397, 399
    in Maya culture, 389
caliph, 247, 256–257, 873
calligraphy, 218–219v, 231v, 258, 454–455
Calvin, John, 435, 442
Cambodia, 210–213v, 499v, 613, 825
    and France, 676
camel, 167v
Camp David Accords, 855
campesinos, 726
Canada, 505, 625, 650–651, 660–661
Candide, 570
cannon, 298, 349, 491
Canterbury Tales, The, 281
Capa, Robert, 759
Cape Colony, 675
Cape of Good Hope, 490v, 493
Cape Town, 493
Capital in the Twenty-First Century, 890
capital, 277
capitalism, 492, 569–570, 612, 627–629
    and competition with Soviet Union, 746–747, 799
    and globalization, 863
    in China, 842
Caral, 386
caravan, 367
caravel, 482
carbon dioxide levels, 917v

Cárdenas, Lázaro, 727, 741
Carib, 483
Caribbean island societies, 400, 402–403, 755
Carlisle Indian Industrial School, 660v
Carolingian dynasty, 270, 275
Carpaccio, Vittore, 428v
carpet-bombing, 759
Carranza, Venustiano, 724, 726–729
Carter, Jimmy, 855
Carter, Ruth E., 867
Carthage, 126, 154–155
cartography, 556–558
Caruso, Enrico, 737
caste system, 71, 196, 659
Castro, Fidel, 794, 804v, 806, 831v
catacombs, 175
Çatalhöyük, 4v, 28–29
cataract, 42
Cathars, 295
cathedral, 279, 281–282v
    Notre-Dame, 284–287v
    St. Basil's, 472–473v
Cathedral of Santa Maria Assunta, 282v
Catherine of Aragon, 436–437
Catherine the Great, 475v, 477v, 577
Catholic Church *See* Roman Catholic Church
Catholic Reformation (Counter-Reformation), 440–443
Catiline, 183v
cats, domestication of, 23v
caudillo, 605, 655
cavalry, 55, 250, 450
cave paintings, 20–21
Cavendish, Margaret, 569
Ceaușescu, Nicolae, 837
celadon, 201, 314, 319v
Çelebi, Evliya, 448–449
Central America, 603, 801, 845
Central Intelligence Agency (CIA), 802
Central Powers, 701v, 719
Chaco culture, 393
Chagatai Khanate, 332v, 338
Chai Ling, 843
Chaldeans, 55
Chamberlain, Neville, 761v, 767
Champa kingdom, 207
Champlain, Samuel de, 505
Chandragupta I (Gupta dynasty founder), 194
Chandragupta Maurya, 78
Chang Jiang, 83
Chang'an, 200
Chardin, Jean, 495
chariot, 55, 116v, 125
Charlemagne, 254–255
Charles I of England, 542
Charles II of England, 544
Charles V (Holy Roman Emperor, formerly Charles I of Spain), 437, 438
Chaucer, Geoffrey, 281
Chavín, 386v–387
Chernobyl, 835, 838
Cherokee, 618–619, 659

Cheyenne, 660
Chiang Kai-shek, 723, 757, 808
Chichén Itzá, 254, 391
child labor, 620–621, 663
children's rights, 858
Chile, 384, 844
Chimú, 396
China, 27v, 76v, 82–91
    and industrial growth, 625
    civil war in, 808
    communism, 722–723, 888
    economic growth of, 842, 863
    Han dynasty, 167v, 198, 202v–203, 432v
    influence in East Asia, 318v–321v
    likely to become world's largest economy, 888
    May Fourth Movement, 722, 723
    Mongol invasion and rule of, 327–329, 333
    Nationalist Party, 722
    opium wars, 612v, 632
    People's Republic of China, establishment of, 794, 808–809
    rebellions in, 636–637
    recession in, 887
    renaissance or golden age of, 432v
    Song dynasty, 204, 308–313
    Tang dynasty, 204–205, 308, 432v
    Tiananmen Square, 722, 842–843v
    Tibet and, 851
    weapons in, 255v
    Wuhan, 908
    See also Ming dynasty, Qing dynasty
chinampas, 395
Chinese Exclusion Act, 662
chinoiserie, 321v
Chivalry, Code of, 293
Chola kingdom, 196v–197
cholera, 620
Chopin, Frédéric, 599
Churchill, 761, 798v, 800
Christianity, 60, 170–171, 187
    and Crusades, 290–295
    and Germanic tribes, 270
    and help for poor and vulnerable people, 663
    and slave trade, 520–521, 527
    Armenian Church, 442, 713
    Church of England, 437, 541, 542
    Coptic Christians, 375, 442
    expansion to Slavic people of Eastern Europe, 236–237
    Iconoclastic Controversy, 236–237, 435
    icons, 234–235v
    in Africa, 511, 668, 671–672
    in Ethiopia, 375
    in India, 634–635
    in Japan, 469
    in medieval Europe, 280–281
    Luther, Martin, 434v–435, 440
    pilgrims, 176–177

INDEX R20

Roman persecution, 178–179, 181
Schism of 1054, 275v
spread of, 174–179
See also Catholic Reformation, Eastern Orthodoxy, Protestant Reformation, Roman Catholic Church
chronometer, 559v
Chulalongkorn, 633, 685v
church and state, relationship between, 268–271, 655, 725, 749
Church of Gabriel-Raphael, 376v
Church of the Gesù, 412–413v
Church of the Holy Sepulchre, 168–173v
Churchill, Winston, 767
Ci Xi (empress), 637v
Cibola, 496
Cicero, 183v
Cincinnatus, 153
Circus Maximus, 163
Cistercian monks, 289
cities, origins of, 36v
city-states, 37
Florence, 410, 414–415, 429
in Aztec Empire, 395
in Greece, 128–129v, 138–139
in Italy, 410, 413–414v
in Phoenicia, 126
in United Arab Emirates, 864
Maya, 166v, 389
civil disobedience, 750–751
civil liberties, restrictions on, 777, 884
civil rights, 860
civil service, 310–311v, 315, 317
in China, 341
in Korea, 207
in Vietnam, 319v
civil war
in Angola, 825
in England, 542
in Libya, 883
in Mexico, 655, 724
in Muslim Empire, 252
in Rome, 158, 180
in Russia, 719
in Saint-Domingue, 588–589
in Somalia, 883
in the United States, 644–646
in Yemen, 878–879
civilians, targeting of during wartime, 778
civilization, 34, 42–43v, 68–69, 94
clan, 208, 361
classical learning, 279, 546
Claudius, 161
Cleisthenes, 130
Clement II, 289
Clement V, 299
Cleopatra VII, 49, 53v
climate change, 688, 895, 899, 911
climate, 544–545
Clinton, Bill, 855v
Clotilda, 529
cloud computing, 898
Clovis point, 384–385v
Clovis, 270
Cluny, 289
Code of Justinian, 227, 238–239

code of laws, 41, 227, 238–239
Code Talkers, 778v–779
codex, 389
coins, 98v, 104, 133v–134
and Commercial Revolution in Europe, 277
in Byzantine Empire, 220v
in China, 311
in India, 195, 456
in Mughal Empire, 411v, 459
in Roman Empire, 161
in Umayyad Empire, 253
lack of in Japan, 317
Spanish reales, 500v
See also currency, paper money
Cold War, 796–829, 844, 845, 882
Coleman, Bessie, 735v
collectivization, 747, 809
College of Cardinals, 299
Colosseum, 150–151v, 187
Columbian Exchange, 488v–489
Columbian Exposition, 653
Columbus, Christopher, 339, 357v, 403, 411, 482–483v
and Northwest Passage, 532
impact of on Portuguese exploration, 490
comic books, 867v
Commentaries on the Laws of England, 583
Commercial Revolution, 277, 281, 310
Committee of Public Safety, 587
Common Era, 864
common law, 583
Commonwealth of Independent States, 841
communism, 613, 722–723, 743
after World War II, 798
and Berlin Wall, 836–837
and Nazism, 744–745
and political aggression, 758
containing, 800
in Cambodia, 825
in China, 808–809, 888
in Cuba, 805
in Soviet Union, 746–747, 834–835
Joseph McCarthy and, 801
Truman Doctrine and, 794, 800
Communion, 178
Communist Party, 719, 720, 757
Compendium of Chronicles, The, 331
Complete History, The, 331
complete revolution, 605
complex societies, 34, 386v–387, 396–399v
compulsory education, 395
computational geneticist, 487
computers, 896–899
concentration camps, 674v–675, 745, 780–781, 784, 790
Concert of Europe, 593
Condivi, Ascanio, 445
Confederacy, 644–645
conflict minerals, 896–897v
Confucianism, 86–87, 254, 314
in China, 202, 340–341, 464, 636–637
in Japan, 317

in Vietnam, 207, 319v
Neo-Confucianism, 311
Confucius, 86
Congo, 672
Congo Free State, 682
See also Democratic Republic of the Congo
Congress (U.S. government), 583
Congress of Angostura, 601
Congress of Vienna, 592–593
connectivity, 898
conquistadors, 484
Conrad, Joseph, 672
conscription, 475, 704, 707
conservation, 608, 893
conservative ideas, 604
Constable, John, 598
Constance, Council of, 299
Constantine the Great, 169, 180–181v
Constantine V, 235
Constantinople, 180, 220v, 224–225v, 228–231v
and Crusades, 290, 293, 295
and Evliya Çelebi, 448
and Ottoman Empire, 345, 348–349
and World War I, 706
See also Istanbul
Constitution of the United States, 583
constitutional government, 283
constitutional monarchy, 540, 585, 592, 627, 718
constitutionalism, 583
consumption (economics), 468
containment policy, 800
Continental Congress, 582
contras (counterrevolutionaries), 845
conversion in Muslim Empire, 251
Cook, James, 537, 554
Cooney, Kara, 52v
Cooper, Jago, 403v
Copernicus, Nicolaus, 536, 546–547
copper, 109, 880–881
Coptic Christians, 375, 442–443
Coral Sea, Battle of the, 769
Córdoba, 242–243v, 253
Coronado, Francisco Vásquez de, 496
coronavirus, 487, 908–909
Cortés, Hernán, 484v
cosmonaut, 794v, 803
See also astronaut
cost-benefit analysis, 863
cottage industry, 618
cotton gin, 612v, 618, 646, 649
cotton, 646v–649v, 673, 755
Council of Trent, 440–441
counterculture, 717
covenant, 59–60
COVID-19, 908–909
cowrie shells, 514
cradle of civilization, 35
Crane, Hart, 717
Creek (Native American people), 618–619
crematoria, 783
Crete, 124v–125

Crimean War, 630v–631
criollos, 600, 603
Crisis, The, 755
Croatia, 697
Cromwell, Oliver, 542, 544
crop rotation, 276
cross-cultural exchanges, 339, 494–495
Crusades, 266v, 290–295v
cryptography, 899
Crystal Palace, 622–623v
Cuba, 654, 677, 794, 804–807
and Sandinistas, 845
and United States, 882
Cuban Missile Crisis, 794v, 805, 831
Cueva de las Manos, Argentina, 21
Culhane, T.H., 912v–913
cult of personality, 747, 809
cultural diffusion, 81
cultural hearth, 24v
cultural heritage, 56, 168v–172, 806v–807v, 876, 881
Cultural Revolution, 810
Cummings, E. E., 717
cuneiform, 36v, 39, 556
Curie, Marie, 717
currency, 161, 180, 238, 277
cowrie shells, 514
euro, 863
in China, 311
in Japan, 317
on Silk Roads, 201
Cusco, 396
Custer, George (general), 660
cybercrime, 898
Cyprus, 850
Cyril, 236–237v
Cyrillic alphabet, 237
Cyrus II (the Great), 104–107v, 114, 116
Czech Republic, 321, 841
Czechoslovakia, 798, 800, 824, 837
Czechs, 698

D

D-Day, 693, 764–765v, 771, 774
da Gama, Vasco, 490
da Vinci, Leonardo, 175v, 418, 422–423
Dahomey, 528
Dai Viet, 315, 341
daimyo, 317, 468–469, 633
Dakota (indigenous people), 659
Dalai Lama, 851v
Dalits, 750
Damascus, 252, 293, 715, 879
Dante Alighieri, 281
Dao de Jing, 86–87
Daoism, 86–87, 207, 254
dar-al Islam, 366
Dardanelles, 706
Darfur, 883
Darius III, 98v, 140
Darius the Great, 110–111, 114
Dark Ages, 280
Darwin, Charles, 537, 613, 627
David (king of the Israelites), 61, 280v
David, Jacques-Louis, 139, 590, 597

Day of Six Billion, 864
de Anda, Guillermo, 390–391v
de la Cruz, Sor Juana Inés, 497
de Las Casas, Bartolomé, 497, 506
de Lespinasse, Julie, 572
death camps, 782–783
    See also concentration camps
debt peonage, 654, 659
Declaration of Independence, 582–583, 663
"Declaration of Sentiments and Resolutions," 663
Declaration of the Rights of Man and of the Citizen, 537, 584, 585
    See also Bill of Rights (U.S. government) and English Bill of Rights
de Condorcet, Nicolas, 572
de Gaulle, Charles, 767, 774, 812
de Gouges, Olympe, 586
de Grouchy, Sophie, 572
de Klerk, F.W., 815
de La Salle, Sieur, 505
de Sahagún, Bernardino, 485
Declaration of the Rights of Women, 586
decolonization, 812–813
deductive approach, 549
deindustrialization, 634
deism, 573
deity, 133
Delacroix, Eugène, 598
Delaroche, Hippolyte-Paul, 302
Delhi, 456–457v
Delian League, 138
delta, 42, 47
demilitarized zone, 821v
democracy
    according to Rousseau, 569
    in Athens, 129–131
    in Greece, 144
    perceived weakening of, 882–884
    spread of democratic ideas, 604–605, 860
d'Épinay, Prosper, 301
Democratic Republic of the Congo (DRC), 406, 813, 896–897v
demographics, 309, 888
Deng Xiaoping, 811, 842–843, 863, 888
Denmark, 500, 767
deportation, 713
depth charge, 778
Descartes, René, 549
Description of Foreign Peoples, The, 312–313
despotism, 340, 587
détente, 834
Dewan, Leslie, 894v–895
Dhaka, 889v
dharma, 71
dhimmitude, 251
dhow, 375
dialect, 309
Dialogue Concerning the Two Chief World Systems, 536
diamonds, 666, 668, 674–675, 813
Dias, Bartolomeu, 490
diaspora, 17, 60v–61, 476–477, 866

Díaz, Porfirio, 655, 657, 724, 726–727
Dickens, Charles, 612, 621
dictator, 153, 158–159, 605, 655, 719
    Duvalier, Francois "Papa Doc," 825
    Franco, Francisco, 758–759
    Hitler, Adolf, 745, 744–745, 771
    Mussolini, Benito, 742v–743, 757, 770, 777
    Pinochet, Augusto, 844
    Somoza family, 845
    Stalin, Joseph, 721, 746v–747, 760–761, 770, 798v–799, 809
dictatorship, 721, 724
Diderot, Denis, 570–571, 574–575
Diocletian, 180
diplomacy, 48, 798
Directory, the, 591
discrimination, 629, 645
disease, 489, 589, 620–621, 652, 908–909
    See also epidemic, plague
disenfranchisement, 584
dissident, 442, 780, 860, 883
diversity
    under Süleyman I, 450–251
    in cities, 870–871v
    in India, 635
    in Muslim Empire, 250–251
Divine Comedy, The, 281
divine right, 576
division of labor, 34, 36v, 617–618
Division of the North, 727
Djoser, 45
doctrine, 289
dogs, domestication of, 23
Dome of the Rock, 253v, 290
domestication, 23
dominion, 651
domino effect, 800
Donatello, 410
Dos Passos, John, 717
Double Disasters, 237
Douglas, Aaron, 432v
dowry, 458
dragons in art, 341
Drake, Nadia, 216
drama, 132–133, 146–147v, 468
Dreadnought, 704
Dresden, 778
Drew, Charles R., 909
drones, 875
Du Bois, W.E.B., 710v, 755
Dubai, 865v
Dubček, Alexander, 824, 826
Dubois, Paul, 300
duchy, 271
Duma, 718–719
Dunkirk, 767
Dunlop, John, 683
Duomo, 414–415
Dürer, Albrecht, 420
Dutch East India Company, 492–493
Dutch Republic, 492
Dutch West India Company, 502–503
Dutch West Indies, 755
Duvalier, Francois "Papa Doc," 825

dynastic cycle, 84
dynasty, 44

E

e-commerce, 864v
Earhart, Amelia, 735, 738v–739
earthquake, 228–230v, 900–901
East Germany, 799–801, 836–837, 840–841
East-West Schism, 221v
Easter Island, 400–402
Eastern Orthodoxy, 275, 349, 375, 442, 697
Eastern Roman Empire (Byzantine Empire), 180, 183
eBay, 864
Ecloga, 238–239
economic dependency, 656
economics, 24, 124, 134–137
    after World War I, 717
    and communism, 627
    and fall of Western Roman Empire, 183
    and Industrial Revolution, 624, 628–629
    consumption, 468
    depression, 653, 740–741
    economic challenges, 862–863
    economic nationalism, 741
    economic warfare, 704
    female economic empowerment, 903
    Gini coefficient, 891
    government intervention in, 741
    government planning of, 799
    gross domestic product (GDP), 890
    in the Soviet Union, 720, 747
    inflation, 455, 464, 500, 709
    Keynes, John Maynard, 741, 886
    Marshall Plan and, 799
    recession, 886
    sanctions, 757
    Smith, Adam, 569–570, 617
    stock market crash, 692, 740–741, 795, 886
    stock, 492
    See also free-market economy
Eden, Anthony, 819
Edessa, 292–293
Edict of Nantes, 439, 541
Edicule, 168–173
Edison, Thomas, 623
education
    in Aztec Empire, 395
    in China, 310
    in medieval Europe, 278–279
Edward III, 298
Edward, Prince of Wales (the Black Prince), 299v
Egeria, 176–177
Egypt, 27v, 32–33v, 42–47v, 141
    and Arab Spring, 874
    and Israel, 853
    during World War II, 770
    resistance to Britain, 673
    Suez Canal, 613v, 777, 818–819
    under Muslim rule, 250, 369
    Zabaleen, 913

Eiffel Tower, 623
Eightfold Path, 72
Einstein, Albert, 744
Eisenhower, Dwight D., 770, 771, 802, 819, 824
El-Alamein, Second Battle of, 770
electricity, 623, 747, 892, 912
Elements, The, 141, 203, 427
Elizabeth I, 439, 540v–541, 548v
Ellis, Steven, 165v
Elmina Castle, 503v
embargo, 646, 768, 805
empires, 39, 166
    after World War I, 715
    Han, 166–167v
    Japanese, 748
    Kushan, 166–167v
    Muslim, 250v–251
    Parthian, 166–167v, 180
    Roman, 158–167v
encomienda, 497
Encyclopedia, 570–572, 575
Endeavour, 554
energy, 617, 892–895
Engels, Friedrich, 613, 627
engineering
    Byzantine, 228–231v
    Inca, 398
    in Britain, 616–617, 622–623v
    in Florence (building of dome), 414–415v
    Maya, 388
    Roman, 162–163, 185v, 187
England
    colonies, 504–505
    competition with the Dutch, 492
    Glorious Revolution, 544–545
    Hundred Years' War, 298
    Protestant Reformation, 436–437
    See also Britain
English Bill of Rights, 544, 576, 583
    See also Bill of Rights (U.S. government) and Declaration of the Rights of Man and the Citizen
English Channel, 298, 767
English Civil War, 542
Enigma machine, 779
enlightened despots, 576–577, 591
enlightenment, 72
Enlightenment (philosophical movement), 564–565, 568–571, 584, 600–601, 604–605
    and Weimar Republic, 744
enslavement See slavery
entrepreneur, 465
environmental refugia, 13
envoy, 339
epic, 37, 183, 389
Epic of Gilgamesh, 5v, 37, 62–63
epidemic, 487, 621, 908–909
    See also disease, plague
"ethnic cleansing," 848–849v, 859
equality, 577, 663, 711
equatorial Africa, 755
Equiano, Olaudah, 518v–519, 527
Erasmus, Desiderius, 425, 435
Eratosthenes, 141
Erdogan, Recep Tayyip, 883

INDEX R22

Erik the Red, 273
Eriksson, Leif, 273
Eritrea, 684, 883–884
estates (French social classes), 584
Estates-General, 299m 585
Estonia, 840–841
Ethiopia, 375–377v, 684–685, 743, 757, 883–884, 902
ethnography, 554
Etruscans, 153
Ettlinger, Harry, 784v
Etzanoa, 393
Euclid, 141, 203, 427v
eugenics, 780
Euphrates River, 34
Euripides, 133
Europe
    Austria-Hungary, 692, 697, 698, 701
    Belgium, 671, 767, 813
    Bosnia and Herzegovina, 697, 698, 849
    Bulgaria, 837
    Crete, 124v–125
    Croatia, 697
    Cyprus, 850
    Czech Republic, 321, 841
    Czechoslovakia, 798, 800, 824, 826
    Denmark, 500, 767
    economic and political domination by, 566–567v, 668–673
    Estonia, 840
    European Union, 862v–863, 882, 883, 884
    Greece, 120–149, 770, 800, 886–887
    Iceland, 886–887, 895
    increasing global dominance of, 627, 630
    Ireland, 629, 886
    Ireland, Republic of, 848
    Kazakhstan, 841
    Latvia, 840
    Lithuania, 840
    Luxembourg, 767
    Netherlands, 420, 492–493, 502–503, 767
    Northern Ireland, 848
    Norway, 767
    Prussia, 542–543, 628
    Romania, 782, 837
    Scotland, 161, 298, 566
    Slovakia, 841
    Thirty Years' War, 542
    Yugoslavia, 841, 848–849v
    See also Austria, Britain, England, France, Germany, Hungary, Italy, Poland, *individual European countries*
European Age of Exploration, 339, 482–483
European Central Bank, 863
eurozone, 886
evolution, 537, 627
excommunication, 275, 289
Exodus, 59
expatriate, 717
    See also immigration

Exploration of the Valley of the Amazon, 657
extraterritoriality, 632–633
extremists, 872–873, 876

F

Facing Mt. Kenya, 755
factory system of production, 617
Faisal al-Hashemi, 715
Falkland Islands War, 835, 844
famine, 267v, 296v, 629
    during and after World War I, 701
    in Bengal, 634
    in China, 637, 810
    in Ireland, 910
    in Russia, 704, 720–721
    in the Congo, 672
    in the Philippines, 679
    in the Soviet Union, 747
    in Vietnam, 778
farming, history of, 22–25v, 94
    and Columbian Exchange, 488–489
    and free trade, 863
    and Industrial Revolution, 628–629
    improvements in, 619
    in Africa, 361
    in Americas, 386v–387
    in China, 310, 340, 465
    in Japan, 316
    in medieval Europe, 276–277, 281, 283
    in Soviet Union, 747v
    in Vietnam, 315
    See also agriculture
fascism, 742–743, 758–759
    possible return to, 884
"Final Solution," 780–781
fashion, 737
fauna, 554
Faust, 598
February Revolution, 719
Fedele, Cassandra, 429
federal, 583, 605
feminism, 663
Ferdinand (Spanish king), 294–295v, 483
Ferdinand II (Holy Roman Emperor), 542
Ferdinand Maximilian Joseph (Mexican emperor), 655v
Ferris wheel, 623, 653
feudalism, 276, 317, 638
figurehead, 257, 314, 317
filial piety, 86
firebombing of Dresden, 778
First Balkan War and Second Balkan War, 697
First Nations, 385, 505, 651, 660–661
First Opium War, 612v
First World War *See* World War I
fiscal austerity, 886–887
Fitzgerald, F. Scott, 717
Five-Year Plan, 746
Flanders, 298
flood narrative, 62v
flora, 552
Florence, 410, 414–415, 429

flying buttresses, 284
food of the future, 915v
food security, 552–553, 910–911, 913
For Whom the Bell Tolls, 759
Forbidden City, 324–325v, 341
forced migration, 55, 397, 399, 748–749
fossil fuels, 617, 629, 892–893, 895
Four Books, The, 311
Four Noble Truths, 72
Fourteen Points, 708
Fox, Keolu, 15
fracking, 892
France, 534–535v
    and absolute monarchy, 540–541
    and Algeria, 822
    and Hundred Years' War, 298
    and Mexico, 655
    and World War I, 698
    and World War II, 767, 774
    Asian colonies of, 613v, 822v–823
    during Age of Napoleon, 590–593
    student movement in, 826
    see also French Revolution
Francis of Assisi, 289, 416v
Franco-Prussian War, 697
Franco, Francisco, 758–759
Frankenstein, 571, 598
Frankfurt Assembly, 627
Franklin, Benjamin, 572, 604v
Franklin, John, 532
Franks, 270
Franz Ferdinand, 692v, 696, 698
Franz Joseph II, 628, 698
Frederick the Great, 467, 576v, 577
Frederick William I of Prussia, 543
Free French, 767, 776
free press, 747, 835
free speech, 572–573, 842–843, 900–901
free-market economy, 569–570, 626, 704, 777, 799
    after the collapse of the Soviet Union, 841
    and neoliberalism, 863
    in China, 842
free trade, 863
French and Indian War, 505, 582, 585
French Equatorial Africa, 776
French Indochina, 676, 678, 755, 822v–823
French Polynesia, 685
French Revolution, 584–587, 591
    and Notre-Dame Cathedral, 284
fresco, 124v, 156v, 185, 197, 454v
    during Renaissance, 412–413v, 416v, 418, 426v–427v
    in Maya culture, 388v
    in Mexico, 728–729v
Freud, Sigmund, 744
Friedrich, Caspar David, 598, 607
Frobisher, Martin, 532
Fujin, 320v
Fukushima, 892
fumarole, 895
fundamentalist, 857

G

Gaffney, Owen, 918
Gagarin, Yuri, 794, 803
Galen, 550
Galerius, 179
Galilei, Galileo, 536, 547
Gallipoli, 706
Gandhi, Mohandas K. "Mahatma," 750v–753, 777, 860
Gang of Four, 811
Ganges River, 68–69v, 193
Gao (Mali), 512v
Garibaldi, Giuseppe, 613v, 628
Garrett, Ken, 580_581
garrison town, 203
Garvey, Marcus, 755v
gas chambers, 783
Gaul, 153, 161, 270
Gautama, Siddhartha, 72–77
gays and lesbians, 883, 904–905v
gender, 905
General Agreement on Tariffs and Trade (GATT), 863
Geneva, 436
genocide, 675, 712–713, 781, 783, 790
    in Cambodia, 825
    in Yugoslavia, 849
    United Nations and attention to, 859
Genghis Khan, 267v, 327v–333
Genocide Watch, 790
Genpei War, 264–265v
gens de couleur, 588–589, 605
Gentileschi, Artemisia, 425v
geocentric theory, 546
geocentric universe, 339
Geoffrin, Marie Thérèse, 572
geoglyph, 396
geographic information systems (GIS), 559
geography, 124, 316–317v
geology, 629, 895
geometry, 46, 141
George III, 467, 552
geothermal energy, 892, 894–895
ger (tent), 326v
Gerber, Tony, 608
German South West Africa, 675, 701
Germanic tribes, 180, 270
German Expressionism (art movement), 745v
Germany, 420
    and Great Powers, 697
    and New Guinea, 685
    and New Imperialism, 671
    and Protestant Reformation, 436
    and refugees, 875
    and Spanish Civil War, 758–759
    and World War I, 700–701, 704–705
    and World War II, 764–767, 770–772, 774–787
    Peace of Westphalia, 542
    preparing for World War II, 766–767
    reunification of, 836v–841
    unification attempt, 627
    unification of, 628

See also Berlin, Nazi Party
Gestapo, 774, 781
Gevorgyan, Yepraksia, 712v
Ghana, 254–255v, 362, 379
    Elmina Castle, 503v, 536v
    independence, 812
ghazi, 344
ghetto, 294, 745, 781, 782, 790
Ghost Dance, 660
Gibbon, Edward, 238
Gilbert, William, 548v
Gilded Age, 652–653
Gilgamesh, 5v, 37
Gini coefficient, 891
Giotto, 416v–417
Giza, 46
gladiator, 163
glasnost, 795, 834–835
Global Positioning Systems (GPS), 898
global warming, 629, 899
    See also climate change
globalization, 625, 627, 629, 863, 869
    emerging economic players and, 888–889
    responses to, 884
Glorious Revolution, 544–545
Glover, Jerry, 913–914
Goa, 491
Göbekli Tepe, 4v, 28–29v
Godfrey of Bouillon, 290, 292
gods and goddesses, 53
    in Rome, 157v
Goering, Hermann, 784
Goethe, Johannes Wolfgang von, 598
gold, 134–137, 368, 406
    in Australia, 677
    in Brazil, 502
    in Democratic Republic of the Congo, 813, 896–897v
    in South Africa, 629, 668, 674–675
    in the United States, 659
Golden Horde, 332v, 338
Golden Horne, 421
Goldman, Emma, 663
Gompers, Samuel L., 662–663
Good Friday Agreement, 848
Goodall, Jane, 608v
Goodyear, Charles, 680, 682
Gorbachev, Mikhail, 795v, 834, 836–837, 840–841
Gospels, 174
Gothic (art style), 281
government
    constitutional, 283
    during Enlightenment, 574–575
    in Abbasid Empire, 257
    in Greece, 144, 886–887
    in India, 197
Goya, Francisco de, 597
Gramsci, Antonio, 743
Gran Colombia, 601
Granada, 294, 483
Grand Canal, 341
Great Acceleration, 629, 918
Great Canon of the Yongle Era, 341
Great Cloud Sutra, The, 204

Great Depression, 692, 740–742, 744, 748, 755
    and political aggression, 758
"green revolution" in food production, 893
Great Divergence, 625
Great Enclosure, 364v–365
Great Exhibition (of London), 622–623
Great Famine of 1315–1322, 296v
Great Leap Forward, 810–811
Great Powers, 696–698v
Great Purges, 747
Great Recession, 795, 884, 886–887
Great Schism of 1378, 299
Great Wall of China, 66–67v, 198, 328, 343
Great War *See* World War I
Great Zimbabwe, 357v, 364–365v
Greco-Persian Wars, 103, 114–115v, 116
Greco-Roman culture, 174–175, 238–239v
Greco, El, 420
Greece, 120–149, 770, 800, 886–887
Greeks in Turkey, 748–749
green building, 893
greenhouse gases *See* climate change
Gregory VII, 289
Gregory XI, 295
griot, 361–362
gross domestic product (GDP), 890
ground-penetrating radar (GPR), 391
Guadalcanal, 772
Guam, 772
Guangzhou, 722, 842
Guatemala, 801, 845
guerilla warfare, 675, 678, 679, 726, 804
    in Afghanistan, 825
    in China, 808
    in Kenya, 813
Guernica, 758–759
Guevara, Ernesto "Che," 804, 806
guild, 277, 414
guillotine, 587v
Gula, Sharbat, 880v
Gulag Archipelago, The, 747
Gulag, 721, 747
gunpowder, 255, 298, 309
    in Japan, 317
    in Mongol Empire, 339
    in Ottoman Empire, 345, 450
Gupta dynasty, 99v, 194–195
Gusky, Jeff, 703
Gutenberg, Johannes, 417
Guttenfelder, David, 805
Guynemer, Georges, 735
Gypsies *See* Roma

H

habeas corpus, 283
Habsburg dynasty, 438, 451, 453–454, 492
hacienda, 497, 603, 726
hacker, 898
Hadrian, 161, 180

Hagia Sophia, 220v, 227, 228–231v, 349
Hague Convention, 698
Hague, The, 859
haiku, 468, 479
Hailie Selassie, 757v
Haiti, 537, 587–589, 605, 825
hajj, 245, 343
Hakka ethnic group, 636
Hamas, 854–855
Hammurabi, 40–41
Han dynasty, 202v–203
Han Empire, 167v, 198
    and Korea, 206
Hangzhou, 309
Hannibal, 155
Happiness index, 891
Harappan civilization (Indus Valley civilization), 69, 81, 94
Harlem Renaissance, 432v
Harold (English king), 274–275
Harrison, John, 559
Hastings, Battle of, 275
Hathor, Temple of, 32–33v
Hatshepsut, 48, 52v
Hausa, 514
Havel, Václav, 837
Hawaii, 400–401, 432v, 677, 679, 688
    Pearl Harbor, 693, 768–769
Haymarket Riot, 653
Heyn, Piet, 502
Heart of Darkness, 672
Hebrew Bible, 59v–60, 62v–63, 106–107
heliocentric theory, 547
Hellenistic culture, 142, 145v
Hellenization, 140
helot, 129
Hemingway, Ernest, 716, 717, 759
Henry III (Holy Roman Emperor), 289
Henry IV (Holy Roman Emperor), 289
Henry the Navigator, Prince, 482, 489v, 490
Henry VIII (English king), 429, 436–437
Herero, 675
heresy, 300
heretic, 294, 299, 435, 547
heritage, cultural, 56, 168–172
Herndon, William Lewis, 657
Herodotus, 102v–103, 110–111, 114, 117
Herschel, Caroline Lucretia, 551
Herschel, William, 551
Heydrich, Reinhardt, 781
Hezbollah, 854–855, 875
Hidalgo y Costilla, Father Miguel, 602v–603
Hiebert, Frederik, 200, 529
hieroglyphs, 46
Hijrah, 245
Hildegaard of Bingen, 279
Himalaya, 68
Himmler, Heinrich, 784
Hind Swaraj (book), 753
Hind Swaraj (Indian self-rule), 750
Hindu-Arabic number system, 195, 259

Hinduism, 63, 71, 192–193
    and Angkor Wat, 210–211
    in India, 634–635, 751
    in Vietnam, 207
hip-hop, 866v
Hirohito, 748, 768, 773
Hiroshige, Utagawa, 469
Hiroshima, 693, 773
Hispaniola, 588
Histories, The, 103, 110–111, 114, 117
historiography, 8
History and Description of Africa, 515
History of the World Conqueror, The, 331
Hitler-Stalin Pact, 760–761
Hitler, Adolf, 733, 767, 770–772, 784, 786
    rise of, 744–745
Hittites, 54–55
HIV, 908
Ho Chi Minh (Nguyen Ai Quoc), 710–711, 822–823v
Hobbes, Thomas, 565
Holocaust, 782–783
Holocene, 629, 918
Holtun cenote, 391
Holy Communion, 178, 288
Holy Land, 290
Holy Roman Empire, 254, 542
Holy Sepulchre, Church of the, 168–173
holy war, 290
Homage to Catalonia, 759
home front, 704, 717, 777
Homer, 125, 144
homosexuality, 744, 780, 883
Hong Kong, 632v, 792–793v
Hong Xiuquan, 636
Hongwu, 338, 340–341
Hooke, Robert, 550
Hopewell, 392
hoplite, 129
Houël, Jean-Pierre, 586
horses
    domestication of, 23–24
    importance to Chinese, 432v
    importance to Mongols, 326–328
Huang He, 83
Huayna Capac, 357
Hudson, Henry, 493
Huerta, Victoriano, 724, 727
Hugo, Victor, 286
Huguenots, 439, 541
Hull House, 663
Human Genome Project, 909
human record, 56
human rights, 713, 853, 858–859, 875, 903
human sacrifice, 395, 397, 443, 485
humanism, 424–425, 428–429
humans, earliest, 8–11
Hundred Flowers Campaign, 809
Hundred Years' War, 267v, 298, 300
Hungary, 628, 783, 819, 824–825v, 836–837
    and refugees, 875
Hunt, Patrick, 155
Hunt, Terry, 401v

INDEX **R24**

hunter-gatherers, 13, 166, 385, 674
Hurston, Zora Neale, 432*v*
Hus, Jan, 435
Hussein, Saddam, 857, 873
Hutu, 790
Hyksos, 47–48
hypothesis, 549

I

Iberian Peninsula, 253
Ibn al-Athir, 331
Ibn Rushd, 259, 427*v*
Ibn Sina, 259
Ice Age, 384, 629
icon, 234–235*v*, 241*v*
iconoclast, 235
Iconoclastic Controversy, 236–237*v*
Igbo, 511
Ignatius of Loyola, 441
il Giovane, Palma, 348
Iliad, 98*v*, 125, 144
Ilkhanate, 332*v*–333, 338
illuminated manuscript, 280*v*, 291
Imhotep, 45
immigration, 477, 605, 624, 629
    during Gilded Age, 652
    populist reaction to, 884
    to Palestine, 714
    to the United States, 662, 884
    See also migration, forced *and* migration, human
Imperial Academy, 202, 319*v*
Imperial Palace (China), 341
imperialism, 668–673, 678–679, 685, 697, 714–715
Inca, 357, 396–399*v*, 410*v*
    and Spanish conquest, 485
    silver, 501*v*
income inequality, 890–891
    See also inequality
indentured servants, 505, 629
India, 27*v*, 94
    anti-colonial nationalism of, 750–753
    British India, 634–635
    economic power of, 888
    Goa, 491
    Great Depression and, 740–741
    Hind Swaraj, 750
    Kashmir and, 849–850, 882–883
    Maurya Empire, 78–79
    Mughal Empire, 456*v*–459*v*, 634–635
    partition of, 816*v*–817
    Taj Mahal, 446–447*v*, 460–463*v*
    textiles, 618, 751
    World War I, 706–707*v*, 750
Indian National Congress, 635, 685, 750, 752, 777
Indian Ocean, 341–342*v*, 357, 374–375, 511
Indian Removal Act, 659
indigenous peoples' struggles for rights, 658–661, 677, 724, 726
Indo-Aryans, 69–71, 80, 192
Indonesia, 406, 677, 817
inductive approach, 549
indulgences, 434
Indus River, 68–69*v*

Indus Valley civilization (Harappan civilization), 69, 81, 94
Industrial Revolution, 536, 566–567, 616–633, 641
    in Africa, 672
    in Britain, 610–611*v*, 620–623
    in Latin America, 654
    in the United States, 644, 652
industrialization, 746–747, 810
inequality, 552–553, 613, 627, 653, 662–663
    after Great Recession, 887
    and globalization, 863
    in China, 842
    income inequality, 890–891
inflation, 455, 464, 500, 709
information revolution, 310
infrastructure, 315
Ingres, Jean-Auguste Dominique, 595
Innocent III, 294
Inquisition, 294–295, 440
Institutional Revolutionary Party (PRI), 844
institutions, 35, 36*v*
Interesting Narrative of the Life of Olaudah Equiano, or Gustavus Vassa, the African, The, 518–519
International Criminal Court (ICC), 859, 883
International Monetary Fund, 799, 863, 903
International Workers' Day, 653
Internet, 864, 889
internment camps, 777
Inti, 397
intifada, 855
Iran, 100–107, 110–117, 452–453, 487
    and Arab Spring, 874
    conflict with Iraq, 856–857
    during World War II, 771
    revolution, 856–857
    See also Isfahan
Iraq, 714, 856–857, 873
Ireland, 629, 886
irezumi, 430*v*
Iron Curtain, 800, 836
Iron Pillar of Delhi, 195
iron, 54–55, 128, 310, 617
irrigation, 35, 43, 196
Isabella (Spanish queen), 294–295, 483
Isandhlwana, Battle of, 674
Isfahan, Iran, 218–219*v*, 452–453*v*, 477, 495
Isis (goddess), 43*v*
    See also Islamic State of Iraq and Syria (ISIS)
Islam, 60
    and Africa, 511
    and anti-colonial resistance, 685
    and Bosnia, 697
    and Crusades, 290–295
    and India, 634–635
    and Mongol Empire, 339
    and Ottoman Empire, 344
    and World War I, 707
    conquering of Arabian Peninsula, 250–251

    dar-al Islam, 366
    divisions within, 442
    Five Pillars of, 246–247
    in India, 634–635
    Islamic Golden Age, 258–259
    origins of, 244–245
Islamic State of Iraq and Syria (ISIS), 873, 875
Islamist, 515, 856, 883, 903
Island Caribs, 403
island hopping (military strategy), 772
isolationism, 761
Israel, 55, 61, 794, 819, 852–853
    conflicts with Arabs, 854*v*–855
    Israel-Egypt Peace Treaty, 855
Istanbul, 220*v*, 228–231*v*, 349, 421
    See also Constantinople
Italy, 222–223*v*, 408–409*v*, 628*v*, 684
    and World War I, 701
    and World War II, 770
Iturbide, Augustín de, 603
Ivan III, 338
Ivan IV (the terrible), 471*v*
Ivory Coast, 682
ivory, 671*v*–672*v*
Iwo Jima, Battle of, 772
Ix Naah Ek' (Maya queen), 389

J

Jackson, Andrew, 659
Jacobins, 586
Jainism, 71*v*
James I of England, 541
Jamestown, 411, 504*v*
janissary, 450
Japan, 316–317*v*
    and Commodore Matthew Perry, 633
    and World War I, 701
    and World War II, 768–769, 771–772, 799
    annexation of Okinawa, 685
    early history, 208–209
    economic strengths and weaknesses, 863
    folk crafts movement, 431*v*
    Fukushima, 892
    gardens of, 318*v*
    Hiroshima and Nagasaki, 693, 773
    Meiji Restoration, 638–639
    nationalism in, 748
    recession in, 887
    student protests in, 826
    tattoo art, 430*v*
    Tokugawa shogunate, 468–469
    zaibatsu, 639, 748
Jahangir, 458
Jamaica, 603, 631, 706
Jayavarman VII, 210
jazz, 737
Jebel Irhoud, Morocco, 9
Jefferson, Thomas, 582–583, 585
Jehovah's Witnesses, 744, 780
Jericho, 28
Jerusalem, 60, 168–172, 176–177*v*, 877
    and Crusades, 290–293
Jesuits, 412, 441, 464, 467

Jesus Christ, 170, 173, 238*v*
    and Crusades, 290–293
    teachings of, 174–175, 290
Jews
    after World War I, 709, 714, 760
    and Israel, 852–853
    and philosophy, 146
    and Roman Empire, 174
    fleeing Germany, 744–745
    freeing of by Cyrus II, 105–107
    in Russia, 476, 629
    in Soviet Union, 747
    religious differences from Muslims, 244
Jhansi, queen of, 635
Jiang Jieshi *See* Chiang Kai-shek
Jiang Qing, 811
jihad, 685
Jim Crow laws, 662
Jin dynasty, 328
Jing Di, 90
Jiuzhang Suanshu (*Nine Chapters on the Mathematical Art*), 203
Joan of Arc, 267*v*, 300*v*–303*v*
Johannesburg, 674–675
Johdpur, India, 27*v*
John (English king), 283*v*
John II (French king), 299*v*
John of Damascus, 235
John of Leyden, 436
John Paul II, 836
Johnson-Tekahionwake, Pauline, 651, 661
Johnson, Lyndon, 795, 823
joint-stock company, 492
Joliet, Louis, 505
Joseph II, 577
Juárez, Benito, 655*v*
Judah, 61
Judaism, 58–61
Judeo-Christian tradition, 174–175, 187
Julius II, 425, 426
Jungle, The, 663
Jurchen, 308–309
Justinian I, 220*v*, 225–227*v*, 228, 232–233
Jutland, Battle of, 704
Juvaini, Ala-ad-Din Ata-Malik, 331

K

Kaaba, 244–245*v*
kabuki, 468
Kadesh, Battle of, 55
Kaifeng, 308*v*–309, 311
Kalahari Desert, 360, 675
Kalibangan, 94*v*
Kalidasa, 195
Kallanai dam, 196
Kamakura period, 317
kami, 316, 320*v*
kamikaze, 772–773*v*
kana, 209, 319
Kangnido, 558*v*
Kangxi, 464–465
kanji, 209
Kant, Immanuel, 549
kapu, 402
Karakorum, 328
karma, 71, 193
Karman, Tawwakol, 903

Kashmir, 849–850v
Kawae, Yukinori, 45
Kazakhstan, 841
Kemal, Mustafa (Atatürk), 748v–749
Kennan, George, 679
Kennedy, John F., 803, 831
Kennedy, Robert F., 828
Kennin-ji, 318v
Kenya, 755, 794v, 813, 906
Kenyatta, Jomo, 755, 813
Kepler, Johannes, 550
Keukenhof, 493
Kew Gardens, 553v
Keynes, John Maynard, 741, 886
KGB, 802, 841
Khadijah, 245
Khama III, 668v–669
Khanate of the Great Khan, 332v–333
khanate, 328
Khayyam, Omar, 258
Khazan, 472
　　Khazars, 471
Khmer Empire, 210
Khmer Rouge, 790, 825
Khomeini, Ayatollah, 856v–857
Khrushchev, Nikita, 805, 809, 819, 831v
Khufu, 46
Kiev, 328, 471
Kievan Rus, 273, 471
Kilwa, 374v–375, 379, 511
Kim Il-sung, 820–821
Kim Jong-un, 882
King, Martin Luther, 826v, 828, 860
Kinjeketile, 673
Kipchak Khanate, 332v
Kipchaks, 328
Kipling, Rudyard, 679
Kirchner, Ernst Ludwig, 745
Knesset, 853, 854
knight, 276, 298, 317
Koguryo chiefdom, 206
Kolkata, 247v
Kongo (kingdom), 346, 511, 528
Korea, 206–207, 314, 558, 639
Korean Peninsula, 266v
Korean War, 794, 820–821
Koryo, 266v, 314
Koumbi-Saleh, 362
Krishna, 71
Kristallnacht, 745, 780
Ku Klux Klan, 645
Ku, Kathy, 551v
Kublai Khan, 332–333, 338, 349
kulaks, 747
Kurds, 715, 873, 875
Kush, 43, 47
Kuwait, 857

L

L'Anse aux Meadows, 273
Laas Geel, Somaliland, 21
labor, 276, 617, 620–621, 626–629, 653
　　and unions, 662–663
　　in Latin America, 656–657
Lagarde, Christine, 903
Laika, 803
laissez-faire, 569–570
Lakota, 658
Lalibela, 375–377v
land bridge, 11
land reform, 724–727
languages, 54, 69, 183, 817
　　African, 360
Laos, 613, 676, 685
Laozi, 86
lapis lazuli, 113
lar (household god), 157
Larmer, Brook, 406
Lascaux Caves, 21v
latex, 680–683
latifundia, 654
Latin America, 602–603, 654–657, 844–845
　　Cuba, 654, 677
　　See also Central America, South America
Latin East, 292
Latin language, 183, 280–281
Latvia, 840
Lawrence, Jacob, 588
laws, 40–41
　　Abbasid Empire, 256
　　Byzantine Empire, 227
　　China, 88–89, 204
　　Code of Justinian, 227, 238–239
　　code of laws, 41, 227, 238–239
　　common law, 583
　　in Greece, 129
　　in Japan, 209
　　in medieval Europe, 283
　　in Mongol Empire, 330
　　in Rome, 153, 159, 187
　　Judeo-Christian, 174–175
　　Napoleonic Code, 591
　　natural law, 279
　　under Süleyman I, 451
League of Nations, 708, 710–711, 714, 757
Leakey, Louise, 9v
Leakey, Meave, 9v
Lebanon, 714
Lee, Christine, 205v
leftist, 845
Legalism, 88, 202
legionary, 162
Lelang, 206
Lenin, Vladimir, 692v, 718, 720v, 731, 746v, 796–797v
Leningrad, Siege of, 778
Leo Africanus, 379, 515
Leo III (emperor), 235, 238–239
Leo III (pope), 270
Leo V, 235
Leonidas, 115
Leopold II, 671–672, 682
Lesser Antilles, 403
Leviathan, 565
Lewis, Lucy, 431v
LGBTQ (lesbian, gay, bisexual, transgender, and questioning or queer) rights, 904–905v
See also gays and lesbians
Li Peng, 843
Li Yuan, 204
liberalism, 626, 709
Liberation Army of the South, 727
libraries
　　in Abbasid Empire, 256
　　in Florence, 415
　　in medieval Europe, 280
Libya, 757, 883
light-detection and ranging technology (LiDAR), 8, 173, 391
Likud, 854
Liliuokalani, 678v–679
Lin Zexu, 632
Lin, Albert, 329
Lincoln, Abraham, 644–645v, 653v, 665
Lindbergh, Charles, 735, 739
Line of Demarcation, 483
Linear A and Linear B, 125
linear perspective, 426
Lingayats, 196
linguistics, 15
Linnaeus, Carl, 536, 552
Lipo, Carl, 401v
Lisbon, 489v
Lister, Joseph, 621
Liszt, Franz, 599
literacy, 196, 310, 445v
literature, 37, 62v–63, 70–71
　　Chinese, 341
　　Greek, 125, 132–133
　　Muslim, 258–259
　　Romantic, 596–598
Lithuania, 840
Little Bighorn, Battle of the, 660
Little Ice Age, 532, 544–545
Liu Bang, 99v, 202
Livingstone, David, 671
llamas, 386
Locke, John, 536, 565, 582, 604
loess, 83
Lohengrin, 599
Lombards, 270–271
London Peace Conference, 698
London, 870–871v
Long March, 757
Long Shadow of Chernobyl, The, 836
longevity, 909
longitude, 554, 559
"Lost Generation," 716–717
Louis IX, 293
Louis XIV, 505, 536, 540–541v, 555, 564–565
　　and lighting of Paris, 573
　　"I am the state," 577
Louis XV, 543
Louis XVI, 583–586
Louis XVIII, 592
Louis Philippe, 627
Louisiana Purchase, 592
Loutherbourg, Philip James de, 610–611
Luddites, 617v
Ludwig, Gerd, 838–839
Lumumba, Patrice, 813
Lusitania, 705v
Luther, Martin, 434v–436
Luxembourg, 767
Ly dynasty, 314–315, 320v
Lydia, 104, 135

M

MacArthur, Douglas, 769, 772, 820–821
Maccare, Cesare, 183v
MacDonald, John, 651
Macedonia, 115, 137, 140–141
Machiavelli, Niccolò, 429
Machu Picchu, 398–399v
Madero, Francisco, 724v, 727
Madison, James, 583
madrasa, 369
Madres de la Plaza de Mayo, 860v
Maduro, Nicolas, 883, 911
Mafia, 804
Magellan, Ferdinand, 484
Maginot Line, 767
Magna Carta, 283, 846
Magness, Jodi, 61v
Magyars, 271, 471, 698
Mahabharata, 63, 71, 192
Mahavira, 71v
Maiben-Owens, Thelma, 528v
Maimonides, 253
maize, 386, 488
Maji Maji Revolt, 673
Malacca, 491, 493, 495
malaria, 486–487, 589, 671, 908
Malay Annals, 495
Malaya, 678, 755
Malaysia, 495, 629
Mali (country), 516–517v
Mali Empire, 358–359v, 362–363, 512
Malinche, La, 485
Malinke, 362
Mamluk Empire, 357v, 369
mammoths, 384–385
Manchuria, 341, 464, 722, 748, 757
Mandate of Heaven, 84
Mandate System, 714
Mandela, Nelson, 795v, 814–815, 846v–847
Manifesto of the Communist Party, The, 613, 627, 720
Manila galleon, 498
manorialism, 276, 296
mansa, 362
Mansur, 256
manumission, 518
Mao Zedong, 723v, 757, 794v, 808v–811
Maori, 400, 677, 678
maps See cartography
Maratha confederacy, 634
Marathon, Battle of, 114v
March of the Women, 585
Marco Polo, 333, 339, 349
Marconi, Guglielmo, 736
Marcos, Ferdinand, 861
Marcus Aurelius, 180
Maria Theresa of Austria, 577
Marie Antoinette, 585–586
Marius, 158
Marmontel, Jean François, 572
Marne, First Battle of the, 700, 717
maroon communities, 527
Marquette, Jacques, 505
Mars, 865v
Marshall Islands, 772
Marshall Plan, 799
Marshall, Mary, 661
Martel, Charles, 270
Martí, José, 654
Marx, Karl, 613, 627, 718, 720

.2
...us), 284,
...d, 439v, 541
...land, 544
..., 736
ma... ...ety, 736–737
Massachusetts Bay colony, 442
Massie, Mark, 895
Masvingo, 365
material culture, 318v–321v
mathematics, 46, 80, 141, 185
    and astrolabes, 557
    in China, 203
    in Greece, 146–147
    in Inca Empire, 399
    in India, 195
    in Italy, 551
    in Maya culture, 389
    in Muslim world, 258–259
    in World War II, 779
Matsumoto Castle, 306–307v
Mau Mau, 794v, 813
Maurya Empire, 78–79v
mausoleum, 459
Maximian, 180
May Fourth Movement, 722, 723
Maya, 166v, 254v, 354–356v, 389–391v, 659
    in Guatemala, 845
Mayflower, 442
Mayo (indigenous people), 725v, 727
Mazzatenta, O. Louis, 90
McCarthy, Joseph, 801
McClellan, George (general), 645v
McCormick, Cyrus, 612, 619, 622
McCurry, Steve, 879–880v
Mecca, 244
mechanical reaper, 612
Medes, 104
Medici family, 415, 429
Medici, Cosimo de, 415
Medici, Lorenzo de (the Magnificent), 415, 420
medicine, 81, 259
    during Crimean War, 631
    during U.S. Civil War, 644
    during World War I, 717
    in Mongol Empire, 339
    quinine, 671
    recent breakthroughs, 980–909
medieval, 227, 270, 280–283, 271
Medina, 220v, 245, 449
megafauna, 384–385
Mehmed II (the Conqueror), 349, 421
Meir, Golda, 852v–853
Menelik II, 684v, 687, 743
Menelik, 375
Meng Tian, 198
Mengele, Josef, 783
Mensheviks, 718
mercantilism, 483, 492
mercenary, 154, 256, 345
merchant, 257, 277, 491
meritocracy, 88
Mes Aynak, 880v–881v
Mesa Verde, 393v
Mesoamerica, 385, 496, 680

Mesopotamia, 34–41v, 62, 81
mestizos, 497, 724
metallurgy, 195, 389, 396, 406, 613
Methodius, 236–237v
Métis, 651, 660–661
metric system, 591
Mexica, 394
Mexican-American War, 655
Mexico, 382–383v
    cenotes in, 390–391
    Hidalgo y Costilla, Father Miguel, 602v–603
    immigration from, 885
    independence of, 537
    Institutional Revolutionary Party (PRI), 844
    land reform in, 724–727
    Mexican Revolution, 724–729
    Mexico City, 497
    Olmec and Zapotec, 386v–387, 680
    Palenque, 389
    political divisions in, 654–655
    student protests, 828
    Teotihuacán, 386v–387
    Yucatán, 659
Michael III, 235
Michelangelo Buonarotti, 418–419v, 423, 445
Michnik, Adam, 861
microplastics, 688
Middle Ages (of Europe), 270, 283
    See also medieval
Middle East, 876
    See also Southwest Asia
Middle Kingdom of Egypt, 43, 47
Middle Passage, 518, 520–521v
Midway, Battle of, 693, 769, 772
migration, forced, 55
migration, human, 10–11v, 13, 14–15, 55
    from Greece, 129
    in Americas, 384–385v, 795v
    in Caribbean, 403
    in China, 309
    Pacific, 400v
Milan, 413
Milgram, Stanley, 790
militarism, 639, 697, 698, 748
Mill, John Stuart, 626
Miller, Greg, 532
Miller, John, 552
Milosevic, Slobodan, 849
Minamoto, 264–265v, 317
minaret, 252, 258
Ming dynasty, 338, 340–343, 464
mingei (art form), 431v
Minoans, 124–125
missionary, 175, 442–443, 496–497
Mississippian culture, 392
mitochondrial Eve, 8
moai, 401–402v
Mobile, Alabama, 529v
mobilize, 698
Mobutu, Joseph, 813
Moche kingdom, 166v, 396
Moctezuma, 394, 484v–485
modern humans, 8–11
modern societies, 630–633

modernism (artistic movement), 744
Modi, Narendra, 885v
Mogao Caves, 74, 200v
Mohawk, 651
Mohenjo-Daro civilization, 69, 94
Moluccas (Spice Islands), 491–493
monarchy, 44, 159, 298–299, 585, 719
monastery, 271, 278–279, 288v–289
money *See* coins, currency, paper money
Mongke, 332
Mongkut, 633, 684–685
Mongol Empire, 326–334, 338–339, 344, 369
monks, 278–279
monotheism, 59–60, 244, 247
monsoon, 81
Mont-Saint-Michel, 268–269v
Monte Verde, 384
Montesquieu, Charles-Louis de Secondat, Baron de, 568, 570v, 574–575, 583
Monument to the Discoveries, 489v
Monuments Men, 784–785v
Moon Jae-in, 882
moon landing, 803, 829v
More, Thomas, 429
Morgenthau, Henry, 713
moriscos, 439, 542
Morocco, 9, 362, 515
Morse code, 736
Morse, Samuel, 625
mosaic, 38v, 61v, 239v
Moscow, 719, 796–797v
Moses, 59
mosque, 230, 242–243v, 247
    and Islamic Golden Age, 258
    and Ottoman court, 421
    and Süleyman I, 451
    Great Mosque of Djenne, 358–359v
    Great Mosque of Samarra, 255v
    Prophet's Mosque, 246v
    Sankore Mosque, Timbuktu, 378v, 515
Mossaddegh, Mohammed, 824
Mossi, 514
mother culture, 387
Mott, Lucretia, 663
Mount Etna, 312v
Mount Fuji, 190–191v, 316
movable type, 310
Mozambique, 910v
Mozart, Wolfgang Amadeus, 576
Muawiya, 252
Mubarak, Hosni, 874
muckraker, 663
mudra, 75–76v
Mughal Empire, 446–447v, 456v–459v, 479v, 491
    and Britain, 634
Muhammad, 220, 244–247, 448, 873
Muhammad, Askia (the Great), 512–515
Muhammad Rabi ibn Muhammad Ibrahim, 495
mujahideen, 825

multinational corporations, 863, 884, 889
mummy, 45, 430v
Mumtaz Mahal, 459
munitions, 694–695v
mural, 728–729v
Murdock, William, 619
Musa, Mansa, 368v
Musharraf, Pervez, 883
Muslim Brotherhood, 818
Muslim Empire, 250v–253
Muslim League, 751
Muslims, 244–247, 250–259
    and Crusades, 290–295
    and Mamluk Empire, 369
    and philosophy, 259
    in Ghana, 379
    Rohingya, 883–884v
    Tatars, 476
Mussolini, Benito, 742v–743, 757, 770
Myanmar, 677v, 883
Mycenaeans, 125, 136v
mystic, 279, 441

N

Naadam Festival, 470v
Nagasaki, 693, 773v
Namibia, 675, 701
Nanjing, 756–757
napalm, 778, 823
Naples, 408–409v
Napoleon I, 534–535, 537, 590v–593, 595v
Napoleon III, 628, 655, 676
Napoleonic Code, 591
Nara, 209
Nasca culture, 166v, 396
Nasser, Gamal Abdel, 818v
nation-building, 845
nation-state, 591–592, 884
National Aeronautics and Space Administration (NASA), 802
National Assembly, 585, 587
National Association for the Advancement of Colored People (NAACP), 755
National Convention, 586
nationalism, 591–592, 604, 613, 685, 742–743
    Africa and, 812–813
    after World War I, 709, 715
    China and, 722
    fascism and, 742–743
    Great Powers and, 698
    Japan and, 748
    Northern Ireland and, 848
    Southeast Asia and, 755
    Soviet Union and, 835
    Turkey and, 748–749
nationalization, 720, 725, 741, 747, 749
    in Cuba, 804
    in Egypt, 818–819
    in Nicaragua, 845
Native Americans, 497
    Apache, 660v
    Black Seminoles, 528
    Cahokia, 356v, 392
    Carlisle Indian Industrial School, 660v

Cherokee, 618–619, 659
Cheyenne, 660
Choctaw, 659
Creek, 618–619, 659
Dakota, 659
Ghost Dance, 660
Lakota, 658–659
Little Bighorn, Battle of the, 660
Navajo, 778v–779
Sioux, 659
Wounded Knee Massacre, 660
See also Aztec, First Nations, Inca, Maya
Native Land Act, 675
nativism, 469
Natufians, 22
natural law, 279
natural resources, 47–48, 134, 893, 896–897v
natural rights, 565, 568, 574–575
naturalism, 418
navigation, 341, 400, 482, 556–559
Nazi Party, 732–733v, 744–745
Ndebele, 673
Neanderthals, 15, 878v
Nefertari, 51v
Nefertiti, 48, 50–51v
Nehru, Jawaharlal, 751, 752v–753, 817
Neo-Confucianism, 311
neoclassical architecture, 562–563v
neoclassicism, 596–597v
neocolonialism, 812–813, 816–817
neoliberalism, 863
Neolithic Revolution, 22, 385
Nepal, 76v
Neri, Margarita, 727
Nero, 175, 178
Nerva, 180
Netherlands Antilles, 503
Netherlands, 420, 492–493, 502–503, 767
New Amsterdam, 503
New Deal, 741
New Economic Policy, 721
New France, 505, 650–651
New Guinea, 685, 769
New Imperialism, 668–685
New Kingdom of Egypt, 48–49
New Mexico, 497, 727
New Testament, 174
New York City, 503, 642–643v, 652
New Zealand, 400, 663, 677, 902
Newcomen, Thomas, 567
Newton, Isaac, 550
Ngo Quyen, 314–315
Nicaragua, 845
Nicene Creed, 181
Nicholas II, 718–719
Niger River, 511
Niger, 514
Nigeria, 673, 754
Nightingale, Florence, 631v
Nile River, 42–43v, 44, 673
Nimitz, Chester, 772
Nine Chapters on the Mathematical Art (Jiuzhang Suanshu), 203
ninety-five theses, 434
nirvana, 72
Nixon, Richard, 811, 823
Nkrumah, Kwame, 812

Noah, 62v–63
Noah, Trevor, 814v
Noble Eightfold Path, 72
nomad, 69, 200, 326, 470
nonaggression agreement, 761
nonalignment, 816–817
nongovernmental organizations (NGOs), 858–859, 884, 909
See also transnational organizations
nonintervention, 760
nonviolence, 750–751, 814–815, 824, 860–861
Noonan, Fred, 738–739
Nooyi, Indra, 903
Normandy, 274–275, 764–765v, 771
Normans, 274–275, 290
Norte Chico, 387
North Africa, 252–253
North America
  Bahamian Archipelago, 403
  Caribbean island societies, 400, 402–403, 755
  early civilizations, 392v–393
  Greenland, 899v
  New France, 505
  rebellions of indigenous peoples, 658–661
  See also Canada, Cuba, United States, Mexico
North American Free Trade Agreement (NAFTA), 863, 885, 888
North Atlantic Treaty Organization (NATO), 800, 849
North Korea, 820–821, 882
North-West Rebellion, 661
Northwest Passage, 493, 532
Norway, 767
Notre-Dame Cathedral, 284–287v
Novgorod, 471
Ntaiya, Kakenya, 904v
Nubia, 43, 47–49
nuclear accident, 835
nuclear disarmament, 827
nuclear power, 892, 894–895
nuclear war, fear of, 802, 849–850
numerals, 195v, 259, 389
nuns, 278, 817v, 845
Nur Jahan, 458–459
Nuremberg Laws, 745
Nuremberg Trials, 786
Nuremberg, 732–733v
nutrition, 386
Nzinga, 511

O
Obama, Barack, 815, 886
Obregón, Álvaro, 724–725
Octavian See Augustus
October Revolution, 719
Ocuila, 727
Odyssey, 125, 144
Ogata Korin, 320v
Ogodei, 328, 331
oil, 663, 665, 682, 725, 741
  and Suez Canal, 819
  in Angola, 825
  in Democratic Republic of the Congo, 813

in Iran, 824
in Libya, 757
in Mexico, 844
in Southwest Asia, 876
in Soviet Union, 747, 770
Japan's need for, 768
oil spill, 892
price of, 856
Okinawa, 685
Okinawa, Battle of, 772
Old Kingdom of Egypt, 43–47
oligarchy, 129
Oliver Twist, 612v
Olmec culture, 166v, 356v, 386v–387
Olympics, 737, 829v
Oman, 511
Omdurman, Battle of, 673
On Liberty, 626
On the Origin of Species, 537, 613, 627
On the Revolution of the Heavenly Spheres, 549
Operation Barbarossa, 770
opium, 612, 632
optically stimulated luminescence (OSL), 13
optics (field of scientific study), 546
Optics, 427
oracle bones, 83
oral tradition, 125, 361, 389
oratory, 183
Organization of American States, 801
Organization of the Petroleum Exporting Countries (OPEC), 856
Orhan, 345
Orléans, 300
Orozco, José Clemente, 655
Orthodox Church See Eastern Orthodoxy, Russian Orthodox Church
orthodoxy, 542
Orwell, George, 759
Osiris, 45–46v
Oslo Accords, 855
Osman, 344–345
Otto the Great, 271
Ottoman court, 421
Ottoman Empire, 344–345, 439, 448–451
  and Armenian genocide, 712–713, 781
  and Balkans, 697
  and control of the Nile, 592
  and Crimean War, 630v–631
  and Cyprus, 850
  and Southwest Asia, 876
  and World War I, 701, 706–707
  persistence of, 454–455
outsourcing, 863
Owen, Robert, 627
Oxus Treasure, 113v, 116v
Ozinsky, Alison, 861
ozone layer, 893, 918

P
Pacal the Great, 389
Pachacuti, 397, 398
Pacific Island societies, 400–403
Paekche chiefdom, 206

Pahlavi, Mohammad Reza, 824, 857
Pakistan, 94, 816–817, 825, 849–850, 879–880
  Pervez Musharraf and, 883
Palenque, 389
paleoanthropologist, 13
Palestine Liberation Organization (PLO), 854–855
Palestine, 290–295, 714, 852–853, 877
Palmares, 527–528
Palmyra, 57v
Pan-African Congress, 710–711, 813
Pan-Africanism, 685, 812
pandemic, 908–909
Pantheon (Roman temple), 163, 185v
pantheon of gods, 157
panzer, 766
paper money, 311
paper, 202, 389, 417
Papua New Guinea, 738v–739
papyrus, 46
Paracas, 396
Parcak, Sarah, 273
Parente, Alan, 173
Paris Agreement on climate change, 899
Paris Peace Conference, 710–711, 758–759
Paris, 284–287v, 534–535v, 572–573v, 573v, 873
Parker, Laura, 688
Parkinson, Bill, 122–123v
Parliament, 283, 299, 540, 542, 545v
  and Enlightenment, 576
  and Glorious Revolution, 544
Parthenon, 120–121v, 132v–133
Parthian Empire, 166–167v, 180
Parthians, 115
Pascal, Blaise, 550
passive resistance, 846–847
Pasteur, Louis, 621
patriarchy, 156
patricians, 153, 156, 158–159
patron, 415
Paul (apostle), 175
Paulze-Lavoisier, Marie, 572
Pax Mongolica, 333
Pax Romana, 159
Paxton, Sir Joseph, 623
PayPal, 864
Peace of Westphalia, 542
peace symbol, 827v
peaceful protest, 750–751, 847, 860
Pearl Harbor, 693, 768–769
peasants, 276, 679
  and Great Famine of 1315–1322, 296
  and Industrial Revolution, 628
  in China, 636, 723, 808–811, 842
  in France, 584, 586
  in India, 741, 753
  in Japan, 639
  in Mexico, 724–729
  in Ming dynasty, 464

INDEX R28

, 719,
, 746–747
...sty, 333
...War, 435

Pelo...esian League, 138
Peloponnesian War, 138–139, 146
peninsulares, 600, 605, 659
Pentagon, 872
People Power Revolution, 861
People's Crusade, 294
perestroika, 834–835
Pericles, 131–133
Periplus, 81
Perry, Matthew (commodore), 633
Persepolis, 100–101v, 111v
Persia, 100–107, 110–117, 140–141
Persian Gulf War, 857
Peru, 346, 386–387, 406, 657
    and geothermal energy, 895
    and Spanish conquest, 485
Peter (apostle), 181
Peter the Great (tsar), 472
Peter the Hermit, 294
petition, 476
Petrarch, 424v
Petrograd *See* St. Petersburg
phalanx, 114, 162
pharaoh, 43, 44
Philip II (of Macedon), 137, 139
Philip II (of Spain), 421, 439v, 542
Philippi, 96–97v
Philippines, 439, 498, 677, 678, 772
    revolution in, 861
Philo Judaeus, 146
philosophes (French social critics), 568
Philosophical Dictionary, A, 570
philosophy
    deism, 573
    in China, 85–87
    in colonial Mexico, 497
    in Europe, 424–425, 428–429, 626–627
    in Greece, 144–146
    in Muslim world, 259
    in Rome, 185
    natural law, 279
    of good and evil, 790
    scholasticism, 279
Phoenicians, 98v, 126–127v, 135
phonograph, 737
physiography, 316
Picasso, Pablo, 717, 758–759
piety, 441
Piketty, Thomas, 890
pilgrimage, 176–177v, 201, 290, 451
    by Evliya Çelebi, 448–449
    in early North America, 392
Pinkerton, Allan, 645v
Pinochet, Augusto, 844
pirates, 439, 527
Piscitelli, Matthew, 387v
Pizarro, Francisco, 410, 485
plague, 226–227, 233v, 267v
    Black Death, 297, 347v, 367
    in Florence, 414–415
    smallpox, 485, 487, 489, 674

See also disease, epidemic
Plan of Ayala, 727
plantations, 526, 605, 659
plastic, 688
Plato, 146, 565
plebeians, 153, 156, 159
Plessy v. Ferguson, 662
Pliny the Younger, 164, 179
poetry, 37, 183, 258, 281
    by members of the "Lost Generation," 717
    in India, 195
    in Japan, 323, 468
    "Ode to Mukden," 467
    Romantic, 596–597
    sonnet, 424
pogrom, 294
poison gas, 757
Poitiers, Battle of, 299
Poland, 719, 761, 766–767, 771, 774
    after U.S.S.R. breakup, 841
    after World War II, 798
    anti-Soviet protests, 824
    during World War II, 780, 782–783
    Solidarity movement, 836v, 861
    Warsaw Ghetto Uprising, 782–783
    Warsaw Pact, 800
polis, 128
political cartoon, 584v, 662v, 665v, 687v, 831v
political prisoners, 721
Politics (book by Aristotle), 146, 565
poll tax, 835
pollution, 460v–463v, 620
Polynesian societies, 400–402
polytheism, 38, 244, 362, 397
Pompeii, 164v–165
Ponce de Leon, Juan, 496
Popol Vuh, 389, 391, 405
popular culture, 736
popular sovereignty, 583, 605
population, growth of, 24, 276, 636, 911, 918
populism, 804, 884
porcelain, 314, 319v, 343
portraits of leaders, 594–595v
Portugal, 346, 490–491, 495
    and Angola, 825
    and Brazil, 502, 603
    and competition with Dutch, 493
postal service, 116–117, 331, 339
potatoes, 386, 629
potlach, 660
Potosí, 497
Potsdam, 798, 820
pottery, 314, 319v, 343, 431v
poverty
    in 18th-century Europe, 552–553
    in Latin America, 656–657
    in Rome, 158
    in the United States, 663
Prague Spring, 824, 826, 827v
Prague, 321, 435
Praise of Folly, The, 425
Prayuth Chan-ocha, 883

Priestly, Joseph, 680
Prince, The, 429
Princip, Gavrilo, 698
printing of books, 266, 310, 410
    and Scientific Revolution, 549
    Gutenberg, Johannes, 417
    Martin Luther and, 434–435
    with metal type, 314, 417, 425
    with woodblocks, 205
privatization, 835
Proclamation of 1763, 582
Procopius, 232–233
proletariat, 627, 719, 720, 747
propaganda, 591, 718v, 743–744, 747, 777
    against immigrants, 875
    as evidence at Nuremberg Trials, 784
Protestant Reformation, 434–438, 442v–443
Protestants, 436, 685, 848
proxy war, 802, 813
Prussia, 542–543, 577, 627
psychology, 744, 790
Ptolemy (Greco-Roman mathematician and astronomer), 427v, 532, 557
Ptolemy (ruler of Egypt), 141
public works, 40, 88, 745
Pueblo, 356v, 393, 431v
pull factor, 477, 885
Punic Wars, 154–155
Puritanism, 436, 442, 542, 544
push factor, 477, 885
Putin, Vladimir, 841, 883
Putnam, George, 739
pyramids, 44–46v, 382–383v, 405v
Pythagorus, 427v

Q

qadi, 256
Quebec, 650
Quetzalcoatl, 394–395v, 485
"Quit India" campaign, 777
qi, 86–87, 311
Qianlong, 465–467v
Qin dynasty, 88–89
Qing dynasty, 411v, 464–465, 566–567, 632
    and Boxer Rebellion, 637
    end of, 722
Quakers (Society of Friends), 518, 531
Quanzhou, 312–313
Quechua, 397
quinine, 671
quipu, 399
Quito, 396
quorum, 131
Quran, 60, 220v, 246–247, 259, 367, 449
    and calligraphy, 454
Qutb Minar, 457v

R

Rabin, Yitzhak, 855v
racism, 521, 629, 662, 714, 742–743, 754
    and Josephine Baker, 775
    and populism, 884

    and World War II propaganda, 777
radar, 387, 391, 778
radio, 735–736
radioactivity, 895
Raijin, 320v
railroad, 619, 625, 638v, 653
Rajaraja, 197
Rajendra, 197
Ramayana, 71, 192
Ramses II (the Great), 49v, 51v
Rapa Nui, 400–402
Rape of Nanjing, 756–757
Raphael, 426v–427v
rationing, 777, 834v
Ravenna, 222–223v, 238v
Reagan, Ronald, 834–837, 845
Réal del Sarte, Maxime, 301
reason, 564–565
Rebellion of 1857, 634–635
recession, 886
Reconquista, 294
Reconstruction, 645
Records of the Grand Historian (Shiji), 198
Red Army, 719, 747, 770
Red Guard, 810–811
redistributive economy, 124–125, 655
referendum, 812
reform movement, 196, 655
Reforma, La, 655
Reformation *See* Catholic Reformation, Protestant Reformation
refugees, 61, 208–209, 784, 795v, 849v
    fleeing Syria, 875
    photographing, 906–907
    refugee crisis, 884–885
Reichstag, 744–745
Reign of Terror, 587
reincarnation, 71, 193
relief (art form), 56v, 187, 255
religion, 38, 59–63
    Abrahamic, 261v
    Anabaptists, 436
    deism, 573
    in Mongol Empire, 329–330, 339
    in Muslim Empire, 250–253
    in Roman Empire, 187
    in Vedic society, 71
    Jainism, 71
    Judaism, 58–61
    Judeo-Christian tradition, 174–175, 187
    monotheism, 59–60, 244, 247
    polytheism, 38, 244, 362, 397
    Puritanism, 436
    voudun, 589
    Zoroastrianism, 104, 113v, 116–117
    See also Buddhism; Christianity; Eastern Orthodoxy; Islam; Protestants; Roman Catholic Church
religiosity, 885
religious fervor, 254–255
religious syncretism, 443, 497
religious tolerance, 253, 349

in Enlightenment Europe, 573
in France under Napoleon, 591
in Gupta dynasty, 194
in Mali Empire, 362–363
in Middle Colonies, 505
in Mughal Empire, 458
in Prussia, 577
in Qing dynasty, 467
Rembrandt van Rijn, 784v
remilitarization, 760
Renaissance, 410v, 416–417, 418v–421v
renaissances in different cultures, 430v–433v
reparations, 708–709, 740, 799
republic of letters, 604
republic, 153, 583, 589
Republic, The, 146
resistance fighters, 774v–775v, 782
revenue, 458
revolutionary ideas, spread of, 604–605, 860
Rhee, Syngman, 820–821
Rhineland, 760
Rhodes, Cecil, 675
Rhodesia, 673, 675
Ricci, Mateo, 343
rice, 488, 676, 678, 707
Richard the Lionheart, 293
Richthofen, Manfred von (Red Baron), 734–735
Rickenbacker, Eddie, 735
Riel, Louis, 661
Rig Veda, 70
Rigaud, Louis, 595
Riis, Jacob, 652
Rimsky-Korsakov, Nicolai, 631
Ring of Fire, 316
Rivera, Diego, 728v–729
Riyadh, 906v–907v
roads
　Anasazi, 393
　Belt and Road Initiative in China, 336v
　Inca, 398–399
　Mongol, 333, 335, 339
　Mughal, 456
　Persian Empire's Royal Road, 110v–111
　Qin dynasty, 88
　Roman, 162–163, 187
　Vietnamese, 315
　See also Silk Roads
Robespierre, Maximilien, 586–587
Robinson, Charles, 496
Rockefeller, John D., 663, 665v
Rohingya Muslims, 883–884v
Roma, 709, 744, 780–781
Roman army, 162–163, 183
Roman Catholic Church, 181, 187
　and art, 426v
　and Croatia, 697
　and Crusades, 290–295
　and Great Schism of 1378, 299
　and Inquisition, 294–295
　and Louis XIV, 541
　and Reformation, 434–437
　art and architecture of, 281, 437v
　changing roles of, 288–289
　in Britain, 626

in Central America, 845
in France, 584–585, 591
in South America, 605
Schism of 1054, 275v
under Charlemagne, 270
Roman Empire, 158–167v
　and Christianity, 174–176, 178–179, 181
　collapse of, 203
　decline of the empire, 180–181
　division of, 180
　Eastern Roman Empire (Byzantine Empire), 180, 183, 349
　end of the Republic, 158–159
　expansion of the Republic, 154–155
　founding and emergence of, 152–153
　legacy of, 184–187
　Western Roman Empire, 180, 182v–183
Roman Forum, 152v, 178v
Romanesque (art style), 281
Romania, 782, 837
Romanov dynasty, 411, 472–475v, 477, 719
Romanticism, 596–599
Rome Statute, 859
Rome, city of, 412–413v, 414
Romero, Matías, 657
Romero, Oscar, 844v–845
Romey, Kristin, 170
Romulus and Remus, 152
Roosevelt, Eleanor, 858
Roosevelt, Franklin Delano, 741, 767, 768, 778, 784
　Four Freedoms speech, 789
　Yalta conference, 798v
Rose, Jeffrey, 12v–13
Rosetta Stone, 46
Rossetti, Dante Gabriel, 267v
Rothenburg ob der Tauber, 277v
Rouen, 301–302
Rousseau, Jean-Jacques, 569, 571v
Royal Road, 111, 116
rubber, 671–672, 676, 677, 680–683, 707
　and Great Depression, 740–741, 755
Rumi, 258
Run-D.M.C., 866v
Russia, 112
　and Armenians, 713
　and Crimean War, 630
　and Golden Horde, 338
　and Great Powers, 697
　and Japan, 469, 639
　and LGBTQ rights, 904
　and Qing dynasty, 465
　and Vikings, 273
　and World War I, 701
　in 21st century, 883
　modernization, 631
　Napoleon's attack on, 592
　Romanov dynasty, 411, 472–475v
　steppes, 470–471
　See also Russian Revolution, serfs

Russian Orthodox Church, 472
Russian Revolution, 692, 718–719
Russo-Japanese War, 697–698, 718
Ruzo, Andrés, 894v–895
Rwanda, 790, 859

S

Sabeti, Pardis, 486v–487
Sacra di San Michele, 288v
Sadat, Anwar, 855
Sáenz, Manuela, 603
Safavid dynasty, 450–453, 495
Sahara, 360–361, 368–369
Sahel, 42, 360–361v, 515
Saint-Domingue, 588
Sak K'uk, 389
Saladin, 293v
salons, 572–573, 717
Salopek, Paul, 16–19, 94v, 334–337
Salt March, 751
salt, 362, 366, 368, 370–373v
Salvation Army, 663
Samori Toure, 685
Samudragupta, 194
samurai, 317, 468
San Martín, Jose de, 603
sanctions (economic), 757, 815, 847
Sandinistas, 845v
sans-culottes, 585
Sanskrit, 69–71
Santa Anna, Antonio López de, 655
Santayana, George, 298
Saratoga, Battle of, 583
Sargon of Akkad, 5v, 39
Sassanians, 115
satellite states, 799
satire, 133, 425
satrap, 104–105, 111
satyagraha, 750–751
Saudi Arabia, 246v, 857, 906v–907v, 909
Saul (king of the Israelites), 61
Schism of 1054, 275v
schism, 295, 299
Schliemann, Heinrich, 136
scholasticism, 279
School of Athens, 426v–427v
Schubert, Franz, 599
Schutzstaffel (SS), 781, 782, 784
science, 81
　and epidemics, 486–487, 621, 908–909
　before the Scientific Revolution, 546–547
　botany, 552–555
　chemistry, 717
　ethnography, 554
　evolution, 627
　geology, 629
　in 18th-century Europe, 550–551
　in Greece, 146–147
　in medieval Europe, 283
　in Mongol Empire, 339
　in Muslim world, 259
　in Rome, 185
　physics, 717, 744
　primate research, 608
　scientific method, 548–549

scientific rationalism, 5
science fiction, 867v
Scipio, 155
Scotland, 161, 298, 566
scribe, 46, 204, 280, 389, 417
　in Aztec Empire, 395
script (form of writing), 153, 375
scriptorium, 280
Scythians, 112
Seacole, Mary, 631v
Second Sino-Japanese War, 757
Second World War See World War II
Secret History of the Mongols, The, 327
secret police, 719, 721, 774, 800
sectionalism, 644
secular clergy, 288
secularism, 262
segregation, 645, 662–663, 776, 814–815v
Selena, 866v
self-determination, 708, 713, 714
self-rule, 750, 754, 836
Seljuk Turks, 290
Senate, 153, 158
Seneca Falls Convention, 663
Senegal, 372–373v, 706v–707v
"separate but equal," 662
separation of powers, 568–569, 591
sepoy, 635
September 11 attacks, 872v–873
Seracini, Mauricio, 422v–423
Serbs, 698, 701, 849
serf, 276, 472, 475, 631
Serious Proposal to the Ladies, A, 569
settlement, 28–29v
Shah Jahan, 447, 459
shah, 452, 824, 857
Shaka, 674
Shakespeare, William, 540
shamanism, 339
Shandong Peninsula, 722
Shang dynasty, 83
Sharansky, Natan, 853v
sharia law, 516, 856
shariah, 246
Sharpeville Massacre, 847
Shawki, Nora, 47
Shea, Christopher, 352
Sheba, Queen of, 375v
Sheets, Millard Owen, 741
sheikh, 244
shell shock, 717
Shelley, Mary, 571, 598
Shi Huangdi, 67, 88v–91, 202
Shiite, 247, 442, 715, 856–857
　and power balance, 873
Shiji (Records of the Grand Historian), 198
Shikibu, Murasaki, 99v, 209
Shinto, 254, 316–318, 320v, 469
　in early Japan, 208
ships and sailing
　Age of Exploration, 480–481v
　caravel, 482
　Chinese ships, 341–343
　chronometer, 559v

INDEX **R30**

, 400
, 704
ps, 492
our, 554
ships, 115
ironclads, 644
longitude, 554, 559
Manila galleon, 498
Roman ships, 154
U.S.S. *Enterprise*, 826–827v
war canoes, 512–513
World War I battleships, 703–704
Shiva, 192–193, 197
Shoah, 783
shogun, 317, 468–469, 633
Shona, 357v, 365
Shotoku (prince), 209
Siam *See* Thailand
Siberia, 747
siege, 298, 778
Siegler, Ted, 688
Siem Reap, 212
silk, 201, 238, 455
Silk Roads, 74, 77, 167, 198
and modern China, 335v
and Mongol Empire, 339, 347v
and Ottoman Empire, 345
and Uzbekistan, 334, 338v
and Yuan dynasty, 333
early history of, 200–201v, 203
Silla chiefdom or kingdom, 206–207, 314
silt, 35, 83
silver, 498v–501v
Sima Qian, 198v–199
Sin, Jaime, 861
Sinai Peninsula, 819
Sinan, Mimar, 421, 451
Sinclair, Upton, 663
Sindi, Hayat, 909v
Singapore, 676, 863
Siqueiros, David Alfaro, 728–729
Sistine Chapel, 419v, 445
Sitting Bull, 659v–660
Six-Day War, 854–855
slash-and-burn agriculture, 388
slavery, 157–158, 256–257, 368
abolition of slavery, 519, 572, 577, 603, 656
and cotton, 618–619, 648v
and Dutch East India Company, 493
and Haitian Revolution, 588–589
and industrial growth, 625
and U.S. Constitution, 583
Atlantic slave trade, 411, 518–519, 531, 536
debt peonage, 654
during World War II, 778
in Aztec culture, 395
in Brazil, 502
in English colonies, 505
in Jamaica, 603
in Maya culture, 389
in Songhai Empire, 514
in Soviet Union, 747
in Spanish colonies, 497, 600

in United States, 605, 618–619, 644–645, 665
Middle Passage, 518, 520–521v
reestablishment of slavery, 591
resistance to slavery, 526–529
slave narrative, 518
Slavs, 273, 470, 698, 761
Slovakia, 841
smallpox, 485, 487
Smith, Adam, 569–570, 612v, 617
Smith, Tommie, 827v, 829v
Snow, Dean, 21
Snowden, Edward, 883
social class, 35, 36v
and communism, 613, 627, 744
and Haitian Revolution, 588–589, 605
and nationalism, 627
and Nazism, 745
and outreach to poor, 663
and socialism, 627, 657
bourgeoisie, 572–573, 584, 627
caste, 750
in Abbasid Empire, 256–257
in Africa, 361
in Athens, 130
in Aztec Empire, 395
in Babylonian Empire, 41
in Britain, 620
in British-Indian society, 634
in Byzantine Empire, 235
in Cambodia, 825
in Caral, 386
in Egypt, 43, 47
in English colonies, 505
in Ethiopia, 684
in Europe after Napoleon, 593
in France, 584–585
in Inca society, 397–398
in India, 196, 750
in Japan, 638
in Latin America, 656–657
in Maya society, 389
in medieval Europe, 276–278
in Mexico, 655, 726
in Mongol Empire, 327
in Mughal Empire, 458
in Muslim Empire, 250–251
in Roman society, 153, 156–157, 165
in Russia, 630–631
in Safavid Empire, 453
in South America, 605
in Spanish colonial societies, 497, 600–601
in Vedic society, 70–71
proletariat, 627, 719
See also peasants
social contract, 565, 582
Social Contract, The, 569
social criticism, 621
social Darwinism, 627, 639, 685, 761
social justice, 874
social media, 874, 884, 889, 898
socialism, 722–723, 746, 799, 805, 824
Society of Friends (Quakers), 518, 531
Socrates, 138–139v, 427v
Sogolon, 362

Sokoto caliphate, 673
soladera, 727v
solar energy, 892–893v
Solomon, 61, 375v
Solon, 130
Solzhenitsyn, Aleksandr, 747
Somalia, 883
Somme, Battle of the, 703, 716
Song dynasty, 204, 308–313, 333
Songhai, 368, 410v, 508–509v, 512–515v
Soninke, 362
Sophocles, 133
South Africa, 629, 666–667v, 674–675, 814–815, 828
Nelson Mandela's oppression and rise, 846
South African War, 674–675
South America
and European exploration, 483
Argentina, 656v, 657, 844, 860v
Bolivia, 497
Chile, 384, 844
Gran Colombia, 601
Inca, 357, 396–399v, 410v
San Martín, Jose de, 603
Venezuela, 537, 600–601, 883
See also Argentina, Brazil, Latin America, Peru
South Korea, 820–821, 863
South Sudan, 883
Southeast Asia, 676v–677v, 680, 707, 740–741
anti-colonialism in, 754–755
Southeast Asia Treaty Organization, 821
Southwest Asia, 876v–881v
Soviet bloc, 800
Soviet Union, 720–721, 770, 825, 834–835, 840–841
soviet, 719
Soweto, 815
space archaeology, 273
space race, 802–803
spacewalk, 803
Spain
armada, 439, 496v, 497, 540
Basques, 759
Spanish Civil War, 758–759
Spanish Empire, 438–439, 496–497
Spanish Inquisition, 440
Spanish Renaissance, 420–421
Spanish Armada *See* Spain
Spanish-American War, 677
Sparta, 115, 129, 138–139
Spartacus, 158
speech, human, 10
spheres of influence, 672
sphinx, 44
Spice Islands (Moluccas), 491–493
spices, 80–81, 296, 347, 492, 494v
spies, 774v–775v, 800, 802, 841, 898
Spirit of St. Louis, 735
Spirit of the Laws, The, 568–570, 575
Spiritual Exercises, 441
sports, 737, 906v
Sputnik I, 802

St. Bartholomew's Day massacre, 439, 541
St. George's Church at Lalibela, 375, 377v
St. Peter's Basilica, 434
St. Petersburg, 472, 474v, 562–563v, 719
stagnation, 227
stalemate, 700
Stalin, Joseph, 721, 746v–747, 770
Hitler-Stalin Pact, 760–761
influence on Mao Zedong, 809
Stalingrad, Battle of, 770
Standard of Ur, 38v
Stanley, Henry Morton, 671
Stanton, Elizabeth Cady, 663
Stasi, 800, 802
steam engine, 567, 612, 617
steamship, 619, 624–625, 632, 672
steel, 54, 310, 613, 617, 747
Stein, Gertrude, 717
stela, 41, 389
steppe, 326, 470–471
stereotype, 494
Stilke, Hermann Anton, 302
stock (economics), 492
Strait of Hormuz, 491
Strategic Arms Limitation Talks (SALT), 802
strike, 653, 656–657, 725, 847
Stuart, Gilbert, 595
student protests, 826–829v, 842–843
stupa, 76
subjugation, 668
submarine, 704–705, 778
See also U-boat
subprime mortgages, 886
succession, 512
Sudan, 673, 883
Sudetenland, 761
Suez Canal, 613v, 625, 676–677, 818–819
suffrage, 663
See also voting, women's roles and status
Suffragette, The, 303
Sufism, 254
sugar, 488, 497, 502, 520–525v, 526
and Cuba, 805
and Haitian Revolution, 588
and Maya revolt, 659
in Java, 678–679
in Mexico, 726–727
Suharto, 817
Sui dynasty, 204
Sukarno, Ahmed, 817
Süleyman I (the Magnificent, the Lawgiver), 450v–451
sultan, 345, 369, 375, 678
sultanate, 375
Sumatra, 677
Sumer, 38–39v
Summa Theologica, 279
Sun Yat-sen, 722
Sundiata, 357, 362
Sunni, 247, 442, 450, 715, 856–857
and power balance, 873
Sunni Ali, 410, 512–513
surplus, 28

surveillance, 873
Suryavarman II, 210
sustainable, 892–893
Swahili Coast, 378
Swahili, 375, 511
synagogue, 61
Syria, 57v, 710–711, 714–715, 873–875
    and destruction of war, 879
Systema Naturae, 536v, 552

T

Ta Prohm, 212
Tabula Rogeriana, 558v
Taejo, 314
Taghaza, 366, 514
Taharqa, 49
Tahiti, 554
taiga, 470
Taíno, 403, 483
Taiping Rebellion, 636v
Taira, 264–265v
Taiwan, 465, 722, 808, 863, 905v
Taizong, 204
Taj Mahal, 446–447v, 459, 460v–463v
Taklamakan Desert, 198, 203
Talaat Pasha, Mehmed, 713
Tale of Genji, The, 209
Tale of the Heike, The, 264–265v
Taliban, 857v, 872–873, 883, 903–904
Tamil Nadu, 197
Tamil, 196
Tang code, 204
Tang empire, 204–205
Tanzania, 608
Tanzimat Reforms, 630–631
tariff, 626, 717, 863
Taro, Gerda, 759
Tatars, 476
tattoos, 430v
taxes, 111
    in Athens, 130
    in British colonies, 582–583
    in Byzantine Empire, 234, 236
    in China, 204
    in France before revolution, 583–584
    in Germany, 435
    in Ghana, 362
    in Japan, 468, 638–639
    in Mughal Empire, 456–458
    in Muslim Empire, 250–251
    in Roman Empire, 161, 180
    income, 717
    of beards, 472
    under Alexander the Great, 140–141
Tchaikovsky, Peter Ilych, 599, 631
tea, 632
tea ceremony, 319v
technology, 35, 36v, 54–55
    and archaeology, 273
    and art, 422–423
    and books, 310
    and colonialism, 668
    and communication, 619, 625, 859, 863
    and farming, 310, 315, 612, 619
    and globalization, 863
    and hunting, 384
    and imperialism, 668, 671
    and Industrial Revolution, 566–567, 616–619
    and Luddites, 617
    and sailing, 309
    and Silk Roads, 201
    and transportation, 619
    and warfare, 255v, 298, 472
    exhibitions of, 623
    in medieval Europe, 276–277, 281–283
    revolutions in, 898–899
telegraph, 625, 672
telescope, 538–539v, 547, 550
temple, 32–33v, 39
    Angkor Wat, 210–211v
    El Castillo (Belize), 354–355v
    Hindu temples, 193v, 196–197
    Temple of Literature, 320v
Temujin *See* Genghis Khan
Ten Commandments, 59v–60, 252
tenement, 652
Tenochtitlán, 357, 394v–395, 484v–485
Teotihuacán, 386v–387, 394
Teresa of Ávila, 441v
Teresa, Mother, 817v
Tereshkova, Valentina, 803
terra-cotta warriors, 89–91
terrace, 387, 388
terrorism, 872–873, 889
TerrSet, 559
Tet Offensive, 823
tetrarchy, 180
Texas, 655
Thailand (formerly Siam), 77, 495, 633, 676, 684–685
    Prayuth Chan-ocha and, 883
"too big to fail," 886
Thatcher, Maraget, 834–835v
theater, 540, 544
Thebes, Egypt, 27v
theocracy, 61, 453
Theodora, 226v–227
Theodosius (emperor), 99v
thermoluminescence, 9
Thermopylae, Battle of, 115
Things Fall Apart, 673
third gender, 905
Third World, 816
Thirty Years' War, 439, 542
Thornton, Christopher, 108v–109
Thoth, 36
Thousand and One Nights, The, 259
Thracians, 500
Three Kingdoms, 206–207
Three Teachings, 207
Thucydides, 146
Tiananmen Square, 722, 842–843v, 888
Tiber River, 152–153
Tibet, 851
Tigris River, 34
Timbuktu, 362, 379, 512–517v
Timur, 338, 341, 345v
tithe, 288
Tito, Josip Bro (Marshal Tito), 848–849
Tiwanaku, 396
Tiye, 52v
toilets, 622
Tojo Hideki, 768, 773
Tokugawa Ieyasu, 411
Tokugawa shogunate, 468–469, 638
Toledo, 420–421
tolerance, 116
Tollan, 394
Tolstaya Mogila, 112
Toltec civilization, 26v, 394v
Topará, 396
Torah, 60
torture, 440, 471, 679, 721
Toshiko, Kishida, 639
total war, 702, 704, 706–707, 757, 761
    during World War II, 776–777
totalitarian, 743, 746, 749
totalitarianism, 742–749
Toussaint L'Ouverture, 588v–589, 595v
trade, 47, 55
    and Age of Exploration, 494–495
    and Mongol Empire, 339
    and opium wars, 632
    and plague, 297v, 339
    and Qing dynasty, 465
    Atlantic slave trade, 411, 518–519, 531, 536
    between Korea and China, 314
    between Vietnam and China, 315
    during Crusades, 295
    during Renaissance, 416–417
    European domination of, 566–567v
    in Abbasid Empire, 256–257
    in Africa, 365, 510–511
    in China, 309
    in Ghana, 362, 536v
    in Indian Ocean, 80–81, 357, 374–375, 493, 511, 520–521v
    in Italy, 413
    in Mali Empire, 362–363
    in New France, 505
    in Roman Empire, 160v–161
    in Songhai Empire, 514
    in Vietnam, 207
    in Yuan dynasty, 333
    Middle Passage, 520–521v
    routes, 346–347v
    Silk Roads, 74, 200–201, 203, 339
    spice, 296
    trans-Saharan, 368–369, 381v, 516–517v
    triangular trade, 520–521v
Trajan, 178, 180
transgender, 905
transnational organizations, 889
    See also nongovernmental organizations
trans-Saharan trade, 368–369, 381v
Travels to Persia, 1673–1677, 495
Travels, The, 366
treason, 199, 542
Treaty of Nanjing, 632
Treaty of Tordesillas, 483, 502
Treaty of Versailles, 708–*t* 760
Treblinka, 783
trench warfare, 700–701, 706, 716–717
tribunal, 784
tribune, 153
tribute, 194, 309
Tripitaka Koreana, 314–315v
Triple Alliance (Aztec), 394
Triple Alliance (European), 697
Triple Entente, 697, 701v
trireme, 115
Troja Palace, 321v
trolls, 899
Trotsky, Leon, 719, 720v, 746
Truman Doctrine, 794, 800, 820–821
Truman, Harry S., 773, 798, 820–821
Trump, Donald, 882, 884–885
Trung Nhi, 207
Trung Trac, 207
tsar, 471
tsunami, 892
Tuareg, 514, 516
Tubman, Harriet, 527v
tulips, 493v
Tun Sri Lanang, 495
tundra, 470
Tunisia, 874
Tupaia, 554
Turing, Alan, 779
Turkey, 28, 54–55, 102
    and Ottoman Empire, 344v–345, 348–349, 455
    modern, 748–749, 883
    Seljuk Turks, 290, 344
Turner, J.M.W., 598
Tuskegee Airmen, 776
Tutankhamen, 48
Tutsi, 859
Tutu, Desmond, 847
Twain, Mark, 653, 679
Twelve Apostles, 175
Twelve Tables, 153, 187
Two Treatises of Government, 536, 565
two-state solution, 853
tyranny, 565
Tyrrhenian Sea, 408–409v

U

U-boat, 692, 704–705
Udayagiri Caves, 194v
Uganda, 370–371, 551
Uichon, 314
Ukraine, 112, 719, 721, 747, 798–799
    and Crimea annexation by Russia, 882
ukulele, 432v
ultranationalist, 748
Umayyad Caliphate, 252–253
Umayyads, 247, 254–255v
umma, 245, 250
unemployment, 740–741, 745, 755, 763
union, 626–627, 653, 662–663, 759, 836

INDEX **R32**

on workers,

Socialist Republics
Soviet Union
Emirates, 864v
ons, 798, 819, 820,

and Day of Six Billion, 864
and global human rights, 858–859
and globalization, 867
United Nations Industrial Development Organization (UNIDO), 406
United Negro Improvement Association (UNIA), 755
United States
   Africatown, 529
   Alaska, 661
   California, 496
   Civil War, 644–646
   Colorado, 663
   early civilizations, 392v–393
   federal system of, 605
   Florida, 496
   Gilded Age, 652–653
   Great Depression and, 740–741
   Harlem Renaissance, 432v
   Hawaii, 400–401, 432v, 677, 679, 688, 693
   historically black colleges and universities, 815
   Hudson River, 493
   illegal slave trade, 529
   independence of, 537
   Indian Removal Act, 659
   Indian Territory, 659
   Indiana, 627
   Industrial Revolution, 618–619
   inequality in, 662–663
   internment camps, 777
   Jamestown, 411, 504v
   Louisiana Purchase, 592
   Massachusetts Bay colony, 442
   Mexican-American War, 655
   Montana, 660
   New England colonies, 505
   New Mexico, 497, 727
   North Carolina, 734v
   Pennsylvania, 872
   Texas, 655
   Trail of Tears, 659
   transcontinental railroads, 625–626, 651
   war for independence, 582–583
   World War I, 701, 704–705, 731
   World War II, 768–769
   Wyoming, 663
   See also Native Americans
Universal Declaration of Human Rights, 858–859
university, 278–279, 320
   and Ottoman Empire, 349
   in Europe, 424
U.S. Armed Forces in the Far East (USAFFE), 769
U.S.S. *Enterprise*, 826–827v
Upanishads, 71
Urban II, 290, 294
urbanization, 652
Uruk, 5v, 34, 35, 37

Ustyurt Plateau, 335
Utopia, 429
utopian community, 627
Uzbekistan, 334v–335, 841

V
V-E Day, 693v
V-J Day, 693v
vaccination, 487, 909
Valley of the Kings, 48
Valley of the Queens, 50
values of Greeks and Romans, 157
van Eyck, Jan, 420–421v
Vanderlyn, John, 483
vaqueros, 726–727
Varanasi, 193
Vargas, Getúlio, 749
Varma, Anand, 658
varna, 71–72
vassal, 276
Vedic, 70
"Velvet Revolution," 837
Venezuela, 537, 600–601, 883
Venice, 413
Verdun, Battle of, 702–703
vernacular, 281, 417
Vernet, Horace, 626
Versailles, Palace of, 541, 564v
Vesalius, Andreas, 550
Via Appia, 162–163
Via Salaria, 371
viceroy, 497
viceroyalty, 497
Vichy France, 767m 822
Victoria (queen), 620, 622, 632, 635, 668
Vienna, 451, 454v, 774
Vietcong, 823
Vietnam, 207, 314–315, 320v, 613v
   and France, 676, 678
   and Great Depression, 755
   and Industrial Revolution, 629
   and Paris Peace Conference, 710
   diplomatic terms with Western countries, 882
Vietnam War, 795v, 822v–823
Vikings, 266v, 272–273v, 274–275, 352v
Villa, Pancho, 726v
Vindication of the Rights of Woman, A, 569, 575
Vinland Sagas, The, 273
Vinland, 273
Viollet-le-Duc, Eugène-Emmanuel, 286
Virgil, 183
Virgin of Guadalupe, 443, 602
virtuoso, 421
Vishnu, 192, 194v
Vita, Kimpa, 511
vizier, 43, 45, 256
Vladimir of Kiev, Prince, 471
Voltaire, 466–467, 475, 540, 569–570v, 573
   views on monarchy, 574v
von Bora, Katharina, 434v
von Petzinger, Genevieve, 20–21
voting, 586, 620, 663
voudon, 589
vulcanization, 680, 682, 683

W
Wadi, 109
Wagner, Richard, 599
wak'a, 397
Wake, Nancy, 774v
Waldseemüller, Martin, 506v
Wales, 161
Wałęsa, Lech, 836
Waller, James, 790
Wannsee Conference, 781
war criminals, 784
Warner, Charles Dudley, 653
"War on Terror," 872–873, 883
Warren, Mercy Otis, 607
Warring States Period, 84–86
Warsaw Ghetto Uprising, 782–783
Warsaw Pact, 800, 840
Washington, George, 582v, 595v
Waterhouse, Jon, 661v
Waterloo, Battle of, 592
Watt, James, 567, 612, 617
wattle, 378
Wealth of Nations, The, 569–570, 612
wealth, distribution of, 604, 887
weapons, 255v, 298, 309
   and Industrial Revolution, 625
   chemical, 701, 857, 875
   in Americas, 384, 392
   in Prussia, 543
   in U.S. Civil War, 644
   in World War I, 702–703
   of mass destruction (WMDs), 873
Weckeiser, Dieter, 838–839
Weimar Republic, 708, 744
West Bank, 852–855
West Germany, 836–837, 840–841
Western Roman Empire, 180, 182v–183
Westminster Cathedral, 282v
Whang-Od, Apo, 430v
Wheatley, Phillis, 531
Wheatstone, Charles, 625
wheel, 35
White Army, 719
Whitney, Eli, 612, 618, 646
Wickham, Henry, 682
Wiesel, Elie, 782v
Wikileaks, 898–899
Wilberforce, William, 577
Wilhelm II, 671, 697, 708
William II of England, 544
William the Conqueror (Duke of Normandy), 274–275
Wilson, Harold, 852v
Wilson, Woodrow, 705
wind farm, 892–893
windmill, 283
Winged Victory of Samothrace, 145v
Winroth, Anders, 352
Winter Palace, 474v
Wittenberg, 434–435
Wollstonecraft, Mary, 569, 571v, 574–575, 577
women's roles and status, 41, 70–71
   among Abbasids, 257
   among African peoples, 361

   among Aztecs, 395
   among Chinese, 99v, 204, 310
   among early Buddhists, 73
   among Egyptians, 48–53
   among Greeks, 129, 133
   among Hakka, 636
   among Inca, 398
   among Japanese, 209, 468, 639, 799
   among Mongols, 327
   among Muslims, 245
   among Nazis, 745
   among Romans, 156, 159
   among Vietnamese, 207
   as nuns, 278–279
   desire for equal rights, 575
   during Enlightenment, 569, 572
   during European Renaissance, 429
   during World War I, 704
   during World War II, 776v–777
   education of women, 903, 906–907v
   food security and, 914
   headscarves, wearing of, 885
   Igbo Women's War, 754–755
   in Afghanistan, 857
   in African slave trade, 528
   in Argentina, 860v
   in art and as artists, 300v–303v, 420v, 425v
   in aviation, 735, 738–739
   in Byzantine Empire, 226, 239
   in colonial Mexico, 497
   in Ethiopia, 883–884
   in France under Napoleon, 591
   in Iran, 857
   in Kenya, 904
   in Mughal Empire, 458
   in Safavid Empire, 453
   in salons, 572
   in Saudi Arabia, 857, 904
   in science and mathematics, 550–551, 608
   in the United States, 663
   in Turkey, 749
   leadership by women, 902v–905v
   March of the Women, 585
   pay rates for women, 903
   sports, 906v
   United Nations and, 858
   women's suffrage (ability to vote), 303, 626, 663, 749
Women's Social and Political Union, 303v
woodblock printing, 205, 420, 469
Wordsworth, William, 596
workhouse, 621
Works Progress Administration, 741
World Bank, 799, 863
World Health Organization (WHO), 909
World Trade Center, 872v
World Trade Organization, 863
World War I, 303, 690–691, 694–711, 714–717
   casualties from, 731
   technology and, 734–736
World War II, 693, 764–787, 779
World Wide Web, 864

R33 INDEX

Wounded Knee Massacre, 660
Wright, Orville and Wilbur, 734v
writing, history of, 20, 36v
    alphabet, 126–128
    in China, 202
    in Crete, 125
    in Egypt, 46
    in Ethiopia, 375
    in Japan, 209, 319v
    in Latin, 153
    in Maya culture, 389
    in medieval Europe, 280v–281
    in Mexico, 727
    in Mongol Empire, 330
    in Sumer, 39
    in Turkey, 748v
    Islamic, 218–219v
Wu (emperor), 198, 203
Wu (empress), 99v, 204
Wudi, 202

Wuzong, 205
Wycliffe, John, 435

X
xenophobia, 875
Xerxes I, 103, 115–116
Xi'an, 91
Xiongnu, 203
Xunantunich, 354–355v

Y
Yaa Asantewaa, 673
Yalta Conference, 798v–799
Yamato clan, 208
Yanagi, Soetsu, 431v
Yaqui, 727
yellow fever, 589
Yeltsin, Boris, 840–841v
Yemen, 878–879, 903
Yiddish, 476
yin and yang, 86–87

YMCA, 663
Yongle, 341
Yorimoto, 317
Yorktown, Battle of, 583
Yoshimune, 468
Yousafzai, Malala, 903v–904
Yuan dynasty, 333, 338
Yucatán Rebellion, 659
Yugoslavia, 841, 848–849v

Z
Zabaleen, 913
zaibatsu, 639, 748
zakat, 251
Zambezi River, 365
Zanzibar, 671
Zapata, Emiliano, 726v
Zapatistas, 729
Zapotec, 386v–387, 655
Zelensky, Volodymyr, 882

Zen Buddhism, 317–3
zero, concept of, 195, 389
Zewde, Sahle-Work, 902
Zhang Qian, 203
Zhao Rugua, 312–313
Zheng He, 341–343, 346, 351, 410v
Zhengtong, 343
Zhou dynasty, 84–86v, 204
Zhu Di, 341
Zhu Yuanzhang, 338
ziggurat, 39
Zika virus, 908
Zimbabwe, 675
Zimmerman telegram, 705
Zionists, 714, 853
Zoroaster, 427v
Zoroastrianism, 104, 113v, 116–117
Zulu Empire, 674
Zurich, 436
Zwingli, Ulrich, 436

SKILLS INDEX

A
Analyze, 199
Analyze Cause and Effect, 11, 41, 99, 109, 115, 118, 123, 129, 165, 188, 195, 197, 212, 214, 240, 245, 259, 260, 297, 299, 304, 311, 315, 317, 333, 339, 349, 350, 380, 389, 391, 399, 417, 423, 435, 437, 443, 444, 445, 453, 459, 469, 478, 483, 491, 493, 497, 503, 505, 506, 515, 529, 530, 545, 549, 560, 578, 587, 599, 603, 606, 607, 613, 619, 637, 640, 663, 664, 669, 675, 686, 705, 730, 741, 761, 795, 803, 809, 813, 815, 830, 837, 851, 853, 857, 916
Analyze Language Use, 475, 905
Analyze Perspective, 49
Analyze Point of View, 89, 235, 449, 541, 555, 679, 686, 743, 762, 895
Analyze Sources, 103, 349, 485, 565, 601, 713, 775, 783, 787
Analyze Visuals, 53, 56, 77, 806, 901
Ask and Answer Questions, 273, 365, 449

C
Categorize, 253, 380, 725, 887
Compare and Contrast, 27, 41, 43, 92, 113, 125, 129, 155, 157, 161, 177, 181, 188, 193, 203, 214, 221, 239, 260, 271, 275, 279, 295, 303, 317, 321, 323, 345, 363, 385, 393, 404, 433, 441, 445, 475, 477, 478, 485, 493, 506, 511, 519, 529, 530, 559, 565, 571, 578, 589, 601, 606, 629, 633, 640, 664, 675, 685, 693, 721, 737, 741, 749, 762, 775, 788, 799, 830, 841, 867, 869, 915

D
Describe, 11, 30, 69, 71, 83, 87, 92, 175, 193, 205, 277, 449, 459, 471, 478, 516, 530, 547, 555, 599, 637, 762, 788, 805, 815, 830
Determine Chronology, 205, 411, 606
Distinguish Fact and Opinion, 260
Draw Conclusions, 11, 24, 30, 47, 49, 73, 79, 81, 92, 105, 113, 118, 125, 127, 133, 153, 163, 165, 183, 187, 188, 207, 225, 233, 239, 240, 245, 251, 260, 267, 277, 283, 289, 293, 304, 322, 329, 350, 357, 363, 375, 376, 380, 387, 395, 404, 415, 417, 425, 441, 444, 487, 489, 506, 529, 530, 571, 578, 589, 593, 607, 621, 623, 629, 640, 645, 651, 655, 661, 664, 699, 707, 713, 719, 721, 723, 730, 737, 745, 747, 749, 757, 759, 762, 767, 769, 773, 777, 783, 787, 788, 799, 819, 830, 841, 845, 847, 853, 855, 859, 868, 873, 885, 889, 895, 905, 909, 916

E
Evaluate, 55, 65, 79, 117, 118, 187, 188, 197, 227, 240, 257, 260, 293, 350, 367, 380, 389, 463, 541, 551, 573, 578, 664, 669, 679, 730, 739, 751, 762, 788, 811, 875, 881, 916
Explain, 69, 214, 240, 380, 515, 560, 699, 730, 755, 819, 825, 881

F
Form and Support Opinions, 30, 55, 65, 92, 117, 118, 131, 139, 147, 148, 173, 188, 199, 214, 230, 240, 245, 259, 304, 322, 350, 380, 404, 489, 506, 530, 551, 553, 555, 560, 578, 593, 603, 607, 640, 705, 745, 759, 762, 821, 851, 859, 869, 873, 881, 889, 893, 899, 916

H
Hypothesize, 640

I
Identify, 11, 15, 39, 61, 89, 131, 315, 369, 404, 423, 477, 543, 560, 673, 893
Identify Main Ideas, 511, 717
Identify Main Ideas and Details, 15, 29, 37, 73, 83, 199, 247, 253, 260, 273, 283, 421, 439, 583, 587, 599, 605, 727, 773, 781, 788, 837, 843
Identify Problems and Solutions, 13, 37, 61, 159, 214, 227, 237, 260, 309, 404, 415, 439, 469, 560, 621, 640, 709, 727, 730, 801, 811, 817, 823
Identify Supporting Details, 233, 451, 471, 549, 553, 677, 868
Integrate Visuals, 286, 809
Interpret Charts, 195
Interpret Maps, 24, 37, 43, 81, 103, 111, 115, 127, 141, 155, 161, 166, 175, 177, 183, 201, 203, 209, 225, 237, 251, 254, 257, 271, 275, 293, 297, 329, 333, 343, 345, 346, 361, 367, 387, 393, 399, 403, 443, 451, 453, 465, 483, 491, 497, 505, 515, 519, 521, 543, 566, 593, 619, 629, 669, 673, 677, 701, 715, 757, 767, 773, 801, 813, 821, 823, 855, 863, 901
Interpret Visuals, 426, 828

M
Make Connections, 27, 61, 87, 143, 148, 309, 321, 350, 395, 404, 433, 545, 547, 559, 573, 583, 605, 606, 619, 625, 635, 639, 640, 661, 664, 715, 743, 761, 837, 843, 845, 851, 868, 899, 915, 916
Make Generalizations, 30, 47, 64, 133, 148, 240, 304, 367, 444, 455, 530, 607, 705, 887
Make Inferences, 24, 39, 47, 64, 71, 77, 85, 92, 105, 111, 118, 139, 147, 148, 153, 157, 159, 163, 181, 187, 188, 201, 209, 235, 260, 279, 283, 303, 304, 343, 350, 361, 365, 369, 375, 380, 385, 421, 435, 437, 455, 459, 465, 487, 503, 506, 521, 530, 537, 571, 577, 578, 623, 633, 635, 645, 651, 653, 655, 661, 663, 664, 699, 701, 707, 709, 725, 730, 747, 777, 779, 781, 784, 788, 805, 847, 857, 901, 905
Make Predictions, 148, 188, 289, 329, 343, 404, 475, 625, 633, 639, 685, 686, 717, 723, 751, 755, 769, 863, 867, 875, 885, 916

P
Pose and Answer Questions, 909

S
Sequence Events, 207, 295, 299, 304, 323, 587, 719, 803
Summarize, 30, 577, 640, 868, 916
Synthesize, 64, 85, 118, 141, 147, 188, 311, 322, 339, 350, 403, 404, 426, 478, 506, 530, 653, 664, 686, 779, 788, 817, 825

ACKNOWLEDGMENTS

National Geographic Learning gratefully acknowledges the contributions of the following National Geographic Explorers and affiliates to our program:

Sam Abell, National Geographic Photographer
Lynsey Addario, National Geographic Photographer
Robert Ballard, National Geographic Explorer-in-Residence
Ari Beser, Fulbright-National Geographic Fellow
Jimmy Chin, National Geographic Photographer
Kevin Crisman, National Geographic Explorer
Jason De León, National Geographic Explorer
Leslie Dewan, National Geographic Explorer
Jeffrey Gusky, National Geographic Photographer
David Guttenfelder, National Geographic Photographer
Kevin Hand, National Geographic Explorer
Fredrik Hiebert, National Geographic Archaeologist-in-Residence
Kathryn Keane, Vice President, National Geographic Exhibitions
Bill Kelso, National Geographic Explorer
Michael Nichols, National Geographic Photographer
Paul Nicklen, National Geographic Photographer
Sarah Parcak, National Geographic Fellow
William Parkinson, National Geographic Explorer
Sandra Postel, National Geographic Freshwater Fellow (2009–2015)
Robert Reid, National Geographic Digital Nomad
Andrés Ruzo, National Geographic Explorer
Tristram Stuart, National Geographic Explorer

PHOTOGRAPHIC CREDITS

Illustration: All illustrations are owned by © Cengage.

Cover Atakorn/iStock/Getty Images, Marco Bicci/Alamy Stock Photo, kathykonkle/DigitalVision Vectors/Getty Images, coolbiere photograph/Getty Images; **i** Atakorn/iStock/Getty Images; **iii** (tl) Victoria Sanchez, California State University, Long Beach, (cl) Mary Lynne Ashley Photography/Cengage, (bl) Mark Thiessen/National Geographic Image Collection; **iv** (tl1) Dan Westergren/National Geographic Image Collection, (tl2) © Lynsey Addario, (tc1) (tc2) Sora Devore/National Geographic Image Collection, (tc3) White House/Zuma Wire/Shutterstock.com, (tr1) Alexandra Verville/National Geographic Image Collection, (tr2) Bryan Bedder/Getty Images Entertainment/Getty Images, (cl1) National Geographic Image Collection, (cl2) Courtesy of Ari Beser, (cl3) Jimmy Chin/National Geographic Image Collection, (c) Robert Clark/National Geographic Image Collection, (cr1) © Kara Kooney, (cr2) Shutterstock.com, (cr3) (cr3) Randall Scott/National Geographic Image Collection, (cl1) Mark Thiessen/National Geographic Image Collection, (cl2) © Guillermo de Anda, (cl3) Courtesy of Leslie Dewan, (c) Universal History Archive/Universal Images Group/Getty Images, (cr1) Paul Morigi/Getty Images Entertainment/Getty Images, (cr2) Steven Ellis/National Geographic Image Collection, (bl1) © George Ohrstrom, (bl2) Courtney Rader/National Geographic Image Collection, (bl3) Courtesy of Kavita Gupta, (bc) © Jeff Gusky, (br1) David Guttenfelder/National Geographic Image Collection, (br2) Mark Thiessen/National Geographic Image Collection, (br3) Courtesy of Patrick Hunt; **v** (tl1) (cl1) Courtesy of Terry Hunt, (tl2) (tc) (tr2) (bl2) Randall Scott/National Geographic Image Collection, (tl3) Mark Thiessen and Rebecca Hale/National Geographic Image Collection, (tr1) KMK/National Geographic Image Collection, (tr2) © Peg Keiner, (tr3) © Amanda Koltz, (tl1) Kathy Ku/National Geographic Image Collection, (tl2) Sora Devore/National Geographic Image Collection, (tl3) (tr3) (bc) Mark Thiessen/National Geographic Image Collection, (tc) © Emmanuel Habimana, (tr1) Mark Thiessen/National Geographic Image Collection, (cl2) Gerd Ludwig/National Geographic Image Collection, (cl3) © Jim Haberman, (c) O. Louis Mazzatenta/National Geographic Image Collection, (cr1) Felix Hörhager/picture alliance/Getty Images, (cr2) Sharon Farmer/National Geographic Image Collection, (cr3) Courtesy of Kakenya Ntaiya, (cl1) © Freddie Claire, (cl2) Alan Parente/National Geographic Image Collection, (cl3) Brian Nehlson/National Geographic Image Collection, (c) Courtesy of Matt Piscitelli, (cr1) © Kristin Romey, (cr2) Scott Degraw/National Geographic Image Collection, (cr3) Courtesy of Andrés Ruzo, (bl1) Damon Winter/The New York Times/Redux, (bl2) (bl3) (br2) Rebecca Hale/National Geographic Image Collection, (br1) Nora Shawki/National Geographic Image Collection, (br3) Mauricio Handler/National Geographic Image Collection, (bl1) © Jen Shook, (bl3) Colby Bishop/National Geographic Image Collection, (bc) © Bruno Calendini, (br1) Dillon von Petzinger/National Geographic Image Collection, (br2) Sora Devore/National Geographic Image Collection, (br3) © Allegra Boverman/MIT News; **vi** George Steinmetz/Corbis Documentary/Getty Images; **vii** (tl) John Stanmeyer/National Geographic Image Collection, (tr1) Ender Bayindir/iStock/Getty Images, (tr2) marcos alvarado/Alamy Stock Photo; **viii** Reynold Mainse/Design Pics/Shutterstock Offset; **ix** (tl) Menahem Kahana/AFP/Getty Images, (tr) China: A sleepy cameleer resting on his Bactrian camel, Tang Dynasty, c.7th-9th century CE/Pictures from History/Bridgeman Images; **x** Lars Schreiber/Robert Harding; **xi** (tl) Emad Aljumah/Moment/Getty Images, (tr) Ivy Close Images/Alamy Stock Photo, (c) Merghoub Zakaria/Shutterstock.com; **xii** Fighting between samurai, detail byobu (screen) scenes from war Gempei 12th century, Japan Tosa School, Edo Period, early 17th century/De Agostini Editore/Bridgeman Images; **xiii** (tl) © Freddie Claire, (tr) © The Metropolitan Museum of Art, (c) zhangshuang/Moment/Getty Images; **xiv** Henry Georgi/Aurora/Getty Images; **xv** (tl) © The Metropolitan Museum of Art, (tr) Paul Nicklen/National Geographic Image Collection, (cl) Ariadne Van Zandbergen/Alamy Stock Photo; **xvi** View of Naples/Wittel, Gaspar van (Gaspare Vanvitelli) (1653-1736)/Fratelli Alinari S.P.A./Palatine Gallery, Pitti Palace, Florence/Bridgeman Images; **xvii** (tl) Dave Yoder/National Geographic Image Collection, (tr) Marco Ferrarin/Moment Unreleased/Getty Images; **xviii** Martial Colomb/Photographer's Choice RF/Getty Images; **xix** (t) Testelin, Henri (1616-95), "Jean-Baptiste Colbert (1619-1683) Presenting the Members of the Royal Academy of Science to Louis XIV (1638-1715)". c.1667. Oil on Canvas. Chateau de Versailles, France, Lauros. Giraudon/The Bridgeman Art Library, (cl) John Kellerman/Alamy Stock Photo, (cr) Julian Elliott/Robert Harding; **xx** Coalbrookdale by Night, 1801 (oil on canvas)/Loutherbourg, Philip James (Jacques) de (1740-1812)/Science and Society Picture Library/Science Museum, London, UK/Bridgeman Images; **xxi** (t) Gavin Hellier/Robert Harding, (cl) Everett Collection, (cr) Biosphoto/Alamy Stock Photo; **xxii** ED/CM/Richard Lea-Hair/Camera Press/Redux; **xxiii** (tl) © Jeff Gusky, (tr) Keystone Features/Hulton Archive/Getty Images; **xxiv** pa_Yon/Moment/Getty Images; **xxv** Steve Winter/National Geographic Image Collection; **xxvi** Robert Clark/National Geographic Image Collection; **xxxii** CLempe/National Geographic/Kobal/Shutterstock.com; **1** CLempe/National Geographic/Kobal/Shutterstock.com; **2-3** (spread) George Steinmetz/Corbis Documentary/Getty Images; **4** (tl) Mohammed Kamal/United Press International (UPI)/Jebel Irhoud/Morocco/Newscom, (tr) Nancy Brown/Photolibrary/Getty Images, (bl) Nathan Benn/Corbis Historical/Getty Images, (br) Chris McGrath/Getty Images News/Getty Images; **5** (tl) © The Metropolitan Museum of Art, 66.173, (tr) (bl) Dea Picture Library/De Agostini/Getty Images, (br) kaetana/Shutterstock.com; **6-7** (spread) Emad Aljumah/Moment/Getty Images; **9** (t) Kenneth Garrett/National Geographic Image Collection, (bl) Marc Steinmetz/Visum für Geo/Redux; **12** National Geographic Television/National Geographic Image Collection; **14** Zoonar GmbH/Michal Bednarek/Alamy Stock Photo; **15** Ian S Foulk/National Geographic Image Collection; **16** John Stanmeyer/National Geographic Image Collection; **19** (t) (b) John Stanmeyer/National Geographic Image Collection; **20** © Dillon von Petzinger; **21** (tr) Ferrero-Labat/ard/AGE Fotostock, (cr) Beth Wald/Aurora Photos, (br) HomoCosmicos/iStock/Getty Images; **22** Erich Lessing/Art Resource, NY; **23** (t) Yadid Levy/Aurora Photos, (br) Christophel Fine Art/Universal Images Group/Getty Images; **24** Dea/G. Dagli Orti/De Agostini/Getty Images; **26** (cr) The Lady and the Unicorn: 'Sight' (tapestry) (detail of 172864)/French School, (15th century)/Musee National du Moyen Age et des Thermes de Cluny, Paris/Bridgeman Images, (bl) Head of an animal with a human head in the open jaws, found at Tula, Hidalgo, Mexico, Early Post-Classic (900-1250) (pottery with mother-of-pearl mosaic)/Toltec/Museo Nacional de Antropologia, Mexico City, Mexico/Bridgeman Images; **27** (tl) oversnap/E+/Getty Images, (cr) Cyril Ruoso/Minden Pictures, (bl) Jayne Russell/Alamy Stock Photo; **29** Vincent J. Musi/National Geographic Image Collection Magazines/Getty Images; **32-33** (spread) Nick Brundle Photography/Moment/Getty Images; **35** Bronze Axes, Bronze Age (bronze)/Bronze Age (2000-600 BC)/AISA/Museo Episcopal de Vic, Osona, Catalonia, Spain/Bridgeman Images; **36** (tl) Balage Balogh/Art Resource, NY, (tr) Tablet from Jamdat Nasr in Iraq, listing quantities of various commodities in archaic Sumerian (early cuneiform script) c.3200-3000 BC (clay) (recto, for verso see 113701)/Ashmolean Museum, University of Oxford, UK/Bridgeman Images, (c) The Picture Art Collection/Alamy Stock Photo, (bl) Erich Lessing/Art Resource, NY, (bc) Dea/G. Dagli Orti/De Agostini Picture Library/Getty Images, (br) Werner Forman/Universal Images Group/Getty Images; **38** The Trustees of the British Museum/Art Resource, NY; **39** Cuneiform tablet, c.2300 BC (clay)/The Trustees of the Chester Beatty Library, Dublin/Bridgeman Images; **40** Image Asset Management/AGE Fotostock; **41** Réunion des Musées Nationaux/Art Resource, NY; **43** Werner orman/Universal Images Group/Getty Images; **44** Kenneth Garrett/National Geographic Image Collection; **45** Tobias Tonner/National Geographic Image Collection; **46** J.D. Dallet/AGE Fotostock/Alamy Stock Photo; **47** Nora Shawki/National Geographic Image Collection; **49** Dea/A. Vergani/De Agostini/Getty Images; **50** (t) Oscar Elias/Alamy Stock Photo; **50-51** (spread) Thomas J. Abercrombie/National Geographic Image Collection; **51** (b) Universal History Archive/Universal Images Group/Getty Images; **52** (tl) Peter Horree/Alamy Stock Photo, (cr) Kenneth Garrett/National Geographic Image Collection, (bl) © Marissa Stevens; **53** (tl) Dea/S. Vannini/De Agostini/Getty Images, (br) Wooden statue of Ahmes Nefertari, wife of Amenhotep I, from Deir el-Medina, detail, the bust, New Kingdom, Dynasty XIX/De Agostini Editore/Bridgeman Images; **54** Ender Bayindir/iStock/Getty Images; **55** Gianni Dagli Orti/Rex/Shutterstock.com; **56** (tc) Mark Thiessen/National Geographic Image Collection, (bl) adam eastland/Alamy Stock Photo; **57** Joseph Eid/AFP/Getty Images; **58** Witt Pierre/hemis.fr/AGE Fotostock; **59** The Tablets of the Law with biblical citations in the border/British Library/British Library, London, UK/Bridgeman Images; **61** (tr) © Jim Haberman, (br) Mark Thiessen/National Geographic Image Collection; **62** Noah supervising the construction of the ark; God tells Noah to enter the ark with his family and the animals/British Library/British Library, London, UK/Bridgeman Images; **66-67** (spread) zhu difeng/Shutterstock.com; **68** Dea/W. Buss/De Agostini/Getty Images; **70** AKG Images; **71** © Purchase, Florence and Herbert Irving Gift, 1992/The Metropolitan Museum of Art; **73** marcos alvarado/Alamy Stock Photo; **74** Marcin

Szymczak/Shutterstock.com; **75** (tl) (tr) Godong/Robert Harding, (br) Manfred Bail/Robert Harding; **76** (t) Don Smith/Robert Harding, (br) Seated Buddha with flaming shoulders, Chinese Six Dynasties Period, Northern Wei dynasty, 3rd-5th century (gilt bronze)/Chinese School/Harvard Art Museums/Arthur M. Sackler Museum, Harvard University Art Museums, USA/Bridgeman Images; **77** (t) Gabriel Perez/Moment/Getty Images, (bl) Ian Griffiths/Robert Harding; **79** Dinodia Photos/Alamy Stock Photo; **81** Dea/A. Dagli Orti/De Agostini/Getty Images; **82** Istvan Kadar Photography/Moment/Getty Images; **84** Roman Sigaev/Shutterstock.com; **85** Munsey Fund, 1931/The Metropolitan Museum of Art; **87** tumteerasak/iStock/Getty Images; **88** Photo 12/Universal Images Group/Getty Images; **89** zorazhuang/E+/Getty Images; **90-91** (spread) O. Louis Mazzatenta/National Geographic Image Collection; **94** John Stanmeyer/National Geographic Image Collection; **96-97** (spread) Reynold Mainse/Design Pics/Shutterstock.com; **98** (tl) James L. Stanfield/National Geographic Image Collection, (tr) Siglos of Darius the Great (metal)/Achaemenid, (550-330 BC)/Bible Land Pictures/Private Collection/Bridgeman Images, (bl) Album/Alamy Stock Photo, (br) Heritage Images/Hulton Fine Art Collection/Getty Images; **99** (tl) Gianni Dagli Orti/Rex/Shutterstock.com, (tc) Paleo-Christian, (4th century)/Bridgeman Image, (tr) China: Wu Zetian (Empress Wu), 624-705, Empress Regnant of the Zhou Dynasty (r.690-705)/Pictures from History/Bridgeman Images, (bl) The Metropolitan Museum of Art, (br) De Agostini Picture Library/De Agostini/Getty Images; **100-101** (spread) BornaMir/iStock/Getty Images; **102** DeAgostini/Superstock; **105** Prisma by Dukas/Universal Images Group/Getty Images; **106** Musee des Beaux-Arts, Orleans, France/Bridgeman Images; **107** AP/Rex/Shutterstock.com; **108** Courtesy of Chris Thornton; **111** Borna_Mirahmadian/Shutterstock.com; **112** (cl) Crescent shaped pectoral from Tolstaya Mogila (gold)/Greek School, (4th century BC)/Historical Museum, Kiev, Ukraine/Bridgeman Images, (br) Two Scythians sew a shirt cut out of an animal skin (gold) (detail of 343656 and 343171)/Greek School, (4th century BC)/Historical Museum, Kiev, Ukraine/Bridgeman Images; **113** (tl) Radiokukka/iStock/Getty Images, (cl) Rogers Fund, 1954/The Metropolitan Museum of Art, (cr) Album/Alamy Stock Photo; **114** Dea Picture Library/De Agostini/Getty Images; **116** Erich Lessing/Art Resource, NY; **117** Garcia Julien/hemis.fr/Getty Images; **119** Darius I with Scythian prisoners, The Behistun Inscription, Kermanshah Province, Iran 521 BC (photo)/Bible Land Pictures/Bridgeman Images; **120-121** (spread) SHansche/iStock/Getty Images; **122** © William Parkinson; **123** National Geographic Image Collection; **124** Dea/G. Dagli Orti/De Agostini/Getty Images; **125** Scala/Art Resource, NY; **126** Detail of the inscription from the sarcophagus of Eshmunazar recounting how he and his mother Amashtarte (servant of Astarte) built temples to the gods of Sidon (basalt)/Phoenician, (5th century BC)/Louvre, Paris, France/Bridgeman Images; **129** Gianni Dagli Orti/Rex/Shutterstock.com; **130** Gianni Dagli Orti/Shutterstock.com; **132** Michael Avory/500px; **133** Dea/A. Dagli Orti/De Agostini/Getty Images; **134** Jose Cabezas/Reuters; **135** mikulas1/E+/Getty Images; **136** World History Archive/Alamy Stock Photo; **137** Dea Picture Library/De Agostini/Getty Images; **138** Phas/Universal Images Group/Getty Images; **139** © The Metropolitan Museum of Art, 31.45; **140** bpk Bildagentur/Art Resource, NY; **145** Universal History Archive/Universal Images Group/Getty Images; **147** Anne-Christine Poujoulat/AFP Contributor/AFP/Getty Images; **150-151** (spread) Bjorn Holland/The Image Bank/Getty Images; **152** Laszlo Szirtesi/Getty Images News/Getty Images; **155** National Geographic Image Collection; **156** Dea Picture Library/De Agostini/Getty Images; **157** N. J Saunders/Universal Images/Superstock; **158** Corbis Historical/Leemage/Getty Images; **159** Mikel Bilbao Gorostiaga- Travels/Alamy Stock Photo; **161** Boadicea haranguing the Britons (oil on canvas)/Opie, John (1761-1807)/Christies Images/Private Collection/Bridgeman Images; **162** Gary Ombler/the Ermine Street Guard/DK Images; **163** Luis Domingo/AGE Fotostock/Getty Images; **164** Photo Italia LLC/iStock/Getty Images; **165** © Steven Ellis; **168-169** (spread) Menahem Kahana/AFP/Getty Images; **170** Thomas Coex/AFP/Getty Images; **174** (t) Rebecca Hale/National Geographic Image Collection, (b) National Geographic Image Collection; **175** Dea/M. Ranzani/De Agostini/Getty Images; **178** James Emmerson/Robert Harding; **181** Vito Arcomano/Alamy Stock Photo; **184** Catiline Orations 63 BC: at roman senate, Cicero denounces plot organized by Catiline to take the power, mural painting by Cesare Maccari, 1882-1888/PVDE (RDA)/Bridgeman Images; **185** robertharding/Alamy Stock Photo; **186** Noppasin Wongchum/Alamy Stock Photo; **190-191** (spread) Tawatchai Prakobkit/EyeEm/Getty Images; **192** Jose Fuste Raga/AGE Fotostock; **193** (tl) vladj55/iStock/Getty Images, (tc) Mishella/iStock/Getty Images; **194** Jon Arnold Images Ltd/Alamy Stock Photo; **197** Raj Singh/Alamy Stock Photo; **198** De Agostini Picture Library/De Agostini/Getty Images; **199** View Stock/Getty Images; **200** Prisma by Dukas Presseagentur GmbH/Alamy Stock Photo; **204** China: A sleepy cameleer resting on his Bactrian camel, Tang Dynasty, c. 7th-9th century CE/Pictures from History/Bridgeman Images; **205** (tc) Rick Zhang/National Geographic Image Collection, (br) O. Louis Mazzatenta/National Geographic Image Collection; **206** Artit Tongvichit/Shutterstock.com; **207** David Henley/Pictures From Asia/Newscom; **208** GraphicaArtis/Archive Photos/Getty Images; **210-211** (spread) Robert Clark/National Geographic Image Collection; **212-213** Robert Clark/National Geographic Image Collection; **218-219** (spread) Lars Schreiber/Robert Harding; **220** (tr1) (c) (bl) © The Metropolitan Museum of Art, (tr2) Emad Aljumah/Moment/Getty Images, (br) RMN-Grand Palais/Art Resource, NY; **221** (tl) (br) © The Metropolitan Museum of Art, (tr) The populace pays allegiance to the new Abbasid Caliph Al-Ma'mun, detail, c.1593 (opaque w/c & gold on paper)/Indian School, (16th century)/San Diego Museum of Art/San Diego Museum of Art, USA/Bridgeman Images, (bl) esherez/Shutterstock.com; **222-223** (spread) Dea/A. Dagli Orti/De Agostini/Getty Images; **224** Adam Woolfitt/Robert Harding; **226** (tr) Ivy Close Images/Alamy Stock Photo, (br) B.O'Kane/Alamy Stock Photo; **228-229** (spread) Tetra Images/Robert Harding; **230** Tetra Images/Getty Images; **231** Matthew Williams-Ellis/Robert Harding; **232** Heritage Image Partnership Ltd/Alamy Stock Photo; **234** Izzet Keribar/Lonely Planet Images/Getty Images; **235** The Metropolitan Museum of Art/Art Resource, NY; **237** AKG Images; **238**

perspectivestock/Shutterstock.com; **239** (tr) (cr) Dea/A. Dagli Orti/De Getty Images, (br) Federica Grassi/Moment Open/Getty Images; **241** St. M (tempera on panel), Byzantine, (14th century)/Byzantine Museum, Athens, Greece/Bridgeman Images; **242-243** (spread) Michael Busselle/Robert Harding; **245** Merghoub Zakaria/Shutterstock.com; **246** orhandurgut/Alamy Stock Photo; **247** Debarshi Mukherjee/EyeEm/Getty Images; **248** Gianni Dagli Orti/Rex/Shutterstock.com; **249** (tr) The Metropolitan Museum of Art, (cr) Oscar Garriga Estrada/Shutterstock.com, (br) Roland & Sabrina Michaud/AKG Images; **251** Werner Forman/Universal Images Group/Getty Images; **253** Gavin Hellier/Robert Harding; **258** Tim Gerard Barker/Lonely Planet Images/Getty Images; **259** The doctor's visit to his patient, scene from 'The Maqamat' by Al-Hariri (gouache on vellum)/Persian School, (14th century)/Indivision Charmet/Osterreichische Nationalbibliothek, Vienna, Austria/Bridgeman Images; **262** Sacramento Bee/Tribune News Service/Getty Images; **264-265** (spread) Fighting between samurai, detail byobu (screen) scenes from war Gempei 12th century, Japan Tosa School, Edo Period, early 17th century/De Agostini Editore/Bridgeman Images; **266** (tc) AKG Images, (tr) French School, (14th century)/Bridgeman images, (bl) Werner Forman/Universal Images Group/Getty Images, (bc) The Metropolitan Museum of Art/Art Resource, NY; **266-267** (spread) A. Burkatovski/Fine Art Images/Superstock; **267** (tl) Rainer Hackenberg/Alamy Stock Photo, (tr) Joan of Arc, 1882 (oil on panel)/Rossetti, Dante Gabriel Charles (1828-82)/Fitzwilliam Museum/Fitzwilliam Museum, University of Cambridge, UK/Bridgeman Images, (br) Rat leaving a ship/English School, (20th century)/Look and Learn (A & B images)/Private Collection/Bridgeman Images; **268-269** (spread) Luis Davilla/Robert Harding; **270** Mondadori Portfolio/Hulton Fine Art Collection/Getty Images; **272** ewg3D/iStock unreleased/Getty Images; **273** © Freddie Claire; **274** Erich Lessing/Art Resource; **277** Prisma by Dukas Presseagentur GmbH/Alamy Stock Photo; **278** joe daniel price/Moment/Getty Images; **280** Mms 9961-2 Historiated Initial 'B' from the Peterborough Psalter depicting King David playing the harp, English, (c.1310-20) (vellum)/English School, (14th century)/Didier Lenart/Bibliotheque Royale de Belgique, Brussels, Belgium/Bridgeman Images; **282** (t) Movementway/Robert Harding, (b) John Warburton-Lee/Danita Delimont Stock Photography; **283** Heritage Image Partnership Ltd/Alamy Stock Photo; **284-285** (spread) Gilles Rolle/Rea/Redux; **286** Julien Fromentin/Moment/Getty Images; **287** Godong/Universal Images Group/Getty Images; **288** Luca Antonio Lorenzelli/Alamy Stock Photo; **289** St. Francis of Assisi preaching to the birds (oil on panel)/Giotto di Bondone (c.1266-1337)/Louvre, Paris, France/Bridgeman Images; **291** Siege of Antioch in Turkey during the 1st Crusade in 1098, manuscript/Tallandier (RDA)/Bridgeman Images; **293** AGE Fotostock/Alamy Stock Photo; **295** Ferdinand II of Aragon and Isabella I of Castile (oil on panel)/Spanish School, (15th century)/Jurgens Osteuropa-Photo/Convento Agustinas, Madrigal, Avila/Bridgeman Images; **296** The Triumph of Death, c.1562 (oil on panel)/Bruegel, Pieter the Elder (c.1525-69)/Prado, Madrid, Spain/Bridgeman Images; **299** Ms 6 f.221v Battle of Poitiers - the King of France surrenders to the Black Prince, 1356, from 'St. Alban's Chronicle' (vellum)/English School, (15th century)/Lambeth Palace Library/Lambeth Palace Library, London, UK/Bridgeman Images; **300** nikonaft/iStock/Getty Images; **301** (tl) De Agostini Picture Library/De Agostini/Getty Images, (tr) Centre Historique des Archives Nationales, Paris, France/Bridgeman Images, (bl) Sylvain Sonnet/Corbis Documentary/Getty Images, (br) alxpin/iStock/Getty Images; **302** (tl) Musee des Beaux-Arts, Rouen, France/Bridgeman Images, (tr) Joan of Arc's Death at the Stake, 1843 (oil on canvas)/Stilke, Hermann Anton (1803-60)/State Hermitage Museum, St. Petersburg, Russia/Bridgeman Images, (br) Joan of Arc, 1879 (oil on canvas)/Bastien-Lepage, Jules (1848-84)/Superstock Inc./Private Collection/Bridgeman Images; **303** (tl) Herbert Dorfman/Corbis Historical/Getty Images, (tr) Universal History Archive/Universal Images Group/Getty Images, (br) 'The Suffragette', 1912 (colour litho)/English School, (20th century)/Museum of London/Museum of London, UK/Bridgeman Images; **306-307** (spread) February/Moment/Getty Images; **308** zhangshuang/Moment/Getty Images; **311** China: A palace examination at Kaifeng. Song Dynasty painting (960-1279 CE)/Pictures from History/Bridgeman Images; **312** Antonio Zanghì/Moment/Getty Images; **315** Eye Ubiquitous/Universal Images Group/Getty Images; **316** JTB Photo/UIG/AGE Fotostock; **318** Robert Harding Picture LIbrary; **319** (tl) Westend61/Getty Images, (cr) Japan: 'A Young Woman Practicing the Kanji', Meiji Period woodblock print by Toyohara Chikanobu (1838-1912), 1897/Pictures from History/Bridgeman Images, (bl) The Trustees of the British Museum/Art Resource, NY; **320** (t) Jason Langley/Robert Harding, (b) The Thunder God Raijin (left) and the Wind God Fujin (right), four panel folding screen, c.1700 (colour on gold leafed paper)/Korin, Ogata (1658-1716)/Pictures from History/Tokyo National Museum, Japan/Bridgeman Images; **321** (tr) Erich Lessing/Art Resource, NY, (cl) © The Jack and Belle Linsky Collection, 1982; **324-325** (spread) Jose Fuste Raga/AGE Fotostock; **326** Egmont Strigl/Robert Harding; **327** Jon Arnold/Danita Delimont; **329** Ben Horton/National Geographic Image Collection; **330** Battle between Mongolians and Egyptians, miniature from manuscript 1113, folio 236, Persia, 14th century/De Agostini Editore/Bridgeman Images; **333** Universal History Archive/Universal Images Group/Getty Images; **334-337** John Stanmeyer/National Geographic Image Collection; **338** Mel Longhurst/AGE Fotostock; **339** © The Metropolitan Museum of Art; **340** © Purchase, Sir Joseph Hotung and The Vincent Astor Foundation Gifts, 2001; **342** National Geographic Maps/National Geographic Image Collection; **345** Interfoto/Alamy Stock Photo; **348** Erich Lessing/Art Resource, NY; **351** Dennis Cox/Alamy Stock Photo; **354-355** (spread) Henry Georgi/Aurora/Getty Images; **356** (tl) Richard Hewitt Stewart/National Geographic Image Collection, (tr) Ira Block/National Geographic Image Collection, (bl) Mayan/Getty Images, (br) gift of Mr. and Mrs. Meredith Long/Tonto style jar (olla) with checkerboard and sun designs, Ancestral Pueblo, c.1300 (earthenware with slip)/Anasazi School (1100-1300)/Museum of Fine Arts, Houston/Museum of Fine Arts, Houston, Texas, USA/Bridgeman Images; **357** (tc) Candlestick, Mamluk dynasty, mid 14th century (brass)/Egyptian School (14th century AD)/Cincinnati Art Museum/Cincinnati Art Museum, Ohio, USA/Bridgeman Images, (tr) GL Archive/Alamy Stock Photo,

ACKNOWLEDGMENTS **R36**

ıages/Getty Images, (br) DEA/De Agostini/Getty Images; ır/Alamy Stock Photo; **361** (tc) Spani Arnaud/hemis.fr/ ıi Arnaud/hemis.fr/Getty Images; **363** George Steinmetz/ y/Getty Images; **364** Christopher Scott/Alamy Stock Photo; **365** ımy Stock Photo; **368** Abraham Cresques/Art Images/Getty ıe Metropolitan Museum of Art; **370-371** (spread) Yannick Tylle/ entary/Getty Images; **372-373** (spread) Finbarr O'Reilly/Reuters; oering/Robert Harding; **375** Bridgeman-Giraudon/Art Resource, NY; 3. w McConnell/Robert Harding; **377** WitR/Shutterstock.com; **378** Ariac Van Zandbergen/Alamy Stock Photo; **382-383** (spread) John Coletti/ Photolibrary/Getty Images; **385** Phil Degginger/Alamy Stock Photo; **387** Courtesy of Matt Piscitelli; **388** AKG Images; **390** Paul Nicklen/National Geographic Image Collection; **391** © Karla Ortega; **393** Michael Runkel/Robert Harding; **395** PHAS/ Universal Images Group/Getty Images; **396** AGE Fotostock/Alamy Stock Photo; **398-399** (spread) Sean Caffrey/Lonely Planet Images/Getty Images; **401** (t) © Terry Hunt and Carl Lipo, (cl) (bl) Courtesy of Terry Hunt; **402** Stephen Alvarez/ National Geographic Image Collection; **403** (tr) © Jago Cooper, (cr) Shutterstock.com; **405** (tr1) Gavin Hellier/Robert Harding, (tr2) Nick Brundle Photography/ Moment/Getty Images; **406** Randy Olson/National Geographic Image Collection; **408-409** (spread) View of Naples/Wittel, Gaspar van (Gaspare Vanvitelli) (1653-1736)/Fratelli Alinari S.P.A./Palatine Gallery, Pitti Palace, Florence/ Bridgeman Images; **410** (tl) 1763 copy by Mo Yi Tongof a map of the world drawn by Zheng He (1371-1433) chinese explorer c. 1421. On r is America, so Zheng He may have discovered America before Christopher Colombus during on of his travels ordered by chinese emperor Zhu Di/PVDE (RDA)/Bridgeman Images, (tr) AGE Fotostock/Alamy Stock Photo, (bl) San Giorgio, marble, detail/Donatello, (c.1386-1466)/Fratelli Alinari S.P.A./Museo Nazionale del Bargello, Florence, Tuscany, Italy/Bridgeman Images, (br) The Trustees of the British Museum/Art Resource, NY; **410** (tl) Album/Alamy Stock Photo, (tr) Robert Clark/National Geographic Image Collection, (bl) A figure of a lion on rockwork (cloisonne enamel)/Chinese School, Qing Dynasty (1644-1912)/Paul Freeman/Private Collection/Bridgeman Images, (br) Art Directors & Trip/Alamy Stock Photo, (c) Mughal Coin from Agra, 1556-1605 (silver)/Mughal School/Ashmolean Museum/ Ashmolean Museum, University of Oxford, UK/Bridgeman Images; **412-413** (spread) Mondadori Portfolio/Hulton Fine Art Collection/Getty Images; **415** (tr) Fernando G. Baptista/National Geographic Image Collection, (br) Lorenzo Mattei/ Robert harding; **416** Fratelli Alinari Idea S.p.A./Corbis Historical/Getty Images; **417** © The Gutenberg Bible, digitised by the HUMI Project, Keio University and National Library of Scotland; **419** (t) Mondadori Portfolio/Hulton Fine Art Collection/Getty Images, (bl) Art Collection 2/Alamy Stock Photo; **420** The Picture Art Collection/Alamy Stock Photo; **421** (tl) Peter Willi/SuperStock/Getty Images, (tr) Fine Art/Corbis Historical/Getty Images; **422** Dave Yoder/National Geographic Image Collection; **424** Stock Montage/Archive Photos/Getty Images; **425** Portrait of a Young Woman as a Sibyl, c.1620 (oil on canvas)/Gentileschi, Orazio (1565-1647)/Museum of Fine Arts, Houston, Texas, USA/Bridgeman Images; **426** Heritage Images/Hulton Archive/Getty Images; **427** Heritage Images/Hulton Archive/Getty Images; **428** Courtesy National Gallery of Art; **430** (tl) Man with traditional Japanese Irezumi tattoo, c.1880 (hand coloured albumen photo) (detail of 398090)/Japanese Photographer, (19th century)/Prismatic Pictures/Private Collection/Bridgeman Images, (cr) Ira Block/National Geographic Image Collection, (bl) Jorge Fernández/LightRocket/Getty Images; **431** (tl) Chuck Place/ Alamy Stock Photo, (tr) Courtesy Charles S. King, (bl) De Agostini Picture Library/De Agostini/Getty Images; **432** (tl) Vanni Archive/Art Resource, NY, (cr1) (cr2) © Thomas Walsh, (bl) Museum Associates/Lacma/Art Resource, NY; **433** (tr) Mario Carrieri/Mondadori Portfolio/Getty Images, (bl) Everett Collection Inc/ Alamy Stock Photo, (br) Interfoto/Alamy Stock Photo; **434** Cranach, Lucas, the Elder (1472-1553)/Bridgeman Images; **437** (tl) DEA/S. Gutierrez/De Agostini/Getty Images, (tr) David Lyons/Alamy Stock Photo; **439** Philip II and Mary I, 1558/ Eworth or Ewoutsz, Hans (fl.1520-74)/Russell Ash Limited/Trustees of the Bedford Estate, Woburn Abbey, UK/Bridgeman Images; **440** Hulton Archive/Getty Images; **441** Dea Picture Library/De Agostini/Getty Images; **443** TAO Images Limited/ Alamy Stock Photo; **447-448** (spread) Foofa Jearanaisil/Shutterstock.com; **450** Sultan Suleiman Khan I, 10th Sultan of the Ottoman Empire, 1815 (colour litho)/ Young, John (1755-1825)/Stapleton Collection/Private Collection/Bridgeman Images; **453** Marco Ferrarin/Moment Unreleased/Getty Images; **454** Scala/Art Resource, NY; **455** A prayer arch of red satin, embroidered in gilt and silver threads and applique with brocades (satin, giland silver thread)/Turkish School, (19th century)/Christies Images/Private Collection/Bridgeman Images; **456-457** (spread) Education Images/UIG/AGE Fotostock; **458** bpk Bildagentur/Museum fuer Islamische Kunst, Staatliche Museen, Berlin, Germany/Hans Kraeftner/Art Resource; **459** Emperor Akbar conversing with Jesuit missionaries, Indian School, (16th century)/Private Collection/De Agostini Picture Library/Bridgeman Images; **460-461** (spread) Jean-Baptiste Rabouan/laif/Redux; **462-463** (spread) © Atul Loke/The New York Times; **465** The Metropolitan Museum of Art/Art Resource; **466** Ch'ien-Lung, Chinese School/Private Collection/Peter Newark Pictures/ Bridgeman Images; **469** Japan: Winter: Atagoshita and Yabu Lane. Image 112 of '100 Famous Views of Edo'. Utagawa Hiroshige (first published 1856-59)/Pictures from History/Bridgeman Images; **470** Thomas L. Kelly/Media Bakery; **471** Tsar Ivan IV Vasilyevich 'the Terrible' (1530-84) 1897 (oil on canvas) (detail of 89327)/ Vasnetsov, Victor Mikhailovich (1848-1926)/Tretyakov Gallery, Moscow, Russia/ Bridgeman Images; **473** Igor Sinitsyn/Robert Harding; **474** Jose Fuste Raga/Corbis Documentary/Getty Images; **475** Dirk Renckhoff/imageBroker/AGE Fotostock; **477** Portrait of Catherine II, also known as Catherine the Great (Stettin, 1729-Pushkin, 1796), Empress consort of Peter III of Russia (1728-1762), c.1770/Rokotov, Fedor Stepanovich (c.1735-1808)/De Agostini Editore/Museum of History, Moscow, Russia/Bridgeman Images; **480-481** (spread) Jean Paul Villegas/iStock/Getty Images; **483** © Architect of the Capitol; **484** (bl) (br) Dea/G. Dagli Orti/De Agostini/ Getty Images; **485** © The Metropolitan Museum of Art; **486** (t) Damon Winter/The New York Times/Redux, (bl) Eye of Science/Science Source; **489** Purepix/Alamy Stock Photo; **490** HandmadePictures/iStock/Getty Images; **492** Erich Lessing/Art Resource, NY; **493** Pete Saloutos/Image Source/Getty Images; **494** Frank Bienewald/imageBroker/AGE Fotostock; **496** The Picture Art Collection/Alamy Stock Photo; **498-499** (spread) Stuart Forster/Alamy Stock Photo; **500** The Trustees of the British Museum/Art Resource, NY; **501** (tl) Gundestrup cauldron, decorated silver vessel/De Agostini Editore/Nationalmuseet, Copenhagen, Denmark/Bridgeman Images, (cr) The Metropolitan Museum of Art, (bc) Museum of Fine Arts, Houston, Texas, USA/Gift of Alfred C. Glassell, Jr./Bridgeman Images; **503** John Elk III/Alamy Stock Photo; **504** Bill O'Leary/The Washington Post/Getty Images; **507** Album/Alamy Stock Photo; **508-509** (spread) Joe Penney/ Reuters; **510** Novarc Images/Alamy Stock Photo; **512** John Macdougall/AFP/Getty Images; **514** Joe Penney/Reuters; **516-517** (spread) Tyler Hicks/The New York Times/Redux; **516** (bl) Benoit Tessier/Reuters; **518** Universal History Archive/UIG/ Shutterstock.com; **521** Stowage of the British Slave Ship 'Brookes' Under the Regulated Slave Trade Act of 1788 (engraving)/American School, (18th century)/ Stapleton Collection/Private Collection/Bridgeman Images; **522-523** (spread) Robert Clark/National Geographic Image Collection; **524** narvikk/E+/Getty Images; **525** Sreekanth G/EyeEm/Getty Images; **526** BnF, Dist. RMN-Grand Palais/ Art Resource, NY; **527** Library of Congress, Prints & Photographs Division, Reproduction number LC-DIG-ppmsca-54230 (digital file from original item, front) LC-DIG-ppmsca-54231 (digital file from original item, back); **528** AP Images/Collin Reid; **529** Emily Kask/The New York Times; **532** Courtesy of the Osher Map Library/ University of Southern Maine; **534-535** (spread) Martial Colomb/Photographer's Choice RF/Getty Images; **536** (tr) Historical/Corbis Historical/Getty Images, (cl) Sebastien Durand/Shutterstock.com, (tr) Historical/ Corbis Historical/Getty Images, (cr) Loom designed by Joseph Marie Jacquard (1752-1834) (mixed media)/French School/CNAM, Conservatoire National des Arts et Metiers, Paris/Bridgeman Images, (b) John Warburton-Lee/Danita Delimont Stock Photography; **537** (tl) Kumar Sriskandan/Alamy Stock photo, (tr) adoc-photos/Corbis Historical/Getty Images, (c) Patrick Kovarik/AFP/Getty Images, (bl) De Agostini Picture Library/De Agostini/Getty Images, (br) Design Pics/Reynold Mainse/Perspectives/Getty Images; **538-539** (spread) Babak Tafreshi/National Geographic Image Collection; **540** The Armada Portrait, c.1588 (oil on panel)/Gower, George (1540-96) (attr. to)/Woburn Abbey, Bedfordshire, UK/ Bridgeman Images; **541** Testelin, Henri (1616-95), "Jean-Baptiste Colbert (1619-1683) Presenting the Members of the Royal Academy of Science to Louis XIV (1638-1715)". c.1667. Oil on Canvas. Chateau de Versailles, France, Lauros. Giraudon/Bridgeman Images; **545** knape/E+/Getty Images; **547** (tr) Ms 2200 f.115v. The World, according to Aristotle, miniature from 'De Philosophia Mundi' by Guillaume de Conches (1100-54) 1276-77 (vellum)/French School, (13th century)/ Indivision Charmet/Bibliotheque Sainte-Genevieve, Paris, France/Bridgeman Images, (cr) De Agostini Picture Library/De Agostini/Getty Images; **548** Dr William Gilbert (1544-1603) showing his Experiment on Electricity to Queen Elizabeth I and her Court, 19th century (oil on canvas) (see detail 99460)/Hunt, Arthur Ackland (fl.1863-1913)/Private Collection/Bridgeman Images; **551** (tr) © Spouts, (c) Courtesy of Kathy Ku; **552** Helianthus annus (Sunflower) illustration for an English translation of a botanical treatise by Carolus Linnaeus (1707-78) 1777 from the Plate Collection of the Botany Library (hand-coloured engraving)/ Miller, John (b.c.1750)/Natural History Museum, London/Natural History Museum, London, UK/Bridgeman Images; **553** Adina Tovy/Lonely Planet Images/ Getty Images; **554** De Agostini Picture Library/De Agostini/Getty Images; **556** Print Collector/Hulton Archive/Getty Images; **557** (t) Map of the world, 1486 (coloured engraving)/Ptolemy (Claudius Ptolemaeus of Alexandria)(c.90-168) (after)/Bibliotheque Nationale, Paris, France/Bridgeman Images, (br) Astrolabe from Saragossa, c.1079-80 (brass) (see also 283947)/Islamic School, (11th century)/ Germanisches Nationalmuseum, Nuremberg, Germany/Bridgeman Images; **558** (t) AKG Images, (br) Everett Collection Historical/Alamy Stock Photo; **559** The polar chronometer of HMS Erebus, used by Captain Ross on the voyage to the Antarctic in 1839-43 (wood & brass)/English School, (19th century)/Christies Images/Private Collection/Bridgeman Images; **562-563** (spread) Miles Ertman/Robert Harding; **564** Lemaire Stéphane/AGE Fotostock; **568** The Trustees of the British Museum/ Art Resource, NY; **570** (tl) Christophel Fine Art/Universal Images Group/Getty Images, (cl) Imagno/Hulton Fine Art Collection/Getty Images; **571** (tl) Heritage Images/Hulton Fine Art Collection/Getty Images, (cl) Niday Picture Library/ Alamy Stock Photo; **573** Danita Delimont/Gallo Images/Getty Images; **574** John Kellerman/Alamy Stock Photo; **576** Picturenow/Universal Images Group/Getty Images; **580-581** (spread) © Kenneth Garrett; **582** Washington Crossing the Delaware River, 25th December 1776, 1851 (oil on canvas) (copy of an original painted in 1848)/Leutze, Emanuel Gottlieb (1816-68)/Metropolitan Museum of Art, New York, USA/Bridgeman Images; **584** Revolutionary cartoon about 'Tithes, Taxes and Graft' (coloured engraving)/French School, (18th century)/Musee de la Ville de Paris, Musee Carnavalet, Paris, France/Bridgeman Images; **586** Photo Josse/Leemage/Corbis Historical/Getty Images; **587** AKG Images; **588** 2019 The Jacob and Gwendolyn Knight Lawrence Foundation, Seattle/Artists Rights Society (ARS), New York;The Jacob and Gwendolyn Lawrence Foundation/Art Resource; **590** AKG Images; **593** Julian Elliott/Robert Harding; **594** Augustus of Prima Porta, c.20 BC (marble)/Roman, (1st century BC)/Didier Lenart/Vatican Museums and Galleries, Vatican City/Bridgeman Images; **595** (tl) Portrait of George Washington, 1796 (oil on canvas)/Stuart, Gilbert (1755-1828)/Brooklyn Museum of Art/Brooklyn Museum of Art, New York, USA/Bridgeman Images, (tr) John Parrot/Stocktrek Images/Getty Images, (br) Digital Image: Yale Center for British Art; **597** (tl) Portrait of Madame Raymond de Verninac (1780-1827) 1798-99 (oil on canvas)/David, Jacques Louis (1748-1825)/Louvre, Paris, France/Bridgeman Images, (b) The Clothed Maja, c.1800 (oil on canvas)/Goya y Lucientes, Francisco Jose de (1746-1828)/Prado, Madrid, Spain/Bridgeman Images; **598** Wreck of a Transport Ship/Turner, Joseph Mallord William (1775-1851)/Museu Calouste Gulbenkian, Lisbon, Portugal/Bridgeman Images; **599** Robbie Jack/Corbis

Entertainment/Getty Images; **601** Simon Bolivar (1783-1830) (chromolitho)/ Indivision Charmet/Private Collection/Bridgeman Images; **602** Gale Beery/ Moment Mobile/Getty Images; **603** AKG Images; **604** GraphicaArtis/Archive Photos/Getty Images; **607** Zip Lexing/Alamy Stock Photo; **608** Hugo Van Lawick/ National Geographic Image Collection; **610-611** (spread) Coalbrookdale by Night, 1801 (oil on canvas)/Loutherbourg, Philip James (Jacques) de (1740-1812)/Science and Society Picture Library/Science Museum, London, UK/Bridgeman Images; **612** (tl) Heritage Images/Hulton Archive/Getty Images, (tr) adoc-photos/British ships destroying an enemy fleet in Canton, 1841. First Opium War, China, 19th century./Duncan, Edward (1803-82)/De Agostini Editore/National Maritime Museum, London, UK/Bridgeman Images, (bc) villorejo/Alamy Stock Photo, (br) Mary Evans Picture Library/The Image Works; **613** (tl) Gianni Dagli Orti/ Shutterstock.com, (tr) BE&W agencja fotograficzna Sp. z o.o./Alamy Stock Photo, (bl) Print Collector/Hulton Archive/Getty Images, (br) Universal History Archive/ UIG/Shutterstock.com; **614-615** (spread) Westend61/Getty Images; **616** A Pit Head, c.1775-1825 (oil on canvas)/English School, (19th century)/National Museums Liverpool/Walker Art Gallery, National Museums Liverpool/Bridgeman Images; **617** A. Burkatovski/Fine Art Images/Superstock; **619** Science & Society Picture Library/SSPL/Getty Images; **621** Heritage Images/Hulton Archive/Getty Images; **623** Science and Society/Superstock; **624** Bettmann/Getty Images; **625** villorejo/ Alamy Stock Photo; **626** AKG Images; **630** Glasshouse Images/Everett Collection; **631** (bl) Past Pix/Science and Society/Superstock, (bc) Winchester College/In aid of Mary Seacole Memorial Statue Appeal/Mary Evans/The Image Works; **632** Gavin Hellier/Robert Harding; **633** Glenn Asakawa/Denver Post/Getty Images; **635** Tate, London/Art Resource, NY; **636** China: Taiping forces break through the Qing encirclement at Fucheng (Taiping Rebellion, 1850-1864)/Pictures from History/ Bridgeman Images; **637** China: Official portrait of Empress Dowager Cixi (1835-1908) by court photographer Yu Xunling, c. 1895/Yu Xunling (c.1880–1943)/ Pictures from History/Bridgeman Images; **638** John Stevenson/Corbis Historical/ Getty Images; **639** MeijiShowa/Alamy Stock Photo; **642-643** (spread) Buyenlarge/ Archive Photos/Getty Images; **645** Everett Collection; **646-647** (spread) iStock. com/David Sucsy; **648** Bettmann/Getty Images; **649** Sarah Leen/National Geographic Image Collection; **650** Tim Fitzharris/Minden Pictures; **651** 914 collection/Alamy Stock Photo; **652** Bettmann/Getty Images; **653** Glasshouse Images/Alamy Stock Photo; **655** 3LH/Superstock; **656** History and Art Collection/ Alamy Stock Photo; **658** Anand Varma/National Geographic Image Collection; **659** Historical/Corbis Historical/Getty Images; **660** (tl) (tr) Classic Collection 3/ Alamy Stock Photo; **661** © Mary Marshall; **662** Library of Congress, Prints & Photographs Division, Reproduction number LC-USZC2-1058 (color film copy slide); **663** Wallace Kirkland/Science Source/Getty Images; **665** Photo 12/ Universal Images Group/Getty Images; **666-667** (spread) Jennifer Pillinger/Alamy Stock Photo; **668** Khama and his wife, c.1910 (platinum print)/Hargreave, A. E. (fl.1910)/Michael Graham-Stewart/Private Collection/Bridgeman Images; **671** Carl E. Akeley/National Geographic Image Collection; **672** AKG Images; **674** Boer families in a concentration camp at Eshowe, Zululand, 1900. 2nd Boer War 1899-1902/Universal Images Group/Bridgeman Images; **675** The Art Archive/ Shutterstock.com; **677** Biosphoto/Alamy Stock Photo; **678** Library of Congress, Prints & Photographs Division, Reproduction number LC-DIG-ppmsca-53150 (digital file from original) LC-USZ62-22488 (b&w film copy neg.); **680-681** (spread) Design Pics Inc/National Geographic Image Collection; **682** Sia Kambou/ AFP/Getty Images; **683** Joel Sartore/National Geographic Image Collection; **684** FLHC 84/Alamy Stock Photo; **685** W. and D. Downey/Hulton Royals Collection/ Getty Images; **687** Chronicle/Alamy Stock Photo; **688** Randy Olson/National Geographic Image Collection; **690-691** (spread) ED/CM/Richard Lea-Hair/Camera Press/Redux; **692** (tl) Stefano Bianchetti/Corbis Historical/Getty Images, (tr) Universal History Archive/Universal Images Group/Getty Images, (b) © NARA; **693** (tl) Austria: A Jewish-owned shoe store that was destroyed by the Nazis on Kristallnacht, Vienna, 10 November, 1938 (b/w photo)/Pictures from History/ Bridgeman Images, (tr1) XM Collection/Alamy Stock Photo, (tr2) Keystone/Hulton Archive/Getty Images, (bl) Ted Small/Alamy Stock Photo, (br) Universal History Archive/Universal Images Group/Getty Images; **694-695** (spread) IWM/Getty Images/Imperial War Museums/Getty Images; **696** ullstein bild Dtl./ullstein bild/ Getty Images; **699** Universal History Archive/UIG/Shutterstock.com; **700** Bettmann/Getty Images; **702** Everett Collection Historical/Alamy Stock Photo;**703** (tc) (br) © Jeff Gusky; **705** John Frost Newspapers/Alamy Stock Photo; **706** Postcard depicting a Senegalese soldier, 1915 (coloured photo), French School (20th century)/Private Collection/Archives Charmet/Bridgeman Images; **707** Historical Images Archive/Alamy Stock Photo; **710** Library of Congress, Prints & Photographs Division, Reproduction number LC-DIG-ppmsca-38818 (digital file from original item) LC-USZ62-16767 (b&w film copy neg.); **712** Diana Markosian/ Magnum Photos; **716** Christopher Furlong/Getty Images News/Getty Images; **718** Shawshots/Alamy Stock Photo; **720** IanDagnall Computing/Alamy Stock Photo; **721** Laski Diffusion/Hulton Archive/Getty Images; **723** Chumphon_TH/ Shutterstock.com; **724** ART Collection/Alamy Stock Photo; **725** Library of Congress, Prints & Photographs Division, Reproduction number LC-DIG-ppmsca-38284 (digital file from original item) LC-USZ62-30693 (b&w film copy neg.); **726** Gianni Dagli Orti/Shutterstock.com; **727** AKG Images; **728** Victor De Palma/The Life Images Collection/Getty Images; **729** (tr) 2019 Artists Rights Society (ARS), New York/Somaap, Mexico City; Schalkwijk/Art Resource, NY; **732-733** (spread) Bettmann/Getty Images; **734** The Wright Flyer I makes its first flight of 120 feet in 12 seconds, at Kitty Hawk, North Carolina, 10.35am, 17 December 1903 (b/w photo)/Daniels, John T. (1884-1948)/Ken Welsh/Private Collection/Bridgeman Images; **735** Michael Ochs Archives/Getty Images; **736** ullstein bild Dtl./Universal Images Group/Getty Images; **737** Science History Images/Alamy Stock Photo; **738** (t) Keystone-France/Gamma-Keystone/Getty Images, (b) Clare Trainor/National Geographic Image Collection; **740** ullstein bild Dtl./Getty Images; **741** Library of Congress, Prints & Photographs Division, Reproduction number LC-DIG-highsm-24732 (original digital file); **742** Oscar Manello/Hulton Archive/Getty Images; **745** Leipzig Street with Electric Tram, 1914 (oil on canvas)/Kirchner, Ernst Ludwig (1880-1938)/Marlborough Fine Art/ Museum Folkwang, Essen, Germany/Bridgeman Images; **746** Fine Art Images/ Heritage Images/Hulton Archive/Getty Images; **747** Bettmann/Getty Images; **748** Sueddeutsche Zeitung Photo/Alamy Stock Photo; **749** ullstein bild Dtl./ullstein bild/Getty Images; **750** AKG Images; **751** Popperfoto/Getty Images; **752** AKG Images; **754** AP Images; **755** George Rinhart/Corbis Historical/Getty Images; **756** LIU JIN/AFP/Getty Images; **757** Bettmann/Getty Images; **758-759** (spread) Guernica, 1937 (oil on canvas)/Picasso, Pablo (1881-1973)/Museo Nacional Centro de Arte Reina Sofia, Madrid, Spain/Bridgeman Images; **761** Popperfoto/Getty Images; **764-765** (spread) Everett Collection; **768** Album/Alamy Stock Photo; **769** (tc) Bryan Bedder/Getty Images Entertainment/Getty Images, (br) David Doubilet/ National Geographic Image Collection; **773** (tr) The Asahi Shimbun/Getty Images, (br) Schultz Reinhard/Prisma/Superstock; **774** UtCon Collection/Alamy Stock Photo; **775** Keystone/Corbis Historical/Getty Images; **776** Keystone Features/ Hulton Archive/Getty Images; **777** Wallace/ANL/Shutterstock.com; **778** Bettmann/Getty Images; **779** Kimimasa Mayama/EPA/Newscom; **780** Scott Barbour/Getty Images News/Getty Images; **781** Arno Burgi/picture alliance/Getty Images; **782** H. Miller/Hulton Archive/Getty Images; **783** Roger Viollet Collection/ Roger Viollet/Getty Images; **784** Uli Deck/picture alliance/Getty Images; **784-785** (spread) © The National Archives; **787** James L. Stanfield/National Geographic Image Collection; **789** John Parrot/Stocktrek Images/Getty Images; **798** TASS/ Getty Images; **790** Lynn Johnson/National Geographic Image Collection; **792-793** (spread) pa_Yon/Moment/Getty Images; **794** (tl) Dmitri Kessel/The Life Picture Collection/Getty Images, (tr) Sovfoto/Universal Images Group/Getty Images, (cr) Hulton Deutsch/Corbis Historical/Getty Images, (bl) Education Images/Universal Images Group/Getty Images, (br) John Frost Newspapers/Alamy Stock Photo; **795** (t) Guillermo Arias/AFP/Getty Images, (bl) PhotoQuest/Archive Photos/Getty Images, (bc) Peter Turnley/Corbis Historical/Getty Images, (br) Louise Gubb/ Corbis Historical/Getty Images; **798** TASS/Getty Images ; **803** (t) (c) NASA; **804** Everett Collection Historical/Alamy Stock Photo; **805** David Guttenfelder/ National Geographic Image Collection; **807-808** (spread) © World Monuments Fund; **807** (tl) woodspiral/Alamy Stock Photo, (tr) © World Monuments Fund; **809** Sovfoto/Universal Images Group/Getty Images; **810** VCG/Getty Images; **811** China: Follow the Road to Cooperativisation! A poster from the time of the Great Leap Forward (1958-1961)/Pictures from History/Bridgeman Images; **814** Kevin Mazur/ Getty Images; **815** Bettmann/Getty Images; **816** AP Images/Uncredited; **817** Tim Graham/Corbis Historical/Getty Images; **818** (cr) Rolls Press/Popperfoto/Getty Images, (b) Tim Martin/Robert Harding; **821** David Guttenfelder/National Geographic Image Collection; **822** Dirck Halstead/Hulton Archive/Getty Images; **823** Sovfoto/Universal Images Group/Shutterstock.com; **825** Laszlo Almasi/ Reuters; **828** (tr) tim page/Corbis Historical/Getty Images, (br) Everett Collection Historical/Alamy Stock Photo; **829** (t) Melet Georges/Paris Match Archive/Getty Images, (bl) Rolls Press/Popperfoto/Getty Images, (br) NASA; **831** Library of Congress, Prints & Photographs Division, drawing by Edmund S. Valtman, LC-DIG-ppmsc-07978; **832-833** (spread) Peter Timm/ullstein bild/Getty Images; **834** AP Images/Anatoly Maltsev; **836** mpworks/Alamy Stock Photo; **837** mark reinstein/Shutterstock.com; **838** (tl) (c) Gerd Ludwig/National Geographic Image Collection; **839** (t) (b) Gerd Ludwig/National Geographic Image Collection; **841** AP Images; **843** AP Images/Jeff Widener; **844** Marvin Recinos/AFP/Getty Images; **846** Alain BUU/Gamma-Rapho/Getty Images; **848** Independent News and Media/ Hulton Archive/Getty Images; **850** Manish Lakhani/Alamy Stock Photo; **851** Stephen Chernin/Getty Images News/Getty Images; **852** Rolls Press/Popperfoto/ Getty Images; **853** Terry Ashe/The Life Images Collection/Getty Images; **855** Cynthia Johnson/The Life Images Collection/Getty Images; **856** Stringer/AFP/ Getty Images; **857** Robert Nickelsberg/The Life Images Collection/Getty Images; **859** Fabrice Coffrini/AFP/Getty Images; **860** Alejandro Pagni/AFP/Getty Images; **864** Matthew Horwood/Getty Images News/Getty Images; **865** (tl) NASA, (b) Andrew Madali/500px Prime/Getty Images; **866** (t) Frank Micelotta Archive/ Hulton Archive/Getty Images, (br) Arlene Richie/Media Sources/Getty Images; **867** (tr) Creative Stock/Alamy Stock Photo, (b) Walt Disney Studios Motion Pictures/Everett Collection; **870-871** (spread) Daniela White Images/Moment/ Getty Images; **872** Porter Gifford/Corbis Historical/Getty Images; **873** Gilles Bassignac/Gamma-Rapho/Getty Images; **874** Linda Davidson/The Washington Post/Getty Images; **875** Gokhan Sahin/Getty Images News/Getty Images; **877** Randal Scott/National Geographic Image Collection; **878** Elizabeth Dalziel/ National Geographic Image Collection; **879** Jon Benz/National Geographic Image Collection; **880** Ulrich Perrey/DPA/Getty Images; **881** Shah Marai/AFP/Getty Images; **882** NurPhoto/Corbis News/Getty Images; **884** John Stanmeyer/National Geographic Image Collection; **885** Kevin Frayer/Getty Images News/Getty Images; **887** Oli Scarff/Getty Images News/Getty Images; **889** Larry Towell/Magnum Photos; **893** AP Images/Liang zhen; **894** (t) Lynn Johnson/National Geographic Image Collection, (bl) Steve Winter/National Geographic Image Collection; **896-897** (spread) Finbarr O'Reilly/Reuters; **899** Joe Raedle/Getty Images News/ Getty Images; **900** (tl) Carl Court/Getty Images News/Getty Images, (cr) imageBroker/Superstock, (br) AP Images/Anthony Devlin; **902** Marty Melville/ AFP/Getty Images; **903** Richard Stonehouse/Getty Images Entertainment/Getty Images; **904** Kate Cummings/National Geographic Image Collection; **905** Tyrone Siu/Reuters/Newscom; **906** (tl) © Lynsey Addario, (c) Lynsey Addario/Reportage Archive/Getty Images; **907** (t) (b) Lynsey Addario/Reportage Archive/Getty Images; **908** Li Xiaoguo Xinhua/eyevine/Redux; **909** (tc) Courtesy of Hayat Sindi, (bc) Alexandra Verville/National Geographic Image Collection; **910** Robin Hammond/National Geographic Image Collection; **911** Manuel Hernández/Vizzor Image/Getty Images News/Getty Images; **912** (t) T.H. Culhane/National Geographic Image Collection, (bl) Courtesy of TH Culhane; **914** Jim Richardson/ National Geographic Image Collection; **915** (t) Patrick Aventurier/Getty Images News/Getty Images, (cr) Westend61 GmbH/Alamy Stock Photo; **918** NASA Earth Observatory image by Robert Simmon.

ACKNOWLEDGMENTS **R38**

TEXT CREDITS

031 (top right) Yuval Noah Harari, "Why humans run the world" | TED2015.; **037** (top right) Source: Epic of Gilgamesh, translated by Maureen Gallery Kovacs, electronic edition by Wolf Carnahan, 1998.; **041** (top left) Source: Hammurabi's Code, translated by L. W. King.; **059** (top right) Source: Ten Commandments By rabbi ronald h. Isaacs.; **062** (top left) Source: Genesis Chapter 7 In the beginning by Mechon Mamre.; **063** (top left) Source: The Epic of Gilgamesh, translated by Benjamin R. Foster, 2001.; **063** (center left) Source: The Mahabharata of Krishna-Dwaipayana Vyasa, translated by Kisari Mohan Ganguli, 1883-1896; **065** (top right) Source: Book of the Dead in Ancient Near Eastern Texts Relating to the Old Testament, edited by James B. Pritchard, Third Edition, 1969.; **071** (center left) Source: "The Triumphant Wife," from the Rig Veda, translated by Wendy Doniger.; **079** (top left) Source: Asoka and the Decline of the Mauras, ed. By Romila Thapar, 1973, pp. 251-252.; **086** (bottom left) Source: Confucius, Analects: With Selections from Traditional Commentaries translated by Edward Slingerland; **092** (center left) Source: Confucius, Analects: With Selections from Traditional Commentaries translated by Edward Slingerland; **094** (center) Source: Paul Salopek, "Cities of Silence".; **103** (top right) Source: Herodotus: The Histories, translated by Aubrey de Selincourt.; **107** (top left) Source: From the Cyrus Cylinder, New translation by Irving Finkel, Curator of Cuneiform Collections at the British Museum.; **107** (bottom left) Source: Holy Bible, Revised Standard Version, The Book of Ezra, 1:1–3; **111** (center left) Source: Herodotus, The Histories, translated by Aubrey de Sélincourt.; **117** (center right) Source: Herodotus, The Histories, translated by Aubrey de Sélincourt.; **119** (center left) Source: Herodotus, The Histories, translated by Aubrey de Sélincourt.; **131** (center right) Source: JSTOR, Early Journal Content, New York Latin Leaflet, vol. 1, "The Funeral Oration of Pericles" by David H. Holmes, 1901; **146** (bottom left) Source: Plato, Book V of The Republic, c. 380, translated by Benjamin Jowett.; **153** (center right) Source: From The Twelve Tables, Table VII. Naphtal Lewis and Meyer Reinhold, editors, Roman Civilization, The Republic and the Augustan Age, Volume 1; **175** (bottom right) Source: Holy Bible, Revised Standard Edition, The Gospel According to Luke 10:30-34.; **176** (bottom left) Source: Letters of Egeria, John Wilkinson, Egeria's Travels, Liverpool University Press, 1999; **179** (top left) Source: The Annals by Tacitus, Translated by Alfred John Church and William Jackson Brodribb; **179** (center left) Source: R. Knipfing, John, Edict of Toleration, Belgian review of philology and history, issued by Emperor Galerius.; **189** (bottom left) Source: Holy Bible, Revised Standard Edition, The Gospel According to Matthew 5:10-11; **195** (bottom right) Source: Ramayana, from a retelling by William Buck.; **198** (bottom left) Source: Ssu-ma Ch'ien, Grand Historian of China, by Burton Watson.; **209** (bottom right) Source: The Tale of Genji, by Murasaki Shikibu, edited and translated by Royall Tyler.; **215** (bottom left) Source: Lessons for Women, by Ban Zhao, Pan Chao: Foremost Woman Scholar of China, by Nancy Lee Swann, New York: American Historical Associate, 1932, pp. 84-85; **216** (center) Source: Nadia Drake, "How 'The Land of the Stars' Shaped Astronomy (and Me)"; **227** (top right) Source: The Institutes of Justinian; **233** (center right) Source: From "The Wars of Justinian" by Procopius, History of the Wars, 7 Vols., trans. H. B. Dewing, Loeb Library of the Greek and Roman Classics, (Cambridge, Mass.: Harvard University Press, 1914), Vol. I, pp. 451-473; **241** (bottom left) Source: S. G. Mercati, "Sull'epitafio di Basilio II Bulgaroctonos," Bessarione 25 (1921), 137-42; "L'epitafio di Basilio Bulgaroctonos secondo il codice modenese greco 324," Bessarione 26 (1922), 220-2; both reprinted in: S. G. Mercati, Collectanea Byzantina , II (Bari, 1970), 226-31, 232-4; **261** (bottom left) Source: The Uthmanis, by Al-Jahiz; **262** (center) Source: Gabe Bullard, "The World's Newest Major Religion: No Religion"; **281** (top right) Source: The Project Gutenberg EBook of Chaucer's Works, Volume 4 (of 7) — The Canterbury Tales by Geoffrey Chaucer (Middle English version) pp. 85-86; **292** (bottom right) Source: Alexiad, by Anna Comnena, Book I, Chapter XIV, ca. 1148. Edited and translated by Elizabeth A. Dawes. London: Routledge, Kegan, Paul, 1928.; **305** (center left) Source: Rosemary Horrox, trans. and ed., "The Persecution of the Jews," in The Black Death (Manchester, U.K.: Manchester University Press, 1994), p. 208; **310** (center left) Source: Patricia Buckley Ebrey, "The Women in Liu Kezhuang's Family", Modern China 10, no. 4, 1984; citation pn p. 437.; **313** (top left) Source: Friedrich Hirth and W.W. Rockhill, Chau Ju-Kua: His Work on the Chinese and Arab Trade in the Twelfth and Thirteenth Centuries, Entitled Chu-fan-chi (St. Petersburg: Imperial Academy of Sciences, 1911), pp. 149, 153–154, 162–163; **313** (center left) Source: Friedrich Hirth and W.W. Rockhill, Chau Ju-Kua: His Work on the Chinese and Arab Trade in the Twelfth and Thirteenth Centuries, Entitled Chu-fan-chi (St. Petersburg: Imperial Academy of Sciences, 1911), pp. 149, 153–154, 162–163; **313** (bottom left) Source:Friedrich Hirth and W.W. Rockhill, Chau Ju-Kua: His Work on the Chinese and Arab Trade in the Twelfth and Thirteenth Centuries, Entitled Chu-fan-chi (St. Petersburg: Imperial Academy of Sciences, 1911), pp. 149, 153–154, 162–163; **313** (bottom left) Source: Allen, Terry "Byzantine Sources for the Jami' al-tawarikh of Rashid al-Din." Ars Orientalis 15 (1985), pp. 121–36.; **323** (top right) Surce: Ono no Komachi, ca. 833-857, translated by Michael R. Burch Watching wan moonlight illuminate tree limbs, my heart also brims, overflowing with autumn.; **331** (top left) Source: The Complete History, by Ibn al-Athir, Edward G. Browne, A Literary History of Persia, (Cambridge: Cambridge University Press, 1902), Vol. II, pp. 427-431.; **331** (center left) Source: The History of the World-Conqueror by Ala-ad-Din Ata-Malik Juvaini, translated from the text of Mirza Muhammad Qazvini by John Andrew Boyle, Ph.D., Volume 1 (Manchester: Manchester University Press, 1958), p. 33.; **349** (top right) Source: History of Mehmed the Conqueror by Kritovoulos, Charles T. Riggs, translator, History of Mehmed the Conqueror, Praeger, 1954.; **351** (bottom left) Source: The Travels of Marco Polo, by Marco Polo and Latham, Penguin Classics, 1958; **352** (center) Source: Christopher Shea, "Did the Vikings Get a Bum Rap?"; **362** (top right) Source: The History of Africa: The Quest for Eternal Harmony, Molefi Kete Asante, Routledge, pages 130–131. Quoted material is from Sundiata: An Epic of Old Mali, Djibril Tamsir Niane, London: Longmans, 1965.; **365** (top left) Source: The History of Africa: The Quest for Eternal Harmony, Molefi Kete Asante, Routledge, page 154. Original source is quoted as "Mallows 1984, 39, 41,56.; **366** (center right) Source: From H. A. R. Gibb, The Travels of Ibn Battuta A.D. 1325–1354, The Hakluyt Society, pp. 918, 144.; **367** (bottom right) Source: Travels by Ibn Battuta, The Story of Swahili, John M. Mugane, Ohio University Press, 2015, page 23. Note in book: Ibn Battuta, quoted in Freeman-Grenville (1975, 29–30).; **379** (top left) Source: Kingdom of Ghana, Al-Bakri, The Book of Routes and Realms, cited in Levitzion and Hopkins, Corpus of Early Arabic Sources for West African History, (Cambridge University Press, 1981) pp. 79-81.; **379** (center left) Source: Dames, Mansel Longworth, trans. The Book of Duarte Barbosa, Volume 1 (London: Bedford Press, 1918, pp. 17–18).; **379** (bottom left) Source: Leo Africanus, A Geographical Historie of Africa, Paul Brians, et al. Reading About the World, vol. 2, 3rd ed. (Harcourt Brace College Custom Books), 1999; **405** (bottom left) Source: Popol Vuh. Translated into English by Delia Goetz and Sylvanus Griswold Morley from Adrian Recino's translation from Quiche into Spanish. Plantin Press, Los Angeles, 1954, p. 86.; **406** (center) Source: Brook Larmer, "The Real Price of Gold"; **429** (top left) Source: Cassandra Fedele, "An Oration . . . in Praise of Letters", Letters and Orations, edited and translated by Diana Robin, University of Chicago Press, 2000.; **429** (center left) Source: The Prince by Niccoló Machiavelli, translated and edited by Angelo M. Codevilla, Yale University Press, 1997.; **429** (bottom left) Source: Utopia by Thomas More, introduction by Jenny Mezciems, Random House, 1992.; **435** (top right) Source: Martin Luther, "Against the Robbing and Murdering Hordes of Peasants", E.G. Rupp and Benjamin Drewery, Martin Luther, Documents of Modern History (London: Edward Arnold, 1970), pp. 121-6.; **445** (center left) Source: Literacy Rate in Europe, Our World in Data.; **445** (top right) Source: "Account of Michelangelo", Ascanio Condivi, The Life of Michelangelo, translated by Alice Wohl (1976).; **449** (top right) Source: Robert Dankoff and Sooyong Kim, translation and commentary, An Ottoman Traveller: Selections from the Book of Travels of Evliya Çelebi (London: Eland Publishing, 2010).; **449** (bottom right) Source: Robert Dankoff and Sooyong Kim, translation and commentary, An Ottoman Traveller: Selections from the Book of Travels of Evliya Çelebi (London: Eland Publishing, 2010).; **467** (top left) Source: Letter from Voltaire to Frederick the Great, Bronson, Bennet, and Chiumei Ho, Splendors of China's Forbidden City: The Glorious Reign of Emperor Qianlong, Merrell Publishers Limited in association with the Field Museum, 2004, p. 274; **467** (center left) Source: Letter from Voltaire to Marquis de Condorcet, Voltaire in His Letters: Being a Selection from His Correspondence, by Voltaire, translated by S.G. Tallentyre, pseud. Evelyn Beatrice Hall. G.P. Putnam's Sons, New York, 1919. pp. 242-243; **467** (bottom left) Source: Letter from Qianlong to King George III, Backhouse, E. and J.O.P. Bland, Annals and Memoirs of the Court of Peking, Houghton Mifflin, Boston, 1914. pp. 322-331; **479** (center left) Source: "Frog Haiku" by Matsuo Basho, loose translation by Michael R. Burch; **485** (top left) Source: General History of the Things of New Spain by Bernardino de Sahagun, Stuart B. Schwartz, Victors and Vanquished: Spanish and Nahua View of the Conquest of Mexico, New York, Bedfore/St. Martin's, 2000.; **491** (top right) Source: Book of Useful Information on the Principles and Rules of Navigation by Ahmad Ibn Majid, cited in Aramco World (July/August 2005; vol. 56, no. 4), "The Navigator Ahmad Ibn Majid"; **495** (top left) Source: Sejarah Melayu (Malay Annals) by Tun Sri Lanang, Aran MacKinnon and Elaine MacKinnon, editors, Places of Encounters: Time, Place, and Connectivity in World History, Volume 1, Westview Press, 2012.; **495** (center left) Source: Travels in Persia 1673-1677 by Jean Chardin, Sir John Chardin, Travels in Persia 1673-1677, London, Argonaut Press, 1927.; **495** (bottom left) Source: The Ship of Sulaimān by Muhammad Rabī ibn Muhammad Ibrāham, Translated by John O'Kane, Columbia University Press, 1972; **507** (bottom left) Source: A Brief Account of the Destruction of the Indies by Bartolome de las Casas, Project Gutenberg, epub format, p. 12.; **515** (bottom left) Source: Leo Africanus, History and Description of Africa, trans. J. Pory and ed. R. Brown, London, 1896, Vol. III, pp. 824–7, and quoted in E.W. Bovill, The Gold Trade of the Moor, OUP, Oxford, 1968, pp. 147–50), History of Africa, Kevin Shillington, Palgrave/Macmillan, page 112.; **518** (bottom right) Source: Olaudah Equiano, The Interesting Narrative of the Life of Olaudah Equiano, or Gustavus Vassa, the African; **518** (bottom left) Source as listed in Voyages, p.568: Olaudah Equiano, The Interesting Narrative of the Life of Olaudah Equiano, or Gustavus Vassa, ed. Vincent Carretta, 2d ed. (New York: Penguin, 2003), pp. 105–109)); **521** (center) Source: Greg Miller, "These Maps Show the Epic Quest for a Northwest Passage"; **527** (bottom right) Source: Sarah H. Bradford, Harriet: The Moses of Her People, copyright by Sarah H. Bradford, 1886; **531** (bottom left) Source: William Cowper, "Pity for Poor Africans", Yale University.; **542** (bottom left) Source: The Trial of Charles I (1649): Selected Links & Bibliography by Lawrence MacLachlan (http://law2.umkc.edu/faculty/projects/ftrials/charlesIlinks.html); **544** (top right) Source: The English Bill of Rights, 1689; **554** (bottom right) Source: Joseph Banks, The Endeavour Journal of Joseph Banks, J.C. Beaglehole, ed., 2nd edition, Vol.1 (Sydney: Halstead Press, 1962, p. 252).; **561** (bottom left) Source: Sir Francis Bacon, quotation, Nature's Government: Science, Imperial Britain, and the "Improvement" of the World, by Richard Drayton. (New Haven: Yale University Press, 2000, pp. 55, 118); **565** (bottom right) Source: Politics by Aristotle, Project Gutenberg, Ebook of Politics, A Treatise on Government, Book III, Chapter VI, translated by William Ellis, A.M. London & Toronto Published By J M Dent & Sons Ltd. & In New York By E. P. Dutton &. Co. First Issue Of This Edition 1912 Reprinted 1919, 1923, 1928.; **570** (center right) Source: A Philosophical Dictionary by Voltaire, University of Adelaide, entry no. 308, "Liberty of the Press".; **571** (top right) Source: "Jean-Jacques Rousseau, Emile, 1762," Liberty, Equality, Fraternity; **572** (top right) Source: Memoirs of Jean François Marmontel by Jean François Marmontel, vol. 2, p. 36, Boston, Houghton, Osgood, 1878.; **572** (top left) Source: The Spirit of Laws by Charles-Louis Montesquieu, Online Library of Liberty, Book 1, Chapter 3. Charles Louis de Secondat, Baron de Montesquieu, The Complete Works of M. de Montesquieu, Volume 1. London: T. Evans and W. Davis, 1777.; **572**

(center left) Source: "A Vindication of the Rights of Woman by Mary Wollstonecraft/With Strictures on Political and Moral Subjects.", Project Gutenberg.; **572** (bottom left) Source: The Encyclopedia by Denis Diderot, Edited and translated by Stephen Gendzier, The Encyclopedia Selections, Harper Torchbooks, 1967.; **579** (bottom left) Source: An Essay Concerning Human Understanding by John Locke, Project Gutenberg, Volume 1 / MDCXC, Based on the 2nd Edition.; **583** (bottom right) Source: Thomas Jefferson, Declaration of Independence; **585** (top right) Source: The National Assembly, Declaration of the Rights of Man and of the Citizen, The Avalon Project, Lillian Goldman Law Library, Yale Law School; **589** (bottom right) Source: The L'Ouverture Project (https://thelouvertureproject.org/index.php?title=Haitian_Constitution_of_1801_ (English)); **591** (top right) Source: Napoleon's Account of His Coup d'État (10 September 1799), A Documentary Survey of the French Revolution. John Hall Stewart. New York: Macmillan, 1951, 763-765. Excerpted in Liberty, Equality, Fraternity: Exploring the French Revolution, Jack R. Censer and Lynn Hunt, eds. American Social History Productions, 2001.; **596** (bottom right) Source: William Blake, "The Tyger", Plate 42 from Songs of Innocence. William Blake. 1789. Copy Z, printed around 1826, is currently held by the Library of Congress; **600** (bottom right) Source: Simón Bolívar, letter to governor of Jamaica, September 1815, Translated by Lewis Bertrand in Selected Writings of Bolivar (New York: The Colonial Press Inc., 1951).; **604** (bottom right) Source: Benjamin Franklin, letter to to Henry Laurens, 25 May 1782, The National Historical Publications and Records Commission, the National Archives.; **607** (top right) Source: Mercy Otis Warren, letter to Catherine Macauley, September 17, 1787; **608** (center) Source: Tony Gerber, "Becoming Jane"; **622** (bottom right) Source: R. Beasland, extract from "London companion during the Great Exhibition"; **641** (center) Source: Statistics on World Population, GRP, and Per Capita GDP, 1–2008 A.D., Angus Maddison, University of Grøningen; **641** (center left) Source: Andrew Ure, The Philosophy of Manufacturers, 1835; **657** (top left) Source: Exploration of the Valley of the Amazon by William Lewis Herndon; **657** (center left) Source: Voyages A-16; Mexican History: A Primary Source Reader, edited by Nora E. Jaffary, Edward W. Osowski, Susie S. Porter, Westview Press 2010, Boulder, CO, p. 257; **657** (bottom left) Source: "First Electoral Manifesto of the Argentine Socialist Worker Party"; **661** (bottom left) Source: "A Cry from an Indian Wife" by Pauline Johnson-Tekahionwake; **665** (bottom left) Source: "House Divided" speech by Abraham Lincoln; **668** (bottom right) Source: King Khama of the Bangwato, quoted in Neil Parsons, King Khama, Emperor Joe and the Great White Queen: Victorian Britain Through African Eyes (Chicago: University of Chicago Press, 1998), p. 103.; **679** (top left) Source: D.R. SarDesai, Souitheast Asia Past and Present, 4th ed. (Boulder: Westview, 1997), p. 92; **679** (top right) Source: Mark Twain, from the New York Herald, October 15, 1900; **679** (top right) Source: Rudyard Kipling, Rudyard Kipling's Verse Inclusive Edition (New York: Doubleday, Page, & Company, 1919), p. 371; **687** (bottom left) Source: G.N. Sanderson, "The Foreign Policy of Negua Menelik" in the Journal of African History, Vol. 5, 1964. Reprinted in Voyages p. 805A.; **689** (center) Source: Laura Parker, "Plastic"; **707** (bottom right) Source: British private Harold Boughton, 1984, "Voices of the First World War: Gallipoli," Imperial War Museum; **711** (top left) Source: General Syrian Congress, "Congress of Damascus Resolution," July 2, 1919, Sources of Global History Since 1900, 2d ed. James H. Overfield (New York: Wadsworth/Cengage, 2012), pp. 102-103.; **711** (center left) Source: "Eight Points," by Nguyen Ai Quoc, 1919, Rhetoric of Revolt: Ho Chi Minh's Discourse for Revolution. Peter Anthony DeCaro. Westport, CT: Greenwood, 2003, Appendix A, p. 101.; **711** (bottom left) Source: Second Pan-African Congress, "To the World," 1921; **713** (top right) Source: Henry Morgenthau, Ambassador Morgenthau's Story, Chapter XXV, "Talaat Tells Why He Deports the Armenians"; **717** (top right) Source: Ernest Hemingway, "Notes on the Next War: A Serious Topical Letter," 1935, Hemingway on War, edited by Séan Hemingway. New York: Scribner, 2003, p. 304; **723** (bottom right) Mao Zedong, "Report on an Investigation of the Peasant Movement in Hunan" March 1927; **731** (bottom left) Source: Vladimir Lenin, "Can the Bolsheviks Retain State Power?"; **743** (bottom right) Source: Antonio Gramsci, from Avanti!, Political Writings 1910-1920 (London: Lawrence and Wishart, 1977), p. 17.; **745** (bottom right) Source: Official Kristallnacht Order, 1938; **763** (bottom left) Source: Sources of Japanese Tradition, ed. William Theodore de Bary, vol 2 (New York: Columbia university Press, 1958) p. 289; **763** (top right) Source: Walter Galenson and Arnold Zeliner, "International Comparison of Unemployment Rates," The Measurement and Behavior of Unemployment (National Bureau of Economic Research, 1957); **767** (bottom right) Source: Winston Churchill, speech before the House of Commons, June 4, 1940; **775** (top right) Source: Nancy Wake, The Autobiography of the Woman the Gestapo Called the White Mouse; **783** (top right) Source: Elie Wiesel, Night, Translated by Marion Wiesel, Hill and Wang, 2006; **787** (bottom right) Source: Robert H. Jackson, Opening Statement before the International Tribunal, Nuremberg, Germany, November 21, 1945; **789** (top left) Source: President Franklin D. Roosevelt, Annual Address to Congress, January 6, 1941, the "Four Freedoms" speech; **791** (center) Source: Yudhijit Bhattacharjee, "The Science of Good and Evil"; **800** (bottom left) Source: Westminster College, Fulton, Missouri, "The Sinews of Peace ('Iron Curtain Speech')", The International Churchill Society, March 5, 1946.; **803** (top left) Source: Bulletin of the Atomic Scientists; **819** (top right) Source: Anthony Eden, address to House of Commons on Suez Crisis, October 31, 1956; **819** (bottom right) Source: Dwight D. Eisenhower, speech on Suez Crisis,; **831** (bottom left) Source: John F. Kennedy, letter to Nikita Krushchev, state.gov,1961.; **831** (bottom left) Source: Nikita Krushchev, letter to John Kennedy, state.gov, 1961; **847** (top right) Source: "Nelson Mandela's Address to Rally in Cape Town on His Release from Prison," 1990; **852** (bottom right) Source: Jewish Virtual Library; **859** (top right) Source: United Nations, Universal Declaration of Human Rights; **861** (top left) Source: Jaime L. Sin, "Guidelines on Christian Conduct During Elections," in The Philippine Revolution and the Involvement of the Church, ed. Fausto Gomez (Manila: UST Social Research Center, 1986), pp. 40-44; **861** (center left) Source: Adam Michnik,

"Letter from the Gdansk Prison," University of California Press, 1987, p86; **861** (bottom left) Source: Alison Ozinsky, "Purple Reign," Upfront, November, 1989. Reprinted in The Purple Shall Govern: A South African A to Z of Nonviolent Action, ed. Dene Smuts and Shauna Westcott (Cape Town: Oxford University Press, 1991), 13-15; **869** (top right) Source: Boutros Boutros-Ghali, "Inaugural Address," Ninth Session of the United Nations Conference on Trade and Development; **889** (center) Source: International Monetary Fund; **891** (top right) Source: CIA World Factbook; **891** (center right) Source: CIA World Factbook; **891** (bottom right) Source: countryeconomy.com; **901** (bottom right) Source: Ai Weiwei Responds To Chinese Authorities Destroying His Beijing Studio; **917** (center left) Source: Hangzhou Declaration from the 5th BRICS Science, Technology & Innovation (STI) Ministerial Meeting, Hangzhou, China, July 18, 2017.; **917** (top right) Source: Luthi, D., et al. 2008; Etheridge, D.M., et al. 2010; Vostok ice core data / J.R. Petit et al.; NOAA Mauna Loa CO2 record.

ACKNOWLEDGMENTS **R40**